THE OXFORD HANDBOOK OF

THE HISTORY OF

CONSUMPTION

Frank Trentmann is Professor of History at Birkbeck College, University of London, and Professor of History and Social Sciences at the Sustainable Consumption Institute, University of Manchester.

THE OXFORD HANDBOOK OF

THE HISTORY

OF

CONSUMPTION

Edited by

FRANK TRENTMANN

OXFORD
UNIVERSITY PRESS

OXFORD
UNIVERSITY PRESS

Great Clarendon Street, Oxford, OX2 6DP,
United Kingdom

Oxford University Press is a department of the University of Oxford.

It furthers the University's objective of excellence in research, scholarship,
and education by publishing worldwide. Oxford is a registered trade mark of
Oxford University Press in the UK and in certain other countries

First published 2012
First published in paperback 2013

Published in the United States of America by Oxford University Press
198 Madison Avenue, New York, NY 10016, United States of America

ISBN 978-0-19-956121-6 (Hbk)
ISBN 978-0-19-968946-0 (Pbk)

Acknowledgements

....

Looking back now at my notes on the initial conception of this volume, I am not sure whether to be touched more by its ambition or by the intellectual generosity and collaborative spirit of the many contributors who helped make it a reality. We all too rarely bring together scholars working on different eras, continents and topics. Of the thirty-six chapters initially planned, thirty-four saw the light of day. One chapter on contemporary spaces fell victim to the demands of higher education politics which became (almost) all-consuming in 2010. The chapter on elderly consumers yet awaits its historian. The aim of this volume was to be thematic and, we hope, refreshing. It is not meant to be a Cook's tour of the entire world. Inevitably, the regional and thematic focus reflects the state of scholarship. Most research on consumption is still conducted in North America, the United Kingdom, and Continental Europe, although this is changing fast. As this volume shows, this does not, however, mean it has to result in a provincial outlook. This book looks to Africa, the Atlantic world, and to Asia as well as to Britain, the Netherlands, and the United States of America, which used to be treated as the consumer society par excellence. As handbooks in history go, this one also suggests some bridges with neighbouring disciplines, with chapters on technologies and practices, status and identity, well-being and everyday life. Between 2002 and 2007 I was fortunate to direct the 'Cultures of Consumption research programme', co-funded by the Economic and Social Research Council and the Arts and Humanities Research Council. The programme planted the seeds for several of the ideas and intellectual friendships that came to fruition in these pages. In addition to my own college, I must also thank the European University Institute, Florence, for awarding me a Fernand Braudel Senior Fellowship which gave me time to get this project rolling. As always, the editors and production team at Oxford University Press have provided just the right touch of professional support.

Frank Trentmann

Birkbeck College, University of London
February 2012

TABLE OF CONTENTS

List of Illustrations   xi
Notes on Contributors   xiii

1. Introduction   1
   FRANK TRENTMANN

PART I TRADITIONS

2. Citizen Consumers: The Athenian Democracy and the
   Origins of Western Consumption   23
   JAMES DAVIDSON

3. Things in Between: Splendour and Excess in Ming China   47
   CRAIG CLUNAS

4. Material Culture in Seventeenth-Century 'Britain':
   The Matter of Domestic Consumption   64
   SARA PENNELL

5. Africa and the Global Lives of Things   85
   JEREMY PRESTHOLDT

PART II DYNAMICS AND DIFFUSION

6. Transatlantic Consumption   111
   MICHELLE CRAIG MCDONALD

7. The Global Exchange of Food and Drugs   127
   FELIPE FERNÁNDEZ-ARMESTO AND BENJAMIN SACKS

8. From India to the World: Cotton and Fashionability   145
   PRASANNAN PARTHASARATHI AND GIORGIO RIELLO

PART III RICH AND POOR

9. Luxury, the Luxury Trades, and the Roots of Industrial Growth:
    A Global Perspective   173
    MAXINE BERG

10. City and Country: Home, Possessions, and Diet, Western
    Europe 1600–1800   192
    DOMINIQUE MARGAIRAZ

11. Standard of Living, Consumption, and Political Economy
    over the Past 500 Years   211
    CAROLE SHAMMAS

PART IV PLACES OF CONSUMPTION

12. Sites of Consumption in Early Modern Europe   229
    EVELYN WELCH

13. Public Spaces, Knowledge, and Sociability   251
    BRIAN COWAN

14. Small Shops and Department Stores   267
    HEINZ-GERHARD HAUPT

PART V TECHNOLOGIES AND PRACTICES

15. Comfort and Convenience: Temporality and Practice   289
    ELIZABETH SHOVE

16. Consumption of Energy   307
    DAVID E. NYE

17. Waste   326
    JOSHUA GOLDSTEIN

18. Saving and Spending   348
    LENDOL CALDER

19. Eating   376
    ALAN WARDE

PART VI STATE AND CIVIL SOCIETY

20. Consumer Activism, Consumer Regimes, and the Consumer
    Movement: Rethinking the History of Consumer Politics in
    the United States   399
    LAWRENCE B. GLICKMAN

21. Consumption and Nationalism: China   418
    KARL GERTH

22. National Socialism and Consumption   433
    S. JONATHAN WIESEN

23. Things under Socialism: The Soviet Experience   451
    SHEILA FITZPATRICK

24. Unexpected Subversions: Modern Colonialism, Globalization,
    and Commodity Culture   467
    TIMOTHY BURKE

25. Consumption, Consumerism, and Japanese Modernity   485
    ANDREW GORDON

26. Consumer movements   505
    MATTHEW HILTON

27. The Politics of Everyday Life   521
    FRANK TRENTMANN

PART VII IDENTITIES

28. Status, Lifestyle, and Taste   551
    MIKE SAVAGE

29. Domesticity and Beyond: Gender, Family, and Consumption
    in Modern Europe   568
    ENRICA ASQUER

30. Children's Consumption in History   585
    DANIEL THOMAS COOK

31. Youth and Consumption   601
    PAOLO CAPUZZO

32. Fashion   618
    CHRISTOPHER BREWARD

33. Self and Body   633
    ROBERTA SASSATELLI

34. Consumption and Well-being   653
    AVNER OFFER

Index   673

LIST OF ILLUSTRATIONS

....

Figure 8.1. Painting of a Rajaput nobleman wearing a red robe and turban. Opaque watercolour on paper, early nineteenth century. Victoria and Albert Museum, IS.115–1960.   149

Figure 8.2. Japanese 'yogi', a thickly padded sarasa cotton textiles imported into Japan by the Dutch from the seventeenth century. Made in the nineteenth century. Victoria and Albert Museum, FE.1550–1983.   152

Figure 8.3. Baju (Jacket) tailored in Sumatra with cloth from the Coromandel Coast of India. Late eighteenth century. Victoria and Albert Museum, IS. 101–1993.   156

Figure 8.4. Fabric used to line a wide-brimmed straw hat worn by the women of Friesland in the Netherlands. The fabric is a calico from the Coromandel Coast of India, c. 1725–50. Victoria and Albert Museum, IS.23–1976.   158

Figure 8.5. Palampore produced on the Coromandel Coast of India. Second half of the eighteenth century. The unusual design with two trees suggests that it might have been made for the French market. Victoria and Albert Museum, IM.85–1937.   160

Figure 8.6. Annual Consumption of Fibre per Capita in Britain, 1798–1861 (in Kilograms).   165

Figure 12.1. Canaletto, *Piazza San Giacomo in Rialto*, c.1740–60. © National Gallery of Canada, Ottowa.   230

Figure 12.2. Herb market in Amsterdam (oil on canvas), Gabriel Metsu (1629–67), Musée du Louvre, Paris. © Giraudon / The Bridgeman Art Library.   234

Figure 12.3. Abraham Bosse, *La Galerie du Palais*, British Museum. © The Trustees of the British Museum.   236

Figure 12.4. After Pieter van der Borcht, 'A Pedlar Robbed by Apes', c.1660, published by Robert Pricke. © The Trustees of the British Museum.   239

Figure 12.5. Ambrogio Brambilla, 'Ritrato de quelli che vano vendendo et lavorando per Roma con la nova agionta di tutti quelli che nelle altre mancavano sin al presente', Rome 1582,

etching with some engraving. © The Trustees of the
British Museum.   241

Figure 12.6.   Detail of Ambrogio Brambilla, 'Ritrato de quelli che vano
               vendendo et lavorando per Roma con la nova agionta
               de tutti quelli che nelle altre mancavano sin al presente',
               Rome 1582, etching with some engraving. © The Trustees
               of the British Museum.   242

Figure 12.7.   Benedetto Ceruti, *Musaeum Francesco Calceolarii*, Verona, 1622.
               © The British Library, London.   244

Figure 34.1.   Percentage shares of consumer expenditure in the UK and USA.   655

Figure 34.2.   Life expectancy at birth, 1980 (173 countries), and 2000
               (191 countries).   659

Notes on Contributors

Enrica Asquer is a postdoctoral research fellow at the University of Sassari, Italy. Her publications include *La rivoluzione candida: Storia sociale della lavatrice in Italia, 1947–1970* (Rome, 2007) and articles on consumer culture and family life in contemporary Italy. She is completing a research project called 'Gender, generations and consumption in the second half of the twentieth century: multiple paths in Southern Italy', with the help of research grant L. R. 7/2007 RAS for the promotion of scientific research and innovation.

Maxine Berg is Professor of History, University of Warwick. Her publications include *Luxury and Pleasure in Eighteenth-Century Britain* (Oxford, 2005) and 'In Pursuit of Luxury: Global Origins of British Consumer Goods', *Past and Present*, 182 (2004).

Christopher Breward is Principal of Edinburgh College of Art, Vice Principal of the University of Edinburgh and Professor of Cultural History. He was formerly Head of Research at the Victoria & Albert Museum. His publications include *The Hidden Consumer: Masculinities, Fashion and City Life 1860–1914* (Manchester, 1999), *Fashioning London: Clothing and the Modern Metropolis* (Oxford, 2004), and *Fashion's World Cities* (edited with David Gilbert) (Oxford, 2006).

Timothy Burke is Professor of History at Swarthmore College. His publications include *Lifebuoy Men, Lux Women: Consumption, Commodification and Cleanliness in Modern Zimbabwe* (Durham, NC, 1996), 'The Modern Girl and Commodity Culture', in Lynn Thomas et al. (eds.), *The Modern Girl Around the World: Consumption, Modernity and Globalization* (Durham, NC, 2008), 'Our Mosquitos Are Not So Big: Images in the Making of Mass Communications in Colonial Zimbabwe', in Paul Landau and Deborah Kaspin (eds.), *Pictures and People in Africa* (Berkeley, 2002), and the weblog *Easily Distracted*.

Lendol Calder is Professor of American History at Augustana College, Illinois. He is the author of *Financing the American Dream: A Cultural History of Consumer Credit* (Princeton, 1999).

Paolo Capuzzo is Professor of Contemporary History at the University of Bologna. His publications include *Genere, generazione e consumi. L'Italia degli anni Sessanta* (Rome, 2003, editor), *Culture del consumo* (Bologna, 2006), and 'Spectacles of Sociability: European Cities as Sites of Consumption', in: Mikael Hård and

Thomas J. Misa (eds.), *Urban Machinery: Inside the Modern European City* (Cambridge, MA, 2008).

Craig Clunas is Professor of the History of Art at the University of Oxford. His publications include *Superfluous Things: Social Status and Material Culture in Early Modern China* (Cambridge, 1991), *Pictures and Visuality in Early Modern China* (London, 1997), and *Empire of Great Brightness: Visual and Material Cultures in Ming China, 1368–1644* (London, 2007).

Daniel Thomas Cook is Associate Professor of Childhood Studies and Sociology at Rutgers University, Camden, New Jersey, USA and serves as an Editor for the journal *Childhood*. He is author of *The Commodification of Childhood* (Durham, NC, 2004), editor of *Lived Experiences of Public Consumption* (Basingstoke, 2008) and co-editor (with John Wall) of *Children and Armed Conflict* (New York, 2011).

Brian Cowan is the Canada Research Chair in Early Modern British History at McGill University, Montreal. His publications include *The Social Life of Coffee: The Emergence of the British Coffeehouse* (New Haven and London, 2005) and *The State Trial of Doctor Henry Sacheverell* (London, forthcoming 2012).

James Davidson is Professor of Ancient History at the University of Warwick. His publications include *Courtesans and Fishcakes: The Consuming Passions of Classical Athens* (London, 1997) and *The Greeks and Greek Love: A Radical Reappraisal of Homosexuality in Ancient Greece* (New York, 2007).

Felipe Fernández-Armesto is the William P. Reynolds Professor of Arts and Letters in the Department of History at Notre Dame University, and author of *Food: a History* (London, 2001); *The World: a History* (Harlow, 2006); and *The Americas: a Hemispheric History* (New York, 2003).

Sheila Fitzpatrick is Bernadotte E. Schmitt Distinguished Service Professor in Modern Russian History at the University of Chicago. Her publications include *Everyday Stalinism: Ordinary Life in Extraordinary Times: Soviet Russia in the 1930s* (Oxford, 2000), *Tear off the Masks! Identity and Imposture in Twentieth-Century Russia* (Princeton, 2005), and *Beyond Totalitarianism: Stalinism and Nazism Compared* (edited with Michael Geyer) (Cambridge, 2009).

Karl Gerth teaches modern Chinese History at Oxford University. His latest book is *As China Goes, So Goes the World: How Chinese Consumers are Transforming Everything* (New York, 2010). He is also the author of *China Made: Consumer Culture and the Creation of the Nation* (Cambridge, MA, 2004).

Lawrence B. Glickman is Carolina Trustee Professor of History at the University of South Carolina. He is the author of *Buying Power: A History of Consumer Activism in America* (Chicago, 2009) and *A Living Wage: American Workers and the Making of*

Consumer Society (Ithaca, 1997). He has also edited *Consumer Society in American History: A Reader* (Ithaca, 1999).

Joshua Goldstein is an Associate Professor of Modern Chinese History at the University of Southern California. His publications include *Drama Kings: Players and Publics in the Re-Creation of Peking Opera 1870–1937* (Berkeley, 2007) and *Everyday Modernity in China* (edited with Madeleine Yue Dong) (Seattle, 2006).

Andrew Gordon is Lee and Juliet Folger Fund Professor of History at Harvard University. His publications include *Fabricating Consumers: The Sewing Machine in Modern Japan* (Berkeley, 2011), *The Wages of Affluence: Labor and Management in Postwar Japan* (Cambridge, MA, 1998) and *A Modern History of Japan: From Tokugawa Times to the Present* (Oxford, 2009).

Heinz-Gerhard Haupt is Professor of European History at the University of Bielefeld and at the European University Institute, Florence. His publications include *Control of Violence: Historical and International Perspectives on Violence in Modern Societies* (with W. Heitmeyer et.al.) (New York, 2010), *Comparative and Transnational History* (with J. Kocka) (New York and London, 2009), and *Die Konsumgesellschaft in Deutschland 1890–1990* (edited with C. Torp) (Frankfurt/Main 2009).

Matthew Hilton is Professor of Social History at the University of Birmingham. His publications include *Smoking in British Popular Culture* (Manchester, 2000), *Consumerism in Twentieth-Century Britain* (Cambridge, 2003), and *Prosperity for All: Consumer Activism in an Era of Globalisation* (Ithaca, 2009).

Dominique Margairaz is Professor of Modern History at Université Paris 1-Panthéon Sorbonne and a member of the CNRS research group on the institutions and historical dynamics of the economy. Her publications include *Foires et marchés dans la France préindustrielle* (Paris, 1988) and *L'information économique, circulation et usages (XVIe–XIXe siècles)* (edited with Philippe Minard) (Paris, 2008).

Michelle Craig McDonald is Associate Professor of Early American and Atlantic history at Richard Stockton College. Her publications include *Voices from the Tavern: Public Drinking in the Early Modern World* (with David Hancock) (London, 2011) and *Caffeine Dependence: Coffee and the Economy of Early America* (Philadelphia, forthcoming).

David E. Nye is Professor of American Studies at the University of Southern Denmark. His ten books include *Consuming Power: A Social History of American Energies* (Cambridge, MA, 1998), *Technology Matters: Questions to Live With* (Cambridge, MA, 2005), and *When the Lights Went Out* (Cambridge, MA, 2010).

Avner Offer is Chichele Professor of Economic History at the University of Oxford. Recent publications on consumption include *The Challenge of Affluence: Self-control and Well-being in the United States and Britain since 1950* (Oxford, 2006), 'British

Manual Workers: From Producers to Consumers, *c.*1950–2000', *Contemporary British History*, 22 (2008), and 'Obesity Under Affluence varies by Welfare Regimes: The Effect of Fast Food, Insecurity and Inequality', *Economics and Human Biology*, 8 (2010) (with Rachel Pechey and Stanley Ulijaszek).

Prasannan Parthasarathi teaches South Asian and Global History at Boston College. His publications include *The Transition to a Colonial Economy: Weavers, Merchants and Kings in South India, 1720–1800* (Cambridge, 2001), *The Spinning World: A Global History of Cotton Textiles, 1200–1850* (edited with Giorgio Riello) (Oxford, 2009), and *Why Europe Grew Rich and Asia Did Not: Global Economic Divergence, 1600–1850* (Cambridge, 2011).

Sara Pennell is Senior Lecturer in History at Roehampton University, London. Her recent work has focused on the materiality of early modern 'everyday' domestic activity and second-hand cultures, with chapters in Karen Harvey (ed.), *History and Material Culture* (London, 2009), Tara Hamling and Catherine Richardson (eds.), *Everyday Objects: Medieval and Early Modern Material Culture and its Meanings* (Farnham, 2010), and Jon Stobart and Ilja van Damme (eds.), *Modernity and the Second-hand Trade* (Basingstoke, 2010).

Jeremy Prestholdt is Associate Professor of African History at the University of California, San Diego. He is the author of *Domesticating the World: African Consumerism and the Genealogies of Globalization* (Berkeley, 2008) as well as of *Global Icons: Popular Heroes since the Sixties* (forthcoming).

Giorgio Riello is Associate Professor in Global History and Culture at the University of Warwick. He is the author of *A Foot in the Past* (Oxford, 2006) and he is currently completing a monograph entitled *Global Cotton: How an Asian Fibre Changed the World Economy* (Cambridge, forthcoming 2012).

Benjamin Sacks is a Ph.D. candidate at Princeton University in the History of Science program.

Roberta Sassatelli is Professor of Cultural Sociology at the University of Milan. Her recent publications in English include *Consumer Culture. History, Theory and Politics* (London, 2007) and *Fitness Culture* (Basingstoke, 2010). She is also author of *Studiare la cultura* (with M. Santoro) (Bologna, 2009).

Mike Savage is Professor of Sociology at the London School of Economics and a Visiting Professor of Sociology at the University of York. His recent publications include *Culture, Class, Distinction* (with Tony Bennett, Elizabeth Silva, Alan Warde, Modesto Gayo-Cal, and David Wright) (London, 2009) and *Identities and Social Change in Britain since 1940: the Politics of Method* (London, 2010).

Elizabeth Shove is Professor of Sociology at Lancaster University. Publications include *Time, Consumption and Everyday Life* (edited with Frank Trentmann and

Rick Wilk) (Oxford, 2009), *The Design of Everyday Life* (with Matt Watson, Martin Hand and Jack Ingram) (Oxford, 2007), and *Comfort, Cleanliness and Convenience* (Oxford, 2003).

Carole Shammas holds the John R. Hubbard Chair in History at the University of Southern California. Her publications include *The Pre-Industrial Consumer in England and America* (Oxford, 1990), *A History of Household Government in America* (Virginia, 2002), and 'The Housing Stock of the Early United States: Refinement Meets Migration,' *William and Mary Quarterly*, 3rd ser., 64 (2007).

Frank Trentmann is Professor of History at Birkbeck College, University of London, and Professor of History and Social Sciences at the Sustainable Consumption Institute, University of Manchester. Publications include *Free Trade Nation* (Oxford, 2008) and *Consuming Cultures, Global Perspectives* (edited with John Brewer) (Oxford, 2006). He is completing *The Consuming Passion: How Things have Seduced, Enriched and Defined Our Lives, Sixteenth Century to the Twenty-First*, to appear with Penguin.

Alan Warde is Professor of Sociology at the University of Manchester and currently also Jane and Aatos Erkko Visiting Professor at the Helsinki Collegium for Advanced Studies. His books include *Consumption, Food and Taste: Culinary Antinomies and Commodity Culture* (London, 1997), *Eating Out: Social Differentiation, Consumption and Pleasure* (with Lydia Martens) (Cambridge, 2000), and *Culture, Class, Distinction* (with Tony Bennett, Mike Savage, Elizabeth Silva, Modesto Gayo-Cal, and David Wright) (London, 2009).

Evelyn Welch is Professor of Renaissance Studies and Vice-Principal (Arts & Sciences) at King's College London. Her publications include *Making and Marketing Medicine in Renaissance Florence* (with James Shaw) (Rodopi, 2011), *Shopping in the Renaissance* (New Haven, 2005), and *The Material Renaissance* (edited with Michelle O'Malley) (Manchester, 2007).

S. Jonathan Wiesen is Associate Professor of History at Southern Illinois University, Carbondale. His publications include *West German Industry and the Challenge of the Nazi Past, 1945–1955* (Chapel Hill, NC 2001), *Selling Modernity: Advertising in Twentieth-Century Germany* (edited with Pamela Swett and Jonathan Zatlin) (Durham, NC, 2007), and *Creating the Nazi Marketplace: Commerce and Consumption in the Third Reich* (Cambridge, 2011).

CHAPTER 1

···

INTRODUCTION

···

FRANK TRENTMANN

CONSUMPTION is a mirror of the human condition. Our understanding of how people consume has always reflected our views about how they ought to live. There are few subjects that have undergone a similarly profound shift in perspective in the last half-century. Routinely decried for most of the twentieth century as leading to alienation, waste, and selfish materialism, consumption in the 1970s and 1980s appeared in a new, positive light. It was hailed as a source of creativity and meaning central to social relations and identity formation. What had been the object of condescension—a minor, private, or mindless pursuit that at best followed, at worst distracted from work and community—now emerged as the very stuff of history. Consumption stepped out of the shadow of production. *Homo consumens* took the place of *homo faber*.

The repercussions for scholarship have been seismic. Just two generations ago, a handbook like this one would have been inconceivable. True, writers have long studied budget books, diet, housing, and spending patterns but such inquiries were mostly instrumental, a means to illuminate class, health, and poverty and related areas of historical inquiry. The acquisition, use, and waste of things, taste and desire were not part of a shared research agenda. When Joan Thirsk offered the present publisher her 1975 Ford Lectures on late Tudor and Stuart England,[1] the Press worried whether consumption was not too much of an obscure, niche subject. Since then there has been a publishing boom, with a deluge of books and dedicated journals, conferences and research programmes.[2]

---

[1] Joan Thirsk, *Economic Policy and Projects: The Development of a Consumer Society in Early Modern England*, Oxford, 1978.

[2] Readers may turn to the bibliography started by Don Slater: <http://www.consume.bbk.ac.uk/news/progdocs/consumption%20biblio.doc>. Useful anthologies of key readings include: Daniel Miller (ed.), *Consumption: Critical Concepts in the Social Sciences*, 4 vols., New York, 2001; Alan Warde (ed.), *Consumption: Benchmarks in Culture & Society*, 3 vols., New York, 2010. For developments in the social sciences, see Daniel Miller (ed.), *Acknowledging Consumption: A Review of New Studies*, London, 1995; Karin M. Ekström and Kay Glans (eds.), *Beyond the Consumption Bubble*, New York, 2011. See now also the multi-volume *Encyclopaedia of Consumption*, ed. Dale Southerton, New York, 2011.

This engagement has had a significant impact on national historiographies and historical method more generally. Attention to female shoppers, consumer movements, and debates over needs and affluence challenged older narratives and prompted new ones. In the United States, the colonial boycotts against British goods in the 1760s and the rise and redefinition of the citizen consumer in the twentieth century emerged as bookends of a new, more consumer-oriented national history.[3] Even in Germany, where the subject had been all but ignored by historians, consumption was suddenly embraced in the late 1990s as a new master narrative of the twentieth century, 'increasingly presented as the destiny of German history, its refuge and redemption.'[4] Yet the legacy for historical writing went well beyond national narratives. The study of consumption was (and remains) a major point of interface with anthropology, sociology, and geography, stimulating new directions in cultural, global, and material history. Historians have been prompted to think about the production, representation, and circulation of things, and about the nature of symbolic communication, material practices, and identity formation.

In historiography, as in real life, affluence creates problems as well as opportunities. Contemporary analysts speak of the 'diseases' of affluence, such as obesity. In the case of historical studies, the single biggest 'disease' has been fragmentation. As historians have followed goods to ever new regions and eras, the subject has been carved up into separate parts. This fragmentation has cut across time and space and through the very stuff of consumption. We have studies of individual nations, cities, streets, shops, and goods. Comparative efforts, by contrast, are rare.[5] This reflects in part an inherent tension between the subject matter and academic tradition (and job description). Almost everywhere, historians are trained and hired to speak to the particular concerns of a nation or region in a particular time period. Few goods and services are similarly tied down.

Fragmentation also, however, reveals a genuine analytical difficulty in moving between the concrete level of empirical research and a more general level of interpretation and abstraction.[6] Academics (and politicians and publics at large) have come to refer to consumption and the consumer in a free and casual manner as if they are self-evident. What these terms mean, however, is far from obvious and a product of

---

[3] T. H. Breen, *The Marketplace of Revolution: How Consumer Politics Shaped American Independence*, New York, 2004; Lizabeth Cohen, *A Consumers' Republic: The Politics of Mass Consumption in Postwar America*, New York, 2003. Lawrence B. Glickman, *Consumer Society in American History: A Reader*, Ithaca NY, 1999. Cf. David Steigerwald, 'All Hail the Republic of Choice: Consumer History as Contemporary Thought', *The Journal of American History*, 93/2, 2006: 385–403.

[4] K. H. Jarausch and M. Geyer, *Shattered Past: Reconstructing German Histories*, Princeton NJ, 2002; p. 269. Alon Confino and Rudy Koshar, 'Regimes of Consumer Culture: New Narratives in Twentieth-Century German History', *German History*, 19, 2001: 135–61. See also Heinz-Gerhard Haupt and Claudius Torp (eds.), *Die Konsumgesellschaft in Deutschland, 1890–1990*, Frankfurt am Main, 2009.

[5] Exceptions are Heinz-Gerhard Haupt, *Konsum Und Handel: Europa Im 19. Und 20. Jahrhundert*, Göttingen, 2002; Paolo Capuzzo, *Culture Del Consumo*, Bologna, 2006; Peter N. Stearns, *Consumerism in World History: The Global Transformation of Desire*, London, 2001.

[6] John Brewer and Frank Trentmann (eds.), *Consuming Cultures, Global Perspectives: Historical Trajectories, Transnational Exchanges*, Oxford, 2006.

change and contestation. What counts as consumption depends on the observer. For economists it can be a shorthand for aggregate demand. In the 1980s, many pioneering historians associated it with shopping. Since then, the focus has broadened to the before and after of the act of purchase, from the creation of desire through the use of things, to waste and recycling. We may want to call all these stages 'consumption', but clearly they are related to different mental and physical actions and involve a different set of relations and institutions. Consumption is a shorthand that refers to a whole bundle of goods that are obtained via different systems of provision and used for different purposes. There is a world of difference between buying a Ferrari and stepping into the morning shower. Both cost money and involve the use of resources but, in addition to the price tag, one is a matter of choice and comes with symbolic power while the other is a daily routine that is so taken for granted that it virtually slips beneath the radar.

This volume does not seek to offer a synthetic history of consumption.[7] Rather it follows several of the most exciting recent pathways into the subject, re-examines old debates and looks ahead to questions for future research. In the same spirit, this introduction is not trying to give an encyclopaedic overview of a literature that by now runs into many thousand books and articles. Rather, it follows the major fault lines—chronological, spatial, and material—to give the reader a sense of the changing look of the land and to sketch new ways for crossing it.

TIME AND SPACE

Histories of consumption have traditionally had strong chronological preoccupations. They have championed two periods over all others. One has been the apotheosis of 'consumer society' after the Second World War, the other its original birth pangs in the seventeenth and eighteenth centuries. Notwithstanding a gulf of three centuries of human experience separating them, these two research agendas initially shared a good deal of common ground. The model of the consumer society was one of America's main export staples to Western Europe in the era of the cold war. This model came in a variety of guises—the 'affluent society', the 'mass consumption society'—but its core argument can be summarized briefly. Affluence had moved the United States onto a new historical trajectory where consumption fuelled growth, defined identities, and shaped public and private life. The main disagreement in the 1950s and 1960s was not whether there was such a thing as consumer society but whether it was good or bad. It was either celebrated for promoting choice and liberty (W. W. Rostow) or condemned for manufacturing artificial wants and putting shallow individualism in the place of public life

---

[7] I offer one account in my forthcoming book *The Consuming Passion*, London, Penguin.

(J. K. Galbraith; V. Packard).[8] A generation later, the British historian Neil McKendrick led the search for the birth of this social formation.[9] He found it in England in the middle of the eighteenth century but what he was looking for was ultimately framed by the image of an affluent America set in the 1950s and 1960s. The decisive ingredients were choice, markets, fashion, and a rise in discretionary income. Writers influenced by Marx and the Frankfurt School had treated mass consumption as a consequence of mass production. McKendrick reversed the order. Not only did he show how widespread china, tea, cotton, and other consumer goods were by the 1760s. He highlighted the role of fashion magazines and the marketing strategies pioneered by Josiah Wedgwood as early instances of how advertising created demand which, in turn, propelled forward new industries. From here it was a short step to see the consumer revolution as preceding the industrial revolution, perhaps even initiating it.

The 'birth of a consumer society' set off a sustained search through inventories and other records for evidence about exactly who owned what when and where.[10] Thanks to these, we now know in fine detail the precise number of teapots and cotton shirts owned by households and their uneven diffusion across regions, groups and time. This narrowing of focus, however, had some unfortunate consequences for the larger picture. For one, the question of origin made it expressly backward looking. Its self-professed interest was in origins, not what happened between the 1750s and the 1950s. Once consumer society was born and started to walk, so to speak, the problem was solved, as far as eighteenth century historians were concerned. Analytically, the biological metaphor of 'birth' was unfortunate, too. For it imagined consumer society as a single organism and implied a straightforward, linear life story that obscured the many diverse pathways and mechanisms by which societies (including Britain) arrived at consumer culture.

In the last decade, historians have tried to push the moment of 'birth' further and further back, all the way to the middle ages.[11] Perhaps more interestingly, they have also reassessed the mode of consumption. In addition to individual choice, historians of eighteenth-century Britain and France have reaffirmed the complementary role played

---

[8] John Kenneth Galbraith, *The Affluent Society*, New York, 1958; Vance Packard, *The Hidden Persuaders*, New York, 1957; George Katona, *The Mass Consumption Society*, New York, 1964. W. W. Rostow, *The Stages of Economic Growth: A Non-Communist Manifesto*, Cambridge, 1960. Compare: Daniel Horowitz, *The Anxieties of Affluence: Critiques of American Consumer Culture, 1939–1979*, Amherst MA, 2004. Important precursors were Simon N. Patten, *The Consumption of Wealth*, Philadelphia 1889, and Stuart Chase, *The Economy of Abundance*, New York, 1934.

[9] Neil McKendrick, John Brewer and J. H. Plumb, *The Birth of a Consumer Society: The Commercialization of Eighteenth-century England*, Bloomington, 1982. See also John Brewer, 'The Error of Our Ways: Historians and the Birth of Consumer Society' (www.consume.bbk.ac.uk, Working Paper No. 012), June 2004.

[10] Carole Shammas, *The Pre-Industrial Consumer in England and America*, Oxford, 1990; Lorna Weatherill, *Consumer Behaviour and Material Culture in Britain 1660–1760*, 2nd edn., London, 1996; John Brewer and Roy Porter (eds.), *Consumption and the World of Goods*, London and New York, 1993.

[11] Christopher Dyer, *An Age of Transition? Economy and Society in England in the Later Middle Ages*, Oxford, 2005.

by social customs, reciprocity, and gifting.[12] Renaissance scholars, equally, have followed the circulation of goods between social groups in northern Italian cities through auctions, pledges, and private loans.[13] Consumption was enmeshed in civic life, social norms, and customs. The problem with the original 'birth' thesis, it is now clear, was that it presumed a far too tight link between consumption, individual choice, discretionary spending, and markets.

The chronological bifurcation between twentieth-century 'consumer society' and the early modern world matters because it has left behind a gulf of silence separating these two research communities. Twentieth-century historians continue to find it difficult to appreciate that popular access to more and more various goods was not the invention of 'mass society'. By comparison with work on the early modern period, the model of consumer society lives on in contemporary history.[14] Contemporary historians have been much slower to wean themselves off the cold war paradigm. This is, arguably, in part because contemporary research continues to work in the shadow of a larger public debate about sustainability and the limits to growth which, following in Galbraith's footsteps, still treats consumption as a new world order, defined in terms of individual choice, purchase, and 'affluenza'.[15]

The chronological divide has had consequences, too, for spatial scope. Historians working on the twentieth century and those working on earlier periods have followed quite different geographical routes. The 'consumer society' was a resolutely American model. It put the United States on display as the first of a new species. In their reader on *The Consumer Society* (2000), the sociologists Juliet Schor and Douglas Holt tellingly entitled their introduction 'Are Americans consuming too much?' Consumerism and Americanization became virtually synonymous. This kind of approach has favoured a diffusionist story, which traces the global advance of consumption outward from its American core.[16] Even historians who stress the selective adaptation of the American way of life in Western Europe after the Second World War ultimately follow influences

[12] John Styles, *The Dress of the People: Everyday Fashion in Eighteenth-Century England*, New Haven CT, 2007. Daniel Roche, *The Culture of Clothing: Dress and Fashion in the 'Ancien Régime'*, Cambridge, 1994 (1989).

[13] Evelyn Welch, *Shopping in the Renaissance: Consumer Cultures in Italy 1400–1600*, New Haven CT, 2005. John Goldthwaite, 'The Empire of Things: Consumer Demand in Renaissance Italy', in Francis Kent and Patricia Simons (eds.), *Patronage, Art and Society in Renaissance Italy*, Oxford, 1987.

[14] For a recent example, see Andreas Wirsching, 'From Work to Consumption: Transatlantic Visions of Individuality in Modern Mass Society', *Contemporary European History* 20, 2011: 1–26. Cf. Frank Trentmann, 'Consumer Society—RIP', *Contemporary European History* 20, 2011: 27–33.

[15] Barry Schwartz, *The Paradox of Choice: Why More Is Less*, New York, 2005; Juliet B. Schor, *The Overspent American: Why We Want What We Don't Need*, New York, 1999; Tim Jackson, *Prosperity without Growth: Economics for a Finite Planet*, London, 2009; Neal Lawson, *All Consuming: How Shopping Got Us into This Mess and How We Can Find Our Way Out*, London, 2009; Oliver James, *Affluenza*, London, 2007. Compare: Avner Offer, *The Challenge of Affluence: Self-Control and Well-Being in the United States and Britain since 1950*, Oxford, 2006.

[16] Bruce Mazlish, 'Consumerism in the Context of the Global Ecumene', in Bruce Mazlish and Akira Iriye (eds.), *The Global History Reader*, New York, 2005, 125–32. Cf Frank Trentmann, 'Crossing Divides: Consumption and Globalization in History', *Journal of Consumer Culture* 9/2, 2009: 187–220.

in one direction.[17] Western Europeans might debate the merits of rock'n' roll and communists tried to boycott Coca Cola. Still, in the final analysis, consumer culture flowed from America to the rest. Historical research sometimes reads like a sequel to contemporary debates about the 'American invasion'.[18] There can be no doubt about the cultural appeal as well as material power of the United States in its heyday. What this perspective does, however, is to ignore the range of other currents. That American consumer culture was dynamic does not mean that European or Asian societies had been static or frozen.[19] The United States did not enter virgin territories of asceticism and plain living in the 1950s. Goods, tastes, habits, and ideals of material civilization had been circulating through imperial and transnational networks.[20] In addition to indigenous histories of material desire, comfort, and commercial life, therefore, we need to recognize translateral as well as reciprocal flows of influence, from the export of the Frankfurt kitchen, to Europeans touring Swedish self-service co-operative stores. The United States imported as well as exported ideals of modernity. That America inspired a particularly resource-intensive way of life of cars, air-conditioning, and shopping malls does not mean it was the only society that generated rising levels of consumption.

As the American century is giving way to the Asian century, such US-centred narratives look increasingly dated. Clearly, democracy and a credit card are not the only paths to affluence. State power, nationalism, and saving can also do the job, as demonstrated by Japan and South Korea in the 1950s to 1980s and more recently by China.[21] Historical investigations of the different institutional and cultural highways to affluence in the late twentieth century are only now slowly de-centring the American narrative and replacing it with a history of multiple consumer societies.

Interestingly, historians studying the sixteenth to eighteenth centuries were among the first to recognize the potential virtues of consumption. In part, they were ahead

---

[17] Victoria de Grazia, *Irresistible Empire: America's Advance through 20th-Century Europe*, Cambridge MA, 2005; Sheryl Kroen, 'Negotiations with the American Way', in Brewer and Trentmann (eds.), *Consuming Cultures, Global Perspectives*, 251–77. Detlef Siegfried, *Time Is on My Side: Konsum und Politik in der Westdeutschen Jugendkultur der 60er Jahre*, Goettingen, 2006.

[18] Richard F. Kuisel, *Seducing the French: The Dilemma of Americanization*, Berkeley CA, 1993.

[19] Uwe Spiekermann, *Basis der Konsumgesellschaft: Entstehung und Entwicklung des Modernen Kleinhandels in Deutschland, 1850–1914*, München, 1999; Erika D. Rappaport, *Shopping for Pleasure: Women and the Making of London's West End*, Princeton NJ, 2000; Karl Gerth, *China Made: Consumer Culture and the Creation of the Nation*, Cambridge MA, 2003; Frank Dikötter, *Things Modern: Material Culture and Everyday Life in China*, London, 2006; Harry Harootunian, *Overcome by Modernity: History, Culture and Community in Interwar Japan*, Princeton, 2000.

[20] Brewer and Trentmann (eds.), *Consuming Cultures, Global Perspectives*; Timothy Burke, *Lifebuoy Men, Lux Women: Commodification, Consumption, and Cleanliness in Modern Zimbabwe*, Durham NC, 1996. Benjamin Orlove (ed.), *The Allure of the Foreign: Imported Goods in Postcolonial Latin America*, Michigan, 1997.

[21] Sheldon Garon and Patricia L. Maclachlan (eds.), *The Ambivalent Consumer: Questioning Consumption in East Asia and the West*, Ithaca NY, 2006; Laura C. Nelson, *Measured Excess: Status, Gender, and Consumer Nationalism in South Korea*, New York, 2000; Karl Gerth, *As China Goes, So Goes the World: How Chinese Consumers Are Transforming Everything*, New York, 2010.

because they were far less troubled by the moral weight of the American empire. Where twentieth-century accounts have tended to paint consumption in dark colours of manipulation and privatism, conformity, and pain, early modern accounts see a rainbow of creativity, self-fashioning, exotic novelty, and (yes) pleasure. The early modern world became history's laboratory of diversity and hybridity.

As late as the 1980s, in the pioneering histories by McKendrick and Fernand Braudel, the advance of consumption in Britain and France still signalled a civilizational lead on the road to modernity. Europe had fashion, Asia did not.[22] This Eurocentric perspective has since given way to more nuanced transnational and global approaches. Several stimuli were at work. One was comparative. Just how distinctive really was Europe's culture of consumption? After all, China had its own rich culture of things, scholars pointed out. It may even have had its own early modernity, Craig Clunas suggested.[23] Trade, possessions, and desire were on the rise in late Ming China. A second came from questions about reception, assimilation, and emulation. European scholars became interested in the lure of tea and coffee, cotton, and exotic luxuries, and their influence on European taste, identity, and lifestyle. Chinese porcelain was not a passive import but changed the way Europeans thought about themselves and the world and spurred them on to acts of emulation, copying, and innovation.[24] A third current followed the things themselves. Things had a social life, sociologists and anthropologists stressed. As they moved from producer via merchant to consumer they changed their meaning and role in society. Following their passage offered a way to link together societies and continents in circuits of exchange. Sidney Mintz's history of sugar offered historians the model of a commodity biography.[25] A final thrust against the European core model came from societies previously relegated to the margins of the world economy: Africa. Studies of West and East Africa showed how pre-colonial Africa played its own active part in the global flow of goods, connecting Zanzibar with India and Salem, Massachusetts. Pre-colonial Africa might not have occupied a position of equal size and force in the world of consumption,

[22] Braudel entitled his discussion of the lack of fashion in China 'When society stood still', in *Civilization and Capitalism*, Vol. 1: *15th–18th century*, New York, 1981, 312.

[23] Craig Clunas, *Superfluous Things: Material Culture and Social Status in Early Modern China*, Chicago, 1991; Craig Clunas, 'Modernity Global and Local: Consumption and the Rise of the West', *American Historical Review*, 1999: 1497–1509. Timothy Brook, *The Confusions of Pleasure: Commerce and Culture in Ming China*, Berkeley, 1998.

[24] Maxine Berg and Elizabeth Eger (eds.), *Luxury in the Eighteenth Century: Debates, Desires and Delectable Goods*, Basingstoke, 2003; Maxine Berg, *Luxury and Pleasure in Eighteenth-Century Britain*, Oxford, 2005; Robert Batchelor, 'On the Movement of Porcelains: Rethinking the Birth of the Consumer Society as Interactions of Exchange Networks, China and Britain, 1600–1750', in Brewer and Trentmann (eds.), *Consuming Cultures, Global Perspectives*; Timothy Brook, *Vermeer's Hat: The Seventeenth Century and the Dawn of the Global World*, London, 2008.

[25] Sidney Mintz, *Sweetness and Power: The Place of Sugar in Modern History*, New York, 1985. See further Arjun Appadurai (ed.), *The Social Life of Things: Commodities in Cultural Perspective*, Cambridge, 1986; Wim M. J. van Binsbergen and Peter L. Geschiere (eds.), *Commodification: Things, Agency, and Identities (the Social Life of Things Revisited)*, Münster, 2005; Robert J. Foster, 'Tracking Globalization: Commodities and Value in Motion', in Christopher Tilley, et al. (eds.), *Handbook of Material Culture*, London, 2006.

but it contributed to its modernity nonetheless.[26] Consumption, in brief, ceased to be a First World subject.

The fascination with flow, diversity and hybridity in the early modern world, on the one hand, and the resilience of the American model of mass consumption for the twentieth century, on the other, deserves a brief comment. This bifurcation is something peculiar to historical writing. In the social sciences more generally, scholars since the 1970s have studied the creative, ambivalent nature of consumption and reclaimed it as a fertile ground for subcultures, hybridity, self-fashioning, and transgressive identity politics in contemporary societies.[27] When it comes to historical work, however, such accents appear more readily at work on the early modern period, often cast in an heroically anti-Whiggish contrast to contemporary society. The eighteenth century can thus appear as the last flowering of a proto-global moment of creativity and connoisseurship before the fully-fledged global world of modern capitalism made everyone want the same mass-manufactured product.[28] Whether consumption really flipped in this dramatic fashion is debatable; numerous studies and ethnographies highlight the creative use and appropriation of things today.[29] What it indicates rather is that historians interested in diversity and self-fashioning have looked for it in earlier centuries. This orientation resulted from the particular political and historiographical constellation in which cultural history took off. For historians, like other social scientists, 1968 shook the foundations of established paradigms. The dismal view of consumer culture favoured by the Frankfurt School came tumbling down with the collapse of Marxism. Unlike social scientists who discovered creativity and resistance in contemporary everyday life, however, historians looked for the exotic, taste, and the pleasures of consumption in the distant past. The cultural turn offered an escape from a present where histories of class had lost their political centrality and purpose.[30]

MATTER AND MODELS

Consumption consists of a bundle of goods, practices, and representations. Which bits historians have investigated has depended in no small degree on their underlying assumptions of what consumption is about. And these, in turn, are indebted to rival models in

[26] Jeremy Prestholdt, *Domesticating the World: African Consumerism and the Genealogies of Globalization*, Berkeley CA, 2008. See also Daniel Miller (ed.), *Worlds Apart: Modernity through the Prism of the Local*, London, 1995; Richard Wilk, *Home Cooking in the Global Village: Caribbean Food from Buccaneers to Ecotourists*, Oxford and New York, 2006.

[27] Michel de Certeau, *The Practice of Everyday Life*, Berkeley CA, 1984; John Fiske, *Reading the Popular*, Boston and London, 1989; Dick Hebdige, *Subculture: The Meaning of Style*, London, 1979; Frank Mort, *Cultures of Consumption: Masculinities and Social Space in Late Twentieth-Century Britain*, London, 1996.

[28] C. A. Bayly, '"Archaic" and "Modern" Globalization in the Eurasian and African Arena, *ca.* 1750–1850', in A. G. Hopkins (ed.), *Globalization in World History*, London, 2002, 45–72.

[29] Daniel Miller, *Material Culture and Mass Consumption*, Oxford, 1987; Ulf Hannerz, 'The World in Creolization', *Africa*, 57, 1987: 549–59; Russell W. Belk, *Collecting in a Consumer Society*, London and New York, 2001; Daniel Miller, *The Comfort of Things*, Cambridge, 2008.

[30] François Dosse, *L'histoire En Miettes: Des Annales À La Nouvelle Histoire*, Paris, 1987.

the social sciences. We can loosely identify three approaches that have been particularly influential. In one, consumption is about status, social hierarchy and inequality. In a second, it is about the production and manipulation of taste and lifestyle in capitalist society. In a third it is about symbolic communication between individuals and groups.

The first perspective privileges highly visible forms of consumption as instruments of social power. Historians most frequently draw on the idea of 'conspicuous consumption' advanced by the heterodox economist Thorstein Veblen a century ago and on the concepts of 'distinction' and 'habitus' introduced by the sociologist Pierre Bourdieu in the 1960s. Both models alerted historians to the ways in which consumption (and not only work or income) produced social rank and reproduced social inequality. Far from frivolous, goods and taste, from jewellery to fine art and J. S. Bach, wove together the fabric of society. Consumption embodied taste and was a source of 'cultural capital'. For Veblen and Bourdieu, these were not neutral observations. Veblen lamented the 'waste' of conspicuous consumption which directed resources away from more productive, socially worthy use. Bourdieu treated consumption as a form of 'symbolic violence'.[31]

While Veblen and Bourdieu are popular points of references, they are just two models amongst many. Almost all major sociologists had something to say about consumption and status, but they differed in approach and conclusion. Veblen worked with a universalist conception of human nature, whereas Werner Sombart, for example, was interested in change and, in *Luxus und Kapitalismus*, diagnosed an intensification of distinction from the seventeenth century.[32] In the words of a recent commentator, the study of distinction has been the story of 'endless rediscovering', resulting from a reluctance to engage with the writings of earlier theorists.[33] While useful in prompting questions and working hypotheses, these models are far less useful as a general guide to historical reality. Veblen derived his ideas from observing the particular culture of a particular mid-Western elite at a particular point in time. It is similarly doubtful whether Bourdieu's insights from his research on 1960s Paris and Lille can be transplanted to other settings, leaving aside the question of whether the original interpretation overstated the data.[34] Sociologists since have debated whether consumption has lost its structuring force in late modern society, where all sorts of taste communities are now competing with each other. What is clear is that 'distinction' does not only work in a top-down direction but sideways, producing inequalities across society, along lines of ethnicity, gender, generation, and locality.[35] These myriad effects deserve much greater attention from historians. It is not that class cultures are fictions, but by drawing on Veblen and Bourdieu historians may have looked only for class-based tastes, missing classless ones. How neatly did tastes for music, sport, food and literature separate classes in the past?

---

[31] Thorstein Veblen, *The Theory of the Leisure Class: An Economic Study of Institutions*, 2nd edn., New York, 1899 (1953 edn.); Pierre Bourdieu, *Distinction: A Social Critique of the Judgment of Taste*, Cambridge MA, 1979; Engl. trans. 1984.

[32] Werner Sombart, *Luxus Und Kapitalismus*, Munich, 1912.

[33] Jean-Pascal Daloz, *The Sociology of Elite Distinction*, Basingstoke, 2010, 44.

[34] Cf. Bernard Lahire, *La culture des individus: Dissonances culturelles et distinction de soi*, Paris, 2004.

[35] Tony Bennett, Mike Savage, Elizabeth Silva, Alan Warde, Modesto Gayo-Cal and David Wright, *Culture, Class, Distinction*, London, 2009.

Emulation has been a shorthand to explain the pull of consumer culture. In eighteenth-century England, contemporaries routinely blamed the rise of an acquisitive culture on the lower orders' desire to imitate their superiors. Historians followed their lead. For McKendrick, 'the mill girl who wanted to dress like a duchess' was the engine of demand.[36] 'Keeping up with the Joneses' was the twentieth-century equivalent. There is something appealing in these simple, common sense formulations, and they continue to inform public anxieties about 'consumerism'.[37] It is therefore important to stress that emulation and status-seeking, however universal a part of human nature, have taken radically different material forms, past and present. Distinction is an inherently contingent and flexible mechanism. In contemporary Nigeria, for example, anyone wanting to impress will ensure that his car has visible markers of status, such as indications of engine type and model number on the boot, and, with the help of official support or a bribe if necessary, number plates of 1, 11, or 111, to show one's primacy. In Switzerland, by contrast, such conspicuous marks are deemed vulgar and would backfire. Anyone worth anything will prefer a sleek, anonymous ride.[38] Status-seeking, in other words, can be either showy or restrained, and how much and which kind of consumption is employed to achieve it is set by the cultural context. By using emulation as a shorthand, historians have deduced motivation from people's possessions, ignoring the cultural context and the various other reasons for which people acquired goods, from functional use and fitting in to pleasure and aesthetics.

The middle decades of the twentieth century witnessed the rise of a Marxist approach to mass consumption. First, Theodor Adorno and Max Horkheimer, then Herbert Marcuse extended Marx's critique of commodification to consumer culture itself. Marx had located the dialectics of capitalism in industry and the extraction of surplus value from wage labour. Adorno and Horkheimer linked mass production to the mass consumption of culture. 'Culture today is infecting everything with sameness,' they wrote in their 1944 Dialectic of Enlightenment. 'Film, radio, and magazines form a system.' Standardized movies, popular hits and advertising were the channels by which bourgeois society diffused its commodified way of life across society. The result was standardization, a drugged existence, and conformity. Consumer culture involved the 'withering of imagination and spontaneity'. It was inauthentic. Audiences were passive sheep: 'film denies its audience any dimension in which they might roam freely in imagination.'[39] The core elements of this diagnosis were in place before 1933. The fascist seizure of power only seemed to bear out the affinity between mass consumption and totalitarian politics, providing the Frankfurt School of Social Research with public appeal and urgency in their American exile. The culture industries did not just dumb down taste. They hollowed out

[36] Neil McKendrick, 'Home Demand and Economic Growth', in N. McKendrick (ed.), Historical Perspectives, London, 1974, 209.
[37] See references at Note 15.
[38] Daloz, The Sociology of Elite Distinction, 76–7.
[39] Max Horkheimer and Theodor W. Adorno, Dialectic of Enlightenment: Philosophical Fragments, Stanford CA, 1944; Engl. trans. 2002, 94, 100.

humanity from the inside, destroying the faculty for critical thought and civic action, preparing the way for servitude. What had happened in Berlin could happen anywhere.

This Marxist cultural analysis set the tone of public debate in the 1950s and 1960s. Marcuse's *One-Dimensional Man* (1964) was a bestseller—a must on the bookshelf of any self-respecting student. In the 'affluent society', Marcuse wrote, the sale of goods 'has been accompanied by moronization, the perpetuation of toil, and the promotion of frustration.'[40] Such judgements drew strength from longer traditions. That advertisers created dangerous 'false needs' had been a regular charge among early socialists and radicals. The spectre of passive conformity harked back to the Enlightenment critique of luxury as the mother of slavery. In many ways, the Frankfurt School capitalized on long-standing communitarian fears that consumption sucked the life out of citizenship and virtue, and updated them in Marxist language. The post-1945 suspicion of the culture industries also chimed with the dystopian picture of 'the consumer society' popular at the time, where manufacturers, advertisers, and *Hidden Persuaders*, as Packard called them in his 1957 bestseller, planted ever new artificial desires in the bosom of pliable consumers.

This Marxist tradition was dealt a serious knock by cultural studies, anthropological research and economic sociology, which reclaimed consumption as an active, creative, and authentic practice in the 1970s and after. Jean Baudrillard gave Marxism a semiotic direction in which consumers figured as pawns in an economy of signs.[41] Victoria de Grazia's *Irresistible Empire* offered a belated historical account of the culture industries, charting the advance of American marketing, Hollywood, and supermarkets through twentieth-century Europe.[42] But, in general, emphasis now shifted from the production of desire by producers and advertisers to consumers themselves. Qualitative research on radio audiences by Paul Lazarsfeld and colleagues were already challenging the presumed passivity of media audiences in the 1940s.[43] A more active view of consumption was gaining ground in the 1960s and 1970s. A decade later, it was in the ascendance. Instead of being impersonal, a host of studies showed market relations, commodification, and shopping to be social.[44] 'False needs' were excised from the vocabulary, making room for subcultures and ruses, and a more general respect for popular culture and the material dreams and lives of ordinary people. Arguably, this pendulum swung so much to one side that it became easy to overlook that consumer culture did involve a major

[40]   Herbert Marcuse, *One-Dimensional Man: Studies in the Ideology of Advanced Industrial Society*, London, 1964; Engl. trans. 2002, 247.

[41]   Jean Baudrillard, *La société de consommation*, Paris, 1970; transl. as *English—the Consumer Society: Myths and Structures*, London, 1998.

[42]   De Grazia, *Irresistible Empire*.

[43]   Paul F. Lazarsfeld and Frank N. Stanton, *Radio Research 1942–1943*, New York, 1944.

[44]   Viviana Zelizer, 'Culture and Consumption', in Neil J. Smelser and Richard Swedberg (eds.), *The Handbook of Economic Sociology*, Princeton NJ, 2005; Daniel Miller, *The Dialectics of Shopping*, Chicago, 2001; Paul DiMaggio and Hugh Louch, 'Socially embedded consumer transactions: for what kinds of purchases do people most often use networks?', *American Sociological Review* 63, 1998: 619–37; Elizabeth M. Chin, 'Purchasing Power: Black Kids and American Consumer Culture', *American Anthropologist*, 104/4, 2002: 1234–5.

asymmetry between the resources of corporate firms, media, and advertisers, on the one hand, and consumers and consumer groups on the other.

Signs, meanings and the creative consumer caught the attention of writers from disciplines across the social sciences and the humanities in the 1970s and 1980s. Perhaps most fruitful for historians was the anthropological approach of Mary Douglas and Baron Isherwood. In *The World of Goods* (1979), they presented goods as an 'information system'. Far from dull and trivial, eating and other ordinary consumption practices were revealed to be powerful rituals of symbolic communication which made social life possible. They created identity, meaning, and relationships. And they were means of social inclusion and exclusion. 'Consumption', Douglas and Isherwood wrote, was 'the very arena in which culture is fought over and licked into shape.'[45] This way of looking at consumption made it enormously attractive to a new generation of cultural historians. How people ate and drank and the representations of objects and practices offered a window on who they thought they were. This interest in meaning and symbolic communication had profound implications for historical method as well as argument, perhaps nowhere executed to greater effect than in Simon Schama's portrayal of seventeenth-century Dutch culture in *The Embarrassment of Riches*.[46] Using iconography in conjunction with textual readings, Schama recreated a society preoccupied with goods, taste, and pleasure that could not have been more at odds with the picture of austere, disciplined Puritan proto-capitalists held up by Max Weber.

For the historical study of consumption, the cultural turn involved a dramatic shift in perspective and substance. The focus moved from the producer and retailer to the end-user, and, with it, from the point of purchase to what people did with things once they had them. The anthropological interest in symbolic meaning and ritual practices also swept aside an older, hierarchical order of consumption, so central to social investigations and welfare policies, which contrasted 'basic needs' with higher, more experiential wants and desires. Food and eating were not just calories. They, too, were rich in meaning. In contrast to an older fixation with luxury goods and conspicuous consumption, ordinary stuff became interesting. What emerged was a relational view: goods acquired value together in a shared system of meaning.

These shifts played themselves out in a number of ways in historical research. One group of scholars turned to the consumption of culture and examined how in the eighteenth century new genres and practices of reading, listening and viewing shaped self-identity and sociability.[47] The domestic interior attracted a second cluster of research. The arrival of these subjects in the historical literature were the immediate consequence of the lines of inquiry opened up by gender studies. The household and its material culture, and getting and spending were recognized as sources of social life and identity as

---

[45] Mary Douglas and Baron Isherwood, *The World of Goods: Towards an Anthropology of Consumerism*, 2nd edn., London, 1996, 37.

[46] Simon Schama, *The Embarrassment of Riches*, Berkeley and Los Angeles CA., 1988.

[47] John Brewer, *The Pleasures of the Imagination*, New York, 1997; Ann Bermingham and John Brewer (eds.), *The Consumption of Culture 1600–1800: Image, Object, Text*, London, 1995.

important as the male sphere of paid work. Consumption—including the female labour of budgeting and housekeeping to make it possible—now lost many of its earlier associations as passive, frivolous, or irrelevant. Consumption ceased to be a footnote in a history of class society based on male industrial work and, instead, advanced into one of the main foundations of the historical record. Cupboards, dresses and wallpaper were retrieved as symbolic sources of women's identity.[48] In recent years, research has shown how dress, pipes, carriages, and other consumer goods were critical to men as well.[49]

This rehabilitation of consumption had implications for our understanding of public as well as private life. Separate gendered spheres suddenly looked more porous than in the Victorian ideal. In the eighteenth century, tea, china, and the novel were the material trappings of a culture of sociability and sympathy which assigned women a special civilizing role in an expanding social sphere. Enlightenment accounts of this culture by David Hume and Lord Kames attracted a fresh look from historians. For studies of the late nineteenth century the dominant figure was the female shopper. The study of shopping shifted from manipulation and 'moronization' to agency and liberation. Department stores like the Bon Marché in Paris and Selfridges in London opened up social spaces. Feminists established tea shops, restaurants, and toilets for female customers, and women's associations organized urban leisure tours that legitimated shopping as part of a cultured day out. In the years around 1900, consumer culture furnished some of the mental and material undercurrents of the more explicitly political movement for greater equality between the sexes.[50]

Changing views of consumption simultaneously reflected and contributed to the intellectual ferment of the late twentieth century. In the 1970s and 1980s, during the heyday of postmodernism and cultural studies, it looked as though the study of consumer culture might turn into a study of signs and representations. Historians were interested in what goods meant to people in the past. Consumption concerned identity and social relations. Not infrequently, material culture was a refuge from politics for scholars. Since the 1990s, there has been a dramatic reorientation. What had initially started

---

[48] Laurel Thatcher Ulrich, 'Hannah Barnard's Cupboard: Female Property and Identity in Eighteenth-Century New England', in Ronald Hoffman, Mechal Sobel, and Fredrika J. Teute (eds.), *Through a Glass Darkly: Reflections on Personal Identity in Early America*, Chapel Hill, 1997, 238–73; Amanda Vickery, *The Gentleman's Daughter: Women's Lives in Georgian England*, New Haven CT, 1998; Amanda Vickery and John Styles (eds.), *Gender, Taste, and Material Culture in Britain and North America, 1700–1830*, New Haven CT, 2006; Ann Smart-Martin, 'Makers, Buyers, and Users: Consumerism as a Material Culture Framework', *Winterthur Portfolio* 28, 2/3, 1993: 141–57; Ann Smart Martin, *Buying into the World of Goods: Early Consumers in Backcountry Virginia*, Baltimore, 2008. For later periods, see Victoria de Grazia and Ellen Furlough (eds.), *The Sex of Things: Gender and Consumption in Historical Perspective*, Berkeley CA and London, 1996.

[49] Amanda Vickery, 'His and Hers: Gender, Consumption and Household Accounting in 18th Century England', in Lyndal Roper and Ruth Harris (eds.), *The Art of Survival: Essays in Honour of Olwen Hufton*, Oxford, 2006; Christopher Breward, *The Hidden Consumer: Masculinities, Fashion and City Life 1860–1914*, Manchester, 1999; Brent Shannon, 'Refashioning Men: Fashion, Masculinity, and the Cultivation of the Male Consumer in Britain, 1860–1914', *Victorian Studies*, 46/4, 2004: 597–630.

[50] Rappaport, *Shopping for Pleasure*; Lisa Tiersten, *Marianne in the Market: Envisioning Consumer Society in Fin-De-Siècle France*, Berkeley CA, 2002.

out as a disillusionment with conventional politics (and political history), turned into a discovery of new kinds of politics. If feminist appreciations of shoppers kick-started this process, contemporary interest in the ethics of consumption, a new wave of local and global activism, and neo-liberal policies to 'consumerize' public services gave it fresh momentum. A string of publications charted the evolution of the consumer as citizen in national, imperial, and global politics.[51]

Looking back at the changing fortunes of the study of consumption in the twentieth century, it is tempting to hail it as a story of flourishing growth and innovation. This would be unhelpful for several reasons. Once derided or ignored, consumption stepped out of the shadow of production. This is true, but at the same time it changed its complexion. We now see consumption everywhere but what we see is mainly the private end-consumer. Early twentieth-century observers, by contrast, still had a more ecumenical understanding, including various acts of public and, indeed, industrial consumption.[52]

It is worth stressing, moreover, that a good deal of the work sketched above involved rediscovery. Recent histories of material comfort in Renaissance Italy, for example,[53] return to a central theme in Jacob Burckhardt's classic history completed a century and a half ago. Interest in the consumer as urban spectator and flâneur take their inspiration from Walter Benjamin's studies in the inter-war years. We have previously noted Sombart's work on luxury a century ago and that of Enlightenment thinkers interested in politeness and sympathy two and a half centuries ago. The list could go on. What this suggests is that, rather than seeing the 1970s–1980s as a break and new beginning, it might be better to see the twentieth century as one of ebb and flow, where early engagement with consumer culture was followed by contraction and re-engagement.

We should also recognize the selective, even lop-sided nature of this re-engagement. Historians emphasized meaning and representation but at the expense of saving

[51] Susan Strasser, Charles McGovern and Matthias Judt (eds.), *Getting and Spending: European and American Consumer Societies in the Twentieth Century*, Cambridge, 1998; Cohen, *A Consumers' Republic*; Martin Daunton and Matthew Hilton (eds.), *The Politics of Consumption: Material Culture and Citizenship in Europe and America*, Oxford, 2001; Frank Trentmann, *Free Trade Nation: Commerce, Consumption, and Civil Society in Modern Britain*, Oxford, 2008; Alain Chatriot, Marie-Emmanuelle Chessel, and Matthew Hilton (eds.), *Au nom du consommateur: Consommation et politique en Europe et aux États-Unis au XX siècle*, Paris, 2004; Frank Trentmann (ed.), *The Making of the Consumer: Knowledge, Power and Identity in the Modern World*, Oxford and New York, 2006; Charles F. McGovern, *Sold American: Consumption and Citizenship, 1890–1945*, Chapel Hill, 2006; *Annals of the American Academy of Political and Social Science*, 611, 2007; S. Jonathan Wiesen, 'Creating the Nazi Marketplace: Public Relations and Consumer Citizenship in the Third Reich', in Geoff Eley and Jan Palmowski (eds.), *Citizenship and National Identity in Twentieth-Century Germany*, Stanford, 2008, 146–63; Kate Soper and Frank Trentmann (eds.), *Citizenship and Consumption*, 2007; Matthew Hilton, *Prosperity for All? Consumer Activism in an Era of Globalization*, Ithaca NY, 2009; Lawrence Glickman, *Buying Power: A History of Consumer Activism in America*, Chicago, 2009.

[52] See Frank Trentmann, 'The Modern Genealogy of the Consumer: Meanings, Identities and Political Synapses', in Brewer and Frank Trentmann (eds.), *Consuming Cultures, Global Perspectives*, 19–69.

[53] Marta Ajmar and Flora Dennis (eds.), *At Home in Renaissance Italy*, London, 2006.

and credit, which only in the last few years has received the attention they deserve.[54] Historical research on consumption developed a strong interface with anthropology and cultural studies, and, to a lesser extent, with sociology and geography. Yet, curiously, given the pecuniary basis of much consumption, the gulf between history and economics is probably bigger than ever before, certainly when compared to the heydays of historical institutionalism and economic sociology a century ago, not to mention the eighteenth century. One exception is Jan de Vries' thesis of the 'industrious revolution' which, drawing on Gary Becker's economistic model where households make a rational choice about how to best allocate their time, sees families in seventeenth-century Holland and eighteenth-century Britain reallocating their time away from leisure and self-provisioning to wage labour and the purchase of goods in the marketplace;[55] this thesis is yet another rediscovery and application of contemporaries' ideas of consumer behaviour, which, it needs to be stressed, reflected normative and prescriptive views of social and material progress.

Scepticism of economics echoes historians' more general scepticism of individualistic models of choice and their 'imperialism' in the social sciences and public policy. It is, therefore, worth stressing that not all economists are the same. Some, like James Duesenberry in the late 1940s, were interested in how habits shaped future consumption.[56] None other than Alfred Marshall, the founder of the discipline two generations earlier, imagined a ladder of consumption where one step led to the next, as habits and desires bred new ones. William Jevons, who put the consumer squarely at the centre of value creation in the 1870s, was not only interested in individual choice but already traced consumption all the way from desire to waste, something that still features all too rarely in historical work.[57] Since the 1990s, behavioural economics has made great strides, but so far only a few economic historians have applied their tools to examine the impact of affluence on well-being in the past.[58] Historical engagement with psychology, philosophy, and law has been similarly patchy even though habit formation, ethics, regulation, and governance go to the core of debates about consumption and sustainability today.

In the last twenty years, historians have mined the department store, the domestic interior, luxury, food, and fashion, and, most recently, consumer politics. These now represent established bodies of knowledge and research orientations. What new fields and

---

[54] Lendol Calder, *Financing the American Dream: A Cultural History of Consumer Credit*, Princeton NJ, 1999; Margot C. Finn, *The Character of Credit: Personal Debt in English Culture, 1740–1914*, Cambridge, 2003; Garon and Maclachlan (eds.), *The Ambivalent Consumer*.

[55] Jan de Vries, 'The Industrial Revolution and the Industrious Revolution', *Journal of Economic History* 54/2, 1994: 249–70.

[56] James Duesenberry, *Income, Saving and the Theory of Consumer Behavior*, Cambridge MA, 1949.

[57] W. Stanley Jevons, *The State in Relation to Labour* (London 1882); Alfred Marshall, *Principles of Economics* (1890; London, 1920, 8th edn). An exception is Susan Strasser's trilogy on the United States: Susan Strasser, *Never Done: A History of American Housework*, New York, 1982; Susan Strasser, *Satisfaction Guaranteed: The Making of the American Mass Market*, New York, 1989; Susan Strasser, *Waste and Want: A Social History of Trash*, New York, 1999.

[58] Offer, *The Challenge of Affluence*.

questions will excite the next generation of researchers? I think there are four clusters that promise to be especially fruitful and relevant: diversity, public consumption, temporal and spatial scales of meaning, and material use.

It is now widely recognized that globalization has not meant homogenization. Recent studies have traced the transnational circulation of novelties and consumer goods in the early modern world and their selective appropriation and embedding in local cultures.[59] We need to know much more about how this story continued and how, why, and in which ways societies developed diverse material cultures, all the way to the present. This calls for macro as well as micro levels of analysis, and requires a greater integration of political economy with cultural inquiry. Clearly it makes a difference whether a country's consumption amounts to 35 per cent of GDP (China, today) or 70 per cent (the United States of America). To use the singular 'consumer society' model is not especially helpful. Attention to diversity and change similarly needs to extend to individual nations. In addition to regional contrasts at any given time, societies have undergone considerable oscillation and transformation over time. References to national types are of limited value—in less than a single generation, supposedly frugal societies like Japan and South Korea switched from super-savers into credit card spenders in the 1990s and 2000s. 'The American way of life', similarly, is a powerful ideal but of limited use when it comes to analysing and understanding how Americans lived their life. Arguably, the United States has a more fragmented and heterogeneous consumer culture than Continental Europe. Sociological analysis of time use suggests Americans differ more widely in their leisure practices.[60] The strong 'national' bias of the historical profession has probably made it more difficult to grapple with these external and internal forms of differentiation than in other disciplines.

Consumption today is so widely associated with the private act of purchase in the market that it is easy to forget that huge chunks have been public (and in many ways continue to be)—in public hospitals, armies, schools, subsidized university canteens and kindergartens. Companies and institutions, similarly, are spaces of consumption as well as work. The author of this text does not pay for the university computer and the energy it consumes—at least, at the time of writing. Still, looking back at the twentieth century (including the United States in the age of affluence), it is striking how the rise of private consumption has been accompanied by the rise of the state.[61] State spending

[59] Maxine Berg, 'In Pursuit of Luxury: Global History and British Consumer Goods in the Eighteenth Century', *Past and Present*, 182/1, 2004: 85–142; Prasannan Parthasarathi and Giorgio Riello (eds.), *The Spinning World: A Global History of Cotton Textiles, 1200–1850* Oxford, 2009; Brook, *Vermeer's Hat*.

[60] Alan Warde, Dale Southerton, Shu-Li Cheng and Wendy Olsen, 'Changes in the Practice of Eating: A Comparative Analysis of Time-Use', *Acta Sociologica*, 50/4, 2007: 363–85; Dale Southerton, Shu-Li Cheng, Wendy Olsen and Alan Warde, 'Trajectories of Time Spent Reading as a Primary Activity: A Comparison of the Netherlands, Norway, France, UK and USA since the 1970s', CRESC Working Paper 39, 2007.

[61] For a discussion of collective consumption as a 'commitment device', see Avner Offer, 'Why has the Public Sector Grown so Large in Market Societies? The Political Economy of Prudence in the UK, c. 1870–2000', Oxford Economic and Social History Working Papers, No. 2002-W44, http://www. economics.ox.ac.uk/index.php/staff/papers/offer.

on public consumption has been complemented by credit policies and investments in infrastructure that made private consumption possible in the first place. We would need to worry less about sustainability if states had not built roads and motorways in the first place. There is still sometimes a danger in the historical literature of treating market societies as 'normal' consumer cultures and socialist and planned societies as pathological misfits. But this presumes a single highway to a shared destination of 'the consumer society' that bypasses the many different roads societies have taken. At a time when a Communist Party state steers markets and is transforming the lives of 1.3 billion Chinese, such alternative forms of governance deserve more critical attention.

One victim of postmodernism and neo-liberalism has been 'commodification', the concept that had dominated Marxist analysis of consumption and discourse more generally. There were some good reasons for this exit. Karl Marx was clearly wrong to presume that just because things were produced by wage labour and made for sale (rather than for personal use) they were stripped of their essence and meaning. Thanks to anthropologists in particular we now have a host of studies that shows how goods continue to be emotional containers and vehicles of social life.[62] Still, if Marx's conclusion was as simplistic as it was grandiose, the question behind it was all but silly. It asked about the relationship between particular forms of production and distribution and the meaning of an object for the consumer. As historical questions go, this is a rather good one. It alerts us to the diverse forms of knowledge, associations, and identity that objects have conjured up for individuals and societies in the past. Anthropologists and geographers have examined this mutation in the life cycle of particular products as a commodity changes meaning as it travels through conduits of commerce, from producer all the way to the end-consumer.

But such changes also happen across larger temporal and spatial scales. Coffee and chocolate, prized for their exoticism in the seventeenth century, mutated into national mass products by the end of the nineteenth. Consumer culture, in other words, involves the historical rescaling of knowledge, value, and politics.[63] What ideas and values did goods convey about their origin and the people who made and handled them at different points in time? Which factors and processes helped to inscribe some meanings and erase others? These questions also concern the ethical reach of consumption, that is, in what relationship consumers see themselves to producers, near and far.

Our final observations concern materiality and practices. While the commodification thesis has cracked, it is nonetheless still common to hear that the West was consumerist because it was human-centred and lacked the East's respect for things—that is the reason, we are told, Western merchants were able to trick Eastern islanders, commodify their products, and impose capitalism.[64] What we now know about the success and dynamism of traders in the Indian Ocean and elsewhere in the early modern world

---

[62] From the rich literature, see Miller, *The Comfort of Things*; Appadurai (ed.), *The Social Life of Things*.

[63] For a suggestive discussion, see Trentmann, *The Consuming Passion*.

[64] Igor Kopytoff, 'The cultural biography of things: commoditization as process', in Appadurai (ed.), *The Social Life of Things*, ch. 2. See also Bruno Latour, *We Have Never Been Modern*, Cambridge MA, 1993.

raises all sorts of problems for this story. Another issue, and one relevant here, concerns the status of things more generally. Seventeenth- and eighteenth-century Europe did indeed give rise to traditions of critical reason which proceeded from a reflective, immaterial self, but they also generated rival traditions which were much friendlier to things and saw them as integral to human life, creativity, and sociality. There is no reason why we should fit our histories of consumer culture in the West around René Descartes and Karl Marx rather than, say, William James or Martin Heidegger, who had a more organic view of humans in the material world. The presumed dichotomy may simply reflect what scholars have presumed things are good for. If objects are treated as signs, it is tempting to see people and things as separate entities, with the former mentally appropriating the latter in acts of self-fashioning and identity formation. If, by contrast, goods are treated as instruments for getting something done—the execution of tasks—then it is much easier to see humans and things as interdependent actors. In that latter view, human existence is thoroughly 'thinged'. Things are part of us. Of course, many things perform both these functions (and many others). A teapot can be an object of desire and identity, and a container which keeps a beverage hot and, with a bit of skill, allows for pouring the liquid into a cup. Still, it has been the former that has dominated the scholarly libraries on consumption at the expense of the latter. Most consumption practices require a successful coordination of user, object, and competence, to use sociological terminology.[65]

What this alerts us to is the significance of materiality itself. An earthenware teapot handles differently and keeps heat less well than one made of china. Skis made of carbon-Kevlar are lighter and stronger than planks made of wood with metal edges and allow for a faster, smoother downhill ride. New materials and technologies constantly transform practices, from electronic gaming to microwaving. Some see a future of virtual, thing-less consumption where books, music, and sensations float freely, unmoored from a culture of possessive individualism, freely shared in social networks. That might be rather too optimistic. For the moment, most 'virtual' consumption rests on material foundations. They are simply hidden away in mainframes, cables, air-conditioning units and electronic and energy networks.

The organization of this volume is thematic and chronological. It is designed to offer readers different pathways into the rich literature. In addition to dedicated discussions of particular aspects of consumption in a certain time and place, the volume is meant to stimulate specialists to look beyond their own terrain of expertise to neighbouring fields of research. Like the other handbooks in history, this volume is not meant to be encyclopaedic and exhaustive but selective, thematic, and exploratory. Part One offers a window

---

[65] Theodore R. Schatzki, Karin Knorr-Cetina and Eike von Savigny (eds.), *The Practice Turn in Contemporary Theory*, London, 2001; Alan Warde, 'Consumption and Theories of Practice', *Journal of Consumer Culture*, 5/2, 2005: 131–53; E. Shove and M. Pantzar, 'Consumers, Producers and Practices: Understanding the Invention and Reinvention of Nordic Walking', *Journal of Consumer Culture*, 5/1, 2005: 43–64; Harvey Molotch, *Where Stuff Comes From: How Toasters, Toilets, Cars, Computers, and Many Other Things Come to Be as They Are*, New York, 2005; Frank Trentmann, 'Materiality in the Future of History: Things, Practices, and Politics', *Journal of British Studies*, 48/2, 2009: 283–307.

on several rich traditions of material culture that existed prior to modernity with which consumer society is often conflated. Chapters in this section examine the public as well as private face of consumption, in relation to public life and social order as well as the organization of households and social groups. Part Two turns the focus to the movement of goods between societies and to questions of global exchange and diffusion in the early modern world. Luxury and necessity are examined in Part Three, with chapters on the luxury wars, patterns of possessions and diet in town and country, and changes in the standard of living. Part Four explores the public and retail spaces of consumption from the Renaissance to the present. The doing of consumption receives particular attention in Part Five, with chapters that follow the life cycle of consumption from the desire to consume in the future (saving), to the use of energy to be comfortable and run things, to eating and throwing things away. Part Six looks at the politics of consumption broadly defined and at the different relationships between consumers, the state, and civil society in democratic, nationalist, fascist, socialist, and colonial societies. A final part, Part Seven, examines consumption's role for personal and social identity, with chapters on status, family life, generational identities, fashion, its impact on the body, and well-being.

PART I

TRADITIONS

CHAPTER 2

··

CITIZEN CONSUMERS:
THE ATHENIAN DEMOCRACY
AND THE ORIGINS
OF WESTERN CONSUMPTION

··

JAMES DAVIDSON

PRELIMINARY THOUGHTS AND
PROVISIONAL ASSUMPTIONS

··

The ancient Greek consumer *per se*, in the restricted sense of a purchaser/user of goods and services, has not hitherto been the subject of much concern or debate amongst classicists, certainly at the micro-economic level, and has (therefore) had little or no presence in recent debates about the emergence of a 'consumer society' in Europe. Though there has, of course, been research about consumption in general, and, more recently, marketplaces in particular, feasting, pleasure, the Subject and subjectivities, status-objects, prostitution, gender and performativity, personal morality, money and exchange—things which are not irrelevant to the present subject—and the current author wrote a book about the discourse of appetite and spending in the context of the Athenian democracy, which has been described by Ian Morris as part of a 'new historicist' turn towards the 'economic passions', and which has occasionally been cited by students of early modern consumption.[1]

[1] J. Davidson, *Courtesans and Fishcakes: The Consuming Passions of Classical Athens* (London, 1997); Ian Morris, 'Hard Surfaces', in Paul Cartledge, Edward E. Cohen and Lin Foxhall (eds.), *Money, Labour, and Land: Approaches to the Economies of Ancient Greece* (London, 2002), 8–43, at p. 16. There has of course been research on consumption in general, see most recently Sitta von Reden, 'Classical Greece: Consumption', in Walter Scheidel, Ian Morris and Richard Saller (eds.), *The Cambridge Economic*

Such neglect seems at first sight odd. Ancient Greece is one of the very earliest societies to provide a range of data about consumer-activity, and certainly the earliest of those societies to fall under the 'Western'/'European' rubric. Its art and texts have served as an important point of reference for Western philosophy and culture since the late middle ages, while its *demokratiai* have served as both etymon and originary myth for Western political systems since the nineteenth century, on both occasions often in implicit or explicit opposition to the Ancient Near East. Indeed the Greeks are widely seen as originating Europe's orientalist discourse with their construction of a Greek identity in self-conscious opposition to the timeless/indolent, slavish, luxurious, and/or effeminate Barbarian Other.

Hardly surprising then that since the early modern period, Western discourses about luxury, autarky, trade and the economy, society and the individual, personal morality and self-control, the spiritual and the material, the elite and the masses have habitually looked back to ancient Greek authors for foundations and inspiration, in order either to aggrandize their arguments or to emphasize their originality. Moreover one polis in particular, Athens, is often credited with becoming not only the world's first democracy but concurrently the world's first proper or 'full-fledged' 'money economy', most or all of whose citizens were familiar with a silver coinage in a very wide range of denominations, including *kermata*, 'small change'—individual coins have been discovered with a miniscule weight of 1/16 of an obol and, at the other extreme, of 10 drachmas; since 1 drachma = 6 obols this represents a *potential* range of 1:960 denominational units— and with prices denominated in that coinage.[2] Athenians were also amongst the first people in recorded history familiar with a central permanent marketplace, centred on the *agora* and filled with a range of goods offered by competing retailers/producers, with the experience not only of shopping—in a sense not totally dissimilar to the way it might be understood today—but of shopping around.

Whether or not this co-development of a particular kind of consuming economy with a particular kind of democratic politics was structural and necessary—and one contributory factor, the discovery of a large silver seam in southern Attica in 483BC, was certainly coincidental—there were in practice profound links between the two. It was the democracy that monitored the mint, authorized the currency, maintained its integrity, and insisted upon its use, that standardized weights and measures through officials called *metronomoi*, and regulated the market through officials called *agoranomoi*, that put coins in people's pockets through cash payments to very large numbers of jurors, to citizens who attended its Assemblies and, in the fourth century BC, its festivals,

---

History of the Greco-Roman World (Cambridge, 2007), 385–406, and in addition some lingering debate about the notion of the ancient city as a capitalism-inhibiting 'consumer-city' in contrast to the medieval city, cf. Kostas Vlassopoulos, 'The consumer city: ancient vs. medieval/modern', in Kostas Vlassopoulos, *Unthinking the Greek Polis; Ancient Greek History beyond Eurocentrism* (Cambridge, 2007), 123–42.

   [2] H. S. Kim, 'Small change and the moneyed economy', in Cartledge, Cohen and Foxhall (eds.), *Money Labour and Land*, 44–51.

that brought thousands of citizens from the country into town several times a month to attend Assemblies, and indeed into the *agora* itself, to attend trials and council-meetings; indeed, in the latter case, it obliged them to take up residence there for several weeks on end.[3]

Finally, like many exemplary early modern consumer societies, the Athenian democracy was also for most of its history a great naval power, and one that was engaged in two mighty struggles against very different kinds of state, the Persian and the Spartan. These were struggles that contributed a powerfully symbolic, even ideological element to its self-awareness as a particular kind of society with a particular way of organizing itself, a self-awareness that frequently mixes discourses of shopping and consuming with discourses of maritime supremacy, freedom, and democracy alongside the more familiar links to discourses of native versus foreign, town versus country, past versus present, and war versus peace.

This means that any study of the consuming subject in the Athenian democracy is bound to be both provisional and perilous. It is provisional because not much has been done in the way of sorting the data, let alone reaching conclusions. It is nevertheless perilous because of the bear-traps pre-laid in this virgin territory, thanks to Athens's importance in modern debates about the ancient economy, and its symbolic role in still powerful Western genealogies. These bear-traps are dangerous not merely because one might thoughtlessly fall into them and end up for instance banally asserting *nihil novi sub sole* or blithely co-opting the citizens of the world's first democracy as the world's first 'full-fledged' Western consumers, but equally because by thoughtfully avoiding such traps one might miss revealing similarities between ancient and modern ways of consuming and end up contributing to a myth of modern exceptionalism or reverting to the Whiggish narrative that sees the past as a failed or incomplete present: 'primitivism'.

The approach I have adopted is in the first place to give some indications of the kinds of data available for the study of the consumer in Athens, organized in what seems to me the most simple-minded fashion and without too much sifting out of 'irrelevant' material in the immediate context. I can already see that the kinds of data available are going to consist for the most part of public discourses, above all comic/satirical, forensic and philosophical discourses about goods, their purchase, their possession, and their consumption. Such discourses do however provide some factual information as to the shape of Athenian consumption, and, *qua* public generalized and structured (i.e. repetitive and cliché-ridden), are themselves important elements in a consuming context, what we might call an Athenian 'consumerscape', which might be expected to mould the Athenian consumer's behaviour, and, by representing, replicating and structuring particular consumer desires, expectations, and anxieties, to produce a particular kind of consuming subject.

---

[3] On 'redistributions' through state payments in the fifth century, see Lisa Kallet, 'The Athenian Economy', in L. J. Samons II (ed.), *Cambridge Companion to the Age of Pericles* (Cambridge, 2007), 70–95, at 77–9.

A City Full of Goods

For a long period Attic comedies which were written for festival competitions in honour of exuberant Dionysus included exuberant descriptions of available abundance in the here and now, rarely without some comic anomalies or satirical point, especially since the *agora* was both marketplace and civic centre:

> Speaker A: For in Athens everything is sold together in the same place, figs—B: witnesses for a summons (*klētēres*)—A: grapes, turnips, pears, apples—B: trial-witnesses (*martures*)—A: roses, medlars, haggis, honeycombs, chickpeas—B: lawsuits—A: beestings, beestings-pudding, myrtle—B: jury-selection machines (*klērōtēria*)—A: hyacinth, lambs—B: speech-timers, laws, indictments.[4]

In encomia of 'beautiful Athens' the marketplace could be seen as a display case for the excellence of the city's *terroir* and its peculiarly mild climate:

> Speaker A [= Athena?]: In the middle of winter you will see cucumbers, grapes, fruit, wreaths of violet…The same man sells thrushes, pears, honeycombs, olives, beestings, haggis, russet figs, crickets, foetal meats. And you would see country-baskets of figs and myrtle covered in snow.
> Speaker B: They sow squash at the same time as turnip so that no-one knows what time of year it is.
> A: What could be better than getting whatever you want all year round?
> B:…If they couldn't get it, they wouldn't want it, and wouldn't have to fork out for it either….You have turned their Athens into Egypt.[5]

Other such *laudes Athenarum* focus instead on the range of merchandise imported from the near and far abroad to Athens and its port of Piraeus, placing Athens at the symbolic centre of the world of goods, as the *agora* itself was the centre of Athens. The markets of Athens even get a mention in Thucydides' version of Pericles' Funeral Speech delivered in 430 BC to honour those who died serving their country in the first year of the Peloponnesian War. Immediately after the preamble comes a much-quoted glorification of the city for which they died—'the school of Hellas' etc.—what it represents, why it is worth dying for. This celebration places democratic Athens, a city as liberal in its inter-personal relations as in its politics, open to outsiders, etc. in opposition to illiberal oligarchic Sparta sealed off from the world—and its goods. This is Thomas Hobbes's translation of 1629:

> We have also found out many ways to give our minds recreation from labour [*ponoi*] by public institution of games and sacrifices for all the days of the year with a decent pomp and furniture of the same by private men, by the daily delight whereof we

[4] Eubulus fr. 63, ap. Ath. 14.640bc, from *Olbia*. Although there was a problem with bought witnesses, the second speaker does not seem to be making a satirical point, but simply playing the buffoon, cf. R. L. Hunter *Eubulus. The Fragments* (Cambridge, 1983), ad loc.
[5] Aristophanes fr. 581, ap. Ath. 9.372bd. The fragment may be mocking Euripides' patriotic *Erechtheus*, cf. C. Collard, M. J. Cropp and K. H. Lee, *Euripides: Selected Fragmentary Plays* I (Warminster, 1995), 155, and Kassel-Austin, ad loc.

expel sadness. We have this farther by the greatness of our city that all things from all parts of the earth are imported hither [*epeserchetai...ek pasēs gēs ta panta*] whereby we no less familiarly enjoy the commodities [*ta agatha* 'good things'] of all other nations than our own.[6]

Exactly the same theme but from a very different perspective crops up in a probably contemporary pamphlet called *The Constitution of the Athenians* by an anonymous opponent of the democracy labelled Pseudo-Xenophon or the 'Old Oligarch'. Here the Athenian *agora* is associated with decadent novelties, cultural impurity and loss of identity:

> If there should be mention also of more minor matters [*smikroterōn*] maritime supremacy has had the following results. First they have discovered ways of indulging themselves by mingling with different people in different places. Whatever the delicacy in Sicily, or in Italy, or in Cyprus, or in Egypt, or in Lydia, or in the Black Sea, or in the Peloponnese or anywhere else—all these things they pile up in one place because of their maritime supremacy. Second, hearing every kind of dialect they have taken this from that and that from this. The Greeks tend to have their own dialect, way of life, and type of dress, but the Athenians use a mixture taken from all, whether Greek or Barbarian.[7]

The most often-quoted illustration of the kind of things Pericles was referring to is from a nearly contemporary fragment of Hermippus' *Phormophoroi* (*Basket-bearers*). It begins in high burlesque style in epic hexameters, indeed with the same invocation to the Muses that introduces Homer's *Catalogue of Ships*.[8] Instead of a list of what each part of Greece contributed to the expedition against Troy, however, there follows a catalogue of 'all the good things for mankind' (*hoss' agath' anthrōpois*) Dionysus has 'shipped' (*nauklērei, ēgage*) to Athens ('here'):

> From Cyrene, silphium stalk and ox-hide, from Hellespont mackerel and preserved fish of all kinds, from Italy groats and ribs of beef. From Sitalces [king of Thrace] a skin condition to make the Spartans itch, from Perdiccas [king of Macedon] a fleet-load of lies. Syracuse, providing pigs and cheese...From Egypt rigging of sails and papyrus, from Syria frankincense. Fair Crete supplies cypress-wood for the gods, Africa, much ivory to buy, and Rhodes, raisins and dried figs that dreams are made of. And from Euboea, pears and fleecy apples, from Phrygia, slaves, from Arcadia, soldiers for hire. Pagasae supplies servants and runaway rogues. Hazelnuts

---

[6] Thuc. 2.38, cf. Nicole Loraux, *The Invention of Athens* (Cambridge MA, 1986), 86–7, R. Meiggs, *The Athenian Empire*, (Oxford, 1972) 264. The speech is explicitly Thucydides' version of 'the kinds of things' Pericles said in his speech.

[7] Pseudo-Xenophon 2.7–8; for a recent discussion, H. B. Mattingly, 'The Date and Purpose of the Pseudo-Xenophon Constitution of Athens' *CQ*, 47 (1997), 352–7. cf. Marx-Engels *Communist Manifesto*: 'An die Stelle der alten, durch Landeserzeugnisse befriedigten Bedürfnisse treten neue, welche die Produkte der entferntesten Länder und Klimate zu ihrer Befriedigung erheischen.'

[8] Hermippus fr. 63, ap. Ath. 1.27e–28a. Alongside those cited Note 4 above, cf. Dwora Gilula, 'Hermippus and his catalogue of goods (fr. 63)', in D. Harvey and J. Wilkins (eds.), *The Rivals of Aristophanes* (London, 2000), 75–90, Margaret C. Miller in a chapter titled 'Cultural Exchange Through Trade', *Athens and Persia in the Fifth Century BC: A Study in Cultural Receptivity* (Cambridge, 1997), 63–5, R. Brock, 'Athens, Sparta and the Wider World', in K. Kinzl (ed.), *The Blackwell Companion to the Classical Greek World 478–323 BCE* (Oxford, 2006) 84–98, at p. 65 drawing a contrast with sealed-off Sparta.

and glossy almonds Paphlagonians provide, for they are the feast's embellishments. Phoenicia, the fruit of the palm and finest flour, Carthage, rugs and fancy-woven pillows.[9]

Amidst these comic, vituperative and celebratory generalizations there is one relevant statistic; like most ancient cities, Athens imposed a 2 per cent tax, the *pentekostē*, 'the fiftieth', on imports and exports. We learn from a speech by one of the tax-farmers, that right at the end of the fifth century, shortly after Athens's catastrophic defeat in the Peloponnesian War it was nevertheless worth slightly over 36 Talents (= 216,000 drachmas). This indicates a huge amount of import-export activity, and doubtless the black market—not something that ancient authors seem particularly anxious about—would have increased that amount very considerably, although we probably cannot extrapolate from this any kind of figure for the average Athenian consumption of imported goods.[10]

THE ORDER OF THINGS

Such lists are organized chaotically in order to emphasize abundance and diversity: slaves, hazelnuts, palm-fruits, flour, pillows. In fact although there were some 'all-buy' general stalls (*pamprasia*), the market in Athens was organized into permanent sections, a model, according to Xenophon, for how a wife should organize her household goods:

> For we know that the city as a whole has ten thousand times more things than we do, but nevertheless if you ask any kind of servant to go and buy something from the agora and fetch it home, not one would have any difficulty, because every one of them clearly knows where to go to each kind of thing. Now there is no other reason for this than that it is to be found in its assigned place.[11]

This type of organization led to a peculiar idiom, one which is quite familiar to English-speakers arranging to meet in a department store today—'meet you in the books'—but that intrigued Roman-era students of classical Attic:

[9] Hermippus fr. 63, 4–24. Writing more than half a millennium later, Athenaeus, the source for the quote, links this with the trope of 'the best X comes from Y', but Hermippus, like Pericles, stresses the marvellous local availability of the quintessentially extra-local—African ivory, Lebanese frankincense (*libanōton*), Egyptian papyrus, Phoenician palm-products (<*Phoinikē d' au*> *karpon phoinikos*) etc.—constructing the marketplace of Athens as a kind of epitome of the world.

[10] Edward M. Harris, 'Workshop, marketplace and household', in Cartledge, Cohen and Foxhall (eds.), *Money Labour and Land*, 67–99, assumes the *pentekostē* is a tax on imports only, which, given a total population of around 300,000, would mean, '40 drachmas worth of imports per person every year' (p. 79). There is a good discussion of the uses of this datum in arguments about the ancient economy in M. H. Hansen, 'The Concept of the Consumption City applied to the Greek polis. Appendix 2, Andoc. 1.133–34 and Athenian overseas trade' in Thomas Heine Nielsen (ed.), *Once Again: Studies in the Ancient Greek Polis* (Stuttgart, 2004), 9–47, at 40–41.

[11] Xen. *Oec.* 8.22. On general stalls, apparently assigned their own place in the market, see R. E. Wycherley, *The Athenian Agora* III. *Literary and Epigraphical Testimonia* (Princeton, 1957), 613 with notes.

and the term 'the books' [*ta biblia*] is used on its own; for in this way Attic writers referred to the place where books were, just as they named the other places after the things sold there…in the words of Eupolis [fifth-century BC comic poet] 'I went round to the garlic and the onions and the frankincense, and through the aromatics and round the knick-knacks [*ta gelgē*].[12]

There are numerous examples of this idiom collected by later writers that enable us to go some way to reconstructing the marketplace. Alongside other references, they reveal on the one hand some higher-level organization—'the women's (*agora*)' (*hē gunaikeia* (*agora*)), 'the fresh fish' or 'fish-market' (separated from the preserved fish, *tarichē*), 'the furniture/utensils' (*skeuai*, also called *kukloi*, 'rings', presumably because of the way the stalls were arranged), 'the vegetables', 'the carrion market' (*kenebreion*), the clothes market (*himatiopōlis agora*) and a mysterious but centrally located 'rogues' market' (*agora Kerkōpōn*) named after a pair of mythical tricksters, which one later writer interpreted as a market for stolen goods. Referred to by the Roman-era medical writer Galen as a 'false place', it may well be a phantom, a misunderstood joke.[13] There were also areas where services or things could be hired: 'the chefs' (*ta mageireia*) was where one went, apparently, to hire a chef, while there was also a place where chefs went to hire cookware (or dinnerware).[14]

These references also provide much evidence for a remarkable degree of marketplace specialization. So apart from sections apparently solely devoted to the sale of 'onions' or 'the garlic', we hear of an area devoted to ass-meat (*memnoneia*), presumably part of the carrion market, to 'the sprats' (*membradas* 'small fish'), a sub-section of 'the fish', to 'the lupin-seeds [*thermous*]', 'the sesame', and 'the myrtle-berries', as well as a section devoted specifically to 'the myrtle-wreaths'. In this way the extravagance of a wife can be expressed in terms of the number of the mob of different traders who plague a husband to demand a settlement of accounts: separate purveyors of different-coloured clothes—the sellers of flame-coloured, violet, mallow, quince-coloured, saffron clothes—of different parts of garments—sleeve-makers, border-makers, fringe-makers, embellishers—etc.[15]

It does seem, moreover, on those rare occasions when we have enough evidence to confirm, that these really are sections of the market where multiple traders gathered. The sources imply several myrtle-wreath-sellers in 'the myrtle-wreaths' and more than one 'small fish-seller' in 'the small fish'. This extreme specialization is in part a reflection

[12] Pollux 9.47, Eupolis fr. 327, with Kassel-Austin, *Poetae Comici Graeci* ad loc. The idiom was also used in Ionian cities, Pollux 10.19. There seems to be some confusion about the meaning of *arōmata*, see Wycherley, *The Athenian Agora* III. *Literary and Epigraphical Testimonia* (Princeton, 1957), 202.

[13] Although one ancient commentator glosses 'the *opson*' as 'a place in the agora; here *opsa*, that is all foods, are sold' (Schol Aeschin. 1.65), opening up the prospect of an even higher level of organization, it seems clear from contemporary usage that the term usually denoted the section devoted to fish/ seafood.

[14] Alexis fr. 259.

[15] Plautus, *Aulularia*, 508–21, widely believed to be a version of a play of Menander, A. W. Gomme and F. H. Sandbach, eds. *Menander: A Commentary* (Oxford, 1973), Introduction, 4. The reference to a 'prefect of women's morals', i.e. *gynaikonomos*, and *corcotarii*, specialists in saffron-coloured dress, confirms that much of this was to be found in the Greek original.

of the specialized and small-scale character of ancient production, the simplicity of manufacture, and the diversity and bittiness of ancient property holdings—tiny parcels of land all over the place each perhaps producing just one crop, or ownership of a single slave with one particular skill, like the slaves inherited by the politician Timarchus: 'a woman skilled in working amorgine cloth, who took fine stuffs (*erga lepta*) to the market, and a man who did fancywork (*andra poikiltēn*)'.[16] Nevertheless it produced a very particular consumerscape.

Another reason for the degree of specialization of shops was that Athens had one permanent giant marketplace serving nearly the whole of Attica. There were also temporary markets at sanctuaries during festivals and we hear of at least one itinerant trader (of fish!), but we know for sure of only two other permanent classical period marketplaces in Athenian territory: the Piraeus, of course, which by the fourth century had been assigned half of the state's ten market-commissioners, and in the far south at Laurium. Indeed comic poets talk of the extra-urban space as a shop-free zone; one character can claim that in his home parish of Acharnae, a very substantial place, but not very far from Athens, you never heard the call 'Buy!'[17] The implication is that the Acharnians did not need to go shopping at all, but since the democracy encouraged and indeed required mass participation and therefore frequent trips from the country to town to attend scrutinies, meetings, trials, festivals, etc., a single central market could well have served an unusually wide area. Moreover, thanks to its transparent organization and size, the marketplace will have encouraged very competitive pricing, well worth the journey.

GENERIC QUALITY AND LABEL-BRANDING

Of course such a market must also have competed on quality. Some of the sub-sections we hear of seem already to be distinguished by criteria of quality, i.e. luxury vs. economy sub-sections within a particular zone of the market: 'the soft wool' or, on the other hand, 'the small fish'. Whether or not they had their own position in the market, further distinctions of generic quality in goods were made according to materials/varieties/methods of manufacture etc., often *associated with*, though not necessarily imported from, particular places. Just as we might distinguish 'Egyptian cotton', '1,100 thread-count', 'Burgundy', 'Bordeaux', so Greeks might vaunt clothes 'of Amorgos' or 'of Cos', 'Milesian-worked' couches, and 'Chian', 'Thasian', or 'Mendaean' wine.

Further than that, the closest we come to particular brands (and even something a little like brandmania) is with horses, in particular 'the sellers of good horses', where

---

[16] Paul Millett, 'The Economy', in R. Osborne (ed.), *Classical Greece* (Oxford, 2000), 33–4, C. Mossé, 'The Economist', in J-P. Vernant (ed.), *The Greeks* (Chicago, 1995), 35–6, Aeschin 1.97.

[17] Ar. *Ach* 34–6, cf. fr. 402. The itinerant fishmonger: Antiphanes fr. 69, cf. 127, Astrid Möller, 'Classical Greece: Distribution', in Scheidel, Morris and Saller (eds.), *The Cambridge Economic History of the Greco-Roman World*, 362–84, at 371, but cf. Alain Bresson, *L'économie de la Grèce des cités*. II *Les espaces de l'échange* (Paris, 2008), 19–20.

Theophrastus' 'Fraud' (a man who indicates he is vastly wealthy when he is not) pretends to be interested in making a purchase.[18] Data on these horse-brands—some of which endured for centuries—comes from sixth–and fifth–century BC vase-paintings, fifth-century comedy, and catalogues of the cavalry discovered in the *agora* and Ceramicus, dating to the later fourth and third centuries, with descriptions and evaluations of each cavalryman's steed. The most esteemed were those branded with the letter Koppa ('Corinthian'?) and San ('Sicyonian'?) both good for chariot-racing, apparently, and the *Boukephalai* of Thessaly, branded with an 'ox-head' (*boukephalaion*). In Aristophanes' *Clouds*, Strepsiades sends his racing-mad son who dreams of chariots and swears by Poseidon, god of horses, to learn sophistry from Socrates in order to wriggle out of the debts he has incurred buying Koppa- and San-branded horses. Alexander's war-horse, a Bucephalas from the stables of Philonicus of Pharsalus in Thessaly, is said to have cost 96,000 drachmas. But the cavalry's evaluators seem to have taken 1,200 drachmas as the maximum, and that is the sum Pheidippides owes for his son's Koppatias.[19] How were these brands certificated/policed? By far the most likely explanation is that, like wines, horses were *Appellations d'origine contrôlées*, marks that were policed by the cities/communities that produced them in much the same way as the polis of Thasos controlled the brand of 'Thasian Wine' by imprinting the name of the authorizing magistrate on distinctively shaped amphorae.[20]

Beyond these generically quality-certified goods, there is next to no evidence in the literature for consumer preference for particular 'producer-brands' of manufactured goods, unless one includes Thearion the breadmaker, who appears in a discussion of excellence in Plato's *Gorgias* (518b). On the other hand, one product in which Athens itself excelled was fine decorated pottery which was exported to all corners of the Mediterranean and the Black Sea. From an early date some producers signed some of their pots before firing: 'X made and/or painted it', especially in the first decades of the democracy and those immediately prior, c.520–480 BC. This would function as advertising as soon as the vase was brought out at a social occasion and would seem to assume at least some consumer brand preference. Moreover, there are one or two examples of painters disparaging other painters' skills, some 'licensing' of a 'brand' (i.e. painter's) name to others in the workshop, one certain forgery, a few vases with images of people using cups signed by particular painters, and one large mixing-bowl signed by the painter after firing, probably at the request of the (original) purchaser. But only a tiny percentage of vases were signed, most of the better artists never signed at all, and we know too little about the buying and selling of

[18]   *Characters* 23.7, 'alazoneia'. I am convinced by J. Diggle (ed.), *Theophrastus: Characters* (Cambridge, 2004), ad loc., that *eis* must be deleted, thereby removing the strange notion that there was a permanent sub-section of the marketplace devoted to the sale of 'the good horses'.

[19]   John H. Kroll 'An Archive of the Athenian Cavalry', *Hesperia*, 46 (1977), 83–140; K. Braun, 'Der Dipylon-Brunnen B1: Die Funde', *AthMitt*, 85 (1970); Ar. fr. 42–3; *Eq* 603; *Nub.* 23, 48, 122, 1298; Pliny *NH*, 8.44; cf. Isaeus 5.43, [Lysias] 7.10, Xen. *Anab.* 7.8, 6, Diggle ad Theophrastus *Char.*, 23.7.

[20]   François Salviat, 'Le vin de Thasos, amphores, vin et sources écrites', in J-Y Empereur and Y. Garlan (eds.), *Recherches sur les Amphores Grecques*, BCH Suppl 13 (École Française d'Athènes, 1986), 145–95.

these occasionally magnificent works of art—written sources are largely silent—to say much more about it.[21]

SYMBOLIC TOPOGRAPHY

The marketplace was centred on the *agora* proper, a flat area to the north of the acropolis clearly demarcated by boundary-stones, but the market spread out from there, in particular towards the main gate of the city, the Dipylon, and beyond. In a later period the *agora* proper was surrounded by expensively marbled stoas, long shaded colonnades devoted to shops/workshops, but in the classical period only one stoa was known as a stoa for goods, the *stoia alphitopōlis*, for barley-meal, and it was perhaps in Piraeus.[22] Instead, the sources refer to 'booths', *skēnai*, or 'tables', sometimes arranged in 'rings' (*kukloi*). There was some symbolic resonance in the location of some sections, so the bronze-workers were located near the temple of their divine patron Hephaestus. There was also a distinction between centre and periphery: 'the majority of you frequent those establishments nearest the agora, the fewest of you those furthest away.' 'Learning that [the virtuous Stripling (*meirakion*)] Euthydemus did not go into the agora because of his youth but sat in the reins-maker's near the agora if he wanted anything doing, Socrates went there himself with some of his group.'[23] The peripheral Ceramicus area around the Dipylon Gate and partly in the extra-urban zone, with its smoky potteries, cemeteries, dirty bathwater, and travellers by land from who-knows-where, seems to have acquired a reputation for more insalubrious exchanges, as the place for brothels and wine shops. It is clearly significant that Aristophanes' insalubrious 'Sausage-seller' sets out his stall there.[24]

There is a great deal of evidence that Athenians were expected to while away many hours each morning in particular sections of the *agora* or particular shops—'you are all accustomed to frequent some shop or other and spend time there'—and it was a mark against one's character if one did not: '[Aristogiton] does not even frequent any of these barbershops or perfume-shops in the city, not one; instead he is intractable, anti-social (*ameiktos*), of no fixed abode, graceless, friendless...'[25] For this reason the *agora* figures

---

[21] The pre-classical mixing-bowl, *Beazley Archive* # 310402, Villa Giulia M446, was found in Italy at Cervetri, cf. M. Robertson's reconstruction of the transaction: 'Epainetos came to Exekias' shop and said "I'll take this one, but I want your signature...",' 'Adopting an Approach I', in T. Rasmussen and N. Spivey (eds.), *Looking at Greek Vases* (Cambridge, 1991) 1–12, at 8. On signatures, J. Boardman, *History of Greek Vases* (London, 2006), 129, 'It is certainly nothing to do with advertisement in the modern sense', although he does allow one Nikosthenes, who aimed at the Etruscan export market, as a 'possible exception'.

[22] Ar. *Ecc.* 686, with R. G. Ussher (ed.) Aristophanes, *Ecclesiazusae* (Oxford, 1973), ad loc.

[23] Lysias 24.20, Xen *Mem* 4.2,1.

[24] Here the *agora* and the Dipylon are opposed: Ar. *Eq.* 1245–7: 'In the agora or at the gate?' 'At the gate...'

[25] Lysias 24.20, Dem 25.52.

regularly in Theophrastus' *Characters* of 319BC, as a civic theatre for the observation of character-types, notably several varieties of penny-pincher.[26]

Particular groups of people could consistently be located in specific areas. Those whose (ancestral?) parish was Decelea frequented a particular barbershop by the Herms, whereas exiled Plataeans met at 'the green cheese' on the last day of every month.[27] Sources are overwhelmingly consistent that Socrates held court in the *agora*—'at the tables'—probably in the shop of one Simon the shoemaker, who seems to have been a real person, even if the discourses ascribed to him are spurious. Later philosophers made much of this and probably the location of Socrates' group was indeed symbolic, indicating a particular kind of humble, local 'fondness for wisdom' (*philosophia*, something Pericles in the Funeral Speech claims was a peculiar feature of the Athenians in general), as opposed to the high-falutin' 'sophistry' of famous foreign intellectuals in the salons of rich men, such as Callias, as described in Plato's *Protagoras*.[28] Another trader has to defend himself from the charge that his shop has become a place where large numbers of bad men (*poneroi*) gather, men who have wasted their own estates and plot, presumably through litigation, to get their hands on the estates of others.[29]

The speaker never says what kind of shop he owns. But we can think of a few candidates. For although this practice of hanging out in the same shop did not necessarily imply buying anything—reins, shoes, green cheese—the nature of the goods sold might reflect on the people who gathered there. In the fifth century, 'the perfume', probably located just outside the south-east corner of the *agora* proper, was the 'assembly-point' (*sunedrion*) where the age-class of beardless Striplings (*meirakia*: roughly 18–20) sat and chatted, more suitable for Dionysius tyrant of Sicily than for a 'rustic'.[30] But one section above all was the object of the *agora*'s gaze: 'the fish'. Those seen there were liable to the charge of *opsophagia* (excessive fondness for fish /gourmandize), a dangerous thing for those who avoided taxes by pretending to be poor, and especially for those with a public position, whose visits could be used as evidence for acceptance of bribes or embezzlement. Hyperides was risking his reputation when he allowed himself to be seen walking around the fish section each morning. Aeschines can appeal to the gaze of the *agora* for clear proof that Timarchus and Hegesander have been conspiring together (to embezzle

---

[26] e.g. 2.7–9, 3.3, 4.15, 5.7, 6.9, 9.4, 10.12, 11.4–8, 16.10, 18.2, 21.8, 22.7 and 10, 23.7–8.

[27] Lysias 23.2–3, 6.

[28] cf. John Sellars, 'Simon the Shoemaker and the Problem of Socrates', *CPhil*, 98 (2003), 207–16. Thuc. 2.40,1.

[29] Lysias 24.19. The disabled man is pleading poverty in order to retain his small state pension, but his defence implies his shop is central (20), which is why it is so busy (19), and brings him into contact with wealthy men (5), who seem to be able to lend him horses (10); it seems to be the nature of the business that leads to the accusation that it is a hang-out for wicked spendthrifts.

[30] Ar. *Knights* 1375–6, Pherecrates fr. 70, Eupolis fr. 222, Polyzelus fr. 11, with Kassel-Austin ad loc. This age-class had a reputation for foppishness, coquetry, partying and chasing after women. Moreover, if Striplings, such as Plato's Euthydemus were expected to keep out of the *agora* proper in the fifth century, then the location of 'the perfume' right on the edge, a place it may have held from the late archaic to the Hellenistic period, (cf. Susan I. Rotroff, 'Hellenistic Pottery: The Plain Wares', *The Athenian Agora*, 33, (2006), 139–40, may explain why it was chosen as a meeting-point for this age-class.

state-funds): 'You all know that what I say is true. You must have seen them at the fish-stall (*toupson*) spending their money.'[31]

THE CONSUMING SUBJECT

This remarkable emphasis on shopping for fish in the Athenian discourse of consumption is highly revealing about the *dispositif* that constructs the consuming subject in classical Athens. In the first place, fresh fish, especially the larger specimens, seems to have been expensive and highly prized and inasmuch as it was purchased, seafood was a kind of gourmandize that was highly visible to the rest of the population. Moreover, fish occupied a particular position in the structuring of food in Greek culture. The Greeks, like the Chinese and other cultures, divided food into the staple—*sitos*—and *opson*, the relish. The staple, eaten with the left hand, was the sustaining element, the *opson*, eaten with the right hand, was the pleasurable element, and one that was closely identified with purchase and therefore with monetary exchange; hence shopping for food was called *opsōnein* and the word for 'salary' was *opsōnion*. Since fish was considered the most purely pleasurable food it came to be considered *the* relish: 'Though there are many poets, it is only one of them, the foremost, whom we call "the poet"; and so, though there are many *opsa*, it is fish which has won the exclusive title "*opson*"…because it has triumphed over all others in excellence.'[32]

Secondly, a very high proportion of the protein consumed by Athenians came in the form of boiled beef, goat, pork, and mutton distributed at sacrifices—indeed it seems probable that by and large sacrifice was the *only* source of such meat, a religious principle, like halal, but one that served to keep meat out of the marketplace.[33] This kind of consumption was experienced as part of a ritual of honouring the gods and of participation in a group or a community, so that being invited to share a sacrifice—or not being invited—could be used as proof of intimacy or kinship: 'He never made any sacrifice without us' (Isaeus 8.15). The smallest of such sacrificial groups was the *oikos*, the household, often, it seems, including women, slaves, and intimates. Naturally, wealthy men would be expected to sacrifice more generously than poorer men, and the quality of the victim would be noted. 'Shares' of sacrificial meat (*merides*) might also be sent to friends and family who were not able to be present.[34] Private religious associations, *thiasoi*, also pooled resources for communal sacrifices.

---

[31] On the tax-dodger, Ar. *Ran.* 1068; on Hyperides, Philetaerus fr. 2, Timocles frr. 4, 17, Hermippus 68aII, 68b (Wehrli); [Plu] *Vit X. Orat.* 849e; on Timarchus, Aeschines I. 65, cf. J. Davidson, 'Fish, sex and revolution in Athens', *CQ*, 43 (1993), 53–66, at 54–5.

[32] Plu. *Mor.* 667f.

[33] *Mageiros* can mean cook or butcher, but its primary reference is to the man who wields the knife at the sacrifice. There are no references to 'meat-selling' *kreopōleia* until after the classical period with the possible exception of Theopompus of Chios *FGrHist* 115 F 111.

[34] Robert Parker, *Polytheism and Society at Athens* (Oxford, 2005), 43 with notes.

But Athens was also distinguished for the number of public sacrifices that were celebrated either at the city level or at the level of the deme (parish). From a study of the few surviving deme calendars and from inscriptions recording the sale of the hides of victims in Athens, it has been calculated that there were something like 16 city sacrifices and about 20 deme sacrifices per year, although many of these would have been far too small to feed the whole community.[35] Again, rich men might sponsor these sacrifices—and have their names recorded as sponsors on inscriptions—in order to win the support of the parish or simply to seem pious and generous, but sponsorship of some sacrifices was a 'liturgy'—an obligatory public service—and others were paid for out of public funds, which meant the democracy itself was taking on the role of benefactor. As the Old Oligarch puts it: 'The city sacrifices a large number of victims at public expense and it is the *demos* that enjoys the feast and shares out the victims.' (2.9)

Fish as a market-supplied delicacy was symbolically opposed to this kind of ritually symbolic meat, a contrast quite explicit in an early fragment of Menander:

> Well then, our fortunes correspond, don't they, to the sacrifices we are prepared to perform? At any rate, for the gods, on the one hand, I bring an offering of a little sheep I was happy to pay ten drachmas for. For flute-girls, however, and perfume and girls who play the harp, for wines of Mende and Thasos, for eels, cheese and honey, the cost scarcely falls short of a talent; you see, you get out what you put in, and that means ten drachmas' worth of benefit for the sheep, if, that is, the sacrifice is auspicious, and you set off against the girls and wine and everything, a talent's worth of damages...At any rate if I were a god, I would never have allowed anyone to put the entrails on the altar unless he sacrificed the eel at the same time....[36]

Similarly fish could be seen, rather bizarrely, as the exemplary food of (decadent) contemporary life, in opposition to the simple, manly, roasted beef of the heroic age: 'Where has Homer ever spoken of any Achaean eating fish?'; 'You know that when his heroes are campaigning he doesn't give them fish to feast on, even though they are by the sea in the Hellespont...'[37] Finally, market-supplied fish was associated with the city, its sophistication, decadence, and deceit in opposition to the simple gastronomic pleasures of the country where one can 'have chaffinches and thrushes to eat instead of hanging around for little fishies from the market, two days old, overpriced and tortured at the hands of a lawless fishmonger'.[38]

On another level, the Athenians talk about consumption above all as an indicator of degrees of self-control. This means that the discourse of consumption remains strongly tied to the pleasures of the flesh: food, drink, and sex. The paradigmatic consuming

[35] These are the calculations of V. J. Rosivach, *The System of Public Sacrifice in Fourth-Century Athens* (Atlanta, 1994), 34, 64; see also, 'Sacrifice and animal husbandry in Classical Greece', in C.R. Whittaker (ed.), *Pastoral Economies in Classical Antiquity* (*PCPhS*, suppl. 14) (1988), 87–119, P. Schmitt Pantel, *La cité au banquet: Histoire des repas publics dans les cités grecques* (Paris/Rome, 1992).

[36] Menander fr. 264 Koerte.

[37] Eubulus fr. 118, Plato *Rep.* 404bc, cf. J. Davidson, 'On the Fish missing from Homer', in J. Wilkins (ed.), *Food in European Literature* (Exeter, 1996), 57–64.

[38] Antiphanes fr. 69, cf. 127, Aristophanes fr. 402.

subject is one who literally consumes or, by a common extension of the metaphor, one who has to satisfy a sexual appetite: 'If only one could satisfy one's hunger', said Diogenes the Cynic as he pleasured himself, 'by rubbing one's stomach.'[39] Words for consuming were also deployed as vivid and productive metaphors for wasting one's property—'eating it up' (*katesthiō*), 'gobbling it down' (*katabrōchthizō*), 'downing it in one' (*katapinō*).[40] As something both eaten and purchased, seafood combines these two elements of consuming—appetite and expenditure—in exemplary fashion.

Moreover, there is an important element of urgency in fish consumption, related to its evanescence as a product. You need to get to the marketplace early—while the fish is fresh, before all the best specimens are gone: 'and in fact, we don't say that those, like Hercules, who love beef are *opsophagoi*…but those who peel back their ears for the market-bell and spring up on each occasion around the fish-mongers'. In Aristophanes' *Peace*, someone imagines the reaction of a fish consumer arriving too late for the eels: 'Woe is me, woe is me, bereaved of my darling in beet-bed confined.'[41] Every morning at the fish stall is pictured as a first day at the sales. Similarly at a banquet, the fish consumers behave like out-of-control addicts, snatching seafood out of the pan and swallowing it whole, men like the *parasitos* nicknamed Crayfish 'who alone of mortal men is able to gulp down whole fish-slices from bubbling casseroles, so that nothing whatsoever is left'; as one comic fisherman explains: 'the fruit of our efforts is snatched from the dish without so much as a "by your leave" and disappears directly from the pan'.[42] Fish consumption becomes the paradigmatic consumption because fish appears and disappears so quickly, thereby adding urgency to purchase and dramatizing the evanescence of its consumption and of the wealth that is expended on it.

SEXUAL SERVICES AND SEMI-DURABLES

Sex also figures prominently in the discourse of extravagance and wasting estates. Here we must be aware of an important distinction between sex as a commodity-exchange and sex as a gift-exchange: *pornai* ('common prostitutes') were associated with the former and *hetairai* ('courtesans', 'mistresses') with the latter. This fragile and highly self-conscious distinction is further muddied by the existence of a large group of women and boys who could be hired for an evening (with or without sexual services assumed to be included in the fee) or for a period of weeks or months, among whom we should include the *mousourgoi*—oboe-girls (*aulētrides*), harp-pluckers, dancing-girls, cithara-boys, necessary accompaniments to a drinking-party or *symposion*. Socrates in *Protagoras* complains that demand for their services makes oboe-girls expensive and by the time of

[39] D.L. 6.2,69, cf. J. C. B. Gosling and C.C.W. Taylor, *The Greeks on Pleasure* (Oxford, 1982), 71 and 80.
[40] J. Davidson, *Courtesans and Fishcakes*, 209–10.
[41] Plu. *Mor.*667f., Ar. *Peace* 1013–14. (It seems that it was customary in many Greek cities to announce the arrival of the catch with a bell, cf. Strabo 14.2.21).
[42] Eubulus fr. 8, Anaxandrides fr. 34, and in general, see Athenaeus 3.100c, 104d, 8.339f–340a.

Aristotle, the maximum fee for hiring *mousourgoi* off the street for an evening was set at 2 drachmas (not cheap). City officials called Astynomoi enforced the limit by using a lottery to decide between competing purchasers of the services of *mousourgoi* in an attempt to prevent an inflationary auction. Nevertheless his 'enslavement' to oboe-girls was one of the factors, along with *opsophagia* and expensive dinner parties etc. that led to Timarchus' 'consuming' of his estate, according to Aeschines at any rate.[43]

By far the most lavish and dangerous sexual expenditure, however, involved paying off cuckolded husbands to avoid the severe penalties laid down for adultery or engaging in relationships with courtesans: buying them presents to keep them sweet, maintaining them in lavish style, or, most extravagant of all, buying them outright or paying for them to be freed. This kind of exchange is a long way from what would normally be included under the heading 'consumerism'. Indeed in this context, sexual consumerism, i.e. the cash transactions of the brothel, could be seen as cheap and uncomplicated ways of letting off sexual steam, a finalizable one-off payment for a specific commoditized service that liberated one from the open-ended ongoing expenditures involved in love affairs with *hetairai*.

In accordance with this emphasis on bodily appetites, there is little in the Athenian discourse of consumption relating to durables and semi-durables, such as clothes and household goods, although such goods have been the focus of some of the most interesting work on early modern shopping and the source of some of the greatest anxieties regarding postmodern consumerism. In fact, despite the ready use of the metaphor of 'consuming property', I can discover no foreshadowings in Athenian discourse of the classical period for the seventeenth-century extension of the concept of 'consuming' to 'the purchase/use of goods' in general, i.e. consumption as the necessary flipside of production.

Such goods were of course purchased and used. Although much cloth was supposed to be homespun, there was also a substantial clothing industry in Athens and a *himatiopōlis* section in the marketplace.[44] One particular kind of cloak, the *chlanis*, frequently crops up as a meaningful possession, a sign of wealth. It is not clear what was distinguished about it, but you could spot it from afar. In Menander's *Dyskolos*, Gorgias and Daos discuss wealthy Sostratos as 'the one with the *chlanis*' (257), while a newly impoverished man finds himself suddenly friendless: 'It was my *chlanis* not me they used to approach; now no-one speaks to me'.[45] Demosthenes notes that his enemy Meidias brought along *chlanides*, when he reported for military duty, as well as a saddle with silver trimmings imported from Euboea (21.133).

The closest we can get to someone actually visiting the clothes market, however, is Theophrastus' Fraud—the man who pretends to be vastly wealthy: 'Going to the couches (?) he selects clothing (*himatismon*) up to the value of 12,000 drachmas [a quite incredible sum] and then quarrels with his slave because he came along without the gold.' Theophrastus also supplies us with the best example of consumption in the general context of 'showing off', although the actual title of this character trait has

---

[43] Plato *Protagoras* 347cd, [Aristot.] *Ath.Pol.* 50.2, cf. Hyp.iv *Eux.* 3, Suid. . 528, Aeschin. 1.42.

[44] The evidence for home vs. commercial manufacture is usefully collected by Wesley Thompson, 'Weaving: A Man's Work', *CW*, 75 (1982), 217–22.

[45] Posidippus 33 K-A, cf. Dem. 36.45.

been lost: 'He doesn't neglect to keep a pet ape, and to acquire an oriental pheasant and Sicilian pigeons and gazelle-horn knucklebones and Thurian oil-flasks of the spherical sort and twisted walking-sticks from Sparta, a tapestry embroidered with Persian scenes and a little wrestling ground with sand and a boxing arena.'[46] Something similar can perhaps be found again in Demosthenes' attack on Meidias:

> He has built at Eleusis a house so big it casts a shadow over the neighbourhood; he drives his wife to the Mysteries, or anywhere else that he wishes, with a pair of white horses from Sicyon [i.e. San-branded]; he swaggers about the market-place with three or four acolytes, describing goblets and drinking-horns and offering-bowls loud enough for the passers-by to hear.(21.158)

Even here, however, we can see the consumption of hardware being reattached to the discourse of bodily appetites: the physical 'consuming' of drink and sex.

Such brief excerpts only highlight the general absence of the discourse of the consumption of goods, so familiar from other eras and other cultures, in classical Athens. Both Plato in *Protagoras* and Xenophon in *Symposium* describe visits to the house of Callias in the years when he was supposed to be the richest man in Athens, but there is no description of the lavishness of his furniture or household goods. Instead the (implicit) focus is on his sponsoring of sophists in the former case and of elaborate entertainments by *mousourgoi* in the latter. Xenophon is more voluble in his description of Socrates' visit to the house of the courtesan Theodote:

> Socrates noticed that she was expensively adorned, and that her mother at her side was dressed and accoutred in a far from haphazard fashion; and she had a great many maids, attractive and hardly more shabby, and that in other respects too her household was maintained with no expense spared.(*Mem.* 3.11,4)

Athenian readers were probably supposed to interpret the very generalized lavishness of Theodote's household as wasted expenditure on the part of her *admirers*, and of one famous admirer in particular: Alcibiades. In this way expenditure on clothes and household goods is tied once more to the pleasures of the flesh. Likewise 'excessive' male clothing attracts comment inasmuch as it denotes an adulterer (*moichos*) or *kinaidos* (lewd effeminate): 'if a man is dolled up and wanders about at night he is a *moichos*.'[47]

---

[46] Theophrastus *Characters* 23.8 and 5.9, with Diggle ad locc. Diggle emends 'the couches' (*tas klinas*) to *skēnas*, 'booths'; for luxury bird-fancying, cf. P. Cartledge, 'Fowl play: a curious lawsuit in classical Athens', in Paul Cartledge, Paul Millett and Stephen Todd (eds.), *Nomos Essays in Athenian Law, Politics and Society* (Cambridge, 1990), 41–61; the tapestry is literally embroidered 'with Persians' (or 'with Persepolis', cf. Ath. 12.541ab, P. Briant, *From Cyrus to Alexander: A History of the Persian Empire*, (Winona Lake, Indiana, 2002) 208.

[47] Aristotle *Rhet.* 2.24, 7, cf. Aeschines 1.131. According to Phylarchus, 'among the Syracusans there was a law that a woman should not put on gold ornaments or wear bright-coloured dresses or have garments with purple borders unless she admitted she was a prostitute; he also says there was another law that a man might not make himself look beautiful (*kallōpizesthai*) or dress elaborately (*esthēti periergōi*) and conspicuously (*diallattousēi*) unless he confessed to being a *moichos* or a *kinaidos* and a free woman was prevented from going out after sunset unless as one about to commit adultery', *FgrHist*, 81 F 45, ap. Ath. 12. 521b.

The 'Severe Style' and Democratic Constraints on Consumption

Students of Athens have sometimes argued that the reason for the poverty of a discourse describing material luxury is that there was not much to describe: 'On voit l'extrême pauvreté de cette civilisation si ingénieuse, son pauvre luxe, son luxe des pauvres.'[48] One of the criticisms of the democratic Athenians made by the Old Oligarch is that their slaves and metics (resident aliens) are disrespectful. This, he infers, is because you cannot hit them. Why? Because if it was customary to hit a slave, you might hit an Athenian citizen by accident, for 'the attire of the people of Athens is no better than the dress of slaves and metics nor are they better looking in appearance.' Indeed throughout the Greek world men do seem to have undergone a dressing down in the course of the fifth century, 'the more prosperous bringing their way of life into line with the majority' as Thucydides puts it, adopting a simple severe 'classical' style of dress, consisting of a single piece of woollen cloth the *himation*, worn over a short shift, *chitōn*, or, preferably, nothing. That was in noted contrast to the archaic style of fine long linen *chitōnes* and long hair fitted with golden grasshoppers. Doubtless this was the result of a self-conscious Hellenic simplicity prompted by the struggles against Persia but also, as Thucydides indicates, of Spartan influence. But the effect was striking: 'The cloaks like the blue boiler suits of the Chinese in the 1970s suggest, to an outsider at any rate, an evenness and equality in dress.'[49]

As the Old Oligarch points out, the Athenian version of classical style may have been more 'democratic' than in other parts of Greece, but the democratic tax system also added to the constraints of fashion and ideology. The rich were tapped for their wealth through a system of 'liturgies' (*leitourgiai*) which included sponsorships of festival choruses (*khorēgiai*) and of warships (trierarchies). In addition, from 428 BC at the latest, they were expected to make contributions to occasional tax levies (*eisphorai*). There is still much dispute about the evolution of the system but it is clear that in the fifth century magistrates would nominate someone from some kind of 'rich list', and at a later date both citizens and resident aliens were required to submit property assessments (*timēmata*).[50] Those nominated for liturgies could nominate someone supposedly richer to take their place; if the substitute refused, the nominator could call his bluff by insisting on the bizarre process of *antidosis*, basically swapping properties with the supposedly wealthier man.

An equally, if not more, important factor was that Athens was a highly litigious polis, and judgements usually depended on large numbers of judge/juries—*dikastai*,

---

[48] Paul Veyne, quoting one of his students, *Le pain et le cirque* (Paris, 1976), 198.

[49] Pseudo-Xenophon 1.10, Thuc. 1.6,4, A. G. Geddes 'Rags and Riches: The Costume of Athenian Men in the Fifth Century Author(s)', *CQ*, 37 (1987), 307–31, at 313.

[50] Matthew Christ offers a recent discussion with relevant bibliography in 'The evolution of the *eisphora* in classical Athens', *CQ*, 57 (2007), 53–69.

the 'Wasps' of Aristophanes' comedy—selected from all citizens in the over-Thirties age-grade. Property was often at issue in such cases and opportunistic prosecutors (labelled *sykophantai*, 'fig-denouncers' [i.e. 'triviality-denouncers']) could often benefit even if they had no direct interest. In addition there were frequent confiscations of property by the state, imposed as a punishment, and inevitable disputes about whether a family of a miscreant was concealing his wealth in order to minimize losses. Without any official independent register of assets, tax and penalty avoidance was a major concern. How wealthy one *seemed* played a very important role in arguments about how wealthy one really was, producing a rich discourse on the epistemology of wealth with frequent references to the slippery distinction between visible (*phanera*) and invisible (*aphanēs*) property: 'Tax evasion was a way of life'.[51]

In other words, conspicuous consumption of material goods for one's own private pleasure was seriously disincentivized by the tax system and the judicial system. In fact, because of one famous series of confiscations, we may be able to move beyond discourse and get some idea of what kind of durables and semi-durables wealthy Athenians consumed at the end of the fifth century. In *c*.414 BC, the property of members of the elite denounced for mocking the Eleusinian Mysteries and vandalizing the statues of Hermes was confiscated and auctioned off. The state auctioneers, *Pōletai*, published marble inscriptions in Eleusis of what was sold and of the tithes paid to the goddesses from the sale, tithes from which the actual sale prices can be calculated. The inscriptions were known to writers of the Roman period such as the word-collector Pollux, and there was some excitement when fragments of the original inscriptions were rediscovered. When put alongside Pollux's information it seemed that the fragments even included the inventory relating to the sale of the property of Alcibiades, supposed to be not only one of the wealthiest but also one of the most extravagant Athenians of the fifth century.

Disappointment followed. There were, to be sure, plenty of cloaks, blankets, rugs, pillows, couches, chairs, tables, pots, and pans, but nothing special, and when the prices were worked out most of it was amazingly cheap. Ordinary couches were valued at around 6 drachmas, the top-end 'Milesian-made' couches about 8 drachmas. The most valuable item in fact was a pair of doors (doors counted as furniture) at 23 drachmas 1 obol, closely followed by a chest for somewhat more than 21 drachmas. As W. K. Pritchett, the editor of the inscriptions comments:

> Our record of the sale of confiscated furniture seems to show that there was little sense of personal luxury in Athens in the last quarter of the fifth century, even among men of wealth....Greek furniture makers knew how to make pieces that were costly as well as beautiful, but such elaborate products were not intended for private use. Stools of ebony, couches inlaid with ivory, chests of rare woods, tables

---

[51] Matthew R. Christ, *The Bad Citizen in Classical Athens* (Cambridge, 2006), 204, cf. 143–204 and id., 'Evolution...' nn. 13, 17, 56, V. Gabrielsen, '*Phanera* and *Aphanes Ousia* in Classical Athens', *Classica et Mediaevalia*, 36 (1986), 99–114.

with golden legs, and others covered with silver, are carefully listed as such in the temple inventories of Athens, Eleusis and Delos, but the furniture from the houses of the companions of Alkibiades was for the most part made simply of wood.

He detects in the sources 'a kind of distaste for any exhibit of private wealth, a distaste which must have been prevalent enough at the close of the Periclean age to influence even the circle of Alkibiades in its manner of living.'—a *pauvre luxe* indeed.[52]

As Pritchett here indicates, the lack of private material luxury was balanced by extravagance in the religious sphere. If private houses were small and poorly furnished it only served to emphasize the grandeur of the houses of the gods, not least Pericles' Parthenon with its giant statue of Athena covered in ivory and gold. According to the same principle, if the wealthy generally eschewed lavish attire they were permitted to vaunt themselves when they had a role as sponsors of religious festival performances (*chorēgoi*), that 'public institution of games and sacrifices for all the days of the year with a decent pomp and furniture of the same by private men' as Pericles/Thucydides puts it in the Funeral Speech.

Xenophon in his *Oeconomicus* indicates that everyone would have 'festival clothing', in the women's quarters (9.5). Even the ostentatiously modest Demosthenes has a special outfit made for the choregic procession, which he insists on calling 'sacred apparel', including, apparently, a gold-embroidered *himation* prepared by a goldsmith in the *agora* (21.16, 22). We observe that when Demosthenes' enemy Meidias brings out his chariot harnessed to a pair of San-branded Sicyonian horses it is with the excuse, as even Demosthenes at first admits, of taking his wife to the Mysteries (ibid., 158); and when we are told that Alcibiades used to 'trail sea-purple robes through the agora' it is almost certainly because he was on his way to or from such an event; one could add to this list of the piously splendid or splendidly pious any number of decent Athenian matrons caught in possession of an expensive saffron-dyed *krokotos*. On these occasions personal luxury is termed 'brilliance' (*lamprotēs*) or 'appropriate magnificence' (*megaloprepeia*). On other occasions an individual so accoutred could be accused of *hubris* ('abusive arrogance'/ 'arrogant abuse'), a very serious crime, as myth tragedy and the law itself concurred, a crime moreover that could incur envy (*phthonos*) and the wrath of the gods.[53] The very existence of this kind of discourse often in the context of criticism or apology means that the appeal to piety did not provide complete protection, any more than an early modern man or woman could protect him/herself from accusations of luxurious adornment by appealing to the concept of 'Sunday Best', but the fact that the appeal to pious festality was so often available to be invoked on these occasions proves that it remained an effective alibi. One could easily argue therefore that, outside the festival context, there was a consequential moral, cultural and religious inhibition on this kind of personal material luxury in ancient Greece.

---

[52] W. K. Pritchett, 'The Attic *Stelai*: Part II', *Hesperia*, 25 (1956), 178–317, at 210.
[53] Plu., *Alc.* 16.1, Satyrus ap. Ath. 12.534c, cf. P. Wilson, *The Athenian Institution of the* Khoregia, (Cambridge, 2000), 98.

Conclusion: Greek Consumerism, Athenian Consumerism, Democratic Consumerism

What I have tried to do in this chapter is to present students of consumerism with some evidence for the character of consumption in a very particular time and place: the city-state of the Athenian democracy in the two centuries between about 500 and 300BC. I hope such a picture will be interesting and useful in itself simply for purposes of comparison, but I have also argued that this particular time and place should be especially interesting on a priori grounds: because of the place classical Athens holds in European / Western genealogies, because Athens was a democracy rather than a monarchy or an oligarchy, because it has been called the first 'full-fledged' 'money economy', because it was one of the first states with a large, permanent, central marketplace offering a wide range of goods. Unfortunately the data available is too impressionistic and fragmentary to offer anything amounting to a rounded and nuanced picture of the Athenian consumer, let alone of Athenian consumerism. What we can do is to present a picture of the general consumerscape, its topographies, distinctions, anxieties, emphases, and of a handful of real, fictional, or satirical consumers moving around that consumerscape.

Much of what we can find will be familiar but no less unexpected for that. Thucydides' version of Pericles' Funeral Speech, a speech supposed to have been delivered in 430 BC connects the marketplace directly to Athens's maritime supremacy (2.38), but already gives the wonderful accumulation of the world's goods in Athens an ideological significance that goes far beyond pride and convenience. For immediately before the sentence about the marketplace is a statement about politics, freedom and individualism:

> We have a form of government not fetched by imitation from the laws of our neighbouring states (nay, we are rather a pattern to others, than they to us) which, because in the administration it hath respect not to a few but to the multitude, is called a democracy...And we live not only free [*eleutherōs*] in the administration of the state but also one with another void of jealousy touching each other's daily course of life [*tōn kath'hēmeran epitēdeumatōn*], not offended at any man for following his own humour [*ei kath' hēdonēn ti drai*] ...[54]

As early as the mid-fifth century BC, therefore, shopping opportunities find a place at the heart of a celebration of what we might now call 'Western/democratic values'.

Other more or less contemporary discourses on the same theme from comic playwrights and the Old Oligarch introduce other familiar, albeit more negative, tropes, the marketplace as out of harmony with nature and the seasons, the marketplace as a threat to local culture and identity, the marketplace as a quintessentially urban space, a site of

---

[54] Thuc. 2.37,1–2, trans. Hobbes.

cheating and deceitfulness, of artificiality in opposition to the simplicity, honesty, and authenticity of the country.

When we move from generalization to facts, we do indeed find evidence that Athens possessed a remarkable shopping centre. It seems to have been huge, extending from the acropolis to the Dipylon Gate and beyond with a fixed permanent place for minute specializations—the myrtle-wreath market, the lupin-seed market, the ass-flesh market. We hear of only two other permanent marketplaces in all of the territory of Attica (*c*.1,000 square kilometres)—one in the harbour of Piraeus, one in Thorikos at the southern end of the peninsula—and sources imply that outside these areas Attica was a shopping-free zone—although this is *a priori* hard to believe and a little evidence, e.g. for an itinerant fishmonger and for 'local' *kapēleia* (taverns), complicates the picture. This extremely centralized marketplace depended upon and may have been produced by centralizing policies of the democracy: the organization of the people into ten tripartite *phylai*, composed of equal parts 'city', 'inland', and 'coastal' parishes, payments and penalties to encourage frequent visits to the centre to attend meetings, musters, scrutinies etc.

Alongside goods, from an early date and certainly by the end of the archaic period *c*.500 BC, there was a well-developed market for services: musical entertainers, cooks, and cooking-ware for hire, as well as teachers of music and letters and physical trainers attached to private gymnasia. The market was well-policed with numerous officials monitoring weights measures, and coinage as well as maximum prices for some goods and services, although where this can be tested, e.g. the maximum of 2 drachmas for hiring musical entertainers, it does not seem to have been very effective.

The marketplace, and in particular the formal *agora* to the north of the acropolis demarcated as such with boundary-stones, had a more than merely geographical centrality in the democratic city. It was also the site for democratic institutions, notably the people's law courts and the Council of 500 (citizens annually selected by lot). This mingling of civic business with trade, like Parliament on Oxford Street, was seen as itself democratic; comic playwrights frequently played upon the spatial overlap and philosophers of an anti-democratic tendency, such as Plato, worried about it, proposing a quite separate non-commercial civic *agora*.

In this context, the to-us-very-familiar linking of democracy and the marketplace produces some rather less familiar tropes. Whereas citizens of oligarchic poleis such as Sparta avoided the marketplace and were indeed forbidden from bringing purchased food to their dining-clubs, the citizens of the democracy were *expected* to while away long hours there, different groups meeting in different shops: the Striplings at the perfume, Socrates and co. at Simon's shoe-shop. In the fourth century, Aristogiton could be criticized for *not* attending, his absence cited as proof that he is *ameiktos* (unmingled). Comic playwrights often introduce political rhetoric into the marketplace, especially the fish-market: high prices are compared to Persian royal tributes, one speaker claims it is 'undemocratic' for one man to buy so much fish. The joke, of course, is the anomalousness of the rhetoric and of the cheapening of political discourse. But shopping also finds its way into political discourses of a rather more serious intent as proof of ill-gotten gains, corruption, treachery, and conspiracy. The least we can say is that the marketplace is presented as a zone of free informal democratic participation, but it is clear, reading between the lines, that it was also presented as a place where one was always being watched.

When we turn from the marketplace and the goods available to be consumed to the discourse of consumption itself, one striking feature is the emphasis on consuming in the most literal sense, i.e. eating and drinking as well as the consumption of sexual services and products. In the same way and in contrast with other famous shopping cities in the historical record there is much less than we might expect on material luxury: furnishings and dress.

We need to be careful about the conclusions we draw from this deficiency. What is missing from discourse may not be missing from life. It may be that there was simply more anxiety about the pleasures of the flesh or that the discourse of wasteful expenditure, of consuming estates, preferred to focus on the literal consuming of more evanescent goods, most bizarrely of fresh fish. There is no sign of anything like a dictatorship of fashion in the field of semi-durables in classical Athens nor therefore for the ideas of outmodedness, obsolescence, and waste. Material luxury may well have been, and often clearly was, viewed as a store of, rather than as a drain on, household wealth.

On the other hand, the inscriptions that record the property of the Herm-bashers, including the notorious dandy Alcibiades, indicate that there was little conspicuous consumption of material goods among the elite in the late fifth century; there really was a 'poverty of luxury'. A few references to conspicuous consumption in the field of armour, saddlery and horses, and of festal attire are exceptions that prove the rule, inasmuch as all these things could be considered as consumption in the service of the state and the gods.

A number of reasons could be adduced for this inhibition: a general cultural moral inhibition centred on the concept of *hubris* as promulgated in myth, poetry, and tragedy; a move to Spartan-influenced simplicity among mainland Greeks after *c.*480, a self-conscious change of style that was reflected in Thucydides' comments about the more luxurious style of a previous generation and literary references to the '*archaia truphe* [luxurious self-indulgence of earlier times]', most notably in a whole genre of anecdotes about the effete citizens of Sybaris (*sybaritikoi logoi*), a city destroyed at the end of the archaic period (*c.*510 BC). It seems very likely that this change to a more severe classical style was also driven by a self-conscious opposition of Greek simplicity to Eastern luxury, a contrast that intensified in the 490s and 480s during the period of the Persian invasions, when those who affected Persian style were suspected of harbouring Persian sympathies—the accusation of 'medizing' covers both. For since Athens's archaic tyrants or dictators, the Pisistratid family, had allied with the Persians and indeed had sought to return in the wake of the Persian invasion force of 490, medizing became a potent accusation in the internal politics of Athens, connected with undemocratic tyrannical tendencies. In addition to this national-democratic ideological opposition to material luxury, the democracy provided straightforward financial disincentives, since those who *seemed* wealthy could be required to pay taxes and to perform expensive services (*leitourgiai*) for the state in the form of sponsoring triremes or festivals. It was also believed that the rich were vulnerable to 'malicious prosecution' (*sykophantia*) in the people's courts.

Therefore, alongside the remarkably precocious linkages between democracy, freedom, individualism, and shopping opportunities that seem to be part of some kind of universalizing or at least very familiar discourse, it is also easy to argue that the peculiarities of the Athenian consumerscape were the consequence of locally contingent conditions: recent history, politics, taxes, laws, and wars.

Finally, although the metaphor of consuming was frequently extended to consumption of sexual services on the one hand and to the 'gobbling up' of property on the other, there is little evidence that it was ever extended to 'the purchase and use' of semi-durables such as household furnishings and clothes. This may be more than simply a failure to extend a metaphor. Athenian lists of property consistently place productive utensils and e.g. slaves who manufacture things to be sold in the marketplace alongside non-productive slaves, non-productive property, and wealth, without discrimination. Moreover production was, on the whole, of a very simple nature and therefore the movement from domestic production to commercial production—from e.g. making clothes for the household to making clothes for the market, growing food for the household to growing food for sale—was both an easy transition in practice and also unremarkable. This raises a very big question and reconnects the subject of consumption to the study of the ancient economy as a whole (and the extensive scholarship on the subject). It raises the question of how any particular consumerscape relates to any particular producer-scape and ownerscape. I have no intention of answering this enormous question in the current chapter but I suggest that the key issue here is the degree to which production in any given culture and society presents a different face, the degree to which it is Other to the rest of society, or even the degree to which production is elaborately structured, obnoxious, separable, and indeed separated from the rest of the community. The classical Athenians certainly categorized some kinds of tradespeople as *banausoi* (roughly, 'people who work sitting down at a furnace'), and metal-workers, potters, and fullers clearly belonged to a different sphere of the community from an early date. But more research needs to be done on the historical construction of the opposition of obnoxious production to amenable consumption. I suggest that the very concept of consumption as we now understand it depends upon that opposition in the first place.

BIBLIOGRAPHY

Bresson, Alain, *L'économie de la Grèce des cités*. II *Les espaces de l'échange* (Paris, 2008)

Cartledge, Paul, Edward E. Cohen and Lin Foxhall (eds.), *Money Labour and Land: Approaches to the Economies of Ancient Greece* (London, 2002)

Davidson, J. *Courtesans and Fishcakes: The Consuming Passions of Classical Athens* (London, 1997)

Geddes, A. G., 'Rags and Riches: The Costume of Athenian Men in the Fifth Century', *CQ*, 37 (1987), 307–31

Harris, Edward M., 'Workshop, marketplace and household', in Paul Cartledge, Edward E. Cohen and Lin Foxhall (eds.), *Money Labour and Land: Approaches to the Economies of Ancient Greece* (London, 2002), 67–99

Kallet, Lisa, 'The Athenian Economy', in L. J. Samons II (ed.), *Cambridge Companion to the Age of Pericles* (Cambridge, 2007), 70–95

Millett, Paul, 'The Economy', in R. Osborne (ed.), *Classical Greece* (Oxford, 2000), 23–51

Möller, Astrid, 'Classical Greece: Distribution', in Walter Scheidel, Ian Morris and Richard Saller (eds.), *The Cambridge Economic History of the Greco-Roman World* (Cambridge, 2007), 362–84

Mossé, Claude 'The Economist', in J-P Vernant (ed.), *The Greeks* (Chicago, 1995), 23–52

Reden, Sitta von, 'Classical Greece: Consumption', in Walter Scheidel, Ian Morris and Richard Saller (eds.) *The Cambridge Economic History of the Greco-Roman World* (Cambridge, 2007), 385–406

Wycherley, R. E. *The Athenian Agora* III. *Literary and Epigraphical Testimonia* (Princeton, 1957).

CHAPTER 3

....

THINGS IN BETWEEN: SPLENDOUR AND EXCESS IN MING CHINA

....

CRAIG CLUNAS

WHEN in 1491 the teenage Italian aristocrat Beatrice d'Este went out shopping, 'in order to buy those things which are available in the city', and ended up brawling in the streets with local market women, it was a rare and startling enough event for the Duke of Milan to record it in a letter to her older sister.[1] But his tone (and that of Isabella d'Este's reply) is one of jocularity, recording a form of transgressive fun which was *so* far from the way an aristocratic woman might be expected to acquire and to consume that it posed no threat at all to the status of Beatrice or of her companions. Just as high-spirited and equally transgressive, but ultimately seen as more troubling and disruptive of a proper order of things, was the behaviour of Zhu Houzhao, born in the very year of Beatrice's escapade, who reigned as emperor of the Ming dynasty (1368–1644) from 1505 to 1521, under the reign title Zhengde, 'Upright Virtue'. The title is more than usually ironic, since in the historical record controlled by the Chinese bureaucratic elite Zhu Houzhao is firmly nailed down as a Bad Emperor, one whose memory is associated more with exotic foreign concubines, louche monks and thuggish drinking companions, cripplingly expensive and rapacious touring of his domains, inappropriate fondness for militaristic posturing, and even rumours of conversion to Islam, than it is with rectitude in government.[2] An 'unofficial history' of his reign gathers together a number of the more lurid anecdotes about

---

[1] Evelyn Welch, *Shopping in the Renaissance* (New Haven and London: Yale University Press, 2005), 19–20.

[2] James Geiss, 'The Cheng-te reign, 1506–1521', in Frederick W. Mote and Denis Twitchett (eds.), *The Cambridge History of China*, Vol. 7: *The Ming Dynasty, 1368–1644, Part I* (Cambridge: Cambridge University Press, 1988), 403–39.

his behaviour, including one which has him turning the world upside down in a most startling way:

> He once wandered over to the Baohe Store [a palace storehouse], and ordered his eunuchs to display at its door all the goods it contained, while he dressed in a shop-keeper's garb, with a melon-shaped hat on his head, and in all the Six Stores from the Baohe to the Baoyan he carried out trading with an account book and abacus in hand, bawling and questioning like who knows what. And he also ordered them to set up a market place to go along with this, with a crowd of stallholders, the stallholders being those eunuchs who kept wine shops in the [palace] lanes. Amidst the racket of every musical instrument, he placed himself right among the tavern women, who came out and dragged at the sleeves of the customers who entered in swarms...All the market place sports such as tumbling monkeys, tricks on horseback, cockfighting, and hunting with dogs were gathered all around, with palace women 'at the balustrades' [a euphemism for prostitution], playing at urging people to drink, and he was so drunk that he slept where he was, carrying on with this for several days.[3]

Between playing at shopping and playing at shops, pretending to buy and pretending to sell, there seems to lie a world of difference. This world of difference could too easily be spun into another thread in the faded old tapestry of absolute antithesis between East and West, with the latter joyously embracing the rich possibilities of the world of goods, while the former is stuck in a place where only the worst of rulers would embrace the abjection of a shopkeeper's hat and the tools of commerce, or would befoul the sacred precincts of the imperial palace with the clamour of the marketplace. The spatial opposition between young Beatrice roaming out of the castle into the vibrant streets of Milan and the simulacral debauchery involved in having to bring pretend streets into the space of a cloistered young man could also too easily be invoked as a metaphor for the opposition between an outward-looking West, on the verge in 1491 of the Age of Discovery, and a China about to be discovered, immured behind its mental and actual walls. There is a sense in which this dichotomy between a vibrant, consuming West, and a fecund, productive, but unconscious East is one of the classic orientalist tropes, feeding into European discussions of consumption from the early modern period itself and not wholly expunged today. More recent work, which will be discussed towards the end of this essay, suggests a required revisiting of this issue.

However, like many orientalist tropes, there are some indigenous strands in its DNA. If the historian chooses to take this line about China, it would be too easy to point to canonical texts of political economy which were known to all educated people in the Ming period, which retained relevance into the twentieth century, and which structured society into the *si min*, 'four categories of the people', a hierarchy which ran downwards from 'officials' at the top through 'peasants' and 'artisans' to 'merchants' at the bottom.[4]

---

[3] Anonymous, *Ming Wuzong waiji*, Zhongguo lishi yanjiu shiliao congshu edn (Shanghai: Shanghai shudian, 1982), 13.

[4] Craig Clunas, *Empire of Great Brightness: Visual and Material Cultures of Ming China* (London: Reaktion Books, 2007), 141–4. For twentieth-century use see Karl Gerth, *China Made: Consumer Culture and the Creation of the Nation* (Cambridge MA and London: Harvard University Asia Center, 2003), 161.

With the former two categories seen as the *ben*, the 'roots' of the social order, the latter two were seen as the *mo*—the word means 'branches', but carries connotations of twigginess and insubstantiality. Or at least such was the theoretical model, which cast the makers of things and even more those who arranged to move them from makers to consumers as disposable or inessential. But despite the horror of the chronicler's censorious gaze, there is plenty of evidence that in Ming China the enjoyment of the fruits of commerce was not so frowned upon as the texts of orthodox morality and political economy might imply. If we read the texts written as funerary eulogies for certain contemporaries by the Ming dynasty calligrapher, writer and painter Wen Zhengming (1470–1559), we get a sense of the complexities through which trade, commodities, and social status were mutually intertwined. Wen was from an elite landowning background, a native of the great commercial city of Suzhou, one of the economic powerhouses of the Ming economy, with a reputation for high-quality textile production which was some centuries old. In 1532 he was commissioned to write a eulogy for one of its textile merchants, Shi Han (1458–1532), whose 'father raised up the family through hemp and silk, it became even wealthier with him, and the business became more flourishing. Their caps and belts, robes and shoes covered the empire, and they were praised whenever patterned weaves were mentioned'. Seven years later he wrote about a man named Shen Xiang (1479–1539), whom he confesses he has never met, but of whom he writes:

> At the age of eighteen he crossed the Yangtze, travelled into Huai and Si, progressed through Yan and Ji to Beijing before returning. Wherever he went he inquired into the prices of goods, aimed at an accordance with the fashion, and was known as an excellent trader between the Yangtze and Huai rivers.

We then hear how Master Shen bought land and how 'his silk, lacquer and rush matting were carried to the four directions', how he grew mulberries for silk and fine teas until 'after several years he was praised for his success at enriching himself'.[5] The reason the families of Shi Han and Shen Xiang were willing to pay for Wen Zhengming's eulogies of their deceased members lay in his reputation as a cultural luminary; he came from a family with members of the 'official' class (highest of the four types of people), and he had himself held a fairly lowly but locally very prestigious position in the imperial capital, where he had worked on the official chronicle of the reign of the Zhengde emperor. Thus he may have even had a hand in the drafting of the passage quoted above, detailing Zhu Houzhao's social cross-dressing and general failure to behave. Between the chronicle's horror and Wen's celebration of commercial acumen lies a vast range of attitudes to the relationship between things and people in the Ming textual record, one which cannot be reduced to a simple characterization of Ming China as being 'pro' or 'anti' commercial prosperity and its concomitant consumption practices.

What is highly likely (though ultimately unprovable) is that Ming China had by 1500 more stuff to think about, or even to think with, than the rest of the world.

---

[5] Craig Clunas, *Elegant Debts: The Social Art of Wen Zhengming, 1470–1559* (London: Reaktion Books, 2004), 115.

The enormous quantities of surviving Ming material culture, which are continuously being augmented by archaeology (since people were buried with goods for use in the afterlife), range from secular and religious buildings, the paintings and calligraphy produced and consumed by the elite, through printed books, furniture, metalwork, textiles, jewellery, carving in a variety of materials from jade to bamboo, ceramics to weapons and tools. There are of course differential rates of survival; Ming textiles are much less common than Ming ceramics, which fill the museums and private collections of the world, and are found in archaeological contexts from Prague to California, East Africa to Australia. The famous blue and white porcelain of the huge factories of Jingdezhen could be thought of as the very first global 'brand'.[6] However, and despite the survival of so much of the material culture of the Ming period (still only a tiny fraction of what was produced at the time), we have no real means of studying consumption behaviour in any of the ways which would be acceptable today to economic or social historians. What we have instead, to set alongside surviving objects of consumption themselves, are a vast range of representations of consumption, in both texts and images. These representations exist alongside and interact with the similarly large range of representations of social status and of good and bad forms of behaviour, in ways which allow us to perceive how the complex of activities and agencies which we now bundle together under the rubric of 'early modern Chinese consumption' appeared to contemporaries.

The representation of the variety and profusion of commodities available in the marketplace is a theme which long predates the Ming period, for example being prominent in the literature of nostalgia written around the fallen Southern Song capital of Hangzhou after the Mongol conquest of 1279.[7] It is a cliché of the writing of those early foreign visitors to China who recorded their impressions, from Marco Polo to Ibn Battuta in the thirteenth and fourteenth centuries. Within the Ming period itself it certainly predates the late Ming (generally dated from after c.1550), which has been the focus of most of the recent scholarship to be discussed below. Dialogues in a handbook of the spoken Chinese language which was already circulating in fifteeenth- or even late fourteenth-century Korea assume that the foreigner visiting Beijing will need an extensive vocabulary in order to cope with the range of things available in the market.

---

[6] Robert Batchelor, 'On the Movement of Porcelains: Rethinking the Birth of Consumer Society as Interactions of Exchange Networks, 1600–1750', in John Brewer and Frank Trentmann (eds.), *Consuming Cultures, Global perspectives: Historical Trajectories, Transnational Exchanges* (London: Berg, 2006), 95–122. Timothy Brook, *Vermeer's Hat: The Seventeenth Century and the Dawn of the Global World* (London: Profile Books, 2008), 54–83.

[7] Jacques Gernet, *Daily Life in China: on the Eve of the Mongol Invasion, 1250–1276* (London: Allen & Unwin, 1962), originally published in French in 1959. Gernet worked from 1955 to 1976 as Director of Studies in the 6th Section of the École pratique des hautes études, founded by Fernand Braudel in 1947. <http://www.efeo.fr/biographies/notices/gernet.htm>, accessed 7 September 2009. Peter Burke, *The French Historical Revolution: The Annales School 1929–89* (Cambridge: Polity, 1990), 100. Craig Clunas, 'Trade Goods, Commodities and Collectables: Some Ways of Categorising Material Culture in Sung-Yuan Texts', in Maxwell K. Hearn and Judith G. Smith (eds.), *Arts of the Sung and Yuan* (New York: Metropolitan Museum of Art, 1996): 45–56.

WANG: Elder Brother who sells satin, [do you have]: sky-blue sleeveless jackets, willow-blue knee-wraps, duck green edging with clouds, parrot-green floral designs; dark-green heavenly flowers inlaid with eight treasures, grass-green-bees flying around plum blossoms, green cypress with flowers of the four seasons, onion-white clouds; peach-red capes; blood-red peony with entwined branches, glittering yellow Chinese writing brush flowers, goose-yellow with four clouds, willow-yellow threaded with colourful male phoenixes, musk-deer brown knee-wraps, moxa-brown jade bricks and steps, shimmering honey-browns, eagle-back-brown hippocampus, and dark tea-brown flowers? Do you have all these types of thick silks and thin silks?

SHOPKEEPER: Customer, do you want it from Nanjing, from Hangzhou, from Suzhou?[8]

The casual trumping of the customer's list of types with the offer of three centres of production (and this is only one of many such litanies of goods in the text) builds up a picture in the reader of China as an almost inexhaustible source of profusion and variety in the material world. 'See China and buy stuff' is one of its central messages, or certainly the central task for which it assumes a reader needs to be equipped. Whether it be kinds of bows, kinds of dishes, or the huge list of things to be taken back to Korea for sale there, a list which begins with 'one hundred pounds of red tassels' and ends up with copies of *The Romance of the Three Kingdoms* (a popular historical novel), quantity and variety of goods are central to the construction of 'China' and to the experience of going there as a consumer.[9]

The concepts of 'consumption', 'consuming', and 'the consumer' are however as anachronistic as they are in the case of Europe at this same period of history, and are alien to the discourse of goods in texts and images of the Ming period, whether those generated inside the empire itself or those imposed on it by outside observers. The modern Chinese word for 'consumption', *xiaofei*, is likely in its present sense to be a neologism of the late nineteenth to early twentieth century, and like so much of the vocabulary of the social sciences in modern Chinese it may well be a loan word from Japanese.[10] What we do find in Ming texts are ways of talking about what we now call 'consumption' in ways which are either negative or positive, but which are never detached from a discourse of morality, of good (or bad) governance, and ultimately of a universal order which links humanity and its actions to wider cosmic matters of harmony or disjointedness. Thus words like *sheng*, 'prosperity', or *fan*, 'splendour', are essentially a good thing, as visible and material manifestations of a world well ruled. These are the words which appear in the titles of two paintings of urban scenes, now rare survivals of a genre which was

[8] Svetlana Rimsky-Korsakoff Dyer, *Grammatical Analysis of the* Lao Ch'i-ta: *With an English Translation of the Chinese Text* (Canberra: Faculty of Asian Studies Australian National University, 1983), 430–1. I have made minimal alterations to the translation.

[9] Rimsky-Korsakoff Dyer, *Grammatical Analysis of the* Lao Ch'i-ta, 351–4. On listing see Clunas, *Empire of Great Brightness*, 112–36, 'Pictures in the Chinese Encyclopaedia: Image, Category and Knowledge'.

[10] Luo Zhufeng (ed.), *Hanyu da cidian*, 2nd edition (Shanghai: Shanghai Dictionaries Press, 2001), Vol. 5b, 1206.

probably once much more common. One, entitled *The Splendour of the Imperial Capital* (*Huang du ji sheng tu*) shows the northern imperial capital of Beijing, while the other, entitled *Thriving Southern Capital* (*Nan du fan hui tu juan*) is of the secondary southern capital of Nanjing.[11] Neither is dated, though both were probably painted around 1600, when the textual record also registers a heightened interest in goods, in selling, and getting. In the former scroll, numerous tradesman can be seen exposing their wares for sale outside the gates of the imperial city, some in substantial booths, some on mats spread on the ground. We see sellers of stationery, of books, of antiques, of locks and other small metal items, of combs, of Buddhist images, and of socks, as well as strolling vendors of feather fans, of towels, of old clothes. We see numerous buyers, Ming *flâneurs*, though all of them are male, and the space of shopping is portrayed as an entirely homosocial one (no room for a Chinese Beatrice here). The Nanjing scroll is dominated by a religious festival procession, which is being watched, one might even say consumed, as a spectacle by a large audience, with men and boys at street level, and women and girls watching from the balconies of buildings. Many of these buildings are in fact shops, and several carry prominent banners advertising the goods and services available there: shops for grain, for leather goods, for gold and pearls, and one offering to supply (according to its signage) 'All the Goods of the Eastern and Western Oceans'. It is worth remarking that the visual evidence of such scrolls is purely on the positive side of the debate, where 'splendour' and 'prosperity' are unequivocally good.

The negative side of consumption is conveyed in the Ming in words, by a totally different vocabulary, that of *chi*, 'wastefulness; excess', and *she*, 'luxury; extravagance'. These negative terms could be applied to exactly the same phenomena as are elsewhere praised as indexes of 'prosperity', and sometimes by the same people. It is this moralizing literature of complaint over 'excess' and 'extravagance' which has formed a mainstay of modern historical writing about the late Ming period in China as one of a rising consumer culture, and which is extensively quoted in what have by now become the key works in the debate. A small sample will be sufficient to give a flavour:

> The customs of the present age have reached an extreme of extravagance, they are 'different every month and dissimilar every season'...Nowadays the wealth and goods of the empire are concentrated in the capital, yet half of them are produced in the south-east. (Zhang Han [1511–93], *Treatise on Merchants*)[12]

The same author complains in another text, in which we see clearly the linkage of anxiety over inappropriate consumption behaviour and instability of the social order:

> The dynasty has clear regulations for the dress and ornaments of women of official families...As times changed and customs became more lavish, people all set their

[11] Both scrolls are illustrated in *A Journey into China's Antiquity*: Vol. 4: *Yuan Dynasty, Ming Dynasty, Qing Dynasty* (Beijing: Morning Glory Publishers, 1997), and discussed in Wang Zhenghua, 'Guoyan fanhua—Wan Ming chengshi tu, chengshi guan, yu wenhua xiaofei de yanjiu', in Li Xiaodi (ed.), *Zhongguo de chengshi shenghuo* (Taipei: Lianjing chubanshe, 2005), 1–57.

[12] Translated in Timothy Brook, 'The Merchant Network in 16th Century China', *Journal of the Economic and Social History of the Orient*, 24 (1981), 165–214.

resolve on venerating riches and excess and, as if they no longer knew there were clear prohibitions, rather set about trampling on them...Nowadays men dress in brocaded and embroidered silks, and women ornament themselves with gold and pearls, in a case of boundless extravagance which flouts the regulations of the state. (Zhang Han [1511–93], 'Account of the Hundred Crafts')[13]

One of the longest and most detailed jeremiads against the new tyranny of fashion is found in the work of another late sixteenth-century writer, Fan Lian:

Customs go quickly from sound to flimsy, like the irreversible falling downwards of the rivers. It has been regretted since ancient times. Our Songjiang was always called extravagant, dissolute, crafty and overbearing in custom and already had no chance of a reversal to soundness and simplicity. Together with that, from the Jiajing and Longqing reigns [1522–72] on, powerful and high-ranking houses have led the way in extravagance and excess. Those who wear ceremonial sashes and scholars' caps excel in craftiness and arrogance. Every day they give rise to strange stories, every year they start a hundred new enterprises. (Fan Lian [b. 1540], 'Eyewitness Record of Songjiang')[14]

The meticulous detail with which Fan Lian catalogues in this text the detailed changes in men's hats and gowns, in women's hairdos, and in dozens of other forms of luxury from foodstuffs to the special picnic boxes which contained them, suggests a fascination at least as great as the distaste which is his ostensible motivation for writing. Clothing, and the shift from frugality to extravagance is also the focus of complaint in the writing of a man from a third urban centre, Yangzhou:

In the Hongzhi and Zhengde eras [1488–1521] it was still the style to esteem agriculture and devote oneself to practical matters. Most gentry living at home wore clothes of simple weave and hats of plain black fabric. Students prided themselves in the study of texts; they also wore plain robes and unadorned footwear...Now the young dandies in the villages say that even silk gauze is not good enough and lust for Suzhou embroideries, Song-style brocades, cloudlike gauzes, and camel serge, clothes high in price and quite beautiful. (Chen Yao [jinshi degree in 1535])[15]

Quotations of this type could be (and have been) multiplied from a range of Ming authors, and complaints of this type must form a reasonably large percentage, perhaps even the majority, of the archive of Ming discourse concerning the issues we would now bracket as 'consumption'. Much rarer in the Ming textual record, so much rarer that it was over 50 years ago the subject of a special study by the economic historian Liensheng Yang, is the 'uncommon idea' that lavishness and luxury are of positive benefit to the body politic. Lu Ji (1515–52) deployed a rather modern-looking argument, hinting

---

[13] Translated in Craig Clunas, *Superfluous Things: Material Culture and Social Status in early Modern China* (Cambridge: Polity Press, 1991), 153–4.

[14] Translated in John Meskill, *Gentlemanly Interests and Wealth on the Yangtze Delta* (Ann Arbor: Association for Asian Studies, 1994), 142 (with romanization amended to Pinyin).

[15] Translated in Timothy Brook, *The Confusions of Pleasure: Commerce and Culture in Ming China* (Berkeley/Los Angeles/London: University of California Press, 1998), 220.

at though not explicitly stating Mandeville's 'private vices and public virtues' of some 150 years later, to the effect that more economic activity was a good thing, and that one man's lavish spending was another man or men's employment opportunity. He begins:

> Those who discourse on government as a rule wish to prohibit extravagance, assuming that restricting spending will enrich the people. However, as an early worthy has observed, as to the wealth produced by Heaven and earth there is a fixed amount. One person's loss becomes the gain of another. I do not see how extravagance is capable of impoverishing the whole world.[16]

Unusual as this argument may be in Ming terms, it shares with critique the fact that it is part of a discourse around consumption, rather than material for the study of it. It tells us what contemporaries thought was happening, and what they thought about what they thought was happening. It does not tell us what was happening, or at least it does so only partially. And in fact we may have to accept that the material will never exist for a satisfactory study of 'consumption in Ming China', since the kind of historical evidence on which such an argument could be based does not and never did exist. That does not mean that the discourse of 'prosperity' (and its dark side, 'extravagance') is of no importance, but it is important that we understand the evidence for what it is, and not try to shoehorn it into a set of categories in which it can never be effectively meaningful.

Pictures of prosperous cityscapes and polemics about silken trousers are far from being the only material we have, but we have very little (especially by comparison with early modern Europe) of the evidence which would allow us to tie specific acts of consumption to specific individuals. In what has been cited above, it is always the faceless and generic consumer who goes overboard for the flashy novelty. Although, as mentioned above, Ming tombs (which necessarily contain named individuals) do to a degree link some specific people with some specific things, the set of practices around burial goods are too distinctive to give much insight into lifetime behaviour. What gives an edge, in terms of specificity, to work on sixteenth- and seventeenth-century Europe is the distinctively European practice of the will and the inventory, usually associated with death and the transfer of property. To regret their absence in the Chinese context is most definitely *not* to subscribe to classic orientalist notions that China lacked a concept of private property, it is simply to acknowledge that private property generated a different range of scribal and individual practices and forms of record-keeping. Thus something like the *Diary from the Water-Tasting Studio* (*Wei shui xuan ri ji*) kept from 1609 to 1616 by Li Rihua (1565–1635) is an unusually valuable testimony, given that it appears to have been maintained as a purely personal record (it was not published until centuries later). Li was typical of the urban-based land-owning class, living in one of the commercially developed cities of the lower Yangtze region, who entered the imperial bureaucracy through the examination system.[17]

---

[16] Lien-sheng Yang, 'Economic Justification for Spending—An Uncommon idea in Traditional China', *Harvard Journal of Asiatic Studies*, 20 (1957), 36–52.

[17] Biography in L. Carrington Goodrich and Chaoying Fang (eds.), *Dictionary of Ming Biography, 1368–1644*, 2 vols. (New York and London: Columbia University Press, 1976), 826–30.

His diary does give us some sense of what a male member of the late Ming elite thought it was appropriate to record about what we would call his own consumption behaviour, and it is particularly interesting to set it alongside a list which Li produced in a more public context, and which he titled, 'A Ranking of Antique Objects'.[18] In this context 'antique' does not have to mean chronologically old, but is also itself a type of moral value, embodying a sense that the object so described materializes elite values of engagement with antiquity (*gu*) as a cultural category. The list begins not surprisingly with the most valued (and commercially valuable) of antiquities in the Ming art market, 'Calligraphic pieces of the Jin and Tang dynasties', then proceeds through 'Paintings of the Five Dynasties' to various other categories of calligraphy and painting, which between them take up the first ten rankings on the list. Only at number 11 do we get 'Brilliant examples of bronze vessels and red jades before the Qin and Han', followed by more jades, inkstones, Qin zithers and swords, early printed books, 'Strange rocks of a rugged and picturesque type', other types of plant, then exotic imports such as 'Imported spice of a subtle kind', 'Foreign treasures of a rare and beautiful kind', foodstuffs such as 'Excellent tea well prepared', 'Rare and delicious food from overseas', and ending up with 'Shiny fine white porcelain and mysterious coloured pottery, old and new'. A coda adds (and here we get objects which are certainly not 'antique' in the colloquial English sense):

> In addition to these, white rice and green dishes, and cotton robes and rattan canes are exquisite objects for the literati to use. They should be aware of the ranking of these objects, like the ranking of scholars in the Lingyan Hall of the Han Dynasty, which was arranged by the wisdom of a just ruler.[19]

The analogy between ranking things and ranking people is made very explicit here, and is repeated in a number of Ming texts (and not just Ming texts, it both precedes and post-dates the Ming as a practice). Arguably, the 'master ranking' of Ming culture was that of the examination system, through the results of which elite males were selected for entry to the imperial bureaucracy; it tested both classical textual knowledge and awareness of policy issues, and provided a template for all sorts of listings.[20] But this analogy also cannot be allowed to pass without drawing attention to one very important aspect of Ming thinking about these matters, which is very significant in the light of some of the recent theorizing about material culture studies, and in particular the issue of the boundaries between things and persons.[21] For Li Rihua, as indeed for all Ming intellectuals (we are much less well informed about popular understandings of the issue), the category *wu*, which has the modern dictionary meaning of 'things', necessarily includes

---

[18] Translated in Chu-tsing Li, 'The Artistic Theories of the Literati', in Chu-tsing Li and James C. Y. Watt (eds.), *The Chinese Scholar's Studio: Artistic Life in the Late Ming Period* (New York: Thames and Hudson, 1987), 14–22, at 15–16.

[19] Li, 'The Artistic Theories of the Literati', 16

[20] Clunas, *Empire of Great Brightness*, 132–6.

[21] For a review of the topic see Frank Trentmann, 'Materiality in the Future of History: Things, Practices and Politics', *Journal of British Studies*, 48 (2009), 283–307.

within it living things, and most definitely encompasses the category of *ren*, 'humanity'. As one earlier writer put it:

> There is a thing (*wu*) of one thing. There is a thing of ten things. There is a thing of a hundred things. There is a thing of a thousand things. There is a thing of ten-thousand things. There is a thing of a million things. There is a thing of a billion things. Isn't man the thing of a billion things?

The explicit point of this passage, as its modern exegetes point out, is the unity of man with other forms of materiality, and the fact that 'it is precisely because man is a thing that he can know things so well'.[22]

What then can Li Rihua's diary tell us of the interaction between a specific man and things in the late Ming period? In fact, and unsurprisingly, there is a reasonably good overlap between the categories on his formal 'public' list and the types of object with which we see him interacting in the relative privacy of his diary. He makes extensive records of the visits of dealers to his house, and of his own visits to commodity contexts both grand and modest, where, as we might expect, it is the key categories of calligraphy (both actual writing and its preservation through rubbings), paintings, archaic bronzes and jades, and ceramics which make up the bulk of the things described in varying degrees of detail.[23] We also see him buy, or consider buying, books, and carvings in wood, rhinoceros horn, agate, and amber. Some categories of purchase are of things not on the list, but very much within the ambit of taste in the 'antique'. We see him buying an ink-stone, which is measured and described in detail, and which he then tries out for the first time using a cake of ink manufactured by the celebrated and fashionable maker of such commodities, Fang Yulu (fl. 1570–1619).[24] He writes about buying gems, and visiting the shop of a gem-dealer who also deals in pictures.[25] On a number of occasions Li describes himself buying rocks and other things for his garden:

> Someone from Wukang brought forty rocks, the big ones like crouching lions, the small ones like creeping foxes; he exchanged them for rice and went away. I put them in the courtyard of the Meiyinxuan, and strolled among them from morning to night—something of the atmosphere of a mountain gully.[26]

---

[22] Kidder Smith Jr., Peter K. Bol, Joseph A. Adler and Don J. Wyatt, *Sung Dynasty Uses of the I Ching* (Princeton: Princeton University Press, 1990), 134. On the 'ten-thousand things' see Lothar Ledderose, *Ten Thousand Things: Module and Mass Production in Chinese Art* (Princeton: Princeton University Press, 2000).

[23] Craig Clunas, 'The Art Market in 17th Century China: the Evidence of the Li Rihua Diary', *History of Art and History of Ideas*, 1 (2003), 201–24. Craig Clunas, 'Commodity and Context: Wen Zhengming in the Late Ming Art Market', in Naomi Noble Richard and Donald E. Brix (eds.), *The History of Painting in East Asia: Essays on Scholarly Method*, Papers presented for an International Conference at National Taiwan University 4–7 October, 2002 (Taipei, 2008), 315–30 looks in detail at Li's engagement with the art of one earlier artist in a market context.

[24] Li Rihua, *Wei shui xuan ri ji*, Song Ming Qing xiaopin wenji jizhu (Shanghai, 1996), 17, [Wanli 37/3/30].

[25] Li Rihua, 23, [Wanli 37/5/17].

[26] Li Rihua, 533, [Wanli 44/5/24; for other rock purchases (some for the desk rather than the garden) see 79, [Wanli 38/2/5], 109, [Wanli 38/6/13].

And once he bought a talking parrot, from the more southerly coastal province of Fujian, a very expensive purchase, but the bird died of the cold after a month.[27]

Li records interaction with foreign rarities (which presumably fall under the rubric of 'Foreign treasures of a rare and beautiful kind'); these include, alongside Japanese lacquer and Japanese metalwork, both much admired for their craftsmanship, what must be pieces of imported blue glassware, possibly Islamic or even Venetian, 'brought by barbarian ships from the south seas, things transformed in fire in a barbarian country'.[28] They also include a 'sea egg' brought by merchants from Guangdong province, a giant egg which is impressively hard and white but which disappointingly fails to glow in the dark. Although Li speculates that it is the egg of a dragon, an ostrich sounds like a more likely source.[29]

It is therefore the case that almost the only 'things' which are culturally visible to Li Rihua are the things which now come into the categories of 'artworks', including 'decorative arts' or 'crafts'. Only very occasionally do we get a glimpse of interaction with what we might call 'commodities', or just with things not on the list, such as when 'a bolt of black and green velvet' forms part of the payment (along with four antique porcelain cups, a piece of calligraphy, and a painting) which is offered to induce Li Rihua to compose a six-sheet funerary elegy for the mother of one caller.[30] On another occasion he enthuses about a lacquered couch inlaid with panels of patterned stone, the innovation of a local entrepreneur, and once he speaks warmly about the pewter teapots of a renowned local craftsmen, but only in the context of being asked for a funeral elegy for the man, not with regard to his own purchase of one.[31] Perhaps he most 'ordinary' thing he chose to record buying in his diary was a lantern decorated with ' various immortals worshipping the Southern Polar Star, for my father's birthday'.[32] The importance of the occasion probably rendered the purchase more memorable. Another time he records how his boat tied up at Changmen, a gate of the city of Suzhou, where he bought between forty and fifty large ceramic pots, presumably fairly everyday items, so that he could collect water for brewing tea wherever he wished.[33] The connoisseurly consumption of water was of particular importance to Li, and provided him with the name of his studio and the diary he composed there, 'Water-Tasting Studio'; the diary also records sessions of water connoisseurship.[34] Consumption in the sense of ingestion was undoubtedly important to Li Rihua; one diary reads in its entirety: 'Tasted the oranges from my own garden. Excellent.'[35] Li sometimes drank heavily, and did not scruple to record his hangovers in the diary. Presumably he cared about what he drank but we never see him choose

---

[27] Li Rihua, 438, [Wanli 43/1/20].
[28] Li Rihua, 84, [Wanli 38/2/21].
[29] Li Rihua, 140, [Wanli 38/10/24].
[30] Li Rihua, 54, [Wanli 37/11/3].
[31] Li Rihua, 481, [Wanli 43/run/6–7]; 441, [Wanli 43/1/29].
[32] Li Rihua, 511, [Wanli 44/1/13].
[33] Li Rihua, 101, [Wanli 38/4/14].
[34] Li Rihua, 534, [Wanli 44/6/2].
[35] Li Rihua, 414, [Wanli 42/9/30].

alcohol for his cellar, just as we never see him choose his clothes, which almost certainly mattered to him a lot too. It is not that consumption of these items did not matter, but that only some acts of consumption were *culturally* visible even to the consumer himself. Even less visible in this sense than the consumption of certain goods was the consumption of *all* services, with the servants, courtesans, chefs, and professional entertainers who were essential to the elite lifestyle all being equally shadowy figures in the diary. We might reasonably suspect that the estates from which Li drew his wealth were very important to him, and we can be absolutely sure that they involved a considerable body of (now lost) textual practices: rent books and leases, account books, deeds, and tax certificates. Nevertheless the diary contains only the rarest of glimpses of this side of life, as when he writes, 'From the 16th to the 30th, a whole half month, I have been managing estate affairs [literally 'fields and rents'] every day, and there is nothing to record.'[36]

Although he records his own consumption behaviour (and very occasionally the prices which he paid for things, or which he had heard others had paid for things) in a manner which eschews moralizing comment, Li Rihua was perfectly prepared to draw on that discourse when it suited him. He spurns an offer of an antique Qin zither (the musical instrument which was a key marker of elite status) on the grounds that there is something not quite right about such an instrument being made of metal: 'In the end not an elegant item, and I returned it.'[37] The opposite of 'elegant' for Li and his contemporaries was 'vulgar', as in the laconic diary entry for one bad night out: 'A banquet with vulgar guests.'[38] And Li is as willing to tut-tut about the vast and licentious excess of a popular religious festival as is he to remark on the extravagant nature of the sweetmeats taken with tea in the (significantly merchant-dominated) culture of Xiuning in Anhui province.[39]

However the criteria of 'elegance' and 'vulgarity' which were so meaningful to Li and his contemporaries increasingly must have seemed to be not the stuff of 'proper' history, and by the time the *Diary from the Water-Tasting Studio* was published for the first time in 1923 the understanding of historical processes in both China and outside it had turned its gaze in other directions. Over a century of imperialist assault and dynastic decline, and the tumult surrounding the birth of the Chinese Republic in 1911, made the etiolated discriminations of the Ming elite seem irrelevant if not offensive to contemporary sensibilities. Some scholars of the Republican period chose to draw on a tradition, which went at least as far back as the eighteenth century, if not to the fall of the Ming in 1644, of seeing too fastidious a concern with the exact cut of hats or with which type of rocks which would make a garden truly 'elegant' as being in some sense a cause of dynastic collapse, and hence an extremely bad historical role model in China's painful transition to modernity.[40] However others saw the self-reflexive sensibility of late Ming

---

[36] Li Rihua, 552, [Wanli 44/10/16].
[37] Li Rihua, 69, [Wanli 37/12/28].
[38] Li Rihua, 536, [Wanli 44/6/15].
[39] Li Rihua, 98, [Wanli 38/4/2] and 385, [Wanli 42/4/20].
[40] Clunas, *Superfluous Things*, 168–71.

writers as being in some sense a harbinger of that modernity, in the literary and cultural, if not in the political or economic, sense, thus ensuring that the late Ming was through the twentieth century a vibrant field of enquiry.[41]

At first, that enquiry was fairly firmly directed towards production, rather than consumption, most notably through the historiographical controversy over the so-called 'sprouts of capitalism' (*zibenzhuyi mengya*). Although strongly associated, indeed almost uniquely associated after 1949, with Marxist historiography, this linked set of arguments about the existence or otherwise of an indigenous motor of economic development in China, seen as burgeoning particularly strongly in the late Ming, was by no means in its origins the product of Marxist historians only. Prominent conservatives such as Tao Xisheng (1899–1988) weighed in to argue that the development of commercial capital in China was not necessarily corrosive of the 'feudal' economy and its social structures.[42] Historians of the mid-twentieth century argued over late Ming commercial developments, such as the growth of cities and of handicraft production, and the increasing involvement of China in global networks of trade which brought silver in unprecedented quantities from the Americas, and whether these did or did not prove that China was tending (via the iron laws of history) autonomously towards a capitalist state. However they tended to do so on the basis of the same bodies of evidence, reading the glass as half-full or half-empty, and praying in aid the kinds of statements Ming writers have left us about 'extravagance' and 'fashion', even as they carried out valuable work on excavating such other evidence as exists in sources like local gazetteers, a genre of chorographic writing which deals with the specificities of place. So Fu Yiling (1911–88) noticed as early as 1957 (coincidentally the very same year in which it was translated by Lien-sheng Yang) the essay of Lu Ji on the economic value of extravagant spending which is cited above, including it on one of only a couple of pages dealing with consumption (a 'Bad Thing' in Chinese Marxist historiography of the period).[43]

The most recent survey of the literature on the history of consumption in China, with special reference to the Ming period, is contained in a volume entitled *Pinwei shehua: Wan Ming de xiaofei shehui yu shidafu*, ('Taste and Extravagance: Late Ming Consumer Society and the Gentry') by the Taiwan-based historian Wu Renshu, who entitles the first chapter 'From the Study of Production to the Study of Consumption'.[44] There he credits scholars working in English with a prominent role in this turnabout, drawing on the revival of consumption as a topic particularly within British historiography of the 1970s and 1980s, but also bringing a range of new perspectives from sociology and anthropology to bear on the evidence. One book he cites, the present author's

[41] Wai-yee Li, 'The Collector, the Connoisseur, and Late-Ming Sensibility', *T'oung Pao*, 81 (1995), 269–302.

[42] Timothy Brook, 'Capitalism and the writing of modern history in China', in Timothy Brook and Gregory Blue (eds.), *China and Historical Capitalism: Genealogies of Sinological Knowledge* (Cambridge: Cambridge University Press, 1999), 110–57, at 150–2.

[43] Wu Renshu, *Pinwei shehua: Wan Ming de xiaofei shehui yu shidafu* ('Taste and Extravagance: Late Ming Consumer Society and the Gentry') (Taipei, 2008), 3.

[44] Wu Renshu, *Pinwei shehua*, 1–22.

Superfluous Things: Material Culture and Social Status in Early Modern China (1991) was certainly written consciously in the light of the scholarship on eighteenth-century Britain, and sought to draw attention to ways in which the early modern European experience might not be unique.[45] It did so by attending to a specific type of late Ming text, and most centrally to the *Treatise on Superfluous Things* by Wen Zhenheng (1585–1645), which provided guidance on correct consumption, structured along the parameters of 'elegance' and 'vulgarity'. Wu Renshu's second landmark in the English-language scholarship is Timothy Brook's 1998 volume *The Confusions of Pleasure: Commerce and Culture in Ming China*, which has a wider compass, and arguably goes some way to addressing the problem raised by Frank Trentmann in a review of the field, where he sees a 'widening gulf between material culture, focused on identities and representations, and material politics and political economy'.[46] The same might be true of Wu Renshu's other examples, with the work of S. A. M. Adshead and Kenneth Pomeranz, which—particularly the latter—puts a new spin on the 'roots of capitalism' question by using the work of Clunas and others to link (in one chapter title), 'Luxury Consumption and the Rise of Capitalism', and to argue, 'But this [European] "rise of consumer society" was not unique…China also became increasingly crammed with paintings, sculptures, fine furniture and so on'.[47] It might be claimed that the 'gulf' has been less of a problem in the literature focusing on China, where there has perhaps not been the same imbalance within material culture studies between the study of culture and the study of material; this is identified by Trentmann as particularly acute in the case of British scholarship on the issue, when he claims, 'In short, historical material culture studies have been more about culture than about material'.[48] Recent work such as that of Dorothy Ko, for example, on the material culture of footbinding and gender identities in China is rigorous in its address to both.[49]

The continuously developing literature on consumption, material culture, and status in China has faced in two directions. It is often united in its opposition to any perceived European exceptionalism (perhaps typified by the continued citation of Fernand Braudel's *Capitalism and Material Life, 1400–1800*, despite the fact that this is generally marked by lamentable and willed ignorance of the material on China).[50] This is often

---

[45] Craig Clunas, *Superfluous Things: Material Culture and Social Status in Early Modern China*, 2nd edition (Honolulu: University of Hawai'i Press, 2004), xi–xvi explains some of the genesis of the book. Wu Renshu perhaps chooses to overlook a quantity of scholarship from the People's Republic of China which draws on the classical tradition for positive affirmations of consumption, and which was produced in the context of the post-Maoist economic transformation.

[46] Trentmann, 'Materiality in the Future of History', 285.

[47] Kenneth Pomeranz, *The Great Divergence: China, Europe and the Making of the Modern World Economy* (Princeton and Oxford: Princeton University Press, 2000), 130; S. A. M. Adshead, *Material Culture in Europe and China, 1400–1800: The Rise of Consumerism* (Houndsmills and London, Macmillan, 1997).

[48] Trentmann, 'Materiality in the Future of History', 288.

[49] Dorothy Ko, *Cinderella's sisters: a revisionist history of footbinding* (Berkeley/Los Angeles/London: University of California Press, 2005).

[50] Craig Clunas, 'Review Essay—Modernity Global and Local: Consumption and the Rise of the West', *American Historical Review*, 104/5 (1999): 1497–1511.

explicitly comparative work, exemplified most clearly by something like Pomeranz's *The Great Divergence: China, Europe and the Making of the Modern World Economy* (which was published, it should be noted, in a series entitled 'The Princeton Economic History of the Western World'). But it is also internally engaged in lively debate about some of the central premises of the work cited by Wu Renshu, which is now decades old. There have been effective challenges to what might be called '*late Ming* exceptionalism', citing developments both before and after the period which tend to erode claims made for the distinctive nature of the century 1540–1640. For example, Kathlyn Liscomb's work on the archaeological evidence from the tomb of a prosperous merchant who died in 1494 tends to challenge the claims, implicit in Clunas's *Superfluous Things*, that it is only after about 1550 that elite forms of luxury consumption spread to a newly assertive merchant class.[51] Jonathan Hay has argued that it would be wrong to see the late Ming moment as some sort of failed or stalled modernity, pointing out instead that the kinds of consumption behaviour over which late Ming moralists fretted may have become so embedded and so common by 1700 that they were no longer worthy of notice. And more recently Hay has engaged with the tradition of phenomenology to look at the material world of the luxury object in China.[52] Kathlyn Liscomb and Jonathan Hay are by disciplinary affiliation art historians, and it could perhaps be argued that it is the ongoing involvement in the debate of art historians and museum curators, who necessarily engage personally with surviving material objects from China's past, which has kept the argument grounded in concerns around the artefact itself.[53] For many art historians now, the 'agency' of things, an idea which a number of social scientists would ascribe to Bruno Latour and to actor-network theory, requires no scare quotes, given that they are likely to be much more familiar with Alfred Gell's *The Agency of Art* (1998), and to the subsequent debates around it. Gell polemically rejects the idea that anything other than language has 'meaning', insisting instead that, 'In place of symbolic communication I place all the emphasis on *agency, intention, causation, result* and *transformation*.'[54] Even those art historians who do not subscribe fully to Gell's 'methodological philistinism' (and it would be professionally hard for them to do so) have found his insistence on doing, rather than meaning, useful in opening up a dialogue with anthropologists and social scientists of other kinds.

Writing in Chinese in 2008, the historian Wu Renshu explicitly seeks to build on the tradition of Braudel and Neil McKendrick to produce an account of late Ming

[51] Kathlyn Liscomb, 'Social Status and Art Collecting: The Collections of Shen Zhou and Wang Zhen', *Art Bulletin*, 78.1 (1996), 111–35.

[52] Jonathan Hay, *Shitao: Painting and Modernity in Early Qing China* (Cambridge: Cambridge University Press, 2001), 339; Jonathan Hay, *Sensuous Surfaces: The Decorative Object in Early Modern China* (London: Reaktion Books, 2010).

[53] Not that there is no involvement of art historians in the study of Western material culture, see Michelle O'Malley and Evelyn Welch (eds.), *The Material Renaissance* (Manchester and New York: Manchester University Press, 2007).

[54] Alfred Gell, *Art and Agency: An Anthropological Theory* (Oxford: Oxford University Press 1998), 6. On Gell see Mathew Rampley, 'Art history and cultural difference: Alfred Gell's anthropology of art', *Art History*, 28/4 (2005), 524–51, also Robin Osborne and Jeremy Tanner (eds.), *Art's Agency and Art History* (Oxford: Blackwell Publishing, 2007).

consumption which is both more nuanced and more detailed. This is attempted through a series of case studies, in chapters entitled: 'Consumption and the Symbolics of Power—the Example of Sedan Chair Culture'; 'The Formation of Fashion—the Example of Clothing Culture'; 'Consumer Taste and Status Discrimination—the Example of Travel Culture'; The Commodification and Singularisation of Objects—the Example of Furniture Culture'; 'The Development and Extension of Scholar Taste—the Example of Food Culture'. Wu's extensive reading of the broadest possible range of Ming sources is meticulous in its care about the terminology used at the time. He unpacks, for example, the term *fu yao*, which means literally something like 'weirdness in clothing', and which had been in use for millennia as a technical term in prognostication, where weirdness in clothing was a sign of impending personal or national disaster. By the Ming, the term was used alongside others to mean also 'fashion victim', 'fashionista', but without ever losing its sense that the material and the cosmic were aligned for good or for evil.[55]

But this Ming terminology is not the only technical language which is explained by Wu Renshu. As is the case with academic writing in Chinese since at least the early twentieth century, neologisms or translations of English technical terms have the original English printed within the Chinese text, a reading knowledge of English being correctly assumed to be widespread among intellectuals. The words which are so treated in the introduction to his book (excluding proper names and titles) are: 'modernity'; 'consumer culture'; 'early modernity'; 'consumerism'; 'fields'; 'wage-rate'; 'the bottom up'; 'consumer society'. Not one of those terms would have been familiar to the writers of the late Ming whose works form the underpinning of the argument. However the 'discrimination' (*pinwei*) and 'extravagance' (*shehua*) of the book's main title have longer pedigrees, indeed would have meant something to a Ming reader, while the status term *shidafu* certainly would, and is correspondingly almost impossible to translate satisfactorily into modern English. *Matthew's Chinese English Dictionary* gives 'gentry; officials; upper classes', but all are contestable. This title of a modern Chinese scholarly work (and one unlikely to enter the wider conversation through translation) might therefore stand as a metaphor for a field of enquiry which is delicately, even precariously, balanced between a set of emic concerns which were intensely meaningful to social actors in China centuries ago, and those etic concerns with development and global historical processes which any 'history of consumption' must address, in the full range of their variety and specificity.

There now seems little point in continuing the argument as to whether China 'also' was developing a consumer society in the Ming period. The quantity of empirical evidence is certainly there to make such a case, and enough of it now exists in English to make further claims of European exceptionalism look increasingly defensive and ultimately slightly perverse. However although *strategically* there was a considerable point to writing Ming China into the history of a global 'early modern' (it is after all the move which gains the present essay a place in this book), the problems and inconsistencies of

[55] Wu Renshu, *Pinwei shehua*, 160–5. On the role of fashion in China see Antonia Finnane, *Changing Clothes in China: Fashion, History, Nation* (London: Hurst, 2007).

such an inscription are by now well understood, and elegantly laid out in the work of Dipesh Chakrabarty, among many others.[56] To carry on insisting that Ming China is 'just like' early modern Europe seems as unproductive as arguing for its total difference—as if that too had not been tried, in fact for some centuries now, and with results which are tediously familiar, not to mention being also supportive of a contemporary Chinese nationalism always at risk of tipping into chauvinistic claims of exceptionalism of their own kind. How then to move forward from either/or, same/different? Although this is acknowledged right at the outset as special pleading, perhaps there is something to be found in art history's own history, and in its long process of extrication from the ahistorical construct of Beauty (which as Bruno Latour observes is 'more easily seen as a construction than is Truth'). Latour has further argued that art history is by its nature, and by its attention to the pleasure derived from the multiplication of mediations, particularly well-suited to 'be constructivist and realist at the same time'.[57] If this claim is true, then perhaps an attention to the full range of mediations materialized in surviving things is equally a way of enjoying the benefits of both those standpoints.

BIBLIOGRAPHY

Brook, Timothy, *The Confusions of Pleasure: Commerce and Culture in Ming China* (Berkeley, Los Angeles, and London: University of California Press, 1998).

———, *Vermeer's Hat: The Seventeenth Century and the Dawn of the Global World* (London: Profile Books, 2008).

Clunas, Craig, 'Review Essay—Modernity Global and Local: Consumption and the Rise of the West', *American Historical Review*, 104.5 (1999): 1497–1511.

———, *Superfluous Things: Material Culture and Social Status in Early Modern China*, 2nd edition (Honolulu: University of Hawai'i Press, 2004).

———, *Empire of Great Brightness: Visual and Material Cultures of Ming China* (London: Reaktion Books, 2007).

Finnane, Antonia, *Changing Clothes in China: Fashion, History, Nation* (London: Hurst, 2007).

Li, Chu-tsing and Watt, James C. Y. (eds.), *The Chinese Scholar's Studio: Artistic Life in the Late Ming Period* (New York: Thames and Hudson, 1987).

Li, Wai-yee, 'The Collector, the Connoisseur, and Late-Ming Sensibility', *T'oung Pao*, 81 (1995), 269–302.

Pomeranz, Kenneth, *The Great Divergence: China, Europe and the Making of the Modern World Economy* (Princeton and Oxford: Princeton University Press, 2000).

Yang, Lien-sheng, 'Economic Justification for Spending—An Uncommon Idea in Traditional China', *Harvard Journal of Asiatic Studies*, 20 (1957).

---

[56] Dipesh Chakrabarty, *Provincializing Europe: postcolonial thought and historical difference* (Princeton: Princeton University Press, 2000). On the specific problems of applying the term 'early modern' to China see Søren Clausen, 'Early Modern China: A Preliminary Postmortem', electronically published 4 April 2000, <http://www.hum.au.dk/ckulturf/pages/publications/sc/china.htm>, accessed 9 October 2009.

[57] Bruno Latour, 'How to be Iconophilic in Art, Science and Religion?', in Caroline A. Jones and Peter Gallison (eds.), *Picturing Science Producing Art* (New York and London: Routledge, 1998), 418–40, at 423.

CHAPTER 4

....

MATERIAL CULTURE IN SEVENTEENTH-CENTURY 'BRITAIN': THE MATTER OF DOMESTIC CONSUMPTION

....

SARA PENNELL

> We must not think of the [early modern] consumer society simply in
> terms of the licence to acquire more. It was, perhaps more crucially, the
> development of new values which helped people transcend that very
> licence to acquire more.[1]

In the thirty or so years since the new wave of historical consumption studies first buffeted social and economic historical accounts of early modern Britain, the call made
by Roy Porter in his own contribution to one of the seminal volumes in that new wave,
Consumption and the World of Goods (1993), has not always been heard. On the one hand,
the 'more' which 'consumer society' brought with it, has been mapped (although many
terrae incognitae remain), and the motivations for desiring the 'more' essayed among
certain groups (including women, the urban middling 'sorts', colonial Americans,
Irish elites; still excluding most of the 'poor', children and adolescents, rural communities, the Welsh and Scots in general, to name but a few).[2] And yet we still falter in our

[1] Roy Porter, 'Consumption: disease of the consumer society?', in John Brewer and Roy Porter (eds.),
Consumption and the Worlds of Goods (London: Routledge, 1990), 58–81, at 71.
[2] Key works covering these groups in early modern Britain are: Lorna Weatherill, *Consumer Behaviour
and Material Culture in Britain, 1660–1760* (London: Routledge, 1988); Peter Earle, *The Making of the
English Middle Class: Business, Society and Family Life in London 1660–1730* (London: Methuen, 1989);
Carole Shammas, *The Pre-Industrial Consumer in England and America* (Oxford: Clarendon Press,
1990), Toby Barnard, *Making the Grand Figure: Lives and Possessions in Ireland, 1641–1770* (London: Yale
University Press, 2004); Timothy Breen, *The Marketplace of Revolution: How Consumer Politics Shaped*

understanding of the full range of values which individuals and communities engaged with in the making and maintaining of their material existences. This necessitates a reworking of Porter's statement: it is the development and negotiation of values old and new which helped people accommodate that very licence to acquire more.

In this chapter, I will focus on three issues: the historiographies which have made the period prior to that in which Neil McKendrick confidently told us a 'consumer revolution' occurred both a necessary staging post en route to revolution and a prelapsarian era in striking contrast to it; the relative absence of 'mundane materiality' within these accounts; and consumption as a matter of practice, rather than as an abstract phenomenon in the 'long' seventeenth century in Britain (c.1600–1720).[3] In this I follow Joan Thirsk in her important 1975 Oxford University Ford Lectures, in accepting Jacobean and Stuart Britain (or at least England) as very much concerned with production for the ends of domestic consumption, in both senses of the word 'domestic'.[4]

Academic reluctance to materialize early modern British history until relatively recently has been concerned in part with disciplinary boundaries between history, archaeology, and other social sciences. But it is also bound up with museological conventions that have tended to privilege the luxurious and artful artefact and, above all, the complete and perfected artefact. Through the case studies of objects very rarely found in public museum displays thanks to their 'everyday' qualities,[5] I will argue for a re-evaluation of non-elite consumption within the domestic sphere as significant within any story we might wish to tell of changing consumption practices across the seventeenth century.

CONCERNING CONSUMPTION

The seventeenth century is problematic for historians of consumption whose frameworks for analysis have mainly derived from eighteenth-century-focused studies. The earlier century clearly lacks some of the key requirements for revolutionizing consumption

American Independence (Oxford: Oxford University Press, 2004). For exceptions to the exclusions, see J. H. Plumb, 'The new world of children', in Neil McKendrick, John Brewer and J. H. Plumb, The Birth of a Consumer Society: the Commercialization of Eighteenth-Century England, pbk edn. (London: Hutchinson, 1983), 286–315; Paul Courtney, 'In small things forgotten: the Georgian world view, material culture and the consumer revolution', Rural History, 7/1 (1996), 87–95; Mark Overton et al., Production and Consumption in English Households 1600–1750 (London: Routledge, 2004); Jonathan White, 'The labouring-class domestic sphere in eighteenth-century British social thought', in John Styles and Amanda Vickery (eds.), Gender, Taste and Material Culture in Britain and North America 1700–1830 (London and New Haven: Paul Mellon Centre for Studies in British Art and Yale University Press, 2006), 247–63.

[3] Neil McKendrick, 'Introduction' and 'The consumer revolution of eighteenth-century England', in McKendrick, Brewer and Plumb, Birth of a Consumer Society, 1–6 (see opening sentence), 9–33; Sara Pennell, 'Mundane materiality: or should small things still be forgotten?', in Karen Harvey (ed.), History and Material Culture (Abingdon: Routledge, 2009), 173–91; Frank Trentmann, 'Materiality in the future of history: things, practices and politics', Journal of British Studies, 48/2 (2009), 283–307.

[4] Published as Economic Policy and Projects (Oxford: Clarendon Press, 1978).

[5] Their absence could be because of collecting policies, but also simple scarcity; these were goods seen as consumable, to the point of destruction or reuse.

and making 'consumers': an expanding press for advertising in; a developed urban retail culture in both metropolis and provinces through which a wider spectrum of potential consumers could access goods; the technological know-how and developments to manufacture and distribute more and different goods; and a less fraught moral relationship with the concept of luxury and its materialization in non-necessary goods.[6] This latter idea of consumption as societally beneficent was undoubtedly alien in contemporary discourses at the beginning of the century; we need only look to the words of Gervase Markham, in the opening paragraphs of his widely circulated, much-reprinted *English Hus-wife* (first published in 1615 as Book II of his *Countrey Contentments*), to capture the sense of domestic order at risk from material excess:

> In her apparel and diet [which] she shall proportion according to the competency of her husband's estate and calling, making her circle rather strait than large, for it is a rule if we extend to the uttermost we take away increase, if we go a hair breadth beyond we enter into consumption.[7]

Yet, if we look to Thirsk's pioneering work, to Margaret Spufford on early modern clothing and, more recently, to Linda Levy Peck's writings, then the landscape changes dramatically.[8] This is a century in which innovations clearly do happen: trade encounters exponentially expand mercantile opportunity (while legislation prioritises English advantage within such trading), and, especially in the post-Restoration period, the fiscal demands of the emerging state and the collective self-interest of the more influential mercantile community produce new ways in which to finance and protect new commercial, industrial, and speculative ventures. Indeed, as Paul Slack has recently emphasized, the shift from consumption as a counsel of evil, so clearly understood by Markham, to being viewed as a potentially munificent engine of change and common good (as expressed in the works of Sir William Petty, Nicholas Barbon, and others) within political economic thought and commentary occurs well before 1700.[9]

This reinstatement of consumption as an active force throughout the seventeenth century still has its limitations, however. These include the magnetism of the metropolis as *the*

---

[6] cf. 'Commercialization and the economy', Part II of McKendrick, Brewer and Plumb, *Birth of a Consumer Society*, 9–194; Maxine Berg, *The Age of Manufactures: Industry, Innovation and Work in Britain 1700–1820* (Oxford: Oxford University Press, 1985); idem, *Luxury and Pleasure in Eighteenth-Century Britain* (Oxford: Oxford University Press, 2005), esp. 21–45.

[7] Gervase Markham, *The English Housewife*, ed. Michael R. Best, pbk edn. (Montreal: McGill-Queen's University Press, 1994), 7. See also Joyce Appleby, 'Consumption in early modern social thought', in Brewer and Porter (eds.), *Consumption and the World of Goods*, 162–74; cf. Jonathan White, 'A world of goods? The "consumption turn" and eighteenth-century British history', *Cultural and Social History*, 3/1 (2006), 93–104.

[8] Thirsk, *Economic Policy*; Margaret Spufford, *The Great Reclothing of Rural England: Petty Chapmen and their Wares in the Seventeenth Century* (London: Hambledon, 1985); Linda Levy Peck, *Consuming Splendor: Society and Culture in Seventeenth-century England* (Cambridge: Cambridge University Press, 2005). See also Christine MacLeod, *Inventing the Industrial Revolution: the English Patent System, 1660–1800* (Cambridge: Cambridge University Press, 1998), chs. 1 and 2.

[9] Paul Slack, 'Material progress and the challenge of affluence in seventeenth-century England', *Economic History Review*, 62/3 (2009), 576–603.

'centre of conspicuous consumption'; the lure of the luxurious or, more precisely, the luxurious 'exotic'; the emphasis on newness (not only novel, but also new, rather than reused,
goods); the sense that, in the seventeenth century, all industry apart from 'heavy' concerns
such as mining and shipbuilding, for example, was somehow still 'proto'-industrial, rather
than fully industrialized by late eighteenth-century standards; and that such technological developments that proved to be more than just short-term 'projections' were primarily industrial, agricultural, or natural philosophical in application, rather than impacting
directly upon the domestic environment, in the same way that eighteenth-century technological innovations, such as English porcelain, printed cottons, and decorative metalwares, did.[10] Thirsk's conclusions, pointing to the early to mid-seventeenth century as the
crucible of domestically-based and -focused production of 'cheap goods', and the foundation of a home demand which was only to strengthen in the eighteenth century (bolstered
by colonial demand), appear indeed to have been consumed by splendour.[11]

Here I will revisit a couple of Thirsk's conclusions and suggest some further gauges for
evaluating the character and velocities of household consumption before c.1700. I want to
reiterate Thirsk's important emphasis on the pre-1700 production and consumption of both
necessary and convenient products: developments which underpinned the much-discussed
eighteenth-century middling and even labouring sense of entitlement to owning 'decencies',
or semi-luxury commodities. Moving beyond Thirsk nevertheless requires attention to how
the sorts of innovation she detailed (technological, agricultural, industrial) entered into and
was accommodated within the 'enigmatic realms' of the non-elite household, a 'black box'
in so many respects.[12] This in turn requires us to think about matters which have surfaced
only very recently in the historiography of eighteenth-century consumption practices, such
as the values placed on utility, material durability, and decorum within early modern economic thinking and the materialized practices which embodied these ideas.[13]

THE MATTER OF MATTER

The historian's 'turn' towards material culture in Britain as both source and methodology in the past decade has also been intimately tied up with the historiography of
consumption across the long eighteenth century.[14] That historiography has been in no

---

[10] F. J. Fisher, 'The development of London as a centre of conspicuous consumption in the sixteenth
and seventeenth centuries', *Transactions of the Royal Historical Society*, 4th series, 30 (1948), 37–50;
Maxine Berg, *Luxury and Pleasure in Eighteenth-Century Britain* (Oxford: Oxford University Press,
2005), esp. chs. 2, 4 and 5; Peck, *Consuming Splendor*, chs. 1, 4 and 8.

[11] Thirsk, *Economic Policy*, esp. 176–80.

[12] Citing Ann Smart Martin, *Buying into the World of Goods: Early Consumers in Backcountry
Virginia* (Baltimore: Johns Hopkins University Press, 2008), 52.

[13] John Styles and Amanda Vickery, 'Introduction' in idem (eds.), *Gender, Taste and Material
Culture*, 1–34; Trentmann, 'Materiality', 296–9.

[14] Karen Harvey, 'Introduction: practical matters', in idem (ed.), *History and Material Culture*, 1–23,
at 8–9; Trentmann, 'Materiality', 286–7, 293.

small part bolstered by the frequent material survival in public and private collections of the sort of 'demi-luxe' and luxury goods featured in metropolitan advertisements and trade catalogues which attract so much attention in histories of Georgian consumption.[15] To take an obvious example, the reputation of Josiah Wedgwood looms much larger in this historiography than his earlier counterparts. Yet the Elers brothers, also working in Staffordshire but in the 1690s, produced fine red stonewares in imitation of imported Chinese redwares, which Wedgwood would later emulate. Wedgwood certainly produced more and in greater variety; but his continued fame is also because he was able to construct a commercial persona and, equally important, the idea of a collectable product through media channels simply not available to the Elers siblings.[16]

Wedgwood's reputation has also been enhanced by the trends for decorative arts collecting in England manifest from the eighteenth through to the early twentieth centuries. Aesthetic preferences for Renaissance artefacts, eighteenth-century furniture, neoclassical objets, fine imported and domestic ceramics, and so on have also strongly influenced what we see on public display, and thus what we can study about the material cultures of the British past in museums like the Victoria and Albert (London). There are different but equally problematic concerns within archaeology and its museology, where until relatively recently the idea of investigating the 'post-medieval' era seemed little more than an act of providing the objectscape for accepted text-based accounts of material progress, if it were undertaken at all. As a result, in many public displays of archaeological material, those very centuries (c.1500 to the present day) are overshadowed by medieval and earlier finds and their interpretation.[17]

Even if Richard Grassby's assertion that 'in early modern England, people were more occupied with things than with abstractions' were true (and I am not convinced it is), those things have survived, above ground at least, in relatively small numbers.[18] The 'soft...decorative' material worlds of the high Georgian and Victorian domestic interior, presented in the later British Galleries at the V&A, are simply less in evidence for the period before 1700, and as the one-time research assistant for the 'Tudor and Stuart' sections of the same British Galleries, I can vouch for the difficulties of curating a rounded, artefactually diverse narrative of pre-Georgian 'British decorative arts'. The economic conditions of a mainly pre-industrial society that simply produced less stuff, but more

[15] Neil McKendrick, 'Josiah Wedgwood and the commercialization of the Potteries' and 'George Packwood and the commercialization of shaving', in McKendrick, Brewer and Plumb, *Birth of a Consumer Society*, 100–145, and 146–94; Pennell, 'Mundane materiality', 176–7.

[16] Lorna Weatherill, *The Pottery Trade and North Staffordshire 1660–1760* (Manchester: Manchester University Press, 1971), chs. 4–6; McKendrick, 'Wedgwood'; Helen L. Phillips, 'Elers, John Philip (1664–1738)', *Oxford Dictionary of National Biography*, Oxford University Press, 2004, <http://www.oxforddnb.com/view/article /8621>, accessed 3 July 2010.

[17] Dan Hicks and Mary C. Beaudry, 'Introduction: the place of historical archaeology', in idem (eds.), *The Cambridge Companion to Historical Archaeology* (Cambridge: Cambridge University Press, 2006), 1–9.

[18] Richard Grassby, 'Material culture and cultural history', *Journal of Interdisciplinary History*, 35 (2005), 591–603, at 594.

museological issues (for example, furniture 'faked' to be Elizabethan/Jacobean), conspire to limit the range of objects available for interpreting and displaying.[19]

Museums with a more explicit social history agenda, underpinned with strong archaeological collections, can and do provide greater chronological and social depth than a collection targeting all that is best about British art and design (the V&A's remit). But this can also confuse. The medieval galleries at the Museum of London do much to substantiate recent assertions by medievalists that, in London and the Home Counties at least, a consumption-oriented economy was in evidence from the beginning of the fourteenth century at the very least.[20] Yet the Museum of London's new (2010) post-1660 displays stress that the texture of London's material life grew significantly more complex and rich after 1660 (the date the new galleries begin), taking the seductive circumstance of the devastating Fire of London as a 'new presentation' of the city. While the Fire of London certainly transformed *some* of London's built environment, 1666 might not mark a significant point of departure for its domestic material cultures, any more than say 1700 or indeed, as Lena Cowan Orlin's edited volume, *Material London* (2000) titularly suggests, 'circa 1600'. This is not to ignore the pre-1660 paucity of useful documentary records beyond parochial and institutional materials, which hinders the sort of textual analysis of material diversity and improvement carried out on later Stuart London inventories by Weatherill and Earle. Yet this documentary dearth contrasts with the archaeological riches of the Museum of London's pre-1700 collections, which are now accessible at the museum's open storage facility.[21] As a result of this disparity between classes of evidence, we do need to be cautious about a major step-change in consuming practices with the coming of the Restoration.

Here, the disciplinary, as well as geographical, divides within British academia become starkly apparent. Archaeologists can see that there is extensive and socially diverse consumption of ceramics, both domestic and imported, well before 1700. Yet historians of consumption tend to rely on the very tailored artefactual collections museums offer up, and documentary accounts of the ceramic trade and its innovations, which put the weight on the very late seventeenth and early eighteenth centuries.[22] Interestingly, the title of a 1998 collected volume of archaeological studies of material change in England

[19] Trentmann, 'Materiality', 287. See also Anthony Burton, 'British decorative and fine art at the V&A before the British Galleries', John Styles, 'History in the galleries', and Nick Humphrey, 'Case study: developing a display', in Nick Humphrey and Christopher Wilk (eds.), *Creating the British Galleries at the V&A: a Study in Museology* (London: V&A Publications/Laboratorio museotecnico Goppion, 2004), 5–17, 29–36, 127–44.

[20] Derek Keene, 'Material London in time and space', in Lena Cowan Orlin (ed.), *Material London, c.1600* (Philadelphia: University of Pennsylvania Press, 2000), 55–74, at 59; Maryanne Kowaleski, 'A consumer economy', in Mark Ormrod and Rosemary Horrox (eds.), *A Social History of England, 1200–1500* (Cambridge: Cambridge University Press, 2006), 238–59.

[21] <http://www.museumoflondonarchaeology.org.uk/english/ArchiveResearch>, accessed 27 September 2010.

[22] Most notably in Berg, *Luxury and Pleasure*, 126–30; cf. Geoff Egan, *Material Culture in London in an Age of Transition: Tudor and Stuart Period Finds c.1450–c.1700* (London: English Heritage/Museum of London Archaeology Service, 2005); Kowaleski, 'Consumer economy', 254.

states the 'age of transition' as being 1400–1600, and not the long eighteenth century. There is a further geographical divide within archaeology itself, too: British archaeologists are circumspect about the notion of an eighteenth-century consumer 'revolution' at all, while American historical archaeologists have based the development of their field in no small part on its existence.[23]

The systematic inflation of what is mainly English (and urban), to be 'British' across the extant historiography of early modern consumption, muddies the interpretive waters further. A good example is Maxine Berg's *Luxury and Pleasure in Eighteenth-Century Britain*: it mentions Ireland and Scotland almost as afterthoughts, even though Dublin was far from a backwater when it came to supplying the wants and needs of both Catholic and Protestant consumers from at least 1660.[24] Speaking strictly geographically, what may be transformative about *eighteenth-century* experiences of new goods, materials and modes of consuming them, is that they were to be had in most corners of the realm: yet the joined-up scholarship to support this notion fully is wanting. Conversely, I would argue that what may be distinctive and differentiating about new or innovative consumption practices in the seventeenth as opposed to the eighteenth century (with the clear exception of tobacco-smoking) is precisely that their take-up was limited to specific cities, towns, and regions within England, with some limited exposure in the major urban centres of its principalities and emerging Caribbean and American colonies before 1700.

This essay will now turn to four arenas of domestic and social practice that might help us renegotiate those chronological hurdles, '1700' and even '1660', in our accounts of consumption practices. They are: the accommodation of industrial and technological change, represented in the adoption of new hearth goods related to coal-burning and metallurgical developments; the adoption of new mass cultural practices, in the material culture of smoking; the wider production of, and access to, non-luxury goods using new manufacturing techniques, through the history of the English engine-made brass thimble; and the material management of possessions, concerned with laundering, mending, and repair. These objects/commodities are not the usual suspects in the most recent account of seventeenth-century consumption—they are as far from Bernini tombs as it is possible to travel.[25] Yet their histories do suggest that, while McKendrick was perhaps right to see the eighteenth century as the era of commercialization of consumption, as was Berg to celebrate the febrile inventiveness of men like Matthew Boulton, the distinctiveness of the later period, in order to constitute it as *the* era of *the* consumer 'revolution', is much less apparent.

---

[23]   David Gaimster and Paul Stamper (eds.), *The Age of Transition, The Archaeology of English Culture 1400–1600* (Oxford: Oxbow Books, 1998); cf. Dennis J. Pogue, 'The transformation of America: Georgian sensibility, capitalist conspiracy or consumer revolution?', *Historical Archaeology*, 35/2 (2001), 41–57, esp. 51–3.

[24]   Berg, *Luxury and Pleasure, passim*; cf. Barnard, *Making the Grand Figure*.

[25]   Peck, *Consuming Splendor*, ch. 7.

TECHNOLOGICAL AND INDUSTRIAL CHANGE AT THE DOMESTIC LEVEL

Perhaps the greatest transformation in the consumption practices of British households across the seventeenth century is the one most usually consigned to the near-ghetto of early modern economic history: the exponential increase in domestic coal use.[26] While John Evelyn's 1661 *Fumifugium* may be read at one level as a manifesto for clearing the choking clouds of sectarianism, it is first and foremost a diatribe against the burning of sea coal, which had become so 'pernicious' and omnipresent by mid-century.[27] In counselling caution about the true exceptionality of London as an 'engine' of material transformation before the seventeenth century, Derek Keene nevertheless singles out domestic coal use as perhaps the only truly dramatic shift in metropolitan consumption patterns across the sixteenth century.[28] Even in inland, rural areas proximity to a coal pit and reasonable transportation links enabled modest and even pauper households to access coal by the end of Elizabeth's reign.[29]

Yet, the adoption of coal as a domestic fuel was by no means inevitable or welcomed.[30] Adapting to coal required several decisions on the part of the householder, since coal burns best raised off the hearth floor, in a narrower area than necessary for wood-burning, and with more restricted chimney flues.[31] Inserting or improving a chimney (rebuilding in brick/stone rather than wood or other more semi-durable materials; refining the flue design) is then a practical response to that pernicious smoke and soot within the domestic interior, as well as a marker for changing conceptions of 'comfort'.[32] Yet, how the incidence of the insertion/improvement of brick/stone chimneys in the English regions maps onto domestic coal consumption is yet to be quantified.[33]

What we do know is that amongst the flow of patents and publication of 'secrets' from the Jacobean decades onwards were several dedicated to reducing the polluting qualities

[26] John Hatcher, *The History of the British Coal Industry: Volume 1: Before 1700* (Oxford: Oxford University Press 1993), 409–18.

[27] J[ohn] E[velyn], *Fumifugium, or, The Inconveniencie of the Aer and Smoak of London* (London: W. Godbid for Gabriel Bedel, 1661), 15. See also Mark Jenner, 'The politics of London air: John Evelyn's *Fumifugium* and the Restoration', *Historical Journal*, 38/3 (1995), 535–51.

[28] Keene, 'Material London', 68.

[29] Margaret Spufford, 'Chimneys, wood and coal', in P. S. Barnwell and Malcolm Airs (eds.), *Houses and the Hearth Tax: the later Stuart House and Society* (York: Council for British Archaeology, 2006), 22–32, at 28. See also Barrie Trinder and Jeff Cox, *Yeomen and Colliers in Telford: Probate Inventories for Dawley, Lilleshall, Wellington and Wrockwardine, 1660–1750* (London: Phillimore, 1980), 109; Overton et al., *Production and Consumption*, 98–9.

[30] Spufford, 'Chimneys', 30–1.

[31] Hatcher, *Coal Industry*, 412–13.

[32] John Crowley, *The Invention of Comfort: Sensibilities and Design in Early Modern Britain and America* (Baltimore: Johns Hopkins University Press, 2001), ch. 1.

[33] R. W. Brunskill, *Vernacular Architecture: an Illustrated Handbook*, 4th edn. (London: Faber, 2000); Spufford, 'Chimneys', 25.

of sea coal in domestic environments, and to fashioning more efficient fire furniture, such as enclosed furnaces and 'fire cages'.[34] Such adaptations are already notable in early seventeenth century inventories from coal-producing areas, but also elsewhere. The Sudbury (Suffolk) clothier John Warner recorded the modifications he made to his main hearth in the middle of the century quite precisely: on 2 December 1659 he laid out £1 16s 'to Mr Milsop for a payr of cooll [coal] irons at 4s the pound'; four years later he purchased an iron fire back for the hearth, and paid to have the coal-irons lengthened to meet the fireback, creating what was effectively a coal grate.[35]

Inventory analysis has also demonstrated a decline in the ownership of cooking pots traditionally hung over a wood fire, notably cauldrons, and smaller tripod cooking pots, such as posnets used over wood embers, complemented by an increasing presence for flat-bottomed vessels, such as kettles, saucepans and stewpans. In the recent edition of probate inventories from seventeenth- and eighteenth-century Marlborough (Wiltshire), posnets are widely evident in inventories up until the third quarter of the seventeenth century, when saucepans start to appear to take their place.[36] Changes in naming might not always denote changes in form, but where appraisers altered inventory entries, to rename items, there was perhaps realization that the use of a vessel may have shifted; thus in one 1677 Marlborough vintner's inventory the appraisers delete 'one cast skillett', substituting ' 1 sauce pann' in its stead.[37]

That cast Wiltshire 'sauce pann' also embodies many of the developments in metallurgical extraction and processing, and the expanded manufacture of brass and associated alloys occurring in Britain by 1700. These depended in part upon the substitution of wood and charcoal by coal, but also upon declining institutional restrictions upon production (for example, the end of the monopolizing Mines Royal), and crises in continental production.[38] This is not to dethrone Abraham Darby I (1678–1717) and his sons and the advances of the early eighteenth century in and around Coalbrookdale, but there are clearly signs in the late seventeenth-century inventory record of the growing impact of domestic iron-casting and brass-founding, in the form of iron and brass kettles, frying pans, mortars, and skimmers. The same can be said of indigenous tin plate-working, before the much-publicized development of John Hanbury's Pontypool tin plate works in the late 1720s. To take but one example amongst very many, John Stevens, who died in Marlborough in late 1692, had amongst his £27 9s 6d's worth of household goods a tin candle-box, two tin pans, and a tin colander, none worth more

[34] Hatcher, *Coal Industry*, 414, 417.

[35] Spufford, 'Chimneys', 23; Suffolk Record Office (Bury St Edmunds), MS HA519/589: Memorandum and account book of John Warner of Sudbury, c.1630–75, fo. 11v.

[36] Sara Pennell, 'The material culture of food in early modern England, c.1660–1750' (unpublished Oxford D.Phil., 1997), ch. 4; Overton et al, *Production and Consumption*, 98–101; Lorelei Williams and Sally Thomson (eds.), *Marlborough Probate Inventories, 1591–1775* (Chippenham: Wiltshire Record Society, 2007), *passim*.

[37] Williams and Thomson, *Marlborough Inventories*, 150.

[38] Roger Burt, 'The transformation of the non-ferrous metals industries in the seventeenth and eighteenth centuries', *Economic History Review*, 48/1 (1995), 25–48.

than a few pence each.[39] Regional, rather than nationally distributed, production is key here. The high frequency of tin plate wares in late seventeenth-century Telford (Staffordshire) inventories probably indicates that Andrew Yarranton and others, producing tinwares in Worcestershire in the early 1670s, had a ready local market.[40]

So, around all but the poorest domestic hearths by 1720 were to be found an accumulation of metalwares which, although clearly 'everyday' goods, also embody significant industrial, technological, institutional, and geopolitical shifts within and beyond the British economy. Such goods were not only artefacts of these processes, but also of new domestic behaviours and consumption practices. Saucepans enabled the preparation of novel sauce-based 'made' dishes, such as fried salmon 'the French way' with its sauce of lemon, anchovy, and butter, a recipe in *The Gentlewoman's Delight in Cookery* (London, *c*.1690). This was one of the cheap 'Penny Merriments' collected by Samuel Pepys, that advertised itself as the compendium of choice for 'English and French ways in dressing Flesh in the best, modish and advantageous manner: *with their proper Sawces* and Garnish.'[41]

These dishes could then be served to the table, and as importantly kept warm on that table, by useful (but not essential) 'gadgets' such as tin plate dish-covers. Keeping food warm was a convenience that in turn contributed to more sociability and less formality around the dinner table; dining 'in company' was not reserved to elites, be they aristocratic, genteel, or corporate, as entries in the early Proceedings of the Old Bailey show.[42] Yet at the same time, the coming of coal and its 'pernicious' soot posed problems for domestic laundering, just as copper and lead-based vessels required regular re-tinning (whereas iron did not), in order to prevent contamination of both food and consumer. These adaptations to domestic practice suggest that the path towards 'consumer satisfaction' with these new commodities was not necessarily straight, nor smoothly navigated.

New Cultural Practices: the Material Cultures of Tobacco-Smoking

Emphasizing elites' luxury consumption as an engine of transformation in early modern urban and country house England is not misplaced, but it does obscure those areas in which shifts in non-elite consumption were occurring well before the Restoration era.

---

[39] Pennell, 'Material culture of food', ch. 4; cf. Burt, 'Non-ferrous metals industries', 34; Williams and Thomson, *Marlborough Inventories*, 318–9.

[40] Trinder and Cox, *Yeomen and Colliers*, 29.

[41] My emphasis: *The Gentlewoman's Delight in Cookery... Very Beneficial for all Young Gentlewomen and Servant-Maids* (London: printed for J. Back, n.d. [*c*.1690]), sigs. A2r–v.

[42] e.g. case of Thomas Wicks, found guilty of housebreaking while his victims were at their neighbours 'at supper', tried on 17 January 1681: see <http://www.oldbaileyonline.org, ref. T16810117a-3> accessed 27 September 2010.

In dress, particular clothing trends (gloves, beaver hats, handkerchiefs, lighter-weight fabrics) were not solely a metropolitan phenomenon; nor were they limited to elite groups, as sermons, satires, and strictures bewailing such affectations in the early seventeenth century reveal.[43]

But far more important, in terms of economic and mercantile history, indeed to the history of the early Stuart development of the Anglo-American and Caribbean colonies, is the trajectory of tobacco, as a new good developing new habits amongst new, non-elite audiences. Although research into its impacts on Jacobean and Caroline political, fiscal, and literary culture abounds, and its phenomenal mercantile and colonial territorial impact has been well served by scholars of the colonial Atlantic economy, the uptake of tobacco is still relatively marginal in most standard accounts of early modern English consumption.[44] This is partly explained by the economic trajectory tobacco production and consumption follows across the period c.1600–1900; its spectacular growth, both in terms of production and consumption, came before 1700. As a potential strand in the story of consumption across the long eighteenth century, tobacco had arguably already burnt out.[45] Tobacco consumption also does not conform to the interpretive frameworks beloved of historians of consumption: it generated a minimal and mundane (as well as mostly, but not exclusively, masculine) material culture; and was predominantly (although again not exclusively) consumed within sociable environments such as taverns, barbers, and coffee houses, again differentiating it from feminized and domesticated consumption in the eighteenth century.[46]

Nevertheless, the material culture of seventeenth-century tobacco-smoking is one of the best represented in surviving artefacts from the period. The clay tobacco-pipe is, because of its omnipresence in the archaeological record, the 'ideal type fossil': the pre-eminent means of dating excavated strata, thanks to the minute but swiftly adopted

[43] Spufford, *Great Reclothing*, esp. 98–104, 118–46; Roze Hentschell, 'Moralising apparel in early modern London: popular literature, sermons and sartorial display', *Journal of Medieval and Early Modern Studies*, 39/3 (2009), 571–95.

[44] The exception is Shammas, *Pre-Industrial Consumer*, although she swiftly moves on to focus upon sugar, and the other so-called 'new groceries': 78–81. See also Tanya Pollard, 'The pleasures and perils of smoking in early modern England', in Sander L. Gilman and Zhou Xun (eds.), *Smoke: A Global History of Smoking* (London: Reaktion, 2004), 38–45; Todd Butler, 'Power in smoke: the language of tobacco and authority in Caroline England', *Studies in Philology*, 106/1 (2009), 100–18. For Atlantic economy-focused studies, see James Horn, 'Tobacco colonies: the shaping of English society in the seventeenth-century Chesapeake', in Nicholas P. Canny (ed.), *The Origins of Empire: British Overseas Enterprise to the Close of the 17th Century* (Oxford: Oxford University Press, 1998), 170–92; Jon Kepler, 'Estimates of the volume of direct shipments of tobacco and sugar from the chief English plantations to European markets, 1620–1669', *Journal of European Economic History*, 28 (1999), 115–36; Douglas M. Bradburn and John C. Coombs, 'Smoke and mirrors : Reinterpreting the society and economy of the seventeenth-century Chesapeake', *Journal of Atlantic Studies*, 3/2 (2006), 131–57.

[45] Shammas, *Pre-Industrial Consumer*, 79–80.

[46] Pollard, 'Pleasures and perils', 43; Brian Cowan, *The Social Life of Coffee: the Emergence of the British Coffeehouse* (London and New Haven: Yale University Press, 2005), 28–9, 82–3.

changes in form deployed by clay-pipe-makers.[47] The tobacco-pipe-making industry in Jacobean England developed incredibly swiftly; the first incorporation of clay-pipe-makers in Westminster dates to 1619, less than 50 years after the first introduction of tobacco into England. Tobacco-smoking also spread extremely quickly beyond the capital and key ports; pipe manufacturing was established in almost every corner of England, Scotland, Wales, and the American and Caribbean colonies, before 1700.[48]

There are of course other artefacts of smoking—tobacco boxes and horns, stoppers or tampers, for example[49]—but none provides so well the scale, geographic distribution, or indeed public and domestic ubiquity of seventeenth-century smoking as the tobacco-pipe. Indeed, it must be viewed as both the first mass-consumed and mass-produced (albeit not by standardized or particularly mechanized means) commodity of the early modern era, after print. It is impossible to know how many pipes were manufactured annually, but it must have run into hundreds of thousands. They were thus extremely cheap: in the November 1688 inventory of Llewellin Evans, a Bristol tobacco-pipe-maker, his stock of 'one hundred gross of pipes at 10d per gross' (that is, *14,400 pipes*) were appraised at £4 4s, or less than a penny *per dozen*.[50] Even if this were a wholesale price, the cost to the consumer at retail would still have been negligible. The prices of associated items was also modest: in the 1661 inventory of another Bristolian, this time chapman John Austen, latten tobacco-boxes were valued at 6d per dozen (i.e. 1/2d per box) and brass stoppers at 8s per gross, or 2/3d per stopper.[51]

Because of such low costs, the tobacco-pipe was amongst the first 'essentially disposable' commodities outside of printed ephemera, 'its life in use…normally measured in hours or days'.[52] The pipe could be, and was, as ephemeral as the tobacco smoked within it; if it was dropped, cracked, broken by being tucked into one's belt (a common way of carrying),[53] or left behind on a tavern table, its inherent cheapness did not impede further consumption. In the title-page engraving by William Marshall to *The Smoaking Age, or the Life and Death of Tobacco* (London, 1617), it may well be a broken, discarded

---

[47] Peter J. Davey, 'The archaeology of the clay tobacco pipe', in David Davison and Martin Henig (eds.), *British Archaeological Reports: Past, Present and Future* (Oxford: Tempus Reparatum, 1996), 65–72, at 65; see also Museum of London, 'Clay Tobacco Pipes Makers' Marks from London' project database (London: Museum of London, n.d.): <http://www.museumoflondon.org.uk/claypipes/index.asp>, accessed 1 May 2010.

[48] Peter J. Davey et al., *The Archaeology of the Clay Tobacco Pipe*, 12 vols (Oxford: BAR, 1979–); Davey, 'Archaeology'.

[49] e.g. for a wooden tobacco tamper stolen by a highwayman, see *London Gazette*, 14 March 1678, p. 2 col. 2.

[50] Transcribed in Edwin and Stella George (eds.), *Bristol Probate Inventories 1657–89*, Bristol Record Society Vol. 57 (Bristol: Bristol Record Society, 2005), 171–2.

[51] Ibid., 6–8.

[52] See Anon., 'Clay Pipes and the Archaeologist' (London: Museum of London, n.d.): <http://www.museumoflondon.org.uk/claypipes/pages/claypipesandthearchaeologist.asp>, accessed 1 May 2010; Davey, 'Archaeology', 65.

[53] As shown in the 1663 engraving of Jack Adams, the 'Cunning Man of Clerkenwell Green', British Museum, Prints and Drawings, 1848,0911.369.

pipe sitting on the table before the right-hand figure, Captain Snuffe; the stem is certainly much shorter than those held by Snuffe and his two co-smokers.[54] Smoking in seventeenth-century England thus provides us with a practice, materially borne out as widespread and mundane, that embodies many of the key criteria of eighteenth-century consumption: mass-produced and mass-consumed, dependent on global trade, and with exotic (but quickly domesticated) associations, the tobacco-pipe should challenge the teacup as an epitome of 'consumer revolution'. That it has not to date should make us re-examine our frameworks of understanding for early modern British consumption.

SUPPLYING THE MUNDANE

If tobacco-smoking needs to be recuperated as a phenomenon of pre-1700 but post-medieval consumption, so too do other quotidian (rather than luxury) goods produced in greater quantities and through new processes. A classic narrative of a luxury good which was subject to innovative reinvention (and, as importantly, domestication) in our period is supplied in the development of English drinking glass production from the late sixteenth century, a narrative which can be found in Peck, Berg, and, of course, the V&A's British Galleries.[55] But there was also a premium set upon those inventions and discoveries which supplied the necessary and met the developing needs of society, or which, in Sir William Petty's words were of 'universal use', evident in communications such as the Royal Society's *Philosophical Transactions* and John Houghton's publications.[56] As we have already seen, developments in metallurgical and mineral extraction and processing transformed the Restoration hearth and kitchen, but there were many other innovations on this domestic scale. Yet you will search in vain in Peck, Weatherill, indeed probably any recent account of early modern British material culture for my next object. It is however present in Bristol chapman John Austen's inventoried merchandize: the brass thimble.

The mechanization of brass thimble production in later seventeenth-century England epitomizes the processes which the Royal Society's committees on mechanics and the 'History of Trades' in its early years were concerned with improving. The thimble itself is an ancient object, but its use in England has not been traced earlier than the fifteenth century, with the majority of thimbles in this and the next two centuries imported from northern Europe.[57] Prior to the late seventeenth century, the production of metal

---

[54] British Museum, Prints and Drawings, Gg, 4U.13.

[55] See also Hugh Willmott, *Early Post-Medieval Vessel Glass in England, c.1500–1670*, CBA Research Report 132 (York: Council for British Archaeology, 2002), 10–34; cf. Berg, *Luxury and Pleasure*, 119–26.

[56] British Library, Add. MS 72,891, Petty Papers, fo. 8v: cited Peck, *Consuming Splendor*, 316, cf. 322. For Houghton, see *A Collection for Improvement of Husbandry and Trade* (London, 1692–1703), reprinted in 4 vols. (Farnborough: Gregg International Publishers Ltd, 1969).

[57] Edwin F. Holmes, *A History of Thimbles* (New York/London: Cornwall Books, 1985), 19, 37.

thimbles was entirely by hand, with the holes for pushing the needle through fabric created by hand-punching.[58] This was to change in England with the engineering efforts of a Dutch émigré, John Lofting (c.1659–1742), who had arrived in London before 1686.[59] Lofting, who specialized in building water-powered engines, created a horse-powered engine (for which a patent was granted in April 1693), enabling the mechanical stamping of thimble indentations. He set up a manufactory using this technology in Islington by the end of 1695, and by the close of the century is believed to have been producing yearly in excess of 2 million thimbles, having moved manufacturing to Marlow, Buckinghamshire (in Houghton's account of his work in July 1697). This scale of production however scarcely registers in the material history of the seventeenth century: excavated thimbles are difficult to date, and do not bear the sorts of manufacturing marks which enable clay pipes to be chronologically and geographically placed.[60]

That Lofting's thimble production was seen as both valuable and important can be gauged by an advertisement in *The Post Man and the Historical Account* of 26 May 1705:

> All Merchants, Haberdashers and other Dealers in Thimbles, that have occasion for any quantity, may be furnished with the best English thimbles of brass or steel, cheaper than they can be imported, at Mr Christopher Greenwood's, merchant, on St Dunstan's Hill, or at Mr Suttonsharp's, at the sign of the Gate in Crooked Lane, London, who will also pay 5 Guineas to such persons as shall inform them of thimbles made contrary to the patent granted to Mr J. Lofting, on condition that they discover the Makers and their accomplices, and make proof against them, so as they may be prosecuted according to Law.[61]

That Lofting applied his engineering expertise to the manufacture of thimbles, as opposed to something more luxurious and high value, is also noteworthy. He invested in thimbles because he recognized a good that was both in wide demand and relatively cheap to manufacture, but which was mainly produced overseas and was subject to heavy duties: as his own patent stated, this latter fact 'doth much discourage the merchants from bringing the same over, so that the price of that commodity will come to be enhanced upon our subjects.'[62]

Like shoe buckles in the following century, thimbles represent a good that is not entirely necessary (one can sew without one), but the utility of which is increased by their accessibility, affordability, and aesthetic qualities.[63] Although Lofting's thimbles may not have embodied the latter value (unlike contemporary silver thimbles, prized

[58] Holmes, *Thimbles*, 21.

[59] K. R. Fairclough, 'Lofting, John (c.1659–1742)', *Oxford Dictionary of National Biography*, Oxford University Press, September 2004; online edn January 2008, <http://www.oxforddnb.com/view/article/16933>, accessed 8 June 2010.

[60] Ibid; Houghton, *Collection*, 23 July 1697, Vol. II, No. 260, 1; Holmes, *Thimbles*, 137–8.

[61] *The Postman and the Historical Account*, 26 May 1705, 2.

[62] John Houghton records 304,000 thimbles coming into London in the three months between March 1691/2 and June 1692: *Collection*, 30 April 1692, 4; 28 May 1692, 2; 25 June 1692, 2; patent 391, cited by Holmes, *Thimbles*, 189.

[63] Berg, *Luxury and Pleasure*, 159, 167–8.

possessions indeed), they certainly met the first two criteria. Lofting's thimbles were sold by their maker for 4 or 5s per gross, each thimble costing a fraction of a penny; they were also packed up into easily transportable packets for chapmen to carry.[64] Thimbles also belong to that category of feminized good that, although small, could be personalized and thus transformed from good into possession. The lady who lost her (admittedly silver) thimble in a flowered damask pocket, along with other small things, 'of but small value', nevertheless thought it worth advertising her loss via the dubious services of thief-taker Jonathan Wild in February 1718.[65]

While Maxine Berg suggests that it was techniques like 'rolling, stamping, and moulding…division of labour, powered machinery' that fuelled 'eighteenth-century invention', these are all evident in the production of Lofting's brass thimbles; and his was certainly not an isolated example of pre-eighteenth-century mechanized mass production, if Houghton's accounts can be trusted.[66] Yet, in the historiography of eighteenth-century consumption, technological ingenuity and market orientation appear to have been freshly forged in the Birmingham manufactories of Matthew Boulton, or fired in Wedgwood's Staffordshire kilns; late seventeenth-century Islington and Marlow scarcely feature in this topography of innovation.

MANAGING MATERIALS: MAINTENANCE AND DURABILITY

As an example of the material culture of needlework, but also an artefact of technologies of repair, the thimble leads to our last area of concern: the maintenance, repair, and recirculation of goods in the seventeenth-century household. The view that 'clothes in a drawer have no meaning' is indeed mistaken.[67] Studying material storage, cleaning, and repair can help identify attitudes to preservation and durability that were potentially open to erosion by wider availability, turnover, and the cheaper cost of goods across the range of consumer items—from clothing to teacups—by the beginning of the nineteenth century. It is this shift, from an appreciation of and value set on durability, to an appreciation of and value set on variability and novelty, which arguably sets apart the sixteenth and seventeenth centuries from those that follow.

Even in the early eighteenth century, concerns about material durability often outweighed the visual appeal of new goods. Without secure supply of replacement goods (and even with it, in a burgeoning centre like London), maintenance and adaptation continued as key virtues of the economic householder. Preserving and renewing, rather

---

[64] Houghton, *Collection*, 23 July 1697, 1.

[65] *Daily Courant*, 7 February 1718, 2.

[66] Maxine Berg, 'From imitation to invention: creating commodities in eighteenth-century Britain', *Economic History Review*, 55/1 (2002), 1–30, at 26; Houghton, *Collection, passim*.

[67] cf. Grassby, 'Material culture', 597.

than making (or buying) new, marked out the frugal housewife from her spendthrift counterpart, not only in conduct books, but in real life: Edward Belson, a Reading distiller, bewailed 'how exceedingly chargeable is married life' when his wife Rachel purchased yet more new linens in August 1728.[68] This is not to say that nineteenth-century consumers of domestic goods were not also concerned with preservation and conservation of their material worlds; but that the seventeenth century in England marks a period in which certain objects *in their own right* (that is, not as religious relics or as carriers of intrinsic economic value, such as silverwares) came to be seen as extensions of the self and of familial identity, and thus worthy of preservation. An account of conservation in the pre-industrial period to complement that of consumption is thus needed to historicize these cultures of repair and reuse, and assess whether attitudes to these practices did change with the greater availability and variety of new goods.[69]

Materially, this subject is rather difficult to pursue for the seventeenth century, as indeed for the entire period up until the end of the Second World War: broken and repaired objects are not easily found in publicly accessible museum displays.[70] While our own culture of re-consumption is mainly concerned with supplying materials for recycling beyond the household via charity shops, electronic auctions, or the local dump, earlier generations practised extensive in-house repurposing and reuse. When a linen shift could no longer be worn, it could be cut down into cloths for cleaning, handkerchiefs, or sold as rags for papermaking. When a pewter pot was dented, it could be banged out by an itinerant tinker, or melted down and recast.[71] Even non-domestic items could be refashioned into household objects: witness Elizabeth Pepys's reuse of a standard flag as possible linings for bed curtains, 'or for twenty uses, to our great contentment', in February 1664.[72]

This reuse and recirculation of domestic goods in Britain is however becoming more visible historically.[73] There was a lively market for second-hand furnishings, kitchen goods, and occupational equipment (especially agricultural) by the end of the seventeenth century, in areas like Kent and north-west England. Sales of second-hand goods were not solely the realm of the bankrupt or the needy, however: domestic downsizing, the desire of the family to liquidate an estate, and moving away were equally common

---

[68] Berkshire Record Office, D/EZ/12/1&2, Account and memorandum book of Edward Belson, *c*.1707–22, up.

[69] Susan Strasser, *Waste and Want: A Social History of Trash* (New York: Henry Holt and Co., 1999), ch. 1; Sara Pennell, 'For a crack or flaw despis'd: thinking about ceramic durability and the "everyday" in late seventeenth and early eighteenth-century England', in Tara Hamling and Catherine Richardson (eds.), *Everyday Objects: Medieval and Early Modern Material Culture and its Meanings* (Farnham: Ashgate, 2010), 27–40.

[70] Although see 'Making Ceramics', room 143, case 6, in the V&A Ceramics Galleries.

[71] Donald Woodward, '"Swords into ploughshares": recycling in pre-industrial England', *Economic History Review*, 2nd series, 38 (1985), 175–91.

[72] Robert Latham and William Matthews (eds.), *The Diary of Samuel Pepys*, 11 vols. (London: G. Bell and Sons, 1970–82), Vol. 5, 48.

[73] For a recent overview of this work, see J. Stobart and Ilja van Damme, 'Introduction', in idem (eds.), *Modernity and the Second-hand Trade: European Consumption Cultures and Practices, 1700–1900* (Basingstoke: Palgrave Macmillan, 2010), 1–15.

motivations.[74] For the potential purchaser, a neighbour's household sale was a possible source of domestic furnishings, to be set alongside new purchases and inherited goods, especially in rural communities, where other opportunities for purchasing might be limited (by time and geography, as much as by availability per se).

On 22 May 1656, the Sussex clergyman Giles Moore (1617–79) entered into his journal details of the goods he had purchased of one Mr Selwyn, executor to the late Mr Pell:

> an old Presse for cloaths coasting [sic] 5s Two formes, Two shelves and a meat block standing in the dairy, 4s 6d. Two stallages in the Buttery 2s 6d the table dresser Board and block in the kitchin 6s. A beestall 5s the old long Table in the Hall giv'n gratis [sum] 1–3–0.[75]

In assembling his new household in Horstead Keynes, where he had just been appointed to the living, Moore blended old and new purchases alongside those goods retained from his earlier housekeeping at Stanmer. We know from a listing of goods transferred from Stanmer to Horstead that Moore owned next to no kitchen furnishings or equipment, so his purchases from Selwyn were both timely and economically astute.[76] Yet Moore was not impoverished, and thus 'involuntarily' consuming second-hand goods; he chose to purchase these goods in this way, while choosing to purchase others new. The multiple lives of domestic goods in the seventeenth century were thus not simply shaped by either paucity and uncertainty of supply of alternate goods, or by economic constraints upon the consumer, or indeed a specifically pre-modern ethic of frugality.[77]

These multiple 'lives' were nonetheless enabled by strategies of maintenance and repair, and these strategies are resonant of prevailing attitudes to new goods and the property of material 'newness'. Recipes for laundering the hoods, handerkerchiefs, and pockets in luxury and not-so luxury fabrics, which became more widely worn and used across the seventeenth century, appear in numerous manuscript recipe collections now housed at the Wellcome Library, London. The one attributed to Mrs Mary Chantrell, who signed and dated the book (16 January 1690) on its opening pages, has two folios dedicated to laundering fabrics, including recipes to 'scowr calicoes', 'to scowr silkes', to clean all ribbons but black, and two recipes to launder and prepare sarsenet (a type of fine silk) hoods; the last of these is annotated, 'this last receapt of washing sharnett [sic: sarsenet] hoods I larned to wash them my selfe: it's a very good way and they look as well as any new hoods, when they are done.'[78]

---

[74] Sara Pennell, '"All but the kitchen sink": household sales and the circulation of second-hand goods in early modern England', in Stobart and van Damme, *Modernity and the Second-hand Trade*, 37–56.

[75] Ruth Bird (ed.), *The Journal of Giles Moore*, Sussex Record Society Vol. 68 (Lewes: Sussex Record Society, 1971), 264–5.

[76] Bird, *Giles Moore*, 12–13; cf. Amanda Vickery, *Behind Closed Doors: At Home in Georgian England* (London and New Haven: Yale University Press, 2009), ch. 3.

[77] Trentmann, 'Materiality', 294–6.

[78] Wellcome Library, MS 1548, MS recipe book attributed to Mary Chantrell and others, begun in 1690; recipes on fos. 82v–85v; citing from fo. 85v. See also Wellcome Library, MS 4054, dated to c.1690–1710, recipes cited at 111–12; Wellcome Library, MS 2323, dated to c.1691–1738, recipes cited at fos. 43r–52r. All these manuscripts are now freely available to view digitally, via the Wellcome Library webpages.

The emphasis here is upon working up existing goods to look as good as new, which does suggest that the pristine-ness that being new imparted to an object was highly prized. Yet, there is not a sense in this recipe or others like it that already owned goods were, if well maintained 'to look as new', in any way inferior to new-bought goods; new-ness, in and of itself, did not privilege an object. Unwillingness to dispose of still service-able and presentable goods is evident in their relocation around households. In January 1666, when Elizabeth Pepys finally completed sewing 'with her own hands' (as Pepys proudly recorded) the new bed furnishings and en suite hangings for the best cham-ber at Seething Lane, Pepys noted that the 'old red ones' were removed to his dressing room.[79] One suspects that even though a new bed and furnishings were purchased for the same best chamber in November 1668, Elizabeth's handmade hangings did not go to waste; they were probably redeployed elsewhere in the house, or perhaps sold on.

In this retention, we might see more continuities, rather than differences between early and late modern care strategies.[80] But there are concerns with the maintenance of more novel, and indeed more fragile, goods seemingly new to the late seventeenth century which surface in recipes for mending the by then more widely available dec-orative earthenwares and porcelains. Recipes for mending broken glass had appeared in published texts (in English) from the late sixteenth century, but those for mending 'cheny' (the contemporary term embracing both porcelain and fine earthenwares) seem not to appear in print until at least the 1670s, and in manuscript collections around the same time.[81] The manuscript collection attributed to the Lowther family of Marske, and probably begun by Sir William Lowther (c.1670–1705), contains two distinct recipes for mending china; one is entitled 'to glew or fasten china togather', and uses isinglass and brandy boiled together to make a jelly, while the other is a more complex 'sement for broken China or other fin [sic] ware'.[82]

Turning to textiles—in receipt of an extensive scholarship on early modern recycling and reuse—the indigenous calico-printing industry that developed in the late seven-teenth century in and around London presents a useful case study of conflicting atti-tudes to material value and preservation before 1720.[83] It also slightly questions the recent assertion that 'printing and dyeing on cloth was the most important area of *eighteenth-century* innovation in Europe'.[84] The engraver William Sherwin (c.1645–c.1709 or after) secured a patent in 1676 on a process to print colour-fast calicoes, using new mordants (to fix the colours) in the dyeing process.[85] Although Sherwin's printed cloth washed

[79] Latham and Matthews, *Diary of Samuel Pepys*, Vol. 7, 14, 24.

[80] Ibid., Vol. 9, 365, 367; Trentmann, 'Materiality', 295–6.

[81] Pennell, 'For a crack or flaw despis'd', 36.

[82] Wellcome Library, MS 3341, dated to late seventeenth century, attributed to Lowther family, 93, 97.

[83] G. Riello, 'The globalization of cotton textiles: Indian cottons, Europe and the Atlantic world, 1600–1850', in G. Riello and Prasannan Parthasarathi (eds.), *The Spinning World: a Global History of Cotton Textiles, 1200–1850* (Oxford: Pasold Research Fund/Oxford University Press, 2009), 261–90.

[84] My emphasis: ibid., 280.

[85] Antony Griffiths, 'Sherwin, William (b. c.1645, d. in or after 1709)', *Oxford Dictionary of National Biography*, Oxford University Press, September 2004, <http://www.oxforddnb.com/view/article/25396>, accessed 11 June 2010.

poorly, subsequent grants appear to have produced much more durable materials. By 1696, the domestic calico-printing trade was strong enough to help dismiss a bill banning the importation of printed calicoes into England (and which potentially extended prohibition to domestically printed materials); the petition focused on the 'usefulness and cheapness' of their product so 'very beneficial to the public'. In 1711, the directors of the East India Company could write to their subcontinent factors that 'our people here [print calicoes] at one-half the price and better colours and patterns'.[86]

As an important moment in the history of both site-intensive production, and of textile preservation, the development of English calico-printing has been overlooked, in favour of the fabric's more general role as a phenomenon of global trade hybridity.[87] Yet English calico-printing by 1720 was 'a factory industry of the modern type', with factories such as Peter Mauvillon's in south-west London employing over 200 workers in 1719. It was also the target of what we might see as the first instance of machine-breaking, with extensive rioting against calico-print works in London and its environs occurring in 1719–22.[88]

Printed calicoes were initially used for domestic linens (for example, bed and window curtains), and also, increasingly, for petticoats and other articles of clothing, 'wherever appearance was crucial'.[89] Their colour-fastness, as well as colour vibrancy, was highly appreciated, along with the quick drying of the cotton from which they were made. Yet, as with the new ceramics, there were major concerns about the durability of such fabrics. English calico-printing on the scale achieved by 1720 may indeed have contributed to the flooding of the domestic textile market at the lower end, with colourful cloths to adorn the non-elite English home and (to a lesser extent) body, but these were materials the anonymous author of *The Merchant's Ware-house Laid Open, Or, The Plain Dealing Linnen Draper* (London, 1696), declared to be 'naturally a rotton [sic] sort of wear'.[90]

Thus the so-called 'calico craze' of the late seventeenth and early eighteenth centuries is not solely or even about spendthrift, irrational consumers throwing money away on 'tawdry' (a word frequently used by its denigrators) fabrics. The contemporary discourses around calicoes not only concern globalization (a current historiographical 'craze' in itself); as importantly, the material itself bears witness to the tensions between durability and fashionability that so much decision-making about domestic consumption needed (and still often needs) to negotiate. The prospective calico consumer had to weigh up her options, through careful assessment of likely usage and cost, as well as

---

[86]   Parliamentary Archives, HL/PO/JO/10/2/23, Silks (Persia and East Indies) Bill, 31 March 1696, Petition of the calico printers; P. J. Thomas, 'England's debt to Indian handicrafts: an account of the beginnings of calico printing in England', *Indian Journal of Economics*, 12 (1932), 457–72, cited at 468; cf. Riello, 'Globalization', 273.

[87]   Riello, 'Globalization', 273–80.

[88]   Thomas, 'England's debt', 468–9; Muriel Clayton and Alma Oakes, 'Early calico printers around London', *Burlington Magazine*, 96/614 (May 1954), 135–9, at 139. Chloe Wigston Smith, '"Calico madams": servants, consumption and the Calico Crisis', *Eighteenth-Century Life*, 31/2 (2007), 29–55.

[89]   Spufford, *Great Reclothing*, 108–11, 121–2; John Styles, 'What were cottons for in the early industrial revolution?', in Riello and Parthasarathi, *The Spinning World*, 307–26, at 314.

[90]   Cited by Spufford, *Great Reclothing*, 109.

appearance and general appeal: assessments which needed to be rooted in practices of everyday life, as much as in response to contemporary mercantilist debates and projects. One can only wonder how long Mary Chantrell's calicoes lasted as they were 'scowred', and how she, a virtuous housewife, might have felt if they fell, as Daniel Defoe warned in 1727 they would, 'soon to rags'.[91]

CONCLUSION

From a historiography very much rooted in the free market economics of the Reagan and Thatcher eras, to a revisionist agenda attending to use, the cultures of ownership, and even 'making do' and mending, it certainly seems that histories of consumption, at least in and of Britain, reflect the economic climates in which historians write them.[92] Yet this attention to practices, rather than perceptions of desire, is not simply an intellectual response to the twenty-first century 'austerity' sweeping the modern West. It marks the superseding of a cultural history based solely on textual and literary accounts of imagined 'needs and wants', and the coming of age of a more concrete and necessarily more complex history focused upon experience and the materialization of those needs and wants.[93]

One of the perennial concerns of British consumption historiography has been with periodization: which century 'made us' into consumers? But to be forever seeking out a possibly mythical point of consumer take-off is arguably a quest with diminishing returns. Instead we should be seeking out continuities, to understand better when significant change actually occurred within the practices, as well as the ideologies, of consumption. This surely means more attention to the quotidian, which of course is less freighted with desire, and usually less materially present to us now, than to 'luxury' and 'splendour'. That said, the objects/practices discussed above materialize features of seventeenth-century consumption that are not simply and solely captured by adjectives such as 'mundane', 'quotidian' or 'functional'; they embrace display, sociability, and self-making too. Let us return to the lady advertising the loss of her thimble in 1718, where the double meaning of 'value' of such small goods oft forgotten by historians is clear: monetarily, the value is negligible, but to the lady, its value as hers, to her, is immeasurable. Attending to the very matter of consumption in all its varieties should make us think more closely about what truly mattered to seventeenth-century Britons.

---

[91] Cited by John Styles, *The Dress of the People: Everyday Fashion in Eighteenth-Century England* (London and New Haven: Yale University Press, 2007), 130.

[92] Frank Trentmann, 'The modern genealogy of the consumer: meanings, knowledge and identities', in idem and John Brewer (eds.), *Consuming Cultures, Global Perspectives: Historical Trajectories, Transnational Exchanges* (London: Berg, 2006), 19–69.

[93] Grassby, 'Material culture', 602; Trentmann, 'Materiality', 307.

BIBLIOGRAPHY

Berg, Maxine, *Luxury and Pleasure in Eighteenth-Century Britain* (Oxford: Oxford University Press, 2005).

Hamling, Tara and Richardson, Catherine (eds.), *Everyday Objects: Medieval and Early Modern Material Culture and its Meanings* (Farnham: Ashgate, 2010).

Harvey, Karen (ed.), *History and Material Culture* (Abingdon: Routledge, 2009).

McKendrick, Neil, Brewer, John, and Plumb, J. H., *The Birth of a Consumer Society: the Commercialization of Eighteenth-Century England*, pbk edn. (London: Hutchinson, 1983).

Overton, Mark, Dean, Darron and Whittle, Jane, *Production and Consumption in English Households 1600–1750* (London: Routledge, 2004).

Peck, Linda Levy, *Consuming Splendor: Society and Culture in Seventeenth-century England* (Cambridge: Cambridge University Press, 2005).

Shammas, Carole, *The Pre-Industrial Consumer in England and America* (Oxford: Clarendon Press, 1990).

Thirsk, Joan, *Economic Policy and Projects* (Oxford: Clarendon Press, 1978).

Trentmann, Frank, 'Materiality in the future of history: things, practices and politics', *Journal of British Studies*, 48:2 (2009), 283–307.

CHAPTER 5

AFRICA AND THE GLOBAL LIVES OF THINGS

JEREMY PRESTHOLDT

CONSUMER desire stands at a crossroads. It reflects and reinforces social norms, inequalities, and aspirations while translating these into the language of economic exchange. Thus, reflection on the rationales for and consequences of consumption practices can provide insight into shifting social relationships, but much more as well: it offers a window on processes of global interrelation. Holistic approaches to consumption that consider the cultural logics of demand alongside their distant reverberations have yielded new ways of understanding the history of global interdependence.[1] The study of consumption in African societies is instructive in this regard. Inquiries into commodification, social distinction and fashion have offered fresh perspectives on African social relations and cultural formations. They have also contributed to a better understanding of how consumer demand has shaped Africa's relationships with other world regions, particularly before the colonial era. From the vantage point of consumer interests we have begun to gain a better appreciation of how Africa's articulation with global economic trends simultaneously affected Africans and many others around the world.

A focus on patterns of social change and mutual constitution through consumption brings African agency into relief. Such an analytical frame also risks minimizing Africa's economic marginalization. Yet the study of consumption in Africa and longer-term

---

[1] See for instance, Arjun Appadurai (ed.), *The Social Life of Things: Commodities in Cultural Perspective.* (Cambridge: Cambridge University Press, 1986); C. A. Bayly, *The Birth of the Modern World, 1780–1914* (Malden, MA: Blackwell, 2004); Karen Tranberg Hansen, *Salaula: The World of Secondhand Clothing Trade and Zambia* (Chicago: University of Chicago Press, 2000); Jan Hogendorn and Marion Johnson, *The Shell Money of the Slave Trade* (Cambridge: Cambridge University Press, 2003); Marcy Norton, 'Tasting Empire: Chocolate and the Internalization of Mesoamerican Aesthetics', *American Historical Review*, 111/3 (2006), 660–91; Gary Y. Okihiro, *Pineapple Culture: A History of the Tropical and Temperate Zones.* (Berkeley: University of California Press, 2009); Frank Trentmann, 'Crossing Divides: Consumption and Globalization in History', *Journal of Consumer Culture*, 9 (2009), 187–220.

material disparities are intertwined. Imported consumer goods were both elemental to social relationships and a cornerstone of Africa's global interfaces. Reflection on African consumer interests thus promises to enrich our understanding of Africa's position within emerging global hierarchies. Specifically, attention to African cultures of consumption before colonial rule can sharpen our understanding of *why*, by what social and cultural rationales, Africans engaged in the regional and global exchanges that sowed social strife, adversely affected local ecologies, and gave rise to slave-plantation complexes in East and West Africa. While Africa's trade relationships created few opportunities for long-term capital accumulation on the continent, the consumer goods acquired through them were vital to position, belonging, and authority in most African societies before the colonial era.[2] The consumer demands of Africans likewise shaped global economic relationships well into the colonial era, sometimes in ways that colonial administrations could not easily control.

ARTICULATING AFRICAN CONSUMER INTERESTS

African poverty has prompted analysts to ask how the forces of global integration have affected the continent's systems of production. Colonial exploitation and recent structural adjustment programmes figure prominently in this reckoning, but scholars have likewise outlined how the pre-colonial demand for slaves, minerals, ivory, and the produce of burgeoning African plantation systems enriched Europe and the Americas while impoverishing Africa.[3] This line of inquiry is of central import, but it has an epistemological limitation: to address questions of underdevelopment, analysts have often emphasized the interests and initiatives of non-Africans. While European-African relations became increasingly asymmetrical over time, by interpreting pre-colonial African societies through their adaptation (or resistance) to foreign demands, the social rationales for African engagement in transregional and global networks of exchange are easily obscured.

Greater attention to the socio-political matrices of power in pre-colonial African societies has offered a way to address this lacuna. Until recently, Africa's most limited resource was people; labour was scarcer than land. Patron-client relationships defined by mutual obligation were primary social bonds in many African societies. Thus, wealth was commonly located in clients and kinship networks—in the control of people more

---

[2] As Jane Guyer outlines in her study of Atlantic Africa's interfaces with European economies, Africans were often 'capitalist in commercial method but not in the uses of money capital'. *Marginal Gains: Monetary Transactions in Atlantic Africa* (Chicago: University of Chicago Press, 2004), 9.

[3] Walter Rodney, *How Europe Underdeveloped Africa* (Washington, DC: Howard University Press, 1989); Immanuel Wallerstein, *The Modern World-System*, 3 vols. (New York: Academic Press, 1974–89).

than in things, as Jane Guyer has emphasized.[4] In return for their followers' allegiances, political elites offered protection and material rewards. '[G]enerosity', Megan Vaughan writes, 'was the price one had to pay for the exercise of any authority'.[5] Specifically, gifts of cloth, beads, foodstuffs, liquor, or other valuable goods were essential to the maintenance of subjects and, by extension, political power. As a result, objects, along with livestock and foodstuffs, were a means to acquire power and influence over people. Labour, however, remained notoriously difficult to control in most African societies.

The expansion of external markets created social and political opportunities for African leaders to circumvent some of the restrictions imposed by such socio-political conditions. They found that selling to the global market and controlling relationships with foreign merchants was less demanding than managing the productive practices of their subjects. This 'externalization' of wealth creation, and the rise of what Frederick Cooper has referred to as 'gatekeeper' states, was perhaps most evident in the slave trade. Foreign slave buyers offered the promise of, in Cooper's words, 'externalizing the consumption of slave labor—and hence the problem of discipline'.[6] By selling captives, leaders gained the means to placate subjects and subdue enemies. A seeming irony emerged: wealth lay in followers and their productive capacities, yet to gain and retain power one needed the means to distribute gifts and coerce labour. With the expansion of overseas trade, selling people, as opposed to disciplining them, offered the most immediate political returns since it was easier to convert people into useful goods than to extract their labour.

Slave-trading was only one dimension of Africa's global extroversion. By the middle of the nineteenth century a diverse set of global relationships had developed in the wake of the slave trade in West as well as East Africa. For instance, at the height of East Africa's economic expansion in the nineteenth century, ivory and the products of slave labour dominated the export market. As I demonstrate below, the region became more fully integrated into patterns of transoceanic exchange, and this created a dynamic in which control over people was increasingly difficult. More individuals began to accumulate objects such as cloth and beads, items that had important use- *and* exchange-values. These new imports were deployed by an increasing diversity of people to claim position and gain followers, thus weakening the 'gatekeeper' position of the old elite.

African definitions of wealth, difficulties in labour coercion and the profit of controlling interfaces with external markets offer insights into why Africa's pre-colonial global relationships took the shape they did. However, these internal dynamics of Africa's extroversion raise additional questions. For instance, why did African consumer demands take the form of goods such as cloth, beads, brass wire, alcohol, and guns?

---

[4] Jane Guyer, 'Wealth in people, wealth in things: Introduction', *Journal of African History*, 36/1 (1995), 83–8.

[5] Megan Vaughan, 'Africa and the Birth of the Modern World', *Transactions of the Royal Historical Society* 16 (2006), 152.

[6] Frederick Cooper, 'Africa's Pasts and Africa's Historians', *Canadian Journal of African Studies* 34 (2000), 321; Frederick Cooper, *Africa since 1940: the Past of the Present* (Cambridge: Cambridge University Press, 2002); see also Jean-François Bayart, 'Africa in the World: A History of Extraversion', *African Affairs*, 99/395 (2000), 217–67.

Just as importantly, how was it that Africans often found the terms of trade in their favour and thus regularly determined the shape of global interfaces?[7] Moreover, what did African influence over these interfaces mean for the producers of goods exported to Africa? Emmanuel Akyeampong, Philip Curtin, Joseph Inikori, Joseph Miller, and others have addressed these questions by highlighting the importance of African consumer interests in the shaping of the continent's internal and external relationships.[8] Curtin, for example, argues that at the height of the external slave trade in Senegambia French manufacturers went to great lengths to appeal to local tastes. Richard Roberts further demonstrates that French investors founded the first industrial textile mill in India for the purpose of producing cloth that appealed to Senegambian tastes.[9] Studying Liverpool merchants, David Richardson shows that during the era of the transatlantic slave trade the requirements of satisfying the tastes of West African consumers affected suppliers, prices, and even the networks on which Liverpool traders relied. Liverpool firms regularly depended on foreign producers of textiles, beads, and iron since British manufacturers were less successful in producing consumer goods that met West African standards. Richardson's work suggests that African patterns of demand significantly affected the entire structure of the English slave trade.[10]

In this essay I wish to address how the social dynamics of consumer demand in Africa were shaped by, and gave shape to, larger social, economic, and political relationships from the sixteenth to the early twentieth century. Though this approach necessarily

[7] In the case of the Loango coast of West Central Africa, Phyllis M. Martin argued that Africans 'called the tune' of transoceanic exchanges. *The External Trade of the Loango Coast, 1576–1870: The Effects of changing Commercial Relations on the Vili Kingdom of Loango* (Oxford: Oxford University Press, 1972), 144.

[8] Emmanuel Akyeampong, *Drink, Power, and Cultural Change: A Social History of Alcohol in Ghana, c.1800 to Recent Times* (Portsmouth, NH: Heinemann, 1996); Philip Curtin, *Economic Change in Precolonial Africa: Senegambia in the Era of the Slave Trade* (Madison, WI: University of Wisconsin Press, 1975); Joseph Inikori, *Africans and the Industrial Revolution in England: A Study in International Trade and Economic Development* (Cambridge: Cambridge University Press, 2002); Joseph Miller, *Way of death: merchant capitalism and the Angolan slave trade, 1730–1830* (Madison: University of Wisconsin Press, 1988). See also Stanley Alpern, 'What Africans Got for their Slaves', *History in Africa*, 22 (1995), 5–43; Dmitri van den Bersselaar, *The Drink of Kings: Schnapps Gin from Modernity to Tradition* (Leiden: Brill, 2007); Timothy Burke, *Lifebuoy Men, Lux Women: Commodification, Consumption, and Cleanliness in Modern Zimbabwe* (Durham, NC: Duke University Press, 1996); Jean and John Comaroff, *Of Revelation and Revolution*, 2 vols. (Chicago: University of Chicago Press, 1995–97); Ghislaine Lydon, *On Trans-Saharan Trails: Islamic Law, Trade Networks and Cross-Cultural Exchange in Nineteenth-Century Western Africa* (Cambridge: Cambridge University Press, 2009); Justin Willis, *Potent Brews: A Social History of Alcohol in East Africa, 1850–1999* (Athens, OH: Ohio University Press, 2002).

[9] Richard Roberts, 'West Africa and the Pondicherry Textile Industry', in T. Roy (ed.), *Cloth and Commerce: Textiles in Colonial India* (Thousand Oaks, CA: Sage, 1996), 142–74. The story of Dutch wax print cloth and West African consumers offers a similarly complex story of manufacturing to appeal to specific African consumer interests. Ruth Nielsen, 'The History and Development of Wax-Printed Textiles Intended for West Africa and Zaire', in J. Cordwell and R. Schwarz (eds.), *The Fabrics of Culture: The Anthropology of Clothing and Adornment* (The Hague: Mouton, 1979).

[10] David Richardson, 'West African Consumption Patterns and their Influence on the Eighteenth-century English Slave Trade', in A. Gemery and J. Hogendorn (eds.), *The Uncommon Market: Essays in the Economic History of the Atlantic Slave Trade* (New York: Academic Press, 1979), 308, 310.

entails greater concentration on imported goods than on the circulation of regionally manufactured commodities, it underscores the interrelation of African cultural imperatives and histories of globalization. To give tight form to the essay, I will focus on East Africa in the late nineteenth century, an era notable for its dramatic increase in global interconnectivity. East Africa offers fertile ground for reflection because it boasts a long history of economic, cultural, and religious integration into the circuits of the Indian Ocean region. For millennia, East Africa enjoyed links to societies along the Indian Ocean rim. In the nineteenth century, both continental and transoceanic routes of exchange greatly intensified as the result of a regional economic boom. This proliferation of networks grafted over long timescales of transoceanic interaction provides a unique vantage point to survey the logics and meaning of African consumer demand.

I begin with a snapshot of consumer trends before the nineteenth century. Then I shift focus to three dimensions of consumption in the late nineteenth and early twentieth century: marketing consumer objects, the social relations of consumption, and the ways manufacturers accommodated African consumer demand. Taken together, these themes augment our understanding of social change in Africa and contribute to wider reflections on consumption as a mode of trans-societal relation. Additionally, they highlight how manufactured objects can be conceptually and physically transformed throughout their global life cycles. The 'new lives' of consumer objects that I outline below demonstrate the plasticity of consumer goods—as forms reimagined and refashioned in their circulation.

BEFORE THE NINETEENTH CENTURY

Material consumption in East Africa has taken many forms. Regionally produced consumer goods were dominant in most places before European colonization. Staples of regional consumer demand included foodstuffs, locally brewed alcoholic beverages, iron products, pottery, jewellery made from copper and gold, and clothes made from available plant fibres or skins. Archaeological investigations across the region have identified diverse earthen vessels and metal instruments that bear testimony to changing uses. Evidencing Indian Ocean connections, East Africans imported Persian, Indian, Chinese, and many other ceramic wares since antiquity. The use of Chinese ceramics for ornamenting coastal tombs and mosques suggests that for at least 1,000 years East Africans have invested imports with special meaning.[11]

From the sixteenth century, Portuguese records yield a clear picture of consumer practices along the coast, the Zambezi River, and in the Mozambique hinterland. In the sixteenth century the Portuguese attempted to control the gold trade from the Zimbabwe Plateau. Though their influence rarely reached beyond the Zambezi Valley

[11] Mark Horton and John Middleton, *The Swahili: The Social Landscape of a Mercantile Society* (Oxford: Wiley-Blackwell, 2001); Chapurukha M. Kusimba, *The Rise and Fall of Swahili States* (Lanham, MD: AltaMira, 1999).

and a few coastal towns, Portuguese residents described a regional commercial system that relied on the importation of one category of goods above others: personal adornments. Specifically, cloth and jewellery figured prominently in regional exchanges. Accordingly, these were the most easily recognizable symbols of social status. They filled a variety of other social roles as well. Cloth, for instance, was important to codes of modesty, particularly in coastal Muslim societies. Through gifting, cloth was also a means to gain or retain power over others. Monarchs and other political elites cemented the allegiances of their subjects and allies through the distribution of cloth. Cloth thus mediated interpersonal, commercial, and political relationships.

Weavers on the upper reaches of the Zambezi, the Querimba Islands and in many urban centres made cotton cloth. Along the Zambezi and on the Zimbabwe Plateau local cotton textiles, called *machira*, were highly valued for their durability and were standard gifts to ancestor mediums. The *machira* was also commonly worn among political elites at the court of Mwene Mutapa. In the seventeenth century, the popularity of Indian textiles began to pose a severe challenge to regional weavers.[12] Specifically, Gujarati (north-west Indian) cottons dyed in dark-blue hues—called *kaniki* in Swahili—became the standard clothing for both men and women along East Africa's main avenues of exchange. These also became symbols of social respectability. Stressing the social import of *kaniki*, a Portuguese resident of East Africa wrote that while a person may have been 'very poor and have not even sufficient food to eat during their lives' they would 'use every endeavor' to purchase a *kaniki* in which to be buried.[13]

While East Africans wove cloth from local cotton and imported textiles from India, they also remade imported cloth into fashions that appealed to local tastes. In a pattern that would be widely replicated in the nineteenth century, the city-state of Pate became a centre of remanufacture in the seventeenth century. Weavers on the small island near the Kenyan mainland imported Gujarati silk textiles, unravelled them, and wove them into popular styles. Pate's textile industry found eager buyers from Mogadishu to the upper reaches of the Zambezi. Pate silks became such measures of prestige in eastern Africa that Portuguese merchants often found it difficult to travel on the Zambezi River without offering Pate cloth as tribute to local rulers.[14] East Africans added value to imports in other ways as well. For instance, entrepreneurs along the Zambezi purchased *bertangi*, a striped or dyed Cambay-made cotton cloth, unravelled it, wove beads into the fabric, and then resold it.[15]

    [12] Pedro Machado, 'Awash in a Sea of Cloth: Gujarat, Africa, and the Indian Ocean, 1300–1800', in Giorgio Riello and Prasannan Parthasarathi (eds.), *The Spinning World: A Global History of Cotton Textiles, 1200–1850* (Oxford: Oxford University Press, 2009), 173; Malyn Newitt, *A History of Mozambique* (Bloomington, IN: University of Indiana Press, 1995).

    [13] João dos Santos, *Ethiopia Oriental*, Vol. 1 (Lisbon: n.p., 1609), 111.

    [14] Jeremy Prestholdt, 'As Artistry Permits and Custom May Ordain: The Social Fabric of Material Consumption in the Swahili World *ca.* 1450–1600', *Northwestern University African Studies Center Working Paper Series*, 3 (1998), 15–16.

    [15] Elizabeth MacGonagle, 'Mightier than the Sword: The Portuguese Pen in Ndau History', *History in Africa*, 28 (2001), 183.

While Portuguese attempts to control regional commerce in the sixteenth and seventeenth century dampened trade, in the eighteenth century new caravan routes revived the regional economy and contributed to a heightened demand for imports. The establishment of plantations on the French islands of Mauritius and Reunion drew slave traders to the East African coast. This increase in the demand for slaves, later augmented by Brazil, Saint-Domingue, the Cape region and other parts of eastern Africa, opened new long-distance routes of exchange.[16] Direct trade between Mozambique Island and Makua-speaking areas in northern Mozambique, and from Kilwa Kivinje on the southern coast of Tanzania to the Yao region southeast of Lake Malawi, acted as giant conveyer belts bringing human captives and ivory to the coast and delivering consumer goods to the interior.

African demand for Indian cloth was an important engine of this economy, but styles changed quickly and were difficult to predict. For example, in late eighteenth-century Manyika, Indian cotton cloths such as the dark-blue indigo *zuartes*, coarse white *dotis*, and narrow white *samateres* were in great demand. By the end of the century, middlemen trading to the interior only found a market for *zuartes*. To address such shifts in demand, Indian cloth merchants, particularly Gujarati Vaniya from Diu, entered into a long-term dialogue with African middlemen. As Pedro Machado demonstrates, Vaniya cloth merchants, with information supplied by local interlocutors, regularly relayed shifts in East African consumer demand to producers in Gujarat. Indian weavers could thus make adjustments to cloth designs and send the desired articles in the next trading season.[17]

FASHION AND REFASHIONING

The contours of material consumption in East Africa changed significantly in the nineteenth century. As the region became more integrated into expanding global markets, East Africans purchased imported consumer goods in volumes that surpassed previous eras. In the early nineteenth century the East African savannah was one of the few regions where large numbers of elephants remained. East Africa's bush elephant (*Loxodonta africana*) had tusks of soft ivory, the variety coveted by manufacturers of jewellery and other ivory products. The region produced high-grade copal (used for varnish), rubber, and, with the establishment of plantations on the coast and islands, cloves, sesame, sugar, and grains. At mid-century East Africa was also the last major slave-exporting region of the world, though the export slave trade did not play as

---

[16] Edward Alpers, *Ivory & Slaves in East Central Africa* (London: Heinemann, 1975).

[17] Pedro Machado, 'Cloths of a New Fashion: Networks of Exchange, African Consumerism and Cloth Zones of Contact in India and the Indian Ocean in the Eighteenth and Nineteenth Centuries', in Tirthankar Roy, Om Prakash, Kaoru Sugihara and Giorgio Riello (eds.), *How India Clothed the World: The World of South Asian Textiles, 1500–1850.* (Leiden: Brill, 2009), 53–84.

important a role in East Africa as it had in Atlantic Africa.[18] Since Indian, European, and American manufacturers were mechanizing production and overseas firms in Zanzibar —the region's largest entrepôt—were competing with each other for African consumers, the average price of imported consumer goods in East Africa fell during the second half of the century. At the same time, the price for ivory and other East African exports increased. These convergent price curves offered Africans much greater purchasing power.

Omani influence at the coast had been significant since the end of the seventeenth century, but Omani commercial interests, financed by Indian capital, expanded in the early 1800s. To better exploit economic opportunities in eastern Africa, the Busaidi sultan Seyyid Said moved Oman's capital from Muscat to Zanzibar, a small but well-positioned island close to the Tanzanian mainland. The new sultanate then extended its rule to most of the coastal towns. Seyyid Said made Zanzibar a free port and encouraged foreign investment. Zanzibar-based firms, most of which were subsidiaries of Indian financial houses, began offering unprecedented lines of credit. This credit fuelled trading ventures to the interior, increased agricultural production for export and brought more cash into circulation. Simultaneously, enterprising traders in many interior societies pioneered new roads to the coast. For instance, Stephen Rockel has shown how Nyamwezi merchants in central Tanzania augmented an older trade in salt and iron across central Tanzania, with direct links to port towns where they bartered for imported consumer goods.[19]

The region lacked navigable rivers to connect the coast and the interior, but caravans facilitated vast networks of exchange. Roads reached from coastal towns such as Kilwa Kivinje, Bagamoyo, and Mombasa to Lake Malawi, the eastern forest belt, and the Kingdom of Buganda on the shores of Lake Victoria. Caravans with porters numbering into the thousands became mobile markets trading imported cloth, beads, and brass wire for export commodities, provisions, and to a lesser extent slaves. As a result, Indian, British, and American cloth was readily available as far as eastern Congo. In the 1840s and 1850s, American cloth—called *merekani* in Swahili—was an important means of 'tribute', or gifts in recognition of a ruler's authority, in many East African societies. At the same time, American cloth became a common component of bride wealth. As a testament to the interpenetration of use- and exchange-values in East Africa, *merekani* even became one of the region's few broadly recognised currencies.

At the coast, access to credit allowed the elite to spend lavishly; it offered social aspirants the means to accumulate and redistribute wealth in attempts to gain retinues; and it gave manual labourers, such as caravan porters and stevedores, the leverage to buy against future wages. Simultaneously, the expansion of regional commerce made it easier for people across the East African region to market subsistence goods or livestock. Along the caravan routes monarchs and small-scale farmers alike exchanged

---

[18] Frederick Cooper, *Plantation Slavery on the East Coast of Africa* (New Haven: Yale University Press, 1972); Abdul Sheriff, *Slaves, Spices, and Ivory in Zanzibar* (London: Heinemann, 1990).

[19] Stephen Rockel, *Carriers of Culture: Labor on the Road in Nineteenth-Century East Africa*, (Portsmouth, NH: Heinemann, 2006).

local products for imported goods. For instance, the sale of a cow to a passing caravan could deliver a windfall of calico, dyed cloths, tobacco, beads, wire, hoes, knives, or gun-powder.[20] Similarly, Zigua farmers living near the coast of northern Tanzania stored up maize surpluses, and in the dry season carried these to port towns to exchange for cloth and other goods. The proliferation of outlets for local products had far-reaching effects. As Jonathon Glassman has demonstrated, by the middle of the century the consideration of exchange-values began to overshadow the use-values of local products. The region quickly transitioned from a subsistence economy to one increasingly dominated by market transactions. Over the course of the century East Africans devoted ever more energy to the production of commodities as a means of acquiring consumer goods. This process of commodification, or the greater market mediation of social interaction, affected all but the most isolated.[21]

Access to imported goods changed how East Africans dressed, how they related to each other, and how political power was defined. For instance, Stephen Rockel relates that in the 1860s most Nyamwezi women wore cotton cloth, but men often favoured skins. By the 1880s almost all Nyamwezi men wore imported cloth, while only people in very remote areas continued to wear skins. A man without cloth was regarded as a 'strug-gling man', and those who wore skins became objects of derision. The long and arduous trek to the coast was a rite of passage for Nyamwezi men, and cloth became so socially important that poor men saw the journey as a critical means of obtaining cloth.[22] In late nineteenth-century Buganda, most shunned bark-cloth in favour of European or Swahili (coastal Muslim) styles. Neil Kodesh argues that by the beginning of the colonial era imported clothing had become a measure of rank. Baganda women would not culti-vate bananas—Buganda's staple crop—if they were not supplied with coloured clothes or white calicos.[23] Even supernatural beings were hungry consumers of cloth. At the coast and on Lake Tanganyika presents in the form of imported cloth were a common means to appease spirits, or *jini*.[24]

The diversity of consumer goods spurred shifting fashions. Joseph Thomson, a British traveller who visited East Africa in the 1870s, wrote that fashion was as important to East Africans as it was to 'the belles of Paris or London'. 'Each tribe', he explained, 'must have its own particular class of cotton, and its own chosen tint, colour, and size among beads'. Thomson noted the exasperation of traders who discovered how quickly consumer goods

[20] Rockel, *Carriers of Culture*, 139.

[21] Jonathan Glassman, *Feasts and Riot: Revelry, Rebellion, and Popular Consciousness on the Swahili Coast, 1856–1888* (Portsmouth: Heinemann, 1995), 35–8, 45; Juhani Koponen, *People and Production in Late Pre-Colonial Tanzania: History and Structures* (Jyväskylä: Finnish Society for Development Studies, 1998).

[22] Rockel, *Carriers of Culture*, 66–8.

[23] Neil Kodesh, 'Renovating Tradition: The Discourse of Succession in Colonial Buganda', *International Journal of African Historical Studies*, 34/3 (2001), 511–41, at 526.

[24] Alpers, '"Ordinary Household Chores": Ritual and Power in a Nineteenth-Century Swahili Women's Possession Cult', *International Journal of African Historical Studies*, 17/4 (1984), 677–702; Henry Morton Stanley, *How I Found Livingstone: Travels, Adventures, and Discoveries in Central Africa.* (New York: Charles Scribner's Sons, 1887).

could decline in value. Only the specific cloth or bead in fashion could fetch a high price, he wrote, everything else 'will hardly be accepted as a present.'[25] New consumer items even drew emotional reactions. For instance, in the 1840s a women's Indian silk-cotton cloth was popularly called the *pasua moyo*, or the 'bursting heart'. The cloth's name was a metaphor for the excitement and longing it engendered. Trademarks became signifiers of prestige as well. In some parts of East Africa, such as Ukuni in south Unyamwezi, the most prized length of American cloth was that with the blue 'Massachusetts Sheeting' stamp on it.[26]

East African consumer tastes were highly differentiated. Beads imported from as far away as Italy, Austria, France, and China offer insight into the diversity of demand. There were at least 400 varieties of beads circulating at mid-century, each with a different value, name, and particular locale of preference. In 1857, for example, red beads were the only kind saleable in Nyamwezi country, whereas black beads were currency in Gogo areas (midway between the coast and Lake Tanganyika) and worthless everywhere else. 'Egg' beads were valuable at the market town of Ujiji on the eastern shores of Lake Tanganyika, but refused most other places. White beads were popular with Fipa, Sagara (east central Tanzania), and Gogo buyers but disliked by Zigua consumers near the coast. The bright yellow 'ghee' bead was in demand by Chagga and Maasai near Mount Kilimanjaro, yet they found no market further south. A consumer's cultural-linguistic affiliation did not always define the minutiae of their wants, however. One traveller who followed the caravan route from the coast to Mount Kilimanjaro wrote that within social or political blocs, 'scarcely two villages concur in their canons of taste'. A certain colour of bead might be in fashion in a specific community, but each person wanted a different shape or size.[27]

At ports of trade foreign merchants had to deliver goods that fit the parameters of East African tastes. This often meant that in addition to watching fashion trends, merchants had to pay close attention to the ways East Africans used imports. Popular uses of brass wire—the most common import after textiles and beads—offer an intriguing example. In East Africa manufactured brass wire was used as a raw material for jewellery-making. In Unyanyembe, the centre of trade in Nyamwezi country, local artisans made imported wire into armlets, leg bracelets, bells, beads, rings, and inlays for gunstocks or knife hilts. As a result, Zanzibari importers would only buy certain gauges, shapes, and lengths and only wire packaged in ways they knew would satisfy jewellers in the interior. American manufacturers designed brass coil conforming to these specifications, and as a result Indian and European firms in Zanzibar were left with no choice but to buy US-made brass coil to sell in East Africa.

---

[25] Joseph Thomson, *To the Central African Lakes and Back: The Narrative of the Royal Geographical Society's East Central African Expedition, 1878–80* (London, 1881), 35–6.

[26] J. Grant, *A Walk Across Africa or Domestic Scenes from my Nile Journey* (Edinburgh: William Blackwood and Sons, 1864), 87.

[27] Harry Johnston, *The Kilimanjaro Expedition. A Record of Scientific Exploration in Eastern Equatorial Africa* (London, 1886), 45; Jeremy Prestholdt, *Domesticating the World: African Consumerism and the Genealogies of Globalization* (Berkeley: University of California Press, 2008).

Foreign merchants suffered when they did not deliver goods that accorded with current African tastes. British merchants, for instance, played only a minor role in the Zanzibar trade because they did not offer much that appealed to East African consumers. Though the British consul exercised considerable political influence at Zanzibar, British firms exported little beyond luxury goods to Zanzibar, including items such as shoes, umbrellas, and carriages. British cloth did find a market in East Africa, but only after a circuitous itinerary. Most of the British cloth purchased by East Africans had been re-exported from India. Mumbai exporters appealed to African consumers by dying, tailoring, and stamping British cloth with designs that conformed to regional tastes. Mumbai firms were so successful in this re-export trade that it continued well into the colonial era (see below). Indian firms recognized that their success was dependent on their agents' abilities to identify trends and relay information about these to dyers and printers. Other importers recognized this, too. In order to gauge the market so that time and money were not lost in sending the wrong goods to East Africa, manufacturers in the United States, Germany, and France usually forwarded samples to their agents in Zanzibar before exporting large consignments.

Given the sluggishness of communication and travel, and the socio-cultural diversity of the East African region, overseas merchants could not always cater to changing trends. To address the minutiae of consumer demand and add value to imports, artisans in coastal cities as well as inland trade centres altered textile designs. Based on information provided by caravan leaders and porters, they added colours, patterns, and borders onto imported cloth. In the 1850s Zanzibari printers found a market in Unyamwezi for the *kitambi banyani*, or white Indian-made cloth stamped with a narrow red border. Similarly, Zanzibaris gave Surati white cotton loincloths broad border stripes of indigo, red, and yellow for discrete interior markets. One of the most impressive examples of how East Africans remade imported consumer goods is the *leso*, a popular item of Muslim women's fashion in Mombasa. The *leso* was a remanufactured cloth, made from colourful men's handkerchiefs exported from Manchester to Mumbai and then on to Zanzibar. In Zanzibar, the handkerchiefs were stitched together to form large wrappers that gave a stunning play of colour and pattern. The style quickly travelled west along the caravan routes, finding eager buyers in non-Muslim societies. By the 1850s women in many societies along the caravan routes were buying the *leso*. Indian manufacturers even began printing cloths with the distinct multiple handkerchief patterns, and by the twentieth century the word *leso* had become the commonly used term in Kenya for bright, printed cloth.

Islam made only limited inroads beyond the coast in the nineteenth century, but as contact with the Muslim coast intensified so did the appeal of Muslim fashions. At the same time that non-Muslim women embraced the *leso*, men in interior markets were drawn to coastal men's fashions—often referred to as 'Swahili'—such as the turban, waistcoat (*kizibao*) and overcoats of Omani provenance (*joho*). While these styles tended to be more popular in the immediate hinterland than further abroad, demand for them in places as far west as Buganda increased in the latter nineteenth century. This demand reached an apex at the turn of the century (see below). Virtually everywhere

Swahili fashions were found, they were symbols of prestige and access to foreign sources of power. Since items like the *kizibao* and *kanzu* were tailored in Zanzibar, coastal artisans benefited from this increase in demand. Yet even tailors in coastal towns and inland trade fairs could not always stay apace of changing local demands. Fashions changed so quickly that caravan traders often found it necessary to redesign pieces of cloth or restring beads while in transit. One strategy caravan leaders employed was to purchase the kinds of cloth or beads previously reported to be in style in a particular locale. Then just before entering the area, the caravan would pause to assess current trends. If necessary, porters would redesign textiles in a way that appealed to local consumers, adding fringes or brightly coloured cloth strips. Though necessary, such tasks could take caravans several days to complete.[28]

As these examples suggest, attention to the life cycles of imported consumer goods reveals an underappreciated layer of complexity to Africa's global interfaces. We typically think of cloth, beads, and brass wire as finished manufactured goods distinct from the raw materials Africans exported. It is more appropriate to think of most imports as unfinished goods. Before they could be sold in local markets, they often had to be redesigned in India, East African ports or on caravan roads. Refashioning was the only means of addressing the uncertainties of changing consumer demands in an era when both travel and communication were slow. By refashioning imports and manufacturing for market niches, regional artisans responded quickly to shifts in consumer demand and translated imported goods into objects of local desire.

ECONOMIES OF DISPLAY
AND DISTRIBUTION

By representing aspirations publicly, new consumer imports were tools in the constitution of personhood and strategies of distinction. For instance, in Mombasa, where residents placed a premium on the social ideals of prestige and respectability, the ability to convert desires into material things was linguistically inscribed in the objects themselves. The Swahili word for 'ability' or 'power', *uwezo*, was not simply a reference to strength; it was also figurative language for home furnishings and their reflection on the home's owner. The *uwezo wa nyumba*, 'the ability of the house', was said to be reflected in the imported mirrors, glasses, and silver vessels in its receiving room, or the Dutch, French, and Chinese porcelain affixed to its walls.[29] 'Ability' referred both to the perceptual effect—the sign-value—of configuring objects in a particular fashion as well as the

[28]   Jeremy Prestholdt, 'On the Global Repercussions of East African Consumerism,' *American Historical Review*, 109/3 (2004), 755–81.

[29]   For a close analysis of this complex subject, see Prita Meier, 'Objects on the Edge: Swahili Coast Logics of Display,' *African Arts*, Winter (2009), 8–23.

social status of a family, its respectability. Home decor was also part of a larger symbolic system as well. In many East African coastal cities the juxtaposition of mirrors, porcelain, and other ornaments created a standard assortment of domestic consumer objects that symbolized connection to distant markets and engagements with common western Indian Ocean region cultural trends.

Greater access to credit and imports contributed to upward mobility in many East African societies, and this fostered crises of power and distinction. For example, Steven Feierman has shown how the wealth available from regional trade had a dramatic effect on the Kingdom of Shambaa in northern Tanzania. The new trade benefited people like district headman Semboja. While historical methods of securing authority in Shambaa centred on the control of shrines and agricultural production, because of his district's position on a caravan route Semboja was able amass imported goods, including guns. These, in turn, allowed him to build a new base of social power and ultimately unseat the hereditary ruler of Shambaa.[30] In many societies, amassing and distributing imports offered the means for aspirants to challenge figures of authority, creating what Justin Willis has termed 'new paths to autonomy', sometimes taken by force.[31] Many aspirants were willing to use newly acquired firearms and followers to mount military campaigns against rulers or rivals. This contributed to increasing political insecurity and conflict across the region. Violence was not the only means to political power, however. In fact, it was more common for political and social aspirants to legitimize their authority by manipulating pre-existing political ideologies.

Jonathon Glassman argues that in the nineteenth century parvenus destabilized structures of authority in novel ways by enhancing their prestige through access to imported goods.[32] Glassman's research on the towns of the northern coast of Tanzania (Mrima) offers insight into the socio-political tensions created by new sources of material wealth. On the early nineteenth century Mrima, power and authority was contingent on lineage as well as the display and distribution of goods that accorded with high social rank. Rituals of chieftainship, for instance, depended on the presentation of expensive prestige goods, such as fine cloth and umbrellas, seen to represent the authority of the leader. During the economic boom, upstarts and new settlers to the towns were able to acquire and display similar objects, pushing the cost of retaining power higher. Soon the objects and rituals that had once cemented the prestige of the old patricians slipped out of their control. Wealth, not lineage, became the critical determinate for claiming rank, even for the highest local offices. By displaying and distributing luxury goods non-patricians began claiming patrician status regardless of ancestry.[33] Imports had become vital political resources in an economy of display and distribution.

[30]   Steven Feierman, 'A Century of Ironies in East Africa (*c*.1780–1890)', in Philip Curtin et. al., *African History: From Earliest Times to Independence* (New York: Longman, 1995), 352–376; Steven Feierman, *Peasant Intellectuals: Anthropology and History in Tanzania* (Madison, WI: University of Wisconsin Press, 1990).

[31]   Willis, *Potent Brews*, 78.

[32]   Glassman, *Feasts and Riot*, 47, 53.

[33]   Ibid., 37, 154–8, 161–5.

Some rulers responded to challenges to their prestige and authority by creating (or revising) sumptuary regulations. To maintain social distance from the nouveau riche, rulers deemed certain luxury goods off-limits to their subjects. More regularly, political elites attempted to represent their power by acquiring objects that reflected privileged connections to global markets, items such as music boxes, silk cloth, or the latest firearms. Mandara, the hereditary ruler of Moshi (near Kilimanjaro) in the 1880s, demanded only the most unique or technologically sophisticated consumer goods from passing caravans in an effort to draw a strong distinction between himself and his subjects. While the value content of imported commodities was inherently unstable, in Buganda coastal and European fashions did not significantly alter social hierarchies. Instead, they were integrated into pre-existing modes of social differentiation and only added greater variation to the equivalence of status and clothing.[34] Across the East African region, emphasis on imported prestige goods as a mirror of social position encouraged the perception that connections to global markets were a crucial source of power. Buganda's elite might have successfully retained older social hierarchies, but many rulers who cultivated the notion that access to imported objects were a reflection of authority and social standing undermined their own positions because their ability to control access to new markets was often limited.

Some of the most sweeping changes of the era were evident in Zanzibar. First, the sumptuary regulations that once preserved symbols of status for the political elite evaporated. The Busaidi sultan was a transplant from Muscat and so had little interest in maintaining the drums, chairs, and other objects that were common symbols of the earlier Swahili state. At the same time, the demographic diversity of Zanzibar heightened the importance of consumer goods for negotiating social relations. By the 1860s, half of all urban Zanzibaris had been brought to the city as slaves. The other half of Zanzibar's population hailed from places as distant as Muscat, Mumbai, Unyanyembe, and Mogadishu. Most new Zanzibaris were vying for position and social inclusion, and consumer goods offered the most tactile mode of social communication. A diversity of imports, combined with the possibility for some to accumulate modest, even significant, fortunes, meant that forms of status representation were constantly in flux.

Slaves and freed people put a high premium on material consumption. Violently uprooted from their homes and harbouring little hope of returning, most slaves and freed slaves sought social inclusion in coastal society. One means of representing claims to social citizenship in Zanzibar was to acquire symbols of coastal culture. The most important symbol for enslaved and plebian Zanzibaris was clothing. Since slave status was often synonymous with nakedness, slaves used all means available to cloth themselves in local fashions.[35] Freed slaves often spent large sums to signal

---

[34] Kodesh, 'Renovating Tradition,' 526.

[35] Laura Fair, *Pastimes and Politics: Culture, Community and Identity in Post-abolition Urban Zanzibar, 1890–1945* (Athens: Ohio University Press, 2001); Laura Fair, 'Remaking Fashion in the Paris of the Indian Ocean: Dress, Performance, and the Cultural Construction of a Cosmopolitan Zanzibari Identity', in Jean Allman (ed.), *Fashioning Africa: Power and the Politics of Dress.* (Bloomington, IN: Indiana University Press, 2004), 13–30.

their social distance from slavery. For freedmen, a primary symbol of transcending slavery was the *kanzu*, the long shirt indicative of Muslim modesty and made of imported cloth.[36] American and Indian cloth, when fashioned into a *kanzu*, became a vehicle for the relocation and grounding of identity; it signified a cultural elsewhere distinct from freed slaves' home societies and a social position distinct from slavery.

For freed people, aspiration to the fashions of the elite led to the appropriation of many goods that had once been the preserve of a small few. One such item was the *kizibao*, or embroidered waistcoat made from European broadcloth, popular among free men of means in the early nineteenth century. By the mid-nineteenth century the *kizibao* was one of the greatest investments for Zanzibari freedmen of lesser means. It even became popular at trade fairs in the interior. For Zanzibari women, jewellery became so essential to appearances that even the poor spent large sums to obtain earrings and bangles made of precious metals, including gold. But the most ubiquitous and remarkable example of the use of consumer goods to claim social inclusion was that of the umbrella. Umbrellas had long been symbols of the state and male patrician identity in Swahili societies. In early nineteenth-century Zanzibar, however, umbrellas of British, Indian, Chinese, and American manufacture became common accoutrements of South Asian businessmen and wealthy women. By the 1870s, umbrellas had become fashionable among even those of meagre means. Marginal groups in Zanzibar, including slaves, defied conventions by carrying umbrellas. As a result, umbrellas were invested with new meanings. They were no longer symbols of patrician status, but through their local popularization were associated with broader Zanzibari cultural norms. Throughout the region, imported umbrellas came to be seen as a common symbol of Zanzibari cosmopolitanism. The material strategies of Zanzibar's plebian majority thus entailed a double movement: claims to social citizenship in Zanzibar and difference from those of lesser social status, including slaves and non-Zanzibaris. In appropriating the status symbols of the elite, Zanzibaris of lower social status democratized the use of some consumer objects and transformed them into symbols of Zanzibari society.[37]

Much like freed slaves who sought to distinguish themselves from their former slave status, wealthy Zanzibaris searched for objects that could magnify social distance from their poorer neighbours. Simultaneously, they attempted to distinguish themselves from other wealthy people. This dual drive sometimes led to ludicrous extremes, such as investments in expensive carriages when few roads on the island could accommodate them. Commonly, modes of claiming distinction concentrated on clothes and interior decor. Wealthy Zanzibaris invested large sums in silk and silk-cotton clothing. They filled their homes with porcelain, imported curios, and mirrors that magnified their possessions. Perhaps the most iconic objects that the wealthy employed to create

---

[36] For freed women the *ukaya* (muslin head covering), *kisutu* (English square cloth dyed in Mumbai), and *leso* (colourful cloth made from imported handkerchiefs) served similar purposes.

[37] Jeremy Prestholdt, 'Mirroring Modernity: On Consumerism in Nineteenth Century Zanzibar', *Trans/forming Cultures*, 4/2 (2009), 165–204.

distance between them and other Zanzibaris were American and European wall clocks. These were items of conspicuous consumption. Few regulated their day by clocks since prayer times provided the common rhythm of life. Yet because clocks were rare outside coastal cities and their machinations pleased local audiences, clocks became synonymous with urban culture and indispensable objects of display for elites.

The greatest example of the uses of consumer goods to represent personal ability and authority was Sultan Barghash bin Said's Beit al Ajaib, or 'House of Wonders'. Completed around 1883, the House of Wonders was the largest building in the region and positioned at the seafront in Zanzibar as the most prominent symbol of the state. Beit al Ajaib served largely symbolic purposes, as evidenced by its narrow rooms and vast central auditorium. The building entailed the creolization of myriad global symbols, a trend typical of cosmopolitan Zanzibar. British Indian in inspiration, the House of Wonders had wide four-sided verandahs, French doors accented by low-hanging lamps, richly worked wooden overhangs and massive western Indian-designed carved doors. To complete the picture of opulence, Barghash laid the floor of Beit al Ajaib with a French black and white marble and filled the building with large chandeliers. In front of the House of Wonders Barghash built a massive tower, and, as a testament to his close relationship with European powers, furnished it with East Africa's largest clocks.

The contents of the House of Wonders were carefully selected to impress. The reception room boasted Persian carpets, red velvet and gilt wood furniture, as well as ormolu timepieces, aneroid barometers, thermometers, anemometers, telescopes, opera glasses and music boxes. In addition, the Beit al Ajaib housed swords, spears, rifles, pistols, photograph albums, portraits of famous personalities, and sets of photographs of famous sites around the world.[38] Barghash visited London's Hall of the Great Exhibition ('Crystal Palace') in 1875, and it is likely that his visit provided the inspiration for the House of Wonders. Like the Crystal Palace, the House of Wonders was ornamented with objects of manufacture representing new technologies—tools used for measurement and magnification, in particular. Barghash designed the House of Wonders as a museum of the contemporary world, and the sultan was keen to show off the collection to his subjects and foreigners alike. Barghash's House of Wonders equated new consumer objects with the sultan and so offered a dramatic example of the domestication of consumer goods in the service of the state. In this imposing structure, Barghash demonstrated to his subjects that he had the power to possess myriad images and objects collected from across the globe.

In the final years of his life, the sultan would see his regional influence dwindle and his mainland possessions fall into the hands of European powers. By the end of the 1880s, much of East Africa was under direct European rule. The colonial epoch ushered in new concepts of global relation, local power relations, and belief systems, all of which shaped East African consumer demands. In the coastal region many nineteenth-century fashions persisted. At the turn of the century, the abolition of slavery offered new economic and social possibilities to a substantial sector of the population. As in earlier decades, clothing was a primary means of representing social integration into a changing society.

[38] Prestholdt, *Domesticating the World*, chapter 4.

For instance, Laura Fair has shown that the long and colourful Indian printed cloth known as *khanga* came to be a primary sign of a woman's adherence to post-abolition social norms in Zanzibar.[39] In the 1920s the black, full body, women's covering called the *buibui*—which was likely an import from southern Arabia—evidenced an increasing trend of veiling in urban coastal East Africa. Veiling had once been a practice of only the Arab elite. With the *buibui*, the veil quickly gained esteem as a barometer of respectability and adherence to new concepts of proper Muslim attire. While the *buibui* dominated coastal women's fashion across social categories, materials ranging from fine silk to cheap cotton allowed for the maintenance of considerable social differentiation among women in Zanzibar, Mombasa, and Dar es Salaam.[40] Muslim women drew more deeply from Arab social mores in the first decades of the twentieth century, but Muslim men cast off items such as sandals and the *kizibao*, embracing European shoes and jackets in their place. Such sartorial choices came to represent men's greater engagement with European concepts of modern attire as well as the normalization of Western fashions across the Muslim world.

Beyond the coast, Swahili fashions found a broad audience in the early colonial era, bringing to a climax a trend that had begun with the caravan trade. Part of the reason for this increased consumption of Swahili styles was that colonial administrations and missionaries encouraged non-Muslims to wear *kanzus* and *khangas*, among other Swahili clothes. In the eyes of many Europeans, Swahili clothing was more authentically 'native' than European dresses, trousers, shirts, and ties. Some European employers even forced their African workers to wear Swahili fashions, while the government of Kenya Colony issued the *kanzu*, fez and *joho* to its newly appointed chiefs. As a result, many young people across East Africa sought to assert freedom from 'traditional' authority, and even equivalence with European residents, by shunning Swahili styles and wearing Western clothes. This practice, one influenced by the presence of Christian missions and new patterns of labour migration, would signal a remarkable shift in East African consumer interests.[41] Indeed, the self-conscious identification as 'modern'—a term with multiple and ambiguous meanings in East Africa—was nowhere more evident than in the demand for Western-style clothing, particularly in East Africa's burgeoning cities.[42]

The influences of Christianity and perceptions of modernity were most readily apparent in urban East Africa, but many rural people likewise chose to don Western clothes.

---

[39] Fair, 'Remaking Fashion in the Paris of the Indian Ocean'.

[40] Fair, *Pastimes and Politics*, ch. 2.

[41] Margaret Jean Hay, 'Hoes and Clothes in a Luo Household: Changing Consumption in a Colonial Economy, 1906–1936', in Mary Jo Arnoldi, Christraud M. Geary and Kris L Hardin (eds.), *African Material Culture* (Bloomington, IN: Indiana University Press, 1996), 243–61; Margaret Jean Hay, 'Changes in Clothing and Struggles over Identity in Colonial Western Kenya', in Jean Allman (ed.), *Fashioning Africa: Power and the Politics of Dress* (Bloomington, IN: Indiana University Press, 2004), 67–83.

[42] Maria Suriano, 'Clothing and the changing identities of Tanganyikan urban youths, 1920s–1950s', *Journal of African Cultural Studies*, 20/1 (2008), 95–115; For the immediate post-colonial era, see Thomas Burgess, 'Cinema, Bell Bottoms, and Miniskirts: Struggles Over Youth and Citizenship in Revolutionary Zanzibar', *International Journal of African Historical Studies*, 35/2 (2002), 287–313 and Andrew M. Ivaska, '"Anti-Mini Militants Meet Modern Misses": Urban Style, Gender and the Politics of "National Culture" in 1960s Dar es Salaam, Tanzania', in Allman (ed.) *Fashioning Africa*, 104–21.

Margaret Jean Hay has demonstrated how the early colonial era's matrix of social, political, and economic change gained material form through revolutionary shifts in rural consumption patterns. In Nyanza Province (western Kenya), an area less affected by the nineteenth century caravan trade than regions closer to the coast, Hay shows that household spending on objects of personal adornment such as brass wire and beads increased in the early twentieth century. Yet missionary emphasis on minimal jewellery and maximal body coverage ultimately led to the demise of an earlier mode of dress that juxtaposed these imported objects with locally available skins. European clothing reflected new concepts of self-identity contingent on Christian mores, while the expanding colonial labour market both exposed young people to new styles and offered the means to purchase them.

For Luo men who earned wages in cities and on plantations, European hats, pants, and trousers became prominent symbols of wealth and success in the early twentieth century. Migrant labourers (almost exclusively men) also discovered that, despite official policies, some employers paid higher wages to those who wore European-style shirts and shorts, a fact that made European clothes pragmatic. Luo women were largely excluded from the migrant labour market, but increased earnings from the sale of agricultural goods, particularly in the interwar period, offered them access to new fashions. And like their male counterparts, they found that Western clothes paid dividends—as did Christianity. For example, entrance into the community of Christians offered social leverage to challenge elders, notably around the question of arranged marriage. The most obvious means of representing this socio-religious conversion and rejecting senior authority was wearing European clothes, usually dresses and headscarves.

For Luo men and women, European styles were seen as symbols of new sources of authority and influence. They also offered a means of claiming a social identity distinct from the perceived cultural strictures of the past. Thus, European fashions highlighted and exacerbated social frictions inaugurated by the new economy, a radically altered political environment and the appeal of a new religion. By the 1940s, not only had skins and beads all but disappeared in places such as western Kenya, but across East Africa European-style clothing, sometimes in combination with Swahili fashions, had come to define a new generation of East Africans.[43]

AFRICAN CONSUMERS
AND THE GLOBAL ECONOMY

East African consumer interests reflected the era's changing socio-political relationships and the region's deeper integration into global markets. They also affected societies and economies in distant parts of the globe. Pedro Machado demonstrates that in the eighteenth century textiles made in Jambusar (near Surat, north-west India) were popular

---

[43] Hay, 'Changes in Clothing and Struggles over Identity'.

in south-east Africa. With the increasing sale of ivory and slaves, African demand for the cloth became so great that Jambusar manufactured cloth almost exclusively for the African market.[44] Early in the nineteenth century, a similar relationship developed between East African consumers and manufacturers in Kachchh (north-west India, bordering modern Pakistan). Varieties of Kachchhi cloth, particularly the indigo *taujiri*, came into fashion in East Africa and Kachchhi textiles quickly surpassed Gujarati cloth in popularity. This popularity coincided with the dramatic expansion of the East African economy. As a result, from the 1810s to 1840 Zanzibar was the single most important market for Mandvi, Kachchh's largest port.[45] Weaving constituted the city's largest industry and the port city's economy became narrowly focused on East Africa. As profits from the trade with East Africa rose, Kachchhi capital investments in the region helped fuel the further expansion of the East African economy.

In the 1840s, East African tastes shifted again. American merchants based in Salem, Massachusetts had been muscled out of the lucrative China and India markets by more powerful New York- and Boston-based businesses and so ventured into the south-western Indian Ocean. New Englanders wanted East African ivory and copal, and East Africans were eager consumers of American cloth. Though *merekani* was more expensive than Kachchhi cloth and did not boast the same vibrant colours, it was prized for its durability. This mutually beneficial relationship between Zanzibar and the United States resulted in a 'most favoured nation' trade agreement between the two states. Initially, most of the American cloth exported to Zanzibar came from Lowell Mills in Massachusetts. Due to increasing competition for Lowell cottons and the introduction of a railway system between Lowell and Boston, Salem merchants saw the price of Lowell goods rise beyond their profitability in East Africa. In response to the higher prices, Salemites invested in their own textile mill.

On its completion, the Salem mill was the largest in the country as well as the first steam-powered textile factory in North America. Though the factory did not produce exclusively for East Africa, many of its products were specifically designed for East African consumers. Where American merchants had once only sold simple unbleached Lowell sheeting to East Africa, between the 1840s and the 1880s they exported a variety of cloth, including bleached and unbleached varieties of sheeting and drills, linen, red broadcloth and handkerchiefs. In the years leading up to the American Civil War, demand for American cloth not only provided a commercial staple for trade to East Africa, it also assured a primary export market for America's largest textile factory. East Africa proved important to Salem's economy in an era of intense competition from larger Boston and New York firms while playing a key role in Salem's transition from mercantile capitalism to industrialization.

The American Civil War signalled the end of American cloth's dominance in East Africa. English merchants were flooding Indian markets with cheap British cloth, and

[44] Machado, 'Clothes of a New Fashion'; Machado, 'Awash in a Sea of Cloth'.

[45] M. Reda Bhacker, *Trade and Empire in Muscat and Zanzibar: The Roots of British Domination* (New York: Routledge, 1992), 160.

Indian exporters took advantage of the high price of wartime American cottons to substitute English cloths for *merekani*. Though much of this cloth was dyed and printed in India, Mumbai exporters also began to cultivate a market for Mumbai-manufactured textiles by replicating the *merekani*. Recognizing the long-term profits in mechanization, Mumbai financiers invested in expensive European steam power technology. Though most of the cloths produced by the new factories were consumed within South Asia, East Africa became one of the primary overseas markets for industrial manufactured cloth from Mumbai. The new factories wove *kaniki*, lighter cotton *doti*, and copies of the famous *merekani* cloth. They even stamped and folded imitation *merekani* to appear like the original American product.

In the 1870s, the telegraph connected the two cities, making it easier to relay changes in demand. At the same time, the Sultan of Zanzibar purchased several steamships and initiated his own service between Zanzibar and Mumbai in an effort to boost trade between the cities. Though a British company ran a similar service, the sultan offered substantially lower shipping rates than his competitor. As a result, the price of Mumbai-manufactured cloth fell in East Africa. This facilitated even greater East African consumption of Mumbai cloth—as much as 13 million yards of knock-off *merekani* in 1890 alone. In that year, East Africans consumed nearly half of all the unbleached cottons exported from Mumbai. At a time when the Indian textile industry faced great competition from Britain, Mumbai manufacturing received stimulus from East African consumers who had more purchasing power than ever before. As a result of its large South Asian market and burgeoning export trade, by the end of the century Mumbai was the commercial heart of the western Indian Ocean. In part because of East African demand for cloth, Mumbai became the epicentre of India's industrialization.[46]

In the late nineteenth century, colonial rule altered trade routes within the region as well as patterns of exchange with other parts of the world. In German East Africa, British Kenya, and the Protectorate of Zanzibar, Indian trading firms and shopkeepers retained a central role in the economy. At the same time, a variety of European manufactured goods began to make inroads. This was partially the result of complementary colonial policies: the promotion of agricultural production for export and the marketing of British and German products in the colonies. Efforts to restructure the regional economy around the production of cash crops such as coffee, tea, and sisal met with success in the early twentieth century. At the same time, the labour market that serviced these and other sectors of the new economy offered access to cash and credit, while railways and roads linked once isolated locales to growing urban centres such as Nairobi, Kisumu, and Kampala. In the earlier twentieth century colonial administrations succeeded in expanding the production of cash crops for export and stimulating African consumer demand, but their corresponding attempts to influence African consumption patterns met with decidedly mixed results.

Colonial officials' success in shaping consumer choices was often the result of extreme measures. For example, in colonial British East Africa fears of the corrupting effects of

---

[46] Prestholdt, 'On the Global Repercussions of East African Consumerism'.

imported liquor (as opposed to local brews, or what colonial laws termed 'native intoxi-cating liquor') led to a near-complete ban on both the supply of imported alcohol to Africans and their consumption of it.[47] On the other hand, the volume of British manu-factured porcelain, soap, and other household goods increased with the wider accept-ance of certain European cultural mores—evidence of a cultural shift that would also spur demand for second-hand European clothes and cotton cloth. As significant as such cultural trends were, they did not ensure markets for British cloth. Popular European styles were usually tailored locally, much as Swahili styles had been for decades, and so Indian textiles continued to offer stiff competition to British imports.

The most dramatic change in the relationship between East African consumers and foreign producers would, in fact, have little to do with British goods and instead reveal the limits of Britain's ability to shape regional consumer demand. By the late 1920s it had become clear that colonial economic restructuring was fuelling a phenomenal increase in Japanese imports to East Africa. Almost from their introduction in the mid-1920s, Japanese cottons, notable for their durability, vibrant colours, and low prices, found a wide market in East Africa. From Nyasaland to Uganda, sales of Japanese textiles quickly outpaced British and Indian imports. In 1930, East Africans were buying more Japanese piece goods than British and Indian varieties combined, a fact that caused considerable concern in official circles. Colonial administrators and manufacturers anticipated that the appeal of Swahili and European styles among East Africans, when combined with greater purchasing power, would ensure a booming market for the products of British and British Indian industry. Yet for over a decade, Japanese manufacturers reaped the greatest benefits of East African demand for cloth.[48]

In an attempt to address the increasing inability of British and British Indian textiles to compete with Japanese goods in East Africa, the Colonial Office increased tariffs on non-British imports. Kweku Ampiah suggests that the new tariff structure had a geopo-litical dimension as well. Ampiah argues that British policymakers used their ability to restrict Japanese access to vast colonial markets as an indirect means of checking Japan's expanding economy at a time of growing rivalry in Asia and the Pacific. Whatever the rationales for increased tariffs, East African consumer interests trumped imperial pol-icy. The consumption of Japanese imports increased in the 1930s such that by the end of the decade Japanese textiles accounted for a staggering 80 per cent of all imported piece goods in Britain's East African possessions. Since the high prices of Lancashire cloth put it beyond the reach of most East Africans, protectionist policies only ensured that East Africans paid much higher prices for Japanese piece goods than before such meas-ures were put in place, a fact that drew the ire of African consumers.[49] Much as with the American trade in the mid-nineteenth century, only war would upset Japan's economic relationship with East Africa.

---

[47] Willis, *Potent Brews*.

[48] Kweku Ampiah, 'British Commercial Policies against Japanese Expansionism in East and West Africa, 1932–1935', *International Journal of African Historical Studies*, 23/4 (1990), 619–41.

[49] Ibid.

The success of the imperial tariff scheme was limited, but such protectionist policies evidenced a new turn in East Africa's relationship with the global economy: in both the export and import sectors Africans' interfaces with international markets were now mediated by a government over which African subjects exercised little direct influence. It would be a mistake, however, to presume that colonial regimes could dictate consumer trends. Consumption patterns were often far less constricted by government directives than were other aspects of Africans' economic lives under colonial rule.

Conclusion

At the end of the nineteenth century the constraints of interaction enforced by colonial empires restricted African economic possibilities. Yet the notion that the interests of outsiders steered the continent's past for centuries obscures the social complexities of Africa's interface with the global economy before and during colonial rule. The socio-political logics of consumer desire offer some insights into why global trade came to be important to Africans long before most were coerced to produce for the market. One insight we can draw from recent reflections on pre-colonial consumption is that regional fashions were incredibly differentiated. Tastes changed quickly and differed among societies, social groups, and neighbours. Consumer demands were often so specific that regional traders were compelled to develop ingenious ways to address them. Caravans became travelling warehouses that catered to wide audiences, and East Africans refashioned imported consumer goods to suit local demand. This value-adding was essential to the regional economy and, by extension, networks of exchange beyond the region. Processes of refabrication in East Africa were not unique, yet they remain an aspect of global exchange too often overlooked by theorists of global integration. In the case of pre-colonial East Africa, trade was not simply the exchange of African raw materials for imported manufactures. Instead, the constant reinterpretation and transformation of consumer goods was elemental to East Africa's interface with the global market before and throughout the colonial era.

The nineteenth century's expanding world of goods dramatically affected East Africa's socio-political landscape. East Africans used gains from the overseas trade to shore up local power relations. While investments in clients and social distinction may not have paid long-term economic dividends, these were primary concerns in societies where controlling people was of the highest priority and wealth was rarely figured by capital accumulation alone. Wealth in the form of imports also offered the means for aspiring elites to challenge historical patterns of rule by redistribution and force. Greater material differentiation highlighted inequalities in East African societies. Rulers enforced sumptuary regulations to ensure their possession of symbols of authority. But this socio-material distance became increasingly difficult to maintain. The availability of luxury goods in some instances reproduced older social hierarchies, while in other cases it created and reflected new communities of aspiration. In places like Zanzibar, where sumptuary regulations were not enforced after the 1830s, elites collected luxury goods to represent their power and ability. During the era of the slave trade, newcomers to Zanzibar often claimed social citizenship through acquisition of the signs of Zanzibari cosmopolitanism. For many, consumption was a strategy of belonging, one that remained important after the formal abolition of slavery.

Shifts in the social logics of consumption and consumer demand also affected East Africa's trading partners. By responding to changing consumer interests, East Africa, northwestern India, and New England engaged in mutually constitutive relationships, modes of reciprocity that were not premised on gross asymmetries of power. East African interests in cloth, New England demand for ivory, and Indian hunger for cloves oscillated over the nineteenth century, but each shift had distant repercussions. Nyamwezi demand for particular kinds of brass wire shaped Zanzibar's trade relationship with America and the working lives of New Englanders. Ultimately, New England and western Indian responses to East African consumer demands contributed to the industrialization of both regions. In the colonial era, African consumer interests continued to influence global networks of exchange and production. As the case of Japanese textiles suggests, colonial administrations' attempts to harness the power of consumer choice were not always successful. East African demand for Japanese cottons, driven at least in part by a thriving market in locally tailored European clothing, helped bolster the industrial capacity of an imperial rival that by the late 1930s posed a considerable threat to British interests in East and Southeast Asia. This was surely an unintended consequence of Britain's exacting economic policies in Africa.

The study of African consumption patterns offers a window on multiple reciprocities, palimpsest feedback loops spanning time and space. Holistic appraisals of East Africa's history of consumption demonstrate that the minutiae of consumer desire and negotiated transaction have been significant factors in the patterning of global integration. In precolonial East Africa, the consumer object both crystallized socio-political tensions and acted as a vehicle for their articulation with the wider world. Thus, consumer interests were equally personal and relational. They affected bonds between consumers as well as among consumers, producers, and those who remanufactured imports—before and during the colonial era. Yet, as the economies of display and distribution shaped East African societies in the nineteenth century and stimulated mass production in India and the United States, East Africans rapidly depleted local resources and became increasingly dependent on slave labour for the production of exports. While neither economic activity proved beneficial to a region whose economy would be radically altered by colonial policies, reflection on the African interests that defined these trends adds nuance to our appreciation of why global hierarchies emerged and how they have been affected by consumer choices.

BIBLIOGRAPHY

Akyeampong, Emmanuel, *Drink, Power, and Cultural Change: A Social History of Alcohol in Ghana, c.1800 to Recent Times* (Portsmouth, NH: Heinemann, 1996).

Bayart, Jean-Francois, 'Africa in the World: A History of Extraversion', *African Affairs*, 99/395 (2000), 217–67.

Fair, Laura, *Pastimes and Politics: Culture, Community and Identity in Post-abolition Urban Zanzibar, 1890–1945* (Athens, OH: Ohio University Press, 2001).

Glassman, Jonathon, *Feasts and Riot: Revelry, Rebellion, and Popular Consciousness on the Swahili Coast, 1856–1888* (Portsmouth, NH: Heinemann, 1995).

Guyer, Jane, *Marginal Gains: Monetary Transactions in Atlantic Africa* (Chicago: University of Chicago Press, 2004).

Hansen, Karen Tranberg, *Salaula: The World of Secondhand Clothing and Zambia* (Chicago: University of Chicago Press, 2000).

Inikori, Joseph, *Africans and the Industrial Revolution in England: A Study in International Trade and Economic Development* (Cambridge: Cambridge University Press, 2002).

Machado, Pedro, 'Cloths of a New Fashion: Networks of Exchange, African Consumerism and Cloth Zones of Contact in India and the Indian Ocean in the Eighteenth and Nineteenth Centuries', in Tirthankar Roy, Om Prakash, Kaoru Sugihara and Giorgio Riello (eds.), *How India Clothed the World: The World of South Asian Textiles, 1500–1850* (Leiden: Brill, 2009)

Miller, Joseph, *Way of death: merchant capitalism and the Angolan slave trade, 1730–1830* (Madison: University of Wisconsin Press, 1988).

Prestholdt, Jeremy, *Domesticating the World: African Consumerism and the Genealogies of Globalization* (Berkeley: University of California Press, 2008).

Vaughan, Megan, 'Africa and the Birth of the Modern World', *Transactions of the Royal Historical Society*, 16 (2006), 143–62.

Willis, Justin, *Potent Brews: A Social History of Alcohol in East Africa, 1850–1999* (Athens, OH: Ohio University Press, 2002).

PART II

DYNAMICS
AND DIFFUSION

CHAPTER 6

······································

TRANSATLANTIC
CONSUMPTION

······································

MICHELLE CRAIG MCDONALD

THE objects people selected, purchased, and used are an important part of how historians now interpret the Atlantic world, whether in scholarship on metropolitan society and their colonies, or the relationship between moral economy and political action.[1] This attention to specific goods and the individuals who acquired them, however, is relatively recent. As late as the middle of the twentieth century, consumer studies were largely subsumed within analyses of trade patterns or specific commodity industries.[2] When individuals did appear, they were usually from society's upper echelons with the means to acquire quantities and qualities of goods that those below them could envy and only occasionally emulate.[3]

The rise of social history broadened the field in important ways. Rather than focus on commercial trends, this generation of historians explored the means of production, both manufactured and agricultural, and traced diffusion of artefacts up and down the socio-economic scale, and from cities to towns and rural villages. Some, such as Lois Green Carr and Lorena Walsh's pioneering study *Robert Cole's World*, analysed account records painstakingly to reconstruct a single community, while British scholars like

---

[1] As examples, Neil McKendrick, John Brewer, and J. H. Plumb, *The Birth of a Consumer Society: The Commercialization of Eighteenth-Century England* (Bloomington, IN: University of Indiana Press, 1982); Cary Carson, Ronald Hoffman, and Peter J. Albert (eds.), *Of Consuming Interests: The Style of Life in the Eighteenth Century* (Charlottesville, VA: University of Virginia Press, 1994), and T. H. Breen, *The Marketplace of Revolution: How Consumer Politics Shaped American Independence* (Oxford and New York: Oxford University Press, 2004).

[2] Most notably, Richard S. Dunn, *Sugar and Slaves: The Rise of the Planter Class in the English West Indies, 1624–1713* (Chapel Hill, NC: University of North Carolina Press, 1972) and Richard Sheridan, *Sugar and Slavery: An Economic History of the British West Indies* (Mona: University of the West Indies, 1974).

[3] For example, see Richard Pares, 'Merchants and Planters', *Economic History Review*, Supp. 4 (1960), 1–91; later expanded into *Yankees and Creoles: The Trade between North America and the West Indies before the American Revolution* (Hamden, CT: Archon Books, 1968).

Lorna Weatherill used probate records to similar effect in considering early modern, working-class, English consumers more generally.[4] But if class changed, other defining features of buying behaviour, including race, gender, and ethnicity, rarely did and the lines of Atlantic exchange and consumption remained decidedly Anglocentric, focusing on the impact of Europe, especially Britain, on North America.

The parameters of material culture studies of the 1980s and 1990s were influenced in no small part by the concurrent rise of Atlantic history and its emphasis on crossing national, regional, and imperial boundaries. Indeed, it is the circulation of goods, people, and ideas across and around the ocean that defined the field. Early studies traced migration, trade patterns, or specific commodities, but more recent work has focused on less tangible, but critically related, fields to consumption, such as taste and refinement, and adaptation and creolization. Like material culture studies, Anglo-Atlantic scholarship outpaced other aspects of the field until the last decade, but historians and literary scholars have begun to turn the tide and the resulting work has not only challenged ideas about what is a commodity and what can be consumed, but also broken down the traditional 'production-distribution-consumption' pattern, and offered a more multi-directional model in which distributors' and consumers' demands and preferences were as likely to influence production decisions as producers' advertisements were to encourage buyer behaviour.[5] Most importantly, this new work broadened both the Atlantic regions and peoples considered as consumers, including Africa, Latin America and the Caribbean, as well as women, native and enslaved peoples.

FROM HISTORY OF TRADE
TO WHAT WAS TRADED

Economic history as understood today is little more than a century old. Most nineteenth-century historians were more interested in political developments, but by the early 1880s began looking for relationships between technology, state policy, and patterns in prices

---

[4] Lois Green Carr and Lorena S. Walsh, *Robert Cole's World: Agriculture and Society in Early Maryland* (Chapel Hill, NC: University of North Carolina Press, 1991); Gloria Main used probate inventories in her analysis of rural Chesapeake life as well in *Tobacco Colony: Life in Early Maryland, 1650–1720* (Princeton, NJ: Princeton University Press, 1983). See also, Lorna Weatherill, *Consumer Behavior and Material Culture in Britain, 1660–1760* (London and New York: Routledge, 1988).

[5] Both Robert DuPlessis and Laura Johnson, for example, used cloth to identify consumer participation in market decisions. The former argued that distinct French and British colonial preferences emerged by the eighteenth century, and the latter that Native American demands influenced European cloth design and manufacture. See Robert S. DuPlessis, 'Cloth and the Emergence of the Atlantic Economy', in Peter A. Coclanis (ed.), *The Atlantic Economy during the Seventeenth and Eighteenth Centuries: Organization, Operation, Practice and Personnel* (Columbia, SC: University of South Carolina, 2005), 72–94, and Laura Johnson, 'Goods to Clothe Themselves: Native Consumers and Native Images on the Pennsylvania Trading Frontier, 1712–1760', *Winterthur Portfolio*, 43/1 (2009), 115–40.

and wages to explain the complex, industrial societies growing around them in Western Europe.[6] A generation later, early twentieth-century British historians, such as George Ramsey and Walter Minchinton, applied these same principles to the study of empire. Their work depended on the business of numbers such as production values and import and export statistics, and they concluded that Atlantic trade—rather than national industry—led to the development of a modern capitalist system in Britain; their counterparts Charles Andrews and Carl Bridenbaugh suggested much the same for North America. Ralph Davis, however, was the first to consider the problem more broadly, suggesting that links between Spanish, Portuguese, Dutch, British, and French commercial and colonial efforts created an Atlantic financial system that transcended the economies of individual nations or empires.[7]

Commodities, and by extension those who purchased and used them, underpinned much of this work, though they most often appeared as aggregates, measured by volume and traced by trends. Table 4 of Davis's chapter on tropical commodities (portions of which appear on the following page), exemplified this tendency. It compared estimated sugar production from Brazil, the British West Indies, and the French West Indies between 1620 and 1767 and allowed readers easily to judge relative output for various empires. But several other factors remain obscure. It is clear from these figures that Brazil first produced sugar commercially, though its involvement in the industry remained episodic over the next century and a half. Barbados led British sugar production until 1720 when it shifted to Jamaica, presumably in part because of the latter island's larger size and population, though this must be assumed as it is neither stated in the table nor surrounding narrative. It is also evident that the French colony of Saint-Domingue surpassed production of all other individual colonies, and that of most combined, by the mid-eighteenth century though it operated within similar imperial laws, a comparable planter-class society, and the same slave-based labour system.[8] More to the point, Davis's table demonstrated that sugar was produced and shipped, but not where it went, to whom, or for what reasons. These questions were simply not part of his equation. Indeed, 'like nearly all economic history', he acknowledged in the book's preface,

[6] Ralph Davis provided a good summary of the rise of economic history in the late nineteenth century in the forward and preface to *The Rise of the Atlantic Economies* (Ithaca, NY: Cornell University Press, 1973), iv–xiv.

[7] George Daniel Ramsey, *English Overseas Trade during the Age of Emergence: Studies in some Modern Origins of the English-Speaking World* (London: St Martin's Press, 1957); Walter Edward Minchinton, *The Growth of English Overseas Trade in the Seventeenth and Eighteenth Centuries* (London: Methuen Young Press, 1969); Charles Andrews, *The Colonial Period of American History*, 4 vols. (New Haven, CT: Yale University Press, 1934–38); Carl Bridenbaugh, *Cities in the Wilderness* (New York: Knopf, 1960), and especially *Cities in Revolt, 1743–1776* (New York: Knopf, 1955); and Davis, *Atlantic Economies*. These ideas were later adopted by Douglass C. North in *The Economic Growth of the United States, 1790–1860* (New York: W.W. Norton & Co., 1966). Stuart Bruchey took a slightly different tack, willing to acknowledge American investment during the colonial period (what he deemed 'the dependent years') but less so after independence; see *The Roots of American Economic Growth, 1607–1861* (New York: Harper & Row Publishers, 1965).

[8] Davis, *Atlantic Economies*, 267. For an excellent discussion of the strengths and weaknesses of the visual presentation of statistical information, see Edward Tufte, *The Visual Display of Quantitative Information*, 2nd edn. (Cheshire, CT: Graphics Press, 2001).

Table 6.1 Estimates of Sugar Production (Thousands of Tons)

	Brazil	Barbados	Jamaica	Other British West Indies	Martinique Guadeloupe	Saint-Domingue
1620	15					
1655		7				
1670	27					
1700		10	5	7		
1720	20	7	10	7	14	10
1740		7	17	11		40
1767		6	36	25	14	63

his work 'is grounded in statistics; for it is usually concerned with the behavior of very large numbers of people, who cannot be treated as individuals.'[9]

And yet it is precisely the social, personal, and cultural connections between objects and their users that preoccupy consumer historians today. Alternative models with stronger ties between the production of goods and their social and cultural consequences certainly preceded Davis, most notably in Harold Innis's work on Canada's fur and cod fishing industries.[10] Innis developed what became known as the 'staples theory' which held that a dominant commodity—or staple export—fundamentally determined a region's rate of economic development. He used the premise to explain colonial success in what he termed the 'new countries' of the Americas, which had abundant resources but limited labour and capital. The migration of Europeans across the Atlantic, initially tentative but increasingly supported by the discovery of new commodities that appealed to European markets, produced, Innis argued, dialectical trade economies based on metropolitan import of American staples and European exports of manufactures to fulfil colonial needs.[11]

Staples theory did not go unchallenged. Some historians charged that its focus on exported goods directed attention away from domestic production and overemphasized colonial reliance on Europe. Others noted the difficulty in disentangling the impact of a commodity on the system of labour that produced it. While Canadian cod fishing and fur trapping seem far removed from plantation economies, several of the characteristics of staples theory, such as small domestic markets, unskilled labour forces, low urban development, and unequal distribution of wealth had also been cited

---

[9] Davis, *Atlantic Economies*, xiii.

[10] Harold Innis, *The Fur Trade in Canada: An Introduction to Canadian Economic History* (New Haven, CT: Yale University Press, 1930) and *The Cod Fisheries: The History of an International Economy* (New Haven, CT: Yale University Press, 1940).

[11] For a more complete discussion of the impact of Innis's staples model on the history of the American economy, see John J. McCusker and Russell R. Menard, *The Economy of British America, 1607–1789* (Chapel Hill, NC: Omohundro Institute for Early American History and Culture, 1991), 18–34.

as driving forces behind the development of slave societies.[12] Studies that followed in the footsteps of Innis produced excellent, richly textured regional histories, but less often ventured comparative analyses between regions, and while merchants and planters received more scrutiny in some of these works, the faces and motivations of individual buyers remained few and far between.[13]

THE TRANSATLANTIC SLAVE TRADE

Studies of the Atlantic slave trade were the glaring exception to this tendency, perhaps because the moral implications of these particular commodities, and the goods they in turn produced, made it impossible to overlook the culpability of consumers. As noted early on by British abolitionist Hannah More:

> Let the Consumer remember, that he is the real Slave owner; that it is for him, and [onl]y him that the system is kept at work: that it is out of his purse that the wages of Men-stealers, Slave Merchants, Planters, and Drivers are paid. Let the consumer, withdraw his support, and Slavery must fall.[14]

The slave trade has also remained, perhaps not coincidentally, one historical sub-field where statistical analyses have been both critically important and hotly debated. Chattel slaves were among the most profitable, and consistently demanded and consumed, goods of the Atlantic world. In the British Empire alone, at least five Africans landed in American colonies for every two Europeans between 1630 and 1700, while between 1700 and 1780 the ratio increased to four to one.[15] Until very recently, however, historians knew much more about the smaller movement of their European counterparts, primarily because of the nature of available data. Alison Games, for example, carefully mined port registers, passenger lists, indenture contracts, and other colonial papers to recover the lives of 1,360 of the 7,507 migrants who left London in 1635. A spectacular accomplishment, it still represented less than 20 per cent of that year's total, and relied on bookkeepers to

[12] Critiques of Innis's 'staples theory' appear in Barry Curtis and Barry Edginton, 'Uneven Institutional Development and the "Staple" Approach: A Problem of Method', *The Canadian Journal of Sociology/Cahiers canadiens de sociologie*, 4/3 (1979), 257–73; D. Glenday, 'The "Dependencia" School in Canada: An Examination and Re-Evaluation', *Canadian Review of Sociology and Anthropology*, 20/3 (1983), 346–58; and, most recently, Stephen Hornsby, *British Atlantic, American Frontier: Spaces of Power in Early Modern British America* (Lebanon, NH: University Press of New England, 2005).

[13] In addition to Innis's work, early examples of North American commodity studies include: Joseph Malone, *Pine Trees and Politics: The Naval Stores and Forest Policy in Colonial New England, 1691–1775* (Seattle, WA: University of Washington Press, 1965); Gavin Wright, *The Political Economy of the Cotton South: Households, Markets and Wealth in the Nineteenth Century* (New York: W.W. Norton & Co., 1978).

[14] Hannah More, 'British Slavery', in *Female Society for the Relief of Negro Slaves Album* (Birmingham: Hudson, Printer, 1828); Birmingham Archives, MS 361221 IIR62 (10/505).

[15] Figures derived from the introduction of Alexander X. Byrd, *Captives and Voyagers: Black Migrants across the Eighteenth-Century British Atlantic World* (Baton Rouge, LA: Louisiana State University, 2008).

record accurately family names, places of origin, and destinations.[16] Those charged with keeping similar accounts for slavers were notoriously less diligent. Gender, approximate age, and regional affiliation appeared as they appealed to potential buyers who believed slaves from different parts of Africa possessed specific, valuable labour skills, such as rice cultivation, or stronger or more malleable temperaments.[17] The motivations behind such records are thus necessarily very different than those documenting people who chose to migrate. They tended to catalogue enslaved people like other commodities, by conditions affecting saleability rather than characteristics important to identity.

This tension between individual slaves and the commodity traffic of slaving produced some of the most impassioned discussions about the place of statistics in historical study since publication of Philip Curtin's 1969 study *The Atlantic Slave Trade: A Census*. Based primarily on previously published scholarship, Curtin provided the first detailed estimate of the overall volume of the slave trade between 1500 and 1867. His figure of approximately 10 million slaves arriving from Africa was far lower than previously published figures and reactions took one of two forms. Some historians publicly debated the utility of aggregate data, especially in light of a trade in people. Curtin anticipated such criticism in his book's introduction when he noted that his focus on statistical trends would necessarily dehumanize the subjects of study, and responded that 'no possible figure from five million to fifty can make the evils of the trade any less than they were.'[18] These reactions, and Curtin's responses, remain one of the best classroom teaching exercises to illustrate history as construction rather than accumulated fact.[19]

[16] Alison Games, *Migration and the Origins of the English Atlantic World* (Cambridge, MA: Harvard University Press, 2001).

[17] See Daniel Littlefield, *Rice and Slaves: Ethnicity and the Slave Trade in Colonial South Carolina* (Baton Rouge, LA: Louisiana State University Press, 1981); Peter H. Wood, *Black Majority: Negroes in Colonial South Carolina from 1670 through the Stono Rebellion* (New York: W.W. Norton and Co., 1974), and Judith A. Carney, *Black Rice: The African Origins of Rice Cultivation in the Americas* (Cambridge, MA: Harvard University Press, 2001). For a slightly different perspective which examines how historians' desire to see slave contributions may shape their interpretations of New World plantation labour, while not disputing the idea that slave purchasers may have believed such was the case, see David Eltis, Philip Morgan, and David Richardson, 'Agency and Diaspora in Atlantic History: Reassessing the African Contribution to Rice Cultivation in the Americas', *American Historical Review* 112/5 (2007), 1329–58.

[18] Philip Curtin, *The Atlantic Slave Trade: A Census* (Madison, WI: University of Wisconsin Press, 1972); quotation from Philip Curtin, 'Measuring the Atlantic Slave Trade: A Comment', *The Journal of African History*, 17/4 (1976), 596. Since Curtin's book was published, historians have continuously modified the numbers; current figures are slightly higher than Curtin's projections and estimate that approximately 12 million slaves arrived in the Americas.

[19] Sample responses include: J.E. Inikori, 'Measuring the Atlantic Slave Trade: An Assessment of Curtin and Anstey', *The Journal of African History*, 17/2 (1976), 197–233, and 'Measuring the Atlantic Slave Trade: A Rejoinder', *Journal of African History* 17/4 (1976), 607–27. See also, Paul E. Lovejoy, 'The Volume of the Atlantic Slave: A Synthesis', *The Journal of African History*, 23/4 (1982), 473–501, and David Eltis and David Richardson, 'The "Numbers Game" and Routes to Slavery', *Slavery & Abolition*, 18 (1997), 1–15, which was expanded into David Eltis and David Richardson, *Routes to Slavery: Direction, Ethnicity and Mortality in the Transatlantic Slave Trade* (London: Frank Cass, 1997). The remainder of that 1997 special issue of *Slavery & Abolition* provides an excellent range of perspectives on studying the history of the slave trade, from reassessments of quantification to cultural impact.

Others responded to Curtin by focusing less on the numbers of slaves traded, than on tracing where they went and to whom. Such work on the varied places, work conditions, and social and cultural settings that enslaved people entered helped break down the monolithic structure of 'slavery' into 'slaveries' by acknowledging the variety of their experiences in the Atlantic world. Many of these took the form of commodity studies, such as sugar, coffee, rice, and tobacco, which followed the life cycle of goods created by enslaved hands.[20] As a result, they hold an interesting double place in transatlantic consumer studies as they not only tracked slaves, who were considered commodities, but also the articles of trade produced by plantation labour, a second tier of goods. Other studies focused on plantation owners and operators, acknowledging that such consistent and growing demand for slaves necessitated a more nuanced explication of the motivations and justifications of slaves' consumers. The result has been a complex image of slave labour in agriculture, urban settings, maritime trades, military service, and skilled professions, as well as better analyses of those who owned them—planters and wealthy elite to be sure, but women, middling classes, state governments, and even free and freed blacks.[21]

Meanwhile, quantification of the slave trade continued. While the number of individual slaves whose lives can be recaptured remains small, great strides have been made in historians' understanding of how groups moved throughout the Atlantic region. One development that made this possible, of course, was the computer revolution and related explosion of archival research conducted since the late 1960s. This work, led by David Eltis, Stephen D. Behrendt, David Richardson, and Herbert S. Klein, culminated in the publication of *The Trans-Atlantic Slave Trade: A Database on CD-ROM* in 2000, a tremendous

[20] The relationship between slavery and commodity production is obvious, beginning with Eric William's groundbreaking study of slavery's role in West Indian production, *Capitalism and Slavery* (New York, Russell & Russell, 1961, c.1944). In addition to Dunn, *Sugar and Slaves*, Sheridan, *Sugar and Slavery*, and Littlefield, *Rice and Slaves*, cited above, see: Allan Kulikoff, *Tobacco and Slaves: The Development of Southern Cultures in the Chesapeake, 1680–1800* (Chapel Hill, NC: University of North Carolina Press, 1986). For a broader study of slavery's role in the Atlantic economy, see David Galenson, *Traders, Planters and Slaves: Market Behavior in Early America* (Cambridge: Cambridge University Press, 1986, 2002).
[21] Examples of non-plantation slave labour studies include: W. Jeffrey Bolster, *Black Jacks: African American Seamen in the Age of Sail* (Cambridge, MA: Harvard University Press, 1998); Verene Shepherd (ed.), *Slavery without Sugar: Diversity in Caribbean Economy and Society since the 17th Century* (Gainesville, FL: University of Florida Press, 2002); Peter Blanchard, *Under the Flags of Freedom: Slave Soldiers and the Wars of Independence in Spanish South America* (Pittsburgh, PA: University of Pittsburgh Press, 2008); Christopher Leslie Brown and Philip D. Morgan (eds.), *Arming Slaves: From Classical Times to the Modern Age* (New Haven, CT: Yale University Press, 2006); and an especially strong essay on state use of slavery in Cuba by Evelyn Jennings, 'War as the 'Forcing House of Change': State Slavery in Eighteenth-Century Cuba', *William & Mary Quarterly*, 3rd series, 62/2 (2005), 411–40.
Studies focusing on patterns of slave-ownership include: Catherine Clinton, *The Plantation Mistress: Women's World in the Old South* (New York: Pantheon Press, 1982); Michel-Rolph Trouillot, 'Coffee Planters and Coffee Slaves in the Antilles: The Impact of a Secondary Crop', in Ira Berlin and Philip Morgan (eds.), *Cultivation and Culture: Labor and the Shaping of Slave Life in the Americas* (Richmond, VA: University of Virginia Press, 1993), 124–37; Hilary Beckles, 'Freedom without Liberty: Free Blacks in Barbados', in Shepherd (ed.), *Slavery without Sugar*, 199–223. While Trouillot explores slave ownership by non-whites as an extension of the rising free mixed race population of Saint-Domingue, Beckles suggests that black slave ownership might be considered a resistance strategy, whereby some relatives purchased others to reunite families in bondage.

compilation of almost 30,000 slave ship voyages that required international collaboration, and included records from English, French, Dutch, Spanish, Portuguese, Danish, and
American archives.[22] It did not include slave names and so is of less use to those seeking
to trace family lines, but it has been of incalculable utility to those concerned about the
extent, significance, and influence of the slave trade market.[23] It was also, almost certainly,
the most extensive, detailed, and historiographically significant undertaking combining
transatlantic trade with statistical analysis to emerge in several decades.

But if slavery was now accepted as an essential part of transatlantic history and
economy, it still received less attention from historians of material culture and consumer studies. Historians have recognized slaves' essential role as consumers; far from
marginal, whole industries in North America and Europe, such as salt cod, pork and
certain textiles, depended on slaves for their livelihoods. Indeed, some industries developed solely in response to slave owners' demands, such as the Negro cloth intended as
clothing for plantation field hands.[24] But these were foods and products selected and
purchased primarily by slave owners for their labourers; only a handful of scholars
acknowledged enslaved peoples as active consumers in their own right. Sidney Mintz
and Douglas Hall found evidence that slaves' participated in local Jamaican markets by
selling surplus provisions grown on land set aside for their sustenance on plantations.
Roderick McDonald took a different tack by focusing on economic activity inside plantations. Rather than accept food, shelter, or clothing rations provided by their owners,
slaves offered opinions on the quality of commodities acquired on their behalf. They
also expressed preferences, and with funds earned from hiring out, selling, or barter-
ing ground provisions and other goods, acquired both food and material possessions
that reflected ethnic and religious identities, as well as individual taste. Likewise, Ellen
Hartigan-O'Connor's work on women's participation in South Carolina and Rhode
Island economic activity explored enslaved and free black women's consumer roles from
proxy shoppers to Charleston market's female higglers, slave women so prominent and
successful in their retail operations that other vendors repeatedly sought legislation to
control their behaviour, fearing competition from price undercutting.[25] Such evidence

---

[22] David Eltis, Stephen D. Behrendt, David Richardson, and Herbert S. Klein (eds.), *The Trans-Atlantic
Slave Trade: A Database on CD-ROM* (Cambridge: Cambridge University Press, 2000).

[23] The slave trade database has, like Philip Curtin's earlier work, sustained some criticism for
considering slaves in terms of 'the number of people sent here' rather than as individuals. See Annette
Gordon-Reid, *The Hemingses of Monticello: An American Family* (New York: W.W. Norton & Co.,
2008), 21–2.

[24] Shane White and Graham White, 'Slave Clothing and African American Culture in the Eighteenth
and Nineteenth Centuries', *Past & Present*, 148 (August 1995), 149–86.

[25] Sidney Mintz and Douglas Hall, *The Origins of the Jamaican Internal Marketing System* (New
Haven, CT: Yale University Press, 1959); Roderick A. McDonald, *The Economy and Material Culture
of Slaves: Goods and Chattels on the Sugar Plantations of Jamaica and Louisiana* (Baton Rouge, LA:
Louisiana State University Press, 1994); and Ellen Hartigan-O'Connor, 'Collaborative Consumption
and the Politics of Choice in Early American Port Cities', in John Styles and Amanda Vickery (eds.),
Gender, Taste and Material Culture in Britain and North America, 1700–1830 (New Haven, CT: Yale
University Press, 2006), 125–49. Another excellent collection of essays about slave consumer behaviour
by Woodville Marshall, Dale Tomich, John Campbell, and Roderick McDonald, appears in 'Part 3: The
Slaves' Economy' of Berlin and Morgan (eds.), *Cultivation and Culture*.

of slaves' independent economic activity indicated a certain degree of autonomy that enabled them, albeit within important limitations, to distance themselves from their owners' control. It also encourages further study of how enslaved people used cash, barter, and consumer choice to express materially their society and culture.

CHANGING PROFILE
OF TRANSATLANTIC CONSUMERS

The incorporation of enslaved people into the field of transatlantic consumption was both exciting and path-breaking, as studies on other groups previously overlooked have followed in their wake. Daniel Richter argued that, like enslaved Africans, Native Americans were not passive consumers in their interactions with Europeans. In fact, through the mid-seventeenth century, most native peoples in eastern North America valued European goods primarily as raw materials to be refashioned and repurposed according to local tastes and needs. A kettle, for example, might be 'prized for its copper, not for its carrying capacity' and reworked as an ornament for a headmen's neck to symbolize his powerful connections to European leaders. Even later, as colonies in North America grew and natives began using the goods they offered as originally intended, consumption remained imbedded in political, social, and cultural symbolism. Gift-giving was not only a central function in creating alliances, but also a key tool deployed by Indians to parlay power between British, French, and Spanish colonial authorities.[26] As Native American scholar Kathleen DuVal suggested, 'European goods served many purposes—religious ceremonial, decorative, protective, subsistence, political—for various peoples, places and times.' An object's 'usefulness is', after all, she concluded, 'in the eye of the consumer.'[27]

Gender has also been resuscitated. John Styles and Amanda Vickery's recent volume explored how gender shaped taste and material culture in eighteenth-century Britain and North America. And if the geographic parameters of an Anglo-Atlantic world seem traditional, the kinds of people populating the English-speaking regions in these essays are very different than those in studies done 20 years ago. Ann Smart Martin, for example, argued that Virginia shopkeepers' accounts filled with men's names mask the important contributions of married women in selecting home furnishings. Women's purchases were not just a 'triangulation between merchant, consumer and object' but often filtered through husbands, fathers, sons, and brothers and, as such, their frequency

---

[26] Daniel K. Richter, *Facing East from Indian Country: A Native History of Early America* (Cambridge, MA: Harvard University Press, 2001), esp. Chapter 2, 'Confronting a New Material World'. For a similar discussion of Native American trade patterns and efforts to balance colonial powers in the south, see Peter C. Mancall, Joshua L. Rosenbloom and Thomas Weiss, 'Indians and the Economy of Eighteenth-Century Carolina', in Coclanis (ed.), *The Atlantic Economy*, 297–322.

[27] Kathleen DuVal, *The Native Ground: Indians and Colonists in the Heart of the Continent* (Philadelphia: University of Pennsylvania Press, 2006), 260, note 21.

and financial significance have been obscured by strictly literal interpretations of eighteenth-century accounting practices. And lest gender be defined as solely female, another cluster of studies in the volume explored the intersection of consumer behaviour and masculinity. Linzy Brekke-Aloise aptly noted that several existing scholars address relationships between material culture and early American nationalism, but that 'the historical and scholarly feminization of consumer culture, shopping, and fashion' has hidden from view 'the way goods, particularly clothing, figured in the lives of men' in the late eighteenth and early nineteenth centuries. George Washington and his contemporaries were certainly conscious of how they crafted their public figures, and held that restraint in fashion conveyed similarly conservative stances on politics and economics.[28] Perhaps the best-known book on male consumption is Michael Zakim's *Ready-Made Democracy*, an examination of the rise of the men's ready-made clothing industry in nineteenth-century America. Zakim argues that homespun garments tied the productive efforts of the household to those of the nation, and became one of the most tangible expressions of colonial self-reliance. But over the next century of industrialization, the mass-produced suit—inexpensive, consistent, and accessible—became an equally powerful symbol for the rise of democratic capitalism, and a new geographically and socially mobile middle class.[29]

The objects being consumed have changed as well. Commodities continue to receive significant scholarly and popular attention today. But, unlike commodity studies of the past, which focused on production or distribution, recent commodity studies are hybrids of history, economics, social geography, material culture, and cultural studies that ask where goods travelled, how they moved, in what quantities, who wanted them and, most elusive of all, why were they desirable. Relieved of their roles as mere economic cargoes or anthropological artefacts, commodities—and their circulation and consumption—have gained a new lease of life where, as cultural anthropologist Daniel Miller has noted in *Material Culture: Why Some Things Matter*, the 'social is as much constituted by materiality as the other way around'.[30]

---

[28] Linzy Brekke-Aloise, '"To Make a Figure": Clothing and the Politics of Male Identity in Eighteenth-Century America', in Styles and Vickery (eds.), *Gender, Taste and Material Culture*, 228.

[29] Michael Zakim, *Ready-Made Democracy: A History of Men's Dress in the American Republic, 1760–1860* (Chicago: University of Chicago Press, 2006). Brian Luskey explored similar intersections between material culture and men's self-fashioning for one profession in particular, the white-collar clerk, in *On the Make: Clerks and the Quest for Capital in Nineteenth-Century America* (New York: New York University Press, 2010).

[30] Daniel Miller, *Material Cultures; Why Some Things Matter* (Chicago: University of Chicago Press, 1998), 17. Anthropologist Mary Douglas and economist Baron Isherwood similarly argued in *The World of Goods* that economics alone could not explain commodities' appeal: 'It is standard ethnographic practice to assume that all material possessions carry social meanings and to concentrate a main part of cultural analysis upon their use as communicators.' Mary Douglas and Baron Isherwood, *The World of Goods: Toward an Anthropology of Consumption* (New York: Routledge, 1979), 59. A more recent example of this same teleology appeared in Frank Trentmann, 'Materiality in the Future of Things: Things, Practices, and Politics', *Journal of British Studies*, 48 (2009), 283–307, which suggests a 'material turn' in contrast to—indeed, in reaction to—the past generation's literary turn in scholarship.

So now, in addition to such durable standards as furniture, cookware, or clothing, or even consumables like sugar, coffee, or codfish, scholarship has tackled the transatlantic consumption of politics, taste, design, and behaviour. Robert Blair St. George, for example, compared passages from novels with small, personal rooms, or 'closets', and the books they contained. His analysis of libraries and other domestic reading spaces in New England homes is one of several studies that examine the rising importance of reading as a scholarly and leisure activity in both the United States and Europe. Julius Scott, a Caribbean historian, also studied the spread of ideas, though of a decidedly more politicized nature. His essay 'The Common Wind: Currents of Afro-American Communication in the Era of the Haitian Revolution' offers a detailed and thoughtful critique of enslaved populations' appropriation of French revolutionary rhetoric both in the French colony of Saint-Domingue and elsewhere throughout the Atlantic world.[31]

Such studies of consumers and that which they consumed demand that scholars approach evidence with open minds, with a certain degree of creativity, and a willingness to make intuitive leaps. Weaving together narratives about slave clothing preferences, for example, might mean reading planters' correspondence against the grain, to disentangle what slaves desired from what their owners thought they wanted or should have wanted, and comparing this information with a handful of accounts in travel narratives, satirical prints, or private sketches, and perhaps one amazing sample book of cloth created for the African trade in an archive in Madrid.[32] This is fundamentally different evidence than the port records or Naval Office Shipping Lists on which consumption studies were previously based, and at times the lens of contemporary inquiry narrows to one city, one storekeeper, and even one object.[33] It should not be surprising, then, that as consumers become more diverse and individual, historians' evidence for them becomes more narrative than statistical.

[31] Robert Blair St. George, 'Reading Spaces in Eighteenth-Century New England', in Styles and Vickery (eds.), Gender, Taste and Material Culture, 81–106; Julius S. Scott, 'The Common Wind: Currents of Afro-American Communication in the Era of the Haitian Revolution', in Laurent DuBois and Julius S. Scott (eds.), Origins of the Black Atlantic: New Histories (New York: Routledge Press, 2010). DuBois provided a similar explication of the same circulation of French rhetoric from the perspective of ex-slaves in the French colony of Guadeloupe when Napoleon reinstated slavery in A Colony of Citizens: Revolution and Slave Emancipation in the French Caribbean, 1787–1804 (Chapel Hill, NC: University of North Carolina Press for the Omohundro Institute of Early American History and Culture, 2006).

[32] Many thanks to Laura Johnson, a doctoral student at the University of Delaware and the 2009/10 Barra Dissertation Fellow in Art and Material Culture at the McNeil Center for Early American Studies for sharing her references to cloth produced for the African trade: 'Quince muestras de géneros bastos de algodón y guimaras indígenas, remitidos por el gobernador de Filipinas en la fragata Astrea y Urca Santa Inés con destino al comercio africano' (loosely translated as, 'Fifteen samples of kinds bastos of cotton and guimaras native, shipments by the governor of Philippines in the frigate Astrea and Holy Ram Inés bound for the African commerce'), Archivo General de Indias, Ministerio de Cultura, Gobierna de Espana, film no. C–7461.

[33] Ann Smart Martin, Buying into the World of Goods: Early Consumers in Backcountry Virginia (Baltimore, MD: Johns Hopkins University Press for the Program in Early American Economy and Society, 2008), especially ch. 6, 'Suckey's Looking Glass: African Americans as Consumers', 173–93.

CHANGING DIRECTION OF
TRANSATLANTIC CONSUMPTION

As historians acknowledged a broader pantheon of purchasers, consumers in general were re-empowered. Homes and store counters were no longer final destinations in a linear march from production to consumption, but a kind of middle ground where what was consumed was tested and evaluated, sometimes accepted, and at other times returned for redesign or refashioning. Sidney Mintz first approached consumption as the natural outgrowth to his work on Caribbean production, but quickly realized that the problem was not nearly as straightforward as he had imagined. Consumer historians noted sugar's increasing popularity over centuries 'without regard to where the sugar came from', while labour and production historians were just as guilty of failing to follow 'where the tropical products go, who uses them, for what, and how much they are prepared to pay for them'.[34] It was not sufficient to line processes up as they might appear in chronological sequence because, especially in imperial studies, doing so led to the unsatisfying tendency for metropoles to appear as refined consumers and outlying colonies as raw product producers, when the relationship was in reality far messier.

Instead, Mintz began to puzzle over what 'demand' really was and to what extent it could be considered natural. He also re-examined words like 'taste', 'preference', and even 'good', and interrogated how they worked. Just because sugar was sweet did not necessarily mean, in other words, that it would become desirable. Instead, production and consumption operated under a larger rhetoric of power—power over taste, demand access, and certainly over labour, because if a commodity's existence did not necessarily ensure its popularity, control over the means of production at least ensured it would exist and have a chance to become so. It is how things were used, where, and by whom, he concluded, that imbued them with social meaning and made them worth acquiring.

Almost a decade passed before the question of consumption's relationship to production arose so explicitly again, this time in Cary Carson's extended chapter 'The Consumer Revolution in Colonial British America: Why Demand'.[35] Carson's footnotes alone make the piece worth reading, as he painstakingly recounted how different historical subdisciplines noted increasing consumption during the eighteenth century, and summarized each historiography with extended annotation. Economic historians looked at the

[34] Sidney W. Mintz, *Sweetness and Power: The Place of Sugar in Modern History* (New York: Penguin Books, 1985), xvii.

[35] Cary Carson, 'The Consumer Revolution in Colonial British America: Why Demand?', in Carson, Hoffman, and Albert (eds.), *Of Consuming Interests*, 483–697. Other work on consumption appeared during the 1980s, of course, including Joel Mokyr, *The Economics of the Industrial Revolution* (Totowa, NJ: Rowman and Allenheld, 1985); McKendrick, Brewer and Plumb, *The Birth of a Consumer Society*; Carole Shammas, *The Pre-Industrial Consumer in England and America* (Oxford: Oxford University Press, 1990); John Brewer and Roy Porter (eds.), *Consumption and the World of Goods* (New York and London: Routledge, 1993).

rise of durable goods, and literary scholars at books, pamphlets, and sermons on luxury and its denigrating effects. Art historians counted the number of portraits and paintings that not only appeared with greater frequency in the homes of middling families, but also depicted lifestyle changes in their foregrounds and backgrounds. Cultural historians pointed to the proliferation of etiquette literature to guide the newly initiated in the arts of social behaviour and proper use of the trappings of gentility, and architectural historians to the diffusion of pattern books that promoted consistent versions of classical architecture just as vernacular building styles declined in popularity. There was, in other words, a perfect storm of commodities, behaviour, and standardization that seemed to portray consumers as uneducated masses desperate both for acquisition and proper instruction.[36]

But this would be confusing the symptoms for the underlying cause. Each of these literatures very clearly outlined important changes in transatlantic consumption—and even the preconditions that made such changes possible—during the eighteenth and early nineteenth centuries, but fewer speculated about why these changes occurred when they did. They assumed that increases in disposable income necessarily led to greater spending, a presentist viewpoint if every there was one. Instead, Carson suggested that consumer trends reflected both a growing distinction between living standard (literally, how one lived) and lifestyle (a cohesive force uniting like-minded people to reaffirm their similarities), as well as a growing number of people who presented themselves and behaved in ways more class- than culture-bound. Underlying these assumptions, however, was careful attention to demography; Carson returned again and again to the notion that changes in living standards depended on a critical population mass, a group against which individuals measured themselves and by whom they were judged.[37]

In so doing, he recombined consumer studies with the best statistical analyses that social history had to offer. Admittedly most of this quantification appeared in the chapter's footnotes so as not to disrupt narrative flow, but they did appear. So too did recognition of material culture's value in filling documentary voids. While Carson described its significance primarily in terms of class, authors cited in earlier segments of this chapter used goods just as effectively for other markers of identity. As Leora Auslander more recently noted, including material culture expands 'the range of our canonical resources' and 'will provide better answers to familiar historical questions as well as change the very nature of the questions we are able to pose and the kind of knowledge we are able to acquire.'[38] If there was one critique of Carson's framework, it was its steadfast adherence to North America and Britain, but perhaps this is unfair given the parameters of the book in which it appeared; even he gestured towards the need to appreciate 'the true internationalist character' of consumer changes. His model not only advocated understanding larger phenomena through the lens of individuals, but also demanded that

---

[36] Carson, 'Why Demand?,' 491–3, notes 9–17.

[37] For distinctions between living standard and lifestyle, and class and culture, see: Ibid., 503, 513. For discussion of population size, see. 508 and 516.

[38] Leora Auslander, 'Beyond Words', *The American Historical Review* 110/4 (2005), 1015.

such connections remained explicit and defined, rather than stated in an introduction and assumed for the rest of the piece.

New Directions

The history of transatlantic consumption is uniquely poised to explore both individuals and the larger social, cultural, and geographic contexts in which they lived their lives. Consequently, it seems a promising solution to the problem of melding micro- and macro-economic studies, as both are necessary to describe developments that take place before and after changes in consumer patterns. Economic historians, after all, are used to analysing events in stages of growth and development. Cultural historians are less so. But cultural historians have redefined the nature of evidence and its relationship to argument, and in this way have liberated historians facing topics that do not come with extensive, well-ordered records spanning decades.

So what might some future topics look like that bridge these traditional disciplinary divides and explore less charted regions of the field? Three possibilities come to mind. The first revisits the concept of barter, a well-explored topic in early modern society which all but disappears in scholarship by the mid-eighteenth century and certainly by the early nineteenth century. Recent work indicates, however, that non-cash transactions persisted well into the nineteenth century in urban centres as well as rural towns, indicating that consumption remained more complicated than a simple monetary transaction might lead one to believe. It often involved something given, either another good, time, or skill in the form of a service provided, for something gained. Thinking of consumption in this context makes each purchase part of a larger complex web of decisions and social agreements.

In today's age of ebay and craigslist, second-hand goods seem another obvious choice for melding individual consumer choice with market trends and forces. As Wendy Woloson convincingly demonstrated in her article 'In Hock: Pawning in Early America', whole industries developed to cater to those purchasing used goods, as pawnbrokers, auctioneers, and even privateers aided in their recirculation between empires, cities, and social classes. In fact, most of the goods North Americans purchased before the Civil War had passed through the hands of at least one previous owner. Woloson weaves together individual stories of those down on their luck to recreate what was an essential way to obtain ready cash for everyone but the privileged few, and 'was therefore a mainstream economic activity'. These small, short-term cash loans provided by pawnbrokers supplemented labourers' insufficient wages, and reinforced the industrial capitalist system within which they operated. Historians' inclination to separate the 'marginal' from the 'mainstream', and couch consumption in terms of modern-day new and disposable goods has downplayed this interconnectedness.[39]

---

[39] Wendy Woloson, 'In Hock: Pawning in Early America', *Journal of the Early Republic*, 27/1 (Spring 2007), 35–81. See also: Wendy Woloson, *In Hock: Pawning in Early America from Independence through the Great Depression* (Chicago: University of Chicago Press, 2010).

Finally, a new economic/cultural consumer history might link the study of things to one central historical problem. Indeed, some already are. Instead of a more traditional commodity life cycle, Brian Schoen uses cotton to understand the intersection of Southern cultural identity and moral economy. Similarly, David Hancock's book on Madeira is more than the story of one wine; it traces the origins of globalization and market differentiation back to the seventeenth century. And my own work, still in progress, argues that Americans' reliance on coffee—both for domestic consumption and re-export—created a regional economic dependence on first the Caribbean and then Latin America through the eighteenth and nineteenth centuries in contrast to the more traditional notions of the nation's political or cultural independence. Individuals and their choices appear in all of these studies, but so too does significant investment in understanding the market forces and networks which created the options in which such decisions were exercised.[40]

BIBLIOGRAPHY

Breen, T. H., *The Marketplace of Revolution: How Consumer Politics Shaped American Independence* (Oxford and New York: Oxford University Press, 2004).

Brewer, John and Porter, Roy (eds.), *Consumption and the World of Goods* (New York and London: Routledge, 1993).

Carson, Cary, Hoffman, Ronald and Albert, Peter J. (eds.), *Of Consuming Interests: The Style of Life in the Eighteenth Century* (Charlottesville: University of Virginia Press, 1994).

Davis, Ralph, *The Rise of the Atlantic Economies* (Ithaca: Cornell University Press, 1973).

Douglas, Mary and Isherwood, Baron, *The World of Goods: Toward an Anthropology of Consumption* (New York: Routledge, 1979).

Eltis, David, Behrendt, Stephen D., Richardson, David and Klein, Herbert S. (eds.), *The Trans-Atlantic Slave Trade: A Database on CD-ROM* (Cambridge: Cambridge University Press, 2000).

Hancock, David, *Oceans of Wine: Madeira and the Emergence of American Trade and Taste* (New Haven: Yale University Press, 2009).

McCusker, John J. and Menard, Russell R., *The Economy of British America, 1607–1789* (Chapel Hill, NC: Omohundro Institute for Early American History and Culture, 1991).

McDonald, Roderick A., *The Economy and Material Culture of Slaves: Goods and Chattels on the Sugar Plantations of Jamaica and Louisiana* (Baton Rouge: Louisiana State University Press, 1994).

McKendrick, Neil, Brewer, John and Plumb, J. H., *The Birth of a Consumer Society: The Commercialization of Eighteenth-Century England* (Bloomington: University of Indiana Press, 1982).

Miller, Daniel, *Material Cultures: Why Some Things Matter* (Chicago: University of Chicago Press, 1998).

[40] Brian Schoen, *The Fragile Fabric of Union: Cotton, Federal Politics and the Global Origins of the Civil War* (Baltimore, MD: Johns Hopkins University Press, 2009); David Hancock, *Oceans of Wine: Madeira and the Emergence of American Trade and Taste* (New Haven, CT: Yale University Press, 2009); Michelle Craig McDonald, *Caffeine Dependence: Coffee and the Early American Economy* (Philadelphia: University of Pennsylvania Press, forthcoming).

Mintz, Sidney W., *Sweetness and Power: The Place of Sugar in Modern History* (New York: Penguin Books, 1985).

Shammas, Carole, *The Pre-Industrial Consumer in England and America* (Oxford: Oxford University Press, 1990).

Styles, John, and Vickery, Amanda (eds.), *Gender, Taste and Material Culture in Britain and North America, 1700–1830* (New Haven, CT: Yale University Press, 2006).

Weatherill, Lorna, *Consumer Behavior and Material Culture in Britain, 1660–1760* (London and New York: Routledge, 1988).

CHAPTER 7

THE GLOBAL EXCHANGE
OF FOOD AND DRUGS

FELIPE FERNÁNDEZ-ARMESTO
AND BENJAMIN SACKS

FOOD and drugs—which, taken together, form the culture we ingest—have a paradoxi-cal place in the history of the exchange of goods. On the one hand, people treat them conservatively, resenting foreign intrusions in experiences as profoundly formative of identity as eating, healing, and psychotropic practices. On the other hand, exotic prod-ucts and fashions often permeate cuisines and pharmacopoeias with surprising ease. By Jean Brillat-Savarin's day, 'a meal such as may be had in Paris [was] a cosmopolitan whole, in which every part of the world [was] represented by its products.'[1] Today, we feed in a globalized world where dishes and ingredients are swapped with enthusiasm, while the drugs trade, both licit and illicit, is one of the largest-scale and longest-range earners. It is tempting to represent this as the culmination of a story of horizons widened by improv-ing communications. That would be false—or, at least, oversimplifying to the point of distortion. There are few more intriguing problems in the history of consumption than that of how cultural barriers to the transmission of foods and drugs have been traversed or broken. Food and drugs are best dealt with together because both are consumed inside the body and because, at the margins, they are hard or impossible to distinguish.

The obstacles to cross-cultural ingestion go a long way back in history, and deep in individual psychology. Personal taste is hard to modify. Children are tenaciously resist-ant to experiments in eating. Cheap tourism shrinks from gastronomic horizons. People return to familiar flavours. Migrants resist the food and drugs of host communities. Households with limited budgets refrain from experiment to limit waste.[2] Curers and shamans form, typically, hereditary elites, deeply invested in their traditional specifics

---

[1] Jean-Antoine Brillat-Savarin, *The Philosopher in the Kitchen* (Harmondsworth: Penguin, 1970), 275.
[2] Marjorie L. De Vault, *Feeding the Family: The Social Organization of Caring as Gendered Work* (Chicago, University of Chicago Press, 1991).

for healing the body and altering the mind. A few sources of influence that have helped overcome these inhibitions can be briefly acknowledged. Hunger or some analogous emergency, such as war or extreme sickness, can dispose people to accept intake which in other circumstances they might reject as foreign. In the sixteenth century, for instance, sweet potatoes became acceptable in China and Japan after introduction in times of famine. The progress of potatoes across northern Europe kept pace with the march of armies.[3] Taste for spam, introduced as American food-aid, outlasted the Second World War in Britain. Today, surpluses that developed countries dole out to refugees of distant wars come from wheat 'mountains' and dairy 'lakes': they convert lactose-hostile cultures to milk products and gruel-eaters to bread. Similarly, economic self-interest can persuade people to change diet in the case of exceptionally exploitable foodstuffs. In the late eighteenth century, Maoris began production of pork and potatoes—foodstuffs previously unknown to them—to sell to European naval and whaling ships. Tourism in the twentieth century is often plausibly credited with effecting mass changes of taste.

Environmental change, too, is a crucial part of the background of global exchanges of food and drugs. The process we have come to know as 'the Columbian exchange' of the last half-millennium—an unprecedented ecological turnaround in world history, as a result of the enormous extension of global shipping routes in the early modern period—made it possible to transplant crops to new climates, by a mixture of adaptation and accident. Changes in the disease environment, meanwhile, have stimulated demand for previously unfamiliar therapeutic drugs. Shifts of religion can also play a big part. The need for shamanic ecstasies is one source of demand, sometimes strong enough to cross political borders and geographical obstacles, for hallucinatory and extremely psychotropic substances. Poisons (though outside the scope of this piece) form a category that overlaps with food and drugs and constitute a trade that overspills frontiers. The foods religions worship or privilege in rites travel with their missionaries. There is also an unaided power of culture which is capable of transmitting taste: what might be called cultural magnetism, in cases where communities ape the foodways or medicine of cultures of superior prestige.

In these pages, the focus will be first, briefly, on imperialism and migration, which are inescapable parts of the background of trade, and then on trade itself, which is probably the biggest single influence on the global exchange of the commodities under consideration.

EMPIRES AND MIGRANTS

Empires' main role in the history of consumption is as arenas for the promotion of trade and cultural exchange. A common motive for the expansion of empires is the programme of diversifying diet by imposing ecological collaboration on regions that specialize in

---

[3] William H. McNeill, 'The Introduction of the Potato into Ireland', *Journal of Modern History*, 21 (1948), 218–21; Hermann J. Viola and Carolyn Margolis (eds.), *Seeds of Change: A Quincentennial Commemoration* (Washington, DC: Smithsonian Institution Press, 1991).

different foodstuffs. Andean imperialism, for instance, from the age of Tiahuanaco to that of the Incas and Spaniards, has been based on enforced exchanges of food and, when necessary, labour, between producers at different altitudes or among the different micro-climates that are characteristic of terrains of mountains and valleys. For much of Chinese history, the empires that have united the contrasting environments of northern and southern China have been bound by the supply of southern rice for northern consumption. The Roman Empire worked because provinces specialized in the supply of basic products to the rest—Egypt, Sicily, and the north African littoral were the 'granaries' of the empire, Betica its olive grove. In the Aztec Empire, shifts of tribute between ecologically specialized zones supported the hegemony of a few communities in and around Lake Texcoco. Over 7,000 feet above sea level, where local agriculture was confined to garden mounds dredged and piled from the lake bottom, the lakebound environment was incapable of feeding the huge population—variously estimated but probably at least 80,000 people—concentrated in the capital at Tenochtitlan. The city's tribute rolls show 240,000 bushels a year of maize, beans, and amaranth levied from subject-communities. The cacao needed for the elite drink, essential for every ceremonial occasion, would not grow in the region at all and had to be brought in by bearers in vast quantities from the 'hot lands' of the far south.[4]

Empires can sometimes be powerful enough to enforce a metropolitan taste on a peripheral area, and they usually promote migration and colonization. These in their turn transmit eating habits alongside other aspects of culture, or re-educate the palates of expatriates who become vectors of new tastes when they return home. The tides of empire run in two directions: first, the flow outwards from an imperial centre creates metropolitan diversity and 'frontier' cultures—cuisines of miscegenation—at the edges of empires. Then the ebb of imperial retreat carries home colonists with exotically acclimatized palates and releases the forces of 'counter-colonization', dappling the former imperial heartlands with enclaves of sometime subject peoples, who carry their cuisines with them.[5] Thus Japan adopts tempura from Portuguese visitors and returns it to Europe with migrants of its own; croissants and baguettes become common at café tables in Brazzaville and Ho Chi Minh City, while tajines and Bun Oc invade the notoriously nationalistic restaurant culture of France; *rijsttafel* graces the table of the 'widow of the Indies' and vindaloo becomes an alternative English 'national' dish, while British soldiers take kushuri from India to Egypt, and Mexican migrants spread tortillas and tacos through the United States. High cuisines form at the nodal points of empire, which sweep ingredients, styles, and dishes from all over the regions of conquest into the central menu: runners took fish to Cuzco for the supreme Inca's table; African silphium was a delicacy in Rome; the Mughal court feasted on melons and grapes.

---

[4] *Codex Mendoza*, ed. Frances Berdan and Patricia Anawalt (Berkeley: University of California Press, 1992).

[5] Sami Zubaida, 'National, Communal and Global Dimensions in Middle Eastern Food Cultures', in Sami Zubaida and Romar Tapper (eds.), *Culinary Cultures of the Middle East* (London and New York: I.B. Tauris, 1994), 33–48.

Turkish cuisine is the outstanding example of how imperial centres attract ingredients from the edges of empire. Though gourmets and food historians are rediscovering the delights of regional and pre-imperial Turkish foods, the menu that has made Turkish food famous and established it as one of the world's great cuisines was concocted in Ottoman Constantinople among a court-aristocracy and, above all, in the Topkapi Palace. The scale of everything in the palace attested to the size of the empire and the reach of Ottoman rule but the statistics of the kitchen management beggar all others. In the sixteenth century, the kitchens were equipped to serve 5,000 diners daily and 10,000 on holidays. The head cook had a corps of fifty sous-chefs, the chief confectioner thirty assistants, and the chief taster a hundred subordinates. These figures grew as the empire enlarged, the dishes grew more refined, the range of culinary influences expanded, and the work became more specialized. By the mid-eighteenth century there was a dedicated kitchen for each of six kinds of halva, each with its own chef and a hundred assistants. Daily deliveries of dates, plums, and prunes arrived from Egypt, honey from Romania or—for the sultan's own table—from Candia, oil from Coron and Medon, and butter from the Black Sea, packed in ox-hides. The cookery of the Topkapi was both imperial and metropolitan—a sort of fusion food—because it combined ingredients from all over the empire in new dishes.[6]

The last great category of colonists' cuisines is that of exiles. Outside lands contiguous with China, the Chinese state has never promoted emigration. The spread of Chinese cooking around the world has therefore been colonial but not imperial, carried by peaceful migrants in self-imposed 'economic exile'.[7] At least, this is true of most recent Chinese migration, though that of the last century was genuinely imperial in another sense, as European governments shunted the conscripted labour of coolies and laundrymen around their own empires. It has produced hybrids of its own, of which the most notorious is 'chop suey'—a mixture, say, of bamboo shoots, bean sprouts, water chestnuts, and other vegetables with slivers of meat: an invention of pioneer Chinese restaurateurs in nineteenth-century North America.[8] Most of the Vietnamese who have carried their cuisine to the West since the 1950s have been political refugees. So were the victims of the Russian Revolution who made Russian food fashionable in Paris after the First World War.

TRADE: SALT

Foodstuffs and drugs travel, sometimes beyond the range of commerce, with the shifts of migrants and other biota; but trade remains at the heart of the story. Goods brought from afar at trouble and cost, or exchanged as gifts with alien plenipotentiaries, derive prestige from their journey out of all proportion to their intrinsic value or their practical merits. They are received as blessings from the divine horizon, or treasured as mirabilia,

---

[6] Ayla Essen Algar, *Classical Turkish Cooking* (New York: HarperCollins, 1991); Norman M. Penzer, *The Harem: Inside the Grand Seraglio of the Turkish Sultans* (New York: Dover, 2005).

[7] Jack Goody, *Food and Love: A Cultural History of East and West* (London: Verso, 1998), 162.

[8] F. T. Cheng, *Musings of a Chinese Gourmet* (London: Hutchinson, 1962), 24.

or prized, initially, for their exclusivity. This is similar to the added interest which travellers acquire as they go, according to how far they journey: pilgrims gain sanctity, leaders charisma, warriors fearsomeness, and ambassadors attention if they come from afar. Unfamiliarity forestalls contempt.[9]

One measure of a great cuisine is the diversity of provenance of its ingredients. This was a fact already appreciated in antiquity. 'Tell me now, muses,' commanded Hermippus (to take a European example, which could be paralleled in other cultures) 'how many good things Dionysus has brought here to men in his black ship since he has plied the wine-dark sea.' From Cyrene, came silphium; from the Hellespont, mackerel and all sorts of salt fish; from Thessaly, wheatmeal and ox-ribs. 'The Syracusans send pigs and cheese...Rhodes raisins and dreamy figs.' Pears and fat apples came from Euboea. Phoenicia provided dates.[10] For most of history long-range trade in ingestibles has been limited to luxury items of these kinds, because every society grows its own staples and essentials, unless and until they can be imported cheaply.

The big exception is salt. It is essential to sustain life. Most metabolisms seem to crave it in quantities far above what is strictly necessary. Its role as a preserving agent, which kills bacteria and suppresses decay, makes it essential in seasonal food management strategies. Where there are no mines or salt pans, it has to be extracted from sea water, or coaxed from plants such as coltsfoot or samphire which absorb salt from the earth. Some peoples cannot obtain adequate supplies locally; all demographically buoyant communities have to import it as soon as their population exceeds a certain threshold. As an item of trade, even salt cannot be traced back in the archaeological record beyond nine or ten thousand years, but some of its more recent historic effects are well known: the role of salt taxes in the making of medieval monarchies, the triggering of the French Revolution, the career of Gandhi. These episodes seem of slight significance, however, compared to the way the existence of two great salt-deficient markets of the past warped world history into new directions: the west African market in the late middle ages and the huge food-salting industry of northern Europe—especially of the Netherlands—in the seventeenth century. The first of these sustained the medieval trans-Saharan gold trade; the second profoundly influenced the course of early long-range maritime imperialism.

When Ibn Battuta, the widest-ranging pilgrim of the middle ages, crossed the Sahara in 1352, he accompanied a salt caravan from the mining centre of Taghaza, bound for Mali, where salt reputedly traded for gold at parity, ounce for ounce.[11] Much of the gold generated by this trade ended up in Christendom, which had little gold of its own: bullion deficiency in Western Europe was one of the great motors of change in the late medieval world, stimulating the voyages that eventually led European mariners across the Atlantic and

[9] Mary. W. Helms, *Ulysses' Sail; an Ethnographic Odyssey of Power, Knowledge and Geographical Distance* (Princeton: Princeton UP, 1988); Felipe Fernández-Armesto, 'The Stranger-effect in Early-modern Asia', *Itinerario*, xxiv (2000), 8–123.

[10] Andrew Dalby, *Siren Feasts: A History of Food and Gastronomy in Greece* (London and New York: Routledge, 1996), 105.

[11] H. A. R. Gibb and C. F. Beckingham (eds.), *The Travels of Ibn Battuta, AD 1325–1354*, 4 vols., (London, 1994), iv, 946–7.

around Africa. An even more urgent shortage, in northern Europe, was of salt—especially when the population began to rise in the sixteenth century and the food industry struggled to keep up. In the early seventeenth-century Netherlands, especially in the north-eastern provinces that came to form the Dutch Republic, food-processing was an industry of major importance: above all, herring-salting and the making of salted butter and cheese.

Poland, France and parts of the Baltic had extensive salt deposits, on which Dutch industries had traditionally drawn, but these were getting expensive and supply was unreliable in time of war. The most coveted supplies were controlled by the Spanish monarchy, in Portugal and the Caribbean, where salt said to be particularly suited to herring was produced. It was also cheap. Dependence on Spanish salt dominated Dutch relations with Spain, provoking war or prompting peace according to the fluctuations in supply. The quest for salt was a principal reason for the establishment of the Dutch West India Company in 1621, when the peace with Spain finally broke down, and the company's claim to a salt monopoly was one of the main causes of the ensuing dissension in the republic. In January 1622, twenty-seven ships from Hoorn and Enkhuizen—two of the most prominent herring industry centres—landed a large force at the rich Venezuelan salt-pans of Punta de Araya, with the aim of seizing them and turning them into a Dutch imperial outpost; but like subsequent expeditions, they were bloodily beaten back.

In the late 1620s, the beleaguered Dutch food industry was saved by the exploitation of new salt-pans at Tortuga, where Spanish rule had never been firmly established. In 1632, however, the Spaniards flooded the pans and over the following few years seized or destroyed all the Dutch garrisons in salt-producing areas of the Caribbean. The Dutch herring fleet was nearly wrecked by the ensuing crisis. By allying with Portuguese rebels, the Dutch were able to recover control of trade in Portuguese salt, which they had been in danger of losing altogether to German competitors.[12] By 1648, hostilities with Spain were over: the Dutch position was recognized in Madrid as unassailable. But salt did not cease to determine the pattern of diplomacy: the Dutch remained interested in getting a share of Caribbean salt and the long, slow, ultimately successful effort to effect a rapprochement between Spain and Holland, between 1648 and 1677, would have been unthinkable without this inducement.[13]

TRADE: SUGAR AND SPICE

By comparison with the high-bulk, high-value, vital trade in salt, a luxury commerce such as that in spices ought to be less important. But pepper, which accounted for about 70 per cent of the world's spice trade in the sixteenth and seventeenth centuries, was close to being a vital product, for the menus of the world's elites demanded it. The other

[12] Jonathan Israel, *The Dutch Republic and the Hispanic World* (Oxford: Oxford University Press, 1986), 25, 45, 92, 123–4, 136, 203, 214, 288–9.
[13] Manuel Herrera-Sánchez, *El acercamiento hispano-neerlandes, 1648–78* (Madrid: Consejo Superior de Investigaciones Científicas, 2002), 110–25.

main constituents of the trade—cinnamon, mace, and nutmeg—were exchanged in relatively small quantities but commanded such high profit margins for the merchants who
shipped them that they acquired a disproportionate importance in the marketplace. Salt
cannot be said to have changed food cultures: its effect is to enhance flavour, not subvert
the integrity of traditional cuisines; spices, however, contributed to the creation of new
food cultures in the areas that received them by way of trade. Moreover, the history of
the spice trade relates fundamentally to the biggest problem in global history: that of the
nature and shift of the balance of wealth and power between the West and the Orient—
the rival civilizations at opposite ends of Eurasia.

The trade was already thousands of years old. Cinnamon and its inferior cousin, cassia,
were among the products shipped to Mesopotamia along the Persian Gulf from the Arab
kingdoms of Dilmun and Magan, the exact whereabouts of which are still not known but
which probably corresponded to Bahrain and perhaps Yemen. Similar exchanges belong
to the context of ancient Egyptian trade with the mysterious land of Punt—an exchange
of staples for luxury aromatics and flavourings. We do not know where Punt was, but the
route involved a long and hazardous voyage down the Red Sea. To the ancient Egyptians,
it was a magnet for adventure and a spring of riches. The products were small objects of
desire; but the Egyptians had to send five ships to get them because the products offered
in return were of small unit value and great bulk.[14] Whereas Punt specialized in luxuries,
Egypt was a mighty food producer, with an economy single-mindedly geared to massive, intensive agriculture. The mission to Punt was more than a cultural encounter: it
was a meeting of contrasting ecologies and an occasion of exchange between them.

Punt possessed 'all marvels', while Egypt offered 'all good things'. Punt's principal
products were the incense trees that yielded myrrh for rites of worship and death; these
are clearly depicted in the wall paintings in Hatshepsut's temple. The gold of Punt was
measured out with bull-shaped weights, and the live incense trees were potted and
carried aboard the Egyptian vessels. The Egyptians paid for them with 'bread, beer,
wine, meat, fruits'.[15] There was, however, no clear line between sacrifice and cookery or
between aromatics and spices at the Egyptian court: pharaonic food was divine.

The Arabian and African spice trades of the Sumerians and Egyptians ultimately
reached Greece and Rome. Yemen was 'where men burn cassia and cinnamon for their
everyday needs'.[16] The earliest surviving report of a Greek explorer of the Arabian seas
raved about the fragrance exuded by the coast of south-west Arabia:

> It is not the sort of pleasure that is derived from spices that have been stored and
> become stale nor that produced by a plant separated from the stem which bore and

[14] On trade with Punt, see Louise Bradbury, 'Kpn-boats, Punt Trade, and a Lost Emporium', *Journal
of the American Research Center in Egypt* 33 (1996): 37–60. On the mysteries of Punt, see Jacke Phillips,
'Punt and Aksum: Egypt and the Horn of Africa', *The Journal of African History* 38.3 (1997), 423–57.

[15] Edouard Naville, *The Temple of Deir el-Bahari*, 5 vols. (London, 1894–1906), i, 21–5; Catherine H.
Roehrig (ed.), *Hatshepsut: from Queen to Pharaoh* (New Haven: Yale University Press, 2005); Joyce A.
Tyldesley, *Hatshepsut: the Female Pharaoh* (New York: Viking, 1996).

[16] Felipe Fernández-Armesto, *Near A Thousand Tables: A History of Food* (New York and London:
the Free Press, 2002), 154.

nourished it, but that of one blooming at its divine peak and giving off from its own natural sources a wondrous scent so that many come to forget human blessings and think that they have tasted ambrosia, seeking a name for the experience that matches its extraordinary character.[17]

The obviously romantic and mythical elements in this rhapsodizing do not suggest first-hand acquaintance; and it may be that Arab middlemen—the Sabaeans, Gerrhaeans and Minaeans of Greek texts—deluded their customers about the provenance of their wares. The plant we now call cinnamon, for instance, is not known to have grown in Arabia. As ancient gazetteers 'of the Erythraean Sea' extended their range to embrace much of the western Indian Ocean, the name came to be reserved for a product Arabs imported from India and Ceylon.[18]

These broadened contacts are reflected in the exoticism of Roman recipes. Of the sixty condiments recommended in the recipes of Apicius, only ten came from outside the empire. But some of them—especially Indian ginger, cardamom, and pepper, heavily used in the Apician tradition—represented the remotest reaches of the spice trade. One of Pliny's objections to spice-rich food was that it enriched the Indian economy and impoverished the Roman. 'They arrive with gold and depart with pepper,' as a Tamil poet put it.[19] The mystery of the spice market deepened, and the value of its products increased, because production was a highly specialized and regional business. Cassia was available from native sources in Arabia in antiquity, but in the middle ages true cinnamon became a Ceylonese near-monopoly. For pepper, merchants went to the Malabar coast of India. Nutmeg, mace, and cloves were produced in only a few places in the Indian Ocean and what is now Indonesia—above all, in the twin 'Spice Islands' of Ternate and Tidore. The vast bulk of the products of all these lands was exported to China, where the market was biggest and the economy richest. Marco Polo reckoned 1,000 lb of pepper a day entered Hangchow in his time. But if the European market was of small importance to the producers, it mattered greatly to the Western merchants who tried to take part in it.

The idea that the demand for spices was the result of the need to disguise tainted meat and fish is one of the great myths of the history of food: an offshoot of the myth of the progress—the assumption that people in earlier times were less competent, or less intelligent, or less capable of providing for their needs than we are today. Fresh foods in the Middle Ages were often fresher than today, because they were locally produced. Preserved foods were just as well preserved in their different ways—by salting, pickling, desiccating, and conserving—than ours are in the age of canning, refrigeration, and freeze-drying (a technique known in antiquity and developed to a high degree by Andean potato-growers in what we think of as the Middle Ages). Both fresh and

---

[17] Agatharchides of Cnidus On the Erythraean Sea, ed. S. M. Burstein (London, 1989), 162.

[18] Lionel Casson, 'Cinnamon and Cassia in the Ancient World', in Lionel Casson (ed.), *Ancient Trade and Society* (Detroit: Wayne State University Press, 1984), 224–41.

[19] James Innes Miller, *The Spice Trade of the Roman Empire* (Oxford: Clarendon Press, 1969); Dalby, *Siren Feasts*, 137.

preserved foods were probably healthier in those days because they were not grown with chemical fertilizers. In any event, taste and culture determined the role of spices in cooking. Spice-rich cuisine was expensive and, therefore, socially differentiating. For those who could afford it, this made it an ineluctable luxury. It was a defining characteristic of medieval Europe's haute cuisine, imitated from the Arabs.[20]

The nature of the European love of spices—rhapsodical, romantic, enlivened by imagination—is captured by the story told by Jean de Joinville, Louis IX's biographer, of the fishermen of the Nile, whose nets filled with ginger, rhubarb, and cinnamon dropped from the trees of the earthly paradise.[21] In the most successful recipe book of the era, the *Menagier de Paris* advised cooks to add spices to their dishes at the last possible moment so that none of the flavour was impaired by heat. The profits that beckoned anyone ingenious or determined enough to buy spices at or near source inspired heroic efforts by medieval merchants to penetrate the Indian Ocean. The routes all involved hazardous encounters with potentially hostile Muslim middlemen: you might try to cross Turkey or Syria to the Persian Gulf or, more usually, attempt to get a passport from authorities in Egypt to ascend the Nile and transfer, via desert caravan, to the Red Sea at Massaweh or Zeila. Not surprisingly, few of these attempts succeeded and the merchants who did manage to effect them became part of the existing trading networks of the Indian Ocean. The great change which converted the world of the traditional Eastern spice monopolies into a new world—a global system in which Western powers controlled the trade and, to a great extent, the production of spices—happened in three stages: first, the westward transfer of the world's main centres of sugar production, which started in the late middle ages; then, in the sixteenth and seventeenth centuries, the development of new trade routes to which Western merchants had privileged access; finally, from the seventeenth century onwards, the progressive takeover of control of production by Western powers, deploying violent methods.

The switch started with sugar, because, uniquely among the exotic condiments favoured in Latin Christendom, this sweetener could grow in the Mediterranean with relative ease. Sugar is not normally classified as a spice today—it is, at best, an anomalous spice, since it has little fragrance; but, in antiquity and the middle ages, it was an exotic condiment obtainable only at great cost by way of trade. Eventually, merchants eluded the expensive end-purchaser role by growing it themselves. This was the basis of the Venetian experiments in sugar production in the Kingdom of Jerusalem in the twelfth century and of the Venetian Cornaro family's vast sugar operation in fourteenth-century Cyprus. The first Genoese-owned sugar estates on a commercially influential scale seem to have been in Sicily, from where, in the fifteenth century, the crop was taken first to the Algarve, then to the newly colonized archipelagoes of the eastern Atlantic, where (in Madeira, the western Canaries, the Cape Verde Islands, and those of the Gulf of Guinea) it became the basis of the islands' economy by the end of the fifteenth century.[22]

---

[20] Paul Freedman, *Out of the East: Spices and the Medieval Imagination* (New Haven: Yale University Press, 2008).

[21] Jean-Louis Flandrin and Massimo Montanari, *Histoire de l'alimentation* (Paris: Fayard, 1996), 63.

[22] Charles Verlinden, *Les Origines de la civilisation atlantique* (Paris: Albin Michel, 1966), 167–70.

Sugar was the only Atlantic product which could compete as a high-value condiment with the spices of the East. The Atlantic centres of production formed together a sort of rival spicerie—sugar islands of the west, rivalling the spice islands of the east. It may have been one of those cases where demand follows supply, for in the last quarter of the fifteenth century, when Atlantic sugar production 'took off' with the development of new sugar-lands in the Canaries, sugar confections were still luxuries, featuring prominently, for instance, in the household accounts of Isabella the Catholic as Christmas gifts for the royal children. But, as with tea and coffee in the eighteenth century and chocolate in the nineteenth, taste responded, at rates that varied from place to place and class to class, to increased supply. Cane sugar replaced honey as the Western world's everyday sweetener. By the time Piero de Cosimo painted his imaginative reconstruction of *The Discovery of Honey* in 1500, api-culture was, in a sense, already a thing of the past, a primitivist image, which could be used to typify a remote age. A few years later, the first sugar mill on Hispaniola opened and the slow transfer of the industry to the Americas began. In 1560 Henry II's physician reported that 'There is hardly anything today prepared for the stomach without sugar.'[23]

By then Vasco da Gama had opened a new route to the spice trade of the Indian Ocean, around the Cape of Good Hope, in 1497. By demonstrating the viability of direct trade with Indian pepper producers, he did not deflect trade from traditional routes. On the contrary, under the stimulus of improved communications, the total volume of the spice trade continued to grow and the amount handled along the traditional routes, via central Asia or the Persian Gulf or Red Sea, was higher in the sixteenth century than ever before. When it faltered, it was because of political instability in central Asia, which interrupted the peaceful conditions on which caravans relied, rather than because of Portuguese competition. The Portuguese handled 10 per cent of the output of Malabar pepper in a good year. This was enough to supply Western European demand but left the old trade to the Middle East untouched.

Spices would never make a major difference to the world balance of trade and power until Europeans succeeded in controlling supply as well as securing trade. The revolution in spice production was gradual, but it had specific critical moments. In the early seventeenth century Portuguese practice on Ceylon, the island which produced most of the world's cinnamon, demonstrated the possibilities. By heavily garrisoning the perimeter of the island and imposing production quotas and monopoly terms, Portugal was able to regulate supply to the point of virtual control. But this was a highly exceptional operation: generally, the Portuguese relied on local collaborators to supply their needs and kept costs down by accepting the constraints of the existing markets and submitting to the conditions imposed by native rulers.

When the Dutch broke into the Indian Ocean circle in the early seventeenth century, it looked as if their operation would merely be a more efficient version of what the Portuguese had already done. They cut costs by making as few stops en route as possible. In the second decade of the century they developed a new, fast, efficient route across the Indian Ocean, with the roaring forties and the Australia current—a great, sweeping arc,

[23] J.-B. Buyerin, *De re cibaria* (Lyons, 1560), 2.

relying, for the outward voyage, on fixed winds and bypassing the monsoons with their slow seasonal rhythms and long turnaround times spent waiting for the wind. From 1619 the Dutch station at Batavia became the gateway to the new route.[24]

Pricing was the essence of the competitive edge the Dutch achieved: their strategy was to drive down costs and maximize profits. Paradoxically, this committed them to escalatingly expensive political and military interventions in the market. The fate of Bantam, the Dutch residency in Java, demonstrates the trajectory that became typical. It boomed with the increased demand for pepper in China and Europe. Land was converted to pepper production until the island became a net importer of food. When the Dutch arrived they found a trade already established on a vast scale. Sancho Moluco, the leading native trader, could supply 200 tons of pepper at a time. Islanders dealt on a vast scale with Chinese and Gujarati merchants. The Dutch could not handle, at most, more than about a quarter of the island's production, but they could not remain indifferent to the power of their competitors in the marketplace, nor to the freedom producers enjoyed to adjust the market to suit themselves. After a series of disputes the founder and governor of Batavia, Jan Pieterszoon Coen, decided to destroy Bantam's trade. The war waged intermittently but ruthlessly for most of the 1620s. Over that period, the island's production fell by more than two-thirds. Ironically, Lim Lakko, the sultan's Chinese adviser who had organized the cartel that provoked the Dutch, was obliged to move to Batavia, 'utterly down and out' to found a new fortune trading with Taiwan. Bantam switched to making sugar for the Chinese market. When pepper production revived for English customers in the 1670s, the Dutch moved in again in force and imposed a humiliating treaty on the sultan at gunpoint in 1684.[25]

Meanwhile, an even more dramatic case of production wrested by force occurred further east. Makassar was a small sultanate on Sulawesi. In the first half of the seventeenth century its economy boomed with the work of refugees from Dutch aggression elsewhere. Malays filled its ships' crews. Moluccans brought savoir-faire in spices. Expelled from their principal emporium at Melaka (also called Malacca), Portuguese introduced their long-range contacts. It became their 'second and better Melaka'. The Kunstkammer of the ruler included a library of Spanish books, a globe, and a striking clock. Like other trading communities of maritime Asia, the Makassarese were not particularly interested in the European market: it was too small and distant to be worth their while. For European traders in the east, however, their own rivalries were all-important. By the mid-seventeenth century, the Dutch had already invested so much in the forcible elimination or restriction of Portuguese (and, to a lesser extent, English) rivals that they could not tolerate a native state which effectively acted as a surrogate and refuge for continued Portuguese profiteering.

'Do you believe,' the sultan asked them, 'that God has reserved for your trade alone islands which lie so distant from your homeland?' The first war they provoked against Makassar, from 1652 to 1656, left the sultanate with 'no powder left, no munitions, nor

[24] Hendrik E. Niemeijer, *Batavia: een koloniale samenleving in de zeventiende eeuw* (Amsterdam: Balans, 2005).
[25] Johan Talens, *Een feodale samenleving in koloniaal vaarwater: staatsvorming, koloniale expansie en economische onderontwikkeling in Banten, West Java (1600–1750)* (Hilversum: Verloren, 1999).

anyone who could supply them'. The most heavily gunned fleet in the history of the Indian Ocean assembled in Batavia to finish the sultanate off. The Dutch renewed the war in 1659. On 12 June 1660—an almost forgotten date, but one which deserves to be remembered as a turning-point in world history—Makassar fell when a Dutch landing-party seized the fortress. The sultanate was reduced to subservience. The Dutch had now completed their ring of force around the spice islands. They could control supply at the source of production as well as the first level of distribution. According to their reading of the fluctuations of the market, they devastated lands, burned plantations, uprooted crops, and destroyed competitors' ships. Plantings of clove, nutmeg, and mace rapidly fell to a quarter of their former levels. In 'depopulated lands and empty seas', south-east Asia's 'age of commerce' came to an end as indigenous cultivators 'retreated from the world economy'. Previously, the new routes tacked to world trade by European interlopers in the East had supplemented the traditional system and expanded its total volume, without modifying its essential character or shifting its main axis. Now a valuable slice of the gorgeous East really was held in fee and the economy of part of the Orient was impoverished for the benefit of the stockholders of the Dutch East India Company. This was a reversal of the aeons-old balance of trade, which had enriched the East at Western expense.[26] The results can still be seen on the Heerengracht of Amsterdam, the avenue of merchant palaces lining a canal, where the spice-rich elite concealed what Simon Schama famously termed their 'embarrassment of riches'—luxurious living behind unpretentious façades.

While it slipped into European control, the production of oriental luxuries for the food trade remained regionally specialized. There were still 'spice islands' and 'pepper coasts'. Ceylon still specialized in cinnamon, Amboina in nutmeg, Ternate and Tidore in cloves and mace, Malabar in pepper. The expectation started by Columbus, that the New World would yield new, undiscovered spiceries, had proved disappointing. Gonzalo Pizarro lost an army seeking a 'land of cinnamon' in Peru. Chilies were more piquant than oriental black pepper and ginger but could only supplement them—extending the culinary repertoire without replacing traditional dishes. In west Africa, Portuguese venturers had discovered 'malaguetta pepper' in the fifteenth century, but this had never succeeded in the European market. So although the distribution of the profits changed in the seventeenth century, and the routes multiplied, the general direction of the spice trade remained much the same as ever.

TRADE: PSYCHOTROPIC BEVERAGES

Where sugar and spices led, coffee—and, ultimately, tea and chocolate—followed. The increase in demand for these substances seems also to have been led by an increase in supply. By 1640, the coffee of Yemen rivalled or exceeded pepper as the main trading

---

[26] Anthony Reid, *South-east Asia in the Age of Commerce*, 2 vols. (New Haven: Yale University Press, 1988–93), 277–303.

commodity of the Arabian Sea. It continued to boom, supplying markets in Persia, where coffee consumption quadrupled to nearly a million pounds a year by the end of the century. Even larger amounts—about 17 million pounds—went to the Ottoman Empire via the Red Sea and Egypt. Coffee arrived in France in 1644 with a returning ambassador from Turkey, along with old porcelain cups of great beauty and small napkins of fine cotton muslin, embroidered in gold, silver, and silk. The coffee-drinking habit soon found patrons. In 1657, Jean de Thévenot noticed that Parisian aristocrats hired Moorish and Italian coffee-makers. Armenian importers and street-brewers popularized coffee drinking in France.[27] Within half a century, coffee became the West's favourite addictive stimulant. In his satirical domestic comedy, the *Coffee Cantata*, Bach credited it with the potential to break up marriages because so many husbands stayed away from home to drink coffee in cafés.

Once the popularity of the new beverage was established, the next stage was to transplant it to new lands where Europeans could control the supply. The great coffee boom of the eighteenth and nineteenth centuries took it to Brazil, to the French islands of the Indian Ocean, and to Saint-Domingue. One of the most enduringly successful of the new coffee lands was Java, where the Dutch introduced the plant in the 1690s, gradually expanded production during the eighteenth century, and, in the nineteenth fought wars to boost production on ever more marginal soils.

While coffee spread across the world from the Middle East, chocolate followed a similar path from a starting place in Mesoamerica. It took longer than coffee to penetrate European markets. In a work of 1648, credited with introducing chocolate to the English-speaking world, Thomas Gage described how colonial Mexico liked it—mixed with Old-World flavours, such as cinnamon, cloves, and almonds, as well as in the stews of bitter chocolate and chillies that were traditional Mesoamerican recipes. As, perhaps to a lesser extent, with coffee and tea, Europeans—after initial revulsion from an unfamiliar flavour—adopted and adapted not only the beverage but also ways of preparing it from the cultures of origin.[28] As the new drink became fashionable in Europe, the cacao from which chocolate was made was transplanted to West Africa, where Danish plantations helped supply the growing trade in the eighteenth century. Tea also contributed to the growth of global trade, but not to the ecological exchange. China was able to supply almost the whole of world demand until the nineteenth century when the British established tea plantations in India and Sri Lanka. Taken—as they commonly were by Western workers—with copious infusions of sugar, tea, coffee, and chocolate (especially when industrial processing turned the last into cheap, sweet chocolate bars) were mildly psychotropic, making bearable the long hours, hard work, tedium, and poor nutrition of early industrial workers. These were the real 'opiate of the masses' and helped to make Western industrialization possible.

[27] Jean Leclant, 'Coffee and Cafés in Paris, 1644–93', in Robert Forster and Orest Ranum (eds.), *Food and Drink in History* (Baltimore: Johns Hopkins University Press, 1979), 86–97.

[28] Marcy Norton, 'Tasting Empire: Chocolate and the European Internalization of Mesoamerican Aesthetics', *American Historical Review*, cxi (2006), 660–91.

THERAPEUTIC AND RECREATIONAL DRUGS

Explicitly therapeutic and recreational drugs enjoyed a similar boom in the enhanced environment of global trade in the early modern era. In antiquity and the middle ages drugs rarely seem to have been traded over long distances. Opium and hemp as a source of narcotics were used in ancient Egypt, but extracted from local sources. Almost all the substances Dioscorides listed came from within the Roman Empire. Those recommended by Galen included few exotics, most of which could be imitated locally.[29] Still, local concoctions were often sold as if they were exotic imports, in ancient Rome and China alike, and there was always a strong presumptive association between power and remote provenance. The increased scale and range of trade in the late middle ages and early modern period made genuine exotica accessible, while physicians' interest in drugs grew.

Not everyone shared the growing enthusiasm for drug-based prophylactics. 'Strive to preserve your health, and in this you will the better succeed in proportion as you keep clear of the physician,' Leonardo da Vinci advised, 'for their drugs are a kind of alchemy concerning which there are no fewer books than there are medicines.'[30] To find this magic, one had to look no further than the local chemist. Cornelius Agrippa wrote in the 1520s that drug stores substituted one thing for another 'or else make medicine of rotten, stale and mouldy drugs', or 'oftentimes give a deadly drink instead of a wholesome medicine'.[31] Debate concerning the efficacy of drugs continued throughout the Enlightenment. Thomas Rowlandson's 1816 illustration *Death Sitting on a Globe* represents drugs as unknown poisons, situated beside duelling pistols, amongst flasks of compounds, gunpowder, opium, and arsenic.[32] In general, however, drugs' ascent to supremacy in Western medicine was unstoppable, aided by the insufficiencies of surgery and patients' faith in a fix.

Meanwhile, with demand assured, one of the biggest influences on the global circulation of drugs was the opening of the New World to exploitation and commerce. The curriculum of the Colegio de Santa Cruz de Tlatelolco included '*Aztec* [not European] medicine'.[33] Bernardino de Sahagún, the pedagogue of Tlatelolco, who was among the first and greatest ethnographers of the Aztec world, noticed the natives' use of excitants and stupefacients in periods of celebration.[34] The persistence of pre-Colombian medicines and medical practices was indicative of the durability of Aztec and Inca traditions.

---

[29] Vivian Nutton, 'The Drug Trade in Antiquity', *Journal of the Royal Society of Medicine*, 178 (1985), 138–45.

[30] Philip Ball, *The Devil's Doctor: Paracelsus and the World of Renaissance Magic and Science* (New York: Farrar, Straus and Giroux, 2006), 164.

[31] Ball, *The Devil's Doctor*, 168. Agrippa, *Of the Vanitie and Uncertaintie of Artes and Sciences* (1530), ed. C. M. Dunn (Northridge, California: California State University Press, 1974), 314.

[32] R. Porter, *Blood and Guts: a Short History of Medicine* (New York: Norton, 2002), 2.

[33] Frank Thone, 'America's Earliest Herbal', *The Science News-Letter*, 28.758 (1935), 250.

[34] Frans Blom, 'On Slotkin's 'Fermented Drinks in Mexico', *American Anthropologist*, new series, 58.1 (1956), 185–6.

Although Church officials attempted to curtail the use of indigenous remedies and magic (e.g. the use of peyote from 1620 onwards), such regulation rarely had much effect— Spaniards and natives alike saw little conflict in the fusion of their two medical worlds. When, in 1592, the influential Spanish doctor Augustín Farfán published *Tratado breve de medicina*, he recommended the use of over sixty Aztec concoctions for the treatment of various European and American illnesses.[35] Sahagún made detailed depictions of Aztec medicinal remedies, solutions, and treatments.

Quinine was the most powerful discovery European ethnobotanists—in this case, Jesuits in late sixteenth-century Peru—took from the native pharmacopoeia. It was a more effective specific for high fevers than anything previously known in the Old World, and a uniquely virtuous suppressant of the symptoms of malaria. Until the discovery of quinine, the only remedies known in Europe were magical mumbo-jumbo—putting a peach stone in an orange, for instance, or having a young virgin tie magic paper around your neck with a long string. It remained, however, a rare and costly export from Peru until the mid-nineteenth century, when Charles Ledger observed, while working with llamas and alpacas in Bolivia, a stock of the highest-quality fever tree seeds the world had ever seen. Previous efforts to propagate the miracle-seeds outside the Andean region had largely failed. But Ledger's seeds throve in Java, where they kept Dutch soldiers alive and the Dutch Empire operative. A pension from the Dutch Government sustained Ledger until his death in a suburb of Sydney, senseless with senile dementia, at the age of 87, in 1906.[36] The importance of his breakthrough for the future history of the world can hardly be overestimated: European armies could now function in the tropics, and extend European imperialism over previously inaccessible swathes of the Earth.

If any drug equalled or exceeded quinine in importance it was opium. As with sugar and hot beverages in the same period, the reasons for increasing demand are mysterious and may have been another case of the reversal of the normal laws of economics: increasing supply seems to have stimulated demand. In the mid-fifteenth century, Xu Boling's *Yingjing Juan* celebrated opium: 'It is mainly used to treat masculinity, strengthen sperm, and regain vigour. It enhances the art of alchemists, sex and court ladies. Frequent use helps to cure the chronic diarrhoea that causes the loss of energy....Its price equals that of gold.'[37] In the sixteenth century, opium sustained Portuguese soldiers in the strenuous margins of empire and in the seventeenth became a big element in the European pharmacopoeia. Growing demand, especially in China, created new production and marketing opportunities, which British merchants were

---

[35] Amos Megged, 'Magic, Popular Medicine and Gender in Seventeenth-Century Mexico: the Case of Isabel de Montoya', *Social History*, 19 (1994), 189–207, at 194; Carlos Agustín Rodríguez Paz and Rosa María Carreón Bringas, 'Dr. Agustín Farfán: cirujano novohispano del siglo XVI', *Revista médica del Hospital General de México*, l56 (1993), 161–5.

[36] Gabriele Gramiccia, *The Life of Charles Ledger* (London: Macmillan, 1988); Fiammetta Rocco, *The Miraculous Fever-tree* (New York: HarperCollins, 2003).

[37] Zheng Yangwen, *The Social Life of Opium in China* (Cambridge: Cambridge University Press, 2005), 10–11; Zheng Yangwen, 'The Social Life of Opium in China, 1483–1999', *Modern Asia Studies*, 37.1 (2003), 1–39.

increasingly able to exploit in the eighteenth century, as the East India Company gained privileged access to opium-growing regions in India. Along with the British Isles and the Indian subcontinent, China formed an important link in what was the most economically powerful trading triangle of the nineteenth century.[38] 'Opium was no hole-in-the-corner petty smuggling trade,' Michael Greenberg stated, 'but probably the largest commerce of the time in any single commodity.'[39] The annual value of the opium that reached China rose fivefold in the 20 years preceding the mid-1830s. Western customers devoured the drug, 'as a cure-all for complaints, some trivial, some serious.'[40] Between 1840 and the 1860s, British and other Western invasions responded to Chinese attempts to ban the trade by literally forcing China into accepting increased imports of opium. For a while London established a near-monopoly over the trade.[41] The most significant consequence for the world economy was the Westerners' conquest of previously impenetrable Chinese markets. Now they had a product to sell and a means of obtaining trading privileges. By the 1870s, for the first time, China's balance of trade with the West turned unfavourable.

FOOD AND DRUGS IN THE ERA OF GLOBAL TRADE

In the context of nineteenth-century mechanization, urbanization, militarization and imperialism, global trade in food and drugs conformed to common patterns: the volume of existing trades grew, while geographical specialization worldwide turned staple foodstuffs into 'primary products', grown in dedicated environments, and shipped or freighted by rail, with the assistance of steam power, for processing to industrializing centres. Improved technologies of preservation—canning early in the century, refrigeration towards its end—made specialized production possible on a genuinely global scale. In many cases—West African palm oil and ground nuts, Assamese and Ceylonese tea, Central American and Caribbean bananas, Canarian tomatoes and bananas, Hawaiian

[38] Gregory Blue, 'Opium for China: the British Connection', in Timothy Brook and Bob Tadashi Wakabayashi (eds.), *Opium Regimes: China, Britain, and Japan, 1839–1952* (Berkeley, Los Angeles, and London: University of California Press, 2000), 31–2.

[39] Jacques M. Downs, 'American Merchants and the China Opium Trade, 1800–1840', *The Business History Review*, 42/4 (1968), 418, and quoted from Michael Greenberg, *British Trade and the Opening of China, 1800–1842* (Cambridge: Cambridge University Press, 1951), 104.

[40] Max Clarke, 'Opium Smoking and the Politics of Association in England, Hong Kong, and Mainland China', *Tufts Historical Review*, 2.1 (2009), 78; Virginia Berridge and Griffith Edwards, *Opium and the People* (New York: St Martin's Press, 1981), 21.

[41] Paul C. Winther, *Anglo-European Science and the Rhetoric of Empire: Malaria, Opium, and British Rule in India, 1756–1895* (Lanham, Maryland; Boulder, Colorado; New York; and Oxford: Lexington Books, 2003), 5.

pineapple, Argentine beef, Brazilian coffee—the products and their climes became synonymous. 'Business imperialism' and, in some cases, monopolistic corporations tended to control most of the trade and much of the production: the most impressive transformation of a previously underexploited environment was, perhaps, the US prairie—formerly known as 'the Great American Desert'—which became the greatest granary of the world. Distribution struggled to match demand, and supply struggled to keep up with soaring global population. Though increases in efficiency, extent, and intensity of food production ratcheted up output, and while the discovery of new sources of industrial lipids eased the mid-nineteenth-century crisis in the availability of dietary fats, famines increasingly ravaged areas reliant on their own staples, as specialization became ever more exclusive.

Twentieth-century innovations—chemical fertilizers and pesticides, complemented by the 'Green Revolution' of the 1960s–1980s, which introduced highly efficient new species of staple grains—solved the problem of famine but accentuated the previous patterns of trade. Producers of the new crops—condemned, in effect, to produce cheap staples for a global market—were locked into a relationship of dependency on consumers in richer economies. With continuing boosts to production, food prices tended to fall, and the value of food—measured by the proportion of income consumers in rich countries spent on it—plummeted. The effect was to impoverish producers further. The global nature of the market made the distribution of specialized production independent of that of consumption. By the early twenty-first century, India—a rice-eating culture—was the world's seventh largest exporter of wheat. Guyana and Argentina were the fastest growing exporters of rice. Despite the dominance of rice in the diet of most of China and India, those countries became major producers of potatoes. Vietnam—a country that never featured in coffee production until the end of the twentieth century—was the world's second biggest exporter of coffee in 2009. Japan, where bovine livestock were extremely few until late in the twentieth century, became an exporter of high-value beef.

Primary producers of drugs—especially the coca and opium that were in high demand and commanded high prices—had the advantage of a valuable product, but the terms of the drug trade came to be even more skewed than those of foodstuffs. Drugs that consumers tended to class as recreational attracted bans on their trade or use, especially if they were addictive; as a consequence, producers tended to be at the mercy of criminal gangs who controlled the trade. Therapeutic drugs, meanwhile, experienced a surprising boom. Despite rival therapies—including enhanced surgery and psychotherapy, drugs became entrenched as the medical professions' chief recourse worldwide. They gained their added value as a result of industrial processing and investment-intensive marketing, so that the primary producers remained at an economic disadvantage, unable to cash in on the profitability of the business. At the beginning of the twenty-first century, the imbalance of global trade could be summarized, crudely but not misleadingly, in a simple formula: food was too cheap, drugs too costly for the good of the world, and, in particular, for the good of primary producers.

PROSPECTS

Although the broad lineaments of the story are clear, its details need filling out—with more exact quantitative data than hitherto, if possible—and its lurches remain unexplained. Future research might clarify the reasons for the huge changes in demand in early modern and modern times that brought sugar, spices, the constituents of hot beverages, opium, and coca-based drugs into prominence in global trade. There is enormous scope to carry into 'deep time' the stories of how humans and their hominid and hominin predecessors obtained and consumed food and drugs, and for pursuing interdisciplinary approaches that embrace anthropology, paleoanthropology, primatology, archaeology, genetics, and biology, as well as nutritional science.[42] Above all, two great mysteries lie at the heart of the history of consumption: why has it increased out of all proportion to the increase of population (and, in the case of food and drugs, out of all proportion to the nutritional value of food and the psychotropic efficiency of drugs)? And—allowing for the influence of differential rates of increase of wealth—why has demand for food and drugs grown at widely, even wildly different rates in different parts of the world?

BIBLIOGRAPHY

Davenport-Hines, Richard, *The Pursuit of Oblivion: A Global History of Narcotics* (New York: Norton, 2002).

Escohotado, Antonio, *Historia General de las Drogas*, 3 vols. (Madrid: Alianza, 2006).

Fernández-Armesto, Felipe, *Near a Thousand Tables: A History of Food* (New York: Free Press, 2003).

Flandrin, Jean-Louis and Montanari, Massimo, *Histoire de l'alimentation* (Paris: Fayard, 1996).

Freedman, Paul, *Out of the East: Spices and the Medieval Imagination* (New Haven: Yale University Press, 2008).

Goody, Jack, *Food and Love: A Cultural History of East and West* (London: Verso, 1998).

Helms, Mary W., *Ulysses' Sail: An Ethnographic Odyssey of Power, Knowledge and Geographical Distance* (Princeton: Princeton University Press, 1988).

Ornelas, Kriemhild C. and Kiple, Kenneth F. (eds.), *The Cambridge World History of Food*, 2 vols. (Cambridge: Cambridge University Press, 2002)

Mintz, Sidney, *Sweetness and Power: The Place of Sugar in Modern History* (Harmondsworth: Penguin, 1986).

Nützenadel, Alexander and Trentmann, Frank (eds.), *Food and Globalization: Consumption, Markets and Politics in the Modern World* (London: Palgrave Macmillan, 2008).

Porter, Roy, *The Greatest Benefit to Mankind: A Medical History of Humanity from Antiquity to the Present* (London: Fontana, 1999).

Yangwen, Zheng, *The Social Life of Opium in China* (Cambridge: Cambridge University Press, 2005).

---

[42] See Andrew Shryock and Daniel Lord Smail (eds.), *Deep History: the Architecture of Past and Present* (Berkeley: University of California Press, 2011).

CHAPTER 8

....

FROM INDIA TO THE WORLD: COTTON AND FASHIONABILITY

....

PRASANNAN PARTHASARATHI
AND GIORGIO RIELLO

INTRODUCTION

....

Cotton has long been the pre-eminent fibre when it comes to consumption and trade in textiles. It holds this position because it yields a cloth that can be comfortably worn in a wide variety of climates: it suffices as the primary garment in the heat and humidity of the tropics and serves as underclothing or as a colourful accessory in the colder temperatures of temperate zones. Cotton takes and holds dyes well, which allows for the manufacture of colourful and elaborately patterned cloths that are easily washed. Finally, although the evidence is not conclusive, it appears that the prices of cotton cloths have historically been low in comparison with its competitors, namely wool and silk, although cottons were more expensive than many varieties of linen. Due to these qualities, since at least the nineteenth century, cotton has been the most important textile fibre in the world. In 1913, cotton accounted for 80 per cent of global fibre consumption: cotton consumption for textile uses was about 4 billion kilograms while that of wool, the second most important fibre, was about 700 million kilograms.[1] In 1990, even after the rise of synthetic fibres, which accounted for 38 per cent of global fibre use in textiles, cotton accounted for 48 per cent of world fibre share and wool had slumped to the low proportion of 4.9 per cent.[2]

---

[1] Donald Coleman, 'Man-Made Fibres before 1945', in David Jenkins (ed.), *The Cambridge History of Western Textiles* (Cambridge, 2003), vol. 2, p. 939.

[2] Giorgio Riello, 'Counting Sheep: A Global View on Wool, 1800–2000', in Giovanni Luigi Fontana and Gérard Gayot (eds.), *Wool: Products and Markets, 13th–20th Century* (Padua, 2004), pp. 113–36.

Cotton is also of global importance because it was from the late eighteenth century critical to the industrialization of Europe. Few today would concur with Eric Hobsbawm's conclusion that 'whoever says Industrial Revolution says cotton.'[3] Nevertheless, it must not be forgotten that in the 1830s cottons accounted for almost a fifth of the value added in British manufacturing.[4] The invention of machinery, including the jenny, water-frame and mule, for spinning cotton in the late eighteenth century truly revolutionized the world. At the same time, however, cotton had a long non-European pre-history and played a major role on the global stage for centuries before the rise of a European cotton industry. For more than a millennium cotton cloth, mainly from the Indian subconti-nent, was traded over long distances, creating a complex web of trade, consumption and production.[5]

Evidence for the long-distance trade in Indian cotton cloth comes from Roman times where cotton fragments, which have been traced back to the Indian subcontinent, have been excavated by archaeologists. A trade between western India and ports of the Red Sea commenced around the same time.[6] Over the next 2,000 years the trade in Indian cottons grew in size, scale, and distance. In the medieval period, the subcontinent sup-plied markets and consumers in the Indian Ocean and in the sixteenth century the reach of these goods expanded to Europe and the Americas.[7] From the mid-sixteenth century the trade in cottons expanded steadily as American silver fuelled the wheels of global commerce.

The appeal of cotton lay in its fashionability. We use the term fashionability because we seek to move the discussion of 'fashion' beyond twentieth-century notions and under-standings. Fashion as a complex system of production, marketing, and consumption is a creation of the twentieth century and can not be projected into earlier periods for the simple reason that there is no evidence for the sophisticated networks of communication and information that make the contemporary fashion system possible. Nevertheless, even in earlier epochs, consumers across the globe sought to be of the style, to be at the cutting edge, and to sport the novel. These desires we label fashionability.

Fashionability was often associated with the exotic, the hard to get, the item that came from afar. Cotton textiles, many from the Indian subcontinent, satisfied these fashion desires for the rare and the unusual. Before the nineteenth and twentieth centuries, a sense of fashion derived from the cloth itself rather than its cut or stitching (and of course in many regions of the world tailoring was not a part of dress). In these contexts, cottons played a major role in creating the new. Cotton textiles played this role because

[3] Eric Hobsbawm, *Industry and Empire: From 1750 to the Present Day* (new edn., New York, 1999), p. 34.

[4] N. F. R. Crafts, *British Economic Growth during the Industrial Revolution* (Oxford, 1985), p. 22.

[5] For an overview of this history see Giorgio Riello and Prasannan Parthasarathi (eds.), *The Spinning World: A Global History of Cotton Textiles, 1200–1850* (Oxford, 2009).

[6] John Peter Wild and Felicity Wild, 'Rome and India: Early Indian Cotton Textiles from Berenike, Red Sea Coast of Egypt', in Ruth Barnes (ed.), *Textiles in Indian Ocean Societies* (London and New York, 2005), pp. 11–16.

[7] Giorgio Riello and Tirthankar Roy, 'The World of South Asian Textiles, 1500–1850', in Giorgio Riello and Tirthankar Roy (eds.), *How India Clothed the World: The World of South Asian Textiles, 1500–1850* (Leiden, 2009), pp. 1–27.

of the sheer variety of cloths that could be achieved with the fibre. Cotton yielded very fine muslins that rivalled silk at times. Cotton yielded elaborately painted and printed calicoes of exquisite design and colour. Cotton yielded plain cloth dyed a deep blue with indigo which possessed a particular smell and feel that appealed to buyers around the world.[8] And cotton woven with dyed yarns yielded complex checks and stripes that were consumed from Japan to West Africa. The staggering variety of cottons was unmatched.[9]

The appeal of cottons led not only to its consumption around the globe but also its production. Textile manufacturers in many parts of the world turned their hands to reproducing the exotic fabrics that held such wide appeal. Many of these cloths, but by no means all, came from the Indian subcontinent. The case of cottons, then, is an example of the ways in which consumer desires can lead to large-scale transformations in systems of production. While the industrialization of eighteenth-century Britain is very well known, attempts by local manufacturers to imitate the imported exotic cotton cloth spanned the world after the year 1200.

COTTON TEXTILES IN INDIA

The cotton plant had long been cultivated in many regions of the Indian subcontinent and from the Punjab to the heartland of north and west India and to Bengal and south India it was essential to peasant crop rotations and peasant strategies for survival. The skill and knowledge to convert the cotton boll into yarn and then into cloth, and then to bleach, dye, or paint or print the fabric was similarly widespread. However, these manufacturing processes were of great importance in several regions. In medieval and early modern times, the coastal regions of Gujarat, Coromandel, and Bengal stood out for their cotton manufactures and were major exporters of a variety of cotton cloths. Gujarat was the pre-eminent source of cottons for much of this period and had long supplied markets in the Indian Ocean and from the sixteenth century even beyond that ocean. For many centuries the Coromandel Coast supplied cotton goods to South-East Asia and it too expanded its reach from the sixteenth century. And Bengal became world famous from the early seventeenth century for its fine muslins and mixtures of silk and cotton. While these three regions are the best known because of the vast volume of their exports and their locations on the Indian Ocean, the Punjab and the heartland of north India were also thriving textile centres. Cotton cloth from these two regions entered into oceanic networks of trade as well as the caravan trade into Iran and Central Asia.[10]

---

[8] Rosemary Crill, *Indian Chintzes* (London, 2007).

[9] John Guy, *Woven Cargoes: Indian Textiles in the East* (London, 1998).

[10] Ruth Barnes, 'Introduction', in Barnes (ed.), *Textiles in Indian Ocean Societies*, pp. 1–10. See also K. N. Chaudhuri, 'The Structure of Indian Textile Industry in the Seventeenth and Eighteenth Centuries', *Indian Economic and Social History Review*, 9/2 (1974), pp. 117–82.

Thousands of varieties of cloth were manufactured in the Indian subcontinent in the medieval and early modern centuries and lists and lexicons of cloth types can run to hundreds of pages. The profusion of cloth types reflects the diversity of tastes within the subcontinent, which varied by region, social status, and aesthetic preference and also changed over time.[11] While much of the cotton woven in the subcontinent was relatively coarse stuff and fitted the budgets of ordinary people, finer goods were also produced in large quantity. The middling orders purchased medium-quality cloth for their clothing, bedding, and decorative needs, and these calicoes, as they came to be referred to by Europeans, formed the raw material for much cloth printing as they took designs better than finer material.

The wealthy demanded fine-quality muslins for their clothing needs and for centuries these fine cottons were much appreciated across the Indian subcontinent. In the early fourteenth century the great Persian poet Amir Khusrau wrote that these fine cloths were 'like a pleasant gift of a springtide and sit as lightly on the body as moonlight on the tulip or a dewdrop on the morning rose'.[12] Even the middling classes incorporated muslin into their dress. Men, for instance, used these finer weaves for turbans and other accessories. G. S. Ghurye has provides a description of the dress of a Brahmin 'beau', as he labels him, in eighteenth-century Gujarat: 'His angarkha was of thin, Dacca muslin, tight-fitting and embroidered. His dhoti came from Nagpur, and had the broad red-silk border which even the rich coveted...He never went out of doors without first donning a newly dyed and fresh-folded deep-red turban from Nadiad' (Figure 8.1).[13]

There are three things of note in this passage. First, there was a clear sense of male fashionability in eighteenth-century Gujarat and it was closely linked to the qualities of cottons as fabrics and their finishing, not to the form or cut of the clothing, such as the angarkha. Second, the fashionability of the Gujarati beau's attire derived in part from the exoticism of the fabrics. Of the three textiles in the description, only that for the turban had its origins in Gujarat, in the town of Nadiad. The dhoti, with its rich red-silk border, came from the central Indian city of Nagpur. And the thin muslin that made up his angarkha came all the way from Dacca in Bengal, which was the most famous centre of muslin weaving in the eighteenth-century world. It would appear that Dacca was as famous in Gujarat as it was in England, France, or Turkey. Finally, much of the desirability of these cottons derived from their finishing. The Dacca muslin was embroidered, work which may have been done in Bengal or in Gujarat. Both were famed for the quality of their embroidery work, but especially the latter. An even more striking element of the finishes in this description is the depth and richness of the colours, in this example the reds of the dhoti's border, albeit of silk, and the red of the turban. Countless paintings from late medieval and early modern India attest to the vibrancy and variety of colours that made up clothing and dress, which points to the critical role that the abilities of Indian cloth-finishers played in creating cotton materials that were fashionable.

---

[11] See, for instance, Moti Chandra, *Costumes, Textiles, Cosmetics & Coiffure in Ancient and Mediaeval India* (Delhi, 1973), ch. 5 and G. S. Ghurye, *Indian Costumes* (Bombay, 1951), ch. 6.

[12] Cit. in Chandra, *Costumes, Textiles*, p. 138.

[13] Ghurye, *Indian Costumes*, p. 138. An angarkha is a coat-like outer garment.

FIGURE 8.1 Painting of a Rajput nobleman wearing a red robe and turban. Opaque watercolour on paper, early nineteenth century. Victoria and Albert Museum, IS.115–1960.

The finishing of the cloth—whether it was dyeing, printing, painting, or, to a lesser extent embroidering—was critical to the appeal of Indian cottons for fashion-conscious consumers outside the subcontinent as well. For centuries, textile manufacturers in Gujarat, Coromandel, and elsewhere were adept at embellishing their cloths to satisfy the tastes of far-flung buyers. Jean-Baptiste Tavernier reported in his *Six Voyages* (1679) that the city of Sironj in Gujarat produced cheap stuff for Persia and Turkey where 'the workers print their calicoes according to the design given by the foreign merchants'.[14] Even for low-quality goods, great care was taken to supply goods that suited consumer preferences. Tavernier further commented on the variety of products in Sironj, which included bed-covers, tablecloths, pillowcases, pocket-handkerchiefs, and waistcoats both for men and women, much of this destined for markets in Iran. From Burhanpur brightly coloured chintzes were sold across Asia as scarves to put on one's head or around one's neck. Baftas dyed in Agra and Ahmedabad were sold in East Africa, especially Mozambique, as well as Abyssinia and Arabia. The better versions of these cloths were traded to the Philippines, Borneo, Java, and Sumatra.[15]

DIFFUSION IN AFRICA AND ASIA

As Tavernier indicated, Indian cotton textiles were not just a key commodity for Indian consumers. From as early as the first century AD they reached the ports of the Red Sea and by the eleventh/twelfth century they were also found in Sung China.[16] In the centuries that followed, Indian cottons influenced textile consumption habits in large parts of Asia and Africa and defined new modes of fashionability.[17] The success of these textiles was due not just to their material properties (bright colours; good workmanship; and relative affordability) but also because they were easily exchanged for other products that entered long-distance trade. Cottons expanded the choices of consumers across the Indian Ocean, and especially in the populous Indian subcontinent, as they facilitated the flow of commodities such as rice, wheat, butter, sugar, oil, hemp, leather, and slaves from the Malay peninsula; pepper, camphor, spices, sandalwood, Chinese porcelain, silks, and metals from the entrepôt of Malacca; cinnamon, pepper, cowry shells, and areca from Sri Lanka and the Maldives; silver from Pegu; and rice from Burma.[18]

[14] Rudolf Pfister, 'The Indian Art of Calico Printing in the Middle Ages: Characteristics and Influences', *Indian Art and Letters*, 13 (1939), p. 15.

[15] Jean-Baptiste Tavernier, *Travels in India*, ed. William Crooke (Oxford, 1925), vol. 2, p. 5.

[16] Rudolf Pfister, *Les toiles imprimées de Fostat et l'Hindoustan* (Paris, 1938), pp. 12–13.

[17] Ruth Barnes, *Indian Block-Printed Textiles in Egypt. The Newberry Collection in the Ashmolean Museum, Oxford* (Oxford, 1997). See also Id., 'Indian Trade Cloth in Egypt: the Newberry Collection', in *Textiles in Trade* (Washington, 1990), pp. 178–91.

[18] M. A. P. Meilink-Roelofsz, *Asian Trade and European Influence in the Indonesian Archipelago: Between 1500 and About 1630* (The Hague, 1962), p. 68; S. Arasaratnam, 'Some Notes on the Dutch in Malacca and the Indo-Malayan Trade 1641–1670', *Journal of Southeast Asian History*, 10/3 (1964), p. 481.

The caravan trade carried Indian textiles to Ethiopia, especially cheap striped textiles, along with silver and gold, and embroidered luxury cloth as regal gifts.[19] As early as the fourteenth century, East Africa exchanged raw materials for Asian cottons, other fine textiles, beads, copperware, Islamic earthenware, glass, and Chinese porcelain.[20] In the western part of the Indian Ocean, Bandar Abbas was an important trading centre and Indian textiles were transported from there to Baghdad, Basra, and further north to Istanbul.[21] Places such as Basra were centres for commerce in locally produced cloth, imported Indian cotton cloths, and textiles from nearby locations, such as muslins from Mosul, bayrami cloth from Qatif and Bahrain and cottons from Yazd in Persia.[22]

In a number of places in the Indian Ocean, Indian textiles supplemented the products of local manufacturers. In some places, including parts of South-East Asia such as the Malay Peninsula, the dry season was not long enough to grow cotton, which made these areas reliant upon imported cotton textiles. Historians, and in particular trade specialists, tend to emphasize the long-distance exchange of cloth, but there was also intra-regional trade over shorter distances. And the Indian subcontinent was not the only source for cloth in these networks of exchange, as illustrated by the case of Java which by the fifteenth century was exporting cotton cloth to northern Sumatra. In the seventeenth century Java was supplanted by South Sulawesi as the leading exporter of cloth to the archipelago.[23] Malaya imported cloth from not only India but also Java and Sulawesi, South Sumatra and Borneo.[24]

In other cases, as in Thailand, imported cotton cloth supplemented local consumption and was re-exported to other areas. *Sarasa* textiles (Gujarati for 'excellent' or 'beautiful') were found in abundant quantities in places such as Ayuthya (near present-day Bangkok) and were sold locally or re-exported to China, the Philippines, and Japan (Figure 8.2). The Indian *sarasa* cloth that appeared as an accessory in Japanese tea ceremonies in the early seventeenth century probably came from Thailand.[25] Europeans considered Japan to be a particularly promising market for Indian textiles. Traditionally the island had relied on silk textiles for the dress of the elite and cheaper hemp, arrowroot,

[19] S. P. Sangar, 'Export of Indian textiles to Middle East and Africa in the Seventeenth Century', *Journal of Historical Research*, 17/1 (1974), p. 5.

[20] N. Chittick, 'East African Trade with the Orient', in D.S. Richards (ed.), *Islam and the Trade of Asia. A Colloquium* (Oxford, 1970), p. 103.

[21] W. Foster (ed.), *The English Factories in India. A Calendar of Documents in the India Office, British Museum and Public Record Office.* (Oxford, 1906–27), vol. iv, pp. 124–5. See also R. W. Ferrier, 'The Trade between India and the Persian Gulf and the East India Company in the 17th Century', *Bengal Past and Present*, 89/1, no. 167 (1970), pp. 189–98.

[22] Sangar, 'Export of Indian Textiles', p. 2; Dina Rizk Khoury, 'Merchants and Trade in Early Modern Iraq', *New Perspectives on Turkey*, 5–6 (1991), p. 65.

[23] Anthony Reid, *Southeast Asia in the Age of Commerce, 1450–1680. Volume One: The Lands Below the Winds* (New Haven and London, 1984), p. 95.

[24] Reid, *Southeast Asia in the Age of Commerce*, p. 91.

[25] Lotika Varadarajan, 'Syncretic Symbolism and Textiles: Indo-Thai Expressions', in Om Prakash and Denys Lombard (eds.), *Commerce and Culture in the Bay of Bengal, 1500–1800* (New Delhi, 1999), p. 367 and note 25.

FIGURE 8.2 Japanese 'yogi', a thickly padded sarasa cotton textile imported into Japan by the Dutch from the seventeenth century. Made in the nineteenth century. Victoria and Albert Museum, FE.1550–1983.

wisteria, and Japanese linden textiles for the poorer classes.[26] Cottons provided an alternative that was appreciated for both colour and softness. They were also exotic and new, which suited the Japanese, because they were 'people desiring change', commented one seventeenth-century European.[27]

Indian cottons figured among the products traded between the Indian subcontinent and Africa well before the sixteenth-century arrival of the Portuguese in the Indian Ocean. In East Africa, Indian cottons came to supplement an already articulated supply of locally woven cotton cloths, especially those produced in the plains of Kilwa in Tanzania.[28] Commercial links between Cambay in Gujarat and East Africa were strong. As early as the fourteenth century, ivory, gold, and slaves from Africa were exchanged for cloths, both of cotton and silk, for apparel and decoration. Cotton cloth was also exchanged in the trans-Saharan trade for gold, copper, and ivory from West Africa.[29] This trade expanded when European traders, in the first instance the Portuguese in the sixteenth century, brought Indian goods to the west coast via the Cape route, thus supplementing the offer of European and North African textiles that had been sold in Guinea and São Jorge da Mina from the late fifteenth century. By the first half of the sixteenth century, this Portuguese trade to West Africa included cottons such as *pano da India*, but also *caudeis*, a Bengali muslin, and *mantises*, a variety of cotton produced in Gujarat.[30]

Moving to East Asia, cotton textiles from the Indian subcontinent were traded to China in the first millennium AD, if not earlier. Contact with Indian textiles might have prompted local attempts to produce them and by the end of the ninth century the cultivation of cotton was widespread in the area of Fujian on the south-east coast of China.[31] By the twelfth century cotton manufacturing was an established sector of the Chinese economy, and the textiles came in a variety of qualities ranging from the elaborate 'three-shuttle cloth', 'floral cloth', normally woven in complicated patterns, to the 'standard cloth', 'T-cloth', and 'mid-loom' cloth that were plain or ordinary cloths produced mostly by rural households.[32] Woven cotton textiles appealed to the high end of the market, while dyed and printed fabrics (*yaobanbu*) produced by using stencilling,

[26]   Reiko Mochinaga Brandon, *Country Textiles of Japan: The Art of Tsutsugaki* (New York, 1986), p. 38.
[27]   Cit. in Mattiebelle Gittinger, *Master Dyers to the World: Technique and Trade in Early Indian Dyed Cotton Textiles* (Washington DC, 1982), p. 167.
[28]   Chittick, 'East African Trade', p. 103.
[29]   Prithvish Nag, 'The Indian Ocean, India and Africa: Historical and Geographical Perspectives', in Satish Chandra (ed.), *The Indian Ocean: Explorations in History, Commerce and Politics* (New Delhi, 1987), pp. 152–3, 157.
[30]   John Vogt, 'Notes on the Portuguese Cloth Trade in West Africa, 1480–1540', *International Journal of African Historical Studies*, 8/4 (1975), p. 644.
[31]   Michel Cartier, 'À propos de l'histoire du coton en Chine: approche technologique, économique et sociale', *Études Chinoises*, 13/1–2 (1994), p. 421.
[32]   Mi Chü Wiens, 'Cotton Textile Production and Rural Social Transformation in Early Modern China', *Journal of the Institute of Chinese Studies*, 7/2 (1973), p. 520. See also Masatoshi Tanaka, 'The Putting-Out System of Production in the Ming and Qing Periods: With a Focus on Clothing Production (I)', *Memoirs of the Research Department of the Toyo Bunko*, 52 (1994), p. 32.

resist dyeing, and block printing in imitation of Indian textiles catered to the middle segments of the market, and cheap, coarse varieties to the low.[33] Unlike Indian textiles, however, until the late eighteenth century Chinese cottons were not popular beyond the borders of the empire.

What makes the trade in Indian textiles so remarkable is not just its geographical reach but also its breadth in terms of quantities and qualities. Top-quality cloth was used to ease diplomatic relations and to gain a toehold in foreign markets as it convinced local elites of the superiority of the Indian goods. In many cases both high- and low-quality textiles were produced to suit the tastes of buyers of different means, something often noted by European traders.[34] We should not however reduce the trade of textiles across the Indian Ocean to pure economic transactions involving anonymous commodities, i.e. objects whose value was expressed only in monetary terms. Lotika Varadarajan reminds us of the importance of the 'meaning' attached to textiles and observes that cottons were exchanged 'within a cultural matrix in which the semiotics of the object traded provided it with a value which could not at all times be expressed in terms of the price paid'.[35] Indian cottons were fashionable, but they were also treasured and handed down from one generation to the next as heirlooms and ceremonial objects. Kenneth Hall has shown the ways in which the use of Indian cottons in South-East Asia went well beyond simple consumption in its modern, functional sense. 'Foreign cloth' was used to cure disease; to celebrate death and other rites; to sanctify icons; to pay for services or taxes; and to establish diplomatic relations. Indian cottons were integral to ceremonial celebrations as well as rituals legitimating power. And narrations of historical change drew upon their designs and representations.[36] Personal consumption might have been the final outcome, but cotton cloth was no less important in processes that were social and involved ritual and material bonds with other individuals or groups, especially between superiors and subordinates. Cotton cloth featured prominently as a diplomatic gift that united, albeit temporarily, different states, as in the case of the gifting of 1,000 bolts of cotton textiles by the Ming Emperor to the Maharaja of Malacca in 1412.[37] In Jambi, in South-East Asia, imported textiles—including cottons called 'Biru' from India—played a key role in the relationship between the king and his subjects located in the interior. In the islands of Indonesia, cotton textiles were considered precious heirlooms with magical properties that connected multiple generations.[38]

[33] Nishijima Sadao, 'The Formation of the Early Chinese Cotton Industry', in Linda Grove and Christian Daniels (eds.), State and Society in China. Japanese Perspectives on Ming-Qing Social and Economic History (Tokyo, 1984), pp. 52–3.

[34] Varadarajan, 'Syncretic Symbolism', pp. 368–9.

[35] Ibid., p. 361.

[36] Kenneth R. Hall, 'The Textile Industry in Southeast Asia, 1400–1800', Journal of the Economic and Social History of the Orient, 39/2 (1996), pp. 92–4.

[37] Lee Chor Lin, 'Textiles in Sino-South East Asian Trade: Song, Yuan and Ming Dynasties', in Rosemary Scott and John Guy (eds.), South East Asia and China: Art, Interaction and Commerce (London, 1995), p. 177.

[38] Fiona Kerlogue, 'The Early English Textile Trade in South East Asia: The East India Company Factory and the Textile Trade in Jambi, Sumatra, 1615–1682', Textile History, 28/2 (1997), pp. 150–1.

Anthropologists have analysed the meanings that these 'foreign' textiles had in different cultures and explored the long historical roots of many present-day customs and traditions. They have also made productive use of artefacts as sources of valuable information. The trading world of the Indian Ocean is not rich in written documentation and archival materials detailing the trade and use of cotton textiles is abundant only for the case of the European East India companies. This is why the analysis of the surviving artefacts is a major research tool. In South-East Asia, for instance, local textile designs contain Indian and Chinese motifs which suggest significant commercial and cultural links with both these regions. Stylistic analysis, often coupled with etymological studies, reveals the existence of complex relationships between textiles produced and consumed in different areas of the Indian Ocean.[39] For instance, the Gujarati term *sarasa* was commonly used in India to denote a patterned cotton cloth. The same term came to be used in Japanese to signify any textiles produced through the mordant and dye techniques.[40]

Anthropological methods have also made historians aware that the very meaning of textiles can be the fruit of material and cultural interaction. As underlined by textile expert Robyn Maxwell, 'The textile arts of Southeast Asia reflect [...] diverse influences: the ancestor figures of earlier legends, the sacred *mandala* of the Hindu-Buddhist world, the zodiac menagerie of Chinese iconography, the flowing calligraphy of Islam and the lace of the West'.[41] This passage points to the capacity of textiles materially to embody a variety of cultural, design, and aesthetic influences and to yield products that are both hybrids and multi-layered repositories of meanings. An example might be a Baju jacket such as the one in Figure 8.3: the cloth was produced on the Coromandel Coast, but the garment was tailored in Sumatra. The floral design, however, shows a strong European influence. At a first glance, therefore, one might think that it was produced according to local taste, but a more attentive analysis shows that this type of garment is linked to the spread of Arab and Indian dress in South-East Asia.[42]

The case of the Baju jacket shows how consumers in different parts of Asia expressed different preferences. For instance, the already mentioned *sarasa* cloth was demanded in several parts of South-East Asia and to suit local taste and uses it was manufactured in long lengths (6.5 metres) and typically unfinished, which allowed it to be used as hangings and banners rather than for clothing.[43] In the eighteenth century, textile producers in Ahmedabad, in Gujarat, manufactured printed textiles in imitation of patola for sale in Indonesia (Sumba, Bali, and North Sulawesi), where they were in high demand as heirlooms and for ceremonial occasions.[44] Hall also suggests that imported textiles

---

[39] Varadarajan, 'Syncretic Symbolism', pp. 370–1.

[40] Gittinger, *Master Dyers*, p. 28.

[41] Robyn Maxwell, *Textiles of Southeast Asia: tradition, trade and transformation* (Melbourne, 1990), p. 20.

[42] See Deepika Shah, *Masters of the Cloth: Indian Textiles Traded to Distant Shores* (New Delhi, 2005), p. 18.

[43] John Guy, 'Sarasa and Patola: Indian textiles in Indonesia', *Orientations*, 20/1 (1989), p. 50.

[44] Gittinger, *Master Dyers*, p. 139.

FIGURE 8.3 Baju (Jacket) tailored in Sumatra with cloth from the Coromandel Coast of India. Late eighteenth century. Victoria and Albert Museum, IS. 101–1993.

might have sparked textile manufacturers in South-East Asia to imitate Indian goods in order to secure local supplies at lower prices.[45]

Historians admit that our understanding of the complex trade and consumption of cotton textiles in the Indian Ocean before the arrival of European traders remains incomplete. What seems likely is that the arrival of European traders in the early sixteenth century did not substantially alter the textile trade there.[46] First the Portuguese, and then after 1600 the Dutch, the English, and other East India companies, entered the trade in textiles from India to the maritime areas of Asia and sought to monopolize the trade in Asian goods back to Europe. The Dutch East India Company (VOC) was particularly successful at exporting Indian cloth to South-East Asia. The Dutch trade in Bengal cottons (mostly coarse cloth) to markets in Asia was less than 3,000 pieces a year in the late 1660s, grew to 10,000 in the early 1690s, and to a staggering 50,000 pieces in the early 1710s. This constituted the backbone of what was termed the 'country trade' (i.e. the intra-Asian trade) of the European companies. Bengal cloth was sold in Arakan and Pegu, in Tenasserim in Siam, in Sumatra and the Malay Peninsula, and in Manila.[47] However, even the large quantities traded by the VOC in the Indian Ocean are likely to have been only a fraction of the enormous quantities of Indian textiles demanded in South-East Asia and other Asian ports.[48] The more important contribution of the European East India companies was to introduce consumers in Europe to new products from Asia, the most important of which were Indian cotton textiles.

---

[45] Hall, 'Textile Industry', p. 88.

[46] S. Arasaratnam concludes, perhaps slightly over-optimistically that 'Indian traders were able to take advantage of the commercial and political rivalries and strengthen their trade in ports outside the control of the Dutch', but still supports the idea of an Indian declining participation caused by the increasing importance of private European 'country trade'. Arasaratnam, 'Some Notes', p. 490.

[47] Om Prakash, 'Asian Trade and European Impact: A Study of the Trade from Bengal, 1630–1720', in Blair B. Kling and M. N. Pearson (eds.), *The Age of Partnership: Europeans in Asia Before Domination* (Honolulu, 1979), pp. 49–50.

[48] Prakash, 'Asian Trade', pp. 51, 53.

EUROPE AND THE ATLANTIC
WORLD AS LATECOMERS

Indian cotton textiles reached Europe in substantial quantities relatively late. The East India companies, active in the trade of cottons within the Indian Ocean, were the main conveyors of these commodities to European ports such as London, Amsterdam, and Lorient where the cloth was sold via auction. The late eighteenth-century calico-printer Oberkampf attended English and French East India Company auctions in London and Lorient to acquire the plain white Indian cotton cloths that he printed in his famous workshops at Jouy-en-Josas near Paris.[49] At these auctions cloth was also purchased by large wholesalers who distributed the textiles to shopkeepers, smaller retailers, and hawkers and peddlers. Through this capillary system of distribution Indian cottons reached even remote parts of Europe.[50] In 1669, for example, a chapman in Cheshunt, Hertfordshire, in England, had a dozen calico hoods in his stock.[51] It was the same in Continental Europe, where imported cotton textiles were not the preserve of only rich or metropolitan consumers, but were found in the wardrobes of farmers and workers in both rural and urban locations. An example of the widespread use of Indian cottons in Europe is their incorporation within what we would now define as 'folk dress' (Figure 8.4). Eighteenth-century Frisian women's hats, an important part of their local costume, are conspicuous for their use of bright and heavily decorated chintz imported from the Coromandel Coast of India.[52]

Why were Indian cotton textiles so successful among European consumers? Today we are used to wearing cottons. Indeed most of the textiles that surround us are either cottons or synthetics imitating cottons. But in the early modern period, the vast majority of Europeans who could not afford expensive and highly decorated silks had to be content with linen and woollen cloths. Linens were used in bedding and tableware as well as for shirts and undergarments. Woollens were used mostly as overgarments in the form of jackets, britches, and gowns but were also occasionally worn next to the skin. Cotton was a material that could easily replace both linen and wool (and needless to say silk) and yet had a much warmer and softer feeling, especially when next to the skin. Those cottons that were used for display normally came in a variety of designs and colours whose vibrancy was unmatched by either linens or woollens. Only silks with their

---

[49] S. D. Chapman and Serge Chassagne, *European Textile Printers in the Eighteenth Century: A Study of Peel and Oberkampf* (London, 1981), pp. 156–8.

[50] Beverly Lemire, *Fashion's Favourite: The Cotton Trade and the Consumer in Britain, 1660–1800* (Oxford, 1991).

[51] Id., 'Fashioning Cottons: Asian Trade, Domestic Industry and Consumer Demand, 1660–1780', in David Jenkins (ed.), *The Cambridge History of Western Textiles* (Cambridge, 2003), vol. 1, p. 497.

[52] *Férie indienne: des rivages de l'Inde au royaume de France* (Paris, 2009), pp. 166–7; Giorgio Riello, 'The Globalization of Cotton Textiles: Indian Cottons, Europe, and the Atlantic World, 1600–1850', in Giorgio Riello and Prasannan Parthasarathi (eds.), *The Spinning World: A Global History of Cotton Textiles, 1200–1850* (Oxford, 2009), pp. 271–2.

FIGURE 8.4 Fabric used to line a wide-brimmed straw hat worn by the women of Friesland in the Netherlands. The fabric is a calico from the Coromandel Coast of India, c. 1725–50. Victoria and Albert Museum, IS.23–1976.

vivid colours and spectacular patterns of flowers, fantastical beasts, and exotic representations of Indian and Chinese people could outdo cottons. But silks cost several times more. The colours of imported cottons from India were also 'fast', i.e. they did not fade after exposure to light or after washing. Europeans appreciated and were dazzled by the 'brightness and life of colour or in their continuance upon the cloth' of Indian cotton textiles.[53] Historians long believed that cottons found easy markets in Europe because they were cheaper than other available textiles. In reality, cottons were not as cheap as previously imagined. In Britain for most of the eighteenth century imported cotton textiles were twice the price of cheap linen or canvas cloth and 25 to 30 per cent more than middling linen. At the same time they were half the price of good-quality linen, a third of top-quality Holland linen, and a third to a quarter of good-quality woollen cloth and broadcloth.[54]

The late seventeenth-century passion for imported Indian cottons was seen as a 'calico craze', but not all in Europe were pleased with these developments. While Indian cottons enriched the East India companies as well as the merchants, traders, and shopkeepers connected to the trade in these new cloths, they aroused the opposition of manufacturers of woollen and silk cloth who argued that the import of calicoes, the generic term for Indian cottons, decreased the wealth of the nation. Growing numbers of European

---

[53] John Ovington, *A Voyage to Surat in the Year 1689*, ed. H. G. Rawlingson (London, 1929), p. 167.

[54] Giorgio Riello, 'The Indian Apprenticeship: The Trade of Indian Textiles and the Making of European Cottons', in Riello and Roy (eds.), *How India Clothed the World*, pp. 344–5.

consumers abandoned home-produced textiles for the Indian imports, which had to be paid for with precious metals, additional grist for critics of the trade. Demands for a ban on the Indian imports were pressed forward and most European states between the 1680s and the early 1720s banned the use of Indian cloth. The calico craze had generated a mercantilist 'calico closure' of Europe's borders, which was to remain in place for the next several decades. Consumers were banned not just from buying but also wearing printed colourful calicoes and it became risky to wear cottons. In 1719, just before the total ban in England, Dorothy Orwell, claimed to have been 'Assaulted by a Multitude of Weavers in Red-Lion-Fields in Hoxton, who tore, cut, and pull'd off her [cotton] Gown and Petticoat by Violence, threatened her with vile Language, and left her naked in the Fields'.[55]

Until recently this account of a late seventeenth-century triumph of Indian cottons in Europe was largely unchallenged. It was backed by the figures compiled by K. N. Chaudhuri in the 1970s showing that the quantities of cottons imported into London by the English East India Company increased rapidly after 1660 and reached a very high plateau in the 1690s. Similar figures for the Dutch East India Company seemed to confirm the hypothesis that it was in the late seventeenth century that cottons penetrated not just European minds but also crept onto their bodies. More recently, historians such as Beverly Lemire and John Styles have questioned this narrative, which sees the late seventeenth century as representing a watershed in the history of cotton in Europe. One might argue, as Lemire does, that Indian cottons achieved popularity as early as the second half of the sixteenth century when they could be found in even remote Iberian locations. She cites a witness from the town of Renteria testifying 'that many Portuguese men were going in this Province selling some clothes that they called *calicús*'.[56] On the other hand, John Styles, in his analysis of garments reported as stolen in London, suggests that cottons might have been less common than previously thought before the late eighteenth century.[57] What is becoming clear is that the import of Indian cottons set off a slow shift to that fibre in Europe, but the full triumph of cotton would await the nineteenth century.[58]

How much did cottons contribute to the diffusion of what we today call fashion? Contemporaries observed that cotton was not as long-lasting as woollens and worsteds and therefore had to be replaced more often. Cottons were also appreciated in Europe for their brilliant colours and variety of designs. One might say that compared to South-East Asia where part of the cottons imported from India—and surely those of higher

---

[55] Old Bailey Proceedings Online, Trial of Peter Cornelius, July 1720 (t-17200712-28), <http://www.oldbaileyonline.org>. Cit. in Chloe Wigston Smith, '"Callico Madams": Servants, Consumption, and the Calico Crisis', *Eighteenth-Century Life*, 31/2 (2007), pp. 33–4.

[56] Beverly Lemire, 'Revising the Historical Narrative: India, Europe, and the Cotton Trade, *c*.1300–1800', in Riello and Parthasarathi (eds.), *The Spinning World*, p. 213.

[57] John Styles, 'What Were Cottons for in the Early Industrial Revolution?', in Riello and Parthasarathi (eds.), *The Spinning World*, pp. 307–26. See also Id., 'Indian Cottons and European Fashion', and Prasannan Parthasarathi's 'Response' to Styles's essay, in Glenn Adamson, Giorgio Riello, and Sarah Teasley (eds.), *Global Design History* (Abingdon, 2011), pp. 37–46, 47–9.

[58] The shift to cottons is evident from inventories of wardrobes. See, for instance, Daniel Roche, *The Culture of Clothing: Dress and Fashion in the Ancien Régime*, trans. Jean Birrell (Cambridge, 1994), pp. 121, 135.

FIGURE 8.5 Palampore produced on the Coromandel Coast of India. Second half of the eighteenth century. The unusual design with two trees suggests that it might have been made for the French market. Victoria and Albert Museum, IM.85–1937.

quality—were taken to be 'important' objects in ceremonies and familial and communal practices, in Europe cottons assumed in the first instance a decorative function. They were consumed as items of furnishing in the shape of bedspreads and wall-coverings. Palampores, often with representations of intricate plant branches and foliage, were highly appreciated as decorative items especially in rich households (Figure 8.5).[59] They complemented other exotic objects such as Turkish carpets (which were used as heavy tablecloths), blue and white porcelain, and smaller objects of ivory, as well as European-made imitations and reinterpretation of Chinese and Japanese furniture.[60]

[59] Their use as bed-hangings can be traced back to at least 1623. Gittinger, *Master Dyers*, p. 186.
[60] Maxine Berg, 'In Pursuit of Luxury: Global History and British Consumer Goods in the Eighteenth Century', *Past and Present*, 182 (2004), pp. 85–142.

It is important to note that Asian cottons held great appeal for Europeans but were not immediately donned as clothing.[61] Innovation in consumption is not always as uncomplicated as marketing historians suggest. Two factors are worth remembering about seventeenth-century European consumers. First, they were cautious when it came to wearing new products. Perhaps actual physical contact with a new and—we might say—'uncertain' object made them wary. Second, they were at times conservative in their tastes and preferences and favoured existing products over new ones. In one such case, in 1682 the East India Company ordered 200,000 ready-made cotton shirts and shifts from Madras to 'introduce the using of Callicoe for that purpose in all these Northern parts of the world'.[62] While the English company was convinced that cheap cotton garments would find eager buyers, consumers were not interested. Historians have duly noted that the quality of the garments may have been low and that the novelty of these products might have diminished rather than enhanced consumers' appreciation for them.[63]

European consumers were also particular in their design and colour preferences. As we have seen earlier, producers in India were experienced in customizing products for different markets. Europeans traders were particularly keen on cloth that was either white or printed or painted with floral or striped motifs. White cloth could be sold in Europe and printed there in the newest style, but cloth that was already decorated had to fit the specific aesthetic preferences of European consumers. One might say that the engagement with the 'exotic' was good as long as it could be sufficiently domesticated to fit within a pre-existing visual, tactile, and artistic sensibility. European consumers, for instance, preferred to use textiles with white backgrounds rather than the more traditional products of western India which typically contained dark or red backgrounds. The English East India Company was already in the 1640s clarifying in letters to factors in India that they wanted textiles with lighter backgrounds. One such letter in the year 1693 spelled out what was demanded in London:

> As much variety as may be, but 50 at least of each work, some purple, and some dark grounds, some red grounds and a few green; but the greatest quantities white grounds, some purple flowered, some red flowers. Note, half the quantity upon stripes, and half upon flowers and some both striped and flowered.[64]

It is difficult to account for this European preference although one might recall the fact that in textiles whiteness was a sign of cleanliness, as in the use of white linen. Even today lighter fabrics tend to be characterized by lighter colours.

From Europe, Indian cottons diffused to other parts of the Atlantic. Cotton cloth was widely used as a medium of exchange for slaves in West Africa from at least the sixteenth century, and in substantial quantities from the late seventeenth century. In the closing

[61] Indian cottons started to be used as apparel by men, not women, in the early 1660s. Gittinger, *Master Dyers*, p. 187.
[62] Cit. in Riello, 'The Indian Apprenticeship', p. 329.
[63] John Styles, 'Product Innovation in Early Modern London', *Past and Present*, 168 (2000), p. 137.
[64] Cit. in George Percival Baker, *Calico Printing and Painting in the East Indies in the XVIIth and XVIIIth Centuries* (London, 1921), p. 33.

decades of the seventeenth century the Gold Coast imported 20,000 metres of European and Asian cloth per year, which complemented an intra-continental trade (estimated at 5,000–10,000 metres annually) in cloth, much of it from Benin.[65] In the second half of the eighteenth century France exported from Rouen annually goods worth 750,000 *livres* to Africa, a third of which consisted of cottons.[66] The rising French cotton industry (revived after the repeal of the ban on the manufacturing and wearing of cottons in 1759) was heavily reliant on African markets.[67] The same was true for the production of cheap 'Guinea' cloth in England. Between 1699 and 1800 Indian and English cotton cloth accounted for forty to fifty per cent of all commodities traded from England to Africa.[68] African consumers, especially in the Atlantic-facing area of West Africa, were not easy to please. The Dutch trader and Captain Ludewig Ferdinand Rømer wrote in 1760 that 'the Blacks' were keen on cottons, gingham, salempuris, calavap, and other textiles but that they were also whimsical consumers: 'A sensible ship's captain knows, at whatever place on the Coast he is, which of his [textile] goods are in demand. But he does not know which goods will be in demand when he goes fifty mile further along the Coast.'[69] African consumers purchased these textiles with slaves, a practice that might have had a negative impact on the availability of skilled labour in textile-producing areas of West Africa.[70]

European and Indian cottons were also in high demand in the Americas. In the late 1640s fabrics arriving in Boston included cottons, fustians, and calicoes.[71] By the mid-eighteenth century various types of cotton textiles (blue, India, 'negro', as well as printed and painted) were being exported from England to the American colonies in large quantities.[72] Robert DuPlessis's analysis of inventories shows that cotton penetrated into the wardrobes of colonists in both French and British possessions in North America and the Caribbean. In the absence of restrictions on the consumption of cottons, which were widespread in Europe, American buyers seemed to have discarded heavyweight woollens and to a certain extent linens in favour of white or coloured cottons. This is most striking in the warm climes of the Caribbean, but also in places as varied as New France, Pennsylvania, South Carolina, and Louisiana where by the 1760s cottons accounted for

[65] Carolyn Keyes Adenaike, 'West African Textiles, 1500–1800', in Maureen Fennell Mazzaoui (ed.), *Textiles: Production, Trade and Demand* (Aldershot, 1998), p. 257.

[66] Ann DuPont, 'Captives of Colored Cloth: The Role of Cotton Trade Goods in the North Atlantic Slave Trade (1600–1808)', *Ars Textrina*, 24 (1995), p. 180.

[67] Maureen Fennell Mazzaoui, 'Introduction', in Mazzaoui (ed.), *Textiles*, p. xxxviii

[68] Marion Johnson, *Anglo-African Trade in the Eighteenth Century: English Statistics on African Trade 1699–1808*, ed. J. T. Lindblad and Robert Ross (Leiden, 1990), pp. 28–9; Colleen E. Kriger, '"Guinea Cloth": Production and Consumption of Cotton Textiles in West Africa before and during the Atlantic Slave Trade', in Riello and Parthasarathi, *The Spinning World*, p. 123.

[69] S. Axelrod Winsnes (ed.), *A Reliable Account of the Coast of Guinea (1760) by Ludewig Ferdinand Rømer* (Oxford, 2000), p. 191.

[70] This is a subject of debate. See in particular Joseph E. Inikori, 'English versus Indian Cotton Textiles: The Impact of Imports on Cotton Textile Production in West Africa', in Riello and Roy (eds.), *How India Clothed the World*, pp. 85–114; and Kriger, '"Guinea Cloth"', esp. 111–125.

[71] Pamela V. Ulrich, 'From Fustian to Merino: The Rise of Textiles using Cotton Before and after the Gin', *Agricultural History*, 68/2 (1994), p. 223.

[72] F. Mason Norton *John Norton & Sons, merchants of London and Virginia, being the papers from their counting house for the years 1750 to 1795* (Newton Abbot, 1968), pp. 22, 72, 103, 125, 150, 190, 218.

at least 20 to 30 per cent of total textile consumption.[73] The establishment of direct trade between America and India in 1784 increased supplies of Indian cotton textiles and Bengali cotton cloths became the most important item traded by the newly independent United States until the imposition of protective tariffs in 1816.[74] The import of these goods created a fashion for fine muslin dresses and colourful bandanna handkerchiefs.[75]

Latin America was similarly an important market for cotton textiles. A cursory analysis of casta paintings, which detail ethnic mixing and diversity, shows that Indian and European cottons were used in multiple ways.[76] They adorned not just women but also men who used cottons for their banyans and other informal robes[77] Even before they were traded via the Atlantic, Indian cottons and silks reached Latin America via the Pacific, a route which was opened in the 1570s by the Spaniards and connected the entrepôt of Manila with Acapulco. Indian cottons fuelled fashion and a taste for luxury in Spanish America, which led to raised eyebrows among legislators and clerics and prompted the imposition of sumptuary laws in the seventeenth and eighteenth centuries.[78] Unlike the North American market, which was disconnected from European networks and purchased cottons directly from India and then later developed a local cotton industry, Latin America in the nineteenth century came to rely heavily on imports of European-made cottons. In 1820 Britain exported 51 million metres of cotton cloth to Latin America and the figure reached 255 million metres just two decades later. By this time Latin American consumers used 9 metres of British cottons per person on average, an indicator of the receptiveness of Latin America to cottons and to imported textiles.[79]

CONCLUSION: THE GLOBAL TRIUMPH OF COTTONS

By the early eighteenth century cotton textiles had achieved a global reach. Whether made locally or imported from the Indian subcontinent or elsewhere, cotton had reshaped tastes, refined a sense of fashionability, and reordered the textile system. Global

---

[73] Robert S. DuPlessis, 'Cottons Consumption in the Seventeenth- and Eighteenth-Century North Atlantic', in Riello and Parthasarathi (eds.), *The Spinning World*, pp. 227–46.

[74] Susan S. Bean, 'Bengal Goods for America in the Nineteenth Century', in Rosemary Crill (ed.), *Textiles from India: The Global Trade* (Calcutta and London, 2006), pp. 217–32.

[75] Ibid., pp. 222–8.

[76] Rebecca Earle, 'Clothing and Ethnicity in Colonial Spanish America', in Giorgio Riello and Peter McNeil (eds.), *The Fashion History Reader: Global Perspectives* (London, 2010), pp. 383–5; and Magali M. Carrera, *Imagining identity in New Spain: Race, Lineage, and the Colonial Body in Portraiture and Casta Paintings* (Austin, Texas, 2003).

[77] On banyans see: Beverly Lemire, 'Fashioning Global Trade: Indian Textiles, Gender Meanings and European Consumers, 1500–1800', in Riello and Roy (eds.), *How India Clothed the World*, esp. 371–86.

[78] Marta V. Vicente, 'Fashion, Race, and Cotton Textiles in Colonial Spanish America', in Riello and Parthasarathi (eds.), *The Spinning World*, pp. 267–70.

[79] Arnold J. Bauer, *Goods, Power, History: Latin America's Material Culture* (Cambridge, 2001), p. 130. In the case of Peru, cotton textiles accounted for 95 per cent of all its imports in the first decade of independence of the country.

reach was not identical with global triumph, however, and the latter may be dated from the closing decades of the eighteenth century. That triumph would reach its zenith in the early twentieth century when, as noted, cotton accounted for 80 per cent of world textile fibre consumption. In the early eighteenth century wool, hemp, and linen were still rivals to cotton, especially in the areas in Europe and the Atlantic world that were latecomers to Indian cloth.

In England the manufacture of wool textiles was considered to be the economic motor of the realm. Daniel Defoe, who championed wool against 'foreign' calicoes in the 1719 campaign for a ban on Asian textiles, wrote that wool was central to the very notion of the British nation: 'all the World wears it [wool], all the World desires it, and all the world envies us the Glory and Advantage of it'.[80] As late as 1772, Arthur Young estimated that the annual output of the English cotton industry came to no more than £900,000, which made it one-twentieth the size of the woollen industry.[81] From Russia to Silesia and Flanders, to Northern Italy as well as in Ireland and Scotland flax and hemp were the most common fibres. The production of linen textiles was a labour-intensive process based on the putrefaction of vegetable raw material that was put through several stages of refinement followed by spinning, weaving, and finishing, but nevertheless it dwarfed cotton production before the nineteenth century.

The nineteenth-century triumph of cotton is shown in the following graph of per capita consumption of wool, flax, and cotton in Britain between 1798 and 1861 (Figure 8.6). The consumption of flax remained more or less constant; that of wool fell slightly and then rose, going from a little under 3 kilograms a year to about 4; that of cotton exploded, increasing fifteenfold in six decades and going from about 1 kilogram per person in 1798 to a little less than 16 in 1861. The graph also shows that cotton did not gain at the *expense* of wool or flax. It simply left the competing fibres behind as it gained an expanding consumer following.

The Industrial Revolution and the mechanization of textile manufacturing were critical for the rapid growth of cottons in nineteenth-century Britain, but they alone cannot explain its triumph. The breakthroughs in spinning which sparked the process of mechanization were designed for cotton and first put to work in cotton manufacturing, but they were quickly adapted for wool and linen. Even with machine production, however, the consumption of these two fibres barely changed in the first decades of British industrialization.

One explanation for this divergence in fibre consumption centres on the supply of raw material and argues that the plantation complex in the United States South provided the land and labour for the cultivation of the cotton plant, which kept the mills of Manchester supplied with abundant and cheap material. This argument assumes that

[80] D. Defoe, *A Plan of the English Commerce, Being a Compleat Prospect of the Trade of this Nation* (London, 1730), p. 190. Cit. in R. L. Sickinger, 'Regulation or Ruination: Parliament's Consistent Pattern of Mercantilist Regulation of the English Textile Trade, 1660–1800', *Parliamentary History*, 19/2 (2000), pp. 213–14.

[81] A. Young, *Political Essays Concerning the Present State of the British Empire* (London, 1772), p. 197.

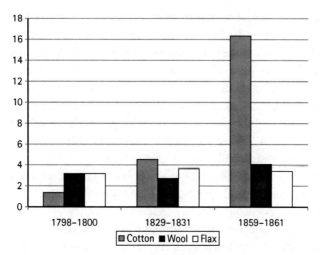

FIGURE 8.6 Annual Consumption of Fibre per Capita in Britain, 1798–1861 (in Kilograms).

Source: T. Ellison, *The Cotton Trade of Great Britain* (London, 1886), p. 120.

no such equivalent land or labour were available for the expansion of sheep breeding or flax growing. While this assumption may hold for flax, which required a long and labour-intensive processing, it may be less applicable to wool. Pat Hudson argues that there were plentiful supplies of domestic and foreign wool in Britain in the eighteenth and nineteenth centuries. In the nineteenth century, the land available for sheep breeding expanded as the animals were raised in New Zealand and Australia. And improved breeding methods led to more wool output per animal.[82]

In the absence of clear-cut supply advantages for cotton, the explanation for its triumph must be located in the demand for the material. Cotton's versatility and desirability gave cotton cloth a global reach in the seventeenth and eighteenth centuries and came to be associated with fashionability across the world. When these consumer preferences were combined with industrial methods of production cotton was propelled to a dominant position and to its global triumph. In Europe and North America, areas that had come late to cotton cloth, the last vestiges of resistance were overcome in the nineteenth century and cotton's protean nature led to its adoption in a number of areas, from bedding to outerwear, where linen and wool had predominated.

The case of cotton and its fashionability is a striking instance in which the preferences and tastes of consumers propelled dramatic changes in methods of production. An accumulating body of evidence is linking the development of textile manufacturing in eighteenth-century Europe and the invention of machinery for making cloth to

---

[82] Pat Hudson, 'The Limits of Wool and The Potential of Cotton in the Eighteenth and Early Nineteenth Centuries', in Riello and Parthasarathi (eds.), *The Spinning World*, pp. 327–50.

European attempts to imitate Indian cottons. The effort to manufacture calicoes to the standards set by Indians propelled the rise of cloth printing throughout Europe. The desire for an all-cotton cloth that matched the products of Indian looms led to a search for machines with which yarn of the requisite quality could be spun. The competitive desire to match Indian goods in quality advanced both technique and technology. The buyers of cotton cloth, whether in Europe, Africa, Asia, or the Americas, set the standards of quality, which had they had learnt from long experience with Indian and other cotton cloths, which had also set the grade for fashionability. With the esteemed position that cottons achieved globally in the eighteenth century, the British technical breakthroughs of the 1770s and 1780s, which made possible far greater levels of production, catapulted cotton to a hegemonic position in the nineteenth century.

Historians have long debated if the late eighteenth-century technological innovations in spinning, followed by further innovations in weaving, were the cause or the effect of a widening of the market for cotton textiles. As we have chronicled, by the eighteenth century the market for cottons came to encompass the whole of the Atlantic world which was the major market for European traders and manufacturers. The growing taste for cottons in the Atlantic began in Europe and West Africa, but then extended to North and South America. The authors of this paper support the idea that it was the 'globalization' of cotton, its becoming a product consumed across the globe and not just in Eurasia, that influenced its production in Europe and not vice versa. As this paper has shown, cotton textiles, Asian and later European, were already in high demand well before the European industrialization of their manufacturing in the late eighteenth century.

This paper has introduced the term fashionability in order to move the discussion of fashion away from twentieth-century understandings. The use of the term fashionability—as opposed to fashion—also expands the discussion of consumer desires for the new and exotic beyond the confines of Europe and the North Atlantic, which are often taken to be sites of fashion-oriented forms of consumption. While this paper rejects the claims to the uniqueness of European fashion and consumption, the forms and practices of fashionability in Asia, Africa, and South America remain to be studied in greater detail, however. Similarly, the relationship between cloth and fashionability, and in particular with the use of cottons and silks, as opposed to the twentieth-century fashion emphasis on cut and style, is still poorly understood. Fashionability opens new vistas, but they still must be explored and charted.

BIBLIOGRAPHY

Adenaike, Carolyn Keyes, 'West African Textiles, 1500–1800', in Maureen Fennell Mazzaoui (ed.), *Textiles: Production, Trade and Demand* (Aldershot, 1998), 251–61.

Arasaratnam, S., 'Some Notes on the Dutch in Malacca and the Indo-Malayan Trade 1641–1670', *Journal of Southeast Asian History*, 10/3 (1964), 480–90.

Baker, George Percival, *Calico Printing and Painting in the East Indies in the XVIIth and XVIIIth Centuries* (London, 1921).

Barnes, Ruth, 'Indian Trade Cloth in Egypt: the Newberry Collection', in *Textiles in Trade* (Washington, 1990), 178–91.

Barnes, Ruth, *Indian Block-Printed Textiles in Egypt. The Newberry Collection in the Ashmolean Museum, Oxford*, 2 vols. (Oxford, 1997).

Barnes, Ruth, 'Introduction', in Ruth Barnes (ed.), *Textiles in Indian Ocean Societies* (London and New York, 2005), 1–10.

Bauer, Arnold J., *Goods, Power, History: Latin America's Material Culture* (Cambridge, 2001).

Bean, Susan S., 'Bengal Goods for America in the Nineteenth Century', in Rosemary Crill (ed.), *Textiles from India: The Global Trade* (Calcutta and London, 2006), 217–32.

Berg, Maxine, 'In Pursuit of Luxury: Global History and British Consumer Goods in the Eighteenth Century', *Past and Present*, 182 (2004), 85–142.

Brandon, Reiko Mochinaga, *Country Textiles of Japan: The Art of Tsutsugaki* (New York, 1986).

Carrera, Magali M., *Imagining Identity in New Spain: Race, Lineage, and the Colonial Body in Portraiture and Casta Paintings* (Austin, TX, 2003).

Cartier, Michel, 'À propos de l'histoire du coton en Chine: approche rechnologique, économique et sociale', *Études Chinoises*, 13/1–2 (1994), 417–35.

Chapman, S. D., and Chassagne, Serge. *European Textile Printers in the Eighteenth Century: A Study of Peel and Oberkampf* (London, 1981).

Chandra, Moti, *Costumes, Textiles, Cosmetics & Coiffure in Ancient and Mediaeval India* (Delhi, 1973).

Chaudhuri, K. N., 'The Structure of Indian Textile Industry in the Seventeenth and Eighteenth Centuries', *Indian Economic and Social History Review*, 9/2 (1974), 117–82.

Chittick, N., 'East African Trade with the Orient', in D.S. Richards (ed.), *Islam and the Trade of Asia. A Colloquium* (Oxford, 1970), pp. 97–104.

Coleman, Donald, 'Man-Made Fibres before 1945', in David Jenkins (ed.), *The Cambridge History of Western Textiles* (Cambridge, 2003), vol. 2, 933–47.

Crafts, N. F. R., *British Economic Growth during the Industrial Revolution* (Oxford, 1985).

Crill, Rosemary, *Indian Chintzes* (London, 2007).

DuPlessis, Robert S., 'Cottons Consumption in the Seventeenth- and Eighteenth-Century North Atlantic', in Giorgio Riello and Prasannan Parthasarathi (eds.), *The Spinning World: A Global History of Cotton Textiles, 1200–1850* (Oxford, 2009), 227–46.

DuPont, Ann, 'Captives of Colored Cloth: The Role of Cotton Trade Goods in the North Atlantic Slave Trade (1600–1808)', *Ars Textrina*, 24 (1995), 177–83.

Earle, Rebecca, 'Clothing and Ethnicity in Colonial Spanish America', in Giorgio Riello and Peter McNeil (eds.), *The Fashion History Reader: Global Perspectives* (London, 2010), 383–5.

Férie indienne: des rivages de l'Inde au royaume de France (Paris, 2009).

Ferrier, R. W., 'The Trade between India and the Persian Gulf and the East India Company in the 17th Century', *Bengal Past and Present*, 89–1/167 (1970), 189–98.

Foster, W. (ed.), *The English Factories in India. A Calendar of Documents in the India Office, British Museum and Public Record Office*, 13 vols. (Oxford, 1906–27).

Ghurye, G. S., *Indian Costumes* (Bombay, 1951).

Gittinger, Mattiebelle, *Master Dyers to the World: Technique and Trade in Early Indian Dyed Cotton Textiles* (Washington D.C., 1982).

Guy, John, 'Sarasa and Patola: Indian textiles in Indonesia', *Orientations*, 20/1 (1989), 48–60.

Guy, John, *Woven Cargoes: Indian Textiles in the East* (London, 1998).

Hall, Kenneth R., 'The Textile Industry in Southeast Asia, 1400–1800', *Journal of the Economic and Social History of the Orient*, 39/2 (1996), pp. 87–135.

Hobsbawm, Eric, *Industry and Empire: From 1750 to the Present Day* (New York, 1999).

Hudson, Pat, 'The Limits of Wool and The Potential of Cotton in the Eighteenth and Early Nineteenth Centuries', in Giorgio Riello and Prasannan Parthasarathi (eds.), *The Spinning World: A Global History of Cotton Textiles, 1200–1850* (Oxford, 2009), 327–50.

Inikori, Joseph E., 'English versus Indian Cotton Textiles: The Impact of Imports on Cotton Textile Production in West Africa', in Giorgio Riello and Tirthankar Roy (eds.), *How India Clothed the World: The World of South Asian Textiles, 1500–1850* (Leiden, 2009), 85–114.

Johnson, Marion, *Anglo-African Trade in the Eighteenth Century: English Statistics on African Trade 1699–1808*, ed. J. T. Lindblad and Robert Ross (Leiden, 1990).

Kerlogue, Fiona, 'The Early English Textile Trade in South East Asia: The East India Company Factory and the Textile Trade in Jambi, Sumatra, 1615–1682', *Textile History*, 28/2 (1997), 149–60.

Khoury, Dina Rizk, 'Merchants and Trade in Early Modern Iraq', *New Perspectives on Turkey*, 5–6 (1991), 53–86.

Kriger, Colleen E., '"Guinea Cloth": Production and Consumption of Cotton Textiles in West Africa before and during the Atlantic Slave Trade', in Giorgio Riello and Prasannan Parthasarathi (eds.), *The Spinning World: A Global History of Cotton Textiles, 1200–1850* (Oxford, 2009), 105–26.

Lemire, Beverly, *Fashion's Favourite: The Cotton Trade and the Consumer in Britain, 1660–1800* (Oxford, 1991).

Lemire, Beverly, 'Fashioning Cottons: Asian Trade, Domestic Industry and Consumer Demand, 1660–1780', in David Jenkins (ed.), *The Cambridge History of Western Textiles* (Cambridge, 2003), vol. 1, 493–512.

Lemire, Beverly, 'Revising the Historical Narrative: India, Europe, and the Cotton Trade, c.1300–1800', in Giorgio Riello and Prasannan Parthasarathi (eds.), *The Spinning World: A Global History of Cotton Textiles, 1200–1850* (Oxford, 2009), 205–26.

Lemire, Beverly, 'Fashioning Global Trade: Indian Textiles, Gender Meanings and European Consumers, 1500–1800', in Giorgio Riello and Tirthankar Roy (eds.), *How India Clothed the World: The World of South Asian Textiles, 1500–1850* (Leiden, 2009), pp. 365–90.

Lin, Lee Chor, 'Textiles in Sino-South East Asian Trade: Song, Yuan and Ming Dynasties', in Rosemary Scott and John Guy (eds.), *South East Asia and China: Art, Interaction and Commerce* (London, 1995), pp. 171–86.

Maxwell, Robyn, *Textiles of Southeast Asia: tradition, trade and transformation* (Melbourne, 1990).

Mazzaoui, Maureen Fennell, 'Introduction', in Maureen Fennell Mazzaoui (ed.), *Textiles: Production, Trade and Demand* (Aldershot, 1998), pp. xiii–l.

Meilink-Roelofsz, M. A. P., *Asian Trade and European Influence in the Indonesian Archipelago: Between 1500 and About 1630* (The Hague, 1962).

Nag, Prithvish, 'The Indian Ocean, India and Africa: Historical and Geographical Perspectives', in Satish Chandra (ed.), *The Indian Ocean: Explorations in History, Commerce and Politics* (New Delhi, 1987), 151–73.

Norton, F. Mason, *John Norton & Sons, Merchants of London and Virginia, Being the Papers from their Counting House for the Years 1750 to 1795* (Newton Abbot, 1968).

Ovington, John, *A Voyage to Surat in the Year 1689*, ed. H. G. Rawlinson (London, 1929).

Parthasarathi, Prasannan, 'Response to John Styles', in Glenn Adamson, Giorgio Riello and Sarah Teasley (eds.), *Global Design History* (Abingdon, 2011), 47–9.

Pfister, Rudolf, 'The Indian Art of Calico Printing in the Middle Ages: Characteristics and Influences', *Indian Art and Letters*, 13 (1939), 23–9.

Pfister, Rudolf, *Les toiles imprimées de Fostat et l'Hindoustan* (Paris, 1938).

Prakash, Om, 'Asian Trade and European Impact: A Study of the Trade from Bengal, 1630–1720', in Blair B. Kling and M. N. Pearson (eds.), *The Age of Partnership: Europeans in Asia Before Domination* (Honolulu, 1979), 43–70.

Reid, Anthony, *Southeast Asia in the Age of Commerce, 1450–1680. Volume One: The Lands Below the Winds* (New Haven and London, 1984).

Riello, Giorgio, 'Counting Sheep: A Global View on Wool, 1800–2000', in Giovanni Luigi Fontana and Gérard Gayot (eds.), *Wool: Products and Markets, 13th–20th Century* (Padua, 2004), 113–36.

Riello, Giorgio, 'The Globalization of Cotton Textiles: Indian Cottons, Europe, and the Atlantic World, 1600–1850', in Giorgio Riello and Prasannan Parthasarathi (eds.), *The Spinning World: A Global History of Cotton Textiles, 1200–1850* (Oxford, 2009), 261–87.

Riello, Giorgio, 'The Indian Apprenticeship: The Trade of Indian Textiles and the Making of European Cottons', in Giorgio Riello and Tirthankar Roy (eds.), *How India Clothed the World: The World of South Asian Textiles, 1500–1850* (Leiden, 2009), 307–46.

Riello, Giorgio and Parthasarathi, Prasannan (eds.), *The Spinning World: A Global History of Cotton Textiles, 1200–1850* (Oxford, 2009).

Riello, Giorgio and Roy, Tirthankar, 'The World of South Asian Textiles, 1500–1850', in Giorgio Riello and Tirthankar Roy (eds.), *How India Clothed the World: The World of South Asian Textiles, 1500–1850* (Leiden, 2009), 1–27.

Roche, Daniel, *The Culture of Clothing: Dress and Fashion in the Ancien Régime*, trans. Jean Birrell (Cambridge, 1994).

Sadao, Nishijima, 'The Formation of the Early Chinese Cotton Industry', in Linda Grove and Christian Daniels (eds.), *State and Society in China. Japanese Perspectives on Ming-Qing Social and Economic History* (Tokyo, 1984), 17–77.

Sangar, S. P., 'Export of Indian textiles to Middle East and Africa in the Seventeenth Century', *Journal of Historical Research*, 17/1 (1974), 1–5.

Shah, Deepika, *Masters of the Cloth: Indian Textiles Traded to Distant Shores* (New Delhi, 2005).

Sickinger, R. L., 'Regulation or Ruination: Parliament's Consistent Pattern of Mercantilist Regulation of the English Textile Trade, 1660–1800', *Parliamentary History*, 19/2 (2000), 211–32.

Smith, Chloe Wigston, '"Callico Madams": Servants, Consumption, and the Calico Crisis', *Eighteenth-Century Life*, 31/2 (2007), 29–55.

Styles, John, 'Product Innovation in Early Modern London', *Past and Present*, 168 (2000), 124–69.

Styles, John, 'What Were Cottons for in the Early Industrial Revolution?', in Giorgio Riello and Prasannan Parthasarathi (eds.), *The Spinning World: A Global History of Cotton Textiles, 1200–1850* (Oxford, 2009), 307–26.

Styles, John, 'Indian Cottons and European Fashion', in Glenn Adamson, Giorgio Riello and Sarah Teasley (eds.), *Global Design History* (Abingdon, 2011), 37–46.

Tanaka, Masatoshi, 'The Putting-Out System of Production in the Ming and Qing Periods: With a Focus on Clothing Production (I)', *Memoirs of the Research Department of the Toyo Bunko*, 52 (1994), 21–43.

Tavernier, Jean-Baptiste, *Travels in India*, ed. William Crooke (Oxford, 1925).

Ulrich, Pamela V., 'From Fustian to Merino: The Rise of Textiles using Cotton Before and after the Gin', *Agricultural History*, 68/2 (1994), 219–31.

Varadarajan, Lotika, 'Syncretic Symbolism and Textiles: Indo-Thai Expressions', in Om Prakash and Denys Lombard (eds.), *Commerce and Culture in the Bay of Bengal, 1500–1800* (New Delhi, 1999), 361–78.

Vicente, Marta V., 'Fashion, Race, and Cotton Textiles in Colonial Spanish America', in Giorgio Riello and Prasannan Parthasarathi (eds.), *The Spinning World: A Global History of Cotton Textiles, 1200–1850* (Oxford, 2009), 247–60.

Vogt, John, 'Notes on the Portuguese Cloth Trade in West Africa, 1480–1540', *International Journal of African Historical Studies*, 8/4 (1975), 623–51.

Wiens, Mi Chü, 'Cotton Textile Production and Rural Social Transformation in Early Modern China', *Journal of the Institute of Chinese Studies*, 7/2 (1973), 515–34.

Wild, John Peter and Wild, Felicity, 'Rome and India: Early Indian Cotton Textiles from Berenike, Red Sea Coast of Egypt', in Ruth Barnes (ed.), *Textiles in Indian Ocean Societies* (London and New York, 2005), 11–16.

Winsnes, S. Axelrod (ed.), *A Reliable Account of the Coast of Guinea (1760) by Ludewig Ferdinand Rømer* (Oxford, 2000).

Young, A., *Political Essays Concerning the Present State of the British Empire* (London, 1772).

PART III

RICH AND POOR

LUXURY, THE LUXURY TRADES, AND THE ROOTS OF INDUSTRIAL GROWTH: A GLOBAL PERSPECTIVE

MAXINE BERG

LUXURY'S MODERN IDENTITIES

Luxury and its discontents have become key areas of debate on our social condition in the late twentieth and early years of the twenty-first centuries. Luxury has become the common parlance of advertising and branding. It is part of the upscaling of consumer aspirations, and a turning away from the mass consumerism which underpinned consumer society from the 1960s to the 1980s. Luxury in recent years has been associated with celebrity culture, and with this goes a belief in access and aspiration. With affluence, we now find not just more consumption or even a widening distribution of consumption, but new desires for consumption that are distinctive, diverse, and individual. But with this shift in the types and levels of consumption we also have growing social inequalities within Western societies, and widening social divisions between the richer and poorer parts of the world. The gap between the top 1 per cent of earners and the rest of society has increased, and we are aware of both new levels of hedonism and conspicuous consumption driving up prices of 'positional goods'. Such goods with a fixed supply and high elasticity of demand are part of the hidden lives of the very rich: works of art, the exclusive golf club or gym, or an uninhabited island. And at all levels of society savings have declined since the 1980s and debt levels are at record levels in the United States and Europe.

This luxury spending in recent years has also globalized. Many of those desirable and distinctive goods, from crafted fashion textiles to tropical holidays, have been produced in poor parts of the world for high-income earners in the West. But new wealth generated in the rapid growth trajectories of the last ten years in China, India, and South-East Asia has created new groups of the super-rich and of aspirant middle classes. This current phase of luxury spending is also a phase of critique, of retrenchment, and recycling in face of environmental change, and of luxury taxes.

Why has luxury both become a wider aspiration, and its levels been ratcheted up during the past two decades? How historically contingent is it? Were there earlier historical phases of hedonism, excess consumption, and critique of these? How do we explain the extension of luxury spending and, alongside this, a preference for this excess consumption over other possibilities of more leisure time?

Keynes, in 1929, did not envisage such a choice among his countrymen or even his social peers. Instead he predicted that rising productivity meant that a fifteen hour work week would suffice to provide most with their necessities and most of the superfluities they desired. But goods in the meantime were upgraded, quality differences extended, luxury branding developed, and new products invented. This process responded to psychological and sociological characteristics of status differentiation that made the demand for quality universal and inexhaustible.[1] Keynes ignored the creation of new and endlessly variable consumer goods that would continue to motivate individuals to earn enough to afford them. Consumption of material goods was also habit-forming. A consumer, excited by a new product, once its possessor quickly became accustomed to it, and moved on to aspire after the next thing.[2] This psychology of 'self-consuming passion' is now, and has been in the past, stimulated by external industrial and commercial forces—advertising and the mass media, and by planned obsolescence.[3] Consumer choice becomes the key marker of social inclusion and exclusion. Aspirations are associated with luxury and designer goods, with lifestyle choices of affluence and distinction. Manufacturers brand their products, seeking to obscure homogeneity. They give nearly every category of good they produce a premium brand; their products signal distinction and the pursuit of status.[4]

SOCIAL SCIENCE THEORY AND LUXURY

This phenomenon of upscaling, branding, and status-seeking through consumer goods has intensified dramatically since the 1980s, but it has also been with us a very long time. Definitions of luxury have varied over time, references to 'rarity' and 'conspicuous

---

[1] Robert Frank, 'Context is more important than Keynes realized', in Lorenz Pecchi and Gustavo Piga (eds.), *Revisiting Keynes. Economic Possibilities for our Grandchildren* (Cambridge, Mass.: MIT Press, 2008), 143–50, 146. Also see Robert Frank, *Luxury Fever. Why Money Fails to Satisfy in an Era of Excess* (New York: Free Press, 1999).

[2] Gary S. Becker, and Luis Rayo, 'Why Keynes Underestimated Consumption and Overestimated Leisure for the Long Run', in Pecchi and Piga (eds.), *Revisiting Keynes*, 179–84, 182–3.

[3] Richard Sennett, *The Culture of the New Capitalism* (New Haven: Yale University Press, 2006), 140.

[4] Avner Offer, *The Challenge of Affluence* (Oxford: Oxford University Press, 2005), 280.

consumption' must always be contexualized as 'relative': a luxury to one may be a necessity to another. Our recent usage refers to goods that are widely desired because they are not yet widely consumed, but the word also invokes qualitative attributes of things and activities; they are 'pleasing', or they offer a 'refinement' on more generic necessities.

Yet, interestingly, luxury has only periodically attracted the notice of economists. Economic theory defines luxury goods as those with income elasticities greater than one. Economic theory has traditionally regarded such goods as exceptions; economic historians have followed in perceiving such goods as relating only to the consumption of elites, and therefore not central to their concerns. Donald Winch has commented that even the mass consumer society which emerged in the later nineteenth and twentieth centuries had little influence on the thinking of professional economists. It did affect the dissidents and those of heterodox views; Veblen, Ruskin, and Hobson introduced discussion of 'conspicuous consumption', they discussed pathologies of consumption and 'under-consumption'.[5]

It was not until the 1960s and 1970s that economists developed theories connected to mainstream economic theory to analyse the demand for luxury goods. But the subject still remained on the margins of the discipline. While product development and branding were developing rapidly, economists dwelt on productivity change. They could not easily incorporate product development and quality differences into their time series. Their consumption functions focused on price and quantity, with tastes assumed to be fixed or consigned to exogenous factors. Lancaster and Ironmonger, however, argued in the 1960s and 1970s that the actual characteristics of consumer goods did matter. Consumers selected among characteristics, and their tastes were something economists could analyse. They argued that product and taste formation were interdependent. The want-satisfying powers of commodities depended on their qualities and on the nature of the wants they served.[6]

Another position, set out in Scitovsky's *The Joyless Economy*, conveyed the importance of novelty to consumer choice. Scitovsky argued that where all the needs of an organism were satisfied, there was neither pleasure nor comfort, only boredom. Habituation needed to be punctuated by novelty and uncertainty. Novelty, variety, complexity, and surprise all aroused the senses and stimulated pleasure.[7] More recently, economists have adapted this analysis to argue the part played by the 'active' consumer who chooses sensual satisfaction over everyday convenience or even necessity. This active consumer is not a passive price taker, but takes part in taste formation, responds to new goods, and combines goods in new ways to create a social identity and a lifestyle.[8] These approaches in turn have relied on

---

[5] Donald Winch, *Wealth and Life: Essays on the Intellectual History of Political Economy in Britain, 1848–1914* (Cambridge: Cambridge University Press, 2009).

[6] Kelvin Lancaster, *Consumer Demand. A New Approach* (New York and London: Columbia University Press, 1971), 2–12; Duncan Ironmonger, *New Commodities and Consumer Behavior* (Cambridge: Cambridge University Press, 1972), 1–13.

[7] Tibor Scitovsky, *The Joyless Economy: The Psychology of Human Satisfaction* (New York: Oxford University Press, 1977).

[8] Bianchi, Marina (ed.), *The Active Consumer: Novelty and Surprise in Consumer Choice* (London: Routledge, 1998), 64–86.

'hedonic indexes' developed by psychologists to measure cycles of pleasure, their stimulus, and intensity. Psychologists have also argued that novelty too had to be 'bounded': it was interesting while it was fresh and innovative; but it was also itself exhausted in the act of consumption. Tastes needed to develop in order to 'recognize' novelty and to 'discover' new characteristics in goods. Goods thus became fashionable because they connected with other networks of goods and their social and cultural frameworks.[9]

The interdependence of consumer preferences was also a key point of Hirsch's concept of 'positional goods'. He too made his case in the 1970s, arguing that goods in fixed supply with a high elasticity of demand were 'those things whose value depends relatively strongly on how they compare with things owned by others'. Such positional consumption was highly visible and marked by its quality of 'superfluousness'.[10]

While economists have treated luxury consumption as a special case, anthropologists have contributed a great deal on this aspect of consumer society. For they have recognized the special occasions in all communities celebrated by rare consumption. Anthropologists see luxuries as social valuables. Mary Douglas characterized such goods by highly specific powers of acquisition, by controls on distribution, patron-client relations of production, and reproduction of status systems. Symbolic attributes were followed by semiotic codes. Appadurai has placed luxuries within a special 'register' of consumption with rhetorical and social uses. This register included elite consumption, specialized knowledge for acquisition, and appropriate consumption, including regulation by taste or fashion, semiotic virtuosity, and a high degree of linkage to the body, person, and personality.[11]

Luxury goods as 'social valuables' have been redefined by cultural critics as 'incarnated signs'. Luxury as status-seeking consumer behaviour is a universal feature, they have argued in both traditional and modern societies. They have argued that demand is socially regulated in either type of society, either by fashion, or by more directly regulated sumptuary or customary systems. Location and historical context, however, shape the relative significance of goods accorded luxury status. Urban consumers in less developed countries spend more than their rural counterparts with similar incomes on relatively expensive and observable goods such as infant formula, imported soap and detergents, and crystal sugar. Even within rural areas, villages closer to towns placed greater value on easily transportable and demonstrable goods—dress, pens, gold watches, and bicycles—than on status-enhancing weddings of more remote villages.[12]

[9] Maxine Berg, *Luxury and Pleasure in Eighteenth-Century Britain* (Oxford: Oxford University Press, 2005), 250–1.

[10] Fred Hirsch, *Social Limits to Growth* (London: Routledge, 1977).

[11] Mary Douglas and Baron Isherwood, *The World of Goods: Towards an Anthropology of Consumption* (Harmondsworth: Penguin, 1978); Mary Douglas, *Thought Styles: Critical Essays on Good Taste* (London: Sage, 1996); Arjun Appadurai, 'Commodities and the Politics of Value', in Appadurai (ed.), *The Social Life of Things: Commodities in Cultural Perspective* (Cambridge: Cambridge University Press, 1996).

[12] Jeffrey James, 'Positional Goods, Conspicuous Consumption and the International Demonstration Effect Reconsidered' (1993), in Daniel Miller, *Consumption: Critical Concepts in the Social Sciences* (London: Routldge, 2001), vol. iii, 289–318, at 304.

Together with anthropologies of luxury goods we have sociologies and cultural accounts of consumer society which in very different ways address the place of luxury. John Brewer sets these out as the fantasist consumer of the department store, the manipulated consumer of the Frankfurt School, the utility rationalizing consumer of the economists, and the identity-creating and resisting consumers of cultural studies.[13] Whatever account we choose, luxury consumption forms a part of all of these, but has dominated discussion in singular ways over different historical contexts.

LUXURY'S HISTORICAL CONTEXT

Luxuries underpinned global grade in the Bronze Age and ancient world. Archaeologists have analysed such luxuries as exotic and foreign goods; luxury goods evoke associations with external markets, with artefacts produced and traded by strangers. From early times they have been endowed with artistic, religious, and magical properties, and traded over long distances. Yet our twentieth-century accounts connect luxury with 'the modern'. They contrast 'traditional societies' and their simple, functional, and internally provided needs with 'modern' societies and their complex wants, irrational desires, and globally sourced luxury goods. This modernity during the 1980s and 1990s was about rapid social mobility, about access to individuality and differentiation as cultural and political desirables. Consumption became a part of the debate on modernity; lifestyle and affluence were about 'choice'. But that contrast between 'modern' and 'traditional' also opened a political debate over consumption. The excess and choice now associated with modern consumption disrupted production systems in both the West and the Third World. Critics decry not just social division, but the loss of pre-lapsarian traditional codes of consumption among those in poor countries.

Such debates on the political framework of luxury emerged from parallel frameworks in the 1950s on economic growth and political regimes. Affluence was connected to democracy in Seymour Martin Lipset's *Political Man*. W. W. Rostow's 'open society' led to an 'age of high mass consumption'. Key commodities became signifiers of democratic or autocratic political regimes; consumption as ownership became a measure of politics. Cold war models both of free market capitalism and of economic planning sought end points of 'high mass consumption'. Increasingly through this period, however, critics had also raised questions over the welfare value of economic growth. This was the time of J. K. Galbraith's *The Affluent Society* (1958), of E. J. Mishan's *The Costs of Economic Growth* (1967), of Vance O. Packard's *The Hidden Persuaders* (1960) and *The Wastemakers* (1960).

But the post-war golden age had its counterpart in other frameworks for debates on connections between consumption and politics. Susman's essays on America in the

---

[13] John Brewer, 'The Error of our Ways', Working Paper No. 12, ESRC Cultures of Consumption Programme, <http://www.consume.bbk.ac.uk/publications.html>.

1930s and 1940s opened a sociology of a depression-born, consumption-fuelled labour militance. The pervasive promise of American consumerism, and the mass experience of homecoming after the First and Second World Wars inspired this militance. War mobilization operated on private themes appealing to consumer aspirations; these private desires in turn constructed notions of public rights. Working-class consumer expectations were thus cast in terms of political or proto-political entitlements.[14]

Prior to these critical political perspectives on wider consumer society, heterodox voices converged between the end of the nineteenth century and the First World War to analyse, deconstruct, and criticize a period of rapid growth of new wealth and luxury expenditure in Europe and America. Luxury goods, excess consumption, and collecting were manifestations of Europe's and America's new super-rich bourgeois classes. Banking and industrial families built palatial residences to be filled with all manner of globally sourced luxury goods, and they collected antique objects and pictures and other art objects. There was a whole *fin-de-siècle* debate on the decline of capitalism, moral corruption, and social division. Sombart, Simmel and Veblen all published their critical texts during this period.[15] Mandeville's *The Fable of the Bees*, first published early in the eighteenth century, reappeared in a new American edition published by Kaye, and it was at the same time translated into German.

Werner Sombart's *Luxury and Capitalism*, published in 1913, argued that personal luxury 'springs from purely sensuous pleasure. Anything that charms the eye, the ear, the nose, the palate, or the touch, tends to find an ever more perfect expression in objects of daily use. And it is precisely the outlay for such objects that constitutes luxury.'[16] Sombart took his analysis of luxury back to the eighteenth century, associating it especially with Paris, and drawing on Mercier's accounts of disgust and desire. Sombart, like Mercier before him, connected women with luxury, arguing that vanity, fashion, and sexuality stimulated consumer demand. Personal luxury was fundamentally erotic: 'In the last analysis, it is our sexual life that lies at the root of the desire to refine and multiply the means of stimulating our senses, for sensuous pleasure and erotic pleasure are essentially the same.'[17] The 'female vice' shaped accounts of sensuality and sexual appetite, of fashion and emulation. Sombart built his analysis of the eighteenth century around the key parts played by courtesans and female domestic servants who in their endless quest for novelties had a devastating impact on wider society. Sombart described the second half of the eighteenth century as a period of 'objectification', a time in which there 'is a greater expenditure of human labour on a specific object'. The effect was to widen the scope of capitalist industry. Sombart's analysis set

[14] See Warren J. Susman, *Culture as History: the Transformation of American Society in the Twentieth Century* (New York: Pantheon Books, 1984), cited in Jean Christophe Agnew, 'Coming up for Air: Consumer Culture in Historical Perspective', in John Brewer and Roy Porter (eds.), *Consumption and the World of Goods* (London and New York: Routledge, 1993), 19–30, esp. 30–1.

[15] G. Simmel, *The Philosophy of Money* (first publishefd 1900), ed. D. Frisby, trans. T. Bottomore and D. Frisby, 1978, 2nd edn. (London: Routledge, 1990).

[16] Werner Sombart, *Luxury and Capitalism* (1913), (Ann Arbor, Michigan: Universitiy of Michigan Press, 1967), xxi, 61.

[17] Ibid., 61.

up to offer a critique of the super-rich of his own day, delved into the eighteenth-century, the debates on luxury conveyed by Mercier, its expression in the growth of capital and court cities, especially Paris, and recounted a full discussion of a number of luxury industries and globally traded goods. He concluded, 'Luxury, then, itself a legitimate child of illicit love—as we have seen—gave birth to capitalism.'[18]

Sombart's psychology of the senses was later turned by Norbert Elias into a social psychology.[19] Elias, focusing less on the goods that were bought than the behaviour surrounding them, argued that the manners and rituals of sixteenth-century court society created a form of self-restraint that became part of the personality. Luxury spending was about cultural displays of power, with such luxury goods as instruments of rule. It was also constrained by the dictates of 'court rationality'. Such rationality reached out to a cult of durable consumer goods to convey family status. These luxuries also demonstrated taste. Craftsmanship transformed objects into high culture, that expressed an elite not just of wealth, but of taste and refinement.

Sombart's 'sensuous luxury' was Veblen's 'emulative consumption', consumption of goods which would elicit the attention of 'observers whose good opinion is sought.' In Veblen's biting analysis of the status-seeking and ostentation of the super-rich, Sombart's Paris had its counterparts in late nineteenth-century American cities.

> It is not that the city population is by nature much more eager for the peculiar complacency that comes of a conspicuous consumption, nor has a rural population less regard for pecuniary decency. But the provocation to this line of evidence, as well as its transient effectiveness, are more decided in the city...in the struggle to outdo one another the city population push their normal standard of conspicuous consumption to a higher point.[20]

THE LUXURY DEBATES

Luxury goods have, of course, been with us from prehistoric times, and debates over luxury have also been continuous since the ancient world. Aristotle's *Nicomachean Ethics*, Book IV, in 355BC elaborated on the concept of '*liberalità*', virtue with the object of moral beauty. He contrasted this with the vices of prodigality and avarice. Renaissance Florence celebrated the virtues of 'splendour' and Philip the IV's Spain of '*magnificencia*'. Debates over luxury were integral to emerging definitions of state and civic power.[21]

[18] Sombart, *Luxury and Capitalism*, 171.
[19] Norbert Elias, *The Process of Civilization* (original German edition 1939), (Oxford: Blackwell, 2000).
[20] Thorstein Veblen, *The Theory of the Leisure Class* (1899) (New York: Macmillan, 1912), cited in James, 'Positional goods', p. 301.
[21] Guido Guerzoni, '"Liberalitas, Magnificentia, Splendor": The Classic Origins of Italian Renaissance Lifestyles', in Neil De Marchi and Craufurd D. W. Goodwin (eds.), *Economic Engagements with Art* (Durham NC and London: University of North Carolina Press, 1999).

It was in the eighteenth century, however, that luxury became a key issue of Enlightenment ideas and economic discourse.

Why was luxury the debate of the age during the Enlightenment? We might explain this by economic and social context: the new access to Asian consumer societies and exotic foods and raw materials of the New World; imported exotica were becoming Europe's consumer goods. Certainly, mercantilist debates of the seventeenth and eighteenth centuries warned of the dangers of French and Chinese manufactures. Definitions of luxury goods changed over the course of the later seventeenth and the eighteenth centuries. The expansion of worldwide trade and commerce in the wake of Europe's East India Companies and greatly expanded private trade both in Asia and the Atlantic world brought a broadening of the world of luxury commodities. There was both a more open debate on the advantages of trade and a more cosmopolitan development of the senses.

The debate on luxury increasingly distinguished between 'new' and 'old' luxury or between 'modern' and 'ancient' luxury. New luxuries were created out of the division of labour and the expansion of commerce; old luxuries conveyed excessive displays with large bodies of retainers. Now discussion shifted to commerce, utility, taste, and comfort, and the language of luxury turned from 'excess' to 'surplus', and from 'vanity' to 'refinement'.

We can follow this shift from old to new luxury in philosophy and political economy. Bernard Mandeville's *The Fable of the Bees* undermined contemporary complacencies on modern manners by revealing the world of the passions, the psychology of self-interest, pleasure-seeking, and vanity. He brought into British and European economic and political debate the Augustinian philosophic analysis of the passions of self-interest and self-love or *amour-propre* as discussed by the Jansenists and Pierre Bayle. Through Mandeville the luxury question would become of the first importance to newly emerging political economy in the work of Jean-François Melon, Montesquieu, David Hume, James Steuart, and Adam Smith.

Mandeville discussed luxury as part of the search for self-identity through fantasy, possessions, and the restless pursuit of novelty. Luxury became part of commercial expansion and consumer society. The moral discourse critical of 'old luxury' shifted to a new political economy of trade and industry. Sir James Steuart (1767) argued that luxury encouraged 'emulation, industry and agriculture'.[22] Montesquieu in the 1770s compared Persian and Parisian luxury, then went on to praise English luxury as the epitome of modern luxury. The Abbé Raynal at the same time compared the commercial Arabs of the Middle Ages who cultivated the arts and literature with the 'barbaric ostentation' of the French nobility under feudalism. David Hume and Adam Smith endorsed the advantages of new luxury, associating it with commerce, convenience, and consumption.[23] Hume defended luxury on what today's economists call 'second-best' grounds.

[22] James Steuart, *An Inquiry into the Principles of Political Oeconomy [1767]*, ed. Andrew S. Skinner (Edinburgh and London: Oliver and Boyd, 1966), 1,266; Jan de Vries, 'Luxury in the Dutch Golden Age', in Maxine Berg and Elizabeth Eger (eds.), *Luxury in the Eighteenth Century* (Basingstoke: Palgrave, 2003), 41–56.
[23] Maxine Berg and Elizabeth Eger, 'The Rise and Fall of the Luxury Debates', in Berg and Eger (eds.), *Luxury in the Eighteenth Century*, 7–27.

Luxury was certainly a poison, but one that was an antidote to worse poisons. Agrarian lethargy was much worse than a luxury which prompted that 'quick march of the spirits' that went with the rise of manufacturing, the arts, and civilization.[24] Such a commercial society directed the passions away from war, violence, and wretched excess. Adam Smith, while praising the luxuries created as durable consumer goods, and arising out of commercial society and the division of labour, also argued that prudence and frugality contributed to capital accumulation and a surplus. Over a static argument of the paradox in favour of luxury focused on the recirculation of wealth, he presented a dynamic distinction between productive and unproductive labour. New luxuries were durable commodities, adding to the surplus and amenable to gains in productivity through the division of labour, rather than the displays and indulgence paid for out of the surplus.[25]

Yet despite these compelling arguments from political economy, luxury remained a paradox throughout the eighteenth century. Rousseau with other critics of luxury put it at the root of national social problems. He argued that luxury consumption destabilized the social order; it brought moral corruption and ruined taste. The Seven Years War followed later by the French wars revived old denunciations of French luxury. Luxury entered the language of late eighteenth-century radicalism and revolutionary virtue as well as conservative country politics. Agrarian autarchy remained embedded in the aspirations and utopian fantasies of both sides of the political spectrum. Adam Ferguson argued that the spread of luxury among the poor corrupted manners in a commercial society. Fielding blamed addiction to new vices of tea, sugar, gin, and fashionable clothing for rising crime rates among the labouring poor. The late eighteenth-century radicals, Thomas Spence, William Godwin, Richard Price, and Charles Hall blamed it for inequality, and sought redemption in simple agrarian community.

Cities and women were at the heart of the debate. The Dutch in the seventeenth century saw the growth of their cities and towns as the setting for new luxury goods and private domestic comfort. Luxury went with the sociability of cities. For Mandeville, early eighteenth-century London was both the 'great maw', a shopping centre, and a great stage for the display of endless varieties of goods and peoples. Mandeville found a new cultural setting for luxury in populous cities where most individuals were unknown to one another. The anonymity opened the possibilities of fantasy and self-fashioning; the desire to distinguish oneself redoubled because there was more expectation of succeeding. The enlarged public sphere of the city invited the cultivation of 'politesse' or later 'politeness'. For Hume cities were sites of civility, the arts, and refinement. Adam Smith found the proliferation of new commodities created by industry and the division of labour and consumed by the middling orders in rapidly expanding industrial and commercial towns.

Luxury was also the female vice. The language of arousal was never far distant in the debate. Exposure to urban life and access to imported goods awakened desire. The classical debate on luxury had associated women with excess and desire; and luxury was

---

[24] Donald Winch, *Riches and Poverty: an Intellectual History of Political Economy in Britain 1750–1834* (Cambridge: Cambridge University Press, 1996).
[25] Berg and Eger, 'The Rise and Fall of the Luxury Debates', 8, 12, 13.

long connected with effeminacy and weakness. In the eighteenth century many of the contestants in the debate still argued that vanity, fashion, and sexuality underpinned consumer markets that were also capricious, inconstant, and unstable. But new arguments acknowledged women's part in fostering sociability, their role in the civilizing process, and the education they provided to the senses and to taste.[26]

LUXURY AND THE GLOBAL ECONOMY

There is a long legacy connecting luxury with foreign imports, and this passed into the mercantilist debates of the seventeenth and eighteenth centuries. Those ancient luxuries were associated with sociable settings for the display of precious goods. The ancient Greek symposia displayed and used gold and silver drinking vessels and wine craters. Wealthy merchants and elites in Renaissance Italy conveyed their status through a taste in ancient oriental ceramics, imitated in fine majolica and in silverware and glass. The accoutrements of private splendour in refined hospitality at table made glass and ceramics into international luxury goods. They were quintessential markers of taste.[27]

But it was not just imports, but imports from the East that gave luxury its particular caché in the later seventeenth and eighteenth centuries. Silk was Europe's classic ancient luxury import from China. The fabled Silk Route conveyed all manner of luxury and other goods, but silk marked its identity with exotic luxury. Chinese silk continued to be imported into Europe throughout the early modern period and the eighteenth century, though Italy had long become the major producer for the West from the fifteenth century onwards. By the later seventeenth century there were new imports of cotton calicoes and muslins, of porcelain and lacquerware. These attained great popularity during the eighteenth century, and were soon imported in large quantities by Europe's East India Companies and sold as decent, high-quality semi-luxuries available in a wide range of patterns, styles, qualities, and prices.

Asian models also stimulated Europeans to produce their own imitations in both production processes, designs, and marketing strategies. For Asian luxury goods were highly successful transmitters of technology, designs, and aesthetics. Such goods transmitted cross-cultural characteristics across great distances. Porcelain services replaced silver plate during European and civil wars. In Islamic lands they substituted for the gold and silver proscribed as materials for eating vessels under Koranic traditions. Indian calicoes adapted to tastes for chinoiserie: designs and markets adapted readily to an already established fashion for Chinese art. Merchants placed orders for patterns picked out on a white ground rather than the traditional Indian red or coloured backgrounds. Lacquerware furnishings had a seductive appeal, especially the cabinets with

---

[26] Berg, *Luxury and Pleasure*, 35–7; Berg and Eger, 'The Rise and Fall of the Luxury Debates', 18–19.
[27] Maxine Berg, 'Luxury Goods', in Joel Mokyr (ed.) *The Oxford Encyclopedia of Economic History* (Oxford and New York: Oxford University Press, 2003), vol. 3, 400–4.

two doors enclosing a set of small (sometimes secret) drawers and a small central cupboard, a suitable vessel for holding ornamental and exotic collectables or secret and private correspondence and small or intimate treasures.[28]

The Eastern provenance of these luxury goods also aroused the interest of Europe's savants, travellers, producers, and merchants. Enlightenment writers, natural historians, and travellers investigated and recounted the customs and manners of the peoples of the Middle East and North Africa, of China, India, and South-East Asia, including the cultures of the courts, the transformation during the early modern period of huge cities from Istanbul to Edo, and their varied and highly sophisticated consumer cultures drawing on all the world's commodities. European curiosity in these cultures extended to investigation of production processes capable of supplying large domestic populations as well as extensive wider world trade in high-quality goods. Luxury goods, often perceived at the time as the master works of single craftsmen, were discovered to be the outputs of large-scale production units organized with intense division of labour, such as Jingdezhen, the porcelain city; or the composite products of a whole series of tribal, religious, and caste communities, again highly specialized through an intense division of labour. Yet the porcelain was harder and finer than any European substitutes; writers marvelled at muslins so delicate they could hardly be seen, and cottons printed in unusual colour palettes with dyes unaccountably fixed.[29]

The exotic in these consumer cultures and production systems was brought into Europe's knowledge systems; manufacturers experimented and adapted, and in the process they created new products, imitations and import substitutes. They used different raw materials and worked on mechanizing the labour-intensive repetitive processes they could not afford to replicate in Europe. Asian knowledge and example acted not just to transform Europe's material culture, but played a significant part in stimulating those key transformations in division of labour, mechanization and factory processes that underlay the making of Europe's own consumer goods sector.[30]

Europe's trade in Asian luxury goods was also transformed over the course of the seventeenth and eighteenth centuries. The rise of Europe's East India Companies, monopolies to be sure, but competing with each other and considerably bolstered by significant private trade, brought more luxury goods to Europe, made them accessible to broader

---

[28] Berg, *Luxury and Pleasure*, 51–6; Oliver Impey, *Chinoiserie: The Impact of Oriental Styles on Western Art and Decoration* (Oxford: The Ashmolean, 1977), 20–6; Robert Finlay, 'The Pilgrim Art: the Culture of Porcelain in World History', *Journal of World History*, 9 (1998), 141–89, 178–9; Giorgio Riello, 'The Indian Apprenticeship: the Trade in Indian Textiles and the making of European Cottons', in Giorgio Riello and Tirthankar Roy (eds.), *How India Clothed the World* (Leiden: Brill, 2009), 309–47.

[29] K. N. Chaudhuri, *Asia before Europe: Economy and Civilization of the Indian Ocean from the Rise of Islam to 1750* (Cambridge: Cambridge University Press, 1990), 304–9; E. L. Jones, *Growth Recurring: Economic Change in World History* (Oxford: Oxford University Press, 1998), 80–2, 158; Finlay, 'The Pilgrim Art', 156; Beverly Lemire, *Fashion's Favourite: the Cotton Trade and the Consumer in Britain 1660–1800* (Oxford: Oxford University Press, 1991), 18.

[30] Maxine Berg, 'From Imitation to Invention: Creating Commodities in Eighteenth-Century Britain', *Economic History Review*, 45 (2002), 1–30; Maxine Berg, *Luxury and Pleasure*, 77–84; Maxine Berg, 'Quality, Cotton and the Global Luxury Trade', in Riello and Roy, *How India Clothed the World*, 391–414.

groups of the wealthy elites, and in Britain and the Netherlands to the middling and sometimes artisan classes. Such luxuries became cheaper relative to staples, thus increasing the relative incomes of the wealthy even as those of the poor declined.[31]

The Asia-Europe trade considerably developed the institutions and organization of international markets, and in the realms of economics, reduced transactions costs over the period. The East India Companies functioned as early versions of multinational corporations, both in developing markets for Asian luxury goods, and in organizing supply and shipping. Merchants developed and adapted designs in anticipation of European taste, and interacted in Asia with go-betweens, and Hong merchants, using pattern books, textile swatches, musters and models to transmit to the manufacturing communities on the ground. They imported large quantities, judging quantities and markets on information gathered at the quarterly East India Company auction sales. Textiles made up over 80 per cent of English East India Company imports from Asia in the mid-eighteenth century, with average imports of 772,000 pieces. The British imported 1 million, rising in some years to 2 million pieces of porcelain a year in the early eighteenth century.[32] Companies made stark choices among speed, tonnage, and trade routes to reach the factory trading bases first, and return to Europe in good anticipation of auction dates.[33]

Selling the goods in Europe was in the first instance highly centralized, and traders were few in numbers and large in scale. Auctions in Amsterdam, London, and Lorient sold the goods in large lots to middlemen who then sold them to dealers advertising large consignments in the provincial press. London's china and earthenware dealers—there were a minimum of 250 of them before 1780—frequently had stocks valued at £2,000–3,000; and even smaller provincial dealers kept stocks at the considerable values of £300–700.[34] This repeated the pattern set by the Dutch. There were also small numbers of large-scale buyers at the Dutch Zeeland auctions—one in the period 1724–48 frequently bought 50,000–100,000 pieces; there were other dealers who took 20–40,000 pieces.[35] This highly centralized marketing and distribution also set the

[31] Jan de Vries, *The Industrious Revolution. Consumer Behavior in the Household Economy, 1650 to the Present* (Cambridge: Cambridge University Press, 2008), 122–83; Jan de Vries, 'Connecting Europe and Asia. A Quantitative Analysis of the Cape-route Trade, 1497–1795', in Dennis Flynn, Arturo Giráldez and Richard von Glahn (eds.), *Global Connections and Monetary History 1470–1800* (Aldershot, Hants: Ashgate, 2003), 35–106.

[32] N. Steensgaard, 'The Growth and Composition of the Long-Distance Trade of England and the Dutch Republic before 1750', in J.D. Tracy (ed.), *The Rise of Merchant Empires* (Cambridge: Cambridge University Press, 1990), 102–52, 106, 118; Lorna Scammell, 'Ceramics', in Mokyr, *Oxford Encyclopedia of Economic History*, vol. 1, 379–83.

[33] F. S. Gaastra and J. R. Bruijn, 'The Dutch East India Company's Shipping 1602–1795 in Comparative Perspective', in F. S. Gaastra and J. R. Bruijn, *Ships, Sailors and Spices: East India Companies and their Shipping in the Sixteenth, Seventeenth and Eighteenth Centuries* (Amsterdam: NEHA, 1993), 177–208, Table 7.2, p. 182.

[34] Lorna Weatherill, 'The Growth of the Pottery Industry in England, 1660–1815', *Post-Medieval Archaeology*, 17 (1983), 15–46, at 17; Hilary Young, *English Porcelain 1745–95* (London: V&A, 1999), 154–7; Aubrey Toppin, 'The China Trade and Some London Chinamen', *English Ceramics Circle Transactions*, 3 (1935), 37–57.

[35] Christian J. A. Jörg, *Porcelain and the Dutch China Trade* (The Hague: M. Nijhoff, 1982), 131.

terms for how domestic quality chinaware came to be sold in the latter half of the eighteenth century.

The impact of the rapid growth of and considerable extent of this trade in luxury goods from Asia to Europe between the later seventeenth and later eighteenth century was to transform what Europeans formerly perceived as exotic Eastern curios into quality commodities in a great variety of designs and grades of fineness. These not only graced the bodies of the rich and provided the paraphernalia of the bourgeois tea table, but sometimes as imports and more often as imitations they integrated into the dress and the necessary utensils of the daily routines of life of rich and poor alike. The impact of that Asian luxury goods trade was to provide the model for consumer markets in Europe for quality goods that were not high luxuries for elites only.

LUXURY AND CONSUMPTION: THE SEVENTEENTH AND EIGHTEENTH CENTURIES

Luxury consumption in early modern Europe, as in the social and cultural life of Asia, Africa, the Americas and the Pacific was constrained by sumptuary laws and codes or customs. The sumptuary laws imposed by European governments were directed to preventing public display above one's social station. The use and display of rare and precious objects, frequently acquired through long-distance trade were marks of elite status. But merchants and others acquiring new wealth frequently clashed with local sumptuary structures. The laws grew extensive in the later Middle Ages just as commerce expanded. Tensions focused especially on the divide between indigenous and foreign goods; and sumptuary laws became associated with protectionist economic regulation. Injunctions centred on silk, furs, gold, silver and jewels, and exotic commodities from India, China, and Persia. Excessive display at family rites of passage from christenings to funerals was tightly controlled, and increasingly challenged in Italian cities and north European towns.[36] Silks were especially proscribed for uses outside the princely courts and the Church, but by the early modern period these regulations were increasingly undermined. Chinese, Indian, and Persian silks spread via Venice through the Mediterranean and Continental Europe. Sea routes to Asia by the beginning of the sixteenth century created another entrepôt through Lisbon. It was impossible to stem the flow of these Eastern luxuries. By the beginning of the seventeenth century in England sumptuary laws were a dead letter, the Netherlands never had them, and while they held on in some other parts of Europe they were increasingly difficult to enforce. A number of Italian cities were producing their own silk by the early sixteenth century

---

[36] Beverly Lemire and Giorgio Riello, 'East & West: Textiles and Fashion in Early Modern Europe', *Journal of Social History*, 41 (2008), 887–916, at 890.

in quantities accessible well beyond the elites; they were soon followed by other centres in Spain and France.[37]

Luxury goods encountered a new fashion dynamic by the later sixteenth century. Some historians have drawn sharp distinctions between luxury and fashion goods. Clearly some fashionable articles of clothing were not luxuries, and court ritual and ecclesiastical ceremony deployed inherited tradition, not fashion. Grant McCracken contrasted the aesthetics and taste for 'patina', which represented status before the eighteenth century, with a fashion system deploying new goods after this. Distinctions then developed out of continual changes in style.[38] Fashion goods also emerged out of the markets and institutions for luxury goods. Charles II in the last third of the seventeenth century introduced the English to oriental and French goods along with a stylish way of living. Paris by the late seventeenth century was Europe's fashion capital, and consumerism there was led by the Court. Luxury goods producers integrated a fashion production cycle into their practices, and workshop inspectors guaranteed their quality, with the result that French goods soon claimed a cultural cachet throughout Europe.

But silks, now manufactured, brocaded, and embroidered in Europe 'became a disputed medium of style'; their 'fashioning' was still labour-intensive.[39] A closely approximate imitation arrived with the new wave of Asian-European seaborne trade: printed and painted cotton calicoes. The fabrics were light like silk, the colours vibrant, and the patterns and designs infinitely variable. These new goods from the East shook the old framework of the sumptuary dispute. Such goods came from afar, but they were not the rarities represented by silk; their value and status from the start was ambiguous, and they quickly moved to the forefront of new priorities over novelty and fashion.

By the eighteenth century fashion was part of the language of luxury. Fashion dictated values. Fashion goods in turn drew on imitative impulses, product innovation, and creative adaptation. The key goods which came to feature in the consumer revolution, clothing and domestic items, were furthermore connected to sociability: fashionable clothing; the glass, chinaware, and silver accoutrements of the tea and dining table; the mirrors, ornamental ware, and seating furniture of dining and drawing rooms. These reflected the rise of middling groups and urban politeness. Innovation in ceramics focused on the domestic setting rather than the courtly display cabinet. Polite culture was an ethos for the urban middling classes as well as modern commercial polities. Fashionable goods conveying good taste were marks of inclusiveness and creditworthiness. Among urban tradesmen they ornamented one's shop and graced one's person, and by extension one's household.

[37] Ibid., 891; see also Alan Hunt, *Governance of the Consuming Passions. A History of Sumptuary Law* (New York: St Martin's Press, 1996); N. B. Harte, 'State Control of Dress', in D. C. Coleman and A. H. John (eds.), *Trade, Government and Economy in Pre-Industrial England* (London: Weidenfeld and Nicholson 1976), 132–65; De Vries, *The Industrious Revolution*, 46, 136.

[38] Maxine Berg, 'French Fancy and Cool Britannia: The Fashion Markets of Early Modern Europe', *Journal for the Study of British Cultures*, 13 (2006), 21–46, at 30; Grant McCracken, *Culture and Consumption* (Bloomington IN: Indiana University Press, 1988); Carlo Poni, 'Fashion as Flexible Production. The Strategies of the Lyons Silk Merchants in the Eighteenth Century', in Charles Sabel and Jonathan Zeitlin (eds.), *Worlds of Possibilities: Flexibility and Mass Production in Western Industrialization* (Cambridge: Cambridge University Press, 1997), 37–74, at 39.

[39] Beverly Lemire and Giorgio Riello, 'East & West', 75–103.

How far down the social scale did this reach and what divided luxuries from necessities? Taxation provided a key platform for the debate over luxuries and necessities. Colonial and Asian groceries were taxed by most European states, yet over the course of the eighteenth century also acknowledged as part of the consumption of the common people. These foodstuffs and hot drinks were very recent imports. Tea was not imported into the Dutch, French, and Baltic ports before the early seventeenth century; similarly coffee only entered the regular sales of the VOC (Dutch East India Company) in the 1690s. But by the end of the 1730s tea and coffee accounted for a quarter of all VOC sales in Amsterdam, second only to silk and cotton textiles. Tea and coffee wares were also then ubiquitous throughout the Dutch towns. The Dutch tax authorities believed the consumption of tea and coffee to be universal by the mid-eighteenth century.[40]

Such goods provided fresh opportunities for government revenue as states exploited new, indirect methods of taxation through customs and excise, stamp duties, and taxes on luxury goods. Adam Smith proposed taxing the 'luxuries and vanities of life', such as mansions and carriages. Tariff policies discriminated against foreign manufactured imports, as they did against 'luxurious' additives to the diet (tea, coffee, sugar, rum, tobacco, wines and spirits) over basic foodstuffs. Smuggling was rampant, focused on luxury goods of high value and subject to high tariff rates. This applied especially to silks and laces, French spirits, tea, and tobacco.[41] Taxation policies also provoked much debate on the extent to which such goods were luxuries or necessities. Governments defended their taxes as justified if they fell on luxuries rather than the necessities of the poor. They frequently assumed imported goods to be superfluous; those who chose to consume such goods should be taxed for it. Taxes on such 'luxury goods' were also enacted as a deterrent on goods perceived to undermine labouring-class morals—tobacco, alcohol, and subsequently tea. Tea drinking, long accepted as part of polite sociability among the middling and trading classes, was by the later eighteenth century, if not well before this, entering into the diets of the labouring classes. Many condemned an irrational use of time and money, and the effeminacy they associated with tea drinking. Taxing such contentious luxury goods from the later eighteenth century entered a radical political discourse over taxing a wide range of consumer goods, goods of 'subsistence' and of 'comfort'; luxuries and necessities. Disputes over luxury thus entered into campaigns for liberty for the people, for rights, and for the vote.[42]

Political debate and economic policy over the divide between luxuries and necessities pushes us to enquire into changing household structures and behaviour over the

[40] Ann McCants, 'Poor Consumers as Global Consumers: The Diffusion of Tea and Coffee Drinking in the Eighteenth Century', *Economic History Review*, 61 (2007), 172–200; de Vries, *The Industrious Revolution*, 154–64.

[41] John Brewer, *Sinews of Power: War, Money and the English State 1688–1783* (London: Routledge, 1989); Maxine Berg and Helen Clifford, 'Luxury, Consumer Goods and British Taxation in the Eighteenth Century', in *Proceedings of the Instituto Internazionale di Storia Economica "F.Datini"* (Prato), 2008, 1105–18; William Ashworth, *Customs and Excise: Trade, Production and Consumption in England 1640–1845* (Oxford: Oxford University Press, 2003).

[42] Patrick O'Brien, 'The Political Economy of British Taxation 1660–1815', *Economic History Review*, 41 (1988), 1–32, at 13; Ashworth, *Customs and Excise*, 350; Berg and Clifford, 'Luxury, Consumer Goods and British Taxation', 1116–17.

early modern period. Jan de Vries termed the complex of changes in household behaviour associated with urban life, trade, and the social power of women an 'industrious revolution'. This was a consumption-driven phenomenon that paved the way for the industrial revolution.[43] But it was not consumption in general that was crucial to the 'industrious revolution', but consumption of new marketed goods, goods acquired from outside the local region, and especially goods imported from afar. Superfluous goods, new colonial groceries, and fashionable items of clothing and of domestic interiors were special attractions. Consumption decisions led especially by women in the household stimulated more labour on marketed production, longer working days, and more members of the household working for wages. The 'industrious revolution' connected rising consumption to higher labour supply, and explained this as a shift in household behaviour.[44] It was thus that consumer demand and not just population growth drove forward those fundamental changes that increased both labour supply and industrial production in the period just prior to industrialization.

STATES, MARKETS, AND GLOBAL EXPORT WARE

The food, drinks, and medicines of the East and the New World, and the exotic manufactures of the Portuguese emporia trade, and soon of Europe's East India Companies soon sparked a scramble for both the world's Eastern and Western commodities. It also prompted states to look to their own domestic industries, and mercantilist policies fostered prestige quality manufactures at home. States competed in developing court manufactures and workshops. European regions developed specialist skills in all manner of luxury goods from glass and fine ironware to silk-weaving and goldsmiths' work. European diasporas of skill spread with religious dissent among engravers and designers, clockmakers, goldsmiths and silversmiths and cabinetmakers. A trade in European luxury goods provided a positive economic image of manufacture.

New commodities imitating Eastern luxuries developed. These relied on domestic raw materials or materials from colonial hinterlands. They conveyed something in their designs that connected with the Eastern luxury goods, but importantly developed new design frameworks. The blue and white of Chinese export porcelain became Wedgwood's blue jasper-ware. Fine Japanese lacquerware was transformed into English japanned metalwares. Luxury goods of many types were imitated in this way through developing new metal alloys and the rolling, stamping, and moulding mechanical techniques to deploy novel designs on surfaces that looked like the gold, silver, or precious stones of old luxury goods. In Britain, silver plated ware, brassware, all manner of wood

---

[43] De Vries, *The Industrious Revolution*, 72.
[44] De Vries, *The Industrious Revolution*, 100–15.

and metal varnishes, lead glass crystal, cylinder-printed cotton calicoes, Axminster imitation Turkey carpets, cut-steel jewellery and buckles, and fine Staffordshire earthenware were imitations that became new luxuries, commodities accessible among the middling classes, and newly desirable English export ware.[45]

The luxury goods imported from Asia brought to Europe a new knowledge of an export ware sector. These goods introduced to Europe lessons of complexity and of simplicity in product design and technology. Asia produced fine cottons, silks, porcelain, and other fine goods for world markets, deploying complex skills and adapting designs to capture the tastes of consumers from Malacca to Cairo, and from Lisbon to Amsterdam. These products offered a new design complexity that seemed readily adaptable to different cultures and fashions. Yet most of China's export ware porcelain was produced in one large centre, in large-scale units with extensive division of labour and assembly line processes. This was a simplified production system which produced a quality and design complexity, but within limits to meet world market demands for expected and similar designs. Europeans transformed these lessons of Asian export ware, not in their own new porcelain works, but in developing north Staffordshire cream-ware into a new world product also branded with quality, standardization, and reliability.

The case of cotton was even more telling. The most significant of new goods developed as a response to Eastern luxury were printed cotton calicoes. European textile manufacturers urgently sought to produce the fabrics, colours, and designs to rival Asian competitors. India's finest muslins and its patterned and painted fine cotton calicoes offered a complexity of versatile designs to Europe's new-emerging fashion markets. This Asian export ware worked, however, to the advantage of Europe and the disadvantage of India. These fabrics and designs arose out of longstanding artisan expertise focused on highly specialized markets and minute and complex divisions of labour through the caste system. Dynasties of craftspeople produced unique forms of quality; such specialty markets led into the rigidities of endlessly proliferating niche markets. Such quality was, however, neither consistent nor predictable; though Europe's East India Companies tapped into the quality and variety which might also be directed to meet European tastes, access to these products in Europe was always uncertain. Retailers fought a constant battle to get the right textiles at the right time. The global trade in this export ware luxury good drove India deeper into specialization and opened her to vulnerabilities.[46] These luxuries for Europe became India's 'luxury in a poor country'.

In response to this Indian ascendancy in world textile markets, Europe's manufacturers lobbied governments to increase tariffs or impose import restrictions on printed and painted cottons. State intervention in the form of high tariffs and outright import bans cleared the way for European producers. Fashion markets, centres of innovation, and diasporas of skilled engravers, dyers, and printers stimulated a new industry in France, Switzerland, Catalonia, and particularly in Britain. Manufacturers especially sought to

[45] Maxine Berg, 'From Imitation to Invention', 1–30.
[46] David Washbrook, 'India in the Early Modern World Economy: Modes of Production, Reproduction and Exchange', *Journal of Global History*, 2 (2007), 87–112.

develop a quality good as they competed with India.[47] They lacked the cheap labour and long traditions of carefully honed skills of India. Instead they pursued new production systems, division of labour, workshop and factory organization, and above all mechanization to produce a product which, though it could not match the highest-quality Indian goods, could provide good quality, could equal the Indian adaptability to fashion markets and produce the required variety and novelty, and above all could reach merchants and retailers in good time in the quantities and dimensions desired. European producers now matched Indian luxury by providing other desirable characteristics: high output at affordable prices, variety and novelty, rapid turnover, warehouse selling, precision, exactness and order. Luxury now had an alternative, a high-quality cotton in a varied product mix produced by machinery. Luxury and a global history of those goods from the East, long neglected by economists and economic historians, thus played a key role in the industrialization of the West.

That shift from a world where Asia's luxury products drove the search for the technologies and industrial organization leading into the industrialization of Europe and North America was followed by two centuries of Western domination of world manufacture. The twenty-first century has seen a new Asian ascendancy: Europe has lost those manufacturing catalysts of textiles, ceramics, and metal goods back to Asia. And the West, now facing the manufacturing and technological challenge of China and the rising capacity of India, is also experiencing new anxieties over its place in the world economy. New issues of world recession have connected consumption and production in ways hitherto unimagined. Luxury brands once rooted in Europe, for example Wedgwood pottery, are now manufactured in distant parts of the world. Consumption crises raise questions over the location of global manufacturing and the fates of industrial workforces. These issues of globalization have a deep history; any history of luxury and consumer goods must form part of the long history of connections among the great regions of the world.

Much research pursued between 1990 and 2005 on aspects of luxury and consumer culture needs to be recast against new questions arising from globalization, economic recession, and the politics of consumption, and new issues of material culture centred on taste and design. We can ask, for example, did the trade in luxury goods become a drive to empire? And to what extent has the study of the objects of luxury consumption opened new directions in the history of global connections? New contexts of recession and of new consciousness of environmental costs and waste have raised a new politics of luxury. Is luxury the indicator of sharply increasing social divisions in our societies? Yet we still have so little knowledge of the history of luxury and even wider consumer cultures in many parts of Europe, and indeed wider parts of the world. Has the moral economy of luxury in the wider public and among historians themselves hindered

---

[47] James Thomson, *A Distinctive Industrialization: Cotton in Barcelona, 1728–1823* (Cambridge: Cambridge University Press, 1992); Giorgio Riello, 'The Globalization of Cotton Textiles: Indian Cotton, Europe, and the Atlantic World 1600–1850', in Giorgio Riello and Prasannan Parthasarathi (eds.), *The Spinning World: A Global History of Cotton Textiles, 1200–1850* (Oxford: Oxford University Press, 2009), 261–90; Maxine Berg, 'Quality, Cotton and the Global Luxury Trade', 391–414.

historical writing on the subject: is this more marked in some parts of Europe and Asia than in others? Finally, we need to know much more about the role of luxury in everyday life, and its manifestation in material culture. What do we know of the part played by luxury goods in the everyday life and material culture of Europeans and Asians in the early modern period? What factors transformed an 'exotic curiosity' into an export ware consumer good? And what social and cultural practices transferred the commodities of ships and warehouses to cupboards and bodies? We need to understand the objects of luxury, their perception, and their use and display. Are the real issues of luxury consumption now about aesthetics, and taste, quality and value?

BIBLIOGRAPHY

Berg, Maxine, *Luxury and Pleasure in Eighteenth-Century Britain* (Oxford: Oxford University Press, 2005).

Berg, Maxine, 'Luxury Trades', in Joel Mokyr (ed.), *Oxford Encyclopedia of Economic History*, (Oxford: Oxford University Press, 2003), 400–5.

Berg, Maxine, 'In Pursuit of Luxury: Global History and British Consumer Goods in the Eighteenth Century', *Past and Present*, 182 (2004), 85–142.

Bianchi, Marina, *The Active Consumer: Novelty and Surprise in Consumer Choice* (London: Routledge, 1998).

de Vries, Jan, *The Industrious Revolution. Consumer Behavior and the Household Economy 1650 to the Present* (Cambridge: Cambridge University Press, 2008).

Riello, Giorgio and Parthasarathi, Prasannan (eds.), *The Spinning World: A Global History of Cotton Textiles, 1200–1850* (Oxford: Oxford University Press, 2009).

Washbrook, David, 'India in the Early Modern World Economy: Modes of Production, Reproduction and Exchange', *Journal of Global History*, 2 (2007), 87–112.

CHAPTER 10

......

CITY AND COUNTRY: HOME, POSSESSIONS, AND DIET, WESTERN EUROPE 1600–1800

......

DOMINIQUE MARGAIRAZ

CITIES, particularly capital cities, have played a crucial role in the study of the changes affecting consumption in the early modern period. While cities lost some of their unskilled industrial activities to the hinterland, they became from the seventeenth century focal points for dramatic changes on the demand side, laboratories for new consumer behaviour, and orbits for new fashions and advertising.[1] At first sight, town and country appear polar opposites when it comes to ways of life and consumption, the environment, the activities and services available, the age, gender, and occupational distribution of the population, and emerging social groups, professions, and trades. Material wealth, power, and knowledge were concentrated in cities. Cities were communication and transport hubs. They served as centres of material and intellectual exchange.[2] And they were open to exchange and innovation in ways that challenged traditional norms and models of behaviour.

This picture is not the product of contemporary sociology or historiography. Already in the early modern period, urban elites defined the city as a place of civilization and cultural progress in stark opposition to the brute nature and barbarism associated with the countryside. Economic commentators were interested in consumption-related phenomena and enriched this image. In the mid-eighteenth century, Richard Cantillon assigned cities and urban property holders a key function in the evolution of commerce and economic dynamism.[3] The physiocrats, meanwhile, blamed their influence for rural underdevelopment. Jean-Baptiste Moheau, in his *Recherches et considérations sur la*

......

[1] Stephen R. Epstein, *Town and Country in Europe, 1300–1800* (Cambridge, 2001), Introduction.
[2] Bernard Lepetit, *Les villes dans la France moderne* (Paris, 1988).
[3] Richard Cantillon, *Essai sur la nature du commerce en général*, 1755 (Paris, 1997).

population de la France (1778), developed at length the contrast between the frugality of rural food habits and their wealth and diversity in cities.

This description is brutally at odds with that of those moralists who castigated the taste for luxury which was supposed to be widespread, even in the countryside. Such a fantasy of universal luxury, however, did not withstand the gaze of contemporary social observers, who were at the very same time trying to piece together the budget of the lower classes, and who were stressing the destitution of the lower sort in the countryside, which was worse even than that of city workers in the textile or building trades.

This stark contrast has been subjected to significant revision by recent historians. From his research on the Tuscan countryside, Paolo Malanima has reached a more balanced picture. By the middle of the eighteenth century, there were signs of modest opulence for well-off tenant farmers who lived in the vicinity of Florence and neighbouring towns. More distant rural homes, too, benefited from material gains. Home or auto-consumption—still widespread in the first half of the century—declined thereafter, as new goods imported from the city found their way into rural homes or as ornaments into male and female dress.[4] Such a picture would certainly have come as a surprise to a traveller coming from the United Provinces. In Holland, in the Frisian countryside analysed by Jan de Vries, peasants were already widely committed to a process of productive specialization by the first half of the seventeenth century. Investment in the farm was paralleled by a transformation of daily life, as farmers acquired furniture, clocks, mirrors, and made their homes more comfortable. Peasants went to the market to sell their own products or to buy foodstuffs and manufactured goods. According to De Vries, these material changes marked the progressive integration of the Frisian countryside into urban cultural norms.[5]

What earlier authors and contemporary historians share is a view of the destiny of the early modern countryside following that of the city, a story of delayed evolution, and of a narrowing civilizational gap. The introductory examples illustrate what is at stake in the differentiation between town and countryside. First, to what extent is it possible to generalize about the differences in material surroundings and daily life between city and country? Second, are these differences, where they exist, the result of different attitudes and behaviour with regard to consumption? These questions raise the issue of the relationship between home consumption and the degree to which households were integrated into the market, but they point also to the consumption choices and preferences which can be seen in the probate inventories of material goods owned by urban and rural populations. Lastly, we need to examine the role played by location. The level of consumption and the orientation of consumer preferences are governed by so many

---

[4] Paolo Malanima, *Il lusso dei contadini: consumi e industrie nelle campagne toscane del Sei e Settecento* (Bologna, 1990).

[5] Jan De Vries, 'Peasant Demand Patterns and Economic Development: Friesland 1550–1750', in William Parke and Eric Jones (eds.), *European Peasants and their Markets* (Princeton, 1975), 205–40. See also Johan Kamermans, *Materiële cultuur in de Krimpenerwaard in de zevventiende en achttiende eeuw* (Wageningen, 1999).

factors that it is difficult to isolate the contribution made by location. Is greater consumption the result of individual wealth, of differences in status or profession, or does it simply record that a person lives in a town rather than in the country? Few studies have examined this thorny issue in a rigorous manner. However, we do have qualitative studies that at least provide some useful comparisons between equivalent social groups, such as peasants and craftsmen, inhabiting different locations.

What is at stake, therefore, is the merit of the binary opposition between town and country. Several initial observations prompt us to minimize it. First, defining a city as a certain kind of lifestyle easily leads to a tautology. Urban lifestyle ends up being both an exogenous and a dependant variable. Second, town and country often were not radically separate spaces in the early modern period. Urban walls were being demolished, and while fiscal barriers remained, suburbs spilled over into the countryside and retained agricultural activity. Agriculture, too, could be found at the heart of cities. Gardeners, pig and poultry farmers, and wine-growers could still be found in Paris in the seventeenth century.[6] Moreover, neither town nor country were homogenous units. While the hierarchy of towns was still defined through tertiary or service activities, economic, social, and cultural disparities between cities were considerable. Capital cities such as London, Paris, or Madrid, which included a royal court, or a large port city like Antwerp[7] were worlds apart from the many smaller towns. Similarly, there was not *one* but *many* countrysides, with highly diversified socio-economic profiles and different levels of prosperity and development. From the outset, therefore, we must keep in mind that contrasts between towns (or between rural areas) were in many ways just as pronounced as those between town and country. Regional location was often decisive, as in England where a rich county like Kent enjoyed a level of consumption well above that of most cities in poor Cornwall.[8]

Finally, we need to distinguish between the different kinds of commercial activity. An active seasonal or transient trade, such as fairs or peddling, allowed for the diffusion of goods from the city all the way to the most distant rural areas.[9] The sharp increase in the number of rural shops and merchants in the early modern period magnified further the availability of all sorts of goods, from textiles and pottery to regional and exotic foodstuffs such as tea.[10] The difference between town and country thus lies not in the presence or absence of commercial services, but rather in their quality. In the Lyon area, for example, there existed a significant gap between the textile shops in town, which offered a rich array

---

[6] Clément Gurvil, *Les Paysans de Paris du milieu du XVᵉ siècle au début du XVIIᵉ* (Paris, 2010).
[7] Baetens Roland and Bruno Blondé, 'À la recherche de l'identité sociale et de la culture matérielle de la bourgeoisie anversoise aux temps modernes', *Histoire, économie et société*, 13 (1994), 531–41.
[8] Marc Overton et al., *Production and Consumption in English Households, 1600–1750*, (London, 2004), Tables pp. 158 and 160.
[9] Laurence Fontaine, *Histoire du colportage en Europe XVᵉ–XIXᵉ siècle* (Paris, 1993); Dominique Margairaz, *Foires et marchés dans la France préindustrielle* (Paris, 1988).
[10] Ronald Berger, 'The development of retail trade in provincial England, *ca.* 1550–1700', *Journal of Economic History*, 40 (1980), 123–8; Hoh-Cheung Mui and Lorna H. Mui, *Shops and Shopkeeping in Eighteenth-Century England* (Kingston and London, 1989).

of goods and special types of cloth, and rural selling places, where cloth was sold next to all sorts of other goods and in a narrower range of quality and choice.[11] Similarly, fairs operated as an outlet for unsold goods that had been unable to find a market in the cities. One study of France's commercial geography suggests that the diffusion of goods was less determined by the rural or urban character of an area than by its wider regional fortune.[12]

CROWDED CITIES, SPACIOUS COUNTRYSIDE?

In the contemporary imagination, crowded cities are opposed to a spacious countryside. In reality, dwelling was more complex in early modern Europe. While large property operations did take place in big cities as early as the seventeenth century, leading to the spread of a primarily horizontal mode of housing, vertical housing remained widespread. In seventeenth-century Paris, almost three-quarters of all apartments consisted of one to three rooms; a third had a single room. However, this did not necessarily mean living in crowded quarters. The most frequent occupants of single-room dwellings were singles, widows and childless couples. Large dwellings, whether apartments or private mansions, were the exception, benefiting an affluent minority.[13]

Were country people better off? In England during the sixteenth and seventeenth centuries, the transformation of rural dwelling could be observed, as buildings turned to bricks, chimneys appeared, and separate rooms were introduced.[14] These changes reached well beyond the aristocracy to yeomen and husbandmen. The percentage of one-room dwellings fell significantly even among the less well off, to below 50 per cent in Worcestershire, for instance, by 1700. At the same time, the number of inhabitants in dwellings with four rooms or more in the county climbed to 27 per cent in 1670, slightly higher than in the East End of London (24.5 per cent).[15]

In Continental Europe however, the picture was different. Seigneurial manors, a symbol of the power exercised by their owners, lost their military attributes and, in exchange, gained ornamental features and gardens. Various improvements also broke with the tradition of the single living room still widespread in the sixteenth century, the large multi-function hall with its ceremonial role doubling up as a food-preparing space and

[11] Françoise Bayard, 'De quelques boutiques de marchands de tissus à Lyon et en Beaujolais aux XVIIᵉ et XVIIIᵉ siècles', in Geneviève Gavignaud-Fontaine, Henri Michel, and Élie Pélaquier (eds.), *De la fibre à la fripe. Le textile dans la France méridionale et l'Europe méditerranéenne (XVIIᵉ–XXᵉ siècle)* (Montpellier, 1998), 429–58.

[12] Thomas Le Roux, *Le commerce intérieur de la France à la fin du XVIIIᵉ siècle* (Paris, 1996); Guillaume Daudin, 'Domestic Trade and Market Size in Late-Eighteenth-Century France', *Journal of Economic History*, 70 (2010), 716–43.

[13] Annick Pardailhé-Galabrun, *Naissance de l'intime*, (Paris, 1988).

[14] William Hoskins, *Provincial England: Essays in social and economic history* (London, 1963), 131–48.

[15] Carole Shammas, *The Pre-industrial Consumer in England and America* (Oxford 1990), Table p. 196.

sleeping area with one or two bedrooms on the side.[16] The homes of the people, however, did not undergo a similar transformation until the very end of the eighteenth century. In the Vexin, a prosperous rural area at the margins of the Paris region, until 1770 there was a remarkable continuity in the prevalence of thatched roofs, single living spaces, small openings letting in little light, and single chimneys providing insufficient heat. In the Perche, where proto-industry was widespread, housing took up a significant share of the household budget. A simple cottage with a garden consumed 25 to 30 per cent of a cloth-maker's annual earnings. Outbuildings, cellars, stables, or barns were only found in the houses of merchant manufacturers or master clothiers. But even these more privileged groups made do with similarly basic living quarters. Almost all households lived together in a single room that jointly functioned as kitchen, common room, and bedroom. The average number of rooms used for housing marginally increased with income and social status, but the differences were small. A separate room dedicated to the children, for instance, was found only in the houses of a few merchant manufacturers and master clothiers.[17] Considering that at the same time, in Chartres, a declining town with around 12,000 inhabitants, wage-workers enjoyed on average two and a half rooms and master craftsmen three and a half rooms, it is clear that overcrowding was a rural as much as an urban phenomenon.[18]

The organization and furniture of domestic space points to additional parallels. Obviously the ability to devote rooms to a specific purpose (e.g. dining room, library, boudoir, living room) and to separate working quarters from living quarters, or areas where public reception could take place away from those devoted to intimacy, directly depended on the actual number of rooms available, and took place mostly in town. The rationalization of storage spaces, for example, made possible by the replacement of the traditional trunk by wardrobes equipped with shelves, can be observed in the countryside as well as in town. The same is true for the decline of the single bed shared by the whole family, or the spread of cupboards. The countryside was often slower in adopting such new furniture, but it did follow the same trajectory. In eighteenth-century Poitou for instance, wardrobes in rural probate inventories jumped up to 18 per cent, compared to 50 per cent in Poitiers.[19] In Brie, they appeared in 30 per cent of the inventories as early as 1750 and in 60 per cent a generation later. In Lorraine, they had reached 94 per cent by the 1770s.[20]

---

[16] M. Nassiet, 'Inventaire du manoir breton de La Chesnaye (1541)', *Histoire et sociétés rurales*, 2 (1994), 191–204.

[17] Françoise Waro-Desjardins, 'Permanences et mutations de la vie domestique au XVIIIᵉ siècle: un village du Vexin français', *Revue d'Histoire moderne et contemporaine*, 40 (1993), 1–29.

[18] Benoît Garnot, 'La culture matérielle du peuple de Chartres au XVIIIe siècle', *Annales de Bretagne*, 95 (1988), 401–10, and 'Le logement populaire au XVIIIe siècle: l'exemple de Chartres', *Revue d'histoire moderne et contemporaine*, 36 (1989), 185–210.

[19] Jacques Perret, 'Les meubles ruraux en haut Poitou au XVIIIᵉ siècle d'après les inventaires après décès', in Joseph Goy and Jean-Pierre Wallot, *Évolutions et éclatement du monde rural. France et Québec, XVIIᵉ–XXᵉ siècles* (Montréal and Paris, 1986), 488–98.

[20] Tony Volpe, 'La civilisation matérielle dans les campagnes lorraines (XVIIᵉ–XVIIIᵉ siècles)', *Annales de l'Est*, 49 (1999), 71.

The same can be said of some new technologies, which tended to show that more thought had started to be given to material comfort, even though we cannot be sure that it was seen that way at the time. By the seventeenth century, every Parisian household benefited from at least two sources of light, for three rooms on average. In Brie most households boasted at least one. In the course of the eighteenth century, urban homes advanced their lead. Fixed and mobile light fixtures diversified. In the countryside, meanwhile, the plain tallow candle gave way to a copper chandelier; in Brie, 60 per cent of the inventories listed one in 1780. Once again, the main contrast with urban culture concerned quality and range.

Heating was a second marker of the growing desire for material comfort. The stove appeared earliest in areas with cold winters, and was already widespread by the sixteenth and seventeenth centuries in Germany, Switzerland, and the Low Countries. French cities, by contrast, favoured open hearths, which gave inferior heat but were unanimously praised for being more attractive. In 1750 Paris, two out of three rooms had a hearth. Stoves only became real competition in the next two decades; even then, they were mostly found in shops and workshops. The countryside, by contrast, was less well equipped. Very often homes only had a single source of heat, the hearth in the main living room, where food was prepared. The stove was basically unknown until the end of the eighteenth century. Day and night, the surrounding cold was mitigated through mobile accessories such as warming-pans, bed-warmers and foot-heaters. These instruments, already widespread in the city, only made a slow, uneven appearance in the countryside. Half the household recorded them in Brie in the 1770s, but they were virtually unknown in the Geneva countryside. Curtains and indoor screens to fight draughts were nowhere to be found in the countryside, except in the homes of the very wealthiest households. Country dwellers made do with bedspreads, woollen blankets or eiderdowns. The bed, often a box-bed, was the main and most expensive piece of furniture, and for most the sole defence against the cold.[21]

Notwithstanding the rationalization of space, the homes of many rural merchants and urban middling groups were characterized by heaps of furniture. Rooms were frequently cluttered with several wardrobes, dressers and writing desks, two or three tables, and over 15 chairs.[22] What is clear from these mountains of stuff is that purchase and inheritance proceeded within a cultural framework that had not yet been affected by the idea of renovation. Recycling and repair were still part and parcel of a mental world that looked at accumulation (not choice and replacement) as a marker of material progress. Only upon the death of the owner, was this movable capital scattered, either distributed among the heirs or recycled through auctions for second-hand circulation.[23]

[21] Daniel Roche, *Histoire des choses banales* (Paris 1997); Roland Baetens and Bruno Blondé, *Nouvelles approches concernant la culture de l'habitat* (Antwerp, 1989); Micheline Baulant, Anton J. Schuurman, and Paul Servais (eds.), *Inventaires après décès et ventes de meubles: apports à une histoire de la vie économique et quotidienne, XIVe–XIXe* (Louvain, 1988).

[22] Alain Croix, 'Le clergé paroissial, médiateur du changement domestique?', *Annales de Bretagne et des Pays de l'Ouest*, 94 (1987), 459–74; Philippe Haudrère, 'Esquisse d'une histoire des intérieurs angevins au XVIIIᵉ siècle', *Annales de Bretagne et des Pays de l'Ouest*, 99 (1992) 227–42.

[23] See also the chapter by Evelyn Welch in this volume.

THE WORLD OF THINGS

In her seminal study of Britain in the years 1660–1760, Lorna Weatherill found that the number of objects listed in probate inventories was on average higher in cities than in the countryside, but she was careful to add that the degree depended on the kind of possession. The difference was limited for basic articles. It was more pronounced for books, mirrors, and household linen, and even more so for new goods that appeared after the mid-seventeenth century, such as china or table cutlery.[24] In their more recent study of Cornwall and Kent, Marc Overton, Jane Whittle, and colleagues reached a similar conclusion. At the same time, they stressed that city residence had limited predictive value for the ownership of such goods. The main discriminating variables were wealth, social status, and occupation.[25] In other words, it is dangerous to presume exclusively urban versus rural profiles of consumption.

Put alongside each other, regional case studies point to some general trends and observations. Across the seventeenth and eighteenth centuries, the countryside did participate in the overall multiplication of possessions and in the transformation of the material environment. Every study available for Western Europe shows an increase in the number of objects found inside households. Some even point to a higher rate of increase of household objects in the countryside due to a phase of catch-up in those goods most widespread in the seventeenth century (basic household tools), and due to the diffusion of some rare items found in seventeenth century urban probate inventories, but only occasionally in rural ones. In Brie, to the east of Paris, small peasant sharecroppers, wine-growers, and day labourers increased their basic household goods such as beds, tables, chairs, tongs, coal-pans, and irons by 40 per cent in the period, compared to an increase of 10 per cent for all probate inventories; the phenomenon did not affect the upper levels of the peasantry, large and mid-sized farm owners who were already well-equipped with the basics, so much as the local elite and craftsmen of the town of Meaux. The diffusion of less common goods was, similarly, more marked in rural households, if only because their initial rate of penetration had been so low. From 1750, one finds more table linen, bed linen and pillows, pottery and earthenware, drinking glasses, forks, armchairs, and mirrors. Yeomen farmers and smallholders made rapid strides. Thus in a century and a half, a large number of goods became common in town and countryside and the earlier quantitative gap narrowed for those goods already widespread at the start of the period. The poorest rural probate inventory from the second half of the eighteenth century is roughly equivalent to the wealthiest urban probate inventory around the period 1600–1650.[26]

---

[24] L. Weatherill, *Consumer Behaviour and Material Culture in Britain, 1660–1760* (London and New York, 1988).

[25] Overton et al., *Production and Consumption in English Households*, 137–69.

[26] Micheline Baulant, 'L'appréciation du niveau de vie. Un problème, une solution', *Histoire & mesure*, 4 (1989), 267–302.

Quantities matter, but it is important to remember that goods were tied to a way of life. Thus the fireplace trammel, the one household item which was found in every inventory at the beginning of the period, gave way to grills and spits in urban homes in France. One mode of cooking was being replaced by another, and the urban elite's taste shifted from the traditional stew to roasts and grilled dishes. At the same time, some objects and materials were disappearing in the city while they were still gaining ground in neighbouring villages. Pewter—the traditional material used in pots, goblets, plates, and for measuring tools—was being replaced by copper or earthenware, based on usage. Urban dwellers, who could afford it, replaced their straw chairs with padded ones that offered greater comfort and aesthetic pleasure. The appearance of new goods and materials was thus accompanied by the obsolescence of others. When it came to the former, the head start of the cities is beyond doubt. In the 1780s, tinplate goods still featured in half the rural probate inventories in France, but there was not a single china piece, rotating spit, umbrella, tea set, or coffee pot. Chimneys and grandfather clocks were a notable exception, found in 60 per cent of the farms in Brie. The urban-rural gap is just as wide when it comes to cultural goods. Almost every urban elite household owned books, paintings, and ornaments. They were rare in the countryside. In the 1780s, the diversification and accumulation of objects had resulted in a new gap between town and country. A minority of rural dwellers, the country squires and yeomen farmers, were more or less on a par with urban elites and craftsmen respectively in terms of their possessions. Still, some goods like upholstered furniture were shunned even by the rural elite. Whether such distinct regional uptake reflects contemporary fashions, different ways of life, or entirely different world views, is a subject for future historical research.

One way forward is to compare different regions. If we move to the north-east of the *Bassin parisien* to rural Vexin we find broadly similar trends, albeit with a delay in the material change of ordinary homes.[27] Until the 1770s, austerity was dominant, except among the aristocracy and the richest yeomen farmers. In most cases, the home was sparsely furnished, with few tables and little bed linen. Homes lacked pillowcases, handcloths and dish towels. Kitchen implements were traditional, pewter widespread. The most frequent terms found in inventories are 'used', 'bad', 'old', 'faded', 'and worn'. The countryside was still a parsimonious world, based on conservation, repairing, and recycling. Only from 1770 is it possible to observe a diffusion of basic household tools and new materials such as earthenware, a diversification of objects, and, on the tables of the wealthiest, specialized items like salad bowls, soup bowls, fruit bowls, salt shakers, and mustard pots. The new focus on ornamentation and convenience is apparent even among more modest households, which start to own more mattresses, pillows, bedspreads and covers, and warming pans. It was now that the coffee pot took off. The speed and depth of the transformation was a direct function of status and wealth, and proceeded from the nobility to the yeomen farmer and then to the labourer. Only the very poorest day labourers missed out. The trend in Vexin and Brie suggests that the bridging

---

[27] Waro-Desjardins, 'Permanences et mutations de la vie domestique', 1–29.

of the gap between levels and modes of consumption was merely a question of time and income.

Other research, however, stresses the cultural singularity of rural and particularly peasant surroundings. One study of late eighteenth-century Catalonia compared three samples of peasant probate inventories, one in Barcelona and its suburbs, another in the small town of Villafranca, roughly 30 kilometres away, and one in the surrounding countryside of Penedes. Urban surroundings strongly influenced consumption habits. Ownership of napkins, forks, chocolate-makers, silverware, jewellery, ornamental pieces, and refined furniture increased with the rate of urbanization. Mirrors, clocks, writing desks, and dressers, for instance, figured in 30 per cent of the Barcelona probate inventories, but in only 6 per cent of those from Villafranca, and a tiny 1 per cent of those from the lowlands around; calicoes appeared in 61 per cent of Barcelona's inventories, compared with 39 per cent in Villafranca, and 24 per cent in the lowlands.[28] It is debatable how much these discrepancies were a result of urban living and how much of income and economic development. The Barcelona peasants cultivated smaller plots, but carried out irrigation, and sold grain, wine, vegetables, and fruits at the urban market, while their wives were almost always textile workers for craftsmen and manufacturers in town. What is most striking, therefore, is the relative backwardness of the Barcelona *pagesos* compared to the artisans and other inhabitants of the city, whose probate inventories list a much higher number of chocolate-makers, forks, books, and luxury furniture. Thus, whatever their place of residence, the peasant mode of consumption seems to have been characterized by common traits, in Barcelona as in Vexin: a taste for sturdy objects over glass, china, and fragile showcases; and a reluctance to follow fashion, as manifest in the refusal to adopt upholstered furniture and in the continued reliance on trunks instead of wardrobes.

These trends have been observed elsewhere in Europe. In the wealthy countryside near Geneva in the late eighteenth century, there was a striking contrast between the sober appearance of rural interiors, and the sophisticated surroundings of town burghers and craftsmen, notwithstanding their reputation for moral austerity. Rural dwellers refused to adopt tin and brass, bourgeois kitchen implements, and table settings; only the coffee pot managed to cross the threshold. Tools for convenience and hygiene were far less widespread here, even though Geneva was next door and bourgeois inhabitants came to retire or vacation in these nearby country seats. Urban ways were not completely unknown but they had to fit into a material culture that stressed sturdiness and usefulness, as illustrated by the frequency of coffee grinders without corresponding coffee pots, or a rejection of the concern with appearances.[29]

[28] Belén Moreno Claverías, 'Lugar de residencia y pautas de consumo: El penedes y barcelona, 1770–1790' ('Place of residence and consumption patterns: the Penedés and Barcelona, 1770–1790'), *Revista de Historia Industrial*, 15 (2006), 139–66.

[29] David Hiler and Laurence Wiedmer, 'Le rat de ville et le rat des champs: Une approche comparative des intérieurs ruraux et urbains à Genève dans la seconde partie du XVIIIᵉ siècle', in Micheline Baulant, Anton J. Schuurman and Paul Servais (eds.), *Inventaires après décès et ventes de meubles: apports à une histoire de la vie économique et quotidienne, XIVᵉ–XIXᵉ siècle* (Louvain, 1988), 131–51.

We can explore this insight further by moving back to England.[30] In the period 1675–1725, a clear conclusion can be drawn from the comparison of the diffusion in the cities and the countryside of a dozen items representative of the new consumer trends over eight different regions. There, the distribution of these objects was very uneven, and large cities, small towns, and villages were hierarchized regardless of the social group one considers. A finer categorisation, taking into account criteria of wealth and occupational status, does modify the distribution outcome significantly for four key items— pewter, potteries, clocks, and mirrors. In the two counties of Cornwall and Kent, the following trend emerges for the period 1600 to 1740: while rarer and novelty goods, such as mirrors, padded furniture, tea or coffee sets, and books, were found earlier and more frequently in the cities, some rural groups equalled or in some cases surpassed their urban counterparts. Thus, Cornwall yeomen accumulated books in the seventeenth century. In both counties, it was farmers who practised a mix of subsistence and commercial agriculture who appear to have been particularly open to innovation; already in 1650 clocks, books, and plates were found more frequently in their homes than in the cities. A finer comparative analysis of yeomen farmers and urban craftsmen shows that there were important gaps, depending on which good or period was considered. In Kent, yeomen farmers held an early lead over craftsmen in spits and padded furniture at the beginning of the seventeenth century, but ended up trailing at its end. At the beginning of the eighteenth century, tea or coffee sets could be found in roughly equal percentages among both groups, but throughout the period artisans had more mirrors. Regressions reveal that status and urban residence were more decisive influences on consumer behaviour than wealth as such. Still, even these factors were dependent on the particular good and period under consideration.[31]

In the final analysis, ownership resulted from a process of accumulation over several generations as well as of individual choices linked to personal life paths and histories. Together, these produced a much more diversified, complex picture than one determined only by occupation and residence. This is why inventories do not give us much information about what it means to own and consume goods.[32] Historians often associate the city with ostentatious behaviour, individualism, and status-seeking as opposed to a rural adherence to community, tradition, and hierarchy. The same historians, however, also stress the accumulation of linen in the trunks of the wealthiest farmers as a clear sign of status-seeking. A 'big laundry' symbolized social power. In Avignon bed sheets were used to decorate the streets during public festivals. Goods, similarly, marked the major events in the life cycle of the family—weddings and funerals, the baptism and churching of women—where the shroud of the deceased, the hope chest of the young bride, the bed sheets of the mother delivered of a new baby, the

[30] Lorna Scammell (Weatherill), 'Town versus country: the property of everyday consumption in the late seventeenth and early eighteenth centuries', in Jon Stobart and Alastair Owens (eds.), *Urban Fortunes: Property and Inheritance in the Towns, 1700–1900*, (Aldershot 2000), 35–49.

[31] Overton et al., *Production and consumption in English households*, Tables pp. 195–200.

[32] Dominique Poulot, 'Une nouvelle histoire de la culture matérielle?', *Revue d'histoire moderne et contemporaine*, 44 (1997), 344–57.

tablecloths and napkins of the wedding feast, were public manifestations of their own-er's rank.[33] Other historians have stressed the usefulness of objects in rural areas,[34] but use-value, exchange-value, and symbolic value were inextricably intertwined. Precious metals in the form of useful (cutlery or goblets), decorative (chandeliers), or religious objects (crucifixes) were at the same time assets and investments. Was their decline in the countryside in the eighteenth century, a sign of the conversion of rural dwellers to consumer culture, a consequence of a process of substitution that favoured house-hold linen, or of the growing uptake of government bonds? Probate inventories do not tell us about how or why a good is owned. What they do enable us to do is to identify the 'cultural intermediaries' leading the diffusion of new goods. A French study has highlighted the central role of local priests in the diffusion of furniture and books in Brittany.[35] English historians have identified the gentry as trendsetters when it comes to the adoption of new objects in the eighteenth century, followed by the professions and other groups linked to the commercial and service sectors—all mobile and in touch with city life in the eighteenth century.[36]

URBAN AND RURAL DRESS

In his seminal work on Paris, Daniel Roche identified several stages and mechanisms in the transformation of clothing practices between the late seventeenth and late eighteenth centuries.[37] In Paris, the share of clothes in the household budget increased for all social groups, rising by up to 172 per cent in constant prices. According to Roche, the sharp increase reflected Paris' lead over provincial towns that were them-selves breaking away from their surrounding countryside, where the dominant econ-omy was still one of wear and tear and second-hand. This evaluation fits with contemporary judgements, such as that of the Baroness of Oberkirch, whose autobi-ography stressed the gap between the capital city and the provinces, even though the latter were kept informed of Parisian fashion through myriad channels, from private correspondence to specialized gazettes.[38] Paris thus can be used as a point of entry to

---

[33] Madeleine Ferrières, *Le bien des pauvres: la consommation populaire en Avignon (1600–1800)* (Seyssel, 2004), 148–9.

[34] Lorena Walsh, 'Urban Amenities and Rural Sufficiency: Living Standards and Consumer Behavior in the Colonial Chesapeake, 1643–1777', *Journal of Economic History*, 43 (1983), 109–17; Gérard Béaur, Christian Dessureault and Joseph Goy (eds.), *Famille, Terre, Marchés. Logiques économiques et stratégies dans les milieux ruraux (XVIIᵉ–XXᵉ siècles)*, (Rennes, 2004); David Hiler and Laurence Wiedmer, 'Le rat de ville et le rat des champs', p. 146–7.

[35] Alain Croix, 'Le clergé paroissial'; Overton et al., *Production and Consumption in English Households*, 166–7.

[36] Overton et al., *Production and Consumption in English Households*, 166–7.

[37] Daniel Roche, *La culture des apparences: Une histoire du vêtement XVIIᵉ–XVIIIᵉ siècle*, (Paris 1989).

[38] *Mémoires de la baronne d'Oberkirch sur la cour de Louis XVI et la société française avant 1789*, ed. and annotated Suzanne Burkard (Paris, 2000), 304.

assess the discrepancies between the respective dynamics of consumer behaviour, from the elite's extravagant accumulation, on the one hand, to the clothing strategies of the most humble, on the other.

Two basic elements characterized the Parisian clothing economy during the Enlightenment. First, we see a double move towards the unification as well as diversification of clothing. Unification, because some pieces of clothing became generalized. Five main pieces formed the basis for women's clothes: the dress, the petticoat, the coat, the apron, and the bodice or *corps de robe*. These pieces were already set by the sixteenth century. Although coat and dress remained rare among wage earners and craftsmen, dress and bodice, as well as the short coat became generalized during the eighteenth century. The number of pieces of clothing also increased in the wardrobes of all Parisians.[39] Diversification, at the other extreme, resulted from the multiplication of patterns, an accompanying profusion of new terms to describe variations, and the proliferation of accessories and ornaments which allowed the wearer to update an outfit in accordance with seasonal fashion. It also grew out of the variety of new materials and colours which, just as with variations in shape and design, expressed refinement and distinctiveness. Cotton and calico, long forbidden, introduced lightness and softness even in lower-class wardrobes.[40] Shoes, which started to replace clogs, were still a rarity, except amongst the rich. The evolution of the male wardrobe followed a similar pattern. The formal components initially common to all (doublet, vest, and breeches) were slightly modified with the doublet fading out, and the spread of the waistcoat and of the frock coat. Still, the main trend was one of generalization of these basic forms, a multiplication of accessories, and a diversification of colours and materials.

A second marker of the unification of clothing codes can be found in the spread of the underwear, shirt, and stockings, for men as well as women. Here again, social differences were reflected in the number of pieces owned, which enabled more or less frequent changes, and an ability to put new conventions of hygiene into practice. Similarly, the demand for white linen—costly to maintain—was a clear sign of wealth and status.[41] Differentiation was reinforced by a diversification of nightcaps, nightshirts, and negligees. The price of stockings ranged from 1 to 15 *livres* a pair, depending on whether they were made of wool, cotton, or silk.

Women played an increasingly decisive role in this economy of fashion. In the reign of Louis XIV, the wardrobes of the wives of the nobility was on average worth twice that of their husbands. They set a trend for the rest of society. In the lower classes, among wage earners or craftsmen, as well as among the bourgeoisie, women assumed an increasingly important pioneer function in the course of the eighteenth century. Whereas among the lower classes, men's and women's wardrobes were of approximately

---

[39] Roche, *La culture des apparences*, Tables pp. 123 and 189 (for women and men).
[40] Ibid., Tables pp. 127 and 137.
[41] Ibid., Table p. 162

equal value in 1700, women's were worth 92 *livres* on average a century later, almost three times that of men's.[42]

The triumph of appearance thus had contradictory results. The gap between the richest and the rest widened. At the same time, the diffusion of fashions and tastes made it more difficult to read social hierarchy of clothes. There was greater individual choice. Since the rich were required to renew their wardrobes, they put in motion a whole secondary circuit.[43] Servants received clothes as gifts from their masters and turned some of them over to second-hand dealers. From here novelties and fashions diffused across society. This circulation was not yet powerful enough to create a universal popular style—many craftsmen and wage earners hung onto sturdy and durable materials in dark colours—but it did create a popular channel for new fashions and materials.

Neither the provincial towns nor the rural world remained untouched by this change. What varied was the particular form and intensity of the experience. Averages can be misleading and comparisons, to be useful, need to involve equivalent status and income. No provincial town could equal Paris' concentration of elites and their wealth; in 1700, in the capital, 50 per cent of the nobility's movable property exceeded 50,000 *livres tournois*. On average, the wardrobe of a Parisian nobleman was worth 37 times what a journeyman earned in a year.[44] Let us compare this to Count Boyer from Albi, in the south of France, a provincial town of 11,800 souls. Boyer lived in grand style on a yearly income of 18,000 *livres tournois* in the 1780s. The countess's *livre de raison* (account book) showed a strong taste for finery; she was a lady up to date with Paris fashion. Her rich wardrobe contained a variety of dresses, fitted coats, shirts, camisoles, corsets, petticoats, party novelties, *négligés*, ornamented aprons, stockings by the dozen, hats and headdresses galore; a range of valuable material: taffeta, satin, silk, calico, lawn, cambric, muslin, and gauze. What set the provincial aristocrat apart from the Parisian *élégantes* was the slower pace of fashionable consumption. Two dresses, four pairs of stockings, four or five pairs of shoes a year, a pelisse every five years, and two aprons every ten years: none of these matched the extremes of the Parisian courtiers.[45]

Let us now compare the lower classes in metropolis and provinces. Chartres (12,000 inhabitants in 1700, 10,700 in 1780), the cathedral town about 100 kilometres south-west of Paris, offers a good example. In 1700 masters and wage earners here had a smaller

---

[42] Ibid, p. 111.

[43] Ibid, p. 111; Beverly Lemire, 'Consumerism in Pre-Industrial and Early Industrial England: The Trade in Second-hand Clothes', *Journal of British Studies*, 27 (1988), 1–24; Jutta Zander Seidel, 'Ready-to-wear clothing in Germany in the sixteenth and seventeenth centuries: new ready-made garments and second-hand clothes', and Bernard du Mortier, 'Introduction into the used-clothing market in the Netherlands', in *Per una storia della moda pronta* Atti del V Convegno Internazionale del Centro Italiano per lo studio della Storia del Tessuto, (Florence, 1991), 9–16, 117–25; Madeleine Ferrières, 'Le circuit de la fripe à Avignon', in Geneviève Gavignaud-Fontaine, Henri Michel, and Élie Pélaquier (eds.), *De la fibre à la fripe: Le textile dans la France méridionale et l'Europe méditerranéenne (XVIIᵉ–XXᵉ siècle)* (Montpellier 1998); Laurence Fontaine (ed.), *Alternative Exchanges: Second-Hand Circulations from the Sixteenth Century to The Present* (New York and Oxford, 2008).

[44] Roche, *La culture des apparences*, 97.

[45] Ibid., 196–7.

number of clothes than their Parisian counterparts.[46] For women, this picture must be qualified: the number of skirts in inventories was similar. Indeed, in Chartres, crafts-men's wives had more dresses. In the course of the eighteenth century, men in Chartres were catching up though still lagging behind in the number of items owned. Women had almost as many skirts as those in Paris, and a greater number of aprons. While corsets tended to replace *corps de robe* in Paris, the latter was still much in use in Chartres, particularly among wage earners' wives. Here the revolution of fabrics had barely begun: wool still dominated, together with strong fabrics like broadcloth, hemp for shirts. Grey, brown, and black remained the most popular colours. Except for headdresses, the lower orders in Chartres had few accessories. In sum, a wide gulf in quality and variety separated the clothes of the people in Chartres from those of the fashionable capital.

Some 50 kilometres to the west of Chartres lies rural Perche, one of the pre-industrial regions of cloth-making.[47] Its population was made up of more or less independent craftsmen who did some farming on the side, and of labourers who were hired by a small elite of rural merchant-manufacturers. In the first half of the eighteenth century, the average male wardrobe in Perche ranked below that of Parisian masters but above that of craftsmen in Chartres. Waistcoats arrived in the 1730s together with collars; dou-blets disappeared. With the exception of dependent weavers, in the next half century all groups enjoyed a further increase in the number of the various items and accessories owned. The men of Perche had more shirts, trousers, and coats than Parisian masters. The number of collars, leggings, and other novelties rose sharply, while ties and under-pants were on the wane. What differentiated social groups was quantity and quality. Merchant-manufacturers played the most active role in renewing fabrics and adopting new colours, even though cottons were still marginal in the 1770s and 1780s. Change was brought about first by the rural petit bourgeoisie, whose mobility connected them to the towns. Still, change was uneven and gendered. The change of women's dress allows us to address the reach of the industrious revolution in a region marked by rural industrial work. In 1700, skirts, for example, were much less frequently mentioned in Perche than in either Paris or Chartres. Dresses and *corps*, by contrast, were widespread. The female consumer in Perche could call a greater number of shirts and stockings her own, some probably home-made. Shoes were mentioned in 54 per cent of the inventories, on a par with Parisian working women. In the second half of the century, Perche broke with the urban trend in the female wardrobe. The *corps* became more widespread, while the pet-ticoat declined. The women of Perche wore more aprons than anywhere else and they adopted scarves. At the same time, they wore fewer shoes—probably swapping them for clogs, which were so cheap that they were not recorded in inventories. In general, the number of shirts owned declined. The universalization of dress was paid for by each

[46] Benoit Garnot, 'Le vêtement populaire féminin à Chartres au XVIIIe siècle', in *112e Congrès national des Sociétés savantes* (Lyon, 1987) ; and *Sociétés, cultures et genres de vie dans la France moderne XVIe–XVIIIe siècles* (Paris, 1991), 104–5.

[47] Claude Cailly, 'Structure sociale et consommation dans le monde proto-industriel rural textile: le cas du Perche ornais au XVIIIe siècle', *Revue d'Histoire Moderne and Contemporaine*, 45 (1998), 746–74.

woman owning one of each new item. Again, social differentiation was a result of quality as much as quantity. Old fabrics like wool and hemp continued to dominate while skirts, *corps*, and handkerchiefs were becoming more colourful.

In the Vexin countryside, by contrast, change came later, but when it did women were at the helm.[48] Until about 1770, dress consisted of little more than a few hemp shirts, a couple of skirts, one or two pairs of wool stockings for women, and clogs for most. Only landlords' wives had dresses and corsets. Labouring men on average owned 13 hemp shirts, one or two suits (trousers, jacket, and doublet), a hat, one pair of shoes, and no coat. The textile revolution got underway in 1770. *Corps* disappeared, while accessories such as shawls made their entry. The number of pieces owned shot up, as did the number of coloured, striped, and checked fabrics. Woollen fabrics had to compete with softer and lighter materials with a mix of cotton. Linen was still rare except for shirts, but the rise of headdresses and bonnets was spectacular. For men, the changes were less noticeable but no less real: waistcoats and collars spread. Brighter colours took the place of dark or poorly dyed fabrics. Nonetheless, the pace of change was of a different order than that in Paris, as testified by the frequent use of 'worn' or 'used' in inventories. Clothes did not only have be fashionable, they had to be worn out before they were replaced, and thanks to the better-off change moved in at a rather slow rate.

Can we conclude from these itineraries of town and country that the consumers' profiles and structural determiners were different? In 1700 Paris, the mean value of the working-class wardrobe was the equivalent of 9 per cent of a nobleman's. By 1789, this figure had dropped to 1.4 per cent. Meanwhile, in Perche the inventory with the lowest value of clothes continued to amount to 25 per cent of that with the most costly wardrobe across the whole period. In other words, inequalities advanced most radically in a big city. The regime of novelty and fashion had a far less significant impact on the countryside.[49] Novelty did reach the provinces but with different effects. Hans Medick showed how at Laichingen, a small town of 2,000 people in Wurttemberg, the arrival of blue colours helped perpetuate an older culture of respect and consideration, in which clothes assigned social rank.[50] Only a micro-analysis can shed light on whether novelty was appropriated as an instrument of conservation or choice and emancipation. Ostentatious behaviour was not an exclusive trait of cities. Country folk could use new fabrics and accessories or fabrics for their own distinct forms of hierarchy and differentiation.

---

[48] Waro-Desjardins, 'Permanences et mutations de la vie domestique'. See also for another example Volpe, 'La civilisation matérielle'.

[49] Cissie Fairchild, 'Determinants of Consumption Patterns in Eighteenth-Century France', in Anton Schuurman and Lorena Walsh (eds.), *Material Culture: Consumption, Life-style, Standard of Living, 1500–1900* (Milan, 1994), 55–67.

[50] Hans Medick, *Weben und Überleben in Laichingen, 1650–1900*, (Göttingen, 1997), 427–46; or Hans Medick, 'Une culture de la considération: Les vêtements et leurs couleurs à Laichingen entre 1750 et 1820', *Annales, Histoire, sciences sociales*, 50 (1995), 753–74.

FEEDING ONESELF IN TOWN
AND COUNTRYSIDE

In contrast to research on the nineteenth and twentieth centuries, work on the early modern period lacks the data that would allow us to offer an aggregate picture of food consumption in town and country. We have to rely on scattered documentation, including *livres de raison*, account books of lay or Church authorities, and registers recording the entries of those taxable goods legally imported into the towns. Any comparison between town and country needs to bear in mind several points. First, home consumption was not exclusively a country practice: townspeople also consumed produce from their own lands, especially wine, poultry and game, cheese, and fruit and vegetables. Towns benefited from gardens and livestock which offered independent sources of supply. Second, home consumption did not uniformly decline in the seventeenth and eighteenth centuries. For example, while auto-consumption declined in Cornwall, homemade bread, dairy products, and alcohol increased in Kent.[51] Third, the end of homemade production was not necessarily a question of choice, nor was it the preserve of the well off: changes in the agrarian economy and the proletariarization of the small peasantry prevented a number of farmers from keeping a vegetable garden, a cow, or poultry. Large-scale farmers with marketable surpluses, by contrast, could partly live off the produce of their farm, even though grain was generally no longer ground domestically. In towns, meanwhile, the rich used home consumption to underscore their rank as property owners with vineyards and estates in the countryside.

We know more about those food items that were produce for the market. Big metropoles like London and Paris benefited from a striking abundance and diversity of goods. Grains, flour, breads, wine and beer, meats, poultry, fish and shellfish, eggs, butter, cheeses, fruits, spices, exotic foodstuffs, and drinks were sold in specialized markets or shops.[52] Delivering such massive quantities into Paris required a market ready to absorb them. It also necessitated that, overall, the population enjoyed a richer and more diversified diet. The question is, just how rich and diversified it was, and to what degree it set towns more generally apart from the country?

For most Europeans the staple food was the same in town and country. They ate cereals in the form of breads or gruels—more or less depending on their complementary diet of vegetables, fat, meat, eggs, and fish. In Paris, the average person consumed 500g of bread—in Toulouse even 600g. Direct comparisons with the countryside, however, are difficult. Bread in cities was generally of higher quality and more nutritious. Meat was largely the preserve of town dwellers. Quantities varied from city to city. Towards

---

[51] Overton al., *Production and consumption in English* households, Table p. 193–4.
[52] Reynald Abad, *Le grand marché: l'approvisionnement alimentaire de Paris sous l'Ancien Régime* (Paris, 2002).

the end of the eighteenth century, the average person in Grenoble ate 26kg of meat per year, that in Caen around 32kg. In Paris and Geneva, meanwhile, inhabitants consumed more than double that amount.[53] In general, the long-term trend was downward. Eighteenth-century Europeans ate less meat than their medieval ancestors. In the country, most people had to settle for bacon boiled in soup, and ate pork or tripe on holidays. Fish, which was plentiful in towns, only reached rural consumers who lived near the sea. Drink and beverages were equally differentiated. Unless it was spring water, unboiled water was avoided since rivers and wells were often contaminated. In the country, cheap wine, cider, and pear brandy quenched the thirst. Wine spread more broadly in towns where by the eighteenth century it was a common drink for the lower sorts. In Lyon, for example, everyone drank on average 0.3 litre a day. The average Parisian enjoyed just over half a litre. This general picture, however, needs some qualification. This average is based on the entire population, including children, although this does not mean that the children drank wine. Also, in the country many lords and clergy enjoyed a rich table. In the Auvergne in the eighteenth century, rich landlords too consumed exotic foodstuffs and fruits, coffee, sugar, and citrus fruits.[54] This was a far cry from the diet of ordinary country folk. Still, even lower social groups were never completely cut off from the culinary world of the local aristocracy thanks also to a culture of gifting and redistribution.

In city and country, people shared one common feature in their diets: imbalance. The general diet was short in animal proteins and relied excessively on carbohydrates. Most people suffered from a lack of lipids and minerals, especially calcium. The nutrition of the rural poor, who often relied on bread alone for 80 per cent of their diet, accompanied by the rare piece of bacon or cheese, was seriously deficient. The result was stunted growth and a weak immune system.[55] Yet even elites who enjoyed greater abundance and variety suffered from deficiencies in vitamins and in lipids found in oils, dairy products, and oily fish. Irrespective of whether they ate decent meals or ate too little, early modern Europeans were rarely well fed.

Where an urban lifestyle was most conspicuously different was in the way food was prepared, served and cooked. Kitchens in Geneva included a variety of utensils designed for kneading, mincing, and pounding that were unknown in the countryside. Urban cooking relied heavily on grilled and roasted food, and meals incorporated a new etiquette of dining and table manners, reflected in the various grades of crockery, cutlery, glassware, and table linen. The eating rhythms changed as supper and dinner started to

[53] Bartolomé Bennassar and Joseph Goy, 'Contribution à l'histoire de la consommation alimentaire du XIVᵉ au XIXᵉ siècle', Annales ESC, 30 (1975), 402–30; Anne-Marie Piuz, 'Le marché du bétail et la consommation de la viande à Genève au XVIIIᵉ siècle', Annales ESC, 30 (1975), 575–83.

[54] Pierre Charbonnier, 'La consommation des seigneurs auvergnats du XVᵉ au XVIIIᵉ siècle', Annales ESC, 30 (1975), 465–77.

[55] Paolo Malanima, 'Changing Patterns in Rural Living Conditions: Tuscany in the Eighteenth Century', in Anton Schuurman and Lorena Walsh (eds.), Material Culture, 118; Jacques Vedel, 'La consommation alimentaire dans le haut Languedoc aux XVIIᵉ et XVIIIᵉ siècles', Annales ESC, 30 (1975), 478–90.

be served later and later in town. New eating places such as restaurants and cafés sprang up which provided a space for new forms of sociability.

CONCLUSION

What general conclusions can be drawn from the variety of local contrasts and uneven terrains we have encountered? The difficulty of reaching a synthetic picture points to the importance of the scale of observation used. It also highlights the danger of an easy assumption that the type of location must have had a decisive influence in structuring consumer behaviour and lifestyle. Recent historical work has brought out significant contrasts between rural regions as well as between cities of comparable size, such as Glasgow and Edinburgh.[56] The advance of urbanization no longer looks as straightforward as it once did. Researchers, therefore, need to be clear about the unit of observation that they employ when investigating rural and urban material culture. Only then is it possible to embark on appropriate qualitative and quantitative lines of inquiry.

What is clear is the contribution of the countryside to new forms of consumption that were emerging in the early modern period. This concerned not only the acquisition of new objects but the obsolescence of certain other goods and practices. The expanding empire of fashion was especially important in extending the scope of purchase and participation in this new consumer culture. Some authors have envisaged this process in terms of diffusion, from metropoles to provincial cities and then to the countryside. It is worth noting that such a general scheme is derived from a few particular cases, such as the role of Paris or the model of the gentleman farmer.[57] The fact remains that we know far too little for large areas of Europe to know whether this diffusionist model has general explanatory power. Our knowledge is pointillist and fragmented, by region and topic. Some scholars pinpoint the frequency of the appearance of certain items, others pay attention to the value of goods/property/possessions, and still others that it is represented in the furniture fortunes. An integrated discussion of lived material culture is rare. At the quantitative level, too, synthesis is difficult, at best partially successful. Inventories are unevenly distributed across time periods and regions and reflect the different standards and codes of the legal cultures. One way forward is to operationalize working hypotheses, such as those of the dynamics of emulation or the industrious revolution. Another is to follow more rigorously the changing rhythms and modalities

---

[56] In addition to Weatherill's and Overton and Whittle's work, see also Carole Shammas, 'Food Expenditures and Economic Well-Being in Early Modern England', *Journal of Economic History*, 43 (1983), Tables p. 93 and 98. Stana Nenadic, 'Middle-Rank Consumers and Domestic Culture in Edinburgh and Glasgow 1720–1840', *Past & Present*, 145 (1994), 122–56. Compare Shammas's chapter in this volume.

[57] Marco Belfanti and Fabio Giusberti, 'Clothing and Social Inequality in Early Modern Europe: Introductory Remarks', *Continuity and Change*, 15 (2000), 359–65.

of consumption, and not to confuse the act of consumption, as recorded in *livres de raison*, with the possession of goods.[58] How new fashion regimes are diffused and socially stratified in small towns and the countryside, their means of distribution and their hierarchy, for example, is still insufficiently known, with the partial exception of England and France.[59] The provision of new and second-hand goods in smaller cities and rural Europe remains a subject for future research. There remains plenty to do for comparative historians of town and country.

Bibliography

Kamermans, Johan, *Materiële Cultuur in de Krimpenerwaard in de zeventiende en achttiende eeuw. Ontwikkeling en diversiteit* (Wageningen: Landbouwuniversiteit Wageningen en verloren, 1999).

Malanima, Paolo, *Il lusso dei contadini: consumi e industrie nelle campagne toscane del Sei e Settecento* (Bologna: il Mulino, 1990).

Meyzie, Philippe, *Histoire de l'alimentation en Europe* (Paris: A. Colin, 2010).

Overton, Mark, Whittle, Jane, Dean, Darron and Hann, Andrew, *Production and Consumption in English Households, 1600–1750* (London: Routledge, 2004).

Pardailhé-Galabrun, Annick, *Naissance de l'intime* (Paris: PUF, 1988).

Revista de Historia Economica 2003, *Consommations textiles*, special number, Vol. 21, Supplement S1 (April 2010).

Roche, Daniel, *La culture des apparences. Une histoire du vêtement XVIIe–XVIIIe siècle* (Paris: Fayard, 1989); English edn.: Daniel Roche, *The Culture of Clothing: Dress and Fashion in the 'Ancien Régime'* (Cambridge: Cambridge University Press, 1994).

Roche, Daniel, *Histoire des choses banales* (Paris: Fayard, 1997); English edn.: Daniel Roche, Daniel, *A History of Everyday Things: The Birth of Consumption in France 1600–1800* (Cambridge: Cambridge University Press, 2000).

Shammas, Carole, *The Pre-industrial Consumer in England and America* (Oxford: Clarendon Press, 1990).

Wiegelmann, Gunter and Mohrmann, Ruth E. (eds.), *Nahrung und Tischkultur im Hanseraum*, (Münster: Waxman, 1996).

[58] An example of exploitation of an account book, that of Barbara Johnson, a clergyman's daughter, who notes all his expenses from 1757 to 1825: Beverly Lemire, *Fashion's Favourite: The Cotton Trade and the Consumer in Britain, 1680–1800*, (Oxford, 1991). See also, eadem, *The Business of Everyday Life: Gender, Practice and Social Politics in England, c. 1600–1900* (Manchester, 2005), ch. 7.

[59] Natacha Coquery (ed.), *La boutique et la ville: Commerces, commerçants, espaces et clientèles, XVIe–XXe siècles* (Tours, 2000).

CHAPTER 11

....

STANDARD OF LIVING, CONSUMPTION, AND POLITICAL ECONOMY OVER THE PAST 500 YEARS

....

CAROLE SHAMMAS

THE words 'standard of living' are closely identified with a more than century long debate in both the popular press and academic journals about the effects of the early stages of industrialization on the working class, especially in nineteenth-century Britain. According to Eric Hobsbawm, one of the primary combatants during the 1950s instalment of the controversy, the debate originated with the *pessimists*, Marx being one of the most famous and earliest. The fact that Western European and North American nations were experiencing a dramatic growth in their manufacturing sectors explains the rising popularity of the term as opinions differed as to the costs and benefits of this economic transformation. *Pessimists* contended that nineteenth-century industrialization brought greater wealth to capitalists but a lower standard of living to the families of nineteenth-century workers. Picking up momentum during the interwar period and into the Cold War when communism seemed a growing threat in the world, the *optimists* argued against that position, citing long-term wage increases and price declines that improved consumption for all. They looked instead to causes unrelated to capitalism to explain what they considered dips in living standards.[1] For both sides, standard of living largely meant gauging the proportion of disposable income that average or poor households spent on the consumption of material goods, especially food, clothing, shelter, and fuel. Gradually those studying earlier periods and other continents made use of the concept,

---

[1] E. J. Hobsbawm, 'The British Standard of Living 1790–1850', *Economic History Review* 10/1 (1957), 46–68.

and while the term continues to be employed in the post-industrial period, the measurement of it has changed substantially. Per capita gross domestic product (GDP) has become a substitute for both household budget data and real income (income adjusted by the cost of a market basket of goods) statistics in many cross-national comparisons due to its broad availability. Also, indicators of longevity, health, and education of the population have been added to the measurement of standard of living and in scholarship often take precedence over income and expenditure data.

In this chapter, I discuss when and why the consumption of material goods became the measure of the 'standard of living' and, secondly, what has led to its displacement in more recent times. These shifts provide insight into changing assumptions about the desirability of household accumulation. I track the state of our knowledge about transformations in living standards from the early modern period on, and discuss whether a longer and broad historical view has demoted industrialization as a causal factor.

Promoting Well-Being by Limiting Consumption

The fact that 'standard of living' did not commonly roll off the lips or the presses prior to the nineteenth-century does not mean that people earlier lacked a concept of 'life's necessaries', a word that does appear frequently, at least in English language publications.[2] It does reveal, however, the absence of governmental criteria for well-being and the timidity of welfare advocates to put forward a pro-consumption agenda. What instead appears in both medieval and early modern Europe and Asia are policies intended to limit consumption of food and clothing, most notably through sumptuary laws. While some of the motivation for sumptuary regulations that only permitted certain classes to have dietary delicacies, large numbers of courses at meals, specific kinds of clothing, and particular construction materials might have been to support a hierarchical social structure, the principal justification was to prevent people from squandering their money on luxuries, especially imported ones, rather than attending to their basic needs.[3] Furthermore, governments employed a variety of other measures to restrict mass consumption and spread around work and goods, including the imposition of wage ceilings on artisanal and agricultural labour, and price controls on 'necessaries' such as bread and grains to stop those who tried to corner the market in times of shortages. Kin and local communities in some countries were forced to share their resources with the impoverished by restricting migration and the assessing of taxes on villages rather than

---

[2] Statement based upon a search of *Early English Books Online, Eighteenth-Century Collections Online, American Periodical Series, Proquest Historical Newspapers.*

[3] Such laws were very common globally as can be seen by the bibliography in Alan Hunt, *Governance of the Consuming Passions: A History of Sumptuary Law* (New York, St Martin's Press, 1966).

individual households, meaning the economically viable households had to make up for the indigent ones. Those unable to support themselves had to submit to servitude in a household that could feed and clothe them. As I have noted elsewhere,[4] demand and distribution were hierarchically structured, with heads of households making consumption decisions for family members, servants, and retainers. Customs and excises taxes, while primarily instituted for revenue purposes, at times were also instituted to curtail consumption. The Christian Church and religious orders in Europe took responsibility for those whose illness, disabilities, or age prevented them from being employed.

Policies of curtailing individual household consumption of necessities were consistent with a belief that the measure of a country's and a ruler's power and wealth was the size of its population: more people available to pay taxes and more men available to bear arms.[5] That belief meant that government policy aimed at keeping the maximum number of people alive through the enforced frugality of the generality: discourage consumption and hope through sumptuary regulations, wage and price controls, and as a last resort charity and parish subsidies to keep numbers up. Needless to say, individual households did not necessarily share these objectives. The attack on Catholic institutions during the Reformation also brought to the fore the situation of the poor. Local governments in Protestant countries gradually supplemented charitable giving with support payments for 'worthy' unfortunates and constructed workhouses for the 'sturdy' poor. In the process governments found it necessary to define minimum standards of living.[6]

While the view that a polity's strength was a function of its population size enjoyed amazing staying power, one can see erosion in the policies supporting the principle as early as the seventeenth century, at least in some Western European countries. Sumptuary laws, for example, disappeared and officials less regularly issued and policed wage and price caps. At the same time, treatises and pamphlets in the new field of political economy, or as the English called it, political arithmetic, surfaced and presented conceptions of a country's well-being that went beyond just number of people.[7] In these writings, authors not only argued about how governments should respond to the dramatic growth in global trade and colonization but buttressed their arguments with

[4] Carole Shammas, *The Pre-Industrial Consumer in England and America* (Oxford, Clarendon Press, 1990, reprinted Figueroa Press, 2008), ch. 7.

[5] Stanley L. Engerman, 'The Standard of Living Debate in International Perspective: Measures and Indicators', in Richard H. Steckel (ed.), *Health and Welfare during Industrialization* (Chicago, University of Chicago Press, 2008), 20–1.

[6] Shammas, *The Pre-Industrial Consumer* ch. 7; E. Merrick Dodd, 'From Maximum Wages to Minimum Wages: Six Centuries of Regulation of Employment Contracts', *Columbia Law Review*, 43/5 (1943), 643–87; the James Z. Lee and Cameron D. Campbell, and Noriko O. Tsuya and Satomi Kurosu articles in Robert C. Allen, Tommy Bengtsson, and Martin Dribe (eds.), *Living Standards in the Past: New Perspectives on Well-Being in Asia and Europe* (Oxford, Oxford University Press, 2005); Ole Peter Grell and Andrew Cunningham (eds.), *Health Care and Poor Relief in Protestant Europe 1500–1700* (London, Routledge, 1997); and Ole Peter Grell, Andrew Cunningham, and Jon Arrizabalaga (eds.), *Health Care and Poor Relief in Counter-Reformation Europe* (London, Routledge, 1999).

[7] On sumptuary law decline see source in note 2. On all of these changes, see Shammas, *Pre-Industrial Consumer*, ch. 5.

estimates of annual incomes and expenditures.[8] Whether applauding the increased affluence brought by commerce and expanded empire or fearing the indulgence of some in luxury, commentators fixated on consumption and that fixation ultimately led to an examination of the standard of living. It might be recalled that in 1695 political arithmetician Tory Gregory King drew up his famous 'A Scheme of the Income and Expenses of the Several Families of England calculated for the Year 1688' to show the Williamite Whig government how war against Louis XIV had impoverished the population.[9] Poverty, moreover, was a public issue because the costs of parish relief were paid through local taxation.

POLITICAL ECONOMY, INDUSTRIALIZATION AND THE EMERGENCE OF A STANDARD OF LIVING DEBATE

As indicated by Gregory King's 'Scheme', quantitative investigation into the consumption of the general population pre-dated any debate about industrialization and its effects on the families of workers, and instead emerged out of the new practice in the empires of trade to link politics and economics. Even actual surveys rather than estimates of household expenditures pre-dated mass industrialization. The first ones that I am aware of were taken in 1790s' England by two observers holding rather different theories about the causes of a low standard of living, and neither tied the problem specifically to manufacturing. David Davies, a minister, hoped the impoverished condition of the agricultural labourers he queried would pressure landlords and farmers to raise their compensation. On the other hand, Frederick Morton Eden believed his surveys of poor households in both town and country and his lists of wages and prices would demonstrate that better dietary habits and more frugal practices could solve the distress of the poor suffering from the high cost of food. Eden, though, did not go so far as his contemporary Malthus, who wanted the poor to raise their standard of living by postponing marriage and thus lowering fertility.[10] Hobsbawm classifies Malthus as a *pessimist* and certainly his message was the opposite of upbeat in terms of material progress, but, unlike later *pessimists*, he did not look to the inequalities produced by industrialization. Instead he laid out a complete refutation of the population as wealth theory, then on its last legs, and in so doing became the poster boy for the liberal, proto-optimist strain in

---

[8] Paul Slack, 'Material Progress and the Challenge of Affluence in Seventeenth-Century England', *Economic History Review*, 62/3 (2009), 576–603.

[9] Tom Arkell, 'Illuminations and Distortions: Gregory King's Scheme Calculated for the Year 1688 and the Social Structure of Later Stuart England', *Economic History Review*, 59/1 (2006), 32–69.

[10] Donald Winch, 'Eden, Sir Frederick Morton, second baronet (1766–1809)', *Oxford Dictionary of National Biography* (Oxford, Oxford University Press, 2004) [<http://www.oxforddnb.com/view/article/8450>, accessed 7 Dec 2009].

the nineteenth century: the market would take care of the workers' standard of living as long as they saved, stopped drinking, and curbed their sexual appetite. All of the old proscriptions against consumption designed to counter starvation while allowing the population to grow—sumptuary laws and price and wage controls—seemed archaic, and direct welfare payments, seen as redistribution from the rich to the poor, came under sustained attack as well. The irony of Malthus's observations are that demographic evidence suggests that the western European population had come to the same conclusions about postponement of marriage much sooner, as early modern brides on average married and conceived their first child at a considerably later age than women in other places around the world. The governing elites and the political economists had become obsessed with a generational blip that would have been barely noticeable if global comparisons had been made.

Through the nineteenth and early twentieth century, as national and provincial statistical departments grew in importance, household budget surveys of the working class became common instruments to gauge the standard of living in Europe and the United States and then came to be applied to the rest of the world, mainly by those trained at American universities or associated with the professionalized civil services of the European empires.[11] Political crises like those over the Corn Laws in Britain and the plight of the Irish peasant stimulated interest in establishing the fairness of the economic system.[12] Ernst Engel working for the Saxon and then Prussian state drew attention to one statistic from household surveys of consumption that could be compared between classes, cross-nationally, and over time, the proportion of a household's expenditure devoted to food. His famous curve charting the relationship showed that as expenditure or income rose, the percentage a household spent on food declined. The estimates of what share food and other budget categories constituted of total expenditures can then be linked to commodity prices to determine the cost of living. Subsequent research has generally confirmed his findings about the relationship between income and food expenditure, although it also shows that in periods of very high food prices, the lowest income category may have a lesser proportion going to diet than the next higher income group just because other necessaries such as payments for rent, fuel, and apparel could not be avoided without walking the streets naked and homeless. Such instances of lower income groups as outliers from Engel's curve may, in fact, signal a very nutritionally stressed population. Another problem with household budget analysis is that expenditure categories outside of those for food, rent, and apparel differ widely from survey to survey, greatly affecting the percentage households are shown as expending on food. Even in pre-industrial times European families spent some money on health care, education, transportation, fuel, and household furnishings,

[11] Carle C. Zimmerman, *Consumption and Standards of Living* (New York, Van Nostrand Co., 1936) provides a comprehensive account of the history of budget surveys.

[12] Perusal of the Gale Cengage British Library Newspaper database suggests that the actual term standard of living does not appear until the 1820s and the first sustained use is *c.*1840, during the movement to repeal the Corn Laws.

but often these categories are poorly represented, which leads to surveys that show 80 per cent of expenditures being on food. Surveys taken in times of crisis such as wartime also exaggerate the dietary proportion. Close analysis of the tallies show that the labouring classes in Britain in the early modern period through the nineteenth century usually devoted no more than 50–60 per cent of their outlay to diet given their other expenses and their counterparts in the United States 40–50 per cent.[13] A more sociological approach to household surveys such as that favoured by Frederic Le Play and later Carle Zimmerman faults the rigid materialist criteria of the Engel approach, especially as it was applied in later budget analyses, and its failure to acknowledge adequately cultural preferences.[14]

After Eric Hobsbawm re-invigorated the *pessimist* position in the late 1950s, economic historians, largely of the *optimist* persuasion, responded with a steady stream of articles that looked back at the early industrial period and the information on wages, prices, and household budgets that had been collected over the years, submitting them to increasingly sophisticated econometric analysis. Jan de Vries has recently summarized where he feels the debate over the standard of living during early industrialization now stands. He considers the work of Charles Feinstein, who has spent a lifetime working on British national accounts, to have demonstrated that in Great Britain at least no substantial increase in real wages (i.e. wages adusted for rises in the cost of living) occurred until the mid-nineteenth century, with the period from 1770 until 1830 showing clear stagnation. Research on a number of other northern European cities demonstrates even weaker real wage growth. De Vries declares the *pessimist* case the winner but 'not for the reasons they had originally advanced', the exploitative nature of rapid industrialization.[15]

Stretching out the Standard of Living Debate

As implied by de Vries's comment, the take-off theory of British industrialization, the notion that manufacturing experienced a huge growth spurt in a couple of decades around 1800, is more or less dead. Not only have economists revised downwards their estimates of early nineteenth-century national income growth, but historians point to notable changes in the pre-industrial standard of living. In other words, changes in diet, clothing, and housing antedated the appearance of factories and power-driven machinery. My own book *The Pre-Industrial Consumer in England and America* discusses these changes, many of which were linked to products brought into Western

---

[13] Shammas, *Pre-Industrial Consumer*, 123–31. Zimmerman, *Consumption and Standard of Living*, ch. 5, provides more examples.

[14] Zimmerman, *Consumption and Standard of Living*, 537–80.

[15] Jan de Vries, *The Industrious Revolution: Consumer Behavior and the Household Economy, 1650 to the Present* (Cambridge, Cambridge University Press, 2008), 85.

Europe by the empires of trade or came out of the wealth from the carrying trade in the commodities. In the North Atlantic, where one has the most available and detailed early modern evidence, many changes that contemporary consumers believed bettered their living standards pre-date industrialization. Diets became more varied thanks to global trade, cotton fabric entered the clothing market, and textile prices appear to have dropped significantly. Brick and stone construction with tile or slate roofs replaced wood and clay in many centre cities and glass windows became near universal. Interior improvements beginning with bedding and at the end of the pre-industrial period extending to furniture, lighting, and coal heating stoves became commonplace. Robert Allen argues that an important factor in promoting urbanization and then industrialization was the stimulation the British economy received from the British Empire, boosting wages in commercial centres. As the cost of grains did not decline, other than for European immigrants moving to the Americas, the acquisition of better material goods is usually attributed to higher real income, lower cost of durables and semi-durables, or better utilization of household labour.[16]

Rather than looking to the effects of trade and colonization, de Vries examines, as had most European economic historians before him, the domestic economy, but in his case it is truly the domestic, as in household. He posits an industrious revolution preceding industrialization that emerged as early as the seventeenth century in places such as the Netherlands. It put more family members at work producing *for* the market in order for households to buy more semi-durables and durables *in* the market.[17] Demonstrating greater productivity in the early modern household, however, is a difficult proposition, even for a historian as gifted and diligent as de Vries, given the paucity of sources for studying work patterns in the period and those in the preceding medieval era when the work was supposedly less market-oriented. Also complicating this story is the fact that the best documented examples of early modern 'industriousness' occur among household members on plantations who were enslaved or indentured.

Besides going back in time in Europe, more recent contributions to the standard of living debate have taken a new look at the situation in early modern Asia. A long tradition in Western European and American scholarship dating back to the classical economists holds that low Asian wages, early marriage, poor protection of property rights, and other governmental policies condemned the Chinese and others around them to a lower living standard than Europeans. The California School of historians of China have challenged these assumptions over the past decade. For example, Kenneth Pomeranz in his book *The Great Divergence* argued that if one compared like with like in the eighteenth century—that is, China's most advanced regions like the Yangtze Delta with Europe's—little contrast in the standard of living could be discerned in the eighteenth century although some new evidence suggests the Yangtze peasant's Golden

---

[16] Shammas, *Pre-Industrial Consumer*, ch. 5 and 6, For an up-to-date list of the work done on early modern consumption see the bibliography in de Vries, *Industrious Revolution*. Robert C. Allen, *The British Industrial Revolution in Global Perspective* (Cambridge, Cambridge University Press, 2009).

[17] de Vries, *Industrious Revolution*, ch. 4.

Age had passed and a decline could be observed by 1820.[18] This question of East versus West standards of living inspired an edited volume, *Living Standards in the Past: New Perspectives on Well-Being in Asia and Europe*.[19] After reviewing the contributions, the editors concurred with Pomeranz to the extent that the volume's research found, largely by comparing food costs, 'no systematic differences in living standards between Europe and Asia before the Industrial Revolution'.[20] Rather, inequality within Europe and Asia exceeded the contrast between the two continents. In Europe the success of urban commercial populations in England and the Netherlands from the late seventeenth century on could not be matched in southern Europe, and the real wages of rural populations declined almost everywhere by the end of the eighteenth century.

HUMAN CAPITAL, PUBLIC GOODS, AND THE STANDARD OF LIVING

In 1820, when Karl Marx was a toddler, German and British life expectancy at birth, according to historical demographers, stood at 40 years. Today most scholars writing on the standard of living are from countries where life expectancy is twice as long. From the early twentieth century, observers in Europe and America recognized mortality had significantly dropped, but recognition of the decline as a global phenomenon was post-1950.[21] It is not surprising, therefore, that measures of life expectancy, morbidity, and education have gained importance in the indices used to compare nation-states in the last 25 years. Economic growth is attributed to investment in human capital—public goods, whereas for the nineteenth century, investment in power-driven machinery and other producer durables usually get the credit. Any shortfall in obtaining a good standard of living rested with the bosses paying an inadequate wage if one were a *pessimist* or with inadequate incentives for capital if one were an *optimist*.[22] As Richard Easterlin noted in a 2000 review of the worldwide standard of living over time, even as late as the 'post-World War II period, the standard of living was typically conceived in purely material terms—the goods and services at one's disposal' and so GDP per capita became the favoured yardstick, even though critics immediately pointed out the inability of that

---

[18]   Kenneth Pomeranz, *The Great Divergence: China, Europe, and the Making of the Modern World* (Princeton University Press, 2000); Roy Bin Wong, *China Transformed: Historical Change and the Limits of European Experience* (Ithaca, Cornell University Press, 1997); and Robert C. Allen, 'Agricultural Productivity and Rural Incomes in England and the Yangtze Delta, *c.* 1620–*c.*1820', *Economic History Review*, 62/3 (2009), 525–50.

[19]   Allen et al (eds.), *Living Standards in the Past.*

[20]   Ibid., 17.

[21]   James C. Riley, *Rising Life Expectancy: A Global History.* (New York, Cambridge University Press, 2001), 7.

[22]   Life expectancy at birth of 33 years means that high infant mortality is bringing down the figure. If one survived childhood, life expectancy in pre-industrial times could reach 60 or 65.

measure to expose inequality and reveal investment in human capital. Currently most analyses and indices of well-being skip over household budgets and real wages. Easterlin considered GDP, life expectancy, fertility rate, and democratic institutions. The UN has developed a Human Development Index (HDI) that has three dimensions—longevity (life expectancy at certain ages and by sex), knowledge (years of schooling), and per capita GDP—as an indicator of 'decent standard of living'. Household surveys only come into the calculations of a supplemental index that adjusts the HDI for inequality.[23]

When life expectancy enters the measurement of standard of living, the twentieth century looks exceedingly good, even globally, and the nineteenth century rather dismal. It is difficult to identify any steady upward movement in Western Europe or in the United States prior to the 1880s.[24] In fact, many scholars studying European and America communities at mid-century report a rise in the death rate as urban areas grew. The best series of data are for England where life expectancy at birth from 1550 to 1799 fluctuates between 35 and 40 years. Numbers on Sweden in the second half of the eighteenth century range between 34 and 44, ending in 1800 at 40. Scholars show Denmark's life expectancy at between 36 and 42 years in the last two decades of the eighteenth century. Figures for France register the most steady improvement but they begin in the 1740s at a much lower number, 26 years, and only reach 32 years by 1800. Community studies of European migrants and creoles in British colonies on the North American mainland show a great divergence in life expectancy at birth depending upon region. Some New England townships during the seventeenth and early eighteenth century had life expectancy at birth nearly double those for European nations, but over time these communities slid downwards. In contrast, British colonies in the American South had seventeenth-century life expectancy numbers half of those in England but did gradually improve over the eighteenth century. Historians attribute the New England numbers to low density and the Southern numbers to the disease environment. Life expectancy for New France for the entire colonial period up to 1760 has been estimated at 36 years, more in keeping with Old World numbers, although notably better than France's during the same time frame.

Little in the way of life expectancy figures have been produced for the colonial African-American population, but the assumption is that they were worse than those for European Americans, the pattern observed later in the nineteenth and twentieth centuries. The trend in mortality for the indigenous population of the Americas has been the subject of intense interest over the past century, and about the only consensus that has emerged is that it was disastrous, so disastrous that the total population living within what would eventually be the continental United States probably did not equal the pre-contact population until 1800, and those living in Mexico did not regain their numbers any earlier than the late-nineteenth century. No prolonged forward march like that post-1880 can be identified

[23] Richard A. Easterlin, 'The Worldwide Standard of Living Since 1800', *Journal of Economic Perspectives*, 14/1 (2000), 7–26. United Nations, *Human Development Report 2010*, 215–219 at http:s//hdr.undp.org/en/reports/global/hdr2010/.

[24] On timing see Riley, *Rising Life Expectancy, passim*, and Easterlin, 'Worldwide Standard of Living since 1800', 12–14.

in the 1500 to 1800 period.[25] Moreover skeletal evidence suggests that medieval era men from North Atlantic Europe attained greater height than did their early modern counterparts or their mid-nineteenth century countrymen undergoing urbanization. The superior heights of North Americans also took a hit at this point.[26] After 1880, water and sewage systems installed in cities are credited with reducing the incidence of disease and thus infant mortality, while germ theory resulted in better hygienic practices in hospitals and homes. The impact of medicine comes afterwards and has little global impact pre-1940.[27] Life expectancy figures, of course, depend heavily on the collection of vital statistics, particularly age at death, and complete, reliable censuses. Because most governments did not have one or either before 1900, national trends are open to question.

Studies going beyond life expectancy and investigating past health status, or nutritional status as it is sometimes called, have mushroomed in the last couple of decades. J. M. Tanner's 1981 book on body weight and height (auxology) studies became very popular with influential economic historians like Robert Fogel, stimulating a considerable amount of research, because data on heights of soldiers, inmates, and slaves covers a much broader spectrum of economic groups than do other kinds of health sources and do not require as elaborate a government collection system as do life expectancy tables.[28] Historians and anthropologists have also teamed up to match documentary sources with skeletal analysis which goes beyond analysis of heights and studies decay and trauma to bones. Collaborators on *The Backbone of History: Health and Nutrition in the Western Hemisphere* constructed a health index that ranked Native American, European American, and African-American populations from prehistoric times until the early 1900s. Surprisingly, in the pre-conquest period, the more sedentary and agriculturally advanced Meso-American population had lower health status scores than smaller Indian polities of the Atlantic seaboard.[29]

Recent volumes on the history of the standard of living reflect this greater focus on life expectancy, health, and education and a reduced emphasis on wages, prices, and

[25] Life expectancy figures for Europe taken from a compilation in Hoffman et al., 'Sketching the Rise of Real Inequality', in Allen et al. (eds.), *Living Standards in the Past*, 134–6. Those for North America from Robert V. Wells, 'The Population of England's Colonies in America: Old English or New Americans?', *Population Studies*, 46 (1992), 85–102; Michael R. Haines, 'The White Population of the United States, 1790–1920', in Michael R. Haines and Richard H. Steckel, *A Population History of North America* (Cambridge, Cambridge University Press, 2000), 305–370; Hubert Charbonneau, Bertrand Desjardins, Jacques Légaré and Jubert Denis, 'The Population of the St. Lawrence Valley, 1608–1760', in Ibid., 99–142; Lorena S. Walsh, 'The African American Population of the Colonial United States', in ibid., 191–239; Robert McCaa, 'The Peopling of Mexico from Origins to Revolution', in ibid., 241–304; and Zadia M. Feliciano, 'Mexico's Demographic Transformation: From 1920 to 1990', in Ibid., 601–30.

[26] Richard H. Steckel, 'Health and Nutrition in the Pre-Industrial Era: Insights from a Millennium of Average Heights in Northern Europe', in Allen et al. (ed.), *Living Standards in the Past*, 227–54.

[27] Riley, *Rising Life Expectancy*.

[28] Roderick Floud, Robert W. Fogel, Bernard Harris, and Sok Chul Hong, *The Changing Body: Health, Nutrition, and Human Development in the Western World since 1700* (Cambridge, Cambridge University Press, 2011).

[29] Richard H. Steckel, 'Biological Measures of the Standard of Living', *Journal of Economic Perspectives*, 22/1 (winter 2008), 129–52, and Richard H. Steckel and Jerome C. Rose (eds.), *The Backbone of History: Health and Nutrition in the Western Hemisphere* (New York, Cambridge University Press, 2002).

household consumption.[30] One of the most important findings from this research is a dip in stature mimicking the mortality data, indicative of not just higher infant mortality but poorer childhood health and nutrition during the period of mass industrialization in Europe and the United States. Most consider this dip as primarily due to the adverse effects of urbanization, as the farming population grew taller than city dwellers, who were more likely to suffer from infectious diseases and poorer diets. In some ways, this finding echoes the work on American Indians, where greater economic and political sophistication prior to the twentieth century did not always translate into better health due to the effects of increased density and inequality.[31] It is also consistent with the *pessimist* position.

What differs from the original debate, which primarily focused on the purchasing power of wages paid by capitalist classes to labour, is that health and education are most often public goods and frequently viewed as the responsibility of government. An important study by Peter Lindert set out to measure the growth in social spending by European and North American governments over the past two centuries.[32] Some of the social spending involved supplements to wages—unemployment insurance, pensions etc.—that would go to paying for food, rent, and other material goods. Other expenditures were for public goods like health care and education. He contends that social transfers occurred most often where political pressure could be exerted by non-elites, or elites found it in their self-interest to make the transfers. An ageing population also contributed, an example where an initial boost in life expectancy had additional benefits. Governments redistributed miniscule amounts from the affluent to the rest of society during the nineteenth century except in the case of education. Growing electoral power changed the picture after 1930 as more and more of the population exerted their political will. Social spending in most nations did not hamper economic growth because nations still provided tax incentives for investment, and pension payments become less generous as the elderly become a higher proportion of the population.

Standard of Living, Poverty Lines, and Consumer Sovereignty

The concept and measurement of standard of living in the past has changed dramatically over the last few decades and seems to be moving away from both GDP per capita and household budget shares. The first has raised criticisms because it hides so much

---

[30] See Robert E. Gallman and John Joseph Wallis, *American Economic Growth and Standards of Living Before the Civil War* (Chicago, University of Chicago Press, 1992); Tommy Bengtsson, Cameron Campbell, James Z. Lee et al., *Life Under Pressure: Mortality and Living Standards in Europe and Asia 1700–1900* (Cambridge, MA, MIT Press, 2004); and Allen et al. (eds.) *Living Standards in the Past.*

[31] John Komlos, 'Access to Food and the Biological Standard of Living: Perspectives on the Nutritional Status of Native Americans', *American Economic Review*, 93/1 (2003), 252–5, and Steckel, 'Biological Measures of the Standard of Living', 141–5.

[32] Peter H. Lindert, *Growing Public: Social Spending and Economic Growth since the Eighteenth Century* (Cambridge, Cambridge University Press, 2004). Also see, Claudia Goldin and Lawrence F. Katz, *The Race between Education and Technology* (Cambridge, MA, Harvard University Press, 2008).

inequality. The second, which depended on large variations in the percentage of expenditures devoted to diet, has lost some of its utility as the spectrum of differences among income groups has narrowed and families in many countries have reduced significantly the proportion spent on foodstuffs. Also determining what is good or bad about spending more or less on a category of goods interferes with consumer sovereignty, a right considered basic by many in the world. During the twentieth century, Communist governments acted to restrain and mould consumption through centralized management of their economies. Scholars frequently attribute much of the failure of the Soviet Union and Eastern Bloc countries to this policy of preferencing industrial and especially military production over consumer goods and micromanaging the kind of material goods people could buy.[33] Capitalist belief in letting the market decide favours a hands-off policy regarding consumer choice. Consequently, redistribution is not based upon cost of some market basket of commodities but one's relative status in the income structure. The European Union utilizes a *relative measure of poverty* whereby those individuals whose income is less than 60 per cent of median income are considered to be living below the poverty line because their resources make it impossible to subsist at the current average level, even though some decades earlier it might have been the norm.[34] Inequality, rather than some set notion of adequate consumption level, is what triggers support.

Nevertheless government collection of household budget information has by no means ceased, as expenditure patterns are of prime importance in understanding the economy. Also, some nations such as the United States still ascribe to *an absolute measure of poverty* in making welfare disbursements. Back in 1965 with the launch of the Johnson administration's War on Poverty, the Government established a poverty line based on decade-old data on the proportion of after-tax income an average family of three or more spent on food. That proportion was one-third. The government then took that expenditure amount and multiplied by three to establish a poverty threshold. Those making below that amount were declared to be in poverty. Subsequently the cost of purchasing that same market basket of food has risen, but not nearly as fast as other prices, as indicated by the fact that today a similar sized family only spends about one-fifth not one-third on food. Poverty line income therefore has not kept up with the cost of living. A variety of reasons for why it has been so difficult in the United States either to move to a relative poverty measure or to change the multiplier in the current absolute measure have been put forward. Mostly they involve political opposition to welfare state policies. But the impasse does point up the theoretical problems involved in determining standards of living.

---

[33]   Gertrude Schroeder, 'Soviet Living Standards in Comparative Perspective', in Horst Herlemann (ed.), *Quality of Life in the Soviet Union* (Boulder, CO, Westview Press, 1987), 13–20; Mark Landsman, *Dictatorship and Demand: The Politics of Consumerism in East Germany* (Cambridge, MA, Harvard University Press, 2005).

[34]   Rebecca M. Blank, 'Presidential Address: How to Improve Poverty Measurement in the United States', *Journal of Policy Analysis and Management*, 27/2 (2008), 233–54.

DEMOTION OF INDUSTRIALIZATION
AS THE PRIME MOVER IN CHANGING
LIVING STANDARDS?

The later twentieth-century emphasis on longevity and human capital inputs has a tendency to move from centre stage the accumulation of industrial products as a marker of an improved standard of living and thus downplays the role of industrialization. Gains in human capital have been attributed not simply to increased economic growth through industrialization but to political pressure put on governments by parties, unions, and electorates to institute redistributive social programmes. In some cases, industrialization is viewed as being at odds with improved life expectancy and health.[35]

Similarly, the increased attention to changing standards of living in the early modern period, as discussed in this chapter, stretches out the time period in which one can track increased household consumption and potentially reduces the importance of nineteenth-century industrialization in the long-term accumulation of material goods. That rapid industrialization in the early nineteenth century substantially enhanced the life of the working classes has been more or less rejected as industrialization has turned out not to have been that rapid. Wars and demographic pressures at the end of the eighteenth and beginning of the nineteenth century also probably brought most of the immizeration for low-income families, and, finally, early modern households may have had their own rise in the standards of living that make any changes in the nineteenth century less remarkable.

At the beginning of this essay, I linked the emergence in Western Europe of an interest in standard of living issues to commercial expansion overseas and its effect on concepts of an empire's wealth and importance. The demand for tropical goods and Asian manufactures that created the Western European empires of trade also gave the world political economists. Discourse on the objectives of empires moved away from regarding population size as the sole measure of state power and well-being. Concern for a population's standard of living was an outgrowth of this political arithmetic although it took a long period of time before serious measurement of people's consumption took place.[36] Measures of the standard of living were heavily based on subjects' material goods—food, clothing, shelter, fuel—as shown by the first surveys of household expenditures at the end of the eighteenth century, not on public goods such as water systems, schooling, and health care, and that more or less remained the case through the nineteenth century.

The argument for a meaningful change in the early modern standard of living rests mainly on transformation in diet, greater choice in apparel (especially the spread of cotton clothing), and greater investment in housing and furnishings bringing greater

[35] For more on this subject, see the contribution by Avner Offer in this volume.
[36] See de Vries, *The Industrious Revolution*, 275–313, and his bibliography for research indicating new levels of consumption in early modern Europe.

comfort. Lower prices for semi-durable and durable consumer goods and a reorganization of household labour are the factors that have been suggested as reasons for this improvement. The former have been easier to document than the latter.

Some, however, put forward a line of argument about these early modern consumption advances roughly comparable to the old *pessimist* position regarding the Industrial Revolution, namely that the improved living circumstances benefited the few not the many. Aside from the governing elites and urbanized populations in north-west Europe, the real incomes and thus the living standards of all other Europeans, like their counterparts in India, China, and Japan, show no secular rise, to these investigators, and in some cases actually decline over the pre-industrial period.[37] It has even been contended that inequality grew in early modern Europe. During long swings food, which constituted a higher percentage of expenditure for poorer households, grew more expensive while luxury or less necessary goods fell in cost. In addition, increases in rents benefited the landlord elite.[38] Even the advances in consumption have been questioned as they involved dietary items that were proven in the twentieth century to be health hazards. The substitution of white bread for brown, butter for cheese, and sugar, tea, coffee, and cocoa for beer, the addition of distilled liquor and tobacco, and the diminution of dairy products and meat raise nutritional and health concerns.[39] Lower-income subjects lacked the political clout of later nineteenth- and twentieth-century citizens.

While real income calculations, depending so heavily on scarce wage and price data, can miss the kinds of changes those showing increased consumption document, that still leaves the mortality issue, another *pessimist* stalwart. The biggest obstacle to claiming an earlier rise in standard of living is not the question of material goods accumulation but with the estimates made of early modern life expectancy that suggest no sustained rise anywhere, including Europe or North America, until the end of the nineteenth century. Considering the life expectancy estimates and heights data used to indicate health status, declarations of a rise in the standard of living ring hollow, even though the population of many countries expanded their ownership of consumer goods and believed themselves to be living better than their ancestors.

Somewhat complicating or contradicting this rather grim biological picture of pre-twentieth-century life, though, are the estimates of world population over time. Granted, the numbers are highly speculative, but all the calculations point to a near doubling of population between 1500 and 1800 due to strong population growth in Asia and Europe,

---

[37] Stephen Broadberry and Bishnupriya Gupta, 'The Early Modern Great Divergence: Wages, Prices, and Economic Development in Europe and Asia, 1500–1800', *Economic History Review*, 59/1 (2005), 2–31.

[38] Philip T. Hoffman, David S. Jacks, Patricia A. Levin, and Peter H. Lindert, 'Sketching the Rise of Real Inequality in Early Modern Europe', in Allen et al (eds.), *Living Standards in the Past*, 131–72; Shammas, *Pre-Industrial Consumer*, ch. 5.

[39] Shammas, *Pre-Industrial Consumer*, ch. 5; Gregory Clark, Michael Huberman, and Peter T. Lindert, 'A British Food Puzzle, 1770–1850', *Economic History Review*, 48/2 (1995), 215–37, and Robert William Fogel, *The Escape from Hunger and Premature Death 1700–2100* (Cambridge University Press, 2004).

increases much greater than in any comparable time span previously, and a much better documented soaring of numbers in the nineteenth century.[40] Demographers over the past fifty years have gone back and forth as to whether the increase can be entirely explained by fertility growth or whether mortality did improve as well, with some modest declines in mortality now more often being viewed as plausible.[41] Also under-explored has been the impact of new crops from the Americas such as maize, beans, and potatoes that were spread around the globe, and the increased acreage given over to wheat, corn, and rice in the Americas, much of which was exported to Europe and parts of Asia. If the world population and grain supply grew in size and households had more 'stuff', might not that argue for better times earlier for many even if the elites were skimming the best off for themselves? Current affairs suggest the latter problem has not exactly disappeared, yet access to material goods has continued to spread among the broader population. All in all there is a need to examine further the effects on the global standard of living that came out of the first era of world trade.

Future historical work on the standard of living will undoubtedly pay increased attention to populations outside of the North Atlantic and be interested in how well the trends in wealth, health, and human capital there match the experience found elsewhere. While the debates on whether European commercial expansion, industrialization, and Cold War politics resulted in a zero sum game favouring the West or great leaps forward for everyone will certainly continue, the focus of that kind of research will most likely shift towards a fuller investigation of how factors within nations or regions, not just the actions of the West, affected a population's living standards.

BIBLIOGRAPHY

Allen, Robert C., Bengtsson, Tommy, and Dribe, Martin (eds.), *Living Standards in the Past: New Perspectives on Well-Being in Asia and Europe* (Oxford, Oxford University Press, 2005).

de Vries, Jan, *The Industrious Revolution: Consumer Behavior and the Household Economy, 1650 to the Present* (Cambridge, Cambridge University Press, 2008).

Engerman, Stanley L., 'The Standard of Living Debate in International Perspective: Measures and Indicators', in Richard H. Steckel (ed.), *Health and Welfare during Industrialization* (Chicago, University of Chicago Press, 2008).

Floud, Roderick, Fogel, Robert W., Harris, Bernard, Chul Hong, Sok, *The Changing Body: Health, Nutrition, and Human Development in the Western World since 1700* (Cambridge, Cambridge University Press, 2011).

[40] Colin McEvedy and Richard Jones, *Atlas of World Population History* (Harmondsworth, Penguin Books, 1978), 342, Figure 6.2, and 353, and Massimo Livi Bacci, *A Concise History of World Population*, 3rd edn. (Oxford, Blackwell, 2001) 27; Table 1.3 derived from J. N. Biraben, 'Essai Sur L'evolution due Nombre des Hommes', *Population*, 34 (1979), 16.

[41] Peter Razzell, *Population and Disease: Transforming English Society, 1550–1850* (London, Caliban Books, 2007); E. A. Wrigley, R. S. Davies, J. E. Oeppen, and R. S. Schofield, *English Population History from Family Reconstitution 1580–1837* (Cambridge, Cambridge University Press, 1997); and Hoffman et al. 'Sketching the Rise of Real Inequality', 133–8.

Hobsbawm, E. J., 'The British Standard of Living 1790–1850', *Economic History Review*, 10/1 (1957), 46–68.

Lindert, Peter H., *Growing Public: Social Spending and Economic Growth since the Eighteenth Century* (Cambridge, Cambridge University Press, 2004).

Pomeranz, Kenneth, *The Great Divergence: China, Europe, and the Making of the Modern World* (Princeton, Princeton University Press, 2000).

Shammas, Carole, *The Pre-Industrial Consumer in England and America* (Oxford, Clarendon Press, 1990, reprinted Figueroa Press, 2008).

Steckel, Richard H., 'Biological Measures of the Standard of Living', *Journal of Economic Perspectives*, 22/1 (2008), 129–152.

Zimmerman, Carle C., *Consumption and Standards of Living* (New York, Van Nostrand Co., 1936).

PART IV

....

PLACES OF
CONSUMPTION

....

....

CHAPTER 12

SITES OF CONSUMPTION
IN EARLY MODERN EUROPE

....

EVELYN WELCH

ENTRY-POINTS

....

In 1535, the Venetian patrician Francesco Priuli began a new account book for his household's daily expenditure.[1] Despite his elevated standing, he kept it in his own hand, noting with precision how his money was spent, where, when, and on what. From this detailed record, we find Priuli, his servants, and his family paying for everyday and luxury purchases using multiple means and in many different spaces. In some cases there were long-standing credit arrangements with local shopkeepers who made regular deliveries to the home. In others, Priuli went out to the city's central markets to buy fruit and fish; he bid for second-hand clothes at the city's street auctions and bought jewellery for his wife (along with a cap for a young servant) in the city's Jewish ghetto. At home, his servants, his young son, and occasionally his mother left the house to buy daily provisions, while his wife, Cecilia, led a much more sheltered existence. Although she did pay for items delivered to the door of their palazzo, her only major outing to make a purchase was to Venice's *Sensa* fair in Piazza San Marco.

There are a number of things to note about this patrician family's behaviour. Firstly, a major mercantile city such as Venice already offered a wide range of shopping spaces and opportunities in the early sixteenth century (and had for many years). At one end of the spectrum were the large public marketplaces and warehouses such as the Rialto or the Fondaco dei Tedeschi (Figure 12.1). At the other stood the temporary fairs and transitory sales offered by auctions and the often itinerant pawnbrokers, second-hand

---

[1] Archivio Marcello Grimani Giustinian, Donà 171; and Evelyn Welch, *Shopping in the Renaissance: Consumer Cultures in Italy, 1400–1600* (New Haven: Yale University Press, 2005), 235–43.

Figure 12.1 Canaletto, *Piazza San Giacomo in Rialto*, *c*.1740–60. © National Gallery of Canada, Ottawa.

dealers and peddlers; in-between were the numerous shops that could be found in both the city centre and scattered throughout the local neighbourhoods.

Secondly, forms of payment varied and could take place long after the goods had been transferred. Priuli enjoyed good credit; having made a purchase, he would not make any payment, either in cash or in kind, until many months later. When he did use coin it was either because he did not know the other party well or because the mechanisms involved, such as an auction, required an immediate settlement.

Thirdly, we need to note the very different ways in which Priuli and his wife accessed the spaces of Venice's commercial world. While it was rare for Francesco to spend a day without buying something, it was almost unheard of for Cecilia to make a direct purchase herself. This did not mean that she was not a consumer, simply that her consumption was mediated through third parties.

Finally, Priuli's purchases (and his occasional sales) make it clear that as well as offering the materials required for an elegant lifestyle, Venice's large second-hand markets provided economic security. Although it is often assumed that the well-documented increase in household possessions in the sixteenth century signalled increased wealth, the simultaneous rise in the recirculation of goods suggests more serious underlying problems of financial liquidity. Families may have made investments in things both because they were desirable and because they were more reliable than money.

CONSUMPTION QUARRELS

In many ways, the Priuli family could be regarded as a model of early modern household management. During the last two decades of the twentieth century, numerous scholarly studies argued that such market-based, male consumption patterns would be superseded by more sophisticated, dynamic forms of acquisition.[2] In Paris and London, new arcades and elegant interiors allowed a wider clientele to congregate in ways that had previously been impossible; printed trade cards and newspaper advertisements drew attention to shops that once might have been only known to the local community.[3] These new spaces encouraged respectable women to leave their homes to make their own purchases of imported novelties such as china, calico, tea, and coffee. Eventually, with the growth of the department stores in the nineteenth century, bargaining would give way to fixed prices while credit, pawning, and delayed payments and credit would become far rarer.[4]

This broad narrative was of course immediately contested by scholars of other periods and places. But instead of challenging the concept of a consumer revolution, they simply tried to shift its location and push it back in time. Thus some studies identified the spark of a new consumerism in fourteenth-century Siena or in fifteenth-century Florence, others in seventeenth-century Amsterdam or Antwerp; consumption is

[2] Joyce Appleby, 'Consumption in Early Modern Social Thought', in Roy Porter and John Brewer (eds.), *Consumption and the World of Goods* (London: Routledge, 1993), 162–73; Woodruff D. Smith, *Consumption and the Making of Respectability, 1600–1800* (London: Routledge, 2002); Daniel Roche, *A History of Everyday Things: The Birth of Consumption in France, 1600–1800* (Cambridge: Cambridge University Press, 2000); and by the same author, *The Culture of Clothing: Dress and Fashion in the Ancien Régime* (Cambridge: Cambridge University Press, 1996) and 'Between a "Moral Economy" and a "Consumer Economy": Clothes and their Function in the 17th and 18th centuries', in Robert Fox and Anthony Turner (eds.), *Luxury Trades and Consumerism in Ancien Régime Paris: Studies in the History of the Skilled Workforce* (Aldershot: Ashgate, 1998), 219–29.

[3] Carolyn Sargentson, *Merchants and Luxury Markets: The Marchands Merciers of 18th century Paris* (London: V&A Press, 1996). On the physical environment of eighteenth-century shops, see P. D. Glennie and N. J. Thrift, 'Consumers, Identities and Consumption Spaces in Early-Modern England', *Environment and Planning*, 28 (1996), 25–46; Andrew Hann and Jon Stobart, 'Sites of Consumption: The Display of Goods in Provincial Shops in Eighteenth-Century England', *Cultural and Social History*, 2 (2005), 165–88; Claire Walsh, 'Shop Design and the Display of Goods in Eighteenth-century London', *Journal of Design History*, 8 (1995), 157–76; and J. Stobart, A. Hann and V. Morgan (eds.), *Spaces of Consumption and Leisure in the English Town, 1680–1830* (London: Routledge, 2007) and Nancy Cox, *The Complete Tradesman: A Study of Retailing*, (Scolar Press, Aldershot, 2000). For a critique and discussions of earlier shop forms and fittings see the essays in B. Blondé, P. Stabel, J. Stobart, I. Van Damme (eds.), *Buyer & Sellers: Retail Circuits and Practices in Medieval and Early Modern Europe* (Turnhout: Brepols, 2006) and Welch, *Shopping in the Renaissance*, 4–5.

[4] Carl Gardner and Julie Shepherd, *Consuming Passion: The Rise of Retail Culture* (London: Unwin Hyman, 1989); Rosalind Williams, *Dream Worlds: Mass Consumption in Late Nineteenth-century France* (Berkeley: University of California Press, 1982); and Margot Finn, *The Character of Credit: Personal Debt in English Culture, 1740–1914* (Cambridge: Cambridge University Press, 2003).

now a major topic for the study of the early modern Ming dynasty and the Ottoman empire.[5]

In one particularly influential study of 1993, Richard Goldthwaite argued for an Italian Renaissance economic boom, one that was generated by high levels of bullion passing through the peninsula, a broader middle class, and a growing demand for the increasing number of material objects that are recorded in household inventories and account books.[6] In his view, the Priuli were not at all traditional in their wants and needs, but a family whose desire for luxury goods had prompted a consumer-led Italian Renaissance.

Yet these attempts to construct a single framework for changing consumption practices run the risk of assuming that all historical roads lead to the twenty-first-century supermarket. There is also the danger in simply translating the experiences of the elite into those of the wider community. Such studies tend to ignore the disjunctions and the anxieties created by consumption and the spaces in which it occurred. This chapter tries to offer an alternative by examining the frameworks, both physical and moral, within which purchases took place in the urban and rural centres of Italy, France, and England. Instead of assuming that the shift from the market stall to an elegant shop interior was either unproblematic or linear, it explores the ways in which men and women of all social groups had to negotiate both the sites of their consumption and their own reputations. It argues that the conventional divisions between places of production and those of purchasing and use (often categorized as the workshop, the shop, and the home) are particularly unhelpful for pre-industrial Europe.[7] Indeed the very divide between producers and consumers is difficult to sustain for the early modern period.

DIVIDING LINES

As described above, the Priuli family's division of labour depended on physical and moral constraints, one in which male and female spheres were seen as separate domains. When the (unmarried) fifteenth-century Italian humanist writer Leon Battista Alberti wrote his treatise on the family, he stressed that 'it would hardly win us respect if our

[5] See Susan Mosher Stuard, *Gilding the Market: Luxury and Fashion in Fourteenth-century Italy* (Philadelphia: University of Pennsylvania Press, 2006). On Antwerp and Amsterdam, see Patrick O'Brien, Derek Keene, Marjolein 't Hart, and Herman van der Wee (eds.), *Urban Achievement in Early Modern Europe: Golden Ages in Antwerp, Amsterdam and London* (Cambridge: Cambridge University Press, 2001). For work done on cultures outside of Europe, see Ariel Salzmann, *The Age of Tulips: Confluence and Conflict in Early Modern Consumer Culture (1550–1750)*, in D. Quataert (ed.), *Consumption Studies and the History of the Ottoman Empire, 1550–1922: An Introduction* (Albany: State University of New York Press, 2000), 83–106, and Craig Clunas, *Superfluous Things: Material Culture and Social Status in Ming China* (Cambridge: Polity Press, 1991). For useful correctives, see Amanda Vickery and John Styles (eds.), *Gender, Taste and Material Culture in Britain and North America, 1700–1830* (New Haven: Yale University Press, 2006).
[6] Richard Goldthwaite, *Wealth and the Demand for Art in Italy, 1300–1600* (Baltimore, 1993).
[7] Jane Whittle, Mark Overton, Darron Dean and Andrew Hann, *Production and Consumption in English Households 1600–1750* (Routledge, 2004).

wife busied herself among the men in the marketplace, out in the public eye. It also seems somewhat demeaning to me to remain shut up in the home among women when I have many things to do among men...'.[8] A century later in 1586, Stefano Guazzo insisted on a similar divide, providing a long list of tasks that women needed to manage within the home, including:

> hangings, and other textiles for the use and ornament of the house, keeping the furniture clean, doing needlework, spinning, winding wool, raising silk-worms, visiting the cellars, the granary, the pantry, garden and poultry shed...and keeping track of the laundry, crockery, cooking ordinary food, and the preserving for the year.[9]

This was not only an Italian ideal. In 1619, an Englishman could write about the need for a clear differentiation between male and female responsibilities, arguing that, 'It is unseemly and doth both disgrace, when either doth usurp the other's place.'[10] But even in this narrative the interpenetration of production and consumption proved more complex. Although the good housewife was theoretically expected to look after the goods that her husband provided, there were considerable overlaps between domestic production and materials destined for the marketplace. The numerous recipe and household management books produced across Europe in the period assumed that a conscientious housewife had the capacity to make up conserves, sweets, and medicines, or turn linen into embroidered coifs, elegant chemises, and cushions.[11] New treatises taught her how to raise silkworms or produce lace on a piecework basis, while spinning, weaving, and even the production of dyes such as verdigris were done at home.[12] Indeed, the economic historian, Jan de Vries's convincing explanation for the growth of the early modern economy is what he terms 'an industrious revolution', where the household was integral to the marketplace.[13] In his analysis, which builds on that of earlier scholars such as Joan Thirsk, the growth in early modern consumption cannot be correlated either to rises in wages or to a fall in prices. Instead, he points to an increased purchasing power that was primarily due to the combined productivity of family members; as the

[8] Natalie Tomas, 'Did Women have a Space?', in Roger J. Crum and John T. Paoletti (eds.), *Renaissance Florence: A Social History* (Cambridge: Cambridge University Press, 2006), 318.
[9] Stefano Guazzo, *La civil conversatione del Sig. Stefano Guazzo, nouvamente corretta e ampliata* (Venice: 1586), f.132v, cited in Ann Matchette, 'Unbound Possessions: The Circulation of Used Goods in Florence; c.1450–1600' (unpublished PhD, University of Sussex, 2005), 56.
[10] Bernard Capp, *When Gossips Meet: Women, Family and Neighbourhood in Early Modern England* (Oxford: Oxford University Press, 2003), 50.
[11] Elaine Leong, 'Making Medicines in the Early Modern Household', *Bulletin of the History of Medicine*, 82 (2008), 145–68; Sandra Cavallo, 'The Artisan's Casa', in Marta Ajmar-Wollheim and Flora Dennis (eds.), *At Home in Renaissance Italy* (London: V&A Publications, 2006), 71; and Elizabeth Cohen, 'Miscarriages of Apothecary Justice: Un-Separate Spaces of Work and Family in Early Modern Rome', *Renaissance Studies*, 21 (2007), 480–504.
[12] David Hussey and Margaret Ponsonby (eds.), *Buying for the Home: Shopping for the Domestic from the Seventeenth Century to the Present* (Aldershot: Ashgate, 2008).
[13] Jan de Vries, *The Industrious Revolution: Consumer Behaviour and the Household Economy, 1650 to the Present Day* (Cambridge: Cambridge University Press, 2008); Joan Thirsk, *Economic Policy and Projects: The Development of a Consumer Society in Early Modern England* (Oxford: Clarendon Press, 1975).

FIGURE 12.2 Herb market in Amsterdam (oil on canvas), Gabriel Metsu (1629–67), Musée du Louvre, Paris. © Giraudon / The Bridgeman Art Library.

household became more effective at collectively supplying the market, it achieved the cash surpluses needed to buy better-quality goods.

But what was this industrious housewife's relationship to the physical marketplace when the gendered divisions described above were so well articulated? One thing that is clear is that while all European communities were eager to ensure that purchases were made in public sites, there was a spectrum of concerns about the market as a space for social encounters, particularly between men and women. Gender divisions were not always uniform. In some cities, such as Amsterdam and Antwerp, women and servants generally did the marketing (Figure 12.2)—in others, the market was primarily a male preserve.[14] In Venice, for example, being seen to operate as a careful consumer was a

[14] Elizabeth Honig, *Painting and the Market in Early Modern Antwerp* (New Haven: Yale University Press, 1998).

sign of elite male behaviour. In the late sixteenth century, one Venetian ambassador to England noted with surprise how in contrast to his own home, 'the Englishwomen have great freedom to go out of the house without men-folk…many of these women serve in the shops.'[15] In 1593, the Englishman Fynnes Moryson was similarly intrigued to find that in Venice, 'only the men, and the masters of the family, go into the market and buy the victuals, for servants are never sent to that purpose, much less women.'[16] This shocked his fellow Englishman Thomas Coryate, who commented that:

> I have observed a thing amongst the Venetians that I have not a little wondered at, that their Gentlemen and greatest Senators, a man worth perhaps two million of duckats, will come into the market, and buy their flesh, fish, fruites and other things as are necessary for the maintenance of their family; a token indeed of frugality, which is commendable in all men; but methinks it not an argument of true generosity, that a noble spirit should deject itself to these petty and base matters, that are fitter to be done by servants than men of a generous parentage.[17]

Of course, there were some women (particularly poultry sellers and vegetable vendors) in the Rialto market and the sight of young girls in London's Cheapside streets was more problematic than the Ambassador assumed. Nonetheless, the comparison underlines how very differently the market was perceived in each city and how crucial social status was to informing consumer behaviour. In Venice, patrician men would shop for groceries; in London this was a task for female servants. This meant that when Pierre Hirondelle wrote a short manual to teach well-to-do Englishwomen how to speak French in the early seventeenth century, he had to configure his pupils' scenarios with considerable care.[18] In his vocabulary for 'cheapening', he took his would-be speaker to the New Exchange in London. Constructed in 1609 by Cecil, Lord Salisbury as a rival to the Royal Exchange based in the City, this was a site devoted exclusively to high-value goods.[19] Here, the young woman was instructed in how to bargain with a mercer and a goldsmith rather than haggle over cheese or fruit. Although the site was novel for London, the New Exchange was based on much earlier continental examples such as the Bourse in Amsterdam, the various Pands in Bruges and Ghent, the *merceria* and Rialto markets in Venice or even the so-called '*Coperto dei Figini*' built in the fifteenth century in Milan.[20] Their common features lay in a single owner, individual, or institutional, who built the commercial structure; there was little if any domestic

[15] Welch, *Shopping in the Renaissance*, 218.

[16] Welch, *Shopping in the Renaissance*, 218.

[17] Welch, *Shopping in the Renaissance*, 23.

[18] Pierre Erondelle, *The Frenche Garden for English Ladyes and Gentlewomen to walke in: or a Sommers days labour* (London, 1605).

[19] Alison Scott, 'Marketing Luxury at the New Exchange: Johnson's Entertainment at Britain's Burse and the Rhetoric of Wonder', *Early Modern Literary Studies*, 12 (2006), 1–19.

[20] Donatella Calabi, *The Market and the City: Square, Street and Architecture in Early Modern Europe* (Harmondsworth: Ashgate, 2004). On comparisons between London, Antwerp, and Amsterdam, see O'Brien, *Urban Achievement in Early Modern Europe*.

Figure 12.3 Abraham Bosse, *La Galerie du Palais*, British Museum. © The Trustees of the British Museum.

accommodation involved; and there was a considerable emphasis on attracting an elite clientele.

At first sight, therefore, these new spaces do seem to signal a new approach to consumption, and they were widely celebrated in prints, correspondence, and performances. In 1609, for example, Ben Jonson wrote a play to commemorate the opening of Cecil's New Exchange. Corneille did the same in France, producing his play *La Galerie du Palais* in 1632, a work which was then published in 1637.[21] The latter was set against the backdrop of the *Galerie du Palais Royale* in Paris with scenes taking place at the stalls of a mercer, linen-draper and bookseller. The same site was depicted in an almost contemporary engraving of 1638 by the French engraver Abraham Bosse (Figure 12.3). In the print, young well-dressed aristocratic men and women gather in the covered *Galerie*

---

[21] On Jonson see Ben Jonson, *The Key Keeper*, ed. James Knowles (Tunbridge Wells: Foundling Press, 2002). On Corneille see Pierre Corneille, *La Galerie du Palais, ou l'Amie Rivalle* (Paris: A. Courbé, 1637) and the discussion in Ricahrd E. Goodkin, 'Comedy Reading the Novel: Corneille's *La Galerie du Palais* and *La Suite du Menteur*' *French Forum*, 27 (2002), 15–29. Corneille's scenes revolve around visits to the bookseller, *lingerie*, and mercer who had stalls next to each other in the *Galerie*. On Bosse see, Maxime Préaud et al, eds., *Abraham Bosse: Savant graveur* (Paris: Bibliothèque Nationale du France, 2004).

to explore the goods on offer. Examining books, gloves, fans, and lace collars, the print seems to initially celebrate the more elegant forms of sale, particularly since a box in the mercer's stall marked 'eventails de Bosse' make it clear that these were the printed fans that we know were produced by the engraver himself in that same year. Here we seem to have moved to a more contemporary notion of shopping as a leisure activity for men and women alike. But the print's caption offers a warning. Although it celebrates the fact that all of human ingenuity is represented in the Galerie, the meeting between male 'courtisans' and the beauties whom they are trying to attract with galanteries is overlaid with sexual overtones.[22] The flirtatious discussions over the 'trifles' on sale are in stark contrast to the worthy classical tomes that they should be purchasing. It cannot be a coincidence that the item shown by the young bookseller to her customer is not one of the serious philosophical texts listed but a play entitled 'Mariane: Trajédie' which was first published in 1637 (the same year as Corneille's play was printed) with a frontispiece by Bosse.[23] Likewise the woman walking through the Galerie wears both a watch and a mirror on her girdle, symbols of vanity and the passage of time, as well as signs of fashionable status. We need to be wary, therefore, of seeing this print as an unproblematic celebration of elegant acquisition. It is also a very traditional warning about the dangers of worldly goods. The appearance of new spaces did not signal the erasure of old anxieties.

THE SPECTACLE OF CONSUMPTION

In Hirondelle's dialogues, Corneille's play, and the Bosse print, the clients are all mobile while the vendors remain stationary. As Linda Levy Peck has shown, by the early seventeenth century, it was perfectly respectable for the twenty-year-old Margaret Spencer to shop regularly in such spaces in London, purchasing fabrics, silks, ribbons, gloves, and hats and organizing the re-tinting of an old fan and the dyeing of ten pairs of silk stockings to extend their life.[24] She undoubtedly took a coach or carriage to move from her home to the Exchange and the privacy afforded by this new means of transport enhanced women's access to the street in important and still understudied ways.

It is important, however, to realize that mobility worked both ways. If men and women could not be seen in the marketplace, market goods could come to them. In city

---

[22] The inscription on the print reads: *Tout ce que l'Art humain a jamais inuenté / Pour mieux charmer les sens par la galanterie, / Et tout ce qu'ont d'appas la Grace et la beauté, / Se descouure à nos yeux dans cette Gallerie. // Jcy les Caualiers les plus aduantureux / En lisant les Romans, s'animent à combatre; / Et de leur passion les Amans langoureux, / Flattent les mouuemens par des vers de Theatre. // Jcy faisant semblant d'acheter deuant tous / Des gands, des Euantails, du ruban, des danteles; / Les adroits Courtisans se donnent rendez-vous, / Et pour se faire aimer, galantisent les Belles. // Jcy quelque Lingere à faute de succez / A vendre abondamment, de colere se picque / Contre des Chiccaneurs qui parlant de procez / Empeschent les Chalands d'aborder sa Boutique.*

[23] François Tristan l'Hermite, *Mariane: Trajédie* (Paris: chez Augustin Courbé, 1637).

[24] Linda Levy Peck, *Consuming Splendour: Society and Culture in Seventeenth-Century England* (Cambridge: Cambridge University Press, 2005), 69–70.

streets and country roads, chapmen or pedlars carried small-scale wares such as knives, mirrors, scissors, buttons, beads, hooks, ribbons, gloves, belts, cloth, and clothing (both new and second-hand), as well as books, printed playing cards and pamphlets, ensuring the rapid distribution of items that allowed for greater comfort and fashion.[25] As with the engravings of new shopping spaces, the wide variety of goods sold on the street and at the door in both urban and rural environments were celebrated with numerous sixteenth- and seventeenth-century images pinning down these most transient of vendors.[26] An English print (which played on a long tradition) of a sleeping pedlar carried the inscription (Figure 12.4):

> And as hee slept the Apes gott to his pack
> They make fine work among his toyes & glasses
> They wonder at the sight of every knack
> Which he had theare to please the co[u]ntry lasses.[27]

Again, behind the amusement of the imagery lay more serious concerns. The pedlar had access to 'country lasses' who might have little knowledge either of the quality of the goods on offer or their price. In the late sixteenth century, the Milanese mercers' guild attacked pedlars who went about the streets, 'with boxes in order to sell headbands, snoods, ribbons, cloth and other such things'.[28] They were particularly concerned about such vendors' access to women:

> How easy it is to deceive women, everyone knows. Because they are vagabonds and do not have a fixed shop in the city...they commit frauds and then they cannot be found to be punished and moreover as they have the occasion to enter into anyone's house, under the guise of selling ribbons and caps, they commit evil deeds.[29]

Likewise, the 1597 English act against rogues, vagabonds, and sturdy beggars outlawed, 'all juglers, tynkers, peddlers and petty chapmen'.[30] Pedlars, particularly Jewish pedlars, were similarly regulated and stereotyped as dangerous and seductive.

But itinerant merchants were crucial to the early modern economy and scholars such as Mary Weisner Wood have noted the important role women occupied as vendors in

---

[25] Margaret Spufford, *The Great Reclothing of Rural England: Petty Chapmen and their Wares in the Seventeenth Century* (London: Hambledon Press, 1984); Beverly Lemire, 'Peddling Fashion: Salesmen, Pawnbrokers, Tailors, Thieves and the Second-Hand Clothes Trade in England, 1700–1800', *Textile History*, 22 (1991), and Nancy C. Cox and Karin Dannehl, *Perceptions of Retailing in Early Modern England* (Aldershot: Ashgate, 2007).

[26] Tom Nichols, *The Art of Poverty: Irony and Ideal in Sixteenth-Century Beggar Imagery* (Manchester: Manchester University Press, 2007); Sean Shesgreen, *Images of the Outcast: the Urban Poor in the Cries of London* (New Brunswick, NJ: Rutgers University Press, 2002). See also Laurence Fontaine, *History of Pedlars in Europe* (Durham, NC: Duke University Press, 1996).

[27] J. B. Friedman, 'The Peddler-Robbed-by-Apes Topos: Parchment to Print and Back Again', *Journal of the Early Book Society*, 11 (2008), 87–120.

[28] Welch, *Shopping in the Renaissance*, 40.

[29] Welch, *Shopping in the Renaissance*, 41.

[30] Spufford, *The Great Reclothing of Rural England*, 8.

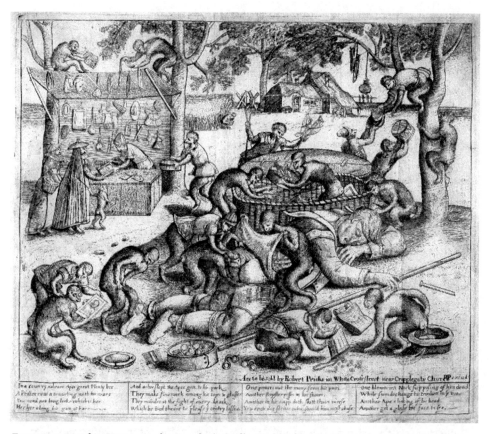

FIGURE 12.4 After Pieter van der Borcht, 'A Pedlar Robbed by Apes', c.1660, published by Robert Pricke. © The Trustees of the British Museum.

early modern Nuremberg, acting as key figures for small-scale distribution networks.[31] Nonetheless, most of her data comes from the regular stream of prosecutions for illegal house-to-house sales in the sixteenth century, with claims that pedlars were breaking rules on hygiene, sumptuary laws, and the censorship imposed on books and pamphlets. Similar work on the street sellers of early modern Nantes in France reveals equivalent concerns, while a study of the Portuguese town of Porto in 1626, finds female street sellers accused of forestalling by cornering the market in milk, watering it down, and then selling it at a high price.[32]

With complaints against hucksters and hawkers such as those issued in 1595 against 'an exceeding great number of lewd and wicked women called fishwives, which swarm about in all parts of this city', English regulators and shopkeepers were keen to disassociate 'respectable' shopping from these transitory and often theatrical modes of

[31] Merry Weisner Wood, 'Paltry Peddlers or Essential Merchants? Women in the Distributive Trades in Early Modern Nuremberg', *The Sixteenth-Century Journal*, 12 (1981), 3–13.

[32] Gayle K. Brunelle, 'Policing the Monopolizing Women of Early Modern Nantes', *Journal of Women's History*, 19 (2007), 10–35, and Darlene Abreu-Ferreira, 'From Mere Survival to Near Success: Women's Economic Strategies in Early Modern Portugal', *Journal of Women's History*, 13 (2001), 58–79.

salesmanship.[33] Yet at the same time as cities were busy regulating mobile vendors, images of pedlars were being circulated in print while their cries were transformed into poetry and song (Figures 12.5 and 12.6).[34] The interconnection between sales and theatricality (and between the false nature of the market and that of the stage) was a long-standing feature of commercial spaces. The English 1597 ban on vagabonds linked jugglers to pedlars while the origins of Italian street theatre are closely tied to the public performances of mountebanks and charlatans selling medicines.[35] There were similarly strong overlaps between popular and aristocratic forms of entertainment. Thus, just as roving groups of actors were often invited to perform within palaces, so too the songs of pedlars found their way into more conventional compositions. For example, the sixteenth-century French composers Claude de Sermisy and Clément Janequin both produced elegant settings for *Voulez ouyr les cris de Paris?* while Orlando Gibbons set the *Cries of London* for voices and strings in the early seventeenth century.[36]

Although civic markets were supposed to be permanent, highly regulated sites that contrasted with the pedlars' impermanence, these fixed spaces also attracted and promoted spectacles.[37] In 1645, for example, John Evelyn described going to Piazza Navona in Rome, 'to see what Antiquities I could purchase among the people, who hold Mercat there for Medaills, Pictures, & such Curiosities, as to heare the Mountebanks prate, & debite their Medicines'.[38] A number of shops were also celebrated for their intrinsic theatricality. In 1596, a barber in Bologna subscribed to the manuscript *Avvisi*, an early form of handwritten newsletter, and paid for a licence to have them read in his shop.[39] Leonardo Fioravanti described in 1564, how in barber shops:

> one can hear all the news and the facts of private people, because sailors talk about their travels, the great fortunes they had, and the costumes of the many lands they saw; soldiers narrate their battles and their victories; husbands recount how they married, and how they do with their wives; young lovers, how they got in love, and how they follow their beloved ones; and one can hear a thousand jokes.[40]

[33] Natasha Korda, 'Gender at Work in the Cries of London', in Mary Ellen Lamb and Karen Bamford (eds.), *Oral Traditions and Gender in Early Modern Literary Texts* (Aldershot: Ashgate, 2008), 120.

[34] Eric Wilson, 'Plague, Fairs and Street Cries: Sounding Out Society and Space in Early Modern London', *Modern Language Studies*, 25 (1995), 1–42.

[35] David Gentilcore, 'Apothecaries, "Charlatans" and the Medical Marketplace in Italy, 1400–1750—Introduction', *Pharmacy in History*, 45 (2003) 91–4 and by the same author, '"For the protection of those who have both shop and home in this city?" Relations between Italian Charlatans and Apothecaries', *Pharmacy in History*, 45 (2003), 108–21, and *Medical Charlatanism in Early Modern Italy* (Oxford: Oxford University Press, 2006).

[36] Korda, 'Gender at Work in the Cries of London'. See also Wilson, 'Plagues, Fairs and Street Cries', *Modern Language Studies*, 25 (1995), 1–42.

[37] Dave Postles, 'The Market Place as Space in Early Modern England', *Social History*, 29 (2004), 41–58.

[38] Patricia Allerston, 'The Second-Hand Trade in the Arts in Early Modern Italy', in Marcello Fantoni, Louisa C. Matthew and Sara F. Matthews-Grieco (eds.), *The Art Market in Italy* (Modena: Franco Cosimo Panini, 2003), 301. See also Margaret A. Katritzky, 'Marketing Medicine: The Image of the Early Modern Mountebank', *Renaissance Studies*, 15 (2001), 121–53.

[39] De Vivo, *Information and Communication in Venice*, 103.

[40] De Vivo, *Information and Communication in Venice*, 98.

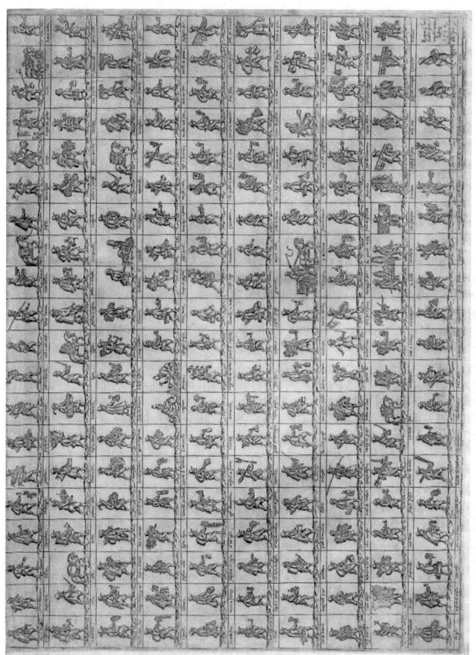

Figure 12.5 Ambrogio Brambilla, 'Ritrato de quelli che vano vendendo et lavorando per Roma con la nova agionta de tutti quelli che nelle altre mancavano sin al presente', Rome 1582, etching with some engraving. © The Trustees of the British Museum.

FIGURE 12.6 Detail of Ambrogio Brambilla, 'Ritrato de quelli che vano vendendo et lavorando per Roma con la nova agionta de tutti quelli che nelle altre mancavano sin al presente', Rome 1582, etching with some engraving. © The Trustees of the British Museum.

But it was not only barbers who offered such opportunities for news and conversation. An early seventeenth-century list of sites where professional informers should be stationed on behalf of the Venetian state included 'bookshops, textile stores, taverns and the premises of mercers and shoemakers, as well as numerous barbers and apothecaries'.[41]

Alongside barber shops, apothecaries proved to be a key site for commercial and social exchange.[42] As Filippo de Vivo has shown, the early modern pharmacy's mixture of clients and its comfortable interior meant that it became an important place for communication.[43] Rumour, political information, and popular songs were all dispensed alongside medical advice, pills, syrups, and electuaries. The Veronese naturalist and apothecary Francesco Calzolari took these opportunities to their logical extension, creating what he called 'a museum or theatre' to testify both to the efficacy of his products and his own personal contacts and learning. Calzolari ran a shop at the Golden Bell in Verona and his products, such as theriac, Armenian boll, and *terra sigillata*, were cure-alls that were often sold by mountebanks. To distinguish himself from these itinerant salesman, Calzolari published descriptions of his various botanical trips, his contacts with famous scholars, and his *teatrum*, a suite that began with a chamber containing the portraits of figures such as Ulisse Aldrovandi. The second room contained a range of equipment designed for the distillation of the simples that went into his famous products, while the final space, described in a lengthy letter by

---

[41] De Vivo, *Information and Communication in Venice*, 97.

[42] Franco Franceschi, 'La bottega come spazio di sociabilità', in Franco Franceschi and Gloria Fossi (eds.), *La grande storia dell'artigianato* (Florence: Giunti, 1999), 65–84; Welch, 'Space and Spectacle in the Renaissance Pharmacy', *Medicina e storia*, 15 (2008), 127–58; and Patrick Wallis, 'Consumption, Retailing, and Medicine in Early-Modern London', *Economic History Review*, 61 (2008), 26–53.

[43] Filippo De Vivo, 'Pharmacies as Centres of Communication in Early Modern Venice', *Renaissance Studies*, 21 (2007), 505–21.

the Veronese doctor Antonio Passieno to Giacomo Scutellari, physician to the condot-
tiere Sforza Pallavicino was:

> a most abundant repository and true treasure of all remarkable medicinal things, in
> which I observed each one placed in wonderful order in most decorative and elegant
> compartments and cases. First, [Calzolari] sought exceptional herbs and then the
> rest from their own distant places and regions, sent to him as gifts from the greatest
> princes and rulers; here it is pleasing to see not a few whole plants and plant roots,
> rinds, hardened or liquid saps, gums, flowers, leaves, fruits, and rare seeds and to
> recognize them as authentic. Also many metals. I omit how many dried terrestrial
> and aquatic animals I was astounded to find that I had never seen before.[44]

Passieno had been shown the collection, with its botanical specimens, stuffed fish and
crocodiles, fossils, and Egyptian papyrus by Calzolari's son. The young man had opened
up boxes, drawers, and cabinets and invited the visitor to smell some of the precious oils
and distillates, making it clear that access was carefully controlled and by invitation only.
In return, the apothecary took care to get his most prestigious guests to leave some form
of testimonial. In 1585, for example, the rooms were seen by two Japanese princes who,
having converted to Christianity, were travelling through Verona on their way to pay
homage to the Pope.[45] Following their visit, they presented Calzolari with an exotic
headdress and garment made from feathers, which joined the collection.

In connecting the efficacy of his products with the attested authenticity of his intellectual connections and access to rare ingredients, Calzolari was part of a growing trend.
However, not everyone was impressed with the exercise in shop display. (Figure 12.7)
The Swiss naturalist Conrad Gessner complained of, 'apothecaries and others who dry
rays and shape their skeletons into varied and wonderful forms for the ignorant',[46] while
William Shakespeare's description of the apothecary shop from which Romeo would
buy his poison was similarly framed:

> I do remember an apothecary—
> And hereabout a dwells—which late I noted [...]
> And in his needy shop a tortoise hung,
> An alligator stuffed and other skins
> Of ill-shaped fishes; and about his shelves
> A beggarly account of empty boxes
> Green earthen pots, bladders and musty seeds
> Remnants of packthread and old cakes of roses
> Were thinly scatter'd to make up a show.[47]

---

[44] Welch, 'Space and Spectacle in the Renaissance Pharmacy', 148–9.

[45] Welch, 'Space and Spectacle in the Renaissance Pharmacy', 149.

[46] Paula Findlen, 'Inventing Nature: Commerce, Art and Science in the Early Modern Cabinet of
Curiosities', in Pamela H. Smith and Paula Findlen (eds.), *Merchants and Marvels: Commerce, Science
and Art in Early Modern Europe* (London: Routledge, 2002), 305.

[47] Lina Perkins Wilder, 'Towards a Shakespearean "Memory Theatre": Romeo, the Apothecary, and
the Performance of Memory', *Shakespeare Quarterly*, 56 (2005), 156.

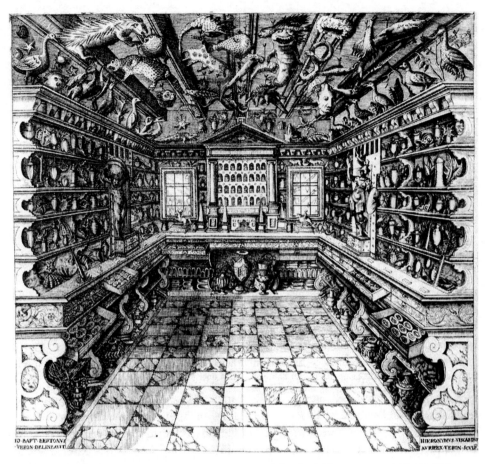

FIGURE 12.7 Benedetto Ceruti, *Musaeum Francesco Calceolarii*, Verona, 1622. © The British Library, London.

As this suggests, clients were already suspicious that extravagant packaging might disguise a poor product. Here again, as stressed above, new forms of display did not allay old suspicions.

CULTURES OF CREDIT

If vendors had to demonstrate the reliability of their products through a combination of investments in their physical appearance and personal testimonials, the same was true of their clients. Credit made commerce possible at every level of society and the same skills required to determine high-quality products were used to identify high-quality consumers. But in circumstances where very powerful and wealthy figures might be as likely to default as poorer families, and with even greater consequences, credit negotiations were far from straightforward. The shop records that survive in considerable numbers across Europe demonstrate a surprising consistency in noting the satisfying moment when the record of a client's debt was struck off with a line through the account.[48] Settlements were guaranteed through a range of mechanisms, including the social connections between buyers and sellers, a legal framework for complaint and redress, and, perhaps most importantly, trust in the material goods that were offered as security for short- or long-term loans or in lieu of payment.[49] Hats and cloaks might cover the expense of a night at an inn; linen might provide a pledge for a bank loan; furniture, jewellery, and very occasionally paintings could be left in return for services rendered.

It has often been thought that this use of pledges and barter was necessary because bullion was both scarce and subject to frauds such as clipping and sweating. But the use of material possessions continued to be crucial even after the import of Spanish silver in the sixteenth century and the development of more standardized coinage production. Indeed, a reliance on tangible goods could be even more important in periods of price inflation.[50] Under these circumstances, a high-quality linen chemise might be a more stable form of payment than unreliable and untrustworthy coins.

But this system of exchange only functioned as long as there were agreed values for goods and when they could be transformed into cash and back again. This meant that early modern communities, both urban and rural, relied on elaborate systems of pawning, resale, and recycling. Despite their association with usury, pawnbrokers provided crucial financial flexibility, transforming the value invested in objects into readily accessible cash. Institutions such as the Italian Monte di Pietà, established by the Franciscans, were designed to prevent the poor from falling into the hands of Jewish moneylenders, but they worked alongside rather than in opposition to the widely available uses of pawn pledges.[51] Moreover, it was not only the poor who took advantage of these arrangements. It was common practice for the elite to use their material goods to raise income: this ensured that they would not have to sell off land in order to pay their debts. During the 1550s, for example, the Roman Baron Paolo Giordano Orsini placed his furniture, tapestries, and plate with a local Roman pawnbroker, redeeming them when he required the items for display.[52] This allowed for safe storage and surveillance of his goods, while giving him some much needed liquidity.

[48] Craig Muldrew, *The Economy of Obligation: The Culture of Credit and Social Relations in Early Modern England* (Basingstoke: Palgrave, 1998); James Shaw, *The Justice of Venice: Authorities and Liberties in the Urban Economy, 1550–1700* (Oxford: Oxford University Press, 2006).

[49] Craig Muldrew, 'Interpreting the Market: the Ethics of Credit and Community Relations in Early Modern England, *Social History*, 18 (1993), 163–83.

[50] Craig Muldrew, '"Hard Food for Midas": Cash and its Social Value in Early Modern England', *Past & Present*, 170 (2001), 78–120.

[51] Anne E. C. McCants, 'Goods at Pawn: The Overlapping Worlds of Material Possessions and Family Finance in Early Modern Amsterdam', *Social Science History*, 31 (2007), 213–38. On the Monte di Pietà, see Carol Bresnnan Menning, *Charity and State in Late Renaissance Italy: The Monte di Pietà of Florence* (Ithaca: Cornell University Press, 1993).

[52] Barbara Furlotti, *Consumption and Baronial Identity in Sixteenth-century Rome: Paolo Giordano I Orsini and his Possessions (1541–1585)* (unpublished PhD, Queen Mary, University of London, 2009), 237–42.

Of course, when owners were not able to redeem their valuables, pawnbrokers had to have some mechanism for recouping their costs. The recirculation of goods, often regarded as a market of secondary importance, is only beginning to receive the full attention required. The life cycle of many objects and, indeed, the lifestyles of many families meant that far from there being one-way traffic from the public arena of shops and markets into the home, goods often made swift exits. Second-hand dealers were crucial in this. They assessed the value of objects which entered the household through marriage, assuring a future husband of the value of a dowry and the wife of what she could expect if and when she became a widow. When death or debt occurred they would then arrange for their resale, either through shops, peddling, or through state-controlled or private auctions. Because of the importance of the resale market to consumer confidence and public credit, auctioneers and dealers were almost always regulated and were often civic officials. The *comandadori* in Venice and Florence, the *boden* of Amsterdam, outropers in London, and *sergeants à verge* and *huissiers* in Paris all operated in different ways but were usually expected to act on behalf of the city rather than for their own profit. In Nuremburg, for example, a post-mortem inventory and appraisal of household property and goods was required after all deaths. This was usually undertaken by a woman, the *unterkeuflin*, who would estimate the resale value of each item. The women did not sell the items themselves (this was a job undertaken by male second-hand dealers) but were expected to have wide experience of market values. Although the land involved was assessed by their male counterparts, even in this situation, women were regarded as having a better understanding of what kitchen equipment, household furnishings, or textiles could fetch under resale conditions.[53]

As this suggests, the existence of resale experts meant that agreed values for second-hand goods could be established with some ease in larger urban markets. The importance of these facilities becomes clear in examining the case of a wealthy Italian widow, the wife of the Mantuan ambassador to Venice, Benedetto Agnello. At her husband's death in 1556, Lucrezia Agnello first had an inventory taken of his goods, arranging for their sale before her departure to Mantua. The more portable items such as clothing, gilt-leather hangings, and paintings were sold at auction in the city's main market, the Rialto. The remainder were auctioned from her own home, including her beds, linens, mattresses, and further paintings. She took some of the profit and used it to redeem a gold-headed marten fur-piece which her husband had used as a pawn in the Jewish ghetto.[54]

Importantly, the widow did not have to set up any of these systems for resale herself; she simply took advantage of the civic structures that controlled the auctions and even the cost of the porters who carried her goods across the city to be sold. But in using this system of resale, she had to be willing to display once private possessions to any potential customer and indeed to any viewer curious enough to stop and watch the sale. In 1581,

---

[53] Weisner Wood, 'Paltry Peddlers or Essential Merchants?', 8.

[54] Evelyn Welch, 'From Retail to Resale: Artistic Value and the Second-Hand Market in Italy (1400–1550)', in Fantoni, Matthew, and Matthews-Grieco (eds.), *The Art Market in Italy*, 289.

the French writer Montaigne described how during his trip to Rome he saw once highly prized personal possessions on display prior to an auction:

> After dinner, the French ambassador sent a footman to tell me that if I wished, he was coming to pick me up in his coach to take me to see the furniture of Cardinal Orsini, which was being sold, since he died this summer in Naples and left as heir to all his vast property a niece of his, a little girl. Among other rare things was a taffeta coverlet lined with swan's down…I saw an ostrich egg, decorated all over and painted with pretty pictures. Also a square box to put jewels in that contained a certain quantity of them; but since the box was most artfully arranged with mirrors all around, when it was opened it appeared much wider and deeper in every direction and seemed to hold ten times as many jewels as were in it.[55]

Here, goods that were once hidden away and only visible to invited guests were now on open view to potential buyers, further blurring the boundaries between the home and the place of sale. It is very likely that the viewing was preliminary to an auction of the Cardinal's goods, a favoured mechanism for rapid disposal. While auctions might signal the shame of bankruptcy, exile, or some other familial disaster, the sale of household goods was not always problematic.[56] Thus the entire wardrobe and furnishings of a mid-level Venetian official, including portraits of his wife and family might end up in the hands of auctioneers at the Rialto, realising a sum that would then be handed over to his widow to ensure her survival or her ability to remarry.[57] In 1549, the Nobili family in Florence sold off a substantial number of their household goods, many containing their armorials, while the Orsini family similarly auctioned servant's liveries, seemingly unconcerned that the connections might be noted.[58]

Auctions continued to flourish throughout the sixteenth century but these traditional forms of circulation were joined by a new mechanism for rapidly transforming goods and property into cash: the lottery. Originally devised as a system of raising money for civic purposes, by the 1520s a group of Venetian second-hand dealers were selling affordable lottery tickets that gave buyers the chance to win carpets, silver plate, jewellery, paintings, and other luxury items. In February 1522, for example, the Venetian diarist Marin Sanudo listed the goods that could be won including 'silk and woolen cloth, paintings, fur-linings of all types, a large amount of silver, many lovely things, large pearls and beautiful jewels of all sorts, amber paternoster beads, and even…horses.'[59] By the

---

[55] Welch, 'From Retail to Resale', 194.

[56] Jacqueline Marie Musacchio, 'The Medici Sale of 1495 and the Second-Hand Market for Domestic Goods in Late Fifteenth-Century Florence', in Fantoni, Matthew, and Matthews-Grieco (eds.), *The Art Market in Italy*, 316.

[57] Jack Hinton, 'By Sale, By Gift: Aspects of the Resale and Bequest of Goods in Late Sixteenth-Century Venice', *Journal of Design History*, 15 (2002), 245–61.

[58] Matchette, 'Unbound Possessions', 91, and Elizabeth Currie, *The Fashions of the Florentine Court: Wearing, Making and Buying Clothing, 1560–1620*, (unpublished PhD, University of Sussex, 2004). See also by Matchette, 'Credit and Credibility: Used Goods and Social Relations in Sixteenth-Century Florence', in Michelle O'Malley and Evelyn Welch (eds.), *The Material Renaissance* (Manchester: Manchester University Press, 2007), 225–41.

[59] Evelyn Welch, 'Lotteries in Early Modern Italy', *Past & Present*, 199 (2008), 71–111.

end of the century, despite considerable civic concern, lotteries were widespread across Italy, France, and the Netherlands while experiments were also under way in England. A series of Roman lotteries from the 1580s give some sense of the sensational nature of the goods that might be involved. In 1584, for example, Claudio Venturini, a Florentine merchant, and nine Roman noblemen advertised their lottery.[60] The first prize was a jewel-handled fan with rubies and diamonds worth 4,000 scudi; the second prize was a sable or marten fur-piece with gold feet and valuable gems worth 3,500 scudi. There were 36 other pieces of jewellery and a further 40 cash prizes. Venturini's decision to hold this lottery was undoubtedly prompted by the fact that he was facing bankruptcy and he was declared insolvent the following year on 20 July 1585. Similarly, the anonymously organized Lotto di Pasquino held by the famous statue of Pasquino in Piazza Navona in the early 1580s offered tableware and clothing such as, 'a marten-head encased in gold with a ruby in its tip and other smaller rubies and emeralds; a silver pepper dish worked with figures; a partly gilded large cup with a cusped food; a string of perfumed buttons; an half-gilded triangular egg dish with a salt cellar.'[61] The 1587 lottery list of the banker Ottavio Gratis, held in the Piazza San Lorenzo by the Campo dei Fiore, listed almost one hundred prizes. These were primarily jewellery and plate, such as 'a necklace with a medal of the Grand Duke of Florence worth 58 *scudi*, a pair of silver candlesticks in the Spanish style worth 38 *scudi* and a gem in the shape of a scorpion worth 170 *scudi*'. But it also included 33 pieces of ancient statuary from the collection of Camillo Crescenzi (one of the backers of Claudio Venturini's earlier lottery). The announcement made it clear that anyone who wished to see these objects before investing in the lottery could view the works at Crescenzi's home.[62]

In a period in which the state itself might default on promised annuities and loans, those playing the lottery seem to have been quite canny about purchasing tickets. As the ability to estimate risk became increasingly domesticated, a broader range of consumers seem to have felt more confident about investing in imagined returns, balancing a need for security with the pleasures of fantasized wealth. At the same time, however, the lottery was not only a social phenomena, it was also a signal of increasing economic pressure. Lotteries were organized by state enterprises, new investment groups such as the joint-stock Virginia Company, or new enterprises such as the founders of the Universities of Harvard and Yale in the early seventeenth century. They were also used

[60]   RASV, Miscellanea, Armadi iv–v, vol. 65, 125, 1584: *Editto sopra il lotto overo ventura da farsi in Roma: Havendo Messer Claudio Venturini ottenuta licenza da Nostro Signore Gregorio XIII di poter fare un LOTTO, overo Ventura in Roma delle infrascritte Gioie, & Denari, le quali sono state diligentemente vedute & stimate da tre Periti sopra ciò eletti & approvati alla presenza del Molto Illustre Signor Ridolpho Bonfiolo Thesoriere Generale di Sua Santità… Qual Lotto ascende alla somma di scudi venti otto millia d'oro in oro, secondo detta stima & denari contanti, & si pagherà uno scudo in oro per voce, overo bollettino in mano di M. Claudio Venturini Mercante in Roma, ricontro all Chiesa di San Celso in Banchi.*

[61]   RASV, Miscellanea, Armadi iv–v, vol. 65, 144: *Benefitiati uscite al bel lotto di Pasquino: Una testa di Zibellino d'oro con un rubino in breccia & altri robini & smiraldi; Una peparola d'argento lavorata con figure; Un Tazzone con il piede a bottoni parte dorato, una filza di bottoni di profumo; un'ovarolo a triangolo con le sue salarine in mezzo dorato.*

[62]   National Library of Scotland, Crawford B 2 (37): 7 April 1587: *Editto Sopra il Lotto di M. Ottavio Gratis, che si fà in Roma nella piazza di San Lorenzo in Damaso innanzi al Spetiale della Corona.*

by individuals or groups of individuals to ensure the rapid liquidity of substantial assets. As such, they point to the increasing pressure to transform the wealth stored in gems, jewellery, clocks, antiquities, and property into the cash required to pay overdue taxes and debts. The pawnbroker, auctioneer, and second-hand dealer all had important roles to play in this well-known cycle, but the lottery had one key advantage. It drew in large amounts of coin over a short period of time, enabling the organizers' own debts to be paid well before the draw had even taken place. Its rapid spread is not always a sign of greed or collective irresponsibility on the part of ticket buyers; it can indicate the need to obtain cash, or at least the promise of cash, before bankruptcy loomed.

CONCLUSIONS

The increasing prevalence of activities such as lotteries and the continuity of second-hand dealers, pawnbrokers, and auctions help to modify some of the current thinking concerning early modern consumption. In his influential works on early modern England, Craig Muldrew has argued for a culture of mutual indebtedness, one where the lack of coin led to both formal and informal networks of credit and trust that in ideal circumstances rarely had to be tested.[63] But while this was equally true of other large European cities and towns, creditors also wanted to know that, if required, debtors could rapidly and effectively realize their assets. This led to an increased emphasis on the mechanisms that allowed those at every level, from poor artisans to aristocratic families, to recoup the investments made in furnishings, wardrobes, silver vaults, or simple cutlery. As such, material goods and the spaces for resale as well as for sale were not marginal to the economy. They were central to the increasingly complex credit systems that linked an ability to pay to the furniture in one's home and the clothes on one's back. Equally importantly, as beds and bedding, shirts, and pots and pans moved between the home, the pawnbroker, and the auction house, they challenged the dividing lines between high- and low-value consumption that were so eagerly sought by early modern moralists. Although the sites where bargaining and exchange might change over time, becoming more elegant, these spaces could never be completely free from the taint of worldly desires and sensuality. New research directions lie, therefore, less in explanatory models of how the pre-industrial economy was transformed into a modern consumer society and much more in the social and material negotiations that took place in the early modern marketplace.

BIBLIOGRAPHY

Blondé, B., Stabel, P., Stobart, J., and Van Damme, I. (eds.), *Buyer and Sellers: Retail Circuits and Practices in Medieval and Early Modern Europe* (Turnhout: Brepols, 2006).

De Vivo, Filippo, 'Pharmacies as centres of communication in early modern Venice', *Renaissance Studies*, 21 (2007), 505–21.

---

[63] Craig Muldrew, *The Economy of Obligation* and '"Hard Food for Midas"'.

de Vries, Jan, *The Industrious Revolution: Consumer Behaviour and the Household Economy, 1650 to the Present Day* (Cambridge: Cambridge University Press, 2008).

Goldthwaite, Richard, *Wealth and the Demand for Art in Italy, 1300–1600* (Baltimore, 1993).

Muldrew, Craig, *The Economy of Obligation: The Culture of Credit and Social Relations in Early Modern England* (Basingstoke: Palgrave, 1998).

Roche, Daniel, *A History of Everyday Things: The Birth of Consumption in France, 1600–1800* (Cambridge: Cambridge University Press, 2000).

Porter, Roy and Brewer, John (eds.), *Consumption and the World of Goods* (London: Routledge, 1993).

Welch, Evelyn, *Shopping in the Renaissance: Consumer Cultures in Italy, 1400–1600* (New Haven: Yale University Press, 2005).

Welch, Evelyn, 'Space and Spectacle in the Renaissance Pharmacy', *Medicina e storia*, 15 (2008), 127–58.

Whittle, Jane, Overton, Mark, Dean, Darron and Hann, Andrew, *Production and Consumption in English Households 1600–1750* (London: Routledge, 2004).

CHAPTER 13

PUBLIC SPACES, KNOWLEDGE, AND SOCIABILITY[1]

BRIAN COWAN

THE concept of 'sociability' was introduced as an analytic term by the German sociologist Georg Simmel, who posited 'Geselligkeit' as an example of what he called 'pure, or formal sociology' in an influential 1911 essay. Simmel thought that Geselligkeit, or sociability, was a form of social interaction that 'is freed from all ties with contents. It exists for its own sake and for the sake of the fascination which, in its own liberation from these ties, it diffuses.' He pointed to behaviours such as coquetry, games, and conversation as exemplary instances of sociability in action, and he thought that these practices reached their height of influence during the ancien régime.[2] As such, it was understood primarily as an elite phenomenon—labourers did not have much time to engage in social interaction for its own sake, and they certainly were not able to articulate their own views about sociability to the same degree as the aristocracy. Court society, with its elaborate but ultimately pointless rules of etiquette, was the epitome of old regime sociability.

The notion of sociability has developed in many different ways since Simmel introduced it nearly one hundred years ago. Most notably, the term no longer applies only to elite social practices: historians have uncovered the many sociabilities of the middling sorts and the labouring classes as well as those of aristocratic and courtly

[1] I would like to thank James Amelang, John A. Hall, Ben Pauley, and Frank Trentmann, as well as all of the participants in the European Science Foundation exploratory workshop on 'The Development of Civil Society in Europe from the Middle Ages until Today', at the University of Antwerp in November 2009, for helpful commentary and additional references for this chapter, although any remaining faults and omissions remain my responsibility.
[2] Georg Simmel, The Sociology of Georg Simmel, trans. and ed. Kurt H. Wolf (Glencoe, IL: Free Press, 1950), 43, 54–5; see also Simmel, 'The Sociology of Sociability', trans. Everett C. Hughes, The American Journal of Sociology, 55/3 (1949), 254–61; and Dietmar Jazbinsek, 'The Metropolis and the Mental Life of Georg Simmel: On the History of an Antipathy', Journal of Urban History, 30/1 (2003), 102–25.

circles.[3] And perhaps just as importantly, historians tend not to see sociable practices as purely formal exercises performed for their own sake, or just for fun. Sociability is often understood as work with a purpose. Despite the veneer of superficiality that encompassed most forms of old regime aristocratic sociability, historians have uncovered the important role played by these forms in maintaining cohesion within social orders and distinction between them, as well as in facilitating the communication of knowledge and information. In other words, understanding old regime sociability does not shed light on the frivolity and aloofness of aristocratic society, it rather helps us understand how old regime society worked—that is, how social cohesion was maintained and how social conflict was negotiated—and whether these sociable practices were successful or not.

Sociability has figured prominently in recent histories of consumer society and material cultures. It has become increasingly clear to historians and social theorists that the places where consumption took place, or where consumer desires were stimulated, and the social milieux in which consumers were located are just as important to understand as the actual acts of consumption.[4] For historians of early modernity, this has led to a renewed interest in 'public' spaces and social situations such as princely courts along with urban institutions such as coffee houses, clubs, salons, shops, and taverns.[5] Theorists and historians of sociability, and the consumption practices encouraged by various forms of sociability, have traditionally focused their attention on either early modern court society or civil society, and in so doing they have tended to reinforce a sense of distinction between the state and civil society, and between aristocratic and bourgeois society. The development of new consumer tastes has often been understood either as the product of a 'trickle down' effect from the courts and aristocratic societies of the old regimes, or it has been argued to be the result of entirely new forms of urban sociability in which aristocratic pretensions were eclipsed or ignored by bourgeois norms of equality. The innovative role of court society for the development of new manners and new consumer tastes has often been associated with the historical sociology of Norbert Elias, whereas the emergence of new forms of civil society and especially its supposed 'bourgeois public sphere' has been singled out by theorists such as Jürgen Habermas as the key to understanding modern consumer sociability. This chapter explores both of these traditions as they developed over the course of the twentieth century.

[3] E. Francois and R. Reichart, 'Les Formes de Sociabilité en France du Milieu du 17e au Milieu du 19e Siècle', *Revue d'Histoire Moderne et Contemporaine*, 34 (1987), 453–72; James S. Amelang, 'La sociabilitat a l'edat moderna: algunes qüestions de mètode', in Carles Santacana, (ed.), *Sociabilitat i àmbit local: Actes del VI Congrés Internacional d'Història Local de Catalunya* (Barcelona: L'Avenç, 2003), 41–54; James S. Amelang, *The Flight of Icarus: Artisan Autobiography in Early Modern Europe* (Stanford: Stanford University Press, 1998), 80–114, 227–8.

[4] For example, Daniel Miller, *The Comfort of Things* (Cambridge: Polity, 2008); Miller, *A Theory of Shopping* (Ithaca, NY: Cornell University Press, 1998).

[5] Paul Yachnin and Bronwen Wilson (eds.), *Making Publics in Early Modern Europe: People, Things, Forms of Knowledge* (London: Routledge, 2009).

I

In the early twentieth century, Simmel's emphasis on the autonomy, the playfulness, and the elitist nature of sociability had great purchase, and explorations of similar themes can be detected in works such as the German Werner Sombart's *Luxus und Kapitalismus* (*Luxury and Capitalism*) (1913); the Dutch historian Johan Huizinga's *Homo Ludens* (1938); and especially the German sociologist Norbert Elias's *Über den Prozeß der Zivilisation* (1939), or *The Civilizing Process*.[6] Elias introduced Freudian insights into human psychology into a 'processual', or sometimes called 'figurational', framework for his historical sociology. In this way, the individual 'psychogenesis' can be related to a broader process of 'socio-genesis' that develops over long periods of time. Elias proposed that the basic human drives and impulses posited by Freud, such as sexual desires and proclivities towards violence, have their own histories, and that by understanding how these drives have been socialized over time we can understand how important long-term social changes, such as the development of the modern state, took place.

Like Simmel, Elias focused on old regime elites as the ideal subjects for explaining how his civilizing process worked. European court society provided the arena in which elite social mores were transformed from the warrior ethos of the medieval knights into the civilized etiquette of the early modern courtier. Although a precise point of origin cannot be identified for this civilizing process, Elias located it generally in the emergence of Renaissance courtesy manuals for princes and courtiers, such as Desiderius Erasmus's *De Civilitate Morum Puerilium* (1530). Manuals such as these gave explicit instructions for the preceptors of aristocratic youth on how to regulate their table manners; their bodily functions such as urination, defecation, spitting, or flatulence; proper states of dress or undress; sexual mores; and proper habits of speech and address. In short, the modern civilizing process owed its origins to the development of courtly etiquette in the Renaissance and its further elaboration in the courts of old regime Europe.

There is an imitative aspect in Elias's description of his civilizing process: civilization would never spread and develop if other courtiers did not ultimately imitate and follow the trends set by their already civilized peers. But Elias's is rather more nuanced than other social emulation models such as the model of conspicuous consumption advanced by the American sociologist Thorstein Veblen in his *Theory of the Leisure Class* (1899). Elias proposed a model of society as a 'network of interdependencies among human beings' which form 'a structure of mutually oriented and dependent people', or a 'figuration'.[7] Social actors do not slavishly imitate one another so much as react to one

---

[6] Werner Sombart, *Luxury and Capitalism* (1913; Ann Arbor: University of Michigan Press, 1967); Johan Huizinga, *Homo Ludens: A Study of the Play-Element in Culture* (1938; Boston: Beacon Press, 1955); Norbert Elias, *The Civilizing Process: Sociogenetic and Psychogenetic Investigations*, trans. Edmund Jephcott, rev. Eric Dunning, Johan Goudsblom, and Stephen Mennell (1939; Oxford: Blackwell, 2000).

[7] Thorstein Veblen, *The Theory of the Leisure Class*, (1899; New York: Penguin, 1994); Elias, *Civilizing Process*, 481–2.

another's behaviours and adjust their own actions and ideals in reaction to them. This figuration is at the heart of long-term social change.

Although it was published in 1939, the inauspicious issue date and language of his work meant that it had little influence on sociological thought or historical research until the first part was finally translated into French in 1973–75, and later into English in 1978–82.[8] Despite the delayed reception of Elias's works until the later 1970s and 1980s, it has had a major impact on the history of sociability and knowledge formation in more recent years, particularly as the history of early modern courts and courtly patronage has advanced and developed into its own distinct field of enquiry.

Early modern French historians remain deeply divided with regard to the validity of Elias's arguments about the importance of courtly manners on state-making and the social order of the old regime and its successors. While historians such as Orest Ranum and Roger Chartier were quick to make use of and elaborate on Elias, others such as Emmanuel Le Roy Ladurie and Daniel Gordon have been deeply critical of what they think of as Elias's overemphasis on, and misrepresentation of, early modern court society. Other historians of elite sociability in old regime France however have insisted that Elias's notion of a hegemonic court society is still useful, and indeed more useful than the more recent alternatives that have tried to distinguish sharply between a restrictive and closed court culture and a broader public sphere.[9] Perhaps because the cultural importance of the early modern English court was challenged by the experience of the seventeenth-century revolutions, and perhaps because Elias himself paid little attention to the English case, his work has had less impact on historians of England. One work of English history which has engaged directly with the civilizing process thesis, Anna Bryson's *From Courtesy to Civility* (1998) is highly critical of Elias's unidirectional teleology as well as of the ways in which he tended to read early modern prescriptive literature as descriptions of changing manners and mores.[10]

---

[8]   An exception is H. G. Koenigsberger, 'Dominium Regale or Dominium Politicum et Regale: Monarchies and Parliaments in Early Modern Europe' (1975), in Koenigsberger, *Politicians and Virtuosi: Essays in Early Modern History* (London: Hambledon, 1986), 1–26.

[9]   Orest Ranum, 'Courtesy, Absolutism, and the Rise of the French State, 1630–1660', *Journal of Modern History*, 52/3 (September 1980), 426–51; Roger Chartier, *Cultural History: Between Practices and Representations*, trans. Lydia Cochrane (Ithaca, NY: Cornell University Press, 1988), 71–94; Daniel Gordon, *Citizens Without Sovereignty: Equality and Sociability in French Thought, 1670–1789* (Princeton: Princeton University Press, 1994); and Emmanuel Le Roy Ladurie with Jean-François Fitou, *Saint-Simon and the Court of Louis XIV*, trans. Arthur Goldhammer (1997; Chicago: University of Chicago Press, 2001); see also Daniel Gordon, 'The Canonization of Norbert Elias in France: A Critical Perspective', and Roger Chartier, '"The Oldest Hath Borne Most": Response to Daniel Gordon', with Gordon, 'Response', *French Politics, Culture and Society*, 20/1 (2002), 68–100; Antoine Lilti, *Le Monde des Salons: Sociabilité et Mondanité à Paris au XVIIIe Siècle* (Paris: Fayard, 2005), 52; and Lilti, 'The Kingdom of Politesse: Salons and the Republic of Letters in Eighteenth-Century Paris', *Republics of Letters: A Journal for the Study of Knowledge, Politics, and the Arts*, 1/1 (2009): <http://rofl.stanford.edu/node/38>.

[10]   Anna Bryson, *From Courtesy to Civility: Changing Codes of Conduct in Early Modern England* (Oxford: Oxford University Press, 1998); compare Peter Burke, Brian Harrison, and Paul Slack, *Civil Histories: Essays Presented to Sir Keith Thomas* (Oxford: Oxford University Press, 2000).

Elias's emphasis on the impact of spreading codes of civility and polite conduct from the court societies has been most deeply elaborated upon by historians of early modern science. Particularly since the publication of Steven Shapin's and Simon Schaeffer's *Leviathan and the Air-Pump* (1985), historians of science have been concerned to explore the impact of contemporary prejudices regarding effective persuasion as the key to understanding how conventions of scientific reasoning and scientific proof developed after the mid-seventeenth century. While Shapin and Schaeffer owed more to later developments in the sociology of knowledge and they did not cite Elias directly in their work, their emphasis on the importance of codes of civility and gentility in the making of scientific persuasion has an affinity with Elias's arguments, and other historians of early modern science have been more explicit in their use of his work. Historians who have worked on science in the early modern courts now insist that courtly patronage, favouritism, and etiquette were not opposed to the making of scientific knowledge: to the contrary, court society made it possible.[11]

The rediscovery and, to a certain extent, the reinvention of Elias's arguments about the courtly origins of modern sociability coincided with a renewed appreciation of the role of court culture in the making of early modern forms of knowledge, be they artistic, literary, scientific, or political.[12] This trend has perhaps reached its pinnacle in the work of Daniel Roche, whose pioneering studies of French provincial academies in the old regime demonstrated both their pervasiveness and their deep integration with the social and political orders of the old regime. It is now well known that the majority of French academicians were nobles rather than the bourgeoisie, and that their ranks were comprised primarily of state servants and clergymen. While the idea of the academy itself was a product of court culture, the diffusion of the academic model in the long eighteenth century saw it become integrated with other forms of urban intellectual sociability such as Freemasonry, salons, and agricultural societies.[13] The history of the old regime academy, in other words, is a case study for the movement of intellectual authority and knowledge production from the court towards civil society.

---

[11] Steven Shapin and Simon Schaeffer, *Leviathan and the Air-Pump: Hobbes, Boyle, and the Experimental Life* (Princeton: Princeton University Press, 1985); Steven Shapin, *A Social History of Truth: Civility and Science in Seventeenth-Century England* (Chicago: University of Chicago Press, 1994); Mario Biagioli, *Galileo Courtier: The Practice of Science in the Culture of Absolutism* (Chicago: University of Chicago, 1994); Paula Findlen, *Possessing Nature: Museums, Collecting, and Scientific Culture in Early Modern Italy* (Berkeley and Los Angeles: University of California Press, 1996); Adrian Johns, *The Nature of the Book: Print and Knowledge in the Making* (Chicago: University of Chicago, 1998).

[12] For an Eliasian study of a non-courtly society, see Stephen Mennell, *The American Civilizing Process* (Cambridge: Polity, 2007).

[13] Daniel Roche, *Le Siècle des Lumières en Province: Academies et Academiciens Provinciaux, 1680–1789*, 2 vols., (Paris: École des Hautes Études, 1978); Roche, *Les Républicains des Lettres: Gens de Culture et Lumières au XVIIIe Siècle* (Paris: Fayard, 1988); see also Stéphane Van Damme, *Paris, Capitale Philosophique: De La Fronde à La Révolution* (Paris: Odile Jacob, 2005); and Lawrence Brockliss, *Calvet's Web: Enlightenment and the Republic of Letters in Eighteenth-Century France* (Oxford: Oxford University Press, 2002).

II

The history of 'civil society' has been a major growth industry in the last few decades and much of this work has developed under the rubric of explaining and exploring the rise of a 'public sphere' in early modern Europe. The English phrase 'public sphere' derives from a translation of a concept developed by the German philosopher Jürgen Habermas in his 1962 work *Strukturwandel der Öffentlichkeit*, now commonly rendered as *The Structural Transformation of the Public Sphere*.

Unlike Elias, Habermas's work located the origins of modern sociability and civil society outside of the realm of court society. Rather than seeing a civilizing process that emanated outwards from the manners of Renaissance courtiers, Habermas posited the radical emergence of an entirely new form of 'publicness' or *Öffentlichkeit* in the long eighteenth century. For Habermas, this was a bourgeois public, and it arose first as a form of literary and ultimately political publicness that existed in-between the private realm (*Privatbereich*) and the state's sphere of public power (*Sphäre der öffentlichen Gewalt*) in which court society was located. Although Habermas's literary public sphere (*literarische Öffentlichkeit*) first learned the art of 'critical-rational public debate' from contact with court society, it was ultimately transformed as it moved away from the aristocratic court and towards the bourgeois town and civil society. This new public sphere found its characteristic home in new urban social spaces such as the English coffeehouse, the French salon, and German dinner societies (*Tischgesellschaften*). It would also find expression in the rapid development of a commercialized print culture in the long eighteenth century. The emergent bourgeois public sphere would ultimately supersede and replace the outmoded 'representative public sphere' of court society in which power was simply put on display for an admiring but uncritical public. For Habermas, the bourgeois public sphere represented a more legitimate and rational basis for political judgment: it was based on 'people's public use of their reason' and as such it epitomized the best of the Enlightenment's intellectual ideals.[14] There is a normative aspect to Habermas's account: one cannot help but detect his sympathy for the emergence of the bourgeois public sphere, especially since much of the last half of the book is devoted to explaining and lamenting its ultimate decline under the pressures of advanced capitalism.

Like Elias, Habermas's strikingly original work was neither received nor assimilated very quickly by many historians, and it was particularly ignored by those writing

---

[14] Jürgen Habermas, *Strukturwandel der Öffenlichkeit: Untersuchungen zu einer Kategorie der burgerlichen Gesellschaft* (Darmstadt and Neuwied: Hermann Luchterhand Verlag, 1962), 44–5; compare Habermas, *The Structural Transformation of the Public Sphere: An Inquiry into a Category of Bourgeois Society*, trans. Thomas Burger (Cambridge, Mass.: MIT Press, 1989), 29–30, 27.

in French or English. While *Strukturwandel* was translated into Italian in 1971, it did not gain much notoriety until its French translation in 1978, but it was only after its English translation in 1989 that the work gained worldwide recognition amongst historians.[15] While Habermas continued to produce many other influential works of social and political theory throughout the 1960s, 1970s, and 1980s, his first work garnered little interest in the historical community, partly because the history of civil society and Enlightenment sociability celebrated by Habermas did not fit with the rather more state-centred and critical histories of state and society relations that were offered by other non-Marxist German historians such as Gerhard Oestreich or Reinhart Koselleck, or by conservative political theorists such as Carl Schmitt.[16] Oestreich's vision of modernization was almost entirely blind to the role of civil society and its ideals and focused instead almost entirely on the 'social disciplining' functions of the militarist state.[17] Koselleck, by contrast, took the emergence of new forms of 'Enlightened' sociability seriously, but he saw them as decidedly equivocal if not dangerous in their threat to social stability.[18]

In time however, Habermas's understanding of the importance of Enlightenment civil society in the making of modern life gathered much more international attention than that of other post-war German theorists and historians.[19] The French translation of *Strukturwandel* initiated an interest amongst historians of private life working in the 'third generation' of *Annales* historiography, and particularly those inspired by the pioneering studies of Philippe Ariès into new topics such as the history of childhood and death. Once again, Roger Chartier played an important role in introducing Habermas to historians in his edition of the early modern volume of Ariès's *History of Private Life* (1985–87); in his later work, he went on to argue that the emergence of a critical

[15] Jürgen Habermas, *Storia e critica dell'opinione pubblica*, trans. Augusto Illuminati, Ferruccio Masini, and Wanda Perretta (Bari: Laterza, 1971); Habermas, *L'espace public: archéologie de la publicité comme dimension constitutive de la société bourgeoise*, trans. Marc B. de Launay (Paris: Payot, 1978). The reception of *Strukturwandel* after its English translation is reviewed in Craig Calhoun (ed.), *Habermas and the Public Sphere* (Cambridge, MA: MIT Press, 1992).

[16] See the account of Carl Schmitt's critique of *Gemütlichkeit* sociability in Jakob Norberg, 'Inget kaffe', *Fronesis*, 24 (2007): 214–25: <http://www.eurozine.com/articles/2007-08-08-norberg-sv.html>; (Eng. trans. 'No Coffee': <http://www.eurozine.com/articles/2007-08-08-norberg-en.html>).

[17] Gerhard Oestreich, *Neostoicism and the Early Modern State*, ed. Brigitta Oestreich and H. G. Koenigsberger, trans. David McLintock (Cambridge: Cambridge University Press, 1982); Peter N. Miller, 'Nazis and Neo-Stoics: Otto Brunner and Gerhard Oestreich before and after the Second World War', *Past & Present*, 176 (2002), 144–86.

[18] Reinhart Koselleck, *Critique and Crisis: Enlightenment and the Pathogenesis of Modern Society* (1959; Oxford: Berg, 1988); Jason Edwards, '*Critique and Crisis* Today: Koselleck, Enlightenment and the Concept of Politics', *Contemporary Political Theory*, 5 (2006), 428–46.

[19] Anthony J. La Vopa, 'Conceiving a Public: Ideas and Society in Eighteenth-Century Europe', *Journal of Modern History*, 64 (1992), 98–115; Dena Goodman, 'Public Sphere and Private Life: Toward a Synthesis of Current Historiographical Approaches to the Old Regime', *History & Theory*, 31 (1992), 1–20; Harold Mah, 'Phantasies of the Public Sphere: Rethinking the Habermas of Historians', *Journal of Modern History*, 72 (2000), 153–82.

public sphere laid the conceptual groundwork for the cultural origins of the French Revolution.[20]

Early modern English historians were somewhat slower than the French to assimilate Habermas's public sphere concept into their research agenda. While the delay can be attributed in some part to the belated English translation of the work, it was also due to the entrenchment of certain Namierite and revisionist prejudices against taking ideology, or indeed any printed work of political persuasion, seriously as politically influential.[21] Unburdened by this interpretative straightjacket, historians of British colonial America and the early republic were quicker to explore the emergence of a Habermasian public sphere in their field.[22] In recent years, historians of early modern Italy have also incorporated and refined Habermas's arguments into their understanding of the period, particularly in their work on the history of communication.[23] Early modern Hispanists too have adopted the public sphere as an important part of their conceptual repertoire.[24]

Despite the initial delays in its reception, the gradual and persistent elaboration of Habermas's public sphere paradigm by historians in nearly every national and chronological field since the 1980s must surely count as one of the greatest success stories of recent historical writing. In early modern European studies, it has now been assimilated into textbook studies and grand narratives of the period, especially under the aegis of Cambridge Professor Tim Blanning, whose synthetic work *The Culture of Power and the Power of Culture* (2002) managed to reiterate Habermas's public sphere notion in a decidedly non-Marxist way that also assimilated it with the prodigious research output

[20]   Peter Burke, *The French Historical Revolution: The Annales School 1929–89* (Stanford: Stanford University Press, 1990), 67–93; Roger Chartier (ed.), *A History of Private Life: Passions of the Renaissance*, trans. Arthur Goldhammer (1986; Cambridge: Cambridge University Press, 1989), 17; Chartier, *The Cultural Origins of the French Revolution*, trans. Lydia Cochrane (Durham: Duke University Press, 1991). See also Brian Cowan, 'What Was Masculine About the Public Sphere? Gender and the Coffeehouse Milieu in Post-Restoration England', *History Workshop Journal*, 51 (2001), 130.

[21]   For elaboration, see Brian Cowan, 'Geoffrey Holmes and the Public Sphere: Augustan Historiography from Post-Namierite to the Post-Habermasian', *Parliamentary History*, 28/1 (2009), 166–78; Peter Lake, 'Retrospective: Wentworth's Political World in Revisionist and Post-Revisionist Perspective', in J. F. Merritt (ed.), *The Political World of Thomas Wentworth Earl of Strafford 1621–1641* (Cambridge: Cambridge University Press, 1996), 252–83; Thomas Cogswell, Richard Cust, and Peter Lake (eds.), *Politics, Religion and Popularity in Early Stuart Britain: Essays in Honour of Conrad Russell* (Cambridge: Cambridge University Press, 2002); and Peter Lake and Steven Pincus, *The Politics of the Public Sphere in Early Modern England* (Manchester: Manchester University Press, 2007).

[22]   Michael Warner, *The Letters of the Republic: Publication and the Public Sphere in Eighteenth-Century America* (Cambridge, MA: Harvard University Press, 1990); David Shields, *Civil Tongues: Polite Letters in British America* (Chapel Hill: University of North Carolina Press, 1997).

[23]   Brendan Dooley, *The Social History of Skepticism: Experience and Doubt in Early Modern Culture* (Baltimore: Johns Hopkins University Press, 1999); Dooley and Sabrina Baron (eds.), *The Politics of Information in Early Modern Europe* (London: Routledge, 2001); and especially, Filippo de Vivo, *Information and Communication in Venice: Rethinking Early Modern Politics* (Oxford: Oxford University Press, 2007).

[24]   William Childers, 'The Baroque Public Sphere', in David R. Castillo and Massimo Lollini (eds.), *Reason and Its Others: Italy, Spain, and the New World* (Nashville: Vanderbilt University Press, 2006), 165–85; and Antonio Castillo Gómez and James S. Amelang (eds.), *La Ciudad de las Palabras: Opinión Pública y Espacio Urbano en la Edad Moderna* (Gijón: Trea, 2010).

in old regime European cultural and political history produced in the four decades since Habermas first published his work.[25] One of the many remarkable achievements of this work is the way in which it brings the state back into its account of the efflorescence of civil society outside the state in old regime Europe. Unlike Habermas, Blanning argues that 'in most parts of Europe for most of the time, the relationship between the public sphere and the state was amicable and mutually supportive. Indeed, one might well go further and argue that the public sphere was both the creation and the extension of the state.'[26] As we shall see, this is an observation that has been largely confirmed by recent research on state and society relations in early modern Europe.

In the hands of a talented historian such as Blanning, the aristocratic court society emphasized by Elias and the bourgeois civil society that Habermas saw as the birthplace for the modern public sphere both receive due attention, and they are shown to be more closely related than a simple model of opposition would imply.[27] Rather than being seen as inimical to one another, many historians now appreciate the complexities of their interrelationships. The representational culture of the old regimes continued right up to the late eighteenth-century age of revolutions that devastated their political foundations; at the same time, the new sociable practices and social spaces of early modern civil society emerged under the carapace of the traditional social order. Modern civil society was less a radical break with the early modern society of orders than it was a natural development out of its pre-existing complexities and contradictions.

III

Historians have now reached what we might call a post-Habermasian moment in their understanding of the ways in which publics and their 'public spheres' were formed, sociability, and knowledge formation in the making of the modern world.[28]

---

[25] T. C. W. Blanning, *The Culture of Power and the Power of Culture: Old Regime Europe 1660–1789* (Oxford: Oxford University Press, 2002); Blanning, *The Pursuit of Glory: Europe 1648–1815* (London: Penguin, 2007); Blanning, 'The Commercialization and Sacralization of European Culture in the Nineteenth Century', in Blanning (ed.), *The Oxford Illustrated History of Modern Europe* (Oxford: Oxford University Press, 1996), 120–47; see also James Van Horn Melton, *The Rise of the Public in Enlightenment Europe*, (Cambridge: Cambridge University Press, 2001); and Hamish Scott and Brendan Simms (eds.), *Cultures of Power in Europe during the Long Eighteenth Century* (Cambridge: Cambridge University Press, 2007).

[26] Blanning, *Culture of Power and the Power of Culture*, 13.

[27] Blanning, *Culture of Power and the Power of Culture*; Blanning, *Pursuit of Glory*; Blanning, 'Commercialization and Sacralization of European Culture'; see also Melton, *The Rise of the Public in Enlightenment Europe*; and Scott and Simms (eds.), *Cultures of Power in Europe*.

[28] Stéphane Van Damme, 'Farewell Habermas? Deux Décennies d'Étude sur l'Espace Public', *Les Dossiers du Grihl* [Online] 'Les dossiers de Stéphane Van Damme, Historiographie et méthodologie', Published 28 June 2007, consulted 10 June 2011. URL: http://dossiersgrihl.revues.org/682; DOI: 10.4000/dossiersgrihl.682.

By post-Habermasian, we should not assume that Habermas's ideas have been entirely rejected or that his scheme for understanding the emergence of modern civil society has been superseded by other challengers. The preceding discussion has shown that, if anything, historians have only become more enamoured with Habermas's terminology and concepts than ever before. But they have also modified his public sphere concept and his arguments about its modern emergence in ways that make their use of his language and ideas very different from their original meanings.

Most significant is the jettisoning of Habermas's Marxist framework for his grand historical theory. Nearly all historians writing today have abandoned the Marxist fixation on class conflict and historical teleology that are central presuppositions of Habermas's original work; although it might be argued that Habermas's text itself evinces some substantial anxieties about these matters as well. Dena Goodman's 1992 declaration that 'in this post-Marxist and post-Cold War world, we can purge Habermas of his Marxism without too much trouble' is typical of the reception and use of public sphere theory amongst historians in the last few decades.[29]

Habermas has been most useful in providing historians with a new framework for discussing the history and significance of sociability. For it was in the emergence of new forms of sociability in the long eighteenth century that Habermas identified his bourgeois public sphere, and it is precisely these forms of sociability that have fascinated growing numbers of historians in recent decades. Here again, however, new research has begun to question the basic details of the original Habermasian story. This is particularly true with reference to the chronology of the emergence of the bourgeois public sphere, an issue that is related to the Marxism of the original work. For Habermas, the bourgeois public sphere had to be in some sense related to the 'bourgeois revolutions' of western Europe and thus its emergence was located roughly in the century between the British Glorious Revolution of 1688—he wrote before English Marxists such as Christopher Hill had made their case for the 1640s and 1650s as the real English bourgeois revolution—and the French Revolution of 1789. Subsequent (and non-Marxist) historians have felt less constrained to fit the public sphere into an age of bourgeois revolutions, and thus there has been a constant push to search further and further back into the past to find the earliest moment in which a Habermasian public sphere might be identified.[30]

The quixotic quest for a precise moment of origin for the modern public sphere is perhaps best abandoned, and historians of late have shown more enthusiasm for exploring the varieties of 'publicness' and the many forms of sociability that have existed in the past. In *The Social Life of Coffee* (2005), I examined the emergence of a new coffeehouse public sphere in seventeenth- and early eighteenth-century Britain, a social form that

[29] Goodman, 'Public Sphere and Private Life,' 8. Compare Jon Cowans, 'Habermas and French History: The Public Sphere and the Problem of Political Legitimacy', *French History*, 13/2 (1999), 134–60

[30] See, for example, Steven Pincus, '"Coffee Politicians Does Create": Coffeehouses and Restoration Political Culture', *Journal of Modern History*, 67 (1995), 807–34; Alexandra Halasz, *The Marketplace of Print: Pamphlets and the Public Sphere in Early Modern England* (Cambridge: Cambridge University Press, 1997); David Zaret, *Origins of Democratic Culture: Printing, Petitions, and the Public Sphere in Early-Modern England* (Princeton: Princeton University Press, 2000).

Habermas had identified as a paradigmatic example for his bourgeois public sphere. I argued that the rise of the coffeehouse was best understood as an extension of the early modern social order and the systems of state governance (both local and national) in which it was situated. The taste for coffee as a desirable commodity developed from an intellectual culture of curiosity cultivated by self-proclaimed virtuosi that managed to adapt coffee drinking into pre-existing consumption habits. In so doing, they managed to domesticate and civilize a hitherto foreign and suspect new drink. Similarly, the coffeehouse survived and flourished as a new social space because it was quickly integrated into the urban economy and was regulated through the familiar forms of licensing that local governments used to manage other public drinking houses such as taverns or alehouses. Without abandoning entirely the public sphere concept, the book revised its use in a way that tried to make it more attentive to early modern concepts of 'publicness'.[31]

A parallel project can be discerned in Antoine Lilti's *Le Monde des Salons* (2005). This monograph sought to refute the neo-Habermasian interpretation of the French salon, another social form which Habermas claimed was the French counterpart to the English coffeehouse as a 'center of criticism', and which has become the object of intense interest amongst old regime French historians in recent years.[32] Lilti's salons are reintegrated into a history of French aristocratic society, one that was perhaps even more deeply influenced by courtly manners and mores than it was by the 'bourgeois' world of urban cafés, fairs, and theatres. French salon society in this account is best understood as an aspect of an elitist *mondain* sociability whose outlook was deeply inward looking and self-obsessed, despite its 'worldly' pretences. Far from being a shelter from court society and the absolutist state, the French salon was an integral part of this world in this account. If neither the English coffeehouse nor the French salon can be understood to have occupied a social role of structural opposition to the early modern state, then the place of the public sphere in old regime society will have to be reconsidered in ways starkly different from the manner in which Habermas presented it.

One major reason for this reconsideration of the Habermasian public sphere schema is that historians have engaged in an even broader rethinking of the nature and role of the early modern state in recent years. This work has been most advanced in studies of the early modern English (and later British) state, but historians of the absolutist French state have also radically revised their understanding of its relationship to French society.[33] Indeed, it might be argued that French historians such as Maurice Agulhon paved the way with their pathbreaking analyses of sociability as a means of explaining

---

[31] Brian Cowan, *The Social Life of Coffee: The Emergence of the British Coffeehouse* (New Haven: Yale University Press, 2005); Cowan, 'The Rise of the Coffeehouse Reconsidered', *Historical Journal*, 47/1 (2004), 21–46.

[32] Lilti, *Le Monde des Salons*; Lilti, 'Kingdom of *Politesse*'; Habermas, *Structural Transformation*, 33; and compare Dena Goodman, *The Republic of Letters: A Cultural History of the French Enlightenment* (Ithaca, NY: Cornell University Press, 1994); Gordon, *Citizens Without Sovereignty*.

[33] William Beik, *Absolutism and Society in Seventeenth-Century France: State Power and Provincial Aristocracy in Languedoc* (Cambridge: Cambridge University Press, 1985); for a review of recent trends, see Beik, 'The Absolutism of Louis XIV as Social Collaboration', *Past & Present*, 188 (2005), 195–224.

the political changes and divisions that emerged in France during its revolutionary century from 1789 to 1871.[34]

Sociability has provided a means of understanding this experience of governing and being governed. If an 'unacknowledged republic' of office-holding was going to work, then local office-holders had to be sociable; this was especially true since offices were held only for short periods of time and thus they rotated amongst a formally egalitarian class of potential office-holders.[35] The early modern term was 'civil' rather than sociable, and the concept of civility has indeed taken centre stage in recent accounts of early modern state formation.[36] It is now clear that Renaissance ideals of civil conversation and rhetoric were just as important to the maintenance of Habermas's civil society as they were to Elias's court society.[37] Speaking and behaving in a civil manner were crucial to the successful performance of authority throughout early modern society, and not just at its very pinnacle.[38]

As the reconceptualization of the state as an entity much less distinct from the rest of the social order than hitherto recognized continues to proceed, our understandings of the commonly recognized civil society elements of the public sphere will also need to be revised accordingly. This has now been achieved for the English coffeehouse and the French salon; much less work has been done on the last element of Habermas's original holy trinity of civil society institutions, the German *Tischgesellschaften*, or dinner societies. This is most likely because these exclusive and nationalist organizations never fit well with the ideals of openness and liberal politics that are often associated with the characteristic institutions of the Habermasian public sphere.[39] Recent work on other voluntary associations such as clubs and Freemasons's lodges, as well as commercialized spaces for public association such as inns, taverns, restaurants, theatres,

[34] Maurice Agulhon, *The Republic in the Village*, trans. Janet Lloyd (1970; Cambridge: Cambridge University Press, 1982); Agulhon, *Pénitents et Francs-Maçons de l'Ancienne Provence: Essai sur la Sociabilité Méridionale* (1968; Paris: Fayard, 1984); Agulhon, *Le Cercle dans la France Bourgeoise 1810–1848: Étude d'une Mutation de Sociabilité* (Paris: Armand Colin, 1977); Carol-Anne Rivière, 'La Spécificité Française de la Construction Sociologique du Concept de Sociabilité', *Réseaux*, 123/1 (2004), 207–31; Stéphane Van Damme, 'La Sociabilité Intellectuelle: Les Usages Historiographiques d'une Notion', *Hypothèses*, 1 (1997), 121–32.

[35] Mark Goldie, 'The Unacknowledged Republic: Officeholding in Early Modern England', in Tim Harris (ed.), *The Politics of the Excluded, c. 1500–1850* (Basingstoke: Palgrave, 2001), 153–94.

[36] Michael J. Braddick, *State Formation in Early Modern England, c. 1550–1700* (Cambridge: Cambridge University Press, 2000); Phil Withington, *The Politics of Commonwealth: Citizens and Freemen in Early Modern England* (Cambridge: Cambridge University Press, 2005); Withington, 'Public Discourse, Corporate Citizenship, and State Formation in Early Modern England', *American Historical Review*, 112/4 (2007), 1016–38.

[37] Withington, *The Politics of Commonwealth*, 124–55; David Randall, 'Epistolary Rhetoric, the Newspaper, and the Public Sphere', *Past & Present*, 198 (2008), 3–32.

[38] Michael J. Braddick, 'Administrative Performance: The Representation of Political Authority in Early Modern England', in Michael J. Braddick and John Walter (eds.), *Negotiating Power in Early Modern Society: Order, Hierarchy, and Subordination in Britain and Ireland* (Cambridge: Cambridge University Press, 2001), 166–87.

[39] Deborah Hertz, *Jewish High Society in Old Regime Berlin* (New Haven: Yale University Press, 1988), 271–5.

and concert halls all point to lapses, lacunae, and problematic assumptions in the Habermasian schema.[40] Above all, Habermas's overemphasis on the 'Enlightenment' as the precise moment for the emergence of civil society and its public sphere no longer seems tenable. As more detailed research proceeds on these characteristic constituent elements of early modern civil society, it is likely that important national and regional differences will emerge. An English coffeehouse was quite a different place than a French *café*, or a German *Kaffeehaus*, for example, and the nature of these places changed over time as well.[41] Disaggregation of the sometimes too often lumped together elements of the public sphere has only just begun, but our understanding of the complex ways in which they were embedded into the social and political structures around them is already much richer than it was when Habermas composed his famous thesis on the topic.

Another area of investigation which has proved immensely fruitful has been the study of the contemporary meanings of common words used to designate forms of social association. Amongst English historians, this work took off when they began to study the terms used by contemporaries to make sense of the early modern social order. Beginning as a search for the origins of a 'language of class', these studies have explored the rich vocabulary of early modern social distinction.[42] In recent years, the approach has been used to interrogate and explicate other contemporary terms of social description, including such key (and diachronically malleable) terms as 'family', 'community', 'public', and 'company.'[43] Research along these lines will be absolutely essential if we are ever to recover an understanding of the historical specificities of past

[40]   Peter Clark, *British Clubs and Societies 1580–1800: The Origins of an Associational World* (Oxford: Clarendon Press, 2000); Michelle O'Callaghan, *The English Wits: Literature and Sociability in Early Modern England* (Cambridge: Cambridge University Press, 2007); Margaret C. Jacob, *Living the Enlightenment: Freemasonry and Politics in Eighteenth-Century Europe* (Oxford: Oxford University Press, 1991); Beat Kümin, *Drinking Matters: Public Houses and Social Exchange in Early Modern Central Europe* (Basingstoke: Palgrave, 2007); Rebecca Spang, *The Invention of the Restaurant: Paris and Modern Gastronomic Culture* (Cambridge, MA: Harvard University Press, 2000); Jeffrey S. Ravel, *The Contested Parterre: Public Theatre and French Political Culture 1680–1791* (Ithaca, NY: Cornell University Press, 1999).

[41]   Brian Cowan, 'Cafés', in Daniel Roche et al. (eds.), *Le Dictionnaire Historique de la Civilisation Européene* (Paris: Fayard, forthcoming); W. Scott Haine, *The World of the Paris Café: Sociability Among the French Working Class, 1789–1914* (Baltimore: Johns Hopkins University Press, 1996); Cowan, 'Publicity and Privacy in the History of the British Coffeehouse', *History Compass*, 5/4 (2007), 1180–1213.

[42]   Keith Wrightson, 'Estates, Degrees and Sorts: Changing Perceptions of Society in Tudor and Stuart England', in Penelope Corfield (ed.), *Language, History and Class* (Oxford: Blackwell, 1991), 30–52; and Wrightson, 'Sorts of People in Tudor and Stuart England', in Jonathan Barry, (ed.), *The Middling Sort of People: Culture, Society and Politics in England, 1550–1800* (Basingstoke: Macmillan, 1994), 28–51; and see now Alexandra Shepard, 'Poverty, Labour and the Language of Social Description in Early Modern England', *Past & Present*, 201 (2008), 51–95.

[43]   Naomi Tadmor, 'The Concept of the Household-Family in Eighteenth-Century England', *Past & Present*, 151 (1996), 111–40; Alexandra Shepard and Phil Withington (eds.), *Communities in Early Modern England* (Manchester: Manchester University Press, 2000); Withington, 'Public Discourse, Corporate Citizenship, and State Formation'; Withington, 'Company and Sociability in Early Modern England', *Social History*, 32/3 (2007), 291–307.

understandings of social life. Indeed, the word 'sociability' itself was an early modern term with currency in English from at least the sixteenth century, and yet the history of the concept awaits further explanation.[44] Contemporary terms such as 'luxury' used to describe or evaluate consumers and their consumption preferences still require further investigation.[45] More work needs to be done: the history of concepts such as shopping, ownership, and possessions, for example, all require further investigation, particularly for the early modern period. This sort of *Begriffsgeschichte*, or conceptual history of early modern social descriptions, will be essential to any understanding of how the experiences of publicness, sociability, and consumption were understood and experienced in the past.[46]

IV

Here we find ourselves returning full circle back to where we started at the outset. For the theorization of sociability did not begin with Simmel in the early twentieth century; indeed, the various meanings and significances attributed to 'sociability' have been a major topic of recent investigation for intellectual historians of Enlightenment Europe.[47] It is now well known that sociability was clearly a topic of major concern for eighteenth-century writers such as Joseph Addison, the third Earl of Shaftesbury, Bernard Mandeville, David Hume, Adam Smith, and Giambattista Vico, to name just a few of the leading figures of the era, but the prehistory of this Enlightenment fixation requires further study. How and why did sociability become such a major topic for discussion and debate in eighteenth-century intellectual culture? Despite a few attempts to link the intellectual history of sociability with its social history, the connection between the two remains very difficult to establish. It can hardly be coincidental that the Enlightenment theorization of sociability was contemporaneous with, and accompanied by, the theorization of consumption and commercial society as well. Sociability, commerce, and

[44] For the French '*sociabilité*' however, see Gordon, *Citizens Without Sovereignty*: for England, see now Phil Withington, *Society in Early Modern England* (Cambridge: Polity, 2010).

[45] John Sekora, *Luxury: The Concept in Western Thought, Eden to Smollett* (Baltimore: Johns Hopkins University Press, 1977); Christopher J. Berry, *The Idea of Luxury: A Conceptual and Historical Investigation* (Cambridge: Cambridge University Press, 1994); John Shovlin, *The Political Economy of Virtue: Luxury, Patriotism, And the Origins of the French Revolution* (Ithaca, NY: Cornell University Press, 2006).

[46] Reinhart Koselleck, *The Practice of Conceptual History: Timing History, Spacing Concepts*, trans. Todd Samuel Presner et al. (Stanford: Stanford University Press, 2002).

[47] John Robertson, *The Case for Enlightenment: Scotland and Naples 1680–1760* (Cambridge: Cambridge University Press, 2005); Lawrence Klein, *Shaftesbury and the Culture of Politeness: Moral Discourse and Cultural Politics in Early Eighteenth-Century England* (Cambridge: Cambridge University Press, 1994); Klein, 'The Figure of France: The Politics of Sociability in England, 1660–1715', *Yale French Studies*, 92 (1997), 30–45; Christopher Berry, 'Sociality and Socialisation', in Alexander Brodie (ed.), *The Cambridge Companion to the Scottish Enlightenment* (Cambridge: Cambridge University Press, 2003), 243–57.

consumption were all theorized in conjunction in the writings of eighteenth-century literati such as Addison, Shaftesbury, Mandeville, and Smith.[48]

By the time that Simmel began to formulate his sociology of modern life in the early twentieth century, the 'old regimes' of the centuries preceding the French Revolution had become the stuff of romantic memory and idealization. Victorian rationalism was haunted by memories of the old regimes of the not so distant past, and so were the historians and social theorists of its age.[49] The era we now call early modern was sufficiently removed from the experience of high modernity to seem different, somewhat strange, and not just a little bit appealing, particularly to critics of modernity such as Simmel.

The challenge for post-Habermasian historians of early modern sociability in the twenty-first century will be to avoid the spectres of our own recent, twentieth-century past. Both Elias and Habermas lived through the Second World War and the cold war that followed. For the Jewish Elias, this experience included the death of his mother at Auschwitz and a permanent relocation to England; while Habermas has managed to see his defeated and divided post-war German homeland reunited and reintegrated into an unprecedentedly effective European Union. He has succeeded in establishing himself as one of Europe's most pre-eminent philosopher-kings and continues to press onwards towards the establishment of a new European constitution in a fashion that would be recognizable to the Enlightenment *philosophes* of his much vaunted public sphere.[50] The history of the relationships between sociability and consumption in what one can only hope will be a new age of cosmopolitanism and international cooperation may offer greater reason for optimism than it did for its founders in central Europe nearly a century ago.

BIBLIOGRAPHY

Agulhon, Maurice, *The Republic in the Village*, trans. Janet Lloyd (1970; Cambridge: Cambridge University Press, 1982).

Blanning, Tim, *The Culture of Power and the Power of Culture: Old Regime Europe 1660–1789* (Oxford: Oxford University Press, 2002).

Cowan, Brian, *The Social Life of Coffee: The Emergence of the British Coffeehouse* (New Haven and London: Yale University Press, 2005).

[48] Lawrence Klein, 'Politeness and the Interpretation of the British Eighteenth Century', *Historical Journal*, 45/4 (2002), 869–98; Anne Goldgar, *Impolite Learning: Conduct and Community in the Republic of Letters, 1680–1750* (New Haven: Yale University Press, 1995); E. J. Hundert, *The Enlightenment's Fable: Bernard Mandeville and the Discovery of Society* (Cambridge: Cambridge University Press, 1994).

[49] Lionel Gossman, *Basel in the Age of Burckhardt: A Study in Unseasonable Ideas* (Chicago: University of Chicago Press, 2000); Brian W. Young, *The Victorian Eighteenth Century* (Oxford: Oxford University Press, 2007); Alan Pitt, 'The Irrationalist Liberalism of Hippolyte Taine', *Historical Journal*, 41/4 (1998), 1035–53; Jazbinsek, 'The Metropolis and the Mental Life of Georg Simmel'.

[50] Jürgen Habermas, 'Why Europe Needs A Constitution', *New Left Review*, 11 (2001), 5–26.

Elias, Norbert, *The Civilizing Process: Sociogenetic and Psychogenetic Investigations*, trans. Edmund Jephcott, rev. Eric Dunning, Johan Goudsblom, and Stephen Mennell (1939; rev. edn. Oxford: Blackwell, 2000).

Habermas, Jürgen, *The Structural Transformation of the Public Sphere: An Inquiry into a Category of Bourgeois Society*, trans. Thomas Burger (1962; reprint Cambridge, MA: MIT Press, 1989).

Lilti, Antoine, *Le Monde des Salons: Sociabilité et Mondanité à Paris au XVIIIe Siècle* (Paris: Fayard, 2005).

Scott Haine, W., *The World of the Paris Café: Sociability Among the French Working Class 1789-1914* (Baltimore: Johns Hopkins University Press, 1996).

Simmel, Georg, *The Sociology of Georg Simmel*, trans. and ed. Kurt H. Wolf, (Glencoe, IL: Free Press, 1950).

Withington, Phil, *The Politics of Commonwealth: Citizens and Freemen in Early Modern England* (Cambridge: Cambridge University Press, 2005).

Wilson, Bronwen, and Yachnin, Paul (eds.), *Making Publics in Early Modern Europe: People, Things, Forms of Knowledge*, (London: Routledge, 2009).

CHAPTER 14

SMALL SHOPS AND DEPARTMENT STORES

HEINZ-GERHARD HAUPT

IN his novel *Au bonheur des dames* (*The Ladies Paradise*) (1883), Emile Zola describes the difference between two worlds of retailing in 1870s Paris. When Denise, the novel's twenty-year-old heroine, arrives in the metropolis, she is confronted by the disparity between her uncle's drapery shop and the newly opened department store. To enter her relative's shop, she has first to go down a flight of stairs which leads her to a humid, dark shop called Vieil Elbeuf. Altogether it employs a handful of shop assistants. The alternative is a much larger and brighter building. It is made of steel and glass and upon entering she faces a broad stairway; a huge variety of goods are displayed: the department store. The plot of *Au bonheur des dames* eventually unites both worlds as Zola concluded the novel with the marriage of Denise and the proprietor of the department store. Unlike Zola's story, however, for a long time historical research on small shops and department stores concentrated on conflict between them.

Historians identified small and large shops as representing discord between traditional and modern, pre-capitalist and capitalist, features of development. For many historians, once this tension had been identified, the implications were inevitable. In the end, small shopkeepers lost ownership of their shops and became another example of proletarianization. Just as Denise's uncle views the department store as a threatening enemy, it was argued that small shopkeepers refused to accept their destiny and defended traditional shops against the modernization of the retail business. In this historiography, the organization and struggle of small shopkeepers against large stores was another example of how the modernization of society produced anti-modernist forces. It drew specific attention to the proximity of such anti-modernist forces to fascist movements and interpreted the actions of small shopkeepers as part of a broader revolt against capitalist industrialization and modernity, suggesting that small shopkeepers were embedded in corporatist, pre-modern structures.

More recent research from the 1980s on has however made the paradigm of opposition redundant. Social and political historians have carefully analysed the role of small shops and department stores, creating a much richer knowledge about both kinds of retail trading. These studies have underlined the heterogeneity of shops, broadening the focus of research to include shops located in proletarian neighbourhoods as well as in established town centres. They have also placed the emergence of department stores within the context of the broader changes which took place in the retail trade. This research has shown how large retail traders had access to greater amounts of capital than small shopkeepers, which allowed them to use new forms of advertising and to reorganize the methods of buying and selling.

In following this approach, changes in the constellation of the retail trade will be highlighted. This chapter will stress the importance of consumer behaviour as both a factor influencing the trade and as a product of changes in the trade itself. In doing so, it will draw attention to the influence of the organization of shops upon consumers and the effect of consumer attitudes upon the structure and appearance of the retailing trade. Furthermore, it will address the questions of how much consumers adjusted to changing conditions of trade and the development of new retailing regimes, as well as the degree to which the trades themselves reacted to conditions in the labour market, the process of urbanization, and changes in consumer preferences.

PREDOMINANCE OF SMALL SHOPS

Statistical analysis of the size of the retail sector focused upon shop size to examine the degree of concentration and capitalization in the distribution sector. One such study at the end of the 1990s, by the European Commission, revealed that even after a century of competition between small shops and large retailers, small units remained overwhelmingly in place. It included the observation that the 'retail trade is characterized by a major fragmentation and a substantial presence of micro-enterprises (1–4 persons employed) which shares over 80 per cent in most of the countries observed.'[1] In European retail sectors there is, however, considerable variation in the survival of small shops. The smallest businesses on average are mainly found in Spain, Italy, and Portugal, and the largest in Germany, Austria, and the Netherlands. The predominance of smaller shops is not however a phenomenon limited to Europe. In Japan in 1972 in a survey which counted 1,494,643 retailers, 990,047 remained as family-run shops. In 1997, even in the rapidly expanding retail market in China, small shops remained the most widespread form of commerce, with 13.5 million small shops counted. The large numbers of small shops should not however be mistaken for their economic independence. During the second half of the twentieth century, small shops were integrated in commercial chains which also imposed merchandising, publicity, sales strategies, and shop-floor plans. Those

---

[1] European Commission, *Distributive Trades in Europe. 1995–1999* (Luxemburg, 2001), 6.

shopkeepers who opposed such integration often went out of business. For example, in West Germany the small family-run shops Tante Emma Laden disappeared during the 1960s when the chain's management introduced self-service and forced the shops to be dependant on it for branded goods and logistics support.

However, analysis which only focuses upon shop size fails to illuminate substantial differences. Crucial other factors which determined the viability of small shops include capital investment, the type of goods sold, and shops' urban or rural locations. Shops selling drapery, confection, or household goods generally required a higher capital investment than those in the food, beverage, or tobacco sector. In general, shops with higher capital investment tend to have a more stable existence. Today this is highest in food shops. During the nineteenth century it was highest in textiles and household furniture. Typically, shops with low levels of investment are managed by families, only employing labour from outside the family in exceptional cases. At the end of the twentieth century, 21.7 per cent of all retailers in the European Union were self-employed. In Greece and Italy the percentage of self-employed retailers was as high as 60 per cent. In Spain and Portugal it was over 40 per cent. In these types of shop the turnover in ownership is and was high. In Bremen, for example, around 1900 two-thirds of shops changed proprietor after only six years.

Important obstacles to the increased concentration and higher capitalization of trade include the size of agrarian populations and their often weak purchasing power. In areas where subsistence agriculture and the direct exchange of goods remained prominent, the importance and concentration of the retailing trade was correspondingly reduced. Examples at the end of the twentieth century include Italy, Spain, or Greece, as well as India, Russia, or China. For example, in China in 2003 the urban market amounted to only 39 per cent of the national population. It was however responsible for 76 per cent of national retail sales. The much larger rural market of 785 million people, spread across the Chinese countryside, accounted for the remaining 24 per cent. The difference between the value of rural and urban retail sales is a result of the strong imbalance between rural and urban purchasing power. Average per capita spending for shopping is estimated at no more than $2 per day in rural China.

One of the most important features of the long-term history of the retail trade is its dualistic urban and rural structure, and alongside this the growth of retailing in the countryside. Currently, the process of sedentarization of the retail trade is taking place in Africa and Asia. For a long time, itinerant traders provided Europe, Japan, and other parts of the world with goods. For example, French *colporteurs* sold needles and cotton to the rural population. They also sold literary products such as almanacs. *Colporteurs* were prominent figures in eighteenth- and nineteenth-century France and they were feared by authorities who suspected them of spreading unwanted news and rumours. A similar kind of itinerant sales took place in Japan at the same time. At the end of the nineteenth century in the rural Hiroshima Prefecture, 62.6 per cent of all commerce was undertaken by mobile traders. The percentage of mobile traders found in Hiroshima town was lower. By 1892, 59.3 per cent of all traders there owned permanent shops and only four years later, this figure had risen to 66.9 per cent. Research suggests that itinerant commerce remained widespread in Japan and in southern Europe for longer than in western Europe. There, its decline occurred earlier, at least by the second half of the nineteenth century. This decline was a result of urbanization and the simultaneous concentration of purchasing power in towns, as well as governments' close control of mobile populations.

In these societies mobile itinerant trade was a sub-proletarian strategy of survival. It usually involved selling vegetables or fruit, which required minimal capital investment. Indeed, it has been shown that itinerant traders often dealt in products which remained unsold at the end of the market day. Those selling these goods were often marginal figures such as the unemployed, widows, or the disabled, some of whom moved their goods in wheelbarrows across towns. The sight of these itinerant traders agitated established shopkeepers. This tension reached its high point at the end of the nineteenth and beginning of the twentieth century. Shopkeepers with fixed premises feared competition from mobile traders and were aggrieved because itinerant traders did not have to pay the same taxes. A Belgian inquiry at the start of the twentieth century revealed that retailers viewed mobile traders as more dangerous competition than the more recent arrival of department stores.

Research by social historians has produced a complex picture of the urban retail trade. In place of the older homogenous image of such trade, social historians have emphasized the importance of unstable neighbourhood shops, run by the shopkeeper or his family. For example, historians of consumption in Weimar Germany have shown that in 1925 shops had an average of only 2.14 employees. Such neighbourhood-based shops were characteristically different from longer established merchants. Crucial differences included their practices of buying and selling, the renting of premises, and above all shop stability. Richer merchants, usually in the confection, drapery, or household sectors, tended to own their stores, employ staff outside the family, and act as providers in direct relation with producers. As a result of their durability, family knowledge was passed from generation to generation, a form of commercial heritage which was unavailable to the much more unstable neighbourhood shop. It was in this commercial environment in the first half of the nineteenth century in Western Europe that we find the first shops which began selling a variety of goods. Remarkably, the employees or merchants of such shops are found among the founders of the first department stores. For example, Boucicaut, who founded the first European department store in Paris, Bon Marché, had worked as an employee before the 1860s.

BIRTH OF THE DEPARTMENT STORE WITHIN THE CAPITALIZATION OF RETAILING

Department stores retained several older practices from the pre-existing retail world. At the same time, because of their size, their splendour, their architecture, and their links to the world of entertainment, department stores were also places of innovation.

Examples of innovation by department stores include extending the range of available products and expanding their sales to cover the whole territory. Beside confection and household goods, in Germany some department stores even sold food products. In Britain, Whiteley's claimed its London department store was a 'Universal Provider'. Department stores extended their market beyond the street and local town by using catalogues and correspondence to sell to national and in some cases even to international markets. As described in *Au bonheur des dames*, the structure of the department store was also innovative. Stores were located in modern buildings and equipped with new technologies. They were usually situated in the centre of towns and cities, contributing to the emergence of the idea of a town centre. Other innovations included the provision of a greater range of services and assistance. To do this, they employed an army of shop assistants. They also directly linked entertainment and consumption, organizing concerts and expositions, and included salons, all of which was intended for an explicitly bourgeois public. These new ways of displaying and selling goods were overwhelmingly successful. The opening of new shops became major public events. For example, in Bremen in 1906, when a new Karstadt was opened, the shop had to be closed due to overcrowding.

Before 1914, the new model of retail provided by the department store was highly successful. Its success may be seen by the way it spread to very different geographical areas, including Cairo, Budapest, Moscow, and by 1917 also Rome, as well as the United States, Argentina, and Japan. The success of the new department stores was made possible by changes in the production of a wide range of consumer goods, the emergence of mass media and the possibilities it offered for advertising. Further fundamental changes included the increase in real wages and mobility. During the inter-war period however, limits to the expansion of department stores in the United States and in parts of Europe began to appear. One-price shops like Woolworths in the United States or Prixunic in France appeared as major competitors to department stores. They could challenge them because they appear to have been economically more successful than the department stores with their high costs and low margins. At the same time, however, the expansion of department stores continued in other parts of the world including Japan and China. During the inter-war period French department stores expanded in Cairo. After the Second World War, there was also a rapid expansion in the number of department stores in Japan. Between 1956 and 1972 their number grew from 177 to 855. In China after 1990 they went through a short period of rapid growth. This honeymoon period appears to have come to an end by 1998, which one commentator described as the 'year of [the] closing door for department stores'.[2]

The emergence of department stores was not the only new form of retail trading which threatened shopkeepers. In the nineteenth century shops created by the co-operative movement slowly emerged across Europe as a serious threat to traditional shops. Co-operatives managed shops' relations with producers and began selling

---

[2] Zhen, *Globalization and the Chinese Retailing Revolution. Competing in the World's Largest Emerging Market* (Oxford, 2007), 77.

large amounts of cheap and healthy goods in packaged form. Only members of the co-operative were permitted to shop in the stores and profits from co-operatives were distributed among members. In Europe, the model of the Rochdale Pioneers in the 1830s was extremely successful in Great Britain, but not so much in other countries. In some places in the nineteenth century, co-operatives did not at first last long. Outside Great Britain, they only achieved stability during the 1880s with the support of working-class social reform movements. This was especially the case in Germany, France, Belgium, and Switzerland, and to a lesser extent in Japan. Co-operatives survived the inter-war period and expanded after 1945, especially in Switzerland, Sweden, and Great Britain. This was in part because they were linked to workers, but also because of the high quality of the goods they offered.

The Confrontation Between Small Shops and Department Stores

As described in Zola's *Au bonheur des dames* traditional shopkeepers contested the emergence of department stores. The antagonism between the two forms of retail is the subject of a great deal of historical research. This research has shown that the fear that the growth of large department stores would destroy traditional small shops was exaggerated. Even as far into the twentieth century as 1939, department stores remained responsible for only a tiny percentage of retail sales. In Japan at this time, department stores realized 9.1 per cent of retail sales. In Britain, they managed only between 4.5 and 5.5 per cent. The number of small shops does not generally reduce but has tended to increase during times of economic crisis, such as following 1929, as periods of rapid growth in unemployment result in increased numbers of small shops. The newly unemployed often opened small shops as a means of surviving the displacement caused by economic crisis. Even today, all over the world, small and mobile shops are still one of the means of an informal economy used by the subaltern classes. In fact, in the long run, the department store was less threatening to small shops than other forms of retail such as chain stores and supermarkets. Indeed, since the beginning of the inter-war period and continuing after 1945, the economic and commercial importance of department stores has been in decline.

Small shops and department stores could co-exist because they targeted different market segments. Small shops sold goods or primary necessities to local neighbourhoods. They provided informal consumer credit and themselves depended upon their relationship with wholesale merchants. Department stores targeted a different market. They attempted to become a form of bourgeois sociability, selling drapery, confection, and other goods to the middle or upper classes. Even department stores targeted specific consumer groups. Among department stores in nineteenth-century Paris this hierarchy described Le Louvre as catering for opulent and upper-class customers, the Bon Marché as 'more middling and provincial in style, the Samaritaine as popular and even working class, while Printemps directed itself at a younger, small and middling bourgeois clientele keen to display its modern taste.'[3] In Japan, department stores such as Mitsukoski and Takushimaya distinguished themselves because of their privileged relationship with the imperial household and nobility. In Germany the hierarchy among department stores was slightly different. Department stores such as Karstadt, Tietz and Schorken had their origins in small provincial towns and also sold food. From the beginning their clientele was not confined to a wealthy elite but included the popular classes.

Department stores were also important spaces for newly emerging gender codes. In all countries department stores attempted to attract bourgeois women as consumers and to offer them a new public space in the late nineteenth century. They posed as morally safe places for bourgeois women. To do so they emphasized their tea salons, concerts, and the brightness of their buildings. Well-dressed shop assistants were instructed to create an atmosphere of affluence and bourgeois lifestyle. However, the way they targeted bourgeois women was not universally accepted. Critics argued that 'Eve's daughter enters the hell of temptation, like a mouse in a trap...As if from Charybdis to Scylla, she glides from counter to counter, dazzled and overpowered.'[4] Some even pointed to shoplifting by middle-class women and claimed that it was evidence of how department stores unleashed the dangerous powers of seduction. Indeed, given that department stores had tried to change the boundaries of private and public, to give more personal freedom to bourgeois women and to make the public more private, they inevitably drew the criticism of all who defended clear-cut social and cultural boundaries. In this way, department stores which because of their signs and language were the very essence of modernity became the subjects of anti-modernist critique.

In the short to medium term the economic viability of department stores was increasingly scrutinized. To many observers it appeared that the costs of huge premises, the wages of large numbers of employees, and the small margins of profit would eventually render department stores economically unviable. The high point of this economic examination occurred in Europe during the inter-war period. Department store managers responded by expanding their clientele to include the lower middle and in some cases even popular classes. They also followed the strategies of other shops aimed at a less elite market. In Liverpool, this change was illustrated by Lewis's proclamation that it was 'Friends of the People' and in Paris the Frere Dufayel chain began providing a credit system aimed at a lower-class public.

From the end of the nineteenth century onwards, department stores and small shops did not really enter into direct competition. They targeted different consumers and sold different kinds of goods. Indeed, over time even certain forms of market sharing emerged. In the neighbourhoods, where the first Parisian department stores were

[3] Geoffrey Crossick and Serge Jaumain (eds.), *Cathedrals of Consumption. The European Department Store 1850–1939* (Aldershot, 1999), 25.

[4] Pierre Perrot, *Fashioning the Bourgeois. A History of Clothing in Nineteenth Century* (Princeton, 1994), 63 (quote from the year 1882).

located, many small shops remained prosperous because they offered goods and services which remained unavailable in the department store. By the end of the twentieth century, it had even become common for self-service department stores to offer retailers the possibility of opening a small shop inside their buildings. Finally, price-fixing was an additional factor which reduced competition between large and small shops. In the Weimar Republic, for example, the price of bread was fixed across the entire country, while in southern Germany local authorities also set the price of meat and milk. At the same time in Italy prices were also controlled. During wars, rationing was also accompanied by price controls. Under these conditions, the competitive advantage of larger shops' purchasing power was reduced and competition between big and small shops was limited to certain specific products.

The Triumph of Self-Service and Supermarkets

The most serious competition for independent shopkeepers and department stores came from chain stores. The first chain stores were founded in the inter-war period, and their numbers expanded rapidly after the Second World War. Examples of this kind of model include Woolworths in the United States, Prixunic in France, and UPIM in Italy. Unlike traditional department stores, they spent far less on costly displays of goods; they also offered a wider selection of goods to the middle class and popular clientele in smaller shops. Because of their purchasing power, they were able to put pressure on producers, demanding standardized products at low prices. Over time they were increasingly successful in reducing the costs of their operations while also gaining an increased market size. This model was first successful in the United States, before it was introduced to Europe, first in Great Britain. During the 1930s, 12,000 chains existed in the UK and they held 7 per cent of the total retail turnover. After the Second World War, the self-service principle they espoused became more and more common in department stores and small shops. In Europe, Switzerland pioneered self-service shops. In Germany, the pressure from chains such as REWE and EDEKA, which had driven the rationalization of selling during the 1960s, overwhelmed traditional forms of shop organization. A similar trend occurred in Japan, where between 1964 and 1977 the numbers of self-service shops increased from 3,620 to 10,634 and their sales nearly doubled. Japanese supermarkets described themselves as *ryohan ten* (mass retailers) because they were both supermarkets and discounters at the same time.

By the final third of the twentieth century, in the global West and also in many other parts of the world, supermarkets had become the dominant form of retail. They had less employees than department stores. Their model was based upon the principle of self-service, they belonged to a chain or were a part of a department store, and they aimed to sell a wide range of cheap goods to as large a public as possible. Wal-Mart is considered to be the prototype of this kind of supermarket. The chain began in the United States in the 1950s. It first targeted smaller rural towns with populations of less than 15,000, offering them a large assortment of cheap goods. The form of the supermarket remains flexible. Supermarkets may operate as a discount outlet, lowering fixed costs and avoiding all extra expenses or display. They may also operate as part of a department store, specializing in food. The growth of supermarkets as the dominant form of retail has resulted in striking changes. Since the 1980s supermarkets have engaged in a process of concentration, and because of their market power they have been able to exercise pressure on producers. As a result of this pressure, many areas in the southern hemisphere have engaged in more and more specialized agriculture and monoculture, destroying the older range of rural activities. As this process destroyed older polycultures, countries in South America, Africa, or Asia have become more and more dependent upon grain imports from the United States. By the end of the twentieth century, dominant supermarket chains sold between 70 and 80 per cent of all food. The same trend is observable in other parts of the world. In Costa Rica, Chile, South Korea, the Philippines, and Thailand, supermarkets share of the market has risen from between 10 and 20 per cent in 1990 to between 50 and 60 per cent only ten years later. Social scientists have characterized this process which 'transforms domestic food markets' as a 'retailing revolution'.[5] Supermarkets themselves have also become subject to a process of transformation. Enlarged supermarkets now exist in the form of malls, for example those found outside US towns, or as hypermarkets such as the French chain Carrefour. Supermarket development began in the United States in the 1930s, before being adopted in Switzerland, Sweden, and Britain during the 1950s. They were established in Western Germany and Japan during the 1960s, and in China after 1990.

SELLING AND BUYING IN DIFFERENT RETAIL TRADES

The price, quality, and availability of goods is at stake in the relationship between buyers and sellers. As a result the selling situation is not determined unilaterally by consumer or retailer. Instead, the selling situation is always the outcome of a process of interaction. Retailers and consumers often shared the common interest of goods' availability. Bad harvests, insufficient distribution of goods, disruptions caused by war, or trade embargoes often changed market conditions, causing increased prices and at times shortages which even resulted in hunger. When this kind of situation occurred, on occasions consumers and retailers would side together against those whom they perceived as

---

[5] Philipp McMichael and Harriet Friedmann, 'Situating the "Retailing revolution"', in David Burch and Geoffrey Lawrence (eds.), *Supermarkets and Agri-food Supply Chains. Transformation in the Production and Consumption of Foods* (Cheltenham and Northampton, 2007), 307.

responsible for the limited availability of goods. At the same time, antagonistic interpretations of the causes of crises could occur. When this happened, both retailers and consumers demanded that the state or the municipal authorities take action to avoid a hunger crisis or violent action. One consequence of this kind of protest was the requirement for millers and bakers to retain reserve supplies of flour. State and municipal authorities also maintained reserve supplies. Other responses to shortages were to increase imports of grain or flour, or market intervention to set prices. When such mechanisms were unavailable, state authorities also reverted to rationing, for example during the First World War.

The strategies used by authorities to avoid social disturbances because of food supply were often insufficient and resulted in conflict over the course of the nineteenth and twentieth centuries. During these disputes, participants were often mobilized by what they understood as a 'fair price'. This idea was used to target those who were accused of manipulating prices against the interests of the popular classes. Historians have often used the concept of the 'moral economy' as a means of conceptualizing crowd and popular responses to price increases. Targets of protest against high prices often included large producers, and intermediaries such as millers, transporters, shippers, and retailers. The forms taken by such protest included acts of symbolic violence, when men and women from the popular classes overturned tables in marketplaces, imposed prices on goods, and destroyed shop windows in bakers, butchers, or other shops as a means of communicating their anger. This tradition of protest over prices may be found across Europe and also in Japan, for example during the 1919 rice riots. The historian Eric Hobsbawn has described these frequent conflicts which were typically solved locally as 'bargaining by riots'. Only later, did such bargaining through physical violence become criminalized as the state monopoly reached the level where it could impose the free circulation of goods and respect for private property.

The quality of goods often also resulted in conflict between shopkeepers and their clients. During periods of shortages, women were often called upon to make more rational use of goods. This response to shortages, found across otherwise different historical situations, usually called on housewives to use goods more carefully, such as vegetables, milk, fat, and meat which were in short supply. Social protest also occurred as a result of the poor quality of goods available. The composition of bread or the splashing or waste of milk were often common starting points for such protests. Beginning at the end of the nineteenth century, consumer co-operatives also encouraged consumers to pay attention to both the quality and the price of goods when shopping. After 1945, consumer organizations continued to scrutinize the quality and price of goods. Since then, the number of state institutions with responsibility for ensuring the quality of consumer goods has also grown considerably. Despite the growth in state control, even after the Second World War, serious problems have occurred as a result of the industrialization and mass production of agricultural products. For example, Steve Kaplan has shown how the production of bread in post-war France did not prevent contamination. In one example, he shows how in the small town of Pont Saint Esprit in 1951 several people were poisoned as a result of the consumption of contaminated bread. By the end of the twentieth century it was the large food chains rather than the state authorities which became increasingly responsible for quality and safety control.

Another fundamental aspect of the relationship between retailers and consumers was payment for goods and services. Even though shopkeepers have often faced immediate demands for cash to pay wholesalers, rent, mortgage, salaries, or other business costs, even after 1945 they were often obliged to provide consumer credit free of charge. This credit was especially necessary during times of economic instability, when there was a sudden increase in unemployment, or when the income of the lower classes was unstable and could be insufficient for long periods. Often consumers could only pay debts at the end of the week or month. This resulted in a situation of mutual dependence: clients depended upon the credit of shopkeepers, who in turn were dependent upon the payments of the popular classes. As a result, shopkeepers could play active roles in the lives of their clients. During times of strikes, shops had to continue to offer credit to striking workers in order not to lose them to competing shops and to ensure that they would eventually recover their overall debts. Consumer co-operatives attempted to avoid the problem of customers' right to credit by insisting on cash payments and by targeting the better-off sectors of the working class. However, the application of this kind of filtering of customers, if applied strictly, limited the number of clients available to co-operatives. Department stores also offered credit to their wealthy clients, and they too complained when they failed to repay on time or in full. In Britain at the end of the nineteenth century some married men even refused to honour the debts of their wives.

Haggling over prices was also common in Europe and markets in Africa, Asia, and South America. It was often a fundamental practice to adapt prices to buyers' low purchasing power. In most small shops, prices were neither fixed nor displayed. This meant that there was room to discuss prices. In Naples, prices agreed in this way were called 'English prices'. From the inter-war period on, however, the practice of fixing prices became increasingly widespread. In Japan, public authorities pressed for fixed prices. Shops in public markets were obliged to show fixed prices.

CHANGES IN RETAIL: ACTIVE AND PASSIVE CONSUMERS

As a result of the changes in retail, some scholars have claimed that consumers have changed from 'active' to 'passive' customers. An active consumer was characterized by his or her proximity to the shop. The shop was located in the customer's own neighbourhood and the consumer was personally known by the shopkeeper. Credit was available and the price and quality of goods was subject to discussion. The customer could also choose between standard, packaged, and other forms of goods. Their visit to the shop might also have been accompanied by conversation about shared non-commercial interests, such as events and problems in the neighbourhood. The 'passive' customer no longer shares in such intimate transactions. In a department store or self-service supermarket, the relationship of the passive customer to the shopkeeper and to the goods is much more anonymous. The shop assistant is not personally known to the shopper. Indeed, the shopper may sometimes simply enter the shop and leave without making a purchase. The goods available to a passive customer are packed, their prices fixed, and the customer has no opportunity to haggle over prices.[6] This contradistinction between active and passive customers does indeed characterize many of the changes which have taken place in retail trading over time. At the same time, however, the conflict between active and passive customers is also too pronounced. For example, in the 1920s Uwe Spiekermann showed that in German traditional shops branded goods amounted to half of the total sales. Customers in department stores and self-service shops also do not fit entirely the model of passivity. Even in these stores they have a range of choice of goods and producers. Indeed, in societies where consumer goods are of poor quality, consumers also face the challenge of having to adapt or transform purchases before using them. For example, attention has been drawn to the fact that in the post-Stalinist Soviet Union purchased goods had to be adapted before use. It is likely, that a similar process may be found to take place in other societies with low levels of income and commercial infrastructure. 'The place occupied in western advertising literature by the exhortation to buy is taken in this (Soviet) literature by the imperative to make.'[7] Yet, even in consumer societies with high levels of income and commercial infrastructure, consumers have often to repair or assemble products in order to use them. Consumers have also had to return, repair, or claim reimbursement for faulty goods. Michel de Certeau has stressed that the relationship between purchased goods and consumers is never simple or unilateral. In his approach, consumers are understood as having always altered or adapted purchased goods, regardless of whether these were material or cultural goods. Even in late imperial Russia, popular consumers did not receive passive goods and market incentives. The 'characteristics of popular culture were…adaptation, appropriation, recycling and hybridization.'[8] The same description may be equally applied to other popular cultures.

THE IMPACT OF RETAILING
ON TIME AND SPACE

The interaction between retailers and consumers resulted in the creation of shared time schedules which had a profound influence upon the urban environment. Henri Lefebvre was one of the first scholars to draw attention to the rhythm of towns.

[6] R. Laermans, 'Learning to Consume: Early Department Stores in the Shaping of Modern Consumer Culture, 1860–1914', *Theory, Culture and Society*, 10 (1993), 79–102.
[7] Susan E. Reid, 'Consumption and Everyday Culture after Stalin', Guest Editor's Introduction, *Russian Studies in History*, 48 (2009), 9.
[8] Steve Smith and Catriona Kelly, 'Commercial Culture and Consumerism', in Catriona Kelly and David Shepherd (eds.), *Constructing Russian Culture in the Age of Revolution: 1881–1940* (Oxford, 1998), 154.

Without doubt, retail trades and consumers contributed fundamentally to the ebbs and flows of a town's rhythm. Their activities depended upon when work stopped and when wages were paid. With the working week ending on a Saturday evening, Sunday was an important time for relaxation, when many consumers engaged in window-shopping. In places as different as Moscow and London at the beginning of the twentieth century, members of the working class were drawn to the attractions offered by department stores, where they could gaze at displays of goods which were beyond their purchasing power. In Europe, there was considerable debate about whether shops should be allowed to open on Sundays. Trade unions and churches opposed shops opening on Sundays. Over the course of time, however, more and more exceptions were granted. In France, for example, before 1914 shops where all the employees were members of the owner's family were permitted to open as they wished. Further exceptions to Sunday-closing were allowed for bakers and greengrocers. In Canada, the failure of ethnic shopkeepers to observe Sunday-closing during the inter-war period reinforced pre-existing ethnic tensions. In Britain and Germany at this time, Sunday-closing was widespread and respected. French observers even depicted the closure of shops as contributing to the horrible grey character of British Sundays. If work stopped on a Saturday evening and workers were also paid then, this was usually the time for workers to pay debts to shopkeepers, and especially for male workers to go to the pubs. With the introduction of the so-called 'English week' before 1914, work stopped on Saturday at lunchtime and the afternoon was left free for shopping or other recreational activities. Shops' opening hours contributed greatly to the rhythm of towns. Later opening during the evening hours contributed to their liveliness. Market days attracted large numbers of visitors to certain town quarters or small towns. These were occasions when commerce and social activity combined.

How space has been used in towns has also been influenced by the retail trade and patterns of consumption. Town centres developed as privileged places for markets, and this was where the first department stores were opened. Fashionable drapery and confectionary shops established their presence in the centre of town. For example, before 1914 in St Petersburg, the Nedvskii Passayh, at the centre of the city, was home to luxury trades. Department stores too wanted to establish themselves near the town hall or close to a privileged means of transport. In Japan, department stores were opened close to private railway stations. They also contributed to the fame and attraction of certain districts within city centres. In Paris the presence of the Bon Marché promoted the sixth *arrondissement*. In Berlin, the Kurfurstendamm became better known because of the Kadewe. With the growth of travel guides, the location of famous department stores also contributed to the way cities were mapped. However, the relationship between department stores and urban geography was not unilateral. After 1945, shopping centres followed the politics of urbanization, just as much as they may have led them in earlier periods. When the middle classes moved from city centres to suburbs, supermarkets and shopping malls followed them. The establishment of new shopping centres in the suburbs destroyed the connection between traditional city centres and retail, often leaving behind city centres which became economically stagnant and depressed.

The experience and space of towns is also influenced by another of consumption's fundamental aspects: advertising. Mural advertising began at the end of the nineteenth century, before becoming widespread at the start of the twentieth. Posters praising products covered the walls of towns and were also found in the countryside. Conservative and right-wing organizations launched campaigns against the growth of the advertisement, describing it as leading to the commercialization of society and the 'denaturalization' of landscape. For example, in Paris, the organization 'Vieux Paris' opposed the placing of advertisements on or near historical monuments and used the issue as a forum for launching an attack on consumer society and modernity. In Great Britain and the United States, similar organizations emerged. Such debates show how commercial enterprise was linked to different cultural values as well as to practices and social groups. Commercial activity did not create cultural values. However, it did contribute to their diffusion and expression within society. In France and Russia, for example, the way department stores used mail to distribute catalogues nationally contributed to the growth of shared tastes and fashions for certain goods across society. Such mailings offered the inhabitants of villages and towns the possibility to purchase goods and make a statement about their own individuality. In late imperial Russia, 'consumer goods were crucial to the assertion of individuality by the younger generation, who joked at the conservatism and conformism of village society.'[9] The way department stores stressed their ability to satisfy human demands through the purchase of certain goods is indicative of this linking of consumption to values. In an early advertisement, Selfridges proclaimed that shopping daily was 'an important part of the day's PLEASURE, a time of PROFIT, RECREATION and ENJOYMENT.'[10]

In a way, this kind of discourse was a response to the continued criticism of these 'cathedrals of consumption', suggesting that they were in fact places which were lighthearted and that consumption was an important part of a pleasant life. The pleasure of consumption was marketed as a part of an aristocratic lifestyle, for example in Hungary. In Japan it was depicted as part of the bourgeois style of life. Consumption was not only open to social coding, but also to national values and citizenship. Often the difference between small shops and department stores was used within the debate about the legitimacy and effects of modernity. In Germany, this division was seen clearly, as small shops were and in some places still are regarded as the defenders of tradition, quality, and *Mittelstand* (middle-class) values. Against the idealization of the small shop, department stores were criticized as the representatives of waste, poor quality, and the loss of individuality in an emerging mass society. In Germany and Austria, the corporate image underlying this kind of attribution of values to forms of retail was rather particular. However, the same coding of department stores with bourgeois values was also found generally in France, Belgium, and Britain.

---

[9] Smith and Kelly, 'Commercial Culture and Consumerism', 112.
[10] Cited in Crossick and Jaumain (eds.), *Cathedrals of Consumption*, 29 f.

THE POLITICS OF RETAILING

At the same time as societies confronted such cultural questions about the meaning of retail, department stores and small shops were also the subjects of politics, or what the French philosopher Michael Foucault has termed the political 'apparatus' (*dispositif*). The political disputes which took place following the emergence of the department store were intimately connected to the emergence of mass politics from the mid-nineteenth century onwards. As political parties targeted wider audiences for support, small independent shopkeepers became an important group. Their collective voice was strengthened as small shopkeepers formed local and national organizations for the protection of their interests. As this was taking place, the politics of consumption became increasingly prominent, as issues such as the price of grain, meat, or coal became subjects of commercial politics. Socialist parties often took the side of consumers, defending their interests against any attempts to raise prices.

Shopkeepers and their organizations lobbied consistently against the expansion of department stores. They called for fiscal and prohibitive restraints upon department stores. To give one example of measures designed to limit the expansion of department stores, in some German states before 1914 the creation of new departments within the large stores, expanding the range of goods on sale there, was subject to a special tax which increased the costs of expansion. Similar debates took place in France, where reform of the '*patente*' (licence) was the subject of discussions by those aiming at the same goal. Over time however, such measures did little to restrict the growth of department stores and are best understood as acts of symbolic politics. In other European countries national politics was less interested in limiting the expansion of department stores. For example, in Britain, local conditions were of greater importance than national policies. In Belgium, the Catholic government promoted a policy of self-help towards shopkeepers who felt threatened by their larger competitors.

Beginning in the inter-war period and continuing after 1945, shopkeepers called for legislation limiting the development of chain stores and other larger retail enterprises. In 1932, German shopkeepers obtained a ban on one-price shops. In the United States under the New Deal, the Robinson Patman Act included provisions limiting the action of chains across state boundaries, although shopkeepers had to prove such transgressions before action would be taken. In Japan in 1938, the expansion of department stores was also banned. After 1945, the prohibition policy underlying such measures was replaced by a more selective regionally based approach. Associations of shopkeepers were permitted to participate in urban planning commissions which were delegated responsibility for decisions concerning the opening of new larger retail units including hypermarkets. This kind of planning formed the basis of the French Royer law of 1969, the Japanese Large Scale Retail Store Act of 1973, and of a Spanish regulation in 1990. The overall impact of this kind of legislation however was limited. In most cases, it had little impact on the changes in structure taking place in the retail trade and was only effective as a means of calming the anger of small shopkeepers.

Although shopkeepers and the owners of department stores from the nineteenth century on organized interest groups, these groups never developed into specific political movements or parties. In this way their political organization differed from that of the peasantry, for whom specific political parties were founded. In the Weimar Republic, shopkeepers supported the Mittelstandpartei, a broad coalition of artisans, proprietors, and shopkeepers. They were thus politically aligned against both the representatives of organized labour and large capital. In France, in 1956, shopkeepers supported the Poujade movement, whose populist policies were aimed at supporting the 'small' shopkeeper against his larger competitors. Small shopkeepers also supported fascist movements and the Nazi Party. However, such support for fascism varied from country to country. For example, in Italy small shopkeepers quickly withdrew support for the Italian Fascist Party because of its control of prices and attacks upon small traders. In Germany, they were an important part of those who voted for the Nazi Party in 1932. Yet, at the same time, in Italy small shopkeepers were disappointed by the regime, as it failed to alter their economic conditions and did not implement its promise to 'destroy' the department stores. As well as general prohibitive measures, there were a number of other political attempts to organize the retail trade. The older tradition of guilds had proved ineffective and disappeared in most European countries by the end of the eighteenth century. Nevertheless, at times during the nineteenth century there were some measures taken to assist certain sectors. For example, in strategic sectors such as bakeries and butcheries, over periods of time, state intervention limited the number of shops and controlled production and distribution. Similar state intervention and control occurred during times of rationing, especially during the First and Second World Wars and their aftermaths.

In Germany and other countries including France and Italy, official authorities supported the self-organization of the retail trade. In Italy and France the Chambers of Commerce were given responsibility for discussing and counselling the political measures touching retail trading. This kind of local organization in which the wholesale and retail trade are normally represented was so successful in some places that it remains in force today. The representative organizations of small shops in German cities like Hamburg and Bremen, where wholesale and overseas trade was dominant, are similar today to those established at the beginning of the twentieth century. At the same time, attempts to establish corporative structures in the retail trade in Germany failed. Such attempts envisaged limiting the right to open shops to those who possessed specific qualifications. After the Second World War, they were supported by the conservative government. The German Constitutional Court however overruled this policy, viewing it as incompatible with the freedom of commerce. Political developments and major events also impacted upon shops and department stores. For example, at the beginning of the First World War, as some sectors of society were engulfed in a wave of nationalist exclusionism, German Maggi shops in Paris were attacked by angry crowds. In times of intense nationalism, retail institutions were judged according to nationalist criteria rather than in economic terms. Early examples of the impact this had upon the retail trade showed in debates on fashion during the nineteenth century. One such debate pitted nationalist politicians and merchants against French fashion. During food shortages, politicians often blamed foreign shopkeepers for problems in supply. In South America and the United States, for example, Chinese shops were specifically targeted after 1945 for boycotts and attacks. In Vancouver, as Chinese retail trading expanded beyond its assigned location, small shopkeepers led a campaign calling for discriminatory licensing of shops. In the Ivory Coast, Lebanese shopkeepers were pressured during the 1980s and 1990s when their commercial penetration of the country was opposed by the government which supported its own clientele. As Catherine Borne has stated, 'commercial sectors across the [African] continent were early…targets of official efforts to "indigenous" control in post colonial economies.'[11] Following the 'national revolution' in Egypt, foreign-owned department stores were attacked and in some cases nationalized during the 1950s.

Jewish-owned shops were often specifically targeted for discrimination and boycott. In Montreal during the inter-war period one agitator blamed the presence of Jewish shops for problems in the retail sector: 'Nous avons laissé le Juif pénétrer dans l'Est, nous voler nos commerces, nos épiceries, nos boucheries, nos magasins de meubles, de merceries, de chapeaux.'[12] As is well known, the Nazi government did not abolish department stores after coming to power in 1933. Instead, measures were taken to expropriate Jewish owners of department stores. Such discriminatory actions were not limited to times of crisis or moments of pogrom. As Edgar Morin has shown in the case of Orleans during the 1950s, Jewish drapery shops were subjected to racist discrimination because of rumours that young women who entered these shops were sold on to slave-traders.

RETAILING AS PART OF GLOBAL HISTORY

Both small shops and department stores depended on goods produced outside the societies where they were established. Even before the industrial and communication revolutions of the nineteenth century, Chinese and Japanese porcelain was sold globally. In Germany, specialist shops—called *Kolonialwarenläden* (translated as colonial goods shops)—were established specifically to sell goods, including spices and rice etc., which originated outside of Europe. International activity was a fundamental part of the purchasing and selling strategies of department stores from their very inception. The owner of Woolworths for example travelled to Germany and the Erzgebirge to buy what were then considered exotic goods for the American market. Wertheim maintained representatives in Istanbul to purchase Turkish rugs. Recently, especially in the global south, supermarket chains concluded privileged trade agreements with producers. As a result

---

[11] Catherine Boone, 'Commerce in Côte d'Ivoire: Ivorianisation without Ivorian Traders', *Journal of Modern African Studies*, 31/1 (1993), 68.

[12] David Monod, *Store Wars: Shopkeepers and the Culture of Mass Marketing 1890–1939* (Toronto, 1996), 41.

older structures of production in these countries have often been destroyed. All of these reasons allow historians to conceptualize the history of small shops and department stores as part of global history.

Indeed, the history of department stores in the century after their first appearance in the 1860s, is a story of international success. The model of the department store emerged more or less simultaneously in France and the United States, before extending to Europe and Russia, although its expansion varied in different geographical contexts. For example, in Italy before 1914 there were only two department stores. The figures for Germany, France, and Great Britain at the same time were considerably higher. Yet, even if the physical presence of department stores was limited in some places, the model illustrates how a particular 'icon' crossed national boundaries. The use of architecturally ambitious and prestigious buildings, the large numbers of employees, and the location of department stores in town centres meant that department stores became symbols of modern retailing and of refined tastes and desires. Furthermore, the styles of clothing they sold became fashionable trendsetters. Selling also occurred globally. Catalogues were used to promote cultural models of clothing and living to the limits of the Russian Empire. In 1894, for example, the Bon Marché in Paris distributed 1.5 million categories of good. Of this figure, 260,000 were sent beyond the borders of France.

Indeed, as Crossick and Jaumain have underlined, French department stores were the most important cultural reference within Europe. Traders and travellers who visited the Parisian Bon Marché were often so impressed that they copied it when they returned home, in some cases even imitating the name in their local language. For example, in Turkey, the department store was named the 'bonmarseler'. Traders also used the experiences of department stores in other locations. In Japan during the inter-war period, European and American retail experiences were copied. For example, Mibukoshi tried to emulate the sale practices of Wanamaker in Philadelphia and Harrods in London.

The establishment of retail chains and department stores was also part of colonial expansion. Before 1914, decision-makers in Paris and Vienna chose to finance department stores in Turkey and in the Arabic world. The famous Orosdi-Bach family promoted the establishment of large shops outside the bazaar in Cairo. Their involvement resulted in the concentration of shops selling European commodities in the Rue des Francs, eventually turning the area into a fashionable shopping centre during the twentieth century. The global nature of their expansion is seen by their presence in Alexandria and Istanbul, as well as by the branches they later established in Bucharest, Salonica, Izmir, and Tunis. After 1918, French department stores including Bon Marché, Le Louvre, Printemps, and Galeries Lafayette established subsidiaries in Cairo. Japanese department stores also followed the expansion of the Japanese Empire. They were a way of selling to the Japanese population in the empire and showcasing the superiority of the Japanese way of life. By 1939, in Korea and China 11 Japanese chains of department stores had opened 70 outlets.

Expansion was not limited to colonial empires. Across the imperial centres, department stores and retail chains contributed to the internationalization of commerce. Before 1914, the German department store Tietz owned shops in Belgium, and Woolworth had founded shops in Canada. During the inter-war period, Woolworths also opened shops in Cuba, Britain, and Germany. In the last 25 years, as is well known, hypermarkets and chains have tried to conquer foreign markets. For example, Carrefour and Wal-Mart were among the first foreign stores to enter the Chinese market. In recent years, historical research specializing in the study of small shops and department stores has shared the general trend for focusing upon cultural rather than social history. At the same time, this trend has been more pronounced in research analysing department stores as places of cultural events and practices. In the case of small shops, complementary studies using a cultural approach could offer rich new insights. Within social studies, it makes sense to move away from the older focus on social structures and to place greater concentration on social practices. Indeed, in depth analysis of consumer expectations and practices generally remains to be completed. Many scholars concur that those undertaking this future research, should do so using anthropological methods. It is also expected that urban studies will place retail trading not just within the city's landscape, but as a more general factor contributing to changes in social relationships, political conflicts, and cultural life.

BIBLIOGRAPHY

Brändli, Sybille, *Der Supermarkt im Kopf. Konsumkultur und Wohlstand in der Schweiz nach 1945* (Vienna, 2000).

Burch, David and Lawrence, Geoffrey (eds.), *Supermarkets and Agri-food Supply Chains. Transformation in the Production and Consumption of Foods* (Cheltenham and Northampton, 2007).

Coquery, Natacha (ed.), *La boutique et la ville. Commerces, commercants, espaces de clienteles, XVIe-XIXe siècles* (Tours, 2000).

Crossick, Geoffrey and Haupt, Heinz-Gerhard, *The Petite Bourgeoisie in Europe 1780–1914* (London and New York, 1995).

Crossick, Geoffrey and Jaumain, Serge (eds.), *Cathedrals of Consumption. The European Department Store 1850–1939* (Aldershot, 1999).

Kupferschmidt, Uri M., 'Who Needed Department Stores in Egypt? From Oraschi-Back to Omar Effendi', *Middle Eastern Studies*, 43 (2007), 175–92.

Punk, Johanna (ed.), *Muslim Societies in the Age of Mass Consumption. Politics, Culture and Identity between the Local and the Global* (Newcastle, 2009).

Spiekermann, Uwe, *Basis der Konsumgesellschaft. Entstehung und Entwicklung des modernen Kleinhandels in Deutschland 1850–1914* (Munich, 1999).

Zhen, Yong, *Globalization and the Chinese Retailing Revolution. Competing in the World's Largest Emerging Market* (Oxford, 2007).

PART V

TECHNOLOGIES
AND PRACTICES

CHAPTER 15

....

COMFORT
AND CONVENIENCE:
TEMPORALITY AND PRACTICE

....

ELIZABETH SHOVE

DESPITE being embedded in the practices and discourses of daily life, comfort and convenience are not terms around which theories and studies of consumption have traditionally revolved. To some extent this is a perfectly understandable consequence of the tendency to focus on moments of acquisition and exchange rather than processes of use; on instances of conspicuous rather than ordinary consumption; and on the world of goods rather than the services and experiences associated with them. So why focus on these topics now?

Over the last decade or so the tides of intellectual fashion have begun to turn, bringing the mundane into view and highlighting previously invisible dimensions of consumer culture. This tendency reflects and contributes to a broader repositioning of consumption and an expansion of the debates of which it is a part and in terms of which intellectual priorities are defined.[1] Lines of enquiry that cast consumption as the flip side of production, and hence as part of the economic ordering of society, or the tangible manifestation of status and distinction have not disappeared, but the field is no longer defined by these concerns alone. As Trentmann has also argued,[2] the turn towards materiality together with renewed interest in the dynamics of social practice has generated different ways of conceptualizing consumption and has consequently changed the kinds of problems addressed.

In this chapter I explore the value of comfort and convenience as sites through which to develop aspects of this new agenda. As I hope to show, historical and contemporary

---

[1] Jukka Gronow and Alan Warde, *Ordinary Consumption*, New York: Routledge, 2001, 3.

[2] Frank Trentmann, 'Materiality in the future of History: things, practices, and politics', *Journal of British Studies*, 48/2, 2009: 283–307.

studies of both topics provide telling, and tellingly different, insight into basic questions about how culturally specific forms of consumption are cast as natural and inevitable; how patterns of consumption evolve beneath the radar of discursive consciousness; and how the hardware of consumer culture configures the form and character of the social practices in which people engage and the conditions in which they live. In reviewing changing interpretations of comfort and convenience I capture some of the processes through which individual habits and routines are reproduced and through which the contours of social life are simultaneously sustained and transformed.

Rather than offering a history of comfort or convenience, I highlight different features of each as a means of interrogating the materially grounded dynamics of ordinary consumption. However, I am also interested in how interpretations of comfort and convenience come to be as they are today, and in understanding the types of consumption and demand they entail. This more substantive angle is important in that contemporary definitions of physical well- being and temporal order imply and rely upon forms of resource consumption that are unsustainable in the longer run or on a global scale.

In pursuing these different tracks I switch between discussion of comfort and convenience as legitimizing discourses important for the naturalization of need and the normative ratcheting and levelling of demand, and as terms that describe specific social, cultural, and material arrangements.

COMFORT

With these ambitions in mind I begin with comfort and with Crowley's thesis that its redefinition as 'self-conscious satisfaction with the relationship between one's body and its immediate physical environment'[3] was a crucial building block in the making of consumer society. To comfort someone is to offer sympathy and support in times of trouble—although this meaning of the word lives on, comfort is no longer exclusively associated with a state of mind or with caring relations between people. In the course of the eighteenth century, comfort acquired a much more physical aspect: 'it developed into a more object bound term, also denoting worldly goods which could enhance mental and physical well-being'.[4] Since then, a multitude of goods and services have been designed, developed, and justified in terms of the goal of providing comfort.

John Crowley contends that this more physical definition was critical on a number of counts. First, it opened up real and imaginary space between the body and the environment into which novel arrangements—smokeless fires, cotton clothing and

---

[3] John E. Crowley, *The Invention of Comfort: Sensibilities and Design in Early Modern Britain and Early America*, Baltimore: Johns Hopkins University Press, 2001, 142.

[4] Wim Heijs, 'The dependent variable in thermal comfort research: some psychological considerations', in N. Oseland and M. Humphreys, *Thermal Comfort: Past, Present and Future*, Watford: Building Research Establishment, 1994, 43.

umbrellas—could be located. Taking a broader view, this is the space in which disciplines like ergonomics have since developed; in which minimum standards for housing and environmental conditions have taken hold; and in which aspects of well-being are reproduced. As Crowley explained, the transition from medieval arrangements and values in which 'definitions of domestic amenity gave priority to social status over personal physical comfort'[5] to those of personalized, individualized and above all embodied comfort brought all manner of material and natural interactions into view. In focusing on matters like those of furnishing, heating and ventilation, Anglo-American political economists, moral philosophers, scientists, humanitarian reformers and novelists converted previously unremarkable conditions into issues of social interest and political concern.[6] In the process, they positioned and represented comfort as a state of affairs to which everyone aspired.

Although specifications of comfort are culturally and historically specific the pursuit of comfort is strongly associated with this implicitly *universalized* sense of human need. The new but apparently self-evident goal of organizing and achieving a satisfactory human-environment relation—typically one that was warm, dry, free of draughts and not too cramped—consequently allowed philanthropic reformers to assert 'a common humanity on the basis of physical comfort'.[7] This association is extremely significant in that the seemingly inherent desire for comfort has the further effect of defining that which is required for its achievement as normal and necessary: as such it justifies and legitimizes consumption for the masses, not just for the few.

In summary, Crowley argues that physically-oriented notions of comfort created problems where none had existed before; underpinning sets of values and understandings that in turn generated and legitimized specific forms of innovation and acquisition. More than that, discourses of comfort established the need for a range of material arrangements, characterizing these as appropriate for all sectors of society. It is on this basis that he makes the case for comfort as a key analytic concept in understanding the consumer revolution. In his words, 'the historical development of the values and material culture of comfort in eighteenth-century Anglo-American society deserves as much attention as other themes in the interpretation of consumption patterns, such as emulation, refinement, self-fashioning, conspicuous consumption and romantic illusions'.[8]

Since comfort and discomfort are conditions arising from the *relation* between people and their surroundings a sensibility to comfort is about more than acquisition: it is also about the comportment of the body, the use of space and the technologies and practices entailed in responding to external conditions. Although Crowley does not develop this theme explicitly, the instruments of comfort are themselves instrumental in redefining the meaning of the concept, and by implication, the course of consumer culture.

---

[5] John E. Crowley, *The Invention of Comfort: Sensibilities and Design in Early Modern Britain and Early America*, Baltimore: Johns Hopkins University Press, 2001, 3.

[6] John E. Crowley, 'The sensibility of comfort', *American Historical Review*, 104/3, 1999: 749–82, 751.

[7] Ibid., 779.

[8] Ibid., 753.

To illustrate this point I turn from the invention of comfort to a somewhat more detailed discussion of the indoor climate. In the process I explore the proposition that discourses and technologies of comfort have contributed to the standardization and the globalization of specific understandings of humans and their habitats, and to the emergence of environmentally unsustainable patterns of demand.

STANDARDS OF COMFORT

Eighteenth century interpretations of comfort served to condense and standardize what had been 'wide, and in large part discretionary, social variations in consumption patterns regarding heating and lighting'.[9] This represents a first step in the specification of optimal indoor climates.

In the UK, the institutional history of the Chartered Institute of Building Services Engineers is cast as a 'Quest for Comfort', suggesting that such a state exists and that innovations from the 1850s to the present day have brought us progressively closer to this goal.[10] In contrast, Gail Cooper's account of Air conditioning American documents the effort entailed in making a workable, and marketable, definition of perfect conditions. She reviews the very real uncertainty that beset the fledgling air-conditioning industry in the first decades of the twentieth century. It was only when it became possible to heat, cool, humidify and ventilate indoor spaces with any precision that the question arose: just what was a healthy, comfortable climate? Should the aim be to emulate a spring morning in the cool mountain air, or a summer day at the seaside? What form should the technology take and who should determine that configuration?[11] Cooper describes the ensuing politics of comfort, cataloguing a process in which complicating social and seasonal variations were ironed out through reference to programmes of physiological research. Laboratory studies of the human body, clad in one standard unit of clothing (technically referred to as the clo), provided a benchmark for the scientific specification of comfort, and in the same move established the need for mechanical heating and cooling around the world. Cooper puts it very clearly: 'When it was shown that no natural climate could consistently deliver perfect comfort conditions, air-conditioning broke free of its geographic limits. When no town could deliver an ideal climate, all towns became potential markets for air-conditioning'.[12]

The representation of comfort as a natural condition, revealed and specified through physiological enquiry, set the scene for the thermal comfort industry we know today,

---

[9]   John E. Crowley, *The Invention of Comfort: Sensibilities and Design in Early Modern Britain and Early America*, Baltimore: Johns Hopkins University Press, 2001, x.

[10]   Brian Roberts, *The Quest for Comfort*, London: Chartered Institute of Building Services Engineers, 1997.

[11]   Gail Cooper, *Air Conditioning America: Engineers and the Controlled Environment 1900–1960*, Baltimore: Johns Hopkins University Press, 1998, 3.

[12]   Ibid., 73.

and for the manufacturing of indoor weather systems that deliver standardized conditions all year round and whatever the weather outside.[13] In reality, not everyone lives in a protected bubble conditioned to a steady 22°C, yet this template of normal is enormously influential: feeding into the design of offices, homes, schools and factories; being embedded in building regulations and codes; adopted as standard in places with contrasting climates, and providing a point of reference in terms of which discomfort is discussed and experienced. As Michael Humphreys reminds us 'If a building is set, regularly at, say, 22°C the occupants will choose their clothing so that they are comfortable at that temperature. If enough buildings are controlled at this temperature, it becomes a norm for that society at that period of its history, and anything different is regarded as 'uncomfortable.'[14] Exactly how this kind of standardization has come about differs from one culture and country to another.

As one might expect, the routes through which air-conditioning enters society vary depending on existing infrastructures and conventions, and on exactly when and how this new configuration takes hold. In America, the diffusion of domestic air-conditioning was linked to the post-war building boom, and to specific innovations in design including standardized, lightweight structures and layouts that presumed and then required mechanical cooling. Between 1962 and 1992, the percentage of American homes with air-conditioning grew from twelve to sixty-four per cent.[15] When mechanical cooling was initially introduced in Japanese homes in the late 1970s it was strongly associated with images of modernity, westernization and American culture.[16] By 2004 eighty-seven per cent of Japanese homes were air conditioned and the technology's initially special connotation had given way to much more functional representations of culturally innocuous necessity. The trajectory was different again in Australia, a country in which the domestic penetration of air conditioners rose gradually until about 1986, remaining fairly stable until the late 1990's before increasing sharply from around thirty-five percent in 2000 to sixty percent in 2005.[17] In each situation the cultural overtones and the implications for related practices depend on the details of timing and sequence and on the character of the traditions and conventions that are redefined along the way.

The general pattern is nonetheless one in which artificial indoor climates, sealed off from the outside and managed in the name of comfort, consistently supplant previously

[13] Elizabeth Shove, *Comfort, Cleanliness and Convenience: the Social Organization of Normality*, Oxford: Berg, 2003.

[14] Mike Humphreys, 'Thermal comfort temperatures and the habits of Hobbits', in Fergus Nicol et al., *Standards for Thermal Comfort*, London: E. & F. N. Spon, 1995, 10.

[15] Willet Kempton and Loren Lutzenhiser, 'Introduction', *Energy and Buildings*, 18, 1992: 171–6, 172.

[16] Harold Wilhite, Hidetoshi Nakagami, and Chiharu Murakoshi, 'The dynamics of changing Japanese energy consumption patterns and their implications for sustainable consumption', in Mark Modera and Diana Shankle (eds) *Human Dimensions of Energy Consumption ACEEE Summer Study on Energy Efficiency in Buildings*, ACEEE, Asilomar, 1996, 8.231–8.238.

[17] Energy Efficient Strategies, *Status of Air conditioners in Australia*, Warragul, Victoria, Australia: Energy Efficient Strategies, 2006, <http//:www.energyrating.gov.au/library/pubs/200509-ac-aust.pdf>, 8, accessed 11 June 2011; Yolande Strengers, 'Comfort expectations: the impact of demand-management strategies in Australia', *Building Research and Information*, 36, 2008: 381–91.

important strategies like those of moving to the hills to avoid the heat of the summer, or having a siesta in the middle of the day. The standardized management of indoor climates also matters for the interpretation of unacceptable conditions, and for representations of the outdoors as a somewhat threatening place. In contrast to previous generations, members of which had a more forgiving approach to heat and humidity, the young Singaporeans interviewed by Lee 'detested' sweat, viewing it as a symptom of ill health, or of failure to maintain an environment in which people can function effectively.[18] Their experiences lend some weight to the contention that air conditioning 'disciplines people so they no longer have any excuse to stop working and gradually come to hate the hot and the wet.' In what seems to be a similar move, the body has become a target for quite specific forms of decontamination,[19] the task of maintaining freshness being of particular concern in contemporary western cultures. In this context, the acquisition and use of products associated with deodorizing, (not)perspiring and sanitizing constitutes comparably defensive forms of civilizing consumption. These different examples represent moments in what Heschong characterizes as a process of alienation in which human bodies are increasingly protected from themselves and from physiological responses like those of sweating, shivering or adapting to the seasons. In Heschong's view this separation is itself harmful, resulting in what she describes as conditions of 'thermal monotony' and sensory deprivation.[20]

Ironically, definitions of comfort as a natural, biologically determined state of affairs have promoted the development and diffusion of goods and services that keep the elements at bay, increasing the distance between narrowly defined conditions of physical well being and the vagaries and challenges of the wider environment. Boundaries between indoors and out are variously well defined in different societies and the character of this relation is important for the details of material culture and consumption within and between these spheres. Traditional architectural forms like covered verandahs represent mediating spaces, modifying conditions indoors and extending the margins of habitable space beyond the walls of the home itself. This gradation is in keeping with a characteristically fluid relation between inside and out. I don't want to overstate the case, but the tendency to standardize indoor conditions appears to have implications for expectations of outdoor life as well. This takes various forms. One is the development of technologies not for mediating or smoothing the boundary, but for comprehensively recreating indoor conditions beyond the building envelope. This is a possibility explored in Hitchings' discussion of the recent diffusion of patio heaters in the UK [21] and

[18]   Russell Hitchings and Shu Jun Lee, 'Air conditioning and the material culture of routine human encasement: the case of young people in contemporary Singapore', *Journal of Material Culture*, 13/3, 2008: 251–65, 262.

[19]   Mary Douglas, *Purity and Danger: An Analysis of the Concepts of Pollution and Taboo*, London: Routledge, 1984; Timothy Burke, *Lifebuoy Men, Lux Women: Commodification, Consumption and Cleanliness in Modern Zimbabwe*, Durham, NC: Duke University Press, 1996; Alain Corbin, *The Foul and the Fragrant*, Leamington Spa: Berg, 1986.

[20]   Lisa Heschong, *Thermal Delight in Architecture*, Cambridge MA.: MIT Press, 1979.

[21]   Russell Hitchings, 'Geographies of embodied outdoor experience and the arrival of the patio heater', *AREA*, 39/3, 2007: 340–8.

suggested by trends in garden heating, lighting and furnishing. A different but related development involves the framing and representation of outdoor clothing as specialized technology designed for those who are willing to brave the elements head on.[22] There is nothing new about the idea of donning a cloak, outdoor coat or jacket, but the mass production and promotion of 'technically advanced clothing' (Rohan), or 'technical apparel' (Patagonia) is intriguing in that it promises to equip consumers with the means to 'rip, ride, or roam without feeling all wetted out, bundled up, or weighed down'[23]—in other words it permits active engagement with the outdoors while maintaining sensory experiences born of a managed indoor climate.

These instances lend weight to the view that experiences of our own bodies, of the weather and of the changing seasons are mediated by an array of consumer goods, technologies and materials all implicated in symbolically and literally separating the comfortable from the wild.

A CRISIS OF COMFORT?

The kind of cocooning described above comes at a cost: in environmental terms, reproducing standardized conditions of comfort all over the world would require energy consumption on a scale and at a rate that is ultimately unsustainable.[24] In modeling future trends, Isaac and Van Vuren anticipate global cooling energy demand to be 'more than 40 times larger in 2100 than in 2000' with the implication that 'associated CO_2 emissions for both heating and cooling increase from 0.8 Gt C in 2000 to 2.2 Gt C in 2100.'[25] This projected escalation is not in itself surprising. After all, 'The systems of knowledge, and of design and construction that spawned comfort science and air-conditioned buildings, required cheap energy, a planetary atmosphere that could be disregarded, an ascendant engineering elite, technological regulation, powerful corporations, and cooperative governments.'[26] The need for drastic reductions in CO_2 emissions associated with heating and cooling buildings are such that these conditions no longer apply. The difficulty, of course, is that understandings of comfort developed during an era of energy-plenty live on in the guise of seemingly natural and therefore non-negotiable conditions that simply must be met.

[22] Mike Parsons and Mary Rose, *Lead User Innovation and the UK Outdoor Trade since 1850* (Institute for Entrepreneurship and Enterprise Development, Lancaster University, 2009.

[23] Mountain Equipment Co-op, *Technical Clothing*, Vancouver, BC., Mountain Equipment Co-op: 2009, <http://www.mec.ca/Main/content_text.jsp?FOLDER%3C%3Efolder_id=2534374302887251&CONTENT%3C%3Ecnt_id=10134198673220743>, accessed 11 June 2011.

[24] Gail S. Brager and Richard J. de Dear, 'Thermal adaptation in the built environment: a literature review', *Energy and Buildings*, 27/1, 1998: 83–96; Fergus Nicol and Mike Humphreys, 'New standards for comfort and energy use in buildings', *Building Research and Information*, 37, 2009, 68–73.

[25] Morna Isaac and Detlef P. van Vuuren, 'Modeling global residential sector energy demand for heating and air conditioning in the context of climate change', *Energy Policy*, 37/2 (2009), 507–21, 513.

[26] Elizabeth Shove et al., 'Comfort in a lower carbon society', *Building Research and Information*, 4/4, 2008: 307–11, 310.

So what of the future? Would it be naïve to anticipate a more medieval approach to the body-environment relation, or a narrowing of the materially mediated gulf between us and our surroundings? Probably so, but given the co-production of conventions, practices and technologies discussed above, it is reasonable to imagine their reconfiguration. It is usual to expect conditions of comfort to be managed and maintained by heating and cooling occupied space within the built environment and to minimize the role of clothing as a means of enhancing insulation or evaporative cooling. In what might be the first sign of a significantly different comfort regime, the Japanese government decided not to heat or cool its own buildings between 20 and 28 degrees C and encouraged staff to adjust their clothing instead.[27] This idea, marketed under the name of Cool Biz, has been picked up by the United Nations, which cut back on air conditioning and simultaneously relaxed diplomatic dress code,[28] and by the prime minister of Bangladesh who 'ordered male government employees to stop wearing suits, jackets and ties to save electricity.'[29] Do these initiatives represent a minor adaptation or are they forerunners of a radical redefinition of comfort? It is not yet clear, but it is possible that future definitions will concentrate more on the body and clothing than on space heating and cooling.

The emergence of more sustainable ways of life almost certainly involves detaching comfort from discourses of natural entitlement and on situating self conscious satisfaction with the relationship between one's body and its immediate physical environment as a thoroughly social achievement. Historical studies of furniture and clothing, and of heating and cooling technologies[30] provide an important reminder: what counts as comfortable in the future is very unlikely to be the same as that which counts as comfortable today. This conclusion undermines a basic logic of comfort-related consumption—that of human need. It is true that people die if they become too hot or too cold and there are real issues of equity and justice to consider. However, those considerations are more, not less, significant once we detach comfort from human biology and attend to the wider politics of where and how notions of physical well being are reproduced, how they circulate and with what consequence for the forms of consumption associated with them.

Crowley argued that comfort was an important but overlooked ingredient in the making of consumer culture. In the eighteenth century, reference to comfort as a universal entitlement legitimized the diffusion of consumer goods across many sectors of society. In this role, discourses of comfort cut through social hierarchies. This continues

[27] Ministry of the Environment Japan, *Results of Cool Biz Campaign*, Ministry of the Environment, Japan, Tokyo: 2005), <http://www.env.go.jp/en/press/2005/1028a.html>, accessed 11 June 2011.

[28] United Nations, *New United Nations climate change campaign to cut emissions, cooling costs at New York headquarters* (2008), United Nations, New York: <http://www.un.org/News/Press/docs/2008/envdev999.doc.htm>, accessed 11 June 2011.

[29] Mark Dummett, 'Bangladesh Suit Ban to Save Power', BBC news, Dhaka, 2009: <http://news.bbc.co.uk/1/hi/world/south_asia/8234144.stm>, accessed 11 June 2011.

[30] Galen Cranz, *The Chair: Rethinking Culture, Body and Design*, New York: W. W. Norton., 1998; Witold Rybczynski, *Home: A Short History of an Idea*, Harmondsworth: Penguin, 1987; Lawrence Wright, *Home Fires Burning: The History of Domestic Heating and Cooking*, London: Routledge and Kegan Paul, 1964.

to be the case. As we have seen, interpretations of the proper relation between the body and its wider environment remain important, humming away in the background of much ordinary consumption and doing vital if invisible work in stitching together trajectories of innovation, patterns of demand and shared understandings of how things should be.

Despite certain standardizing tendencies, definitions of what counts as comfort at any one location or period, and the means by which it is achieved remain diverse. As we have seen, the routes through which air-conditioning or central heating become part of everyday life, and the technologies and arrangements displaced in the process are many and varied. While such trajectories have path dependent qualities, these are not the same in India and China as they are in the UK or the USA. Nor is the narrative one of smooth progression. In all of this the central point is that although definitions evolve, the pursuit of comfort figures as a consistently powerful argument for acquisition and mass consumption. Those who give this concept meaning and shape are consequently instrumental in making markets where none existed before and in helping to specify normal and acceptable relations between people and their surroundings. The result is a process in which reference to comfort has simultaneously underpinned an escalation of demand and its global diffusion, thereby contributing to the development of widely shared, and in that sense level, but also resource intensive expectations. In the next section I comment on forms of consumption related to the pursuit of convenience and on how these reproduce and reflect trends in the temporal ordering of everyday life.

CONVENIENCE AND TEMPORAL ORDER

Until relatively recently the terms comfort and convenience were virtually interchangeable. Crowley's work is again a useful point of reference in that he tracks subtle shifts in the meaning of convenience from the fifteenth and sixteenth centuries when 'convenience (more frequently 'conveniency') had strong connotations of harmony and comformity to a given order, as in 'congruity of form, quality or nature'. Two centuries later, 'this meaning became obsolete, as convenience increasingly referred to open-ended suitability 'to the performance of some action or to the satisfying of requirements".[31] These movements are revealing but for the purposes of this discussion the more important transformation, and the one that clearly sets convenience apart from comfort, occurred in the 1960s, this being the moment when the Oxford English Dictionary first recorded an association between convenience and the use of time.[32]

---

[31] John E. Crowley, 'The sensibility of comfort', *American Historical Review*, 104/3, 1999: 749–82, 762.
[32] Alan Warde, 'Convenient food: space and timing', *British Food Journal*, 101/1, 1999: 518–27, 519.

TIME AND TIMING

Convenience is currently associated with a reduction in the time taken to complete a specific activity and/or with the capacity to rearrange temporal sequences and in a sense shift time. Warde[33] makes use of these two interpretations in distinguishing between modern and hypermodern conveniences, the first category including foods and stores that minimize the minutes taken to cook and shop, the second encompassing things like video and digital recorders, freezers, microwaves and mobile phones all of which promise to increase flexibility in scheduling the day. In both these roles convenience has become a hugely significant sales pitch, invoked and applied in relation to products and services ranging from banking and travel through to many forms of partly and completely prepared food, laptops (the one on which I am currently writing claims to afford 'luxury and convenience'), wireless connections, communication technologies and very much more.

Interpretations that refer back to ease of use still exist but there must be some reason why time is now such a priority—not only in marketing consumer goods but also in the discourses of daily life. One popular explanation is that preoccupations with time reflect the progressive erosion of society's temporal structures.[34] This is an account that might apply as well to periods of intensive urbanization in which seasonal, agricultural rhythms gave way to new forms of coordination, or to situations like those in which gas and electric light facilitated the extension and standardization of the working day. Contemporary formulations focus on the loosening of social and institutional order. Now that shops are open all hours, that radio and television programmes are available on demand, and that arrangements to meet can be made and broken at a moment's notice, the week and the week-end, the evening and the day have lost the grip they once had. As a result, individuals have to find a way through increasingly complex timescapes simultaneously characterized by fragmentation, such that days consist of many small episodes, and expansion. According to research for Yahoo, multi-tasking allows people to pack the equivalent of forty-three hours into the day.[35] The idea of convenience makes little sense in societies characterized by strong shared temporal rhythms, or for people whose timetables are controlled by others. However, its significance increases dramatically when times for eating, playing, working and socializing are less precisely defined and when individuals are free and indeed obliged to construct schedules of their own.

A second explanation is that the need for convenience reflects the *increasing pace* of society. It is, as Southerton says, 'commonly perceived that the pace of daily life is accelerating and that there is an increasing shortage of time. Time famine, the time squeeze, the

---

[33] Ibid.

[34] Dale Southerton, '"Squeezing time"—Allocating practices, coordinating networks and scheduling society', *Time & Society*, 12/1 (2003), 5–25, 7.

[35] Mike Hess, *It's a Family Affair: the Media Evolution of Global Families in a Digital Age*, OMD, New York, 2006: <http://l.yimg.com/au.yimg.com/i/pr/familyaffair_final.pdf>, accessed 11 June 2011.

harried leisure class, the search for quality time: all these are topics of public discussion.[36] There is much debate about whether people really have less free time now than in the past; whether they are caught in a spiral of working-and-spending, or whether the crucial issue is that of intensification associated with the Taylorization of domestic life.[37] It is nonetheless generally agreed that the pursuit of convenience makes sense in response to contemporary pressures associated with de-routinization and speeding up. The more harried we become, the more we value time, the more convenience counts and the more we consume in its name. In many respects these are convincing arguments. However in taking *time* to be the central concern such explanations overlook the rather more complicated relation between convenient solutions and the specific practices to which they relate. Detailed studies of how convenience devices and services are used, especially within the home, bring these issues to the fore.

CONVENIENCE AND COMPROMISE

The busy mothers interviewed by Thompson in 1996 valued meals prepared from scratch over those that were just unwrapped. The idea of eating together as a family was also highly valued and where convenience foods made this possible they were—up to a point—*consistent* with ideals of care and not necessarily opposed to them.[38] While Thompson's respondents struggled to negotiate the pros and cons of convenience, another set of busy mothers, interviewed a decade later by Carrigan and Szmigin were much less ambivalent. As they saw it, 'convenience products were there to enhance their quality of life, essentially freeing them from tasks that were routine and boring.... There was little sense these choices required justification'.[39]

Carrigan and Szmigin's findings may suggest that convenience food—which in any event takes many forms—has become just food and that it is, as such, uncomplicated by notions of compromise or guilt. A related possibility is that keeping on top of sequencing and synchronization have become such central priorities that the fact that food is on the table at the right time is more significant for the reproduction of normal family life than what the meal consists of. Either way, Carrigan and Szmigin conclude that 'women in the UK have evolved in their mothering through harnessing the benefits of convenience'[40] and that convenience products have allowed them to deal

[36] Dale Southerton, '"Squeezing time"—Allocating practices, coordinating networks and scheduling society', *Time & Society*, 12/1 (2003), 5–25, 6.

[37] Arlie Hochschild, *The Time Bind : When Work becomes Home and Home becomes Work*, New York: Henry Holt, 2001.

[38] Craig Thompson, 'Caring consumers: gendered consumption meanings and the juggling lifestyle', *Journal of Consumer Research*, 22, 1996: 388–407, 399.

[39] Marylyn Carrigan and Isabelle Szmigin, '"Mothers of invention": maternal empowerment and convenience consumption', *European Journal of Marketing*, 40/9–10, 2006, 1122–42, 1135.

[40] Ibid., 1136.

with the challenges of fragmentation and temporal disruption and to do so in ways that demonstrate love and care.

If we turn from food to laundering, it is obvious that washing machines, once defined as modern conveniences have become normal parts of household infrastructure. They are no longer seen as appliances that save time and toil, nor does their use imply sub-standard performance. This is so despite the fact that boiling was previously 'considered essential for getting the wash really clean and germ-free'[41] and that these are standards that no machine can match.

These few examples imply that definitions of acceptably convenient goods and services are in a state of symbolic limbo: always teetering on the edge of unremarkable normal-ity but not yet fully absorbed into it. They also underline the impossibility of separating concepts of convenience from evolving meanings of care, domesticity and effective per-formance. In other words, convenience-related consumption is not simply about saving or shifting time as such, but is instead about re-designing and re-negotiating temporal demands associated with the proper accomplishment of specific social practices. In the next section I elaborate on the material aspect of this relationship, focusing on the ways in which products bought and sold in the name of convenience modify the time-profiles of everyday practices and consequently modify the rhythms of society.[42]

CONVENIENCE AND THE TIME-SPACE PROFILES OF PRACTICE

A generation or two ago doing the household laundry was a major undertaking, often occupying the best part of a day. That Mondays were routinely devoted to this task obvi-ously made a difference to what else did and did not happen on that day, and to how the rest of the week was organized. Though they have not necessarily reduced domestic labour, Cowan[43] for one, argues that many labour saving devices failed to have this effect, washing machines have undoubtedly transformed the temporal structure of domestic life. Data from the UK's market transformation programme indicates that washing machines are currently used an average of 274 times a year,[44] each occasion demanding relatively brief moments of attention—loading, turning on, unloading—scattered across a number of hours. For any one individual, the temporal organization of

---

[41] Christine Zmroczek, 'Dirty Linen—Women, class and washing machines, 1920s–1960s', *Womens Studies International Forum*, 15/2, 1992: 173–85, 176.

[42] Henri Lefebvre, *Rhythmanalysis: Space, Time, and Everyday Life*, London: Continuum, 2004.

[43] Ruth Schwartz Cowan, *More Work for Mother: The Ironies of Household Technology from the Open Hearth to the Microwave*, New York: Basic Books, 1983.

[44] Market Transformation Programme, *BNW05: Assumptions underlying the energy projections for domestic washing machines*, 2006, Market Transformation Programme/DEFRA, London: <http://efficient-products.defra.gov.uk/spm/download/document/id/569>, accessed 11 June 2011.

daily life reflects the availability of, and relation between a constantly changing mixture of co-existing appliances, each with their own time-space profiles. In the UK in the mid 1980s, freezers were pretty well established, with around a quarter of households also owning a microwave. This pattern that changed during the following decade such that both appliances were in widespread use across all social classes by the mid 1990s.[45] The freezer, initially alone, and now in combination with the microwave permits the conversion of practices that used to demand longer blocks of concentrated effort into the many fragments that now make up the mosaic of a day.

Coordinating these mini-moments is itself a challenge, hence the need for further solutions to help individuals cope with the demands of organizing personal schedules and of synchronizing with others whose timetables are as fractured and fragmented as their own. The more arranging there is to do and the more flexible this arranging is, the greater the potential for disruption and for changing plans at short notice. This sets in train a cycle in which goods and services that facilitate re-scheduling or reduce the time taken to accomplish specific practices have the cumulative effect of exacerbating the very problems they are intended to address. As with comfort, the result is an escalation of need, but for different reasons. Where might this lead and what is the future of convenience?

In discussing the 'rise and rise of convenience food' Tim Dowling[46] comments on the seemingly ludicrous idea of 'instant baked beans on toast, this being a 'frozen, fused sandwich that goes in the toaster', on partially microwaved bacon—a product that 'shaves precious seconds off your valuable microwaving time', and on tea granules that cut out the time it takes to remove and dispose of a tea-bag. These are perhaps extreme examples but they raise intriguing questions about the prospect of what manufacturers already refer to as super-convenience. In thinking about how far this might go and about what a thoroughly convenient society might look like, it is important to notice that convenience has implications for the amount of time specific practices demand, and for where and when they are enacted. Although popular and commercial references to convenience generally focus on duration and timing, some relate to material qualities like those of weight and portability.

Laptop computers and portable machines for watching films, listening to music or playing games afford convenience by allowing certain practices to colonize moments and previously vacant minutes like those spent waiting for trains, planes or other people.[47] From this point of view, the development and diversification of hand held battery operated devices is part and parcel of a tendency to dis-locate and extend the sites in

---

[45] Andrew McMeekin and Mark Tomlinson, 'Diffusion with distinction: The diffusion of household durables in the UK', *Futures*, 30/9, 1998: 873–86.

[46] Tim Dowling, 'The rise and rise of convenience food', 19 May 2006, The Guardian: <http//:www.guardian.co.uk/lifeandstyle/2006/may/19/foodanddrink.uk>, accessed 11 June 2011.

[47] Juliet Jain and Glenn Lyons, 'The gift of travel time', *Journal of Transport Geography*, 16/2, 2008: 81–9; Heike Weber, 'Portable Pleasures', in Mika Pantzar and Elizabeth Shove (eds.), *Manufacturing Leisure*, Helsinki: National Consumer Research Centre, 2005, 134–59; Giovanni Gasparini, 'On waiting', *Time & Society*, 4/1, 1995: 29–45.

which activities can and do go on. The point that goods and practices are important in defining place has been made before,[48] but this discussion suggests that studies of convenience could provide further insight into the dynamic relation between material culture and the micro-geography of social practice, including issues of location, duration and timing.

The struggles of keeping things together[49] and of keeping work and family life on track are experienced as personal pressures yet there is a sense in which being hurried and harried is a necessary consequence of living with the cast of convenience devices that now populate the lives of many, and that demand and structure moments and places of attention. In a simple sense such devices script responses and configure the temporal and spatial characteristics of the practices of which they are a part.[50] This is not to deny the significance of active integration or resistance. In his study of when and how UK families slotted video and computer technologies into existing rhythms and moral economies, Silverstone demonstrates the many ways in which identical devices are appropriated depending on the 'clocking' or temporal style of different households in the late 1980s.[51] Hand and Shove's analysis of the freezer leads to much the same conclusion. In this case households interviewed in 2006 underlined the practical and symbolic flexibility of the freezer, the purpose of which depended on the regimes and rhythms of food provisioning into which it was inserted.[52] These are important observations yet the point that methods of shifting and saving time are mobilized and used creatively, for instance, being deployed to generate pockets of calm elsewhere in the schedule,[53] does not alter the fact that convenient solutions configure the time-space profiles of specific practices. As Douglas and Isherwood argued quite some years ago, 'any given state of technology and production can be characterized by a particular pattern of consumption periodicities.'[54] While these authors go on to discuss the relation between time, consumption and social status/rank this is not the only route to take. For present purposes, the more general point is that the hardware of consumer culture is directly and actively involved in configuring the rhythm and temporal texture of society and in giving rise to specific forms of scheduling, sequencing, spatial distribution and coordination.

In this there are obvious parallels with comfort in that experiences and expectations of the proper relation between ourselves (our bodies) and our surroundings are configured

[48] Ash Amin and Nigel Thrift, *Cities*, Oxford: Polity, 2002.
[49] Craig Thompson, 'Caring consumers: gendered consumption meanings and the juggling lifestyle', *Journal of Consumer Research*, 22, 1996: 388–407.
[50] Madelaine Akrich, 'The description of technical objects', in W. Bijker and J. Law, *Shaping Technology/Building Society*, Cambridge, MA.: MIT Press,1992.
[51] Roger Silverstone, 'Time, information and communication technologies and the household', *Time & Society*, 2/3, 1993: 283–311.
[52] Martin Hand and Elizabeth Shove, 'Condensing practices: ways of living with a freezer', *Journal of Consumer Culture*, 7/1, 2007: 79–104.
[53] Dale Southerton, '"Squeezing time"—Allocating practices, coordinating networks and scheduling society', *Time & Society*, 12/1 (2003), 5–25, 6.
[54] Mary Douglas and Baron Isherwood, *The World of Goods: towards an Anthropology of Consumption* (London: Routledge, 1996), 82.

and mediated by changing, but at any one moment, 'necessary' forms of material culture. Achieving contemporary standards of comfort and convenience requires increasing amounts of resource consumption and in both cases there seems to be no way back. The examples considered here suggest that expectations of comfort are defined and held in place by a mesh of commercial interests and conventions. The result is indeed sticky in that it is difficult to imagine when or how such thoroughly normalized arrangements might be radically re-defined (Cool Biz aside). Patterns of temporal order appear to be just as firmly embedded, yet the self-fulfilling, self-perpetuating qualities described above suggest that the forms of path dependence involved are not quite the same.

COMFORT, CONVENIENCE, AND CHANGING PATTERNS OF CONSUMPTION

In contemporary usage comfort explains demand for materials and means that allow people to reproduce a specific relation between the body and its wider environment. The value of convenience is also taken for granted, so long as minimum standards of performance are not compromised or undermined. There may be instances in which specific goods signify the latest in comfort or convenience and in which their acquisition constitutes a form of self expression but the more important point is that discourses of comfort and convenience legitimize patterns of demand that are not primarily driven by conscious choice, decision-making or debate, and that are not obvious sites of social display and competition.

Their invisible self-evidence presents certain challenges for understanding and conceptualizing change. At any one moment, interpretations of normality are simply taken for granted yet meanings and related material arrangements continue to evolve. How does this work? Social psychologists like Verplanken and Stern[55] contend that habits only change when individuals become conscious of their routines and, having become conscious, make a deliberate decision to act in some other way. Wilk[56] draws upon similar ideas, and on Bourdieu[57] in arguing that habits have to switch from the realm of what Giddens[58] refers to as practical consciousness into that of explicit, recognized and visible discursive consciousness if they are to change at all. Once modified, new ways of doing and acting become routinized and slip back into the domain of the unnoticed.

---

[55] Bas Verplanken et al., 'Context change and travel mode choice: Combining the habit discontinuity and self-activation hypotheses', *Journal of Environmental Psychology*, 28/2, 2008, 121–7; Paul C. Stern, 'Toward a Coherent Theory of Environmentally Significant Behavior', *Journal of Social Issues*, 56/3, 2000:, 407–24.

[56] Richard Wilk, 'Consumption, human needs, and global environmental change', *Global Environmental Change*, 12/1, 2002: 5–13.

[57] Pierre Bourdieu, *Distinction: A Social Critique of Judgement and Taste*, London: Routledge, 1984.

[58] Antony Giddens, *The Constitution of Society*, Cambridge: Polity Press, 1984.

This account is widely held, and important in shaping policies that seek to influence consumer behaviour. But it does not fit with what we know about the creeping evolution of social and material arrangements or about forms of consumption defined and justified in terms of comfort or convenience.

One limitation is that models of this kind fail to capture or explain collective shifts—for instance in expectations of comfort. Not so long ago, it was common to wake up to frost on the inside of the window in an ordinary English home in winter. Although some people still do, this is no longer an experience that is widely shared. Have new habits and routines of comfort taken hold through a process of conscious reflection and deliberation? Is this a convincing explanation of change? At one level the answer may be 'yes'. Getting rid of the frost almost certainly involved investing in central heating, or insulation, or both. A decision was made. But at another level, the answer is clearly 'no'. The idea that individuals subscribe to one interpretation of comfort for years and then suddenly decide to change their ways is not particularly plausible. Not only is this account overly individualized, as if people switch habits in isolation from each other, it also overlooks the relation between material culture, consumption and practice. In other words, it supposes that consumer habits are detached from the material means of their realization.

The idea that the pursuit of convenience is a consequence of successive moments of recognition and decision is also only partly convincing. While the distinction between that which is taken-for-granted (like using the washing machine) and that which is currently on the edge (like relying on convenience foods) is tangible, the speeding up of laundry processes and food preparation appears to be less a consequence of actions flipping in and out of practical consciousness, and more a matter of ongoing adjustment as people negotiate the demands, constraints, injunctions and obligations of daily life.

If we take a longer term view it may be possible to identify moments of societal transformation occasioned by a mass blip of realization or recognition. To some extent Crowley's argument is that the eighteenth century sensibility of comfort arose from and at the same time represented a collective and evidently discursive re-definition of the relation between people and their immediate environments. The many sites and actors involved in making this sensibility perhaps support this image of a momentary revolution in ideas: a shared instant of discursive consciousness on the topic of comfort. However, this is again not quite enough. The idea of mass entitlement, and hence the legitimacy of comfort-related-consumption, only carries weight when accompanied by, and in a sense carried by, a raft of physical infrastructures and material arrangements. In other words debate about legitimacy and entitlement re-framed the symbolic meaning of homes, furniture, clothing and more, casting them as instruments of comfort-achievement. At the same time, the *substance* of what constitutes a comfortable arrangement is configured by the scripting effects and by the path dependent and path shaping characteristics of historically specific repertoires of material culture. This is important in that the switching of habits and routines takes place in a world already populated by hard and soft infrastructures, elements of which are always on the move.

From the eighteenth century on, comfort has been cast as a condition to which all aspire. Yet the qualities and characteristics of what counts as comfort have changed beyond recognition, and will surely change again in the future. But how, and in what direction? Although the environmental costs of maintaining Western interpretations of body, well being and temporal order are unsustainably high, the prospect of turning the clock back or of advocating 'uncomfortable' conditions is politically out of the question. In addition, and as advocates of slow cities or of slow food are only too well aware, the temporal rhythms that constitute the pace of life and that reproduce and fuel the need for convenience are deeply and multiply embedded. In their different ways, comfort and convenience constitute what we might think of as non-return valves of consumer culture. The forms of path dependence involved are not the same yet both are strongly associated with a sense of inevitability: so much so that the notion of spending an entire day doing the laundry is as odd as that of wearing half a dozen layers of clothing indoors.

Current conventions are so utterly normalized it is no wonder that policy makers focus on the efficiency with which these standards are met, and pay so little attention to the much more significant issue of how meanings of comfort and convenience come to be as they are, and how they might change in the future.[59] Though understandable, it is also short sighted. In shying away from the question of whether conventions of comfort and convenience might be configured along less demanding lines, governments effectively deny their own role in sustaining contemporary expectations. It only takes a moment to realize that culturally specific notions of comfort are reproduced through building codes and regulations and that governments are directly and indirectly involved in shaping the pace of life: for example permitting longer opening hours, seeking to quantify and reduce the time lost to traffic jams, and planning cities, villages and suburban estates in ways that impact on the meaning and use of time. Through these and other routes the state is implicated in reproducing current ways of life and the means required for their effective, and effectively unsustainable, reproduction.

The insights and conclusions of historical and contemporary studies of comfort and convenience have yet to feed into public policy on behaviour, environment and climate change on any scale but what if they did? It is one thing to realize that seemingly inevitable arrangements are unlikely to last forever, but another to understand, let alone influence, plausible and possible future trajectories above and below the radar of discursive consciousness. Although largely avoided at the moment, we might imagine a situation in which topics of comfort and convenience loom large in the environmental agenda. Indeed, the Japanese government's Cool Biz programme might be the first sign of a global debate about the meaning of comfort and entitlement to it. As in the eighteenth century, such discussion might be carried and amplified by novelists, designers, political economists, moral philosophers, scientists and humanitarian reformers. However, this is only part of the story. Studies of consumption, inspired by the material turn, demonstrate the extent to which the hardware of daily life figures in the reproduction and transformation of social practice, and in related patterns of demand.

---

[59] DEFRA, *A Framework for Pro-Environmental Behaviours*, London: HMSO, 2008.

That much is clear, but only in the most general of terms. Comparison of comfort and convenience, broadly defined, suggests that these domains evolve in different ways—but this far we know relatively little about the detailed mechanisms involved: how do new configurations take hold below the radar of discursive consciousness, and do how these processes work out in different societies? Addressing this question is likely to involve new lines of enquiry and methods of analysis capable of detecting connections and relationships between objects typically studied in isolation. For example, understanding the changing qualities of comfort might require an historical analysis of clothing, not as fashion, but as insulation the characteristics of which are defined by also relevant technologies of heating, cooling and building design. Likewise understanding the relentless pursuit of convenience is, in part, a matter of showing how repertoires of consumer goods give shape and form to the practices they sustain, and how these configure the temporal texture of individual lives and the pulse of society as a whole.

Further questions arise when we look ahead: what are the material cultures required or implied by more sustainable interpretations of well being or by substantially less resource intensive rhythms of daily life? And how might these new versions of normality come about? As indicated above, there intellectual resources on which to draw. For historians and sociologists of consumption, the challenge is to mobilize these and to enrich popular and policy understandings of relations between material culture and the practices and discourses of daily life, and of how these persist and change. It is now time to bring my contribution to an end but as these closing remarks make clear, the story has only just begun.

BIBLIOGRAPHY

Brager, Gail S. and de Dear, Richard J., 'Thermal adaptation in the built environment: a literature review', *Energy and Buildings*, 27/1, 1998: 83–96.

Carrigan, Marylyn and Szmigin, Isabelle, '"Mothers of invention": maternal empowerment and convenience consumption', *European Journal of Marketing*, 40/9–10, 2006: 1122–42.

Cooper, Gail, *Air Conditioning America: Engineers and the controlled environment 1900–1960*, Baltimore: Johns Hopkins University Press, 1998.

Crowley, John E., *The Invention of Comfort: Sensibilities and Design in Early Modern Britain and Early America*, Baltimore: Johns Hopkins University Press, 2001.

Gronow, Jukka and Warde, Alan, *Ordinary Consumption*, New York: Routledge, 2001.

Hitchings, Russell and Lee, Shu Jun, 'Air Conditioning and the Material Culture of Routine Human Encasement: The Case of Young People in Contemporary Singapore', *Journal of Material Culture*, 13/3, 2008: 251–65.

Shove, Elizabeth, *Comfort, Cleanliness and Convenience: the Social Organization of Normality*, Oxford: Berg, 2003.

Shove, Elizabeth et al., 'Comfort in a Lower Carbon Society', *Building Research and Information*, 4/4, 2008: 307–11.

Southerton, Dale, '"Squeezing time"—Allocating Practices, Coordinating Networks and Scheduling Society', *Time & Society*, 12/1, 2003: 5–25.

Warde, Alan, 'Convenient food: space and timing', *British Food Journal*, 101/1, 1999: 518–27.

CHAPTER 16

CONSUMPTION OF ENERGY

DAVID E. NYE

HISTORIOGRAPHY

Business historians, anthropologists, and Marxists long treated the consumption of energy as largely a question of supplying a necessity. Business historians sought inspiration in the work of Joseph Schumpeter or Alfred Chandler where entrepreneurs held the centre stage.[1] Historians of coal, oil, and gas focused on extraction, organization, and marketing, and wrote relatively little about end-users. Early studies of electrification dealt with inventions, power generation, transmission, and the formation of monopolies, but said little about how and why ordinary people adopted this new form of energy. Likewise, automotive history before c.1975 focused on invention, production, labour relations, product design, and marketing, with far less about the popular reception and use of automobiles.

Anthropologists working within a functionalist tradition considered energy to be a fundamental need, along with food, water, and shelter. In 1949 Leslie White argued that systems of energy were so fundamental that societies could be classified according to how much light, heat, and power they had mastered.[2] The society with the greatest access to energy was the most advanced. The most primitive were those that controlled nothing more than their own muscle power. The domestication of animals such as oxen and horses thus placed Renaissance Europe at a higher stage of evolution than the Aztecs; the British mastery of steam power placed them above colonial peoples; full electrification lifted American and European societies to a still higher stage. In such theories, societies with atomic energy occupied the highest level, which apparently promised perpetual

---

[1] Joseph Schumpeter *Business Cycles: A Theoretical, Historical, and Statistical Analysis of the Capitalist Process.* 2 vols. (New York: McGraw-Hill, 1939). Alfred D. Chandler, *The Visible Hand: The Managerial Revolution in American Business.* (Cambridge, MA: Harvard University Press, 1977).

[2] Leslie A. White, *The Science of Culture* (New York: Grove Press, 1949).

inexpensive power. Early Marxist authors were not at odds with these assumptions about energy, as they also viewed history in terms of advances in productivity. The hand-mill gave way to water power followed by the steam engine, and each increased the scale of industry. Even when writing about advertising, Ewen (1975) proclaimed that advertisers were *Captains of Consciousness*. Workers and the means of production, not the consumer, played the central roles. All these approaches saw energy primarily in terms of increasing supply and paid less attention to demand. The business historians, anthropologists, and Marxists all tended to see consumers as a passive 'nation of sheep' whom advertising could easily manipulate.

By the 1980s, however, historians began to see consumers as actors whose decisions shaped which products succeeded in the market, as documented elsewhere in this volume. The notion that advertisers controlled consumption collapsed after Roland Marchand's archival work revealed that agencies continually responded to changes in public taste, forced to follow trends beyond their control. Ruth Schwartz Cowan persuasively argued that purchases were negotiations at a 'consumption junction'.[3] Her argument was part of the contextualist approach that Wiebe Bijker, Thomas Hughes, and Trevor Pinch championed in the history of technology.[4] They presented technologies as part of the life-world, and they focused on the cultural factors that shape the invention, use, and interpretation of new objects. A characteristic work (Nye, 1990) examined the social construction of electricity between 1880 and 1940 by ordinary people, who wove it into urban life, factories, the home, the farm, and the sense of the future, as could be seen in newspapers, novels, popular speech, painting, and photography.[5] In such works, consumers were not passive but selective, and they used energies for their own purposes.

While Thomas P. Hughes participated in discussions of 'consumer choice', as early as 1983 he advanced an alternative approach that focused on organizations and institutions.[6] He argued that once a society made initial selections in the design of its energy system and these became institutionalized, a 'soft determinism' set in. The whole complex of machines, installations, personnel, and educational programmes acquired a 'technological momentum' that was difficult to change. Once utilities or oil companies had geared up to supply what millions of consumers had become accustomed to buy, the energy system moved with great force in a single direction. In the industrialized West, by *c.*1920 both the automobile and the centralized electrical system had attained this 'technological momentum'. Even the 1970s energy crisis did little to alter the form of either system in Western countries.

The approach to energy consumption in this essay takes consumer choice seriously but recognizes the constraints of technological systems whose momentum has

    [3] Ruth Schwartz Cowan 'The Consumption Junction: A Proposal for Research Strategies in the Sociology of Technology', in Bijker, et. al., 261–80.

    [4] Wiebe Bijker, Thomas Hughes, and Trevor Pinch (eds.), *The Social Construction of Technological Systems* (Cambridge, MA: MIT Press, 1987).

    [5] David E. Nye, *Electrifying America* (Cambridge, MA: MIT Press, 1990).

    [6] Thomas P. Hughes, *Networks of Power: Electrification in Western Society* (Baltimore: Johns Hopkins University Press, 1983).

been established. These systems are large in scale and embedded in landscapes, where decisions of previous generations are built into the layout of settlement, lighting, transportation, and recreation. This approach assumes that one must look at both institutional and personal energy consumption. It also has environmental implications, because the consumption of energy is not only difficult to modify but it is inseparable from problems of acid rain, smoke pollution, CO_2 emissions, and global warming. Much recent work intertwines the histories of technology, the environment, and consumption.[7]

MUSCLE POWER

From antiquity until the nineteenth century, the majority of the power in society came from the muscles of animals or human beings. Even now this energy regime has not passed away, but can be seen in 'undeveloped' areas or among the Amish in the United States. They eschew most of the energy technologies developed since c.1800, relying mostly on horses, oxen, and human muscle. In their world, energy cannot be consumed by merely flicking a wall switch, turning a knob on the stove, or opening a radiator valve.

Indeed, the all-encompassing word 'energy' is a rather new abstraction that consolidates all forms of light, heat, movement, and force into a single concept. Before c.1875 people did not 'consume energy'. Rather, they produced through their own labour the light, heat, or power needed. Usually this required performance of several tasks, such as chopping wood, carrying it inside, arranging it on a hearth or in a stove, and lighting a fire. For millennia, this person was a servant, serf, slave, or a child. Families wanted many children, who could perform the routine chores of a muscle-power economy. Landowners wanted many tenants, often bound to the land as serfs. The Roman fleet did not rely solely on the wind but instead enslaved rowers. When Europeans created plantations in the New World, they relied on slaves to plant, cultivate, and harvest sugar, rice, cotton, and tobacco. Until the nineteenth century, buying slaves or hiring unskilled 'hands' were common ways to obtain power.

While moral reformers undoubtedly led the movement to abolish slavery, it is vital to understand that during the same period industrialization developed new kinds of power that were less expensive than the muscles of oxen, horses, and men. To the extent that slavery was an investment in muscle power, it was gradually becoming an outmoded investment. Nineteenth-century engineers determined that a healthy man could produce only about one-tenth of a horsepower for any extended period. Even a small steam engine or water wheel could replace the power of many men. By 1849, the average factory commanded 1.15 horsepower per worker, or roughly eleven times what each worker's muscles could provide.[8] This ratio doubled in the second half of the century, making it

---

[7] Ronald Kline, *Consumers in the Country* (Baltimore: Johns Hopkins University Press, 2000); David E. Nye, *When the Lights Went Out* (Cambridge, MA: MIT Press, 2010).

[8] Louis C. Hunter, and Lynwood Bryant, *A History of Industrial Power in the United States, 1780–1930: The Transmission of Power* (Cambridge, MA: MIT Press, 1991), 312.

far cheaper to buy mechanical power than to buy slave power, assuming the same work could be done by each. Furthermore, as one historian concluded, 'a machine (unlike a slave or a horse) is most economically operated when it runs all the time'.[9]

Escape from hard muscular effort was the goal of many early innovations. If a job still required human muscle, mechanical devices performed the most demanding work. To take a simple example, it is possible to grind wheat or other grains using a hand-mill, but this is hard and slow work. A man or woman produces only one-tenth of a horsepower, and needs to rest periodically. In contrast, even a small water-powered grist-mill generates 5 horsepower, and does so continuously. It produces flour far more quickly and easily than a hand-mill, making it a rational choice for a farmer to use his time and a horse's muscle power to take grain to the mill for processing. Indeed, an older child often performed this errand, freeing the farmer for other tasks. Mills thus encouraged division of labour and rational analysis of where muscle power could be avoided or put to better use. Likewise, turning to sawmills to make lumber was a rational choice. Two men at opposite ends of a large saw might produce fifteen long boards in a day, while a mill could do more than this in one hour.

As agriculture and industry mechanized, slavery survived more out of familiarity and technological momentum than due to economic benefit. In the United States, both the industrial North and the agricultural Midwest were more prosperous than the slave South, where one found few steam engines except those used to process agricultural products. With each new labour-saving invention slavery became a worse investment. The pace of innovation had been increasing since the eighteenth century when steam power was improved and spread in Britain, but the dramatic change came during the nineteenth century, with the availability of gas, electricity, and internal combustion engines. These intensifications of power use also facilitated adoption of the abstract idea 'energy' that became disembodied as it was divorced from muscle power. By c.1930 urbanites seldom thought about the physical labour of miners or power plant operators when they wanted to turn on the heat or light.

However, a tight connection between time, work, and energy remained the norm for much of the world's population, even at the end of the twentieth century. In rural Asia, Africa, and Latin America, much farming was still carried out using draft animals and human muscle power, water had to be pumped and carried, and most of the heat and light came from fires. In such societies, millions of unskilled workers offer themselves as sources of energy, whether pedalling a rickshaw or digging in a field. The ability to consume energy without having to produce it is partial and recent. It also has its problematic side. As farms, cities, businesses, and households give up energy self-sufficiency, they become dependent on distant and often anonymous sources of power, whether coal mines, dams, oil wells, or gas fields.

Such superior methods of consuming power were essential to getting more work out of labourers, to producing goods more cheaply, and to freeing more labour for other

[9] James Marsden Fitch, *American Building 2: The Environmental Forces that Shape it* (New York: Schoken Books, 1975), 89.

tasks. European expansionism and imperialism would have been difficult to sustain without improved power systems. Notably, the ocean-going sailing ship dramatically increased the power available to the colonial powers. When the western hemisphere was discovered, Europeans had ships of 100 tons that when sailing at 10 knots delivered 500 to 750 horsepower.[10] This formidable energy could be commanded by sailors, whose muscles alone could produce far less horsepower and only for short periods. Combined with gunpowder and cannon, such ships gave Europeans a decisive military advantage compared to peoples with smaller vessels largely propelled by rowing or paddling. European ships carried raw materials and finished goods between manufacturing centres and the colonial periphery. The later adoption of steamships further increased the European military and commercial advantage. After c.1815, Western gunboats controlled the interior of India, China, and Africa, and steamboats facilitated expansion of European populations into the interiors of North and South America.

URBAN NETWORKS

Before it was possible to think of energy as something to be effortlessly consumed, complex networks of power had to be built into the very structure of cities. As Joel Tarr has shown,[11] these installations often began with water supply systems that usually required a steam-driven pumping plant, followed by other networks. One supplied commercial gas for lighting, which for generations was manufactured from coal and then piped to street lights, businesses, and a few wealthy homes. Gas systems in major European and American cities expanded their customer base to most of the middle class by the 1880s. In the 1840s the telegraph further established the idea of centralized networks that relied on pipes or wires. In the second half of the nineteenth century this idea was extended to systems of fire alarms, police call-boxes, and telephones. In each case, the consumer was directly connected to the system and could receive a service with minimum effort. Fully aware of the need for such a system if electrification were to be profitable, in 1879 Thomas Edison simultaneously invented not only the electric light bulb but also the dynamo, insulated wiring, wall switches, and all the devices needed for a distribution network. The Edison system was modelled on that used by gas companies and designed to become competitive with it.

Perhaps no artefact expresses more clearly the changing patterns of energy consumption in American and European cities in the nineteenth century than the humble coal-wagon. Delivering coal to businesses and homes, it signified the shift from chopping and burning wood to the reliance on distant mines to supply heat. The same wagons, after a

---

[10] William Fred Cottrell, *Energy and Society: The Relation Between Energy, Social Change, and Economic Development* (Westport, CT: Greenwood Press, 1970), 50.

[11] Joel Tarr, *Technology and the Rise of the Networked City in Europe and America* (Philadelphia: Temple University Press, 1988).

bit of scrubbing, often delivered ice during the spring and summer. This harvesting and preservation of winter ice for sale in cities was also a form of energy consumption. In New York alone in the 1880s two-thirds of a ton of ice was sold for each inhabitant of the city. Without it, much produce would have spoiled, and no urban home or apartment was complete without an icebox. Coal and ice were both essential consumer goods until the 1930s in the United States, and until the 1950s in some parts of Europe. After *c.* 1900 ice was increasingly manufactured and preserved using electric compressors, eliminating most of the energy once needed to obtain and ship it. Gradually, however, coal and ice trucks disappeared. Beginning in the 1930s, refrigerators undermined the ice trade, while smoke abatement regulations pressed homeowners to adopt other forms of heating. Most consumers shifted to oil or natural gas, although electric radiators were popular in Norway and some other locations with inexpensive hydroelectric power.

FACTORIES

The same systems that undergirded cities also facilitated the establishment and growth of factories. So long as work was manual, the workplace remained decentralized. Cloth was produced in crofts and by the fireside. Likewise, in most areas of life muscle power was the only motive force available, whether to plough fields, to turn lathes, to run printing presses, or to move tons of earth in construction. There were important exceptions, such as water wheels, which had been known since antiquity, and windmills, that became important only in the late Middle Ages. In the eighteenth and nineteenth centuries new engines emerged that ran on hot air, gas, compressed air, steam, and gasoline. (Electrical motors emerged later and had to compete with these innovations.) These were used to increase productivity, literally making available a greater array of consumer goods. Once it became possible after the 1830s to measure early forms of millwork (shafts, gears, belts, etc.) they were discovered to be terribly inefficient. As Louis Hunter documented in meticulous detail, engineers both improved these transmission systems and created new ones that used not only steam but also wire rope, high-pressure water, and compressed air.[12] All could be distributed from some form of central station to factories, steel mills, ports, and other sites demanding power.

For example, Dublin's port introduced high-pressure hydraulic transmission in 1795, and this method of cargo handling spread to many British ports and also became a power source in a few urban areas as well. Elsewhere, a central water supply could drive small water motors attached to church organs, small machines, appliances that required less than 2 horsepower, and many elevators in commercial buildings. The city of Milwaukee alone in *c.*1880 had 600 hydraulic elevators. Burning illuminating gas to produce power also briefly flourished, but proved uncompetitive. Clean, safe, compressed air was the

---

[12] Hunter and Bryant, *History of Industrial Power* (Cambridge, MA: MIT Press, 1991).

most successful of these systems, particularly in Paris, where in 1899 more than 100 miles of pipe supplied 24,000 horsepower. Another alternative was selling customers the right to attach their belts to a shared driveshaft running through a commercial building. Such systems made economic sense to any business that had only a small or episodic demand for mechanical power.

In retrospect, these transitional systems accustomed consumers to the idea of a centralized distribution network, before they opted for electrical power. But at the time, the alternative systems were sensible choices. In 1891 to transmit water power one mile or less using wire rope cost only half what electricity did. Electricity was more cost competitive with other networked systems when transmitting over long distances. Nevertheless, after 1900 electricity proved so versatile in application and the costs to consumers dropped so quickly that it became the energy of choice for most applications.

PUBLIC LIGHTING

Gas lighting in nineteenth-century cities lengthened the commercial day and increased the sense of security in the central city. Indeed, Peter Baldwin found that by the 1870s New Yorkers assumed that if the gas system failed the city might explode into lawlessness.[13] The first electric lights amazed the public, and they always drew a crowd. Throughout human experience fire and light by definition had been the same thing. In contrast, electric light did not require oxygen, did not blow out or flicker, and remained constant in shape, even if turned upside down. Lighting arrays grew more elaborate at successive world fairs from 1881 in Paris until 1915 in San Francisco. These displays convinced cities and towns to install permanent electric street lighting, which permitted stores to remain open after dark and made streets more appealing to consumers. Businesses put up electric signs and window displays, creating a new night landscape that emphasized prosperous enterprises and main thoroughfares, in effect deleting other areas as unimportant blanks. Urban lighting became even more intense with the spread of the automobile.

Prominent structures, such as the Statue of Liberty, Big Ben, and the Eiffel Tower also began to be floodlighted, soon followed by major commercial buildings. In 1907 the Singer Tower, then New York's tallest, was bathed in light, and became the first landmark visible when approaching the city. Other corporations saw the advantages of such displays, notably the Woolworth Building, completed in 1913. Its 792 ft terracotta tower had 600 special high-intensity bulbs with corrugated reflectors that diffused the light evenly, establishing a new standard for other skyscrapers. Central squares and theatrical districts in most of the industrialized world also embraced decorative illumination and giant advertising signs, notably in Piccadilly Circus, Times Square, and Tokyo's Ginza Strip. Popular with the

[13] Peter C. Baldwin, 'In the Heart of Darkness: Blackouts and the Social Geography of Lighting in the Gaslight Era', *Journal of Urban History*, 30/5 (July 2004), 749–68.

public, these installations became permanent features of urban life and were immediately missed if turned off due to a system failure, utility strike, or wartime blackout. One of the most popular Second World War songs on the Allied side was Vera Lynn's 'When the Lights Come On', which described the joyous return of lights and peace.

DOMESTIC CONSUMPTION

From the late 1870s until 1915, people experienced electric lighting in public, but few had it at home. As late as 1905 only 5 per cent of American houses were wired, even fewer in most other nations. The slowness of adoption was largely due to cost. Not only did a house need to be wired and current paid for, but two light bulbs in 1900 cost about one day's wages. Yet for those who could afford it, domestic electricity was clearly preferable to gas, candles, or lamps. While gas was thought to be a great innovation in c.1835, it provided poor-quality light for reading or detailed work. It produced unwelcome heat in summer and soot all year round. Leaking gas could asphyxiate residents or explode. By comparison, electric light was more even, did not flicker, and produced no soot or noxious by-products. For the same expense, it gave less heat and more light than gas. Should a bulb break, it did not leak electricity. Little wonder that homeowners preferred electricity, and fire insurance companies lowered their rates for buildings that abandoned gas.

In addition, consumers who could afford electricity found that it enabled many services, including at first burglar alarms, doorbells, buzzers, thermostats, and pumps to refill continually a water tank on the roof. After c.1900 many found new heating appliances convenient, notably waffle irons, toasters, water heaters, and irons. Other now familiar appliances were not perfected until a mass market developed for them after c.1920 in the United States but only after the Second World War in most of Europe. The sequence of adoption was roughly the same, however, in roughly the following order: vacuum cleaners, stoves, radios, refrigerators, garbage dispose-alls (primarily in the United States), televisions, freezers, and air-conditioners.

The idea of replacing slaves or servants recurred in advertisements for early consumer appliances. A survey of how electricity was being employed observed that 'Motors have been applied to lawn-mowers, to carpet-sweepers, to shoe-polishers, and, in fact, there is no household operation capable of being mechanically performed of which, through the motor, electricity cannot become the drudge and willing slave'.[14] The electrical goods manufacturers found that this idea appealed to consumers. During the 1920s the National Electric Light Association collaborated with women's organizations to spread the message. The president of the Federation of Women's Clubs declared in 1926 that, by using electrical appliances, 'Housewives must come up from slavery'.[15]

---

[14] Nye, *Electrifying America*, 247.
[15] Mary King Sherman, 'Housewives Must Come Up from Slavery', in *Proceedings of the Forty-Ninth Convention of the National Electric Light Association* (1926).

Westinghouse also emphasized liberation through appliances. One advertisement asked 'Why Be a Slave to a Stove?' and explained how an electric stove with an automatic timer made it possible for a woman to leave home for several hours and let the dinner take care of itself. Women no longer needed to spend much time on sweeping or ironing, because 'electricity has worked their emancipation'. The kitchen supposedly had become a servantless workplace, where the modern woman could remain a lady because her labours were light. General Electric advertisements declared 'any woman who does anything which a little electric motor can do is working for 3 cents an hour'. This slogan was accompanied by images of women bent over washtubs scrubbing clothing or cleaning a carpet by hand. A good woman 'does not rob the evening hours of their comfort because her home is dark. To light a room splendidly, according to modern standards, costs less than 5 cents an hour. Men are judged successful according to their power to delegate work. Similarly the wise woman delegates to electricity…'.[16] Travelling lecturers sent out by the electrical goods manufacturers further hammered home this message, using slide presentations showing contrasting images of physical labour and the modern, electrical replacements. The gas manufacturers made similar arguments.

Ruth Schwartz Cowan has argued that women spent just as many hours at domestic labour after electrification as before.[17] Families with washing-machines had more clothing and did more laundry. Cleaning might be easier, but houses were growing larger. Moreover, men did less domestic work. Where once they had carried rugs outside and beaten them, the housewife alone was expected to vacuum them. The ritual of a spring house-cleaning that involved the whole family gradually disappeared, leaving mother to do the work. While this argument may not apply with equal force to all nations and social classes, it is an important reminder that new technologies do not necessarily liberate anyone.

REACTIONS TO HIGH ENERGY CONSUMPTION

Even as railways and labour-saving machines spread around the globe, many began to worry that a high-energy networked society might enfeeble the young who had never needed muscle power to obtain life's necessities. In response, they began to preserve national parks and discovered the virtues of camping and roughing it. A former soldier who had served in Africa, Robert Baden-Powell founded the Boy Scouts in 1908. Moving between the high-energy world of London and remote areas of the British Empire where muscle power was still essential to most aspects of life, Baden-Powell became concerned that modern life was becoming effete. The Boy Scouts reverted to muscle power in most activities, and learned how to make fires and survive in the wild. Similar concerns led American universities to develop extensive sports programmes and inspired Cecil Rhodes

---

[16] Nye, *Electrifying America*, 270.
[17] Ruth Schwartz Cowan, *More Work for Mother* (New York: Basic Books, 1984.)

to give his famous scholarships only to those who had both intellectual and athletic prowess. Bill Lukin found that later British thinkers such as G. M. Trevelyan, Vaughan Cornish, and Patrick Abercrombie believed 'the periodic bouts of isolation in the wilderness are the only sure means of temporarily healing the wounds attributable to urban civilisation'.[18]

Nevertheless, new forms of energy affected the way that people thought about their bodies. In the world of muscle power, a person was often compared to a horse, whether a thoroughbred, an old nag, a skittish racehorse, or a workhorse. There were also many popular expressions such as 'getting the bit between his teeth' or 'she has a burr under her saddle'. Steam engines inspired quite different metaphors, such as 'he is getting up a head of steam', or 'she is under a lot of pressure'. An 1860 newspaper article, 'The Human Coalburner', declared that 'every man is not only a locomotive but a fuel consumer too',[19] and went on to extol the efficiency of the human body as a machine. In these and many other expressions, human beings, instead of being compared to domestic animals, were reconceived in terms of engines, wires, and motors. The emergence of new metaphors for the self became particularly evident as electrification spread through society. People began to use such expressions as 'getting your wires crossed', 'an electrifying performance', or suffering a 'mental short circuit'. The brain was increasingly understood as an electrical system that had affinities with a battery that could be run down and recharged. This impulse was expressed more formally in the new science of ergonomics, which defined human beings as inefficient machines that needed training to maximize their potential. E. J. Marey argued that, 'As we regulate the use of machines in order to obtain a useful result with the least exertion of work, so man can regulate his movements…with the least fatigue possible'.[20] Similar ideas inspired Frederick Winslow Taylor and other scientific managers, who imposed on the bodies of workers their vision of rationality and efficiency. Thus the consumption of energy had reciprocal effects on consciousness.[21] Not only did the consumer continually adopt new metaphors to understand the self but managers wanted workers to conform to 'rationalized' shops.

TRANSPORT

The most efficient use of muscle power for transportation was the canal, which in the eighteenth century was an important means of carrying bulk cargo, particularly in France and Britain. Adam Smith, in *The Wealth of Nations* (1776), used canals to

---

[18] Bill Luckin, *Questions of Power: Electricity and Environment in Inter-War Britain* (Manchester: Manchester University Press, 1990), 160.

[19] 'The Human Coalburner', *Railway Times* (15 September 1860), 12, 37.

[20] Anson Rabenbach, *The Human Motor: Energy, Fatigue, and the Origins of Modernity* (New York: Basic Books), 1990, 116.

[21] See Frederick Winslow Taylor, *The Principles of Scientific Management* (Harpers, 1911) and Philip Scranton, *Endless Novelty: Specialty Production and American Industrialization, 1865–1925* (Princeton: Princeton University Press, 1997).

exemplify how improved transportation lowered transaction costs. As late as the 1820s, the United States experienced a canal-building boom, creating a network of waterways from the Atlantic coast to the Mississippi that astonished early travellers. A heavy cast-iron stove or a printing press made in Philadelphia that were uneconomical to haul by wagon could be floated inexpensively to St Louis or Chicago. Water transportation moved coal, wood, grain, and other goods so cheaply and efficiently that it remained cost competitive with railroads until at least 1880. Fogel even argued that the railroad was not necessary to integrate the United States into a national market, as canals and rivers would have been sufficient.[22]

The shift from muscle power to burning fossil fuels occurred with the simultaneous invention of steamboats in Europe and the United States c.1800, soon followed by the first steam railway in Britain. These forms of steam transport gradually spread throughout the world, linking raw materials, factories, and consumers into international markets and encouraging manufacturing on a larger scale. The US rail system, already double the size of Europe's in 1850, kept expanding until 1916, when it encompassed 254,000 miles of track and carried most of the freight and 98 per cent of all intercity traffic. As Wolfgang Schivelbusch discovered, early train passengers were thrilled by the speed and scale of railroads but fearful that the bouncing and high velocity damaged their nervous systems.[23] Once the novelty wore off, a justifiable fear of accidents remained. However, by the late nineteenth century, railways had achieved a high level of safety, punctuality, and comfort, notably in the lavish Pullman sleeping-cars. Londoners could get on a Pullman in the evening and arise the next morning in Edinburgh.

In 1890 hardly anyone had seen, much less owned, an automobile, but by 1990 it had become the world's most important consumer good and the source of the largest demand for energy. While the gasoline car now predominates, as Gijs Mom found, in 1900 electric cars were more widespread in Paris or New York than the gasoline car.[24] Electric cars were quieter and non-polluting, but lacked the speed, range, and rapid refuelling of cars with internal combustion motors. Steam cars did not have these drawbacks, however, and the steam engine was familiar to consumers, and it could burn a variety of fuels. However, they took a long time to heat up before starting, and they were much heavier, a considerable problem on muddy roads and rural bridges. Even so, consumers chose the gasoline car in good measure because Henry Ford's manufacturing innovation of the assembly line more than halved the purchase price from over $800 in 1909 to under $300 in 1924. However, consumers rejected Ford's standardization of style and colour, preferring the new hues and annual style changes of General Motors vehicles. In 1927, after manufacturing 15 million Model Ts, Ford was forced to follow suit.

[22] Robert William Fogel, *Railroads and American Economic Growth* (Baltimore: Johns Hopkins University Press, 1964).
[23] Wolfgang Schivelbusch, *The Railway Journey: The Industrialization of Space and Time* (Oxford: Basil Blackwell, 1980).
[24] Gijs Mom, *The Electric Vehicle* (Baltimore: Johns Hopkins University Press, 2004).

Adoption of the car was by no means rapid everywhere. Already in 1925 there was one for every six Americans, and it had become standard family transport. At that time there was only one car for every 100 Germans, fewer in Eastern Europe, more in Britain. Full market penetration only arrived in Europe and Japan after c.1960 and at least a generation later elsewhere. Meanwhile, the United States embraced the automobile almost to the exclusion of buses and railroads, and in the process built cities such as Phoenix and Los Angeles where half the land was devoted to roads, car parks, gas stations, driveways, limited access highways, and other spaces for the automobile. In 1968 one in every six American workers was directly or indirectly employed in manufacturing, selling, or servicing the automobile. Vast commercial strips ringed the cities, including 211,000 gas stations, 114,000 auto repair shops, 40,000 motels, countless diners, fast-food restaurants, drive-in banks, drive-in theatres, miniature golf courses, shopping malls, and other attractions catering to the automotive consumer.[25] After two generations of cruising through this sprawling cornucopia toward their suburban homes, this high-energy environment seemed 'natural' to Americans. It had overwhelming technological momentum and was embedded in the landscape and in the life-world to such a degree that often there were no alternatives. Where a Dutch or Danish consumer could combine the train and bicycle to reach most destinations, the American typically had no choice but the automobile. Moreover, Americans insisted on large cars with poor gas mileage compared to those manufactured in Europe or Japan. When the American Congress legislated to require more efficient vehicles, consumers responded by purchasing millions of small trucks and sports utility vehicles that were not required to meet the higher standards.

DOMESTIC ENERGY CONSUMPTION

By 1930 the electrification of Europe and the United States included every city and was becoming common in the countryside as well. In densely populated countries such as the Netherlands or Britain utilities found it profitable to run transmission lines into rural areas. In the more sparsely settled United States, only one farmer in ten had utility power, mostly on irrigated farms that required electric pumps. But as Ronald Kline discovered, farmers did not passively wait for energy technologies.[26] They adopted the automobile, purchasing Model T Fords as quickly as their city cousins, and they adapted car batteries to play the radio and run small appliances. Rural areas also set up their own telephone exchanges. In the 1930s they seized the opportunity to create electrical cooperatives offered by the Roosevelt administration and rapidly erected transmission lines and wired their farms. Moreover, they showed considerable consumer independence, resisting the blandishments of salesmen intent on selling electric fences and farm

---

[25] Stephen B. Goddard, *Getting There: The Epic Struggle between Road and Rail in the American Century* (Chicago: University of Chicago Press, 1994), 214.

[26] Ronald Kline, *Consumers in the Country* (Baltimore: Johns Hopkins University Press, 2000).

equipment, and instead buying water pumps, indoor plumbing, washing-machines, refrigerators, and other domestic appliances.

By the 1950s rural people everywhere in the industrialized world had full access to modern road and electrical networks, and thereafter participated in the rapid growth of consumer electronics. This story usually emphasizes the invention of the transistor, the miniaturization of computer chips, and enormous increases in memory. However, battery improvement and miniaturization were just as important to making consumer electronics portable. Today people carry electricity with them at all times, in their watches, phones, iPods, and in some cases hearing-aids, and pacemakers. This miniaturization began with portable radios in the 1950s, primarily as a fad among young people. With each passing year more and more functions were added. By 2005 the miniature radio was just one of many functions in phones that also included browsers, calculators, cameras, clocks, email, games, and messaging, packed into a device smaller than the 'miniaturized' radio of 1960. The near universal adoption of these devices and laptop computers intensified battery use, creating toxic waste problems due to the millions of discarded electronic devices, often still containing their batteries.

As the independence of rural consumers and the explosive growth of consumer electronics suggest, advertising and marketing did not always drive the growth of energy consumption. Between 1890 and 1920 Westinghouse, General Electric and Siemens took little interest in the domestic market, and focused on selling large systems, notably for urban lighting and transportation. The new field of home economists and some feminists were then more interested in appliances. Progressive women's organizations studied how to make the best use of electricity, and in the 1920s such user groups served as mediators between production and consumption. They shared practical knowledge of how to make use of new gas and electrical appliances. Home economists helped set up and staff 'all-electric' demonstration homes and displays at state and county fairgrounds.

The centrality of women's expertise in negotiating the consumption junction declined after the Second World War. Corporations had more in-house knowledge of the domestic market and their collaboration with user groups correspondingly declined, replaced by new expertise from advertising and public relations agencies. The consumption junction also changed as the state became a more central actor, both regulating quality and approving new devices. For example, American state regulations determined whether buildings with electric heating or air-conditioning qualified for loans to veterans, and state agencies set safety standards. Thus in the post-war period, female user groups and home economists were squeezed out by in-house corporate experts, psychologists, advertising agencies, and the state.

In the 1960s, however, new user groups appeared at the mediation junction, reacting against this professionalization. Reformers, such as consumer advocate Ralph Nader, became watchdogs, demanding cars and appliances that were safer and used less energy. Counter-cultural groups began to explore alternative technologies that were decentralized. They pooled their knowledge in *The Whole Earth Catalogue* (1968) and in a spate of books on how to live off-grid, build a passive solar house, or use the sun to dry and preserve food. In the early 1970s E. H. Schumacher's bestseller *Small is Beautiful* argued for the benefits of decentralized, small technologies.[27] His book appealed to consumers caught in the energy crises of that era. For a few years investments poured into 'alternative energies' such as solar and wind power. Gasoline rationing was briefly imposed in most of Europe and the United States. Denmark and the Netherlands returned to high rates of bicycle use. Americans demanded smaller cars with better mileage. However, the parsimony of the 'energy crisis' was short-lived. Beginning in the 1980s World Watch issued yearly 'State of the World' reports, pointing out the many social and environmental problems that come with an economy focused solely on growth.[28] Yet such reports and the 1970s ideal of sustainability based on alternative energies did not transform energy practices for many people. As soon as fuel shortages receded, consumers reverted to familiar patterns, including a reliance on automobiles for transportation and high per capita electricity usage.

Yet energy consumption was by no means the same in nations with otherwise comparable standards of living. Americans used twice as much energy as German or French consumers, and almost three times as much as the Japanese. American car ownership and energy use had increased far beyond any conceivable definition of necessity. In 2001 lighting represented only 8.8 per cent of total domestic electricity use. Homeowners used less electricity for lighting than on space heating (10.1 per cent), hot water heating (9.1 per cent), or kitchen appliances (8.9 per cent), and consumed twice as much for air-conditioning (16 per cent). Families had multiple radios and stereos. They used electrical coils to keep waterbeds and outdoor hot tubs perpetually warm. They acquired cable hook-ups, satellite dishes, VCRs, DVDs, cordless phones, answering machines, humidifiers, dehumidifiers, power tools, and outdoor electric grills. Their televisions multiplied and grew from a mere 14in. in the 1950s to 42in. a half century later. Clothes driers, rare before 1960, in 2001 were in 75 per cent of American homes. No one owned PCs in 1970, but three decades later Americans had 200 million, with accompanying printers and peripheral devices.[29] Furthermore, homes kept expanding and had more rooms to heat, cool, light, and fill with gadgets. The typical family of 2001 consumed more electricity each month than a family in 1940 had during an entire year.

FUTURE PATHS

Consumers became more aware of energy (over-)consumption after 2000. Oil prices rose and fell erratically, and climbed to over $150 a barrel in 2008. Rolling blackouts due to excessive demand on the electrical system, an occasional problem in the 1990s,

[27] E. H. Schumacher, *Small is Beautiful Economics as if People Mattered* (New York: Harper and Row, 1973).
[28] World Watch Institute, *State of the World 2004, Special Focus: The Consumer Society* (Washington, World Watch Institute 2004).
[29] US Department of Energy, 'Table US-1. Electricity Consumption by end use in U.S. households, 2001', 22 July, 2009, <http://www.eia.doe.gov/emeu/reps/enduse/er01_us_tab1.html>.

became more common. Complete, accidental blackouts also recurred. In 2003 alone, Copenhagen and London suffered major blackouts, as did 50 million people in the north-eastern United States and lower Canada. People trapped in elevators and subways or forced to sit in dark homes and offices without televisions, computers, or air-conditioning suddenly understood how dependent they had become on electricity. Yet the solution was not simply to produce more. Because much electricity is generated by burning coal, its environmental effects grew more salient every year, notably acid rain, CO_2 emissions, and smoke pollution. The Kyoto Protocol was intended to help reduce pollution and global warming. Signed by most of the world's nations starting in 1997, it came into effect in 2005. However, during this eight-year interval, the signatory nations failed to restrain consumer demand, which galloped ahead each year by an average of 500 billion additional kilowatts. According to the US Energy Information Administration, the world was using one-third more electricity (15,758 billion kWh) in 2005 than it had in 1997. This growth was by no means evenly distributed. Japan, whose economy was stagnant, nearly achieved zero energy growth (4 per cent), in contrast to China's rampant 223 per cent increase. Germany (10 per cent), France (17 per cent), and the United Kingdom (12 per cent) grew rather than shrank their demand, but they were less profligate than Ireland (51 per cent), India (40 per cent), Argentina (39 per cent), or Brazil (27 per cent). Almost everywhere the demand was for more, and no nation had managed to reverse the trend.

The failure to reduce energy use cannot be explained by cost-benefit analysis. US energy efficiency could be improved by 23 per cent through off-the-shelf technologies such as better insulation, replacement of inefficient appliances, and the like.[30] The cost of making these changes would quickly be recovered through large savings on fuel bills. Consumers would also save large sums if they could be persuaded to buy more fuel-efficient cars. But consumer behaviour is hard to change. In contrast, some businesses have become energy efficient. Volkswagen has built factories that minimize their environmental impact. The giant retailer Wal-Mart has developed a sustainability index to evaluate its suppliers, and it is seeking to make itself into a green corporation. Many companies are literally going green, by putting grass and other plants on their roofs, which improves insulation, removes CO_2, and reduces the cost of air-conditioning. The Automobile Club of Southern California reduced its summer consumption of electricity by 4.8MW through an in-house campaign that cost just $1,000 in award money. As John Eggink has shown, when organizations see definite savings from energy efficiency, they usually pursue the benefits, which are long term.[31]

For governments, the gap between green rhetoric and action was partly due to indecision about what path to follow towards greater sustainability. Two quite different models of future energy consumption had emerged by c.2010. Both recognized that fossil fuel consumption is unsustainable. The first model, endorsed by George Bush,

[30] Kate Galbraith, 'Efficiency Drive Could Cut Energy Use 23%', *New York Times*, 30 July 2009.
[31] John Eggink, *Managing Energy Costs: A Behavioural and Non-Technical Approach* (London: Taylor & Francis, 2007).

Gordon Brown, and many corporate leaders, would continue to rely on centralized service, but would rely on nuclear fission instead of burning coal. France exemplifies such a system, generating more than 80 per cent of its electricity in nuclear plants. This model anticipates that windmill and solar generation would supply no more than a quarter of the total energy. For a consumer plugging a device into the wall, this model would require few changes in behaviour.

The second model, developed in variant forms, notably by Hermann Scheer and Al Gore, rejects centralized power stations, including nuclear plants, and calls for radical decentralization, based on a smart electrical grid more akin to the internet than to the distribution network of the past.[32] Large power plants would be phased out in favour of micro-installations, including every home, business, and office building. Electricity would be generated by a combination of wind, solar, geothermal, hydro, and tidal power. Amory Lovins has long advocated decentralization as being resilient against breakdowns or attacks.[33] A smart grid would transform all consumers into producers, who could become self-sufficient or even sell excess power back to the system, rather than merely try to consume less. Such a system is feasible, but its costs would be more widely distributed than building nuclear plants. For example, roughly two-thirds of all US energy needs could be supplied from solar power in the American south-west, but a new transmission system to the rest of the country would be needed.[34] When there was excess solar power, it could be stored as hydrogen to be burned when needed. Likewise, in Germany excess wind power has successfully been stored both through pumped storage of water and as compressed air in abandoned mineshafts. This leaner, smarter system would make energy efficiency potentially profitable to every family. Indeed, well-insulated houses have already been built in Germany with new heat-exchangers that permit good ventilation. They require no energy inputs for heat and generate much of their own electrical power using solar panels.

While an energy transition seems unavoidable, unless consumers and voters exert themselves, the nuclear energy model seems more likely to be adopted in many nations rather than the decentralized, alternative energy model. Choosing the nuclear option does not ask the consumer to install anything new or give much thought to change. In contrast, the public would need to make a psychological adjustment and financial investment to transform homes into energy generators. The problem remains that, since its introduction in the nineteenth century, the centralized energy regime has built up tremendous technological momentum. It includes trillions of dollars invested in gas- and coal-fired central stations, millions of jobs throughout the energy infrastructure, and the ingrained habits of those who use it. Previous energy regimes were not replaced rapidly. For example, it took more than half a century for steam engines to supplant water power.[35]

[32] Scheer, Hermann, *Energy Autonomy* (Washington: Earthscan, 2007).
[33] Lovins, Amory, *Brittle Power: Energy Strategy for National Security* (Andover: Brick House Publishing, 1982).
[34] Ken Zweibel et. al., 'A Solar Grand Plan', *Scientific American* (16 December 2007), 64–73.
[35] David E, Nye, *Consuming Power* (Cambridge, MA: MIT Press, 1998), 79–82.

There are some signs of a widespread shift in consumer awareness. Voluntary curbs on electrical demand occur during the annual worldwide Earth Hour. This movement began in 2007 in Sydney, Australia, and immediately spread to London. Earth Hour then spread to 88 countries during the following two years. Held on the last Saturday in March, individuals extinguish their lights and some appliances for one hour, in a voluntary rolling blackout that moves around the globe. With this symbolic gesture, citizens tell politicians they want to make real reductions in electricity demand.

While millions participate in Earth Hour, a significant number, including Michelle Obama, grow their own vegetables to reduce their impact on the environment. They essentially are using muscle power to replace expensive energy inputs. Food production and consumption together require 17 per cent of all the energy used in the United States. Half of that is for processing, transportation, and preservation. Much of the other half is used in ploughing, planting, cultivating, and harvesting, all typically done using internal combustion engines. Those who garden by hand cut out all fossil fuel inputs and often do not need to use the refrigerator before preparing to eat the food. Home farming provides fresh produce and reduces the gardener's energy footprint, especially compared to, for example, kiwis shipped from New Zealand to London, or apples sent from Chile to New York.

A few comprehensive projects rethink how people consume energy, seeking sustainability. For example, the Abu Dhabi government is investing $22 billion in Masdar City, a project endorsed by the World Wildlife Fund. It will run on solar power and require only one-fifth the energy of a conventional city. Cars will be banned, replaced by electric transport beneath the streets. However, Masdar City might turn out to be an enclave of solar virtue in the midst of high-energy abuse. Indeed, next door a new racetrack is being laid out. For sustainable living that clearly works, one may still need to look to the Amish, who selectively adopt only a few new technologies, and thrive by relying primarily on muscle power.

Future research might focus on three areas. One is the social response to breakdowns, such as electrical blackouts, or adaptation to equipment failure or irregular service.[36] A second area worth investigating is a detailed comparison of energy use, to see to what extent it varies by social class, ethnicity, gender, and nationality. Who has the largest carbon footprint, and why is this so? Such information would provide a nuanced picture of the social construction of energy systems, and it might be helpful in understanding where the resistance is to more sustainable energy use. Such research in turn would help to develop knowledge of a third area, how the various forms of power function within and structure different historical periods and social life-worlds. Research to date has escaped from the narrow confines of Whig history and its narratives of liberation and progress through greater energy consumption. What narratives will historians put in its place? My own sense is that future studies of energy consumption will prove inseparable from environmental history.

[36] Nye, *When the Lights Went Out*; Elizabeth Shove, Richard Wilk, and Frank Trentmann, *Time, Consumption and Everyday Life* (London: Berg, 2009).

BIBLIOGRAPHY

Arsenault, Raymond, 'The End of the Long Hot Summer: The Air Conditioner and Southern Culture', *Journal of Southern History*, 50/4 (1984), 587–628.

Baldwin, Peter C., 'In the Heart of Darkness: Blackouts and the Social Geography of Lighting in the Gaslight Era', *Journal of Urban History*, 30/5 (2004), 749–68.

Bijker, Wiebe, Hughes, Thomas P., and Pinch, Trevor (eds.), *The Social Construction of Technological Systems* (Cambridge, MA: MIT Press, 1987).

Cottrell, William Fred, *Energy and Society: The Relation Between Energy, Social Change, and Economic Development* (Westport, CT: Greenwood Press, 1970).

Cowan, Ruth Schwartz, *More Work for Mother: The Ironies of Household Reform* (New York: Basic Books, 1983).

Cowan, Ruth Schwartz, 'The Consumption Junction: A Proposal for Research Strategies in the Sociology of Technology', in Bijker et al.

Durning, Alan, *How Much is Enough? The Consumer Society and the Future of the Earth* (New York: W. W. Norton, 1992).

Eggink, John, *Managing Energy Costs: A Behavioural and Non-Technical Approach* (London: Taylor & Francis, 2007).

Ewen, Stuart, *Captains of Consciousness* (New York: McGraw Hill, 1975).

Fitch, James Marsden, *American Building 2: The Environmental Forces that Shape it* (New York: Schoken Books, 1975).

Fogel, Robert William, *Railroads and American Economic Growth* (Baltimore: Johns Hopkins University Press, 1964).

Goddard, Stephen B., *Getting There: The Epic Struggle between Road and Rail in the American Century* (Chicago: University of Chicago Press, 1994).

Hoffman, Steven M., and High-Pippert, Angela, 'Community Energy: A Social Architecture for an Alternative Energy Future', *Bulletin of Science, Technology, and Society*, 25/5 (2005), 387–401.

Hughes, Thomas P., *Networks of Power: Electrification in Western Society* (Baltimore: Johns Hopkins University Press, 1983).

Hunter, Louis C., and Bryant, Lynwood, *A History of Industrial Power in the United States, 1780–1930: The Transmission of Power* (Cambridge, MA: MIT Press, 1991).

Kline, Ronald, *Consumers in the Country* (Baltimore: Johns Hopkins University Press, 2000).

Lovins, Amory, *Brittle Power: Energy Strategy for National Security* (Andover, MA: Brick House Publishing, 1982).

Luckin, Bill, *Questions of Power: Electricity and Environment in Inter-War Britain* (Manchester: Manchester University Press, 1990).

Marchand, Roland, *Advertising the American Dream* (Berkeley: University of California Press, 1986).

Mom, Gijs, *The Electric Vehicle* (Baltimore: Johns Hopkins University Press, 2004).

Nye, David E., *Consuming Power* (Cambridge, MA: MIT Press, 1998).

Nye, David E., *Electrifying America* (Cambridge, MA: MIT Press, 1990).

Nye, David E., *When the Lights Went Out* (Cambridge, MA: MIT Press, 2010).

Rabenbach, Anson, *The Human Motor: Energy, Fatigue, and the Origins of Modernity* (New York: Basic Books, 1990).

Scheer, Hermann, *Energy Autonomy* (Washington: Earthscan, 2007).

Schivelbusch, Wolfgang, *The Railway Journey: The Industrialization of Space and Time* (London: Basil Blackwell, 1980).

Schumacher, E. F., *Small is Beautiful* (New York: Harper and Row, 1973).

Shaw, Ronald E., *Canals for a Nation: The Canal Era* (Lexington, KT: University of Kentucky Press, 1990).

Shove, Elizabeth, Wilk, Richard, and Trentmann, Frank, *Time, Consumption and Everyday Life* (Oxford: Berg, 2009).

Tarr, Joel, *Technology and the Rise of the Networked City in Europe and America* (Philadelphia: Temple University Press, 1988).

White, Leslie A., *The Science of Culture* (New York: Grove Press, 1949).

CHAPTER 17

··

WASTE

··

JOSHUA GOLDSTEIN

In 2006 Cheung Yan became the first female to be dubbed the wealthiest person in the People's Republic of China (PRC). Formally known within her company, Nine Dragons Paper, as 'the Chairlady', she became a momentary darling of the financial press under titles like 'The Queen of Rubbish'.[1] The 'Queen''s estimated worth in 2007 was around US$10 billion and her company was selling at over HK$26 per share. On 27 October 2008 that share price plummeted to 81¢; in December, Standard & Poors downgraded Nine Dragons Paper's credit rating to junk bond status. Today Cheung Yan has yet to remount the billionaire charts, but Nine Dragons' stock has begun a steady recovery as global business is returning to usual.

The meteoric rise and fall of Nine Dragons is emblematic of a post-Cold War globalization in which, if Consumption is King, then Trash is Queen. While mass consumption is venerated as the lifeblood of the global economy and monitored compulsively by consumer confidence surveys, trash and waste—the inexorable products of that consumption—go largely ignored. Nine Dragons was a fortune built on trash, specifically on old packing boxes. Several years before starting Nine Dragons, Cheung had founded America Chung Nam, a shipping company specializing exclusively in hauling OCC (Old Corrugated Cardboard) from North America to China; Nine Dragons then turned those old boxes into new ones. The reuse of waste-paper for new paper stock is one of civilization's most venerable recycling processes, but Cheung Yan's empire raised it to an unprecedented spatial and quantitative scale. By 2001 America Chung Nam had become the single largest exporter by volume of freight from the United States; 'In other words, nobody in America was shipping more of anything each year anywhere in the world'.[2] That volume continued to balloon. In 1997 North America had exported around 4 million tons of waste-paper to all of East Asia; by 2007 China alone was importing

[1] Anna Pukas 'The GBP2 Billion Queen of Rubbish', *Wall Street Journal*, 13 October 2006.
[2] Evan Osnos, 'Wastepaper Queen', *The New Yorker*, 30 March, 2009.

20 million tons valued at over US$3 billion.[3] During a decade when the United States' trade deficit with China exploded, waste exports to China grew just as quickly.

The gargantuan growth of the global post-consumer waste trade bespeaks the unrivalled shopping binge that world consumers, and particularly those in the United States, have been on since the 1980s. But more specifically it reveals the interestingly pivotal role of waste in these cycles of production and consumption. From the 1990s to 2008 the United States accumulated a trillion dollar trade deficit with China as it became the main factory floor furnishing the notorious 'Wal-marting' of America. Those goods needed to be shipped in something, hence China's cardboard box boom. Those boxes were in turn carried on container ships, behemoths that chugged to US shores heavily laden with goods, only to return to China on a virtually empty 'backhaul'. An empty backhaul being a clear money-loser for shipping companies, a load of anything at almost any price is preferable. Why not trash? Container ships left China heaped with bulging new boxes and returned stacked with crushed OCC. In the 1990s/2000s it was often cheaper to ship a ton of waste cardboard (or any other scrap) across the Pacific than across the Rockies or down the Mississippi. For Nine Dragons, the shipping cycle born of the global trade imbalance was a virtuous circle sweeping prime materials to China's shores for next to nothing. This virtuous circle became a vicious cycle with the 2008 financial collapse: US consumption stagnated, Chinese factories were shut, and container ships languished in port. The demand for cardboard boxes caved while the 'backhaul' shipping price shot upwards. For Nine Dragons, a bullish company that had ploughed hundreds of millions of dollars into new production lines to keep pace with runaway market expansion, the sudden contraction was devastating.

Nine Dragons' appetite for trash was not unique, and China's post-reform era (post-1978) hunger for scrap has not been limited to cardboard. Take plastics: in 1990 the total global trade in waste plastics came to a little over US$120 million; by 2008 China and Hong Kong combined, alone accounted for over $6 billion in waste plastic imports, over 80 per cent of global market share (a global market that topped 8 million tons). As for scrap copper and aluminum, China imported over twice as much of both these waste metals as any other country during the first decade of the twenty-first century. Add it all together, and China's largest import from the United States over this period, in both quantity and monetary value, was waste and scrap. Those who proudly proclaim that the United State's most influential global export is its consumer culture do not know how right they are.

This chapter on 'waste' aims to set the centrality of post-consumer waste in today's circuits of global trade in some historical perspective, providing an abbreviated look at waste-related histories in general, and touching on a few core areas of inquiry in the literature today, with a bias towards focusing on modern China.

'Waste' as a concept/signifier is not merely a designation of material substances or goods, but is also fundamentally an impressionistic, morally laden, conceptual category.

---

[3] Unless otherwise noted, trade volume statistics are based on those provided by the United Nations Commodity Trade Statistics Database at <http://comtrade.un.org/db/>.

It often carries religious connotations of punishment (laid waste) or abandonment and devastation (wastelands), but retains a kernel of potentially transcendent 'redemption', available to anything from a penitent soul to an empty Coke bottle. Waste's fascination partly lies in this internal tension: it is both destructive and generative, a simultaneous manifestation of superfluity and ruin, excess and poverty. In waste the productive and the barren, the disgusting and the banal, are inseparable and merged. These vital contradictions inflect our understanding of how material wastes figure in cultural and economic systems, foregrounded, for instance, in histories of nineteenth-century sanitation engineering schemes that merged paranoid fantasies of deadly miasmas with utopian visions of turning crap into crops, and garbage into gold.

Defining 'waste' thus produces widely varying meanings depending upon one's discipline and approach. Zsuzsa Gille provides one of the most insightful analytical overviews of the scholarship on waste in her book *From the Cult of Waste to the Trash Heap of History*. As she notes:

> Scholars studying waste in one form or another have been speaking at cross-purposes because they operate with different implicit definitions of waste. Especially unfortunate has been economists' assumption that waste is merely an attribute of efficiency, but public discourse has also been hampered by an environmentalist impulse to reduce the problem of waste to a problem of pollution.[4]

Waste, Gille argues, is not merely 'something that we have failed to use'. Rather she opts for a modification of Mary Douglas's brilliantly simple description of 'dirt' from her landmark *Purity and Danger*:

> Dirt [i]s matter out of place....[This] implies two conditions: a set of ordered relations and a contravention of that order....Where there is dirt, there is a system. Dirt is the by-product of a systematic ordering and classification of matter, in so far as ordering involves rejecting inappropriate elements. This idea of dirt takes us straight into the field of symbolism.[5]

Gille tweaks this idea to emphasizes that waste is not 'merely out of place': it is 'a concept out of order...a liminal or boundary object' marking multiple boundaries— between past and present, public and private, value and its opposite. Waste is disruptive, poorly differentiated, marginalized, and hence (and herein lies a major challenge for the historian) goes unaccounted and often undocumented. Waste is not just un(der)known and un(der)valued because it lies at the edge of our attention and value systems, but because it is intrinsically destabilizing of forms of knowledge and systems of value.

What we designate as 'waste' in our daily lives or in our scholarly analysis is inescapably shaped by value judgments. In classical economics for example, waste designates forms of inefficiency (wastes of time, of labour, of money) and material wastes

---

    [4] Zsuzsa Gille, *From the Cult of Waste to the Trash Heap of History: The Politics of Waste in Socialist and Post-Socialist Hungary* (Bloomington: Indiana University Press, 2007), p. 14.
    [5] Mary Douglas, *Purity and Danger: An Analysis of the Concepts of Pollution and Taboo* (London: Ark Paperbacks, 1984), p. 36.

(by-products of production of little or negative value to their owner—the opposite of 'goods' which can be exchanged through the market). From the perspective of alternative politico-economical critiques, however, many 'goods' might be adjudged wastes: stockpiled armaments, forms of conspicuous consumption or planned obsolescence, forms of insurance and arbitrage, etc. I do not delve into these complex issues of economic theory here, nor into the vast topic of production wastes (mine tailings, industrial effluents, etc.) or atmospheric pollutants (ash, sulfur, CO_2). Rather, the limited pallet of this chapter covers those wastes most directly associated with consumption, namely post-consumer solid(ish) wastes, their disposal, and reuse. Even within this limited range, waste is not only conceptually slippery, it is often slimy, disgusting, and prefigured in one or another form of shit; and shit is where pretty much any overview of post-consumer waste history has to begin.

MOSTLY SHIT: WASTE BEFORE THE NINETEENTH CENTURY

Up until around the nineteenth century throughout the world, post-consumer waste had been mostly organic: ashes, food wastes, animal carcasses, and shit. In rural areas, these wastes occasionally posed headaches, but most often were useful as good soil supplements. Of course there were other forms of solid waste: cracked ceramics, glass shards, tattered clothes, broken furniture, metal bits. Such objects were relatively limited in quantity and nearly infinite in variety. Rather than being merely discarded, most such objects were repaired (collars and coats turned, shoes resoled, tin pots patched) or put to inventive reuse (a broken bowl becomes a scoop, tattered trousers a mop) in an array of marvellous and banal practices that Susan Strasser has dubbed 'the stewardship of objects'.[6]

The most common practice for solid waste disposal through the millennia was simply relegating it to dumping grounds or middens. More deliberate landfills where wastes were placed in large pits layered with earth date back to Minoan Crete (3000–1000 BCE). Channelling water to flush out waste from streets or other urban areas seems to have been a rather universal idea in ancient civilizations, no doubt as an outgrowth of irrigation, drainage, and water provisioning technologies. In Moenjodaro (Sind, Pakinstan, c.5000 BCE) every home had a latrine on the street side with a cesspit that drained into the street's main sewer. Yayoi-era Japan (300 BCE–200 CE), Eastern Zhou-era (800–221BCE) Chinese cities, and Mayan Teotihuacan (200 BCE–800 CE) all had well-developed sewage systems. By far the most famous ancient sewer, largely because it came to symbolize the pinnacle of civilized urban planning among the great sanitary engineers of nineteenth-century Europe, was the Cloaca Maxima of ancient Rome. It is thus slightly ironic that historians today agree the Cloaca Maxima was not

---

[6] Susan Strasser, *Waste and Want: A Social History of Trash* (New York: Holt Paperbacks, 1999), p. 21.

initially a planned sewer at all, but rather a monumental open-air canal that was part of constructing the Forum Romanum in the seventh century BCE, and was only adapted into a drainage system centuries later; modernizing Europe's model of planned civil engineering was, it seems, the product of historical bricolage. Still, under normal conditions, the Cloaca served the Roman Republic well, flushing the wastewater and refuse from Rome's famed public baths and latrines into the waters of the Tiber, stretches of which apparently became so polluted as to be undrinkable.

Pre-modern sewers were primarily intended for street and wastewater drainage, not for disposing the populace's collective faeces. Throughout documented urban history we find repeated ordinances against dumping night soil into the sewers, directing residents to tidy away their refuse for collection or personally to carry it beyond the city walls to be dumped.[7] Urban excrement was too useful to be flushed away; it was collected for use on nearby farmland, and it seems probable that night soil collecting developed almost everywhere urbanization did.[8] In China for example, sources imply that collection of urban wastes for fertilizer dates back thousands of years, while formal markets in night soil emerged in the Song dynasty (960–1279) and were highly developed by the Jiajing era (1521–66) of the Ming dynasty.

Overall, the field of pre-modern waste remains under-explored with little in the way of critical or comparative work. Recent debates sparked by Kenneth Pomeranz's *The Great Divergence* have, at least tangentially, touched off a tempest in a night soil bucket. Pomeranz claims that farmers in China's Jiangnan region in the eighteenth century began replacing local night soil with imported Manchurian bean cake in order to raise productivity and save labour, which he sees as evidence of continued economic 'development'. A scholar named Yong Xue has responded that bean cake quantities were much smaller than Pomeranz claims and did not replace but supplemented night soil, signalling an ecological crisis of soil depletion and economic 'involution' rather than development. In another article Yong Xue describes in vibrant detail how highly specialized the night soil marketing system was in Jiangnan at this time. Night soil quality was strongly tied to the richness (in wealth, and especially in diet) of the urban inhabitants who 'produced' it. The prosperous city of Hangzhou, famous for its consumption of fatty roasted geese, produced the crème de la crème of protein-rich night soils, and farmers who could afford to would boat several days out of their way to get it. Indeed, the extent of differentiation and commoditization found in East Asian night soil markets (similar evidence can be found in areas of Japan as well) almost certainly exceeded those in Europe. It is hard to imagine eighteenth century Hangzhou night soil collectors

[7] In his *History of Shit* Dominique-Gilbert Laporte performs a wonderful analysis of laws regulating faecal disposal in sixteenth-century Paris, though he attributes perhaps too much novelty to laws that have many similarities with those of other cities and eras.

[8] Early colonial US history might be one exception, for it appears many farmers resisted using fertilizer until around the early nineteenth century when the land began showing clear signs of exhaustion. See Joel Tarr, 'From City to Farm: Urban Wastes and the American Farmer', in idem, *The Search for the Ultimate Sink: Urban Pollution in Historical Perspective* (Akron, OH: University of Akron Press, 1996), pp. 293–308.

imitating their Parisian counterparts, who at this time were regularly violating bans by furtively dumping their loads into the city's sewers rather than delivering them to the processing pits at Mountfacon; the Jaingnan market put far too high a premium on night soil for such squandering. There are many interconnected reasons that help explain this difference in how night soils were used and valued: mild winters and an excellent infrastructure of waterways made year-round transport of night soil much more convenient in China's Jiangnan region than in northern Europe; minimally treated liquid night soil is excellent for fertilizing rice paddy, but less ideal for dry wheat farming (for which poudrette, which took one to three years to process from raw night soil, was better); and Chinese peasants, raising relatively few large animals (many pigs, but very few sheep, horses, or cows), faced a corresponding dearth of manure and hence depended more on human wastes for fertilizer.

Why bother with such comparisons? In part they might help frame our understanding nineteenth- and twentieth-century developments. One of the main side-effects of the comprehensive sewer systems that would become a signature of modern urbanism in Europe and the United States was that the night soil cycle (returning organic nutrients to rural production) was disrupted or severed. Thenceforth, shit by the ton would be daily flushed into rivers and out to sea. In Jiangnan China, such a profligate waste of waste would have seemed unthinkable, short of a revolution in agricultural practices; and even when such systems were considered in the twentieth century, the surrounding context of night soil-intensive farming shaped their adoption. Indeed, all the way into the 1990s a dominant portion of Shanghai's shit (averaging 3 million tons annually 1960–95) was collected by porters and trucks, disgorged onto barges, and transported to rural surroundings for use on the fields.[9] In sum, a closer look at pre-modern waste sheds light on broader questions regarding the shifting dynamics of urban and rural development.

DISPOSABILITY STAGE 1: THE SANITARY IDEA IN THE NINETEENTH CENTURY

It was not until around the mid-nineteenth century that waste shifted from being a 'nuisance' subject to patchwork responses and disciplinary edicts ('we command you to delay and retain any and all stagnant and sullied waters and urines inside the confines or your homes': Francis I, 1593), to becoming an urban problem deemed best handled by state-managed systemic solutions.[10] It is in this era that dogmatic

[9] Use of urban excrement as rural fertilizer lasted longer in some parts of Europe than others, with Parisian and Belgian suburbs implementing sewage farming on a diminishing scale even two or three decades after the Second World War. But I know of no capitalist cities systematically encouraging and expanding the rural use of urban excrement as found in China; in Shanghai in the 1950s they even experimented with putting the agricultural bureau in charge of the pertinent portions of urban waste management.

[10] Dominique Laporte, *History of Shit* (Cambridge, MA: MIT, 2000) p. 41.

visionaries like Edwin Chadwick, slick technocrats like Colonel George Waring, and the archetypal civic planner Baron Haussmann take to the field of civil engineering and, backed by the clout of urban governments leveraging massive amounts of public debt, design and implement large-scale projects for waste management. The emergence of the 'sanitary idea' and the urban infrastructure bonanza it inspired are the most discussed topics in waste history, justifiably seen as a turning point in the construction of waste as a social problem. In terms of material disposal this turning point is easily summarized: shit to the sewers. Whether through a combined or separate network of pipes, the purpose of sewers changed from removing urban run-off to include 'spiriting away wastes'.[11] But the confluence of ideas and issues underlying this simple shift in sewage practice were crucial to reframing waste in the colonial modern age.

What drove this shift? The composition of urban waste did not change greatly in the nineteenth century, but its demographics and social coding did. Spurred by industrialization, urban populations grew rapidly, exacerbating age-old problems of cesspool leakage and overflow, and swamping regional economies with a surfeit of human excrement. By the early 1800s, it was said travellers could smell Paris long before they could see it. As Alain Corbin argues in *The Foul and the Fragrant*, the increase in stench was as much perceptual as it was quantitative.[12] Scientific discourses on the miasma theory of disease—claims that disease resulted from the spread of the fumes of poisonous decayed matter—converged with rising bourgeois anxieties to spawn an obsession with deodorization and a missionizing intolerance for 'the stench of the poor'. The perceived threat from putrescence gained a new urgency with the advent of cholera in European cities in the 1830s, outbreaks suddenly striking down thousands with deadly rapidity, and infecting rich and poor alike. Contemporaries sensed a link between cholera and faecal matter, but most thought foul air, not foul water, was the culprit. Ridding urban environs of wastes was vital, and using water to do so seemed expedient. Urban population and industrial growth had already been driving an increase in urban water supply, and this trend only accelerated under the new impetus of waste removal. By mid-century Euro-American cities were in the grips of a veritable water mania, consuming water on a greater scale than ever before: Haussmann and Belgrand's mid-century aqueducts more than doubled Paris' water supply and helped flush the city's streets (though not yet its homes) of refuse; US cities gushed with hundreds of new waterworks meeting the demands of growing populations with a burgeoning appetite for water (per capita water consumption in Chicago shot up over 1,000 per cent from 1856 to 1880);[13] the vogue for flush toilets in London in the 1840s and 1850s flooded the Thames with liquefied wastes, making London one of the first cities to direct the vast bulk of its human wastes down

[11]   Christopher Hamlin, 'Edwin Chadwick and the Engineers, 1842–1854: Systems and Antisystems in the Pipe-and-Brick Sewers War', *Technology and Culture*, Vol. 33, No. 4 (October 1992), p. 704.

[12]   Alain Corbin, *The Foul and the Fragrant: Odor and the French Social Imagination* (Cambridge, MA: Harvard University Press, 1988).

[13]   Martin V. Melosi, *The Sanitary City: Urban Infrastructure in America from Colonial Times to the Present* (Baltimore: Johns Hopkins University Press, 2000), p. 82.

sewers and into the river. Unfortunately, because this sewage went untreated, this trend likely contributed to London's major cholera outbreaks of 1849 and 1853, as well as to the notorious Great Stink of 1858 which drove Parliament to distraction and finally to action, granting upwards of £3 million to build a comprehensive system of intercepting sewers to remove the city's waste well downstream.

City governments, engineers, and sanitarians shared the same goal: to fashion the most economically efficient, healthful, and uniformly consistent infrastructure to handle urban sewage and waste. But specific visions and theories could be deeply at odds. Chadwick envisioned an economically self-sustaining system providing cities with fresh water for consumption, thence using it to channel liquefied human wastes to suburban sewage farms for use as fertilizer. Haussmann, on the other hand, was appalled by the idea that his majestic sewers should be sullied with factotum and proposed an expensive system of collectors and carriages to handle the waste. His contemporary A. Mille had great success using non-human sewage (urban street run-off was highly enriched by large quantities of horse manure) to irrigate the fields of Gennevilliers, transforming it into the vegetable basket of Paris, and so inspiring a short-lived heyday for sewage farming throughout Europe (by the twentieth century rising suburban land prices made such schemes increasingly untenable). Yet even Paris' own 'Great Stink' of 1880 could not convince the government, nor even Louis Pasteur, that 'everything down the sewer' was the proper sanitary solution for Paris, and it was not until the city's cholera outbreak of 1892 (London's last such outbreak had been in 1866, and only in one area where sewage diversion had yet to be completed) that the will was mustered for 'tout-à-l'égout'.

The consequences of these nineteenth-century debates and projects were crucial to shaping modern Western modes of defining and treating wastes. Of most interest to cultural historians has been the powerful architectural and administrative disciplining around habits of hygiene, the rise of bio-politics, and the various social encodings around public and private matters of waste. From the perspective of environmental history, the flushing of human wastes into the sewers was the first major step into a culture of disposability: what had once been a valuable soil conditioner became contaminating refuse, in many respects worse than useless because costly to treat. The replacement of night soil in agriculture, first with imported guano in the 1840s and later with chemical fertilizers, was also a key element in this shift. In any event, the breaking of the night soil cycle clearly shaped the paths of modern urbanization and agricultural.

With shit now relegated to the subterranean realm of liquid waste, the category of Municipal Solid Waste (MSW) as we know it today emerged. We should also note that, though MSW has become a universal concept of urban management today, its late nineteenth-century origin in a matrix of urban infrastructures and disciplinary practices (household-level water/sewerage networks, paved streets, modern rituals of public and private hygiene) was decisively Euro-American and—when enforced elsewhere—colonial. Indeed, the heuristic device of historical stages that I am using in this overview fails to adequately decentre this teleological framework. As we will see below, in cities like Beijing, MSW would continue to include human waste and ash well into the twentieth century (and still does today in many cities throughout the world), testifying to the inequities and insufficiencies of this notion of historical stages.

DISPOSABILITY STAGE 2: MSW THROUGH THE 1980S

The late nineteenth century saw MSW emerge as a distinct concern in European, US and Japanese cities as they continued to grow and expand with unprecedented speed. Well-trafficked boulevards were heaped in horse manure, while city slums, lagging in sewers and other amenities, were often swamped in pestilential refuse. By the 1890s in the United States, few cities could give away their night soil to area farmers, let alone sell it to them.[14] Citizen movements—often led by middle-class women's groups like the Ladies Health Protective Association—demanded solutions to waste's threat to health and civility, and cities adopted a patchwork of approaches ranging from the resourceful to the depraved: 'reduction' factories sifted, boiled, and compressed waste to render its grease, fertilizer, and other compounds for sale; incinerators, when they worked, transformed garbage into electricity; household ash and other wastes were used as construction landfill; and garbage scows dumped untreated waste by the ton into seas and lakes. Domestic waste at the time was overwhelmingly composed of ashes and food scraps (both of which have been largely removed from many MSW streams today through the use of gas heating and kitchen-sink grinders). Little else was discarded. A household's soiled and damaged goods were still typically repaired or repurposed at home (collars turned, worn textiles quilted, rags woven into rugs, glassware and crockery mended with pastes and glues concocted from recipes of lye, egg white, potash, gelatin, and linseed oil). Rags, bones, metal scrap, and rubber bits—scraps all good for industrial and handicraft use—were bartered and sold to tinkers. The remaining junk that finally was discarded came in such relatively small quantities that it was veritably submerged in the flow of organic refuse and ash.

But the handling and contents of MSW was changing. Under a combination of factors—rising industrial production, rail transport, the increasing scale and consolidation of MSW—manufacturers began to take interest in collecting materials through the waste stream. Itinerant tinkers increasingly sold to or worked under small scrap companies, and the number of registered scrapyards and traders grew to supply the industry's demands. Technological change played a pivotal role driving demand for particular materials. The 1870s saw the advent of open-hearth steel-making which digested large quantities of scrap steel. The United State's ferrous scrap trade grew with the nation's steel-based economy: railroads, car manufacture, and construction/demolition all fired

---

[14] In these same decades, night soil was still a favourite fertilizer in many parts of northern Europe, so a single generalization about time periods would be very misleading.

the steel scrap business, and the First World War saw a tenfold leap in the scrap iron trade to a value of over $1 billion. The development of the Hall-Heroult process of aluminum refining around the turn of the twentieth century made aluminum available for large-scale industrial use, and not long after aluminum scrap became a much sought commodity as well.

But the paradigm shift in post-consumer waste 'production' in the Euro-American case arrives with the dawning of mass consumption around the turn of the twentieth century. Catalogue merchandizing was making consumer goods available wherever rails could carry them. In the early 1900s, packaged goods—advertising cleanliness, standardization, and status—rapidly replaced the pickle and cracker barrels at the grocery and encouraged consumers to buy in bulk. As the nineteenth century bourgeois identification with deodorized cleanliness became an aspirational norm, it offered seemingly limitless potential for the marketing of disposable 'hygienic' goods: toilet paper, sanitary towels, paper towels, disposable razors, soaps of all kinds. The automobile, and especially the production of a car that could be marketed to the average consumer, soon gave birth to one of the world's most massive waste streams (and that is without even considering the flood of greenhouse emissions cars produce). Of course, the electrification of homes throughout the century ushered in all sorts of appliances that radically altered consumption practices and the wastes generated therefrom: the refrigerator, the TV (with its comrades the *TV Guide* and the TV dinner), the incandescent light bulb (famed object of planned obsolescence), boxes of cake mix, and vacuum cleaner bags. In the United States, the post-Second World War marketing blitz to promote appliances and cars in a model of everyday suburban commuter living pushed consumer demand for packaged goods into overdrive. 'In 1966 packaging cost the American public $25 billion—3.4 per cent of the Gross National Product—not including the expense of collection and disposal once discarded. In that year packaging material amounted to 52 million tons of waste,' or about a quarter of all the residential, commercial, and industrial waste combined.[15]

By the late 1960s, waste in the OECD nations had generally taken on the forms we know today. The average citizen was producing 1kg (2.2lb) or so of garbage daily—not shit and ash, but mostly paper products, packaging, bottles, cans, food scraps, and increasing amounts of plastic. These were tossed into dustbins, collected and compressed in diesel-powered trucks, and delivered to sanitary landfills, or sometimes incinerators. Recycling of aluminum, glass, and paper waste was systemized according to various schemes that are still being debated today: source separation, deposit and redemption fees, and, most recently, producer responsibility schemes. In any case, recycling processes that in the nineteenth century had been the domain of scavengers, tinkers, and peddlers were now firmly dominated by municipal and national-scale disposal companies and industrialized scrap operations. The handicraft and tinker methods of collecting, reusing, and recycling worn goods (a liminal role that in many ways personified

[15] Melosi, *The Sanitary City*, p. 340.

scrap's intermediacy between consumption/disposal and production) had been replace by industrial processes that completely melted down, shredded, or pulverized old goods to produce utterly new industrial products—a change that was obviously crucial to integrating recycling into a consumer economy geared to selling ever changing batches of identical new products. In sum, the ever increasing MSW stream was channelled rather directly from the consumers' household receptacles into one of two industrial complexes, one managing waste disposal, the other recycling.

I need not rehearse here the various cultural and market(ing) forces that propelled the parade of obsolescence that swelled the waste stream in the West (and the United States in particular) through the latter half of the twentieth century and down to today as this is a staple of histories of consumption explored in this volume. From the perspective of waste history, the fashion cycle in everything from clothes to cars to mobile phones plays a huge part in feeding the beast. But there are other strong cultural and systemic currents compelling waste production. Our commutes between home, work, amusement etc. almost necessitate our using disposable items (fast food or microwaveable lunch, bottle of water or cup of coffee, newspaper, plastic bag for a sandwich); disposability is a function of speed. Moreover, we rely on the safety and reliability of standardized packaged goods; regulating consumer goods (let alone shipping them) would be almost inconceivable without such packaging. In sum, we consumers are enmeshed in, and in many ways interpolated by, cultural and material provisioning systems that make disposability not simply convenient but in some cases gratifying and in others all but unavoidable.

The United States was a global leader in creating novel and prolific amounts of post-consumer waste in the twentieth century, a fact emblematic of US consumerism, but also linked to US geography, agribusiness, and post-automobile urbanization.[16] Some excellent histories on modern US garbage and scrap have been written. Susan Strasser's *Waste and Want* focuses on habits of consumption, the replacement of what she dubs 'the stewardship of objects' in the nineteenth-century home with habits of disposal

[16] Though the US has dominated the per capita waste charts over the last six decades, it is not outside the OECD norm: higher GDP = more MSW remains a rule of thumb which only since 2005 is beginning to *possibly* show signs of changing in a few countries (notably Britain and Germany). Canada and Norway topped US per capita MSW recently, with Denmark and Ireland at over 700kg annually, Australia and Switzerland in the mid-600kg. Indeed, Japan is the only rich country to show consistently low per capita MSW production (around 410kg for decades) in relation to its GDP. Of course, methods of estimating waste production vary, are greatly shaped by collection methods and data availability, and paths are hardly linear historically; still, waste tracks with GDP across the world, especially when comparing rich and poor countries. So, while I do not at all wish to dismiss the importance of variations, considering the global historical scale of this essay, I have opted for lumping the OECD countries (the West) together and using the US as a leading example, and for focusing on what I believe are both quantitatively and qualitatively the most significant differences. Waste studies consistently (though not invariably) bare out: that the poor define waste quite differently from the rich, consuming (using, repairing, and eating) things the better off would discard; that the poor work in waste trades the rich would refuse to engage in; and that poor and racially discriminated against groups are subjected to living and working in greater and more dangerous proximity to known wastes and toxics than the better off.

over the course of the twentieth century and the changing cultural codes, domestic practices, and commercial products that promoted this shift. Using popular sources such as housekeeping manuals and magazines, as well as tracing the marketing of particular products like the tampon, Strasser shows how the habits of daily life were thickly enmeshed with changing domestic ideals, notions of cleanliness, modernity, class, gender, and—through wartime drives to 'Get In the Scrap'—national identity. Martin Melosi's *The Sanitary City* is more of an institutional history, providing an astonishingly comprehensive assessment of the history of US waste-related infrastructures and service delivery, charting and analysing the politics and economics of key debates in waste management—public vs. private, separate vs. combined sewage systems, landfill vs. incineration—and mapping paradigm shifts in the interpretations and technologies of waste handling—the ascendance of the 'sanitary idea' in late nineteenth century, the pre-eminence of ecological concerns in the 1970s etc. Most recently, Carl Zimring's *Cash for Your Trash: Scrap Recycling in America* has sketched a business history of the scrap sector from the horse-cart peddlers of the late nineteenth century through the international brokers of the post-Second World War era. Merely having three such monographs places US waste history far ahead of most other regions on this score. Needless to say, in a field so underdeveloped, there is huge room for further research. Some obvious follow-up questions to the above works might be: What happens when Strasser's gendered insights are applied to durable goods like cars and microwave ovens? How do Melosi's overviews of infrastructure break down when analysed through the lenses of class, neighbourhood, race, red-lining practices, etc.? While Zimring (and others) highlight how the waste trade has shunted towards ethnic groups who face discrimination and abuse as 'dirty' and 'dishonest', what role might the economic logics of the trade play in reinforcing these biases? And Zimring provides little in the way of an environmental history perspective; the recycling industry occupies a fascinatingly paradoxical position, tightly enmeshed with movements for environmental conservation, yet profiting directly from increasing consumption. These are merely some obvious follow-up issues. The more exciting challenge lies in producing synthetic research that integrates the three rather distinct fields of the above monographs (consumer/cultural history; institutional/ environmental/technological history; and business/economic history).

But what of conditions outside the most industrialized countries? These US-European narratives are hardly apt as frameworks for writing the modern histories of waste in other regions, though, as in so many other historical fields, these Western narratives exert an inexorable teleological pull on studies of the non-West. This is not to say that Western histories are meaningless outside the West; colonial era and late capitalist pressures to emulate (and occasionally condemn) the practices of wealthy/'advanced' countries are as significant in the realm of waste history as in any other sphere. But clearly, aside from Japan, the heyday of durable goods consumption and its attendant post-consumer waste boom did not arise in the non-West until decades later. Even today, the waste and recycling sectors in most of the world are overwhelmingly informal domains of poor scavengers and mum-and-dad sorting and processing operations nowhere near the capacity of the mid-sized and large corporations that dominate Western markets.

Nor do narratives of developmental or cultural lag suffice here. Take for example, Ibadan Nigeria, with a population of 2 million, most lacking household sewer connections, producing millions of tons of solid waste including large quantities of both food wastes and plastics, and facing problems with domestic and imported toxic wastes. Clearly, seeing Ibadan as 'lagging' historically is completely inaccurate (plastics and toxic imports are late twentieth-century waste issues, while the shift from cesspits to sewers was, in the West, largely a nineteenth-century issue); imagining Ibadan as some concatenation of several historical periods is equally unhelpful.

Thankfully, some excellent studies on waste in the modern non-West allow us to embark on a path towards 'provincializing' Euro-American waste. Articles by Vijay Prashad (on Delhi), Colin McFarlane (Bombay), Warwick Anderson (Philippines) Spencer Brown (Lagos), Todd Henry (Japanese-colonized Korea), and Dipesh Chakrabarty (India)[17] touch variously on the instrumental role that the discursive construction and disciplinary control of 'native' sanitary habits played in producing/ enforcing power relations between the colonizer and the colonized. Doing a gross injustice to the specifics of each context and each author's work, a few general trends become evident. Technologies and management models were typically adopted wholesale from the West with little consideration of local conditions. Colonizing governments tended to treat the native 'Other' as less capable of internalizing sanitary habits, and sanitation enforcement was often more invasive, violent, and officially supervised than in the metropole. Moreover, while in the metropole sewage and other waste infrastructures were promoted under a democratic ethos (an ideal rarely realized in reality), colonial implementation was often starkly and unapologetically discriminatory, with the foreign enclaves and local elites receiving services from which the average native residents were clearly excluded—a neglect excused by a familiar litany of justifications: lack of sufficient funds, the inured state of natives to the discomforts of illnesses and filthy living, etc. Predictably, the inequity of colonial programmes only served to exacerbate and re-inscribe the racist biases on which they were predicated.

These biased models of discourse and practice did not simply vanish when formal colonialism ended, and Chakrabarty, among others, analyses the continuities between imperialist and nationalist sanitary ideologies—Naipul: 'Indians defecate everywhere'; Gandhi: 'Everybody is selfish, but we [Indians] seem to be more selfish than others...We do not hesitate to throw refuse out of our courtyard onto the street...Where so much

[17] Vijay Prashad, 'The Technology of Sanitation in Colonial Dehli', *Modern Asian Studies*, Vol. 35, No. 1 (2001), pp. 113–55; Colin McFarlane, 'Governing the Contaminated City: Infrastructure and Sanitation in Colonial and Post-Colonial Bombay', *International Journal of Urban and Regional Research*, Vol. 32.2 (2008), pp. 415–35; Todd A. Henry, 'Sanitizing Empire: Japanese Articulations of Korean Otherness and the Construction of Early Colonial Seoul', *The Journal of Asian Studies*, Vol. 64 No. 3 (2005), pp. 639–75; Spencer H. Brown, 'Public Health in Lagos, 1850–1900: Perceptions, Patterns, and Perspectives', *The International Journal of African Historical Studies*, Vol. 25, No. 2 (1992), pp. 337–60; Warwick Anderson, 'Excremental Colonialism: Public Health and the Poetics of Pollution', *Critical Inquiry* Vol. 21, No. 3 (Spring, 1995), pp. 640–669; Dipesh Chakrabarty, 'Of Garbage, Modernity and the Citizen's Gaze', *Economic and Political Weekly*, Vol. 27, No. 10/11 (1992) pp. 541–547.

selfishness exists, how can one expect self-sacrifice?'[18] The association of natives' 'unhygienic' practices with a kind of base selfishness and incapacity for modern civic and nationalistic virtues is a theme shared by colonial officials and nationalist intellectuals alike; rather ironic when we recognize that the modern hygienic virtues being valorized typically go hand in hand with enforcing stricter regimes of private property and capitalist consumerism—hardly the stuff of self-sacrifice. At their most basic these offences to modern hygiene are often about 'matter out of place', or conflicting ideas about the disposition of spaces. Chakrabarty writes:

> People in India, on the whole, have not heeded the nationalist's call to discipline, public health and public order. Can one read in this a refusal to become citizens? If that question is guilty of reading intentions into popular culture, let me put the problem this way. The cultural politics of transforming 'open spaces' into 'public places' require a certain degree of divestment of pleasure on the part of the people. The 'thrills' of the bazaar are traded in for the 'conveniences' of the sterile supermarket. Old pleasures are now exchanged for the new pleasures of capitalism; creature comforts, an insatiable obsession with the body and the self (the pleasures of privacy), and the mythical freedoms of citizenship. When capitalism has not delivered these cultural goods in sufficient quantities—and Indian capitalism has not—the exchange of 'old' pleasures for 'new' remains an understandably limited exercise.[19]

In a different context of 1900s–1940s China, Madeleine Yue Dong's *Republican Beijing, The City and Its Histories* arrives at similar insights. Though not betrayed by the title, Dong's study is at its core an exploration of recycling as a set of material practices and survival tactics for engaging in and comprehending the production of history and modernity. Seemingly everything in republican Beijing was being scavenged for resale and reuse: 'the labor intensive material practices of recycling ranged from the targeting of antiques for sale to wealthy foreigners to the remaking of rags into shoe soles for the poor.'[20] Dong rejects periodizations of republican Beijing that characterize it as 'traditional', in transition but not yet modern, or lagging behind cities like Shanghai. Rather than place Beijing at some mid-point on a teleological timeline towards industrial modernity, Dong argues for an utterly coeval modernity—not an 'alternative' modernity, but a specific engagement with colonial modernity and global capitalism— manifested largely through practices of recycling. She argues that the spatially, temporally, and socio-economically fragmented communities that comprised Beijing were almost literally woven together by recycling. Through recycling, objects circulated across and between realms: a wealthy man's cigarette butt provided waste-paper for barter and some shreds in the tobacco pouch of an indigent picker; destitute Manchu families hawked their decrepit furniture and vases as antiques for the new middle class;

[18] Chakrabarty, p. 541.

[19] Dipesh Chakrabarty, 'Of Garbage, Modernity and the Citizen's Gaze', *Economic and Political Weekly*, Vol. 27, No. 10/11 (1992) p. 544.

[20] Madeliene Yue Dong, *Republican Beijing, The City and Its Histories* (Berkeley: University of California Press, 2003), p. 300.

imperial gardens were refashioned into public spaces to promote citizenly demeanour and earn tourist dollars; bricks from the ancient city walls were cannibalized for home repairs. At Tianqiao, 'Beijing's recycling centre' nestled in the city's southern slums (an enormous open-air market not unlike Chakrabarty's 'bazaar'); every form of second-hand good, patent medicine, and handicraft repair was on display and up for haggling. Dong's descriptions resonate with Chakrabarty's above:

> Tianqiao promised unlimited anonymity. The anonymity of consumers at department stores was sustained and limited by a basic level of economic status; they had at least to look right to shop there. Tianqiao, however, welcomed anyone from homeless beggars to curious foreigners. The commodities at Tianqiao were also anonymous. No one was clear where they came from, where they had been, or whose hands they had passed through. The anonymity at department stores allowed shoppers to role-play but also confirmed the status quo, a combination both amusing and safe, based on an underlying trust [including trust of the products] and an exclusion of certain social hazards such as poverty and dirtiness. But at Tianqiao, a visitor might do business with a criminal or brush up against a beggar with lice; appearances and transactions could not be trusted. Tianqiao's anonymity brought both freedom and threat...If citizenship required self-sacrifice and uniform orderliness, Tianqiao was the opposite: it required selfishness and self-protection from the interests of others at all times.[21]

While it might seem we have entered the realm of consumption and forgotten about waste, recall that the basis of all this is precisely the refashioning and recirculation of what would otherwise be wastes:

> At the heart of the recycling process was the tension not only between the old and the new, but more fundamentally between agency and its lack. The recycling potential of the old commodities themselves was limited by the histories etched into them. Their past could be partly erased, mended, torn, or elaborated, but never eliminated—a product of recycling could only masquerade as new, and rarely convincingly.[22]

While Dong voices no such ambition in her study, I would propose that her description of recycling might be far more apt for describing conditions in many nineteenth- and twentieth-century cities—ranging from Berlin to Bombay—than typical notions of traditional, early modern and the like. Her concept of recycling reinterprets a consumer experience that has typically been glossed as traditional (even by Chakrabarty above) as very much part of modern processes. Finally, recycling as Dong describes it breaks down the over-simplified notion that production, consumption, and disposal are discrete stages or acts in an economic cycle. With our histories of capitalism so imbricated in these terms—to the point that it has produced this volume dedicated to the history of *consumption*—such a recasting is at the very least conceptually refreshing.

[21] Ibid., p. 206.
[22] Ibid.

Before moving into the current era, the example of waste under state socialism deserves attention as it compels us to think critically of the categories we impose on waste history. One might imagine that state socialism's drive to pair rapid industrialization with limited consumption would foster thrift and recycling. Indeed, in both the Eastern bloc and China state-run networks of waste-collecting shops enabled citizens to trade waste materials (metal bits, empty bottles, cardboard boxes, bone, and even human hair) for pocket money. Through these shops as well as regularized campaigns to collect scrap to further national economic development, socialist societies encouraged habits around waste akin to those found in capitalist economies only during war efforts. In her book on waste in modern Hungary, Zsuzsa Gille provides a wonderful portrait of these habits, while at the same time arguing that the obsession with collecting and valorizing wastes in an economy of chronic shortage probably made state socialist industry even more wasteful than its capitalist counterpart. Hungarian factories on the one hand hoarded materials to hedge against shortages (with such materials lying idle, spoiling, and rusting), while on the other they looked upon production wastes as resources and thus apparently had less incentive to seek more efficient production methods. This last irony, a kind of inversion wherein waste becomes more precious than goods, reached tragicomic heights in Maoist China's Great Leap Forward (1958–60), during which thousands of tons of 'waste' iron and steel (including countless perfectly good woks and other goods) were smelted into useless slag in 'backyard' steel furnaces as part of a campaign to overtake the capitalist world in steel production.

GARBAGE GOES GLOBAL

In the decades of decolonization following the Second World War, many newly independent countries adopted production-driven models of development built around import substitution and trade barriers, in large part as an attempt to protect against the kind of foreign domination they had endured as colonies. Since the 1980s, however, this model of development has been generally abandoned if not reviled, attacked as protectionist and dampening to domestic and global consumption. The reigning commonsense of neo-liberal economics (bolstered by the successes of Japan, Taiwan, Korea; unopposed due to the collapse of the Socialist bloc; and all but imposed today by the IMF, WTO, etc.) trumpets export-led growth as the sole path to economic salvation. Consumption makes the economic world go round, and all obstacles to it, especially in the form of trade barriers, must be demolished. The incantation to consume ever faster and more conveniently has spawned its inevitable end-product. Since the 1980s, the trickle of waste materials crossing national boundaries and oceans has grown to flood proportions, and China has become its favourite destination. Scrap had long played a supporting role in global trade (recall the role of the scrap iron trade in the tensions between the United States and Japan in the run up to the Second World War). But the rule of thumb in the waste trade had generally been that shipping was the prohibitive cost: the best market for scrap was the closest one. That logic has been shattered. Cheap labour, grossly uneven environmental regulations, and the relocation of production capacities now shape a globalized geography of waste markets.

The transnational 'trashplosion' is a result of an interlocking set of trends including labour outsourcing, the lowering of trade barriers, breakthroughs in containerization and shipping, and a virtual pandemic of urbanization. The UN estimates that the global proportion of urban population rose from 13 per cent (220 million) in 1900, to 29 per cent (732 million) in 1950, to 49 per cent (3.2 billion) in 2005. The raw numbers, even more than the percentages, throw light on the enormous amplification in demand for manufacturing materials over the last few decades. Enter the new, above ground 'mine' for raw materials: post-consumer waste.

China's meteoric rise to the top of the waste heap began with the economic reforms of the 1980s, and hit its stride during the go-go 1990s (inaugurated by Deng Xiaoping's 1992 'Southern Tour,' whence He gazed down upon the export-led boom of South China and saw that it was Good). A fortuitous mix of domestic and international economic forces have conspired to make China the world's scrap magnet and magnate.

Market Reforms

This deceptively simple term would require volumes to outline and unpack, but the gist of it entailed: promotion of foreign direct investment; instituting profit-driven models of enterprise management (though at times retaining soft budget constraints); the full monetization of previously subsidized sectors (including housing, food, health care, etc.); shattering the urban 'iron rice bowl' of guaranteed employment and subsidies; dismantling rural collectives and instituting a household responsibility system that apportioned land on a per capita basis to rural residents; opening labour to market forces—thereby giving excess labour just freed from rural collectives job opportunities in the cities; and gradually dismantling the *hukou* (household registration) system—all too slowly (and still not completely) removing the many constraints that constituted institutionalized discrimination against rural migrants living in the cities. I will return to this last point below, but suffice it to summarize here that these reforms together made possible China's export-led economic boom, combining a cheap, exploitable, and stable workforce with high levels of domestic and foreign investment.

Rapid Urbanization

Though the growth of China's population from around 1 to 1.6 billion is a factor, equally significant has been the massive rural to urban migration unleashed by the reforms. Statistics are unreliable because migrants constantly move between city and country and bureaucratic definitions of 'urban' have changed somewhat, but the proportion of urban residents has risen from around 20 per cent in 1980 to around 50 per cent today, with anywhere from 300 to 600 million people becoming urban in these three decades. This population shift has unleashed (and also supplied the cheap labour for) an onslaught of infrastructure and construction projects on an historically unprecedented scale. Beijing, with its distinctive ring roads, is conveniently illustrative: through 1990 Beijing's urban core was mainly contained within the second ring road, an area of about 40 square kilometers (15 square miles); that 'core' now reaches to the fifth ring road and covers over 600 square kilometers (230 square miles).

Consumerism

In 2004 China outstripped the United States as the biggest producer of MSW, at 190 million tons (per capita of course the average Chinese produces far less garbage than his or her US counterpart). Predictably, China's rising tide of waste tracks rising income and consumption closely. (This is a nearly universal trend in modern capitalist history, only very recently changing in some European countries such as Germany and the UK.) Per capita GDP measures vary, but the IMF estimates a vertiginous rise in China from US$350 in 1990 to US$3,100 in 2008. Staring into the income gap is also vertigo inspiring. In 2007 China's Gini coefficient topped 0.46, with urban incomes averaging more than three times rural ones; but if remittances from urban migrant workers are excluded (and there are still 100–300 million Chinese not benefiting from migration), the ratio is closer to 5:1 or even 10:1. China now has upper- and middle-class populations that rival those of the United States in size and wealth (even if proportional to China's total population they make up less than 10 per cent), and a much larger 'comfortable' urban class (*xiaokang shehui*) making several thousand dollars per year. These consumers are fully engaged in disposable consumption, with one notable difference: many urban Chinese do not simply dispose of their recyclables—they *sell* them to itinerant recyclers. There are two main reasons for this economic habit, the first being the legacy of the PRC's state socialist recycling system which paid cash for recyclables beginning in the late 1950s and continued to do so right up through the 1990s. This system was challenged and economically defeated by the highly efficient and informal system of itinerant rural migrants in the 1980s and 1990s, who offered equal if not more money for recyclables and far more convenient service than the state. But the other reason that urban consumers can sell rather than merely dispose of their recyclables is that the Chinese market will bear this price because industry's demand for resources is so great.

Limited Resources and Enormous Industrial Demand

In contrast with China's huge, inexpensive, and (up to now) quite stable workforce, the PRC is short on many raw materials, particularly ones that can be supplied through recycling: paper fibre, petroleum (the basis of plastic products), copper, and aluminum. The recycling process is labour-intensive (particularly collection and sorting), but

China's rural migrant labour has been plentiful and cheap, making recycling often the best option for these resources.

Combine these forces and you have a recipe for the booming recycling industry of China today. It began in the mid-1980s with rural migrants picking through urban construction sites and a proliferation of open garbage dumps (it took China's municipal governments well into the 1990s to begin building sanitary landfills to handle the enormous new quantities of MSW generated by the shift to consumerism). Discovering that the newly emerging small factories (mainly township-village enterprises that flourished in the first decades of market reform) would pay well for their materials, migrants began buying recyclables from urban residents at equal or higher prices than the state's recycling companies offered. The state did not cede its monopoly on trash willingly. Using the household registration system as a convenient excuse (rural migrants without the proper registration papers were technically in the cities illegally), police subjected migrant recyclers to systematic discrimination and abuse throughout the country, beating, detaining, extorting, and deporting them by the thousands.[23] Still, this informal, pedal-powered workforce has driven the state-run system nearly out of business.[24] But industry's hunger for recyclable materials grew more rapidly than China's MSW stream could satisfy, and, by the 1990s, the logics of cheap labour and cheap shipping costs (based on the trade imbalance described in the introduction) had scrap heading to China from abroad, to be funnelled into the hands of what were now China's very savvy sorters, processors, and traders. Moreover, the PRC government has been highly proactive in capitalizing the shipping port, highway, and industrial park infrastructures that make raw materials importation convenient, giving China a leg up on many competing developing economies.

Today, China's recycling sector is probably worth anywhere from $50 to $100 billion and employs several million. A handful have struck it rich; maybe 5–10 per cent have become small-time entrepreneurs running small processing shops, junk market stalls, or trucking businesses of one or two vehicles. The vast majority of these millions are factory day labourers, dustbin-picking scavengers, and itinerant recyclers who stack their bike-carts (or perhaps a beat-up diesel truck) with recyclables to haul to the outskirts of a city every day, rain or shine.[25] Mostly these carts are piled with cardboard, plastic containers,

[23] In the 1990s this abuse of migrants, and particularly scavengers, was endemic in China's cities, but declined quite dramatically under Hu Jintao.

[24] Though the scavengers are trouncing the state-owned companies in terms of market share in urban recycling, it is a very uneven battle with the state-owned companies having every political and capital advantage. Indeed, in an historically amusing irony, the government's recycling bureaucracy often refers to the migrant recyclers as a 'guerilla force' (youjidui), precisely what the Chinese Communists were prior to their victory in 1949. Despite the collapse of its collection networks, the state-run recycling system refuses to die and continues to receive hefty subsidies which are invested in large-scale projects like transfer markets, baling stations, and massive industrial parks dedicated to joint venture waste processing enterprises.

[25] Here we see the geography of recyclable waste circulation seeming to reiterate that of shit from a century ago (from city to surrounding suburb/countryside), only now the logic is solely one of real estate values, with waste markets moving ever outward towards the urban fringe as land values in the city centres rise.

cans, etc., but they increasingly include used air-conditioners, TVs, computers and other forms of e-waste. Indeed, e-waste comprises an increasingly large and terribly problematic portion of China's post-consumer waste stream. The town of Guiyu in south China became world famous in 2002 when Greenpeace and the Basel Action Network revealed that it had become a catastrophically polluted centre for the processing of imported e-waste. The open burning of plastics (creating highly toxic dioxins), cooking of circuit boards, and dumping of untreated acid bath wastes into the area's streams has had terrible health consequences in Guiyu, with lead poisoning endemic among the children. Several similar e-waste processing towns have sprung up throughout China but the vast majority of the e-waste they handle is no longer imported from abroad but 'produced' domestically as China's own middle class upgrades to the latest mobile phone, flat screen TV or PC.

Aside from its huge scale, there is little unique about China's recycling sector today. Almost every developing country has a recycling sector peopled mainly by informal scavengers who are plagued by harassment, exploitation, and work-related illness. Waste scavenging has become one of the largest and most ubiquitous economic and employment sectors in the world. Globalization simultaneous universalizes and produces profound inequalities, a contradictory process starkly apparent in the realm of waste. Death by garbage avalanche is an appallingly widespread experience: Pinarbasi, Turkey, 1993, 17 dead; Manilla, Philippines, 2000, 218 dead; Chongqing, China, 2002, 10 dead; Bandung, Indonesia, 2005, 33 dead—and these are only the most publicized cases. Communities of recyclers, almost as a rule, suffer marginalization and discrimination, whether they be lower castes in India, Zabbaleen in Cairo, Henanese in Beijing, Roma in Europe, or 'the homeless' in the United States; in the worst cases (such as Columbia's vicious 'social cleansing' campaign in the 1980s) they are subjected to systematic violence. In response to such treatment, waste-picking communities have begun organizing to defend themselves and their interests, first in urban cooperatives, and more recently in networks and federations on a national scale. In 2008 Women in Informal Employment: Globalizing and Organizing (WEIGO) held a World Conference of Waste-Pickers in Bogota with attendees from Africa, Asia, and Latin America. The conference was followed by the publication of *Refusing to Be Cast Aside: Waste Pickers Organizing Throughout the World*[26], which, among other topics, explores alternative models of modern MSW management that incorporate and recognize the value of waste-picking communities. The struggle to establish such alternative models of modern waste management must compete not only against the powerful interests of well-capitalized MSW management corporations, but also against the history of modern waste management itself, which for nearly two centuries has depicted waste-picking communities as the antithesis of hygienic modernity.

[26] Melanie Samson, ed. Refusing to be Cast Aside: Waste Pickers Organising Around the World (Cambgidge: WIEGO, 2009). Available for download at <http://wiego.org/sites/wiego.org/files/publications/files/Samson-Refusing-to-be-Cast-Aside-Wastepickers-Wiego-publication-English.pdf>

As the waste trade globalizes, so too does the spread of toxic waste and e-waste. The list of countries with well-established markets for imported e-waste includes Ghana, India, Vietnam, Pakistan, South Africa, China, Nigeria, and Egypt, and is growing longer every year. While international treaties and laws ban the e-waste trade, the line between e-waste and second-hand electronic equipment is so blurry and confusing that millions of tons of e-waste evade regulators annually. But as hazardous (and also potentially valuable) as e-waste can be, it is not the only recycled waste that poses environmental hazards. In fact almost every recycling process has the potential to produce large quantities of pollution in the absence of proper safety equipment and treatment facilities. Predictably, in many factories throughout the developing world it is precisely the absence of such equipment and facilities that makes recycling lucrative, and if such equipment were in fact adopted, the profits might well dry up. So, while the picture of waste-pickers wading and sorting through an open landfill might provide the most striking image of the losing end of the commodity chain, it is the workers in the unregulated reprocessing factories and the nearby residents who drink or irrigate with a paper plant's effluent or breath the escaping fumes from a polystyrene shop to whom we are exporting some of our most toxic pollution.

Some Closing Thoughts

The history of waste is vast and almost any topic imaginable merits further exploration. Take the overview I have provided here, with its huge gaps and conceptual deficiencies, as indicative. The absence of discussion of industrial and production wastes in this essay is terribly limiting; the line between production and consumption wastes is arbitrary and problematic, but few studies bridge this gap effectively (Zsuzsa Gille's work again stands out as exceptionally well conceived in this regard). Equally arbitrary are the lines between solid, liquid, and gaseous wastes—my essay on waste might well have been of greater pertinence had it been dedicated to discussing how the history of consumption is linked to sulphur dioxide, CO_2, methane, and other gaseous emissions, rather than to shit, waste-paper and scrap metals. Historical geographies of waste are also of great interest. Decisions over sites of disposal/discharge are always shaped by assumptions about the nature of wastes and by relations of power—the 'ultimate sink', as Joel Tarr has dubbed it, is an ever receding mirage, and the modern search for such solutions inevitably takes marginalized populations and/or environmental phenomena for granted. Histories of how wastes have moved across spaces and environments, how environments shift in and out of being 'wastelands', and how land use and abuse are linked to larger patterns of production and consumption, all could have great relevance today.

Of all the challenges and gaps in the field of waste history, gaining an informed critical purchase on the roles of science and technology may prove the most exciting and confounding. There are plenty of great histories on the cultural consumption of cars and TVs, but few of these entail an understanding of the material engineering of the objects they study. Full-fledged waste studies is impossible without such knowledge, and given the ever increasing complexity of the objects we consume, the range of knowledge needed is flabbergasting. The data gaps and disinformation surrounding waste, and particularly pollution issues, is an added obstacle. And then there is the matter of incomplete knowledge and historical perspective: early plastics producers could not have anticipated the problem of dioxin; Henry Ford cannot be held accountable for smog; drug companies that developed birth control pills or anti-depressants could hardly have predicted that the massive ingestion and excretion of their products would cause deformities in river biota. Waste studies returns us to the historical paradox that we must somehow take responsibility for what we did not understand. It is too late for us to let the dead bury the dead—too many communities are experiencing ongoing poisoning and crisis. This ethical conundrum is central today in policy debates about greenhouse gas emissions (how much responsibility should the United States and Europe take for emissions that occurred decades before CO_2 was a known problem?) and e-waste (can cradle-to-cradle design be achieved without stifling economic development?). These are debates where historians can do deeply relevant work, but relevance demands more than cultural and political critique (which remain indispensible); it also demands basic familiarity with the economic and material science issues that shape these problems.

BIBLIOGRAPHY

Chakrabarty, Dipesh, 'Of Garbage, Modernity and the Citizen's Gaze', *Economic and Political Weekly*, Vol. 27, No. 10/11 (1992), pp. 541–7.

Corbin, Alain, *The Foul and the Fragrant: Odor and the French Social Imagination* (Cambridge, MA: Harvard University Press), 1988.

Dong, Madeliene Yue, *Republican Beijing: The City and Its Histories* (Berkeley: University of California Press, 2003).

Gille, Zsuzsa, *From the Cult of Waste to the Trash Heap of History: The Politics of Waste in Socialist and Post-Socialist Hungary* (Bloomington: Indiana University Press, 2007).

Hamlin, Christopher, *Public Health in the Age of Chadwick: Britain 1800–1854* (Cambridge: Cambridge University Press, 1998).

Laporte, Dominique-Gilbert, *History of Shit* (Cambridge, MA: MIT Press, 2000).

Medina, Martin, *The World's Scavengers: Salvaging for Sustainable Consumption and Production* (Lanham, MD: Altamira Press, 2007).

Melosi, Martin V., *The Sanitary City: Urban Infrastructure in America from Colonial Times to the Present* (Baltimore: Johns Hopkins University Press, 2000).

Pellow, David, *Resisting Global Toxics: Transnational Movements for Environmental Justice* (Cambridge, MA: MIT Press, 2007).

Strasser, Susan, *Waste and Want: A Social History of Trash* (New York: Holt Paperbacks 2000).

Tarr, Joel, *The Search for the Ultimate Sink: Urban Pollution in Historical Perspective* (Akron, OH: University of Akron Press, 1996).

Zimring, Carl, *Cash for Your Trash: Scrap recycling in America* (Brunswick, NJ: Rutgers University Press, 2009).

CHAPTER 18

....

SAVING AND SPENDING

....

LENDOL CALDER

'Before long the question of money came up again.'
Madame Bovary

Money matters. It always has. Of Jesus' thirty-three parables, fifteen are stories about coins, debts, or investments. The Buddha, not normally given to aphorisms about money, nevertheless is represented in the Pali canon as saying the wise and moral man 'should divide his money in four parts; on one part he should live, with two expand his trade, and the fourth he should save against a rainy day.' In feudal China, the merchant-statesman Fan Li amassed an enormous fortune following the advice of his teacher, Ji Ran, who said, 'One must not allow money to be idle.' Fan Li's maxims, still in print 2,500 years later, counsel those who handle money to 'Be vigilant in credit control', 'Don't be penny-pinching', and 'Don't undersave—keep reserve funds strong'. Clearly, money has always mattered, even when there was not a lot of it. The conclusion is seconded by economic anthropologists.[1]

But surely in modern consumer societies money matters more. How it came to matter more, in what ways, and to what effect, historians have only begun to study.

Monetization describes the process whereby money became the dominant means of exchange in developing commercial societies. It is an economic development whose profound social, political, and cultural consequences are not yet well understood. The monetization of household economic life elevated practices that once affected only

[1] J. Parry and M. Bloch (eds.), *Money and the Morality of Exchange* (Cambridge: Cambridge University Press, 1989). The quotation attributed to the Buddha appears in 'The Admonition to Singāla', in R. K. Pruthi (ed.), *Buddhism and Indian Civilization* (New Delhi: Discovery Publishing House, 2004), 132. Ji Ran's maxim appears in HuanZhang Chen, *The Economic Principles of Confucius and His School*, Vol. 2 (PhD diss., Columbia University, 1911), 457. Fan Li's formula for success was written under the name he later adopted, Tao Zhugong, *Golden Rules for Business Success* (Singapore: AsiaPac Books, 2006).

the wealthy—Fan Li's 'golden rules for business success'—to core competencies of living mandatory for everyone. For this reason, concerns about money—how to get it, how to save it, how to invest, multiply, and spend it—have likely sold more books in the last two hundred years than any other subject after religion.

The print culture that helped people make sense of money—through financial advice offered in books, newspapers, magazines, and advertisements—awaits its historian. We do not know whether financial advice over the years has followed a prevailing script or if vernacular economic theory is divided into schools and periods in the manner of its high-brow cousin, the field of macroeconomics. It is not an exaggeration to say that we know more about how the Ford Motor Company financed its business empire than we know about how car buyers scraped up the money to buy Fords. But we do know a few things. We know that handling money is part of the work of modern consumption, a point that gets lost when consumer societies are regarded merely as pleasure grounds for fun and relaxation. The second thing we know is that no one inherits prudence. Every generation has to learn to handle money for itself.

In a 2007 hit song titled 'Can't Tell Me Nothing', hip-hop artist Kanye West sampled a sentiment held by moralists from the beginning of monetization: 'I had a dream I can buy my way to heaven / When I awoke, I spent that on a necklace / I told God I'd be back in a second / Man it's so hard not to act reckless.' Recklessness is a real problem for people living in highly monetized societies, as the global economic crisis of 2008–9 reminds us. To say no to marketeers, to stretch an income, to make money multiply, to use it on one's own terms—such acts call for skills, dispositions, and intelligences that are for the most part not inborn but require education and cultural support. How has money—so necessary, so potent, so hard to *get* in every sense of the word—been lived by people in consumer societies? How have they managed it?

Responses to monetization have varied, of course—from society to society; by class, gender, race, and religion; and over time as well. But the general response to monetization has been to look for money management techniques to help one, in the words of a 1980s credit card slogan, 'master the possibilities'. Thorstein Veblen referred to such techniques as "the intellectual discipline of pecuniary management."[2] Preferring a more limber term, I call them the *financial arts*. Like the liberal arts, the martial arts, the culinary arts, and so forth, the financial arts are a disciplinary realm offering freedom and well-being through the mastery of form. Thus, the financial arts operate as a counterweight to consumer societies' libertine tendencies (which is not to say that the financial arts, like the other arts, are not implicated in acts of hedonic consumerism). This chapter reviews what historians know about the financial arts—that is, the beliefs, skills, dispositions, and practices undergirding how people make sense of money and what they do with it once it comes into their possession.

Some might wonder whether money management really has a history. Is not prudence eternally necessary in human society, recommended in every tradition, if disregarded by

---

[2] Thorstein Veblen, *The Place of Science in Modern Civilization and Other Essays* (New York: B. W. Huebsch, 1919), 321.

nearly all? It is an objection I imagine Mr Micawber making: "'My other piece of advice, Copperfield," said Mr. Micawber, "you know. Annual income twenty pounds, annual expenditure nineteen pounds nineteen and six, result happiness. Annual income twenty pounds, annual expenditure twenty pounds nought and six, result misery.'" If the law of prudence is this unrelenting, the practice of money management can hardly be expected to change over time. Savers prosper; spenders go to their doom. What more is there to say on the subject?

Much more, as it turns out. The Micawber Principle has value as financial advice, but as a historical argument it is deeply mistaken. Contra Micawber, income has not always placed an absolute, binding limit on consumption. In various times and places, consumers have violated conventional understandings of prudence and prospered to tell about it. Some have crashed and burned too, which is an important part of the story. But the point is that the history of money management is not a book with one chapter. If it looks banal, look again. The search for a proper balance between saving and spending, between permissions that unleash creativity and restraints that limit a myopic preference for the present over the future, remains an important project of self-formation for modern people.

Reflecting on the scholarship that has examined saving and spending, I offer the following points as an assessment of where things stand and as a call for more research. First is the rather obvious conclusion that money has always mattered to people. But now, a surprising second point: the significance of money, the fact that people worry about it, that spouses quarrel over it, that consumers scheme day and night to multiply it until money becomes the equal of their desires, all of this might be missed if the only thing one had to read were histories of consumption. For reasons that will need to be considered, historians of consumer culture have not given the financial affairs of consumers the attention the subject deserves. Finally, the historical work that has been done, though sparse, amply demonstrates the rich potential of the financial arts for generating significant problem areas for research. Few other subjects in the glittering universe of consumption lead more directly to the largest questions we can ask about desire, virtue, and the construction of the modern self.

The Known World of Money

In the early 1990s, Jean Christophe-Agnew characterized scholarship on the history of consumption as an 'embarrassment of riches'.[3] There has been no let-up in production since. But if we have learned a great deal about the things money can buy—goods, services, leisure, and entertainments—we are still mostly in the dark about how people

---

[3] Jean-Christophe Agnew, 'Coming Up for Air: Consumer Culture in Historical Perspective', in John Brewer and Roy Porter (eds.), *Consumption and the World of Goods* (New York: Routledge, 1993), 20.

paid for them. Money, the one indispensable thing in a consumer society, has been hard to see for historians.

This is not to say that nothing is known about the history of money itself. Dozens of serious, big-picture histories of money have been written, building on without surpassing John Kenneth Galbraith's *Money: Whence it Came, Where it Went*.[4] Galbraith and his successors answer basic questions about the development of coinage and currency, the ebbs and flows of commodity prices, the specifics of recurring financial crises, the rise of financial institutions such as banking and the agencies that regulate them, and other matters of business and public finance relevant to the study of consumers and their money. But the histories of money written thus far shine little light on the circuitries of money within society's smaller commonwealths, its families and households.

What this means is that the history of the financial arts and how they have been practised is the most under-studied, under-theorized, and under-narrated problem area in the history of modern consumption. Historians have focused so intently on the relations between consumers and goods that they have walked right past the antecedent problem of how consumers managed to afford to buy goods. In a bibliography of the history of money, history has nothing to put up against Flaubert's *Madame Bovary*, Simmel's *The Philosophy of Money*, or Vermeer's *Woman Holding a Balance*. Unlike with advertising, department stores, and signature consumer goods such as the automobile, historians studying saving and spending have yet to generate even a single comprehensive monograph advancing our understanding of how money has been lived.[5]

LEADERS WITHOUT FOLLOWERS

A Rip Van Winkle who fell asleep in 1985 and awoke to read this chapter would probably be confused at this point. He would object, correctly, that early, trailblazing work on the history of modern consumption took household finance very seriously. What happened?

It is true that the first historical studies positing a consumer revolution drew attention to money matters. For example, Daniel Boorstin's *The Americans: The Democratic Experience* sketched the broad outlines of a history of credit financing, which Boorstin considered to be a crucial element for the development of American consumerism. 'It was hardly an exaggeration to say,' observed Boorstin, 'that the American standard of

[4] John Kenneth Galbraith, *Money: Whence it Came, Where it Went* (Boston: Houghton Mifflin, 1975); Niall Ferguson, *The Ascent of Money: A Financial History of the World* (New York: Penguin Press, 2008).

[5] Examples of what history is lacking that can be found in other disciplines include Viviana Zelizer, *The Social Meaning of Money* (New York: Basic Books, 1994); Jonathan Parry and Maurice Bloch, *Money and the Morality of Exchange* (Cambridge: Cambridge University Press, 1989); and Andrew Leyshon and Nigel Thrift, *Money/Space: Geographies of Monetary Transformation* (London: Routledge, 1997).

living was bought on the installment plan.'[6] Likewise, in one of the most influential works of British history ever published, *The Birth of a Consumer Society: The Commercialization of Eighteenth-Century England*, John Brewer discovered while researching his contribution to the volume that he could not get very far exploring the origins of a consumer society in England without looking into financial conduct, the question of how money was managed to facilitate trade and consumption. In his contribution to the volume, John Brewer noted, 'Private indebtedness...has received much less attention from historians [than public credit] despite the fact that it was a persistent and indeed ubiquitous source of anxiety in Hanoverian England.'[7] Generalized beyond England, Brewer's observation remains true today and could serve as an epigraph to everything said thus far. Money and finance matters to people a great deal, and always has, though how it has mattered since the financial arts became a necessary set of disciplines under conditions of complete monetization is not something historians have looked into thoroughly. Boorstin and Brewer drew attention to important subjects, but few followed up.[8]

WHY SO FEW HISTORIES OF MONEY MATTERS?

Before examining some important exceptions to the overall neglect, it may be instructive for the development of future work to pause and consider why historians have been squeamish about examining money. The power of money has been a popular theme in art, literature, and popular music. Why have historians slighted it?

An explanation worth considering comes from Viviana Zelizer, author of *The Social Meaning of Money*, who has observed that in her field of sociology, money has taken a backseat to other inquiries 'as if it were not sociological enough.'[9] Zelizer's eye-opening discoveries of how money worked in people's lives in the United States between 1870 and 1930 led her to believe that almost everything social scientists have assumed about money is wrong. According to Zelizer, the first generation of sociologists suffered from an 'intellectual color blindness' about money. Early theorists viewed monetary transactions as corrosive of personal bonds and culture, rendering social life cold, distant, and

---

[6] Daniel Boorstin, *The Americans: The Democratic Experience* (New York: Random House, 1973), 426.

[7] Neil McKendrick, John Brewer, and J. H. Plumb, *The Birth of a Consumer Society: The Commercialization of Eighteenth-Century England* (Bloomington, IN: Indiana University Press, 1982), 203.

[8] Interestingly, early attempts to present overviews of consumer culture often mention the importance of money management, only to drop the subject after the first paragraph. For examples, see Richard Wightman Fox and T. J. Jackson Lears (eds.), *The Culture of Consumption: Critical Essays in American History, 1880–1980* (New York: Pantheon Books, 1983); Christopher Lasch, 'The Culture of Consumption', in Mary Kupiec Cayton, Elliott J. Gorn, and Peter W. Williams (eds.), *Encyclopedia of American Social History*, 3 vols. (New York: Scribner's, 1993), Volume II: 1381–1390; and Susan Strasser, 'Consumption' in Stanley I. Kutler (ed.), *Encyclopedia of the United States in the 20th Century* (New York: Scribner's, 1995). Strasser went the furthest, beginning with her perceptive claim that credit management and bargaining with cash must be considered part of the 'work' of modern consumption.

[9] Zelizer, *The Social Meaning of Money*, 4.

calculating. Money was said to be 'abstract and impersonal' (Weber), reducing social relations between people to an 'unmeaning,' purely quantitative 'cash nexus' (Marx) in which the 'colorlessness and indifference' of money 'hollows out the core of things' (Simmel). According to Simmel, money's most influential academic interpreter, money possesses a rationalizing logic asking only 'how much', not 'what and how'. Money, Simmel believed, turned the world into 'an arithmetic problem'.[10] Zelizer's conclusion is that these early ideas about money became powerfully influential but made a poor foundation for further analysis. Money was assumed to be a colourless, uninteresting force on a par with gravity and other constants lacking interesting trajectories of historical development. Zelizer summarizes the thinking of twentieth-century social scientists with words from Gertrude Stein: 'Whether you like it or whether you do not money is money and that is all there is about it.'[11] Who would want to study something like that?

Zelizer's explanation for why sociologists disregarded money can account for the similar lacuna found in histories of consumer culture. As a test case, consider William Leach's *Land of Desire: Merchants, Power, and the Rise of a New American Culture*. In this magisterial work, Leach brilliantly describes how Americans' longing for goods was stoked by a new commercial aesthetic that sought to show off goods day and night through astonishing manipulations of colour, light, and glass. In the new cultural order symbolized by department store show windows, 'money was at the heart of it all', maintains Leach. So much so that he lists 'the influence of money' as one of four cardinal features of the emergent culture of consumer capitalism. But whereas the other three cardinal elements are given densely argued narratives to explain their meaning and significance, Leach's sweeping claims about money are largely undeveloped. Thus, when Leach maintains that 'pecuniary values would constitute the base measure for all other values', he assumes that readers will find the claim self-evident. The footnotes show that Leach knows what he knows about money not on the basis of historical analysis but from economists and sociologists, the very people Zelizer identifies as formative for how social science came to understand—or rather, misunderstand—money.[12]

The lesson for those who would pick up where *Land of Desire* leaves off is clear: common assumptions about money thought to end in full points may deserve question marks instead. Do markets really empty human life of moral significance? Has money worked historically to homogenize and flatten social relations? Have the financial arts razed authentic values with a wrecking ball of numerical logic? Future work touching these questions will build on Zelizer's discovery that money is not sterile, but deeply meaningful in people's lives.

---

[10] Ibid., 6–9.

[11] Ibid., 1–2.

[12] For his ideas on money, Leach leans heavily on Charles Horton Cooley, an early president of the American Sociological Association. Glossing Cooley's scorn for pecuniary values, Leach concludes his thoughts on money with a peroration reminiscent of Marx, Weber, and Simmel: 'Increasingly, the worth of everything—even beauty, friendship, religion, the moral life—was being determined by what it could bring in the market.' See William Leach, *Land of Desire: Merchants, Power, and the Rise of a New American Culture* (New York: Vintage, 1994), 3–8, 51.

MODELS OF ENQUIRY

Enquiry along these lines can build on two superb studies that were early exceptions to historians' inattention to money matters—one British, the other American, both published in 1985. Paul Johnson's *Saving and Spending: The Working-Class Economy in Britain, 1870–1939* investigated how English wage earners created a plebeian version of the financial arts to make money work for them. In *The Morality of Spending: Attitudes toward the Consumer Society in America, 1875–1940*, Daniel Horowitz contrasted how Americans spent their income with how social critics thought they should. The landmark status of both these books owes something to the authors' perception that what people do with money says a good deal about what people value.

Should anyone need convincing that the study of money matters can do more than simply fill a hole in the history of consumption, that it can produce fresh interpretations of larger historiographical questions, Paul Johnson's *Saving and Spending* will satisfy all doubts. In this book Johnson took up a familiar problem in labour history, the low wages and unreliable employment of industrial workers. But instead of focusing on workers' relation to trade unions, the response to low wages emphasized by left-leaning historians from Engels to Hobsbawm, Johnson turned away from institutional labour history in order to pay attention to how working-class households spent the little money they had. Working with unused data on working-class savings, insurance policies, and spending patterns, Johnson learned that workers defined themselves at least as much through bourgeois concepts such as status as they did through collective identities like trade unions. 'Although the means adopted were sometimes mutual and collective,' Johnson concluded, 'the goal was always personal and competitive; self-help sometimes, self-interest always.'[13] Without minimizing class consciousness where it could be found, Johnson's attention to money matters led him to challenge the dominant interpretive tradition of British labour studies. Collective economic efforts by workers, he argued, were not necessarily a prelude to trade unionism. On the contrary, the spending patterns of British workers showed that many were less interested in building an industrial democracy than in advancing their social position in the neighbourhood.

Saving and Spending achieved an additional accomplishment, which was to reconstruct the rationality of working-class money management practices roundly condemned by self-help enthusiasts for being wasteful, pointless, and even morally wrong. Against this view, Johnson demonstrated that workers who bought burial insurance and pawned personal possessions valued savings as much as the middle class, though the circumstances of their lives called for different forms and understandings of thrift. Johnson's data showed that the conditions in which working-class households lived made middle-class approaches to saving and spending totally unrealistic for them.

---

[13] Paul Johnson, *Saving and Spending: The Working Class Economy in Britain, 1870–1939* (Oxford: Oxford University Press, 1985), 232.

Deprived of adequate and dependable streams of income, working-class households developed their own financial arts, ingenious methods, and institutions calculated to make the most of intermittent cash flows. *Saving and Spending* is a Baedeker's Guide to these strategies, beginning with insurance plans (the most popular form of savings among workers) and extending to single-purpose savings plans, savings clubs, cooperative retailing, and sources of credit financing such as hire purchase and pawning. In each case, Johnson argued that what appeared to be financial madness to comfortable middle-class observers often made sense in the circumstances faced by workers. Pawning, for example, certainly cost more than drawing from one's own savings account, while the very act of putting possessions in hock suggested a deplorable indifference to the sanctity of private property. But in Johnson's sympathetic view, working-class people considered belongings like luxurious bedding and Sunday clothing as forms of capital that could be given up for cash when bad times required it. Allowing the dynamics of capitalism to invade the sanctity of the home in this way shocked middle-class observers, but as a savings strategy it made sense for workers. To confirm the rationality of working-class saving and spending, Johnson pointed to the decline of pawning after 1909. When state-sponsored pensions, health insurance, and unemployment benefits became available, workers shifted their savings strategies toward investment in old-age endowment policies, exactly the opposite of what one would expect if the working class was profligate by nature, as critics alleged.

A quarter-century after publication, *Saving and Spending* continues to be instructive. Later we will consider how Johnson's defence of working-class shrewdness invites new narratives for the history of thrift based on understandings of saving more capacious than putting one's tuppence in the bank. Also worth emulating is Johnson's adept use of sources. All students of money matters face a difficult problem: while corporations issue annual reports, households do not. To form his conclusions, Johnson worked with statistical and qualitative evidence taken from a vast menu of sources including autobiographies, social surveys, institutional records, and government documents. An even more astonishing command of dissimilar forms of evidence can be found in Margot Finn's *The Character of Credit: Personal Debt in English Culture, 1740–1914*, an important study of formal and informal working-class credit arrangements that adds novels, prison records, and court documents to the mix used by Johnson.[14] On this model of source material, historians of the financial arts must be positively omnivorous.

A different way to proceed can be found in Daniel Horowitz's *The Morality of Spending*. Like Johnson, Horowitz surmised that people's values are revealed in how they spend their money. Trusting that this insight could open up new ways to contribute to debates scholars were having about the arrival and impact of consumer society, Horowitz pulled together two main sources of evidence: a set of landmark budget studies published between 1875 and the late 1930s, and the writings of those who commented on them. Of his sources, Horowitz observed, 'Household budget studies are rich reservoirs

[14] Margot Finn, *The Character of Credit: Personal Debt in English Culture, 1740–1914* (Cambridge: Cambridge University Press, 2003).

of information that historians are only now beginning to tap.'[15] A quarter-century later these words are still true, and Horowitz remains the best guide to these indispensable sources.

Empirical documentation of how rural, industrial, and, later, middle-class households spent their money began in the early years of social science. In France, the mining engineer Frederic le Play published in 1855 his monumental *Les Ouvriers Européens*, a set of thirty-six fine-grained studies of the material and moral lives of European families representing various nationalities and social groups. Le Play's methods were widely influential. One admirer was Carroll D. Wright, head of the Massachusetts Bureau of Statistics of Labor (MBSL), who in 1875 conducted the first major American investigation into the expenditures of working-class households. Wright's 1875 report is the first of twelve budget studies examined by Horowitz.

In the beginning, Horowitz hoped that study of budget data would reveal changes in patterns of household expenditure over time. It did: by the end of the period surveyed, families spent proportionally less on food compared to items in the 'miscellaneous' category (i.e., other than food, clothing, and shelter), with the biggest shift occurring between 1875 and 1907.[16] But the more Horowitz lingered over the budget studies, the more potential he saw in them for addressing other questions, and he predicted:

> Once more fully regained as sources, analysis of the data can sharpen the debate over when the United States became a consumer culture; help reveal the changing styles of life of different social and ethnic groups; enable us to chart more precisely the development of a market economy; make it possible to enhance the examination of the contributions of husbands, wives, and children to the family economy; and shed light on the balance between defensive and acquisitive patterns of spending.[17]

This list scratches only the surface of possibilities for using budget studies to investigate money matters.

Reading *The Morality of Spending* is like following a social worker a century ago into tenements and bungalows to look in on families while they are eating. For example, in the 1875 MBSL study of 397 families, we learn that Household #223, a French-Canadian family composed of two parents and five children, ate 'bread, butter, gingerbread, molasses, tea' for supper. The family's income that year was $650. Of that amount, $385 came from the father's mill job and the rest from the two older boys, who were sent out to work. All but $24.58 of the family's income was spent on food, clothing, and shelter. The budget shows that the family was debt free, but there is no indication of savings. 'Family dresses poorly', noted the investigator, 'and looks pale and unhealthy'. Overall, about half of the families in the MBSL survey reported putting money aside; the average amount saved was 3 per cent of income. The most commonly reported spending on 'sundries' went on newspapers, organizational memberships, and church contributions.

[15] Daniel Horowitz, *The Morality of Spending: Attitudes toward the Consumer Society in America, 1875–1940* (Baltimore: Johns Hopkins University Press, 1985), xx.

[16] Ibid., 173–4.

[17] Ibid., xx.

Only a few families spent money on recreation, travel, consumer durables, or health care. Other budget studies examined by Horowitz report similar kinds of data for a variety of types of households: working-class families in New York City in 1907, salaried middle-class families from across the nation in 1912, Berkeley college professors in 1927, and so on. Incredibly rich data sources, budget studies could keep social historians busy for a long time.

But they have to be used cautiously. Horowitz recognized that budget studies are not objective documents at all but 'morality plays' dramatizing the attitudes of the researchers behind them. Horowitz concluded that before he could use budget studies to write a social history of saving and spending, it was necessary to apply the questions and methods of intellectual history to surveys of household expenditure. The researchers who compiled the budget studies thought their rigorous methods were value free. But the very categories they used to describe spending behaviours, as well as the spending they noticed and the kinds of spending they ignored (not to mention the revealing notes they scribbled in the margins of their reports), all betrayed attitudes about consumption that say as much about how investigators thought people should spend their money as they say about actual household spending. For this reason, Horowitz decided to make the investigators' moral outlook the primary focus of his study.

This means *The Morality of Spending* is not a straightforward social history. On the other hand, it is not a purely intellectual history either, and herein lies a strength of the book as a model. Horowitz recognized that traditional categories of historical work fit his subject and sources poorly. Therefore, he hoped to accrue dividends from a blending of approaches, methods, questions, and disciplinary fields, a cross-cutting approach that has become characteristic of work done on money matters.

At the time Horowitz was working on *The Morality of Spending*, a strong consensus among historians had developed around a powerful narrative explaining the growth of a culture of consumer capitalism in the United States. The dominant narrative described the 1920s as a watershed moment in American history, the tipping point when a nineteenth-century 'producer ethic'—an ethos of restraint, thrift, and work, arising from conditions of scarcity—was surpassed by a twentieth-century 'consumer ethic' that took abundance for granted and found expression in lifestyles of release, therapeutic indulgence, and fun. In this linear account of the past, Horowitz expected to find that attitudes toward saving and spending were recalibrated in the 'Prosperity Decade' from unbending condemnations of thriftlessness toward a more relaxed acceptance and even celebration of freer spending. But this is not what he found. At least, it was not a sufficiently rich account of the evidence.

Horowitz allowed that between 1875 and 1940, budget investigators and social critics did change their thinking considerably on the persistent question of what a rising standard of living meant for American lives and culture. But the shift in attitudes was not from opposition to acceptance. Rather, Horowitz argued, elite observers exchanged one type of moralism for another, hoping in both cases that better spending habits would elevate the moral lives of others. Traditional moralists such as Carroll Wright focused on the alleged profligacy of workers' and immigrants' households. In contrast, modern moralists, such as the progressive social critics Robert and Helen Lynd, became alarmed by what they saw as the vacuous conformity of the middle class. Traditional moralists looked at the convivial drinking of working men and expressive ethnic customs of immigrants and worried about the loss of self-control. Modern moralists witnessed the integrity of working-class life and immigrant folk cultures being replaced by an insipid, homogenized middle-class way of life; they feared the power of greedy corporations and mass society. Traditional moralism attended to individuals; modern moralism directed criticism against institutions and social systems. Traditional moralists wanted to instruct households in the virtues of character, hard work, and restraint, and train them for the proper enjoyment of leisure, disdaining the false pleasures of commercial goods and experiences for the true joys of a so-called higher life found principally in Culture. Modern moralists hoped to liberate the gullible masses by introducing them to non-commercial lives passionately lived, viewing Culture as a revitalizing force for bohemian individuality. What both traditions of moralism shared was a belief that affluence is corrupting. Both believed in a higher life threatened by commercialism and wealth. Both shared a narrow view of the function of goods, believing commercial goods and experiences to be therapeutic devices that compensated for lack of access to a good life, which traditional moralists defined as personal virtue and modern moralists conceived of as fulfilling labour. 'For both sets of observers,' Horowitz concluded, 'the danger was that people selected escape, not renewal; false pleasures, not true ones.'[18] After *The Morality of Spending*, simple, linear accounts of a 'revolution in manners and morals' relating to consumption and spending became increasingly recognized as untenable.

Modern moralism did not expire in 1940. Horowitz followed *The Morality of Spending* with additional explorations of money matters, presenting an intellectual history of the moral consequences of post-Second World War affluence and a biography of the 1950s social critic Vance Packard. Though Americans are often stereotyped as carefree consumers, until someone corrects Horowitz, *ambivalence* is the key word for describing how Americans have responded to the moral quandaries of money.

For those interested in studying the social history of money management, *The Morality of Spending* (which might have been better titled *The Immorality of Spending*) can be read as a cautionary tale about the limitations of a moralistic outlook. A deep anxiety about the moral consequences of wealth is an old and enduring part of the American national tradition, as Daniel Shi made clear in *The Simple Life: Plain Living and High Thinking in American Culture*.[19] This finding is corroborated in *The Morality of Spending* when Horowitz identifies a common language Americans (and others) have used to talk about consumption, a way of thinking and talking about money whose key idioms are decadence, self-control, corruption, and the need to get back to aspirations higher than getting and spending. Those who study the financial arts from the precincts of the liberal arts often write from within this tradition, which in unguarded moments shows

[18] Ibid., 166.
[19] See the introduction and epilogue to Daniel Shi, *The Simple Life: Plain Living and High Thinking in American Culture* (New York: Oxford University Press, 1985).

itself in sneering references to Wal-Mart shoppers, SUV drivers, and the super-sized citizens of a fast-food nation. Although criticizing how other people spend their money may be a therapeutic way of reaffirming one's own commitment to righteous ideals and sophisticated forms of Culture, Horowitz's critique of modern moralism reveals the limitations of such an outlook. For one thing, a condescending eye inevitably blinds critics to the social meanings people give to their consumption. As an alternative to moralism, Horowitz's proposal for a *reciprocal model* offers a better approach, 'one that emphasizes the power of the economic system and elites to set the framework of consumer culture but does not forget the ability of people, within limits, to shape the meaning of their consumption patterns.'[20]

In addition to recommending a fruitful way of thinking about money matters, *The Morality of Spending* offers numerous jumping-off places for future research. Budget analyses will be an important source of information for future studies, allowing us to learn more about the gendering of money management as well as the financial practices of immigrant, ethnic, and other unstudied groups. A stunning example of the possibilities comes from John McClymer, who used data taken from the 1902 Report of the Massachusetts Bureau of the Statistics of Labor to learn what material culture working-class families aspired to have and what strategies they used to afford what they wanted. The MBSL data is eye-opening for what it reveals about American dreams and workers' realities. The average gap between family expenditures and paternal wages was $253, a hefty 29.9 per cent of total spending. Conventional wisdom, in line with Mr Micawber, dictated that families should live within the bounds of the paternal breadwinner's earnings. But few families in McClymer's sample were content to live within their means. What did people do? About a third put children out to work. Another third took in boarders. In all cases, housewives found various ways to take up the slack. This means that since at least 1900, the main breadwinner's income has been inadequate to realize an American standard of living. McClymer's findings also imply that consumer credit can be viewed as the historical replacement for income-enhancing strategies such as child labour.[21]

An important question that needs following up is the extent of the influence of financial advice givers, which remains unclear. The financial arts have had many teachers. We will not know how representative or influential Horowitz's moralists were until we know more about other sources of moral authority on money matters, including ministers, novelists, editors, popular economists, psychologists, business writers, teachers, songwriters, and the self-appointed apostles of thrift. At the end of Father Abraham's sermon on 'The Way to Wealth', Benjamin Franklin has Poor Richard observe: 'The people heard it, approved the doctrine, and immediately practised the contrary.' Franklin's pessimism notwithstanding, the influence of financial advice literature like the advice books of Samuel Smiles or Fan Li's long-lived *Golden Rules for Business Success* is an important subject that remains to be explored.

---

[20] Horowitz, *The Morality of Spending*, 168.
[21] John F. McClymer, 'The "American Standard" of Living: Family Expectations and Strategies for Getting and Spending in the Gilded Age', *Hayes Historical Journal*, 9/3 (1990), 20–43.

Also needed are micro-histories that can illuminate and supplement what we already know about general patterns of saving and spending. The black box of the household economy will be hard to unlock without data and testimony from householders themselves. Here the horizon of possibility is suggested by recent studies in retailing history making use of account ledgers and records belonging to particular merchants. These fine-grained studies hold many surprises for understanding past worlds of goods and commercial relations.[22] As an example of the promise of micro-history approaches, consider the letters of Walter T. Post, a late nineteenth-century American railroad clerk whose correspondence takes us inside one household's financial decision-making.[23]

Born on a Michigan farm in 1867, Walter Post attended a Detroit business college and took a job in 1889 as an accountant with the Northern Pacific Railroad. From the day he arrived in St Paul, Minnesota until losing his job seven years later, Walter wrote weekly letters to his parents recounting his thoughts, activities, and finances, sometimes with monthly budget figures recording outlays to the penny. The correspondence offers a window into the money management of a household over important shifts in the life cycle of a young man, and then a woman, who aspired to bourgeois respectability.

Conspicuous in the letters is the Posts' confident use of credit, which will surprise those who believe in a golden age of American thrift when middle-class people supposedly never went into debt. Walter Post made use of credit from the first day he arrived in St Paul. By the spring of 1895, the Posts owed money to the dentist, the doctor, the grocer, the butcher, a tailor, the hardware store, and a sewing-machine agent. They owed money on their furniture and stove, renewing loans to a department store several times over. To satisfy some creditors Walter tapped a brother for loans. Walter's disposable income that spring was about $10 a month; the Posts' debts totalled $78.50. Were the Posts atypical? Walter thought so. He portrayed himself as the *thriftiest* of the dozens of clerks who worked in the St Paul office, clerks who were occasionally fired for drunkenness, for gambling, and for having their wages garnished by lenders. Walter probably exaggerated his prudence to justify himself to his parents. Still, the 1890 US census calculated that American households on average that year owed about $880. This is a remarkable amount of debt given that the average annual wage of workers at the time was $475, and that the figure, based on recorded mortgages, does not include the kinds of debts carried by Walter and Lilly Post. Post's letters bring alive a saying of the late nineteenth-century celebrity preacher Henry Ward Beecher: 'If a young man will only get in debt…and then get married, these two things will keep him straight, or nothing will.'[24]

But the most striking feature of the letters is Walter Post's thinking on financial management. Perusing the debt totals, we might accuse the Posts of wasteful overspending. But that is not how Walter interpreted his spending and borrowing. In a letter to his

[22] See Anne Smart Martin, *Buying into the World of Goods: Early Consumers in Backcountry Virginia* (Baltimore: Johns Hopkins University Press, 2008); Diane E. Wenger, *A Country Storekeeper: Creating Economic Networks in Early America, 1790–1807* (University Park, PA: Pennsylvania State University Press, 2008).
[23] Walter T. Post letters, Box P1040, Minnesota Historical Society, St Paul, MN.
[24] Beecher, quoted in P. T. Barnum, *Dollars and Sense* (Boston: Eastern Publishing Co., 1890), 49–50.

brother Charlie, Walter confided: 'I have to do some awful close figuring to make ends meet, and then they don't meet.' To his father, Walter complained: 'We were paid off today but all the money is spoken for before I get it almost.'[25] The impression left by Walter's letters is not that of a reckless spender but more of a frazzled budgeter applying all the financial arts he knows to the difficult problem of affordability. Despite his money worries, Post felt that the debts he incurred were beneficial for achieving the life he and Lilly wanted. Comparing the costs of renting a house versus boarding, Post conceded that a few more years of boarding would have enabled the couple to put aside $150 of his salary at a savings bank. 'But now we have $202.80 worth of furniture,' he countered. 'And we might have had to use some of the money in the Bank so you see we are ahead a good deal.'[26] It is an interesting logic. Though the Posts still owed money on their tables and chairs, Walter regarded their furniture as a form of savings, and he recognized that the liquidity of a bank savings account was to him a constant temptation to fritter money away on insubstantial expenditures. On display in the letters, then, is an important shift in the middle-class understanding of thrift, a transformation happening well before advertisers, economists, and credit advocates in the 1920s began promoting 'spending-to-save' credit plans.

To say that borrowing money can be thrifty sounds odd, but only if we assume a static definition of thrift. The reality is that thrift has a history, and the rise of consumer credit is a chapter in that story. The history of thrift is one of several problem areas to emerge in the scattering of work on money matters that followed Horowitz's *The Morality of Spending* and Johnson's *Saving and Spending*. 'Scattering' is the key word here; the history of money matters is less an industrious exchange in which scholars build on each other's work than a lonely dance floor where a few bold souls sally forth looking for someone to hook up with. Still, problem areas can be discerned, beginning with the concept of thrift and how it has changed over time. A second focus of enquiry asks comparative questions. With regard to saving and spending, have consumer societies moved in similar directions? How have they differed, and why? In both problem areas, historians have called into question well-known assumptions about the history of saving, debt, and credit, offering new insights that are relevant to public policy on personal finance.

THE HISTORY OF THRIFT

Many believe today's overspent Americans are in headlong retreat from a thriftier past, when people saved their money and lived within their means. 'People have changed their view of debt,' wrote John Kenneth Galbraith in *The Affluent Society*. 'Thus there has been an inexplicable but very real retreat from the Puritan canon that required an individual to save first and enjoy later.' Narratives describing a decline in the moral culture of

---

[25] Post letters, to Charlie, 20 January 1896; to his father, 2 April 1895.
[26] Post letters, to his father, 2 April 2 1895.

economic decision-making were popularized in the 1920s by Horowitz's modern moralists. They gained legitimacy from historian David Tucker's *The Decline of Thrift in America*, which argued that 'installment buying required a moral revolution against the Puritan ethic.' Most famously, Daniel Bell asserted in *The Cultural Contradictions of Capitalism* that 'the greatest single engine in the destruction of the Protestant ethic was the invention of the installment plan, or instant credit.'[27] The belief that thrift today is on life support, that the story of American saving and spending is the story of a fall from the heights of thrift on which previous generations lived and contributed to national great-ness, is such a powerful narrative for understanding the history of saving and spending that it is helpful to give it a name. I have called it 'the myth of lost economic virtue.'[28]

That thrift has declined seems beyond obvious. Oddly, dating the decline is not. Some recall a golden age of saving before the 1990s, before pay day lending and home equity loans that allowed mortgage holders to treat equity investments as a personal ATM machine. Others believe thrift died in the 1960s, killed off by credit cards. Some date the end of the golden age of financial prudence quite precisely to 1966, the year National Thrift Week quietly expired. But if we ask why National Thrift Week was necessary in the first place, why the YMCA and thousands of savings banks mobilized annually after 1919 for campaigns of savings evangelism, it is possible to interpret the *creation* of National Thrift Week as a sign that long before credit cards the nation already had a problem with thrift. Promoters of National Thrift Week blamed the demise of thrift on the instalment plan, which made ownership of consumer durables a hallmark of American consump-tion. Many factors, then—the appearance of new forms of consumer credit, the expan-sion of a 'buyosphere' oriented to spending, pleasure, and fun, along with the very real dismantling of a cultural apparatus for the promotion of savings—have made it easy to believe in a past golden age of thrift.

But the myth of lost economic virtue has not held up well under recent historical scrutiny. Historians looking into saving and spending in the United States are replac-ing declension narratives with interpretations more respectful of contrary evidence and more sensitive to the survival of thrift as a surprisingly adaptable ethos operating across time and economic contexts.

For starters, it has become increasingly hard to locate a time in the past when American households were not using credit—often reluctantly, sometimes zealously—to solve the problem of affordability. Bruce Mann summarizes dozens of social histories when he observes that 'debt was an inescapable fact of life in early America', evident in the pervasiveness of debts owed and owing in probate inventories, the predominance of debt actions in civil litigation, the vast number of surviving account books for indi-viduals and merchants, and the fact that promises to pay were a major medium of

[27] Preston William Slosson, *The Great Crusade and After, 1914–1928* (Macmillan Co., 1930), 181; John Kenneth Galbraith, *The Affluent Society* (Houghton Mifflin, 1958), 200; David Tucker, *The Decline of Thrift in America* (Praeger, 1991), vii–ix, 99–155; Daniel Bell, *The Cultural Contradictions of Capitalism* (Basic Books, 1976), 21.

[28] Lendol Calder, *Financing the American Dream: A Cultural History of Consumer Credit* (Princeton, NJ: Princeton University Press, 1999), 22–31.

exchange. This river of red ink flowed well into the nineteenth century, as I showed in *Financing the American Dream: A Cultural History of Consumer Credit*. The dilemma for Americans, Mann points out, was that owing other people money is the antithesis of the revolutionary ideal of independence, yet in a 'republic of debtors' few have escaped the creditors' nets.[29]

Even the most unassailable presumption of the myth of lost economic virtue—that the ethos of thrift is a legacy from Puritan Christianity—appears to need correction. Stephen Innes and others have underlined crucial differences between the Puritan moral economy and visions of thrift that came later. Unquestionably, Puritans on both sides of the Atlantic valued an ethos of restraint that had something to do with the legitimization of capitalistic practices. But unlike Franklinian acolytes of saving, Puritan merchants and tradesmen did not understand thrift as 'the Way to Wealth' or as a technology of moral perfection. In the Puritan culture of discipline, the imperative to save was always defined and restricted by moral and theological ends that distinguish it from the modern capitalist's self-oriented motivation to save. Thus, when modern moralists decry the loss of the so-called Puritan ethic in saving and spending, it is doubtful they are thinking about Puritan thrift at all.[30]

The crucial point here is that thrift has a history, though it has not had historians. No concept has been more important than thrift for shaping the moral culture of economic life under capitalism. Thrift is a habit that the Puritans correctly recognized as having deep theological and anthropological implications, finding expression in a multitude of practices and dispositions grounded in an ethos of care. Standing on more capacious understandings of thrift, historians will find it possible to move beyond familiar rise-and-fall narratives in which parsimonious saving is invented by the Puritans, achieves its greatest influence among the Victorians, and then in the late twentieth century withers away and dies. In the place of such overly simple Anglo-American histories of ascent and decline, we need more complex narratives of institutional and cultural realignment in which the meaning and practice of thrift ebbs and flows across time and from place to place, buffeted by historical transformations yet capable of being revived and realigned in manifold, often cross-cutting ways of restraint and release. If thrift is understood as the making of wealth out of scarcity, then it will be possible to see how dynamic and versatile thrift has been, as relevant to uses of time, natural resources, manpower, and human passions as it is to money. Thrift will then belong not just to Puritans and moralists, but also to peasants, monks, revolutionaries, conservationists, environmentalists, civil rights activists, philanthropists, social protestors, and others

[29] Ibid.; Bruce H. Mann, *Republic of Debtors: Bankruptcy in the Age of American Independence* (Cambridge, MA: Harvard University Press, 2002), 1–5.

[30] Stephen Innes, *Creating the Commonwealth: The Economic Culture of Puritan New England* (New York: Norton, 1995); James Calvin Davis and Charles Mathewes, 'Saving Grace and Moral Striving: Thrift in Puritan Theology', in Joshua J. Yates and James Davison Hunter (eds.), *Thrift and Thriving in America: Capitalism and Moral Order From the Puritans to the Present* (New York: Oxford University Press, 2011).

committed to an ethos of restraint. When thrift is historicized, we will find it has been reimagined many times and is a more malleable concept than generally recognized.[31]

A striking example of the adaptability of thrift comes from the work of scholars examining the development of consumer credit in the United States. In *Financing the American Dream*, I contested the common view that instalment buying undermined financial prudence by making it easier for people to live hedonic lives oriented to instant gratification. In my research, I noticed that users of instalment credit often maintained that, for the duration of their repayment periods, they were forced to cut out expenditures on fancies of the moment, put aside money for the monthly bills, and work diligently at one or more jobs to guarantee a dependable supply of income. Impressed by their testimonies, I shifted my attention from the moment of sale to the lived experience of credit over time, which led me to argue that the greatest contribution consumer credit made to American consumer society is the way it enforced discipline, hard work, and the channelling of productivity toward the acquisition of durable goods. Once consumers step onto the treadmill of regular monthly payments, it becomes clear that consumer credit is not about 'easy payments' or a rejection of thrift, but is a new form of self-discipline supporting new variants of thrift. 'Easy payment!' exclaimed an immigrant housewife to a journalist in 1912. 'Hard payment it is! Easy payment with everybody workin' their nails out!'[32]

The evidence I offered for the view that consumer credit represents a new kind of thrift was suggestive, but thin. I made use of arguments from authorities such as the economist E. R. A. Seligman, whose massive study of consumer finance in the 1920s demonstrated that money spent on the instalment purchase of consumer durables was a genuine form of saving.[33] I related anecdotes about individuals who used credit to discipline their spending, including Walter Post, who in 1895 complained to his parents, 'I have to pay $10 this month on my stove.…We have to squeeze and pinch awful hard to make ends meet until we get everything straightened up.' But the evidence I presented left the case for credit-as-thrift merely plausible, not certain. And did the argument hold up at all once revolving credit and universal credit cards entered the picture?

Since *Financing the American Dream*, succeeding histories of American consumer credit have extended and deepened the linkage between credit and thrift. Studies by Josh Lauer and Donncha Marron confirm the disciplinary power of credit as a means of social restraint and self-control, arguing that credit management has become an important technique for the formation of the self. Lauer's history of credit reporting describes far-flung systems of disciplinary surveillance that since the 1850s have effectively regulated commercial and consumer behaviour. Lauer argues that the omnipresent gaze

---

[31] At the time of writing, a major collection of interdisciplinary scholarship on the history of thrift is forthcoming from Oxford University Press: Joshua J. Yates and James Davison Hunter (eds.), *Capitalism and Moral Order: A Social History of Thrift in America from the Puritans to the Present*.

[32] Mary Fields, 'The Drama of Wages', *The American Magazine*, 74 (November 1912), 76.

[33] Edwin R. A. Seligman, *The Economics of Instalment Selling: A Study in Consumers' Credit*, 2 vols. (New York: Harper & Bros., 1927), 1:272–4, 277.

of the credit reporter made human beings legible and accountable to others in novel ways, generating a 'financial identity' or 'credit consciousness', a new vision of the self, that promoted consumer spending while simultaneously supporting the virtue of self-control expressed as 'credit morality'. The message of credit morality—pay on time, refrain from overspending, follow a budget, think ahead—'was a peculiar form of counter-propaganda set amid a sea of advertising designed to incite consumer desire.' Borrowing from Foucault, Lauer presents modern credit education as an ideological discourse of self-government or 'soul training', a technique for self-formation that carries higher expectations for personal responsibility than older ways of household finance that allowed running up bills at stores and perhaps never paying at all.[34]

Similarly, Donncha Marron finds consumer credit to be a 'regime of enforced saving', making credit buying not an abandonment of thrift but a tighter embrace of the Puritan desire for self-discipline. According to Marron, credit accomplishes for consumers what Frederick Taylor's industrial engineering did for workers: it optimizes individual performance. The curious thing is that what workers perceived as repression, consumers on a budget experience as a kind of freedom, a liberty based on the disciplined mastery of money, credit, and desire. Extending his historical sociology of consumer credit into the new millennium, Marron presents an ingenious argument to the effect that the credit score is to consumers today what the savings account passbook was to previous generations: a register for the moral evaluation of the self, measuring an ethos of personal peak performance. This means that even as credit cards have shifted the nature of credit purchasing away from investments in durable goods, and even as lenders have discovered incentives to keep credit customers perpetually on the hook as a source of profit, the popular fascination with, and misunderstanding of, credit scores ensures that consumer credit continues to exercise an effective discipline on consumer behaviour. Like Lauer, Marron regards the credit score to be a lynchpin of personal identity formation. Far from encouraging hedonism, Marron concludes that consumer credit in the era of the credit score 'has as its corollary a more all-round, finely grained management of the self.'[35]

Recognizing the disciplinary function of credit is important because it corrects a common misconception about the culture of consumption. Consumer societies are often represented as endless carnivals of freedom for the desiring self, offering boundless opportunities for pleasure, comfort, self-expression, and fun. But viable cultural orders cannot be purely hedonic. In every society a balance must be maintained between releases and restraints. The history of saving and spending reveals how the culture of consumption has generated its own mechanisms of restraint. Consumer credit is one of them.

[34] See Chapter Five in Josh Lauer, 'The Good Consumer: Credit Reporting and the Invention of Financial Identity in the United States, 1840–1940' (PhD dissertation, University of Pennsylvania, 2008). Available from ProQuest: Paper AAI3328606 http://repository.upenn.edu/dissertations/AAI3328606. See also Josh Lauer, 'From Rumor to Written Record: Credit Reporting and the Invention of Financial Identity in Nineteenth-Century America', Technology and Culture, 49 (2008), 301–24.
[35] Donncha Marron, Consumer Credit in the United States: A Sociological Perspective from the 19th Century to the Present (Basingstoke: Palgrave Macmillan, 2009), 182–185, 193–210.

Thrift lives on in other ways, too. Saving pennies is one way to be thrifty, but it is not the only way to extract abundance from scarcity. Once time came to be counted as money, the desire to manage time with 'time-payment plans' proved irresistible. The new thrift imagined by Walter Post, defended by Seligman, and analysed by Lauer, Marron, and others simply extends the older thrift ethos from physical space—that is, from land, soil, resources, and money—to non-spatial time. But the dynamics of capitalism are not the only explanation for the development of time thrift: there is also the inexorable fact of human mortality. No one knows how much time they really have. Hence, the desire to be thrifty with time, to turn its deficits into abundance, is at bottom a desire to cheat death, sickness, and debility of their inevitable victories. Traditional thrift recommends waiting and doing without, but in its obsession with space it ignores a truth about time that everyone feels: there may not be enough time to wait, and the postponement of gratification has its own costs. Saving to buy a house, one has to pay rent. Saving to buy a wedding ring, lovers risk second thoughts. 'Buying on time' became popular because it removed the wait from wanting, producing surpluses in the present, whereas previously linear time was felt as a deprivation. Of course, time thrift, like traditional money thrift, can be mishandled to the point it becomes dysfunctional. Taken too far, penny-pinching becomes miserliness; too much buy now pay later yields a harried life. But this is just another reason to regard credit-based time thrift as a new variant of the thrift ethos. The sweet spot for thrift has never been easy to find.

Revisionist histories of thrift are finding traction with other scholars. In *Rebirth of a Nation: The Making of Modern America, 1877–1920*, Jackson Lears takes money matters very seriously in a dazzling account of the transformation of American yearnings. Lears discards the classic assumptions about monetization criticized by Viviana Zelizer, the suppositions that segregated money from human values, emotions, and relationships. On the contrary, Lears maintains, money was 'more than merely a means of keeping people afloat, more even than the key to new realms of pleasure; it was also a mechanism for reinventing the self.' For Lears, the connections between money management and the self become clearer once one gives up declension narratives charting a fall from saving to spending, from thrift to hedonism. In history, Lears reminds us, virtues are not replaced by their opposites but by new amalgamations of old ideas. What replaced Victorian thrift was not hedonism, he argues, but the ideal of 'personal efficiency'. According to Lears, ideals of selfhood promoting personal peak performance rest on a new understanding of the psyche. Older notions of thrift emerged from a psychology of scarcity that elevated concerns for the conservation of money and energy. But economic prosperity generated a psychology of abundance that reimagined thrift along the lines of a high-performance ethos. Under this new dispensation of the self, one needs more energy and discipline, not less.[36]

Still, newer understandings of thrift have not travelled very far beyond the history seminar. Social scientists continue to be influenced by the myth of lost economic virtue, often portraying the 'credit card nation' as a land of maxed-out, hyper-consumerist debtors deprived of an evaporating cultural heritage that once upon a time made household

---

[36] Jackson Lears, *Rebirth of a Nation: The Making of Modern America, 1877–1920*, (New York: HarperCollins, 2009), 56.

income an absolute limit on spending decisions.[37] Despite their historical naivety, some of the studies in this vein show there is life yet in narratives of decline. For example, Avner Offer, in *The Challenge of Affluence: Self-Control and Well-Being in the United States and Britain since 1950*, marshals a wealth of interesting data to argue that 'affluence breeds impatience, and impatience undermines well-being.' In other words, prosperity has undercut prudence. Humans have always struggled to control their 'myopia', Offer concedes, meaning that it is natural to prefer present satisfactions to future ones. But Offer believes that consumers in the past dealt with their myopia by exercising self-control and, when that was insufficient, by enlisting the aid of 'commitment technologies' enforced by third parties, such as savings clubs, payroll deduction plans, and, presumably, such obligations as home mortgages and automobile loans. What has happened since the Second World War, Offer argues, is that credit-driven prosperity has negated many of the older commitment technologies, because 'under affluence, the environment changes faster than commitment strategies can keep up with it.'[38]

While some of his conclusions have been challenged by fellow economic historians, Offer's fresh analysis and mobilization of data is impressive. Offer's distinction between internal disciplines and external restraints or 'commitment devices' are a useful organizing principle for future histories of saving and spending. But it is his thesis that should shake things up for historians of money matters. A reviewer commends the book for making 'the charge of immoral consumerism freshly devastating.' If so, then Offer should be read in conjunction with *The Morality of Spending*, in which Horowitz faults modern moralists who believe everything is going to the dogs for misunderstanding the social dimensions of consumer spending. It may be that Offer's bleak point of view on affluence needs leavening from cultural history. Cultural historians, if they know anything, know at least this: somewhere between nostalgia for the past and belief in the myth of progress, two things are always happening. Things are getting worse, like Offer says. And they are getting better.

COMPARATIVE SAVING AND SPENDING

The history of thrift is obviously not just an American story. As Sheldon Garon reminds us, organized, state-sponsored thrift promotion was an international movement of the nineteenth and much of the twentieth centuries.[39] So a second problem area for scholars

---

[37] See Robert D. Manning, *Credit Card Nation: The Consequences of America's Addiction to Credit* (Basic Books, 2001); Brett Williams, *Debt for Sale: A Social History of the Credit Trap* (University of Pennsylvania Press, 2005); Teresa Sullivan, Elizabeth Warren, and Jay Westbrook, *The Fragile Middle Class: Americans in Debt* (Yale University Press, 2001); George Ritzer, *Expressing America: A Critique of the Global Credit Card Society* (Pine Forge Press, 1995).

[38] Avner Offer, *The Challenge of Affluence: Self-Control and Well-Being in the United States and Britain since 1950* (Oxford: Oxford University Press, 2006), 1, 49, 74.

[39] Sheldon Garon, 'Savings-Promotion as Economic Knowledge: Transnational Insights from the Japanese Experience', in Martin Daunton and Frank Trentmann (eds.), *Worlds of Political Economy: Knowledge and Power in the Nineteenth and Twentieth Centuries* (Basingstoke: Palgrave Macmillan, 2004), 168.

of money matters raises questions inflected with a comparative perspective. Across time and place, how have patterns of saving and spending matched up transnationally? Another question follows: do developments in any one society, particularly the United States, foretell for others converging paths to a common future? Thus far, comparative studies have documented significant differences among consumer societies with regard to savings rates and people's willingness to incur debt. But the picture is complicated and firm conclusions are far from clear.

What do we know about cross-country patterns of saving and borrowing? A considerable literature on this subject has been built up by economic historians attempting to identify stable transnational differences. The policy orientation motivating this enquiry means that scholars have wanted to determine not just the what, but also the how and the why of variables affecting household decisions to save or to spend. Does the provision of a social safety net cause household savings to increase or decrease? Does it matter for savings rates what kind of social welfare is provided: means-tested or universal, health insurance or public pensions? What matters more to explain high levels of household debt—the provision of an old-age pension system, which reduces the need to save for retirement, or the availability of credit and a relaxation of strictures against borrowing? And so on. So far, on questions such as these there is little consensus. It calls to mind the old joke: ask three economists for an explanation, and you get four opinions. But some things are known.

Charles Horioka of Osaka University has summarized data on saving and indebtedness from the G7 nations (the world's seven major industrialized countries) for the recent past, 1985–2000. The first surprise is that for most of this period the world's most relentless borrowers were not the Americans but the Japanese, whose debts exceeded their disposable income in most of the years (in one year by 135 per cent!). During this period Americans were only average users of debt products with respect to the ratio of total liabilities to disposable income. As for the other countries, households in Canada and Great Britain out-borrowed those in the United States, while the French and Germans borrowed less than the Americans. Italian households borrowed least of all.

The overall picture changes when household assets (savings and property) are set against liabilities. Compared to Americans, the Japanese have much higher net wealth, as do the Italians and the British. Americans, Germans, and the French have relatively fewer assets to balance against their borrowing, and the Canadians have least of all. Thus, from 1985 to 2000, the Japanese borrowed the most, saved the most, and were the most financially healthy. Canadians borrowed a lot and possessed the least wealth to repay their debts, making them the least financially secure. The other countries traded places from year to year, somewhere in between.[40]

This summary of G7 data suggests how extraordinarily complicated it is to work with transnational comparisons. Also, when a clear picture does emerge, it often surprises.

---

[40] Charles Yuji Horioka, 'Japan and the Western Model: An Economist's View of Cultures of Household Finance' (working paper presented at the 'Cultures of Credit' workshop, German Historical Institute, Washington D.C., 5–6 February 2010).

Just as the history of thrift has been energized by the discovery that conventional wisdom on the subject is unreliable, comparative studies of saving and spending have likewise run up against deeply entrenched orthodoxies. For example, it is commonly believed that Americans are one-of-a-kind borrowers. At the same time, a popular theory of modernization presents the United States as an early adopter of economic innovations bound to be copied by other societies coming along behind. Thus the history of cross-national saving and spending challenges both a myth of American exceptionalism and a myth of Americanization. The trick has been to confront one version of conventional wisdom without supporting the other.

Going up against this opposed pair of orthodoxies, historians have contributed to a growing collection of country by country histories of saving, spending, and borrowing that challenges much of what people suppose. For example, everyone is aware that Asians, the Japanese in particular, are prolific savers. But Sheldon Garon has shown that Japanese households were not always thrifty; they had to be made that way. At the beginning of the twentieth century, Japanese saving rates trailed both the Americans and the British. To change this, the Japanese state and allied groups worked assiduously to shape the financial and moral habits of the people by sponsoring savings and frugality campaigns that underwrote Japan's military and nation-building projects. Even so, we should not get the wrong idea about the Japanese, urges Andrew Gordon. Despite their socialization into the ways of thrift, Gordon finds that consumer credit in Japan has a surprisingly long history of use. Indeed, in Gordon's telling, the history of consumer borrowing in Japan loosely parallels the development of consumer credit in the United States. It is striking to learn, for example, that E. R. A. Seligman's landmark 1927 defence of consumer credit was read and studied in Japan within months of its publication in the United States. In fact, the Tokyo Chamber of Commerce went even farther than Seligman in recognizing the disciplinary benefits of instalment credit, which they lauded as 'not only extremely useful in order to live a disciplined life, planning a monthly budget of expenses; it also raises standards of living by allowing purchases of goods otherwise too expensive.' By 1959, Japanese consumers were buying half their durable goods on time, an amount comparable to the American figure.[41]

Turning to Germany, the stereotype of the thrifty German has been unpacked by Jan Logemann, who wonders why during the 1950s and 1960s the bourgeois ideals of saving and restraint in consumption persisted in West Germany even though credit availability was rapidly expanding. Logemann finds an answer in a combination of reasons: public policy (the West German state prioritized rebuilding a shattered infrastructure over household consumption), retailers' apathy (they were not enthusiastic about following American models), bankers' caution (another stereotype, but perhaps a true one),

[41] Sheldon Garon, 'Fashioning a Culture of Diligence and Thrift: Savings and Frugality Campaigns in Japan, 1900–1031', in Sharon A. Minichiello (ed.), *Japan's Competing Modernities: Issues in Culture and Democracy, 1900–1930* (Honolulu: University of Hawaii Press, 1998), 312–34; Andrew Gordon, 'From Singer to Shinpan: Consumer Credit in Modern Japan', in Sheldon Garon and Patricia L. Maclachlan (eds.), *The Ambivalent Consumer: Questioning Consumption in East Asia And the West* (Ithaca, NY: Cornell University Press, 2006), 137–62.

and householders' attitudes (bourgeois Germans were reluctant to use financial tools associated with poverty and destitution). But the interesting thing noted by Logemann is that while German savings rates remained very high, the purpose of saving shifted from traditional thrift to a new ethos of 'saving to spend.' In other words, savings went from being an end in themselves to being an alternative means to consumption. Why? Logemann argues that the building of a social safety net meant that Germans did not have to save for retirement or illness, meaning they were free to save for consumption. Americans, by contrast, were not. Minimal social welfare in the United States meant that American households had to save for life's eventualities, making credit financing for consumption more tempting than in West Germany.[42]

Findings such as these move us beyond cultural stereotypes of thrifty Germans, improvident Americans, and timeless Asian values in which thrift has pride of place. But to question essentialist myths is not to say that peoples everywhere are all the same, approaching money matters as calculating, rational actors following an identical logic of self-interest. If this were true, then the history of transnational money management would reveal a single track to the future with the most advanced economic societies leading the way, providing support for the myth of Americanization.

However, this is not what historians have found. In the case of West Germany, so many older notions of money management lived on into the Wirtschaftswunder, Jan Logemann concludes that the United States must be considered less a model for others than an outlier. Logemann speaks for virtually all studies of transnational saving and spending when he writes:

> One can hardly speak of an 'Americanization' of West German consumer society with regard to credit. While some proponents of consumer credit in Germany did look to the United States as a model for 'modern' forms of consumption, many others rejected this model. As it moved toward affluence in the postwar decades, West Germany—like many other European and Asian countries—struck a balance between elements of modern consumption and older notions of restraint and saving.[43]

A key theme, then, in comparative histories of money management is distinctiveness. In Japan, Sheldon Garon has uncovered the same ambivalence described by Logemann: 'consumerist America loomed sometimes as a role model, but often as the undesirable Other.' Garon argues that Japanese thrift promotion campaigns, originally inspired by British models for encouraging saving, show that post-war Japan did not simply follow the American example. In the United States, the last year for National Thrift Week was 1966. In Great Britain, the government abolished the 62-year-old National Savings Committees in 1978. But in Japan, even with the slow economic growth since the 'lost decade' of the 1990s, institutions for promoting and investing household saving remain largely intact, despite criticism from American economists that the Japanese

---

[42] Jan Logemann, 'Different Paths to Mass Consumption: Consumer Credit in the United States and West Germany in the 1950s and '60s', *Journal of Social History*, 41 (2008), 525–59.

[43] Logemann, 'Different Paths to Mass Consumption', 546.

are over-savers.[44] Significantly, Garon's emphasis on distinctive Japanese patterns of consumption is echoed by Andrew Gordon, the historian whose studies of consumer credit in Japan reveal surprising interactions and parallels between Japan and the United States. Gordon, too, insists that Japanese borrowing has gone its own way. Historically, most consumer credit in Japan was single-purchase instalment credit. For years banks are restricted from offering revolving credit, and consumers were required to clear accounts monthly. Though the regulatory system was liberalized in 1992, and use of credit cards has skyrocketed, Japanese credit users continue to act as if the regulations are still in place. In 2007, 71 per cent of Japanese credit card bills were paid off in full at the end of the month, with most of the rest structured as traditional instalment debt. The number of Japanese who run a credit card balance in the American style is miniscule.[45]

In debates over coca-colonization, then, comparative histories of money management come down squarely on the side of those believing there has never been such a thing as *the* culture of consumption. Looking ahead, other questions beckon.

Chief among them is the brute problem of household finance and prosperity. Of all the problem areas in the history of consumption, few rival money matters for direct relevance to public policy. What is the proper balance between saving and spending? Are some kinds of indebtedness better than others for sustaining economic stability and growth? What variables explain why some societies and social groups save more than others? Where and how should the financial arts be taught? Questions such as these are too important to be left to economists and money management gurus, many of whom are influenced by nostalgia for a lost golden age of economic virtue. Historians have a role to play in public conversations about money matters, as Sheldon Garon has recognized. At the beginning of an essay on the production of what he calls 'economic knowledge', Garon asks, 'Could a government or groups, for instance, mould a "culture of thrift" that values high levels of savings while discouraging "excessive consumption"?' Garon answers affirmatively based on the case of Japan, ruefully observing that few Anglo-American economists today would consider such a question. Or historians, for that matter.

But maybe they should. In the wake of the global economic crisis of 2008–09, some are saying the time has come when people should expect less of economists and more of economic history. The fact is, for all their sophisticated models, economists were unable to see the crisis coming. Indeed, they contributed to it with flawed theories of market behaviour. Since the crisis, there has been little agreement among economists about its ultimate causes. In a widely circulated essay, economist Robert J. Shiller of Yale University admitted that the best explanation of the financial crisis is not a work of economic analysis at all, but a history: *This Time is Different: Eight Centuries of Financial*

---

[44] Sheldon Garon, 'Japan's Post-war "Consumer Revolution", or Striking a "Balance" Between Consumption and Saving', in John Brewer and Frank Trentmann (eds.), *Consuming Cultures, Global Perspectives: Historical Trajectories, Transnational Exchanges* (New York: Berg, 2006), 191; Garon, 'Savings-Promotion as Economic Knowledge', 184.

[45] Gordon, 'From Singer to Shinpan', 161–2.

Folly, by Carmen M. Reinhart and Kenneth S. Rogoff.[46] This book is almost entirely innocent of economic theory. If economists are going to pull back from mathematical models in order to make use of knowledge gleaned from psychology, neuroscience, sociology, and history, then the history of money matters should have something to contribute. In the real world, money matters are influenced by layers of emotion, social relationships, desire, and notions of the good. Here, mathematical models can only take one so far. Ultimately what is required is the kind of 'fuzzy logic' historians are trained to exercise, recognizing that the moral and social yearnings of human beings are not reducible to universal laws, but better captured in the richly braided narratives that are the hallmark of historical enquiry.

FINANCIALIZATION

Money management has always been hard. But over time it has also become complicated. This is a third problem area—in addition to thrift and comparative money management—that calls for historical analysis. In uneven ways, for some more than others, the era of monetization is yielding to a new age of financialization. Whereas people once counted their money on two hands, today money flows through people's lives in a bewildering variety of forms and the techniques for managing it grow ever more complex and difficult to master.

As a macroeconomic concept, financialization refers to a process whereby financial markets, institutions, and elites gain greater influence over economic policy and economic outcomes. There is less consensus about what financialization means at the level of households. This is less a problem for historians than an opportunity to help determine whether financialization is a faddish misstep corrected by the global meltdown of 2008, or a late stage of monetization, or a new era altogether. At bottom, the financialization of society refers to the elevation of financial management and Weber's 'calculating attitude' to the self's highest vocation. Under monetization, workers brought home a pay cheque and the problem was how to disburse it. In the era of financialization, wages and salaries are paid electronically through direct deposit and the problem is how to make income multiply though investments, speculations, and other strategic deployments. For the middle class, financialization imagines a reversal of the home as a haven from the heartless world of economic striving. Instead, it aims to remake private life on the model of a business. Labour is replaced by risk. Repose is given up for speed, connectivity, and access to information. Randy Martin sums up financialization this way: 'Without significant capital, people are being asked to think like capitalists.'[47]

[46] Robert Shiller, 'A Crisis of Understanding', *Project Syndicate—A World of Ideas*, March 12, 2010, <http://www.project-syndicate.org/commentary/shiller70/English>, accessed 15 April 2010.
[47] Randy Martin, *Financialization of Daily Life* (Philadelphia, PA: Temple University Press, 2002), 12.

Put the central question of this chapter—how have people managed money?—to friends and someone will answer wryly, 'Not well.' The mismanagement of money becomes a default narrative as financialization advances. The fact that failure is so readily acknowledged in this area suggests that the financial arts, like the liberal arts, have a high cognitive threshold. Also, rather high expectations for the will.

To see how much is expected of people in a financialized world—and to suggest something of the extent of the problem area available for historical exploration—consider the pedagogy of modern financial planning. The world's largest financial planning website is CNNMoney.com. Owned by the Fortune Money Group, a division of Time Warner, CNNMoney.com drew 10.8 million unique visitors per month in 2006. At CNNMoney.com, consumers are coached to replace common 'rules of dumb' with finer-grained economic intelligence on the myriads of money matters that confront all but the poorest. How does one estimate monthly mortgage payments? Calculate net worth? Determine how much insurance is enough? Ascertain when it makes sense to retire? For complex questions such as these, CNNMoney.com offers calculators to assist rational thought. If that is not enough, the financially befuddled can submit questions to an expert. Or, if the college years were wasted studying literature or history, one can go back to school for a remedial course in economics.

'Money 101' is CNNMoney.com's version of a college-level course in personal financial management. Offering 'a step by step guide to gaining control of your financial life', the syllabus guides financial novices through twenty-three lessons covering topics such as 'Making a budget', 'Controlling debt', and 'Investing in bonds.' Exams at the end of each unit test for comprehension of key terms, concepts, and strategies:

4. The capitalized cost of a lease is:
- The value of the car at the start of the lease.
- The value at lease end.
- The interest charge.
- How much value was lost over the lease term.

Hundreds of such questions define what it means to be economically literate in the early twenty-first century. What is the difference between a simple interest rate, a note rate, and the annual percentage rate (APR)? When does it make sense to consider a 401(k) versus a Roth IRA (USA), a bAV (Germany), a Japanese-version 401(K) (Japan), or to supplement one's BSP and S2P with a PA (UK)? In a financialized world the questions are not easy to answer or even, for the financially illiterate, to understand. But as Niall Ferguson points out in *The Ascent of Money*, 'The rewards for "getting it" have never been so immense. And the penalties for financial ignorance have never been so stiff.'[48]

Experts can be consulted but their knowledge comes with a price. 'How costly?' asks Avner Offer in *The Challenge of Affluence*: 'Well, precisely $149.95.' Offer refers to the cost of ESPlanner, a financial planning software program developed by Laurence J. Kotlikoff,

---

[48] Ferguson, *The Ascent of Money*, 14.

chair of the Department of Economics at Boston University, and Jagadeesh Gokhale, a former senior adviser to the Federal Reserve Bank of Cleveland. The economists' software uses 'a patented dynamic programming method' to maximize household living standards by applying the life cycle model of saving and consumption for which Franco Modigliani won the Nobel Prize for Economics in 1985. Patented computer programming? Dynamic methods? Inter-temporal consumption models? We have travelled a long way from the Micawber Principle. When did financial planning become rocket science? Must life really be an endless business school curriculum? Noting ESPlanner's high cognitive demands, Offer marvels, 'It is just a tool, willpower is not included. And what did people do before it was invented?'[49]

That is an excellent question. When historians can provide a complete answer, it will fill in an enormous blank spot in the history of consumer societies.

CONCLUSION

The history of the financial arts can be compared to a jigsaw puzzle that has been dumped on a table. A few border pieces are in place, but it is not yet clear how other pieces fit together. Readers should know that I have not described every piece of scholarship useful for understanding the history of saving and spending. Rather, to make sense of an inchoate topic, I have drawn attention to a few landmark enquiries worth emulating and pieced together several themes in which scholars are building on each other's work. Although work on money matters lags behind other key subjects in the history of consumption, the good news is that there are more scholarly pieces to the puzzle than I have been able to mention. Moreover, it is encouraging to note that interest in money matters appears to be growing. Several important monographs appeared too late to be included in this survey and more are on the way. It will not be long until the state of the field looks very different than it does now.

For the time being, though, the most important thing to know about the study of saving and spending is this: nearly forty years after Daniel Boorstin's pioneer treatment of consumer credit in the United States, we lack comprehensive accounts of how money came into people's lives, what they thought about it, how they managed it, and what monetization and financialization have meant for modern societies. The bold, synthetic treatments I am calling for, similar to what has been done with advertising and retailing, may have to wait until more forays have been made to explore slices of the problem. Thus far the lion's share of attention has been given to debt, credit, lending, and borrowing, but these topics are far from exhausted. Meanwhile, the history of thrift and comparative analyses of transnational patterns of saving and spending offer promising avenues for additional research. Greatly needed are histories examining financial literacy and the pedagogy of the financial arts, beginning with the literature of money

---

[49] Offer, *The Challenge of Affluence*, 52.

management advice and its reception by readers. Finally, we have much more to learn about how social identities have affected how money has been experienced, including variables such as gender, race, ethnicity, age, and religion. Here especially researchers will not start from ground zero since much useful information has already been uncovered by social historians working on problems apart from the history of consumption.

If there is any truth to the saying, 'money talks', then the finances of the household are a promising frontier of discovery. Without money, consumer societies are unimaginable. Without more histories of money matters, consumer society will be forever unfathomable.

BIBLIOGRAPHY

Brewer, John, and Porter, Roy (eds.), *Consumption and the World of Goods* (New York: Routledge, 1993).

Calder, Lendol, *Financing the American Dream: A Cultural History of Consumer Credit* (Princeton, NJ: Princeton University Press, 1999).

Finn, Margot, *The Character of Credit: Personal Debt in English Culture, 1740–1914* (Cambridge: Cambridge University Press, 2003).

Horowitz, Daniel, *The Morality of Spending: Attitudes toward the Consumer Society in America, 1875–1940* (Baltimore: Johns Hopkins University Press, 1985).

Johnson, Paul, *Saving and Spending: The Working-Class Economy in Britain, 1870–1939* (Oxford: Oxford University Press, 1985).

Logemann, Jan, 'Different Paths to Mass Consumption: Consumer Credit in the United States and West Germany during the 1950s and '60s', *Journal of Social History*, 41/3 (2008), 525–59.

McKendrick, Neil, Brewer, John, and Plumb, J. H., *The Birth of a Consumer Society: The Commercialization of Eighteenth-Century England* (Bloomington, IN: Indiana University Press, 1982).

Reinhart, Carmen M., and Rogoff, Kenneth S., *This Time is Different: Eight Centuries of Financial Folly* (Princeton: Princeton University Press, 2009).

Yates, Joshua J., and Hunter, James Davison (eds.), *Capitalism and Moral Order: A Social History of Thrift in America from the Puritans to the Present* (Oxford: Oxford University Press).

CHAPTER 19

....

EATING

....

ALAN WARDE

In this chapter I first review recent scholarship in the field of eating and then I use the lens of the globalization thesis to explore how goods, people, and ideas have come to circulate in ways that affect eating habits. I argue that scholarship on eating per se has been comparatively weak, and that recently, rather than being driven by the theoretical concerns of social science, the focus has been on popular anxieties about food.

CONSUMPTION AND FOOD STUDIES

....

Consumption is something of a chaotic concept. It has two semantic roots. In economics it indicates almost exclusively purchase in market exchange. Economists are concerned with 'demand' in the abstract. However, it has much wider application to how people use and dispose of items, a meaning emerging from Latin into early English with a negative connotation—to destroy, to waste, to use up. The two meanings, one signalling interest in the changing value of items being exchanged, the other the purposes to which goods and services might be put, exist in tension. By concentrating upon eating we signal a focus on the second of these meanings.

Among the copious research on consumption in the last couple of decades, historians and historical accounts have made some most trenchant and fruitful contributions (e.g. Brewer and Trentmann 2006; Cohen 2003; De Grazia 2005; Hilton 2000; Trentmann 2009). However, our improved understanding of the operation of, for want of a better concept, consumer culture has, despite its apparent potential, had limited impact on the analysis of eating.

Eating is worthy of study for many reasons, not least its current political visibility in the context of food scares and the 'crisis' of obesity, but also because it is a fine test bed for analytic consideration of social change. Substantively, the literature on food is deeply contradictory. On the one hand, it is believed that eating habits are among the most resistant to change: culinary traditions remain recognizable over centuries (Mennell 1985; Kjaernes 2001), childhood tastes persist (Counihan 2004), and food behaviours are among the last to be abandoned by migrants (Gabaccia 1998). On the other hand, radical transformations of food practices, usually considered retrograde, are repeatedly announced; individualization, the demise of the family meal, the disintegration of valued national cuisines, and the emergence of new hazards are key issues which even the most sceptical reviewers of food trends must consider seriously (Ascher 2005; Ashley et al. 2004; Poulain 2002b). Disagreement results partly simply from the multiplicity of dimensions along which food behaviour can change, but also from restricted data sources and inadequate methods of analysis.

The social scientific study of food is highly fragmented. It is served by many disciplines (anthropology, economics and political economy, psychology, sociology, cultural, and literary studies). As yet, no combination of them provides a persuasive integrative framework for understanding eating. Wilk (2004), addressing the thorny problem of definition of consumption through the examination of the metaphors used to describe it, postulated that 'the more an act is like eating, the more it seems like real consumption'. If eating is 'the prototype' of consumption, then it is disappointing how little the study of eating has advanced theoretical understanding of consumption. Belasco (2002: 6), seeking to explain the low academic status of food studies, observes that social scientists usually study food not for its own sake but in response to other research agendas. In addition, the outputs of medical sciences and marketing often shape the popular understanding more than do social sciences. Moreover, eating is a topic upon which professional food writers have probably had more impact than academic scholars and for them theory building and the application of theory is not a priority.

Studies addressing national or regional histories comprise the most prominent form of scholarship on eating. Some of these analyses are magnificent but are not necessarily well equipped to advance general understanding (e.g. Anderson 1988; Burnett 1989, 2004; Capatti and Montanari 2003; Levenstein 1988, 1993). Panoramic global accounts may be more ambitious, but are necessarily schematic and short on the detailed evidence with which to make systematic comparisons (e.g. Flandrin and Montanari 1996; Tannahill 1988).

Some works from the social sciences have grand theoretical ambitions. Poulain (2002a: 190) helpfully maps approaches to eating along two dimensions. The first contrasts universalist with developmental explanations. Some scholars try to account for the role of food anywhere and everywhere, an approach which is more common in anthropology, though other disciplines offer accounts which describe the functions that eating plays in human societies. Of the most widely celebrated theorists, Levi-Strauss (1965) and Douglas (1984) tend to the pole of invariance, while Elias (1969[1939]), Harris (1985), Mennell (1985), and Goody (1982) focus on historical processes generating variation. Poulain's second dimension concerns the degree to which the autonomy of the social is posited, with Bourdieu (1984) and Grignon (1993) examplars of sociological accounts of consumption, as opposed to a focus on individuals, for example Fischler (1980). When the social theories in use are classified by social scientists reviewing the scope of the field (e.g. Mennell et al. 1993; McIntosh,1996), it is surprising how few of the potentially relevant alternative theoretical currents in social sciences are represented.

Early studies of food consumption were narrow in focus. Empirical research was for a very long time simply a study of whether people got enough, or enough of the right kinds, of food to remain healthy. Tied to policy issues of poverty and inequality, the social circumstances of malnutrition were the primary focus of study. In addition, economists were interested in the effects of industrialization or affluence on patterns of spending, with corroboration of Engel's Law being the primary focus. Anthropologists found in food habits and rituals important sources of cultural meaning and diversity which revealed patterns of social organization (Douglas 1984). Sociologists showed some interest in the social arrangement of the meal as an institution (Simmel 1994 {1910]) for the drawing of the boundaries of sociability and, increasingly, as a means of social differentiation.

The expansion of social scientific research in the last third of the twentieth century produced a new set of themes and theoretical considerations. Structuralist anthropology and semiotics created new understandings and approaches to the symbolic significance of eating; the culinary triangle and a semiotic deconstruction of steak and chips were noteworthy contributions (Levi-Strauss 1965; Barthes 1993). Political economy, if somewhat hampered by the economistic assumptions of neo-Marxism, generated work which had residual effects on the understanding of consumption, with the Regulation School (Aglietta 1979) at one pole, and Mintz's *Sweetness and Power* (1985) at the other. Mintz's examination of the integral connection of production and consumption in the history of the spread of sugar remains a beacon of synthetic analysis. Materialist accounts were supplemented by studies like Mennell's *All Manners of Food* (1985), an application of Elias's theory of the civilizing process which contrasted eating habits in Britain and France since the Middle Ages. In addition, a magnificent section in Bourdieu's *Distinction* (1984 [1979]) documented the role of eating in symbolizing social hierarchy in Paris and Lille. These were major pioneering works in the sociological and developmentalist paradigms.

After the mid-1980s, however, few studies exhibited the equivalent level of vision or innovation. A burgeoning literature on food included an increasing number of empirical studies. But with respect to consumption, this normal science seemed neither to clarify and consolidate existing positions, nor to create conceptual integration and new syntheses. The political economy of the agro-food industry continued to make the most progress, using versions of a theory of the food chain, but without saying much explicitly about the stage of eating (see below). The other major field of activity arose from 'the cultural turn' of the social sciences, which begat cultural studies, postmodernism and cultural economy. Drawing flexibly on neo-Marxist, semiotic, and mass communications theories, it dealt with some, though a limited range, of issues associated with the symbolic meanings of foodstuffs. Increasingly revolving around the concept of identity, the association between nation, ethnic group, and food choice was examined for the ways in which eating expressed and represented personal and group belonging. The preferred and expanding topics came to be personal and ethnic identity, nation-building and national identity, food scares, eating out, consumer movements, and migration, all of which were wrapped up more or less in the phenomenon of globalization. As a result, attention shifted away from famines, food riots, Engel's Law, poverty, credit and debt, etiquette, meals and class differences. Emphasis shifted from social relations and resources to culinary cultures. Arguably, the new writings made limited theoretical progress and added comparatively little to pre-existing theoretical understandings.

In most respects, recent developments in food studies have been driven less by the logic of theoretical inquiry than by a mission to respond to public anxieties about food consumption. These anxieties may be put into three categories. The first concerns the deteriorating quality of foodstuffs arising from fears about the system of industrial manufacture of food—additives, chemical fertilizers, and new breeding techniques, for example. This concern is frequently addressed through the risk society thesis (see Beck 1992), supplemented by accounts from political economy focusing on the role of profit in the food chain (e.g. Nestle 2006). Second, there are worries about the destructuring of meal arrangements. The meal, central to sociological accounts of eating (Wood 1995), has been thought to be under assault from the individualizing potential of convenience foods and informalization processes apparent since the 1960s. In Britain this is symbolized by the decline of the family meal and typically explained by time pressure (Southerton 2003). The third issue involves a crisis of meaning, most memorably captured by Fischler's (1980) neologism, 'gastro-anomie', which refers to an escalating and potentially unmanageable choice among wide varieties of available foods. Once there is no compulsion to eat from a single, established, validated, or traditional menu then the practical and aesthetic rationale for selection becomes, it is argued, highly troubling.

In the last decade the major foci of research have been products and production, and the cultural consequences of globalization. The former produced commodity biographies and additional work on the political economy of the agro-food system. The latter produced studies of the mobility of people and ideas, and the consequences for self-identity, cuisine, and textual (and visual) representations of eating.

EATING IN THE ERA OF GLOBALIZATION

Globalization has driven much of the social scientific research over the last decade (see Inglis and Gimlin 2010; Nuetzenadel and Trentmann 2008). An often confusing term, the nature of the process has aroused much controversy. Theoretically, the nature of globalization is usefully captured by Appadurai (1990, 1996) who offered an early and effective appreciation of the multi-dimensional aspects of globalization which identified five types of 'flow' in the contemporary world: people, money, messages, ideas, and commands. I follow Appadurai (1990, 1996) by taking globalization in its current phase to mean that more social entities are moving more frequently, further and faster than before, with consequences for networks of interaction and social relations in different places across the world. This is not inconsistent with Mintz's (2008) observation that the transportation of foodstuffs across state boundaries, including specifically into Europe, has occurred continuously over hundreds of years, from the transporting of new plants, to the trading of spices, through the extraction of staples from colonies overseas, to the integrated transnational regime of the industrialized food corporations of today. As Nuetzenadel and Trentmann (2008: 4) argue, putting a date on the beginning of globalization is controversial, and they suggest a multiple, rather than a singular, process. In the following sections I therefore consider, in turn, flows of things, people, and ideas, reflecting the operation of global institutions of economy, politics, and mass communication.

Moving Things

Recent research has concentrated, perhaps excessively, on 'things'. One of the main developments in the study of consumption has been the material culture approach (see *Journal of Material Culture*; Miller 1998). In food studies the product biography has become de rigeur. And while by no means inevitable (witness Mintz 1985), product biographies often pay little attention to consumption and eating. Associated with the political economy approaches of agro-food studies, extensive use is made of the metaphor of a chain to account for the process of production of food in modern societies. Accounts of the global commodity chain, the commodity system, and systems of provision have gradually refined a comparatively simple Marxist account of the 1970s. While recognizing the importance of consumption, the chain being organized for the purpose of providing foods to sell to an end consumer, most nevertheless account for consumption in terms of production. The most recent generation of scholars working out of political economy and commodity chain perspectives find this problematic and have issued calls for better understanding of processes of consumption and more effective theoretical analysis of the connections between production and consumption (e.g. Goodman and DuPuis 2002).

For two decades sociology and anthropology have devoted much energy towards developing frameworks for understanding the social functions and uses of consumption (compare: Lury 1996; Miller 1995; Sassatelli 2007). Consumption has been shown to play many roles including classifying people, relating people to goods, anticipating the future, and pursuing pleasures. Cultural studies, for its part, has emphasized especially the extension of aesthetic value into new spheres of everyday life through consumption, manifest as expression of personal identity and the proliferation of style. A great deal is now known about how people appropriate commodities as part of the conduct of their everyday life. But it is an increasingly repeated criticism that this has often resulted in a divorce between production and consumption no less damaging than that of earlier economistic accounts. One of the more important insights from anthropologists like Appadurai (1986) and Kopytoff (1986) is that goods produced as commodities do not necessarily retain their commodity status, as they are singularized through use. Commodity status is a temporary condition which might be superseded as products enter a different domain or mode of provision, as for example with domestic food preparation or food aid.

The commodity biography, often also production-centred, became a very common approach (e.g. Cook 2004; Dixon 2002; Freidberg 2004; Schivelbusch 1993).The product focus permits the simultaneous grasp of material, biological, economic, social, and symbolic aspects of particular foodstuffs. Product biographies are particularly good at capturing the fact that foodstuffs have biological and chemical properties, and that there is a material substructure (a very complex one in the contemporary world) to the availability of any of the many products that we expect to find in the supermarket. For example, Harvey et al. (2002) trace human engagement with the tomato, through processes of domestication, fabrication, and modification, which resulted throughout the twentieth century in its continual biological, economic, and social transformation. They capture the specific material properties of tomatoes, the means of their economic exploitation, and their changing culinary role. Focus on products can also lead to proper appreciation of the role of technological innovation in the formation of contemporary dietary regimes. Freidberg's *Fresh: A Perishable History* (2009) is a study of food preservation and transportation during the industrial era in the USA. She shows that what counts as being 'fresh' changes over time, and 'that freshness depends less on time or distance than upon the technology that protects it' (2009: 5). Refrigeration has affected the production and distribution of most categories of food—meat, fruit, eggs, milk, vegetables, and fish—with variable consequences for strategies for defining and representing the items as 'fresh'. Since people now mostly prefer not to think of their food as being anything but fresh, because of its association with the good and the natural, the ways in which food is processed have often been a matter of public concern. Food scares offer prominent examples of the controversies that Beck (1992) found typical of the 'risk society', where people are aware of the uncomfortable fact that many modern hazards are the consequence of scientific and technological transformation of natural processes.

MOVING PEOPLE

If movement of goods is one important impetus to the transformation of eating habits, the movement of people is another. Relocation affects what is eaten where, and with whom. To the extent that labour power is a commodity, then the geographical movements of workers are effects of commodification in capitalist societies. However, people primarily, though not simply, migrate in search of better economic opportunities. As Diner (2001) shows, Italians, severely restricted in the availability of foodstuffs by their social class system, left for the USA in the late nineteenth and early twentieth centuries specifically because food was known to be abundant there. Italians typically were more concerned with eating than other migrant groups and devoted a greater proportion of their income to it.

International Migration

The effects of population movements on tastes and habits provide an interesting natural experiment for how food behaviour changes. Research around globalization has prioritized studies of international migration. Two issues have been closely examined; the first concerns how migrants adapt to their new environments, while the second considers their impact on the eating habits of the host population.

Migrants very often go to great lengths to get access to the foods of their homeland, foods which they know and like. Recent studies have compared the eating habits of migrants in their country of origin with the behaviours adopted in the country of reception (e.g. Diner 2001; Ray 2004). The processes of adaptation of first generation migrants have some common features. They initially attempt to replicate the tastes and eating habits of the country of origin—if in the case of Italians in the USA, according to Diner, the tastes and habits of the rich rather than the basic diet of the peasantry and working classes to which they had themselves been accustomed. This involves sometimes small-scale domestic production, usually the setting up of businesses to import favoured foodstuffs which are locally unavailable, and the selling of prepared meals through small catering outlets (e.g. Panayi 2008, for Britain; Diner 2001, and Ray 2004 for the USA). The resulting culinary practice is often a novel hybrid, a compromise arising from the insecurity of supply of the products that were typical of home.

Unintended consequences also arise for the host society, for contact with the 'exotic' raises questions of the identity of the familiar, and facilitates syncretic effects of combination. Gabaccia (1998), in a study of successive migrations to the USA since the colonial era focusing on culinary practice in five cities in different regions of the USA, contests the view that it is only recently that culinary eclecticism and consumer individualism have replaced the conservative and ethnically rigid eating habits of the past. Rather, the sale of new ethnic specialities on the wider American food market has been repeated regularly, as waves of small immigrant entrepreneurs in food production and marketing sought to expand their businesses beyond a given enclave. This has characterized American food practice for at least three centuries. Such specialities lose their ethnic specificity as they are adapted to popular taste and incorporated into a creolized national culinary field. This happens almost automatically once they are taken up by large corporations, which is a major part of the story of the twentieth century. She concludes that, 'Americans have no single national cuisine. But we do have a common culinary culture. What unites American eaters culturally is how we eat, not what we eat. As eaters, all Americans mingle the culinary traditions of many regions and cultures within ourselves.' (Gabaccia 1998: 225–6) Hers may be a rather optimistic view (cf. Mintz, 2001). Nevertheless, there are many examples of national cuisine emerging through syncretic and fortuitous processes, one of the best accounts of which is Wilk's (2006) study of the small Central American state of Belize.

Wilk brings refreshing analytic clarity to issues about how and when global forces impact upon local cuisine. He shows that Belize has been subject to such influences since the sixteenth century, as contact with Europeans was mediated first by pirates, then by slaves and slave owners, subsequently by colonial administrators, and most recently by tourists. Each had characteristic effects on diet, but not ones which would support the common conviction 'that colonialization and globalization are forces for homogeniza-tion' or of 'the domination of local cultures by modernization and globalization' (Wilk, 2006:10). While not a matter of effortless mixing of ingredients, tastes, and techniques, as implied by the term 'creolization', Wilk identifies many of the processes which have resulted in the current diversity of cuisine in Belize. Emphasizing that tourism is one force which encourages diversity, recent history saw the incorporation of imported foods and tastes alongside an appreciation of the local specialities that international tourists from rich countries expect to experience as authentic to the locale. There is, he says, 'no incompatibility between being global and being local' (Wilk 2006: 9).

Suburbanization

If being geographically mobile affects what one eats, it also affects whom one eats with. While recently more attention has been paid to international movements, mobility of native populations within countries remains equally important. Opportunities for food consumption change when moving house or going on holiday. Urbanization, and subse-quently suburbanization, has everywhere had major impacts. Moving to the suburbs effected major changes in shopping, provisioning, cooking, and thus eating. Brought to light by feminist scholars in the 1980s, the changing character of domestic life, and its pri-vatization in nuclear family households, clearly impacted upon eating. Household organ-ization and domestic routines were transformed as new technologies, suitably miniaturized for small households, and new part-prepared foods were introduced, partly in response to demand from the middle classes who could no longer employ domestic servants (e.g. Cowan 1983). Suburbanization entailed new modern infrastructures, a much increased reliance on the automobile for shopping and, critically for the practice of eating, much less frequent return to home for midday meals for those in employment.

Eating has to be repeated frequently, and in the past was often embedded in fixed annual, weekly, and daily routines. In many contexts meals perform the function of a Zeitgeber, a marker of the phases of the day. Institutions—monasteries, military bar-racks, factories, and schools—punctuate the day regularly with meal breaks (Zerubavel 1985 [1981]). But similar principles also operate in less formal contexts. Domestic pat-terns are mostly structured by employment obligations which then require tempering to household and family logics (Grignon 1993). Time-use studies show that the patterns vary by country. For example, in Spain workers still take long and simultaneous lunch breaks which may accommodate a siesta; the French typically spend less time at lunch, though they mostly eat at the same hour; while Britons and Americans eat more irregu-larly and often at their desks or in their cars (Warde et al. 2007). As economies become more flexible in their working hours, with more shift-work now reflecting the '24/7' arrangements of service industries, opportunities for household members to coordinate their schedules in order to eat together diminish (Southerton 2003).

The meal is perhaps the principal concept for the sociological understanding of eating (Wood 1995). It is a major institution of social organization, for families and for societies. Meals can be, and usually are, highly rule-governed, with rules covering, to different degrees, what, where, when, with whom, how, and why we eat. Rules thus orchestrate social interactions and underpin judgments about affect and respect. Conduct repeatedly performed and reproduced generates relationships, bonds, commitments, understandings, and rationales for practices. The sociological and anthropological literature demonstrates trenchantly the symbolic role of interactions around the supply and consumption of food in nuclear family households. As Marjorie DeVault in *Feeding the Family* (1991) most persuasively demonstrated, the care and love expressed in the production of meals, mostly by women, is a major source of family cohesion. This role for the meal is a product of the consolidation and diffusion of the ideals of the bourgeois family in the nineteenth century, where the family, and mothers especially, were seen as bulwarks against social disorder (Kaufmann 2005). The family meal is simultaneously a source of patriarchal domination, inter-generational conflict, and a symbol of care, love, bonding, and solidarity.

Greater irregularity in meal patterns (snacking, fast food, skipping meals) has become a source of anxiety lest valued social relationships are undermined. The UK has seen repeated moral panics about the collapse of the family meal. Many investigations have been conducted since the 1970s to estimate the extent and character of that collapse. The social scientific consensus is, as Anne Murcott (1997) neatly demonstrated, that there is rather little evidence of recent collapse, but a long history back into the nineteenth century of fears of imminent collapse. In France, the dismantling of the pattern of sharing domestic meals has also attracted substantial social scientific attention since the 1970s, though for somewhat different reasons. Whereas in Britain the anxiety is primarily about the fragility of marriage and instability of the family, in France the problem is posed more as one of the destructuration of the meal as an institution, with negative consequences for culinary traditions or the sociable pleasures of eating (Poulain 2002b; Ascher 2005). Explanations are often couched in terms of individualization, the instantiation of the ideology of consumer choice and the declining force of collective conventions (Ascher 2005: 48–50). Others stress underlying trends like greater participation of women in the labour market and time pressure. Nevertheless, the ideal that family members should eat together regularly at home seems as strong as ever (Marshall and Anderson 2002; Poulain 2002a).

Another reason for concern with meal patterns is their influence on diet. Kristensen and Holm (2006), in a qualitative study in Denmark, show that the temporal organization of meals directly affects not only types of food consumed, but even the feeling of being satisfied. There is no biological, geographical, or commercial explanation for why, for instance, Danes and Norwegians eat cold lunches while Swedes and Finns eat hot food in the middle of the day (Kjaernes 2001). Rather, it would seem that there are powerful conventions, nationally variable, which associate particular foods with temporally (and spatially) defined eating events. How much and what people eat depends upon their definition of the occasion and local conventions of appropriateness.

THE MEETING OF GOODS AND PEOPLE

While some people have eaten away from home in all societies, this usually occurred out of necessity. Now, however, eating out is increasingly important to the agro-food system because it is no longer just a side effect of working at a distance from home, but one of the most popular of contemporary leisure activities. At least in America and Europe, customers are spending more of their time, and more of their food budgets, in restaurants than ever before (Warde et al. 2007). No longer is paying to dine out for pleasure the preserve of a small rich minority, it is increasingly common to all strata of the population (Burnett 2004). It is subject to ever more publicity, as the merits of chefs, restaurants, dishes, and cuisines are widely discussed by the cultural intermediaries of television, magazines, and guidebooks.

There is limited research on eating out and in general it suffers from the same deficiencies as that on the food system more generally; the better part is about production, on the orchestration of activities of business units, and on labour conditions (e.g. Fine 1995, Leidner 1993). Indeed, arguably the main source of information about eating out is generated as market research to serve the interests of producers of food; for there is no doubt that the distributors, and increasingly the producers, think about the end consumer in a more calculated and purposive manner than in the past. There is some rudimentary understanding of socio-demographic and psychographic structural variation and some historical interpretation of what has appeared on menus (e.g. Driver 1983; Jacobs and Scholliers 2003), but little theoretical guidance on the activities and experiences involved (but see Finkelstein 1989; Warde and Martens 2000).

From the point of view of 'consumers', eating out involves spending time and money, mostly on a highly discretionary basis (for there are alternative modes of provision), in an activity offering variation across sites, formats, time slots, styles of cuisine, symbolically identifiable and valorized dishes, companions, prices, and much else. Ascher (2005) finds it a prototypical and emblematic activity of a burgeoning consumer culture, a domain ripe for exploring some of the tendencies diagnosed by contemporary social theory as typical of the cultural trajectory of high modernity or postmodernity (see also Beriss and Sutton 2007). Individuals can choose among very many restaurants, and then select from menus according to their personal preferences. These features should not, however, be overemphasized for they co-exist with many constraints, including expense, socially learned tastes, the preferences of companions, the nature and reason for the event. In addition, tastes are differentiated along lines of gender, class, education, and generation (Warde and Martens 2000). But that is not to deny the immense variety of the provision, as the cuisines of the world are served up nearby for urban populations in rich countries. Despite national variations, people in these societies are making increasing use of restaurants (Cheng et al. 2007) and devoting more of their food expenditure to eating out. In the USA about half of all food dollars go to the catering trade, compared with 30 per cent in the UK (Stewart et al. 2004; Warde et al. 2007).

Restaurants expose many of their customers to new and different dishes and cuisines. Cafés, restaurants and takeaway shops have been crucial in the adaptation and the incorporation of new foods (and retention of old ones). Consider the rapid acceptance of 'ethnic' food in Britain from the 1970s. This is partly a consequence of the entrepreneurial endeavours of immigrants and the fact that the catering trades are a major source of employment for migrant workers (Panayi 2008; Trubek 2000). Imperial connections and preferred destinations of migrants influence the spread of particular cuisines and new tastes. Perhaps the mobility occasioned by tourism alters the culinary landscape; Ray (2008) argues that mass holidays taught visitors tastes for foreign food, and 'gastro-tourism' has become an industrial niche market. However, while in the UK change coincided with the growth of international tourism as the price of air travel fell, holiday destinations do not correspond to favourite cuisines; for example, Great Britain is a major tourist destination but there is no indication that Europeans or Asians acquire a fondness for British cuisine which they seek to reproduce upon their return home. Nevertheless, even the most conservative of eaters, and those who eat out rarely, cannot avoid exposure to a wide range of ideas about novel items that might be highly palatable and which are increasingly available courtesy of the global economy.

MOVING IDEAS

The circulation of ideas about what is good to eat is another important impetus to the persistence and reformulation of eating habits. The amount of information in circulation is now enormous. The nature of recommendations varies from positive injunctions about what is good for you, or what is the best available, to less insistent suggestions about what it might be interesting to try on occasion. Much emanates from government agencies proffering nutritional advice, and large food corporations promoting products through marketing campaigns. It is often remarked that such messages convey changing and often contradictory advice about what to eat. Other sources include a long tradition of gastronomy, writing explicitly about the qualities of food and the 'art' of eating, but also cookery books, diet books, newspapers, magazines, restaurant guides, not to mention television and the internet, which provide a vast amount of information and advice. In addition, people learn as much from each other, informally through contacts with family, neighbours, and friends, and in a more organized manner when they join social movements and organizations. In the next sub-sections I deal with accounts of how such vehicles for the circulation of ideas represent and influence eating behaviour.

Eating Texts: Gastronomy and Restaurant Guides

The third current crisis, 'gastro-anomie', diagnoses a lack of certainty about what it is most appropriate to eat. This was much less of a problem a few decades ago because of the longstanding international reputation in the West for the excellence of French haute cuisine. International elites shared a conviction that the techniques and tastes of France set a universal culinary standard. Gastronomy, a minority interest, is the work of enthusiasts and connoisseurs; arguably a specifically French pursuit (Poulain 2002a), it has had an extensive effect upon what people think is good to eat. Gastronomy thrived in France partly because Paris was the source of the modern restaurant (Spang 2000). From the first observers and commentators, like Grimod de la Reynière and Brillat-Savarin, writing about restaurant provision has had an impact on the definition of good taste. Indeed, Ferguson (2004) argues that haute cuisine was established as much because of the circulation of ideas in France than as an effect of the availability of restaurants, or the inherent quality of products or cooking. She stresses the role of writing, describing a copious literary mode, part gastronomic, part didactic, resulting in a shared sense of culinary tradition, one derived from the practice of the restaurant rather than the household.

Gastronomy emphasizes the aesthetic dimension of eating, and aestheticization is frequently declared to be a corollary of globalization. In recent years periodicals focusing on gastronomy and gourmet dining have proliferated, along with reviews in newspapers and specialized restaurant guides, their analysis providing evidence of changing patterns of eating out (e.g. Rao et al. 2005; Ray 2008; Warde 2009b). The restaurant guide is the cultural intermediary par excellence; an artefact, itself a commercial product in a competitive market, it performs a service of conveying strategic and symbolic messages between producer and consumer. Besides fulfilling a regulatory function in relation to a particular market, the restaurant guide acts as a tool of recommendation for consumers and plays a key part in establishing relevant ideas about boundaries and identities.

For many years Michelin has published the most influential guides to food excellence. Karpik (2000) provides a very instructive account to the way in which the Michelin *Red Guide* developed; initially primarily a guide to the location of garages in the French countryside for motorists, it became the definitive authority on superior cooking. Its professional inspectorate, its secrecy about its procedures and criteria, and the limited information that the guides give about menus in chosen restaurants makes it an intriguing phenomenon whose fortunes reveal cultural change. Whereas Michelin could have been sure of its standards in the 1950s, a raft of innovative developments has induced uncertainty and allowed variety to flourish. Nouvelle cuisine represented the earliest major challenge to the dominance of haute cuisine. Not insignificantly, it was championed by a competing guide, *Gault Millau*, which sought to establish new, alternative culinary principles (Rao et al. 2003; Johnston and Baumann 2007). Many subsequent challenges emerged as the catering industries diversified, especially by incorporating tastes and techniques from other parts of the world. Currently, inventive chefs everywhere experiment with hybrid mixtures of ingredients, flavours, and textures that preclude attempts to establish authoritative national cuisines or any single standard of excellence. The eclecticism which Gabaccia (1998) attributed to the USA has become a feature of professional cooking in many countries, and regular visitors to restaurants typically experience a plurality of cuisines (Warde 2009a).

Eating Texts: Cookery Books

If gastronomic texts and restaurant critics circulated ideas about how to eat out, it was cookery books, often supported by mass circulation women's magazines, which framed domestic tastes. A vast amount of what we know about eating in the past arises from the inspection of recipe books. As Humble in her excellent *Culinary Pleasures* (2005) acknowledges, because they may never be used for cooking and because they are addressed to different sections of the population, they are potentially misleading about historical differences in practice. Ironically, recipe books provide very sound evidence about many things, but not about what people actually ate or cooked.

To date, recipe books have proved useful means of identifying the adoption of new technologies; Humble (2005) noted that the diffusion of the blender and the freezer can be dated by reference to them. They also record the availability of new foods and ingredients; Humble observed that a 1970s book referring to the avocado 'pear' indicated lack of familiarity with it in British kitchens. She also charted changing class relations through references to the management of home, as instructions shift from how to direct the cook to how to do the cooking. Interestingly, Wansink (2006) examined recipes for the same dishes in a popular multi-edition American cookbook to show that portion sizes had increased very substantially since the 1930s, which may explain in part the current obesity epidemic.

Cookery books have been used extensively for studies of national identity and nation-building, and of the reception of ethnic cuisines. Appadurai (1988) makes a good case for the idea of nationhood in India having been cemented among the middle class through construction of a national cuisine, though the process does not seem to have been the same in Italy (Capatti and Montanari 2003). Indeed, it was arguably less the unification of Italy and more the work of expatriates in the USA in the late nineteenth and early twentieth century that created an identity for Italian cuisine.

Panayi argues that the idea of national cuisines is a relatively recent one. His extensive survey of cookery books published in England since the mid-nineteenth century problematizes the notion of 'British' food, avowing that although some authors tried to celebrate the specificity of British or English cookery, most took little notice of the national associations of recipes. It was not until the 1950s that cookery books presenting the cuisines of other nations become commonplace, and only then did 'foods develop nationalities' (Panayi 2008: 36). For while recipes have long circulated internationally, it was only after the Second World War that repertoires of dishes came to be classified by their nationality, this being a precondition for the contemporary 'situation where "multicultural" food is the norm' (Ibid.: 216). Books with recipes specifically and exclusively of French, Italian, Middle Eastern, and Chinese food began to be published. In partial reaction, books on British cookery emerged. Moehring (2008) documented a similar process and chronology in Germany.

Finally, when it comes to formation, confirmation, and corroboration of what is good to eat, word of mouth remains a primary source of the circulation of ideas. While not everyone continues to like the foods of their childhoods, they rarely forget them and usually use their memories meaningfully to order their adult dietary habits. Generations of women have typically learned from their mothers how to cook, which, along with tastes established in childhood, provides a mechanism for the perpetuation of communal culinary traditions and norms (Sutton 2006). But collective, public mobilizations of eaters, often seeking change, also shape eating. Consumer associations, vegetarian societies, the Slow Food Movement, Weight Watchers, and the like, provide contexts for personal interaction directed towards establishing shared definitions of good food. Popular movements seeking to overcome the anonymity of economic exchange—currently symbolized by local food and farmers' markets—harmonize with action to achieve a sustainable diet in the face of climate change and environmental degradation (Belasco 2006). To the extent that consumption becomes more politicized—as repeated invocation of the role of the consumer-citizen implies (e.g. Cohen 2003)—collective action will supply fresh impulse for the modification of eating habits. Research on social movements around food, mostly arising from popular anxieties, delivers an understanding of forces for change.

AGENDA

Scholars should be cautious about their evidence and the examination of promotional texts should not be overdone. The extent to which people act in accordance with such advice, even when it is more or less unanimous, as for example with the broad current international consensus on the basics of human nutrition, is highly variable. For example, the vast majority of Britons know about the value of eating fruit and vegetables and avoiding too much sugar, salt, and fat, but nevertheless many of them do not follow the prescribed guidelines. The disjunction between messages sent and messages received means that we cannot predict or explain actions on the basis of textual material. Nonetheless, much has been learned by social scientists about eating from what is written about food. Varying from country to country, texts entrench the global as much as they grasp the local, and in a potentially confusing world, cultural intermediation is crucial.

Analysis of eating is perhaps best framed as a matter of understanding the formation, persistence, and change of habits (Ilmonen 2001). In my view, three avenues of research could be especially fruitful. First, we should consider applying a broader range of social scientific theories specifically to eating. Rare forays by exponents of theoretical traditions like symbolic interactionism, actor network theory (e.g. Cochoy 2007), ethnomethodology (e.g. Teil and Hennion 2004), conventions theory (e.g. Murdoch and Miele, 2004), and practice theory (e.g. Warde, 2004) show promise. Of these, theories of practice offer particularly attractive features. Their appeal for the analysis of consumption is that they are neither individualist nor holist. They portray social organization as something other than individuals making decisions, emphasizing instead the role of routine, on the one hand, and emotion, embodiment, and collective solidarities on the other. They insist on giving equal consideration to doings and sayings. Practice theories also accord techniques, technology, and infrastructure an important place, one which is not exactly captured in product biographies. Eating can be viewed through such a lens because, while consumption of food—its sequence, duration, structure of meals, preferences for ingredients, modes of provision, context of consumption, etc.—is regimented, repetitious, regularized, and routinized, it has also changed very perceptibly in recent years. Methodical examination of national food systems could isolate relevant causal conditions and causal configurations lying behind such changes. The theoretical pay-off would be a better account of how institutionalized practices change.

Second, we could learn more about the social relations and relationships surrounding the activity of eating. Central aspects of the sociological heritage have been relegated; the lapsing of interest in domestic roles—including the household division of labour and the role of eating in the maintenance of social relationships—accompanies a longstanding dearth of research on domestic hospitality. Exceptions indicate the effectiveness of ethnographic study of practices which analyse actions in social and historical context. For example, Counihan (2004) combined participant observation and extended interviews with three generations of a Florentine family, about 35 people in all, to chart their daily behaviour, their collective involvement in food production, and their accounts of how eating had changed through the twentieth century. Older family members' reflections on changes to their habits indicated the tensions associated with transition from a peasant diet—which for all its privations was viewed as satisfying, decent, and tasty—to a modern, much more varied, and abundant, yet somehow disappointing one. Interviewees', reflections on the (slowly) changing role of gender relations in the household also anchored consumption in its social context. In another fine example of the use of autobiographical accounts, Sutton (2001) used extensive anthropological fieldwork on the Greek island of Kalymnos to describe the role of memory, and particularly sensory memories, underlying the changing social meanings of meals and meal content. In addition, the comforts and the irritations of the activities of mutually sharing space and a way of life deserve attention (though see Kaufmann 2005). When most of the driving questions about food concern change, we need ethnographies, observation, time-use studies, in-depth interviews, autobiographical interviews, and their equivalents to capture what people do, i.e. how they actually organize the activity of eating. This might not only offset over-dependence on textual evidence for understanding eating, thus reducing our reliance on recipe books, but also, in turn, reconnect with theoretical concerns of sociological and anthropological traditions addressing the social arrangements of modern societies.

Third, we should exploit and learn from the comparative analysis of the institutional arrangements that generate manifest differences in experience and taste between groups and categories of people—classes, ethnic groups, generations, nations. Despite many very informative case studies, no programme of research to concentrate and learn from them exists. Individual cases could be used to explore the causes of differences; and more ambitious collations of survey and documentary sources might enhance the explanatory potential of comparative analysis (e.g. Fischler and Masson 2008; Kjaernes 2001; Kjaernes et al. 2007). However, comparative studies are few. Extended investigation of globalization has shown that the rapid flows of the current epoch are, contrary to expectation, responsible in significant part for the creation and promotion of cultural diversity. It is thus necessary to study the defining features of contexts—regulation, monopoly powers, balance of power between key actors, local geography, historical movements of population, family arrangements, etc.—in order to distinguish the relatively invariant features of eating habits from their specific institutional integuments. Therein lies a programme of research based on the collaboration of historians, geographers, sociologists, and anthropologists.

BIBLIOGRAPHY

Aglietta, M (1979), *A Theory of Capitalist Regulation* (London: Verso).

Anderson, E. N. (1988), *The Food of China* (New Haven CT: Yale University Press).

Appadurai, A. (1986), *The Social Life of Things: Commodities in Cultural Perspective* (Cambridge: Cambridge University Press).

Appadurai, A. (1988), 'How to make a national cuisine: cookbooks in contemporary India', *Comparative Studies in Society and History*, 30(1): 3–24.

Appadurai, A. (1990), 'Disjuncture and difference in the global cultural economy', *Theory, Culture & Society*, 7 (2–3): 295–310.

Appadurai, A. (1996), *Modernity at Large* (Minneapolis MN: University of Minnesota Press).

Ascher, F. (2005), *Le Mangeur Hypermoderne: une figure de l'individu éclectique* (Paris: Odile Jacob).

Ashley, B., Hollows, J., Jones, S., and Taylor, B. (2004), *Food and Cultural Studies* (London: Routledge).

Barthes, R. (1993), 'Steak and chips', in *Mythologies* (London: Vintage), 62–4.

Beck, U. (1992), *Risk Society: Towards a New Modernity* (London: Sage).

Belasco, W. (2002), 'Food matters: perspectives on an emerging field', in Belasco, W. and Scranton, P. (eds.), *Food Nations: Selling Taste in Consumer Societies* (New York: Routledge), 2–23.

Belasco, W. (2006), *Meals to Come: a History of the Future of Food* (Berkeley CA: University of California Press).

Beriss, D., and Sutton, D. (eds.), (2007), *The Restaurants Book: Ethnographies of Where We Eat* (Oxford: Berg).

Bourdieu, P. (1984[1979]), *Distinction: a Social Critique of the Judgement of Taste* (London: Routledge & Kegan Paul).

Brewer, J., and Trentmann, F. (eds.) (2006), *Consuming Cultures, Global Perspectives: Historical Trajectories, Transnational Exchanges* (New York: Berg).

Burnett, J. (1989), *Plenty and Want: a Social History of Food from 1815 to the Present*, 3rd edition (London: Routledge).

Burnett, J. (2004), *England Eats Out: a Social History of Eating Out in England from 1830 to the Present* (Harlow: Longman).

Capatti, A., and Montanari, M. (2003[1999]), *Italian Cuisine: a Cultural History*, trans. A. O'Healy (New York: Columbia University Press).

Cheng, S-L, Olsen, W., Southerton, D., and Warde, A. (2007), 'The changing practice of eating: evidence from UK time diaries, 1975 and 2000', *British Journal of Sociology*, 58(1): 39–61.

Cochoy, F. (2007), 'A sociology of market-things: on tending the garden of choices in mass retailing', in Callon, M., Yuval, M., and Muniesa, F. (eds.), *Market Devices* (Oxford: Blackwell), 109–29.

Cohen, L. (2003), *A Consumer's Republic: the Politics of Mass Consumption in Postwar America* (New York: Knopf).

Cook, I. (2004), 'Follow the thing: papaya', *Antipode*, 36(4): 642–64.

Counihan, C. (2004), *Around the Tuscan Table: Food, Family, and Gender in Twentieth-Century Florence* (New York: Routledge).

Cowan, R. Schwartz (1983), *More Work for Mother: the Ironies of Household Technology from the Open Hearth to the Microwave* (New York: Basic Books).

De Grazia, V. (2005), *Irresistible Empire: America's Advance through 20th-century Europe* (Cambridge MA: Harvard University Press).

DeVault, M. (1991), *Feeding the Family: the Social Organisation of Caring as Gendered Work* (Chicago: Chicago University Press).

Diner, H. (2001), *Hungering for America: Italian, Irish and Jewish Foodways in the Age of Migration* (Cambridge MA: Harvard University Press).

Dixon, J. (2002), *The Changing Chicken: Chooks, Cooks and Culinary Culture* (Sydney: University of New South Wales Press).

Douglas, M. (ed.) (1984), *Food in the Social Order* (New York: Russell Sage Foundation).

Driver, C. (1983), *The British at Table, 1940–80* (London: Chatto & Windus).

Elias, N. (1969 [1939]), *The Civilizing Process, Vol. I. The History of Manners*, (Oxford: Blackwell).

Ferguson, P. (2004), *Accounting for Taste: the Triumph of French Cuisine* (Chicago: Chicago University Press).

Fine, G. (1995), *Kitchens: the Culture of Restaurant Work* (Berkeley: University of California Press).

Finkelstein, J. (1989), *Dining Out: a Sociology of Modern Manners* (Cambridge: Polity).

Fischler, C. (1980), 'Food habits, social change and the nature/culture dilemma', *Social Science Information*, 19: 937–53.

Fischler, C. and Masson, E. (2008), *Manger: Français, Européens et Américains face a l'alimentation* (Paris: Odile Jacob).

Flandrin, J-F., and Montenari, M. (1996), *Histoire de l'Alimentation* (Paris: Fayard).

Freidberg, S. (2004), *French Beans and Food Scares: Culture and Commerce in the Anxious Age* (Oxford: Oxford University Press).

Freidberg, S. (2009), *Fresh: A Perishable History* (Cambridge MA: Harvard University Press).

Gabaccia, D. (1998), *We Are what We Eat: Ethnic Food and the Making of Americans* (Cambridge MA: Harvard University Press).

Goodman, D., and Du Puis, E. (2002), 'Knowing food and growing food: beyond the production-consumption debate in the sociology of agriculture', *Sociologia Ruralis*, 42(1): 6–23.

Goody, J. (1982), *Cooking, Cuisine and Class: A Study in Comparative Sociology* (Cambridge: Cambridge University Press).

Grignon, C. (1993), 'La règle, la mode et le travail: la genèse social du modèle des repas français contemporains', in Aymard, M., Grignon, C. and Sabban, F. (eds.), *Le Temps de Manger: alimentation, emploi du temps et rythmes sociaux* (Paris: Maison de Sciences de l'Homme), 275–324.

Harris, M. (1985), *Good to Eat: Riddles of Food and Culture* (New York: Simon & Schuster).

Harvey, M., Quilley, S., and Beynon, H. (2002), *Exploring the Tomato: Transformations of Nature, Society and Economy* (Cheltenham: Edward Elgar).

Hilton, M. (2000), 'Consumer politics in post-war Britain', in Daunton, M., and Hilton, M. (eds.), *The Politics of Consumption: Material Culture and Citizenship in Europe and America* (Oxford: Berg), 241–60.

Humble, N. (2005), *Culinary Pleasures: Cookbooks and the Transformation of British Food* (London: Faber and Faber).

Ilmonen, K. (2001), 'Sociology, consumption and routine', in Gronow, J., and Warde, A. (eds.) (2001), *Ordinary Consumption* (London: Routledge), 9–24.

Inglis, D., and Gimlin, D. (eds.) (2010), *The Globalisation of Food* (Oxford: Berg).

Jacobs, M., and Scholliers, P. (eds.) (2003), *Eating Out in Europe: Picnics, Gourmet Dining and Snacks since the late Eighteenth Century* (Oxford: Berg).

James, A. (1996), 'Cooking the books: global or local identities in contemporary British food cultures', in Howes, D. (ed.), *Cross-cultural Consumption: Global Markets, Local Realities* (London: Routledge), 77–92.

Johnston, J., and Baumann, S. (2007), 'Democracy versus distinction: a study of omnivorousness in gourmet food writing', *American Journal of Sociology*, 113: 165–204.

Karpik, L. (2000), 'Le guide rouge Michelin', *Sociologie du Travail*, 42(3), 369–89.

Kaufmann, J-C. (2005), *Casseroles, Amour et Crises: ce que cuisinier veut dire* (Paris: Hachette).

Kjaernes, U. (ed.) (2001), *Eating Patterns: a Day in the Lives of Nordic Peoples*, SIFO Report No.7 (Oslo).

Kjaernes, U., Harvey, M. and Warde, A. (2007), *Trust in Food: an Institutional and Comparative Analysis* (Basingstoke: Palgrave Macmillan).

Kopytoff, I. (1986), 'The cultural biography of things: commoditisation as process', in Appadurai, A. (ed.), *The Social Life of Things*, 64–94.

Kristensen, S. and Holm, L. (2006), 'Modern meal patterns: tensions between bodily needs and the organization of time and space', *Food and Foodways*, 14:151–73.

Leidner, R. (1993), *Fast Food, Fast Talk: Service Work and the Routinization of Everyday Life* (Berkeley CA: University of California Press).

Levenstein, H. (1988), *Revolution at the Table: the Transformation of the American Diet* (Oxford: Oxford University Press).

Levenstein, H. (1993), *The Parodox of Plenty: a Social History of Eating in Modern America* (Oxford: Oxford University Press).

Levi-Strauss, C. (1965), 'The culinary triangle', *Partisan Review*, 33: 586–95.

Lury, C. (1996), *Consumer Culture* (Cambridge: Polity).

Marshall, D., and Anderson, A. (2002) 'Proper meals in transition: young married couples on the nature of eating together', *Appetite*, 39: 193–206.

McIntosh, A. (1996), *Sociologies of Food and Nutrition* (New York: Plenum Press).

Mennell, S. (1985), *All Manners of Food: Eating and Taste in England and France from the Middle Ages to the Present* (Oxford: Blackwell).

Mennell, S., Murcott, A., and van Otterloo, A. (1993), *The Sociology of Food: Eating, Diet and Culture* (London: Sage).

Miller, D. (ed.) (1995), *Acknowledging Consumption: a Review of New Studies* (London: Routledge).

Miller, D. (ed.) (1998), *Material Cultures: Why Some Things Matter* (London: UCL Press).

Mintz, S. (1985), *Sweetness and Power: the Place of Sugar in Modern History* (Harmondsworth: Penguin).

Mintz, S. (2001), 'Eating American', in Counihan, C. (ed.), *Food in the USA: a Reader* (New York: Routledge), 23–34.

Mintz, S. (2008), 'Food, culture and energy', in Nuetzenadel, A., and Trentmann, F. (eds.), *Food and Globalization*, 21–36.

Moehring, M. (2008), 'Transnational food migration and the internalization of food consumption: ethnic cuisine in West Germany', in Nuetzenadel, A. and Trentmann, F (eds.) *Food and Globalization*, 129–52.

Murcott, A. (1997), 'Family meals—a thing of the past?', in Caplan, P. (ed.), *Food, Identity and Health* (London: Routledge), 32–49.

Murdoch, J., and Miele, M. (2004), 'Culinary networks and cultural connections: a conventions perspective', in Amin, A., and Thrift, N. (eds.), *The Blackwell Cultural Economy Reader* (Oxford: Blackwell), 231–48.

Nestle, M. (2006), *What to Eat* (New York: Macmillan).

Nuetzenadel, A., and Trentmann, F. (eds.) (2008), *Food and Globalization: Consumption, Markets and Politics in the Modern World* (Oxford: Berg).

Panayi, P. (2008), *Spicing up Britain: London: the Multicultural History of British Food* (London: Reaktion Books).

Poulain, J-P. (2002a), *Sociologies de l'Alimentation: les mangeurs et l'espace social alimentaire* (Paris: PUF).

Poulain, J-P. (2002b) 'The contemporary diet in France: "de-structuration" or from commensalism to "vagabond feeding"', *Appetite*, 39: 43–55.

Rao, H., Monin, P., and Durand, R. (2003), 'Institutional change in Toque Ville: nouvelle cuisine as an identity movement in French gastronomy', *American Journal of Sociology*, 108(4): 795–843.

Rao, H., Monin, P., and Durand, R. (2005), 'Emergence of nouvelle cuisine in France', *American Sociological Review*, 70: 968–91.

Ray, K. (2004), *The Migrant's Table: Meals and Memories in Bengali-American Households* (Philadelphia PA: Temple University Press).

Ray, K. (2007), 'Domesticating cuisine: food and aesthetics on American television', *Gastronomica*, 7(1): 50–63.

Ray, K. (2008), 'Nation and cuisine: the evidence from American newspapers *ca*.1830–2003', *Food and Foodways*, 16: 259–97.

Sassatelli, R. (2007), *Consumer Culture: History, Theory and Politics* (Oxford: Berg).

Schivelbusch, W. (1993), *Tastes of Paradise: a Social History of Spices, Stimulants and Intoxicants* (New York: Vintage).

Simmel, G. (1994[1910]), 'The sociology of the meal', trans. M. Symons, *Food and Foodways*, 5(4): 345–50.

Southerton, D. (2003), 'Squeezing Time': allocating practices, co-ordinating networks and scheduling society, *Time & Society*, 12(1): 5–25.

Spang, R. (2000), *The Invention of the Restaurant: Paris and Modern Gastronomic Culture* (Cambridge MA: Harvard University Press).

Stewart, H., Blisard, N., Bhuyan, S., and Nayga, R. (2004), *The Demand for Food Away From Home: full-service or fast food?*, United States Department of Agriculture, Agricultural Economic Report No.829., <http//:www.ers.usda.gov/publications/aer829/aer829.pdf>.

Sutton, D. (2001), *Remembrance of Repasts: an Anthropology of Food and Memory* (Oxford: Berg).

Sutton, D. (2006), 'Cooking skills, the senses and memory: the fate of practical knowledge', in Edwards, E., Crosden, C., and Phillips, R. (eds.), *Sensible Objects: Collections, Museums and Material Culture* (Oxford: Berg).

Tannahill, R. (1988), *Food in History*, 2nd edition (Harmondsworth: Penguin).

Teil, G., and Hennion, A. (2004), 'Discovering quality or performing taste?: a sociology of the amateur', in Harvey, M., McMeekin, A., and Warde, A. (eds.), *Qualities of Food* (Manchester: Manchester University Press), 19–37.

Trentmann, F. (2009), 'The long history of contemporary consumer society: chronologies, practices and politics in modern Europe', *Archiv für Sozialgeschichte*, 49: 107–28.

Trubek, A. (2000), *Haute Cuisine: How the French Invented the Culinary Profession* (Philadelphia PA: University of Pennsylvania Press).

Wansink, B. (2006), *Mindless Eating* (New York, Bantam).

Warde, A. (2004), 'La normalita del mangiare fuori', *Rassegna Italiana di Sociologia*, 45(4): 493–518.

Warde, A. (2009a) 'Globalisation and the challenge of variety: a comparison of eating in Britain and France', in Inglis, D., and Gimlin, D. (eds.), *The Globalisation of Food*, 227–42.

Warde, A. (2009b), 'Imagining British cuisine: representations of culinary identity in the Good Food Guide', *Food, Culture and Society*, 12(2): 149–71.

Warde, A., and Martens, L. (2000), *Eating Out: Differentiation, Consumption and Pleasure* (Cambridge: Cambridge University Press).

Warde, A., Cheng, S-L., Olsen, W., and Southerton, D. (2007), 'Changes in the practice of eating: a comparative analysis', *Acta Sociologica*, 50(4): 365–88.

Wilk, R. (2004), 'Morals and metaphors: the meaning of consumption', in Ekstrom, K., and Brembeck, H. (eds.), *Elusive Consumption* (Oxford: Berg), 11–26.

Wilk, R. (2006), *Home Cooking in the Global Village: Caribbean Food from Buccaneers to Ecotourists* (Oxford: Berg).

Wood, R. (1995), *The Sociology of the Meal* (Edinburgh: Edinburgh University Press).

Zerubavel, E. (1985 [1981]), *Hidden Rhythms: Schedules and Calendars in Social Life* (Berkeley: University of California Press).

FURTHER READING

Belasco, W. (2002), 'Food matters: perspectives on an emerging field', in Belasco, W., and Scranton, P. (eds.), *Food Nations: Selling Taste in Consumer Societies* (New York: Routledge), 2–23.

Counihan, C. (2004), *Around the Tuscan Table: Food Family and Gender in Twentieth Century Florence* (New York: Routledge).

Diner, H. (2001), *Hungering for America: Italian, Irish and Jewish Foodways in the Age of Migration* (Cambridge MA: Harvard University Press).

Harvey, M., Quilley, S., and Beynon, H. (2002), *Exploring the Tomato: Transformations of Nature, Society and Economy* (Cheltenham: Edward Elgar).

Humble, N. (2005), *Culinary Pleasures: Cookbooks and the Transformation of British Food* (London: Faber and Faber).

Inglis, D., and Gimlin, D. (eds.) (2010), *The Globalisation of Food* (Oxford: Berg).

Nuetzenadel, A., and Trentmann, F. (eds.) (2008), *Food and Globalization: Consumption, Markets and Politics in the Modern World* (Oxford: Berg).

Poulain, J-P. (2002), *Sociologies de l'Alimentation: les mangeurs et l'espace social alimentaire* (Paris: PUF).

Warde, A., and Martens, L. (2000), *Eating Out: Differentiation, Consumption and Pleasure* (Cambridge: Cambridge University Press).

Wilk, R. (2006), *Home Cooking in the Global Village: Caribbean Food from Buccaneers to Ecotourists* (Oxford: Berg).

PART VI

....

STATE AND CIVIL SOCIETY

....

CHAPTER 20

....

CONSUMER ACTIVISM, CONSUMER REGIMES, AND THE CONSUMER MOVEMENT: RETHINKING THE HISTORY OF CONSUMER POLITICS IN THE UNITED STATES[1]

....

LAWRENCE B. GLICKMAN

I

....

The historiography of consumer society in the United States has matured in the last decade. As David Steigerwald noted in an influential review essay in 2006, 'consumer interpretations of American history have come of age.' These interpretations prominently emphasize the politics of consumption. Indeed, Steigerwald made his claim about the state of the field largely on the basis of an analysis of the paradigm-shifting books of T. H. Breen on 'how consumer politics shaped independence' (2005) and Lizabeth Cohen on 'the politics of mass consumption in postwar America' (2003). Breen suggests that shared practices of consumption (and later non-consumption) shaped American identity during the Revolutionary era. Cohen argues that the United States in the postwar decades can be best understood as a 'Consumers' Republic', fostered by the state

[1] The portions of this essay on consumer activism and the consumer movement are drawn from Lawrence B. Glickman, *Buying Power: A History of Consumer Activism in America* (Chicago: University of Chicago Press, 2009).

and business interests, often to the detriment of the public sphere.[2] Most of the recent major works in consumer history, on a wide variety of subjects, have also employed the framework of consumer politics.[3] In their efforts to identify a 'politics of consumption' historians have looked in a wide variety of places and described numerous phenomena as falling under this rubric. Historians mean different things when they talk about American consumer politics, however, and it will be the job of this essay to examine the taxonomy and flesh out those differences.

In particular, this chapter will explore and disaggregate three core elements of consumer politics: what I call *consumer activism*, the *consumer movement* and *consumer regimes*. Although, as we will see, there is some overlap among these categories, they represent distinct sites of politics. 'Consumer activism' refers to bottom-up protests by non-state actors; the classic activities of consumer activists are boycotts and 'buycotts'. The 'consumer movement' refers to efforts through advocacy and lobbying to protect and advance the 'consumer interest'. The term 'consumer regime' refers to the often overlooked state politics of consumption, the ways in which the nation-state fosters and shapes patterns of consumption and, not insignificantly, acts as a consumer in its own right. By distinguishing among the politics of the grass roots, organized lobbies, and the state we can better understand the breadth of the intersection of consumption and the public sphere in the United States. Because scholars have attended more to consumer activism and the consumer movement and less to consumer regimes, this essay will emphasize the latter, with the hope that consumer regimes will put in new perspective the former two aspects of consumer politics.[4]

Before we discuss the differences among the various types of consumer politics, we should note that in the not too distant past historians questioned the very legitimacy of the topic, disclaiming any positive correlation between consumption and politics.

---

[2] David Steigerwald, 'All Hail the Republic of Choice', *Journal of American History*, 93 (September 2006), 385–403; T. H. Breen, *The Marketplace of Revolution: How Consumer Politics Shaped American Independence* (New York: Oxford University Press, 2005); Lizabeth Cohen, *A Consumers' Republic: The Politics of Mass Consumption in Postwar America* (New York: Knopf, 2003).

[3] A sampling of this burgeoning literature includes Kathleen G. Donohue, *Freedom from Want: American Liberalism and the Idea of the Consumer* (Baltimore: Johns Hopkins University Press, 2003); Kristin Hoganson, *Consumers' Imperium: The Global Production of American Domesticity, 1865–1920* (Chapel Hill: University of North Carolina Press, 2007); Meg Jacobs, *Pocketbook Politics: Economic Citizenship in Twentieth-Century America* (Princeton: Princeton University Press, 2005); Charles F. McGovern, *Sold American: Consumption and Citizenship, 1890–1945* (Chapel Hill: University of North Carolina Press, 2006).

[4] For early uses of the concept of consumer regimes or 'regimes of consumption', see Lawrence Glickman, 'Twentieth-Century Consumer Activism and Political Culture in America and Germany', in Roland Becker, Andreas Franzmann, Axel Jansen, and Sascha Liebermann (eds.), *Eigeninteresse und Gemeinwohlbindung. Kulturelle Ausformungen in den USA und Deutschland* (Konstanz: Universitätsverlag Konstanz, 2001), 115–36; Victoria De Grazia, *Irresistible Empire: America's Advance through Twentieth-Century Europe* (Cambridge MA: Harvard University Press, 2005); idem, 'Changing Consumer Regimes in Europe, 1930–1970: Comparative Perspectives on the Distribution Problem', in Susan Strasser, Charles McGovern, and Matthias Judt (eds.), *Getting and Spending: European and American Consumer Societies in the Twentieth Century*, (New York: Cambridge University Press, 1998), 59–84.

'In a culture of consumption,' wrote Christopher Lasch in 1993 summarizing the conventional wisdom, 'the citizen disappears into the consumer' and politics becomes impossible since 'consumers have no interests in common.' As Meg Jacobs has noted, historians have long believed that the politics of consumption was an 'oxymoron.' Given this assumption, it is not surprising that very few historians examined what they took to be a non-existent relationship. Jennifer Mittelstadt observed in 2005 that consumption is 'a topic that political historians have largely bypassed.' David Potter's 1954 study of consumption and American national character was widely admired, but few historians followed up on his claims or else they took him (inaccurately) to be celebrating abundance as a sign of the superiority of the free world.[5]

The recent spate of studies of consumer politics would thus seem to mark an abrupt change in perspective. Yet in fundamental ways consuming practices have long been central to interpretations of American political culture. Well before consumer history was recognized as a field and long before there were self-identified historians of consumption, political analysts employed American consumer practices as key explanatory devices. As Charles McGovern writes, 'By 1930, commentators would proclaim that consumption was not only the symbol but also the guarantee of democracy in America.'[6] Indeed, the idea of 'American exceptionalism' largely rested on the importance, ubiquity, and uniqueness of American consumerism. Alexis de Tocqueville, considered by many to be the founding exceptionalist, wrote:

> A native of the United States clings to this world's goods as if he were certain never to die; and he is so hasty in grasping at all within his reach that one would suppose he was constantly afraid of not living long enough to enjoy them. He clutches everything, he holds nothing fast, but soon loosens his grasp to pursue fresh gratifications.[7]

Tocqueville was thus among the first commentators to understand mass consumption as central to American political culture; the pursuit of abundance he noticed was a feature of democracy, not a bug. In answer to his 1906 rhetorical question, 'Why Is There No Socialism in the United States?', the German sociologist Werner Sombart answered, continuing in the tradition of Tocqueville, 'reefs of roast beef and apple pie.' Under conditions of American abundance, Sombart concluded, 'socialistic utopias of every sort are sent to their doom.' For these reasons, unlike the working classes of Europe, Americans

---

[5] Christopher Lasch, 'The Culture of Consumption', in Mary Kupiec Cayton, Elliott J. Gorn, and Peter W. Williams (eds.), *Encyclopedia of American Social History* (New York: Scribner's, 1993), Vol. 2, 1381–90, at 1388; Meg Jacobs, 'The Politics of Plenty in the Twentieth-Century United States', in Martin Daunton and Matthew Hilton (eds.), *The Politics of Consumption: Material Culture and Citizenship in Europe and America* (Oxford: Berg, 2001), 223; Jennifer Mittelstadt, 'Consumer Politics: A New History of the Rise and Fall of the New Deal Order', *Reviews in American History*, 33/3 (2005), 431–8, at 431. On Potter, see Daniel Horowitz's excellent analysis in *The Anxieties of Affluence: Critiques of American Consumer Culture, 1939–1979* (Amherst MA: University of Massachusetts Press, 2004), 79–100.

[6] McGovern, *Sold American*, 103.

[7] Alexis de Tocqueville, 'Why The Americans Are So Restless In The Midst Of Their Prosperity', in *Democracy in America* (New York: Alfred A. Knopf, 1945), Vol. II, Ch. 13, 136–9 <http://xroads.virginia.edu/~HYPER/DETOC/ch2_13.htm> (accessed 9 June 2011).

felt no need to turn to socialism because of the consuming opportunities their material wealth provided them.[8]

Historians followed suit in explaining the supposed lack of radical politics in the United States as a function of its abundance, which made socialism both unnecessary and unappealing. In short 'rising consumption compensated for—and thereby helped to suppress workers' consciousness of their rising exploitation.'[9] In this exceptionalist framework, consumer society diverted Americans from militance both on the shop floor and at the ballot box. This line of scholarship posited a close causal connection between consumption and politics, although that connection was understood entirely in the negative: consumption precludes politics. Arnon Gutfeld's recent study of American exceptionalism is fittingly subtitled 'The Effects of Plenty on the American Experience'. Conversely, Andrew Bacevich has recently rejected the concept of exceptionalism primarily because it sanctions an 'empire of consumerism', that is, a foreign policy dictated by a desire to supply consumers in the United States with cheap goods. His solution to the problem of empire is to knock conspicuous consumption off its pedestal.[10] For these interpretations, politics properly understood lay in the realm of production, not consumption. Consumption was not a form of politics or a gateway to civic life but an antipolitics that foreclosed meaningful public-spirited activism. The fact that this view was not fully corroborated by the historical evidence did not limit its explanatory power.

The negative relationship between consumption and politics was essentially recapitulated by the first generation of self-defined historians of American consumer society, and was especially reflected in the work of Stuart Ewen. Consumption was not seen as a political arena itself but as one that diverted attention from the political issues. More precisely, the creation of consumer society was the construction of big business and its surrogates in the nascent advertising industry. Those cohorts of historians who examined consumer society in the 1980s generally steered clear of explicitly political frameworks. Most of them focused on popular culture, commercial leisure, and advertising. To be sure, the majority of these scholars favoured a 'cultural studies' framework that was broadly political, especially in their focus on inequalities of race, class, and gender. But they made few attempts to link consumer society to social movements, the state, or electoral politics.[11]

[8] Werner Sombart, *Why is There No Socialism in the United States?* (New York: Sharpe, 1976). See also Eric Foner's prescient essay, 'Why is There No Socialism in the United States?', *History Workshop Journal* (1984), 17: 57–80.

[9] Stephen Resnick and Richard Wolff, 'Exploitation, Consumption and the Uniqueness of US Capitalism', *Historical Materialism*, 11 (2003), 210.

[10] Arnon Gutfield, *American Exceptionalism: The Effects of Plenty on the American Experience* (Brighton: Sussex Academic Press, 2002). Andrew Bacevich, *The Limits of Power: The End of American Exceptionalism* (New York: Metropolitan Books, 2008), 29. See also Seymour Martin Lipset, *American Exceptionalism: A Double-Edged Sword* (New York: W. W. Norton, 1997), 84.

[11] Stuart Ewen, *Captains of Consciousness: Advertising and the Social Roots of the Consumer Culture*, 25th anniversary edition (New York: Basic Books, 2001). For an extension of this point, see Lawrence B. Glickman, 'Born to Shop? Consumer History and American History', in Lawrence B. Glickman (ed.), *Consumer Society in American History: A Reader* (Ithaca NY: Cornell University Press, 1999), 9–10.

The new generation of historians of consumer politics has overturned these assumptions. Much as the 'cultural turn' of the 1990s led historians to define the political arena broadly and to find 'politics' everywhere, historians of consumption have used a broad definition of politics to enrich our understanding of the intersection of consumption and politics. And indeed it is still the case that culturally oriented historians have taken up this topic far more than strictly political historians. Whereas previous generations did not generally interpret the history of consumption in political terms, the recent generation of scholars—regardless of their focus—see politics everywhere. The purpose of this essay is not to challenge the new broadly construed category of political consumerism but rather to tease out the various aspects of this label and to distinguish among them.

II

Drawing a tripartite distinction among consumer politics is important not just for terminological reasons. It has implications for our understanding of the development of consumer society and political culture. To understand what Matthew Hilton has called 'the full range of consumer politics' requires a long-term perspective because when and how each component emerged points to important differences in this spectrum.[12] Viewing consumer politics over the entirety of United States history helps us examine continuities, changes over time, and to trace distinctions among various forms of consumer politics, and also to distinguish American consumer politics from those of other countries.

By and large, historians of consumer politics have endorsed a 'three-phase' model, which focuses on outbreaks of politically oriented consumerism in the Progressive era, New Deal period, and 1960s. This leads them to miss the origins of consumer politics in the eighteenth and nineteenth centuries, and to elide important distinctions among various forms of consumer politics. These scholars generally highlight the consumer movement, which was a largely twentieth-century development. But the evolution of the founding elements of consumer politics—consumer regimes and consumer activism—can only be understood over a long historical frame. Moreover, a too narrow focus on the three-phase model can lead to the elision of consumer activism with the consumer movement and to a more monolithic view of consumer politics than is warranted. For example, Michael McCann writes that 'traditional consumer politics sanctioned and served citizen desires for private wealth as the greatest promise of modern society' and 'was limited to concerns for more, better, and cheaper goods.' An examination of American consumer activism over the course of US history, however, reveals that this position was not traditional at all but a radically new, and by no means uncontested, component of consumer politics, one that developed only in the twentieth century.[13]

---

[12] Matthew Hilton, 'Consumers and the State Since the Second World War', *Annals of the American Academy of Political and Social Science*, 611 (2007), 66–81, at 67.
[13] Michael W. McCann, *Taking Reform Seriously: Perspectives on Public Interest Liberalism* (Ithaca NY: Cornell University Press, 1986), 135.

A long historical perspective shows that Americans inherited some traditions of consumer politics but also made major contributions to the development of all three categories. Both consumer activism, in the form of grass roots protests, and consumer regimes, in the form of states setting the parameters of consumption, long preceded the founding of the United States. Through their innovations—expanding the range of boycotts beyond one locality, inventing the 'buycott', developing product testing, to name only a few—Americans can plausibly be considered the founders of modern consumer activism and the consumer movement. And although the American state was relatively small in the first century of the nation's history, through targeted expenditures, federal and local law, and policies it shaped and promoted uniquely American forms of consumption from the beginning, not least through the state-sanctioned institution of chattel slavery, which underwrote the American consumer economy.

A more variegated long-term history of American consumer politics also challenges the view of American exceptionalism that associates its commitments to capitalist imperatives with unbridled, unregulated private consumption. Critics of American exceptionalism have long argued for the radicalism of home-grown political traditions and, as I show in what follows, consumer politics played an important role in the making of these traditions, providing an important frame of reference for understanding the broader political culture of the United States.

III

Although consumer activists have generally worked at the grass roots level, they have often intersected with the state. Indeed, the United States was founded—the nation born—through the actions of consumer activists, who challenged British imperial policy. In the first half of the nineteenth century American abolitionists, Southern white nationalists, and supporters of evangelical reform invoked consumer power and responsibility in new ways, and set consumer activism on its modern course. In each of these cases, consumer activists sought to change state policy: by seeking the end of slavery (or its extension), or by calling for new laws and prohibitions against alcohol. In the early twentieth century African-American boycotters of Jim Crow streetcars sought to overturn new municipal policies which mandated that transportation firms segregate their facilities.[14]

At the same time, boycotters of the nineteenth century developed a concept of political action that took place within the marketplace rather than the halls of government. Their imagined community of political actors was determined by the size of the market for the product being boycotted; sometimes it was local, other times it was co-extensive with the nation and sometimes supranational. Rather than being thought of as a discrete and bounded place, each point of consumption began to be conceived of as a node linking individual shoppers to what was becoming a nationwide (and, in some cases,

---

[14] For extensive documentation see Lawrence B. Glickman, *Buying Power: A History of Consumer Activism in America* (Chicago: University of Chicago Press, 2009).

even worldwide) web of producers, manufacturers, other consumers, environments, and even nation-states. We tend to think of the networked world as a new thing, but the linked nature of the United States, and much of the rest of the world, was the condition through which these groups sought to build a new politics of solidarity.

This networked world of solidarity and publicity frequently built on the ligaments of state power or developed in relation to transnational linkages. The word boycott, coined in 1880, points to the impact of transatlantic modes of commerce and communication. Its coiner, James Redpath, derived its name from the British land agent, Charles Cunningham Boycott, who was the target of anti-colonial protest of Irish peasants. Redpath made clear, however, that he gained first-hand knowledge of 'the terrible power of social excommunication' during his time as a US government official in the era of Reconstruction.[15] Redpath had witnessed boycotting *avant la lettre* as a school superintendent in Charleston, South Carolina, and Northern journalists, including Redpath himself, had reported on them. 'No Northern man is welcomed in the South if he believes in the principles of the Republican party and votes and acts in accordance with his creed', as Redpath wrote in 1876. 'He is ostracized in society and business by native whites.'[16] Describing these acts of ostracism as an 'American boycott whose history has not yet been written', the journalist Arthur Dudley Vinton in 1886 labelled the 'policy of social ex-communication with which the south met the emigrants or "carpetbaggers" from the north after the civil war' as 'the immediate parent of the policy of social excommunication which the Irish adopted and to which they gave the name of boycott.' Vinton noted that 'this policy was first recommended to the Irish people by Mr. James Redpath', claiming that Redpath's experience of ostracism in the South explained why the boycott should be considered 'an American custom with an Irish name.'[17]

In this context, we can appreciate the aptness of Vinton's comment that 'we lent the policy to Ireland and she returned it to us with a name.' Vinton argued for the importance of studying 'the travels of the boycott', since to freeze the practice to one place was to lose sight of its meaning, of its transatlantic derivation, and its uses by the 'downtrodden people of other nations.' The boycott was a travelling institution, in many senses of the word, one that developed in a transatlantic (and, as we will see, trans-Pacific) context. Not only did word of the Irish boycotts travel immediately via the various newspapers for which Redpath wrote, but the web of print culture also set off immediate responses from distant places. Less than a month after the Irish boycott had begun, an American woman telegraphed Father O'Malley, the Irish priest who worked closely with Redpath to develop the boycott name and to popularize the tactic, with an offer to pay the arrears of the tenants, as the Chicago *Daily Inter-Ocean* reported, thereby publicizing this course of action and perhaps encouraging others to do the same.[18]

---

[15] James Redpath, 'Mr. Redpath's Letter', *Daily Inter-Ocean*, Chicago, 29 October 1880, 1.

[16] Quotation from James Redpath, 'The Stake in America', *Independent*, 23 March 1876, 1.

[17] Redpath's debt to his Southern experience is discussed in Arthur Dudley Vinton, 'As to Its Origin: Something about the Term Boycott', *Atlanta Constitution*, 29 July 1890, 9.

[18] Arthur Vinton, 'As to Its Origin', *Daily Inter-Ocean*, Chicago, 19 November 1880, 4. O'Malley turned the offer down, noting that it was the British landlord's responsibility to settle with the tenants.

The global movement of peoples and goods also played a significant role in the first decades of the boycott. Although many of the Americans who took up the boycott can accurately be described as 'downtrodden', one of the most frequently boycotted groups in the early years were generally impoverished immigrants. Among the earliest and, without a doubt, the largest boycotts, 'the most gigantic boycott ever known in this country', according to *John Swinton's Paper*, were anti-Chinese protests led by working-class groups in the western United States. Indeed, the first article in the *New York Times*, in the spring of 1882, on the boycott's migration to the United States, noted that California workers were proposing that the Chinese be 'severely left alone'. Calling on fellow workers to 'drive out the Chinese by refusing to hire them or buy of them', the *Times* quoted a boycott leader who, drawing on the heritage of Revolutionary boycotters, called for 'a non intercourse act' against the Chinese. It is important to note that the boycott went in the other direction as well, and also at a very early date. As early as 1882, and for the next several decades, many Chinese, both in China and throughout the global diaspora, threatened to boycott American goods because of America's treatment of Chinese immigrants and passage of the Chinese Exclusion Act.[19]

If Americans of different ethnicities and backgrounds were the targets in this case, Americans frequently used the weapon against other countries as well. For example, after the Dreyfus Affair, a number of American newspapers called for a boycott of the French Exposition at the World's Fair in 1899. American women also called for a boycott of 'frilly' French fashions. The boycotts of Perrier and other French goods in the wake of France's refusal to join the coalition fighting in the Iraq War in 2003 was not the first time that Americans had taken such action against that country.[20]

If we shift our gaze from those who were boycotted to examine those who used the boycott in the early years, we find that many early boycotters were working-class immigrants or their children, most often of Irish or German ancestry. When critics denounced boycotting, as they regularly did, as a foreign institution, they were correct to the extent that these actions were a product of global migrations. The boycott was 'imported from Ireland', not just because the phrase was invented there but because people of Irish ancestry pioneered the labour boycott in the United States. If the migration of peoples played a role in the history of boycotting, the global movement in commodities and ideas did as well. Many of the products boycotted in the 1880s and 1890s had a transnational history of their own and those that did not, such as beer, cigars, newspapers, saloons, and bakeries, usually had a transnational workforce and appealed to an immigrant audience.[21]

[19] 'A Gigantic Boycott', *John Swinton's Paper*, 11 July 1886, 1; 'A Gigantic Boycott', *Workmen's Advocate*, 18 July 1886, 3; 'Boycott the Chinese', *New York Times*, 1 March 1886, 5. The 'leave alone' quotation is from 'American Boycotters', *New York Times*, 7 May 1882, 8. On Chinese boycotts see, 'Chinamen are Angry', *New York Times*, 5 January 1882, 5.
[20] 'Boycott the French Exposition' *Denver Evening Post*, 10 September 1899; 'Boycott France! Whole World Rings with Execration of Dreyfus's Verdict', *Boston Daily Advertiser*, 11 September 1899; '"The Dreyfus Blot"': Movement to Boycott the Paris Exposition Unless Justice Prevails', *Arkansas Democrat*, 12 September 1899; 'The Dreyfus Boycott', *Weekly Rocky Mountain News*, 21 September 1899, 4; 'Shall American Women Boycott French Frills? Some of the Matrons of Milwaukee in Favor of Teaching the French People a Lesson', *Milwaukee Journal*, 21 May 1898, 5.
[21] 'Latest Definitions', *Life*, 8 Apr 1886, 206.

IV

Unlike consumer activism and consumer regimes, the consumer movement came about only in the twentieth century, when consumer politics came to be characterized by a conception of 'the consumer' as needing protection. Moreover, self-described consumer organizations—groups that saw their task as representing, defending, and lobbying for consumers—emerged, establishing consumers as an interest group in a pluralistic society, one making demands on the state. Those groups coalesced in the 1930s into something known as the 'consumer movement', an organized political effort on behalf of consumers, whose chief aim was, as Helen Sorenson described it in her 1941 book, *The Consumer Movement*, 'protecting and promoting the consumer interest.' What distinguished the 'consumer movement' from previous and contemporaneous movements of consumers was precisely this emphasis on consumers themselves as the chief beneficiaries of political activism. These groups claimed to represent the 'consumer interest', an interest which, for the first time, became seen as within the purview of federal regulation. At the municipal level, however, American society was highly regulated by public and private law in the nineteenth century (Novak 1996). From the Pure Food and Drug Act of 1906, through the various consumer advisory boards of the New Deal, through the President's Special Assistant for Consumer Affairs, begun under President Lyndon Johnson in the 1960s, the federal government came to understand the protection of consumers interest as one of its duties. By contrast, consumer activists did not see themselves as part of a 'consumer movement.' Rather, these groups mobilized consumers not for the benefit of consumers but on behalf of the nation, the slave, the worker, or the poor.[22]

The central idea of the consumer movement was the recognition that consumers were a distinct group with their own interests, rights, and responsibilities, one which required a lobby to protect its interests. Unlike other interests requiring lobbies, however, proponents of the consumer movement believed that consumers were not a narrow minority but representative of all Americans. It became an article of faith among leaders of the consumer movement that consumers needed protection that could be achieved via a combination of technical expertise, lobbying assistance, and—here is the connection to consumer regimes—a responsive state. Consumer activists, as we have seen, had invoked the centrality of consumption and consumer power ever since the late eighteenth century. Highlighting the force of consumption was different from acknowledging a separate consumer interest. In the nineteenth century, consumer activists had called upon citizens in their capacity as consumers to act collectively on behalf of a great many causes and people but 'consumers' were not among them. To be sure, they saw consumers as

---

[22] Helen Sorenson, *The Consumer Movement: What It Is and What It Means* (New York and London: Harper and Brothers, 1941), 111; William J. Novak, *The People's Welfare: Law and Regulation in Nineteenth-Century America* (Chapel Hill: University of North Carolina Press, 1996). On the ebb and flow of this duty, see Michael Pertschuk, *Revolt Against Regulation: The Rise and Pause of the Consumer Movement* (Berkeley: University of California Press, 1982).

the central moral agents in an interconnected world of markets; but they did not posit consumers as the key group to be served by this vision of moralized consumption.

V

Consumer regimes are the least studied and understood form of consumer politics. Yet the state has long played a key role in shaping, regulating, and demarcating consuming practices. Tocqueville was one of the first to point out that states shape private consumption. On his famous visit to the United States in 1831, he noted that American democracy tended to produce people who wanted more than they could afford and that mass consumption was a part of the nation's democratic character. He also observed the indirect role of the American state compared with many European nations where, 'the State consumption of manufactured produce is always growing larger, and these commodities are generally made in the arsenals or establishments of the government.' Tocqueville's great insight was that the American government fostered mass consumption but did so indirectly through subsidizing, creating a legal framework, providing infrastructure for, and otherwise supporting private enterprise.[23]

Scholars of twentieth-century America have hinted at parts of this picture but they have tended to define the American consumer regime as a relatively recent development and have insufficiently described its reach. For example, Andrew Bacevich writes that only since 1965 has consumerism defined the nation's domestic and foreign policy:

> For the United States, the pursuit of freedom, as defined in an age of consumerism, has induced a condition of dependence—on imported goods, on imported oil, and on credit. The chief desire of the American people, whether they admit it or not, is that nothing should disrupt their access to those goods, that oil, and that credit. The chief aim of the U.S. government is to satisfy that desire, which it does in part through largesse at home...and in large part through the pursuit of imperial ambitions abroad.

Bacevich is correct to highlight the relationship between the government and private consumption, but the relationship is both more complicated and longstanding than he suggests.[24]

It is important to note that consumer regimes shape the parameters of consumption in vastly different ways. Not all consumer regimes seek to promote private consumption or the interests of consumers, and certainly none do at all times. (Think of the United States

[23] Alexis de Tocqueville, 'That Amongst The European Nations Of Our Time The Power Of Governments Is Increasing, Although The Persons Who Govern Are Less Stable', *Democracy in America* (New York: Alfred A. Knopf, 1945), Vol. II, Sec. IV, Ch. V, <http://xroads.virginia.edu/~Hyper/detoc/ch4_05.htm> (accessed 9 June 2011). For intriguing analysis, see Richard Swedburg, *Tocqueville's Political Economy* (Princeton: Princeton University Press, 2009), 21, 38, 69.
[24] Bacevich, *The Limits of Power*, 173, 29.

during the Second World War, when it encouraged conservation and rationed many consumer goods.) To be sure, the United States, perhaps more than any other country, has viewed consumption as central to the economic health of the nation, and therefore has often sought ways to encourage it. The business columnist James Surowiecki has written that, in contrast with other countries, in particular China, 'The American economy revolves around the consumer', and that, as a result, 'enhancing consumer welfare is the ultimate goal.'[25] While the first clause is inarguable, the conclusion about the paramount place of consumer welfare is inaccurate. An historical analysis of the American consumer regime shows us why. To say that the federal government has long promoted consumption is not the same as saying that it has always promoted the consumer interest. From its inception the American state set out to protect and promote economic systems that lubricated the system of consumption and that assisted purveyors of items of mass consumption. In other words, to say that America's governing regime has kept consumption at the forefront from the beginning of the nation's history is not to say that it has done so because of its deep commitment to consumer welfare, a concept that only emerged in the late nineteenth century and matured in the twentieth century. Even in the twentieth century, the idea of consumer protection faced virulent opposition from the business community, and, while many significant pieces of legislation were passed, many more, such as the push to create a consumer protection agency in the 1970s, have languished or been defeated. Promoting mass consumption then is not identical to pushing for consumer welfare.

A basic point but one under-examined by historians of consumer society, who have tended to focus on individuals and businesses rather than the state, is that governments are major purchasers; from a macroeconomic point of view, government spending is a significant percentage of total consumption, which makes governments consumers writ large. Even in the nineteenth century the federal government made significant spending decisions, especially involving internal improvements and westward expansion. As Lawrence Hines observed, early national proponents of development saw government spending as a 'public investment.' Federalists used the government to encourage manufacturing, in part hoping that farmers drawn into industry would be effective consumers of agricultural surpluses and that agricultural folk would buy manufactured goods. Government thus played a crucial role in the creation of what Gordon Wood has called 'commercial modernity', which was defined by a government-supported infrastructure of industry, laws, markets, and credit, all of which facilitated the growth of a nation of consumers.[26]

Governments can also do the opposite by withdrawing their spending, creating what is essentially a federally coordinated and enforced boycott. One especially powerful tool of governmental consumer activism is the embargo, a prohibition on certain kinds of or all trade with a foreign nation. Ever since 1809, when the United States enforced a

[25] James Surowiecki, 'The Financial Page: The Frugal Republic', *The New Yorker*, 7 December 2009, 35.

[26] Lawrence G. Hines, 'The Early 19th Century Internal Improvement Reports and the Philosophy of Public Investment', *Journal of Economic Issues*, 2/4 (October 1968), 384–92; Gordon S. Wood, *Empire of Liberty: A History of the Early Republic, 1789–1815* (New York: Oxford University Press, 2009), 101.

policy of 'non intercourse' with France, government policy has often been joined with individual practices of boycotting. Americans have often organized 'a boycott coincident with an embargo' or a 'boycott-embargo'. This is one of the ways in which consumer activism and consumer regimes have intermixed. James Redpath argued that Irish American workers 'see that the tariff is a legal and national method of boycotting England'. Before the United States government embargoed fascist Japan in 1940, leaders of the grass roots boycott of Japanese silk claimed that government officials endorsed their actions. And of course, the state has also directly launched boycotts under its own name, as in the 1980 Olympic boycott, which the United States called in protest at the Soviet invasion of Afghanistan.[27]

One virtue of the consumer regime framework is that it challenges a tendency of some historians to overemphasize the autonomy of the private consumer and to underemphasize the framework governments set on consumer behaviour. Often, American consumer society is ascribed to seemingly immutable and eternal aspects of national identity or the 'American character', such as individualism, abundance, and an affinity for 'shopping too much'. Few scholars have followed Tocqueville in emphasizing the extent to which political architecture shapes individual consuming practices. Although they are not often paired, the rise of the McDonald's hamburger restaurant chain and the Holiday Inn hotel chain—and the new kinds of mass consumption they pioneered—can be understood in part as a product of the $76 billion dollar Interstate Highway Act of 1956. The federal government invested heavily, and even produced a good chunk of the infrastructure of mass consumption, from the era of canal building through the age of the internet. The United States became a 'fast food nation' in large measure due to federal subsidies to agribusiness, especially corn producers. Lizabeth Cohen and Meg Jacobs have brilliantly examined some of the ways in which the state has shaped consuming practices—by subsidizing suburban housing or fighting inflation, for example—but more work remains to be done in this area, particularly for the pre-twentieth-century years.[28]

The important point here is that the state plays a crucial role in shaping consuming practices that commentators often assume to be a product of individual choice or even luck. The 'vibrancy of the market' in America, as the columnist David Brooks recently wrote, 'grew up accidentally...but it was nurtured by choice.' What Brooks calls an 'accident', however, was the product of the use of the state, which made the 'choice' he celebrates possible. The federal government played a crucial role in shaping the examples Brooks cites of actions which created free markets across great distances, including railroads, land-grant colleges, and antitrust regulations. During his campaign for health

---

[27] G. W. Daniels, 'American Cotton Trade with Liverpool Under the Embargo and Non-Intercourse Acts', *American Historical Review*, 21 (January 1916), 276–87; Burton Crane, 'What Would Boycott Do To Japan?', *New York Times*, 10 October 1937, 71; A. Redpath, quoted in 'A Brilliant Discovery', *Brooklyn Daily Eagle*, 18 August 1884, 2.

[28] This is an implicit theme of David Halberstam, *The Fifties* (New York: Ballantine, 1994); see, for example, 178. On subsidies see, Eric Schlosser, *Fast Food Nation* (Boston: Houghton Mifflin, 2001), 7–8; Michael Pollan, *The Omnivore's Dilemma: A Natural History of Four Meals* (New York: Penguin, 2006), 52; Cohen, *Consumers' Republic*; Jacobs, *Pocketbook Politics*.

care reform, President Barack Obama highlighted the government's role in shaping consumption:

> We could set up a system where food was cheaper than it is right now if we just eliminated meat inspectors, and we eliminated any regulations on how food is distributed and how it's stored. I'll bet in terms of drug prices we would definitely reduce prescription drug prices if we didn't have a drug administration that makes sure that we test the drugs so that they don't kill us, but we don't do that.[29]

States shape markets in a wide variety of ways, which affect, directly and indirectly, all aspects of consumption.

Since the Second World War there has been recognition that federal spending and support for 'the politics of mass consumption' have played major roles in our economy. In the mid-1950s, the United States government was accurately dubbed 'the world's largest consumer'. Since the recession that began in the autumn of 2008, some commentators have pointed to the essential role of federal spending in promoting recovery. As the political blogger Matthew Yglesias wrote in the fall of 2009, 'The economy is suffering from a catastrophic collapse in overall spending with households, businesses, states, and municipalities all pulling back. If the federal government pulls back too we're going to go down the drain.'[30] Since most state governments are hamstrung by balanced budget laws and an abiding aversion to tax increases, federal stimulus spending has been the most effective way to spur the economy.

The nation-state has a history as a significant spender, facilitator, and regulator of consumption that goes back much further than is commonly supposed. In his farewell address, George Washington called for the government to promote 'the progressive improvement of interior communications by land and water.'[31] Just as modern consumer activism developed during the era of the market revolution, so too did an American consumer regime emerge in the first decades of the nineteenth century. Despite the mythology of the free market, the federal government played a crucial role in developing the infrastructure that shaped the simultaneous transportation, market, and consumer revolutions of the first half of the nineteenth century. As George Rogers Taylor noted in his classic study of the transportation revolution, there was 'little or no prejudice against the state enterprise' and the federal government was an 'active and extremely important economic factor in the industrial development of the time.' America's mass production-mass consumption economy was abetted by federal support for railroads, canals, and turnpikes. As Alexander Hamilton's 1791 *Report on Manufacturers* declared, 'The

---

[29] David Brooks, 'The Democrats Rejoice', *New York Times*, 23 March 2010. Obama made these comments during the Health Care Summit, 25 February, 2010.

[30] Matthew Yglesias, 'Nelson: Bad Economy Means We Should Wreck Economy, Destroy Planet, Let Health Care Languish', 6 November 2009, <http://yglesias.thinkprogress.org> (accessed 9 June 2011). 'Biggest consumer' is from Willard L. Thorp, 'The Tariff and the Consumer', *Consumer Reports* (June 1953), 267–71, at 269.

[31] Carter Goodrich, 'National Planning of Internal Improvements', *Political Science Quarterly*, 63 (March 1948), 16–44, at 26.

General Government alone' can 'shorten distances, facilitate commercial and personal intercourse, and unite...the most remote quarters of the United States.' Government policy, not the invisible hand, created 'extensive domestic markets' in the early republic.[32]

Many early American politicians, especially those advocating continental expansion, recognized that markets did not arise automatically but required federal assistance. The idea of 'internal improvements', Carter Goodrich noted, 'may be taken to mean the adoption by government or community of deliberate and concerted policies which are designed to promote economic expansion or prosperity and in which positive action to provide favorable conditions for economic activity is emphasized.' Associating markets not with laissez-faire but with federal coordination, one proponent of westward expansion claimed:

> The great evil, and it is a serious one, indeed, under which the inhabitants of the western country labor, arises from the want of a market. There is no place where the great staple articles for the use of civilized life can be produced in greater abundance or with greater ease, and yet as respects most of the luxuries and many of the conveniences of life the people are poor.

The solution, he and many others believed, was a system of internal improvements that would allow Americans to, as John C. Calhoun put it, 'conquer space.' Even before the late nineteenth century, the federal government provided the visible hand that favored private economic transactions.[33]

The force of consumer regimes in shaping consuming practices is hardly limited to government spending. Two US national projects in particular, slavery and imperialism, did as much, if not more, to make modern American consumer society than the department store and the advertising industry. Yet consumer historians have written far more about the latter than about the former. It was the system of slave labour that first made goods such as sugar, coffee, tobacco, and cotton textiles items of mass consumption. Slavery was not an uniquely American project, of course, but in the nineteenth century, the United States became the largest slaveholding country in the world, one sustained by the compact that the slave South made not only with consumers in the North but also with the people who benefited (and suffered) from the global system of trade that it spawned. At bottom, slavery, one abolitionist noted pointedly, was a system that existed 'for the express purpose of furnishing products to the consumer.' The purchase of slaves itself was a state-sanctioned system of consumption. Moreover, clothing and feeding slaves and providing implements for their labour all became part of a system of mass production in the North and mass consumption in the South. Slave labour in turn produced staples that filled the emporiums of the North. The saturation was so complete

[32] Frank Bourgin, *The Great Challenge: The Myth of Laissez-Faire in the Early Republic* (New York: HarperCollins, 1990). Hamilton is quoted in Goodrich, 'National Planning of Internal Improvements', 18. George Rogers Taylor, *The Transportation Revolution, 1815–1860* (New York: Holt, Rinehart and Winston, 1951), 382–3; Wood, *Empire of Liberty*, 101.

[33] Charles Sellers, *The Market Revolution: Jacksonian America, 1815–1846* (New York: Oxford University Press, 1990), Ch. 3, 78. Goodrich, 'National Planning of Internal Improvements', 16.

that when abolitionists in the free produce movement sought to boycott slave-made goods, their critics within the abolitionist movement pointed out that this was simply impossible since few goods in the United States did not bear the mark of slavery.[34]

Another crucial way in which the American state shaped consumption was in its foreign policy, especially in its search for raw materials, cheap labour, and markets. As Jackson Lears notes, 'imperialism underwrote expanding mass consumption.' After continental expansion was complete by the late nineteenth century, Americans pursued a policy of expansion outside of national borders. Both forms of expansion were deeply rooted in the quest to find consumers abroad and make consumers at home. Simon Patten, the political economist and prescient observer of consumer society, observed that cheap bananas from Latin American had become 'a permanent addition to the labourer's fund of goods.' 'Sugar, which years ago was too expensive to be lavishly consumed by the well-to-do,' Patten wrote in 1907, now 'freely gives its heat to the workingman.' Domestic furnishings increasingly reflected America's global possessions and trade.[35]

Nation-states also formulate and enforce policies that shape the economics of consumption in a polity. Even more important than the US government's role as a spender were the ways in which it shaped consumption choices through legislation, offered (or withheld) consumer protection, and shaped industry through land grants, tax abatements, subsidies, and foreign policy, especially through the pursuit of empire, and through immigration policies that made goods and peoples part of the American system of production and consumption. States serve as facilitators of consumption, setting the parameters for the kinds of consumption that are rewarded (through tax credits), dissuaded (through sin taxes or high tariffs), or made illegal (for example, by the prohibition of alcohol or narcotics). Political scientists and sociologists have been attuned in recent years to ways in which the state shapes market cultures. Rather than viewing the market as an ahistorical abstraction, they have shown that 'market culture' is a product of a combination of forces, which differs in each country and era. The sociologist Douglas S. Massey, for example, questions whether 'in the absence of human "interference" markets will spring into existence smoothly' and claims instead that 'markets are constituted by the society in which they are embedded.'[36]

Just as the era of modern consumer activism began in the early nineteenth century, in that period lay the origins of America's consumer regime, which, as with consumer activism, built on eighteenth-century precedents. As the market revolution—abetted

[34] Quote from 'Products of Slave Labour', *Non Slaveholder* (April 1847), 84–9. James Walvin, 'Slavery and Mass Consumption and the Dynamics of the Atlantic World: An Overview', in Douglas Hamilton and Robert J. Blyth (eds.), *Representing Slavery: Art, Artifacts and Archives in the Collections of the National Maritime Museum* (Aldershot: Ashgate, 2007), 18–27.

[35] Simon N. Patten, *The New Basis of Civilization* (New York: Macmillan, 1907), quoted in Jackson Lears, *Rebirth of a Nation: The Making of Modern America, 1877–1920* (New York: Harper Collins, 2009), 282–3. Charles Maier, *Among Empires: American Ascendancy and its Predecessors* (Cambridge, MA: Harvard University Press, 2006), 238–4.

[36] Douglas S. Massey, *Return of the 'L' Word: A Liberal Vision for the New Century* (Princeton: Princeton University Press, 2005), 44–5.

by government policy—separated production and consumption, it presented new dilemmas for consumers, who could no longer vouch from direct experience for the quality and safety of the food they ate, the clothing they wore, and the durables that increasingly entered their homes. Many of these dilemmas were due to lack of information about products that had previously been crafted in the home or community. This lack of information redounded in two directions for consumers. While consumer activists focused on the responsibility shoppers bore for those who made the goods they bought, many citizens came to believe that the state needed to protect them from the potential (and often invisible) dangers of goods. 'With the transportation revolution came the gradual disappearance of the family cow,' wrote George Rogers Taylor, 'and this fact led to the necessity of protecting the common milk supply.' In his special address on consumer protection in 1967, Lyndon Johnson, pointing to the precedent of laws prohibiting fraudulent use of the mail, noted that consumer protection already had a century-old history.[37] The federal government began to regulate food and drugs in 1906, but some individual states and municipalities regulated food and drink in the nineteenth century. As *Harper's* reported in 1892, food was often:

> rendered impure and something else than that which the consumers think they are buying. It has become so common a practice that many merchants indulge in these adulterations as a matter of course, and with no thought that it is dishonest in itself and made criminal by the laws of many of the States.[38]

Local governments, following the late medieval practice, continued to regulate the price and size of loaves of bread, a doctrine known as the 'assize of bread', well into the nineteenth century. The commissioners of Mobile, Alabama, for example, levied a 'tariff for bakers' in 1814, fixing the weight of the loaf in accordance with the price of flour. (They regularly changed the required weight to account for changing prices of raw materials.) The Common Council of New York City enforced an assize until 1821 and long afterwards required that bakers sell a standard loaf. As late as 1841, the Alabama Supreme Court upheld the assize as constitutional since, 'the great end [urban bread supply] is better secured by licensing…than by leaving it to the voluntary acts of individuals.'[39]

Another way in which the US government claimed to protect consumers came in its enactment of anti-trust legislation, particularly the Sherman Act of 1890. According to one scholar in 1912, the purpose of this legislation was the 'protection of the consumer from extortion by monopoly.' Indeed, the idea of 'consumer protection' first emerged in discussions of anti-trust laws (and, as we will see, in tariff debates as well). Anti-trust legislation did not promise protection from dangerous or poisonous goods but simply

---

[37] Taylor, *The Transportation Revolution*, 379; 'Text of President Johnson's Special Message to Congress on Consumer Protection', *New York Times*, 17 February 1967, 24.

[38] 'Food Adulterations', *Harper's Weekly*, 11 June 1892, 570–1.

[39] 'An Assize of Bread in Mobile, Alabama', *Quarterly Journal of Economics*, 21 (February 1907), 330–2; Sean Wilentz, *Chants Democratic: New York City and the Rise of the American Working Class, 1788–1850* (New York: Oxford University Press, 1984), 139. See also Taylor, *Transportation Revolution*, 378–9; Novak, *The People's Welfare*, 90.

from the high prices which could result from the existence of monopolistic firms.[40] This was consumer protection through federal enforcement of market competition.

Throughout the nineteenth century one of the central policy issues and one of the only topics of fundamental political disagreement was the protective tariff. Indeed, the debate over a tax on imports marked one of the few clear differences between Democrats and Republicans in the post-Civil War era. The debate about the tariff is usually understood through a productivist lens but seeing it from a consumerist viewpoint adds an important perspective. Free traders in particular emphasized that the consumer interest lay at the heart of their vision but was 'subordinate' in the protectionist world view.[41] In his history of the tariff, Frank William Taussig proclaimed that the tariff 'brings a burden on the domestic consumer.'[42] 'No tariff ever guards consumers' rights,' wrote Will Atkinson in a defence of free trade in 1929. 'Tariffs always and everywhere plunder consumers.'[43] One of the first uses of the phrase 'consumer protection' came in an address by Grover Cleveland, the ex-President, in a 1902 address on the benefits of a downward tariff revision.[44] Similarly, a front page cartoon in *Harper's Weekly* entitled 'The Consumer Consumed' showed a shopper victimized by the protective tariff on imported goods and the trusts on domestic goods. The cartoonist called for the government to step in to protect the consumer in both cases.[45]

The idea of a state-promoted 'consumer interest' was popularized in the course of the tariff debate. 'We have long been accustomed to the view that the consumer's interest is a subordinate one,' wrote Jesse Orton in 1909, initiating a new era in which calls for government recognition of and advancement of the consumer interest became a mainstay of political discourse. He did so, as did most of contemporaries, by talking about the tariff.[46] The home economist Elizabeth Hoyt shared the view that 'Up to the present, practically all the action on tariffs has been taken by producers.' For Hoyt this denied the importance of a consumer identity and of the true importance of consumption. 'Yet every producer and every wage earner is a consumer, and consuming is, after all, the end and goal of producing.' By 1961, in an article on tariff reform, a reporter for the *New York Times* was noting that both sides referred to consumers as 'the great mass of unorganized citizens whose needs and wants keep the economy humming.' By that time, this privileging of consumers as a group had long become the conventional wisdom, although many business leaders and politicians responded to this need not with consumer protection

---

[40] 'For the Benefit of Consumers', *New York Times*, 11 May 1892, 9; 'Mr. Sherman's Views Again', *New York Times*, 13 Sep 1890, 4; 'Anti-Trust Amendment: Scheme of Senator Nelson to Protect Consumers and Vendors of Sugar', *New York Times*, 19 June 1897, 3; Charles A. Boston, 'The Spirit behind the Sherman Anti-Trust Law', *Yale Law Journal*, 21 (1912), 341–71, q uotation at 347.

[41] Jesse Orton, 'Tariff Revision from a Consumer's Standpoint', *Popular Science Monthly* (1909), 463–7.

[42] Frank William Taussig, *The Tariff History of the United States*, 6th edn. (New York: G. P. Putnam's Sons, 1914), 398. See also 53, 186, 227, 279, 300, 421, 422.

[43] Will Atkinson, 'Guarding the Consumer', *New York Times*, 29 June 1929, 8.

[44] 'Grover Cleveland On Tariff Reform', *New York Times*, 31 October 1902, 5.

[45] *Harper's Weekly*, 7 April 1888, cover.

[46] Jesse F. Orton, 'Tariff Revision and the Consumer', *Independent*, 11 March 1909, 524–8, at 524.

but with business-friendly policies that they claimed would ultimately redound to the consumer's benefit.[47]

VI

Consumer politics is not entirely contained by the nation-state. American consumer activism, for example, was born in part through the legacy of what I have called 'early modern' consumer protests, such as ostracism and bread riots; events that dotted the landscape of Britain's American colonies and continued to dominate colonial protest through the early phases of the American Revolution. Furthermore, consumer activism, as we have seen, has often taken diasporic forms. The boycott itself was a transnational development, practised first by Irish peasants, coined by a (Scottish-born) American journalist, and popularized in the 1880s by the mostly immigrant American working class. In the twentieth century, the anti-Nazi and Japanese silks boycotts were international, carried out in many countries. The consumer movement too moved beyond the nation-state. The product-testing arm of the consumer movement was born in the United States but was quickly exported to other industrialized countries. In the 1950s and 1960s, leaders of the American consumer movement helped to build an international consumer movement. And, of course, the American state worked hard to create other consumer regimes in its own likeness and interest.[48]

At the same time, consumer politics has taken distinct forms in the United States, in large part because of American's longstanding recognition—even invention—of consumption as a political act. Moreover, all three of its core elements have been consistently powerful forces and inextricable parts of American political culture. Finally, the parameters set by the American consumer regime shaped not only consumer practices but consumer politics. As the nation-state encouraged consumption and recognized a consumer interest, grass roots groups and lobbyists were able to use the power of consumption for different purposes and to redefine the meaning of consumer welfare. Occasionally all of these forces intersected, as in 1885 when the 'Gas Consumers' Association' of New York City held an 'indignation meeting' and 'resolved to black list every legislator who did not vote as they liked and to support or oppose every candidate for the Senate or Assembly next Fall, according as he did or did not promise to vote as they wished.' Here we have a group of consumer activists mobilizing into a consumer movement making demands upon the consumer regime.[49]

[47] Elizabeth E. Hoyt, 'Tariffs and the Consumer', *Journal of Home Economics*, 26 (February 1934), 82–6, at 82; Brendan M. Jones, 'Consumer Stake In Tariff Noted', *New York Times*, 10 December 1961, F1.

[48] Emily S. Rosenberg, *Spreading the American Dream: American Economic and Cultural Expansion, 1890–1945* (New York: Hill and Wang, 1982); Victoria de Grazia, *Irresistible Empire: America's Advance through Twentieth-Century Europe* (Cambridge MA: Harvard University Press, 2005); Matthew Hilton, *Prosperity for All: Consumer Activism in an Era of Globalization* (Ithaca NY: Cornell University Press, 2008).

[49] 'New York Gas Consumers Association,' *Brooklyn Daily Eagle*, 6 June 1885, 4.

Distinguishing among forms of consumer politics, then, should not lead us to ignore the overlaps and connections among them. But doing so helps us understand both the historical and conceptual development of the politics of consumption, and it allows us to examine these developments from many different points of view. As we have seen, the consumers' perspective was not always foremost in the minds of state actors. Even consumer activists were wary of overt concern for the consumers' point of view; they cared more about consumer responsibility. Proponents of the consumer movement, on the contrary, believed in the necessity of representing and lobbying for the consumer viewpoint, but even they defined the 'consumer interest' in a variety of ways. Historians of consumer politics should, like the actors they study, seek to understand these distinct points of view. And they should aim to consider these distinct missions and viewpoints as they explore the politics of consumption.

Bibliography

Breen, T. H., *The Marketplace of Revolution: How Consumer Politics Shaped American Independence* (New York: Oxford University Press, 2005).

Cohen, Lizabeth, *A Consumers' Republic: The Politics of Mass Consumption in Postwar America* (New York: Knopf, 2003).

de Grazia, Victoria, *Irresistible Empire: America's Advance through Twentieth-Century Europe* (Cambridge MA: Harvard University Press, 2005).

Donohue, Kathleen G., *Freedom from Want: American Liberalism and the Idea of the Consumer* (Baltimore: Johns Hopkins University Press, 2003).

Glickman, Lawrence B., *Buying Power: A History of Consumer Activism in America* (Chicago: University of Chicago Press, 2009).

Hoganson, Kristin, *Consumers' Imperium: The Global Production of American Domesticity, 1865–1920* (Chapel Hill: University of North Carolina Press, 2007).

Jacobs, Meg, *Pocketbook Politics: Economic Citizenship in Twentieth-Century America* (Princeton: Princeton University Press, 2005).

McGovern, Charles F., *Sold American: Consumption and Citizenship, 1890–1945* (Chapel Hill: University of North Carolina Press, 2006).

CHAPTER 21

....

CONSUMPTION AND NATIONALISM: CHINA

....

KARL GERTH

THE topic of *consumption and nationalism* combines two of the most important historical forces in modern history and, unsurprisingly, of recent historical studies. While *consumption* occurs in all times and places, *consumerism* is an historically more recent and precise phenomenon that refers to consumption of branded, mass-produced goods and services, the proliferation of media images about them, and the orientation of social life around them. That is, consumerism involves the creation or reproduction of social identity through the consumption of such things, rather than through family, generation, ethnicity, gender, place of work, or class, though, of course, these forms of identity are never mutually exclusive. Consumption and nationalism have intersected with efforts by nation-states, business leaders, patriotic students, and other figures to define buying and use as a political statement through the non-consumption of things from other countries and the consumption of one's own nation's goods and services.

The modern Chinese experience reveals the range of activities linking consumption and nationalism. Indeed, as I have argued elsewhere, the politicization of consumption at the end of the nineteenth and start of the twentieth century became a key way in which intellectuals and politicians *defined* and the general population *experienced* nationalism.[1] In China and throughout the globe, consumption has served as a battleground in the creation of the modern nation. This essay traces the changing manifestations of these historical connections between consumption and nationalism across modern Chinese history up to the present, focusing on the most conspicuous form of economic nationalism in the twentieth century, boycotts, as well as a newer form, brand nationalism.

[1] For an extensive discussion on the introduction, spread, and political uses of economic nationalism throughout urban society in China before the Second World War, see Karl Gerth, *China Made: Consumer Culture and the Creation of the Nation*, (Cambridge, MA: Harvard University Press, 2003).

China provides a useful basis of comparison for scholars of other nations. After all, China was not the only country to attempt to nationalize its nascent consumer culture by constraining individual consumer behaviour in the name of national interests.[2] The *swadeshi* (belonging to one's own country) and non-cooperation movements in India (1904–8, 1920–22) are the best-known and best-studied equivalents of China's efforts.[3] Likewise, scholars of American history have been aware of links between consumerism and nationalism since late colonial times to the present.[4] Indeed, Chinese seeking to link nationalism and consumption regularly sought to justify such links with reports on the activities of similar campaigns in other countries, often arguing that economic nationalism is the foundation of Western power and not simply a reaction against Western domination of trade.

Thus economic nationalism in China should be seen as one among many forms rather than as a unique phenomenon. What makes the Chinese case particularly interesting for comparative purposes is that the country was not formally colonized yet lacked many aspects of sovereignty, including the ability to set tariffs, the most straightforward way states push citizens to consume certain products, by making imports prohibitively or simply unattractively expensive. To use the common Chinese term for the country's situation, China was 'semi-colonial' (*ban zhimindide*). And, for this reason, the Chinese efforts to promote patriotic consumption were not, nor could have been, solely state directed.

LINKING NATIONALISM AND CONSUMERISM VIA BOYCOTTS

Although Chinese intellectuals were developing ideological and state policy forms of economic nationalism in the late nineteenth century, in the early twentieth century boycotts became the most visible—and violent—aspect of the Chinese attempts to nationalize consumption. A key problem facing those who wished to link consumption and nationalism in any nation, then as now, was how to convince one's compatriots to 'buy domestic', or, more fundamentally, how to persuade people to think of products in terms

---

[2] On the intersection of nationalism and consumerism in Latin America, see Benjamin S. Orlove (ed.), *The Allure of the Foreign: Imported Goods in Postcolonial Latin America* (Ann Arbor: University of Michigan Press, 1997).

[3] For a good overview of the better studied Indian case, see C. A. Bayly, 'The origins of Swadeshi (Home Industry): cloth and Indian society, 1700–1930', in Arjun Appadurai (ed.), *The Social Life of Things: Commodities in Cultural Perspective* (Cambridge: Cambridge University Press, 1986), 285–321; Sumit Sarkar *The Swadeshi Movement in Bengal, 1903–1908* (Cambridge: Cambridge University Press, 1973).

[4] For a survey of efforts to link nationalism and consumption in America from the Boston Tea Party to the present, see Dana Frank, *Buy American: The Untold Story of Economic Nationalism* (Boston: Beacon Press, 1999).

of their nationality—to divide the world of goods into 'foreign' and 'domestic' products—and then enlist consumers to buy goods based on nationality rather than other criteria such as price or quality.

During and since the twentieth century, boycotts have played a pivotal role in instilling, sometimes even forcibly, the notion that every product has a nationality and that product nationality should determine consumers' purchasing decisions. In the first third of the twentieth century, boycotts precipitated or accompanied major turning-points in China's relations with the imperialist powers, affecting not only consumers but also merchants and manufacturers as the former removed or disguised imported products and the latter purged foreign materials or design elements from their goods to make them appear as Chinese as possible. Significant consumer boycotts of foreign goods took place every few years between 1905 and 1931 and then nearly continuously into the Second Sino-Japanese War in 1937–45.[5] The policies behind the boycotts may have even provoked the war with Japan, which Japan fought to ensure access to Chinese markets.[6]

In several ways, the nationalistic boycotts of foreign consumer products that began before the Sino-Japanese War followed a predictable pattern. They invariably began after a specific 'national humiliation' (or *guochi*, as the Chinese label such incidents then and now) prompted a popular protest that included a boycott. They generally ended when government suppression from above, inertia from below, and the profit motive of merchants who priced imports irresistibly inexpensively undermined the commitment of participants. Yet these individual boycotts should not be seen—as they usually are in textbooks and monographs alike—as suddenly emerging from nowhere as an emotional response to an act of foreign aggression, but rather viewed as simply the most conspicuous aspect of a broader, continuous effort to combine nascent nationalism and consumer culture by teaching the Chinese to differentiate 'Chinese products' from 'foreign products'. Although boycotts always included opportunists such as hooligans and petty government officials who used the events to shake down merchants, their core supporters remained active between boycotts, cultivating the basis of economic nationalism more generally. Even when boycotts inevitably failed to ban the targeted imports, they played a pivotal role in developing Chinese nationalism and anti-imperialism.

Take, for example, the anti-American boycott of 1905. Like subsequent boycotts, this one had an identifiable spark: the increasingly restrictive US immigration measures

---

[5] The most comprehensive survey of anti-imperialist boycotts remains Charles F. Remer, *A Study of Chinese Boycotts, with Special Reference to Their Economic Effectiveness* (Baltimore: John Hopkins University Press, 1933). Remer's study differs from my own in that he views boycotts as recurring but only loosely connected events rather than part of a broader web of economic nationalist activity and institution-building. The best study of the economic impact of various boycotts remains Kikuchi Takaharu, *Chūgoku minzoku undō no kihon kōzō: Taigai boikotto no kenkyū* (The Historical Background of the Chinese National Movement: a Study of Anti-foreign Boycotts) (Tokyo: Daian, 1974), who does a better job intensifying the key merchant organizations behind boycotts.

[6] This link between boycotts and the war is made in Donald A. Jordan, *Chinese Boycotts Versus Japanese Bombs: The Failure of China's 'Revolutionary Diplomacy', 1931–32* (Ann Arbor: University of Michigan Press, 1991).

toward the Chinese. To express their outrage and pressure the United States to change its policies, Chinese merchants in cities throughout China began to boycott American products. This boycott was critical to the development of a sustained economic national-ist movement for four reasons: it initiated a long series of anti-imperialist boycotts, was national and even international in scope, cut across class lines, and created new ways and co-opted others to foster popular participation. These methods included modifying popular songs, destroying stocks of American products, soliciting pledges, tearing down advertisement posters for American goods, spreading rumours (e.g., that American cig-arettes contained poison), and using advertisements to identify products as Chinese and encourage their consumption. Protestors used different media to reach as many people as possible: newspapers for the cultural elite; songs, lectures, slogans, drama perform-ances, and cartoons of mistreated Chinese for a wider audience; and handbills, leaflets, and placards written in the colloquial language for intermediate groups. In short, the boycott, which gradually dissolved by 1906, began to force a link between consumption and nationalism by promoting a sense of empowerment through consumption choices.[7]

The protests surrounding the Versailles Peace Conference (1919), which grew into the larger May Fourth Movement, provide another example of how boycotts furthered the development of Chinese nationalism. Again, a specific 'national humiliation' was at the centre of these protests, in this case a shift in foreign control of Shandong province. Since the late nineteenth century, the province had been part of Germany's 'sphere of interest' in China. During the First World War, however, Japan took it over and required China to recognize its interests there as part of the Twenty-One Demands the Japanese had pre-sented to Chinese president Yuan Shikai in 1915. China, however, had expected to recover control of the Shandong concessions as a reward for entering the war against Germany, an expectation heightened by Woodrow Wilson's rhetoric of self-determination. But Japan had carefully laid the groundwork for assuming control with secret agreements, and the publicizing of these agreements during the Versailles Peace Conference sparked Chinese demonstrations. On 4 May, several thousand students gathered in Tiananmen Square at the entrance to the Forbidden City to advocate the return of Qingdao and denounce the Versailles settlement. In the following weeks and months, the inhabit-ants of some two hundred Chinese cities in more than twenty provinces participated in strikes and boycotts that aimed to translate humiliation into retaliation by boycotting Japanese products, ships, and currency. For more than a year, new humiliations con-tinually stoked anti-imperialist sentiments and kept the boycotts alive.

Chinese politicians also tacitly or openly encouraged boycotts to politicize con-sumption. By 1925, the Nationalist Party (Guomindang) had begun to strengthen its relationships with organizations advocating economic nationalism, and the boycotts it

---

[7] On the many forms of protest adopted and created by participants in this first nationwide boycott, see Wang Guanhua, In Search of Justice: The 1905–1906 Chinese Anti-American Boycott, East Asian Monograph series (Cambridge, MA: Harvard University Press, 2001). For a thorough account of how Chinese and foreign businesses positioned themselves during boycotts, see Sherman Cochran, Big Business in China: Sino-Foreign Rivalry in the Cigarette Industry, 1890–1930 (Cambridge, MA: Harvard University Press, 1980).

supported in 1928 and 1931 were the most effective to date.[8] Although the Nationalists were able greatly to extend the scope of these boycotts, they never completely controlled them.[9] In fact, it can be said that proponents of economic nationalism used the Nationalist government as much as the other way around, as when they used an official government campaign against cigarette-smoking in the mid-1930s as a pretext for confiscating foreign cigarettes. Ultimately, heavy pressure from Japan and the policy of 'first internal pacification, then external resistance' convinced Nationalist leader Chiang Kai-shek (Jiang Jieshi, 1887–1975) to withdraw his party's support for boycotts. Nevertheless, even after his government tried to suppress the May 1932 boycott by, among other things, banning the popular term 'enemy products' (*dihuo*), many Chinese continued to pressure merchants by picketing stores, confiscating goods, sending intimidating anonymous letters and postcards, disrupting distribution channels, pasting posters on store fronts, and forcing shopkeepers to place advertisements vowing not to sell imports in local newspapers.

NATIONALISM AND COMMODITY SPECTACLES

A more subtle mode of linking consumerism to nationalism in the early twentieth century was an interlocking set of nationalistic commodity spectacles that included modern imaged-based advertising, museums, department stores, and exhibitions that all articulated and propagated this link through a nationalistic visuality.[10] Once again, China provides an interesting contrast with Western cases. While the idea of such commodity spectacles may have been borrowed from Western countries and Japan, in China they were taken a step further and transformed to promote nationalistic consumption through museums devoted to displaying national products, markets and stores that sold only national products, and an advertising culture that constructed and emphasized product nationality. Collectively, these efforts projected onto commodities such nationalistic aspirations as unity against foreign imperialism and domestic division, economic strength and self-sufficiency, and, above all, the possibility of following a modern lifestyle without surrendering to imperialist economic penetration.

Chinese advocates of nationalistic consumption appropriated commodity spectacles from Europe and America, often by way of Japan. As with many other modern institutions, Japan helped introduce industrial exhibitions to China. The Japanese government

---

[8] On these links between the Nationalists and business organizations, see Joseph Fewsmith, *Party, State, and Local Elites in Republican China: Merchant Organizations and Politics in Shanghai, 1890–1930* (Honolulu: University of Hawaii Press, 1985), which also contains a very helpful account of early economic nationalist ideology in the late nineteenth and early twentieth centuries.

[9] Gerth, *China Made*, especially ch. 4. A central argument of this book is that boycotts should not be viewed as isolated incidents that arise out of nowhere and recede to nowhere after they sputter out. By the same token, this does not mean that that are creations of the Nationalist government, as contemporary foreign observers loudly argued.

[10] See Gerth, *China Made*, especially chs. 5 and 6.

began organizing industrial exhibitions and smaller bazaars (*kankōba*) within Japan around the time of the 1868 Meiji restoration.[11] Early Chinese reformers such as Kang Youwei, a leader of the Hundred Days Reforms of 1898, which tried to revive China's struggling Qing dynasty, suggested that China follow Japan's lead by holding trade fairs.[12] Indeed, from government officials to merchants to students, Chinese who promoted the idea of economic nationalism consistently referred to the need to emulate the Japanese use of commodity spectacles to promote nationalistic consumption. They saw such displays not only as an element in Japan's rise to industrial power but also as a tool in its imperialistic designs on China by winning over consumer loyalties. Now China sought to appropriate these same institutions.

At the same time as major cities throughout the world were holding cosmopolitan events intended to showcase products from as many countries as possible, China began hosting dozens—even hundreds—of exhibitions limited strictly to 'national products' (*guohuo*), as such products were now called.

The study of economic nationalism via consumers and consumption is a potentially rich field of historical and contemporary investigation. Despite the emergence of consumer nationalist movements throughout the globe, historians have neither devoted much attention to them nor suggested that they are key aspects of nation-making. When mentioned at all, the nationalization of consumer culture is treated as a natural by-product of the creation of nation-states. In fact, the causes and consequences of nationalizing commodities played a crucial role in creating nations. Perhaps modern nation-states did not precede the notion of each nation having its own 'national products'. Rather, the two constructs may have evolved together dialectically. Nation-making included learning, or being coerced, to shape preferences around something called the nation and away from items deemed 'foreign'—a problematic process reinforced by institutional elaborations, and driven by consumer nationalists.

AFTER 1949: NATIONALIZING CONSUMPTION VIA THE STATE

By far the least studied period of economic nationalism in twentieth-century China is the period from the formation of the People's Republic of China in 1949 until the death of Mao Zedong in 1976. This period sees fundamental changes in the manifestations of economic nationalism in China. In short, the new state soon ends the ease with which consumers could choose foreign products, making earlier social movements to promote patriotic consumption of Chinese 'national products' unnecessary and irrelevant.

---

[11] Yoshimi Shun'ya, *Hakurankai no seijigaku: manazashi no kindai* (The Politics of Exhibitions: a Look at Modernity) (Tokyo: Chūkō shinsho, 1992).

[12] Hsiao Liang-lin, *A Modern China and a New World: K'ang Yu-wei, Reformer and Utopian, 1858–1927* (Seattle: University of Washington Press, 1975).

Unsurprisingly, popular expressions of economic nationalism focused on consumption fade while Mao Zedong's regime attempts to turn cities known for their consumption into centres of production instead, emulating the Soviet Union's economic model that emphasized state-owned heavy industry over consumer goods. China also gradually forces foreign multinationals to leave China, thereby eliminating most foreign products from store shelves. After some initial hesitation that allowed bourgeois consumer life-styles to persist into the mid-1950s, the state appropriated all private enterprises, and consumer culture was virtually outlawed.

Thirty years later, after the death of Chairman Mao in 1976, China once again dramati-cally changed political course, which allowed for the re-emergence of older forms of eco-nomic nationalism.[13] Since the start of China's market reforms under Deng Xiaoping in 1978, imports from capitalist countries have once again arrived in ever greater numbers. As China has reintegrated itself into global capitalist markets, boycotts have re-emerged as an economic and political weapon in the face of increased competition with estab-lished Chinese economic interests and a growing consumer movement, which is ever ready to call a boycott against companies and countries deemed to have treated Chinese consumers unfairly.

With the start of Deng Xiaoping's economic reforms and the policy known as 'open-ing to the outside world', or simply the Open Door Policy, China slowly began to per-mit the importation of consumer goods, reasoning that allowing imports was a small price to pay for access to foreign consumer markets for their own products. But over the past three decades, as the range and volume of imports has grown, the tension between Chinese 'national products' and 'foreign products' has periodically re-emerged in Chinese attitudes. Beginning with the lead-up to China's ascension to the World Trade Organization (WTO) in 2001, nationalistic consumer activism has grown, for several reasons. First, WTO commitments that allowed multinationals easier access to the Chinese market rendered countless domestic enterprises uncompetitive and created millions of unemployed workers. Second, a new generation of patriotic students has continued to invoke the language of economic nationalism and call for boycotts, as in the widespread boycotts of the French retailing giant Carrefour in China in the spring of 2008 in retaliation for the disruption of the Olympic torch relay in Paris. Finally, domes-tic consumers periodically call for boycotts of specific foreign products when they feel they have collectively been treated poorly by multinational companies. Such actions demonstrate doubts among the Chinese about the wisdom of leaving national well-being to the 'free market'.

It is clear, then, that the strong connection between consumption and nationalism did not end with China's entry into the WTO in 2001. Especially since the global finan-cial crisis began unfolding in 2008, political and business leaders around the world have increasingly called upon Chinese consumers to rescue the global economy by saving less

---

[13] For a discussion of these new and re-emergent forms of economic nationalism since 1989, see Joseph Fewsmith, *China since Tiananmen: The Politics of Transition* (Cambridge: Cambridge University Press, 2001).

and consuming more. China's leaders have had their own reasons for wanting to promote domestic consumption and to shift China from a producing to a consuming society. In 2008, Li Keqiang, a rising political star, voiced the conventional wisdom among top Chinese policymakers that 'boosting domestic demand is essential for propping up growth', especially in the face of global economic weakness.[14] Thus Chinese leaders have implemented policies designed to dismantle barriers to increased consumption, particularly of domestic goods and services, including macroeconomic policies such as making it easier for banks to lend money by easing credit and reserve restrictions and discouraging savings by lowering interest rates. With a vast potential consumer market outside China's major cities, officials have also attempted to stimulate rural consumption by improving the power grid and subsidizing the costs of mobile phones, washing-machines, and flat-screen televisions.[15] To encourage indirectly consumers to tap into their 'rainy day savings', they have also begun to re-strengthen social welfare provisions by introducing health insurance and ensuring minimum income (*di bao*). They have also increased buying power by giving civil servants pay rises, abolishing agricultural taxes, and allowing the Chinese currency to appreciate within limits.[16]

These policies have been implemented with a growing sense of alarm. Wanting to avoid the stagnation experienced by other Asian export-led economies such as Japan, Korea, and Taiwan, Chinese leaders have identified domestic demand as the key to long-term economic security. They have long feared that the country has become too dependent on overspent US consumers and that a political backlash in America over surging imports and the growing trade deficit could lead the United States to restrict China's access to its markets. To counter this, China's policymakers hope to increase the country's annual average consumption rate from 35 per cent of GDP—already down from the mid-1980s, when it stood at 50 per cent, and the lowest for any major economy—to something closer to the US and world average of 70–80 per cent.

The Chinese government has also enacted specific policies to promote leisure spending as it anxiously pushes its economy away from an over-reliance on polluting and energy-intensive heavy industry and towards service industries. China has implemented weekend or 'double leisure days' (*shangxiu ri*) and the five-day, forty-hour work week, and promoted the relatively new notion of vacationing as patriotic. The government's intention, as announced by former Vice Premier Wu Yi at the 2006 Hangzhou World Leisure Expo, is to see that leisure activities do not become 'the privilege of a minority of people' but, rather, popular and widespread.[17] The most high profile of these efforts has been the creation of Japanese-style Golden Weeks, three seven-day annual national holidays around Chinese Lunar New Year, Labor Day, and National Day Golden Week

---

[14] 'China's vice premier urges demand boost: state media', *Agence France-Presse*, 20 August 2008.

[15] Andrew Jacobs, 'China's economy, in need of jump start, waits for citizens' fists to loosen', *New York Times*, 2 December 2008; Elaine Kurtenbach, 'China boosts subsidies for car, appliance buyers', *Associated Press*, 19 May 2009.

[16] Kathy Fong, 'China wants to boost consumer spending', *China Daily*, 9 January 2006.

[17] 'Wu Yi: Jiji fazhan xiuxian fuwu, buduan tigao shenghuo zhilian' ('Wu Yi: The positive development of leisure and service, steadily improve the quality of life'), *Xinhua*, 23 April 2006.

(commemorating the establishment of the People's Republic of China on 1 October 1949). These weeks have provided a huge boost to domestic tourism, so much so that the government recently discontinued them in an attempt to spread Chinese travel more evenly throughout the year. During the first National Day Golden Week in 1999, some 28 million Chinese took to the road; eight years later, the number had climbed to over 120 million. The increased promotion of leisure activities and travel have led to the overnight creation of a massive tourist industry in China, now a critical and deeply entrenched part of the economy. Travel agencies, once few and state-run, have become ubiquitous. Likewise, Hainan Island, once a sparsely populated and underdeveloped hinterland off the coast of Vietnam, is becoming for the Chinese what Hawaii is to Americans.

The policy shift of moving from a labour- and energy-intensive economy to one focused on services and consumerism has led to new forms of economic nationalism. In China, branding—always a central feature of modern consumer cultures—has now become much more overtly an issue of economic nationalism than in the United States and elsewhere.[18] In China, consumerism is not simply a product of the free market, something that developed naturally once the Chinese state got out of the way, but rather a consequence of ongoing policy decisions by China's leaders. Chinese leaders see stimulating domestic consumer demand as the key to the country's long-term economic (and therefore political) well-being. In addition to its decision to join the WTO and allow multinational companies much greater access to Chinese consumers, China's government has committed its influence and resources to building internationally competitive China-based brands. Building or buying such brands is considered a matter of national economic security and national pride. The success of Chinese brands depends, first of all, on convincing Chinese consumers to buy them, as opposed to ensuring consumer loyalty to domestic manufacturers as had been the case since 1949—by protecting China's markets, banning imports, limiting access to the foreign currency needed to buy imports, and levying tariffs so high that foreign goods became prohibitively expensive. In effect, then, the logic of China's economic development strategy is leading it to urge both state and private companies to spend billions building brands.

Having caught up with its foreign competitors as a global manufacturing superpower, the Chinese recognize that their country now needs to move up the value chain and also become a brand superpower. Chinese government and business leaders view domestic ownership of global brands and intellectual property as symbolic of national wealth and power, the economic equivalent of hosting the Olympics, but much more permanent. China wants its own domestic companies to join the list of prominent global brands associated with powerful countries such as the United States (Microsoft, Boeing, Starbucks, Google), Germany (BMW), Japan (Honda, Nintendo, Sony), and Korea (LG, Samsung). The government also wants to develop competitive brands across the

---

[18] I explore these newer forms and manifestations of economic nationalism in *As China Goes, So Goes the World: How Chinese Consumers are Transforming Everything* (New York, NY: Hill & Wang, 2010), especially Chapter 5.

spectrum of consumer products and services, including high-tech consumer electronics, and to revive 'established brands' in traditional areas such as medicine. This push to create Chinese-owned brands also applies to the service sector, where the Ministry of Commerce has set ambitious targets for developing restaurant and hotel brands and prominent brands in the beauty, laundry, and home service industries.[19] To help accomplish these goals, state policies have promoted the creation of large-scale, horizontally integrated, multinational corporations to compete against foreign multinationals. In the 1990s, the state selected a 'national team' of 120 industrial groups to receive state assistance and promoted 925 top domestic brands.[20]

That this government-directed movement has had some success in weaning Chinese consumers from a preference for international brands can be seen in the growing popular indignation at what is seen as the inferior treatment of Chinese consumers by foreign companies. As domestic product quality has improved and demand for higher-quality products and luxury goods has grown, so have expectations of brand performance. Consumers, no longer content with First World market leftovers, have felt increasingly aggrieved, arguing that multinationals do not respect Chinese consumers, take market access for granted, cut corners on safety and quality, ignore Chinese laws, and dump their low-end products in the country. The Chinese media, sensitive to such slights and feelings, inevitably highlights the foreignness of a company and its commodities whenever any consumer scandal related to imported goods breaks out. In 2003, for instance, media stories about a Shanghai-based company that claimed to have been overcharged by Dell for computers, led to a public campaign against Dell and other foreign companies, forcing Dell to compensate customers. In 2005, quality problems and recalls undermined the reputation of several major international brands, such as KFC, Heinz, Nikon, Sony, and Nestlé. In contrast, powerful domestic brands are sometimes protected from similar consumer scandals. For instance, in 1997, the head of the Beijing *Youth Daily* was fired after publishing a report claiming that yoghurt drinks manufactured by the state-owned Hangzhou Wahaha Group had fatally poisoned several children.[21]

As China becomes increasingly inundated with new waves of products and brands, Chinese consumers demand that the government protect Chinese brands against international rivals, even as those same consumers simultaneously often prefer and buy foreign products. Chinese companies sometimes take advantage of these sentiments to boost business, building bigger businesses and creating nationalistic-minded consumers at the same time. Take online gaming, where imports account for 90 per cent of China's $500 million market. This led a Chinese software company to collaborate with the China Youth Union, the Communist Party's youth division, to develop an online game called

[19] 'Zhonghua laozihao' Bejing Zuiduo, Shangwubu muqian gongbu shou pi mingdan' ('China's established brands: Beijing has the most'), *Beijing yule xinbao*, 8 October 2006.

[20] An Li, '925 ge chanpin de juhui' ('A gathering for 925 products'), *Zhongguo zhiliang yu pinpai*, 1 (2006). Cambridge University Professor of Management Peter Nolan has written extensively on the subject of China's 'national team'; see, for instance, his *China and the Global Economy* (New York, 2001).

[21] 'Consumer rights—buyers bite back', *China Economic Review*, 23 January 1999.

Anti-Japan War, set in the 1937–1945 war between the two nations. Players begin as farmers or workers who aspire to become soldiers in the Chinese Communist Party's Eighth Route Army by rescuing anti-Japanese guerrillas and elderly citizens endangered by Japanese soldiers. The Beijing-based company Huagizixun similarly marketed a line of domestically developed and manufactured digital cameras by naming them after significant events in the war against Japan. The Patriot V (Aiguo V) series included models such as the V815, named after the date of the end of the Second World War (15 August).

In 2002, the Chinese state further strengthened its control over large companies by creating the very powerful State Assets Supervision and Administration Council (SASAC), which owns and runs over 150 enormous corporations, including eight of the fourteen mainland Chinese enterprises listed on the Fortune 500. Since the early 1990s, the Chinese government has used SASAC to entice Chinese companies to 'go global' with favourable policies, including the abolition of foreign currency restrictions for overseas investment.[22] Through these new, internationally prominent brands, China intends to remake the perception of Chinese brands, and hence of China itself, around the globe. The effects of the Chinese government's pressure on the nation's biggest companies to sell more branded products abroad is most visible in developing markets, where the Chinese already sell branded appliances, consumer electronics, and even automobiles, but these initiatives are simply a dry run for competition in developed markets such as the United States. China's biggest appliance maker, Haier, already sells refrigerators under its own name in the United States and is aggressively trying to acquire established white goods brands, including a failed attempt to buy Maytag in 2005 and a subsequent effort to buy GE's white goods division.

In other words, although international pressure and its entry into the WTO forced China's leaders to remove formal barriers to foreign products, that has not stopped them from playing both a direct and indirect role in promoting a new form of economic nationalism centred on brands. For instance, in 2003 the former chief negotiator in China's efforts to join the WTO, Long Yongtu, claimed that encouraging Chinese consumers to purchase Chinese products 'will violate neither the WTO rules nor the market economic rules.'[23] Likewise, in the summer of 2008, the national government even incorporated the establishment, protection, and management of national brands into its National Strategy.[24] Government-sponsored promotion of Chinese brand consciousness has also included setting up new mechanisms to help domestic consumers identify Chinese products among the torrent of brands now available. In anticipation of stiff foreign competition after entry to the WTO, the State General Administration for Quality

---

[22] P. Bellabona and F. Spigarelli, 'Moving from open door to go global: China goes on the world stage', *International Journal of Chinese Culture and Management*, 1/1 (2007), 93–108; 'SASAC Director Li Rongrong: Only the best state-owned enterprises should make acquisitions in Europe and the United States', *Zhongguo zhengquan bao*, 27 September 2008.

[23] "Official: Consumption of Chinese Products should be Encouraged," *China Daily*, 19 September 2003.

[24] 'Guojia zhishi chanquan zhanlüe gangyao' ('The guiding principles of national intellectual property strategy'), <http://baike.baidu.com/view/1736822.htm>, accessed 5 June 2009.

Supervision and Inspection and Quarantine, China's watchdog for product quality, set up a 'China brand name strategy promotion commission' and awarded 57 brands from 45 enterprises the title of 'China's Top Brand'. The goal was to alert Chinese consumers to high-quality domestic brands.[25] In a move reminiscent of China's anti-imperialist nationalist economic campaigns of the early twentieth century, the government now organizes exhibitions for 'established brands' (*laozihao*) to increase national brand awareness among consumers.

Another advantage Chinese companies have over their international competitors is that the huge and highly competitive Chinese market forces multinationals to adapt international brands to local tastes, which becomes ever more essential as Chinese consumers, now confronting choice rather than scarcity, become pickier about what they buy. International companies have learned that they cannot target 'the Chinese' as a homogenous market of largely identical consumers. The resulting move toward market segmentation—the recognition that subgroups within a market have common characteristics within them that set them apart from each other—is forcing international companies to expand their product offerings to accommodate regional, generational, class, and other preferences. To meet regional taste preferences, for instance, KFC sells 'Old Peking Style Chicken Rolls' with sweet bean sauce and mushroom chicken porridge.[26] Consuming segment-specific branded products has become a way for Chinese consumers to manifest differences in wealth, education, and regional identity.

A half-century ago, Chinese leaders and media conducted a nationalist economic campaign that urged the Chinese to buy Chinese products and extolled the success of home-grown businesses such as that of Wu Yunchu, known as the 'MSG king' for successfully competing against the Japanese in the market for food flavouring. Today, Lenovo offers the Chinese a story of a home-grown company that is so successful that it was able to buy the most famous international computer brand, a corporate rags to riches tale. Founded in 1984 with $24,000, Lenovo, a state-owned enterprise that originated in the Chinese Academy of Sciences, began as a distributor of computer brands, including IBM. In 1990, it began manufacturing its own computers, profiting from state commissions and little competition. By 1997, it controlled over a quarter of the Chinese market, making it the largest-selling brand of PCs in China. In 2000, it followed the government edict to 'go global' and began selling overseas.[27] In April, 2003, because of copyright conflicts in other countries where the company's original English name, Legend, was already registered, the company renamed itself Lenovo.[28] (In Chinese and in China, it is still called *Lianxiang*.) It became the world's third-largest producer of computers in

---

[25] '45 businesses scoop top brand gongs', *Xinhua*, 8 September 2001.

[26] See Jing Wang, *Brand New China: Advertising, Media, and Commercial Culture* (Cambridge MA: Harvard University Press, 2008), p. 67.

[27] Ling Zhijun, *Lianxiang fengyun: Jiemi lianxiang jituan guanli neimu* (*The Inside Story of the Lenovo Group's Management*) (Beijing: Zhongxin chubanshe, 2005).

[28] 'China steps up efforts to forge world name brands', *Xinhua*, 6 January 2004; Xin Bei, 'Lenovo deal a huge step for Chinese brands', *China Daily*, 10 December 2004.

December 2004 by spending $1.25 billion to acquire the PC arm of IBM, which was then three times its size and much more recognizable worldwide. Now Lenovo sells billions of dollars worth of computers under its own global brand.[29]

This purchase proved a harbinger of what was to come, as a stronger yuan made it possible, and even strategically necessary, for Chinese companies to buy iconic foreign assets. There have been many such acquisitions, particularly of established but struggling international brands, such as Nanjing Auto's purchase of MG-Rover and Dongxiang's acquisition and successful marketing of the Kappa brand—most closely associated with British football hooligans but now a leading fashion brand in China—and of Phoenix, a Japanese ski-wear brand. Li Ning, China's top domestic sports brand, entered into an alliance with Lotto Sport Italia, and Peace Mark, Asia's biggest watch retailer, bought Swiss watch brand Milus.[30] The Chinese are subjected to endless media coverage of these successful acquisitions. Within Chinese pop culture, these branding efforts represent heroic successes in China's struggle to move from a previously semi-colonized country to an economic superpower in the era of global capitalism.

Despite government investments and policies that favour China's own products, Chinese companies face a number of challenges as they make the transition from its earlier fragmented, state-run, and production-oriented economy to one driven by creating consumer desires and meeting consumer demands. The first of these challenges is one China faced a century ago when Japan overtook it as the world's largest exporter of silk and the British in India took a commanding share of the global tea trade: consistency in mass production. Under the productivist paradigm of the Maoist era, consistency was much less important than supply; demand was assumed and, thanks to shortages, was assured. But with the country's reintegration into global capitalist markets, China's political and business leaders want to consolidate and standardize domestic products before foreign companies' rival products replace or acquire them. Take the tea industry, where one would assume China would have a competitive advantage. China has over 1,000 varieties of tea, many of which are renowned throughout the world, but yet no national ones. Thanks to climate and soil conditions as well as traditional preferences, most Chinese tea brands are regional and many are still produced by families, making it nearly impossible to ensure their quality. These problems, combined with a growing Chinese appetite for trustworthy branded products, have confirmed the government's fears of aggressive foreign expansion by the Anglo-Dutch Unilever Group's Lipton brand.

Other Chinese companies have had a difficult time making the transition from state patronage and the prestige derived from a lack of access for other producers or monopoly situation to market competition and advertising. Take Maotai, the famous Chinese liquor distilled from fermented sorghum and manufactured exclusively in the southwest province of Guizhou (like Champagne, Maotai is trademarked by place). Maotai, used to toast at important state occasions, was a favourite liquor of Chinese leaders Deng Xiaoping, Zhou Enlai, and Mao Zedong. Because of its high profile and the fact that

[29] Pepe Escobar, 'Selling China to the world', *Asia Times*, 15 January 2005.
[30] Robin Kwong, 'Luxury brand ownership on rise in Asia', *Financial Times*, 29 April 2008.

one needed written permission to obtain it, Maotai never needed to advertise. Although Maotai is now affordable, available, and heavily advertised, intense competition in the liquor industry has undermined its status and therefore the value of the brand.[31] Cognac is the liquor of choice today, thanks to its position as a status symbol among China's newly rich.

Despite government efforts to help officially designated established brands compete, the companies behind these brands still often make basic mistakes of brand management based on socialist-era assumptions; indeed, branding itself is often considered a waste of money. In 1990, the former Ministry of Commerce awarded the title 'old and famous brands' to 1,600 shops and enterprises in the clothing, medicine, and food and beverage industries. These nationalized hangovers from the pre-Maoist eras had never needed to turn a profit, and even household names like Quanjude's Peking Duck, Tongrentang's traditional Chinese medicine, and Wuyutai's tea have faced difficult transitions. Twenty per cent of these designated famous brands have been operating at a loss for years and are nearly bankrupt, while another 70 per cent are barely profitable. Thus these former pillars of Chinese consumer consciousness have begun to disappear. In January 2003, for instance, Wangmazi Scissors, a Beijing institution founded in 1651, sparked a national debate on traditional brands by announcing its bankruptcy.[32]

Officials and business leaders acknowledge that products associated with China have had difficulties overcoming negative images as old-fashioned (or even pre-fashion) and lacking innovation and style. State-owned monopolies like the mobile phone company China Mobile have also had to fight image problems connected with state ownership. When China Mobile was established in Guangzhou in 1987, it was unconcerned with branding, but by the 1990s company managers worried that the name invoked an image of an unresponsive state-owned, bureaucratic enterprise, uninterested in product improvements or customer service. Its success, however, suggests that it is possible to vitalize the state-owned image, as subscribers grew from 20,000 in 1990 to 3.65 million in 1995 and 100 million in 2002. But the true test only began when foreign competition arrived.

CONCLUSION

Among the consequences for Chinese consumers of this national obsession with creating national brands is the increasing standardization of brands across the nation, a foundational element of a national consciousness through consumerism. One might view this as a Chinese McDonaldization or internal Coca-colonization—as China, like America in the early twentieth century, goes from having countless local brands to having a handful of national and international ones. To compete, Chinese brands will have

[31] 'Maotai liquor: from drink of officials to drink of ordinary people', *China Daily*, 29 September 2002.
[32] 'Brands may not live forever', *China Daily*, 4 May 2004; 'Old firms need brand protection', *China Business Weekly*, 9 August 2004.

to do all the obvious things. They will have to provide a value for whatever they change, including making high-quality, innovative products. They will also have to make their brands household names with positive associations though advertising in all its wondrous forms, from the yeoman bus-stop poster to subtle product placement in popular movies and TV shows.

China's leaders, like the leaders of market economies, wanted 'consumerism'—an economy with high value added via the marketplace for branded products. What the world has got is a Chinese government with an updated version of economic nationalism channelled into the state-sponsored creation of global brands that will challenge those of the rest of the world. Since the late nineteenth century, China's leadership (if not necessarily its housewife-on-the-street consumers) has developed a strong sense of economic nationalism and demonstrated a willingness to make any sacrifice to develop world-class industries in the name of 'national survival', including sacrificing the well-being of its workers and the health of its environment. In the current post-industrial world, Chinese leaders see ownership and control over world-class brands as the next battleground, the key to continued economic development. Thus one can confidently predict that scholars studying the intersection of nationalism and consumption will find this new intersection of the two in brands a productive area of research for the foreseeable future.

BIBLIOGRAPHY

Cochran, Sherman, *Big Business in China: Sino-Foreign Rivalry in the Cigarette Industry, 1890–1930* (Cambridge, MA: Harvard University Press, 1980).

Fewsmith, Joseph. *China since Tiananmen: The Politics of Transition* (Cambridge: Cambridge University Press, 2001).

Frank, Dana, *Buy American: The Untold Story of Economic Nationalism* (Boston: Beacon Press, 1999).

Gerth, Karl, *China Made: Consumer Culture and the Creation of the Nation* (Cambridge, MA: Harvard University Press, 2003).

Gerth, Karl, *As China Goes, So Goes the World: How Chinese Consumers are Transforming Everything* (New York, NY: Hill & Wang, 2010).

Jordan, Donald A. *Chinese Boycotts Versus Japanese Bombs: The Failure of China's 'Revolutionary Diplomacy', 1931–32* (Ann Arbor: University of Michigan Press, 1991).

Orlove, Benjamin S. (ed.), *The Allure of the Foreign: Imported Goods in Postcolonial Latin America* (Ann Arbor: University of Michigan Press, 1997).

Remer, Charles F. *A Study of Chinese Boycotts, with Special Reference to Their Economic Effectiveness* (Baltimore: John Hopkins Press, 1933).

Trentmann, Frank. *Free Trade Nation: Commerce, Consumption, and Civil Society in Modern Britain* (Oxford: Oxford University Press, 2008).

Wang, Guanhua, *In Search of Justice: The 1905–1906 Chinese Anti-American Boycott*, East Asian Monograph series (Cambridge, MA: Harvard University Press, 2001).

CHAPTER 22

....

NATIONAL SOCIALISM
AND CONSUMPTION

....

S. JONATHAN WIESEN

IT is tempting to associate consumption exclusively with political democracy. Many important works in the field of consumer studies focus on the United States and post-Second World War Western Europe, and the former is often cast as the paradigmatic example of consumer society.[1] Notwithstanding the disruptions of the Great Depression and less severe business cycles, these societies offer plentiful images of bustling stores, widening economic opportunities, and the emergence of politicized citizen-consumers.[2] Consumption, however, is not limited to democratic settings. It also existed, even thrived, under fascist dictatorships, and this fact offers a number of challenges to the historian. First, it disrupts a linear narrative of progress. Because the fascist movements of twentieth-century Europe culminated in catastrophic defeat, we cannot consider them mere phases in an overall success story. Their grandiose visions gave way to bombed-out cities, broken infrastructures, and starvation, and as wartime consumption withered, the consumer, in effect, ceased to exist. Second, the unique violence of the movements—whether manifested in the militant machismo of Mussolini

---

[1] See, e.g., Lawrence Glickman, *Consumer Society in American History: A Reader* (Ithaca: Cornell University Press, 1999), and Victoria de Grazia, *Irresistible Empire: America's Advance through 20th Century Europe* (Cambridge, MA and London: Harvard University Press, 2005). For post-war Europe see, e.g., Martin Daunton and Matthew Hilton, *The Politics of Consumption: Material Culture and Citizenship in Europe and America* (Oxford: Berg, 2001). For Germany, see Michael Wildt, *Am Beginn der 'Konsumgesellschaft': Mangelerfahrung, Lebenshaltung, Wohlstandshoffnung in Westdeutschland in den fünfziger Jahren* (Hamburg: Ergebnisse, 1994); Alon Confino and Rudy Koshar, 'Régimes of Consumer Culture: New Narratives in Twentieth-Century German History', *German History*, 19/2 (2001): 135–61. For an effective questioning of terms like 'consumerism' and 'consumer society', see Frank Trentmann, 'Beyond Consumerism: New Historical Perspectives on Consumption', *Journal of Contemporary History*, 39/3 (2004): 373–401.

[2] See Lizabeth Cohen, *A Consumer's Republic: The Politics of Mass Consumption in Postwar America* (New York: Knopf, 2003).

or the genocidal thrust of National Socialism—sets fascism apart from other twentieth-century developments. While consumption always serves political aims, under fascism it served particularly brutal ones.

This essay attempts to answer some of the questions that emerge from a consideration of fascism and consumption. In particular, it focuses on National Socialist Germany, where consumption served a uniquely harsh end. How did Nazism envision buying, selling, and consuming? To what extent was consumption shaped by the state's ideological priorities? Did Nazi society diverge from other modern settings in offering opportunities for mass consumption? Finally, how did the consumer 'on the ground' engage in daily acts of consumption and experience the regime's dictates?

NAZI VISIONS OF CONSUMPTION

In some respects, consumption stood at the centre of the fascist vision. Because it emerged during a time of economic distress, fascism was inherently (and at times explicitly) premised on the creation of an abundant society, in which average citizens could partake of the riches once enjoyed by an elite social stratum. The bellicose vitality of Mussolini's Fascism was linked to the dream of a *Pax Italiana*, in which military might, modern technology, and egalitarian social schemes would create a materially plentiful utopia.[3] In Nazi Germany, too, the promise to pull the country out of the Great Depression and bring material comforts to the average citizen was Adolf Hitler's chief source of appeal. In the case of National Socialism, consumption was not only tied to economic recovery. If this were so, its vision would have differed little from those of other political regimes struggling to emerge from the world economic crisis. Rather, consumption for Hitler was tied to the goal of establishing hegemony over Europe. The Nazi leadership often linked its quest for '*Lebensraum*'—living space in which racially accepted Germans could propagate—to the promise of a higher standard of living. Occupied Europe, in the Nazi vision, was not only a site of racial and economic revival. It was also a scene of consumer culture that would elevate the racial and national power of a revived German nation.[4]

Adam Tooze, who has written a definitive work on the Nazi economy, has shown that the Nazis aimed not simply to better the lives of average Germans, but to overtake the United States in the country's standard of living.[5] The United States represented an easy

[3] On Italian Fascism and consumption, see, e.g., Adam Arvidsson, *Marketing Modernity: Italian Advertising from Fascism to Postmodernity* (London: Routledge, 2003), 1–64; Victoria de Grazia, *The Culture of Consent: Mass Organization of Leisure in Fascist Italy* (Cambridge: Cambridge University Press, 1981).

[4] Alan S. Milward, *War, Economy, and Society, 1939–1945* (Berkeley: University of California Press, 1977), 8–14.

[5] Adam Tooze, *The Wages of Destruction: The Making and Breaking of the Nazi Economy* (New York: Viking, 2006), 138–47.

foil for Germany with its ethnic diversity and social tensions, and National Socialism devised an alternate vision of a racially and socially homogenous consumer society. The Nazis sought the abundance of consumer society without the crassness, racial diversity, and cultural hybridity associated with mass culture in the United States. While Hitler's promise of future abundance bespeaks a positive orientation toward consumption, the Nazis were in fact more ambivalent. If party economists asserted people's right to consume all goods produced, they did so with some trepidation. Thorstein Veblen had famously bemoaned conspicuous consumption in 1899, and the Nazis shared a fear of overindulgence.[6] In the 1920s, they adopted essentially an anti-consumption stance: too much commerce fostered cosmopolitan (Jewish) distractions from higher commitments to the state and the leader. This hostility was greatly tempered by 1933, as the public clamoured for relief from the Depression, but the party still warned against treating consumption as 'an end in itself.' Nor should consumption take the form of 'wasteful spending' (*Verschwendung*).[7] Rather, consumption was to serve a higher purpose, namely the enrichment of the *Volk* (German people) during its struggle for global and racial dominance. In this respect, goods and services had a national, even moral, purpose. Party leaders did not deny the dangers inherent in the homogenization of tastes or in the 'creation of needs' fostered by modern marketing. But they recognized that they presided over an advanced economy whose economic strength required a vibrant sphere of consumer activity. If Veblen had, in Lisa Tiersten's words, tied 'the advent of the modern market to moral decline,'[8] the Nazis sought to link the market to moral rehabilitation.

It is perhaps useful to understand consumption as part of the Nazis' larger effort to build a *Volksgemeinschaft* or 'racial community' in Germany. The *Volksgemeinschaft* was in many respects an inclusive vision. Germans of all social classes, professions, and milieus were to be bound together through their racial homogeneity and their ability to access goods and services. As the regime attempted to overcome the class divisions of the 'bourgeois' or 'liberal' era, it designated certain goods as particularly useful to the body politic and thus worthy of protection and subsidization. *Volks*-radios, *volks*-vacuum cleaners, and *volks*-refrigerators were to complement the Volkswagen as affordable goods that would open up new vistas for the population.[9] The radio would allow each person to receive the messages of unity from the Propaganda Ministry; the time-saving household appliances would free up the *Hausfrau*, the head of the *Volksfamilie*, to attend to her children; and the Volkswagen would enable mass motorization. A racially unified people would be on the move, criss-crossing the German-controlled continent for leisure and pleasure.[10]

[6] Thorstein Veblen, *The Theory of the Leisure Class* (New York: Macmillan, 1912): 66–101.

[7] Bruno Kiesewetter, 'Kartell, Marktordnung, Recht auf Verbrauch', *Die deutsche Volkswirtschaft*, 6/17 (2 June 1936): 536–8.

[8] Lisa Tiersten, *Marianne in the Market: Envisioning Consumer Society in Fin-de-Siècle France* (Berkeley and Los Angeles: University of California Press, 2001), 9.

[9] Wolfgang König, *Volkswagen, Volksempfänger, Volksgemeinschaft: 'Volksprodukte' im Dritten Reich: Vom Scheitern einer nationalsozialistischen Konsumgesellschaft* (Paderborn: Schöningh: 2004).

[10] Rudy Koshar, *German Travel Cultures* (Oxford: Berg, 2000), 115–34.

Historians have paid close attention to the Volkswagen and its place in the Nazis' vision because it bespeaks the fundamental modernity of their worldview. It has been a long time since scholars portrayed National Socialism as merely a backward-looking reaction to modernity—as a flight into a Teutonic past at the expense of technological advancement. But if they now acknowledge the 'reactionary modernism' of National Socialism, historians are still distilling the specific nature of this modernity.[11] As a component of the Nazis' larger mass leisure programme, 'Strength Through Joy' (*Kraft durch Freude*—KdF), the 'people's car' stands as a testament to the centrality of mass production, mass consumption, and mass mobility in the Nazi vision. The shiny new Volkswagen factory in Wolfsburg, Germany, never produced cars for the civilian sector until after the Second World War. But the KdF programme did send millions of Germans from all social classes on comfortable vacations within Germany and on cruises through the fjords of Scandinavia and around the warm-water beaches of the Mediterranean. According to Shelley Baranowski this mass leisure programme bound Germans emotionally to the *Volksgemeinschaft* and, ultimately, to the regime.[12]

Historians Frank Bajohr and Michael Wildt have stressed that the *Volksgemeinschaft* was not only based on inclusion but equally, if not more so, on exclusion, and here we encounter a fundamental component of consumption in the Third Reich.[13] Social, political, and racial undesirables were to be shut out of the future consumerist utopia. Jews served as the villainous counterpoint to the Nazi ideal, and the 'rules' of consumption were always premised on their economic and social ostracization. The 1 April 1933 boycott of Jewish shops, which the Propaganda Ministry planned despite little enthusiasm from the populace, was primarily about severing daily acts of consumption from Jewishness, now linked to moral and racial danger. So too was the pogrom of November 1938, when the sites of morally suspect commerce, namely Jewish shops, were vandalized and rendered off limits to the 'Aryan' consumer. The Aryanization of Jewish business throughout the 1930s and the exclusion of Jews from the economy were meant to protect Germans from impure racial elements. In the process, the Nazis could 'sanitize' the entire process of market exchange in Germany.

With the help of propagandists, the Nazis prescribed 'correct' forms of consumption. Under the auspices of the Propaganda Ministry, the regime established the Advertising Council for the German Economy (Werberat der deutschen Wirtschaft). The Advertising

---

[11] Jeffrey Herf, *Reactionary Modernism: Technology, Culture, and Politics in Weimar and the Third Reich* (Cambridge: Cambridge University Press, 1986). On Nazism and modernity, see Riccardo Bavaj, *Die Ambivalenz der Moderne im Nationalsozialismus: Eine Bilanz der Forschung* (Munich: Oldenbourg, 2003); Paul Betts, 'The New Fascination with Fascism: The Case of Nazi Modernism', *Journal of Contemporary History*, 37/4 (2002): 541–58; Mark Roseman, 'National Socialism and Modernisation', in Richard Bessel (ed.), *Fascist Italy and Nazi Germany: Comparisons and Contrasts* (Cambridge: Cambridge University Press, 1996), 197–229; and Norbert Frei, 'Wie modern war der Nationalsozialismus', *Geschichte und Gesellschaft*, 19 (1993): 367–87.

[12] Shelley Baranowski, *Strength through Joy: Consumerism and Mass Tourism in the Third Reich* (Cambridge: Cambridge University Press, 2004), 9.

[13] Frank Bajohr and Michael Wildt (eds.), *Volksgemeinschaft: Neue Forschungen zur Gesellschaft des Nationalsozialismus* (Frankfurt am Main: Fischer, 2009), 7–23.

Council tried to create a new form of '*Deutsche Werbung*' (German advertising) that would be stripped of the supposedly decadent features of international advertising and would promote the racially pure *Volksgemeinschaft*.[14] In particular, it targeted advertisements it believed offended *völkisch* sensibilities, took commercial advantage of Nazi ideology, or tarnished the landscape. Starting 1 January 1936, the Advertising Council banned advertising on the radio, which the regime saw as a precious propaganda tool not to be mixed with commerce. Pictures of swastikas or SS men, as well as portraits of the Führer and Nazi phrases, were also prohibited from advertisements and store fronts, and the Advertising Council eventually prohibited roadside billboards, product plugs in editorials, and the unauthorized use of celebrities and politicians in advertisements.[15] This purification of advertising would supposedly keep the population focused on the ideological tasks at hand—particularly the push for economic self-sufficiency.

Despite its name, the Advertising Council's remit was much broader than advertising as such. While it devoted much time to regulating 'commercial propaganda', it also placed under its purview the broader practice of consumption. For example, by severely limiting the number of trade fairs and exhibitions in the Third Reich, the Advertising Council made it clear that (over-)consumption could serve as a distraction.[16] The commercialization of public and private space risked distracting the *Volk* from its mission. Here we confront a paradox. Even though the Advertising Council tried to enact a specifically Nazified form of commerce, the visual culture of consumption looked much as it did before 1933. To invoke Ernst Fraenkel's concepts, the Advertising Council tried to make sure that the 'prerogative' state of National Socialism channelled consumption along ideological lines. But marketeers and consumers still functioned in the 'normative' market—trafficking in goods and services much as they had before 1933.[17]

This continuity with the Weimar Republic is significant; in the importance they lent to consumption and in their quest to regulate its social and ethical effects, the Nazis were not exceptional. In the 1920s, when consumers came to be recognized as key social and political actors, a range of elites decried the seemingly negative effects of their presence: a pecuniary mindset, profligacy in the marketplace, and a cultural and spiritual levelling. Calls for the moral education of shoppers were rife, and municipal authorities went to great lengths to cleanse cities of exaggerated forms of consumerism: flashy billboards, blaring loudspeakers, and jostling customers.[18] Politicians recognized that social order

[14] On the Advertising Council, see Matthias Rücker, *Wirtschaftswerbung unter Nationalsozialismus: Rechtliche Ausgestaltung der Werbung und Tätigkeit des Werberats der deutschen Wirtschaft* (Frankfurt am Main: Peter Lang, 2000); and Uwe Westphal, *Werbung im Dritten Reich* (Berlin: Transit, 1989), 50–7.

[15] Dirk Reinhardt, *Von der Reklame zum Marketing: Geschichte der Wirtschaftswerbung in Deutschland* (Berlin: Akademie, 1993), 429–41, 447; Hartmut Berghoff, ' "Times Change and We Change with Them": The German Advertising Industry in the Third Reich—Between Professional Self-Interest and Political Repression', *Business History*, 45/1 (2003): 128–47.

[16] Hans Ruban, 'Das deutsche Messe- und Ausstellungswesen', *Deutsche Volkswirtschaft*, 9/8 (1940): 210–12.

[17] Ernst Fraenkel, *The Dual State: A Contribution to the Theory of Dictatorship* (New York and London: Oxford University Press, 1941).

[18] Molly J. Loberg, 'Berlin Streets: Politics, Commerce and Crowds, 1918–1938', Ph.D. dissertation (Princeton University, 2006).

depended on widening consumer opportunities (thus the growing interest in the 'standard of living' measurement) but also on restraint. Self-sufficiency, the rejection of luxury, and—especially during the Depression—making do with less were common tropes of Weimar-era consumption politics.[19]

While these pre-1933 preoccupations carried over into the Third Reich, they took on a different ideological resonance. In the Weimar Republic, the political parties used measures of consumption to inform their specific visions of the good life, and they wrestled with the meaning of consumer capitalism for the health of the nation. But the Nazis gave these discussions a racial imprimatur. The state was no longer concerned with provisioning the population and bettering the lives of 'Germans' as such; rather it was interested in guaranteeing material satisfaction to only the biologically worthy.

REALITIES OF CONSUMPTION
IN THE THIRD REICH

On a superficial level, consumption represented an uncomplicated feature of Nazi ideology; the aim was to increase the purchasing power of Aryans and take away that of non-Aryans. The regime proclaimed its goal of providing the German population with a bounty of goods and services in an expanded, racially pure German Reich. But these Nazi visions were always tempered by realities, and it is therefore worth looking more closely at consumption 'on the ground'. In the Third Reich the politics of consumption was marked by, in Hartmut Berghoff's words, 'the constant juxtaposition of enticement and deprivation.'[20] On the one hand, several market sectors seen as politically or ideologically vital—such as radios, movies, furniture, and telephones—saw increased sales; the state's support of mass entertainment and its pro-family schemes allowed these industries to flourish. On the other hand, in other sectors, such as foodstuffs, the promise of plentiful goods was never met by reality. Consumption suffered under the reality that Nazi economic policy was overstretched: providing jobs, building loyalty, safeguarding precious raw materials, and preparing for German hegemony in Europe took precedence over providing bountiful consumer opportunities. Managed consumption in the service of war—rather than unfettered access to the joys of material goods—was the reality for most Germans in the Third Reich.[21]

Indeed, the importance of war to Nazi-era consumption habits must not be underestimated. While the regime's make-work projects, such as constructing highways

[19] On Weimar consumption, see Claudius Torp, 'Das Janusgesicht der Weimarer Konsumpolitik', in Heinz-Gerhard Haupt and Claudius Torp (eds.), *Die Konsumgesellschaft in Deutschland, 1890–1990: Ein Handbuch* (Frankfurt am Main: Campus, 2009), 250–67.

[20] Hartmut Berghoff, 'Enticement and Deprivation: The Regulation of Consumption in Pre-War Nazi Germany', in Daunton and Hilton, *Politics of Consumption*, 165–84.

[21] On managed consumption in the Third Reich, see Reinhardt, *Von der Reklame zum Marketing*, 446; and Westphal, *Werbung im Dritten Reich*, 137.

and draining swamps, led to almost full employment and pulled Germany out of the Depression, it was more to the benefit of the military sector than the civilian.[22] Despite increases in jobs, real wages remained stagnant and the prices of necessities rose.[23] In every respective year between 1933 and 1945, the cost of living in Germany increased, and during the Second World War per capita consumer spending registered an annual decline, such that by 1944 it was only 70 per cent of its 1938 level.[24] Despite an overall increase in economic activity during the 1930s and 1940s, military expenditure constituted an ever larger proportion of Germany's GDP.

This is not to diminish the psychological boost that came with re-employment and rearmament; after 1945 West Germans tended to associate any hardships under Hitler with the war years (especially the more severe strictures after 1943) rather than the pre-war years.[25] Far from being smug over Germany's 'awakening', however, consumers consistently grumbled about shortages and lower product quality in the 1930s.[26] Inflation was the last thing the Nazis wanted to add to this mix, and to address this concern, the leadership implemented a price freeze in autumn 1936, followed by extensive rationing.[27] Both forms of economic control would stay in effect for the rest of the Third Reich, and they only confirmed the view held by some that military producers, not civilian manufacturers or consumers, were enjoying the lion's share of national wealth.

The regime's anticipation of war meant not only depriving consumers of coveted goods, but also preparing them psychologically for such sacrifices. While price freezes were initiated to protect against inflation, the Nazi government asked companies, advertisers, and consumers to do their part in regulating themselves in an economy of scarcity. In 1936, the National Committee for Economic Enlightenment led Germans in a 'Kampf dem Verderb' ('Struggle against Waste'), whereby housewives learned to store fruits, vegetables, and other perishables correctly during the winter.[28] Other campaigns throughout the late 1930s, which entailed the production of colourful brochures, flyers, and films, indicate the extent to which the state tried to regulate private behaviour. Saving soap, battling garden and household pests, and washing laundry correctly all became the business of the government in its attempt to save precious resources.[29]

---

[22] R. J. Overy, 'Cars, Roads, and Economic Recovery, 1932–1938', *Economic History Review*, 28/3 (1975): 466–83.

[23] André Steiner, 'Zur Neuschätzung des Lebenshaltungskostenindex für die Vorkriegszeit des Nationalsozialismus', *Jahrbuch für Wirtschaftsgeschichte*, 2 (2005): 129–52.

[24] Werner Abelshauser, 'Guns, Butter and Economic Miracles' in Mark Harrison (ed.), *The Economics of World War II* (Cambridge: Cambridge University Press 1998), 122–76, at 154; and Tim Kirk, *The Longman Companion to Nazi Germany* (New York: Longman, 1995), 99.

[25] Ulrich Herbert, 'Good Times, Bad Times: Memories of the Third Reich,' in Richard Bessel (ed.), *Life in the Third Reich*, 2nd revised edition (Oxford: Oxford University Press, 2001), 97–111.

[26] Tim Kirk, *Nazi Germany* (Basingstoke: Palgrave, 2007): 65–6.

[27] Fritz Blaich, *Wirtschaft und Rüstung im 'Dritten Reich'* (Düsseldorf: Schwann, 1987), 21–6.

[28] König, *Volkswagen, Volksempfänger, Volksgemeinschaft*, 137–50. On the 'Fight against Waste' and other measures, see Jill Stephenson, *Hitler's Home Front: Württemberg under the Nazis* (London: Hambledon Continuum, 2006), 166. See also Nancy Reagin, *Sweeping the German Nation: Domesticity and National Identity in Germany, 1870–1945* (Cambridge: Cambridge University Press, 2007), 152.

[29] Westphal, *Werbung im Dritten Reich*, 142–5.

The latter campaign would consume the energies of private companies, Reich business groups, the German Women's Bureau (Deutsches Frauenwerk), and private advertisers, who calculated to the exact Reichsmark how much clothes damaged by poor domestic habits cost the national economy.[30]

The Second World War represented a turn toward the deprivation side of Berghoff's 'enticement/deprivation' binary. By 1939, an inflation- and depression-weary population was enjoying the fruits of economic recovery, and the last thing it wanted was disruption. Consumers greeted Germany's invasion of Poland with trepidation and, according to one report, a 'flight into material assets.' With bountiful memories of the 1923 currency collapse, Germans spent the autumn of 1939 hoarding consumer goods in case money became worthless. Popular brand names flew off the shelves—from Salamader shoes to Wolff and Sohn toiletries. Urban dwellers snapped up camping stoves, and farmers bought one or even two grand pianos so that they could own something of lasting value.[31] By Christmas, the market had settled down. But the rest of the war saw mounting levels of consumer frustration. Continuing a pre-war trend, civilian goods contracted on behalf of military goods, leaving Germans with excess purchasing power. Shortages of raw materials and the diversion of oils and fats to military usages meant the disappearance of favourite brands. Coffee was replaced by ersatz malt drinks, which Germans found distinctly unflavourful, and popular products like Persil laundry detergent were pulled from the market, replaced by inferior wash powders. As the war proceeded, the euphoria that had accompanied Germany's military victories in 1940 and 1941 was replaced by the daily making do. With the bombing of German cities, concerns about having to use ersatz products gave way to the fundamental desire to stay alive.

The Nazi regime understood that this decline in consumer goods could have negative effects on morale, and it encouraged alternate forms of gratification to supplant the desire for commodities. As consumer goods disappeared, Germans directed their excess purchasing power toward movies and radio programmes. Until it was discontinued in 1941, the *Wunschkonzert für die Wehrmacht* was an immensely popular call-in radio show that allowed the public to request their favourite hits.[32] The 1940 movie of the same name, *Wunschkonzert*, was the second most popular film in wartime Germany, after 1942's *Die große Liebe* (*The Great Love*). In general, the radio and film industries did remarkably well during the war. The number of cinema admissions peaked in 1943 and stayed constant through 1944, representing an increase in the popularity of film over

---

[30] Aufklärungs-Aktion des Waschmittel-Einzelhandels über das Thema Wasche Wäsche Weiss (Propaganda campaign on the theme 'Wash your Laundry White'). Bundesarchiv Berlin, 18 July 1939, R5002/26.

[31] Archiv of the Gesellschaft für Konsumforschung, Nuremberg, 'Verbraucher und Markenartikel in den ersten Kriegsmonaten', December 1939, S 1939 015, p. 12.

[32] Corey Ross, *Media and the Making of Modern Germany: Mass Communications, Society, and Politics from the Empire to the Third Reich* (Oxford: Oxford University Press, 2008), 356–7; and Brian Currid, *A National Acoustics: Music and Mass Publicity in the Weimar and Nazi Germany* (Minneapolis: University of Minnesota Press, 2006), 54–8.

the pre-war years, and movie houses witnessed a rise in ticket scalping and scenes of tumult in their foyers.[33] At the 'higher' end of the spectrum, orchestral music and literature found a ready audience of Germans eager to escape from the daily pressures on the home front.[34]

While acknowledging the disruptions to consumption, the regime ultimately depicted them as temporary inconveniences. Soon enough, it promised, this New Order would witness a 'cultural and economic blossoming' (kulturelle und wirtschaftliche Blüte), offering people throughout Nazi-dominated Europe the experience of personal security and the joys of buying cars, consumer durables, and a bounty of food items.[35] The combination of military victory, the privations of war, and the vision of a post-war utopia constituted a powerful tool for social control. The economy in the present was marked by shortages, but its future would be marked by an abundance earned through sacrifice. This dialectic between deprivation and wealth, between reality and promises, helped maintain the loyalty of the population during the war years.

MARKETING IN THE THIRD REICH

The story of consumption under National Socialism has often focused on a protagonist, the consumer. But the story is also about the producer, who arguably had the most at stake. How did the institutions that depended on consumption go about their business? What did consumption mean to company leaders and market professionals, who were responsible for moving goods from the factories to the homes of consumers? When looking at advertising, marketing, and merchandising in Nazi Germany, one is struck by the tremendous continuity with the prior years. While the consumer economy remained stagnant in Nazi Germany, this did not mean that the profit motive disappeared, and advertisers and economists freely explored the latest methods and rationales for selling their products. Experts in branding and corporate publicity continued to discuss the applicability of business practices from the United States, where there flourished the mass democracy that the Nazis formally critiqued. Companies relied on a combination of psychological mechanisms and standard marketing strategies: Siemens called upon advertising specialistst to design logos that would penetrate the 'mass brain';[36] hot-air balloons bore the image of the 'Bayer Cross'; companies christened ships bearing their names; and business leaders led Nazi leaders, visiting foreign dignitaries, and Olympic

[33] Ross, Media and the Making of Modern Germany, 366.

[34] On classical music during the Nazi years, see Misha Aster, The Reich's Orchestra, 1933–45 (New York: Mosaic Press, 2007).

[35] 'Um die neue Ordnung Europas', Die deutsche Volkswirtschaft, 8/29 (2 October 1939): 993–4; Jakob Werlin, 'Motorisierung in Europa', Die deutsche Volkswirtschaft, 9/30 (1940): 970–2.

[36] This is a term that Siemens advertiser Hans Domizlaff used. See Rainer Gries, Volker Ilgen, and Dirk Schindelbeck (eds.). 'Ins Gehirn der Masse kriechen!' Werbung und Mentalitätsgeschichte (Darmstadt: Wissenschaftliche Buchgesellschaft, 1995), 45–73.

athletes on factory tours.[37] At its peak in 1938, the Henkel chemical company led 80,000 visitors on such tours, where they could watch workers at their stations and view high-budget promotional films that they might have missed in their local cinemas.[38] All of these gestures at once reinforced confidence in a company name and contributed to the visual spectacle that accompanied economic renewal in the 1930s.

The area that witnessed the greatest innovation was consumer research, which combined the latest findings in applied psychology with in-home interviews of consumers. The Society for Consumer Research (Gesellschaft für Konsumforschung, GfK), Germany's largest market research organization today, was established in 1934 under the auspices of Professor Wilhelm Vershofen, economist, novelist, poet, and seasoned America observer. Vershofen built around him at the University of Nuremberg a circle of economists that included, most famously, future West German chancellor Ludwig Erhard. The GfK was also the brainchild of Wilhelm Mann, a director of IG Farben and future sales director of Bayer AG. As President of the GfK, Mann worked with an advisory board that included executives and owners from Dr Hillers, Kaffee Hag, Dr Oetker, Kaufhof, and AEG, to name a few. These individuals came together not simply to talk about the business of consumer research, but also to confront the larger implications of mass consumption. They defended brand names against cheap imitation products, assessed the positive and negative effects of advertising, probed the nature of consumer desire, and debated the merits of applied psychology in consumer research.

Throughout the 1930s and, indeed, during the Second World War, large and mid-sized firms hired the GfK to gauge the reception of their products and to chart the resonance of the company name. Correspondents went undercover into chemists and perfume shops, interviewing customers or mentioning a product name to see what reaction they would get. The GfK prepared reports on the popularity of Persil soap and Opel cars, on popular brands of cigarettes, on the favourite products for personal hygiene, and on the importance of the Bayer Cross logo in marketing. The goal of all these reports was to hear, according to the leitmotiv of the organization, 'the voice of the consumer' ('*die Stimme des Vebrauchers*').

The GfK was careful not to present 'German consumers' as an undifferentiated mass. Rather, in its reports GfK researchers reproduced dozens of quotations from people representing all walks of life. Homemakers, teachers, plumbers, retirees—all were given a voice in GfK publications. Moreover, the GfK took care to differentiate people based on income, region, and gender. Indeed it rejected any notion that the consumer was coded female. The organization spent much time exploring the difference between men's and women's shopping habits and desires. In the Nazi leadership's vision, gender roles were organic and traditional; the woman was the shopper and homemaker, the man was the breadwinner. But the GfK discovered a persistent reality: women also brought home

---

[37] See Bayer Archiv, Leverkusen, 'Olympide-'*Bayer*'-Tag: Programm für die Fabrikbesichtigung', 168.2.29.

[38] Wilfried Feldenkirchen and Susanne Hilger, *Menschen und Marken: 125 Jahre Henkel, 1876–2001* (Düsseldorf: Henkel, 2001), 257.

money and men also shopped for toiletries and clothes. In the 1950s, marketers spoke of men as the 'hidden consumer', but twenty years earlier, the GfK was already trying to bring him to light.[39]

This focus on men as consumers was not specific to the GfK. If much historical literature tends to portray women as prototypical consumers, market professionals in the Third Reich recognized the prominent place that men occupied in the *völkisch* economy. While the family father might cede some everyday purchasing decisions to his wife, he did not surrender the privilege of being a shopper in his own right. Nazi economic periodicals showcased fancy watches and accessories that would lend status to the 'high-performing' business executive; clothing magazines and daily newspapers offered the latest in suits and ties; and window displays invited men to indulge in the joys of shopping.[40] This focus on the male consumer mirrored international advertising trends, and despite their promotion of 'German' forms of marketing, Nazi leaders readily drew upon this and other developments from beyond the borders of the Third Reich.

Even in the midst of total war, Germans were engaged with developments in international marketing. When American bombs were raining down on German cities, the GfK was studying American popular periodicals and department store catalogues (such as those of Sears Roebuck and Montgomery Ward) to see how widespread mass-produced household appliances were in the United States and if they would be compatible with Germany's producer-centred ethos. At the same time, despite its fascination with the American market, GfK associates believed they were working in a distinct German intellectual vein—not, as such, working for big business. The GfK enterprise, they claimed, belonged to the humanities—far removed from the scientific empiricism that, they felt, defined the American approach. Importantly, too, they looked askance at the hyper-individualism bred by American mass consumption. Rejecting a *Homo Economicus* model, they instead saw their work as a means of capturing people in all their 'intellectual-spiritual complexity' ('*geistig-seelischen Komplexität*'). The *Mensch*—the human being—who stood at the centre of the GfK enterprise was a figure who maintained his rights as an individual consumer—with needs and desires for material comforts—but who remained grounded in the community.[41]

The GfK was not the only institution to engage in consumer and market research. During the Third Reich, companies expanded their in-house advertising branches, the Nazi regime established a national school of advertising, and market professionals who had begun their careers in Weimar Germany continued to practise their trade. In short, Nazi Germany witnessed a modernization of marketing, even as the state increasingly

---

[39] 'Verschiedenheiten in der Verbraucherhaltung der beiden Geschlechter', *Vertrauliche Nachrichten*. 4 (September 1937): 1–6, GfKA.

[40] See, e.g., the magazine of Rotary clubs in Germany, *Der Rotarier* (1933–37); and Irene Guenther, *Nazi Chic? Fashioning Women in the Third Reich* (Oxford: Berg, 2004), 25, 80, 159.

[41] On the history of the GfK, see, Georg Bergler, *Die Entwicklung der Verbrauchsforschung in Deutschland und die Gesellschaft für Konsumforschung bis zum Jahre 1945* (Kallmünz and Oberpfalz: Michael Laßleben, 1959).

dictated what could be produced and sold. In a setting where visual propaganda saturated public space, companies—in their attempt to sell products and services—found a comfortable home.

CONSUMPTION AND CONSENT: A DEBATE

These developments in marketing, set against the backdrop of decreasing consumer goods, provide a conundrum for the historian. How can we reconcile these dueling images of stagnation and advancement? Some scholars do so by emphasizing an overall progressive trend—a 'modernization of consumer culture'—during the Nazi years, despite the shrinking of consumer opportunities.[42] Rather than representing a backward interregnum in the otherwise progressive unfolding of a consumer society, Germans in the Nazi years created a commercially advanced society and accustomed themselves to economic comforts and rich leisure opportunities after the scourges of the First World War, inflation, and depression. Certainly, developments in marketing suggest a 'modern' scene of companies vying for customers and consumers exercising their power of the purse. Other historians, however, emphasize the limitations of the consumer economy, the false promises of abundance, and privations of war. Which view is correct? The question is important, as its touches on wider debates about Germans' support for the Nazi regime. If the Nazis did indeed provide rich consumer opportunities to Germans, then we are perhaps closer to understanding the regime's popularity and, in turn, its ability to succeed in its genocidal aims with little protest. If, on the other hand, the consumer economy was less than dynamic, we must look elsewhere to explain the origins of popular support for the regime.

The relationship between consumption and consent has been the source of particularly heated debate since 2005, when a prominent German historian, Götz Aly, published a controversial book called *Hitler's Beneficiaries*.[43] In this book and elsewhere, Aly has argued that Nazi Germany was anything but a society in need. By focusing less on the consumer economy than on broader Nazi policies he sees as having been enormously favourable to middle- and lower-income Germans, he depicts the Third Reich as very kind to the consumer. Progressive tax codes, an expansive welfare state, and the influx of wartime booty gave Germans a high standard of living and ultimately provided the basis for overwhelming support for the 'consensus dictatorship' of Nazi Germany. Far from dismissing Nazi Germany as an economic aspirant, Aly sees the material benefits as voluminous and, indeed, much more decisive a factor than Nazi ideology or racism in explaining popular support for National Socialism. The cumulative effect of Aly's views

---

[42] Dagmar Herzog, *Sex after Fascism: Memory and Morality in Twentieth-Century Germany* (Princeton: Princeton University Press, 2005), 16.

[43] Götz Aly, *Hitler's Beneficiaries: Plunder, Racial War, and the Nazi Welfare State* (New York: Metropolitan, 2007).

is to place Nazi Germany on a forward path toward the social market economy and mass consumer society of West Germany.

Aly's critics have seen the Nazi economy as anything but consumer-friendly. Adam Tooze paints a picture of a country beset by shortages and unhappy consumers. In the 1930s, Germany's per capita income, Tooze argues, was more akin to that of present-day Iran than to the inter-war United States, and financial crises abounded throughout the Third Reich.[44] With reference to the wartime period, critics have also taken Aly to task for his depiction of the Third Reich as a 'kleptocracy', which paid for its aggression through stolen goods. They question Aly's numerical calculations that allowed him to conclude that key parts of the German war effort were funded by expropriations from Jews, forced labourers, and the looting of occupied territories. While they do not deny that cratefuls of stolen property, indeed from Jews, made their way back to the Reich and even into German households, they dispute that this amounted to a significant source of revenue to fund the war. They also see average Germans as carrying a much higher burden of wartime debt than Aly's picture of wartime comfort would suggest.[45]

Aly's work touched a nerve not because of his questionable number crunching, but because it drew sweeping conclusions about the nature of consent and complicity in Nazi Germany and because it looked to the Third Reich for the origins of the West German welfare state. During the war, Aly writes provocatively, Germans became 'well-fed parasites' who rewarded the regime with loyalty.[46] Aly is not the only person to see consumption as enabling support for the regime. Kristin Semmens, who has written about tourism in the Third Reich, see mass consumption as providing a semblance of normality in a highly racist and aberrant state.[47] As long as people had access to consumer necessities and even some luxuries, they could credit the state with looking out for their best interests. Whether or not this translated into active support for the Nazis' more radical and racist aims is difficult to ascertain but, at the very least, consumption, according to this argument, engendered a level of tacit support.

It is beyond dispute that many Germans supported the Nazi regime.[48] But the nature of this support is open to this debate. Did they like the racist aspects of National Socialism? Did they grant support at times and withhold it at others? These are

---

[44] Tooze, Wages of Destruction, xxiii.

[45] Of the numerous reviews, see Martin Vogt, et al., 'Essays zu Götz Alys 'Hitlers Volksstaat', Neue politische Literatur, 50/2 (2005): 185–217; Michael Wildt, 'Vertrautes Ressentiment: Der moderne Sozialstaat hat mit dem "Volksgemeinschafts"-Konzept des Nationalsozialismus nichts zu tun. Eine Antwort auf Götz Aly', Die Zeit (4 May 2005), http://www.zeit.de/2005/19/P-Aly, accessed 10 June 2011; J. Adam Tooze, 'Einfach verkalkuliert', die Tageszeitung, 13 (12 March 2005), http://www.taz.de/index.ph p?id=archivseite&dig=2005/03/12/a0289, accessed 10 June 2011.

[46] Aly, Hitler's Beneficiaries, 324.

[47] Kristin Semmens, Seeing Hitler's Germany: Tourism in the Third Reich (Basingstoke: Palgrave, 2005), 191.

[48] See, e.g., Robert Gellately, Backing Hitler: Consent and Coercion in Nazi Germany (Oxford: Oxford University Press, 2001); and Frank Bajohr, 'The "Folk Community" and the Persecution of the Jews: German Society under National Socialist Dictatorship, 1933–1945', Holocaust and Genocide Studies, 20/2 (2006): 183–206.

interpretative questions that cannot be answered definitively. An individual's support of the regime could be tempered with anger about the war, frustration over the lack of preferred goods, and optimism about the future. Moreover, using consumption to gauge opinion requires accessing consumer expectations both before and after 1933—not an easy exercise. The Second World War provides a unique challenge. If Götz Aly writes of a fundamental level of satisfaction during the war, we are forced to question what it means to be satisfied during a period of rationing, wartime controls, and dying loved ones.

Related to this question of satisfaction and support for the regime is Aly's explanation for *why* the public was happy. Aly has come under fire for offering a crassly materialistic account.[49] In the last two decades, historians of National Socialism have emphasized the importance of ideology to our understanding of consent in the Third Reich. Rather than simply being grateful for the country's economic recovery and their improving personal fortunes, individuals, according to this view, actually bought into the premises of the *Volksgemeinschaft*.[50] It was not simply a marriage of convenience between an anti-Semitic state and a materially needy public. Rather, Germans backed the regime because of, not in spite of, its beliefs, and thus bear a measure of guilt for its crimes. Aly is, of course, not denying a broad complicity: indeed he offers a very harsh portrait of a populace fully indebted to National Socialism. But, for Aly, the reason is strictly un-ideological: the public was, in effect, bought off. Such a view radically downplays the importance of both coercion and ideology and thus misses a key dynamic of Nazi Germany. Yes, the people may have felt good about their lives in the Third Reich, but this was as much based on their belief that Germany was undergoing a spiritual awakening as it was on better job situations, the possibility of upward mobility, or ill-gotten gains. Moreover, these feelings of optimism existed alongside the knowledge that the state would brook no opposition to its policies. In short, satisfaction, fear, and frustration existed alongside each other in the Third Reich.

This historical dispute about consumption and consent is partly an empirical one, and thus we await more nuanced studies of how Nazi policies affected consumers in different regions and from varied social backgrounds. Class divisions remained in Nazi Germany, and material comforts varied according to occupation and family wealth. Certainly, rich people found Nazi policies quite favourable to them; members of 'high society' found numerous luxuries under fascism.[51] But even if average Germans never enjoyed the economic opportunities or living standards of the United States, they still took advantage of a modern consumer economy—one that provided both creature

---

[49] Hans-Ulrich Wehler, 'Engstirniger Materialismus', *Der Spiegel*, 14 (4 April 2005), http://www.spiegel.de/spiegel/print/d-39916224.html, accessed 10 June 2011.

[50] See Claudia Koonz, *The Nazi Conscience* (Cambridge: Belknap Press, 2003); and Peter Fritzsche, *Life and Death in the Third Reich* (Cambridge: Belknap Press, 2008).

[51] Fabrice D'Almeida, *High Society in the Third Reich* (Cambridge: Polity, 2008); on the thriving of high fashion, see Guenther, *Nazi Chic?*

comforts and national pride. In the Third Reich, Germans could never attain as many goods and services as were available in richer, less regulated economies, but this did not stop them from trying. Despite the strictures of the Nazi marketplace (regulations of corporate publicity, price controls, and a war economy), economists and business leaders forged ahead with their project of building a consumer society, which entailed creating a Germany that at once protected its ethos of quality production and catered to the material needs of the masses. They engaged in advertising, public relations, and consumer research, and they discussed the meanings of mass culture and society. They in turn found a willing audience in a population eager to experience the material gains that came with economic recovery.

Thus while Götz Aly's reductive materialism may rightfully be critiqued, his focus on the popular resonance of the economy remains essential. The empirical reality of shortages did not stop Germans from exulting in a perceived improvement in their fortunes as consumers. The real problems that the Nazi economy confronted in the pre-war years did not dispel popular visions of a thriving consumer marketplace. To be sure, as war loomed, a full return to prosperity would need to be deferred to an undefined 'post-war' period. But Germans engaged in the 'virtual consumption' (to use Hartmut Berghoff's term) of goods no longer on the shelf,[52] and promises of delayed gratification sustained most people as they experienced imminent military victory in 1940 and 1941 and later eventual defeat.

LEGACIES OF CONSUMPTION UNDER FASCISM

When National Socialism collapsed in the spring of 1945 so too did the last vestiges of 'normal' consumption. While the war had witnessed increasing misery on the home front, structures had still been in place for the provisioning of the population. The state's rationing of food and clothes, for example, had guaranteed a basic level of comfort for Germans. The summer and winter after Germany's defeat, however, was marked by iconic images of children playing in rubble and once hearty citizens scrambling for food. Given the deprivation, the economic recovery that followed in the 1950s has appeared to scholars and lay people as 'miraculous'. Merely five years after the end of the war, the West German economy began to witness extraordinary growth rates, and consumer products that had been off the shelves for a decade flooded back into stores and shops.

In trying to understand this rapid recovery, historians have looked for links between the pre- and post-1945 periods. They have found, for example, that Germany's industrial capacity was not nearly as damaged by aerial bombing as the Allies had hoped and that

---

[52] Berghoff, 'Times Change and We Change with Them'.

factories resumed production relatively quickly after 1945. In their search for continuities, scholars have looked not only at production but also at consumption. While Nazi consumption policies do not have a causal relationship to the post-war boom, it is now clear that 1945 was less of a break than once assumed. Hans-Ulrich Wehler portrays the West German combination of planning and market economics as the logical result of 1930s policies. By this he means that Nazism unleashed German consumers' high expectations, which could only be met after 1945 by a generous capitalist welfare state.[53] In addition, twentieth-century Germany witnessed continuities in 'consumption personnel', as some of the same people who had worked for the state and private industry to promote a 'managed consumption' under fascism went on to pursue vibrant careers in the Federal Republic.[54] Under Nazism, these economists and market professionals had portrayed consumption as the most important component of the economy. After 1945 they conveniently shifted allegiance from a state-run economy to a free market system. Likewise, continuities in consumer research practices, marketing, and branding strategies reveal the extent to which Nazi consumerism was not, as such, as aberration. The Society for Consumer Research maintained some of the same clients, asked the same questions, and employed some of the same people after 1945. Such continuities were not only limited to West Germany. Like the Nazis, successive East German governments tried to regulate consumption and protect the public from its moral threats. While the shortages of consumer goods in the GDR had parallels in the Third Reich, the Nazis did not go so far as the East German regime, which in 1976 banned outright the advertising of consumer goods in an attempt to lower demand.[55]

The most important continuity, however, was in attitudes about consumption. If, according to Wolfgang König, the Third Reich was a 'failed consumer society', this was not for want of trying.[56] Coming on the heels of the Weimar Republic, which saw a flowering of consumer culture, the Third Reich also witnessed earnest attempts to maintain high levels of consumption but to guide it toward the aims of a racial state. On a superficial level, this resembled attempts to link high consumption lifestyles to the health of the anti-communist West during the Cold War era. According to Michael Geyer, '[The] social contract of an acquisitive society was formed in the consuming passions of the 1930s and 1940s, rather than in the postwar years.'[57]

[53] Wehler's position is summarized in Stefan Schwarzkopf, 'Kontrolle statt Rausch? Marktforschung, Produktwerbung und Verbraucherlenkung im Nationalsozialismus zwischen Phantasien von Masse, Angst und Macht', in Árpad von Klimó and Malte Rolf (eds.), *Rausch und Diktatur: Inszenierung, Mobilisierung und Kontrolle in totalitären Systemen* (Frankfurt: Campus, 2007), 193–209.

[54] Advertiser Hanns Brose, for example, put his experience with 'communal advertising' to work in the 1950s on behalf of *Die Waage*, a state and industry-sponsored initiative to sell the merits of the market economy to West Germans. Mark E. Spicka, *Selling the Economic Miracle: Economic Reconstruction and Politics in West Germany, 1949–1957* (Oxford and New York: Berghahn Books, 2007), 114.

[55] Pamela L. Swett, S. Jonathan Wiesen, and Jonathan R. Zatlin, *Selling Modernity: Advertising in Twentieth-Century Germany* (Durham NC: Duke University Press, 2007), 16.

[56] König, *Volkswagen, Volksempfänger, Volksgemeinschaft*.

[57] Michael Geyer, 'The Stigma of Violence, Nationalism, and War in Twentieth-Century Germany', *German Studies Review*, 15 (Winter 1992): 75–110 (p.102).

In the end we must understand consumption under National Socialism in the broader global context of twentieth-century consumer capitalism. The 1930s witnessed two transformative historical events. On the one hand, it saw the rise of consumer-driven economies throughout capitalist states. On the other, it saw the ascent of fascism, which gained the support of shopkeepers, farmers, and others who saw hyper-capitalism as a threat to their livelihoods. This confluence created a core dilemma for the National Socialist regime. The Nazis condemned mass consumption as decadent, American, Jewish, and as a force that threatened to undermine the integrity of the German nation. But they also recognized, correctly, that consumer society still embodied the dreams of many Germans. The regime responded to this dilemma by crafting a uniquely National Socialist vision of mass consumer society, based on racial purity and sanitized commercial practices. But this vision was contradictory, even schizophrenic, marked as it was by both an attraction to and repulsion toward consumer culture. The Nazis envisioned a peaceful, affluent society, but they used violent means to obtain it. They imagined a future rich in consumer opportunities but relegated consumption to a low priority. In short, National Socialism offered a brutal, conflict-ridden, and ultimately failed response to global capitalist developments.

BIBLIOGRAPHY

Aly, Götz, *Hitler's Beneficiaries: Plunder, Racial War, and the Nazi Welfare State* (New York: Metropolitan, 2007).

Baranowski, Shelley, *Strength through Joy: Consumerism and Mass Tourism in the Third Reich* (Cambridge: Cambridge University Press, 2004).

Berghoff, Hartmut, 'Enticement and Deprivation: The Regulation of Consumption in Pre-War Nazi Germany', in Martin Daunton and Matthew Hilton, *The Politics of Consumption: Material Culture and Citizenship in Europe and America* (Oxford: Berg, 2001), 165–84.

Berghoff, Hartmut, '"Times Change and We Change with Them": The German Advertising Industry in the Third Reich—Between Professional Self-Interest and Political Repression', *Business History*, 45/1 (2003), 128–47.

Confino, Alon, and Rudy Koshar, 'Régimes of Consumer Culture: New Narratives in Twentieth-Century German History', *German History*, 19/2 (2001), 135–61.

De Grazia, Victoria, *Irresistible Empire: America's Advance through 20th Century Europe* (Cambridge, MA and London: Harvard University Press, 2005).

König, Wolfgang, *Volkswagen, Volksempfänger, Volksgemeinschaft: 'Volksprodukte' im Dritten Reich: Vom Scheitern einer nationalsozialistischen Konsumgesellschaft* (Paderborn: Schöningh: 2004),

Reagin, Nancy, *Sweeping the German Nation: Domesticity and National Identity in Germany, 1870–1945* (Cambridge: Cambridge University Press, 2007).

Reinhardt, Dirk, *Von der Reklame zum Marketing: Geschichte der Wirtschaftswerbung in Deutschland* (Berlin: Akademie, 1993).

Ross, Corey, *Media and the Making of Modern Germany: Mass Communications, Society, and Politics in Germany from the Empire to the Third Reich* (Oxford: Oxford University Press, 2008).

Schäfer, Hans-Dieter, *Das Gespaltene Bewußtsein: Über deutsche Kultur und Lebenswirklichkeit 1933–1945* (Berlin: Ullstein, 1984).

Schwarzkopf, Stefan, 'Kontrolle statt Rausch? Marktforschung, Produktwerbung und Verbraucherlenkung im Nationalsozialismus zwischen Phantasien von Masse, Angst und Macht', in Árpad von Klimó and Malte Rolf (eds.), *Rausch und Diktatur: Inszenierung, Mobilisierung und Kontrolle in totalitären Systemen* (Frankfurt: Campus, 2007), 193–209.

Semmens, Kristin, *Seeing Hitler's Germany: Tourism in the Third Reich* (Basingstoke: Palgrave, 2005).

Tooze, Adam, *The Wages of Destruction: The Making and Breaking of the Nazi Economy* (New York: Viking, 2006).

CHAPTER 23

....

THINGS UNDER SOCIALISM: THE SOVIET EXPERIENCE

....

SHEILA FITZPATRICK

THINGS were not meant to be a problem under socialism. It was capitalism that created problems by making things into commodities to be bought and sold for profit, creating desire, envy, and a 'fetishism' of goods. The unequal distribution of things was one of the basic iniquities of capitalism. But that was easy to correct. 'We no longer have *commodities*, but only *products*', wrote two distinguished Soviet theorists in their *The ABC of Communism* (1920). 'These products are not exchanged for each other; they are neither bought nor sold. They are simply stored in the communal warehouses, and are subsequently delivered to those who need them.'[1] This followed the principle laid down by Marx and Engels: 'From each according to his ability, to each according to his needs.'

But might not an individual's 'needs' prove tricky to determine? What if some people claimed more than they were entitled to? In the theorists' view, this might be a problem for a few decades, requiring a temporary distribution system weighted according to the amount of work an individual performed, but the problem would soon be overcome: socialism would bring abundance, thus abolishing anxiety about getting one's share. Once there is 'an ample quantity of all products', which was only a matter of time:

> our present wounds will long since have been healed, and everyone will be able to get just as much as he needs... Today, for example, no one thinks it worth while when he wants one seat in a tram, to take three tickets and keep two places empty. It will be just the same in the case of all products.[2]

---

[1] N. Bukharin and E. Preobrazhensky, *The ABC of Communism*, ed. E. H. Carr, trans. Eden and Cedar Paul (Harmondsworth, Middlesex, UK: Penguin, 1969), 116.

[2] Bukharin and Preobrazhensky, *ABC of Communism*, 116–17.

Coupled with confidence in future abundance was the recognition that, for the short term, in the wake of the Revolution and before the 'building of socialism' had been completed, things might be tough and goods scarce. So the immediate Revolutionary task was to ensure that those who had formerly been poor in goods became rich, and vice versa. The challenge of early Soviet policy and practice was successfully to accomplish that redistribution.

EARLY SOVIET PRACTICE

At the governmental level, nationalization of private businesses, estates, factories, and financial institutions, and municipalization of dwellings was the first step in the redistribution strategy. This meant that the state took things from the 'bourgeoisie' (the Soviet catch-all term for those it classified as 'class enemies', including the old nobility and service class); and, since the state was, by definition, 'proletarian', that was conceptually much the same thing as putting them in the hands of the people. Direct popular confiscation of bourgeois property also occurred: for example, when peasants drove the landowners off their estates in the summer of 1917 and urban 'Revolutionaries' (some saw them as 'looters') broke into shops and apartments and helped themselves; and again during collectivization at the end of the 1920s, when peasants who participated in the expropriation of 'kulaks' (a category of peasant regarded by the Bolsheviks as exploiters) generally got a share of the spoils. But direct popular action was messy, and the Bolsheviks generally preferred to avoid it. The proper way to confiscate property was to come as an accredited agent of the party or the new Soviet state and make an inventory ('*opis*') of the goods taken. As a result of this Revolutionary usage, a formerly innocent word acquired sinister connotations: *opisi* were what the victims had to sign when a Revolutionary group showed up to take their possessions or, later, when house searches were conducted against suspected 'enemies of the people'. The confiscation of bourgeois things was the beginning of socialism.

The positive aspects of redistribution—that is, the reassignment of the confiscated assets to those who needed them—was carried out in a rough-and-ready way in the early years, primarily through rationing and housing policy. National rationing systems were something many belligerent countries had set up during the First World War, but the bureaucratic challenge had defeated Tsarist Russia, even though it managed to create a national Food Committee for procurement and distribution to local authorities. Ad hoc local rationing schemes, mainly for bread, sugar, and meat, existed in many cities before the collapse of the old regime, but it was left to the Provisional Government to introduce a national system (legislated in June 1917), which was inherited by the new Soviet regime after the October Revolution. The Bolsheviks, however, had their own approach to rationing: in contrast to the Provisional Government's practice (and what would have been the imperial regime's, if it had succeeded in creating a rationing system), it was *not* egalitarian. Rather, it was intended to favour the proletariat, the Revolution's allies, and discriminate against the bourgeoisie, its enemies.[3] The same principle underlay housing policy, where city soviets did their best to achieve redistribution by settling 'proletarians' in spacious 'bourgeois' apartments, along with the old 'bourgeois' owners, who were now relegated to one or two rooms. This was the origin of the later notorious 'communal apartment', where each room was inhabited by a different household, and kitchen, bathroom, and hall were for collective use. The communal apartment was a product of socialist ideology only in the sense that it was part of a confiscatory and discriminatory approach to bourgeois property. Contrary to the impression of many later observers, it was not officially regarded as an experiment in collective living.

In the long term, to be sure, new forms of collective living were on the agenda. Families would eat in communal dining rooms rather than wastefully making their own meals; they would do their laundry in communal facilities and take vacations at communal dachas (country cottages) and resorts. Apartments would be owned by the state, which would probably also supply the furniture. Town-dwellers would travel swiftly and conveniently by public transport; in the villages, there would be a pool of collectively owned horses and carts for everyone's use. Palaces of culture would be created, some of them in the old palaces of the nobility, but these would belong to the people. A few enthusiasts wanted to start building the new 'socialist everyday' immediately, arguing that without it the emancipation of women, which was so important a Revolutionary aim, could not be achieved. Because of their efforts, a few model apartment blocks were built, one example being the modernist Narkomfin Communal House designed by the architect Moisei Ginzburg, whose facilities—rather like the kibbutzim of the early Israel state thirty years later—included a communal kitchen and dining room, communal gymnasium, library, mechanical laundry, and crèche where children would spend their days and nights, leaving both parents free to work.[4]

Avant-garde 'Constructivist' architects, artists, and theorists were among the few people inclined to take things seriously in the 1920s. The Revolution means more than the liberation of workers, the Constructivist Alexander Rodchenko wrote in 1925, it also means 'the new relation to the person, to woman, to things. Our things in our hands must be equals, comrades.'[5] The theorist Boris Arvatov proposed (though not on the basis of observation) that proletarians had a special affinity with industrially mass-produced goods. But nobody had a practical suggestion as to how things might

---

[3] On the imperial and Provisional Government's efforts, see P. V. Struve, K. I. Zaitsev, N. V. Dolinsky, and S. S. Demosthenov, *Food Supply in Russia during the War* (New Haven, CT: Yale University Press and Carnegie Endowment for International Peace, 1930), 161–72. On early Soviet rationing, see Mary McAuley, *Bread and Justice: State and Society in Petrograd 1917–1922* (Oxford: Clarendon Press, 1991), 286–91, and Julie Hessler, *A Social History of Soviet Trade* (Princeton, NJ: Princeton University Press, 2004), 63–9.

[4] The Narkomfin Communal House is the subject of Victor Buchli's *An Archeology of Socialism* (Oxford and New York: Berg, 1999), 68–9. Its planned crèche was never actually built.

[5] Christina Kiaer, *Imagine No Possessions: The Socialist Objects of Russian Constructivism* (Cambridge, MA: MIT Press, 2005), 68–9, at 1.

become comrades, or even how industrially mass-produced goods might be brought to the proletariat (whose things were mainly artisan-produced or home-made) to find out if they liked them. Lenin and Trotsky were impatient with what they saw as the idle chatter of the Constructivists, distracting from real tasks and bringing the Revolution into disrepute.

To most Bolshevik leaders, schemes for the reconstruction of everyday life seemed premature, if not (in the case of the Constructivists) positively harmful. In Bolshevik usage, the very term 'everyday' ('*byt*') was pejorative: *byt* was something that had to be mastered, its natural tendency to undermine the Revolution overcome. Objects were not central in this discourse, apart from their pernicious influence as survivals of the past (*perezhitki*). The important thing was to change behaviour. Leon Trotsky, the leader who was most interested in the everyday, devoted almost all his writings on the subject to educational and behavioural themes: learning to read, learning polite forms of address and proper behaviour to women, learning hygiene, learning efficient work habits and punctuality, learning not to drink.[6] Even Trotsky, a charismatic figure, could not make these tasks seem glamorous to young Communist militants who were interested only in politics and fighting the class enemy.

In general, the Bolshevik leaders' thoughts about things were that the less one thought about them, the better. The approved Revolutionary lifestyle in the 1920s was simple and ascetic, with books the only possession about which one could conceivably boast. This was in line with the pre-Revolutionary radical tradition of contempt for possessions: 'Nobody [in the family] ever owned any real estate or other property', Lenin's wife Nadezhda Krupskaia wrote proudly in an autobiographical entry whose abnegation of self was intensified by being written in the third person.[7] When forced to contemplate the world of things, Bolsheviks of the 1920s were likely to display a slight preference for the functional and mass-produced (as long as it was not too 'American' or associated with eccentric avant-garde artists). They too were proponents of modernity, after all, and thus disapproved of a range of non-modern objects, from the humble goods produced by artisans and craftsmen ('backward' and 'petty bourgeois') to the luxury possessions of the bourgeoisie and nobility. With regard to things, disapproval was generally a stronger Bolshevik reaction than approval. Almost the only things that were wholeheartedly approved and conceptually privileged in early Soviet Russia were those associated with hygiene, like soap, handkerchiefs, and toothbrushes.

---

[6] Leon Trotsky, *Problems of Everyday Life* (New York: Pathfinder Press, 1973). The Russian title of the 1924 edition—*Voprosy byta. Epokha 'kul'turnichestva' i ee zadachi* (Moscow: Gos. izd-vo, 1924)—uses the usually negative term '*kul'turnichestvo*' (meaning cultural work divorced from politics) in a positive sense unusual for a Bolshevik of the period.

[7] N. Krupskaia, 'Avtobiografiia' (mid-1920s), quoted in Sheila Fitzpatrick and Yuri Slezkine (eds.), *In the Shadow of Revolution: Lives of Russian Women from the Revolution to the Second World War*, trans. Yuri Slezkine (Princeton, NJ: Princeton University Press, 2000), 111.

SCARCITY AND PRIVILEGE

It was all very well for the Bolshevik leaders to take a high-minded attitude about things: by virtue of their official positions, they were able to provide themselves with the basics of food, clothing, and shelter. Other people found themselves obsessed by things—their loss and absence, and the constant need to go out looking for them. An Englishwoman soon to marry the future Foreign Minister Maxim Litvinov came to Russia thinking that 'ideas' would be everything and 'things' nothing, but quickly discovered her mistake: 'peering into ground-floor windows I saw the *things* of Moscow huggermuggering in all the corners and realized that they had never been so important.'[8] This was so because of their scarcity. After a brief respite at the end of the Civil War, when optimists thought the Revolution was over and life was returning to normal, the Revolution started up again and scarcity became worse than ever.

The new phrase of Revolution—Stalin's 'revolution from above'—was a state-initiated great leap forward on the economic front, involving a rapid industrialization drive, collectivization of peasant agriculture, abolition of private trade in the towns, and the introduction of central economic planning. Urban living standards declined dramatically over the first Five-Year Plan (1928–32). Rationing was reintroduced for the urban population, a non-egalitarian system, as in the Civil War, but even harder on the lowest category, that of 'social aliens' like traders and priests, who did not even get ration cards. The people best off were those whose workplaces were in priority sectors like heavy industry, for, with the retail system in chaos, a large proportion of the goods distributed by the state came via the workplace. Special 'closed distributors' were set up for Communist and professional elite members.[9] This was not a new practice, since some scholars and artists had been put on a special 'academic ration' during the Civil War, and party officials continued to be issued with food packages throughout the inter-war period. But it was at the beginning of the 1930s that closed stores selling only to elite members 'on the list' became entrenched in Soviet life, and the hierarchy of privilege—which meant privileged access to the goods in state warehouses—consolidated.[10]

The extreme importance of privileged access to goods at this time was related to the desperate food situation produced by collectivization. The point of collectivization was to force peasants to farm and sell their produce collectively, selling to the state at non-negotiable low prices to facilitate the process of 'socialist accumulation' for industrialization. But peasant resistance, and the state's inability to gauge exactly how much could be

---

[8] From a letter to a friend, quoted in John Carswell, *The Exile: A Life of Ivy Litvinov* (London: Faber and Faber, 1983), 101.

[9] On these practices, see Sheila Fitzpatrick, *Everyday Stalinism: Ordinary Life in Extraordinary Times: Russia in the 1930s* (New York and Oxford: Oxford University Press, 1999), 55–6.

[10] See Elena A. Osokina, *Our Daily Bread: Socialist Distribution and the Art of Survival in Stalin's Russia*, trans. Kate Transchel and Greta Bucher (Armonk, NY: M. E. Sharpe, 2000).

taken without dooming the peasants to starvation, ended in a famine in 1932–3 that not only killed millions in the countryside but led millions more to flee to the towns, causing near collapse of the urban rationing system. At this point, given the violence with which the state was collecting agricultural procurements and the pittance it was paying for them, 'procurement' was almost a synonym for confiscation. But there was outright confiscation as well: when kulaks were expropriated and deported at the beginning of the 1930s, their substantial property (horses, agricultural implements) was supposed to go to the collective farms, but their personal property (linen, pots and pans, pillows, boots, shirts, honey) often ended up in the hands of their neighbours. The campaign against kulaks was accompanied by a drive against religion, which brought another kind of confiscation: that of iron church bells, taken to be melted down 'for industrialization'.

As collectivization imperilled the food supply, the accompanying squeeze on artisans and craftsmen was producing other critical shortages. Suddenly nobody could find such ordinary household items as tea-kettles, sacks, nails, boards, paint, spoons, forks, plates, basins, oil lamps, and baskets—all things formerly produced by artisans who had now been put out of business. Leather goods, including shoes, vanished from the market after the mass slaughter of animals by peasants in the early stages of collectivization. There were no buttons, needles, and thread to be had: even in the mid-1930s, when the consumer economy had recovered somewhat and private tailoring was again grudgingly permitted, one had to provide one's own buttons and thread, as well as cloth, in order to have a suit made.[11] Such small items had become consequential: children all over the Soviet Union were running around in the name of industrialization collecting scrap—now dignified with the sinister sounding Latinate neologism util'syr'e. Metal fragments, bone, rags, glass, old boots, cherry pits, corks, tins, and bits of rubber were all grist to their mill, along with human hair (which it was rumoured would be sent abroad in exchange for tractors).

With the rapid influx of population, the towns became yet more crowded: average living space in Moscow was down to 5 ½ sq. m per capita in 1930, and would drop almost to 4 sq.m by 1940. Communal apartments, along with barracks and dormitories, became the basic form of dwelling, and would remain so until the late 1950s. 'Communal' meant intense non-sharing on the part of involuntary neighbours, usually hostile and suspicious of each other. Demarcation lines in the communal kitchen were rigorously monitored, rules of serial access instituted, but still the authorities deplored the prevalence of 'hooligan behavior' in communal apartments, mentioning particularly 'mean tricks (throwing other people's things out of the kitchen and other places of communal use, spoiling food prepared by other residents, damaging property and produce, and so on)'.[12]

If it was each for himself (or rather, his household) in the communal apartment, the same went for provisioning, which required the combined skills of the hunter and

---

[11] Fitzpatrick, *Everyday Stalinism*, 42–5.

[12] Quoted in Fitzpatrick, *Everyday Stalinism*, 48. See also Katerina Gerasimova, 'Public Privacy in the Soviet Communal Apartment', in David Crowley and Susan Reid (eds.), *Socialist Spaces: Sites of Everyday Life in the Eastern Bloc* (Oxford: Berg, 2002), 207–30.

gatherer. Shortages of goods, at first thought to be a temporary problem caused by collectivization and the industrialization drive, turned out to be systemic: it was not necessarily a matter of absolute scarcity (though at numerous times in the turbulent history of the Soviet Union from 1917 to the early 1950s it was that too) but rather of the system's inability to get the goods to the enterprises and individuals that needed them, and the consequent tendency of enterprises and individuals to hoard.[13] *Shirpotreb*, shorthand for *produkty shirokogo potrebleniia*, was the new bureaucratic acronym for consumer goods; the Politburo was alarmed by perpetual *shirpotreb* shortages but seemed unable to do anything about it. But if the system could not get things to you, you had to do it yourself. As well as queueing, buying illegally from 'speculators', and finding a well-supplied workplace, a crucial survival strategy was the system of informal connections known as *blat*: better 100 friends than 100 rubles, as the saying went.[14]

Privilege in the Soviet Union was not a matter of owning things but of having *access* to the things the state had in its warehouses. This facilitated what Bourdieu would call 'mis-recognition'[15] on the part of the new Soviet elite, whose advantages over the rest of the population increased in the course of the 1930s: we did not own things, one high official's wife remembered, so we did not consider ourselves privileged. A car came to take her husband to work and they received special food packages, but even the furniture came out of state warehouses, to which it must ultimately return. 'There was no cult of things in our household,' the daughter of a similarly placed official remembered, even though they had a car for their own use as well as a 'beautiful apartment' and a dacha ('Stalin's little gifts'). They had no 'fancy furniture'. 'All the pieces, except perhaps the bookshelves, had brass tags with inventory numbers on them.'[16]

THE REDISCOVERY OF GOOD TASTE

While the ascetic ethos may have remained dominant among the older generation of Bolsheviks, times were changing. *Things* were making a comeback, along with good taste, for which the Soviet term was *kul'turnost'*, the quality of being cultured. An

---

[13] On this systemic characteristic, see Janos Kornai, *Economics of Shortage, Contributions to Economic Analysis* No.131, 2 vols. (Amsterdam and New York: North-Holland Publishing Company, 1980).

[14] On *blat*, see Alena Ledeneva, *Russia's Economy of Favours: Blat, Networking and Informal Exchange* (Cambridge: Cambridge University Press, 1998), and Stephen Lovell, Alena V. Ledeneva, and Andrei Rogachevskii, *Bribery and Blat in Russia: Negotiating Reciprocity from the Middle Ages to the 1990s* (London: Macmillan, 2000).

[15] Pierre Bourdieu, *Language and Symbolic Power*, 151–3, 169–70, and *passim*.

[16] Fruma Treivas, 'We Were Fighting for An Idea!', in Sheila Fitzpatrick and Yuri Slezkine (eds.), *In the Shadow of Revolution. Lives of Russian Women from the Revolution to the Second World War*, trans. Yuri Slezkine (Princeton, NJ: Princeton University Press, 2000), 326; quotes from Inna Shikheeva-Gaister, 'A Family Chronicle', in ibid., 175–6.

approving newspaper report in 1935 on a customer's discerning purchase of teaspoons in a Moscow department store noted that he spent a long time comparing 'shape, luster, and design', and remarked that 'recently he has been particularly drawn to simple, attractive, and well-made things. Earlier he somehow did not notice crude spoons and bowls in the dining rooms, torn or dirty jackets, ugly ties'.[17] But now the famine was over, rationing had just been lifted, Stalin had made his famous pronouncement that 'Life has become better, life has become more cheerful', and Food Minister Anastas Mikoian was busy bringing ice-cream and Soviet champagne to the people. The newspapers ran lip-smacking descriptions of the many kinds of sausages, cheese, fish, and pastries available (for a price) in a recently reopened luxury grocery on Moscow's main street.[18] Advertisements sang the praises of unheard-of products like ketchup (evidently for educational reasons, as the goods were not available in Soviet stores). Workers in department stores were encouraged to acquire the habits of 'cultured socialist trade', that is, to modify their naturally belligerent and defensive attitude to customers and inform them politely about their products.

For the time being, of course, not everybody could have access to caviar and Soviet champagne; there was simply not enough to go round. But socialism, which the Soviet state was in the process of building, would bring abundance, and then there would be enough for everyone. In the meantime, a minority of the population would have privileged access—a 'vanguard', to conceptualize it in Bolshevik terms, but different from the old 'vanguard of the working class' of Revolutionary days in that it was distinguished not so much by political consciousness as by *kul'turnost'*. Here was another useful misrecognition, translating elite material privileges into a vanguard's cultural superiority. Yet it had its limits, and a degree of elite uneasiness about privilege, and a stronger degree of popular resentment of it, remained. This was manifest during the Great Purges of the late 1930s, when disgraced high officials, now identified as 'enemies of the people', were accused of building themselves expensive dachas and cultivating a luxurious lifestyle of banquets, cars, foreign consumer goods, and expensive clothes.

As token that the beneficiaries of privilege were a cultural vanguard, not a social elite, Stakhanovite workers and peasants—those recognized for outstanding work performance—were among their number, being rewarded with material goods which they proudly listed at public meetings. 'I received a bed, a gramophone, and other cultural

[17] See Sheila Fitzpatrick, 'Becoming Cultured: Socialist Realism and the Representation of Privilege and Taste', in Fitzpatrick, *The Cultural Front: Power and Culture in Revolutionary Russia* (Ithaca, NY: Cornell University Press, 1992), 216–37, at 224; Vadim Volkov, 'The Concept of *Kul'turnost'*: Notes on the Stalinist Civilizing Process', in Fitzpatrick (ed.), *Stalinism: New Directions* (London: Routledge, 2000), 210–30; Jukka Gronow, *Caviar with Champagne: Common Luxury and the Ideals of the Good Life in Stalin's Russia* (Oxford and New York: Berg, 2003); Randi Cox, ' "NEP without Nepmen!" Soviet Advertising and the Transition to Socialism', in Christina Kiaer and Eric Naiman (eds.), *Everyday Life in Early Soviet Russia: Taking the Revolution Inside* (Bloomington: Indiana University Press, 2006), 119–52; Julie Hessler, 'Cultured Trade: the Stalinist Turn towards Consumerism', in Fitzpatrick (ed.), *Stalinism: New Directions*, 182–209.

[18] On the new higher-priced 'commercial stores' introduced in the mid-1930s, along with the ideology of 'cultured trade', see Hessler, *Social History of Soviet Trade*, 197–201.

necessities, a Tadzhik Stakhanovite announced. 'I can report to you that I don't live in my old mud hut anymore—I was awarded a European-style house, I live like a civilized person.' From the south of Russia, a Stakhanovite peasant woman boasted: 'Everything I am wearing I got as a prize for good work in the kolkhoz. As well as the dress and shoes, I got a sewing machine in Nalchik. For the harvest, I got a prize of a silk dress worth 250 rubles.' After three years working in Magnitogorsk, Aleksei Tishchenko, whose possessions and those of his wife had all fitted in a single home-made suitcase when they arrived, received a hunting gun, a gramophone, and a motorcycle as prizes for Stakhanovite achievement, and in addition showed his growing *kul'turnost'* by acquiring furniture, including a couch and a wardrobe, and dress clothes, including two overcoats.[19]

'Cultural goods' had become a special category of things that had definitively escaped the taint of capitalism. Under the heading of 'cultural construction', official statistics were gathered and published on the number of radios, gramophones, sewing machines, watches, alarm clocks, iron bedsteads, bicycles, and motorcycles acquired by the urban and rural population each year—in effect, a quantitative celebration of rising popular *kul'turnost'*.[20]

The Second World War meant another six years of rationing and privation for the Soviet population. But its victorious end brought an orgy of looting as Soviet soldiers marched across Europe, astonished at the array of possessions owned by ordinary citizens. Officers participated too, at a higher level, shipping wagon-loads of 'trophy goods' like grand pianos back home. 'Material craving engulfed postwar society from top to bottom', wrote Vera Dunham, whose sociological study of Soviet fiction revealed a new level of passion for beautiful objects (or, in Dunham's perception, kitsch), as in the embroidered pillow and nightstand 'covered with pink paper, scalloped at the edge' with which a fictional student decorated her corner in the student dormitory, or the 'delicate mauve wallpaper' and 'airy pink lampshade' which graced the living-room of an elite apartment, along with a piano 'upon which was lined up a whole army of knickknacks'.[21]

That piano (a trophy, perhaps?) was now inheritable. Private inheritance of property had been formally abolished, as a capitalist institution, in 1918, though in practice the state seldom exercised its rights as legatee with regard to personal possessions. But by a 1945 law, inheritance was back, much on the pattern of the rest of Europe, and Soviet lawyers were discussing a new concept of personal property (*lichnaia sobstvennost'*), which differed from (capitalist) private property by being limited to things that people

[19] See Sheila Fitzpatrick, *Stalin's Peasants: Resistance and Survival in the Russian Village after Collectivization* (New York and Oxford: Oxford University Press, 1994), 278, and eadem, *Everyday Stalinism*, 103.

[20] See Fitzpatrick, *Everyday Stalinism*, 266–7.

[21] Vera S. Dunham, *In Stalin's Time: Middleclass Values in Soviet Fiction* (Cambridge and New York: Cambridge University Press, 1976), 41–58 (ch. 3: 'Possessions'), at 42, 45. For a disapproving account of speculation on trophy goods by elite wives, see Lidiia Shatunovskaia, *Zhizn' v Kremle* (New York: Chalidze Publications, 1982), 139–52.

personally used. These included dachas, and we hear in the 1940s of the first of many law suits over possession of dachas after death or divorce.[22]

KHRUSHCHEV'S THAW AND THE PROMISES
OF ABUNDANCE

With Stalin's death in 1953, there was a consensus within the leadership that living standards had to be radically and swiftly increased. Khrushchev, a utopian as well as an optimist, predicted that the Soviet Union would catch up with the West in the realm of food supply and consumer goods within a few years; and the 1961 party programme anticipated the advent of communism—not just the preliminary stage of socialism—within two decades. Communism, of course, meant abundance, and people were glad to hear it was on the way. The issue of principle was whether the abundant goods of the future should be in individual (household) hands or the hands of collectives and the state. Khrushchev and his economic advisers had no hesitation in choosing the collective option: 'public consumption funds' would provide the goods and services of communism, and that would have the effect of 'strengthening the collectivist spirit and getting rid of the psychology of private ownership'. With abundance, according to Academician Strumilin, 'the people themselves will throw away personal cars and dachas and individual houses like so much excess baggage.' Why bother having your own car 'when excellent cars of all models and colors (just pick one to suit your taste) are lined up in the public garages, just waiting for passengers?'[23]

Some people, resentful of elite privileges, liked the sound of this, and even recommended immediate collectivization of such valuables as dachas and cars that were currently in individual hands.[24] But these were, perhaps, people who saw no chance of acquiring such goods themselves. The operational practice of Khrushchev's regime, as opposed to its abstract principle, was to put an ever increasing quantity and array of goods into individual or household hands. First on the list were apartments. In the second half of the 1950s, Khrushchev launched a massive housing construction programme, based on the premise that the single family apartment was the ideal. Millions of households were able to move out of communal apartments into separate ones, an extraordinarily important social change: the separate apartment represented one's own

---

[22] Frances Foster-Simons, 'The Development of Inheritance Law in the Soviet Union and the People's Republic of China', *American Journal of Comparative Law*, 33/1 (1985), 33–62; Stephen Lovell, *Summerfolk: A History of the Dacha, 1710–2000* (Ithaca, NY: Cornell University Press, 2003), 169–78.

[23] On popular reactions (from interviews of the 1990s), see Iurii Aksiutin, *Khrushchevskaia 'ottepel' i obshchestvennye nastroeniia v SSSR v 1953–1964 gg.* (Moscow: Rosspen, 2004), 331–7; on public consumption funds (from the 1961 party programme), A. V. Pyzhikov, *Khrushchevskaia 'ottepel'* (Moscow: Olma Press, 2002), 299; Strumilin article in *Izvestiia*, 30 August 1961, 3.

[24] Pyzhikov, *Khrushchevskaia 'ottepel'*, 300.

space, perceived by many as a cherished haven of privacy; and the concept of a private sphere, separate from the public, gained broad currency.[25]

Most of the new apartments were still rented from the state (though now, for the first time, it was possible to buy an apartment in a cooperative building), but dachas could be owned—and increasing numbers of urban families did so. Close to 3 million Muscovites were leaving town on summer weekends for the dacha, and of these almost half a million owned their own. Millions more were adding major appliances to their (previously very short) list of household possessions, notably television sets (a third of all households had them by 1965 and 80 per cent ten years later), refrigerators (a rise over the same period from 17 per cent of households to 77 per cent), and washing-machines (29 per cent to 76 per cent).[26] No wonder that the regime, its eyes fixed on the achievement of communism, was nevertheless forced to recognize 'remnants of the past (*perezhitki*) such as private-property tendencies' still visibly present in the society, perpetuated by 'backward' elements.[27] But this analysis was more and more off key, as people (and not 'backward' but go-ahead types) owned more things and felt an ever growing desire for further acquisition. Indeed, new things generated their own demands. Once in the new apartment, for example, people had to buy new furniture, both because the old did not fit and because the spirit of the age seemed to require something lighter and less ponderous than the old Stalinist models: architects and designers recommended a simple and functional 'contemporary' style, Scandinavian via Eastern Europe in style.[28] The world of socialism expanded to include fashion (Christian Dior was invited to show a collection in Moscow in the late 1950s) and taste professionals. For a while, cars were the sticking-point: private cars were not part of Khrushchev's definition of socialist entitlement, but they were definitely part of the elite's—and, increasingly, the ordinary citizen's—definition. But by the 1970s the line had been breached and the Soviet Union entered the automobile age.[29]

[25] On the housing reform, see Lynne Attwood, 'Housing in the Khrushchev Era', in Melanie Ilič, Susan E. Reid, and Lynne Attwood (eds.), *Women in the Khrushchev Era* (New York: Palgrave Macmillan, 2004), 177–202; Steven E. Harris, 'Moving to the Separate Apartment: Building, Distributing, Furnishing, and Living in Urban Housing in Soviet Russia, 1950s–1960s', Ph.D. dissertation (University of Chicago, 2003); and N. B. Lebina and A. N. Chistikov, *Obyvatel' i reform: Kartiny povsednevnoi zhizni gorozhan v gody NEP'a i khrushchevskogo desiatiletiia* (St Petersburg: Dmitrii Bulanin, 2003), 22–45, 166, 172. On privacy, see Susan E. Reid, 'The Meaning of Home: The Only Bit of the World You can have to Yourself', in Lewis H. Siegelbaum (ed.), *Borders of Socialism: Private Spheres of Soviet Russia* (New York: Palgrave Macmillan, 2006), 145–70, and Steven E. Harris, ' "I know all the Secrets of my Neighbors": the Quest for Privacy in the Era of the Separate Apartment', in ibid., 171–90.
[26] For dacha statistics, see Lovell, *Summerfolk*, 198; other statistics from *Narodnoe khoziaistvo SSSR za 60 let, Iubileinye sbornik* (Moscow: Statistika, 1977), 510.
[27] From a draft resolution of the Polianskii Commission on social parasitism, c.1957, quoted in Sheila Fitzpatrick, 'Social Parasites: How Tramps, Idle Youth and Busy Entrepreneurs Impeded the Soviet March to Communism', *Cahiers du Monde Russe*, 47/1–2 (2006), 390–1.
[28] Iurii Gerchuk, 'The Aesthetics of Everyday Life in the Khrushchev Thaw in the USSR (1954–64)', in Susan E. Reid and David Crowley (eds.), *Style and Socialism: Modernity and Material Culture in Post-War Eastern Europe* (Oxford: Berg, 2000), 81–99.
[29] See Lewis H. Siegelbaum, 'Cars, Cars, and More Cars: The Faustian Bargain of the Brezhnev Era', in Siegelbaum (ed.), *Borders of Socialism*, 83–103.

The problem of deciding to satisfy consumer needs was that it set the Soviet Union on a course of competition with the West which, as it was playing catch-up, it was very likely to lose. That was the Cold War strategy the American sociologist David Riesman had recommended in 1951: bombard Moscow with nylon stockings and dishwashers, and Western victory would be assured. It was a strategy Vice-President Richard Nixon followed successfully in his 'kitchen debate' with Khrushchev at the exhibition of American consumer goods held in Moscow in 1959, where Nixon's pitch for dishwashers, supermarkets, and Coca-Cola carried the day, and Muscovites crowded the exhibition to marvel at American appliances.[30] Some have interpreted the whole downfall of the Soviet Union and the communist bloc as simply the result of Western victory in the competition over things.

The Khrushchev regime was not against exposure to Western culture, as long as it met Soviet standards of *kul'turnost'*. Indeed, the cultural opening to the West initiated with the 1957 Moscow Youth Festival was in the first instance a *state* initiative, though one enthusiastically embraced by the population. The Thaw, it has been said, started with fashion; and acquiring certain Western goods like blue jeans, leather jackets, polo-neck sweaters, books by Hemingway, and Beatles and rock 'n' roll tapes for the new (Soviet-produced) tape recorders was an integral part of the Soviet 'sixties', a term strangely paralleling the American one in its association with cultural liberation that came into nostalgic use in the 1980s.[31] Still, many of these goods (rock 'n' roll as an example) failed to meet the Soviet standard of *kul'turnost'*, thus acquiring a counter-cultural, potentially oppositional, appeal.

EASTERN EUROPE AND 'SOCIALIST MODERNITY'

Eastern Europe was a major conduit for Western goods, as well as Western-style East European goods, to enter the Soviet Union in the post-war period. This was a counter-trajectory to the better known one of 'sovietization' of Eastern Europe after the Second World War. Such 'sovietization' certainly existed, both at the institutional and socio-cultural level. The expropriation of local capitalist bourgeoisies and aristocracies

[30] Susan Reid, 'Cold War in the Kitchen: Gender and the Destalinization of Consumer Taste in the Soviet Union under Khrushchev', *Slavic Review*, 61/2 (2002), 211–52, at 222.

[31] On state initiative in the opening to the West, see Eleonory Gilburd, 'The revival of Soviet Internationalism in the 1950s', in Denis Kozlov and Eleonory Gilburd (eds.), *The Thaw: Soviet Society and Culture during the 1950s and 1960s* (Ithaca, NY: Cornell University Press, forthcoming); on fashion, see Larissa Zakharova, 'Soviet Fashion in the 1950s–1960s', in Kozlov and Gilburd (eds.), *The Thaw*, and Lebina and Chistikov, *Obyvatel'*, 195–228; on the sixties, see Petr Vail' and Aleksandr Genis, *60-e. Mir sovetskogo cheloveka* (Ann Arbor, MI: Ardis, 1988). For new products of the 1950 and 1960s, see entries for *banlon, kapron, tranzistory, magnitofony*, etc. in Nataliia Lebina's entertaining *Entsiklopediia banal'nostei: Sovetskaia povsednevnost', kontury, simvoly, znaki* (St Petersburg: Dmitrii Bulanin, 2006).

was accompanied by the same Communist critique of luxury and puritanical asceticism—or rather, the Communist critique of an earlier epoch in the Soviet Union which, like collectivization of agriculture and proletarian affirmative action programmes, evidently needed to be deployed only in the foundational stages of socialist construction. There were the same promises of future abundance; the same discourse of 'cultured socialist trade', associated particularly with new department stores of 'contemporary' architectural style. The socialist planned economy produced shortages in Eastern Europe, just as in the Soviet Union; indeed, Kornai's classic analysisis no doubt based in the first instance on his observation of his native Hungary.[32] Shortages produced the same kind of hunting and gathering behaviours, and equivalents soon appeared in the local languages for the Russian *blat* and '*defitsitnye tovary*' (deficit goods, i.e. those that were in chronically short supply).[33]

Communism brought a grey and drab lifestyle to Eastern Europe, with objects devoid of vivid colour and style—at least this is what Western visitors always said, and what post-Communist locals reiterate. But Hungary, Poland, Czechoslovakia, and the GDR had their own stylistic commitment to locally produced modernity: the 'socialist modern', as it has been called; export items like Czech furniture and Polish cosmetics brought this style to the Soviet Union. While Western goods had high symbolic value, citizens in Eastern Europe were not without loyalty to their own branded products, like the Schwalbe moped in East Germany. According to official rhetoric, new department stores and apartment buildings, as well as consumer goods, were 'gifts' from the state to the people. The suspicion lingered, however, that these gifts were often cheap and shoddily made.[34]

In Russia, the Soviet order—however irritating and intrusive—was at least 'ours'. This was not so in Eastern Europe, and the cult of the private that developed there had strong oppositional overtones. Urban Poles embraced their apartments, state-owned though they might be, as 'a sanctuary, private in the sense of being a hidden or inaccessible realm', shut away from the gaze of the state; they filled them with things, often the kind of things that contemporary designers thought of as kitsch and the authorities called 'bourgeois'. Czechs fled at every opportunity to the weekend cottage (*chata* in Czech, *dacha* in Russian); the state apparently encouraged this, partly for security reasons, in the wake of 1968, and by the early 1980s, almost a third of all Prague households owned

---

[32] See note 13.

[33] On the Polish version of cultured trade, see David Crowley, 'Warsaw's Shops, Stalinism and the Thaw', in Reid and Crowley (eds.), *Style and Socialism*, 25–47; on hunting and gathering behaviours, see Judd Stitziel, 'Shopping, Sewing, Networking, Complaining: Consumer Culture and the Relationship between State and Society in the GDR', in Katherine Pence and Paul Betts (eds.), *Socialist Modern: East German Everyday Culture and Politics* (Ann Arbor, MI: University of Michigan Press, 2008), 253–86.

[34] Krisztina Fehérváry, 'Goods and States: The Political Logic of State-Socialist Material Culture', *Comparative Studies in Society and History*, 51/2 (2009), 426–59; Ina Merkel, 'Consumer Culture in the GDR, or How the Struggle for Antimodernity Was Lost on the Battleground of Consumer Culture', in Susan Strasser, Charles McGovern, and Matthias Judt (eds.), *Getting and Spending: European and American Consumer Societies in the Twentieth Century* (New York: Cambridge University Press, 1998), 281–99; Pence and Betts, *Socialist Modern*.

their own chata.[35] The 'resistance' aspect to this, especially in the intelligentsias, was noted by contemporary Western observers. According to the anthropologist Katherine Verdery, whose field is Romania, 'consumption goods and objects conferred an identity that set you off from socialism... Acquiring objects became a way of constituting your selfhood against a deeply unpopular regime.'[36]

AFTER COMMUNISM

The collapse of communism in 1989–91 meant that Western goods, long desired but largely out of reach, suddenly became accessible. East Berliners swarmed across the Wall and bought things in the West as their first, liberating gesture. In the Soviet Union, kiosks sprung up overnight selling Western liquor, sausages, leather jackets, fashionable boots, gold jewellery, chocolates and sweets (including the infamous and ubiquitous Snickers). The first reaction was to run out and buy as much as you could carry home. The second reactions were more complicated.

The talk across the Soviet Union and Eastern Europe, at least among intellectuals, was that finally, thank God, we can live 'normal' lives, the lives that socialism denied us. This included having the *things* that socialism denied, to which people now felt entitled. Hungarians, according to an American anthropologist, regarded 'American kitchens' and 'luxury bathrooms' as part of the normal way of life in the West, and thought they should now have them too—but for many, they were financially out of reach. Worse still, at least in Russia, was not being able to afford things that your neighbour had somehow acquired: the nouveau riche 'New Russians', building their ornate villas and conspicuously displaying their expensive leather jackets and gold chains, accompanied by thug-like bodyguards in US Army fatigues, were deeply unpopular.[37]

There was disappointment, too, with the new Western goods. Tomatoes from the Netherlands all but drove locally grown tomatoes off the market in Moscow; Muscovites were at first entranced by the beauty of their unblemished forms, later sharply disappointed by their lack of taste. In the Soviet Union, where the foreign goods were, in fact, often adulterated, the handsome labels on foreign liqueur bottles being the only genuine thing about them, well-founded suspicions of fraud set in: evidently the paradise

---

[35]   David Crowley, 'Warsaw Interiors: the Public Life of Private Spaces, 1949–65', in Crowley and Reid (eds.), *Socialist Spaces*, 181–206, at 187; Paulina Bren, 'Weekend Getaways: the *Chata*, the *Tramp*, and the Politics of Private Life in post-1968 Czechoslovakia', in Crowley and Reid (eds.), *Socialist Spaces*, 123–40.

[36]   Katherine Verdery, *What was Socialism, and what Comes Next?* (Princeton, NJ: Princeton University Press, 1996), 29.

[37]   Sheila Fitzpatrick, *Tear off the Masks! Identity and Imposture in Twentieth-Century Russia* (Princeton, NJ: Princeton University Press, 2005), 303–17 (ch. 15: 'Becoming Post-Soviet'); Krisztina Fehervary, 'American Kitchens, Luxury Bathrooms, and the Search for a "Normal" Life in Post-socialist Hungary', *Ethnos*, 67/3 (2002), 369–400; Caroline Humphrey, *The Unmaking of Soviet Life: Everyday Economies after Socialism* (Ithaca, NY: Cornell University Press, 2002), 175–201 (ch. 9: 'The Villas of the 'New Russians').

of Western consumer goods was just another 'deception' (*obman*), like the promise of abundance under Communism. Consumers started to seek out 'our' goods again, as less risky.[38] The issue of adulteration and deception was less important in Eastern Europe, but there was a comparable sense of disillusion: the things of the West that had seemed so magical at a distance lost their enchantment from close up.[39]

And then there was the humiliation attendant upon the devaluing of a way of life and its objects. 'People here [in the GDR] saved for a lifetime for a spluttering Trabant. Then along comes the smooth Mercedes society and makes our whole existence, our dreams and our identity, laughable.'[40] It was the same experience described by the Soviet dissident Vladimir Bukovsky, who on his departure from Russia, direct from Gulag, twenty years earlier, had 'stood in the airport in Zurich over my bag of prison odds and ends—completely amazed that all my valuables, penknives, razors, and books accumulated over the years by generations of convicts were turning under my eyes into nothing.' To acquire those things, he had deployed all the Soviet and specifically Gulag hunting and gathering skills that were a part of his identity. 'And now all this experience, all your property, collapses in a single instant.'[41]

Perhaps the nostalgia for the old ways that emerged in the Eastern bloc so vividly in the late 1990s was a way of coping with this, re-asserting the worth of 'our' objects in the face of a West that denied it. Brands were lovingly remembered: 'catchwords are enough for mutual recognition [of former GDR citizens]. "Remember the Multimax [drill]?" is enough to start a lively conversation.'[42] Russian television in the 1990s produced a long-running series called *The Old Apartment* (*Staraia kvartira*), where moderators and studio audiences shared reminiscences of the *things* of socialism (each week, a different year): sausage (a new type came in that year), sweets, stores, wall rugs showing a tiger, popular songs, new buildings, streets. As the TV station's website states, 'people came to this apartment not only to remember but to relive the half century of our common history. "Staraia kvartira" was a writing of popular memoirs, where conversation was simple, like neighbors.'[43] Wolfgang Becker's enormously successful 2003 film *Good Bye Lenin*, with its ironic celebration of Eastern bloc products like Globus peas from Hungary, Mocha-Fix Gold coffee, and Spee detergent, did the same thing for an international audience.

But it was not only 'simple, like neighbors'; *Ostalgie*, or nostalgia for the old East, was commercial too. Soviet Army fur hats were sold at Checkpoint Charlie. Trabants, those

---

[38] Humphrey, *Unmaking of Soviet Life*, 40–63 (ch. 3: 'Creating a Culture of Disillusionment: Consumption in Moscow, a Chronicle of Changing Times'); Olga Shevchenko, '"Between the Holes": Emerging Identities and Hybrid Patterns of Consumption in Post-socialist Russia', *Europe-Asia Studies*, 54/6 (2002), 841–66.

[39] Milena Veenis, 'Consumption in East Germany. The Seduction and Betrayal of Things', *Journal of Material Culture*, 4/1 (1999), 79–112.

[40] Quoted in Daphne Berdahl, '"(N)Ostalgie" for the Present: Memory, Longing, and East German Things', *Ethnos*, 64/2 (1999), 196.

[41] Quoted in Humphrey, *Unmaking of Soviet Life*, 43.

[42] Merkel, 'Consumer Culture in the GDR', 296.

[43] *Staraia kvartira* programme website of Channel 5, St Petersburg, <http://www.5-tv.ru/video/504606>, accessed 22 March 2010. For a different, but still nostalgic, approach to the old apartment, see Svetlana Boym, *Common Places: Mythologies of Everyday Life in Russia* (Cambridge, MA and London: Harvard University Press, 1994).

stripped down plastic cars developed in the GDR as a people's car, once treasured by their owners, later despised, were now lovingly refurbished as 'vintage'. Board games on the GDR everyday became popular in Germany; GDR brands were retro fashion. Museums of everyday life appeared in the GDR and the former Soviet Union, where they were usually called 'Staraia kvartira'; there were restaurants, too, decorated with Soviet kitsch and featuring menus enclosed in old Soviet cardboard files (papki).

Once upon a time, socialism was going to provide goods in abundance, and at the same time render them unimportant, free of the fetishism of capitalism. It did not happen. The goods were scarce, and that made them important. Then the goods, along with the old life, vanished or were submerged in a flood of Western goods, seemingly demonstrating their insignificance. And now those old goods are back, fetishized in a new (only partly capitalist) way via Ostalgie. The things of socialism are still 'huggermuggering', as Ivy Litvinov put it, if now largely in memory. In the wake of the collapse of communism in the Soviet Union and Eastern Europe, people struggled to understand what socialism had been all about, as well as what they were getting in its place.[44] It turns out that 'really-existing socialism' was not only about distributing things (the state's function) but—who would have thought it?—about having them, too.

BIBLIOGRAPHY

Boym, Svetlana, Common Places: Mythologies of Everyday Life in Russia (Cambridge and London: Harvard University Press, 1994).

Buchli, Victor, An Archeology of Socialism (Oxford and New York: Berg, 1999).

Crowley, David and Susan E. Reid (eds.), Socialist Spaces: Sites of Everyday Life in the Eastern Bloc (Oxford: Berg, 2002).

Fitzpatrick, Sheila, Everyday Stalinism: Ordinary Life in Extraordinary Times: Soviet Russia in the 1930s (New York and Oxford: Oxford University Press, 1999).

Gronow, Jukka, Caviar with Champagne: Common Luxury and the Ideals of the Good Life in Stalin's Russia (Oxford and New York: Berg, 2003).

Hessler, Julie, A Social History of Soviet Trade (Princeton, NJ: Princeton University Press, 2004).

Humphrey, Caroline, The Unmaking of Soviet Life: Everyday Economies after Socialism (Ithaca, NY: Cornell University Press, 2002).

Lewis, Siegelbaum (ed.), Borders of Socialism Private Spheres of Soviet Russia (New York: Palgrave Macmillan, 2006).

Osokina, Elena A., Our Daily Bread: Socialist Distribution and the Art of Survival in Stalin's Russia, trans. Kate Transchel and Greta Bucher (Armonk, NY: M.E. Sharpe, 2000).

Pence, Katherine and Betts, Paul (eds.), Socialist Modern: East German Everyday Culture and Politics (Ann Arbor, MI: University of Michigan Press, 2008).

Reid, Susan, 'Cold War in the Kitchen: Gender and the Destalinization of Consumer Taste in the Soviet Union under Khrushchev', Slavic Review, 61/2 (2002), 211–52.

Reid, Susan E. and Crowley, David (eds.), Style and Socialism: Modernity and Material Culture in Post-War Eastern Europe (Oxford: Berg, 2000).

---

[44] See the wry title of Verdery's 1996 book, What was Socialism, and What Comes Next?

CHAPTER 24

··

UNEXPECTED SUBVERSIONS: MODERN COLONIALISM, GLOBALIZATION, AND COMMODITY CULTURE

··

TIMOTHY BURKE

SCHOLARS initially engaged in the 'turn to consumption' in early modern European historiography often described themselves as rescuing the subject from long-standing neglect or marginalization by historians and social theorists. A closely connected series of studies ended up suggesting that attention to consumption was not merely a compatible addition to an established paradigmatic understanding of industrialization and modernization in early modern European societies, but a thorough revision, even inversion, of many existing assumptions about the causal roots and consequences of the transition to modernity.[1] In contrast, scholarship on the relationship between consumption and modern colonialism, has not had quite so clear a critique of existing work or even a sense of shared movement. More than a decade after a wave of similar works about consumerism in modern African, Asian, Middle Eastern, Latin American, or Pacific societies appeared in a variety of area studies fields, scholarly attention to consumer practices

---

[1] Perhaps the best single overview of this 'turn to consumption' in early modern historiography, as well as some sharply pointed critiques of its claims, is John Brewer and Roy Porter (eds.), *Consumption and the World of Goods* (London: Routledge, 1993). One particularly interesting description of the marginalization of consumption as a subject of study is given in this volume by Joyce Appleby, who attributes the neglect of consumption not to recent scholars but to a strong 'productivism' in Enlightenment-era political economy and moral philosophy which has carried over into contemporary times. For a particularly strong version of revisionist thinking about the causal importance of consumer desire, see T. H. Breen, *The Marketplace of Revolution: How Consumer Politics Shaped American Independence* (New York: Oxford University Press, 2004) and Lisa Jardine, *Worldly Goods: A New History of the Renaissance*, 1st edn. (New York: Nan A. Talese/Doubleday, 1996).

and commodity culture in many developing societies remains, as Mona Abaza puts it, a 'blind spot'.[2]

In part, this sporadic development of a scholarly conversation is a mirror of diffuse connections between different area studies projects. I also think, however, that scholars studying the history of modern colonialism have been more reluctant to make strongly contrarian claims about consumerism and commodification similar to those made by early modern Europeanists because they are more unsettled by some of the implications of their own studies. As Abaza notes, modern consumer culture is strongly mapped to 'Westernization' and globalization, subjects which are the focus of acute theoretical and political unease in most scholarship devoted to colonial and post-colonial societies, not to mention political life within those societies.[3] It was one thing for a scholar like Lisa Jardine to argue that it was the desire for new goods that caused European expansion in the early modern period. It is another thing for a specialist in a colonial and post-colonial society to suggest that the study of consumption and commodities should spark a comprehensive rethinking of the transformative power or instrumental coherence of colonial governments and globalizing capitalism. Yet in some measure (though with numerous qualifiers) this is in fact what many of the works focused on consumer cultures in modern colonial and post-colonial societies have argued.

There is an inevitable bit of definitional business at the outset of the discussion. Namely, which societies count as 'colonial'? This is an especially vexing question if the specific topic at hand is consumerism and commodification. It is easier to apply sharp delineations of period and region if the topic at hand is the rise, development, and end of formal structures of European imperial rule, or even if the subject is specific moments in the transnational organization of capitalism as a whole, such as the relationship between late nineteenth-century financial speculation and industrialization in the capitalist periphery. When the discussion concerns subjects which are in some fashion or another concerned with culture, the practice of everyday life, or identity and personhood—which certainly describes consumption—setting temporal or spatial boundaries around the conversation is much more difficult.

Does a review of the character of consumption in 'colonial societies' include imperial metropoles as well as regions colonized by Europe, or the expansion of the United States across North America?[4] If so, there is a very large class of scholarly studies which in some respect or another discuss the association between colonialism and consumption

---

[2] Mona Abaza, *Changing Consumer Cultures of Modern Egypt: Cairo's Urban Reshaping* (Leiden: Brill, 2006), p. vii.

[3] See Abaza, *Changing Consumer Cultures*, ch. 2.

[4] For a discussion of how boundaries between empire and metropolis need to be understood as fuzzy or indeterminate, see Catherine Hall, *Civilising Subjects: Colony and Metropole in the English Imagination, 1830–1867* (Chicago: University of Chicago Press, 2002). Also see the essays in Catherine Hall and Sonya O. Rose, *At Home with the Empire: Metropolitan Culture and the Imperial World* (Cambridge: Cambridge University Press, 2007). For a broader theoretical discussion of the modern global system in terms of circulations and 'flows' which encompass and erode some of the distinctions between metropolis and colony, see Arjun Appadurai, *Modernity at Large: Cultural Dimensions of Globalization* (Minneapolis: University of Minnesota Press, 1996).

in nineteenth- and twentieth-century global culture.[5] Even constrained to the Western European states which created or extended formal empires in Africa, Asia, and the Pacific after 1860, studies like Anne McClintock's intricate reading of British commodity culture indicate the extent to which colonial meanings and images were circulating within metropolitan societies.[6] Nevertheless, there are good reasons that work of this kind should not be prominently included in a review of scholarship on colonialism and consumerism besides the sheer unmanageability of this scope of analysis. Bernard Porter has suggested that the cultural ubiquity of empire in the affairs of metropolitan societies has been overemphasized,[7] but even more to the point is Nicolas Thomas's pointed arguments against the generalizing tendencies of work on 'colonial discourse'.[8] Thomas's own markedly original work on the movement of commodities in the colonial cultures of the Pacific, *Entangled Objects*, seems to me to define the location of the boundary between work which is centrally concerned with the entanglement of consumption and colonialism and work on consumer culture where ideas about empire are in some sense present but not centrally constitutive.[9]

A great focus on particularity and on societies subjected to modern imperial domination by Western states puts traditional area studies scholarship at the centre of the analysis, with all of the advantages of its focused form of expertise, but also some of the problems that area studies work tends to pose for comparative or global analysis. Scholars working in area studies traditions sometimes resist or inhibit comparative approaches. Where this struggle between particularity and comparison poses a definitional problem is in deciding which societies were in fact the subjects of modern colonial rule. The regions subjugated by the 'new imperialism' of the late nineteenth century (Africa, parts of South Asia, the Middle East, and much of the Pacific) seem the obvious core cases. Even within those regions, however, there are diverse histories of imperial control. There are long-standing debates about how to compare South Africa's layering of early modern mercantile rule, mid-nineteenth-century expansion by a supposedly liberal British empire which also encouraged white settlement, and emblematic forms of later imperial administration, with something like the more abrupt and violent subjugation of other African societies in the 'Scramble for Africa' after 1870. The similar layering of imperial regimes and practices in India poses similar problems of comparison within South and South-East Asia, and so on.

Even more vexing are questions about societies which were not under direct European territorial control after 1860, but were nevertheless strongly affected by imperial hegemony,

---

[5] Deborah Root, *Cannibal Culture: Art, Appropriation, and the Commodification of Difference* (Boulder, CO: Westview Press, 1996); Mona Domosh, *American Commodities in an Age of Empire*, (New York: Routledge, 2006); Kristin L. Hoganson, *Consumers' Imperium: The Global Production of American Domesticity, 1865–1920* (Chapel Hill: University of North Carolina Press, 2007).

[6] Anne McClintock, *Imperial Leather: Race, Gender, and Sexuality in the Colonial Contest* (New York: Routledge, 1995).

[7] Bernard Porter, *The Absent-Minded Imperialists: Empire, Society, and Culture in Britain* (New York: Oxford University Press, 2006).

[8] Nicolas Thomas, *Colonialism's Culture* (Princeton, NJ: Princeton University Press, 1994).

[9] Nicolas Thomas, *Entangled Objects: Exchange, Material Culture, and Colonialism in the Pacific* (Cambridge, MA: Harvard University Press, 1991).

such as those in China, Thailand, or Latin America. While I have chosen to focus strongly on the core cases of modern colonialism, I will sometimes refer to work on China, Thailand, and other locations outside of that core because of its strong analytic resemblance to work on more narrowly defined examples of colonial societies. There are strong intellectual and theoretical connections linking much of the scholarship on consumption, commodification, shopping, and material culture in China, Thailand, Latin America, or the Caribbean to work on Africa, the Middle East, South Asia, and the Pacific.

CONSTRUCTING THE COLONIAL
AND POST-COLONIAL CONSUMER

If nothing else, non-Western populations have often been similarly constructed as consumers (or non-consumers) by Western actors, with little regard for any differences between them. The distinctive fashion in which colonial subjects or non-Western populations were or were not envisioned as consumers in the discourses of colonial authorities or metropolitan elites has therefore been a powerful starting point for scholars studying these subjects. This very much makes sense as a point of intellectual origin: post-1950 historical and anthropological scholarship on colonial and post-colonial societies was intensely interested from the outset in refuting or attacking the ways in which colonial rulers had depicted their subjects as backward, primitive, lacking history, childlike, violent, and a host of associated stereotypes. The academic study of modern colonialism and its consequences has since extended this critique in a variety of ways: to more specific forms of colonial social construction applied to specific identities or groups, to more specific institutional uses of representation in the domination of colonized populations, or to forms of particular contradiction and tension in the imperial imagination. The historical circumstances under which non-Western societies and individuals have or have not been envisioned as consumers turn out to be potently visible in all three of these extensions, strongly accenting or complicating imperial ideas about class, gender, and ethnic difference in colonial societies while also unsettling their ideas about the passivity of colonial subjects.

The contradictions between imagining modern consumers as imbued with a distinctly modern kind of capitalist agency and imagining colonial or non-Western populations as not-yet-modern and incapable of self-rule appear as fault lines in the earliest moments of the 'new imperialism' of the late nineteenth century. For example, Thomas Richards and Anne McClintock both speak to the extent to which nineteenth-century British culture envisioned the commodity as an instrument of empire, autonomously civilizing or modernizing Africans and other non-Western societies.[10] Some of the most

---

[10] Thomas Richards, *The Commodity Culture of Victorian England: Advertising and Spectacle, 1851–1914* (Stanford, CA: Stanford University Press, 1990); McClintock, *Imperial Leather*.

politically powerful arguments in favour of imperial expansion across Europe and in the United States primarily envisioned African, Asian, and Pacific societies as new markets for manufactured goods, rather than as sources of raw materials for Western industries, the opposite of what actually occurred in the early economic development of most of Europe's new colonial possessions. (Though as Elisabeth Croll notes of China, many of these societies were also long-standing 'dream markets' that had figured in the imagination of Western commerce for far longer.[11])

The reality was unsurprisingly different. When colonial labourers were partially motivated by the desire to accumulate commodities, as in the case of mine workers from Mozambique travelling to South Africa after the initial opening of the Witwatersrand gold fields, the active suppression of wages and increasingly tighter control over the migrant economy severely limited rather than promoted the development of local consumption.[12] In the case of many colonized societies in Asia, East Africa, and the Middle East, the extension of colonial control or of indirect imperial hegemony in the late nineteenth century interrupted or impeded long-standing flows of European imports into local consumer markets. Important new work in recent years has described the degree to which non-Western consumer markets were an active driver both of the early modern world economy and in the industrialization of Europe and the United States.[13] To some extent, the consuming practices and material culture of colonized societies between the late nineteenth century and the middle of the twentieth century remains one of the least explored areas within this general area of study. Sherman Cochran's study of Chinese merchants and consumer culture in China and South-East Asia underscores how little we know about merchants, retailing, and material culture in most colonial societies before 1960.[14] This relative emphasis on more contemporary experiences in scholarly publications may partially be a by-product of the imperial perception of their subjects as always-about-to-consume, an attitude which also affects what kinds of information exist in archives and thus the plausibility or difficulty of studying the topic in the first place.

However, the characteristic double move of forgetting that colonized populations were already consumers with existing relationships to global commodity flows (or were actively interested in becoming so) and depicting those same populations as an always-potential yet to be tapped market for Western consumer goods, has retained most of its force in a continuous fashion, from the establishment of modern European empires through to the contemporary moment, even among scholars. The constant rediscovery

---

[11] Elisabeth Croll, *China's New Consumers: Social Development and Domestic Demand* (London: Routledge, 2006).

[12] Patrick Harries, *Work, Culture, and Identity: Migrant Laborers in Mozambique and South Africa, c.1860–1910* (Portsmouth, NH: Heinemann, 1994).

[13] See for example Jeremy Prestholdt, *Domesticating the World: African Consumerism and the Genealogies of Globalization* (Berkeley, CA: University of California Press, 2008).

[14] Sherman Cochran, *Chinese Medicine Men: Consumer Culture in China and Southeast Asia* (Cambridge, MA: Harvard University Press, 2006).

of this double trope resembles internal tensions associated with other 'civilizing' projects, most notably missionary Christianity. All such projects of modernizing were imagined as always just beginning, never quite actually begun, but consumerism has its own peculiar valences and associations.

The most intense focus on this construction by scholars has been on post-1950s advertising and marketing carried out through mass media in post-colonial or late colonial societies. Studies like Steven Kemper's *Buying and Believing*, Mark Liechty's *Suitably Modern*, Robert Foster's *Materializing the Nation*, William Mazzarella's *Shoveling Smoke*, Daniel Miller's *Capitalism: An Ethnographic Approach*, and my own study *Lifebuoy Men, Lux Women* all focus at some point on the particular construction of specific non-Western populations as consumers through post-1950 advertising and mass media, in Sri Lanka, Nepal, Papua New Guinea, India, Trinidad, and Zimbabwe respectively.[15] Other scholarship focused on advertising outside of the United States and Western Europe, such as Brian Moeran's *A Japanese Advertising Agency*, has also contributed to this body of knowledge by adding ethnographic and sociological texture to the scholarly understanding of transnational advertising.[16]

The relatively consistent observation offered by most of these studies is that in these settings advertising firms (both local and transnational) continually reworked their audiences as *differently desiring* and as *continually converging* towards some kind of cosmopolitan middle-class modernity which would align their desires with global culture. In Zimbabwe, for example, marketing campaigns aimed at African women through various 'women's clubs' in order to sell a parallel version of consumer domesticity which resembled white domesticity but did not converge upon or challenge it. The more interesting question for most scholars has instead been the relationship between media or official constructions of the colonial/post-colonial consumer and the practices and performances of the audiences envisioned or targeted by those representations. In some cases, as Kemper, Mazzarella, and I suggest, local advertisers and their post-colonial middle-class audiences have been socially overlapping, and so the constructions with which they mutually work do not so quickly conform to any simple version of a colonial or globalizing ideology.[17]

---

[15] Steven Kemper, *Buying and Believing: Sri Lankan Advertising and Consumers in a Transnational World* (Chicago: University of Chicago Press, 2001); Mark Liechty, *Suitably Modern: Making Middle-Class Culture in a New Consumer Society* (Princeton, NJ: Princeton University Press, 2003); Robert John Foster, *Materializing the Nation: Commodities, Consumption, and Media in Papua New Guinea* (Bloomington: Indiana University Press, 2002); William Mazzarella, *Shoveling Smoke: Advertising and Globalization in Contemporary India* (Durham, NC: Duke University Press, 2003); Daniel Miller, *Capitalism: An Ethnographic Approach* (Oxford: Berg, 1997); Timothy Burke, *Lifebuoy Men, Lux Women: Commodification, Consumption, and Cleanliness in Modern Zimbabwe* (Durham, NC: Duke University Press, 1996).

[16] Brian Moeran, *A Japanese Advertising Agency: An Anthropology of Media and Markets* (Honolulu: University of Hawaii Press, 1996).

[17] See in particular Part III of Mazzarella's *Shovelling Smoke* and ch. 7 of Kemper's *Buying and Believing*.

MIDDLE CLASSES, NATIONS AND MODERNITY

By far the most central, empirically rich area of focus among scholars studying the relationship between modern colonialism and consumption concerns the role of consumerism and commodities in the social and imaginative life of the colonial and post-colonial middle classes. In some cases, scholars have found their way to consumption as a topic by focusing on the life of the middle class, in others, to the middle class by an interest in commodity culture. Mark Liechty expresses a view common in much of the literature when he writes, 'Cultures of consumerism, media, and youth are not side effects or consequences of middle-class formation. Rather, they are among the most important cultural processes through which an emerging middle class actually creates itself as a sociocultural entity.'[18]

Liechty here identifies not only why the history and anthropology of colonial and post-colonial middle-classes should so strongly involve attention to consumerism and commodities, but also why this attention often runs against the grain of an older historiography. To some degree, both colonial rulers and later anti-colonial critics have viewed non-Western middle classes or aspirant elites as chimeras or phantoms, a group that should not exist or whose social role is debased or compromised. Some studies (including Liechty's book) finesse that challenge by viewing such middle classes as new or emergent, working with globalized or cosmopolitan material culture in circumstances of rapid economic and social change. Other work, however, not only looks at the contemporary circumstances of the post-colonial middle classes but argues that those circumstances have deeper roots in a history that extends back all the way to the outset of the colonial era and in some cases beyond it.[19] One especially influential examination of the early colonial production of new social forms through commodities and consuming practices that were both 'middling' and self-consciously modern is the second volume of Jean Comaroff and John Comaroff's *Of Revelation and Revolution*, which focuses heavily on the uses of material culture by both Nonconformist missionaries and Christian converts in a Tswana chiefdom in nineteenth-century southern Africa. The Comaroffs are insistent that nineteenth-century struggles and collaborations around clothing, domestic space, and other objects and commodities have a strong genealogical connection to more contemporary assertions of middle-class identity and ethnic pride in Botswana.[20] Though many studies in other regions which focus instead on the last two or three decades note some of the historical rootedness both of middling classes

---

[18] Liechty, *Suitably Modern*, 7.

[19] Two historical studies focused centrally on colonial middle-class life are Sanjay Joshi, *Fractured Modernity: Making of a Middle Class in Colonial North India* (New York: Oxford University Press, 2001) and Michael O. West, *The Rise of an African Middle Class: Colonial Zimbabwe, 1898–1965* (Bloomington: Indiana University Press, 2002).

[20] Jean Comaroff and John Comaroff, *Of Revelation and Revolution*, Vol. 2 (Chicago: University of Chicago Press, 1997).

and their uses of goods, the kind of historical depth offered by the Comaroffs is still in relatively short supply.

Whatever period they are focusing on, scholars rarely refer to colonized or post-colonial elites as a single social class in the Marxist sense. As Liechty notes, a Weberian approach to what might be called 'middling classes' often seems more appropriate. These groups were (and often remain) a heterogeneous assembly of people with diverse sources of wealth or social prestige who share a common if loose imagination of themselves as between an elite (whether European colonial rulers, 'traditional' landholders, state rulers, or the extremely wealthy) and the rural and urban poor. Consumer culture, in the view of scholars, has become for these groups a crucial domain of performance and practice, an indispensable tool for crafting and expressing a sense of competency and affiliation with global, cosmopolitan, or modern meanings and objects in order to express a 'middling' identity and position. Indeed, as Maureen O'Dougherty notes, the definition of who counts as 'middle' is an active subject of concern for both 'natives' and observers, and contested actively through consumerism and commodities.[21] Descriptive accounts in various works often resemble the picture sketched by the Comaroffs, in which an increasingly commodified material culture simultaneously becomes a dialogic arena for struggle and collaboration. Communication and performance, on one hand, and consciousness, on the other, are central, repeated themes in this scholarship, often joined to a third, which is attention to the everyday or ritual practices which constitute consumer culture, particularly shopping.

The entanglement of the middle classes with consumer culture is hardly understudied in Euro-American contexts. One difference made by colonialism and its various aftermaths is that the middle classes of colonial and post-colonial societies have to struggle to claim a cosmopolitan identity through consumerism against discursive constructions that make that fashioning invisible, yet to happen, or intrinsically oppositional; that these groups live in places which are represented as absent of modernity or as struggling against the imposition of 'Westernized' global culture, whereas Euro-American middle classes have related to consumer culture as something they are situated always already within, on 'home ground'. Priti Ramamurthy, for examples, has written about how Indian 'modern girls' self-fashioned through and around the representation of local cinematic 'sitara' celebrities like Sulochana in the 1920s and 1930s, on one hand appropriating the styling of American film stars like Clara Bow, on the other inflecting that image with novelty through saris and connections to local performative genres and aesthetics.[22]

Perhaps as a consequence, scholarship details how the colonial and post-colonial middling classes also have struggled with ambivalence about identities fashioned through commodity culture, and the very real limitations that their peripheral position in colonial or global economies has imposed upon their access to manufactured consumer

---

[21] Maureen O'Dougherty, *Consumption Intensified: The Politics of Middle-Class Daily Life in Brazil* (Durham, NC: Duke University Press, 2002).

[22] Priti Ramamurthy, 'All-Consuming Nationalism: The Indian Modern Girl of the 1920s and 1930s', in Alys Eve Weinbaum et al. (eds.), *The Modern Girl Around the World: Consumption, Modernity, and Globalization* (Durham, NC: Duke University Press, 2008).

goods. Those limitations also drive some of the fascination both inside and outside of scholarly circles with consuming practices in the developing world which appear to be financially impossible or dramatically improvident, such as the use of Parisian fashions by Congolese *sapeurs*,[23] or perhaps the most descriptively fetishized form of 'colonized consumption', the cargo cult of Pacific societies. Many scholars working on these often exoticized practices argue that to see them as consumption is a categorical error in the first place, as in Martha Kaplan's careful and critical reconceptualization of cargo cults in Fiji.[24] Even when the practices on hand are not marked off as unusually exotic, scholars writing about middle-class identity and consumption in colonial and post-colonial society often struggle to describe honestly what one collection of essays on Latin America calls 'the allure of the foreign' without succumbing to the concept of 'emulation' as it has sometimes figured in the critique of consumer culture, precisely because the tropes associated with emulation seem so uncomfortably close to the common colonial stereotype of non-Western elites as slavishly and immaturely imitative.[25]

Much of the scholarship in this field seeks to amplify its description of this dilemma through careful attention to specific social locations and circumstances such as urban neighbourhoods, domestic spaces, professional or working life. Mona Russell's essay on consumerism and modernity in the nineteenth- and early twentieth-century Egyptian home is a good example of this angle of approach.[26] Another common way further to specify analysis is through the prism of gender. An especially notable example of this approach is Mary Beth Mills's *Thai Women in the Global Labor Force*, which pays close attention to consumerism as the key domain within which the women she studies construct and interrogate *thansamay* or 'modern' selves simultaneously in reference to their locality, class, work process, and gender.[27] Yet another common form of specification is to focus on the intersection between class, consumerism, and middling-class youth, which is a major part of Liechty's analysis but also informs many other works, such as Chua Beng Huat's *Life Is Not Complete Without Shopping: Consumption Culture in Singapore*.[28]

[23] See Bob W. White, *Rumba Rules: The Politics of Dance Music in Mobutu's Zaire* (Durham, NC: Duke University Press, 2008).

[24] Martha Kaplan, *Neither Cargo nor Cult: Ritual Politics and the Colonial Imagination in Fiji* (Durham, NC: Duke University Press, 1995).

[25] Benjamin Orlove (ed.), *The Allure of the Foreign: Imported Goods in Postcolonial Latin America* (Ann Arbor, MI: University of Michigan Press, 1997). A potent and easily accessible example of racist caricature of colonized peoples consuming in a slavish or imitative fashion can be found in Hergé, *Les Aventures de Tintin: Tintin au Congo (Tintin in the Congo)* (French and European publications, 1931). In many respects, Homi Bhabha's analysis of colonial mimicry is a useful guide for approaching emulation as a trope, but the concept has a separate intellectual history of association with consumerism that traces back to Veblen.

[26] Mona Russell, 'Modernity, National Identity, and Consumerism: Visions of the Egyptian Home', in Ruth Schecter (ed.), *Transitions in Domestic Consumption and Family Life in the Modern Middle East: Houses in Motion* (Basingstoke: Palgrave Macmillan, 2003), 38–62.

[27] Mary Beth Mills, *Thai Women in the Global Labor Force: Consuming Desires, Contested Selves* (Chapel Hill, NC: Rutgers University Press, 1999).

[28] Chua Beng Huat, *Life Is Not Complete Without Shopping: Consumption Culture in Singapore* (Singapore: Singapore University Press, 2003).

Gender is a dominant focus in the historiography of consumerism as a whole in part because of the degree to which consumer practices and consciousness have been envisioned in the West as distinctively feminine. Extending this focus to the experience of non-Western societies in some cases parallels the insights of 'women in development' scholarship, documenting the mis-mapping of Western binaries onto societies which formerly had very different conceptual and social maps of the relationship of gender to labour, spatiality, cultural reproduction, and so on. In other cases, however, study of commodity culture and changing terrains of gender identity and practice have revealed consumption's importance in facilitating new or transformed gender roles within colonial and post-colonial societies.[29]

The constitution of middle-class life in colonial and post-colonial societies is not the only domain where the use or role of consumerism has drawn scholarly attention. Foster, Kemper, Miller, Huat, Abaza, Gerth, Richard Wilk and many other authors in this field have also focused centrally on the relationship between consumption and national identity, on the making of post-colonial nations through commodity culture, mass media, and public space. In many respects, the principal tension evident in middle-class uses of commodities for self-fashioning repeats itself in constructions of the nation. Richard Wilk's work suggests, for example, that the spectrum of commodified performances trying to negotiate the relation between globalizing and local identities is expansive, illustrated in his studies by a close reading of beauty pageants in Belize. Just as colonial and post-colonial middle classes struggle to balance a consuming modernity with the constraints and possibilities of the local, post-colonial nations represent consumer culture both as a homogenizing, Westernizing force which they oppose through cultivating a distinctive local nationality *and* as a tool for achieving legitimacy and parity within global modernity. In Wilk's reading, this struggle for balance is inevitably tilted against post-colonial societies, and, in the end, all 'cultural consumers', who are 'shifted away from participating in culture, and towards treating objectified culture as a consumer good.'[30] Perhaps the single most emblematic example of this deployment of consumption and commodities against the backdrop of colonial rule is the *Swadeshi* movement against the British in India, with its iconic focus on homespun cloth as both political weapon and nation-making tool, but there have since been many other episodes around the world which repeat some elements of this episode.[31]

As Foster makes explicit, a focus on consumption, commodities, and advertising along these lines is in some sense a natural extension of Benedict Anderson's description of artefacts like the census, the map, and print culture as producing national identity.[32]

---

[29] See Weinbaum et al (eds.), *The Modern Girl Around the World*, particularly the two introductory essays and essays by Lynn Thomas, Priti Ramamurthy, Madeline Dong, Ruri Ito, Tani Barlow, and Timothy Burke.

[30] Richard Wilk, 'The Local and the Global in the Political Economy of Beauty: From Miss Belize to Miss World', *Review of International Political Economy*, 2/1 (1995), 134.

[31] See Lisa Trivedi, *Clothing Gandhi's Nation: Homespun and Modern India* (Bloomington: Indiana University Press, 2007); Manu Goswami, *Producing India: From Colonial Economy to National Space* (Chicago: University of Chicago Press, 2004); and Mazzarella, *Shoveling Smoke*.

[32] Foster, *Materializing the Nation*, 64–5.

But as Foster, Kemper, Huat, and other scholars note, defining emerging or developing nations as composed of active consumers also speaks very directly to the history of imperial ideas about the agency of colonial subjects in a manner that is paradoxically both subversive and reassuring to capitalist globalization. Within the public discourse of modern capitalism, the consumer is a *choosing* subject, but only, as Wilk observes, within the often severe limits of a consumer marketplace. Post-colonial nations assertively defining themselves as consuming nations have run the risk of being at once accused by wealthy nations of being both improvident and vulgar, and of being regarded as a threat to existing distributions of wealth, security, environmental quality, and so on. In the past two decades, the most emblematic case to spark this kind of anxiety in Western societies is that of China, and scholars have responded with a wave of studies of new or emerging consumer cultures in China, many of which are attentive to the consequences of weaving together China's international profile, its domestic national identity, and increasingly conspicuous forms of global consumerism within China.[33] But examples can be found anywhere. South African news stories in 2010 and 2011 about the notoriously excessive 'sushi parties' of South African businessman Kenny Kunene, who has boasted that 'he has eaten sushi from the body of a white woman in Cape Town, a black woman in Johannesburg and in the future, will eat off the body of an Indian woman in Durban', were only partially concerned with ruling party corruption and at least as concerned with the proposition that profligate consumption is somehow an even worse or more provocative spectacle when it is embodied in a non-white subject.[34]

Most scholars working in this loose constellation of subjects agree that there are marked excluded areas where little work has been done, such as the consuming habits or material culture of rural populations throughout the developing world. That absence strikes me more as a product of the ways in which we categorize study than as an actual absence. There is a huge body of scholarship on rural life in Africa, South-East and East Asia, and the Middle East which incidentally often describes material culture or everyday life in detail, including the use of imported, foreign, or manufactured commodities. Only rarely does such work define itself as being *about* commodification, however, such as James Ferguson's important essay on 'commodity pathways' in rural Lesotho or Bruce Roberts's account of beer as a commodity in rural Kenya.[35] Ferguson observes, for example, that divergent expressions of agency through consumption in rural communities

---

[33] See Croll, *China's New Consumers*; Karl Gerth and Harvard University, *China Made: Consumer Culture and the Creation of the Nation* (Cambridge, MA: Harvard University Asia Center, 2003); and *Patterns of Middle Class Consumption in India and China* (Los Angeles, CA: Sage, 2008) for only a few examples of this fast-growing area of scholarly enquiry.

[34] See Celia W. Dugger, 'Partying Amid Poverty Stirs a South African Debate', *New York Times*, 15 February 2011, A4, for a summary of the Kunene controversy. For images from Kunene's parties, see 'Kenny Kunene—40th Birthday', YouTube, <http://www.youtube.com/watch?v=buWaqJxgLLk> (accessed 15 February 2011).

[35] James Ferguson, 'The Cultural Topography of Wealth: Commodity Paths and the Structure of Property in Rural Lesotho', *American Anthropologist*, 94/1, New Series (1992), 55–73; Bruce D. Roberts, 'Always Cheaply Pleasant: Beer as a Commodity in a Rural Kenyan Society', in Angelique Haugerud, M. Priscilla Stone, and Peter D. Little (eds.), *Commodities and Globalization: Anthropological Perspectives* (Lanham, MD: Rowman & Littlefield, 2000).

(such as one Lesotho man buying a television, the other buying cattle) are especially likely to be misperceived as fundamental structural differences in social class. To some extent, this categorical rather than descriptive absence reinforces again the importance of the ways in which consumer culture in colonial and post-colonial societies has been constructed in association with modernity—hence, with urban, middle-class, educated, cosmopolitan, and 'national' populations. Another interesting wrinkle in the sociology of consumption in colonial and post-colonial societies is patterned rejections or avoidances of consumerism in general or of specific commodities as a strategy for defining identity or community, as in Amy Stambach's analysis of the contradictory meanings of consumerism for evangelical youth in Tanzania.[36]

THE THINGS THEMSELVES

One of the distinguishing features of the historical and ethnographic study of consumer culture is that such work necessarily directs attention not just to the sociality and practices of consumers, but to the materiality of commodities themselves, and hence not just to how they are used by their owners but also how they are acquired and how they are produced. Advertisers may try to affect how audiences see commodities, manufacturers may powerfully shape what goods are or are not available for consumption, governments may endorse or suppress some products. But commodities themselves also shape consumption practices through their concrete materiality and in terms of the embedded histories of meanings associated with them.

Scholars studying colonial and post-colonial societies have been as attentive to commodities as scholars in other regional and temporal fields of study. In fact, one of the fundamental canonical templates in this area of study is centrally concerned with colonialism, though more with the early modern Atlantic: Sidney Mintz's *Sweetness and Power*.[37] Mintz's study of sugar insists that the production of sugar through slavery, its rising global ubiquity since 1750, and our cultural imagination of sugared foods and objects are always inextricably tied together. On one hand, Mintz's work has arguably given shape to a genre of popular histories of the global production and consumption of a single foodstuff or commodity, such as Mark Kurlansky's *Salt* or Tom Standage's *A History of the World in Six Glasses*.[38] Some of these books trace the history of their object or commodity in relation to modern colonial experiences, generally with little analytic depth, though there are notable exceptions.[39] However, there are also more

---

[36] Amy Stambach, 'Evangelism and Consumer Culture in Northern Tanzania,' *Anthropological Quarterly*, 73/4 (2000), 171–9.

[37] Sidney W. Mintz, *Sweetness and Power: The Place of Sugar in Modern History* (New York: Viking, 1985).

[38] Mark Kurlansky, *Salt: A World History* (Penguin, 2003); Tom Standage, *A History of the World in Six Glasses* (New York: Walker Publishing Company, 2006).

[39] See for one example Pietra Rivoli, *The Travels of a T-Shirt in the Global Economy: An Economist Examines the Markets, Power, and Politics of World Trade*, 2nd edn. (Wiley, 2009).

scholarly works which take on some part of Mintz's blueprint in a more specific context, generally to study a commodity produced for global consumption within a colonial or post-colonial society. Brad Weiss's study of coffee in Tanzania, Yangwen Zheng's social history of opium consumption and exchange in China, and Karen Hansen's study of the circulation of second-hand clothing in Africa are three good examples of this approach, which strives for an integrated account of the production, circulation, and consumption of a globalized commodity in the context of a particular locality.[40]

A slightly different but equally influential blueprint for studying the relationship between particular commodities and colonial and post-colonial societies is the anthology *The Social Life of Things*, edited by Arjun Appadurai. The analysis of Appadurai and his contributors frequently ends up at some of the same junctures as work by scholars who focus on social identity and consumer practice, such as Alfred Gell's essay on how one local South Asian elite feel obligated to avoid conspicuous consumption.[41] Sometimes, however, the road travelled in tracing what Igor Kopytoff calls 'The Cultural Biography of Things' is also importantly different in some key respects.[42] Essays in the volume on carpets, qat, and cloth suggest that a focus on commodities first, consumption practices second, often allows the analysis to follow goods in and out of social contexts, and to observe how meaning is accumulated or redirected in the course of this circulation. Arnold Bauer's *Goods, Power, History* demonstrates the strength of this approach by categorizing various commodities as contact, civilizing, modernizing, developing or global in Latin American history.[43] In many respects, a commodity-focused approach also allows scholars to discuss distinctive cultural subsystems which involve but are not limited to consumer practices, such as fashion in the case of clothing or beauty pageants in the case of cosmetics. Or, as in the case of Thomas's *Entangled Objects*, to trace the circulation of goods between distantly separated localities.[44] Moreover, a commodity-driven analysis often puts materiality into clear focus compared to a heavier emphasis on sociological analysis or representation in treatments of consumerism and advertising, which often adds a crucial missing dimension to those other approaches. Materiality constrains where and how a commodity can be kept or used, where it can travel, how much it costs, and the kinds of social and economic organization needed to produce it. As a result, such work is inviting to comparative analysis, both across regions and time periods, including between modern commodity culture and pre-colonial or premodern

[40] Brad Weiss, *Sacred Trees, Bitter Harvests: Globalizing Coffee in Northwest Tanzania* (Portsmouth, NH: Heinemann, 2003); Yangwen Zheng, *The Social Life of Opium in China* (Cambridge: Cambridge University Press, 2005); Karen Tranberg Hansen, *Salaula: The World of Secondhand Clothing and Zambia* (Chicago: University of Chicago Press, 2000).

[41] Alfred Gell, 'Newcomers to the World of Goods: Consumption Among the Muria Gonds', in Arjun Appadurai (ed.), *The Social Life of Things: Commodities in Cultural Perspective* (Cambridge: Cambridge University Press, 1988), 110–40.

[42] Igor Kopytoff, 'The Cultural Biography of Things', in Appadurai (ed.), *The Social Life of Things*, 64–94.

[43] Arnold J. Bauer, *Goods, Power, History: Latin America's Material Culture* (Cambridge: Cambridge University Press, 2001).

[44] Thomas, *Entangled Objects*.

circulations and uses of the same commodity. While the materiality of a particular good or product can usefully constrain an analysis of consumption, a focus on a particular commodity also often offers an opportunity for a deep hermeneutical reading (something that colonialism often otherwise obscures or makes difficult). Reading meaning from material culture is not as easy as it might seem (an issue with which archaeologists must continually grapple), but comparing the circulation and production of textiles in premodern South Asia or West Africa and the contemporary scene for the same is nevertheless an important strategy for connecting past and present in spite of the intervening presence of modern colonial rule.

The disadvantages of commodity history are most readily visible in popular works following this format. The integration of production, consumption, and circulation for a single commodity runs the risk of disembedding the commodity from all its relations to other commodities, other acts of consumption, and the overall structure of production and circulation, a form of commodity fetishism conferred through exclusivity of focus. At its most problematic, this approach magnifies its chosen commodity to a position of overwhelming historical centrality and supreme self-determining agency, a danger that is mitigated only slightly by the whimsy deployed in many popular Kurlansky-style works. It is easy to forget the uneven and unequal relations of the political economies that lie at different ends of the global circuits defined around and through goods as diverse as coffee, skin-lighteners, popular music, bananas, and second-hand clothing when the focus is on the commodities themselves. Recalling the 'colonial' part of the story with particular emphasis makes it easier to keep this point in view.

CONSUMER AGENCY IN THE CONTEXT OF GLOBALIZATION

In Brewer and Porter's collection of scholarship on early modern European consumption, the practitioners of the 'turn to consumption' are confronted by several forms of criticism. Jean-Christophe Agnew in particular argues that while the newer accounts enhance historians' understanding of early modern European economy and society in many respects, they overestimate the causal power of consumption. More pointedly, Agnew argues that if consumer culture has been dismissed as the antithesis of a society dedicated to democratic liberty and social justice, it is for good reason. In Agnew's view, the long-standing hostility of liberal and left thinkers towards consumerism ought to be only slightly blunted by the insights of scholars studying consumption.[45] Debates between intellectuals about the politics of mass consumption and commodity culture in contemporary American culture have at times been still more sharply drawn, with

---

[45] Jean-Christophe Agnew, 'Coming Up For Air: Consumer Culture in Historical Perspective', in Brewer and Porter (eds.), *Consumption and the World of Goods*, 19–39.

appreciative treatments of the constructive or generative aspects of consumerism often bracketed by sharp critiques from both the right and the left.[46] Indeed, as Joyce Appleby observes in the Brewer and Porter anthology, consumerism figures as both an excluded and condemned construct across the span of early modern social thought, at the root of later conservative and radical traditions.[47]

Scholarship concerned with the intersection of consumption, commodities, and modern colonialism has yet to provoke so sharp a response, but perhaps it is time that it should. I suspect many scholars writing on consumerism in developing societies in the 1990s encountered modest pre-emptive scepticism similar to the kind that early modern Europeanists once complained about. (I recall one historian objecting to a presentation of my own work on consumerism in colonial Zimbabwe on the grounds that since colonialism so thoroughly impoverished Africans, there could be nothing worth studying.) More typically, however, specialists in colonial and post-colonial societies have welcomed work along these lines.

Most recent anthropological and historical studies of consumption and commodities in the modern developing world begin from the assumption that older critical assumptions about the cultural and social impact of globalization and modernization are partially flawed; most crucially, in the view that globalization will inevitably remake the material culture and everyday practices of non-Western societies into a single homogenous world culture modelled on Western norms and ideals. In this, scholars working on consumerism and globalization are not alone: this critical assumption is shared across a broad span of work on 'multiple modernities' in colonial and post-colonial societies. Such work tends to argue that colonial rule and globalization has not produced a single monolithic and homogenous global culture for a variety of reasons: because of colonialism's own ambivalent and contradictory view of such an objective, because colonial and post-colonial societies have resisted attempts to remake them in such a fashion, because the power of global capitalism and colonial rule was and is more limited or fragmented than many modernization theorists assumed, and, most crucially, because global capitalism and modernity are as productive of new forms of difference as they are of homogeneity. Much of this critical response, particularly as applied to material culture and everyday life, has been compactly summarized in John Tomlinson's book *Cultural Imperialism*, frequently cited in this literature. Tomlinson writes:

> It can reasonably be argued that the processes of modernity originated in the West and that the imperialist adventures of Western nations have been central in establishing a context of domination in which 'Western-modern' institutions have been transferred more or less intact. But to blame 'the West' cannot mean to blame a coherent collective project belonging to agents in the West. For we have seen that

---

[46] See for example Juliet Schor, *The Overspent American: Upscaling, Downshifting, and The New Consumer*, 1st edn. (New York: HarperPerennial, 1999) versus James B. Twitchell, *Lead Us into Temptation: The Triumph of American Materialism* (New York: Columbia University Press, 1999).

[47] Joyce Appleby, 'Consumption in Early Modern Social Thought', in Brewer and Porter (eds.), *Consumption and the World of Goods*, 162–76.

agents in the West have been as little able to control the direction of their route out of tradition as are agents in the Third World.[48]

Or as Frank Trentmann writes: 'Modernity created different openings for consumers in different political and cultural spaces, depending on the role of nation, state, traditions of citizenship and social identities. There is no universal history of the consumer, just as there is no essentialist consumer.'[49]

In descriptive terms, what this approach often amounts to is an emphasis on the localization and remaking of consumer culture in colonial and post-colonial societies. Here too this emphasis on the study of consumption and material culture in the developing world resembles scholarship on similar topics, such as mass media and popular culture. Indeed, this emphasis on the localization of global culture and institutions has been so pronounced in the last decade and a half of anthropological and historical scholarship that it is not uncommon to catch a hint of impatience at even having to revisit the view that modernization brings homogenization or that modernity entails any single or fixed set of meanings, practices, and/or social formations.

Yet as a popular discourse in both Western and developing nations, the older tropes of modernization theory retain much of their force and authority. National publics have worked and continue to work with (and are worked upon) the proposition that commodities, advertising messages, and consumer practices are 'Westernizing' or 'globalizing' forces that need to be adapted or fought. Popular works of social criticism such as Benjamin Barber's *Jihad vs. McWorld* continue to use the basic framework of modernization theory and its assumptions about the impact of the spread of consumerism around the world.[50] But these sentiments are not really the other side in a debate which encompasses anthropological and scholarly study of colonialism's entanglement with commodities and consumption. They are more a subject of study, something to reframe and examine; indeed, for Mazzarella, Foster, Kemper, and others, this reframing is perhaps the most central objective of their analysis.

So is there anything in this literature to parallel the provocative inversion of consumption and production in the historiography of early modern Europe? I think there is indeed a gun on the mantelpiece which gets fired by the last act, but it is done quietly and offstage, with considerable ambivalence. If consumerism and commodity culture turn out to be an excellent vehicle for studying both the limits and contradictions of colonial power and globalization on one hand, and richly diverse histories of localization on the other, does not this suggest that many standard critiques of imperialism, neo-liberalism, or capitalist globalization are in need of serious modification or softening?

This prospect is precisely what drives the objections of some scholars to the magnification of local agency and the decomposition of colonial power in much of the 'multiple

[48] John Tomlinson, *Cultural Imperialism: A Critical Introduction* (Baltimore, MD: Johns Hopkins University Press, 1991), 168.

[49] Frank Trentmann, 'The Evolution of the Consumer', in Sheldon Garon and Patricia L. Maclachlan (eds.), *The Ambivalent Consumer: Questioning Consumption in East Asia and the West* (Ithaca, NY: Cornell University Press, 2006), 43.

[50] Benjamin R. Barber, *Jihad Vs. McWorld* (New York: Ballantine Books, 2001).

modernities' literature.[51] Yet many studies which might seem to have a diminished view of colonial or capitalist power and an accordingly magnified vision of local autonomy take some pains to suggest that this is precisely *not* what they are claiming, often by arguing that binary pairings of local/global, Western/non-Western, colonial/colonized are unhelpful or unproductive in the first place. Richard Wilk, writing about beauty contests in Belize, observes:

> a place like Belize has never had very much range for autonomous action; not under British colonialism and not under Cold War discipline. But the growth of a global order of communication and of systems of common difference forces us to think about autonomy and dependence in very different ways. The same processes that destroy autonomy are now creating new sorts of communities, new kinds of locality and identity.[52]

Wilk's move here strikes me as common to this body of literature on commodity culture and modern colonialism, a simultaneous agreement that colonialism, post-1945 internationalism, and globalization exerted enormous power over the developing world, and yet also accidentally or uncontainably spurred the development of novel forms of social and cultural practice which perpetually 'slip the leash' of hegemony or domination, only sometimes because of programmatic resistance by the colonized. Mazzarella puts it in a rather different way, that the problem with advertising in India is not that it is false or deceptive, but that it misappropriates universality, 'cloaks its partiality', and 'reaches into the concrete foundations of our collective experience.'[53]

Put in that way, it is not clear about which forces, institutions, or practices in the modern world this could not be said. There is a certain amount of the having and eating of cake going on in these formulations, of wanting to find commodity culture, advertising, and consumerism guilty of something, culpable in some fashion, but not in a way which obliges the critic to have any alternatives in mind, or a praxis to turn to. This is in some measure because these critics are attempting to map and describe what they think is an existing praxis of response to consumerism which is neither resistance nor submission. At least the old modernization theorists (both on the left and the right) had a clear descriptive view of an alternative traditional or authentic culture in non-Western societies that they claimed consuming modernity had or would displace. At least some of the same critics on the left also took pains to imagine that there could be some future dispensation that would replace consumer culture with a preferable alternative, or that an anti-colonial nationalism might be meaningfully mobilized against Westernization, just as critics on the right have tried to describe a moral, spiritual, and intellectual world we (or they) have lost in a morass of materialism.

I would not argue that the study of consumption and colonialism needs to return to embracing these perspectives. Indeed, I think the move away from such arguments is

[51] See the discussions of Talal Asad's critique of colonial studies in Charles Hirschkind and David Scott, *Powers of the Secular Modern: Talal Asad and His Interlocutors*, first edn. (Stanford, CA: Stanford University Press, 2006) for one example of this scepticism.

[52] Richard Wilk, 'Learning to be Local in Belize', in Daniel Miller (ed.), *Worlds Apart: Modernity Through the Prism of the Local* (London: Routledge, 1995), 130.

[53] Mazzarella, *Shoveling Smoke*, 287.

empirically, theoretically, and politically sound. But I think in some cases, what looks like a highly conditional, partial acknowledgement of the imaginative and material possibilities of commodity culture in the developing world needs to be accepted as such without too many attempts to evade responsibility for making such a characterization. Along with that argument, this scholarship is potentially one of the stronger documentations that colonial power and globalizing transformation were neither as strong nor as instrumentally coherent as they and their critics have frequently imagined them to be. At a global level, the fecundity of consumer culture and bourgeois life-worlds may be a messier and more multiplicious thing than European liberals or conservatives once (or still) imagined they would be, but so much the better. At the conclusion of my own study of commodification and consumption in modern Zimbabwe, I argued that I had written a history of the making of desire, and implied that both colonial rulers and scholarly commentators had underestimated the generative force and subversive meanings of that history. Perhaps it is time to stop doing so.

BIBLIOGRAPHY

Abaza, Mona, *Changing Consumer Cultures of Modern Egypt: Cairo's Urban Reshaping* (Leiden: Brill, 2006).

Appadurai, Arjun (ed.), *The Social Life of Things: Commodities in Cultural Perspective* (Cambridge: Cambridge University Press, 1988).

Burke, Timothy, *Lifebuoy Men, Lux Women: Commodification, Consumption, and Cleanliness in Modern Zimbabwe* (Durham, NC: Duke University Press, 1996).

Cochran, Sherman, *Chinese Medicine Men: Consumer Culture in China and Southeast Asia* (Cambridge, MA: Harvard University Press, 2006).

Ferguson, James, 'The Cultural Topography of Wealth: Commodity Paths and the Structure of Property in Rural Lesotho', *American Anthropologist*, 94/1, New Series (March 1992), 55–73.

Foster, Robert John, *Materializing the Nation: Commodities, Consumption, and Media in Papua New Guinea* (Bloomington: Indiana University Press, 2002).

Friedman, Jonathan (ed.), *Consumption and Identity* (Chur, Switzerland: Harwood Academic Publishers, 1994).

Chua, Beng Huat, *Life Is Not Complete Without Shopping: Consumption Culture in Singapore* (Singapore: Singapore University Press, 2003).

Liechty, Mark, *Suitably Modern: Making Middle-Class Culture in a New Consumer Society* (Princeton, NJ: Princeton University Press, 2003).

Mazzarella, William, *Shoveling Smoke: Advertising and Globalization in Contemporary India* (Durham, NC: Duke University Press, 2003).

Mills, Mary Beth, *Thai Women in the Global Labor Force: Consuming Desires, Contested Selves* (Chapel Hill, NC: Rutgers University Press, 1999).

O'Dougherty, Maureen, *Consumption Intensified: The Politics of Middle-Class Daily Life in Brazil* (Durham, NC: Duke University Press, 2002).

Stearns, Peter, *Consumerism in World History: The Global Transformation of Desire*, 2nd edn. (London: Routledge, 2006).

Weinbaum, Alys Eve et al. (eds.), *The Modern Girl Around the World: Consumption, Modernity, and Globalization* (Durham, NC: Duke University Press, 2008).

CHAPTER 25

....

CONSUMPTION, CONSUMERISM, AND JAPANESE MODERNITY

....

ANDREW GORDON

THE experience of people in Japan offers a rich body of evidence for comparative and global study of consumption from early modern through modern times to our postmodern present. One finds ample grist for the mill of economic historians seeking to measure the extent and the shifts in consumption of all manner of goods and services. One also finds sources in abundance from the seventeenth century onwards speaking to the politics and culture of regulating, lamenting, and celebrating consumption. Building on early modern foundations, consumption expanded in the era of self-conscious modernization that followed the overthrow of the Tokugawa shogunate (1868), with a turn to new goods alongside more widespread use of customary ones. As this happened, attitudes in Japan evolved as part of a global dialogue on consumer life. This was not a balanced dialogue: the transformative impact on thought and behaviour elsewhere of what one historian has called America's 'irresistible' market empire was profound.[1] But the Japanese story is not one of simple absorption or mimicry; local patterns and understandings of consumer life were not stamped uniformly from a single mould. And especially in recent decades, global trends in consumer life have in some measure been 'made in Japan'.

EARLY MODERN CONSUMPTION

....

Decades ago, it was common both in Japan and among foreign scholars to describe the Tokugawa era (1600–1868) in bleak terms as a time of oppressive military rule, tight restrictions on social and physical mobility, and (after about 1700) economic stagnation

[1] Victoria de Grazia, *Irresistible Empire: America's Advance Through 20th-Century Europe* (Cambridge, MA.: Harvard University Press, 2005).

emblematized by famine and the widespread practice of infanticide.[2] Austere sumptuary laws were understood to have restricted dress, food, and other forms of consumption for farmers as well as city-dwellers.[3] The best of these early works acknowledged the flowering from the late seventeenth century of a gaudy urban culture centred on entertainment districts whose heroes were kabuki actors and geisha, and pointed out that the frequent issue of sumptuary laws is good evidence they were not followed.[4] Building on such perspectives, since the 1960s, and with increased force from the 1970s and 1980s, both Japanese and Western-languages scholarship on what has come to be called early modern (rather than late feudal) Japan has described a world of economic vitality and growth. Even infanticide in some cases appears to have been the act not of desperate peasants but of upwardly striving, relatively prosperous farmers seeking to minimize family size to protect their assets for the next generation.[5]

It is possible to take this line of argument too far. The fruits of the growing economy were unevenly distributed. Famines were chronic and at times devastating as late as the nineteenth century; recent work suggests that infanticide took place for diverse reasons in different places.[6] But the new consensus—to me a persuasive one—holds that 'any search for the historical origins of the consumer in Japan must surely begin with the significant growth in the population of towns and cities that set in after the establishment of the Tokugawa regime.' Japan by 1800 was home to 'more large cities than any other country in the world, and its urban populations had come to rely almost entirely on the market' for a vast array of manufactured or processed consumer goods.[7] City-dwellers had access to large and expanding inventories of food and drink, clothing, and personal adornments, and cultural products including imported books (mainly from China) and woodblock prints, as well as services ranging from tea-houses and theatres to lawyers and merchant bankers.[8]

---

[2] Honjo Eijiro, *Economic Theory and History of Japan in the Tokugawa Period* (New York: Russell and Russell, 1965). E. H. Norman, *Japan's Emergence as a Modern State* (New York: Institution of Pacific Relations, 1940), ch. 2.

[3] Mikiso Hane, *Peasants, Rebels, and Outcastes: The Underside of Modern Japan* (New York: Pantheon Press, 1982), p. 7.

[4] Donald Shively, 'Sumptuary Regulations in Status in Early Tokugawa Japan', *Harvard Journal of Asiatic Studies*, Vol. 25 (1964–65), pp. 123–64.

[5] Important early works in this mode in English include Thomas C. Smith, *Native Sources of Japanese Industrialization: 1750–1920* (Berkeley: University of California Press, 1988) and Smith, *Nakahara: Family Farming and Population in a Japanese Village, 1717–1830* (Berkeley: University of California Press, 1977), as well as Susan B. Hanley and Kozo Yamamura, *Economic and Demographic Change in Preindustrial Japan, 1600–1868* (Princeton: Princeton University Press, 1977).

[6] Fabian Drixler, 'Infanticide and Fertility in Eastern Japan: Discourse and Demography, 1660–1880', Ph.D. dissertation (Harvard University, 2006).

[7] Penelope Francks, 'Inconspicuous Consumption: Sake, Beer and the Birth of the Consumer in Japan', *Journal of Asian Studies* Vol. 68, No. 1 (February 2009), p. 142. See also Francks, *The Japanese Consumer: An Alternative Economic History of Modern Japan* (Cambridge: Cambridge University Press, 2009), ch. 3, pp. 47–73.

[8] Mary Elizabeth Berry, *Japan in Print: Information and Nation in the Early Modern Period* (Berkeley: University of California Press, 2007); Jonathan Zwicker, *Practices of the Sentimental Imagination: Melodrama, the Novel, and the Social Imaginary in Nineteenth-Century Japan* (Cambridge, MA; Harvard University Asia Center, 2006), ch. 3.

Many of these goods were made (and increasingly consumed) in a countryside itself becoming more productive and prosperous. Again, care must be taken not to soar to excessive heights of celebration at these trends; alongside wealthy farmers engaged in trade, banking, and production one finds increasingly vulnerable peasants. By the early nineteenth century they were more willing than ever to protest their weakness in the face of the vagaries of the market.[9] But it is clear that by the eighteenth century and more densely in the nineteenth century, producers, sellers, and consumers were linked in networks that not only drew goods from rural centres of specialized production to distant cities (a defining feature of 'proto-industrialization'), but also placed a wide range of goods in the hands of a thickening upper strata of rural society.[10]

One noteworthy new element in consumer life of the late Tokugawa era which supported these developments was the offer of credit for the purchase of daily life goods. In the nineteenth century, indigenous providers of consumer credit were particularly prominent in the lacquer industry which developed in central and south-western Japan, especially Ehime, Wakayama, and Kyushu. Improvising upon a traditional form of mutual credit provision called *mujin* or *kō*, lacquerware was sold to relatively well-off rural households with payment made in quarterly instalments.[11]

It is tempting to clinch the case that Tokugawa Japan was a time of expanding consumption by offering a long list of the goods finding their way into the hands of more and more city-dwellers and country folk. Indeed, this is a favourite (and effective) tactic of historians. Susan Hanley writes that:

> in 1813, one shop in the village of Ōi sold ink, paper, writing brushes, pots, needles, pipes, tobacco and pouches, teapots, various containers and dishes, vinegar, soy sauce, bean paste, salt, noodles, kelp, sake, cakes, tea and teacups, *senbei* (rice crackers), grain, oil, candles, hair oils, hair strings and hairpins, cotton cloth, towels, *tabi* (socks), footgear including zori, *geta* (wooden clogs), and *waraji* (straw sandals), funeral requisites, and 'other everyday necessities'.[12]

Such a list, it is important to note, is not only a rhetorical device of historians. Its production was itself a new and favourite cultural pastime of Japan's early modern era. The

[9] See Stephen Vlastos, *Peasant Protests and Uprisings in Tokugawa Japan* (Berkeley: University of California Press, 1986) on this aspect of peasant protest.

[10] Kären Wigen, *The Making of a Japanese Periphery, 1750–1920* (Berkeley: University of California Press, 1995).

[11] "Nihon geppu hanbai hatten no rekishi" *Geppu kenkyū*, Vol. 1, No. 1 (15 April 1957), p. 3. *Mujin* or *kō* were revolving mutual credit funds where members met monthly, usually for a meal and drinks, and each contributed an agreed sum. The total was given to the winner of a lottery. Subsequent lotteries were limited to those who had not yet won. In the Ehime lacquer innovation, all members of a group received their goods upon an initial pooled payment, and periodic subsequent payments were collected from the entire group. Tetsuo Najita, *Ordinary Economies in Japan* (Berkeley: University of California Press, 2009), ch. 6: 'The Mujin Company', pp. 175–209, offers an important recent discussion of the *mujin*.

[12] Susan Hanley, *Everyday Things in Premodern Japan: The Hidden Legacy of Material Culture* (Berkeley: University of California Press, 1997), p. 17. See also, for example, Wigen, *Making of a Japanese Periphery*, p. 64; Francks, 'Inconspicuous Consumption,' p. 143.

proliferation of all manner of published lists and rankings makes it clear that expanding consumption was beginning to produce 'consumerism', understood as a self-conscious discourse which both celebrated and fretted over the increase in getting and spending. In her brilliant meditation on the proliferation of information as a defining mark of an early modern nation, Mary Elizabeth Berry introduces the genre of the 'urban survey' in which such lists featured prominently. The *Dappled Fabric of Edo*, for example, in its summary of one avenue in the central Nihonbashi area, enumerates as residents:

> Lacquerers, dealers in ink and writing brushes, dealers in silk thread, booksellers, dealers in raincoats, dealers in mirrors, dealers in fans, dealers in Buddhist goods, dealers in swords, mounters and binders [of paintings and books], dealers in Buddhist robes, printers, dealers in koto, dealers in samisen, carvers of bone and horn, cake makers, dealers in mortuary tablets, dealers in paper, dealers in candles, dealers in heavy brushes, dealers in baskets, dealers in lacquer goods, and dealers in Chinese-style straw hats.[13]

She concludes that these surveys 'took as their subject the opportunities of consumers and strangers'. They were woven from a 'warp of streets and wards', and a 'weft of commercial enterprise, historical legacy, and ritual activity' which 'traced images of ambition and power' and in which 'the market rivaled the regime as a source of autonomous power'.[14] It would take the argument too far—and further than Berry herself would go—to say that the market was the primary solvent which brought down the old regime. But it surely played a role in shaking its foundations. And it is certain that a robust world of consumption and a widespread apprehension of its importance were both in place well before Japan's modernizing revolution of the late nineteenth century.

The Emergence of the Modern Consumer

Japan's modern era is conventionally dated from 1868. In this year insurgent samurai overthrew the Tokugawa regime. They installed a new emperor (Meiji) and announced the 'restoration' of imperial rule. Although early changes were cloaked in ancient form, in many respects the years immediately following this event did mark a sharp break with the past. In the decade of the 1870s, old status distinctions and privileges were abolished, including those of the samurai themselves. The 270 semi-autonomous domains ruled by warrior families with hereditary claim to their positions were replaced by a much smaller number of prefectures headed by centrally appointed governors. The new state imposed a unified national tax, a military draft, and compulsory education. Knowledge from and

---

[13] Berry, *Japan in Print*, p. 156.
[14] Ibid.

of the West was embraced by many. In the 1880s a modern constitution modelled on that of Prussia was written and promulgated.

But consumption was one realm where the modern revolution of these two decades had little impact. Susan Hanley, in her study of everyday life in Tokugawa and Meiji Japan, makes a strong case that it was not 'until the twentieth century that the elements of everyday life—the material culture—began to become significantly Westernized or modernized for most people.'[15] To be sure, even in the 1870s leaders of the new government, followed some years later by their wives, donned Western dress in public, and the fashionable Ginza district of red-brick shops (constructed in 1875) drew wide attention and was celebrated in woodblock prints. But the Ginza 'Bricktown' did not emerge as a vibrant commercial district for several decades. In realms of housing, food, and dress into the 1890s, gradual improvement in standards of living mainly took place through the more widespread consumption of traditional goods previously limited to the wealthy. These ranged from ceramic *hibachi* for home heating, to polished white rice (not a healthy shift) and increased use of soy sauce, to straw sandals (by those who had once gone barefoot).[16] These goods were for the most part domestically produced. As in the past, they were sold in the countryside by peddlers or in the city in small shops.

Against this backdrop, the turn of the twentieth century marks the advent of a modern consumer life marked, and indeed defined, by a particularly pronounced tension between discursive and social practices. Key elements of 'modern' consumption included the following. It was centred in cultural imagination on urban, educated, middle-class families. It was typically paid for through monthly salary or wages earned outside the home. Many of its goods were branded, and they were sold in new sites, most notably department stores. They were promoted through advertising in the new media of daily newspapers and monthly magazines. The purchase of these publications was itself perhaps the single most rapidly expanding modern form of consumption in the early decades of the century. Daily readership of both *Asahi* and *Mainichi* newspapers exceeded 1 million by 1924. Monthly magazines soared in popularity, with publications for women prominent among them. In the early 1920s the three most popular women's magazines (*Fujokai* [Women's World], *Shufu no Tomo* [The Housewife's Companion], and *Fujin Kurabu* [Ladies Club]) each claimed circulations in excess of 200,000 copies. Total monthly sales of women's magazines exceeded 1 million copies. The consumption practices these magazines promoted involved goods of modern (Western) industrial civilization, from toothpaste and soap to electric fans and sewing machines, although few could afford the latter. Their spread initiated an ongoing, uneasy negotiation between lifestyles understood to be modern and Western and those presented as traditional or Japanese.

Middle-class consumers were more diverse in social practice than in cultural imagination, for they included shopkeepers, wholesalers, and small-scale manufacturers,

---

[15] Hanley, *Everyday Things in Premodern Japan*, p. 156. Francks, *The Japanese Consumer*, presents a similar argument. See especially ch. 4, pp. 74–107.

[16] Hanley, *Everyday Things in Premodern Japan*, pp. 156–68.

whose occupations and lives had early modern lineage. But observers identified their centre of gravity as wage- or salary-earning office workers, and their families: government bureaucrats and low-ranked clerks, managers in private corporations and financial institutions, and lower-level corporate functionaries or technicians. By the 1920s, such people had reached a critical mass as a significant minority in the vanguard of consumer life and a wider presence in cultural imagination. Occupational surveys show a large increase in the proportion of 'office staff' positions in major cities, in Tokyo from 6 per cent in 1908 to 21 per cent in 1920.[17] The numbers of vocational middle schools increased substantially, and a multi-tiered system of recruitment began to link these institutions, as well as higher schools and universities, to corporate and government employers. The contestants for these jobs included not only the children of former samurai, but also the offspring of the old middle class of urban shopkeepers or manufacturers, or middling farmers in the countryside.[18]

As mass media and department stores dangled new goods in front of these people, commentators and participants engaged in vigorous discussion of the extent and meaning of a new consumer life. In the early 1920s, this centred on 'cultural' life and 'cultural homes' which housed the people and the goods of the modern middle class. Historian Jordan Sand has observed that such discourse 'marked the beginning of an incessant dialectic between consumers' dreams and their frustrated reality that is itself an aspect of the modern condition.'[19] The flourishing media industry offered the arena where this dialectic played out. A rich array of image and text described a gendered consuming world populated by women in a variety of roles, as well as their salaryman husbands or fathers. They partook of new services as well as goods. The first three decades of the century witnessed a dramatic proliferation of milk halls and beer halls, Western-style restaurants for a wide range of budgets, and new forms of leisure from bathing to spectator sports, most famously baseball.[20] In women's magazines of these years, the housewives of the middle class could study cooking and sewing. They could learn of the latest fashions on sale for themselves or their children in the multi-storey department stores recently erected in the major cities. They could read articles about how to earn money in their spare time and tales of the successes, and the tribulations, of the small but growing band of full-time working women with jobs as seamstresses or hairdressers, typists or teachers (stories of the hundreds of thousands of textile spinners were rare).

But the greatest attention was devoted to the character known as the 'modern girl'. She was photographed strolling on the Ginza, lampooned in cartoons, lamented or celebrated in essays of numerous social commentators, and depicted in literary masterpieces (serialized in newspapers) such as Tanizaki Junichirō's short novel *Naomi*. Tanizaki's

[17] Matsunari Yoshie *et al.*, *Nihon no sarariiman* (Tokyo: Aoki shoten, 1974), p. 31.

[18] Matsunari et. al. *Nihon no sarariiman*, p. 35.

[19] Jordan Sand, *House and Home in Modern Japan: Architecture, Domestic Space, and Bourgeois Culture* (Cambridge, MA: Harvard University Asia Center, 2003), p. 226.

[20] See Francks, *The Japanese Consumer*, pp. 112–18, for a more extensive discussion of these leisure trends.

heroine was a café waitress, and in his story, as in the media telling more generally, waitresses flaunted their sexuality and broke convention by choosing their own partners. The sexual services industry continued to thrive in the old setting of licensed quarters which reached back to the seventeenth century, but by the end of the 1920s café waitresses outnumbered licensed prostitutes in Tokyo, and their relative freedom was seen by some as a threat to social order.[21]

This world of the urban middle class was not simply a media concoction. But those who read of the lives of such people far outnumbered those who actually worked in city offices, shopped in department stores, or frolicked in cafés. Some indication of this reality gap is offered by ownership data for the treasured items of middle-class life. Of the products of modern machine civilization, only the bicycle was truly an item of mass consumption by the end of the 1920s; the total number of bicycles in use in Japan rose from about 500,000 in 1910 to nearly 8 million by 1930, an impressive number in a nation of roughly 14 million households.[22]

Bicycles were outdoor goods, and most users in the early twentieth century were men.[23] The most important industrial product making its way primarily into the hands of female consumers was the sewing machine, but the penetration rate was considerably less. Singer dominated this market and sold roughly 500,000 household machines in Japan between 1903 and 1930, establishing a foothold in actual ownership and a much larger presence in image and brand awareness. Advertising, magazine articles, word of mouth, and the ubiquitous presence of thousands of door-to-door salesmen working out of a network of nearly 800 shops throughout the Japanese empire by the early 1930s made this good far better known and desired than possessed. By 1930 perhaps 4 per cent of Japan's households owned these machines.

A single state-administered network (NHK) began radio broadcasts in 1925, but the proportion of households owning radios by 1930 had not passed 5 per cent. With the exception of electric fans and irons, none of the other goods spreading rapidly in the United States, such as refrigerators, stoves, washing-machines, or phonographs, found even this level of use. Indeed, these products remained so firmly in the realm of fantasy that advertisers actually held back from promoting them. A model house on exhibit in the newly developed suburb of Denen-chōfu in 1924 featured an electric stove, washing-machine, and vacuum cleaner, but the executive in charge of the exhibit is said to have removed these goods when he realized how much the electricity to run them would cost the potential homeowners.[24] With or without such treasures inside, only a small minority of Japanese could afford to live in the 'cultural' homes built by railway and real estate developers.

---

[21] On café waitresses, Miriam Silverberg, *Erotic Grotesque Nonsense: The Mass Culture of Japanese Modern Times* (Berkeley: University of California Press, 2006), pp. 73–107, and Sheldon Garon, *Molding Japanese Minds: The State in Everyday Life* (Princeton: Princeton University Press, 1997), pp. 106–111.

[22] Suzuki Jun, *Shin gijutsu no shakai shi* (Tokyo: Chūō kōron shinsha, 1999), p. 205.

[23] In 1905, the fact that 30 or so schoolgirls commuted to class by bicycle was sufficiently remarkable to merit newspaper coverage. Suzuki, *Shin gijutsu no shakai shi*, p. 201.

[24] Suzuki, *Shin gijutsu no shakai shi*, p. 241.

In this context, aspiring consumers spoke in frustrated, anxious terms. During the First World War, Japan's European competitors temporarily disappeared, leaving Japanese producers as the only suppliers for many domestic and Asian markets and sparking an unprecedented economic boom. But inflation surged together with industrial production. Newspapers published laments such as this 1918 letter from an elementary school teacher supporting a family of five. After listing monthly expenses totaling 20.75 yen, he asserts:

> my monthly income after deductions is 18 yen and change. Even 20 yen are not enough. How can we live on 18? There's no choice but to cut our rice costs a little by mixing in barley, more than 50 percent, and once a day making a meal of barley-rice gruel. Because charcoal is expensive, no one in the family has taken a bath for over a month, and we can hardly afford a cup of sake, or a few pieces of meat, or even a single potato. To buy a new kimono is out of the question. Is there anything so pitiful as the life of an elementary school teacher who cannot afford to dress his child in a New Year kimono or even eat *mochi*?[25]

This letter is noteworthy not only for its plaintive tone. It was published in the decidedly modern medium of the daily newspaper. It was written by a salaried man in a job—the public school teacher—itself new to the modern era. But other than eating meat, the goods and practices he saw as appropriate to his status, yet cruelly out of reach, were indigenous. What was new was the expectation that his family eat white rice, bathe regularly at home, drink sake with dinner, and purchase a new kimono for the New Year.

Despite such frustrated desires and the highly uneven spread of goods old and new, consumption did grow steadily through these decades. People generally paid for food, drink, and leisure services in cash. But they increasingly bought the goods which defined the 'cultural' life of modern industrial civilization with money they did not yet have in hand. In this they relied on diverse indigenous and foreign practices which emerged more or less simultaneously around the turn of the twentieth century. What defines them as modern is the fact that borrowers were required to make regular instalment payments linked to the new practice of monthly salaries for office workers.

Indigenous providers of credit in modern times had emerged out of the late Tokugawa lenders in the lacquerware industry. From the 1880s into the 1890s, the more successful seller-lenders built regional networks offering a range of goods, especially furniture and clothing, on monthly instalments. Apprentice merchants split off from their masters, but retained the signature trademark of a merchant house, which placed a *kanji* character such as "i" (井) or "zen" (善) in a circle. The Japanese pronunciation of circle is *maru*, so the company names were as Marui, Maruzen, Marukyo, Marutake, Maruichi, and so forth. These businesses evolved into 'instalment department stores' from the late 1890s, selling household goods such as furniture, bedding, tatami, clothing (including men's Western dress), lacquerware or ceramic ware, moving from the

---

[25] Matsunari et al., *Nihon no sarariiman*, pp. 44–5, cites *Tokyo Asahi Shinbun*, 17 February 1918. *Mochi* are sticky rice cakes traditionally prepared for New Year holiday.

south-west toward the north-east rather gradually. The first such seller opened in Tokyo only in 1915; a number of others immediately followed.[26] These businesses appear similar in customer base and products to the so-called 'borax stores' which spread in the United States from the 1880s.[27]

Foreign corporations provided the second source of modern instalment credit. Among the most important were the Tokyo office of *The Times* (of London), which sold the *Encyclopedia Britannica* in tandem with Maruzen booksellers, and the Singer Sewing Machine Company. Singer was the most significant in systematizing and spreading instalment buying. In contrast to those who patronized instalment department stores, Singer's clientele were middle- to upper-class urban wives and daughters. Unlike most native instalment sellers, some of whom required no contract at all, Singer and the other foreign sellers used detailed signed agreements. Terms of repayment were considerably longer, and the cost of a typical good was higher. A Singer machine represented about two months' wages for an ordinary 'salaryman', making a purchase 'on time' the only way for many to afford it. In the 1920s, roughly two-thirds of annual sales of about 50,000 machines were sold on the instalment plan.[28]

Sellers and buyers understood themselves to be engaged in a progressive new practice of American or British origin, something Japanese people should be proud of doing, and ashamed to fail at. A Singer leaflet from 1908 proclaimed, 'Japan is the country of progress.' Six years earlier, an article in the Jiji newspaper proudly announced that Maruzen bookstore was selling the *Encyclopedia Britannica*, which cost 175 yen paid in cash, for a 5 yen down payment followed by 19 monthly instalments of 10 yen. Jiji cautioned 'that the Times corporation is using this method in Japan proves that it views Japanese and British people as equal and is giving us sufficient trust. Therefore, if anyone somehow breaks the contract, this will wound the reputation of Japan and betray the hopes of the foreigners.'[29]

The first organization in Japan to survey this emerging world of consumer credit in systematic fashion was the Tokyo Chamber of Commerce. Its pioneering 1929 study introduced readers to credit in the United States and Britain, as well as Japan. It drew on E. R. Seligman's important and just published opus, *The Economics of Installment Selling* (1927), for the account of the American scene.[30] It notes that a dramatic expansion of instalment selling had begun in Japan in the mid-1920s.[31] One new entrant was Nihon Gakki (Yamaha), selling pianos and organs since 1924. In addition to a scattering of other household appliances sold on credit, suburban homes were sold on several-year mortgages along the newly opened commuter railway lines.

---

[26]   Tokyo shōkō kaigisho, *Geppu hanbai seido* (Tokyo: Tokyo shōkō kaigisho, 1929), pp. 212–13.

[27]   Lendol Calder, *Financing the American Dream* (Princeton: Princeton University Press, 1999), pp. 56–7.

[28]   Janome kabushiki kaisha, *Janome mishin sōgyō 50 nenshi* (Tokyo: Janome kabushiki kaisha, 1971); Kuwahara Tetsuya, 'Shoki takokuseki kigyō no tainichi toshi to minzoku kigyō', *Kokumin keizai zasshi*, Vol. 185, No. 5 (February 2002), p. 50.

[29]   Cited by Fukushima Hachirō, 'Geppu, wappu, kurejitto', in *Gekkan Kurejitto*, No. 200 (1973), p. 20.

[30]   On Seligman, see Calder, *Financing the American Dream*, pp. 237–48.

[31]   Tokyo shōkō kaigisho, *Geppu hanbai seido*, p. 227.

Although instalment selling was both an imported American practice and a modernized form of an indigenous practice, and was sometimes recognized as both, the imported practice drew more attention. An academic article from 1933 based on a survey of 254 instalment sellers in Osaka and Tokyo claims the salaried urban life 'perfected' in the mid-1920s was a 'cultured life' centred on 'so-called "American goods"' such as sewing machines and pianos.[32] By 1934, according to another survey, conducted by the city of Tokyo, roughly 10,000 of 130,000 retailers in Greater Tokyo offered their goods 'on time'. In all, 8 per cent of Tokyo retail sales were estimated to be made through instalment plans, said to be a remarkably high number for a new practice.[33] The top goods sold on credit were men's Western dress, bicycles, automobiles, shoes, radios, sewing machines, books, medical and scientific equipment (including cameras), watches and jewellery, and Western furniture. Clearly the link between consumer credit and a new consumer life tied to goods of Euro-American origin was intimate. Almost all the items on this list were products of Western material and for the most part industrial civilization.

Through the 1930s (and beyond), both in goods consumed and in the use of credit to buy them, Japan was certainly playing catch-up to the global leaders, beginning with the United States. But as the almost immediate appropriation of Seligman's work on credit suggests, people in Japan took part more fully in the self-consciousness of modern consumerism than in the socio-economic practice of modern consumption. The effort to study these transformations of daily life proceeded in near simultaneity with similar assessments in the consumer societies of the West.

The Tokyo Chamber of Commerce was among the most noteworthy in its prescient perspective. The preface to its 1929 report states that:

> To recover from the long recession...along with urging the rationalization of management...it is necessary to reform the consumer economy, increase the efficiency of consumption, eliminate waste, lower the expense of daily life, and thus rationalize daily life.... The skillful operation of this [instalment credit] system can make a major contribution to rationalization of both management and daily life. From the perspective of the consumer, instalment purchases allow one to buy goods of considerable cost, which is far more economical [in the long run] than purchase of inexpensive shoddy goods with cash...this allows one to level out expenditures over time. It is not only extremely useful in order to lead a disciplined life, planning a monthly budget of expenses; it also raises standards of living by allowing purchase of goods otherwise too expensive.[34]

Most striking in this passage is the appreciation of instalment credit as a form of social discipline not unlike investment or savings. Although Seligman in his classic 1927 defence of consumer credit recognized the disciplining function of instalment credit,

[32] Hirai Yasutaro, 'Honpō ni okeru bunkatsu barai seido no genjō ni oite', *Kokumin keizai zasshi*, Vol. 43, No. 2 (1933), pp. 69–73, 81.
[33] Tokyo shiyakusho, kōgyōkyoku, shōgyōka, *Wappu hanbai ni kan suru chōsa* (Tokyo: Tokyo shiyakusho, 1935).
[34] Tokyo shōkō kaigisho, *Geppu hanbai seido*, pp. 1–2.

he was less explicit than these Tokyo authors in stressing its centrality.[35] The Chamber of Commerce authors find it a strange fact that in the land of the most developed market for instalment purchase, there seems to be more opposition than support.[36] By the late 1920s, Japanese observers were in the forefront of global trends in their insights on the significance of American-style instalment selling.

Opinions on consumer borrowing, it is important to note, also included contrary voices worried that instalment credit might fray the social fabric, make buying too easy, and overextend a consumer beyond the ability to pay. As a rhetoric extolling traditional values gained force along the road to war, one outraged marketing expert wrote in 1938 that 'the American-style system of instalment selling is extremely cruel and completely at odds with the spirit of the Japanese nation and the virtue of Japanese people.'[37]

While debate over credit constituted one stream of the modern discourse of consumer life, another more pervasive flow of words swirled around the effort in a context of rapid change to define or defend a particular Japanese identity in daily life and consumer choices. Discussion was most often directed at the threat or promise of what came to be called the 'two-layered life' (*ni-jū seikatsu*, also translatable as 'double life'). The term refers to the simultaneous presence of goods and practices described as 'Western' and 'Japanese' in realms of food, housing, and dress. Newspapers, magazines—especially those for women—and more academic publications for professionals in fields such as architecture and home economics were full of anxious discussion of the pros and cons of practices such as tatami-sitting versus use of chairs or the merits of Japanese kimono versus Western dress.

The Japanese state played an important part in framing this discussion of the 'two-layered life' and daily life more generally. In the immediate aftermath of the First World War, as the state significantly broadened its efforts to reinforce order in a complex, contentious society, bureaucrats allied themselves with middle-class reformers and experts in various fields. Officials in the Home Ministry and the Ministry of Education played the key role in founding one such initiative in 1919, the League to Reform Everyday Life. Over the following years, in publications, exhibitions, and lectures, the League connected state officials with outside experts and activists. Attentive to each other and to the work of counterparts in Europe and North America in fields ranging from architecture to home economics, they organized more narrowly focused committees concerned with rational and scientific housing, food, and clothing.[38]

The Japan Dress Reform Association was one such organization. Founded in 1921, the Association sought to relieve the burden of the 'two-layered life' by designing reformed versions of Western-style dress which better fit Japanese bodies. To this end, it published a book written by two of its leading members, the husband and wife team of

---

[35] Calder, *Financing the American Dream*, pp. 29–33.
[36] Tokyo shōkō kaigisho *Geppu hanbai seido*, pp. 181–8.
[37] Matsumiya Saburo, *Sugu kiku kōkoku* (Tokyo: Mikasa shobō, 1938), pp. 77–80.
[38] On these campaigns more generally, Garon, *Molding Japanese Minds*, pp. 10–15. On the League's efforts in housing reform, Sand, *House and Home in Modern Japan*, pp. 16–19, 181–202.

Ozaki Yoshitarō and Gen. The work itself was a consumer good of sorts. Titled *Economic Reform: Sewing for the Future*, this nearly 500-page tome sold 70,000 copies. It argued that for reformed dress to prevail, it had to be simple enough to fabricate in the home, with or without a sewing machine, and it had to be economic in its use of fabric. It also had to allow free and active movement.[39]

Hata Rimuko, head of the Singer Sewing Academy, founded by the company to educate both customers and its own cadres of teachers, picked up the thread of this concern in the 1924 preface to the second edition of her bestselling sewing textbook:

> Recently, the numbers of women and children wearing Western clothes has increased greatly. This appears at first to be a welcome trend, but if this is simply a matter of pursuing fashion with no sense of principle, it is most regrettable. The burden placed on the nation by the spread to women of the two-layered life in clothing is fearful even to think about.[40]

She continued by noting that the 'double life' burden could be solved 'if it were possible to simply cease making Japanese dress', but she had to admit 'far into the future, women are not going to abandon Japanese dress.' Given this situation, she offered some options to ease the economic and decision-making burden of the 'double life' in dress: limit Japanese wear to ceremonial occasions; only gradually move from Western dress for work to Western dress for social events; or adopt those Western fashions such as the 'one piece' dress which are similar in fit to Japanese clothing and relatively easy to sew. Hata was well aware that Western dress was more adaptable to sewing by machine than Japanese dress, or at least that users believed this to be true. Her interest as head of the Singer Sewing Academy was unambiguous: the more quickly women moved to Western dress, the better. Her remarkably cautious and defensive advocacy of Western dress despite her self-interest makes clear that dress for female consumers carried a particular burden of defining cultural identity in a changing world.

Hata's dilemma continued to surface in debates concerning the pros and cons of hand versus machine sewing and the merits of Japanese versus Western dress. As such debate took place with growing frequency in the 1920s, some of Japan's best-known writers, such as Tanizaki Junichirō, were writing with elegant nostalgia about what they saw as a sad disappearance of traditional lifestyles in the face of the uncritical embrace of the modern and the Western.[41] Such writing rested on a commonsense binary opposition that in Hata's case set Japanese sewing, hand stitching, kimono dress, and 'tradition' against Western sewing, sewing machines and machine stitching, Western dress, and 'modernity'. But here and in debates over daily life reform more generally, it is misleading to map the struggle as a fight between 'Japanese' tradition and 'Western' modernity.

[39] Inoue Masato, *Yōfuku to Nihonjin: kokumin fuku to iu moodo* (Tokyo: Kōsaidō shuppan, 2001), pp. 143–5, 221. The Japanese name for the Japan Dress Reform Association is Nihon fukusō kaizen kai.
[40] Hata Rimuko, *Mishin saihō hitori manabi* (Tokyo: Hata shoten shuppan bu, 1933). 3rd edn., pp. 3–4, reprints preface to 2nd edn.
[41] Works by Tanizaki that evoke this spirit include *Some Prefer Nettles*, first published in Japanese in 1928 and *In Praise of Shadows*, first published in Japanese in 1933.

Each party to this debate was making a claim for the consumer practices best suited to its particular understanding of a life that was both 'Japanese' *and* modern, one which accepted and often embraced values of rationality, speed, and efficiency, and sometimes freedom of choice even as it celebrated Japaneseness.

The modern discourse of the consumer in Japan was complex not only because those who defended traditional patterns of consumption argued their case on modern grounds. Another significant and enduring complexity of the inter-war discourse of consumption was that some understood the modern consumer as a disciplined subject of the modern nation, others saw her as a legitimate seeker of personal fulfilment and pleasure, and some saw her as both. Consider, for example, a 1936 newspaper advertisement placed by a domestic producer of sewing machines seeking to compete with Singer. Next to the profile of an elegant Caucasian-appearing woman, the ad copy reads: 'You! This year's resolution is to earn a ton with your woman's hand! It's shop 'til you drop, as fast as you can.' The lengthy text goes on to explain that, 'the American woman is the one who plays more, buys more, and earns more than any in the world. In our country as well, in 1936, one new trend for women is to earn without hesitation, and to quickly buy whatever you like without holding back.' However, the reader is asked, how on earth can a woman with obligations to do so much housework find time to earn and then to spend money? The answer is simple: 'the problem is solved perfectly by bringing in science.' If one buys a scientific product such as a sewing machine, one can economize on time and expenses and use the profit to shop to one's heart's content.[42] The ad thus brilliantly juxtaposed the scientific, frugal, and rational aspect of modernity with the face of the pleasure-seeking consumer, and it validated both aspects.

The Consumer and Wartime Modernity

The newspapers which ran such ads already blanketed the nation by the end of the 1920s. Over the next decade the level of media saturation increased sharply due to a combination of new technology, increased prosperity and purchasing power, and the collaborative effort of state and private actors to mobilize for war and chronicle its progress. In a bit more than a decade the newest mass medium, radio, soared in popularity. Subscriber households rose tenfold, from 650,000 in 1929 to 6.6 million by 1941. The number continued to climb through the Pacific War, reaching a peak of 7.5 million in 1944. Geographies of region and of class changed as a result. In the late 1920s, listening to the radio at home was the privilege of the urban middle class. Even at the end of the war, as photographs and accounts of groups listening to the Emperor's surrender broadcast attest, listening to the radio was sometimes a communal activity, especially in the

---

[42] *Asahi Shinbun*, 9 January 1936, p. 5.

countryside. But over the course of the 1930s, radio came to cast a far wider net. In the early 1930s, roughly one in four urban households subscribed to NHK radio broadcasts, but only one in twenty rural homes did so. By early 1940 radio use in the cities had doubled, but use in the countryside rose fourfold; NHK's 'Radio Yearbook' for 1940 reports that one in five rural households were subscribers.[43] The radio was both the most widely owned electric good for use inside the home, and a primary means to bring additional information and dreams, whether of economy, empire, and conquest, of education and culture, or of sports and amusement, into the lives of millions of people.

The surge in radio subscriptions resulted in significant part from intense media competition to cover and to glorify Japan's new imperialism of the 1930s. Sparked especially by the Manchurian Incident in September of 1931, newspapers such as *Asahi* and *Mainichi* competed with each other, and with NHK, to be first with the top stories of the day; they turned to aeroplanes to send reporters and film to and from the continent, and they turned to newsreels and movie theatres, as well as newsprint, to reach a fast-growing mass audience. Spurred by the advent of 'talkies', movie audiences nearly tripled in size in the decade from 1930, surpassing 400 million viewers at 2,363 theatres by 1940, an average of nearly six films per person per year. In sum, as historian Louise Young concludes, the Manchurian Incident sparked a dramatic 'growth spurt' for an already strong news industry, a 'process of innovation and expansion in the mass production of an industrialized mass culture.'[44]

War and entertainment coexisted throughout the decade, and despite rising political tensions between the United States and Japan, the American origin of so much of mass cultural production did not impede its enjoyment. Charlie Chaplin's May 1932 visit to Japan was the focus of huge popular interest, even though it coincided with the assassination of Prime Minister Inukai. Japan's first professional baseball teams began to compete regularly in 1934. That same year, thousands of people thronged to see Babe Ruth play with an American team in 18 exhibition games in 12 major cities during a month-long tour. A capacity crowd of 65,000 jammed the stadium in Tokyo for the first game. Pro baseball continued to be played until November 1944.

The frequent convening of such commercial public spectacles coincided with the proliferation of new forms of retail shopping, and new services and habits of personal decoration, especially for women, part of a quickly changing urban landscape centred on the modern middle-class consumer. Hair salons spread throughout Japanese cities in the 1930s, offering permanents to thousands of middle-class women. By 1939 there were about 850 such hair salons in Tokyo alone. Sewing schools and dress shops likewise expanded in popularity more rapidly in the 1930s than before. By 1943, at the height of the war, no less than 1,282 dress shops (572 owned or operated by women) were in business in Tokyo alone.[45] In tandem with these trends, the sales and ownership rates of

[43] Nihon hōsō kyōkai, *Rajio nenkan* (Tokyo: Nihon hōsō kyōkai, 1940), p. 270.

[44] Louise Young, *Japan's Total Empire: Manchuria and the Culture of Wartime Imperialism* (Berkeley: University of California Press, 1998), p. 68.

[45] Nakayama Chiyo, *Nihon fujin yōsō shi* (Tokyo: Yoshikawa kōbunkan, 1987), pp. 411–25.

sewing machines spiked upward sharply in the 1930s, with the greatest increase in fact coming between 1935 and 1940. By the eve of the Pacific War, nearly one in ten Japanese households owned a sewing machine. And of great fascination for male media and culture critics, as well as of course for women themselves, both on grounds of fashion and of purported rationality, the 1930s saw a significant acceleration in a shift toward women's Western dress. It was said to be more efficient for factory workers, safer for evacuation in case of earthquake or fire, and more comfortable for all manner of daily activity.

In sum, although a wide gap remained between the modern consumer life as dream and as materially owned reality, across the 1930s it began to close; a significantly expanded proportion of people in Japan, especially in the cities, came to possess the objects that defined middle-class modernity. An even greater proportion joined modern life simply by strolling along city streets, reading monthly magazines, going to the movies, or listening to radio broadcasts on subjects ranging from English or sewing lessons to Olympic sports. At the very least, this expansion of the realm of material and cultural modernity took place *in spite of* the drift toward war; one sees a persistent rise in consumption and continued attraction to a life of modern mass leisure despite the increasingly censorious demands of wartime political leaders that people offer patriotic service in a time of emergency, live more simply, and reject American ways.

Ironically, however, this modern life of consuming and leisure also spread *because of* the efforts to cope with Depression and war. First, and most obviously, after the Manchurian Incident the economy recovered smartly from the Depression, sparked in part by war-induced deficit spending, giving more people the means to buy consumer goods and take part in modern leisure activities. Second, as both state and commercial media beat the drums for war, modern media spread their reach ever further. Third, the logic of 'rationalization' first articulated during the recession and Depression from the late 1920s included calls not only for streamlining and frugality, but also injunctions to modernize material life including wartime dress for both men and women.

With luxury the enemy and Hollywood the ever tempting dream, the desires of the modern consumer thus persisted into the dark heart of wartime. But with the year 1939 one turning-point, and 1942–43 a more decisive break, the combination of increasingly stringent economic policies and a growing scarcity of resources came to limit the ability of women and men to pursue their modern pleasures. In an effort to hold down inflation and protect the purchasing power of a labour force mobilized for war, the government imposed price and wage controls in 1939 and put in place rules limiting the free movement of workers. These policies, designed to end the 'wasteful' competition of a market economy and funnel capital and raw materials to military production, made it increasingly difficult to manufacture and sell consumer goods. By 1944–45, a home front nightmare of scarcity, rationing, and fire-bombing turned the story of consumption into a desperate tale of struggle to survive.

Yet, to present consumption in Japan after Pearl Harbor as a linear narrative of inexorable constriction fails to capture the complexity of negotiations to control tastes across realms from music to hair styles to dress which continued at least until 1944, and it misunderstands their outcome. In *Blue Nippon*, E. Taylor Atkins argues that the persistence of jazz in wartime Japan sparked relatively creative efforts, however riddled with contradiction, to devise an 'authentic' Japanese jazz.[46] Echoing the improvisations of jazz, those who designed clothes, taught sewing, or used sewing machines took part in a tortured wartime effort to design an 'authentically' Japanese but functionally modern dress, dubbed 'people's dress' in the case of men and 'standard dress' for women.[47] These efforts to define a 'Japanese' daily life in a time of total war, one can say—at some risk of giving insufficient weight to its ultimate horror—were ironically productive. Amid a flood of rhetoric that condemned the modern and the West for corrupting the purity of the Japanese nation and soul, people were searching not so much for a traditional essence as for an 'appropriately Japanese' modernity.

The Post-war Ascendance
of Consumers

The more recent history of consumption in Japan marks a quantitative break with the past in that levels of consumption soared from the 1950s through the 1990s. But in terms of the actors and their behaviour, the goods desired, and the way they were discussed, the post-war story does not so much break with the past as build upon it. Mass media had been central to the promotion of inter-war and wartime modernity, and the first surge in the post-war return to a 'normal' daily life of modern goods and pleasures came in the production of texts, voices, and moving images. A voracious public consumed all manner of books, magazines, radio broadcasts, popular music, and movies, ranging from the so-called 'dregs literature' obsessed with the erotic, to political satire and analysis, to English conversation manuals and programmes.[48]

For several years thereafter, shortages and rationing inhibited the purchase of the material goods of modern life, but as soon as the means were at hand, renewed growth in consumption further narrowed the gap between the dream of modern life and its material attainment. The new element here was not the particular goods desired, but the fact that these so increasingly—and famously—came to be made in Japan, not only for domestic use but for export. This process began in the years of American occupation with the continued 'mechanization' of the household, a trend that began in the pre-war decades, pre-dating the more famous era of 'household electrification'. One important good in this process was the sewing machine; it allowed buyers, including thousands of

---

[46] E. Taylor Atkins, *Blue Nippon: Authenticating Jazz in Japan* (Durham, NC: Duke University Press, 2001), pp. 127–63.

[47] Andrew Gordon, *Fabricating Consumers: The Sewing Machine in Modern Japan* (Berkeley: University of California Press, 2011), ch. 5; Inoue Masato, *Yōfuku to Nihonji: kokuminfuku to iu moodo* (Tokyo: Kōsaidō, 2001).

[48] John Dower, *Embracing Defeat: Japan in the Wake of World War II* (New York: Norton, 1999), Part II (chs. 3–5), superbly evokes this cultural efflorescence.

war widows, to earn money as seamstresses or homeworkers, even as it was marketed as a scientific object of high technology or as a glamorous, even sexy, symbol of a bright new modern life. In 1951 Japanese makers were selling over 1 million household machines per year, about two-thirds for export; by 1952 domestic sales topped 500,000 machines.[49] Then, from the mid-1950s, as a government White Paper famously declared 'the postwar era is over', the electrification of Japanese households began in earnest. According to one survey, by 1960 the proportion of Japan's 20 million households owning key household consumer goods stood as follows: radios, 89 per cent; sewing machines, 72 per cent; bicycles, 66 per cent; televisions, 54 per cent; cameras, 47 per cent; electric washing-machines, 45 per cent; electric fans, 42 per cent; electric rice cookers, 38 per cent; transistor radios, 25 per cent; electric phonographs, 20 per cent; electric refrigerators, 16 per cent, and motorbikes, 12 per cent.[50]

This nearly vertical take-off of the consumer economy was fuelled by credit. Beginning in 1948 and 1949, manufacturers of bicycles, radios, and sewing machines once again began to offer their goods on the instalment plan. In an important post-war innovation, which anticipated the credit cards of several decades later, newly founded finance companies offered credit tickets to consumers, usually through their employers. A consumer/employee would use the tickets, denominated like paper currency, to purchase goods at participating stores. The store redeemed the ticket for cash with the issuing lender. The lender then collected the face value plus interest in monthly instalments from the consumer. This system offered flexible instalment credit to buy all sorts of goods and even services such as movie tickets. It proved extremely popular.[51] By the end of the decade, purchasing by instalment was the method of choice for consumers seeking the 'cultural' goods that defined the bright new life of peacetime and prosperity. Their collective shopping binge transformed radios and sewing machines, then washing-machines, televisions, refrigerators, vacuum cleaners, cameras, motorbikes, and (later) automobiles from luxuries to virtual necessities of the burgeoning middle-class masses.

Although they sometimes feared that excessive consumption would spark dangerous inflation or erode social discipline, observers at the time echoed and drew upon the precocious appreciation of consumer credit found in pre-war discourse. They noted that such credit fuelled demand and served as an engine of the national economy by connecting manufacturers, lenders, and consumers in a virtuous circle of growth. As early as 1952, the economist Kawauchi Mamoru praised instalment selling for 'bringing latent demand to the surface' and bringing 'planning into daily life and regulating consumption.'[52] The Tokyo Chamber of Commerce echoed Kawauchi as well as its own

---

[49] Tsūsho sangyō shō (ed.), *Nihon bōeki no genjō* (Tokyo: Tsūsho sangyō chōsakai, 1954), p. 59.
[50] Nihon mishin kyōkai (ed.), *Nihon mishin sangyō shi* (Tokyo: Nihon mishin kyōkai, 1961), p. 7.
[51] Andrew Gordon, 'From Sewing Machines to Credit Cards: Consumer Credit in Modern Japan', in Sheldon Garon and Patricia MacLachlan (eds.), *The Ambivalent Consumer: Questioning Consumption in East Asia and the West* (Ithaca: Cornell University Press, 2006), pp. 147–62.
[52] Kawauchi Mamoru, 'Geppu hanbai no keizaigaku', *Nihon mishin Taimusu*, No. 172 (1952), p. 9.

rhetoric of the late 1920s in a publication of 1957, neatly encapsulating the 'Fordist' logic of consumer society and political economy consolidated across the transwar era:

> The installment sales system helps first of all manufacturers, but also retailers, to expand commodity markets. It plays an extremely significant role in sales strategies to insure stable sales volumes. In addition, of course it brings the benefit of raising the standard of living to consumers and rationalizes consumer outlays.[53]

As such claims linked borrowing to social discipline and investment as well as to economic growth, they had much in common with the logic of savings promotion which was powerfully articulated in Japan during these same years. That is, post-war citizens were urged to save as a cornerstone of a responsible and disciplined economic life that would benefit producers by providing needed investment capital, but would also benefit individuals and families by providing the wherewithal for future consumption.[54]

Once the basics of the bright new life were widely possessed, Japan's consumer society arguably entered a new stage, what the sociologist Yoshimi Shunya has labelled the 'post-postwar' era.[55] He identifies the decade from the early 1970s into the 1980s as the transition point. Globally and in Japan, consumer life first came to be marked by a new degree of segmentation into various niches of consumption, and more recently it has been characterized by the rise of 'virtual' consumption of culture through new information technologies. As with consumer goods of the high growth post-war era, key products in 'post-postwar' times, not only hardware but software such as computer games or cell phone novels, were made in Japan and circulated globally. This process reflected a growing local creativity. High-growth era exports by companies such as Sony and Honda, that is, were innovative in quality and in design, but radios and cars had already been invented and developed in the West. In the 'post-postwar' era, Japan began to produce and export cultural goods of local conception, from Hello Kitty paraphernalia and transformer toys to manga to anime. These goods constituted what the journalist Douglas McGray dubbed, in a well-known essay in 2001, 'Japan's Gross National Cool'.[56] Their popularity continued throughout the first decade of the new century. For McGray—who drew on Joseph Nye's analysis of the cultural dimension of national strength—these cultural productions constituted 'a vast reserve of potential soft power.' That contention is difficult to assess. But the circulation of consumer entertainment from and into Japan in recent years has surely played some part in connecting cultural worlds among people in Asia as well as outside it. Millions of young Koreans have come to enjoy Japanese popular music. Millions of Japanese women have thrilled to the exploits of the dashing young Bae Yong Joon, nicknamed Yon-sama, the star of a Korean television drama, *Winter Sonata*. Bae was at the forefront of the 'Korean Wave'

---

[53] Tokyo shōkō kaigisho, *Wappu hanbai ni kan suru jittai chōsa* (Tokyo: Tokyo shōkō kaigisho, 1957), p. 1.
[54] Sheldon Garon, *Beyond our Means: Why America Spends While the World Saves* (Princeton: Princeton University Press, 2012).
[55] Yoshimi Shunya, *Posuto sengo shakai* (Tokyo: Iwanami shoten, 2009).
[56] Douglas McGray, 'Japan's Gross National Cool', *Foreign Policy* No. 130 (2002) pp. 44–54.

of the late 1990s, referring to the growing popularity of Korean popular culture in China, Japan, and South-East Asia as well.

The irony is that this surge in new forms of cultural production and consumption has coincided not only with two decades of relative economic stagnation in Japan, but also with a levelling off in the purchase of 'traditional' modern goods. Most notably, both domestic consumption and, perhaps most significantly, the expressed desire for owning automobiles among young Japanese consumers declined substantially in the first decade of the twenty-first century.[57] This trend is perhaps as good a marker as any of a world of postmodern consumer life.

In writing this chapter, I have relied on works in Japanese as well as a number of excellent recent works in English, noted in the bibliography and for the most part written in the past decade. The appearance of this work indicates a healthy interest in the history of consumption and consumerism in Japan, but there is certainly room for additional work. One fruitful avenue is the study of particular goods—the ways they were sold, the uses to which they were put, the meanings ascribed to them. Items that would repay careful attention include bicycles, radios, and pianos, as well as more personal items linked to changing bodily practices such as stockings and high-tech toilets.[58] Another issue deserving more systematic attention is the spatial configuration of consumption in modern Japan, both regionally— with attention to provincial cities and towns as well as to rural areas—and across the colonial empire. Finally, although the fact that post-war Japan was marked simultaneously by extremely high rates of saving and consistent expansion of domestic consumption has been noted by economic historians, the cultural meaning of this conjuncture has yet to be fully explored.[59] The Japanese case of avid spending alongside devoted saving offers fertile ground for exploring the process by which modern citizens or subjects are not so much liberated as they are disciplined by their consumption practices.

BIBLIOGRAPHY

Berry, Mary Elizabeth, *Japan in Print: Information and Nation in the Early Modern Period* (Berkeley: University of California Press, 2007).
Francks, Penelope, *The Japanese Consumer: An Alternative Economic History of Modern Japan* (Cambridge: Cambridge University Press, 2009).
Garon, Sheldon *Beyond Our Means: Why America Spends While the World Saves* (Princeton: Princeton University Press, 2012).
Gordon, Andrew, *Fabricating Consumers: The Sewing Machine in Modern Japan* (Berkeley: University of California Press, 2011).

[57] 'Atama itai kuruma banare', *Asahi Shinbun*, 28 July 2008, p. 3.
[58] Scholars in Japan have undertaken some impressive efforts already. One pioneering work is Amano Masako and Sakurai Atsushi, *'Mono to onna' no sengoshi: shintaisei, kateisei, shakaisei o juku ni* (Tokyo: Yūshindō, 1992).
[59] For the economic data, Charles Horioka, 'Consuming and Saving', in Andrew Gordon (ed.) *Postwar Japan as History* (Berkeley: University of California Press, 1993), pp. 259–92.

Hanley, Susan, *Everyday Things in Premodern Japan: The Hidden Legacy of Material Culture* (Berkeley: University of California Press, 1997).

Masako, Amano and Atsushi, Sakurai, '*Mono to onna' no sengoshi: shintaisei, kateisei, shakaisei o juku ni* (Tokyo: Yūshindō, 1992).

O'Bryan, Scott, *The Growth Idea: Purpose and Prosperity in Postwar Japan* (Honolulu: University of Hawaii Press, 2009).

Partner, Simon, *Assembled in Japan: Electrical Goods and the Making of the Japanese Consumer* (Berkeley: University of California Press, 1999).

Sand, Jordan, *House and Home in Modern Japan: Architecture, Domestic Space, and Bourgeois Culture* (Cambridge, MA: Harvard University Asia Center, 2003).

Silverberg, Miriam, *Erotic Grotesque Nonsense: The Mass Culture of Japanese Modern Times* (Berkeley: University of California Press, 2006).

Young, Louise, *Beyond the Metropolis* (Berkeley: University of California Press, 2012).

CHAPTER 26

....

CONSUMER MOVEMENTS

....

MATTHEW HILTON

CONSUMERS do not just shop; they organize. Think of all the options open to consumers today if they want to do more than just spend, spend, spend. They can select from an array of magazines to assist them in making ethical consumer decisions. They can show their solidarity with poor farmers and labourers around the world by purchasing fair-trade products. They can choose to opt out of the consumer rat race by supporting local producers, and organic farms, and even make collective decisions to turn entire towns into Slow Food capitals. Alternatively, they can join consumer co-operatives and seek a non-capitalist mechanism for organizing the market and the economy. Indeed, today, worldwide, perhaps as many as 900 million have elected to do just that. And consumers do not just organize to assist their own choices. They do so to set the boundaries and parameters of choice for everybody. They can seek representation on bodies that ensure our essential goods industries and services are regulated. They can lobby corporations and public bodies to ensure the consumer voice is heard. And they can seek to have a say in who gets what, at what price, in what quantity, and through what means.

The phenomena of consumer organizing, consumer protesting, consumer activism, and consumer movements are not just confined to recent decades. Ever since consumer society was 'born'—either in the eighteenth century or even earlier depending on your definition—it seems the rise of the acquisitive collector of material possessions has been accompanied by the politicized purchaser, the conscientious consumer, and the sympathetic shopper. While many consumers have undoubtedly displayed a voracious appetite for getting ever more stuff, others have demonstrated an engaged form of citizenship eager to inject morality and politics into the marketplace. Consumers have boycotted and campaigned against injustice from slavery to apartheid. They have fought for a living wage and the right of themselves and others to participate in the good life. They have cooperated, tested, lobbied, and pressured in order to identify problems in the marketplace and work out solutions, usually without recourse to the political ideologies that have so often motivated other social movements.

Yet for all that the study of consumption has expanded exponentially over the last three decades, it is only relatively recently that our knowledge of these movements has come anywhere close to catching up with what is known about, say, consumer psychology, consumer marketing, consumer economics, or the cultural practices of shoppers. Historians and political scientists have developed the field of consumption studies into areas of activism and social movements. They have uncovered a huge range of motivations that lie behind why consumers organize collectively or have sought guidance for ways in which to shop other than as self-interested individuals. They have gone some considerable way, though there is clearly scope for further research, to demonstrate the importance of consumer agency in shaping the direction and development of consumer society as a whole.

In this chapter I want, first, to set out why scholars of consumption have turned to an analysis of consumer activism. Secondly, I want to offer a broad chronology of consumer movements to show the different types of consumer politics that have emerged over the last 200 years. And, thirdly, I want to set out some of the areas to which future scholars of consumption and social movements might turn their attention. Indeed, so long as consumers continue to find ever new means of engaging with the marketplace ('carrot mobbing'[1] is perhaps the latest form of consumer activism), scholars will maintain their interest in the array of factors that ensure that consumption is about far more than just shopping.

THE STUDY OF CONSUMER MOVEMENTS

Just as sociologists, anthropologists, and cultural studies scholars began to unpack the variety of ways in which consumers interact with the world of goods around them, so too were historians discovering that various types of consumer had occupied a crucial role in shaping the development of consumer society. For some time, social historians had moved away from the realm of the workplace and socio-political movements of labour in order to understand the hopes and desires of ordinary people. This had led to an outpouring of work in the 1970s and 1980s on the history of popular culture and everyday life in Europe and America. It was becoming obvious that how the working classes spent their money was just as important an area of historical analysis as how they earned it. Yet often this scholarship turned its attention to leisure and consumption only in order to explain away other phenomena. For many scholars of popular culture what needed to be understood was the absence of political activity of workers: consumption, here, as in the Frankfurt School, might have been enjoyed by the ordinary man and woman, but essentially it remained a diversion from, to put it simplistically, the 'forward march of labour'.

---

[1] 'Carrotmob is a method of activism that leverages consumer power to make the most socially responsible business practices also the most profitable choices. Businesses compete with one another to see who can do the most good, and then a big mob of consumers buys products in order to reward whichever business made the strongest commitment to improve the world.' See http://www.carrotmob.org, accessed 8 June 2011.

That said, there was emerging in this historical literature a sense too that it was through popular culture, leisure, and consumption generally that identities were being forged, and that these identities were as much an expression of political hopes and aspirations as they were of self-expression. Detailed investigations by American historians found that political attitudes were being developed as much through consumption as they were through production.[2] Lawrence Glickman argued that movements of workers needed to be understood too as movements of consumers. The fight for a 'living wage' in America at the turn of the twentieth century was a product of a political consciousness formed as much by expenditure as by earnings: indeed, the point was that wages and prices, getting and spending, production and consumption, were not thought of as discrete entities in the minds of those who wanted to participate in consumer society.[3]

Such a turn in the literature chimed with those European scholars who had long seen in consumers' cooperation a movement which embraced ordinary people's role as consumers as well as producers.[4] And for many women's historians, it was increasingly observed that not only was consumption an arena through which women could gain access to the political sphere but one which women organized specifically as consumers, either to act as the moral conscience of the marketplace or as citizens fighting for a political contract over the cost of living.[5]

Finally, in a perhaps more unrelated development, political scientists also came to be interested in movements of consumers. Although they remain a minority specialism within a wider field, certain scholars have sought to examine the political role of consumer interest groups, particularly in the post-Second World War period. On the one hand, this interest has emerged out of a globalization and new social movement literature which has explored post-materialist solidarities in, for example, the green movement, the peace movement, and student protests. Over the last two decades, it has been noted how consumers have behaved as political subjects to tackle many of the issues associated with globalization, from boycotting the products of global corporations to choosing fairly traded and ethically manufactured goods.[6] On the other hand, a more established form of political analysis has sought to uncover a neglected group of organized interests in society and politics: that of consumer pressure groups. Important here has been the

[2] Lizabeth Cohen, *Making a New Deal: Industrial Workers in Chicago, 1919–1939* (Cambridge: Cambridge University Press, 1990).

[3] Lawrence B. Glickman, *A Living Wage: American Workers and the Making of Consumer Society* (Ithaca, NY: Cornell University Press, 1997).

[4] Ellen Furlough and Carl Strikwerda (eds.), *Consumers Against Capitalism? Consumer Co-operation in Europe, North America and Japan, 1840–1990* (Oxford: Rowman & Littlefield, 1999); Ellen Furlough, *Consumer Co-operation in Modern France: The Politics of Consumption* (Ithaca, NY: Cornell University Press, 1991); Peter Gurney, *Co-operative Culture and the Politics of Consumption in England, c.1870–1930* (Manchester: Manchester University Press, 1996); Johnston Birchall, *The International Co-operative Movement* (Manchester: Manchester University Press, 1997).

[5] Matthew Hilton, 'The female consumer and the politics of consumption in twentieth-century Britain', *The Historical Journal*, 45/1 (2002), pp. 103–28.

[6] Michele Micheletti, *Political Virtue and Shopping: Individuals, Consumerism and Collective Action* (London: Palgrave, 2003).

work Patricia Maclachlan on Japanese consumer groups and Gunnar Trumbull's exploration of consumer protection regimes in post-war Germany and France.[7]

From all such directions, then, by the end of the 1990s there had emerged a growing recognition that ordinary people have and do mobilize as consumers. Moreover, they have done so, and continue to do so, not because they are somehow trapped in a state of false consciousness, but because consumer activism represents a rational political approach to tackling the sort of everyday concerns that citizens face. Consumer movements have been a significant driver of history. The analysis of them, either in the past or the present, has the potential to unpack both the very meaning of consumer society and the alternative visions and values upon which consumers themselves have hoped consumer society might be based.

A TYPOLOGY OF CONSUMER MOVEMENTS

The history of consumer movements can be roughly divided into three types. Although there is overlap between them, and the types of movement do not always match neatly onto precise historical periods, they do form something of a chronology. The first type of consumer movement that has existed is that which has involved the mobilization of consumers around the concerns of other types of person: for instance, the slave, the worker, the child. If it maps onto a specific period, it was from the end of the eighteenth century to the early twentieth century. A second type of consumer movement is that which sees consumers organize both to protect their own self-interest and to campaign for the rights of all consumers. The two key instances of this form of consumer movement are the consumer co-operative movement which began in the latter half of the nineteenth century and peaked in the mid-twentieth, and the consumer goods and services testing movement which became a global movement in the second half of the twentieth century. A final type of consumer movement is that which has emerged over the last two to three decades and which is associated with ethical consumerism, green consumerism and fair-trade. In many ways, this marks a return to the duties many consumers felt towards the welfare of others that marked many movements in the nineteenth century. But because they have become so prevalent and are predicated upon a consumer consciousness that is focused on not one issue but a whole range of issues (often associated with the umbrella term, globalization), it requires separate treatment and analysis.

The starting point for our first period and type of consumer movement might be the American War of Independence. As T. H. Breen has argued, the boycotts and commercial protests of the American Revolution constituted the first organized consumer

---

[7] Patricia L. Maclachlan, *Consumer Politics in Postwar Japan: The Institutional Boundaries of Citizen Activism* (New York: Columbia University Press, 2002); Gunnar Trumbull, *Consumer Capitalism: Politics, Product Markets and Firm Strategy in France and Germany* (Ithaca, NY: Cornell University Press, 2006).

movement.[8] However, this mobilization of consumer power to serve another political purpose is more usually associated with the duties affluent shoppers felt towards the disadvantaged either at home or abroad. The most widely cited instigator of this form of consumer mobilization was the anti-slavery movement. Women in Britain and America purchased brooches, badges, ribbons, pins, buttons, and jewellery bearing the legend 'Am I not a man and a brother?', in order to protest against the slave trade in the 1790s. Accused of merely purchasing items to engage in fashionable dispute rather than contributing directly to the public sphere of political debate, women consumers especially brought the private into the public as they went on to boycott sugar, the virtue of abstinence here incapable of being dismissed quite so readily as a mere 'feminine trifle'. In the United States, this was followed by a 'free produce' movement, begun by Quakers in the 1820s, which sought to sell basic staples not produced by slave labour.[9]

Not all consumer movements of this period were so socially progressive. In the United States boycotts may well have been launched by abolitionists but they were also instigated by Southern advocates of 'non-intercourse' with the North.[10] Self-interest, too, could be a factor. Later in the century, consumer groups emerged in many British municipalities to campaign for better access to utilities such as water, gas, and electricity. The point is that consumer mobilization could be used to serve a variety of political ends. For women, for instance, political agency could be exercised through consumption in the bazaars, tea parties, and the temperance circles of the Anti-Corn Law League, through discriminating purchasing policies during election campaigns, and in the exclusive dealing campaigns of the Chartist women who put pressure on shopkeepers to vote for radical candidates.[11]

The political actions of groups of consumers were not solely the preserve of the middle class. Glasgow tenants went on a rent strike in 1915 and in 1904 East End Jewish housewives forced bakers to sell bread made by a recognized trade union.[12] In the United States there existed a long tradition of workers' involvement in cost of living campaigns and the fight for a living wage. As American workers conceptualized the pay packet in terms of how it was spent, as well as how it was earned, their struggles were about 'pocketbook politics' that combined both their producer and consumer roles.[13] Obtaining goods that

[8] T. H. Breen, *The Marketplace of Revolution: How Consumer Politics Shaped American Independence* (Oxford: Oxofrd University Press, 2004).

[9] Clare Midgley, *Women against Slavery: The British Campaigns, 1780–1870* (London: Routledge, 1992); K. Davies, 'A moral purchase: femininity, commerce, abolition, 1788–1792', in E. Eger and C. Grant (eds.), *Women and the Public Sphere: Writing and Representation 1660–1800* (Cambridge: Cambridge University Press, 2000); Lawrence B. Glickman, *Buying Power: A History of Consumer Activism in America* (Chicago: University of Chicago Press, 2009).

[10] Glickman, *Buying Power*.

[11] P. A. Pickering and A. Tyrell, *The People's Bread: A History of the Anti-Corn Law League* (London: Leicester University Press, 2000); D. Thompson, *The Chartists* (London: Temple Smith, 1984), p. 137; Frank Trentmann, *Free Trade Nation: Commerce, Consumption, and Civil Society in Modern Britain* (Oxford: Oxford University Press, 2008).

[12] Marcel van der Linden, 'Working-class consumer power', *International Labour and Working-Class History*, 46 (1994), pp. 109–21.

[13] Meg Jacobs, *Pocketbook Politics: Economic Citizenship in Twentieth-Century America* (Princeton: Princeton University Press, 2005); Glickman, *A Living Wage*.

were better value for money and overcoming the unscrupulous tactics of commercial advertisers also proved attractive to European trade unionists. They had earlier joined with other philanthropic, women's, and faith-based organizations to organize consumers in defence of workers' rights. Clementina Black of the British Women's Trade Union Association set up a Consumers' League in 1887. This was a campaign against 'sweat shops' modelled on the efforts of the Knights of Labour in the United States and, although it proved short-lived, it was an inspiration for the later Christian Social Union (established in 1889) which published 'white lists' to guide middle-class shoppers towards stores with union-approved working conditions.[14]

Black's League was also taken up across the Atlantic where a Consumers' League was formed by the Women's Trade Union League in New York in 1890. Other chapters soon appeared across the United States until a National Consumers' League was formed in 1898 headed by the dynamic Florence Kelley, who spearheaded the 'white label campaign'. The idea then travelled back across the Atlantic, helping to inspire the *Ligue Sociale d'Acheteurs* in France in 1902, the *Käuferbund Deutschland* in Germany, and similar organizations in Switzerland, Italy, Belgium, and the Netherlands. As organizations of mainly middle-class women, the consumers' leagues proved popular with philanthropically minded sympathizers of labour. In 1908, for instance, representatives from nine countries attended the International Conference on Consumers' Leagues in Geneva, including members of the British Anti-Sweating League while by the outbreak of the First World War, there were over 30 branches of the *Ligue* in France in alone.[15]

Women's consumer organizations continued to leap to the defence of the worker. In the United States, the League of Women Shoppers opened its first chapter in 1935, claimed 25,000 members by the end of the decade and embarked on a series of high-profile progressive causes, especially over the cost of living. It described itself as an 'auxiliary' of the labour movement, even developing connections with the Communist Party—resulting in future investigations by Senator McCarthy—and demonstrated the close links that were often made between consumer and worker action in the United States.[16] Yet its opposition to certain forms of consumption also fits in with a longer,

---

[14] Matthew Hilton, *Consumerism in Twentieth-Century Britain: The Search for a Historical Movement* (Cambridge: Cambridge University Press, 2003).

[15] Kathryn Kish Sklar, 'The consumer's White Label Campaign of the National Consumer's League, 1898–1918', in Susan Strasser, Charles McGovern and Matthias Judt (eds.), *Getting and Spending: European and American Consumer Societies in the Twentieth Century* (Cambridge: Cambridge University Press, 1998), pp. 17–35; Warren Breckman, 'Disciplining consumption: the debate on luxury in Wilhelmine Germany, 1890–1914', *Journal of Social History*, 24 (1991), pp. 485–505; Marie-Emmanuelle Chessel, 'Consommation, action sociale et engagement public fin de siécle, des États-Unis à la France', in Alain Chatriot, Marie-Emmanuelle Chessel and Matthew Hilton (eds.), *Au nom du consommateur: consommation et politique en Europe et aux États-Unis au XXᵉ siécle* (Paris: La Découverte, 2005), pp. 247–61; Marie-Emmanuelle Chessel, 'Consommation et réforme sociale à la Belle Époque: la conference internationale des ligues socials d'acheteurs en 1908', *Sciences de la Société*, 62 (2004), pp. 45–67.

[16] Tracey Deutsch, 'Des consommatrices américaines trés engages, du New Deal à la guerre froide', in Chatriot et al., *Au nom du consommateur*, pp. 361–75; Lawrence B. Glickman, ' "Make lisle the style": the politics of fashion in the Japanese silk boycott, 1937–1940', *Journal of Social History*, 38/3 (2005), pp. 573–608; Landon R. Y. Storrs, 'Red scare politics and the suppression of popular front feminism: the loyalty investigation of Mary Dublin Keyserling', *Journal of American History*, 90/2 (2003), pp. 491–524.

if sporadic, form of protest—the boycott—which women have in particular mobilized around. Rising food prices, rent hikes, shortages, and perceptions of profiteering have persistently brought women onto the streets, occasionally resulting in more sustained forms of action, at others petering out as the specific problem was resolved.

The point is that many of these organizations were motivated by a sense of duty to protect the interests of others, sometimes consumers but just as often workers, slaves, housewives, children, and the poor generally. The duty of the female consumer, for instance, came to be regarded as even a professional activity. Women professionals in the United States were brought into the Department of Agriculture's Bureau of Home Economics from 1923, where they worked with producers to improve the quality of commercial goods and sought to educate housewives into making more rational family buying decisions. Being a consumer thus came to be associated with good citizenship. In Britain, middle-class, non-feminist organizations such as the Women's Institutes, the National Federation of Townswomen's Guilds, and, during the Second World War, the Housewives' League and the Women's Voluntary Service, spoke on a range of consumer issues, from food to housing to clothing.[17] In Germany, the National League of Housewives' Associations set up its own testing facilities as early as 1925 and, along with the Housewives' Union of the Catholic Women's Leagues, promoted a defensive, protectionist consumer politics which promoted German products over foreign imports and celebrated the skills of the rational housewife.[18] Such groups drew on the professionalization of home economics as an academic discipline, first institutionalized in the American Home Economics Association in 1909. The translation of Taylorist mass production strategies into techniques of household efficiency by pioneers such as Christine Fredericks led to a greater attention to housewifery among European and American women's groups as well as to the redesign of living spaces, most emblematically in the 'Frankfurt Kitchen' with its hyper-rational attention to the orderly movement of women in the home.[19]

In many senses, this form of consumer movement will always exist. Consumers will always seek to use their consumption either to promote the interests of others or to help their own welfare, or both. More distinct are our second type of consumer movements, those which develop the role of the consumer into a more general form of politics and political identity. Here, the co-operative movement has a strong claim to being the oldest, most established and most successful consumer organization. Beginning in the north of England in the 1840s, the dividend-on-purchase, consumer co-operative ethos of the Rochdale Pioneers spread throughout Europe as an alternative to the capitalist marketplace. By the outbreak of the First World War, there were literally thousands of

---

[17] Hilton, 'The female consumer'; Ina Zweiniger-Bargielowska, *Austerity in Britain: Rationing, Controls and Consumption, 1939–1955* (Oxford: Oxford University Press, 2000).

[18] Nancy Reagin, 'Comparing apples and oranges: housewives and the politics of consumption in interwar Germany', in Strasser et al., *Getting and Spending*, pp. 241–62.

[19] Carolyn Goldstein, 'Educating consumers, representing consumers: reforming the marketplace through scientific expertise at the Bureau of Home Economics, United States Department of Agriculture, 1923–1940', in Matthew Hilton, Marie-Emmanuelle Chessel and Alain Chatriot (eds.) *The Expert Consumer: Associations and Professionals in Consumer Society* (Aldershot: Ashgate, 2006) pp. 73–88; Paul Betts, *The Authority of Everyday Objects: A Cultural History of West German Industrial Design* (Berkeley, CA: University of California Press, 2004).

local societies in the United Kingdom, Austria, Germany, France, Russia, and across Scandinavia.[20] These were often the largest retailers in their respective countries and could claim to impact upon the purchasing decisions of large numbers of working-class households.

In certain countries, the movement was divided—as in France, Germany, and Belgium—between the more avowedly socialist organizations and those who wished to concentrate on the more politically neutral forms of retail trading. But, elsewhere, co-operation became a social and political as well as an economic enterprise. Most developed their own propaganda departments (the British co-operative movement even had its own film unit), educational sections, recreational facilities, and they forged strong links with the labour movement. Prominent co-operative ideologues also emerged, such as Anders Örne in Sweden, Charles Gide in France, and George Jacob Holyoake in Britain, who helped establish the principles around which a global movement could develop following the creation of the International Co-operative Alliance in 1895.[21]

Co-operation was subsequently weakened through its own institutional and parochial weaknesses, the interference of totalitarian regimes and the competition of more dynamic capitalist firms, but it was still a vociferous presence in Europe and Japan after the Second World War. Co-operatives played an important role in the establishment of consumer protection systems in Scandinavia, as well as provoking an ongoing debate about their relevance as a third sector alternative to capitalism. But the threat they faced as the leading organization of the consumer movement came with the emergence of the consumer testing organizations.

By the middle decades of the twentieth century, many of the demands of consumer groups about access to a decent standard of living were being met, either directly or indirectly, through the development of social democratic institutions. It enabled many of the specific political issues that consumers had campaigned for to be translated into universal demands for welfare or for entitlements to participation. By 1941, Franklin D. Roosevelt was able to identify 'four essential human freedoms': from fear, of speech, of religion, and from want. This built on the incorporation of consumerist agendas within the institutions of the New Deal, particularly the Consumers' Advisory Board of the National Recovery Administration and the Office of the Consumers' Counsel within the Agricultural Adjustment Administration. These bodies, along with the Office of Price Administration during the Second World War, helped mobilize and institutionalized 'citizen consumers' who fought for their individual rights at the same time as using their economic power for the greater good of the US economic recovery.[22]

[20] Martin Purvis, 'Societies of consumers and consumer societies: co-operation, consumption and politics in Britain and continental Europe, c.1850–1920', *Journal of Historical Geography*, 24/2 (1998), pp. 147–69; Martin Purvis, 'Co-operation, consumption and politics: co-operation in Europe, 1850–1920', in Bill Lancaster and Patrick Maguire (eds.), *Towards the Co-operative Commonwealth* (Manchester: Manchester University Press, 1996).
[21] See note 4 above.
[22] Kathleen G. Donohue, *Freedom from Want: American Liberalism and the Idea of the Consumer* (Baltimore: Johns Hopkins University Press, 2003).

With the establishment of welfare regimes across Europe and North America, the stage was set for the creation of a new form of consumer politics, focused more on rights than on duties. Consumption, or the right to enjoy its pleasures, had become an entitlement for citizens who had made sacrifices in two world wars and expected a share in the societies being reconstructed in their name in the late 1940s and 1950s. The affluent society had to promise more choice for those who could afford it, but also more stuff for those who so far could not. In the United States, the 'consumer democracy' has been argued to have been at the heart of post-war planning, whereby consumers were able to exercise their citizenship not only at the ballot box but on a daily basis through their participation in the marketplace.[23] Consumer democracy might not capture the full range of consumer regimes which emerged in the latter half of the twentieth century, but there was clearly a widely expressed desire to improve standards of living and to ensure that all could participate in the good life. In Germany, Ludwig Erhard declared a social market economy; in Scandinavia, social democracy took account of workers' desires to share in the good life, and even amidst the apparent asceticism of 1950s Britain there existed a sense of universal entitlement to affluence, which surely emerged out of the 'fair shares' policies associated with the foundations of the welfare state.

This shift to a rights-based approach has been most closely associated with the campaigns and tactics of the comparative testing movement. Beginning in the late 1920s in America, Consumers' Research began publishing its *Bulletin* in order to help consumers overcome their relative ignorance in the marketplace. Following a strike in 1936, Consumers' Research split as several disgruntled staff went off to form Consumers Union. Unsurprisingly for an organization founded amidst a labour dispute, Consumers Union would pay close attention to the labour conditions of those who made the products featured in its reports, though for the many millions of shoppers who read *Consumers Reports* over the course of the twentieth century, it was the quality tests themselves that drew them and that explain the organization's tremendous growth and popularity. By the turn of the millennium, the circulation figures of *Consumer Reports* topped 5 million.[24]

The appeal of comparative testing consumerism was not confined to the United States. After the Second World War, consumer groups began to appear across Western Europe as post-war economies shifted into a prolonged period of affluence. First, in France, the *Union Fédéral des Consommateurs* was formed in 1951. It was followed by *Consumentenbond* in the Netherlands in 1953, and then the Consumers' Association

---

[23] Lizabeth Cohen, *A Consumers' Republic: The Politics of Mass Consumption in Postwar America* (New York: Knopf, 2003).

[24] Lawrence B. Glickman, 'The strike in the temple of consumption: consumer activism and twentieth-century American political culture', *Journal of American History*, 88/1 (2001), pp. 99–128; Robert N. Mayer, *The Consumer Movement: Guardians of the Marketplace* (Boston, MA: Twayne 1989); Norman Isaac Silber, *Test and Protest: The Influence of Consumers Union* (New York: Holmes & Meier,1983); Michael Pertschuk, *Revolt Against Regulation: The Rise and Pause of the Consumer Movement* (Berkeley, CA: University of California Press 1982); Charles McGovern, *Sold American: Consumption and Citizenship, 1890–1945* (Chapel Hill, NC: University of North Caroline Press 2006).

of the United Kingdom in 1956, and the *Association des Consommateurs* of Belgium in 1957. These private testing bodies were joined by a range of state-assisted agencies such as the *Arbeitsgemeinschaft der Verbraucherverbände* in Germany (1953), the Norwegian *Forbrukerrådet* (1953), and the Swedish *Statens Konsumentråd* (1957).[25]

More significant still is that this was not just a Western phenomenon. In 1960, the leaders of the main European and US groups came together to found the International Organisation of Consumers Unions (IOCU). Its growth is a testament to the spread of organized consumerism across the developing world. By 1970, IOCU's membership consisted of consumer groups across Asia, Africa, and Latin America, if only in the richest nations of these regions. By 1990, however, IOCU could claim to be truly global, and today it is represented in over one hundred countries. Much of its expansion had been overseen by Anwar Fazal of the Malaysian consumer movement, President of IOCU from 1978 to 1984, though other developing world activists have subsequently directed the global consumer movement from Indonesia, Brazil, and Kenya.

Much of this growth has been predicated upon an operating philosophy of consumer rights. On 15 March 1962, President John F. Kennedy made a speech to the US Congress in which he acknowledged the responsibility of government to respond to the key concerns of consumer activists. Most crucially, he listed four consumer rights which he took to be the heart of the political philosophy of the consumer. These were the right to safety, the right to be informed, the right to choose, and the right to be heard. These four consumer rights were adopted as the central pillars of IOCU policy and the date chosen for World Consumer Rights Day was the anniversary of Kennedy's coming out into the consumerist fold. Moreover, this rights-based perspective became the basis for political consumerism as a whole. These rights can be found at the heart of national consumer protection systems the world over and they form the basis of the UN Guidelines on Consumer Protection.

As these rights have become institutionalized, there are many within the consumer movement who suggest that the movement has achieved almost all that it can achieve. Certainly it has enjoyed some great successes. Beyond the establishment of consumer protection as a central principle of any market economy, the consumer movement became something of a leading player in global civil society in the 1980s, not least through its establishment of key campaigning networks such as the International Baby Food Action Network, the Pesticide Action Network, and Health Action International. Yet since this decade it has been eclipsed by a third form of consumer movement, or perhaps movements, as concerned shoppers bring to their purchasing decisions a range of political, ethical, and moral beliefs.

The origins of this third type of consumer movement was marked by the return to popularity of the boycott. In recent decades, in Britain alone, there have been boycotts against lead in paint (1984), against an amusement park because of its captured whales

---

[25] Matthew Hilton, *Prosperity for All: Consumer Activism in an Era of Globalization* (Ithaca, NY: Cornell University Press, 2009); S. Brobeck, R. N. Mayer and R. O. Herrmann (eds.), *Encyclopedia of the Consumer Movement* (Santa Barbara, CA: ABC-CLIO, 1997), various entries.

and dolphins (organized by Greenpeace, 1984), against Tarmac and MAN-VW over their links with cruise missiles (organized by CND, 1983), and against Schweppes for using non-returnable bottles (organized by Friends of the Earth, early 1970s). Famous international campaigns have included the boycott of Barclays for its activities in apartheid-era South Africa, Nestlé for its marketing of baby milk substitutes, and of Douwe Egberts for processing coffee from Angola. At the end of the 1990s, the *Ethical Consumer* magazine maintained a list of around 40 companies being boycotted, ranging from oil companies such as Esso, Texaco, and Shell, clothes stores such as Gap, Nike, and Marks and Spencer, to perceived perennial offenders such as McDonalds, Philip Morris, and Nestlé. Added to this list were several countries included for their abuses of human rights, including China, Turkey, Burma, and Israel, as well as the United States through the 'boycott Bush' campaign.[26]

Boycotts or buycotts—the targeted purchase of goods and services to reward particular firms for behaviour in accord with the activists' wishes—are but part of a more general trend towards ethical consumer behaviour. Arising out of the boycott movement and the growth of single-issue political groups since the 1960s, green consumerism was seen to have come of age with the publication of *The Green Consumer Guide* in 1988. Aimed at 'a "sandals-to-Saabs" spectrum of consumers', rather than those committed to a 'hair-shirt lifestyle', the *Guide* attempted to build on previous green consumer victories, such as the shift to unleaded petrol, the replacement of 'hard' detergents with 'soft', the greater use of biodegradable products, and the increased demand for health foods and organically grown produce.[27] It drew strength from a survey of environmental organizations, 88 per cent of which believed that individual consumer choice could have a major impact on the direction of the economy. Many of these groups were themselves shifting away from a focus on the boycott as a campaign strategy, to a focus on informed choice and discriminative purchasing. Rather than supporting a state-directed control of the logging industry, Friends of the Earth's *Good Wood Guide* offered information for consumers acting by themselves to switch their preferences in the marketplace from hardwoods grown in tropical forests to sustainable alternatives. Green consumerism was therefore shifting away from ascetism, self-denial, and the retreat from materialism to the point of non-consumerism, and building instead on the growing number of 'lifestyle' shoppers so apparent in the consumption studies literature. By the early 1990s, companies were embracing some degree of green consumerism within their marketing strategies and notable achievements included the declining manufacture of CFC-propelled aerosols and the abandonment of animal testing by several cosmetics manufacturers.

This trend is best encapsulated with the emergence of the Ethical Consumer Research Association (ECRA). ECRA began in 1987 as a research group collecting information on company activities, but began publishing the bi-monthly *Ethical Consumer* in March 1989. Although never as successful as the Consumers' Association (there were just 5,000 subscribers at the end of its first year), it has drawn on a committed subscriber

[26] Hilton, *Consumerism in Twentieth-Century Britain*, pp. 317–28.
[27] J. Elkington & J. Hailes, *The Green Consumer Guide* (London: Gollancz, 1988), p. 2.

membership, many of whom were able to provide ECRA with a £40,000 collective loan in 1991 to finance its expansion. *Ethical Consumer* was able to bring together a whole range of political beliefs which have directed people's consumption decisions, committing itself to the promotion of universal human rights, environmental sustainability, and animal welfare. While the magazine itself informs consumers of these issues in relation to particular goods, ECRA has also continued its research into company affairs. It has maintained a database called Corporate Critic made up of collected publications which are critical of specific company activities and it continues to undertake research projects for other organizations on corporate responsibility and environmental impact analysis, as well as campaigns on specific subjects.

To some extent, this ethical approach has clearly entered the mainstream, perhaps best encapsulated with the modern fair-trade movement. Fair-trade has its origins in the alternative trading organizations pioneered in the 1960s and 1970s by international non-governmental organizations such as Oxfam, faith-based groups and older bodies such as those of the consumers' co-operative movement. In 1992, in the UK, the Fairtrade Foundation was established to 'empower consumers to take responsibility for the role they play when they buy products from the third world'.[28] It was created by several pre-existing groups, namely CAFOD, Christian Aid, New Consumer, Oxfam, Traidcraft, and the World Development Movement, later being joined by the Women's Institute. It has enabled Britain to become the leading fair-trade market worldwide. Sales have been growing at an annual rate of 40 per cent and total sales reached topped £1 billion in 2010. It is no longer associated with alternative values and lifestyles and is a central plank of most supermarkets' marketing strategies.[29]

To ethical consumerism, fair-trade, and boycotting much more could be added. We can also include many local market disputes, exemplified most dramatically by the surge of interest in the trial of José Bové, a French farmer who led a protest against McDonald's in Millau in the Roquefort-making region of southern France.[30] There is too, the Slow Food Movement, particularly popular in Italy as consumers use their purchasing power to express their support for a market based upon a much smaller scale and a less anonymous set of market values.[31] And there are a whole host of anti-globalization protests that have embraced what one political scientist has called 'political consumerism'.[32] All are based upon a set of consuming duties and all are expressly concerned with the interests of others rather than just themselves.

To this extent, the history of consumer activism has come full circle: today's protestors have much in common with the campaigners of the nineteenth century. Yet like

[28] Fairtrade Foundation, *Introducing Fairtrade: A Guide to the Fairtrade Mark and the Fairtrade Foundation* (London: Fairtrade Foundation, 2000), p. 2.

[29] Matthew Anderson, 'The history of the fairtrade movement in Britain', unpublished Ph.D. thesis (University of Birmingham, 2009).

[30] J. Bové and F. Dufour, *The World is Not for Sale: Farmers Against Junk Food* (London: Verso, 2001).

[31] Victoria de Grazia, *Irresistible Empire: America's Advance Through Twentieth-Century Europe* (Cambridge, MA: Balknap, 2005).

[32] Micheletti, *Political Virtue and Shopping*, p. 1.

the affluent shoppers who purchased *Which?* and *Consumer Reports*, today's ethical shoppers are more fully aware that they are consumers. It is not so much that they bring specific political issues to specific acts of consumption. It is more that they recognize that the whole world of consumption is now political and that politics pervades every product and service that is bought and sold. As consumerism (as a cultural description of our age) pervades so many aspects of our lives, so too will it be likely that consumerism (as a political movement) will increase in popularity and scope.

FUTURE DEVELOPMENTS

The recent spate of books on consumer movements suggests that the historical record is by now far more complete than it was just a few years ago. Yet this is perhaps mainly true for a British and American literature and there remain important gaps to be filled both by period and by place. Moreover, if there is a lesson to be learnt from the history of consumer movements it is that the infinite relationships we can have with goods have the potential to create an unlimited number of political interventions through consumption. I began this chapter with a reference to 'carrot mobbing'. No doubt, by the time this volume reaches print another form of activism will have been invented that sees consumers organizing to correct a perceived injustice. This must be the first observation we therefore make about the future scholarship on consumer movements: that it must respond to the tremendous energy found within consumer activism. Scholars will continue to uncover forms of consumer organizing that demonstrate the perpetually moving contours of consumers' engagement with the world of goods.

A second area that will no doubt come under closer scrutiny is in the less attractive forms of consumer organizing. There is something of a progressive bias in the literature in that it is those consumer movements concerned with liberal causes—anti-slavery, workers' welfare, women's rights—that have come under the most academic scrutiny. What the history of consumer movements shows us, though, is that consumers do not unite solely for socially progressive reasons. Often, they unite out of prejudice and a reactionary conservatism, be it to defend the institution of slavery, discriminate against racial groups, or support nationalistic politics. Moreover, institutions exist which appear to represent movements of consumers but which support other interests and agendas. The US-based Center for Consumer Freedom, for instance, likes to position itself as an organization that builds on the type of work conducted by the Consumers Union in seeking to protect the interests of all consumers. As it states on its website, 'The Center for Consumer Freedom is a nonprofit organization devoted to promoting personal responsibility and protecting consumer choices.'[33] What it means by this is a virulent opposition to any form of regulation and any form of intervention by the state on behalf of the public. In this case, we can easily question whether such an organization

[33] <http://www.consumerfreedom.com/about.cfm>, accessed November 2009.

is actually a movement, since further enquiry reveals it to be a body funded largely by private corporations. Yet by having some individual members, it also claims to represent consumers as a whole. It is precisely these 'front' organizations—those which speak as if for consumers but whose interests really lie in representing other political groups—that future researchers will turn their attention towards.

It is likely too, that, as with consumption studies generally, research into consumer movements will extend into a third area, one which lies beyond the affluent West and in the developing world. My own research has examined consumer movements in Malaysia and across the global south. This builds on work conducted on Japan, China, and Asia generally, as well as the former Soviet bloc.[34] In India, for instance, around 2,000 consumer groups have been founded since the passing of the 1986 Consumer Protection Act. And in China, one estimate has suggested that the total number of institutional and supervisory contact points for consumers from the village upwards amounts to over 150,000.[35] Over the past few decades, as these societies have come to experience Western-style forms of consumption, so too have their consumers chosen to act politically and in groups and movements. As scholars engage with questions of climate change, the politics of consumption around the world will become of greater and more urgent interest.

Fourthly, the whole question of the relationship between human rights and consumer rights may well attract attention. Consumer rights, or those which deal with access to basic goods and services, are covered in Articles 22–27 of the Universal Declaration of Human Rights. There are important questions about the individualism said to be inherent to human rights frameworks. The rights-based advocacy of the consumer testing movement, for instance, can be incredibly individualistic, not least in the promotion of the right to choice. But in the right to basic needs, consumer movements have campaigned for collective entitlements reminiscent of the political campaigns that lay behind the formation of welfare regimes around the world in the mid-twentieth century. By contrast, the more recent forms of consumer movement seem to eschew a rights-based approach, emphasizing instead the duties of the consumer—to the environment or to fellow human beings. Yet in the way these moral and political dilemmas are presented, especially in ethical consumer magazines that owe a great debt to the 'best buy' tables of the comparative testers, the decision as to how to promote any one ethical issue over another is left to the individual. Duties as much as rights, as they are currently presented, are therefore just as individualistic.[36]

---

[34] Maclachlan, *Consumer Politics in Postwar Japan*; Hilton, *Prosperity for All*; Matthew Hilton, *Choice and Justice: Forty Years of the Malaysian Consumer Movement* (Penang: Universiti Sains Malaysia Press, 2009); Malgorzata Mazurek and Matthew Hilton, 'Consumerism, solidarity and communism: consumer protection and the consumer movement in Poland', *Journal of Contemporary History*, 42/2 (2007), pp. 315–43.

[35] Jing Jian Xiao, 'Chinese consumer movement', in Brobeck et al., *Encyclopedia of the Consumer Movement*, pp. 104–108.

[36] I explore these issues at greater length in 'Consumer activism: rights or duties?', in Kerstin Brückweh (ed.), *The Voice of the Citizen Consumer: A History of Market Research, Consumer Movements, and the Political Public Sphere* (Oxford: Oxford University Press, 2011), pp. 99–116.

Such a point leads on to a final observation. So long as politicians and governments continue to use the language of consumer rights and consumer choice, academics will be interested in the meaning of the consumer. For those interested in consumer movements, the questions will be about the extent to which organizations of consumers have influenced such political rhetoric, the extent to which they can continue to engage with it, and the limitations of a political movement based around consumption. Too often, the focus on choice limits consumer politics to highly prescribed fields, such that choice becomes synonymous with the far more limited concept of preference. A focus on consumer rights, too, has its limits in terms of how it can address collective issues about resource allocation, social justice and the distribution of wealth. For all the dynamism of consumer movements and their constantly evolving nature, can they really get beyond an individualistic framework or one which deals with problems as and when they arise rather than at source?

A strong steer comes from the historical evidence to answer this question. What becomes apparent is that the more sustainable and successful consumer movements have not been those that deal with specific issues. Certainly, they may well succeed in their aims, but others fail, and fail often. They offer very little continuity from one boycott to the next and no guarantees that such a form of activism will necessarily succeed again, since the context will be very different. Instead, the consumer movements that have become most prominent—the co-operative and the comparative testers—are those which combine self-interest with altruism, rights with duties, individual action with collective solution. Through the dividend and the best buy, both have catered to the acquisitive and the material interests of their members. But both too have campaigned for the interests of all consumers to be considered in the regulation of the economy and in political decisions about resource distribution. If they have defended the rights of any one consumer, they have also, in classic liberal tradition, defended the rights of everybody to enjoy such rights. This is not to argue that these movements are not without their failings and their faults. But it is to suggest that if scholars wish to examine effective political movements they might be better off examining the co-op and the consumers association rather than the culture jammer, the anti-globalizer, the downsizer, the Slow Food advocate, the recycler, the fairtrader, the support of organic farmers' markets—or even the carrot mobber.

BIBLIOGRAPHY

Charles F. McGovern, *Sold American: Consumption and Citizenship, 1890–1940* (Chapel Hill: University of North Carolina Press, 2006).

Gunnar Trumbull, *Consumer Capitalism: Politics, Product Markets and Firm Strategy in France and Germany* (Ithaca, NY: Cornell University Press, 2006).

Lawrence B. Glickman, *Buying Power: A History of Consumer Activism in America* (Chicago: University of Chicago Press, 2009).

Lizabeth Cohen, *A Consumers' Republic: The Politics of Mass Consumption in Postwar America* (New York: Knopf, 2003).

Martin Daunton and Matthew Hilton (eds.), *The Politics of Consumption: Material Culture and Citizenship in Europe and America* (Oxford: Berg, 2001).

Mathew Hilton, *Consumerism in Twentieth-Century Britain: The Search for a Historical Movement* (Cambridge: Cambridge University Press, 2003).

Matthew Hilton, *Prosperity for All: Consumer Activism in an Era of Globalisation* (Ithaca, NY: Cornell University Press, 2009).

Meg Jacobs, *Pocketbook Politics: Economic Citizenship in Twentieth-Century America* (Princeton: Princeton University Press, 2005).

Patricia L. Maclachlan, *Consumer Politics in Postwar Japan: The Institutional Boundaries of Citizen Activism* (New York: Columbia University Press, 2002).

S. Strasser, C. McGovern and M. Judt (eds.), *Getting and Spending: European and American Consumer Societies in the Twentieth Century* (Cambridge: Cambridge University Press, 1998).

CHAPTER 27

....

THE POLITICS
OF EVERYDAY LIFE

....

FRANK TRENTMANN

The great historian will in as full measure as possible present to us the every-day life of the men and women of the age which he describes. Nothing that tells of this life will come amiss to him....In the writings of our historians, as in the lives of our ordinary citizens, we can neither afford to forget that it is the ordinary every-day life which counts most; nor yet that seasons come when ordinary qualities count for but little in the face of great contending forces of good and of evil, the outcome of whose strife determines whether the nation shall walk in the glory of the morning or in the gloom of spiritual death.

Theodore Roosevelt, 1912[1]

Man must be everyday, or he will not be at all.

Henri Lefebvre, 1947[2]

Everyday life is the secret yeast of history.

Agnes Heller, 1970[3]

The everyday is political. Readers today will hardly raise an eyebrow at this statement—after all, the personal is political, too. This was not always so. As recently as 1985, the doyen of social science history in Germany, Hans-Ulrich Wehler, said the study of

---

[1] 'History and literature', Presidential address to the American Historical Association, repr. in Theodore Roosevelt, *History as Literature and Other Essays* (New York, 2006), pp. 27–9.
[2] Henri Lefebvre, *Critique of Everyday Life*, Vol. 1 (Paris, 1947, 2nd edn. 1958; English edn. London, 1991), p. 127.
[3] Agnes Heller, *Das Alltagsleben: Versuch einer Erklärung der individuellen Reproduktion* (Budapest 1970; German edn. Berlin 1978), p. 25, my translation.

everyday life added little more than a bit of 'gruel' to the main course of history.[4] Since then, the turf wars between social history, history from below, and cultural history have themselves become a thing of the past. Big Politics (states, parties, great men) has been joined by little politics, attentive to the subjectivity, power, and resistance of ordinary people in their ordinary lives. From the heights of extraordinary events, the analysis lowered to take in the *'infra-ordinaire'*, as the French novelist Georges Perec called it.[5] The everyday is pretty much taken for granted now. This is the problem that animates this essay. The quotidian, which is about the familiar, has itself become so familiar that it stands in the way of appreciating its historical genesis.

It was during the 1950s–1970s that first sociologists and then 'new social' historians embraced the everyday. The flowering of consumption studies since would be unthinkable without the recognition that everyday life is an important—perhaps the most important—place people find meaning, develop habits, and acquire a sense of themselves and their world. People, we learnt, were absorbed by their daily lives. They registered a change of wallpaper more than a change of government. History books, local museums, school classes, and television shows[6] were not only 'peopled' but 'thinged',[7] giving us a greater appreciation of people's material lives, what they owned, how they got it, how they used it, and how they disposed of it—in short, of the life cycle of consumption.

Fame has come at a price, however. Such is the common sense appeal of the everyday that it can mean everything and nothing to everyone. In part, this problem mirrors the democratic character that made the subject so attractive in the first place. Unlike sitting on a throne or storming the Bastille, everyday life is not something particularly special. Everyone has one. The problem was aggravated by intellectual politics and praxis. Everyone started to talk of the everyday, though they rarely meant the same thing.

The everyday has resisted definition. In 1978, a decade after the quotidian took politics by storm, Norbert Elias wrote a critical note about the sociology of everyday life. In the 1930s Elias himself had written a pioneering account of the civilizing process of manners, but he remained unconvinced by the idea that the everyday was an identifiable subject. He noted eight different meanings in circulation. For some writers, the everyday was made up of ordinary routines in contrast to extraordinary events. For others it stood for a people's history versus that of elites, or, more narrowly, for the work-day of

---

[4] 'Hirsebrei'; Hans-Ulrich Wehler, 'Königsweg zu neuen Ufern oder Irrgarten der Illusionen? Die westdeutsche Alltagsgeschichte', in Franz-Josef Brüggemeier and Jürgen Kocka (eds.), *Geschichte von unten—Geschichte von innen: Kontroversen um die Alltagsgeschichte* (Hagen, 1985), pp. 17–47, at p. 37.

[5] Georges Perec, *L'infra-ordinaire* (Paris, 1990).

[6] For the consumption of history, see Jerome de Groot, *Consuming History: Popular Experience of the Past* (London, 2005).

[7] In addition to the popular wave of biographies of things, see Arjun Appadurai (ed.), *The Social Life of Things: Commodities in Cultural Perspective* (Cambridge, 1986); Bill Brown, 'Thing Theory', *Critical Inquiry*, 28/1 (2001), pp. 1–22; Laurel Thatcher Ulrich, *The Age of Homespun: Objects and Stories in the Creation of an American Myth* (New York, 2001); Susan Hanley, *Everyday Things in Premodern Japan* (Berkeley, CA, 1997); Daniel Roche, *A History of Everyday Things: The Birth of Consumption in France 1600–1800*, trans. Brian Pearce (Cambridge, 2000); Frank Trentmann, 'Materiality in the Future of History: Things, Practices, and Politics', *Journal of British Studies* 48/2 (April 2009), pp. 283–307.

the labourer rather than bourgeois luxury. For yet others it marked out the private from the public. Some associated the everyday with spontaneous and authentic actions as opposed to the conscious and artificial world of art and science, while others saw it precisely as the sphere where false needs and experiences ruled. Clearly, these approaches were incompatible. That they managed to multiply and coexist, Elias argued, reflected that sociology itself was fragmenting. Structural models with an ambition to explain everything had hit a crisis of confidence. This left a vacuum for 'sects', each conducting their own conversation rather than talking to each other.[8]

It would be unfair to levy exactly the same charge at historians—the pioneers of history from below, after all, were locked in heated debate with Weberian historians who studied states, classes, and modernization. Still, Elias's main observation about the cacophony of voices stands, and only gets more confusing once we add history and cultural studies. What prevented these approaches from colliding was not a shared substantive position but a shared suspicion of universal, structuralist, and deterministic models. Everyday life reclaimed whatever conventional approaches had left out. For historians, it became a catch-all for the little man and the little things in life, for agency, and the concrete. It encompassed everything from the spectacle of food protests in the First World War to unspectacular routines of eating and blowing one's nose in sixteenth-century France. Few stopped to ask whether there was such an entity as the everyday in the first place or how it had evolved over time. The political romance of the everyday meant that most historians treated it as a given, a realm of human experience which had always existed and which they had retrieved from obscurity. Ironically, then, studies which prided themselves on rehabilitating the concrete evolved into a body of literature which in method and focus was all but concrete.

The aim of this chapter is not to lay down a universal law about what the everyday is or is not. Its goal is more modest. It seeks to offer an historical account of the changing scope and politics of everyday life. Everyday life is not simply out there. In contrast to recent discussions which have made the everyday appear the product of Western Europe after the Second World War, I am keen to recover the longer history of the everyday and the different politics of modernity which it has inspired. The 1950s–70s have been treated as a natural unit of analysis. The age of affluence, neo-realist film, the Situationist International, and new forms of identity and lifestyle politics provided the historical soil for the seminal studies by Henri Lefebvre and Michel de Certeau, *microstoria*, history workshops, and the appetite for people's history and ordinary artefacts more broadly.[9]

---

[8] Norbert Elias, 'Zum Begriff des Alltags', in Kurt Hammerich and Michael Klein (eds.), *Materialien zur Soziologie des Alltags* (Opladen, 1978), pp. 22–9; Norbert Elias, *The Civilizing Process* (1939, Engl. edn Oxford 1994).

[9] Henri Lefebvre, *The Critique of Everyday Life*, 3 vols. (1947, 1961, 1981; English trans. London, 1991, 2002, 2005); Michel de Certeau, *The Practice of Everyday Life* (Berkeley, CA: University of California Press, 1984; 1st French edn. 1974). Kristin Ross, *Fast Cars, Clean Bodies: Decolonization and the Reordering of French Culture* (Cambridge MA, 1996); John Brewer, 'Microhistory and the Histories of Everyday Life', *Cultural & Social History*, 7/1 (2010), pp. 87–110.

What happens if we move the historical goalposts? Everyday life did not suddenly begin in 1947 with the first volume of Henri Lefebvre's *Critique*. The post-war years were one chapter in a longer story. Not that societies always thought there was such a thing. The everyday is not any day. It was in the decades on either side of 1900 that we can discern a growing fascination with the quotidian, in terms of cultural praxis and intellectual reflection as well as political ambition. The city and the home came into view as the political terrain of everyday life. In this earlier gestation—and in sharp contrast to the later celebration of resistance and individual ruses—everyday life was a utopia of modernization, directed by states, experts, and social movements. Broadening the time-frame, then, also shifts our perspective. The focus on post-war affluence as a formative moment has anchored the history of everyday life in the particular experience of Western Europe as it was coming to terms with the American empire of goods; it is, probably, no coincidence that these years also were the formative years for many recent commentators. This has given the politics of everyday life a geographical centre and linear time-frame but at the cost of creating a convergence history where attention to everyday life appears as a Western European left-progressive response to post-war affluence. Here is yet another irony, for the radical contribution of microhistory and history from below was precisely to tear up such centred, linear scripts and to show how history can be told from multiple perspectives and at different scales. The political ambition to reform everyday life in Japan and in the Soviet Union in the 1920s offer two such additional vantage points. Taking a longer perspective allows other forms of consumption and politics to enter the stage.

In the spirit of this volume, I look back at past debates but also look ahead to outline three directions for future research. One concerns our point of view, another process, and a final one space. In addition to approaching it 'from above' or 'from below', it may be useful to see everyday politics as operating 'in between', a channel open in both directions where the infra- and extraordinary meet and, sometimes, collide. A second, related point is to turn the standard association of the everyday with sameness more into a historical question about process. Sameness is not stasis. Moments of breakdown and disruption allow us to see what is needed to keep ordinary consumption practices going. My final point questions the dominant view of the quotidian as a self-contained sphere, a refuge from the world where people could exercise microbe-like resistance. The evidence for everyday life as a separate realm is thin and doubtful. This, however, does not make it any less important. Rather, a more porous view allows us to consider the interconnections between the politics of the everyday and the national and global.

EVERYDAY LIFE: A SHORT HISTORY

In history as in sociology, the three decades after the Second World War marked a sustained search for everyday life. The search benefited from certain shared contexts—a growing suspicion of technology, grand narratives of progress, and orthodox Marxist models of base/superstructure, on the one hand, and the new wave of gender and identity politics in the 1960s and 1970s, on the other. Together with the expansion of the social sciences and of university places, this created a buoyant market for anthropology, cultural studies, oral history, and the study of consumption. Recent commentators have stressed the shared European moment of the quotidian.[10] The interest in the everyday grew out of a suspicion of big structures and determinist accounts of capitalism and class. It rejected the idea that politics was a battle over the control of the state and institutions. One source of inspiration was the attempt to humanize Marxism. Lefebvre had translated Marx's 1844 manuscripts in the 1930s. Similarly, historians from below in the 1970s turned to the younger Marx and his idea of alienation. How people appropriated their world moved to the centre of analysis. This, however, left room for significant differences about the nature of the everyday, its political content and, for intellectual praxis. Ultimately, political contexts as well as disciplinary preoccupations produced substantially different traditions.

For sociologists and theorists, the intellectual centre was France. Here discussion of the everyday was tied to a public debate about consumer culture. It was a pre-1968 phenomenon.[11] Everyday life appeared ambivalent, simultaneously under siege by consumer capitalism and eluding it. Politics flowed in and out. Historians, by contrast, tended to look at it as a separate sphere. Fernand Braudel, one of the leaders of the French *Annales*, presented quotidian life as almost unchanging, a world apart from politics and markets.[12] In Germany, where everyday life became the province of history from below in the 1970s, historians were more interested in its politics but equally keen to see the everyday as a space apart, with its own rules and logic. Here the context was set by a debate about Nazism, not affluence. The everyday was used to show the limits of fascism and restore agency to ordinary people.

The theoretical point of view was developed most ambitiously by the sociologist-philosopher Henri Lefebvre in his three-volume *Critique of Everyday Life* (1947, 1961, 1981). For Lefebvre, the everyday was not a discrete sphere. Rather it was a 'level' between the grey and stagnant trivial and the realm of decision and events. This 'level' was constantly shifting as goods and technologies entered life, met needs, and created new ones. The everyday was not a universal aspect of human existence but the product of modernity. Earlier societies, Lefebvre insisted, had shared an identical 'style'. It was capitalism and the division of labour that tore apart this unity in the course of the nineteenth century, separating high culture from common culture, leisure from work, masses from classes, and ideology and religion from folk wisdom. It was this split which opened up the everyday. Consumer culture in the 1950s and 1960s deepened those fissures. Technological progress was achieved at the cost of an 'underdevelopment of everyday life'. Happiness was reduced to comfort. Advertisers and the fashion industry manipulated people into consuming out of fear of being excluded; like many European

[10] Brewer, 'Microhistory'. See also Jacques Revel, 'Introduction', in Jacques Revel and Lynn Hunt (eds.), *Histories: French Constructions of the Past* (New York, 1995).

[11] Michael Sheringham, *Everyday Life: Theories and Practices from Surrealism to the Present* (Oxford, 2006).

[12] Fernand Braudel, *The Structures of Everyday Life* (New York, 1981).

commentators, Lefebvre took a leaf out of J. K. Galbraith's *The Affluent Society* (1958). The consumer technologies that invaded the home, Lefebvre wrote, made 'mincemeat of everyday life'.[13] Modernity advanced with a dialectical force, chopping up time and rhythms in the pursuit of progress but at the same time creating repetition, monotony, and the familiar as a side-product. The everyday served as the repository of older rhythms, which 'lagged' behind historical time.

In his study of rhythms, towards the end of his life in 1991, Lefebvre compared modern societies to horse trainers who used 'dressage' to break in animals. Through institutions and rituals like politeness, society instilled repetitive, automatic behaviour. Liberty was an illusion. Social dressage 'determines the majority of rhythms'. Once habits had formed it was difficult to change them. If this meant ideas of individual freedom were overblown, it also explained why totalitarianism and consumerism had failed to conquer ordinary life. The everyday was stubborn. It was this conservatism that made the quotidian so attractive to many scholars in the 1960s and 1970s; some, like Michel de Certeau, focused on creative acts of resistance, while others, like Michel Maffesoli and Richard Hoggart, stressed an ingrained attitude of resignation.[14]

For Lefebvre, the everyday was thus bipolar. It 'drags itself along in the wake of change', yet was never sealed off from politics. Private life, he wrote in 1961, was 'saturated' with public life, while the public was simultaneously becoming ever more private.[15] Thanks to television and magazines, the 'humblest farm-hand "knows" queens, princesses and filmstars'.[16] Ordinary people knew bosses' kitchens, bathrooms, and home interiors as well as their own. That private was now public was, he stressed, an illusion, but this made it no less powerful in a society in which media consumption had become central. Twenty years later, in the final volume of the *Critique*, he went one step further. Consumption was changing the relationship between citizen and state. By treating citizens as users of services, the democratic state had diluted itself to a 'service state'—a prescient prognosis of the 'consumerism' of public services that would capture the imagination of right and left in the 1990s.[17]

Far from separate, the micro was enveloped by the macro. The everyday was thus never a passive object of domination. It also contained the potential for emancipation which, he hoped, would ultimately overcome alienation and fragmentation. The critique of consumption developed in tandem with a search for a more humanist Marx after Stalinism; Lefebvre was expelled from the Communist Party in 1958 and his engagement with the everyday stemmed from his life's project to revitalize Marx. Lefebvre extended the young Marx's analysis of the split between private bourgeois and public citizen to

---

[13] Henri Lefebvre, *Critique of Everyday Life: Foundations for a Sociology of the Everyday*, Vol. II (Paris 1961; English edn. London, 2002), p. 75, and p. 145.

[14] See Sheringham, *Everyday Life*, pp. 212–47.

[15] Lefebvre, *Critique of Everyday Life*, Vol. 2, p. 34, see also pp. 4, 70–4.

[16] Lefebvre, *Critique of Everyday Life*, Vol. 2, p. 91.

[17] Henri Lefebvre, *The Critique of Everyday Life: From Modernity to Modernism*, Vol. III (Paris, 1981; English edn. London, 2005), pp. 79–82, 122–8. Compare, John Clarke, Janet E. Newman, Nick Smith, Elizabeth Vidler, and Louise Westmarland, *Creating Citizen-Consumers: Changing Publics and Changing Public Services* (London, 2007).

consumer society.[18] Consumer capitalism simultaneously exported the everyday to the rest of society and led to a fracture between needs and desires. The study of everyday life, according to Lefebvre, was to show 'how the social existence of human beings is produced, its transition from want to affluence and from appreciation to depreciation.'[19] In 1957 Lefebvre launched his manifesto for a romantic revolution. Three years later he set up the research group on everyday life at CNRS (Centre national de la recherche scientifique). It was here, a year later, that Guy Debord, the leader of the Situationist International, attacked the artificiality of consumer needs and poverty of contemporary life and laid out 'Perspectives for Conscious Alterations in Everyday Life'; in the spirit of the argument, Debord broke with the convention of the lecture and instead communicated with the audience through a tape recording.[20]

The everyday promised a new terrain of revolutionary action after Stalinism. For Lefebvre, its critique required total praxis. 'Changing the world', Henri Lefebvre wrote in his second volume of the *Critique* in 1961, 'means changing the everyday.'[21] Fragmentation and alienation could be overcome. Instead of an old-style, top-down, state-led revolution 'from without', the emphasis was on the transformation of lived experience 'from within'. As is well known, American-style mass consumption was a crucial target and dystopia in this debate.[22] Equally important, the rehabilitation of the everyday entailed a new sensitivity to consumption (as opposed to work) as a source of human identity and (potentially) of human freedom. Consumption, not the means of production, now appeared as the lever of change. The everyday was the new frontier of consumer capitalism. Territorial colonialism, Debord and Lefebvre argued, was being superseded by the colonial conquest of the home and mind. Instead of physical violence, fashion and advertisers exercised the violence of conformity.[23] Jean Baudrillard in 1970 defined consumption as the 'organisation totale de la quotidienneté', a line echoed by Lefebvre.[24] In France, Lacanian psycho analysis provided the everyday with a particularly pronounced, additional gravity that moved the subversive, revolutionary

[18] Compare Henri Lefebvre, *Critique of Everyday Life*, Vol. 1, pp. 170–2 and Lefebvre, *Critique of Everyday Life*, Vol. 2, pp. 79–81 with Marx's 'On the Jewish Question' (1844) in Karl Marx, *Early Political Writings*, ed. Joseph O'Malley (Cambridge, 1994), pp. 28–56.

[19] Henri Lefebvre, *Everyday Life in the Modern World* (New Brunswick, NJ 1971), p. 23.

[20] Guy Debord, 'Perspectives for Conscious Alternations in Everyday Life' (1961), repr. in Ben Highmore (ed.), *The Everyday Life Reader* (London, 2002), pp. 238–45. The relationship between Lefebvre and Debord, however, should not be exaggerated and was more tenuous than sometimes presumed; see the reconstruction by Vincent Kaufmann, *Guy Debord; Revolution in the Service of Poetry* (Minneapolis, 2006) pp. 165–72.

[21] Lefebvre, *Critique of Everyday Life*, Vol. 2, p. 241.

[22] Richard F. Kuisel, *Seducing the French: The Dilemma of Americanization* (Berkeley, CA, 1993); Axel Schildt, Detlef Siegfried, and Karl Christian Lammers (eds.), *Dynamische Zeiten: Die 60er Jahre in den beiden deutschen Gesellschaften* (Hamburg, 2000); Victoria de Grazia, *Irresistible Empire: America's Advance through 20th-Century Europe* (Cambridge, MA, 2005).

[23] For biographical and intellectual connections between Lefebvre, Georges Perec, the experimental novelist of *Les Choses* (1965), and Roland Barthes, who studied the sign power of advertising in these years, see Sheringham, *Everyday Life*.

[24] Jean Baudrillard, *La Société de Consummation* (Paris, 1970), p. 264.

centre of political action further away from class and institutions to the realm of desire. The everyday was the stage where the self rediscovered itself through a set of new, liberating experiences. While consumer culture provided French commentators with a new zone of engagement in the 1950s and 1960s, the sociological and public investment of the everyday in France needs also to be seen as continuation and reworking of a pre-existing cultural tradition where surrealist artists had championed the experience of poetics and arts (not formal political practice) as transformative experience.

The ambition of 'total praxis' received a serious knock in the 1970s from Michel de Certeau, who disaggregated everyday life into an ensemble of individual practices and ways of doing (reading, eating, walking). The study of everyday life, which had originally proceeded from mature Marx to young Marx, now made do without Marx altogether. Still, Certeau—himself a historian as well as sociologist—stopped short of the flight from politics that would characterize much of the 'new history' in this decade. What he did was to lower the sights of political action. Subversion took the place of revolution. While no longer holding the potential of total transformation, the everyday still offered individuals a chance to resist conformity through 'microbobe'-like strategies; this was in marked difference to Pierre Bourdieu's account of habitus where embodied tastes reproduce existing hierarchies.[25] It gave consumption a political dimension of its own. Certeau presented the 'tactics of consumption [as] the ingenious ways in which the weak make use of the strong'.[26] His emphasis on unintended, creative uses, on clever tricks, and on how individuals manipulated and reappropriated goods in the course of practice was an important step towards a recognition of the active consumer.

Historians came late to the everyday, with the exception of a few forerunners in the *Annales*. And when they did, in the 1970s, they did so in a political context where Lefebvre's confidence in romantic revolution had been superseded by a more relativistic and sceptical tone. It mattered hugely that historians' interest in the everyday was largely a post-1968 phenomenon. Politically, it gave it a compensatory function. Mentalities and everyday life took the place of revolutionary utopias. The identity crisis was most pronounced in France, the mother of revolution. '*Nouvelle histoire*' gave a depoliticized nation the chance to find itself in an equally depoliticized past.[27] The quotidian past offered comfort in an uncertain present. Whereas earlier sociologists wanted to expose the familiar as that which was not known—from housewives' columns in glossy magazines to driving habits—the new generation of cultural historians were fascinated by the strange.

Historians preferred to write about the everyday as if it were a given realm, with little interest in its genesis or ambivalence. In the 1970s and 1980s, the everyday started to appear in a wide range of guises, from a virtually depoliticized sphere of cooking, eating, and sleeping all the way to the politically supercharged protests over the price of food and rationing in times of war. Braudel, in his three-volume *Civilization and Capitalism*,

---

[25] Pierre Bourdieu, *Distinction: A Social Critique of the Judgment of Taste* (Paris 1984, engl. edn. Cambridge, MA, 1979).

[26] Michel de Certeau, *The Practice of Everyday Life* (Berkeley, CA, 1984; 1st French edn. 1974), p. xvii.

[27] François Dosse, *L'histoire en miettes: des Annales à la nouvelle histoire* (Paris, 1987); Lutz Raphael, *Die Erben von Bloch und Febvre: Annales-Geschichtsschreibung und nouvelle histoire in Frankreich, 1945–80* (Stuttgart, 1994).

significantly gave *Les Structures du quotidien* (1979) the first volume to themselves, separating them physically as well as analytically from those on commercial capitalism and world domination. Looking back on his life's work, Braudel wrote that 'mankind is more than waist-deep in daily routine. Countless inherited acts...repeated time after time to this very day, become habits that help us live, imprison us, and make decisions for us throughout our lives.'[28] To him the everyday mattered because it pulled us along, not because of agency and politics. By contrast, social historians who took their lead from E. P. Thompson—who himself avoided the term 'everyday'—focused on dramatic clashes over bread, food prices, scarcities, and the black market. This has enriched our understanding of the politics of consumption in Berlin, London, Moscow, and Vichy France in the era of the two world wars.[29] The everyday here, however, is not at all about sameness and routine. Rather it is about suspension and crisis, moments when inherited customs, beliefs, and habits came under pressure or broke down. Admittedly, these were no longer the great events of great men, but they were 'events' nonetheless. They simply broadened the repertoire of events and actors, stretching the terrain of politics from the Cabinet office to the neighbourhood street, including housewives as well as politicians.

History from below went a step further. The quotidian had its own politics and agency, 'new' social historians stressed. Dorothee Wierling, an early gender historian, defined 'the everyday as the sphere in which people through their actions exercise direct influence on their condition,'[30] a broad definition that was equally silent about the production of rhythms and desires that had interested social theorists and about the pull of routines in Braudel. The main target was an older social history. To lump together ordinary people as either heroic rebels or passive conformists was too schematic. Hans Medick challenged Thompson's opposition between plebeian culture (authentic) and commercial capitalism (inauthentic and coerced) in the eighteenth century. Common people, too, participated in fashion, drink, and commercial culture.[31] If industrial capitalism triumphed, it did not snuff out people's everyday life. They continued to find meaning and subjectivity in the family and at the workplace, where they cultivated what Lüdtke called '*Eigensinn*'. Such 'self-will' created a micropolitical universe of its own.[32]

---

[28] Fernand Braudel, *Afterthoughts on Material Civilization and Capitalism* (Baltimore, MD, 1979), p. 7.

[29] Belinda J. Davis, *Home Fires Burning: Food, Politics, and Everyday Life in World War I Berlin* (Chapel Hill, NC, 2000); Maureen Healy, *Vienna and the Fall of the Habsburg Empire: Total War and Everyday Life in World War I* (Cambridge, 2004); Shannon Lee Fogg, *The Politics of Everyday Life in Vichy France: Foreigners, Undesirables, and Strangers* (Cambridge, 2008).

[30] Dorothee Wierling, 'Alltagsgeschichte und Geschichte der Geschlechterbeziehungen', in Alf Lüdtke (ed.), *Alltagsgeschichte: Zur Rekonstruktion historischer Erfahrungen und Lebensweisen* (Frankfurt, 1989), p. 171.

[31] Hans Medick, 'Plebeian culture in the transition to capitalism', in Raphael Samuel and Gareth Stedman Jones (eds.), *Culture, Ideology and Politics* (London, 1982), pp. 84–112; at length, see now John Styles, *The Dress of the People: Everyday Fashion in Eighteenth-Century England* (New Haven, CT, 2007).

[32] Alf Lüdtke, 'Cash, Coffee-Breaks, Horseplay: Eigensinn and Politics among Factory Workers in Germany Circa 1900', in Michael Hanagan and Charles Stephenson (eds.), *Confrontation, Class Consciousness, and the Labor Process* (New York, 1986), pp. 65–95; Belinda Davis, Thomas Lindenberger, and Michael Wildt (eds.), *Alltag, Erfahrung, Eigensinn: Historisch-Anthropologische Erkundungen* (Frankfurt, 2008).

Routinely sneaking off for an illegal coffee-break, pulling each other's moustaches, and other horseplay, all this was political, too, he insisted. It was a very different conception of everyday politics from that of Lefebvre. Instead of reciprocal flows between private and public, it was a world apart. Here ordinary people kept their distance from national politics. In a case study of factory life in Saxony, Lüdtke presented a sheltered micropolitics which allowed workers to retain their self-respect and sense of independence both from the discipline of the factory and from parties and unions. The separation between these political worlds, he argued, reached its greatest point in 1933.[33]

For Marxist historians, feminism was one bridge from structures to subjectivity. As it was women who did the shopping and cooking and who kept the fabric of domestic life together, this was hugely consequential for a scholarly recognition that consumption mattered. In Britain, Raphael Samuel was amongst the first to cross that bridge. Women's stuff, he wrote, was not 'trivia, but a way of challenging centuries of silence... It is unclear why a preoccupation with the material practices of everyday life... is either Utopian or undesirable from a Marxist point of view.'[34]

For these 'new' social historians, the rehabilitation of the everyday was a political act in two major respects. One was to challenge the intellectual division of labour. People's history demanded a more democratic praxis of history—giving ordinary people their voice back and including them in history workshops and oral history projects. The other was to fight consumer capitalism from the bottom up, by getting under the skin of its trivial appeal. In essays resembling Charles Baudelaire and Walter Benjamin, Samuel followed the appeal of retro-chic, heritage, fake 'historic' watches, and arts and crafts wallpaper.[35] The charge that capitalism bred 'false', inauthentic needs lay never far from the surface. It 'is unlikely', he wrote in 1981, 'that we shall ever be able effectively to combat bourgeois ideology until we can see how it arises in ourselves, until we explore the needs and desires it satisfies, and the whole substratum of fears on which it draws.'[36]

These different points of entry explain why the everyday often appeared in such contrasting lights, and why exchange and cross-fertilization between historians and social scientists remained limited. Only Certeau in the 1970s provided a shared point of contact in a post-revolutionary setting. While Lefebvre would belatedly be exported to cultural studies in the United States,[37] he had virtually no reception amongst German historians from below, who looked to the more structuralist Pierre Bourdieu.[38] Anglo-Saxon cultural historians meanwhile took their cue from anthropologists.

---

[33] Lüdtke, 'Cash, Coffee-Breaks, Horseplay'.

[34] Raphael Samuel, 'People's History', in Raphael Samuel (ed.), *People's History and Socialist Theory* (London, 1981), p. xxxi.

[35] Raphael Samuel, *Theatres of Memory* (London, 1994).

[36] Samuel, 'People's History', p. xxxi.

[37] See the special issue edited by Alice Kaplan and Kristin Ross, 'Everyday Life', *Yale French Studies*, 73 (1987).

[38] German sociologists took earlier notice; see Thomas Kleinspehn, *Der verdrängte Alltag: Henri Lefebvres Marxistische Kritik des Alltagslebens* (Giessen, 1975).

German radicals also liked to speak of 'Konsumterror', but however sceptical historians of below were of the American way of life privately, intellectually they were preoccupied with the Nazis, not contemporary fashion and consumer goods.[39] They turned
to the everyday as a way of coming to terms with Nazism by examining the role of ordinary people under the Swastika. In particular, they challenged a simple divide between
consent and coercion; the turn to oral history in Italy followed a similar path.[40] As most
of the 'new' social historians came from the left and labour history, it is not surprising
that their focus was on the workplace and 'kleine Leute', plebeians or little guys. Instead
of homes filling up with goods and gadgets, the German interest was in deprivation and
getting by, more 'Little Man, What Now?' than the women's lifestyle magazines which
caught Lefebvre's attention. Everyday life happened at the edge of a proletarian existence. It was a struggle for survival, about how the poor got by and preserved some
autonomy under totalitarian rule. The study of everyday life, Lüdtke wrote, aimed to
give back 'their own contours to those who had been beaten, exploited and murdered by
and during German fascism.'[41]

These national and political traditions shaped how intellectuals saw their own role and
that of their subjects. Oral history and history workshops were driven by a democratic
impulse to free people from the straightjacket of structural interpretations. Historians
ought to listen to people since they knew their own lives best. Everyday life was simultaneously treated as an object of study and a 'medium of memory'; in this view, quotidian routines left their mark on people's consciousness. Talking about them could unlock
otherwise hidden memories.[42] By contrast, Debord had compared everyday life to 'a sort
of reservation for good natives who keep modern society running without understanding it.'[43] Lefebvre's humanism, too, had limits: 'people in general, do not know their own
lives very well, or know them inadequately.'[44] That is why they needed a sociologist and
philosopher to interpret them.

Let us take stock of the discussion so far with a few interim observations. It is noteworthy how historians' initial focus on production and work led to a more sealed conception of everyday politics, compared to the earlier French debate that evolved around
goods, images, desires, communications, and their consumption. Whether we approach
the everyday as a 'sphere' or as a 'level' influences not only what we see but where we
see it coming from and going to. Intriguingly, when cultural historians and historians
from below took to the everyday they resisted asking too much about its history. This

[39] The historical engagement with Americanization came later; see Alf Lüdtke, Inge Marssolek
and Adelheid von Saldein (eds.), Amerikanisierung: Traum and Alptraum im Deutschland des 20.
Jahrchunderts (Stuttgart, 1996).
[40] Detlev Peukert, Inside Nazi Germany: Conformity, Opposition, and Racism in Everyday Life (New
Haven, CT, 1982); Laura Passerini, 'Work, Ideology and Consensus under Italian Fascism', History
Workshop, 8 (1979), pp. 82–108.
[41] Alf Lüdtke, 'Einleitung', in Alf Lüdtke (ed.), Alltagsgeschichte, p. 10, my translation.
[42] Lutz Niethammer, 'Einleitung', in Lutz Niethammer (ed.), Die Jahre weiss Man nicht wo Man sie
Hinsetzen soll: Faschismuserfahrungen im Ruhrgebiet (Berlin, 1983), p. 20, my translation.
[43] Debord, 'Perspectives for Alterations in Everyday Life', p. 240.
[44] Lefebvre, Critique of Everyday Life, Vol. 1, p. 94.

was, arguably, because the everyday was a weapon in the battle against a unitary history, big structures, and grand narratives. The result was a series of pointillist pictures. What it sidestepped was a basic historical question: if the everyday was a sphere, how did this sphere come about and change over time? John Brewer has recently stressed how the historical turn to the everyday was prepared by neo-realist film in the wake of the Second World War and the aesthetic shift to narrating reality from multiple points of view.[45] For the social sciences more generally, we need to distinguish between a recognition that the everyday was concrete and fragmented, on the one hand, and a critique of linear history on the other. For Lefebvre, the everyday was fragmented and contradictory, but he was nonetheless convinced that it had *a* history and that it contained *a* total truth. This is not to say that we need to subscribe to his account of that history. His evidence for the progressive 'underdevelopment' of everyday life in affluent post-war societies, for example, made a whole range of debatable observations, such as a reduction in tourism and travel, the erosion of cooking, and a 'backwardness' in terms of sex and family planning—at the very moment when most people started to fly to the sun for the first time, discovered new tastes and cuisines, and experimented with new forms of sexual pleasure.[46] Similarly, it is unhelpful to see the invasion of the home by technology and consumer goods as a twentieth-century phenomenon, as Lefebvre liked to do; he invoked an idyllic picture of recent country life and organic community. New coal-burning fireplaces, saucepans, and teapots in the late seventeenth and eighteenth centuries, gas, baths, and toilets in the nineteenth, and, more generally, technologies of comfort and convenience have long transformed domestic needs and rhythms.[47] Still, historians should learn from Lefebvre to ask questions about the genesis of the everyday. What has been the course and extent of the fragmentation between leisure, work, and the everyday? How did it proceed in different times and places? What is the respective contribution of capitalism, nationalism, and ideology? Is the distance always widening, or are there also times of fusion?

EVERYDAY LIFE: A LONGER HISTORY

Integral to these questions is when societies started to reflect on everyday life and for what purpose. Most historians have looked to the age of affluence after the Second World War. This focus has been reinforced by intellectual politics, in particular academic turf wars over the imperial ambition of neoclassical economics. The rise of mass consumption is tied up with the hegemony of rational choice and American power during the Cold War. In this view, accounts of human behaviour that have looked at habits, routines,

[45] Brewer, 'Microhistory and the Histories of Everyday Life'.
[46] Lefebvre, *Critique of Everyday Life*, Vol. 2, pp. 145 f. There is an interesting affinity here with the idea of cultural regression and a decline in 'real' pleasure, including sex, in John Kenneth Galbraith, *The Affluent Society* (New York, 1958), pp. 218–9.
[47] See the chapters by Pennell and Shove in this volume.

and the everyday appear as a recent emancipatory reaction, reclaiming human nature from the clutches of consumer sovereignty and its neo-liberal champions. One historian who has spoken up for the 'habitual, repetitive, [and] unreflective' has confidently declared that 'everyday life... had not been the province of either history or social study before the Second World War.'[48] Whether routines are automatically unreflective is a matter of debate; a recent study has stressed how many people in fact use them for thinking and fantasizing.[49] The point here is that such assertions are based on a paradigm inherited from the Cold War. Everyday life has a longer, more surprising history.

Fascination with the everyday can be traced back to several intellectual traditions in the decades around 1900, the formative moment of the social sciences and academic professionalization. The first point to emphasize is the pluralistic history of the everyday. For French writers after the Second World War, and for later Hungarian thinkers like Agnes Heller, a principal source of inspiration was Georg Lukacs's discussion of Marx and the concept of reification. Lukacs's *History and Class Consciousness* (1923) was the *Ur*text for later Marxist critiques that saw the everyday as a hybrid of alienation and emancipation.[50] The everyday, Lukacs argued, was neither authentic nor inauthentic. It was where commodification was most directly experienced. Consumption united the purchase and use of goods with the proletariat's self-awareness as that group which sold its labour. Commodification and self-knowledge thus worked in tandem. This humanist Marxism would emerge as the dominant voice of studies of the everyday in Western Europe after the Second World War, but at the time it was just one amongst many currents. These ranged from Edmund Husserl's phenomenology of everyday life and the life-world—concepts that later would be picked up by Garfinkel and Habermas—to Alfred Schütz's early sociology of everyday life.[51] Martin Heidegger contributed a nihilistic strand, where '*Alltäglichkeit*' (everydayness) produced the very opposite of emancipation: a conformist mindset.[52] References to the everyday, *Alltag*, and *quotidien* are scattered across the works of intellectuals, novelists, and surrealists in the late nineteenth and early twentieth centuries. These include figures we might expect—like Walter Benjamin and his cultural archaeology of urban spaces and rhythms—but also other more surprising instances. Max Weber, in his classic essay on the three types of

---

[48] Pat Hudson, 'Closeness and Distance', *Cutural & Social History*, 7 (2010), pp. 375–85, at pp. 376–7.

[49] Billy Ehn and Orvar Löfgren, *The Secret World of Doing Nothing* (Berkeley CA, 2010).

[50] Georg Lukács, *History and Class Consciousness: Studies in Marxist Dialectics* (1923; English edn. 1971). See further, Edward Roberts, *Philosophizing the Everyday: Revolutionary Praxis and the Fate of Cultural Theory* (London, 2006).

[51] See Kurt Hammerich and Michael Klein (eds.), *Materialien zur Soziologie des Alltags* (Opladen, 1978).

[52] Martin Heidegger, *Sein und Zeit*, (Tübingen, 1927; 2nd edn. 2001). Lefebvre warmed to Heidegger's later *Holzwege* (1959). Recent attempts at a left-Heideggerianism have been criticized as 'philosophically incoherent'—Geoffrey Waite, 'Lefebvre without Heidegger: Left-Heidegerianism qua contradictio in adiecto', in Kanishka Goonewardena, Stefan Kipfer, Richard Milgrom, and Christian Schmid (eds.), *Space, Difference, Everyday Life: Reading Henri Lefebvre* (New York, 2008), p. 106. This does not diminish their interest as a historical phenomenon. On earlier sociologists, see Hammerich and Klein (eds.), *Materialien zur Soziologie des Alltags*.

legitimate rule, for example, described charismatic rule as '*ausseralltäglich*' (extraordinary) and noted how, once the ruler holding its personal magnetism died, authority had a tendency to be routinized in everyday life ('*Veralltäglichung*')—a very different politics of everyday life from that discussed previously.[53]

Perhaps the most compelling analogue to the humanist Marxist rehabilitation of the quotidian was the liberal tradition of pragmatism. It dominated American public discourse in the first half of the twentieth century, but has since been marginal and has largely dropped off the radar of those writing about the everyday. Pragmatists made meaning and identity an everyday process. Instead of lofty, abstract thought, philosophy and psychology had to be brought down to earth and made concrete. In a 1905 lecture, William James, its pre-eminent spokesperson at the time, declared that 'any philosophical system which does not answer the questions of life—of real, grimy, everyday life—can be called to account as not fulfilling its vocation.'[54] The 'common sense' of the 'common man' became worthy of study.

James's plea for the concrete was not so dissimilar from Lefebvre's half a century later, but it rested on a very different understanding of human behaviour in general, and habit, in particular. James, too, noted how habits tended to embody individual character and conserve social structures. 'Habit', he wrote in *The Principles of Psychology* (1890), was 'the enormous fly-wheel of society, its most precious conservative agent. It alone is what keeps us all within the bounds of ordinance.'[55] It ensured that miners kept on mining in darkness, and fishermen fishing in winter. Once our habits were fixed it was too late to switch to a different path of life. This also prevented 'social strata from mixing.' At the same time, habits also had a progressive, liberating potential. This was for two main reasons. First, James explained, habits set free 'the upper regions of brain and mind', and thus enabled human flourishing. Repetition and training enabled people to carry out at the same time a far greater range of practices than if an action needed the full attention of the conscious will—what today is called multitasking. 'There is no more miserable human being', James wrote, 'than one in whom nothing is habitual but indecision, and for whom the lighting of every cigar ... [is the] subject of express volitional deliberation.'[56] Once they had become embodied sensations, all repeated actions needed was a 'cue' to set off a chain of movements. As a good deal of consuming practices operate in this mode (eating, washing, playing sports, driving), how such habits are learned, passed on, and modified or broken is a subject of enormous importance, although it has received little attention from scholars of consumption until recently.[57]

---

[53] Max Weber, 'Die drei reinen Typen der legitimen Herrschaft', in *Soziologie, universalgeschichtliche Analysen, Politik* (Stuttgart 1973), p. 163.

[54] Lecture at Wellesley College, 1905, repr. in William James, *Pragmatism* (Cambridge MA, 1975), Appendix 2, at p. 275.

[55] William James, *The Principles of Psychology* (New York, 1890), Vol. 1, p. 121.

[56] James, *The Principles of Psychology*, Vol. 1, p. 122.

[57] Jukka Gronow and Alan Warde (eds.), *Ordinary Consumption* (London, 2001); E. Shove, *Comfort, Cleanliness and Convenience: The Social Organisation of Normality* (Oxford, 2003); Elizabeth Shove, Frank Trentmann, and Richard Wilk (eds.), *Time, Consumption, and Everyday Life* (Oxford, 2009).

Habit formation, secondly, was linked to social action and ethical progress. Unlike later commentators, James was interested less in how habits were imposed from the outside and more in how they were cultivated on the inside. For pragmatists, concrete action was the true base of ethical life. James acknowledged that there were many bad habits—drink in particular. Yet, habits could also improve character. James scorned passive entertainment and self-absorbed pleasures of the imagination that bore no practical fruit. 'The habit of excessive novel-reading and theatre-going will produce true monsters.... The weeping of the Russian lady over the fictitious personages in the play, while her coachman is freezing to death on his seat outside, is the sort of thing that everywhere happens on a less glaring scale.'[58] The remedy was to ensure that actions, through repetition, developed into the habitual partner of sentiment. A little daily exercise of doing something for no other reason than that we would rather not, would train our 'habits of the will' and prepare us for that moment when we might be confronted with a serious challenge. Over time, the routine of paying attention in school and work would strengthen the power of judgement. Repetition, in other words, far from making habitual actions trivial or mindless, nurtured critical faculties.

What has this got to do with consumption? A great deal. For this way of looking at behaviour managed to engage with both choice and routine, two modes that later became separated by neoclassical economics and studies of everyday life. Instead of treating choice as an instant, it viewed it more organically as a habit of reflection, something that could be trained and refined over the course of one's life. The home economics movement was one channel which brought this idea into public circulation, teaching thousands in the inter-war years how to develop 'wise consumption choices'.[59]

That habits could be changed through consumption had been an intellectual leitmotiv since the Enlightenment if not earlier. From the late seventeenth century, writers noted how new tastes and goods stimulated industrious habits, and discussed the influence of comfort and convenience on social disposition and cultural refinement. We need to know more about what happened to this discourse after the eighteenth century and its relation to the engagement with habits and everyday things around 1900; William James, for example, had read Sydney Smith, an early nineteenth-century Anglican writer. Political economists continued to discuss 'comfort' and in *The Civilization of the Renaissance in Italy* (1860), the Swiss historian Jacob Burckhardt offered one of the first histories expressly concerned with the material trappings of daily life and new habits of cleanliness and politeness.[60]

---

[58] James, *The Principles of Psychology*, Vol. 1, p. 125. For a more sympathetic account of these cultural practices, see John Brewer, *The Pleasures of the Imagination* (New York, 1997).

[59] Hazel Kyrk, *Economic Problems of the Family* (New York, 1929), p. 391; John Dewey, *Human Nature and Conduct: An Introduction to Social Psychology* (New York, 1922). Compare Mark Bevir and Frank Trentmann, 'Civic Choices: Retrieving Perspectives on Rationality, Consumption, and Citizenship', in Soper, Kate, and Frank Trentmann, eds. *Citizenship and Consumption*: Palgrave Macmillan, 2007. (Basingstoke, 2007), pp. 19–33.

[60] Jacob Burckhardt, *The Civilization of the Renaissance in Italy* (1860, New York 2nd edn. 1958); Wilhelm Roscher, *Principles of Political Economy*, trans. John J. Lalor (New York, 1878), pp. 231–2.

The fascination with the everyday in the years around 1900 owed a good deal to the transformation of comfort and the accumulation of objects, new and old, in previous generations. New research on the Parisian bourgeoisie, for example, has highlighted the great number of material changes that supported new sensibilities and habits in the course of the nineteenth century. Increasingly sophisticated locks on dressers and private bureaus as well as front doors created feelings of security and interiority. Curtains and carpets blocked out noise. The selective introduction of gas changed illumination. The cult of the antique fashioned new tastes and practices, such as collecting, and brought bric-a-brac and exotic objects into the home.[61] In many ways, this preoccupation with 'confort' and advice in popular guidebooks on how best to arrange the interior to reflect one's own personality and taste, continued on tracks that reached back to the eighteenth century and the Renaissance.

What arguably distinguished the quotidian moment of the early twentieth century from earlier periods was the broad public interest in everyday life and the energetic attempts to transform it. Intellectuals and artists were carried along by a much bigger cultural and political current. In part, this was fed by a real material spring. Living standards were rising in the late nineteenth century and new objects, comforts, and domestic technologies were changing American and European homes. Standardization meanwhile triggered an interest in antiques, bric-a-brac, folk customs, and 'authentic' country furniture. Tellingly, one of the earliest and most ambitious collectors of popular everyday objects was Henry Ford, whose collection in Dearborn, Michigan, would stretch across 9 acres. Ethnographic exhibitions put on display American Indians cooking bread and Swedish peasants churning butter. Daily life, it was said, exhibited the civilizational state or 'genius' of a nation.

Which quotidian matters moved into focus depended on the viewer's political lens. In the United States, the everyday was largely seen in democratic outlines. The first living history museum opened in Oakland, California, in 1896 to give visitors a feel for the life and character of people in the past.[62] A democratic society needed a people's history, not a story of great men. Historians, like ordinary citizens, should give their full attention to everyday things, Theodore Roosevelt said. In this broadly progressive vision, everyday life preserved a historical record of the growth of democracy. By contrast, the Soviet Union and Japan took a more aggressive approach in the inter-war years: their aim was to change it.

It is tempting, looking at the literature after the Second World War, to imagine everyday life as a bulwark against modernization, a fortress of true humanity under siege by the anonymous and inauthentic forces of bureaucracy and consumer capitalism.

[61] Manuel Charpy, 'Le Théâtre Des Objets: Espaces Privés, Culture Matérielle et Identité Bourgeoise, Paris 1830–1914', 2 vols., Ph.D. thesis (Université François-Rabelais de Tours, 2010). See also Clive Edwards, *Turning Houses into Homes: A History of the Retailing and Consumption of Domestic Furnishings* (Aldershot, 2005); Deborah Cohen, *Household Gods: The British and Their Possessions* (New Haven, CT, 2006).

[62] Bill Brown, *A Sense of Things: The Object Matter of American Literature* (Chicago, 2003), pp. 108 f., and more generally for the turn to things in this period.

In the years after the First World War, however, everyday life was an object of modernization, not an escape from it. Indeed, in terms of public policy and discourse, it would not be far-fetched to say that everyday life was the child of modernizers. In the Soviet Union, it was a revolutionary conception, in Japan a reformist one. This difference notwithstanding, both looked to everyday life as a nursery of modern habits and mentalities. People would abandon feudal customs and folk beliefs and acquire instead habits of self-discipline and rational calculation.

To be successful, the Russian Revolution had to be followed by a revolution of everyday life, Trotsky announced in *The Problems of Everyday Life* in 1924.[63] People carried with them an outdated material shell. It had to be replaced with one fit for socialism. The future did not only depend on how things were produced, but on how they were consumed. The avant-garde constructivist Boris Arvatov elaborated: bourgeois capitalism had split consumption from production, and high from low culture; socialist everyday life would reunite them, with labourers, artists, and intellectuals working together. Consumption, Arvatov argued, was decisive in shaping a people's 'world-outlook and, more importantly, its world-feeling.' The material everyday created a 'person's cultural type.' The United States, as the highest stage of capitalism, showed the way forward. Here things were 'dynamized' and 'spoke for themselves.' Arvatov listed collapsible furniture, automat restaurants, and reversible outfits as examples. Yet American capitalism still alienated things from nature. The remedy lay with new technologies of consumption. In electricity and the radio, 'for the first time, producing and consuming forms of energy are applied in the same way; nature in its pure form penetrates society and becomes *byt* [daily life].' Socialism would drive this process to its historical conclusion and usher in 'the dominion of Things' where objects and instruments reconnected people and nature.[64]

The reform of the '*byt*' targeted the petit-bourgeois home and the oppression of women within it. Reform strategies reflected the changing realities of power. In the 1920s, party activists and feminists moved deep into the home and tried to eradicate private pleasures and routines. The party promoted communes and housing cooperatives. All socialists were expected to follow the same objective code of everyday behaviour. In the 1930s, official policy began a partial retreat. Instead of suppressing them, Stalin now tried to harness private desires and possessions to the goal of productivity. Stakhanovites, the most productive workers, were rewarded with a gramophone, and Boston suit or crêpe de Chine dress. Housewives were urged to beautify their private home, with needlework and tablecloths, not to smash the chains of their petit-bourgeois oppression.[65] The retreat was never complete, however. The party, it was said, no longer

---

[63] Leon Trotsky, *The Problems of Everyday Life* (1924; engl. edn New York 1973).

[64] Boris Arvatov, 'Everyday Life and the Culture of the Thing (1925), Transl. By C. Kiaer', *October*, 81 (1997), pp. 119–28.

[65] Lewis H. Siegelbaum, *Stakhanovism and the Politics of Productivity in the USSR, 1935–41* (Cambridge, 1988); Sheila Fitzpatrick, *Everyday Stalinism: Ordinary Life in Extraordinary Times: Soviet Russia in the 1930s* (Oxford, 1999); Jukka Gronow, *Caviar with Champagne: Common Luxury and the Ideals of the Good Life in Stalin's Russia* (Oxford and New York, 2003). See also Fitzpatrick's chapter in this volume.

had any business in interfering with 'the trifles of everyday life',[66] as long as people's behaviour still served its interests. Personal cleanliness became the touchstone of socialist civilization, the full, untrimmed beard its enemy. The wives of party leaders swarmed across the country to bring mirrors and razors to work units. It is doubtful they had read William James, but they appreciated how daily habits conditioned the self. Shaving and other daily routines left their mark on internal will as well as external appearance. They embodied self-discipline and self-respect.

In Japan, the reform of everyday life (*seikatsu kaizen*) was led by a coalition of state ministries, professionals, women's groups, and other civic organizations. It combined nationalist and progressive goals. 'Everyday life', a Home Ministry official explained, 'is the expression of the nation's thought, and national thought appears and takes the form of everyday life.'[67] Rationalizing daily life would simultaneously improve social welfare (by cutting waste) and strengthen the nation (by catapulting it from feudalism into modernity).[68] Superstitious customs would be cast off in favour of a more instrumental rationality. Costly weddings and funerals had to stop, personal budgeting to start. Housewives and husbands were asked to pay attention to time, in the sense of being punctual but, equally importantly, of planning ahead for the future. They were urged to improve society by improving themselves, in their hygiene, their clothing, and their domestic comfort. These reform initiatives extended from the everyday life exhibitions of modern dwellings and kitchens in the 1920s to the 'new life' campaigns of the 1950s.[69] The budget book, the savings account, and the modern kitchen, with gas, running water, and functional work units, where the housewife could carry out tasks standing up, were the material manifestations of a 'better' everyday life.

What these initiatives suggest is that we must be careful to avoid simple oppositions. Japanese reformers and many intellectuals in the 1920s and 30s were drawn to everyday life not as a conservative refuge from change but as a modern stimulus to it. Although they have yet to receive serious attention in the general literature, Japanese intellectuals were amongst the pioneers of an ethnography of everyday life. The architect Kon Wajirō, who observed urban life from street corners, dreamt of a new discipline of 'modernologio' (*kokengaku*) that would study the 'abnormal'. Its explicit goal was to change everyday life. Consumption—and American jazz, film, and fashion in particular—was appreciated

---

[66] Rabonitsa, 1936, cited in Victor Buchli, *An Archaeology of Socialism* (Oxford and New York, 1999), p. 78. See also Stephen Kotkin, *Magnetic Mountain: Stalinism as a Civilization* (Berkeley, Los Angeles, and London, 1995).

[67] Tago Ichimin, quoted in Jordan Sand, *House and Home in Modern Japan: Architecture, Domestic Space, and Bourgeois Culture, 1880–1930* (Cambridge, MA, 2003), p. 183.

[68] It broadly looked to a middle-class ideal of domesticity—similar orientations can be found in colonial India and elsewhere, although the global circulation of this domestic ideal deserves further research. See Judith E. Walsh, *Domesticity in Colonial India: What Women Learned When Men Gave Them Advice* (Lanham, MD, 2004); Douglas Haynes, Abigail McGowan, Tirthankar Roy, and Haruka Yanagisawa (eds.), *Towards a History of Consumption in South Asia* (Oxford, 2010).

[69] Sheldon Garon, *Molding Japanese Minds: The State in Everyday Life* (Princeton NJ, 1997).

as a source of subjectivity.[70] The context of modernization in which Japanese intellectuals found themselves thus placed them in a different relation to the everyday and to
past and future than better-known European contemporaries like Walter Benjamin. For
Benjamin, capitalist modernity had cast a dream-like spell over people. Urban spaces
and everyday things were passageways into the past—and for the scholar, therapeutic
routes to wake them up. Benjamin likened shopping arcades to 'caves containing the
fossil remains of a vanished monster: the consumer of the pre-imperial era of capitalism,
the last dinosaur of Europe.'[71] For Japanese writers, by contrast, the everyday embodied
the future. It was the feudal past which had been an inauthentic dream. Some, like
Gonda Yasunosuke, who studied bars, brothels, and cinemas in Tokyo's Asakusa district, feared modernity might result in homogenization, turning the Japanese into slaves
of things. Many others, however, saw the quotidian as liberating. For Kon Wajirō, people
regained agency through things and choice. Unlike feudal customs, which had been top-
down and ceremonial, everyday life was authentic and immediate. The modern home,
street life, and quotidian pleasures were sources of self-awareness and revealed the true
soul of the people. A generation before Lefebvre, the Marxist Tosaka Jun urged philosophers to take clothes and objects seriously. The everyday, he argued, was the true reality
philosophers had failed to see.[72]

The Japanese case further illustrates the danger of approaching habit and choice as
always opposed, one belonging to everyday life, the other to the market. For reformers in Japan, everyday life was about replacing 'bad' customary habits with 'good' modern habits. Routines such as keeping a budget book would help families make informed
choices about saving and spending. It was choice which distinguished everyday life from
custom, and which made consumption the main focus of attention for reformers and
intellectuals.

Harry Harootunian, who has done most to illuminate the Japanese engagement
with the quotidian, has stressed how the everyday emerged in the context of urban
modernity—hence, the focus on cinemas, urban fashion, and the ethnography of street
life. Urban modernity, however, had a private as well as a public side. For the appreciation
of everyday life as well as its praxis, the home played a crucial role. Arguably, domestic and
urban space are best seen as symbiotic. In Japan in the 1920s, reformers wanted dwellings
to be stripped of ornamentation, modified for chairs, and equipped with simple, sturdy
furniture. After the Second World War, new housing introduced functional Western
room design. We know from recent ethnographic work that these material changes did
not lead to a wholesale Westernization of domestic life; in their flats, families created

---

[70] Harry Harootunian, *History's Disquiet: Modernity, Cultural, Practice, and the Question of Everyday
Life* (New York, 2000), esp. pp. 126–8. Several Japanese writers had been influenced by Heidegger.
[71] Walter Benjamin, *The Arcades Project*, trans. Eiland Howard and Kevin McLaughlin (Cambridge,
MA, 1999), p. 540, R2, 3.
[72] Harry Harootunian, *Overcome by Modernity: History, Culture and Community in Interwar Japan*
(Princeton, NJ, 2000), esp. chapters 2 and 3. As Harootunian points out, not all commentators were
progressive. By 1942, the quotidian was also championed by those who wanted an Asian zone ruled by
Japan and looked to it as a glue between past and present.

Japanese-style rooms with tatami mats and built alcoves (*tokonoma*) to house ornaments, souvenirs, and spiritual objects.[73] In Europe, similarly, families moved into modern housing but, once inside, remained immune to the pleas of modernist architects and designers for functional simplicity and Neue Sachlichkeit. At the same time, the urban networks that delivered running water, gas, and later electricity marked a break in many 'ordinary' routines, from cooking and bathing to going to the toilet and reading under a gas light.

In-Between

In *Cultural Revolutions*, one of the few books that explicitly sets out to follow the politics of everyday life, Leora Auslander examines the place of quotidian objects and material habits in the English, American, and French revolutions (1640s, 1760s–1770s, and 1789–1800). All revolutionaries quickly found that changing people's minds required changing material culture. The English banned dancing, Americans donned homespun clothes, and the French sans-culottes made long trousers the republican uniform.[74] Yet, what is, perhaps, equally striking is how marginal the impact of these revolutions was on everyday life in the long run. Once they were over, dress and eating returned to earlier patterns. For a revolution like the French one, which set out to create a new world with its own calendar and language, the legacy on everyday life was miniscule, leaving behind little more than the tricoloured cockade and a national anthem. It fades into insignificance when compared to the transformations brought about by railways, running water, the motor car, or the television set.

If we move forward in time to the Russian Revolution (1917) and China's Cultural Revolution (post-1966), the repercussions are more dramatic. This was, in part, because socialism explicitly targeted the home as the incubator of bourgeois habits and mentalities. Such interventions often had surprisingly unintended consequences. In China, Mao mobilized young men and women against their parents in the hope of diverting their loyalty from the family to the party. What happened instead was that Chinese youths acquired a sense of personal autonomy and material entitlement. The anthropologist Yunxiang Yan has charted the spread of possessive individualism in village communities in Heilongijang province in north-east China. When the local party structures started to wither away in the 1970s, it left behind a culture of 'privatism'. Instead of a communal material culture, the legacy of the Cultural Revolution was homes with individual rooms, possessions, and leisure pursuits. Parents and children started to watch their favourite programmes on separate TV sets in separate rooms.[75]

---

[73] Inge Daniels, *The Japanese House: Material Culture in the Modern Home* (Oxford, 2010).

[74] Leora Auslander, *Cultural Revolutions: The Politics of Everyday Life in Britain, North America and France* (Oxford, 2009). Compare, Richard Wrigley, *The Politics of Appearances: Representations of Dress in Revolutionary France* (Oxford, 2002).

[75] Yunxiang Yan, *Private Life under Socialism: Love, Intimacy, and Family Change in a Chinese Village, 1949–99* (Stanford, CA, 2003).

The politics of everyday life is not limited to the express designs or unintended con-sequences of revolutions, however. Taking their cue from the late Michel Foucault and the social theorist Nikolas Rose, recent historians have moved the inquiry from formal politics to 'governmentality', that is, the practices and mentalities which authorities have used to govern their citizens. Here attention shifts from institutional structures (parties, ministries, trade unions) to the technologies of everyday life, such as gas lighting, post-boxes, abattoirs, and toilets. In nineteenth-century Britain, it is argued, these technolo-gies taught people to discipline themselves according to a liberal ideal of self-regulation. Personal hygiene has been treated as a test case, the private cubicle of the toilet as its material manifestation.[76] There is little doubt that these new urban networks cast social relations in a new political light. Street gas lamps were critical for the ability to see the poor, for example. As Chris Otter has noted in his history of light in Victorian England, the political consequences of these technologies were far from straightforward.[77] While better lighting and transport enhanced freedom by facilitating circulation, it also threat-ened freedom by bringing people and things into collision with each other.

Research on governmentality has been helpful in broadening the scope of politics to include its material articulation. At the same time, the shift from actors and institu-tions to strategies of rule has made it often difficult to know exactly who did what to whom. The relation of 'governmentality' to more conventional forms of political power and ideas remains unclear. How much was the 'liberal' governmentality attributed to gas lighting and water closets, for example, a function of these technologies, how much of the liberal political culture of Victorian Britain? After all, these technologies also spread across nationalist, authoritarian, and, in the inter-war years, to socialist and fascist soci-eties. Governmentality studies work with such a strong theoretical lens that they end up finding strikingly similar techniques of rule in all sorts of historically specific and varying situations, from Victorian cities to urban China today.[78] While governmentality studies therefore are a welcome shift away from conventional political history, they tend to replicate a top-down view that sees the everyday as an object on which experts, archi-tects, and reformers impose desired, new forms of behaviour. The primary attention is on the rationalities of self-rule hidden in the designs of planners and engineers. Actual practices of consumption often disappear from view.

In fact, everyday life has been remarkably porous, open in both directions; politics flows outwards as well as inwards. This double flow has varied considerably across time in terms of force and substance, depending not only on technological innovation but on existing private practices, as well as the public norms and institutions available for collec-tive action. Nineteenth-century conflicts over gas and water illustrate some of the ways new technologies brought politics across the doorstep. The appropriate use of gas was

---

[76] Tom Crook, 'Power, Privacy and Pleasure: Liberalism and the Modern Cubicle', *Cultural Studies*, 21/4–5 (2007), pp. 549–69; Patrick Joyce, *The Rule of Freedom: Liberalism and the Modern City* (London, 2003). For further discussion, see Trentmann, 'Materiality in the Future of History'.

[77] Chris Otter, *The Victorian Eye: A Political History of Light and Vision in Britain, 1800–1910* (Chicago, 2008).

[78] Li Zhang and Aihwa Ong (eds.), *Privatizing China: Socialism from Afar* (Ithaca, NY, 2008).

a constant bone of contention between consumers and providers. Many householders worried about safety. Before going to bed, they would lock their doors and switch off the main valve, against the advice of the gas company. Measuring consumption was a second problem. Engineers were in despair over the many users who misread their meters or, worse, manipulated them with magnets or enlarged the gas openings.[79] Consumers meanwhile were enraged when they were charged the full rate for lights that often only flickered. In a few cases, they were driven to collective action and even set up their own company—Parisians formed a Union des Consumateurs de Gaz in 1879. Generally speaking, however, these conflicts were fought out one by one and rarely spilled over into organized consumer politics.

Water generated a more powerful political current, especially in Victorian England. Water connected new practices and ideals of comfort and cleanliness with thorny issues of public health and a political tradition of the citizen as ratepayer. In Britain, landlords paid for water as citizens of their local government on the basis of their local property tax. Irritation at being overcharged by private monopolies was thus easily translated from an individual into a civic grievance, raising questions of rights and democratic accountability. Some called for a 'water parliament'. In the early 1880s, 'consumer defence leagues' sprang up in London to defend the rights of water consumers.

As the networks changed habits and levels of consumption, other troubles began to bubble to the surface. Baths were a classic problem of the political tensions that could arise from the normalization of a practice. Traditionally, baths had been treated as a luxury, for which water companies were entitled to charge 'extra', over and above the rate for 'domestic' purposes. As baths spread, however, and bathing was accepted as a normal part of domestic life, such premium charges started to look atavistic, a barrier to public morality, cleanliness, and a civilized lifestyle. In Sheffield, respectable townsmen formed a Bath Defence Association and led a consumer boycott.

The arrival of constant supply in the big cities, in the 1880s–1890s, raised political tensions to new heights. In one generation, Londoners, poor and rich alike, became used to having water on demand, night and day. When a series of droughts hit London in the mid-1890s, it forced the water companies to suspend constant supply. People were furious. The companies blamed the drought on 'wasteful' consumers and urged the public to conserve water. Consumers ignored them and blamed profit-hungry companies instead. Workers and housewives, progressives and socialists, joined in widespread protests. A public takeover followed in 1904.[80]

These cases raise substantive as well as methodological questions about the nature of the everyday and its relation to non-everyday processes and power. For one, they point

---

[79] Graeme J. N. Gooday, *The Morals of Measurement: Accuracy, Irony, and Trust in Late Victorian Electrical Practice* (Cambridge, 2004); Martin Daunton, 'The Material Politics of Natural Monopoly: Consuming Gas in Victorian Britain', in Martin Daunton and Matthew Hilton (eds.), *The Politics of Consumption: Material Culture and Citizenship in Europe and America* (Oxford, 2001), 69–88.

[80] Vanessa Taylor and Frank Trentmann, 'Liquid Politics: Water and the Politics of Everyday Life in the Modern City', *Past and Present*, 211 (May 2011). For France, see Jean-Pierre Goubert, *The Conquest of Water: The Advent of Health in the Industrial Age* (Princeton, NJ, 1989).

to the limitations of approaching the everyday as a separate, intimate sphere, parochial, inward looking and instinctively conservative. The terrain of everyday life is more differentiated. New technologies like water pipes, hot baths, flush toilets, and constant running water changed practices of consumption which, in turn, generated norms and expectations that could exert pressure on public life and politics. The clean Victorian who enjoyed the comfort of his home was not only an individual end-user but also a citizen with ideas about his public rights as a ratepayer. By 1900 cleanliness and access to running water had almost become a democratic right that carried with it obligations for public authorities. The creation of urban networks, meanwhile, also tied households together in new interdependent relationships. In Victorian England, a vibrant associational life ensured that these material networks were civic as much as technical affairs.

Everyday life, then, stands in a reciprocal relation to civil society as well as state and economy. The dialogical flow has been well captured by the contemporary historian Paul Ginsborg, who has presented families as the 'agents of everyday life' and nodal points of civil society. Families are distinguished by their 'plasticity', he notes, and their ability to change. This makes their relation to the outside world flexible and contingent. They can be inward looking and withdrawn or they can be 'porous…open not closed, curious and willing to intermingle.'[81] The orientation of everyday life therefore is not given but results from the interplay of family, civil society, and state. How that interface has changed over time deserves greater attention from historians.

A second qualification concerns resistance. The celebration of ruses, horseplay, and resistance has come naturally in a dualistic world view that sees the everyday as the space where ordinary people try to retain their creative individuality against big systems. It is rather less helpful if we want to understand the career of ordinary consumption practices, such as washing, cooking, or driving, that are tied to technological networks. People are not only rebels or victims. Their daily habits ratchet up aggregate demand and help shape the technological systems that try to meet it. They 'co-construct' systems of provision, in the words of science and technology studies.[82] One lesson from the rising levels of water consumption in the modern era is just how impossible authorities have found it to control and modify daily practices; in London, after constant supply was introduced, many householders just left the tap running in the summer to water their gardens overnight. In the years around 1900, municipal authorities and social democrats believed that once water was in public hands, civic spirit would encourage conservation and eliminate private waste and future droughts. Repeated scarcities and water stress in the following decades exposed this belief as naive. Once people developed routines of watering their garden with a water hose, washing their cars, and taking more frequent baths and (later) showers, it was difficult to break such habits. Behind the expanding volume and infrastructure of consumption lurk the everyday practices of millions.

[81] Paul Ginsborg, *The Politics of Everyday Life: Making Choices, Changing Lives* (New Haven, CT and London, 2005), pp. 91–2.
[82] Nelly Oudshoorn and Trevor Pinch (eds.), *How Users Matter: The Co-Construction of Users and Technology* (Cambridge, MA, 2003).

One innovative development in the study of everyday life in recent years has been the turn to practices.[83] Practices—eating, reading, taking photos, holidaying, and so forth—involve the integration of materials, meanings, and skills. An electric oven on its own does not make a meal or shape how a family has dinner. In contrast to governmentality, the practice approach takes seriously that it is ultimately people who have to integrate the different elements for a practice to arise and to continue. At the same time, it recognizes that the accomplishment and coordination of practices are not personal quirks but conditioned by larger societal configurations. Time use studies, for example, record remarkable differences in the distribution of practices. In France, people sit down for a leisurely lunch and dinner whereas in Finland they snack throughout the day. Energy and water use, similarly, follow different cycles.[84] Everyday life ticks to a variety of rhythms in modern societies, depending on a whole range of regionally and socially specific temporal configurations, from different work, commuting, and housing patterns, to holidays and school hours, down to the opening hours of the local shop. New practices can compete and crowd out old practices.

Instead of carving up life into micro-quotidian and macro-structures, research on practices recognizes, as Lefebvre did, that they are entwined, although not always in the same manner. Practices take us into how consumption is done. They are a reminder that we are dealing with processes that involve learning (and forgetting) and require feats of coordination with other practices. Consumption can be seen as a long evolutionary story of the rise, mutation, and diversification of some practices and the extinction of others. These are historical processes, although we still know relatively little about what the normalization of a practice (or its death) precisely looked like.[85] One way forward for research is to use moments of disruption such as water scarcity, electric blackouts, and traffic jams as historical passageways into the creation of normality. The normal does not just happen. Breakdowns reveal the effort needed to integrate technology, meaning, and competence to keep a practice going.[86]

In the debate about consumer society—past and present—the terms have been set by affluence, choice, and variety. It would be foolish to deny their impact on public policies, academic practice, and ideas of the good life. One unfortunate legacy, however, has been to treat consumption as the natural twin of market societies, alien to socialist economies. Proceeding from practices, normalization, and disruption instead of individual

[83] Theodore R Schatzki, Karin Knorr-Cetina, and Eike von Savigny (eds.), *The Practice Turn in Contemporary Theory* (London, 2001); Alan Warde, 'Consumption and Theories of Practice', *Journal of Consumer Culture*, 5/2 (2005), pp. 131–53; Elizabeth Shove, Matthew Watson, Martin Hand, and Jack Ingram, *The Design of Everyday Life* (Oxford, 2007).

[84] Elizabeth Shove, 'Everyday Practice and the Production and Consumption of Time', in Shove, Trentmann, and Wilk (eds.), *Time, Consumption, and Everyday Life*, pp. 17–33.

[85] Some insights are in Daniel Roche, *A History of Everyday Things*; Gail Cooper, *Air-Conditioning America: Engineers and the Controlled Environment, 1900–1960* (Baltimore, MD, 1998). See also the chapter by Shove in this volume.

[86] David E. Nye, *When the Lights Went Out: A History of Blackouts in America* (Cambridge MA, 2010); Frank Trentmann, 'Disruption is Normal: Blackouts, Breakdowns and the Elasticity of Everyday Life', in Shove, Trentmann, and Wilk (eds.), *Time, Consumption, and Everyday Life*, pp. 67–84.

choice and motivation leads to a more ecumenical approach. Bathing, watching television, home improvement, driving, and many other consumption practices spread in
socialist everyday life as well as under capitalism. There may have been fewer brands to
choose from in the socialist bloc in the 1960s–1980s, but Eastern like Western Europeans
were entangled in an historically unprecedented, ever more complex web of consumption practices.

Where socialism made a difference was to their social distribution, coordination,
and politicization. Fewer cars meant less driving, fewer showers less showering. On the
other hand, the shortage of consumer goods gave a special boost to other practices like
home improvement, knitting, and sewing. Above all, socialism exacerbated the challenge of coordination, especially for women. Queuing for goods ate up time that could
have been devoted to other practices. We have earlier pleaded for a more porous conception of the everyday. This also applies to socialist countries like the German Democratic
Republic (GDR), although here it was the state, not civil society, which provided the
political interface. The GDR operated an elaborate petitioning system. Set up to contain
dissent, the petitions developed into a forum for hundreds of thousands of ordinary citizens to voice their frustrations about poor-quality housing, the interminable wait for a
car, shoddy service and queuing in vain for a new pair of shoes for the children. These
petitions did not galvanize organized opposition but it would be equally wrong to discount their political effect. What they did was to foster a political subjectivity by making
citizens articulate what 'normal' daily life should be like, and connect its shortcomings
with the failure of the state to deliver that normality. Was it really 'normal', petitioners
asked, that one had to suspend ordinary life and take a holiday to hunt down a pair of
children's shoes or return a faulty product to the factory for the umpteenth time? The
failure to coordinate everyday practices satisfactorily became the failure of the regime.[87]

In the modern world, conventions of comfort and convenience and the ways of
eating, dressing, and dwelling associated with them, were not only home-grown and
national, but exported by traders, missionaries, and imperialists. The 'civilizing mission'
of the nineteenth century involved the global scaling-up of provincial European norms
and practices. Eating with cutlery and napkins, sleeping in beds in stone houses, washing with soap, and putting on trousers and dresses, these became universal ideals. It is
impossible to make sense of the global distribution of this material civilization without
the role played by empire.

At the same time, global food and commodity chains changed the ethical scale of
everyday life. Eating breakfast and sipping tea now connected consumers in one continent to producers in another. Potentially, the politics of everyday life was now global.
It can be tempting to trace back today's ethical consumer movements to the boycotts

---

[87] Frank Trentmann, 'Kurze Unterbrechung—Bitte Entschuldigen Sie die Störung—
Zusammenbruch, Zäsur und Zeitlichkeit als Perspektiven einer europäischen Konsumgeschichte', in
Sven Oliver Müller, Christina Benninghaus, Jörg Requate, and Charlotte Tacke (eds.), *Unterwegs in
Europa: Beiträge zu einer vergleichenden Sozial- und Kulturgeschichte* (Frankfurt, 2008), pp. 219–46; Ina
Merkel, *Utopie und Bedürfnis: Die Geschichte der Konsumkultur in der DDR* (Cologne, 1999); Jonathan
Zatlin, *The Currency of Socialism* (Cambridge, 2007).

of slave-grown sugar around 1800. Historical reality was less straightforward and progressive. Liberals dreamt of a world where trade connected people and continents in webs of interdependence. But by 1900, few people in the affluent north troubled themselves with the conditions of the millions in the south who sweated to procure the ingredients of their comfort. Coffee, cocoa, and many other colonial products previously prized for their exotic qualities were nationalized, rebranded as national mass consumer goods. Interestingly, it was at the very time that Westerners discovered the consumer in New York, Berlin, London, and Paris that they forgot about the African consumer. In the inter-war years, caring at a distance meant privileged British housewives buying Canadian apples and Kenyan coffee to support their white cousins in the empire.[88]

OUTLOOK

For the study of consumption, everyday life is central since so much is about how people actually use things and services. In the study of everyday life this centrality has taken two forms. While one tradition warned of mind-numbing consumerism and standardization, others have celebrated the everyday for giving rise to creative acts of consumption and resistance. When historians were drawn to everyday life in the 1970s they tended to view it as a sphere separate from politics and commerce, where ordinary people lived their lives according to their own logic. There were compelling historiographical reasons for this approach at the time, but, in retrospect, we can see how it simultaneously separated historical research from the intellectual pre-history of everyday life and from alternative ways of looking at the subject. This chapter has tried to stretch out the topic, historically and conceptually. Everyday life was neither a new product of the Cold War, nor was (or is) it a natural site of resistance to modernization. On the contrary, in the early twentieth century it attracted attention from revolutionaries and reformers as a vehicle of modernization. Like any large concept and phenomenon, the everyday has been conceived differently in different traditions. To treat it as a separate sphere that stands in opposition to state and capitalism is an ideological choice, not some given reality. In fact, everyday practices have often interacted with state and civil society.

Because they are concrete does not mean quotidian practices are 'micro' phenomena that can be studied apart from 'macro' systems. It is a methodological fallacy to collapse size and scale. In ordinary consumption practices such as washing, eating, and driving tiny actions combine with vast networks. Science and technological studies have concerned themselves with their material impact. But their political and ethical scale are perhaps of equal interest. Everyday life is often defined as trivial, but this does not mean

---

[88] Trentmann, *The Consuming Passion (forthcoming)*, chapter. 2; Frank Trentmann, 'Before "Fair Trade": Empire, Free Trade, and the Moral Economies of Food in the Modern World', *Environment and Planning*, D 25/6 (2007), pp. 1079–102.

it is necessarily numbed or unreflective. Trivial acts, especially when they are embodied through eating and drinking, could at times carry enormous ethical force. How and why the ethics of everyday life has changed over time is a rich subject for future historians.

BIBLIOGRAPHY

Auslander, Leora, *Cultural Revolutions: The Politics of Everyday Life in Britain, North America and France* (Oxford: Berg, 2009).

Brewer, John, 'Microhistory and the Histories of Everyday Life', *Cultural & Social History*, 7/1 (2010), pp. 87–110.

Certeau, Michel de, *The Practice of Everyday Life* (Berkeley, CA: University of California Press, 1984; 1st French edn. 1974).

Ehn, Billy, and Löfgren, Orvar, *The Secret World of Doing Nothing*, (Berkeley CA: University of California Press, 2010).

Fitzpatrick, Sheila, *Everyday Stalinism: Ordinary Life in Extraordinary Times: Soviet Russia in the 1930s* (Oxford: Oxford Unversity Press, 1999).

Ginsborg, Paul, *The Politics of Everyday Life: Making Choices, Changing Lives* (New Haven and London: Yale University Press, 2005).

Harootunian, Harry, *History's Disquiet: Modernity, Cultural, Practice, and the Question of Everyday Life* (New York: Columbia University Press 2000).

Highmore, Ben (ed.), *The Everyday Life Reader* (London: Routledge, 2002).

Lefebvre, Henri, *The Critique of Everyday Life*, 3 vols. (1947, 1961, 1981; English trans. London: Verso, 1991, 2002, 2005).

Lüdtke, Alf (ed.), *Alltagsgeschichte: Zur Rekonstruktion historischer Erfahrungen und Lebensweisen* (Frankfurt: Campus, 1989).

Moran, Joe, *Queuing for Beginners: The Story of Daily Life from Breakfast to Bedtime* (London: Profile Books, 2007).

Ross, Kristin, *Fast Cars, Clean Bodies: Decolonization and the Reordering of French Culture* (Cambridge MA: MIT, 1996).

Sheringham, Michael, *Everyday Life: Theories and Practices from Surrealism to the Present*. (Oxford: Oxford University Press, 2006).

Shove, Elizabeth, Trentmann, Frank, and Wilk, Richard (eds.), *Time, Consumption, and Everyday Life* (Oxford: Berg, 2009).

Taylor, Vanessa, and Trentmann, Frank, 'Liquid Politics: Water and the Politics of Everyday Life in the Modern City', *Past and Present*, 211 (2011).

PART VII

IDENTITIES

CHAPTER 28

....

STATUS, LIFESTYLE, AND TASTE

....

MIKE SAVAGE

THE concepts of status, lifestyle, and taste have played a powerful role in the sociological lexicon for well over a century. Their deployment from the later nineteenth century, especially in the thinking of Georg Simmel and Max Weber, was itself a marker of a new modern sensibility that defined the intellectual territory of nascent sociology.[1] This is the period when, as Stephen Kern has explored, a new focus on simultaneity and fragmentation were part of the remaking of cultures of time and space linked to the rise of new electrical technologies, urban growth, and mass migration.[2] In such a context, the idea that taste and lifestyles were both a fragment of modernity, and a means of recovering lost solidarities, proved both appealing and enduring to the project of sociology as a whole. Throughout the twentieth century, the quest for what might be termed 'lifestyle communities' has haunted sociology, presenting the social sciences both with a vision of what has been lost, as well as a challenge for its recovery. Now that it is claimed that we are living in another period of epochal change, associated with the digital revolution and the network society,[3] we are in a position to take historical stock of the ideas of status, taste, and lifestyle afresh, as a means of questioning our understanding of the relationship between past and present.

My approach will therefore be radically historical. Rather than the more familiar approach of taking social scientific ideas at face value and reflecting on their historical reach and scope—an exercise which inevitably leads to empirical qualification of these terms, and thereby reinforces the unfortunate tendency to regard history and the social

[1] See David Frisby, *Fragments of Modernity* (Oxford, 1986).
[2] Stephen Kern, *Cultures of Time and space*. (2nd edn., Cambridge, MA, 2003).
[3] See, for instance, Manel Castells, *The Rise of the Network Society* (Oxford, 1996), and John Urry, *Global Complexity* (Cambridge, 2003).

sciences as different enterprises—I will treat the conceptual formation of status, lifestyle, and taste as themselves historical products. I will show how we must relate them to the circumstances of their time, and more particularly how they are rooted in what the sociologist Zygmunt Bauman has identified as the ambivalence of modernity.[4] The 'grand narratives' of modernity hold status and 'taste communities' to be dissipated by modern complexity, but also reveal a yearning for their recovery. I want to show how this ambivalence is often misunderstood by sociologists who reduce these terms to empirically testable propositions.

In the second part of this chapter I briefly introduce the argument of Pierre Bourdieu, the single most influential figure whose work now commands the central stage in debates related to status, taste, and lifestyle. I will show that although his conceptual repertoire has some superficial similarities with earlier sociological formulations, it is actually substantially different in important ways, notably its refusal of a nostalgic account of status and its insistence on the reworking of forms of cultural power even within the heartlands of modernity. I will show how this perspective is also to be seen as historically rooted through being based on a positioning from 'the margins of modernity', written at a time when metropolitan cultural power seemed all-pervasive and significant.

Having clarified the contrast between these issues in the first part of the chapter, I explore how arguments about the remaking of status, taste, and lifestyle are associated with dramatic social change during the twentieth century associated with the rise of the white-collar middle classes, the cultural industries, and Americanization. I show how the emergence of academic, social scientific reflections on status were themselves implicated in these developments. Their embroilment in these social changes helps to explain why status anxieties have become such a central feature of our self-analysis. This clarification leads, in the final part of this chapter to a resolutely empirical approach to exploring the recent fortunes of what might be termed cultural elitism. Drawing on quantitative survey data, I argue that we have seen the remaking of claims to distinction, away from what I will term the primitive accumulation of cultural capital to its more mature and elaborated form. Whereas historically, during the dominance of aristocracy, status differentiated itself from the popular, today status arises through being able to play with knowledge and information, including elements of popular forms. Rather than the decline of status, we are seeing its reorganization along more subtle, and for this very reason more powerful, axes.

WEBER AND 'STYLES OF LIFE'

The first great theorist of status and lifestyle was undoubtedly Max Weber (1860–1920), the German polymath whose work has proved foundational for twentieth-century sociology. Weber introduced the concept of status into the social scientific armoury, where it

---

[4] See, notably, Zygmunt Bauman, *Modernity and Ambivalence* (Cambridge, 1989).

has remained as a central reference point. There is, however, currently a contentious dispute about Weber's intellectual legacy, which I need to unravel since it bears critically upon how we need to relate the concepts of status and lifestyle to the ambivalences of modernity itself.

In the English-speaking world, Weber has normally been hailed as a founder of positivist sociology, someone who insisted on the need for researchers to be 'value neutral' and to define concepts carefully in order that they can be operationalized as distinctive variables.[5] Here, his distinction between class, status, and party was pivotal in the development of the Anglo-American sociology of stratification, as a means of empirically distinguishing these three separate factors, each of which might generate inequality. What is status? In Weber's celebrated words, whereas class came about when people shared a common economic position, linked to their relationship to commodity and labour markets, 'Status *groups* are normally communities ... In contrast to the purely economically determined "class situation" we wish to designate as "status groups" every typical component of the life fate of men that is determined by a specific, positive or negative, social estimation of *honour*....' Furthermore, 'In content, status honour is normally expressed by the fact that above all else a specific *style of life* can be expected from all those who wish to belong to the circle.'[6]

This formulation is important, firstly for analytically registering the role of status as a kind of honorific community, and secondly for analytically differentiating it from class. This has led to a persistent trend, especially in the United States, to seek measures of status deemed to be independent of class or other economic indicators. At an early stage this fed into the anthropological studies of the Lynds' on Muncie, Indiana, in the interwar years, and Lloyd Warner's 1940s studies of Yankeetown, both of which emphasized the power of status hierarchies. The methodological playing out of this perspective led to the elaboration of quantitative 'status scales' in the second half of the twentieth century, whereby people were allocated a status score on the basis of the esteem in which their occupation was seen to be held by the public.[7] This concern with measuring status was influential in the development of post-war survey research, both in the United States and also in Europe, which quizzed people about what kinds of occupations were regarded as being most desirable.[8] These status scores have undergone a revival in the past decade as social network analysis has allowed an alternative way of measuring status, one which does not rely on asking respondents about which kinds of occupations are more desirable, and instead reports on people's actual friends or relatives—and hence the sorts of social circles that they can be deemed to belong to. One of the most influential of these is the Cambridge Social Interaction and Stratification Scale (CAMSIS), which places occupations in a hierarchy according to the social exclusiveness of their marital partners.

[5] This interpretation arises especially from the way Weber's thought was incorporated into American structural functionalism, and the post-war thinking of Robert Merton.

[6] Weber, 'Class, status, party', in H. Gerth and C. W. Mills, *From Max Weber* (New York, 1950), 187.

[7] H. Lynd and S. Lynd, *Middletown* (New York, 1929) and *Middletown in Transition* (New York, 1937).

[8] See, for instance, K. Hope and J. Goldthorpe, *The Social Ranking of Occupations* (Oxford, 1972).

My main point here is to reflect on the problems of seeking a Weberian warrant to define a 'pure' measure of status as if this can be neatly differentiated from other social relations. German scholars have recently argued that this positivist interpretation misreads Weber's thinking in important ways. Hennis insists on the influence of Nietzsche on Weber, arguing that he was tormented by the failure of scientific value to ultimately account for itself. Science by its very nature can never adequately ground its truths, which are necessarily surpassed by later work and hence prove a fragile and ultimately unstable platform. Weber has little but withering scorn for those who think that modernity has satisfactorily established itself according to scientific, utilitarian, and rational criteria.[9]

These recent critics have emphasized that Weber's main concern was actually with understanding the '*menschentum*', the 'types of life' that are possible in modern conditions.[10] Here, his work shares the ethical reach and preoccupations of many other German-speaking cultural critics of the later nineteenth century, ranging from novelists such as Thomas Mann, to fellow sociologist Georg Simmel, and Marxist literary critic Georg Lukacs. He also foreshadows the cultural pessimism of the Frankfurt School. How, in a fragmented world, where no ultimate value holds sway, does one best comport oneself honourably? This is not a question, Weber insists, that sociology has any answers to, even though it might point out the unintended consequences of certain responses to it. But this does lead to a distinctive approach to status.

First, this re-reading of Weber's work emphasizes that status should not be seen as characteristic of pre-industrial societies, with industrial, market, capitalism marking the pre-eminence of class over status. Such an interpretation sees status as the product of 'tradition', and often focuses on Weber's argument that caste—taken to represent pre-industrial societies—was a particularly marked status-based society.[11] By contrast, the rise of bureaucratic regulation, and the instrumental rationality with which it is associated, is deemed to be symptomatic of the fading away of status.

Although Weber's use of ideal types allows him analytically to distinguish status from class and party, even a cursory reading of his writing makes it clear that he had a more subtle and complex understanding which emphasized the ambivalences of status. So, status can be seen as belonging to communities in the sense of their having shared visions of the world and practices, which function as mechanisms for the 'monopolization' of certain claims to 'social honour' and more generally as mechanisms of 'social closure'. Here status is a mechanism of social closure which is part of all human culture—including amongst the modern. It is also noteworthy that Weber's most extended discussions of status are about the American situation, where he sees status as emerging out of 'elective', even democratic, processes:

[9] Weber, 'Science as a Vocation', in Gerth and Mills, 143.

[10] See the outstanding analysis of Isabelle Darmon, 'The question of the 'human type' in social sciences in Germany at the turn of the 20th century, and its posterity', Ph.D. thesis (University of Manchester, 2011).

[11] 'Where the consequences have been realized to their full extent, the status group evolves into a closed "caste"'(Weber, 'Class, status, party', 188).

In its characteristic form, stratification by 'status groups' on the basis of conventional styles of life evolves at the present time in the United States out of the traditional democracy. For example only the residents of a certain street ('the street') is considered as belonging to 'society', is qualified for social intercourse, and is visited and invited.[12].

Therefore, there is no simple erosion of status in modern industrial capitalism. Modern sub-cultures and lifestyles can all be seen as arising from boundary drawing concerns which arise out of modern market relations. This is a similar argument to that which has been developed recently by American sociologists who see status as arising out of attempts to stabilize the contingencies and uncertainties of market relations.[13] It is also a similar argument to those who show that urban neighbourhoods are strongly informed by status-like considerations, even when these areas are in privately owned or rented housing and organized on a thoroughly marketized basis.[14]

Secondly, Weber differentiated between different modes of status orderings, so making it clear that status was not a variable which could be extracted from its historical context, and juxtaposed with class or party. In most historical 'stande'-based societies, status was organized as something which linked inner states to external conditions through certain kinds of 'life conduct'.[15] Weber argues that modernity sundered this link between inner and outer lives. Precisely because of the limitations of economic and instrumental rationality adequately to account for itself, concerns to re-establish some kind of ordering and closure would emerge, but in very different ways to the mobilization of status in traditional societies.

Weber's view was therefore that status was subtly reworked within modern capitalism. He saw the 'conventional life conduct' of middle-class Americans with their attention to the street of residence or fashion as a hollowing out of an authentic inner culture concerned with composure, and a reliance on shallow signals of display and pomp. He was similarly scornful in his description of the educational strategies of those aspiring to positions in the officialdom in Germany. In a similar manner to Veblen's influential concept of 'conspicuous consumption', Weber points towards an evolution of status group 'life conduct' towards external gesticulation—through forms of consumption and display—and indeed to the subordination of status attributes to material interests (occupation, marriage) and economic advantage, at least amongst those groups belonging to the middle class.

What we see here is what might be termed the tragedy of status, in which the erosion of cultural authenticity creates ever more strident concerns to prove one's standing, though in an increasingly shallow way. Weber's concern grows out of his reflections on

[12] Weber, 'Class, status, party', 188.
[13] J. Podlony, *Status Signals* (Princeton, 2005).
[14] Notably, the influential book by Robert Bellah and his associates, *Habits of the Heart* (1st edn., Berkeley, 1985), which developed the influential concept of 'lifestlye enclave' to recognize the role of those who form communities amongst those who they choose—rather than are historically constrained—to live with. See also M. Savage, G. Bagnall, and B. Longhurst, *Globalisation and Belonging* (London, 2005), for their emphasis on the contemporary role of 'elective belonging'.
[15] Weber's concept of *lebensfuhrung* is sometimes mistranslated as 'lifestyle' rather than 'life conduct', and hence his insistence on the link between inner values and concerns, and external practices, is lost.

historical changes in late nineteenth-century Germany, notably the decline of Junker estates from older 'stande' formations to modern capitalist ones. We need to be cautious, therefore, in banding around the concept of status as some kind of transhistorical object, the extent of which can be quantitatively measured.

Let me now turn to the concept of 'lifestyle', which also has a chequered and complex history which overlaps with that of status. Concerns with 'style' originated from the nineteenth-century art historical analysis of Wolfflin and the hermeneutic thinking of Dilthey.[16] Wolfflin defined style as the cultural coherence which can be found in a range of artefacts from a given historical period. Famously, he emphasized that 'the essence of the gothic can be found in shoes as much as the great cathedrals: styles are not created arbitrarily by individuals but out of the feeling of the *volk*.'[17] He thus deploys the concept of style as a means establishing the systematic coherence of cultural artefacts in order to define particular periods. This argument was then mobilized into the view that in modernity, such epochal cultural coherence—for instance that of the gothic—is lost, due to the fracturing of social worlds associated with what Georg Simmel (1848–1918) identified as overlapping social circles. Here, style became associated with a nostalgic and conservative framing, in which its coherence was held to be dispersed by modern fragmentation. Georg Simmel, along with Weber, critically drew on this argument. Thus Simmel's famous essay on the metropolitan condition argues that the accentuation of shock and nervous overload experienced in the modern city, heartland of the money economy, causes the blasé attitude and more intellectualized apprehensions to emerge as psychological defence mechanisms. Simmel's insistence that lifestyles are remade, rather than dissipated, by modern conditions are nowhere more evident than in his essay on fashion which emphasizes that fashions are subject to renewal as a means of drawing new cultural boundaries.[18]

The same complex politics of nostalgia and hope are marked strongly in Walter Benjamin's influential work. Benjamin also evokes the loss of tradition, though he places this into a distinctive analysis of the loss of 'aura', recognizing tradition to be wedded to a conservative structure in which the viewer is bound up with the ritual and cultic power of the auric work of art. For Benjamin, therefore, the loss of stylistic coherence is far from being an unmitigated disaster, and allows the prospect for hope through the recovery of the utopic moment associated with fleeting 'monads'. In his *Passagenwerk*, his recovery of the lost cultural moments in late-nineteenth century Paris, he seeks to redeem the hopes and desires associated with the fragmentary aspects of nineteenth-century life. Recognizing that such fragments are no sooner created than they are woven back into a teleological tissue which bind them again into tradition, his—hopeless?—aim is radically to blast apart the totalizing power of style itself.[19]

---

[16] See Wilhelm Dilthey and Ramon Betanzos, *Introduction to the Human Sciences: an attempt to lay a foundation for the study of society and history*, (Detroit, 2008); Heinrich Wolfflin, *Principles of Art History, The problem of the development of style in later art*, (London, 1986).

[17] quoted in Joel Schwartz, 'Cathedrals and shoes: concepts of style in Wolflin and Adorno', *New German Critique*, 76, (p 3–47) p 5.

[18] Georg Simmel, *The Sociology of Georg Simmel*, (New York, 1964).

[19] Walter Benjamin, *The Arcades Project* (Cambridge, MA, 2002).

I have shown that concepts of status and lifestyle are not innocent technical concepts that can simply be historically applied by discerning researchers. They carry with them a complex moral and political baggage. Their very existence is the product of historical contestation and dispute. This point is important also, since it should not be thought that my historical excavation only pertains to German thinking of the early twentieth century. We can find a similar conceptual archaeology in different times and places. At the Birmingham Centre for Contemporary Cultural Studies in the 1960s and 1970s, Stuart Hall and Dick Hebdige generated new interests in youth 'sub-cultures', which have persisted to the present as a means of comprehending the increasing visibility of youth lifestyles. The concept of sub-culture also harked back to lost coherent 'cultures', in the case of Hebdige the 'parent' cultures associated with social classes, and notably the working class. Such parent cultures were claimed to be challenged by post-war social change, including de-industrialization and the remaking of urban territory, leading to the generation of sub-cultures as means of symbolically reclaiming what had been lost. Thus the rise of punk could be identified as a sub-culture which was a response to social change amongst the working class. We can thus see the same conceptual formation of loss and recovery at work, even though the Marxist and Gramscian roots of the Birmingham school claimed a different lineage to the German social theorists discussed above.[20]

My point, therefore, is that we need to be wary of seeing claims about status simply as matters of empirical testing and historical application. Rather, concepts of status, taste, and lifestyle play into deep ambivalence about the 'modern condition', being simultaneously accounts of historical change, diagnoses of loss and nostalgia, and encapsulating hope for the future. Thus the idea is that we see the decline of cultivated standards, a failing of civilized levels of taste, tradition, and status, as something that is built into our very conception of modern life, along with a hope for recovery and reinvention in which the social sciences also present themselves as agents of renewal. Seen in this context, we need to understand the historical stakes as not only concerned with the nature of social and cultural change, but also with how certain forms of cultural practice and consumption are legitimated by being deemed aspects of lifestyle groups or cultural communities.

BOURDIEU AND CULTURAL REPRODUCTION

There is an alternative frame of reference to that which I have discussed above, associated with the French post war-sociologist Pierre Bourdieu (1930–2002), whose concepts of cultural capital and distinction have now eclipsed those of Weber and Simmel. It is helpful to understand Bourdieu as a 'pre-modern' sociologist. Rather than reflecting on the modern condition from within its terms of reference, Bourdieu's intellectual project sought to bring into relief the cultural oppositions between modern metropolis and

---

[20] A very similar conceptual architecture also surrounds arguments about the decline of social capital—on which, see Robert Putnam, *Bowling Alone* (New York, 2000).

remote rural province, starkly juxtaposing these, hence revealing the arbitrariness and symbolic violence implicit in the modern 'metropolitan habitus' itself.[21] This unusual perspective was linked to his life history. He was brought up in rural Bearn, in south-west France, during the 1940s, and he was also strongly influenced by his early experiences in the Algerian War in the later 1950s.[22] From these experiences he remained strongly aware of the conditioning power of what he called the habitus', the engrained ways of apprehending and comporting oneself which he saw as characteristic of rural peasants.

Comparing these experiences with metropolitan Paris, he became interested in the symbolic power of a fundamentally different lifestyle, one which celebrated its distance from the 'daily grind', and which could only be enjoyed by the cultivated middle and upper classes who were freed from the workaday world of necessity. Whereas those in grinding poverty had lives marked by cultures of graft and getting by, those in more advantaged positions were freed from such pragmatic considerations and had the capacity to articulate their artistic and cultural superiority. This supremacy was marked by its capacity to intrude into, and judge 'objectively' the habitus of the peasant, so exercising a kind of 'symbolic violence' over others. Writing about farming dances in rural Bearn, Bourdieu mused:

> So, in this small country ball is the scene of the real clash of civilisations. Through it, the whole urban world, with its cultural models, its music, its dances, its techniques for the use of the body bursts into peasant life.... The dances of the old days, which bore the stamp of peasant culture in their names (*la crabe, lou branlou, lou mounchicou* etc.) in their rhythms, their music, and the words which accompanied them, have been ousted by the dances imported from the town.[23]

Bourdieu's subversive strategy was to reverse the normal direction of gaze (such as that found in Weber), so that he reflected on how we might understand the lifestyles of the rich and cultivated not in the way they present themselves—as intrinsically superior to other social groups—but as markers of their own arbitrary habitus—that of the educated bourgeoisie. It is important to insist on this point since Bourdieu draws on the sociology of Weber and Durkheim to study lifestyle not as a part of the project of 'rendering the promise and perils of modernity', but as exposing the contest between urban modernity and its rural, provincial, and popular 'other' as itself the subject of analysis. Whereas Weber sees modern status as shallow and consumer-oriented, lacking a link to inner motivations and life conduct, Bourdieu claims the opposite, that the habitus of educated intellectuals offers a distinctive bodily/mental embrace of the Kantian aesthetic which celebrates the distance from necessity. Whereas Weber remains within the frame of the scholarly intellectual, dismissing the shallowness of contemporary life, Bourdieu seeks to render the intellectual position—in all its seriousness, composure, and self-importance—as itself a problem. This reversing of the telescope allows

[21] The term 'metropolitan habitus' is derived from Tim Butler and Garry Robson, *London Calling* (Aldershot, 2003).
[22] See Pierre Bourdieu, *Sketches for a Self-Analysis* (Cambridge, 2008).
[23] Pierre Bourdieu, *Bachelor's Ball* (Cambridge, 2008), p 83.

Bourdieu fundamentally to rework the terms of debate, presenting status, taste, and life-style communities not as undermined by modernity, but as the vehicle for new kinds of social advantage.

Bourdieu's most celebrated concept is that of cultural capital.[24] Taking his standpoint from peasant society, where the inheritance of landed property is fundamental to social reproduction, Bourdieu was interested in the way that the inheritance of educational privilege becomes a new device for securing inheritance. The affluent middle classes pass on their advantages less through transmitting landed property and more in ensuring that their children perform well in the educational system. This kind of inheritance is however probabilistic and indirect, one which cannot be guaranteed, and which hence hides its biases within a formally meritocratic guise. Much of his analysis in his most celebrated work, *Distinction*, emphasizes that despite apparent educational reform during the 1960s in France, and the development of new kinds of educational institutions, the most privileged are nonetheless able to reproduce their advantages in their children.

Within this perspective, status can be understood as constantly 'worked on' by those in positions of power, rather than as some kind of historical residue, and as necessarily depending on relational contrasts with those defined as lacking such status. In drawing attention to this constantly fraught process, he drew upon the concept of field, in which struggles for taste and lifestyle are part of a 'battlefield'. Rather than the view of positivist sociologists that a widely shared 'status order' could be detected, in which most people recognized and accepted the superior status of legitimate groups, Bourdieu thus argued that there was a constant and ongoing battle to command authority.

Within this framing, an interesting conceptual innovation can be made. Bourdieu excavates the power of the cultural conflict between the townsfolk and the peasant, in which the former define their superiority through contrasting themselves with the natural, primitive peasant. This process of differentiation from what might be termed the 'popular-natural' was profound throughout early phases of capitalist modernity, as the cultivated sought to distinguish themselves from the poor. However, as the educated middle classes grow in number, and the educational attainment becomes a more frequent precondition for access to privileged labour market positions, it is no longer necessary to contrast learning with the 'popular-necessary'. This might be deemed an important historical shift between the primitive and elaborated accumulation of cultural capital.[25]

This argument can be elaborated within Bourdieu's concept of field, which provides an historical analysis of the differentiation of autonomous domains of social and cultural life. Rather than seeing historical change in terms of the 'rise' or 'decline' of different kinds of capital, we can recognize a process in which sub-fields, each with their own 'rules of the game', became more separated from each other during the nineteenth

[24] A good introduction is Eliot Weininger, 'Foundations of Pierre Bourdieu's class analysis', in E. O. Wright, *Approaches to Class Analysis* (Oxford, 2004); see also Bennett et al., *Culture, Class, Distinction* (London, 2009).

[25] M. Savage, M. A. Warde, and F. Devine, 'Capitals, assets, and resources', *British Journal of Sociology*, (2005), 31–47.

and early twentieth centuries, before being challenged by a concern to make the economy more pre-eminent through neo-liberal reforms in the later twentieth century. This kind of historical account thus is attentive to context and specificity, and refuses epochal arguments in a provocative way. Let me see if it might shed historical light in the remainder of this chapter.

DISTINCTION AND SOCIAL CHANGE

Having found our bearings, I now return to our nostalgic sociologists, bewailing the loss of cultural value. As I have argued, such concerns remain as evident today as during Weber and Simmel's time, and are commonplace in cultural studies, sociology, and the humanities more generally.[26] Yet we need to recognize these intellectuals as themselves complicit in the very process that they lament.

Worries about the loss of status are inextricably related to the decline of the aristocracy,[27] taking this to include the titled, landed aristocracy which dominated European nations into the twentieth century, but also involving any practice inscribed around innate, ascribed, and inviolable cultural values (ultimately deriving from birth and blood). Historians have emphasized the endurance, indeed the resurgence, of the landed aristocracy into the world of industrial capitalism.[28] On the eve of the First World War, all European nations possessed a cohesive, socially exclusive nobility which combined economic resources with access to political power, and the trappings of honour and status. This was associated with a vibrant cultural arena which allowed wealthy patrons to partake of consecrated culture of dance, classical music, elite theatre and which proved an enthusiastic audience for museums and art galleries. Centred in courtly capitals and spa resorts catering for the gentry, this world was marked by the rituals of the 'season', in which familial intrigues of courtship and cultivation took place. This arena often overlapped with involvement in elite voluntary associations—literary and philosophical societies, statistical societies, and suchlike. Access to this elite highbrow culture was controlled, being dependent on birth and upbringing.

This kind of status-based community should not be regarded as an historical residue, inevitably diminished by market capitalism. Aristocratic forms were dynamic and highly innovative. In the period between 1880 and 1914, however, two distinctive fractures destabilized the aristocratic embrace. Firstly, there were the first signs of a parting of ways between intellectuals, who had previously been dependent on aristocrats by virtue of patronage, from social aristocracies. In many European nations, modernist avant-garde intellectuals became increasingly critical of the social shallowness of the

---

[26] See the discussion in Celia Lury, *Consumer Culture* (Oxford, 1996).
[27] See David Cannadine, *The Decline of the British Aristocracy* (New Haven, CT, and London, 1990).
[28] See Arno Mayer, *The Persistence of the Old Regime* (London, 2010)

privileged, and translated aristocratic concerns with distinction into the 'pure' world of modernist art and culture. In Britain, an intellectual aristocracy centred on Oxbridge, which increasingly colonized academia, professional hierarchies, and the civil service, became separated from the landed aristocracy itself.[29] This group played a key role in the development of the cultural infrastructure of museums and art galleries. In France, the formation of a distinctively intellectual identity, associated with Zola's mobilization of progressive opinion in the Dreyfus case, was decisive. The most celebrated work of modernist literature, Marcel Proust's *A la recherche du Temps perdu* (written between 1911 and 1922), can be read as a nostalgic paean to the separation of the intellectual in search of the pure aesthetic (represented by the form of the ultimately triumphant narrator) from the worldly seductions of the urban aristocracy (represented by the lavish opulence of the salons of the Faubourg Saint-Germain). In Germany, Weber's own sociological reflections were part of a wider mobilization of educated opinion against aristocratic philistinism.

Secondly, and largely simultaneously, there was a marked consolidation and organization of the activities of the popular classes, through the formation of trade unions, self-help associations, and the emergence of organized leisure ranging from football to cycle clubs.[30] The effects of this process were double-edged. On the one hand, it reinforced elite conceptions of their cultural superiority over the popular classes, underscoring the cultural separation between classes. On the other hand, the flowering of popular culture politicized cultural activity itself, thus making one's leisure interests and tastes a matter of political concern and an object of contestation. It is these double differentiations from the aristocratic figure that explain why sociologists such as Weber and Simmel self-consciously appealed to status, and why 'style' became a matter of overt concern. It was both a means of recovering what was deemed to be lost, and a response to the politicization of cultural life.

During the middle decades of the twentieth century appeals to honour, status, and distinction became differentiated between a series of increasingly separate fields, only loosely bound together. Professional organizations, aristocratic salons, academics, social reformers, landed elites, and bankers all emphasized their claims to status and worth, but increasingly within their own specific fields of activity. The precise working out of these relations varied considerably between nations. In Britain, new forms of modernist culture—represented most emphatically by Bloomsbury—continued to embrace the social aristocracy as its ultimate reference point. Whereas Proust, however sadly, unravelled the separation of the worlds of the intellectual and the aristocrat, writers such as Anthony Powell or Evelyn Waugh, writing between the 1940s and 1960s, continued to see the fortunes of the intellectual as tied up with the aristocratic world.[31] In mainland Europe, revolutionary experience and political disruption eclipsed the

---

[29] The key work here is that of Noel Annan, in *The Dons* (London, 1999), as well as *Our Age* (London, 1991).

[30] See in the British case, Ross McKibbin, *Classes and Cultures* (Oxford, 1998).

[31] See the discussions in Stefan Collini, *Absent Minds* (Oxford, 2006) and M. Savage, *Identities and Social Change in Britain since 1940* (Oxford, 2010).

hereditary power of the aristocracy, which led concerns with status to be directed into other arenas, notably within bureaucratic and professional hierarchies. In the United States, by contrast, given the absence of an old titular aristocracy, the intellectually oriented middle classes proved more powerful, notably in the championing of a socially progressive, pragmatist, programme. As Brint has shown, these professional groups still justified their privileges through their supposed 'social worth', continuing to appeal to status.[32] Sociologist Richard Sennett, writing in the 1960s, could still note the existence of the 'Boston Brahmins', a distinctive, exclusive, business elite which dominated this major city.[33]

It is only during the last third of the twentieth century that these kinds of claims to distinction appear to have radically dimmed. Three factors have been important here. First, the rise of what might best be termed a technocratic, bureaucratic middle class, seen by many as the bearer of instrumental values. This was a class of salaried technicians, lower managers, and senior supervisors, who could not readily be identified with either the working class or the professional classes. The appearance of this class was a source of concern and fascination in equal measure. In the British context, George Orwell saw it as a beacon of hope, sweeping away cultural elitism, whereas the American sociologists C. Wright Mills, and W. H. Whyte identified it as the voice of conformism.[34] It was, essentially, a class which lacked status but enjoyed economic and organizational resources, and thereby pointed to a new kind of managed social world. We see here how post-war affluence challenged the cultural order associated with primitive cultural capital. Before the second half of the twentieth century, those claiming status and distinction defined themselves against the poor and wretched, deemed to be 'outside culture' through the fact of their brutal working and living conditions. Hence, the appearance of an affluent, yet apparently 'uncultured', middle class from the 1950s was deeply unsettling. Cultural illiteracy could not simply be associated with poverty, and status and distinction needed to be seen as social and political products. It was this insight that Pierre Bourdieu drove home in his anatomy of cultural taste.

Second, we need to note the emergence of what might be termed 'culturally saturated' consumer-oriented capitalism. Until the late twentieth century, the activities associated with cultural distinction represented a critique of a capitalism which was deemed to be concerned with large-scale production designed for the mass audience. However, in a process that the geographer Nigel Thrift has identified as 'knowing capitalism',[35] knowledge- and information-gathering processes become incorporated into 'soft capitalism'. Boltanski and Chiapello have discussed in the French context how companies incorporated the cultural critique of capitalism into the productive activities of leading firms, for instance through the eradication of status divisions between '(production)

[32] Stephen Brint, *An Age of Experts* (Berkeley, CA, 1983).
[33] Richard Sennett, *Respect in a world of inequality* (New York, 2003).
[34] C. Wright Mills, *White Collar* (New York, 1951).
[35] Nigel Thrift, *Knowing Capitalism* (London, 2005).

line' and 'staff', quality circles and an emphasis on networks rather than hierarchies. Post-Fordist forms of flexible specialization were aimed at providing quality products, to high degrees of specification, for increasingly discerning consumers. This culminated in reflections about the significance of postmodernity during the 1980s. In neo-liberal consumer-oriented capitalism, where all and any customers were sovereign, it seemed difficult to ground claims to cultural supremacy.[36] In place of modernist forms which imputed cultural value through abstraction, irony, and myth, postmodern culture could only evoke pastiche and superficiality.

The third major shift was the geopolitical decline of capitalist Europe as pivot of the globe and the rise of the American and Soviet spheres of influence. Down to 1914 European culture was the locus from which status was defined. Its complicity in the imperial project permitted it to plunder spoils from other parts of the world, allowing it to present itself as the custodian of civilization. As Said argues, this also allowed non-European cultural activities to be exoticized and used as a mirror to reinforce European self-confidence.[37] I have already emphasized how the very concept of status emerged out of this European intellectual current concerned both to articulate and also defend its view of the world. The decisive weakening of European power which was associated with the aftermath of the Second World War and the Cold War politics which pitted America against the Soviet Union ushered in a new kind of cultural flow emanating from Hollywood, and American markers and advertisers offered a new vision of freedom.[38] From the later 1950s, and spectacularly in the 1960s, popular culture 'came of age', basking in its association with these American motifs of freedom from snobbery and convention.

One important aspect was the restructuring of the city form. The European city, building on its medieval roots, was a visible container of status. Its central public core was dominated by its high-status denizens at the same time that it defined the meaning of the city and urban culture itself. The lack of status of those living in other parts of the urban domain was marked through their differentiation from the urban public elite. Yet during the twentieth century the city lost this central coherence, partly through suburbanization, but more seriously through the rise of the fluid, mobile, and networked urban processes which bypassed central urban cores.[39] The American urban model, organized around weak downtown districts, extensive, semi-autonomous, and defensive suburbs, all made possible through the automization of mass transportation, physically marked a more fluid and dynamic urban and social order.

---

[36] Key reference points here include W.F. Whyte, *The Organization Man*, (New York, 1956); George Orwell, *Essays*, (London, 2000); J-F Lyotard, *The Post-Modern Condition* (Montreal, 1979), David Harvey, *The Condition of Post-Modernity*, (Oxford, 1986), and F. Jameson, *The Cultural Logic of Late Capitalism* (London, 1988).

[37] Edward Said, *Orientalism* (London, 1978).

[38] See Victoria De Grazia, *Irresistible Empire: America's Advance Through Twentieth-Century Europe* (Princeton, 2004).

[39] The literature here is voluminous. See Douglas Rae's *The City: Urbanism and Its End* (New Haven, CT, 2003) for a particularly evocative statement. Also, Ash Amin, and Nigel Thrift, *Reimagining the City* (Cambridge, 2002).

These shifts are fundamental. We can read them, in Weberian fashion, as marking the eclipse of status. Yet in this chapter I have insisted on the need to avoid the appeal of the historicist lament which is embedded in our very conceptual architecture for understanding status. An alternative approach suggests that status is reworked from a primitive to a mature form. Following Bourdieu's anti-modern framing, this might suggest that rather than status being defined in contrast with the 'popular-natural', it is now associated with mobility and proliferation. I pursue this line by reflecting on the interesting and important idea that we have seen the rise of the 'cultural omnivore'.

THE DECLINE OF HIGHBROW TASTE?

Over the past two decades cultural sociologists have devised ingenious and effective methods for analysing changing forms of cultural taste and engagement. The most interesting argument here is that educated middle class 'snob' taste was giving way to 'cultural omnivorousness', in which middle-class interests spanned both high and low culture, so that those who enjoyed classical music and the opera also became more enthusiastic fans of middle- and 'lowbrow' culture.

The concept of the cultural omnivore was introduced by Richard Peterson in the 1990s in his account of the changing nature of American musical taste.[40] He laid out the basic ideas as follows:

> Appreciation of the fine arts became a mark of high status in the late 19th century as part of an attempt to distinguish 'highbrowed' Anglo-Saxons from new 'lowbrowed' immigrants whose popular entertainments were said to corrupt morals and thus were to be shunned. In recent years, however, many high status people are far from being snobs and have become eclectic, even 'omnivorous' in their tastes... This suggests a qualitative shift in the basis of marking status—from snobbish exclusion to omnivorous appropriation.[41]

In this formulation, Peterson was able to use the idea of the omnivore as a means of criticizing Bourdieu's emphasis on cultural capital (a theme taken up by other critics.[42] Yet the concept has also been attractive to those more sympathetic to Bourdieu's arguments, notably Alan Warde, who defines contemporary cultural capital in terms of its omnivorous orientation.[43]

[40] See the discussion in R. Peterson, 'Problems in comparative research: the example of omnivorousness', *Poetics*, 33 (2005), 257–82.

[41] R.A. Peterson, and R. Kern, 'Changing highbrow taste: from snob to omnivore, *American Sociological Review*, 61 (1996), 900.

[42] e.g. T.-W. Chan and J. Goldthorpe, 'Social stratification and cultural consumption: the visual arts in England', *Poetics*, 35 (2007), 168–90; T.-W. Chan, and J. H. Goldthorpe, 'Social Stratification and cultural consumption: the case of music', *European Sociological Review*, 23 (2007), 1–19.

[43] see Bennett et al., *Culture, Class, Distinction*; A. Warde, D. Wright and M. Gayo-Cal, 'Understanding cultural omnivorousness or the myth of the cultural omnivore', *Cultural Sociology*, 1/2 (2007), 143–64.

Peterson's argument proceeds by classifying the musical genres in the American General Social Survey into either 'highbrow' (classical and opera), 'middlebrow' (easy listening, Broadway, big band), or 'lowbrow' (gospel, country, blue grass, rock, and blues), and seeing how far those who liked highbrow music also liked middlebrow and lowbrow forms. Between 1982 and 1992 it became increasingly likely for highbrows also to report more preferences for lowbrow and middlebrow music. This approach has been influential in defining omnivorousness as (a) a kind of score or scale where the more genres that one likes, the more omnivorous one is; and, (b) as linked to mobility across key categorical types defined by the sociologist (in this case, 'high', 'middle', and 'lowbrow').[44]

Let us consider four key issues in this conceptual architecture. First, how useful is it to group musical genres into 'brow' categories? After all, these labels were developed primarily with reference to literary taste. They have also been more influential in the United States than in Europe. Peterson sees the idea of the 'highbrow snob' as tapping into Bourdieu's analysis of cultural capital and legitimate culture which he develops in *Distinction*, but this is not warranted by Bourdieu's own analysis, which focuses on the contrast between the 'Kantian aesthetic' and the 'culture of the necessary'.[45]

Secondly, there is a typical assumption that a liking for classical music is the litmus test for exponents of 'highbrow' culture. Despite disagreements in how popular music is categorized, there is here a common view that 'highbrow' music can be singled out through an appreciation of classical music. Here, we often see a genuflection to Bourdieu's famous arguments about its apparent role in constituting cultural capital. Bourdieu, however, does not regard a taste for classical music as necessarily 'highbrow', or a marker of cultural capital. In *Distinction*, he even regards a predilection for Strauss's 'The Blue Danube' as a marker of popular taste.

This is not a trivial point: once we recognize that classical music itself might not be inherently highbrow, then indicators of omnivorousness might simply be picking up on the remaking of classical music itself. There is evidence that 'light classical' music has increased in popularity in recent years. This is based on the popularization of classical music components in popular culture and the media. Krims focusing on the popularity of popular classical musicians such as Charlotte Church and Sarah Brightman, and the extensive sales of compilations such as *Bach for Relaxation* or *The Most Relaxing Piano Album in the World... Ever!* emphasizes the significance of a new role for classical music as an aspect of interior design'.[46] Further evidence for the pertinence of this kind of orientation is found in the interviews conducted by Savage, Bagnall, and Longhurst, who showed that many middle-class Manchester residents embraced 'light classical' music, but specifically avoided 'difficult' forms of classical.[47] They repudiated

[44] For an example of scale-based approaches, see B. Bryson, ' "Anything but heavy metal": symbolic exclusion and musical dislikes', *American Sociological Review*, 6 (1996), 884–99.
[45] Peterson, 'Problems in comparative research', 258.
[46] See Adam Krims, *Music and Urban Geography* (London, 2007), 148, 150.
[47] Savage et al., *Globalisation and Belonging*.

avant-garde or esoteric classical music in favour of 'easy listening': Mozart or Vivaldi rather than Schoenberg or Stravinsky. In short, rather than people becoming more omnivorous, perhaps genre boundaries have been reworked. Rather than seeing those who like 'light classical' and 1960s rock as omnivores because they seem to straddle genre boundaries, perhaps they are actually genuine enthusiasts for an emergent musical sub-culture associated with new urban spaces which is not accurately captured by standard genre labels.

Thirdly, this leads us to focus further on boundary-making and classificatory processes themselves. Holt insists that we need to examine how boundaries around and within genres are defined, rather than take genre labels at face value.[48] This is an argument amply developed in cultural studies, where writers such as John Frow see genres as constantly evolving or in process, as subject to mutation and hybridization, and as historically mutable. Antoine Hennion has developed this point by emphasizing that genres are constructed through performances involving a range of human, institutional, and technical agencies, so emphasizing the fluidity and complexity of musical process, which cannot usefully be seen in terms of static and all-encompassing 'genre' labels.[49]

Finally, we can identify an even more fundamental issue at stake here. Peterson's argument has the characteristic structure of much Anglo-American social thought.[50] It differentiates a structure (in this case, of genres arrayed into a hierarchy) and then the possibility of individual mobility within this structure (through the figure of the omnivore). One result, paradoxically, is to reproduce the hierarchical categories which it also argues are being transcended. Most individuals prefer to position themselves as mobile between classes, and thus narrate stories of individual and familial social mobility, but in the process they produce accounts of classes as the benchmarks from which mobility can be measured. This conceptual architecture involves a 'variable centred' focus on the characteristics which distinguish the omnivore from the non-omnivore. The problem here is the lack of attention to what might be termed the 'cultural structure' in which mobility is deemed to take place. Hence, the omnivore does not so much undermine status, but proliferate hierarchical cultural categories.

The cultural omnivore, we might thus argue, testifies to a new kind of snobbery, one that does not speak its own name, and claims distinction under a different head. Rather than reject the 'popular-natural' as vulgar, it seeks voraciously to consume both high and low culture. It sets itself against the staid and the conventional. Yet this process of cultural mobility is one which depends on the cultural confidence and resources of privilege. Through these terms we can thus see how status boundaries are re-energized even as they are apparently called into question.

---

[48] Douglas Holt, 'Does cultural capital structure American consumption?', *Journal of Consumer Research*, 25 (1998). See also Bryson, ' "Anything but heavy metal" '.

[49] John Frow, *Genre: the New Critical Idiom* (London, 2006); Antoine Hennion, 'Music lovers: taste as performance', *Theory, Culture and Society*, 18/5 (2001), 1–22.

[50] See Marilyn Strathern, *After Nature* (Cambridge, 1991).

CONCLUSIONS

We have travelled a long way in this chapter. My main argument has been to dispute the longstanding belief that status and distinction has declined. I am fascinated by the way that claim continually reasserts itself in different ways, so registering it as central to our own cultural self-conceptions. The debate amongst quantitative cultural sociologists regarding the rise of the cultural omnivore has a remarkably similar architecture to that framed by German cultural critics of a century before, despite their huge epistemological and methodological differences This teleological narrative neutralizes and naturalizes the relationship between power and culture, seeing ascribed status as always in the past, yet also as marking a cultural decline which inscribes the lost values of aristocracy as somehow pre-eminent.

Taking Weber, Simmel, Benjamin, and especially Bourdieu as my guides, I have argued instead for a more complex and historically nuanced analysis. Battles over status, distinction, and position are ongoing. The apparent decline of 'snob' culture means that markers of status have been repositioned, with the capacity to move between genres and categories becoming the marker of cultivated taste. As 'highbrow' forms of culture—such as classical music—have become diffused and embraced by a wider audience, so status rests in making claims not to abhor the 'popular-natural', but through the capacity to move between forms and repertoires.

My final point, therefore is to refuse the separation of history and social science itself, as a means of resisting teleological framings, and to insist on the way that historical claims about change themselves play in the present. The task is to render both past and present as messy and complex. I hope in this chapter to have contributed to this project by querying the terms in which concepts of status, distinction, and lifestyle have been set up.

BIBLIOGRAPHY

Bennett, T., Savage, M., Silva, E. B., Warde, A., Gayo-Cal, M., and Wright, D., *Culture, Class, Distinction* (London: Routledge, 2009).

Bourdieu, Pierre, *Distinction* (London: Routledge, 1985).

Bryson, B., '"Anything but heavy metal": symbolic exclusion and musical dislikes', *American Journal of Sociology*, 102/3 (1996), 884–99.

Frisby, David, *Fragments of Modernity* (Oxford: Blackwell, 1986).

Gerth, Hans H. and Mills, Charles W., *From Max Weber: Essays in Sociology* (London, Routledge, 1991).

Peterson, Richard, 'Problems in comparative research: the case of omnivorousness', *Poetics*, 33 (2005), 257–82.

Peterson, R. A. and Kern, R., 'Changing highbrow taste: from snob to omnivore', *American Sociological Review*, 61 (1996), 900–9.

Podlony, Joel, *Status Signals* (Princeton: Princeton University Press, 2005)

Savage, Mike, *Class Analysis and Social Transformation* (Milton Keynes: Open University Press, 2000).

CHAPTER 29

DOMESTICITY AND BEYOND: GENDER, FAMILY, AND CONSUMPTION IN MODERN EUROPE

ENRICA ASQUER

WHEREVER historians have located the 'birth of a consumer society',[1] women, family, and domesticity have always featured as central elements. Since McKendrick's pioneering essays[2] and the seminal book edited by John Brewer and Roy Porter in the early 1990s,[3] women's fascination with 'the world of goods' and their intimate experience of it have been tightly linked to transformations in the mechanisms of demand and the 'consumer revolution' in early modern Europe.

As late as a generation ago, a 'productionist' approach to consumption dominated the public and scholarly debate on consumer culture.[4] A conceptual distinction between production and consumption and the primacy of the former, which can be recognized as intrinsic assumptions of nineteenth- and twentieth-century economic and social

[1] Neil McKendrick, John Brewer, and John H. Plumb, *The Birth of a Consumer Society: the Commercialization of Eighteenth-Century England* (London: Europa, 1982).

[2] Neil McKendrick, 'The Consumer Revolution of Eighteenth-Century England', in McKendrick, Brewer, and Plumb, *The Birth of a Consumer Society*, 9–33.

[3] Amanda Vickery, 'Women and the World of Goods: a Lancashire Consumer and her Possessions, 1751–81', in John Brewer and Roy Porter (eds.), *Consumption and the World of Goods* (London and New York: Routledge 1993), 274–301; see also Lorna Weatherill, 'A Possession of One's Own: Women and Consumer Behavior in England, 1660–1740, *Journal of British Studies*, 25/2 (1986), 131–56.

[4] Jean-Christophe Agnew, 'Coming up for Air: Consumer Culture in Historical Perspective', in Brewer and Porter (eds.), *Consumption and the World of Goods*, 19–39; Paul Glennie, 'Consumption within Historical Studies', in Daniel Miller (ed.), *Acknowledging Consumption: A Review of New Studies* (London and New York: Routledge, 1995), 164–203; Frank Trentmann, 'Beyond Consumerism: New Historical Perspectives on Consumption', *Journal of Contemporary History*, 39/3 (2004), 373–401.

theories, treated consumption principally as a range of 're-productive' or 'un-productive' acts, necessarily driven by and subordinate to capitalist mass production. This narrative was substantially gendered: it implied a divide between a male producer, operating in the workplace, and a female consumer, confined to the realm of the family and the home.[5]

The effects of this limiting conceptualization was visible, too, among second-wave feminists, especially those with Marxist and materialist backgrounds. Here, the marginalization of consumption resulted, paradoxically, from the same 'productionist' paradigm: even though feminists criticized the usual underestimation of the crucial and political role of women's domestic work, they found a significant deterrent to dealing with consumption in its potentially manipulative or merely narcissist aspects.[6]

The innovative approach that has emerged since the late 1980s, within the lively debate on the rise of the so-called 'consumer society', brought with it a renovated and more mature attention to gender and family issues. In the light of suggestions provided by cultural studies, historians became more concerned with consumer practices and agency, reconsidering the power of capitalist producers and the effectiveness of their techniques for maximizing profits. In particular, the previous dualistic vision was successfully challenged by Daniel Miller and Michel De Certeau, whose emphasis on the 'productive' nature of consumption has been an important contribution to overcoming rigid separations and interweaving production and consumption in a more complex framework.[7]

A not unrelated tendency amongst earlier histories was to explain consumers' longings for goods as the product of a 'Veblenesque' desire for social emulation, associated particularly with women of the lower middle class.[8] In a simplistic way, they had been interpreted as being 'naturally' devoted to conspicuous consumption in order to emulate the higher classes and to improve their husband's and family's social status. This approach proved to be very limiting, for it reproduced an 'essentializing' explanation, based on a presumed 'natural' and a-historical feminine desire for luxury, and, what is more, it neglected the importance of ordinary consumption and everyday routines, undoubtedly dominant within the politics of consumption. By privileging 'feminine'

[5] Victoria De Grazia, 'Introduction', in Victoria De Grazia and Ellen Furlough (eds.), *The Sex of Things: Gender and Consumption in Historical Perspective* (Berkeley and London: University of California Press, 1996), 1–10. See also Roberta Sassatelli, 'Genere e consumi', in Emanuela Scarpellini and Stefano Cavazza (eds.), *Il secolo dei consumi: Dinamiche sociali nell'Europa del Novecento* (Rome: Carocci, 2006), 141–73.

[6] Judy Giles, *The Parlour and the Suburb: Domestic Identities, Class, Femininity and Modernity* (Oxford and New York: Berg, 2004), 141–65; Joanne Hollows, 'The Feminist and the Cook: Julia Child, Betty Friedan and Domestic Femininity', in Emma Casey and Lydia Martens (eds.), *Gender and Consumption: Domestic Cultures and the Commercialisation of Everyday Life* (Aldershot and Burlington, VT: Ashgate, 2007), 33–48; with reference to shopping, Angela McRobbie, 'Bridging the Gap: Feminism, Fashion and Consumption', *Feminist Review*, 55 (1997), 73–89.

[7] Daniel Miller, *Material Culture and Mass Consumption* (Oxford: Basil Blackwell, 1987); Daniel Miller, 'Consumption as the Vanguard of History', in Daniel Miller (ed.), *Acknowledging Consumption*, 1–57; Michel De Certeau, *L'invention du quotidien: 1. Arts de faire* (Paris: Gallimard, 1980).

[8] Thorstein Veblen, *The Theory of the Leisure Class* (London: Macmillan, 1899). For a critique, Colin Campbell, *The Romantic Ethic and the Spirit of Modern Consumerism* (Oxford: Blackwell, 1987). See also Roberta Sassatelli, *Consumer Culture: History, Theory and Politics* (London: Sage, 2007), 25–30.

individualistic and narcissist attitudes, moreover, it downplayed men's involvement in consumption, contributing to reinforcing the presumed 'natural' link between women, shopping, and 'un-productive' activities.[9]

Since the late 1990s a number of studies have transformed our understanding of gender, consumption, and domesticity. There have been two main growth areas. First, historians have explored the 'public' face of consumption, examining the spread of department stores since the nineteenth century, and tracing the rise of the consumer as a political and self-conscious actor in civil society.[10] A second focus has been on the 'private side' of consumption, in particular on the 'commodification' of domestic space and the significance of home cultures since the eighteenth century.

This chapter offers an overview of these recent historical debates, considering principally modern Europe, and using domesticity as a key concept. Gender history has generally understood domesticity as an ideology that, principally since the nineteenth century, justified the separation between a public sphere, dominated by men and explicated around institutional political activities and economic exchanges within the market, and a private sphere, assigned to women and connected with the day-to-day management of the family and the home. More recently, however, the attention to material culture and ordinary consumption has provided an enlarged—and more sympathetic—view of domesticity, including a wide range of everyday practices within the domestic space and acknowledging consumers' autonomy and creativity. Domesticity has been retrieved as a crucial cultural space which criss-crosses public and private spheres, calling into question at the same time individualistic and civic values, gender and family issues, and discourses and practices associated with the domestic environment.

My analysis is divided into four main sections. In the first, I provide an introductory discussion on the relationship between gender history and the history of the family, especially in the field of consumer studies, and I show the problematic yet fruitful connection between them. In the second section, I concentrate on those works that examine the rise of a 'modern' public sphere, structured around mass consumption and potentially more inclusive with respect to women. Reframing Habermas's account with a gender-conscious approach and recognizing the power of the discourse in shaping historical processes, some of the studies considered here critically utilized the Habermasian assumption that commercial culture caused a radical transformation of the classic bourgeois public realm.[11] Focusing on the contemporary debate about women shoppers and the challenge they posed to the masculine public sphere, these works explore the tensions between different 'publics' that were emerging in the nineteenth century within European societies and the changing ways in which domesticity and motherhood were linked to consumer culture.

---

[9] Margot Finn, 'Men's Things: Masculine Possession in the Consumer Revolution', *Social History*, 25/2 (2000), 133–55.

[10] Frank Trentmann (ed.), *The Making of the Consumer: Knowledge, Power and Identity in the Modern World* (Oxford and New York: Berg, 2006).

[11] Jürgen Habermas, *The Structural Transformation of the Public Sphere: An Inquiry into a Category of Bourgeois Society* (Cambridge, MA: MIT Press, 1989), in particular part V; orig. edn. *Structurwandel der Öffentlichkeit* (Neuwied: Luchterhand, 1962). For a critical reading, Craig Calhoun (ed.), *Habermas and the Public Sphere* (Cambridge, MA: MIT Press, 1992).

In the third section, I turn back to the domestic sphere proper, and discuss a recent set of studies that explores the housewife's creative power within domestic space and the crucial tensions that historical transformations in ordinary domestic consumption generated in the dynamics of gender, family, and consumption. If the works analysed in the second section investigate consumption principally as a phenomenon occurring in the public realm, here the focus will be on the 'public' and 'social' nature of private acts of consumption. These studies explore home as a site of power, in which subjectivities and identities are constructed through the day-to-day conflict between social norms, structural constraints, and consumers' creativity. The organization of domestic space—the ways in which its inhabitants have arranged it since the eighteenth century or in which architects, designers, and 'experts' have suggested doing it—is approached as a contested arena reflecting the complex production of the everyday life.

The last section of the chapter focuses on the politicization of everyday life in twentieth-century Europe. By giving their attention to state politics, women's, and consumers' organizations, and new cultural trends connected with collective traumas like wars and economic crises, historians have investigated the potential link between a progressive 'publicization'—commercialization and politicization—of home cultures and ordinary life, and the increasing political relevance of women as housewives and citizen-consumers. While the relationship between the politics of consumption and gender equality still remains problematic, these processes radically changed the collective perception of 'private' and 'public', suggesting to historiography a more open conceptualization of these critical issues.

GENDER AND FAMILY: A TRICKY
BUT FRUITFUL CONNECTION

As Megan Doolittle noted a decade ago, gender history and the history of the family have rarely been brought together by historians, despite the many aspects they had in common.[12] Both challenged mainstream narratives of historical processes by recognizing the crucial role of family and domestic life. And both criticized the impact of the two main European traditions of political thought, Marxism and Liberalism, which were largely responsible for marginalizing the family and gender identities as historical agents in their own right.[13] Nonetheless, contrasting methods, different sets of sources and concepts, inhibited the dialogue between the two disciplines. On the one hand, the

[12] Megan Doolittle, 'Close Relations? Bringing Together Gender and Family in English History', *Gender and History*, 11/3 (1999), 542–54.

[13] Linda Nicholson, *Gender and History: The Limits of Social Theory in the Age of The Family* (New York: Columbia University Press, 1986), 131–200. More recently, Paul Ginsborg, 'Scrivere la storia delle famiglie del Novecento: La connettività in un quadro comparato', in Enrica Asquer, Maria Casalini, Anna Di Biagio, and Paul Ginsborg (eds.), *Famiglie del Novecento: Conflitti, culture e relazioni* (Rome: Carocci, 2010), 15–38.

demographic approach to family history has often analysed the family as a unit, privileging collective subjects and patterns of behaviour rather than gendered individuals and their unique experiences.[14] On the other hand, gender history identified family as the main reason for women's oppression and thus tended to emphasize the autonomous construction of women's subjectivity *outside* or *against* the family, rather than within it. According to some critics,[15] women historians themselves were trapped in a 'masculinist' theory of modernization. Locating modernity outside the home in the workplace and the public sphere, many saw women's emancipation and domesticity as natural opposites. As a result, the patriarchal nature of the family and of domesticity has been taken for granted rather than treated as a historical question.

Economic historians influenced by neoclassical theories have generally neglected the family as an agent of consumption, privileging the individual and applying an utility-maximizing ideal-typical rationality to him or her. The individual consumer, with a given income, has been assumed to behave as a 'sovereign', perfectly aware of what he/she wanted and capable of evaluating and choosing autonomously his/her own 'utility'. While many critics with different methodological approaches questioned these assumptions for not taking sufficiently into account the role played by the social system in orienting consumer behaviour, and especially the human need for communicating and constructing social ties through consumption,[16] within economics the neoclassical approach to family has been revised since the 1960s with the body of theories called the 'new household economics'. By focusing on the allocation of time within the family, this new approach found that, in past as in modern times, the household realized its economic functions through a rational division of labour shared between its members in order successfully to achieve individual and collective goals.[17] As reaffirmed recently by Jan De Vries,[18] in nineteenth-century northern Europe, for instance, the gender division of labour within the male breadwinner and homemaker households was the product of a rational allocation of time, shared by husbands and wives and made convenient by new cultures of consumption, and in particular by the emergence of new needs—a cleaner house or better nutrition—that imposed a greater amount of domestic work in order to became consumable. In this perspective, then, the housewife was not the product of the patriarchy and the household was the basic economic unit in which the individuals' decision-making took place.

This emphasis on the rational organization of the household, however, needs to be combined with other studies that have revealed deep gender and generational

---

[14] Louise Tilly, 'Women's History and Family History: Fruitful Collaboration or Missed Connection?', *Journal of Family History*, 12/1 (January 1987), 303–15.

[15] Janet Wolff, 'The Invisible *Flâneuse*: Women in the Literature of Modernity', *Theory, Culture and Society*, 2/3 (1985), 37–46; Judy Giles, *The Parlour and the Suburb*, 1–22.

[16] Mary Douglas and Baron Isherwood, *The World of Goods: Towards an Anthropology of Consumption* (New York: Basic Books, 1979).

[17] See in particular, Gary S. Becker, 'A Theory of the Allocation of Time', *Economic Journal*, 75 (1965), 493–517.

[18] Jan De Vries, *The Industrious Revolution: Consumer Behavior and the Household Economy, 1650 to the Present* (New York: Cambridge University Press, 2008), 186–237.

inequalities in the distribution of power over family purchases and resources. Up to the twentieth century, for instance, historians have found within European families an unequal distribution of food, and especially meat, giving priority to the male breadwinner with the justification of the presumed greater hardness of his tasks.[19] Significantly, the same was found by sociologists concerned with the ritual of family meals in 1970s rural France and in some manufacturing towns in the north of England in the 1980s, where family meals were prepared by women in accordance with men's and children's preferences.[20] Studies of domestic budgeting, moreover, have demonstrated that the intra-household allocation of resources in modern Europe largely depends on the social role played by each member within the family. In the early 1980s, for example, Jan Pahl's seminal study of household financial arrangements in Britain emphasized the husbands' greater degree of freedom in personal spending.[21] In this perspective, thus, family emerges as a complex consumer, whose acts derive from a constant tension and negotiation between different and not always symmetrical components within it.

The cultural construction of family identity through domestic consumption and of gender and generational identities has been one of the growth fields of recent research. One thematic focus has been on the link between motherhood, childhood, and consumption. Anthropological research, in particular, provides precious insights into the role of consumer culture in constructing the mother and the child as social subjects, that begins to exist before the birth of the child with the accumulation of specific objects, such as clothes, toys, and other items related to the mother- and the child-to-be.[22] While this is certainly a contemporary tendency, nonetheless a similar role in the cultural construction of motherhood and childhood has been observed in the past with respect to the proliferation of the advice literature, the modern advertising, and the popular press for women that since the nineteenth-century have approached female consumers as mothers and as having the principle responsibility for family well-being. At the end of the nineteenth century, for instance, shopping at Christmas was represented by the popular press in London as a female joyful task providing women with the opportunity to demonstrate their propensity to sacrifice energy and time for children and family.[23]

[19] Edward Shorter, *A History of Women's Bodies* (New York: Basic Books, 1982).

[20] Christine Delphy, 'Sharing the Same Table: Consumption and the Family', in Stevi Jackson and Shaun Moores (eds.), *The Politics of Domestic Consumption: Critical Readings* (Hemel Hempstead: Prentice Hall/Harvester Wheatsheaf, 1995), 25–36 (first published in English in Christopher Charles Harris et al (eds.), *The Sociology of the Family: New Directions for Britain*, Sociological Review Monograph, 28 (1979)); Nickie Charles, 'Family and Food Ideology', in Jackson and Moores (eds.), *The Politics of Domestic Consumption*, 100–15 (first published in Christopher Charles Harris (ed.), *Family, Economy and Community* (Cardiff: University of Wales Press, 1990)). See also Marjorie De Vault, *Feeding the Family: The Social Organization of Caring as Gendered Work* (Chicago: Chicago University Press, 1991).

[21] Jan Pahl, *Money and Marriage* (Basingstoke: Macmillan, 1989).

[22] Janelle S. Taylor, Linda L. Layner, and Danielle F. Wozniak (eds.), *Consuming Motherhood* (New Brunswick, NJ, and London: Rutgers University Press, 2004), see here in particular Anna J. Clark, 'Maternity and Materiality: Becoming a Mother in Consumer Culture', 55–71.

[23] Christopher P. Hosgood, 'Doing the Shop at Christmas: Women, Men and the Department Stores in England, c.1880–1914', in Geoffrey Crossick and Serge Jaumain (eds.), *Cathedrals of Consumption: The European Department Store, 1850–1939* (Aldershot: Ashgate, 1999), 97–115.

By contrast, fatherhood and men's presence in domestic consumption has only belatedly received attention. Some pioneering works have investigated the origins of a 'domestic masculinity',[24] realized through many activities among which are particular consumer acts, such as buying luxurious objects—i.e. paintings, lamps, musical instruments, photographic equipment, or exotic seeds and plants—for decorating the home and the garden in late eighteenth- and early nineteenth-century England,[25] or organizing holidays and cooking special meals—homemade 'pasta' at Christmas for instance—for middle-class families in Milan in the 1960s.[26] These examples show the fruitful connection between family and gender history in the area of consumer studies.

Studies of shopping have highlighted consumption as a central element in the process of women's emancipation from a restrictive ideology of domesticity. In particular, nineteenth-century American and European department stores have been studied as a new public opening for women, transgressing the separation between private and public spheres. Drawing attention to even earlier periods, and focusing on material cultures emerging from an analysis of wills and many other private sources, such as diaries, letters or account books, historians have recognized a strong and gendered link between female consumers' attachment to luxuries, personal, and domestic objects—fine clothes, china, silverware—and the 'construction of a sense of self' in women's domestic life.[27] As shown by Lorna Weatherill, in late seventeenth- and early eighteenth-century England, for example, looking glasses and mirrors occurred more frequently in middle-rank women's probate inventories than in men's ones, reflecting not only women's concern for home and personal appearance, but also 'some degree of self-awareness'.[28] Seemingly, in sixteenth- and seventeenth-century Turin (Italy), Sandra Cavallo has noted, detailed descriptions of goods and gifts in bequests, and the use of possessive adjectives to refer to personal possessions were specific to women. As consumers, women invested personal objects with their particular selfhood and between the seventeenth and the eighteenth century, this tendency increased for a material reason, as:

> the emergence of a view of marriage as a conjugal pact centered around children, and the emergence of the family of marriage as the primary locus of identity...had the effect of giving greater legitimacy to the suppression of women's right over the property they brought into the marital household.[29]

[24] Ralph LaRossa, *The Modernization of Fatherhood: A Social and Political History* (Chicago: University of Chicago Press, 1997).

[25] David Hussey, 'Guns, Horses, and Stylish Waistcoats? Male Consumer Activity and Domestic Shopping in Late Eighteenth- and Early Nineteenth-Century England', in David Hussey and Margaret Ponsonby (eds.), *Buying for the Home: Shopping for the Domestic from the Seventeenth Century to the Present* (Aldershot: Ashgate, 2008), 47–69; Karen Harvey, 'Men Making Home: Masculinity and Domesticity in Eighteenth-Century Britain', *Gender and History*, 21/3 (2009), 520–40.

[26] E. Asquer, 'Rompere senza far rumore: Famiglie dei ceti medi a cavallo del 1968 (Cagliari e Milano)', in Asquer et al., *Famiglie del Novecento*, 211–38.

[27] Sandra Cavallo, 'What Did Women Transmit? Ownership and Control of Household Goods and Personal Effects in Early Modern Italy', in Moira Donald and Linda Hurcombe (eds.), *Gender and Material Culture in Historical Perspective* (London: Macmillan, 2000), 51.

[28] Weatherill, 'A Possession of One's Own', 144. See also Amanda Vickery, *Behind Closed Doors: At Home in Georgian England* (New Haven, CT and London: Yale University Press, 2009), 106–28.

[29] Cavallo, 'What Did Women Transmit?', 38.

A strong attachment to personal effects and moveable domestic objects thus provided women with an instrument for constructing a 'private' sphere *inside* the family.

From early modern consumer practices to nineteenth-century shopping, consumption was therefore part of a constant renegotiation of gender identities and power *inside* and *outside* the domestic sphere. To presume a stark divide between women's emancipation and domesticity runs the risk of overlooking the manifold nature of the former and the complexities of the latter.

COMPETING PUBLICS: MARKETPLACE, NATION, AND CIVIL SOCIETY

From Paris to London, from Berlin to Milan, the spread of mass consumption, epitomized by the monumental temples of shopping that appeared in late-nineteenth-century metropoles,[30] raised intense debates over the nature of the public sphere and bourgeois femininity.[31] Although women were not the only spectators and beneficiaries of this new commercial public space, they were protagonists in the narrative centring on the modernity led by the department stores: journalists and writers, entrepreneurs, politicians, activists, and judges often approached the department store as female territory and shopping as a new pleasure for women.

Commercial culture raised anxieties about new gender identities and shifting boundaries between private and public spheres. In public debate, economic conflicts between traditional specialized shopkeepers and 'universal providers', and in particular between thrift and hedonism, and tensions between liberal individualism and civic values, were all discussed in gendered terms. New opportunities of sociability for female shoppers, provided by tea rooms, restaurants, reading rooms, and resting places within the comfortable and illuminated interiors of the department store, new experiences of urban mobility made possible by the development of public transport, and wives' financial manoeuvres offered by the spread of buying on credit, spawned anxieties about women's changing position in public life.

The female body attracted attention from both the supporters and the adversaries of consumer culture: it was represented as an emblem either of cultural progress

---

[30] For a comparative perspective, Crossick and Jaumain (eds.), *Cathedrals of Consumption*. See also Michael B. Miller, *The Bon-Marché: Bourgeois Culture and the Department Store 1869–1920* (London, Boston, and Sydney: Allen & Unwin, 1981; new edn. 1994); William Lancaster, *Department Store: A Social History* (Leicester: Leicester University Press, 1995); Elena Papadia, *La Rinascente* (Bologna: il Mulino, 2005).

[31] Erika Diane Rappaport, *Shopping for Pleasure: Women in the Making of London's West-End* (Princeton: Princeton University Press, 2000); Lisa Tiersten, 'Marianne in the Department Store: Gender and the Politics of Consumption in Turn-of-the-Century Paris', in Crossick and Jaumain (eds.), *Cathedrals of Consumption*, 116–34; Lisa Tiersten, *Marianne in the Market: Envisioning Consumer Society in Fin-de-Siècle France* (Berkeley and London: University of California Press, 2001).

or, instead, of moral degeneration.[32] As Erika Rappaport has shown, in Victorian and Edwardian London, for example, critics claimed that shopping within the department store could mean the possibility of middle-class women going through the urban crowd without men's protection and feeling free to drink alcohol in public and indulge in other similar 'immoral' pleasures, including prostitution. The bourgeois housewife and her family commitments were central to this discourse. Middle-class respectability, which relied on a clear distinction between family and marketplace, was presumed to be under pressure. Shopping for pleasure was associated by those critics with irrationality and immoral sensuality, that is to say power and disorder.

Here and elsewhere, by contrast, a variety of supporters of shopping and consumer culture was entering the public arena. By proposing an association between department stores and modernity, entrepreneurs and a community of journalists and politicians around them attempted to elaborate a counter-discourse, in which the language of domesticity and family reconciled a 'dangerous' marketplace with a 'moral' and respectable public sphere. The department store was depicted as a comfortable 'semi-public' arena, in which women could experiment with pleasurable activities away from the dangerous temptations of the city. The mingling of genders and classes was proposed as a symbol of cosmopolitanism, instead of a danger, while services to thirsty and tired customers were portrayed as 'necessities' improving city life, and not as luxurious surplus.

The debate about the department store played with different meanings of the 'public'. In late nineteenth-century France, for instance, the main concept of 'public sphere' had at its core a special emphasis on social duty and collective interest, as opposed to individualistic or privatizing inclinations potentially brought about by women's consumption. As Lisa Tiersten's seminal account shows, criticism of consumer culture was intimately tied to the weak penetration of the free trade ideology in France.[33] Unlike in Britain and the United States, in France a contradiction was emerging between the 'public' interpreted as the political community of citizens, devoted to the civic values upon which the Republique was constructed, and the 'public' intended as the marketplace, dominated by the principle of laissez-faire and made up of individual, self-interested consumers. As Tiersten explains, a third conceptualization of the public sphere emerged in this debate, first of all as a consequence of the attempt by department store owners and defenders to reconcile the commercial public with the republican civic public—a feminine form of citizenship, which was represented by the female shopper who, as 'a representative of the family' and as 'the guardian of the nation's artistic prestige', 'acted for the benefit of her family and the nation'.[34] Both family and nation were thus invoked as moral guarantees against the threat of an individualistic culture. While family was the consolidated

[32] Rappaport, *Shopping for Pleasure*, 16–47; Judith Walkowitz, *City of Dreadful Delight: Narratives of Sexual Danger in Late-Victorian London* (Chicago: University of Chicago Press, 1992); see also Elizabeth Kowaleski-Wallace, *Consuming Subjects: Women, Shopping and Business in the Eighteenth-Century* (New York: Columbia University Press, 1997).
[33] Tiersten, 'Marianne in the Department Store', 116–17.
[34] Tiersten, 'Marianne in the Department Store', 125–7 *passim*.

symbol of the social and moral order upon which European bourgeois culture was constructed, 'French taste' was an important, nationalistic, feature of this emerging ideology of citizenship based on consumption. By emphasizing how female shoppers, with their well-educated taste, were the guardians of a national aesthetic patrimony, this representation invested women with a political role. While this public commitment did not challenge women's familial involvement, family, nation, and marketplace were interwoven in a new complex definition of a female-specific public sphere.

These accounts, then, question a theoretical framework based on a simple distinction between private and public spheres. Multiple, competing ideas of public and private were at stake. The French case shows that it was possible for consumer culture to be associated with a (female) individualistic propensity that could affect civic values: private meant individual as opposed to collective. Here, the family, together with the nation, appeared as a collective resource that assigned women a central role and, at the same time, buttressed republican citizenship against unlimited laissez-faire. The reinvented tradition of French good taste was the means that allowed women to enter consumer politics.

Significantly, the British debate followed a different path. Within the 'free trade nation' analysed by Frank Trentmann,[35] the liberal values that supported free competition in the marketplace were not viewed by their supporters (conservatives but also progressive women's movements, the Labour Party, and co-operatives) as being opposed to the collective interest. Rather, the individual consumer advanced public welfare. Free choice, cheap goods, and an open door were seen to buttress civil society, parliamentary democracy, and national strength. Until the First World War, the public debate about consumption and citizenship emphasized the need to shield the private citizen-consumer against the state and capitalist trusts.[36]

In different national contexts, therefore, private and public carried different connotations, reflecting broader cultural and political traditions. These include conservative traditions often missing from earlier accounts concerned with women's liberation. Victoria De Grazia, in particular, has stressed the need to move beyond a perspective concerned with an idea of women's emancipation based on the mere process of entering those spaces provided by department stores and consumption in general.[37] The public presence of female consumers was often supported by a conservative gender division of labour. Prescriptive and asymmetrical roles could be assigned in the public sphere exactly the same way as in the private. In late nineteenth-century Paris, the national relevance of female shoppers was recognized without questioning their exclusion from civic and political rights, such as the right to vote. And the very progressive consumers' association called *Ligue Sociale d'Acheteurs*, too, while developed at the beginning of the twentieth

---

[35] Frank Trentmann, *Free Trade Nation: Commerce, Consumption and Civil Society in Modern Britain* (Oxford and New York: Cambridge University Press, 2008).

[36] Frank Trentmann, 'Bread, Milk, and Democracy: Consumption and Citizenship in Twentieth-Century Britain', in Martin J. Daunton and Matthew Hilton (eds.), *The Politics of Consumption: Material Culture and Citizenship in Europe and America* (Oxford and New York: Berg, 2001), 129–69.

[37] Victoria De Grazia, 'Empowering Women as Citizen-Consumers', in De Grazia and Furlough (eds.), *The Sex of Things*, 275–86.

century in the tradition of 'social Catholicism' and involving women aware of their social duties as consumers, did not join with feminists movements in claiming women's rights and equal treatment to men.[38] Extra-domestic spaces and consumers' associations did not constitute themselves automatically as a *civil society*: that is to say, in the words of Paul Ginsborg, as an associational space distinct from the private sphere, as well as from the market and the state, that was sensitive to gender equality and social justice.[39]

HOME CULTURES: SUBJECTIVITIES AND POLITICS

In a seminal article in 1993,[40] Amanda Vickery challenged the separate spheres paradigm, arguing that it was underpinned by an ideological narrative according to which nine-teenth-century British society witnessed a shift from an idyllic 'golden age' to an era dom-inated by women's domestic seclusion, not overcome until the rise of second-wave feminism in the 1960s and 1970s. Focusing on the British middle classes between the late eighteenth and the mid-nineteenth century, Leonore Davidoff and Catherine Hall argued that crucial links existed between the spread of modern capitalism and urbanism, the emergence of a distinctive middle-class culture and a new emphasis on domesticity as the women's realm.[41] In that period, they found, middle-class women were marginalized from family economic affairs and other public activities, being increasingly involved in a new 'mystique' of domesticity, according to which women as caregivers were functional to the construction of a domestic 'heaven' in the 'heartless world' of bourgeois society. By emphasizing that gender asymmetries pre-existed, Amanda Vickery, by contrast, ques-tioned whether the nineteenth century was an historical turning-point in British women's history. In Georgian England, she showed, crucial transformations involving, in particu-lar, middle-class domesticity and material culture had promoted a growing women's visi-bility. The renovated emphasis on traditional gender norms in the nineteenth century could thus be read as a cultural reaction against these processes.

In her latest book, *Behind Closed Doors*, Vickery reconstructs the 'secret history' of the Georgian home by interweaving architectural history, economic history, family,

---

[38] Marie-Emanuelle Chessel, 'Women and the Ethics of Consumption in France at the Turn of the Twentieth Century: The *Ligue Sociale d'Acheteurs*', in Trentmann, *The Making of the Consumer*, 81–98.

[39] Ginsborg, 'Scrivere la storia delle famiglie', 33; see also Jürgen Kocka, 'Civil Society in Historical Perspective', in J. Keane (ed.), *Civil Society: Berlin Perspectives* (Oxford: Berghahn, 2006), 37–50.

[40] Amanda Vickery, 'Golden Age to Separate Spheres? A Review of the Categories and Chronology of English Women's History', *The Historical Journal*, 36/2 (June 1993), 383–414.

[41] Leonore Davidoff and Catherine Hall, *Family Fortunes: Men and Women of the English Middle Class 1780–1850* (London: Hutchinson Education, 1988); see also Davidoff and Hall, 'Introduction' to 2nd revised edition of this book (London and New York: Routledge, 2002), xii–l; Leonore Davidoff, 'Gender and the "Great Divide": Public and Private in British Gender History', *Journal of Women's History*, 15/1 (2003), 11–27.

and gender history. British domestic space, she finds, was becoming much less a cage for women of the 'middling sort' than ever before. In the course of the eighteenth century, the domestic interior became an 'arena of social campaign and exhibition', through the progressively institutionalized ritual of visiting, the debate over good taste, and the 'commercial construction of the discriminating female consumer and artistic beautifier of the home'.[42] While a gradually more comfortable domestic environment began to separate and protect family intimacy from the outside,[43] at the same time the home became more open to exhibition and public debate, commercially defined, and managed by well-educated homemakers.

Many other studies have explored material culture, from the eighteenth- and nineteenth-century cult of chinaware, whose 'breakability' was supposed to epitomize feminine frailty, to the culture of the parlour, and home decoration.[44] Overcoming a simplistic 'Veblenesque' reading, these accounts try to analyse domestic consumption and women's homemaking in the broader context of a cultural and discursive construction and negotiation of social and gender identities, in which 'taste' is a crucial means.[45]

Of particular interest to historians is the lively debate raised over home design within the community of the European architects in the 1920s and 1930s. The modernist movement, involving architects like Le Corbusier and Ernst May, pioneered a new approach to the domestic space that challenged the bourgeois-style arrangement and harshly criticized the use of the home as a status symbol. In Le Corbusier's words, the house was a 'machine for living in' and should be functionally designed with a rational floor plan and furnished with essential items, in order to satisfy the basic needs of its dwellers and reduce women's domestic work.[46] With this latter aim, in particular, the kitchen had to be separated from the living-dining room and organized as a scientific laboratory, according to the well-known 'Frankfurt kitchen', designed by the Austrian architect Grete Schütte-Lihotsky at the end of the 1920s. In the 1940s and 1950s, the modernist imperatives gained momentum, inspiring European politics of public housing during the post-war reconstruction. While largely supported by the professional and the popular press, however, the architects' demand for a rationalization of domestic interiors in many cases proved to be opposed by the agency of homemakers, not always subordinated and totally obedient to external prescriptions. In the 'new town' of Harlow, near

[42] Amanda Vickery, *Behind Closed Doors*, 7.

[43] Raffaella Sarti, *Europe at Home: Family and Material Culture, 1500–1800* (New Haven, CT and London: Yale University Press, 2004); Martine Segalen, 'Material Conditions of Family Life', in David I. Kertzer and Marzio Barbagli (eds.), *The History of the European Family* (New Haven, CT and London: Yale University Press, 2002), Vol. 2, 3–39.

[44] Vanessa Alayrac Fielding, ' "Frailty, thy Name is China": Women, Chinoiserie and the Threat of Low Culture in Eighteenth-Century England', *Women's History Review*, 18/4 (September 2009), 659–68; Jane Hamlett, ' "The Dining Room Should be the Man's Paradise, as the Drawing Room is the Woman's": Gender and the Middle Class Domestic Space in England, 1850–1920', *Gender and History*, 21/3 (2009), 576–91.

[45] Pierre Bourdieu, *La Distinction: Critique social du jugement* (Paris: Gallimard, 1979).

[46] Christopher Reed, 'Introduction', in Christopher Reed (ed.), *Not at Home: The Suppression of Domesticity in Modern Art and Architecture* (London: Thames and Hudson, 1996), 7–17.

London, on which Judy Attfield focused her pioneering oral history account,[47] as well as in the publicly funded high-rise housing complexes in the Paris area, analysed in a seminal research study carried out in 1955 by the urban sociologist Paul-Henri Chombart de Lauwe,[48] inhabitants and especially housewives shaped their homes creatively, showing that their own needs—an eat-in kitchen for example and a parlour with plenty of decorative items—did not necessarily coincide with those theorized from the outside by architects and designers. By proposing a critical reading of these processes, these studies have tended to overcome the conventional separation between high and low culture, emphasizing the importance of this lively debate on domestic modernization in the light of a growing acknowledgment of home material cultures as a crucial site of power.[49]

Even if these accounts are more concerned with the private realm than with department stores and other public spaces of consumption, it is not hard to recognize here an approach similar to the one analysed in the previous section. With respect to women's agency and empowerment, here connected with the creative power of homemaking, we do, in fact, need to be cautious again. Consumption, from shopping within a spectacular department store to decorating the living-room, has provided women with a means of self-expression that sometimes challenged gender boundaries. However, to interpret these challenges as more general acts of political resistance against power imbalances and inequalities is more debatable. In subverting the dominant rules of home decorating or body fashioning, female consumers did not automatically question domesticity and motherhood as women's primary and 'natural' commitments. Their longing for self-expression and individual creativity, moreover, was not necessarily combined with an active attempt to discourage women's inequality in some other crucial field of citizenship, such as political rights, instruction, or labour conditions.

THE POLITICIZATION OF EVERYDAY LIFE IN TWENTIETH-CENTURY EUROPE

For future historians, a crucial task will be to unravel the cultural, economic, and political processes that made everyday consumption a central political issue, that ultimately challenged the very nature and meaning of politics itself. While feminist critics

---

[47] Judy Attfield, 'Inside Pram Town: a Case Study of Harlow House Interiors, 1951–1961', in Judy Attfield and Pat Kirkham (eds.), *A View from the Interior: Feminism, Women and Design* (London: The Women's Press, 1989), 215–38.

[48] Paul-Henri Chombart De Lauwe, *Famille et Habitation* (Paris: CNRS, 1959 and 1960); Nicole Rudolph, 'Who Should Be the Author of a Dwelling? Architects versus Housewives in 1950s France', *Gender and History*, 21/3 (2009), 541–59.

[49] Daniel Miller (ed.), *Home Possessions: Material Culture Behind Closed Doors* (Oxford: Berg, 2001). See also Hilde Heynen and Gülsüm Baydar (eds.), *Negotiating Domesticity: Spatial Productions of Gender in Modern Architecture* (London: Routledge, 2005).

like Nancy Fraser[50] correctly pointed out that gender blindness was a consistent weakness in the dualistic Habermasian account of public and private, and were right to reaffirm the integrally political dimension of the 'private sphere', it is equally clear that the twentieth century has witnessed a progressive politicization of everyday life that calls for historical explanation. This politicization has come with increasing attention to the role of ordinary life in public opinion, market surveys and opinion polling, and political culture in the broadest sense of the term. While commercial goals have favoured the spread of market research since the first decades of the twentieth century, mainly within the American industries of consumer goods, such as Ford, the political relevance of polling public opinion was mostly recognized in the 1940s, in connection with the growing need of national governments' to monitor civilian morale during the Second World War, as happened with the British 'Wartime Social Survey' established in April 1940. The rebuilding of democracy in post-war Europe, furthermore, was significantly accompanied by a new emphasis on social surveys monitoring people's living conditions, like the parliamentary 'Inchiesta sulla miseria' ('Survey on poverty') in 1950s Italy. During the following twenty years, in many countries the offices for national statistics began regularly to monitor households' patterns of consumption and in 1975 the European Community carried out an important sample survey on 'European Consumers: their interests, aspirations and knowledge on consumer affairs'.

Recent historians have moved the chronological goalposts of this story back from the era of affluence after the Second World War to the early twentieth century. Simon Gunn, for example, traces the shift from a liberal public sphere to a 'consumerist' one to the First World War.[51] Rather than affluence and productivity, it was growing state intervention, nationalistic mobilization, and, especially, economic crises and collective traumas, that invested everyday life with an unprecedented political role during and after the war.[52] Many studies concerned with the inter-war period in Europe have explored how, alongside the spread of the home modernization movement, housewives and women's associations played an active role in elaborating specific politics of domestic

[50] Nancy Fraser, 'What's Critical about Critical Theory? The Case of Habermas and Gender', *New German Critique*, 35 (1985), 97–131.

[51] Simon Gunn, 'The Public Sphere, Modernity and Consumption: New Perspectives on the History of the English Middle Class', in Alan Kidd and David Nicholls (eds.), *Gender, Civic Culture and Consumerism: Middle-Class Identity in Britain 1800–1940* (Manchester: Manchester University Press, 1999), 12–29.

[52] Lizabeth Cohen, 'The New Deal State and the Making of Citizen Consumers', in Susan Strasser, Charles McGovern and Matthias Judt, *Getting and Spending: European and American Consumer Societies in the Twentieth Century* (Cambridge: Cambridge University Press, 1998), 111–25; Lizabeth Cohen, *A Consumers' Republic: The Politics of Mass Consumption in Post-War America* (New York: Knopf, 2003); with reference to Europe, Belinda Davis, 'Food Scarcity and the Empowerment of the Female Consumer in World War I Berlin', in De Grazia and Furlough (eds.), *The Sex of Things*, 287–310; Claire Duchen and Irene Bandhauer-Schöffmann (eds.), *When the War Was Over: Women, War and Peace in Europe, 1940–1956* (Leicester: Leicester University Press, 2000), part I.

consumption in order to support the national economy.[53] Housewives' private acts of consumption were redefined as a duty to the state. Housewives' movements were also mobilized around authoritarian economic policies adopted by totalitarian regimes. In Fascist Italy, autarchic policy rested on the national mobilization of women, who were supposed to conduct their ordinary housekeeping with self-restraint, giving preference to Italian foods in their cooking. Here again, the relationship between consumption and domesticity, and between the private and the public side of consumption, proved to be complex and ambivalent. On the one hand, the assumption of specific patterns of consumption and the reform of domesticity, inspired by the principles of Taylorized home management, was portrayed as an area of co-optation that rested on women's 'natural' housewifery. On the other hand, the active participation required of women was a challenge to the inherited gender imaginary. It provided women with a political role outside the home. The modernization of home management, too, could be interpreted by women themselves as a crucial means of emancipation from a restrictive and humiliating domesticity. Moreover, cultures and practices of consumption were not absorbed and totally monopolized by the Fascist regime: instead, new commodities and especially new commercial pastimes, such as the cinema, became important features of a 'public', yet individualistic, space, partly separated from the authoritarian state and quite divergent from the dominant and rigid codification of gender roles as well.

In the aftermath of the Second World War, the politicization of everyday life became even more accentuated.[54] In Germany and Italy, Paul Betts has shown, modernization and Americanization, the centrality of domestic consumption and family, and the 'aestheticization of privacy and individual pastimes' in the hands of industrial design, emerged out of the specific context of post-war reconstruction after fascism.[55] The experience of a totalitarian mobilization in the inter-war era, with its demands on privacy and freedom, wartime suffering, together with the militant use of domesticity as a weapon in the Cold War battleground, anchored citizenship in private well-being and the home. German industrial design began to abandon the ideal of a domestic Taylorized worksite for an older model of an intimate and quiet place of refuge for the family. In the same way, the popular Italian washing-machine 'Candy' was advertised as an incentive for Italian

[53] Mary Nolan, ' "Housework made Easy": The Taylorized Housewife in Weimar Germany's Rationalized Economy', *Feminist Studies*, 16/3 (1990), 549–77; Nancy Reagin, 'Comparing Apples and Oranges: Housewives and the Politics of Consumption in Interwar Germany', in Strasser, McGovern and Judt, *Getting and Spending*, 241–61; Victoria De Grazia, *How Fascism Ruled Women: Italy, 1922–1945* (Berkeley and Los Angeles: University of California Press, 1992).

[54] See Paul Betts and David Crowley (eds.), *Domestic Dreamworlds: Notions of Home in Post-1945 Europe*, Special Issue, *Journal of Contemporary History*, 40/2 (2005); Richard Bessel and Dirk Schumann (eds.), *Life After Death: Approaches to a Cultural and Social History of Europe During the 1940s and 1950s* (Cambridge: Cambridge University Press, 2003), in particular Pat Thane, 'Family Life and "Normality" in Postwar British Culture', 193–210.

[55] Paul Betts, *The Authority of Everyday Objects: A Cultural History of West German Industrial Design* (Berkeley and Los Angeles: University of California Press, 2007), especially 213–47, at 245; Paolo Scrivano, 'Signs of Americanization in Italian Domestic Life: Italy's Post-War Conversion to Consumerism', *Journal of Contemporary History*, 40/2 (2005), 317–40.

women to participate more actively in family life and happiness. Much less emphasis was put on its potential contribution to women's affirmation outside the home.[56] Efficiency still remained an important claim in 1950s magazines and exhibitions of domestic appliances, but it was supposed to go hand in hand with a new and effective golden age of family leisure. In this context, durability, rather than 'consumability', was the distinctive key value expressed by post-war European material culture, signalling the compromises and hybridization to which American consumer culture was exposed.[57]

Consumption, and in particular domestic consumption, therefore, was progressively established as a common language, through which subjectivities, identities, and political aspirations were articulated. However, the potential competition between consumer culture and democracy remained a very critical point. The crucial process described above, in fact, did not prevent social differences and gender inequalities from arising again. Sociologists are debating, for example, whether within European families domestic labour and the day-to-day caregiving still remain substantially female tasks, or whether consumer culture has not resulted in 'de-genderization'. The process of the 'globalization' of caregiving which is transforming upper and middle-class domesticity in Western countries seems to suggest that the housewife's caregiving role is frequently granted to female migrants, instead of being renegotiated between women and men.

Despite some vital paths of research, the topic 'gender, family, and consumption' continues to be mainly centred around the Victorian period. The debate on the separate spheres in the nineteenth century remains an important starting point. Nonetheless, future research will need to explore more fully the twentieth century, especially the second half. Here, more work needs to be done on domesticity and family from the standpoint of social and cultural history. A greater sensitivity to subjective experiences, which oral sources in particular can provide, might improve significantly our understanding. The 'black box' of the modern family has to be opened with greater investigations of the history of fatherhood, its modernization, and the role played in this process by twentieth-century consumerist lifestyles. Class, too, has to be explored more broadly, well beyond the frequent practice of assuming the middle class as emblematic of the entire society considered, or as a compact homogenous culture. My own research on white-collar families in Italy and their material culture after the economic 'miracle' of the 1960s, for instance, highlights the conflict within the middle classes between consumer culture, with its homologizing and nationalizing strengths, and an older material culture that reflected the need for distinctive social status. Legacies and conflicts between generations is another topic that would benefit from greater attention, especially with the aim to investigate the cultural transformations of the last decades of the twentieth century.

---

[56] E. Asquer, *La Rivoluzione Candida: Storia Sociale della Lavatrice in Italia, 1945–1970* (Rome: Carocci, 2007), 125–41.

[57] Paul Betts and David Crowley, 'Introduction', in Betts and Crowley (eds.), *Domestic Dreamworlds*, 213–36; E. Asquer, 'La Memoria Tralasciata: Per una Storia Intima dei Ceti Medi tra Casa e Ufficio negli Anni Sessanta e Settanta del Novecento Italiano', Ph.D. thesis (Florence: Università degli studi, 2009), 168–80.

BIBLIOGRAPHY

Asquer, Enrica, *La Rivoluzione Candida: Storia Sociale della Lavatrice in Italia, 1945–1970* (Rome: Carocci, 2007).

Betts, Paul, *The Authority of Everyday Objects: A Cultural History of West German Industrial Design* (Berkeley and Los Angeles: University of California Press, 2007).

Betts, Paul, and Crowley, David (eds.), *Domestic Dreamworlds: Notions of Home in Post-1945 Europe*, Special Issue, *Journal of Contemporary History*, 40/2 (April 2005).

Casey, Emma, and Martens, Lydia (eds.), *Gender and Consumption: Domestic Cultures and the Commercialisation of Everyday Life* (Aldershot and Burlington, VT: Ashgate, 2007).

Davidoff, Leonore, and Hall, Catherine, *Family Fortunes: Men and Women of the English Middle Class 1780–1850* (2nd edn., London and New York: Routledge, 2002).

De Grazia, Victoria, and Furlough, Ellen (eds.), *The Sex of Things: Gender and Consumption in Historical Perspective* (Berkeley and London: University of California Press, 1996).

Donald, Moira, and Hurcombe, Linda (eds.), *Gender and Material Culture in Historical Perspective* (London: Macmillan, 2000).

Jackson, Stevi, and Moores, Shaun (eds.), *The Politics of Domestic Consumption: Critical Readings* (Hemel Hempstead: Prentice Hall and Harvester Weatsheaf, 1995).

Rappaport, Erika Diane, *Shopping for Pleasure: Women in the Making of London's West End* (Princeton: Princeton University Press, 2000).

Tiersten, Lisa, *Marianne in the Market: Envisioning Consumer Society in Fin-de-Siècle France* (Berkeley and London: University of California Press, 2001).

Trentmann, Frank, 'Bread, Milk, and Democracy: Consumption and Citizenship in Twentieth-Century Britain', in Martin J. Daunton and Matthew Hilton (eds.), *The Politics of Consumption: Material Culture and Citizenship in Europe and America* (Oxford and New York: Berg, 2001), 129–69.

Vickery, Amanda, *Behind Closed Doors: At Home in Georgian England* (New Haven, CT and London: Yale University Press, 2009).

CHAPTER 30

CHILDREN'S CONSUMPTION
IN HISTORY

DANIEL THOMAS COOK

CHILDREN acted as consumers and were regarded as a market several generations before scholars began to address their participation in commercial life. Commercial goods made specifically for children's use have existed since at least the eighteenth century in England and the United States. Yet, the academic study of children as consumers took root in the 1960s and did not begin in earnest until the 1970s when the paradigm of 'consumer socialization' took hold among psychologically oriented business scholars. In the 1980s, some discussion of the history of children's consumption and popular culture began to appear in edited volumes and journal articles, with full treatments of some aspects of that history coming into view in the 1990s.

The somewhat lengthy inattention paid the child consumer speaks in large part to the marginal status traditionally afforded, until recently, to social and cultural studies of childhood and consumption. Neither was considered a legitimate field or area of study on its own, but derivative of established fields and disciplines—i.e., studies of childhood deriving from developmental psychology, consumer studies from economics and business. Historical research, initially at least, made for an uneasy fit with these fields that favoured contemporaneous knowledge and more or less precise measurement of effects and outcomes.

Even as children's consumer culture takes centre stage in contemporary media reports, political punditry, and academic scholarship, the history of children's consumption remains largely unrecognized in or otherwise marginal to both histories of childhood and histories of consumption. Children's consumer lives or the popular culture of childhood most often occupy a side or subsidiary position in the overall historiography of childhood as in, for instance, recent works by Steven Mintz and Hugh Cunningham.[1]

---

[1] Steven Mintz, *Huck's Raft: A History of American Childhood* (Cambridge, MA: Harvard University Press, 2004); Hugh Cunningham, *Children and Childhood in Western Society Since 1500* (Harlow: Pearson Longman, 2002).

In a similar manner, many 'general' histories of consumption and advertising—like those of Jackson Lears, Rosalind Williams, and Roland Marchand—either ignore completely or offer token discussions of the world of commercial goods, spaces, and meanings for children.[2] When recognized at all, children tend to be discussed as symbols or symbolic figures—clearly important to study—but not as socio-historical beings who have engaged in consumer practices.[3]

The marginality of children's consumption cannot be attributed to being simply an artefact of academic myopia, but must be understood also as a social-historical reality. The materials of childhood and the practices and activities engaged in by children have not, until recently, been thought worthy of being saved or recorded to any great extent by adults. As well, children's items—clothing, playthings, books—tend to be fragile, handled roughly by children and are often handed down to younger siblings until they are no longer useful or have been destroyed though use.[4]

Given these characterizations, it is unsurprising that few themes cut across or unite work in this arena. What scholars do share is the necessity of having to confront and manage the sense of exceptionalism that presents itself whenever children and childhood are at issue. A core preoccupation that underlies studies of children's consumption history revolves around the ever present, felt need of having to assess both the import of childhood to consumer life and culture, and the significance of consumer life and culture to the childhoods of a given time or context. Scholars in this area face the near ubiquitous twin presumptions that children and childhood occupy a marginal place and position with regard to economic life overall, and that consumption is ultimately peripheral to larger, more important factors like labour, the polity, and family structure.[5] Researchers of children's consumption history do not necessarily accept these assertions. They serve, rather, as background interrogations that subtly structure the character of inquiry by making the significance of children's consumption and its history something to be demonstrated in ways not asked of studies of 'adult' consumption and history.

Epistemological Tensions and Quandaries

These points lead to basic and non-trivial questions that speak to the focus of inquiry. What is a child? What are the boundaries of childhood that are relevant to the questions to be investigated? Age and age range matter of course, developmentally as well as

[2] Jackson Lears, *Fable of Abundance: A Cultural History of Advertising in America* (New York: Basic Books, 1994); Rosalind Williams, *Dream Worlds: Mass Consumption in Late Nineteenth-Century France* (Berkeley: University of California Press, 1982); Roland Marchand, *Advertising the American Dream:1920–1940* (Berkeley: University of California Press, 1985).
[3] See Daniel Thomas Cook 'The Missing Child in Consumption Theory', *Journal of Consumer Culture*, 8/2 (2008), 219–43, for analysis on the position of 'the child' in theories of consumption.
[4] Miriam Formanek-Brunell, *Made to Play House: Dolls and the Commercialization of American Girlhood, 1830–1930* (Baltimore: Johns Hopkins University Press, 1993).
[5] See Don Slater, *Consumer Culture and Modernity* (Oxford: Polity Press, 1997).

culturally. Social definitions of age and age categories have transformed in some significant ways over the past 150 years, particularly in industrialized, developed, media-saturated societies of the global north.[6] Age-related and culturally determined notions of the 'adolescent', the 'teenager', the 'toddler', and the 'tween', among others, have arisen as both named phases of the early life course and as marketing/merchandising categories.[7] In the 1920s, 'youth' in American society could include non-married persons well into their late twenties—where 'youth' was as much a matter of behaviour and lifestyle as it was of numerical age.[8]

To presume the definition of 'child' or the boundaries of childhood precludes the ability to inquire about other, equally fundamental issues of analytic import. For instance, what is a 'child's' product? What constitutes 'consumption'? Is 'children's consumption' that which is done for children? By children? By adults ostensibly for children, but which enhances the status of the parents? Historians of children's consumption in large part have not posed these questions in ways that would inform their undertakings.

To understand the history of children's consumption it is necessary to keep an eye on its historiography, which itself entails attending to deep, yet changing, cultural beliefs about the place and position of children in social relations and the meanings of various childhoods. For it is the focus on children that sets the main interpretive frame of the studies undertaken—and for good reason. Consumption is about the acquisition and purchase of material and non-material goods (e.g., images, statuses). Children generally—and young children and infants in particular—tend to be highly dependent on adults and the adult world for the procurement and provisioning of goods and services. They have not had and do not have much money or resources, if any at all, to purchase or otherwise acquire commercial goods (one key reason they have for so long remained outside the purview of the economist).

Hence, children's consumption always implicates and is implicated in the practices, beliefs, and contexts of adults, especially parents, and most often mothers. This fundamental structure of children's economic dependency complicates simple, typical presumptions about the autonomy and individuality of social actors. Investigating the materials, contexts, practices, and industries that have made the child consumer a possible and viable social figure in a given historical time and place requires that researchers extend consideration past the nominal focus on children, conceptualized as individualized actors, and into the relationships between children and adults, between childhood

---

[6] See Howard Chudacoff, *How Old Are you?* (Princeton: Princeton University Press, 1989).

[7] On the invention of the 'toddler', see below and Daniel Thomas Cook, 'The Rise of "the Toddler" as Subject and Merchandising Category in the 1930s', in Mark Gottdiener (ed.), *The New Means of Consumption* (Lanham, MD: Rowman & Littlefield), 200; on teenagers, see Grace Palladino, *Teenagers* (New York: Basic Books, 1996); on the history of the 'tween', especially the tween girl, see Daniel Thomas Cook and Susan B. Kaiser, 'Betwixt and Be Tween: Age Ambiguity and the Sexualisation of the Female Consuming Subject', *Journal of Consumer Culture*, 4/2 (2004), 203–27.

[8] Paula Fass, *The Damned and the Beautiful: American Youth in the 1920s* (Oxford: Oxford University Press, 1977); see also Chudacoff, *How Old Are you?*, 39–72.

and adulthood, and, as well, between child and adult structures and practices like advertising and marketing.[9]

Given these complications, it should not be surprising that scholarship on children's consumption history is spotty, disjointed, and does not yet hold together as a body of knowledge or tradition of research. That is, there is not much evidence that extant studies have built upon or critiqued each others' findings, insights, or approaches to any significant extent. Most certainly, authors reference one another as appropriate, but there exists a felt lack of conversation among those who write the history of children's consumption.

Differing frames of reference, interests, and goals can make dialogue between historians difficult. A recent, edited collection by Dennis Denisoff, *The Nineteenth-Century Child and Consumer Culture*, highlights some of the difficulties noted above. Many of the contributors examine fiction for clues as to how children and childhood were becoming figured and configured in relation to an increasingly commercialized culture. For instance, chapters on Henry James's sexualization of the Victorian girl, wordplay in Lewis Carroll's *Alice in Wonderland*, the increasing presence of images of children and goods in Christmas scenes in the *Illustrated London News*, and reviews of child stage performers all address the increasing interconnections between a growing recognition and acceptance of children as desirers who may consume and children as desirable subjects who may be consumed. Only Liz Farr's account of toy theatres seeks to examine the experiences or practices of biographical subjects.[10]

The point here most definitely is *not* to elevate or denigrate one form of inquiry in relation to another, but to point to the epistemological entanglements encountered when seeking to determine what the field or area of 'children's consumption history' entails. Certainly, the various ways that the child and representations of children have become associated with commodities must be considered informative of any broad understanding of children's consumption in history. The issues and questions raised here, however, are indicative of the difficulties in characterizing the field of study of the 'history of children's consumption'—difficulties which are to some extent definitive of the area of study.

In what follows, I take up these difficulties in an examination of several significant histories that deal with living historical subjects—as opposed to those trained on depictions or representations of these subjects. Certainly, this distinction between

[9] Daniel Thomas Cook 'The Missing Child in Consumption Theory'; Lydia S. Martens, Dale Southerton and Sue Scott, 'Bringing Children (and Parents) Into the Sociology of Consumption', *Journal of Consumer Culture*, 4/2 (2004), 155–82.

[10] Liz Farr, 'Paper Dreams and Romantic Projections: The Nineteenth-Century Toy Theater, Boyhood and Aesthetic Play', 44–62, Michèle Mendelssohn, '"I'm Not a Bit Expensive": Henry James and the Sexualisation of the Victorian Girl', 81–94, Carol Movor, 'Forgetting to Eat: Alice's Mouthing Metonymy', 95–118, Lorraine Janzen Kooistra, 'Home Thoughts and Home Scenes: Packaging Middle-class Childhood for Christmas Consumption', 151–72; Marah Gubar 'The Drama of Precocity: Child Performers on the Victorian Stage', 63–78, all in Dennis Denisoff (ed.), *The Nineteenth-Century Child and Consumer Culture* (Aldershot: Ashgate, 2008).

a 'living subject' and 'representation' cannot be absolute. It is made to distinguish between different foci and registers of research. Of the many ways the studies could be grouped—e.g., chronologically, regionally, by consumer good, or industry—I have chosen to present them in terms of what the authors considered to be the key actor in children's commercial lives: parents, industry, or children.

PARENTS AS PRIMARY CONSUMERS

Most of the historical work on children's consumption understandably favours research in the United States, the UK and Europe, where modern consumer culture originated.[11] In the main, historians of children's consumption focus on the period between about 1890 and 1950. An exception to this periodization can be found in Neil McKendrick, John Brewer and J. H. Plumb's *The Birth of Consumer Society*, one of the earliest historical treatments of children and consumption, published in 1982.

In individually authored chapters, they argue that an overall increase in wealth stemming from the Industrial Revolution helped create monied middle classes in eighteenth-century England. The influx of wealth fed a kind of spending and social emulation 'frenzy' among those in the middle classes anxious to copy the styles and lifestyles of the well-to-do. Wealth and increased consumption both followed and led rapid changes in styles in clothing and other goods that fuelled this process that Thorstein Veblen would theorize at the end of the nineteenth century. It was, however, a change in the acceptance of commercialism in everyday living in the household that allowed the consumer revolution to take root.[12]

There is virtually no mention of the place of children in this revolution in most of a publication that deals with fashion, pottery, men's shaving practices, and politics, except for J. H. Plumb's chapter discussing the 'new world' of children in eighteenth-century England. This new world, argues Plumb, was one where there arose an increased expectation that children would live beyond the first few years of their lives and hence were more amenable to emotional *and* monetary investment. Accompanying the decrease in child mortality among this class were new attitudes toward children. Citing John Locke's notion of the child as a 'slate' which could be written upon, Plumb notes that a preoccupation with the middle-class child's social future (as opposed to religious salvation) came to predominate parental concerns.[13]

---

[11] Outside of Western or global North contexts, children's consumption and its attendant social-moral concerns, have come to the attention of social researcher in recent years. Most notably, the 'Little Emperor' phenomenon in China in Jun Jing, *Feeding China's Little Emperors: Food, Children, and Social Change* (Stanford: Stanford University Press, 2000), and consumption by children and youth in globalizing India in Ritty Lukose, *Liberalization's Children: Gender, Youth and Consumer Citizenship in Globalizing India* (Durham, NC: Duke University Press, 2009).

[12] Neil McKendrick, John Brewer, and J.H. Plumb, *The Birth of a Consumer Society: The Commercialization of Eighteenth-Century England* (Bloomington, IN: Indiana University Press, 1982).

[13] On Locke, McKendrick, Brewer and Plumb, *The Birth of a Consumer*, 287–90.

Here, Plumb contends that a focus on a liberal education for children—both boys and girls in different ways—became seen by parents as a form of intergenerational investment in maintaining and increasing a family's social standing. Children served as the vehicle for a kind of 'capital investment', as illustrated by advertisements for small private academies. In addition, the creation of new kinds of children's literature and expenditures on 'amusements and pleasures' for children together demonstrate that parents regarded their children not as 'sprigs of Adam whose will had to be broken', but as conduits for social display and emulation.[14]

Plumb offers an explanation about increased expenditures on children's education and educational goods from the perspective of upwardly aspirant parents. Middle-class children occupied a place of importance in the development and transmission of the family's status. They appear as something akin to a social object to be wielded rather than as social objects to be engaged. He makes no effort to represent children's experiences nor makes any mention of children's desires, indicating that perhaps, for Plumb, these are irrelevant or presumed to be given. Nor does he give consideration to the different ages of children, although the focus of the research appears to be at the contemporary equivalent of the elementary school level. Children exist in and are subject to regimes of consumption but are not themselves consumers. Consumption appears to be something done for and, perhaps, to them.

The actions and wishes of parents and other adults, as discussed earlier, cannot be avoided or ignored when contemplating the world of children. How adults and parents figure into the explanatory and conceptual mix does vary among scholars. Gary Cross, the most prolific writer on the history of children's consumption, trains much of his effort on the actions, perspectives, and desires of parents.

In *Kids' Stuff: Toys and the Changing World of American Childhood*, Cross offers a history of children's playthings focusing mainly on the period after 1900 in the United States. In ways similar to Plumb, he argues that modern playthings have been 'subject to evolving and conflicting attitudes towards, and styles of, childrearing.'[15] Beginning in the first decades of the twentieth century, an expanding market and industry for children's toys was both restrained by and sought to influence parental attitudes toward play. The industry had to overcome both a lingering premodern concern about play as excess, and a more recent notion that toys served as repositories for tradition, in order for the 'modern toy box' to flourish. A revolution in marketing—i.e., display and advertising—and the accompanying financial success of the toy industry itself may not have taken hold were it not for a 'new empathy of parents toward child's play.'[16]

Over several chapters, Cross outlines what may be thought of as a dance between manufacturers, retailers, and marketeers, on the one side, and parents—more particularly,

[14] Capital investment and quote, McKendrick, Brewer and Plumb, *The Birth of a Consumer Society*, 287 and 292.
[15] Gary Cross, *Kids' Stuff: Toys and the Changing World of American Childhood* (Cambridge, MA: Harvard University Press, 1998), 8.
[16] Ibid., 33.

their changing attitudes toward child rearing—on the other, focusing mainly on the 1900 to Second World War period. Toy manufacturers produced items that reinforced gender norms and catered to children beyond the infant and toddler range, apparently with the assent of parents. Countering the socialization function of most toys, fantasy and novelty toys drew upon folk and literary traditions that invited children into a 'secret' garden' of the imagination. Much less 'productive' than dolls that train for motherhood or tools that train for work, fantasy toys—from teddy bears to kewpie dolls, to Shirley Temple and Mickey Mouse, to those derived from comic book characters—reflected the changing 'meanings and values attributed to childhood by parents.'[17] So-called 'educational toys', for Cross represented the 'perfect symbol of the status conscious middle-class family' whereby parents 'trained children for life.'[18]

The story Cross tells is one of the breakdown of certainty regarding children and parents after the First World War, particularly for the American baby boom generation. He explains the acceptance of the 'rampant consumerism' embodied in the Barbie doll and the destruction and war play encouraged by the G. I. Joe military doll as, in part, a breakdown in 'traditional parent-child roles and a loss in confidence of what the child's path to maturity' should be. In an unacknowledged twist to Plumb's view, Cross sees the parents of baby boomers not 'investing' in their child's future through consumption, but purchasing toys 'because their children wanted them'—something of an acquiescence to a triumphant commercial-media culture.[19]

In his 2004 book *The Cute and the Cool*, Cross defines and strengthens his thesis that children's consumption throughout modern twentieth-century history hinges on the feelings and actions of parents. He distinguishes between sheltered innocence—a protective posture toward children derived from Romantic views of childhood—and wondrous innocence—an adult pleasure in witnessing children's pleasure—arguing that the latter form of innocence has fuelled the rise and proliferation of children's consumerism. Wondrous innocence gained its expression through invocations of the 'cuteness' of children in dolls, stories, and iconographic representations in advertisements and popular venues like the cover of the famed *Saturday Evening Post*. For Cross, the threat of a loss of a pastoral past that associated children with nature and of innocent childhood in the face of social change made middle-class parents long nostalgically for their own childhoods. It was through summoning the 'wondrous child' through gift giving, Christmas, Halloween, and other rituals that such a feeling could be inspired and experienced.[20]

Commercial enterprises in a sense conspired with this parental attitude toward children, playing it for all it could be worth with advertisements and 'appropriate' goods. But the spectre of the 'cool child', who is transgressive, dispassionate, and disobedient, also arose from the commercial milieu of the twentieth century. Seeds of this figure could

---

[17] Ibid., 85.
[18] Ibid., 139.
[19] Ibid., 187.
[20] Gary Cross, *The Cute and the Cool* (Cambridge, MA: Harvard University Press, 2004).

be found in literary genres of fantasy and juvenile fiction in the nineteenth century. The 'cool' kid animated the early comics of the 1930s, migrating into children's television shows in the 1960s, and into edgy comic book characters and video games in the latter part of the century. The result, for Cross, is the development of a commercial 'dream world' for children—embodied in the 'glazed over-intent look' of a child at the controls of a video game—that is beyond the parents' own 'dream world' of cuteness and innocence. The 'cool' kid serves as a foil to innocence, sheltered or wondrous, nurtured by a commercial culture which feeds children's desires that have gotten 'away from parents' control and understanding.'[21]

Like Plumb, Cross places parents at the centre of explanation and action regarding children's consumption and their relation to commercial culture. Unlike Plumb, Cross sees parental 'investment' in emotional rather than financial or legacy terms. Clearly, markets and marketeers play a more central role in Cross's scheme than in Plumb's, given that they are discussing developments that occurred well over a century apart. Cross speaks to children's desires and actions as something ultimately dangerous. It is when children have their desires acted upon and indulged by both parents and corporations that the cool, anti-innocent child comes into social power. No attempt or thought is made to locate children's voices or perspectives in history; these tend to be read from sales and the popularity of goods. As well, in both of these efforts, the ages of the children at issue remain unclear. Cross addresses infants and toddlers at one point, middle school children at another, teenagers at another, and is often unclear as to the ages of the children who are of concern in any given argument or for any given historical period.

INDUSTRY CONCEPTUALIZATIONS
OF THE CHILD CONSUMER

In different ways and to different extents, Plumb and Cross position parents and their motivations centrally in the commercial lives of children in their respective eras and contexts. Both acknowledge and address somewhat how business interests and actions figure into the desires of parents—and, for Cross, of children also. To be sure, Cross's 'cool' kid arises from commercial and media contexts, but it is the changing views of parents ushered in by a new child psychology and child rearing literature that pave the way for those in the middle class to be amenable to the notion of a child consumer in their midst.

A number of historical treatments dealing with the twentieth century in the United States take the practices of those in industry—among them marketers, manufacturers, and advertisers—as necessary rather than contingent to the creation of the construct or conceptualization of the 'child consumer', and indeed of emergent forms of childhood

---

[21] 'glazed over-intent look': Cross, *The Cute and the Cool*, 161; 'away from parents' control': ibid., 163.

itself. In *Raising Consumers*, Lisa Jacobson seeks to elucidate how a 'positive reevaluation of children's consumer identities in the 1920s and 1930s came about', through an examination of how market ideologies and ideologies of the family helped shape and legitimate an emergent children's consumer culture.[22] Making use mainly of parenting, women's, and children's magazines and advertising trade journals, Jacobson analyses the discourses of childhood, money, play, and gender that arise and intermingle during this period.

In contrast to Cross, Jacobson found that parents and educators indeed voiced concerns about children's consumption in the early 1900s. Banks sponsored savings clubs, schools offered training courses on money, and playground clubs emerged that encouraged a sense of thrift on the part of children throughout the early decades of the century. Jacobson sees these efforts as attempts to instil and maintain the values and morals of a culture of self-discipline and sacrifice that was being challenged by one that favoured excess.[23] This excess was promoted and given form by the advertising industry, which had discovered the child consumer in the early 1900s. The industry addressed its messages to the parent, mainly the mother, as well as to the child—finding in the former an eagerness to please her child and in the latter an insatiability for things as well as a keen ability to influence parents into purchasing. Moreover, she asserts that the child in early advertising served as an effective icon in its ability to blend precocity and innocence.[24]

Throughout her excursion into investigating the image of the 'hero' boy consumer, the adolescent girl athletes of the 1920s and 1930s, the increasing entanglements of children's play with consumption, and the radio clubs of the 1930s, Jacobson, like Cross, does not often specify the ages of the children at issue. 'Children' appear to be something of a piece in her descriptions even as they have particular ages in the advertisements she examines and the products and activities associated with them. It is ultimately the power of advertising to 'imagine' children as consumers and 'imagine' the consuming household that helps to usher in a new social order based on consumption. It is an order based on a newly 'democratizing' family whereby children's desires can hold sway for the middle classes in ways that could not have been considered a generation earlier.

Daniel Thomas Cook centres his history on the emergence of the US children's clothing industry, focusing strongly on the discourses of and efforts by apparel (and other) industry members in the construction of children and mothers as consumers. In *The Commodification of Childhood*,[25] Cook examines the establishment of the industry in the 1910s through the lens of key trade journals and supplemental materials. In these, he finds that separate clothing departments for infants and young children in urban department stores did not exist prior to about 1915. Instead, young people's clothing was stocked by type rather than by age—with various sized socks in the sock area, shirts in

---

[22] Lisa Jacobson, *Raising Consumers* (New York: Columbia University Press, 2004), 3.

[23] Jacobson, *Raising Consumers*, ch. 2.

[24] Ibid., 21.

[25] *The Commodification of Childhood: The Children's Clothing Industry and the Rise of the Child Consumer* (Durham, NC: Duke University Press, 2004).

the shirt area, etc. A purposeful effort was made by some in the apparel industry to gather all things needed for infants and young children into one department. It was an arrangement that appealed to the perspectives and motivations of mothers and mothers-to-be that had taken hold and become standard industry practice by the early 1930s. These women, trade observers noted, also happened to serve as purchasing agents for the family, and thus to draw them to one's store for the 'baby's needs' would also keep them there to shop for the rest of the family.

Cook notes an emergent phenomenon in the 1930s whereby entire 'floors for youth' were being arranged with the child's, instead of the mother's, orientation in mind. Child-height fixtures and mirrors, child-oriented iconography and music, as well as layouts favourable to the presumed perspective of the child, were, by the 1940s, standard for clothing and other retail areas for children like toys and furniture. The transition from the mother's perspective to favouring the child's marks a significant historical break, according to Cook, particularly in the way that commercial industries began to recognize, appeal to, and 'speak' (lexically, visually, and spatially) to the child as a consumer in its own right.

Market recognition, symbolized by the capital investment in retail spaces, did not simply acknowledge what had existed, Cook insists, but had a hand in creating some of the categories, transitions, and perhaps emergent meanings of childhood itself. He analyses the changing named phases of childhood, and particularly girlhood, from the 1920s to the 1950s, finding that stages of childhood and clothing size categories increasingly merged into one another. The 'toddler' for instance did not exist to any great extent until the 1930s when it became a clothing size; similarly, the clothing size ranges of 'children's' and 'pre-teen' also became confluent with their counterpart age ranges. These developments, when examined together over time, lead Cook to contend that commercial practices and interests play a necessary but not independent role in the rise of children's 'personhood' status through the twentieth century, which becomes manifest in later decades in such things as the UN Convention on the Rights of the Child and contemporary concerns about 'children getting older, younger.'

In addressing this modern consumer culture of the twentieth century, William Leach offers some contained—i.e., segregated—observations about children. In a small part of one chapter of his *Land of Desire*,[26] Leach emphasizes how toy manufacturers and department store merchandisers began to create a 'child world' of goods and enticements in the 1910s in the United States. The rise of Santa Claus as a commercial icon and the ties forged between department stores and Christmas shopping were deliberate attempts to make department stores, and specifically the toy section, a destination for children and parents. In a separate article, Leach describes what he calls the 'institutional collaborators' that helped usher in a place for children in consumer culture. These collaborators included, in addition to department stores, child welfare agencies and publishers who assisted those in the merchant class to find commercial solutions

---

[26] William Leach, *Land of Desire: Merchants, Power and the Rise of a New American Culture* (New York: Pantheon, 1993).

to problems confronting children, with Baby Weeks and Children's Days that focused on department stores and baby goods but were ostensibly held for children's health and welfare (see below).[27]

CHILDREN'S EXPERIENCES IN AND WITH THE WORLD OF CONSUMPTION

How parents and commercial actors understood, created, and acted upon the figure of the 'child consumer' no doubt represent significant realms of social action and practice. Yet, left unto themselves, these perspectives easily permit caricature of children and their experiences. Even as much of children's lives and practices remain hidden in or have been erased from historical records, there are historians who attempt to determine more directly how children may have understood and experienced commercial life.

In *The Adman in the Parlor*, Ellen Gruber Garvey examines the relationship between magazines and the gendering of consumer culture from the 1880s to the 1910s. Most of the book centres on adults and adult magazines. Significantly, she begins with an examination of children's trade card scrapbooks. Trade cards were small rectangular advertisements imprinted with the name and address of a business, often accompanied by a logo or promotional image, in some ways recalling the 'calling cards' (i.e., cartes de visites) of the well-heeled classes.[28]

Scrapbooks of the 1870s and 1880s were presumably made by children and mostly by girls. Children collected and arranged the trade cards in a variety of ways—some seemed to be simply a collection of cards, others highlighted the appearance of the cards and ignored the message, still others positioned the cards as if to tell a new narrative. As an example of the latter, Garvey describes how images of a scolding woman and sneaky salesman were cut out of one card and pasted onto the scrapbook page so as to comment on images from other cards.[29] In another scrapbook, the compiler takes images of infants and babies and arranges them in reference to each other with the word 'Baby' across the page cut out from another source. Garvey suggests that, in using only mass-produced chromo-lithographed materials, the complier connects the home and the commercial world and 'looks for her family in the marketplace of national advertising.'[30]

[27] William Leach, 'Child-World in the Promised Land', in J. Gilbert et al. (ed.), *The Mythmaking Frame of Mind* (Belmont: Wadsworth, 1993), 209–38. In a somewhat different vein, Nicholas Sammond, *Babes in Tomorrowland* (Durham, NC: Duke University Press, 2005), examines the intertwined histories of Walt Disney, the man, Disney the corporation, and developmental psychologists's views of the 'child' in the 1930–1960 era, and how these entered into an existing 'discursive matrix' that had constructed a universal, generic child.
[28] Ellen Gruber Garvey, *The Adman in the Parlor: Magazines and the Gendering of Consumer Culture, 1880s to 1910s* (Oxford: Oxford University Press, 1996).
[29] Ibid., 32–4.
[30] Ibid., 34.

Manipulating scrap cards and making scrapbooks reveals, according to Garvey, an active engagement with the images and values of an increasingly consumer-oriented society that functions both as a kind of personal record and expression and as a form of gender training. By the late 1800s, advertisers were keen to enlarge upon these practices and were making trade cards specifically for children to collect. Emerging at this time also were advertising contests and advertising games, encouraging young people to direct their attention and imagination to advertising so that the commercial messages would register—a practice in line with the psychology of advertising of the time.[31]

Looking at the material culture of childhood, Miriam Formanek-Brunell writes on dolls and the 'commercialization of girlhood' in *Made to Play House*. Focusing on the 1830–1930 period in the United States, she makes use of fiction, autobiographies, and trade and popular writings on dolls, among other things. The bulk of her book seeks to demonstrate how the production of American dolls moved, in the late 1880s, from being locally and regionally based enterprises that were owned and run by women to a large, national, and industrialized male-dominated industry in the twentieth century. In the 1800s in America, the women's crafts on the whole strove to produce lightweight, durable, and somewhat 'childlike' dolls made specifically for children's identification and play, in contrast to heavy foreign-made fashion dolls of the time that were less amenable to child play. Parents and child observers of the mid- to late nineteenth century positioned doll playing for girls as a form of training in gender roles, including mourning rituals that were depicted with some regularity in child fiction of the time.[32] At the same time, Formanek-Brunell produces ample evidence that girls and boys of the time used dolls in ways that most likely would not have been proscribed by adults, such as abusing them and demonstrating aggression toward them.[33]

By the beginning of the twentieth century, dolls 'cease to be objects of resentment and resistance manifested in previous generations' as doll playing appeared to become accommodated to a 'new domestic ideal.'[34] Formanek-Brunell consults memoirs, autobiographies, and other materials to argue that dolls became important consumer items in girls' lives in this period, as many girls demonstrated a significant discrimination and consumer acumen in their tastes and purchasing of these objects.[35] She points to industry concerns about 'tomboyism' in girls—although quietly tolerated by parents—that threatened sales, leading to more direct and specific appeals to girls in advertising copy and images. These efforts culminated in the industry-sponsored 'Children's Day'—an annual event that sounded like it arose from social reform when in fact it was the brainchild of commercial industry—whereby events emphasizing parenting and child health interwove with commercial products and retailers.[36] The result, according to Formanek-Brunell, was a blurring of child experts with promoters of dolls and toys.

[31] Ibid., 51–67.
[32] Formanek-Brunell, *Made to Play House*, 22–3.
[33] Ibid., 23–9.
[34] Ibid., 162.
[35] Ibid., 163–7.
[36] Ibid., 170–4; see also Cook, *The Commodification of Childhood*, 51–7, on similarly sponsored and run Baby Weeks in the 1910s and 1920.

Historian David Nasaw finds children—working-class children in particular—actively involved in aspects of commercial culture in the early twentieth century. Focusing his efforts on New York City and other urban areas of the American northeast, he discusses some ways that children searched for and found amusements in commercial outlets, especially in the new Nickelodeon theatre houses. Much to the consternation of reformers, children sought out these movie houses where for 5¢ they could be bemused by the new medium of moving pictures. Reformers expressed their concern and outrage that children would be in dark settings, unaccompanied by adults, taking in images of violence and lewdness.[37]

Nasaw notes that these were precisely the selling points for both the children, who sought pleasures outside the surveillance of their parents, and for the theatre owner who recognized that it was the children who virtually 'created' the Nickelodeon. An effort by Jane Addams, the celebrated child reformer from Chicago, to create 'clean' movie houses failed miserably, indicating that the pleasure of the movie house was in part its salaciousness. Children acquired their own money to spend by working as boot-blacks, newsies, and errand boys and girls, and patronized arcades and peep shows as well. Undaunted by newly minted censorship laws and various attempts to keep them out of the movie theatres, children and the theatre owners colluded against the reformers' efforts, and often with a wink and a nod from local police.[38]

Concluding Thoughts

Each of the works discussed contributes a piece to a puzzle, the shape and content of which remains unknown. In many ways, the extant work in this area may be thought of collectively as representing a demonstrative phase of the historiography of children's consumption. That is, the general marginality and invisibility of children in history and in consumption make the historian's first task to demonstrate that indeed commercial goods, messages, and spaces for children have existed and held a significant place in the lives of young persons and adults. Each of these treatments, in its own way, takes some element or aspect of an emergent commercial world and attempts to illustrate the import of it on children's lives. The relative lack of shared knowledge and questions among the authors give indication less of an unfocused field as of one in the process of defining itself and its subject matter.

One area of overlap and general relative agreement among the histories discussed, noted above, involves identifying a turning-point in twentieth-century children's consumer culture. It is noteworthy that three of the scholars discussed—Cross, Jacobson and Cook—all found the 1930s to be a pivotal decade. For Cross, this is the decade

---

[37] David Nasaw, 'Children and Commercial Culture', in Elliot West and Paula Petrik (eds.), *Small Worlds: Children and Adolescents in America, 1850–1950* (Lawrence, KS: University of Kansas Press, 1992), 17.

[38] Nasaw, 'Children and Commercial Culture', 18–25.

of the rise of fantasy toys that ultimately break children from the world of adults; for Jacobson, the democratized family arises strongly in this decades and goes hand in hand with the commercial lauding of child consumers; for Cook, it is the time of transition when the child's perspective gains commercial recognition and expression. All three struggle with the relationship between commercial appeals and everyday practices, as well as with the parents' place in relation to both the commercial culture and their children. None attempt to locate and use children's voices and perspectives to any great degree, with Cross interested more in the parents' perspective, Jacobson reading children's experiences from advertisements, and Cook finding children's voices in how industry members portrayed them to each other. It appears that, in a time of severe economic depression, both parents and commercial actors looked to childhood and the 'child' as promising bearers of hope for the future—an effort that might resemble, though not duplicate, Plumb's analysis of eighteenth-century England. It is a question ripe for concentrated thought, research, and analysis.

As we have seen, intensely focusing research and analysis on children problematizes the often taken for granted understandings of the autonomy and independence of social actors. Parents, in one way or another, figure in every historical analysis discussed. Even if they were not put at the centre of explanation, the spectre of the parent hangs like a shadow over the child in the Nickelodeon and in the playroom, as well as serving as a key addressee for advertised goods for children. The difficulties of locating and representing children's voices and experiences—often erased from the historical record—are highlighted both by the work that sought to feature such experiences and voices (Formanek-Brunell, Garvey, and Nasaw) and by others who examined primarily structural factors or industry actors. It is clear that to investigate children's consumption in history one must be vigilant about balancing attention on the conspicuous, large-scale productions of industries, that might seem to overwhelm children and their worlds, with how children may have engaged with the materials of these industries, while remaining ever aware that children's engagements necessarily take place in the penumbra of family life.[39]

Historians are not alone in their struggles to come to terms with the problems posed when children's lives and experiences reside at the centre of concern. Over the last several decades, sociologists, anthropologists, media scholars, psychologists, literary critics, and others have continually wrestled with the analytic, practical, and political tensions that arise from the recognition of children as both key and marginalized social actors who engage in social practice, and who are, in many ways, uniquely subjected to the structures and definitions of adults and the adult world. Over the past two decades a 'new' childhood studies has taken hold as a paradigm of research, arising mainly from sociology and anthropology, which acknowledges children's experiences as essential

---

[39] Investigations of the place of sibling relationships and peers for children are notably absent from these extant histories. Those who study teenagers and teen culture of the post-Second World War era address peer relations, but the relationship between children's peer relationships and consumption remain to be examined for any time period.

to any social inquiry.[40] This perspective, which seeks to de-marginalize children by privileging their understandings and voices, informs childhood history,[41] debates about children's rights,[42] and issues related to education and family dynamics.[43] Contemporary research on children's consumer and media behaviour remains entangled in the difficulty of determining who or what a 'child' is—beyond simplistic numerical age designations—precisely because the commercial and media worlds of children have a part in changing the definition and boundaries of childhood itself.[44]

With no easy answers in any field, it is not surprising that the works considered here do not uniformly speak to the same issues or in the same register. They may be characterized as much by the questions they do not ask as the ones they do. Future research in this area necessarily will have to confront the fundamental problems of the boundaries and meanings of childhood in different eras and contexts and hence the related questions of what constitutes 'consumption' and specifically 'children's consumption'. Most certainly, studies of children's experiences that make use of their voices will be valuable additions to the corpus of work discussed here. Finally, the future direction of scholarship in this area must engage directly not simply with the ways in which consumption and consumer culture 'commodified' or otherwise commercialized childhood, but also with how children's presence and actions transformed consumption and consumer industries and, as well, with how childhood itself has been transformed irrevocably in the process.

BIBLIOGRAPHY

Cook, Daniel Thomas, *The Commodification of Childhood: The Children's Clothing Industry and the Rise of the Child Consumer* (Durham, NC: Duke University Press, 2004).

Cross, Gary, *Kids' Stuff: Toys and the Changing World of American Childhood* (Cambridge, MA: Harvard University Press, 1998).

Cross, Gary, *The Cute and the Cool* (Cambridge, MA: Harvard University Press, 2004).

Denisoff, Dennis (ed.), *The Nineteenth-Century Child and Consumer Culture* (Aldershot: Ashgate, 2008).

[40] Allison James and Alan Prout, 'A New Paradigm for the Sociology of Childhood? Provenance, Promise and Problems', in Allison James and Alan Prout (eds.), *Constructing and Reconstructing Childhood: Contemporary Issues in the Sociological Study of Children* (London: Falmer Press, 1991), 7–34; and Chris Jenks, *Childhood* (London: Polity Press, 1996).

[41] Karen Sanchez-Eppler, *Dependent States: The Child's Part in Nineteenth-century American Culture* (Chicago: University of Chicago Press, 2005).

[42] Barbara Woodhouse, *Hidden in Plain Sight: The Tragedy of Children's Rights from Ben Franklin to Lionel Tate* (Princeton: Princeton University Press, 2008).

[43] See Peter Pufall and Richard Unsworth (eds.), *Rethinking Childhood* (New Brunswick, NJ: Rutgers University Press, 2004).

[44] see David Buckingham, *After the Death of Childhood: Growing Up in the Age of Electronic Media* (Cambridge: Polity Press, 2000).

Formanek-Brunell, Miriam, *Made to Play House: Dolls and the Commercialization of American Girlhood, 1830–1930* (Baltimore: Johns Hopkins University Press, 1993).

Garvey, Ellen Gruber, *The Adman in the Parlor: Magazines and the Gendering of Consumer Culture, 1880s to 1910s* (New York: Oxford University Press, 1996).

Jacobson, Lisa, *Raising Consumers* (New York: Columbia University Press, 2004).

McKendrick, Neil, Brewer, John, and Plumb, J.H., *The Birth of a Consumer Society: The Commercialization of Eighteenth-Century England* (Bloomington, IN: Indiana University Press, 1982).

Palladino, Grace, *Teenagers* (New York: Basic Books, 1996).

Sammond, Nicholas, *Babes in Tomorrowland* (Durham, NC: Duke University Press, 2005).

CHAPTER 31

....

YOUTH AND CONSUMPTION

....

PAOLO CAPUZZO

THE kaleidoscope of social identity is defined by multiple forces of signification. Gender, ethnicity, and class trace porous borders of the social and symbolic space within which consumption practices unfold, changing, forcing, and sometimes even subverting the apparent fixity of those spaces.[1] If the definition of youth as the stage of life between the condition of dependency of childhood and the autonomy of adulthood is a good conceptual starting point,[2] it opens a field of research on the different ways in which the condition of being young has been historically considered. The transition from child-hood to adulthood is marked by clear biological changes that affect the conduct of life and the ways in which to confront a series of phases in the form of the transformation and maturation of the body. Nevertheless, any attempt to define the condition of youth on the basis of its biological determinants is destined to be frustrated by the great variety which youth has taken over time and in different geographical contexts. Even within the same historical and geographical context, the condition of youth may be marked by various characteristics deeply embedded in other social matrixes of identification, such as gender, ethnicity, or class. The definition of adolescence is part of this complex field of forces and stands at the crossroads of youth, subjective agency, and the representation of youth given from the outside.

In 1928, in *Coming of Age in Samoa*, Margaret Mead opened up a debate within the social sciences on the socially conditioned nature of the experience of adolescence. Mead compared the relative ease of the passage to adulthood within a cohesive culture with very limited sexual taboos such as those of young Samoans, with the traumas and difficulties experienced by young Americans who lived in a complex and contradictory cultural context. Young Americans were subject to multiple pressures and conflicting

[1] M. de Certeau, *Arts de faire. L'invention du quotidien*, Paris, Gallimard, 1990 (1980).
[2] G. Levi and J. C. Schmitt, *Storia dei giovani*, Bari and Rome, Laterza, 1994.

regulations and restrictions, with the American myth of unlimited possibilities feeding the insecurities of youth and feelings of inadequacy.[3]

The idea of adolescence as a troubled and uncertain phase of life was adopted in late nineteenth-century European culture.[4] It had increasing success after the Second World War, when adolescence became a specific field of investigation for the psychological sciences which profoundly affected the intellectual background of educational agencies. If this 'discovery' put into focus the specificity of a phase of life, it also reflected the perspective of the adult world, which identified adolescence as a transitional period rather than focusing on the self-expression of youth.

It is in following these autonomous and expressive aspects that the analysis of consumption practices can be useful in showing how young people define themselves. This analysis, however, must not be separated from the perception of a youth image cultivated by the media and companies seeking to develop a specific market. This distinction between grassroots practices and the semiotic production of a commercial sphere is more analytical than historical because the two elements are inevitably intertwined in historical processes. Although consumption practices are an aspect of subjective expression, they can only be based on a range of connotations already defined or supplied by the commercial system.

Youth consumption takes place in specific spatial and social contexts. When and where specific youth consumption patterns began to develop is still being debated. Historians today agree that this began earlier than the 1950s, previously considered the age of the 'absolute beginners'. There are those who consider the important turning point to be the First World War in England, with the introduction of a welfare system, which protected working-class families from unemployment, and made available to young people a greater share of income compared with the pre-war years, when they had to contribute more to the family budget.[5] Others believe that in advanced urban northern Europe specific tendencies of young consumption developed in the late nineteenth century.[6] In rural areas, forms of control and deference between generations appear to have been more rigid and durable than those in urban regions—the seduction of the entertainment industries was weaker and consumer goods scarcer. In countries such as Italy the first manifestation of youth-specific consumption patterns appeared in the 1930s, in the advanced urban industrial frameworks of Milan and Turin, while the rest of the country had to wait until the post-war period. The same can be said of Spain.

---

[3] Cf. M. Mead, *Coming of Age in Samoa: A Study of Adolescence and Sex in Primitive Societies*, Harmondsworth, Penguin Books, 1961 (1928). See also M. Bucholtz, 'Youth and Cultural Practice', in *Annual Review of Anthropology*, 31 (2002), 525–52.

[4] J. Neubauer, *The Fin-de-Siècle Culture of Adolescence*, New Haven, CT and London, Yale University Press, 1992.

[5] D. Fowler, *The First Teenagers: The Lifestyle of Young Wage-Earners in Interwar Britain*, London, The Woburn Press, 1995.

[6] B. Beaven, *Leisure, Citizenship and Working-Class Men in Britain, 1850–1945*, Manchester, Manchester University Press, 2005.

The availability of resources and the overall economic and social conditions are significant but not sufficient elements to trigger an autonomous youth consumer culture: on the micro-social level there also had to be an opportunity for independent practices. This has, on occasion, resulted in a curious role reversal between young middle-class and working-class youths. The latter, in fact, although poorer in an absolute sense, would have had fewer constraints than the former when it came to the use of their resources. In reality, already earning a living at the age of fourteen, working-class adolescents were able to spend part of their salary on entertainment and socialization along with other youths, while young middle-class students were more subject to parental control.

Gender is a further element of differentiation. The same process of individualization, which middle-class men in the nineteenth century experienced and which was a pre-condition for consumer culture, was more problematic for women who were restrained by family structures. However, women slowly developed their own role as consumers and began to acquire greater independence in the commercial sphere late in the nineteenth century. Commercial premises opened up friendly urban spaces for women,[7] while advertising provided new signs that enabled women to change their social image and adopt a more individualized style of consumption. These processes were never free from disciplinary pressures.[8]

DEVIANTS: CULTURES OF CONSUMPTION AMONG YOUNG WORKERS

Consumption practices of youth have often been related to juvenile delinquency. In England during the late nineteenth century, subversive behaviour by adolescents from working-class neighbourhoods in the big industrial cities caused widespread concern. Social disintegration, lack of family control and, albeit modest, discretionary spending on amusement triggered fear of moral decadence and biological degeneration. Juvenile delinquency was viewed by the conservative press as a symptom of British racial decline.[9]

What differentiates this symbolic challenge from generational conflicts of the early modern period, particularly acute during the carnival in *charivari* and impatience with Church discipline, was that it took the form of a broader social change. The turmoil caused by early modern youth was tolerated in the knowledge that it was a temporary phenomenon, ultimately contained by tradition.[10] By contrast, in industrial urban

[7] Erika D. Rappaport, *Shopping for Pleasure: Women in the Making of London's West End*, Princeton, NJ, Princeton University Press, 2000.

[8] L. Tiersten, *Marianne in the Market: Envisioning Consumer Culture in Fin-de-Siècle France*, Berkeley, University of California Press, 2001.

[9] B. Beaven, *Leisure, Citizenship and Working-Class Men in Britain, 1850–1945*, pp. 88ff.

[10] N. Schindler, 'I tutori del disordine: rituali della cultura giovanile agli inizi dell'età moderna', in G. Levi and J. C. Schmitt (eds), *Storia dei giovani. 1 Dall'antichità all'età moderna*, pp. 303–74.

societies the sub-cultural change led by adolescents was perceived as a threat to social order, an element of corruption and social change.

The famous '*scuttlers*' of Manchester, who gave rise to moral panic and triggered police and judicial repression already during the 1870s, came from the city slums. Still, they were not as impoverished as young workers earlier in the century. They were a juvenile working-class generation that took advantage of a significant increase in real wages after the 1850s.[11] The young people who ended up in court were almost all occupied, relatively free of family control, and had spending power.[12] They purchased their own clothes, a clear sign of collective identification and group membership,[13] and read the so-called penny-dreadful, a brand of pulp magazine published during the 1860s addressed specifically at the emerging working-class youth market.[14] The penny-dreadful, with its tales of urban violence and crime, was a new form of cultural consumption, stigmatized by the Victorian middle class and often blamed for youth violence in these years.[15] These juvenile workers also socialized in pubs and on the streets, following working-class tradition.

Although these were predominantly male groups, the presence of young women also gained in importance—a topic that calls for further research. They were mainly represented as the girlfriends of 'scuttlers' and frequently a source of conflict. Still, they moved within the same social spaces as young men. They often worked in factories, and although they had less free time because of domestic duties, they too enjoyed increasingly independent spending power, at least before marriage. These adolescent females spent their resources on fashionable clothing and going to music halls and dance halls, and at times would even visit pubs, though mostly accompanied by their male partners.[16]

Scuttlers often occupied public spaces in provocative and exhibitionistic manner. In the entertainment districts, where music halls and pubs were concentrated, such as Lower Mosley Street in Manchester, there was a steady stream of complaints about noise and aggressive behaviour by juvenile gangs. Notwithstanding these complaints, the level of violence within British society was significantly lower than during the first half of the century. The behaviour of juvenile gangs rather represented a clash with a hegemonic culture of respectability that had been promoted by the Victorian middle class.[17] The adolescent pursuit of consumption and instant pleasure challenged the rules of

---

[11] S. Horrell, 'Home Demand and British Industrialization', *Journal of Economic History*, 56 (1996), 561–604.

[12] A. Davies, *The Gangs of Manchester: The Story of the Scuttlers, Britain's First Youth Cult*, Preston, Milo Books, 2008.

[13] A. Davies, 'Youth Gangs, Masculinity and Violence in Late Victorian Manchester and Salford', *Journal of Social History*, 32:2 (1998), 353.

[14] G. Law, *Serializing Fiction in the Victorian Press*, Basingstoke, Palgrave, 2000, pp. 23ff.

[15] See, A. Maunder and G. Moore (eds), *Victorian Crime, Madness and Sensation*, Aldershot, Ashgate, 2004.

[16] A. Davies, '"These viragoes are no less cruel than the lads": Young Women, Gangs and Violence in Late Victorian Manchester and Salford', *British Journal of Criminology*, 39:1 (1999), 72–89.

[17] F. Thompson, *The Rise of Respectable Society: A Social History of Victorian Britain 1830–1900*, Cambridge MA, Harvard University Press, 1988; P. Capuzzo, *Culture del consumo*, Bologna, Il Mulino, pp. 205–77.

civilization based on thrift, decorum, and a deferral of desire, central to the dominant culture of consumption.[18]

'Scuttlers' disappeared in the early twentieth century for a number of reasons: repression, slum clearances which erased some of their social spaces, and the parallel emergence of new meeting places such as football grounds, which provided new forms of sociability and identity. The creation of Manchester City was an explicit attempt to channel the energy of these young people towards more civilized targets.

These Victorian fears anticipated patterns that would be apparent throughout the twentieth century. Fears and the will of reform have provided a valuable source of information in the study of youth culture and consumption patterns, but not without problems for the historian. On the one hand, the repeated admonishment of juvenile behaviour left behind a wealth of texts that simultaneously stigmatized youth behaviour and supplied indirect information on its dynamics. On the other hand, the normative character of these texts have left behind a generic, common-sense notion of what youth is like which stands in the way of a more historical view of changes across time and space. First, the focus on deviant behaviour tends to generalize from the most visible aspects of juvenile misbehaviour, even if these never concerned more than a minority of youths. The 'outrageous' lifestyles and consumption patterns of small groups has often been taken as a paradigm for a whole generation. Second, criticism concerning the most visible aspects of lifestyle, such as dress and activities in public, has privileged quite specific consumption practices for identity formation, at the expense of other aspects which would have required a more intimate understanding of the lives of these young people.

That phenomena of youth 'deviance' appeared in many European industrial cities at the beginning of the twentieth century testifies to the strong link between an expanding commercial culture and the generational tensions produced by an urban industrial society. In the Paris neighbourhood of Belleville, gangs of young men appeared at the beginning of the twenieth century, attracting media attention with their violent actions. The so-called *Apaches* adopted a striking look, wearing black shirts underneath flamboyant jackets, scarves and shiny shoes. They frequented dance halls and had a reputation for seducing women. With the help of style, a distinct look and manner, they fashioned an identity that distinguished them from the popular milieu of the *banlieu* from which they came.[19]

In Germany, the phenomenon of youth gangs, often wearing flashy, expensive dress, also caused much apprehension after the First World War.[20] These adolescents from

[18] B. Schwarz, 'Night Battles: Hooligan and Citizen', in M. Nava and A. O'Shea (eds), *Modern Times: Reflections on a Century of English Modernity*, London, Routledge, 1996, pp. 101–27.

[19] M. Perrot, 'Dans le Paris de la Belle Époque, les "Apaches", premières bandes de jeunes', in *La lettre de l'enfance et de l'adolescence*, 67:1 (2007), 71–8.

[20] O. Voß and H. Schön, 'Die Cliquen jugendlicher Verwahrloster als sozialpädagogisches Problem', in Carl Mennicke (ed.), *Erfahrungen der Jungen*, Potsdam, Alfred Protte, 1930, pp. 69–89 and G. Staewen-Ordemann, *Menschen der Unordnung*, Berlin, Im Furche, 1933, pp. 124–37; H. Lessing and M. Liebel, *Wilde Cliquen: Szenen einer anderen Arbeiterjugendbewegung*, Bensheim, Päd. extra Buchverlag, 1981; E. Rosenhaft, 'Organising the "Lumpenproletariat": Cliques and Communists in Berlin during the Weimar Republic', in R.J. Evans (ed.), *The German Working Class 1888–1933: The Politics of Everyday Life*, London, Croom Helm, 1982, pp. 174–219.

working-class neighbourhoods with no education or professional qualifications found themselves in a particularly unstable segment of the labour market at a time of hyper-inflation and high unemployment. The phenomenon, however, had its roots during the war, which freed youths from parental control and moral codes. While criminal gangs were in minority, a commercial culture organized around consumption practices became part of the life of a growing number of youths. In the course of the twentieth century this cycle of juvenile consumer culture, social stigmatization and regulation repeated itself time and again, as urbanization and commercial change unravelled an inherited social fabric, increasingly reaching rural communities as well.[21] If the 'deviant behaviour' involved a minority of young people, mostly from the popular milieu, the phenomenon took on a larger symbolic meaning. Consumer behaviour was treated as subversive, a challenge to middle-class culture and dominant norms and practices.

Bodies, Films, and Fantasies

One of the most obvious, visible features of the generational divide concerns the body and the physical presentation of the self. Following the first successful recording of *Dixie Jazz Band One Step* (1917), which quickly sold a million copies, ballrooms in New York multiplied. Middle-class boys and girls dancing wildly to jazz music alarmed right-thinking adults. In these establishments, new images of being young were defined. This, in turn, fed specific marketing strategies, which targeted boys and girls. Clothes, magazines, cosmetics, film, and cigarettes were the main items of an expanding youth market. Mr and Mrs Scott and Zelda Fitzgerald were icons and symbols of this new trend among young Americans in the 1920s, but they also brought this new style to Europe on their frequent trips. The American flapper transformed the image of the young woman into someone who donned the persona of males, who had short-hair, smoked, was confident when appearing in public spaces but also knew how to provoke sexual attention with the help of cosmetics, skirts above the knee, silk or rayon stockings, gloves and high heels. For these young American women, drinking and smoking in public meant breaking previous taboos—an act of self-affirmation and empowerment. Underneath the dress, the body was freed from corsets, enabling it to move and express itself more promiscuously during the course of the wild dancing to the sound of jazz. This was a source of intense discord between youths and their parents.[22]

---

[21] A. De Venanzi, 'Social Representations and the Labeling of Non-Compliant Youths: The Case of Victorian and Edwardian Hooligans', in *Deviant Behavior*, 3 (2008), 193–224; J. Neuberger, *Hooliganism: Crime, Culture, and Power in St. Petersburg*, Berkeley, University of California Press, 1993.

[22] K. A. Yellis, 'Prosperity's Child: Some Thoughts on the Flapper', *American Quarterly*, 21:1 (1969), 44–64. On the young women of the American roaring twenties, see P.S. Fass, *The Damned and the Beautiful: American Youth in the 1920s*, New York, Oxford University Press, 1977 and A. J. Latham, *Posing a Threat: Flappers, Chorus Girls, and Other Brazen Performers of the American 1920s*, New Hampshire, University Press of New England, 2000; P. Erens, 'The Flapper: Hollywood's First Liberated

In addition to dance and sports, young women in this period gained a more general presence in the workplace and public spaces. Being slim became a distinctive feature of feminine beauty. Advertising helped to shape the social representation of the thin female body with products and publicity. Lucky Strike adverts, for example, used images of elegant and slim women to highlight tobacco's effect in reducing appetite.[23] In the 1920s, companies advertised diets, massage machines, body products and developed marketing strategies around cinema stars, icons from the cinema of the 1920s, such as Clara Bow, who had risen from the slums of Brooklyn to the cream of Hollywood. The so-called *Gibson girl* of the late nineteenth century now gave way to a new feminine shape and standard of beauty, and, with it, signs of psychological tension and anorexia not dissimilar to those reported today.

Unlike the cultural battle triggered by the gangster style in the early twentieth century, this new trend in juvenile consumption and identity came from the middle and upper classes. The bob haircut was established in France by young women from the upper social classes and in bohemian circles at the beginning of 1910s, from where it spread both internationally and socially to the urban middle and lower middle classes, including salesgirls and clerks and the growing number of girls attending college in America.

Films were a fundamental vehicle for the dissemination of this style because they were attended by large female audiences and helped circulate the new image across social classes.[24] Cinemas produced a consumer culture in which generational conflicts were more pronounced than those of class or gender. Cinemas targeted different market segments, but the dissimilarities in price were not insurmountable and films were enthusiastically followed by young people, in particular young girls, more so than adults. The cinema was at the centre of a complex multi-media framework that included the specialist press, which provided information about forthcoming films, and related stories and gossip on film stars. On the screen, films paraded images and tales that fuelled fantasies and offered new sources of identity. The generational character of mass entertainment was defined by such processes of appropriation. Films enjoyed by young people ranged from romantic dramas to Westerns. Many films were set in metropolitan environments that referred to juvenile criminal gangs. One such was *Regeneration* (1915, directed by Raoul Walsh), shot on the Lower East Side, which told the story of a young man who became the leader of a street gang before falling in love with a social worker who redeemed him. The subject of untamed life within the slums and the search for redemption, usually facilitated by a woman, was a successful genre that reached an iconic climax with Marlon Brando in *On the Waterfront* (1954, directed by Elia Kazan).

Woman', in L. R. Broer and J. D. Wather (eds), *Dancing Fools and Weary Blues: The Great Escape of the Twenties*, Bowling Green, OH, Bowling Green State University, 1990, pp. 130–39. See also chapter 15 of J. Savage, *Teenage: The Creation of Youth, 1875–1945*, London, Chatto & Windus, 2007.

[23] P. Tinkler, 'Rebellion, Modernity, and Romance – Smoking as a Gendered Practice in Popular Young Women's Magazines, Britain 1918–1939', in *Women's Studies International Forum*, 1 (2001), 111–22.

[24] E. Altenloh, *Zur Soziologie des Kino. Die Kino-Unternehmung und die sozialen Schichten ihrer Besucher*, Basel, Stroemfeld, 2007 (1914).

Despite this generational culture, subtle social distinctions remained visible. The difference between a tailored suit and an industrially produced suit signalled an unbridgeable gulf in status. Still, there was an undeniable symbolic convergence between the elite and the mass market, promoted by designers of new forms of mass consumption which now stressed a generational rather than class divide. If the American affluence of the roaring twenties was a major influence behind these new currents, the phenomenon did not fail to sweep across Europe, at least in metropolitan centres such as Berlin during the Weimar years. Young girls showed their beauty in line with the aesthetics of *Neue Sachlichkeit*, an art trend that stressed a new modern and objective relationship with the reality. These images were multiplied by advertising, film, and literature, and the successful novels of Irmgard Keun.[25]

In the 1930s, fascist regimes led the attack on these trends in youth consumption. If fascists were not solidly anti-modern, they were vehemently opposed to new gender roles,[26] and shared an aversion to the wild flapper of the 1920s. The flapper's erotic play and their ambiguous relationship with black music and dance did not sit well with fascist ideals of maternity and race. This does not mean that fascist regimes did not make their peace with other, selective aspects of modern urban youth culture, as demonstrated by Italian cinema in the 1930s. *Gli uomini che mascalzoni* (1932, directed by Mario Camerini), is a good example of an entire film genre that accepted modern urban dimensions, glossy magazines, trams, cars, girls who worked outside home, consumption, and advertising. While not demonizing those aspects of modernity, the film warned of the risks of social emulation. Traditional gender roles produced a happy end.[27] The film thus tried to incorporate some of the new elements of consumerism from America within a frame of traditional roles.

In Italy during the 1930s different models of juvenile social behaviour co-existed, ranging from strict controls over the meeting between boys and girls, a pattern still dominant in many rural areas, to more open relationships in cities.[28] If meetings between boys and girls still took place under the watchful eye of parents at home, the darkness of the cinema provided a space of intimacy. Furthermore, the dance floor offered a stage to show off one's body. Many girls were banned from attending dances but, in reality, transgression was widespread. In the 1930s, participation in this form of consumer culture was

---

[25] I. Keun, *Gilgi – eine von uns* (1931) and *Das kunstseidene Mädchen* (1932); on these novels see B. Kosta, 'Unruly Daughters and Modernity: Irmgard Keun's *Gilgi - eine von uns*', *The German Quarterly*, 68:3 (1995), 271–86.

[26] M. Makela, 'The Rise and the Fall of the Flapper Dress: Nationalism and Anti-Semitism in Early-Twentieth-Century Discourses on German Fashion', in *Journal of Popular Culture*, 3 (2000), 183–208; V. de Grazia, *How Fascism Ruled Women: Italy, 1922–1945*, Berkeley, University of California Press, 1992; V. de Grazia, 'Nationalizing Women: The Competition between Fascism and Commercial Cultures Models in Mussolini's Italy', in V. de Grazia and E. Furlough (eds), *The Sex of Things: Gender and Consumption in Historical Perspective*, Berkeley and Los Angeles, University of California Press, 1996, pp. 337–58.

[27] R. Ben-Ghiat, *Fascist Modernities: Italy, 1922–1945*, Berkeley, University of California Press, 2001.

[28] V. de Grazia, *How Fascism Ruled Women: Italy, 1922–1945*, Berkeley, University of California Press, 1992, pp. 201ff.

mainly a middle-class and urban working-class phenomenon. With the Second World War, parental control loosened for the young generation as a whole.[29]

If social pressures focused on women, the cultural industries' influence on boys was viewed with suspicion, too. It was feared that Americanization would bring cultural contamination. In Italy in the 1930s there was a significant increase in the consumption of comics. One of the most successful titles was *L'Avventuroso*, which began publication in 1934 and introduced Walt Disney's cartoons along superheroes such as Flash Gordon, the Phantom, and Mandrake. The preference of young audiences was definitely for American comics, and the attempts of fascism to Italianize these heroes had limited success. There were some exceptions, for instance Dick Fulmine, an Italian-American cop who fought Chinese criminals, black skinned Caribbean bandits and Jewish merchants.

TOWARDS A YOUTH MASS MARKET

In the late 1930s, when consumption begun to recover after the Great Depression, the youth market became a very interesting source for several businesses, in particular record labels. The wide dissemination of swing provoked a wave of moral panic. The concerts of Benny Goodman were attended by throngs of young hysterical juveniles such as they were described by the media. Goodman was the first person to create a mixed band with black and white musicians, and the same miscegenation characterized those at his concerts. At a festival held in Chicago in 1938, a bacchanal of wild dancing broke out in which the protagonist was a whole generation born during the First World War, frightened by the Depression and that finally let go of its vitality in what the press called an hysterical orgy formed of tens of thousands of young people in and out of Soldier Field.[30] It was believed that the wild and primitive rhythms of jazz undermined the psychological balance in the minds of juveniles and adolescents, thus lowering moral restraints and unleashing immediate sexual instinct. However, there were those in defence of swing who deemed it important to have this expression of pubescent vitality and spontaneity among a generation that had proved fruitful and successful in work and the social area.

One element, however, both detractors and supporters were in agreement on, namely, that the fact that the passion for swing resulted in the involvement of young people as a generation, regardless of ethnic segregation, class, gender or geographical origin: even in the reactionary south there were many young swing fans who participated in racially mixed scenes. This increased capacity for integration between different cultures in consumption based on a common generational experience. It was facilitated by important

[29] D. Forgacs and S. Gundle, *Mass Culture and Italian Society from Fascism to the Cold War*, Bloomington, IN, Indiana University Press, 2007, pp. 70ff.

[30] L. A. Erenberg, *Swingin' the Dream: Big Band Jazz and the Rebirth of American Culture*, Chicago, University of Chicago Press, pp. 35ff.

new media technologies, which were to have a major effect after the Second World War. A new wave of colour magazines proved very popular from the 1930s onwards, as did radio broadcasts and juke boxes, which allowed for a rapid and widespread diffusion of new music—as well as attitudes related to it throughout the United States. If the fashion of swing involved young people of different social classes, the bulk of swing fans were college students who, in the late 1930s, began to also come from working-class milieu. A young man from a working-class family of Irish descent in Massachusetts, who had embraced the sub-culture of swing in 1937, expressed himself thus: 'Every aspect of my life and that of my friends, revolved around big bands, jazz, dancing, jitterbugging, in my formative teens...Our heroes, Our dress, looks, styles, morals, sex lives Were based on immersion in the lives bands and They Showed us.'[31]

Swing had an immediate impact on Europe even in the most unlikely places such as Nazi Germany, where some groups of young middle-class jazz fans used a slang thick with foreign words and wore clothes (especially raincoats and hats) that closely resembled those of the stars from American cinema at that time. In the reports taken from the police charged with repressing their activity, they were described as 'anti-German' and stigmatized because of their 'Americanism', the uninhibited sexual promiscuity and their wild 'Negro and bestial' dances. These activities were exposed to certain risks because these young people refused to abide by cultural rules imposed by the regime.[32] However, the mainly upper–middle-class origin of these people made the actions taken by the repressors more cautious, and therefore swing fans managed to continue their parties until the early years of the war. Even in areas of German occupation, especially in northern France, the spread of swing took on an anti-German slant: the so-called *Zazou*, which borrowed the style of young swing, had frequent opportunities to come into conflict with authority and fascist youth organizations.[33]

This extraordinary swing movement presented many features which have been generally associated with the teenagers only from the 1950s onwards. It was a mass movement which had overcome social fragmentation through generational commonalities, or at least it appeared to have done in the eyes of the adult world. These young people relied on music produced by social groups marginalized by the American dream, such as black Americans, although through the mediation of white liberals like Benny Goodman whom for some critics exercised a function of cultural mediation similar to that played by Elvis in the post-war period. However, the timing of this movement was

---

[31] Quoted in Erenberg, p. 39.

[32] G. Helmers and A. Kenkmann (eds), *'Wenn die Messer blitzen und die Nazis flitzen...'. Der Widerstand vom Arbeiterjugendcliquen und –banden im 'Dritten Reich'*, Lippstadt, Leimeier, 1984; W. Breyvogel (ed.), *Piraten, Swings und junge Garde. Jugendwiderstand im Nationalsozialismus*, Bonn, Dietz, 1991; O. Bender and K. Frischmuth, *Swing unterm Hakenkreuz in Hamburg, 1933–1943*, Hamburg, Christians, 1993; A. Kenkmann, *Wilde Jugend. Lebenswelt großstädtischer Jugendlicher zwischen Weltwirtschaftskrise, Nationalsozialismus und Währungsreform*, Essen, Klartext, 2002.

[33] Jean-Claude Loiseau, *Les Zazous*, Paris, Le Sagittaire, 1977, pp. 155–8; K.G. Seward, *Zazou, Zazou Zazou-hé: A Youth Sub-culture in Vichy France, 1940–44*, Victoria, Australia, University of Melbourne, School of Historical Studies, 2007.

not the happiest. The new world war broke out in 1939 and young Americans and young Europeans had a far more tragic fate than that which was promised by the optimistic and progressive wave emulating from swing. The US military presence in Western Europe was an extremely important vehicle for the dissemination of young American consumption patterns, especially in England, as witnessed by numerous Mass Observation surveys. The problem was that young Europeans in the 1940s could only watch at the potentiality of a society based on the expansion of consumption, but had to wait for the 1950s to profit from it.

YOUTH'S GOLDEN AGE

In the late 1950s and in the early 1960s youth consumer cultures reached what may have been the peak of their visibility. This is the best-known and explored period of youth consumption, which for a long time was considered to represent the beginning of a youth culture based on consumption, although, as has been previously discussed, recent research has dated its roots to the end of the nineteenth century. The reorganization of social representation around the generational gap was associated with the decline of traditional class cultures in a phase of expansion in consumption, which saw different social classes converge towards mass consumption patterns. The 'end of the proletariat', a phenomenon stressed by social sciences in several countries in the 1960s, opened the analysis of social articulation according to other divisions than class such as as gender and generation.[34] Boys and girls became central figures of society because of their considerable demographic dimension, but above all because of their materialistic and symbolic practices. These practices subverted common sense and were the target of commercialization processes which, in turn, collected new social and cultural trends and reified them as commercial icons. The relationship between young people and their image established by marketing strategies was very productive, although ensconced in conflict and tension. Thus, the image and identity of juveniles became a battleground in which commercial representation competed with subjective social practices which went beyond them.[35]

The Anglo-American scene had a fundamental role in setting new trends and fashions thanks to the dynamics of consumer-oriented capitalism which characterized it. However, attention must be paid to the process of reception and appropriation and to the extent to which this defined the framework of the social experience of young people and their consumption behaviour. In other words, generalizations and schematics must be avoided.

[34] P. Capuzzo, 'Gli spazi della nuova generazione', in P. Capuzzo (ed.) *Genere, Generazione e consumi: l'Italia degli anni Sessanta*, Rome, Carocci, 2003, pp. 217–47.
[35] L. Grossberg, *We Gotta Get Out of this Place: Popular Conservatism and Postmodern Culture*, London, Routledge, 1992, pp. 183ff.

Rock 'n' Roll came to Italy with the film *Rock Around the Clock* (1956), but the wave of youth hysteria feared by the media—which expressed in detail of events which had occurred in the USA in previous years—did not happen. Record consumption was still quite limited and the spread of new music and dance was thanks to films and juke boxes, which were much cheaper and enabled music to be heard collectively in pubs and milk bars. Between 1958 and 1965 the number of juke boxes in Italian public spaces increased from four to forty thousand. The spread of Rock 'n' Roll and the style which accompanied it followed complex social processes of appropriation. While in the major metropolitan centres such as Milan this style spread among young suburban workers who thereby expressed their generational distinction from adults and their hostility to the dominant pattern of behaviour, in the industrial city of Terni, deep in the countryside and remote from major metropolitan centres, this musical style seemed to be apparent only amongst middle-class juveniles.[36]

As the record industry began to take off in Italy, with specific investment in the youth segment, the adoption of new musical styles developed along peculiar lines. The so-called *urlatori* (shouters), a new generation of singers, defiantly broke with the tradition of melodic Italian song, but although they constituted a fracture in the Italian context, they were a tame version of American Rock 'n' Roll, which proved to be successful in its domesticated version in the form of the Platters and Bill Haley.

A specific film genre—which was short-lived but intense—served to broaden the popularity of this music and generate national singing stars. The so-called *musicarelli*, a sort of new Italian musical, generally developed around a hit song—or one which was promoted to become such—whose content was expanded through a script. Models for these *musicarelli*, which focused on the shouters were certainly taken from American films, with Elvis as the protagonist. After peaking in the mid-sixties, the *musicarelli* were supplanted by television, which began at that time to broadcast on variety shows in which the juvenile idols were finally accepted, wheareas they had previously been rejected after being considered too subversive for the Italian general public.

This relationship with American culture, even though subjected to rigid processes of appropriation, is not specific to Italy, but was experienced throughout Europe. The concept of *Americanization*, which has been used to define a process of European conformation to those cultural patterns shaped by an American cultural industry, has been subjected to much criticism. In fact, the category of Americanization does not pay enough attention to processes of adaptation, reception, and reworking of the American commercial culture which has undoubtedly had a central role in the construction

---

[36] On Terni see A. Portelli, 'Elvis Presley è una tigre di carta (ma sempre una tigre)', in D. Carpitella et ali, *La musica in Italia. L'ideologia, la cultura, le vicende del jazz, del rock, del pop, della canzonetta, della musica popolare dal dopoguerra ad oggi*, Roma, Savelli, 1978, pp. 7–68 and A. Portelli, 'L'orsacchiotto e la trigre di carta. Il rock and roll arriva in Italia', in *Quaderni Storici*, 58 (1985), pp. 135–47 and E. Capussotti, *Gioventù perduta. Gli anni Cinquanta dei giovani e del cinema in Italia*, Firenze, Giunti, 2004, pp. 222ff.

of a consumer society within Europe after the Second World War.[37] If we look at the Netherlands, for example, we are able to see that the influence of American commercial culture did not lead to a process of cultural assimilation, but was rather appropriated by Dutch adolescents in order to change their local cultural framework. This reception process was fragmented along class lines. The appropriation of American cultural elements in the 1950s led to innovative processes that coalesced with the lively hippie counterculture in Amsterdam during the 1960s.[38] This, in turn, became a centre for the diffusion of youth cultural trends across Europe.[39] Cultural relationships and the circulation of fashion and style within youth consumption throughout Europe should be explored in more detail rather than just approaching the cultural dynamics of postwar Europe based solely on the relationship between the USA and Europe.[40] For young Spaniards, the waves of tourists, especially female tourists, who invaded southern Spain from northern Europe in the 1960s seemed to have been just as important as American culture in disseminating new values, styles, and means of representing the body.[41] For young Yugoslavs during the 1970s, the influence of Italian television seemed to have played a primary role in changing popular culture.

The influence of American commercial culture in the early 1950s within Germany was viewed with distaste and suspicion because of its lasting influence of eugenic rhetoric, which had its roots in the early part of the century and viewed social degeneration in unrestrained juvenile consumption. This anti-American sentiment was paradoxically shared by the conservatives of West Germany and by Stalinists of East Germany in an attempt to define a German identity in opposition to American culture.[42] However, in the years that followed, West Germany discovered a more comprehensive interpretation of adolescent behaviour, mainly thanks to psychological theories of young juveniles, which considered this a difficult stage and subject to contradictory impulses and discoveries, that is, a difficult transition towards stable maturity.

This psychology of social phenomena related to youth turbulence was able to weaken any alleged political worthiness in trying to creating them into something more innocuous. Even in East Germany, the emphasis placed by the then regime on juveniles as a driving force in new communist Germany favoured a dialogical approach to new trends

---

[37] On this influence see V. de Grazia, *Irresistible Empire: America's Advance through Twentieth-Century Europe*, Cambridge, MA and London, Harvard University Press, 2006; on the reception of American commercial culture after the Second World War, see Sabrina P. Ramet and Gordana P. Crnkovic (eds), *Kazaaam! Splat! Ploof! The American Impact on European Popular Culture since 1945*, Lanham and New York, Rowman & Littlefield Publishers, 2003.

[38] M. van Elteren, *Imagining America: Dutch Youth and Its Sense of Place*, Tilburg, Tilburg University Press, 1994.

[39] M. Guarnaccia, *Gioco magia anarchia. Amsterdam negli anni Sessanta*, Paderno Dugnano, Colibrì, 2005.

[40] On the Eurovision Song Contest see, I. Raykoff and R. Deam Tobin, *A Song for Europe: Popular Music and Politics in the Eurovision Song Contest*, Aldershot, Ashgate, 2007.

[41] G. Cardona and J. C. Losada, *La invasión de las suecas*, Barcelona, Editorial Ariel, 2009.

[42] See U. G. Poiger, *Jazz, Rock, and Rebels: Cold War Politics and American Culture in a Divided Germany*, Berkeley, University of California Press, 2000.

in youth culture, even though they were influenced by the American commercial culture, and sometimes adapted for a socialist cultural programme.[43]

The 1960s were the years of youth consumption par excellence because of an increasingly sophisticated industry producing consumer goods for young people, the marketing effort in building their image,[44] and a cultural industry that interwove effectively different media (cinema, music, radio, TV, magazines) interacting with grassroots trends in youth behaviour. In the following decade the economic and social crisis made the lines of social division more evident, and subsequently the generational gap became entangled with other distinctive areas in the social mapping of culture consumption.

The increasing interconnection between commercialization and production of subjectivity ended up with the creation of a short circuit within the development of a Fordist society, which relied on the growth of mass consumption, on a certain stability of gender roles and family patterns. Juvenile consumer culture destabilized and subverted this project because it did not comply to the social boundaries set by the mass Fordist society. The youth consumption of the 1960s contributed to the disintegration of the Fordist social model, which completely collapsed in the 1970s, leading to a transformation in the regulation mode of capitalism.

These developments have attracted the interest of scholars who have since developed new approaches to the study of youth culture. Already in the 1920s, the study of youth culture had assumed new dimensions thanks to the Chicago school of sociology and its first elaboration of the concept of sub-culture. The investigation into the city as an ecological system of different worlds based on different sub-cultures meant to reject the notion of deviance as individual defection from shared value systems made possible by the weakening of social authority (according to a tradition going back to Durkheim). Instead, the ecological approach saw groups and sub-cultures establishing moral standards, values, and behaviours as a means in affirming subjectivity within a complex metropolis. The attempt to explain the cultural specificity of different groups and their self-representation led these sociologists to adopt the ethnographic method in order to examine Chicago. Even gangs of juvenile delinquents were therefore based on their cultural codes, which often were aimed at pursuing a symbolic compensation for discrimination suffered from the dominant culture. Respect, pride, and reputation were earned by activities carried out by neighbourhood gangs that would provide the means to overcome the sense of relative deprivation which marked the lives of these young people.[45] Thus, posed a new basis for interpretation of youth consumer culture, Howard S. Becker developed the labelling theory, revealing as the construction of a deviant culture depended on the established cultural relationship of power in society.

---

[43] M. Fenemore, *Sex, Thugs and Rock 'n' Roll: Teenage Rebels in Cold-War East Germany*, New York, Kensington Books, 2009.

[44] A. Arvidsson, *Marketing Modernity: Italian Advertising from Fascism to Postmodernity*, London and New York, Routledge, 2003.

[45] A. K. Cohen, *Delinquent Boys: The Culture of the Gang*, Glencoe, IL, Free Press, 1955.

Youth sub-cultures were built in response to dominant social relationships and were then crystallized and labelled as deviant by those who were able to exert cultural hegemony.[46] These first attempts to investigate youth sub-culture were then taken up and continued by the cultural studies in the 1960s and 1970s.

The cultural studies at the Centre for Contemporary Cultural Studies (CCCS) of Birmingham have gradually overcome the mistrust towards mass culture still present in the 1950s[47] and look at youth consumption culture without the prejudices of critical sociology from the Frankfurt school. The analysis of sub-cultures by the CCCS in Birmingham did not delete the class divisions in the generational divide; on the contrary, they reconsidered it in the context of the restructuring of class relationships in post-war Britain,[48] in relation to inequality in access to resources and as a strategy of resistance to the power structures that governed society. The cultural theory developed in Birmingham gave birth to a series of analysis on sub-cultural agencies in which consumption practices played a central role as a material process as well as a symbolic battlefield. However, even the sub-cultural approach of the Birmingham cultural studies, which had historical significance in the opening of new fields of investigation, also proved to be flawed because of its univocal representation of social groups and its cohesive concept of sub-culture. This weakness appeared to be increasingly evident in the late 1970s as the fragmentation of youth sub-cultures and their internal articulation exposed the limits of a sub-cultural concept that hypostatizes cultural cohesion, neglecting the porosity, flexibility, and contradictory character of subjectification processes. Gender and ethnicity were two major threads in the reconstruction of a youth culture consumption fragmenting the alleged cohesion of the sub-culture.[49] Moreover, the rigid connection between sub-culture and resistance to power began to be seen as too romantic and contrived, neglecting the elements of conformity that marked many youthful transgressions.

At the same time, more attention was paid to the influence of the media and to the marketing semiotics as fundamental elements of sub-cultures that lost autonomy and purity to become, instead, considered as part of a complex semiotic system of society.

The multifaceted social space in post-Fordist capitalism has made social significance and values less and less readable in terms of generational divisions. The advertising reification of youth has provided identification models increasingly disconnected from specific generational references, becoming a container able to contain a multiple of social experiences. These social experiences interact within a globalized media and consumptive world which in turn provides material and symbolic resources.[50]

[46] H.S. Becker, *Outsiders: Studies in the Sociology of Deviance*, New York, The Free Press, 1963.
[47] R. Hoggart, *The Uses of Literacy: Aspects of Working-Class Life, With Special References to Publications and Entertainments*, Harmondsworth, Penguin, 1957.
[48] S. Hall and T. Jefferson (eds), *Resistance through Rituals: Youth Subcultures in Post-War Britain*, London, Hutchinson, 1976.
[49] See A. McRobbie, 'Girls and Sub-cultures', in *Resistance through Rituals*, pp. 209–22; and P. Gilroy, *'There ain't no black in the Union Jack': The Cultural Politics of Race and Nation*, Chicago, University of Chicago Press, 1991 (1987).
[50] A. Ross and T. Rose (eds), *Microphone Fiends: Youth Music, Youth Culture*, New York and London, Routledge, 1994.

The tension between increasingly globalized material and symbolic production systems and the different meanings and functions played by goods in socialization and self-representation of young people is an interesting and emerging topic of research. This has certainly had a centuries-long history—one need only look at the copious literature on the cultural history of consumption in the context of World History[51]—which takes on an even greater significance in world trade dominated by global branding, by a global commercial infrastructures and cultural industries in addition to communication tools such as the World Wide Web. The historiography has recently begun to highlight these issues outside Europe and America. Here are two examples.

After the 1964 revolution which overthrew the sultanate, the new socialist state of Zanzibar engaged in a process of nation-building which required commitment and discipline from everyone, but especially from young people. However, tension grew between this socialist construction and Islamic customs, and the influence which American cinema had imposed on attitudes and habits of young people. The effort to rebuild post-colonial Zanzibar was based on the recovery of intergenerational relationships in deference typical of pre-colonial costume, but with long hair, mini skirts, and casual clothing, young people stressed their autonomous subjectivity, thus sharply conflicting with the stability of subordinate relationships between generations.[52] Despite the mobilization of groups (including youth) linked to the party, the challenge to the regime through autonomous consumption practices never disappeared.[53]

This course of adaptation and reception also affected consumer choices, which was expected to contribute to the standardization and homogeneity of consumer cultures. The research into McDonald's expansion within the Asian marketplace stressed the role of this brand in standardizing consumption throughout the world, thanks to benchmarking in production processes and to the commercialization of food, but it is also maintained that McDonald's was not able to control the social message which was then disseminated throughout the world. The messages represented by Mc Donald's food as well as its commercial premises can be adapt according to the social and cultural contexts through which they spread. They may be rejected as an alien invasion, accepted enthusiastically as a an exciting novelty, but more often than not they are noticeably appropriated in the context of eating habits and in the use of urban space, which is then varied country to country. This suggests that even something so commercially standardized as the brand offered by Mc Donald's may become the object of appropriation and domestication which differentiate its message, and this can be said of several other American and global brands.[54]

[51] J. Prestholdt, *Domesticating the World: African Consumerism and the Genealogies of Globalization*, Berkeley and Los Angeles, University of California Press, 2008.

[52] On the relationship between youth and revolutionary discipline, see T. Burgess, 'Remembering Youth: Generation in Revolutionary Zanzibar', in *Africa Today*, 2 (1999), 29–50.

[53] T. Burgess, 'Cinema, Bell Bottoms, and Miniskirts: Struggles over Youth and Citizenship in Revolutionary Zanzibar', in *The International Journal of African Historical Studies*, 35:2/3 (2002), 287–313.

[54] J.L. Watson (ed.), *Golden Arches East: McDonald's in East Asia*, Stanford, Stanford University Press, 1997.

New approaches in the study of youth consumptions should be able to overcome even the implicit elitism which characterizes the study of youth sub-cultures, namely the focus of research on cultural experience which has represented the vanguard rather than mainstream consumer culture, minority rebels instead of the various forms of conformism or local adaptation, which then characterizes the practices of most young consumers. To look at youth culture becomes part of an attempt to investigate local realities situated within the kaleidoscope of cultural complexity. Space and times in the process of constitution and appropriation of symbolic dimensions require models and figures irreducible to any consistent sub-culture. They therefore refer to the interaction between global landscapes and 'scenes',[55] designed as a local sub-cultural spaces, which are not a fix space to which to belong permanently, but a porous space from which one may get in and out of in continuous movement marked by subjective rhythms of variable intensities.[56] In the complexity of these references, the generational factor does not disappear, but it is increasingly being explored as a value in the process of subjectification, rather than a fact to be discovered. Thus, being young, rather than just phase of life, should become the result of a cultural choice.

BIBLIOGRAPHY

Arvidsson, A., *Marketing Modernity: Italian Advertising from Fascism to Postmodernity*, London and New York, Routledge, 2003.

de Grazia, V. and Furlough, E. (eds), *The Sex of Things: Gender and Consumption in Historical Perspective*, Berkeley and Los Angeles, University of California Press, 1996.

Fowler, D., *The First Teenagers: The Lifestyle of Young Wage-Earners in Interwar Britain*, London, The Woburn Press, 1995.

Fowler, D., *Youth Culture in Modern Britain, c.1920–c.1970: From Ivory Tower to Global Movement: A New History*, Basingstoke, Palgrave Macmillan, 2008.

Hall, S. and Jefferson, T. (eds), *Resistance through Rituals: Youth Subcultures in Post-War Britain*, London, Hutchinson, 1976.

Levi, G. and Schmitt, J. C. *Storia dei giovani*, Bari and Rome, Laterza, 1994.

Mort, F., *Cultures of Consumption: Masculinities and Social Space in Late Twentieth-Century Britain*, London and New York, Routledge, 1996.

Peukert, D., *Grenzen der Sozialdisziplinierung: Aufstieg und Krise der deutschen Jugendfürsorge von 1878 bis 1932*, Cologne, Bund-Vlg., 1986.

Ramet, S. P. and Crnkovic, G. P. (eds), *Kazaaam! Splat! Ploof! The American Impact on European Popular Culture since 1945*, Lanham, MD and New York, Rowman & Littlefield, 2003.

[55] A. Appadurai, *Modernity at Large: Cultural Dimension of Globalization*, Minneapolis, MN and London, University of Minnesota Press, 1996.

[56] M. Maffesoli, *Le temps des tribus. Le déclin de l'individualisme dans les sociétés de masse*, Paris, Le livre de Poche, 1991 (1988).

CHAPTER 32

··

FASHION

··

CHRISTOPHER BREWARD

FASHION CYCLES

···

The late fashion sociologist Fred Davis proffered an anecdote in his book *Fashion Culture and Identity* that perfectly captures the power of fashion change to transform the sense of self in far-reaching ways. He quotes from the journal of an American, working in the fashion industry, who returned home from a visit to the East Asia in 1947 and found herself confronted by a paradigm shift in appearances as she travelled:

> At every airport where we stopped on the way back from China I started watching the women coming the other way. At Calcutta the first long skirt and unpadded shoulders looked like something out of a masquerade party. At the American installations in Frankfurt (also in Vienna) a lot of the newer arrivals were converted and were catching everyone's attention. At the airport in Shannon...I got into conversation with a lady en route to Europe. She was from San Francisco, and told me that they hadn't been completely won over; just as many were wearing the long skirts as not. But as she flew east, she found that just about everybody in New York had gone in for the new styles and she was happy she wasn't staying on or her wardrobe would have been dated. By the time I took the train from New York for home, my short skirts felt conspicuous and my shoulders seemed awfully wide! Two weeks now and I am letting down hems, trying to figure out which of all my China-made clothes can be salvaged, and going on a buying spree![1]

1947 was the year in which the Parisian couturier Christian Dior launched his celebrated New Look, a collection that offered an aspirational alternative to the fabric restrictions and low consumer expectations of post-war austerity—seemingly re-routing fashionable trends in Europe and North America in the space of a season. The diarist had unwittingly become first a witness to and then participant in the mysterious process

[1] Fred Davis, *Fashion, Culture and Identity* (Chicago: University of Chicago Press, 1992), p. 151.

of fashion change—a process that in the static and familiar environment of home often remains hidden and ineffable. Suffering from a version of sartorial jet-lag, she faced an oncoming tide of novelties, fresh versions of the fashion designer's diktat, whilst her own wardrobe remained in another, less contemporary, time zone. She knew that she must adapt or be overtaken. Though it would be difficult to re-enact this precise scenario today or in the more distant past, it does present some generic issues concerning fashion's close relationship with novelty, change, competition, guilt and desire that will be familiar to historians of consumption in the early modern period and the contemporary.[2] Daniel Defoe famously recorded a similar case of the movement of new fashionable goods (in this case Indian chintzes) across places and populations in the *Weekly Review* of 1708:

> The general fansie of the people runs upon East India Goods to that degree, that the chintz and painted calicoes, which before were only made use of for carpets, quilts etc., and to clothe children and ordinary people, became now the dress of our ladies, and such is the power of a mode as we saw our persons of quality dressed in India carpets, which but a few years before that chambermaids would have thought too ordinary for them: the chintz was advanced from lying on their floors to their backs, from the footcloth to the petticoat; and even the Queen herself at this time was pleased to appear in China and Japan, I mean China silks and calico. Nor was this all, but it crept into our homes, our closets and bedchambers, curtains, cushions, chairs and at last beds themselves, were nothing but calicos or Indian stuffs, and in short, almost everything that used to be made of wool or silk, relating either to the dress of the women or the furniture of our houses was supplied by the Indian trade.[3]

However, three centuries later, the speed and complexity of modern communications, the globalization of the media and fashion industries, and the demise of more linear systems of distribution have helped to compress the sensation of a singular sartorial evolution such as might have held sway during the chintz craze of the early eighteenth century or the post-war triumph of the 'New Look'. The twenty-first-century consumer experiences fashion as a more fragmented, simultaneous, and potentially confusing cultural phenomenon, whose effects are not far removed from the viral analogies promoted by brand marketing agencies. In an apparent and rather ironic vindication of classic Marxist economic theory, the almost seamless knitting together of the processes of fashion production and consumption have created the sublimation of the circumstances of production in a mirage

---

[2] Neil McKendrick, John Brewer and John Plumb, *The Birth of a Consumer Society: The Commercialisation of Eighteenth-Century England* (London: Europa, 1982); Lorna Weatherill, *Consumer Behaviour and Material Culture in Britain 1660–1760* (London: Routledge, 1988); B. Lemire, *Fashion's Favourite: The Cotton Trade and the Consumer in Britain, 1660–1800* (Oxford: Oxford University Press, 1991); John Brewer and Roy Porter, *Consumption and the World of Goods* (London: Routledge, 1993); Giorgio Riello, *A Foot in the Past: Consumers, Producers and Footwear in the Long Eighteenth Century* (Oxford: Oxford University Press, 2006).

[3] Christopher Breward, *The Culture of Fashion* (Manchester: Manchester University Press, 1995), p. 126.

of desires where all human values have become commodified.[4] It is then little wonder that some critics have been driven to equate the nature of Fashion, not just with the making, selling, and wearing of clothing, but as a powerful (and often negative) metaphor for the mercenary and materialistic state of modern society and culture in general.[5]

Critical analyses of the processes and effects of fashion consumption, or the use of fashion consumption as a cipher for broader cultural and societal shifts are nothing new, as Defoe's report on the influx of Indian styles makes clear, and it is notable that current fashion theorists continue to draw on this long-established literature, much of it generated in the nineteenth and early twentieth centuries. Following early modern and eighteenth-century discussions of the politics of dress, couched in religious, economic, or moral language, the idea of fashion took on a new academic seriousness in the literary and artistic salons of the Second Empire and *fin de siècle*, exalting what had previously been dismissed as the feminized trivia of popular journalism or the esoteric pursuit of the cleric or dandified aristocrat to the status of a science and a philosophy.[6] This reflective analysing of the luxurious habits of the rich drew on the repeated description and reproduction of its details in gossip columns, magazines, novels, painting, theatre, and latterly film. In Paris its effects can be read in the works of Balzac, Baudelaire, Mallarmé, the Goncourts, and Proust.[7] In London it finds its apotheosis in the satirical voice of Wilde, whose professional interest in the worlds of fashion and entertainment saw him both lampooning its pretensions in his dramatic works whilst fuelling its progress in his role as editor of the progressive journal *The Woman's World*.[8] In Boston and New York, Henry James and Edith Wharton chronicled an 'over-investment in the world of appearances' which was simultaneously dissected in the studies of economist Thorstein Veblen and captured on canvas in the 'Golden Age' portraits of John Singer Sargent.[9] Following the First World War the European artistic avant-garde recognized in the promotion and circulation of fashion a valuable commentary on Modernism, and its slippery characteristics were utilized in the theoretical writings of architects including Adolf Loos and Le Corbusier, the novels of writers such as Franz Kafka and Virginia Woolf, and the imagery of various Futurists, Expressionists, Dadaists, and Surrealists.[10]

More recent fashion theorists, from Roland Barthes onwards, have extended this concern with the character of fashion beyond the conspicuous consuming behaviour of metropolitan elites, towards a consideration of fashion's operation in everyday life,

[4] Marshall Berman, *All that is Solid Melts into Air: The Experience of Modernity* (New York: Simon & Schuster, 1982).

[5] Terri Agins, *The End of Fashion* (New York: William Morrow, 1999).

[6] Aileen Ribeiro, *Dress and Morality* (London: Batsford, 1986); Michael Carter, *Fashion Classics: From Carlyle to Barthes* (Oxford: Berg, 2003); Daniel Purdy, *The Rise of Fashion: A Reader* (Minneapolis: University of Minnesota Press, 2004).

[7] Ellen Moers, *The Dandy: Brummell to Beerbohm* (New York: Viking, 1960).

[8] Rhonda K. Garelick, *Rising Star: Dandyism, Gender and Performance in the Fin de Siècle* (Princeton, NJ: Princeton University Press, 1998).

[9] Clare Hughes, *Henry James and the Art of Dress* (Basingstoke: Ashgate, 2001).

[10] Andreas Huyssen, *After the Great Divide: Modernism, Mass Culture, Postmodernism* (Bloomington: University of Indiana Press, 1986).

as a signifier of more demotic concerns.[11] As an example of this focus, the history of the denim jean has often functioned as a history of more generic issues. Associated over its two hundred year history with the freedoms of the American landscape and the 'American way of life', the jeans soft blue nap has offered a fresh canvas to successive generations of producers, cultural intermediaries, and consumers. In its earliest sixteenth-century incarnation the indigo-dyed, hard-wearing cotton claims connections with both the textile-manufacturing centre Nîmes in France (thus denim) and the port of Genoa in Italy (jean). There certainly seems to be an antecedent in the seagoing breeches of eighteenth-century sailors, though it was the needs of land-workers, gold-diggers and cattle-drivers in the American West of the 1850s that inspired local clothing manufacturers and wholesalers such as Levi Strauss to produce durable overalls and trousers for an active and itinerant workforce who were without ready recourse to tailoring or outfitting shops, or domestic support in the way of laundries and home-sewers. These were seamed with the strong stitches of the new sewing technology and reinforced with the rivets more usually used in the construction of horse-blankets and saddlery. They were cheap, demanded little maintenance in the way of washing and pressing, and travelled well; but their social and aesthetic connotations were lowly—a uniform of labour.[12]

A century later and such connotations had been transformed in line with America's mythologizing of its own recent history as a land of pioneers, newly immortalized in Hollywood. The realities of corporate culture and urbanization, together with agricultural depression in the inter-war years, lent the jean a sentimental and nostalgic patina that had little to do with its original functionalism, but made it the patriotic garment of choice for the increasing leisure hours enjoyed by ordinary Americans. By the 1950s further suburbanization and a virtual worship of mass consumerism meant that the escapist legend of denim came to offer a more oppositional stance. Its unchanging, apparent anti-fashion characteristics and essentializing ties to action and adventure set the jean up as a badge of a more subversive intent, chosen by rebels and outcasts as a marker of difference and refusal. That its neutral coordinates could by the end of the 1960s encompass adherents in the Americas, Europe (west and east), and the South Pacific, as varied as broodingly contemptuous film stars, bohemian intellectuals, left-leaning political radicals, feminists, gay men, students, and teenagers, was a tribute to its malleability and supremely suggestive symbolic qualities.[13]

By the late 1970s such properties had not gone unnoticed by the rapidly globalizing fashion industry. But whereas earlier versions of the garment were largely standardized and fairly undifferentiated in terms of their manufacture and styling, the new variants capitalized on the romantic sense of heritage that companies such as Levi Strauss or

[11] Diana Crane, *Fashion and its Social Agendas: Class, Gender and Identity in Clothing* (Chicago: University of Chicago Press, 2000).

[12] Lee Hall, *Common Threads: A Parade of American Clothing* (Boston: Little Brown & Co., 1992); Leslie Rabine and Susan Kaiser, 'Sewing Machines and Dream Machines in Los Angeles and San Francisco', in Christopher Breward and David Gilbert (eds), *Fashion's World Cities* (Oxford: Berg, 2006).

[13] Stuart Ewen and Elizabeth Ewen, *Channels of Desire: Mass Images and the Shaping of America* (Minneapolis: University of Minnesota Press, 1992).

Wrangler could lay claim to, whilst inventing a multiplicity of reinvented traditions and associations through intensive advertising. Subtle product differentiation, together with the competitive promotion of particular designer brands to niche markets transformed the jean from a fairly functional throw-away item to a 'lifestyle' concept rich in iconic potential and profit.[14] A near saturation of the global market for denim goods by the turn of the twenty-first century has resulted in some extraordinary renegotiations of the staple commodity. Now shorn of its innocence, the once American jean has been consecutively manipulated as a rare collector's item, hived-off to increasingly obscure Japanese and European labels, and re-engineered to meet the aesthetic desires of a generation enamoured of new technologies and customization. And all the while, as recent studies have shown, its ubiquity and close relationship with the body and sense of identity of the wearer have rendered the jean an extraordinary and material capacity to trace deeper, local shifts in the development of consumer cultures.[15]

It could be argued, then, that the history of the jean provides a means of understanding the increasing importance placed on the role of the fashion process (the relationship of object and beliefs and its contribution to formations of consumerism) in the general operation of late capitalism. This reflects a development that many writers on consumption have identified as a broad cultural shift from a society in which a focus on the utility or intrinsic quality of objects and products was prioritized to one in which much greater value is placed on their symbolic and associative worth. Whilst I would suggest that consumers have generally negotiated a more nuanced path between these two positions, valuing both use and symbolic values simultaneously, the early twenty-first century certainly offers a scenario in which the carefully manipulated associations of the fashionable brand and a keen attention to the vagaries of style have transformed the humble equipment of contemporary living into the ephemeral props of ever-changing lifestyle concepts. Though this may well be set to change again, the air traveller of the present, unlike her New Look predecessor, does not confine her worries to the modish state of her wardrobe. Virtually every facet of her existence, from the choice of airline, through mobile phones, food and financial packages, must now accord with the complex directions of global trends. The remit of fashion today has expanded well beyond the design, manufacture, and wearing of a new dress inspired by Paris.

CONSUMPTION AND THE CITY

Though the power of Paris to dictate global trends may have waned since the 1950s, the history and practice of Western fashion is nevertheless still closely related to the history and culture of urban life. Indeed, the importance of ideas of metropolitanism and their

[14] Jane Pavitt (ed.) *Branded* (London: V&A Publications, 2000).
[15] Kitty Hauser, 'The Fingerprint of the Second Skin', in Christopher Breward and Caroline Evans (eds) *Fashion and Modernity* (Oxford: Berg, 2005); D. Miller and S Woodward, 'A Manifesto for the Study of Denim', in *Social Anthropology* 15:5 (November 2007), 335–351.

spatial character to the construction of fashion consumer identities have become a key focus of recent academic literature.[16] As cultural geographer David Gilbert has claimed, this complex relationship between fashion, consumption, and place underpins contemporary understandings of global fashion as a system orchestrated around a sifting network of world cities, particularly Paris, New York, London, Milan, and Tokyo, but also incorporating (at various times) Moscow, Vienna, Berlin, São Paulo, Kuwait City, Cape Town, Barcelona, Antwerp, Sydney, Shanghai, Hong Kong, Mumbai, Stockholm, and many others. The hierarchy of these locations, Gilbert suggests, has to be understood through a history that places fashion at the intersection of key cultural and economic processes that shaped the urban order. These included the consumer revolution of the eighteenth century, the economic and symbolic workings of European imperialism, the growing American engagement with European fashion (specifically via the medium of Hollywood film) and the emergence of a distinctively fashion-focused promotional industry (advertising and magazines, fashion weeks, and runway presentations) based on a few key urban centres.[17] Following Gilbert's lead, this chapter now looks to crucial historical moments in this development that witnessed the consolidation of the idea of the city as a pivotal location in the global organization of both geographical and sartorial relationships, with long-term consequences for the directions taken by a globalized fashion industry and its related consumer cultures in the modern period.

The first European centres of fashion production, distribution, and display prospered because of the concurrent existence of clusters of highly skilled clothing producers; local and international markets for the trading and dissemination of raw materials, finished goods and printed representations of them; and the proximity of magnificent court cultures where the promotion of luxury was a social and moral necessity. These three factors were often inter-dependent, echoing fashion's generic character as an amalgamation of the forces of production, distribution, and consumption. But the emphasis and effect differed from city to city, leading to local distinctions and wider competition. Thus the rising dominance of Burgundian, Venetian, and Spanish sartorial styles in formations of early modern European taste reflected those moments during which their respective courts (and their host cities) enjoyed unchallenged political, economic, and military influence. In fourteenth-, fifteenth, and sixteenth-century Venice, Florence, Madrid, Paris, Bruges, and London, fine textiles and clothes were as significant an indicator of civic power as the streets, squares, guildhalls, and palaces that signified heightened metropolitan status in architectural terms. Furthermore, such sites offered spaces where crowds might congregate, classes of people intermingle, and individuals compete for attention through the modishness of their attire. To be fashionable was to be urban and vice versa.

[16] Breward and Gilbert (eds) *Fashion's World Cities*; John Potvin (ed.) *The Places and Spaces of Fashion, 1800–2007* (Abingdon: Routledge, 2009).
[17] D. Gilbert, 'Urban Outfitting: The City and the Spaces of Fashion Culture', in S. Bruzzi and P. Church-Gibson (eds), *Fashion Cultures: Theories, Explorations and Analysis* (London: Routledge, 2000), p. 15.

By the late seventeenth century the dual systems of mercantile trade and courtly display had produced a convergence. Paris emerged as the prime centre of urban fashionability and the first of fashion's world cities. The nearby court of the 'Sun King' Louis XIV utilized the power of fashion for dynastic and nationalistic propaganda. As Jean-Baptiste Colbert, Louis's most powerful statesman, remarked, 'fashion is to France what the gold mines of Peru are to Spain'. Royal sponsorship of French textile, ceramic, metal, and furniture manufactures as substitutes for Spanish and Italian luxury imports, and the spectacular consolidation of the king's household at Versailles as a carefully managed symbol of absolutism strengthened the idea of French fashion as a vehicle for control and promotion. Ambitious courtiers and subjects were kept in check by a complex system of sartorial regulations, and foreign competitors were awed into submission by the staging of ostentatious fashionable consumption, both personal and ceremonial.[18]

The labour that lay behind this emphasis on the creation of fashionable personae, lifestyles, and happenings was located in Paris and underpinned the transformation of France's economy and international profile. Unsurprisingly, the thousands of weavers, embroiderers, tailors, dressmakers, and milliners employed in the service of the court at Versailles were also able to establish themselves as an alternative source of fashion knowledge, materials, and techniques to local clientele. The demi-monde of wealthy courtesans and actresses at home in the city, the rising Parisian bourgeoisie, and increasing numbers of overseas and provincial visitors formed a new audience for their goods, and a new conduit for trends that operated independently of those trickling down from the monarchy. By the middle of the eighteenth century Parisian tastes, freed from the restrictions of official practice, were also attracting the attention of a younger aristocratic generation. After 1715 Louis XV's circle chose to embrace the chic urbanity of metropolitan modes over fossilized court ceremony. It was in this context that the Paris-based purveyor of fashion gained a new role and prominence in the system of Paris fashion.[19]

The complicated guild regulations that governed the production of Paris fashion in the eighteenth century (preceding the equally severe edicts of the Chambre Syndicale de la Haute Couture in the twentieth century) threw up discrete categories of producer, most notably the *maitresses couturières* (responsible for the cutting-out and construction of the basic garment) and the *marchandes de modes* (who supplied trimmings and had more influence over fashion directions). One of the latter, Rose Bertin of the rue Saint-Honoré was dressmaker to Marie Antoinette; her reputation as a domineering dictator of Ancien Regime style arguably formed the prototype from which later constructions of the Parisian fashion designer developed. Like several of her successors, from Charles Worth in the 1870s to Coco Chanel in the 1930s and Yves Saint Laurent in the 1970s, her expertise lay in a masterful juxtaposing of existing elements sourced from the city's rich supply of exquisitely crafted products, the ability to flatter and anticipate the tastes of her elite clients, and a driving self-promotional force.

---

[18] V. Steele, *Paris Fashion: A Cultural History* (Oxford: Oxford University Press, 1988).

[19] D. Roche, *The Culture of Clothing: Dress and Fashion in the Ancien Regime* (Cambridge: Cambridge University Press, 1994).

The characterization of Bertin and her successors as part-artist, part impresario underlines the continuing importance of the personality of the couturier to enduring ideas of Paris as premier fashion city. But the gradual development of the physical city and its role in the imagination of the fashion consumer further contributed to the creation of a powerful myth of Parisian prestige, endorsed in countless tourist guidebooks and subsequent representations of what Walter Benjamin would come to call the 'capital of the nineteenth-century'. From the 1860s to 1914 Paris itself was transformed into the 'City of Light': a global object of desire and a cipher for high-end consumption.[20] Bertin's world had been located in a rarefied domain of small gilded showrooms and prestigious made-to-measure workrooms which over the decades expanded to incorporate the rue Richelieu and the rue de la Paix. By the 1850s the neighbouring Palais Royal housed a less-refined, but no less opulent collection of ready-made fashion goods for visiting tourists and wealthy locals hungry for the latest 'look'. In contrast, the rue Saint-Denis, with its new and luxurious department stores, was associated with the respectable but stylish purchases of the middle classes; its pavements were equally crowded. Despite their different atmospheres, these districts held in common a blind belief in the global supremacy of Parisian fashion, and a scattering of tenants whose trading names had become synonymous with that same phenomenon.[21] Alongside Worth, couturiers including Doucet and Paquin produced products and ideas that signified elegance and modernity throughout Europe, its colonies, and the Americas.

Yet by the late nineteenth-century the seemingly undisputed domination of Paris as first city of fashion was coming under threat from other versions in Europe and beyond. London, by this time enjoying economic and political world prominence, could also boast an established reputation as the 'home' of gentleman's tailoring: the 'man's city' whose Savile Row-inspired elegance stood in opposition to the French capital's association with glamorous femininity.[22] In Berlin, Barcelona, Brussels, and Vienna, café society and the promotion of artistic bohemianism offered alternative interpretations of fashionable urbanity, premised on aesthetic avant-gardism and social experimentation.[23] And in the United States the fashion retail and manufacturing innovations of Chicago and New York showed the potential for a more democratic understanding of fashion as a commercial endeavour, synonymous with America's youthful metropolitan centres and their expanding populations.[24]

[20] D. Harvey, *Paris, Capital of Modernity* (London: Routledge, 2003) and C. Jones, *Paris, Biography of a City* (London: Penguin, 2006).

[21] P. Perrot, *Fashioning the Bourgeoisie: A History of Clothing in the Nineteenth Century* (Princeton, NJ: Princeton University Press, 1994).

[22] C. Breward, *The Hidden Consumer: Masculinities, Fashion and City Life 1860–1914* (Manchester: Manchester University Press, 1999); C. Breward, E. Ehrman, and C. Evans, *The London Look* (New Haven, CT: Yale University Press, 2004).

[23] R. Stern, *Against Fashion: Clothing as Art 1850–1930* (Cambridge, MA: MIT Press, 2004).

[24] N. Green, *Ready-to-Wear and Ready-to-Work: A Century of Industry and Immigrants in Paris and New York* (Durham, NC: Duke University Press, 1997) and M. Zakim, *Ready-Made Democracy: A History of Men's Dress in the American Republic, 1760–1860* (Chicago: University of Chicago Press, 2003).

To some extent all these established and emergent cities of fashion were linked through the ties of international diplomacy, trade, and labour and reflected a broader colonial context. Their rise coincided with the circulation of widely recognized symbolic codes for the luxurious, the 'primitive', and the 'exotic', which reflected fashion capitals' function as nodal points of an imperialist geography of consumerist supply and demand, where the fashionable goods in production, on show, or in use, conformed to respected hierarchies of taste. Such values could be seen at play in the imaginative uses made of 'orientalist' displays in European and American department stores, or the manner in which the perfect craft and visual flair of elite metropolitan fashions were celebrated as 'art' in the new magazines. These distinctions were naturalized as part of the fabric of Western 'civilization', demonstrating the merits of the 'sophisticated' beauty of urban fashion in the developed world in vivid contrast to the 'savage' simplicity of clothing in subordinated non-urban societies. Immigrant communities, whose presence was also an important contribution to the establishment of modern fashion cities, together with those who resided in the colonies of European empires, provided the labour necessary for the production and distribution of city-specific fashions, and often, the sources of inspiration for the latest lucrative trends (this can be seen, for example, in the translation of the South Asian *boteh* motif into the Paisley shawl craze that hit Europe from the 1840s—a successor to chintz).[25] Local and seasonal patterns of migration and exchange between cities and their rural hinterlands also ensured that fashion capitals in the Industrial Age maintained their reputation as magnetic centres, attracting manpower and wealth, and generating creativity.

By the *fin de siècle*, fashion had thus established itself as one of the currencies by which cities distinguished themselves and competed against each other. The production and consumption of particular genres and styles of fashionable goods sat alongside the promotion of state architecture, the cult of the international exhibition, the imposition of grand street plans and the rise of international tourism as a mechanism for engendering a higher profile in the Western consumer's dream world. A more immediate motivation for those involved in such promotion was greater prosperity in the clothing and advertising trades. By the 1920s and '30s the influence of an American engagement with European fashion (and vice versa) via the instruments of a new mass culture had also become a defining factor in the forging of a popular concept of the fashion city, though often through recourse to nostalgic tropes of metropolitan life created in the previous century. Hollywood film directors and Fifth Avenue magazine editors branded an enduring image of Paris as the eternally elegant city of fashionably dressed eroticism on global consumer consciousness, while New York attained a screen identity as the dynamic and futuristic domain of slick and snappy acquisitiveness that it has subsequently found hard to shed.[26] In this dream-like vision of fashion's complementary

---

[25] E. Paulicelli and H. Clark (eds) *The Fabric of Cultures: Fashion, Identity and Globalisation* (London: Routledge, 2009) and R. Ross, *Clothing: A Global History* (London: Polity Press, 2008).

[26] R. Arnold, *The American Look: Fashion, Sportswear and the Image of Women in 1930s and 1940s New York* (London: I.B.Tauris, 2009).

centres, London featured either as a bastion of tradition and conservatism, or as a gothic nightmare of fog-shrouded alley-ways and hansom-cabs. What is fascinating is the manner in which such stereotyping still endures in the language and imagery of late twentieth- and twenty-first-century fashion industry rhetoric: the extravagance of a Dior couture collection still evokes the sensual overload of a Proustian courtesan's boudoir; successful television and film franchises such as *Sex and the City* with their obvious reliance on commodity-fetishism and materialist values have been taken as an unproblematic representation of Manhattan mores; and the provocative sexuality of a Vivienne Westwood or Alexander McQueen show draw non-ironic comparisons with Victorian melodrama and the world of Jack-the-Ripper.[27]

Where the nineteenth-century conceptualization of the world fashion city was focused on improving infrastructural foundations and establishing representational ideas as part of the broader promotion of cosmopolitan ideals, more recently the identity of the fashion city has been increasingly bound up with the evolution of modern fashion (noted earlier in this chapter) as a universal and aspirational cipher whose meanings extend far beyond the production of luxury clothing.[28] From the 1950s a more finely graded ranking of fashion's key centres has echoed the relative fortunes of national and increasingly international fashion-based industries, and caused the mantle 'fashion city' to be deployed more self-consciously as a form of protectionism, as a promotional tool, or a mechanism for re-branding and regeneration.[29]

Looking forward, the nature of the fashion city looks set to change again as the system of 'fast fashion', with its reliance on far-flung sites of production, disrupts the traditional relationship between time, place, and fashion creativity. Similarly, the rise of Internet fashion portals such as the Worth Global Style Network has made the seasonal display of collections in a few key 'fashion weeks' less relevant when journalists and retailers can identify emerging trends instantaneously online. The specific atmosphere and accrued traditions of established fashion centres appear to dissolve in the virtual world of the web. Such developments have also opened up spaces in which other cities, notably Shanghai, Mumbai, and São Paulo, have been able to challenge the hegemony of Paris, London, New York, Milan, and Tokyo, cities whose claims for international fashion prominence were consolidated in the nineteenth and twentieth centuries. In a postcolonial twenty-first-century it is precisely those places who formerly supplied aesthetic inspiration or manpower to the centres of an older fashion empire that are emerging as competitive sites for the production of new products and ideas. For contemporary Chinese, Indian or Brazilian designers, entrepreneurs, and consumers, the idea of Paris, London, or Milan as the sole generators and guardians of fashion innovation carries far less power than it might have done for previous generations.

---

[27] C. Evans, *Fashion at the Edge: Spectacle, Modernity and Deathliness* (New Haven, CT and London: Yale University Press, 2003).

[28] I. Loschek, *When Clothes Become Fashion: Design and Innovation Systems* (Oxford: Berg, 2009).

[29] D. Gilbert, 'From Paris to Shanghai: The Changing Geographies of Fashion's World Cities', in Breward and Gilbert (eds), *Fashion's World Cities*, pp. 3–32.

What seems less likely, though, is the demise of the nineteenth-century idea of the fashion city as a crucial component of the concept and structural organization of fashion consumption more generally. Contemporary sartorial commodities by necessity operate in a globally understood 'realm of values'. The design and media creatives in the most successful and long-standing fashion cities have always understood this, seeking to project their particular sense of life and culture onto the rest of the world's markets in a responsive and fluid manner. The differentiated and often stereotypical fashion imagery of Paris, London, and New York is now not entirely fixed in its geographical specificity, even though its validity and meaning partly lies in a real industrial history, architectural landscape and cultural heritage inherited from at least a hundred years before. It is precisely the flexible nature of fashion city values rooted in a longer historical trajectory that endows the modern fashion order with the continuing capacity to create and challenge social, material, and aesthetic realities across the globe.

Fashionable Definitions

Fashion's relation to time and space, then, has formed a fascinating context in which to consider the development of consumerism, but how has the nature of fashion itself been addressed by theorists and historians interested in harnessing its properties to unpack the wider characteristics of consumer societies, and how might such studies develop in the future? In his influential and provocative treatise on Western fashion as one of the most potent cultural forms in modern societies, philosopher Gilles Lipovetsky suggests that

> 'in order to conceptualize fashion, we shall have to stop identifying it as a principle that is necessarily and universally inscribed in the evolutionary course of all civilizations, and we must also stop viewing it as a historical constant with universal anthropological roots. The mystery of fashion lies here, in the uniqueness of the phenomenon, in the way it sprang up and took hold in the modern West and nowhere else. Neither an elementary force of collective life nor a permanent principle of social transformation rooted in the human condition in general, fashion is essentially a socio-historical formation limited to a single type of society. We can uncover its fascinating effects not by invoking its presumed universality, but rather by carefully determining the limits of its historical extension.[30]

Lipovetsky's dictums are both compelling and slightly frustrating for the student setting out to marry a history of fashion with a history of consumption. He is helpful in his plea for a focused and nuanced definition of what constitutes 'fashion' as a meaningful social concept (for him it is essentially a European and post-medieval phenomenon), and inspirational in his identification of its mysterious and spectacular qualities. But he is more vague in his attempts to describe the shifting remit of fashion in any material

---

[30] Gilles Lipovetsky, *The Empire of Fashion: Dressing Modern Democracy* (Princeton, NJ: Princeton University Press, 1994), p. 15.

sense. For Lipovetsky it remains an abstract system and is never evoked as a concrete process, which limits the usefulness of his theories to those scholars who have lately become interested in the tracing the development of an empire of 'things'. He agrees that 'the history of clothing is unquestionably the privileged reference for such a problematics', but also concurs that 'other sectors—furniture and decorative objects, language and manners, tastes and ideas, artists and cultural productions—have been won over by the fashion process, with its fads and its rapid shifts of direction'. It is then 'a specific form of social change, independent of any particular object; it is first and foremost a social mechanism characterized by a particularly brief timespan and by more or less fanciful shifts that enable it to affect quite diverse spheres of collective life'.[31]

Lipovetsky was writing in the late 1980s when the academic study of fashion was beginning to extend beyond the specialist realm of costume history, to engage the interest of social and economic historians, anthropologists, sociologists, and cultural theorists.[32] In popular discourse the world of fashion was also gaining value as symbol and measure of a post-Fordist, indeed postmodern moment where the idea of a fashionable identity being intrinsically linked to contemporary subjectivities was gaining a certain urgency, politically and aesthetically.[33] By the time The Empire of Fashion was published in English in 1994 it was, arguably, impossible to discuss the evolution of consumer societies without invoking fashionable clothing and consumer identities as paradigmatic forces in their rise. Yet it has taken a further two decades for fashion historians to arrive at a more precise set of definitions that help elucidate fashion's unique relation to the world of consumption. I cite two recent examples here.

In 2008 business historian Regina Lee Blaszczyk opened the introduction to her edited collection Producing Fashion: Commerce, Culture and Consumers with the question 'What is Fashion'. In laying out an answer, she looked not to philosophy, but to the senior American marketing consultant and former fashion magazine editor Estelle Ellis for her leads:

> In her eyes, fashion found its fullest expression in four areas of culture: 'mode—the way we dress; manners—the way we express ourselves; mores—the way we live; and markets—the way we are defined demographically and psychologically.' Looking at the world through the lenses of these four M's, Ellis understood fashion simply and directly, that is, as a causal agent that constantly reshaped all material things, from 'the fabric environments which surround our bodies' to the 'nature of design and architecture.' Fashion, Ellis persuasively argued, was like a perpetual motion machine, always busy, always moving, and always recontouring 'daily living, whether in the home, office, institution, or community'.[34]

[31] Lipovetsky, Empire of Fashion, p. 16.
[32] Lou Taylor, The Study of Dress History (Manchester: Manchester University Press, 2002), and Fashion Theory: The Journal of Dress, Body and Culture, Special Issue Methodology, 2:4 (1998).
[33] Elizabeth Wilson, Adorned in Dreams: Fashion and Modernity (London: Virago, 1985) and Juliet Ash and Elizabeth Wilson (eds), Chic Thrills: A Fashion Reader (London: Pandora, 1992).
[34] Regina Lee Blaszczyk (ed.), Producing Fashion: Commerce, Culture and Consumers (Philadelphia: University of Pennsylvania Press, 2008), pp. 1–2.

As Blaszczyk affirmed, Ellis's 'ideas may seem too inclusive or evanescent to be useful in historical analysis'. Like Lipovetsky's they deal in generalities that are difficult to test against the evidence; but they do, via their informed-insider perspective, offer a catholic model for

> the analysis of fashion as a form of cultural production, as the richly textured interplay between economic institutions and private individuals, social trends and belief systems, entrepreneurs and tastemakers, marketers and consumers. Historical analysis that pivots on the fundamental premise that fashion affects all types of products has the potential to be remarkably illuminating. It can show how fashion—styles, trends, *modes*, and other manifestations of beliefs, values, ideas, *manners* and *mores*—took hold in all aspects of material life.[35]

Indeed, I had been attempting to arrive at a similar synthesis in my 2003 overview of modern fashion produced for this publisher.[36] Based as I was in a fashion design college, about to move to a national museum, and concurrently engaged on a major cross-disciplinary project on the cultures of consumption as they pertained in post-war London's fashion industry, I felt compelled to offer a reading of fashion that both recognized its historical contingency, emphasized its materiality and function as a creative practice and also acknowledged the medium's adaptability to broader theoretical conjecture (in short to satisfy the perceived needs of readers who might include student practitioners and their lecturers, future curatorial colleagues and academic peers in the humanities).[37] My challenge was to present modern fashion as the outcome of a precarious marriage between the processes of authorship (by designers, manufacturers, and consumers), technologies (of production and representation), and representation (or dissemination); and to reconcile the notions of fashion as idea, object and image. Essentially I was searching for a 'definition of the history of fashion as a history of industrial manufacture and distribution, allied to the growth of a metropolitan sensibility, the energies and tensions of a consumer culture, and the expanded sphere of visual reproduction...developments embedded in the stuff of clothing itself'.[38] A year later, expanding on the role played by fashion in London's longer history I felt emboldened enough to be able to write:

> [Fashion] is a bounded thing, fixed and experienced in space—an amalgamation of seams and textiles, an interface between the body and its environment. It is a practice, a fulcrum for the display of taste and status, a site for the production of objects and beliefs; and it is an event, both spectacular and routine, cyclical in its adherence to the natural and commercial seasons, innovatory in its bursts of avant-gardism, and sequential in its guise as a palimpsest of memories and traditions.[39]

[35] Blaszczyk, *Producing Fashion*, pp. 4–5.
[36] Christopher Breward, *Fashion* (Oxford: Oxford University Press, 2003).
[37] 'Shopping Routes: Networks of Fashion Consumption in London's West End 1945–1979', funded by the Economic and Social Research Council and the Arts and Humanities Research Council as part of the 'Cultures of Consumption' programme.
[38] Breward, *Fashion*, p. 15.
[39] Christopher Breward, *Fashioning London: Clothing and the Modern Metropolis* (Oxford: Berg, 2004), p. 11.

FASHION'S END

Over the course of this chapter, and following on from the citation above, I have attempted to draw on suggestive examples (the fashion cycle, the fashion object and the fashion city: process, materiality, and space) that illuminate the close connections between theories of fashion and theories of consumption and their continuing prominence in recent scholarship. All find common ground in discussions on the nature of modernity and bring us back to Lipovetsky's assertion that fashion is 'a specific form of social change, independent of any particular object; it is first and foremost a social mechanism characterized by a particularly brief time span and by more or less fanciful shifts that enable it to affect quite diverse spheres of collective life'. Fanciful shifts and a sense of flux are concepts that have fascinated cultural theorists since Baudelaire and his claims that fashionable modernity incorporates 'the ephemeral, the fugitive, the contingent'.[40] Via Simmell and Benjamin, right through to the cultural studies project of the 1980s and '90s, this concept of Baudelarian modernity still provides a forceful framework for re-thinking the nature of fashion consumption.[41] But as Lipovetsky suggests, it is also necessary to locate any such study in its proper historical moment, for as other commentators have observed, 'modernity' also suggests the experience of 'feeling modern' or 'being up to date' and it is here that a rigorous consideration of consumer identities in relation to fashion can really prove its worth. In a recent collection of essays on the relationship between fashion and modernity my co-editor and myself recognized the necessity of foregrounding this element of reflexivity as a crucial method of historical and critical analysis in contemporary fashion studies (and the field is constantly expanding to include examinations of, for example, ethical, ecological, religious, and political debates in fashion production and consumption, and the nature of fashion cultures in pre-modern epochs and beyond the West).[42] I continue to feel that this is a primary task for anyone setting out on such an endeavour:

> Fashion is a process in two senses: it is a market-driven cycle of consumer desire and demand; and it is a modern mechanism for the fabrication of the self. It is in this

[40] Charles Baudelaire, 'The Painter of Modern Life', in J. Mayne (trans.), *The Painter of Modern Life and Other Essays* (London: Phaidon, 1964), p. 12.

[41] George Simmel, 'Fashion' and 'The Metropolis and Mental Life', in D. N. Levine (ed.), *On Individuality and Social Forms* (Chicago: University of Chicago Press, 1971); Walter Benjamin, 'On Some Motifs in Baudelaire', in H. Zohn (trans.), *Illuminations* (London: Fontana Collins, 1973); Mike Featherstone, *Consumer Culture and Postmodernism* (London: Sage, 1991); Hal Foster, *The Return of the Real: The Avant-Garde at the End of the Century* (Cambridge, MA: MIT Press, 1996); Anthony Giddens, *Modernity and Self-Identity: Self and Society in the Late Modern Age* (Cambridge: Polity Press, 1991); Frederick Jameson, *Postmodernism, or the Cultural Logic of Late Capitalism* (London: Verso, 1991).

[42] See for example: Alexandru Balasescu, *Paris Chic, Tehran Thrills: Aesthetic Bodies, Political Subjects* (Bucharest: Zeta Books, 2007); Michelle O'Malley and Evelyn Welch (eds), *The Material Renaissance* (Manchester: Manchester University Press, 2007); Giorgio Riello and Prasannan Parthasarathi, *The Spinning World: A Global History of Cotton Textiles 1200–1850* (Oxford: Oxford University Press, 2009); JuanJuan Wu, *Chinese Fashion: From Mao to Now* (Oxford: Berg, 2009).

respect that fashion operates as a fulcrum for negotiating the meeting of internal and external worlds...If fashion is a paradigm of the capitalist processes which inform modern sensibilities, then it is also a vibrant metaphor for modernity itself.[43]

BIBLIOGRAPHY

Agins, Terri. *The End of Fashion* (New York: William Morrow, 1999).

Blaszczyk, Regina Lee (ed.). *Producing Fashion: Commerce, Culture and Consumers* (Philadelphia: University of Pennsylvania Press, 2008).

Breward, Christopher. *Fashion* (Oxford: Oxford University Press, 2003).

Breward, Christopher and David Gilbert (eds). *Fashion's World Cities* (Oxford: Berg, 2006).

Crane, Diana. *Fashion and its Social Agendas: Class, Gender and Identity in Clothing* (Chicago: University of Chicago Press, 2000).

Davis, Fred. *Fashion, Culture and Identity* (Chicago: University of Chicago Press, 1992).

Lemire, Beverley. *Fashion's Favourite: The Cotton Trade and the Consumer in Britain 1660–1800* (Oxford: Oxford University Press, 1991).

Lipovetsky, Gilles. *The Empire of Fashion: Dressing Modern Democracy* (Princeton, NJ: Princeton University Press, 1994).

Purdy, Daniel (ed.). *The Rise of Fashion: A Reader* (Minneapolis: University of Minnesota Press, 2004).

Riello, Giorgio and Prasannan Parthasarathi. *The Spinning World: A Global History of Cotton Textiles 1200–1850* (Oxford: Oxford University Press, 2009).

Steele, Valerie. *Paris Fashion: A Cultural History* (Oxford: Oxford University Press, 1988).

Wilson, Elizabeth. *Adorned in Dreams: Fashion and Modernity* (London: Virago, 1985).

---

[43] Breward and Evans (eds), *Fashion and Modernity*, pp. 2–3.

CHAPTER 33

··

SELF AND BODY

··

ROBERTA SASSATELLI

In his discussion of consumption in eighteenth-century Britain and the changing discourses on the economy and the self, the historian Roy Porter noted a paradox. While a new moral rhetoric of Bernard Mandeville and others reversed conventional wisdom and embraced consumption as good for society, medical rhetoric insisted that consumption did not lead at all to individual health.[1] On the contrary, doctors considered the new consumption patterns as a threat to health, not only because of excess, but also because new practices and ideals of the self and body produced new risks. Porter explores the writings of Thomas Beddoes, a prominent physician, radical campaigner against tuberculosis, and intellectual well connected to a number of Romantic writers. For Beddoes, the subtle changes 'in almost every circumstance of the manner of living' produced diseases both in the working classes—through their own neglect and the unconcern of their masters—and in the consuming classes—by sacrificing health for fashion, image, and a belief that money would buy everything, including health.[2] City life, Porter writes, was conceived as 'high-stress' and 'weakening the nerves' to the point that people 'needed the artificial support of drugs and stimulants, in turn creating a downward spiral of deteriorating health. Coffee, tea, tobacco…had first been used as medicines, but had become reduced to "necessities".[3] Beddoes was indeed adamant that 'our chronic maladies are of our own creating', and that 'the tribute of lives we render to consumption' will only increase lest we 'all learn not to bear to have everything about us—clothes, tables, chairs, pictures, statues—all exquisite in their kind—except our progeny'.[4]

Beddoes's words provide a fitting point of entry to this chapter. The chapter investigates the historical formation and specific configuration of a threefold relation

[1] R. Porter, 'Consumption: disease of the consumer society?', in J. Brewer and R. Porter, *Consumption and the World of Goods*, London: Routledge, 1993, pp. 58–84.

[2] T. Beddoes, 'Essay on the Causes, 1 Early Signs, and Prevention of Pulmonary Consumption for the Use of Parents and Preceptors', in Porter, 'Consumption: disease of the consumer society?', p. 65.

[3] Ibid., p. 69.

[4] Ibid., p. 70.

crucial to contemporary society, that between the body, the self, and material culture. In contemporary, late modern (or post-industrial) societies, this relation has become largely defined through consumer culture. Its symbolic appeal is increasingly shaped by advertisers and marketing, and its commodities are sourced through circuits of commerce increasingly disembedded from local realities. This is itself a novelty. In the past, societies had mainly relied on self-production, barter, and local exchange for daily needs related to the maintenance of the body and on personal relations critical for identity formation. Drawing on historiography, sociology, and anthropology, I will discuss in the next few pages how, from the early modern period, the consolidation of new consumption patterns and values has given way to particular visions of the human being as a consumer, and how, in turn, the consumer has become a cultural battlefield for the management of body and self.

THE HUMAN BEING
AS A CONSUMING ANIMAL

Max Weber defined mature Western capitalism as a type of society in which 'the satisfaction of daily needs' is realized 'through the capitalist mode'.[5] This is to say, ordinary desires and everyday needs are satisfied through the acquisition and use of 'commodities', goods which are produced for exchange and profit and sold in the marketplace. Although there were always various forms of capitalism in all periods, Weber argued, it was only in the modern West that we can find this type of society. In addition, I want to add, we not only satisfy our most elementary daily needs through commodities, we also conceptualize the purchase and use of goods as acts of 'consumption' and we are happy to be addressed as 'consumers'. The 'consumer' has become a crucial social persona, addressed by a plethora of scientific disciplines, public and commercial discourses and social institutions which contribute to delineate what kind of relation to body and self consumers do and should perform.

This process has mirrored a second development: the de-moralization of luxury and the concomitant privatization of a relatively separate sphere of consumption. In early modern times, consumption gradually emerged from the kind of legal-political regime provided by sumptuary laws, and moved into a cultural-economic regime driven by the dynamics of fashion.[6] In the fashion regime, aesthetic judgements such as 'tasteful' and 'tasteless' might work as political and moral tools, to justify social inclusion or exclusion. The de-moralization of luxury did not mean that the cultural repertoires which were deployed in the eighteenth century luxury debate were lost. On the contrary they were often reworked and reframed and have left an important legacy for the moral appraisal

---

[5] M. Weber, *General Economic History*, New Brunswick, NJ: Transaction Books, 1981 (1920).
[6] See the chapter by Maxine Berg in this volume.

of consumption to the present day.[7] Broadly speaking, the de-moralization of luxury has given way to a moralization of the new configuration of economic value that is in line with the entrenchment of capitalist modernity. This configuration sets apart what one consumes as private, and pushes one's own work definitely into the public sphere. The social system came to be described as the interaction of two distinct and different objective and subjective modes of relation with the material world—consumption and production. The characterization of life as a merry-go-round of production and consumption now becomes dominant, with consumption typically in an ancillary position, at least morally. While work is freed of moral restraints, consumption takes on more ambiguous connotations: unequivocally positive for the social body as a stimulus of growth in production and commercial exchange, it has a rather more dubious rule when it comes to the individual body. Consumption, in short, is a paradox: a private vice that is good for the nation, a passion that needs to be tamed into accepted, rational forms of capitalization or self-improvement.

This is the historical context in which the human being is increasingly portrayed as a consuming animal whose needs are infinite and undefined.[8] The consolidation of economics and modern market institutions in the West have naturalized notions of consumption and the consumer to the extent that their prescriptive values may go unnoticed. Adam Smith considered even excessive and luxurious consumption a spring of economic development. The expenditure of the 'great' aided the birth of a class of merchants and bourgeois who drove society towards modern capitalism and who, freed from all personal dependence, guided the whole nation to civil liberty.[9] Even Smith, though, distinguished between appropriate and inappropriate ways of consuming. Merchants are good, well-behaved, rational consumers as opposed to the immoral, irrational, wasteful, and whimsical behaviour associated with the declining nobility. To discriminate among goods, Smith uses the notions of 'convenience' and 'decency'. Decencies indicate goods that can be used for non-ostentatious comfort. They are neither needs nor luxuries. They are a type of consumption which makes the body efficient and the self rational. These are bourgeois comforts: a category of 'durable goods' which make genuine capitalization possible, since they are 'more favourable' than others to 'private frugality' and, consequently, to 'the increase of public capital'. They respond to the 'calm and dispassionate desire' of 'bettering one's own condition', while diverting from the 'passion for present enjoyment'.[10] Smith's thought naturalized (some) goods and their consumption as part of an evolutionary process situated in a particular colonial geopolitics.

---

    [7] M. Hilton, 'The legacy of luxury: moralities of consumption since the eighteenth century', *Journal of Consumer Culture*, 2004, 4 (1): 101–23.

    [8] J. C. Agnew, 'Coming up for air: consumer culture in historical perspective', in Brewer and Porter, *Consumption*; J. O. Appleby 'Consumption in early modern social thought', in Brewer and Porter, *Consumption*. See further R. Porter (ed.), *Rewriting the Self: Histories from the Renaissance to the Present*, London: Routledge, 1997.

    [9] A. Smith, *An Enquiry into the Nature and Causes of the Wealth of Nations*, ed. A. Skinner and R. Meek, Indianapolis, IN: Liberty Classics, 1981 [1776].

    [10] Ibid., pp. 341–9.

Under these conditions, the (Western) consumer-merchant became the foundation of a new social and political order, the sovereign of his own desires to which the market needed to respond. This illustrates the historical background of contemporary consumer culture: a simultaneous valorization of personal gratification, self-control, and individual autonomy. In Western culture, individual autonomy has thus worked in a dualistic fashion. The body not only needed to be controlled and restrained, but also had to be transformed, modified, and expanded by the self.

A self-possessed self may well do to solve the paradox of consumption as public benefit and private vice. However, this paradoxical configuration also gives way to other types of less coherent subjectives. In particular, moral compromises were reached to integrate the values of otherworldly asceticism and rationality with the production of a variety of new commodities which initially appeared superfluous. Extreme contradictions were at work in a lifestyle that favoured commercial exchange. Mandeville, for example, celebrated the lifestyle of Urbano, a fictitious character who incarnated the worldly and civic bourgeois in his combination of industrial rationality and refined hedonism. Urbano is described as a man who 'is employed in heaping up more Wealth the greatest part of the Day; the rest he devotes to his Pleasures', a rational *bon vivant* who knows both how to invest but also how to 'live in Splendour', a pragmatic materialist who 'minds only himself, and lets everybody do as they please'.[11] Such a style of life required a capacity to modulate different attachments, emotions and behaviour, and was mainly found amongst rising social groups. However, the whole population had to adjust to the new relationship between production and consumption, which sees the latter as a sort of liberated enjoyable space where hard-working characters can finally relax from (and refuel for) work discipline. To this day, this new optimistic portrayal continued to call forth radical critique which stressed the dire consequences for the individual from the contradictions of capitalism.

The compromise between entrepreneurial asceticism and hedonistic consumption was reached against the backdrop of the shifting symbolic properties assigned to specific commodities in specific periods and places. Significantly, many new commodities involved body and self. In his history of luxury goods, Wolfgang Schivelbusch considers the diffusion of coffee and cocoa from the end of the seventeenth century to the first half of the eighteenth and shows how these drinks took on different meanings, mixing pleasure and duty, and providing different visions of bodily conduct and identity to social groups in different countries.[12] Across Europe, these beverages were accompanied by another revolution in foodstuffs: the consumption of sugar.[13] The diffusion of sugar and beverages marked and reinforced a particular vision of social actors, who were becoming 'consumers'. As such they had to be capable, beyond their

[11] B. Mandeville, quoted in R. Sassatelli, 'Consuming ambivalence: eighteenth century public discourse on consumption and Mandeville's legacy', *Journal of Material Culture*, 1997, 2 (3): 339–60.

[12] W. Schivelbusch, *Tastes of Paradise: A Social History of Spices, Stimulants and Intoxicants*, New York: Pantheon Books, 1992 (1980).

[13] S. W. Mintz, *Sweetness and Power*, New York: Viking Press, 1985; S. Mintz 'The changing roles of food in the study of consumption', in Brewer and Porter, *Consumption*, pp. 261–73.

specific social position, to procure their own satisfaction in ways that were legitimated by international market circuits. In England and Holland at the end of the seventeenth century and beginning of the eighteenth century, individualist materialism took root. In William Reddy's words, this marked the rise of 'market culture'.[14] The individual desire of Western consumers was constructed through an international division of labour that made the colonies distant reservoirs of exotic and mysterious commodities, as well as irrational selves and tempting bodies. The apparent inexhaustibility of Western consumers' desire matched the abundance brought about by the colonial system—a system that responded to consumers' increased capacity to work through the rules of a rationalized, monetized market. Consumers' desire thus came to appear as the legitimate source of value.[15]

THE BODY, THE MOST BEAUTIFUL OBJECT OF CONSUMPTION

Contemporary societies saturated with commercial massages and images have been described as inviting individuals to take responsibility for their bodies, have fun, and to invest in body maintenance in order to perform culturally appropriate self-presentation.[16] In this view, body and self are conspicuously linked through consumer culture at the expense of the soul. No longer subject to the dangers of sin still prevalent in nineteenth-century culture, the body is said to become the 'visible carrier of the self' in contemporary 'consumer culture'.[17] Indeed, in Jean Baudrillard's words, the human body becomes 'the finest consumer object' of them all—'its "rediscovery", in an era of physical and sexual liberation, after a millennial age or Puritanism; its omnipresence (especially of the female body) in advertising, fashion, and mass culture; the hygienic, dietetic, therapeutic cult which surrounds it; the obsession with youth, elegance, virility/femininity, treatments, and regimes, and the sacrificial practices attached to it all bear witness to the fact the body has today become an object of salvation. It has literally taken over that moral and ideological function from the soul.'[18] Following in the footsteps of

[14] W. Reddy, *The Rise of Market Culture*, Cambridge: Cambridge University Press, 1984.

[15] M. Sahlins, *Culture in Practice*, New York: Zone Books, 2000, part 3.

[16] S. Bordo, *Unbearable Weight: Feminism, Western Culture and the Body*, Berkeley: University of California Press, 1993; A. Howson, *The Body in Society*, Cambridge: Polity Press, 2004; J. O'Neill, *Five Bodies: The Human Shape of Modern Societies*, Ithaca, NY: Cornell University Press, 1985. For a review of the role of the body in contemporary sociological theory see N. Crossley, *The Social Body*, London: Sage, 2001.

[17] M. Featherstone, 'The body in consumer culture', *Theory, Culture and Society*, 1982, 1 (2): 18–33. More broadly on the history of the body see M. Feher, R. Daddaff and N. Tazi, *Fragments for the History of the Human Body*, New York: Zone Books, 1989; R. Porter, 'History of the body', in P. Burke, *Perspectives on Historical Writings*, Cambridge: Polity Press, 1991, pp. 206–32.

[18] J. Baudrillard, *The Consumer Society: Myths and Structures*, London: Sage, 1998 (1970) p. 129.

critical thinkers such as Marcuse, Baudrillard treats the liberation of the body promised by advertisers and retailers as anything but real. In reality, he argued, it amounted to an intensification of power relations, an expansion of the capitalist logic of profit into the domains of intimacy, eroticism and pleasure. Similarly, Christopher Lasch has maintained that in consumer societies, the rewards for constant, disciplined bodywork are no longer either spiritual salvation or well-being, but an improved, more marketable physical appearance.[19]

Baudrillard's and Lasch's arguments resonate with the critical judgements of recent socio-theoretical works that consider investment in self-presentation via consumption as a disease of the will brought about by contemporary Western consumerism, the epitome of the transformation of 'consumers into commodities' and an instance of a deeper 'corrosion of character'.[20] Broadly speaking, in this view the de-politicization and secularization of bodywork has opened the door to a purely materialistic and ultimately vain search for physical perfection. A number of commercially provided goods and activities—from diet products to exercise, from beauty creams to plastic surgery—aimed at caring for and transforming the body have become, as Susan Bordo puts it, 'a project at the service of the body, rather than the soul', directed at purely 'physical enemies' such as 'fat' and 'flab' rather than at gaining self-realization.[21] Advertising images are the prime culprit—they encourage us to pursue whatever ideal appearance might be the order of the day and make us feel inadequate while searching for a superficial, fleeting satisfaction. Women are the favourite prey, their selves being reduced more ruthlessly to their physical appearance. Illnesses such as anorexia and bulimia have become widespread among young females and the norm of a culture in which the consumer sees her body as an alien object that must be constantly controlled.

More broadly, though, the shift away from the soul is a move towards the surface of the body. The rationalized emphasis on performance which is dominant in the sphere of work extends to the domain of consumption. What matters, Mike Featherstone suggests,[22] is the 'look': 'consumer culture permits the unashamed display of the human body... Clothing is designed to celebrate the "natural" human form, a marked contrast to the 19th century in which clothes were designed to conceal the body'. Within consumer culture the 'outer' (appearance, movement, and control) and 'inner' (functioning, maintenance, and repair) of the body are conjoined in an effort of polishing the flesh. The goal of maintaining the inner body focuses on the improved appearance of the outer body. The consumer is expected to assume responsibility for appearance, namely, to engage in bodywork. Failing to do so becomes a sign of moral failure.[23]

[19] C. Lasch, *The Culture of Narcissism*, New York: Norton, 1991 (1979).

[20] Z. Baumann, *Consuming Life*, Cambridge: Polity Press, 2007; R. Sennett, *The Corrosion of Character*, New York: Norton, 1998.

[21] Bordo, *Unbearable Weight*.

[22] M. Featherstone, 'The body', p. 22.

[23] R. Sassatelli, *Fitness Culture: Gyms and the Commercialisation of Discipline and Fun*, Basingstoke: Palgrave Macmillan, 2010.

Such polemic interpretations have had a good deal of support. It would be equally foolish to deny that the display of the human body has a central role in contemporary visual media and advertising, as it would be to ignore the role of media and advertising in promoting universal body ideals. The proliferation of commercial visual culture (movies, photographs, and so forth) increased individuals' awareness of external appearance and bodily presentation. For example, the burgeoning film industry legitimated public bodily display and leisured body building, from sunbathing to fitness training. More specifically, contemporary advertising has made full use of the human body to promote the most diverse goods and services. The body has been turned into a public space, its shape, size, and texture representing body maintenance routines and sexual arousal, and playing with fantasies of bodily transformation. The most hidden parts of the interior have been laid open to public scrutiny via the fictional representation of medical practice and the arts. In past societies, certain physical characteristics were publicly celebrated and associated with high status, but they were also treated as exclusive to the privileged or fortunate. In contemporary consumer culture, bodies that are more accessible to the privileged are idealized through a variety of images in mass advertising and simultaneously coded as a matter of individual will and proof of personal and social success for all. In such circumstances, the body is viewed as a site of domination through commoditization, which ultimately leads to the reproduction of gender, ethnic, and class inequalities.[24]

Such perspectives on consumer bodies and selves can be criticized on several grounds. Not only do they rest on a value-laden opposition between the sphere of consumption and that of work which is being increasingly contradicted in the lives of the new middle-classes engaged in creative professions. They also fail to see that, rather than producing a pathological consumer as its norm, Western consumer culture offers visions of normality that people are asked to engage with. It is through the appropriation of otherwise fairly standardized, distant services and goods that consumers may cope with, and thus effectively come to terms with and reframe, ideals of the body and self. Rather than removing ideologies of asceticism and self-negation and replace them with ideologies of liberation and hedonism, commercial culture has promoted the combination of hedonism and asceticism through commodities that promise balance.[25] It is through the appropriate, tamed but joyous enjoyment of certain goods that consumers can demonstrate their command of themselves and their bodies.

A number of works have taken a more nuanced view of the new hedonistic directions taken by commercial societies. Colin Campbell saw its roots in British romanticism.[26] Chandra Mukerji traced the mixture of hedonism and asceticism to the Renaissance.[27]

[24] A. Wernick, *Promotional Culture: Advertising, Ideology and Symbolic Expression*, London: Sage, 1991; M. Wykes and B. Gunter *The Media and Body Image*, London: Sage, 2005.

[25] R. Sassatelli, 'Tamed hedonism: choice, desires and deviant pleasures', in J. Gronow and A. Warde, *Ordinary Consumption*, London: Routledge, 2001, pp. 93–106.

[26] C. Campbell, *The Romantic Ethic and the Spirit of Consumerism*, Oxford: Blackwell, 1987.

[27] C. Mukerji, *From Graven Images: Patterns of Modern Materialism*, New York: Columbia University Press, 1983.

Many others point to the dawn of the twentieth century. Thomas Jackson Lears has shown for the United States how during the last two decades of the nineteenth century commercial culture promoted the secularization of the protestant ethic.[28] The emergence of a new type of ethic that blended hedonism and asceticism created a climate particularly favorable to consumption: the 'therapeutic ethic of self-realization' that pushed actors to try to develop themselves through goods and services dealing with health and physical appearance. Thus in commercially mediated leisure spaces, especially in the United States after the First World War, it became a virtual duty to 'have fun' and enjoy yourself. Having fun meant using one's body as a vehicle of gratification and pleasure. The body thereby became an arena that had to be explored and was visualized and appropriated for profit. The new ethic took hold of the middle classes. A 'quest for disciplined vitality' and 'for intense experience' was further stimulated by promotion of a variety of new goods (cosmetics, deodorants, make-up, etc.) and services (hairdressers, beauty salon, gyms, etc.).[29] Here was an instance of a larger cultural trend by which commercially mediated objects and techniques were created and deployed to rediscover the body in all its aspects. The body was conceived as a meeting point where the unconscious found expression and external demands repressed it.[30] Whilst still predicated on body-mind/self dualistic premises, this trend opened the way to incorporating into Western consumer culture Eastern notions of subjectivity that sought to transcend this very dualism.

These twentieth-century developments should be viewed as part of a longer historical process. In increasingly rationalized capitalist societies, or, as Norbert Elias would say, in ever more 'unexciting' societies, the 'compensatory' role of 'pleasurable excitement'—organized in specialized institutions and focused on specific practices as a form of 'controlled de-control' of emotions—has greatly increased.[31] The continuous, often strenuous, and never-ending disciplining of taste vis-à-vis one's own material and symbolic engagement with objects and places is intrinsic to the pleasures of consumption. Indeed, as we shall see, the normalization of the consumer as a key social persona has historically happened on the backdrop of an (admittedly unstable) harmonizing of hedonism and asceticism.

A second set of criticism levied at polemic interpretations concerns their textual bias. Textualism develops here at two different levels: at the macro-historical level, where abstract signs or images are given explanatory and causal power; and at the

[28] T. J. J. Lears, *No Place of Grace: Antimodernism and the Transformation of American Culture 1880–1920*, New York: Norton, 1981; T. J. J. Lears, 'From salvation to self-realization: advertising and the therapeutic root of the consumer culture 1880–1930', in W. Fox and T. J. J. Lears, *The Culture of Consumption: Critical Essays in American History 1880–1980*, New York: Pantheon Books, 1983, pp. 3–38.
[29] T. J. J. Lears, *No Place of Grace*, 1981.
[30] G. Vigarello, *Le corps reddressé*, Paris: Delarge, 1978.
[31] N. Elias and E. Dunning, *The Quest for Excitement: Sport and Leisure in the Civilizing Process*, Oxford: Blackwell, 1986, pp. 36ff.

micro-sociological, where consumers' meanings are derived from analyses of objectified promotional texts such as advertising messages and images. With regard to the former, they present a rather flat view of history, one where institutions, people, and social relations are mere shadows of the revolutionary postmodern reign of the commercial sign. Yet, in reality, the history of advertising images has been long and diverse and involved new professional knowledge and figures: advertising executives, marketing experts, shop-assistants—all of whom had quite stringent self and body presentational needs. Marketing and advertising were complemented by a number of other professionalized figures such as designers and fashion journalists. These so-called 'cultural intermediaries' participated in a broad process of institutionalization, which gave way to a variety of diverse collective actors (professional organizations, market watchdogs, consumer movements, etc.) who were busy in adding their portrayal of consumers, their wants and capacities.[32] With regard to the latter level, polemical interpretations have found it difficult to grasp the lived experience of consumers. Consumers are not simply bombarded by advertising images. They have to decode them and will do so in different ways according to locally situated forms of consumption, social relations and institutional contexts.[33] All in all, how we experience the body, manage corporeal identity, participate in social rituals, present ourselves as moral selves and so on is to a great extent mediated by consumer culture. But consumer culture cannot be reduced to a collection of signs or advertising images. Rather, it should be understood as lived culture, unfolding via situated interaction in specific institutional formations that have their own historical depth. As lived culture, consumer culture is made by living, embodied agents. Thus, we need not only to explore commercial images, but also embodiment, practices and their social organization.

TASTES, HABITUS, AND INDIVIDUALIZATION

In most cultures throughout history body decoration practices have been fundamental markers of social identity. In modern Western societies the human body has been invested with instrumental rationality, disciplined as an instrument for work and labour, a utility, a function, while continuing to operate as the paramount symbol for the subject to demonstrate his or her being in possession of a civilized self. Ever more sophisticated bodily markers indicate both 'diffuse social statuses' and individual 'character', that is, a person's 'conception of himself' and his or her 'normality' or 'abnormality'.[34] The process of individualization largely means that the sacred is translated at the level of the embodied self: a particular 'civilized' bodily conduct based on the 'internalization of social

---

[32] P. Bourdieu, *Distinction: A Social Critique of the Judgement of Taste*, London: Routledge, 1984 (1979).

[33] R. Sassatelli, *Consumer Culture: History, Theory, Politics*, London: Sage, 2007.

[34] E. Goffman, *Behaviour in Public Places*, New York: The Free Press, 1963.

controls' has become the norm.[35] A sort of 'air bubble' envelopes the body in ordinary life and helps people project a sacred, 'deep' self.[36] In late modern societies, body decoration, body marking, and various techniques of body modification (from plastic surgery to fitness training) are being commercialized as potent symbols of status and character, both for men and women. A variety of commodities thus serve as an ever more sophisticated identity tool-kit for the celebration of one's own identity. This not only entails unconscious *somatic involvement*—as tastes are embodied through habituation and imitation[37]—but also more reflexive *somatic investment* in the form of body modification strategies and body projects.[38]

For recent scholarship on consumption, the body and the self, Pierre Bourdieu's work has been seminal. Bourdieu has been a key contributor to a broader stream of thought that considers consumption as a ceremonial, communicative act. His unique emphasis, though, is on embodiment. Consumers operate though a sense of distinction which they have incorporated through taste. Consumers not only distinguish between goods in order to distinguish themselves. They cannot do anything but distinguish goods and themselves: that is, these are placed in different categories, included or excluded, according to their capacity for distinction. Although it is expressed in the apparently neutral and innocuous language of individual preference, taste 'marries colours and also people, who make "well-matched couples", initially in regard to taste'.[39] It is, thus, a generative and classificatory mechanism which simultaneously classifies the classifier and helps stabilize his or her social position. Bourdieu proposes a theory of practice whereby human action is constructed as something concrete and human experience is understood in terms of mimesis: to this end he elaborates the notion of *habitus*,[40] a system of dispositions, 'structured structures predisposed to function as structuring structures', which are written into the body through experiences reaching back to the first years of life. They work as an unconscious but extremely adaptable mechanism that orientates actors towards objects, themselves and others. Tastes are subjective realizations of the mechanism of *habitus*, which organizes consumption.

To this complex and finely calibrated description of *habitus*, Bourdieu juxtaposes a hierarchical and linear vision of social structure and its relationship with the structuring of taste. The individual *habitus* and the class *habitus* (defined by structural forms of *capital* derived from one's own professional position, education and social networking) stand in a relationship of *homology* to each other—that is, of 'diversity within homogeneity'. Embodied disposition thus works as symbolic power that naturalizes the existing system of power differences. For Bourdieu, the state of the body is itself the realization of a 'political mythology': lifestyle regimes reflect the cultural genesis of tastes from the specific point within the social space from which individuals originate, and

[35] N. Elias, *The Civilizing Process*, Oxford: Basil Blackwell, 2 vols., 1978/82 (1936/9).
[36] E. Goffman, *Behaviour*, and *Interaction Rituals*, New York: Pantheon Books, 1967.
[37] P. Bourdieu, *Distinction*.
[38] A. Giddens, *Modernity and Self-Identity*, Cambridge: Polity Press, 1991.
[39] P. Bourdieu, *Distinction*, p. 243.
[40] P. Bourdieu, *The Logic of Practice*, Cambridge: Polity, 1990, p. 53.

they are incorporated through the most elementary everyday movements inculcating the equivalence between physical and social space. Even 'in its most natural appearance…volume, size, weight, etc.' the body is a social product: 'the unequal distribution among social classes of corporeal properties' is both realized concretely through 'working conditions' and 'consumption habits', and perceived through 'categories and classification systems which are not independent' of such distribution.[41] Take the example of the contemporary health market. Here we find many different attitudes to the body and its state of health that correspond to different forms of health service consumption. The middle classes, generally speaking, tend to operate around the idea that they can and must control themselves, their bodies and their state of health. They thus have more medical check-ups, resulting in an effectively longer average life-span. By contrast, the working classes tend to adopt a fatalist attitude, not worrying about small illnesses and only reluctantly visiting the doctor in case of emergency, resulting in shorter lives.[42]

While *habitus*, in Bourdieu's theory, is a deep-seated often unconscious mechanism for the matching of taste and material culture, the strategic dimension of identity constitution through goods has been also foregrounded by theories of late modernity. Participation in the market is crucial for the accomplishment of individual identity in an age that Ulrich Beck and Anthony Giddens have called 'reflexive individualization'.[43] Much emphasis has been placed on the purposive individual stylization of oneself and one's body through consumer choices. As opposed to the polemical approaches discussed above, Giddens offers a more positive view of individualization which revolves on the notion of 'body projects': the idea that in late modernity the self becomes a reflexive and secular project which works on an ever more refined level of body presentation. At a time of cultural de-classification and growing emphasis on individuality, consumers can reappropriate symbols and use them in unanticipated ways. This involves unremitting self-monitoring, self-scrutiny, planning and ordering of practices and choices into a coherent display of identity—all of which might have its costs, but equally might allow consumers to resist the tyranny of the marketplace.

This positive view of individualization, however, has its own critical foundation. If for liberalism choice is just freedom, for these theorists choice is somehow compulsory. We are forced into it not so much by the drive of the capitalist economy but by the absence of a stable social and cultural order in post-traditional societies. We have 'no choice, but to choose', according to Giddens.[44] For Beck, '[l]iberalism presupposed a coherent identity, yet identity seems to be precisely the main problem of modern existence and is itself something to be chosen'; the self is thus 'a project which is directed to us by a

[41] P. Bourdieu, *Outline of a Theory of Practice*, Cambridge: Cambridge University Press, 1977, p. 51.

[42] On France see P. Bourdieu, *Distinction*; L. Boltanski, 'Les usages socials du corps', *Annales ECS*, 1971, 26 (1): 205–33; on the UK see M. Tomlinson 'Lifestyle and social class', *European Sociological Review*, 2003 19/ (1): 97–111; and T. Bennett, M. Savage, E. Silva, A. Warde, M. Gayo-Cal, and D. Wright, *Culture, Class, Distinction*, London: Routledge, 2009.

[43] U. Beck, *Risk Society: Towards a New Modernity*, London: Sage, 1992 (1986). Giddens, *Modernity*.

[44] Giddens, *Modernity*, p. 81.

pluralized world and must be pursued within that pluralized world'.[45] Of course, together with choice comes self-responsibility for the chosen self and risk-perception changes accordingly: now risks are in the region of anomy, linked to the incapacity to convincingly perform a positively valued self through one's own choices. As Giddens observes, late modernity confronts the individual with a complex diversity of choices which is 'non-foundational', produces anxiety and offers 'little help as to which options should be selected'.[46] The solution to such risk and anxiety to be found in consumer culture is, for Zygmunt Baumann 'technical':[47] it solves the problem of the durable and coherent self in the face of incessant non-foundational complexity by treating all problems as solvable through specific commodities. Each of them may be suited to a particular task, but they still have to be arranged in a coherent, credible whole. Lifestyle, as a reflexive attempt to create coherence, can be seen as a way in which the pluralism of post-traditional identity is managed by individual consumers and organized (or exploited) by commerce. Again Giddens stresses that in the context of post-traditional societies 'the cumulative choices that combine to form a lifestyle define the nucleus of a person's identity'. The 'very core of self-identity' is 'mobile' and 'reflexive', made of 'routinized practices [...] reflexively open to change'.[48] Lifestyle orders things into a certain unity, reducing the plurality of choice and affording a sense of 'ontological security'. Social reproduction is thus transferred from traditional culture to the market for goods (and labour). The notion of individual wants becomes central to economic growth just as standardized consumption patterns became central to economic stability, reducing risks not only for individuals but also for corporations. This may bring us to conceive of the self as a commodity itself. A process of self-commodification is indeed adumbrated with 'self-actualization [being] packaged and distributed according to market criteria'.[49]

The picture emerging from Giddens appears fairly distant from that offered by Bourdieu, yet both offer an account of the historical specificity of contemporary consumer culture. They have elicited quite different criticisms. One question concerns the peculiarly Western nature of this culture and the different relationship between body and mind-self in no less modern countries like China or Japan. Another concerns the historical continuities and discontinuities of habitus and reflexivity within Western modernity. On a theoretical level, Bourdieu's work on taste and distinction has been accused of providing a fairly hierarchical view of social stratification and determinist picture of reproduction via homology. Sociologists and anthropologists of consumption have called for greater attention to the internal complexity of consumer practices, especially their creativity and their capacity to generate classifications and styles that ultimately contribute to the continuous structuring of *habitus* in their own right.[50] For example, we know that women and teenagers engage with a range of popular cultural

[45] Beck, *Risk Society*, p. 131.
[46] Giddens, *Modernity*, p. 80.
[47] Z. Bauman, *Intimations of Post-Modernity*, London: Routledge, 1992, p. 200.
[48] Giddens, *Modernity*, p. 81.
[49] Ibid., p. 198. See also Z. Baumann, *Consuming Life*, Cambridge: Polity Press, 2007.
[50] Sassatelli, *Consumer Culture*.

commodities—books, films, TV series, music—and produce fan cultures that are inter-nally complex, irreducible to the meanings circulated by the media, and productive of highly specific forms of cultural capital.[51] Whilst far from being the direct expression of self-interested agents, domains or cultures of consumption may consolidate identities and dispositions that are *relatively* autonomous from structural divisions such as class, profession, gender, or ethnicity. In the case of youth sub-cultures or amateur practices, it is the practices of consumption themselves that create a structure for the standardiza-tion of taste. Thus it would be simplistic to say that wine-tasting is a fashionable middle-class practice which responds to middle-class cultural positioning. Participation in the culture of wine-tasting is not only a function of class membership. It produces classifica-tion principles that endow participants with competences other than class distinction.[52] Bourdieu's *habitus* helps us consider that it is not enough to postulate a relationship between embodied taste and the world of things, since the second does not generate the first, or vice versa. Still, we must not exaggerate homological effects. The encounter between embodied subjects and objects is creative: to understand how tastes and mate-rial culture find correspondences and are mutually shaped requires more attention to the local contexts of consumption, and in particular to the institutions which mediate acqui-sition and use, organize interaction and manners in ways which we consider appropriate, and propose narratives for the constitution of accountable, morally acceptable selves.

Attention to self-narratives is central to Giddens's and Beck's theories. They both stress reflexivity—with either a triumphant or a worried voice—as paramount charac-terization of the consumer. While investment in body presentation and self-projection are indeed strongly related to consumption in contemporary culture, theories of reflex-ive individualization run the risk of overemphasizing reflexivity. There is a tendency to provide a fairly abstract characterization of consumer identity to the effect of overlook-ing everyday consumer practices, their differentiation in terms of reflexivity and the entanglement with a variety of body dispositions and social identities not reducible to consumption. For a young, heterosexual Italian woman, for example, wearing a pair of jeans has a lot to do with how she manages her sexuality. At the same time, jeans can be used to neutralize one's own sexual appeal in certain contexts and to stress it in others. Sexualization, then, cannot be reduced to a commodity. Rather it draws on embodied dispositions that are often construed in opposition to commercial materiality.[53] The ten-dency towards the abstract consumer corresponds to a conflation of the normative aspect of identity-building and the practical aspect of agency constitution, which is much more embedded, varied, conflicting and contested, and which feeds back to the consumer as a normative social identity. We thus should be wary of considering consumption as a fairly disembedded reflexive activity and bring such grand theoretical view down to

[51] J. Radway, *Reading the Romance: Women, Patriarchy and Popular Literature*, London: Verso, 1987; S. Thornton, *Club Cultures: Music, Media and Subcultural Capital*, Cambridge: Polity, 1995.

[52] A. Hennion and G. Teil, 'L'attività riflessiva dell'amatore. Un approccio pragmatico al gusto', *Rassegna Italiana di Sociologia*, 2004, 45 (4): 519–42.

[53] R. Sassatelli, 'Indigo bodies: fashion, mirror work and sexual identity in Milan', in D. Miller and S. Woodward (eds.), *Global Denim*, Oxford: Berg, 2011, pp. 127–44.

what different consumers do in different contexts. When we consume, we do not reflect on everything, precisely because we act in practical ways. On the contrary, the meanings we attribute to our practices and the narratives with which we reflexively create our trajectory of consumption and present ourselves at least partly reflect the conditions in which we find ourselves and act. Such *bounded reflexivity* best characterizes the dialectic between consumption and embodied subjects. It corresponds to the fact that consumption not only expresses but also performs identity: through making objects their own, social actors make themselves, both as consumers and as embodied selves with specific and different roles linked to different identity markers such as ethnicity, gender, sexuality, which are loosely coupled with specific styles of consumption. The history of functional items such as hearing-aids offers a telling illustration. During the nineteenth century hearing-trumpets were used only by men even though deafness was also found amongst women. It was only in the twentieth century that hearing-aids were used by women and men. Yet hearing-aids were given gender-specific meanings. Women, advertisements promised, would once again become 'good listeners', while men would 'be able to interact better'. Women would regain 'closeness with their husband and family', while men would overcome their 'lack of authority' and the trials and tribulations of 'work'.[54] Through these objects and their distinct cultural framings, consumers effectively produce an image of themselves for themselves and others, an image which is credible in so far as it is appropriately gendered. Such taken-for-granted identities cannot be reduced to consumption alone.

One way to rectify the shortcomings of Bourdieu's homology and Giddens's reflexivity theses is to play one against the other. Cultural declassification surely allows for increasing possibilities of reappropriation as long-established social hierarchies are crumbling. Yet, reappropriation is not equally accessible to all. People who occupy different social positions and may count on different embodied dispositions appear to have different opportunities for appropriation. The phenomenon of the cultural omnivore is a case in point. Sociologist Richard Peterson has shown that for goods as different as food and music, strategies of consumption are emerging that are no longer expressed through just one genre, style, or taste following a clear distinction between 'high' and 'low' culture, but through an assorted mixing of different genres, forms and products.[55] Such omnivorous style values variety in and of itself. It allows individuals to choose between different commodities in a market where the infinitesimal differentiation of options makes it difficult to create a coherent aesthetic style. It also enables individuals to keep up with as large a number of social groupings as possible, increasing one's chances of being recognized as aesthetically competent. This form of appropriation stresses individuality but does not appear equally across society. In many Western countries today, the working classes appear culturally disadvantaged not because they do not appropriate a standardized culture in their own way, but because they are unable

---

[54] H. Schwartz, 'Hearing aids: Sweet nothings or an ear for an ear', in P. Kirkham (ed.), *The Gendered Object*, Manchester: Manchester University Press, 1996, pp. 64–82.

[55] R. Peterson, 'Understanding audience segmentation: from elite and mass to omnivore and univore', *Poetics*, 21 (1992), 243–58.

to command variety and consume a less varied basket of cultural goods.[56] The most eclectic individuals largely come from favourite social groupings that maintain a sense of hierarchy through their varied practices. We have here a kind of reflexive second-order distinction. They consume all sorts of culture but are careful to construct elaborated topographies of where, when, and with whom they consume different cultural goods. They tend to prefer 'cultured' genres for public, formal occasions and 'popular' ones for private settings.[57] All in all, consumption implies the appropriation of cultural hierarchies, but the capacity to translate and re-enact them in ways that fabricate symbolic capital is unevenly distributed. Conversely, commodities continue to act as markers of social distinction but in ways that are more or less reflexive according to a differentiated social mapping. Grand theoretical views are thus grounded with concrete empirical research, for example, by relating reflexive body projects to the particular self-presentational needs of the new middle class, who compete in job and relationship markets that require high levels of 'physical capital'.[58]

Not only homology and reflexivity are differently intertwined depending on their social mappings, different consumer goods, practices, and institutions also express homology and reflexivity in different degrees. Understanding these relationships thus requires attention to the specific domains of consumption where bodies, selves, and goods finally come together. There are fields of consumption, like sporting activities, where *habitus* is more reflexively worked upon, and one's own embodying certain class/gender dispositions as to self and body is purposively reframed.[59] As I will show below with reference to sport, certain practices are more in line with a theory of homology, others much less so. Thus, another way to revise the homology and reflexivity theses is to take seriously that consumption is a 'relatively autonomous and plural process of cultural self-construction' and 'stands for the diversity of 'local' social networks'.[60] The diversity of local networks is realized in the many consumer spaces and institutions that have come to populate contemporary urban realities. We know how historically the rise of consumer culture is linked to the spread of urban living and its many consumer spaces—from cafés to theatres, from cinemas to tourist villages, from restaurants to fitness centres. Part of their hold on consumers is that they offer situated, embodied experiences of locally relevant structured variety, drawing people into relatively separate realities where they can engage with a specific set of goods, activities, manners and identities. They offer the possibility of getting into organized contexts of involvement which arrange a world

[56] For recent empirical studies that develop and qualify Bourdieu's work, considering also Peterson's suggestions, see T. Bennett, M. Emmison, and J. Frow, *Accounting for Tastes, Australian Everyday Culture*, Cambridge: Cambridge University Press, 1999 and Bennett et al., *Culture, Class, Distinction*.

[57] B. Lahire, *La culture des individus. Dissonances culturelles and distinction de soi*, Paris: La Decouverte, 2004.

[58] P. Bourdieu, *Distinction*. See also M. Featherstone, *Consumer Culture and Postmodernism*, London: Sage, 1991.

[59] G. Noble and M. Watkins 'So, how did Bourdieu learn to play tennis? Habitus, consciousness and habituation', *Cultural Studies*, 2003, 17 (3/4): 520–38; R. Sassatelli, *Fitness Culture*.

[60] D. Miller, 'Consumption as the vanguard of history', in D. Miller, *Acknowledging Consumption: A Review of New Studies*, London: Routledge, 1995, pp. 1–57, esp. p. 41.

of internal rewards that is partly disjoined from broader social rules of relevance and gives vent to the peculiarity of local contingencies. They thus provide for learning experiences which may mobilize bodies and selves.

Consumer spaces are vessels for bounded reflexivity with their ceremonies, meanings, and narratives for self-constitution. They are domains of action mediated by commercial relations where we not only have to command reflexive choice to participate, but draw on a domain's internal repertoire that is largely taken for granted. Such repertoire may be more or less following class and gender distinctions standardized outside, in the broader social structure. Consumption practices thus play a role in how habitus is generated, sometimes more loosely, sometimes more tightly connected to social structures.

The domain of sport illustrates the differences between two contemporary institutions of consumption: the boxing gym and the fitness centre. The boxing gym, studied ethnographically by Loïc Wacquant, is an important space in working-class neighbourhoods where it offers its mainly male clients an 'antidote to the street', a 'dream machine' and a sub-culture of 'controlled violence' whereby the boxing habitus follows class habitus.[61] The fitness centre, which I have studied ethnographically, presents a different case.[62] It covers social groups that are so broad to be hardly distinctive. Indeed, precisely because the fitness gym is part of rather blurred mainstream cultural formations such as commercial body modification techniques (from cosmetics to plastic surgery), promotional imagery, and the representational needs of fashionable urban living, it promotes a habitus that is far less class bound. The carnality of the fitness gym is sanitized, managed excitement: fitness fans have to become 'excited to resist', embracing the joyous strenuousness of a practice that is all training, whereas the boxer has to resist the excitement of violence, learning to control very immediate fears and dangers.[63] In both cases, though, the control of embodied emotions—the capacity to generate pleasure in discipline, or pleasure in danger—is crucial and narratives of self revolve around this. What is more, both cases testify to the historically shifting articulation between specific body practices, their meanings and the hierarchical structure of society. Their class characterization has shifted across history as much as their institutional set-up. While boxing began as a noble, upper-class pursuit in elite clubs, gymnastics was for a long time expression of public health concerns and the military objectives of nation states over lower social strata. In the course of the twentieth century, boxing became increasingly associated with working-class culture and places. Fitness meanwhile evolved largely through feminized aerobics and masculine body-building, with ever new training regimes provided by a variety of commercial institutions geared to a rather universalizing picture of consumers' individual desires, aspirations, and needs. These different histories reveal the way each practice characteristically reflects and shapes structural elements, pointing to the uneven nature and differentiated fit between local, situated cultures of consumption and broader, long-established social structures. They also illustrate that subjects are shaped through pleasure and self-discipline in leisure rather than only through work or political institutions. Finally, they show that habitus stabilizes both through practice

---

[61] L. Wacquant, *Body and Soul*, Chicago: Chicago University Press, 2003, pp. 239–40 and 83.

[62] R. Sassatelli, *Fitness Culture*, pp. 177–8.

[63] Ibid., pp. 125–9.

and through narratives of self and body with which we confront broad cultural ideals, and legitimatize our tastes, accounting for our consuming passions.

In particular, keep-fit training is felt by fitness fans as 'a form of taking responsibility' that involves 'improvements' and 'changes' which are 'earned with your own sweat'.[64] Compared with the kind of epic which is articulated in the narration of the boxing habitus, these claims invoke a different carnality, emotional structure and relational set-up. Fitness gyms are not as closed as boxing gyms.[65] They have the feeling of mainstream urban culture rather than of a sub-cultural site.[66] In the lobby, the bar, and relaxation areas, people engage in small chat about everyday life. To be sure, clients who regularly attend generally improve their own performance. Some fitness fans suggest that they feel very 'gratified' by their trainers' recognition of their abilities. Overall, however, the creation of privileged, exclusive groups seemed to be marginal. Competition between members and the creation of exclusive elites generally remains discreet and is often stigmatized. In contrast to athletics, fitness gyms do not idolize performance, ability, and prizes. Instead, they promote pluralistic *abundance*. Just like contemporary consumer culture through which it is mainly channelled, fitness culture solves the problem of competition by offering non-competitive gratifications predicated on an infinite and diverse horizon of growth. There is always something more, something else, something new in fitness, something which can be adjusted to members' needs. The lack of direct opponents and the difficulty to get one's own achievements recognized in an official hierarchy are replaced by *novelty* and an emphasis on *self-experimentation*. Coming to see and feel one's own body though the regular practice of a variety of new activities is presented as a key feature. Regulars maintain that in order to continue training when exercise capacities improve, they constantly need to find new incentives, try more difficult things and explore modern techniques and trainers. Likewise, fitness trainers and managers insist that clients should consider their gym as a place where each person has to find a 'personal' way of training by using the array of techniques available and by making the most of all novelties. Coupled with the display of joyous commitment to the task, the creation of personalized and continuously renovated training programmes is itself a major device for the provision of non-competitive satisfaction. It cultivates a strong self which has learnt to like what is best for itself.

CONCLUDING REMARKS: THE CONSUMING DUALIS OF BODY AND SELF

We can now return to the normative power of the notion of the subject as a consuming animal. Typically modelled as individual choice, private consumption needs further legitimation, in that choice must be seen as not consuming the choosing self. From Smith

---

[64] Ibid., pp. 68ff and 190ff.

[65] Wacquant, *Body and Soul*, pp. 29ff.

[66] A. M. Klein, *Little Big Men: Bodybuilding Subculture and Gender Construction*, New York: State University of New York Press, 1993.

onward, the portrayal of the consumer as a rational, self-interested, forward-looking and autonomous hedonist who controls immediate pleasures for the sake of a long term project of well-being, has painted a picture of 'normality' that normalizes consumption: to consume properly, people must be masters of their will.[67] Consumers are sovereigns of the market in so far as they are sovereigns of themselves. The consumer's sovereignty is double-edged: hedonism, the search for pleasure, must be tamed by various forms of discipline which stress the subject's capacity to guide that search, to moderate pleasures, to avoid addiction, to be, in a word, recognizable as someone who chooses autonomously. Such normalization itself happens largely on a dualistic premise, where the body is the celebrated object through which the self gains value. Body practices are the crucial, if dangerous, terrain of self fashioning. The peculiarities of individual bodies herald a sense of individuality. This was increasingly appreciated in the late nineteenth century, as commodity standardization appeared as a potential threat to the development of human personality.[68] Bodies are both the source of our natural originality, and the flexible object of our will. They contain desire, the motor of choice, but also the potential of addiction.

The paradigm of 'addiction' helps explain the anxieties associated with consumption in the early modern period as well as today:[69] as fixed social hierarchies of goods and people recede, the fear that commodities will consume the self occupies an increasingly central place in the cultural repertoire used to understand and govern consumer practices. 'Addiction'—conceived as a disease of the will induced by a substance or an object—articulates concerns with disorder and works as 'the other' of autonomous choice with various 'addict identities' providing a dystopic image of the 'consumer'. Thus, while it amounts to a tiny fraction of consumer behaviour, compulsive consumption draws much attention because it stands for the boundary which consumers must not overstep if they want to appear convincing in their role as sovereigns of the market. The kleptomaniac, the immoderate gambler and the alcoholic have been coded as the outcome of an encounter between specific objects and contexts and dangerous social groups (women, working-class people, immigrants).[70] To this day, goods and products are differentiated according to how much they support the image of consumer sovereignty. For example, alcoholic drinks still have an ambiguous status because their consumption can be easily medicalized as pathological dependency. 'Drugs'—a category created to define certain discredited, risky substances—have ended up taking on a quasi-mythic status as generators of addiction.[71] While the boundaries of what is an addictive 'drug' and

---

[67] R. Sassatelli, *Fitness Culture*.

[68] M. Hilton, 'The legacy of luxury'.

[69] R. Porter, 'History of the body'; E. Sedgewick, 'Epidemics of the will', in J. Crary and S. Kwinter (eds), *Incorporations*, New York: Zone Books, 1992.

[70] E. Abelson, *When Ladies go A-Thieving: Middle Class Shoplifters in the Victorian Department Stores*, Oxford: Oxford University Press, 1989; A. F. Collins, 'The pathological gambler and the government of gambling', *History of the Human Sciences*, 1996, 9 (3): 69–100; M. Valverde, *Diseases of the Will: Alcohol and the Dilemma of Freedom*, New York: Cambridge University Press, 1998.

[71] See, for example, the social history of opium, V. Berredge and G. Edwards, *Opium and the People: Opiate Use in Nineteenth-Century England*, London: Allen Lane, 1987.

what is not are subject to ongoing debate, 'addiction' itself is one of the most powerful ways of stigmatizing all and every kind of consumption. The spectre of addiction can be invoked not only with respect to alcohol and drugs; every commodity can be described as causing dependence. The experiences of 'addictive consumers' are increasingly placed under scrutiny as a pathological sign of acquisitive mentality or 'epidemics of the will' said to characterize contemporary life.[72] In current medical practice addict identities have come to be defined in terms of subjective evaluations of a loss of control.[73] In this way otherwise healthy practices like dieting or physical exercise can become 'excessive'. When they spin out of an individual's control, they appear as abnormal or maniacal. Precisely because consumption *must* be constituted as a place for the expression of individual free will, preoccupation grows regarding the effective capacity of consumers to exercise their will in all circumstances. Utopias of total self-sufficiency are always lurking behind the pressure for becoming self-calculating and calculable and, coupled with a body-mind dualism, foster the perception of the body as an instrument of the self even in consumer domains which are predicated on the care of the body or on overcoming the very dualism.

The interconnection between bodies, selves, and consumer culture has been an increasingly central feature in modern societies. This articulation has taken place at three major levels: subjective, representational and institutional. First, how individuals realize themselves as embodied subjects—that is how they manage corporeal identity participating in social interaction and how they experience and perform self and body—is largely mediated via the use and representation of commodities. Second, the imagery associated with consumption has informed visual representation of selves in commercial culture, which in turn has come to revolve around the display of the body. Finally, a variety of consumer spaces, contexts and institutions have emerged that address the individual as a sensuous, embodied subject in search of personal gratification and social improvement. The various processes playing themselves out at these three levels have emphasized individual reflexivity but have nonetheless been tied to specific domains of consumption and their looser or tighter articulation with, at least, class and gender habitus. Consumer practices and cultures have been characterized by a changing mix of hedonism and asceticism that has shifted the direction of dualistic reasoning from repression to expression.

While there is agreement about the overall picture, the precise historical contours of these processes are yet to be explored. We need to know more about which social agents and institutions promoted which mix hedonism and asceticism, and how these have been justified or resisted to produce different images and practices of self and body. (Bounded) reflexivity has yet to be analysed as a historical process, if we want to gain a better understanding of the continuities and discontinuities between past and present,

---

[72] Sedgewick 'Epidemics of the will'; see also S. Eccles, 'The lived experiences of women as addictive consumers', *Journal of Research for Consumer Issues*, 2002, 4: 1–17.

[73] G. Reith, 'Consumption and its discontents: addiction, identity and the problems of freedom', *The British Journal of Sociology*, 2004, 55 (2): 283–300.

as well as internal differences among and between consumers at a given time. We thus need to tease out the limits of reflexivity and the embeddedness of habitus, considering the role that key market institutions like advertising have in the process. There may well be a gap between consumers' own characterization of themselves, their capacity to produce meanings through consumption, and the effects that these meanings have on broader social arrangements; ordinary 'folk' cultures of consumption and market institutions shape competing visions of normality. Finally, there is the need to address the interplay between everyday practices and normative discourses of consumption that relate to forms of embodiment and selfhood. Social agents position themselves differently with respect to dominant images of body, self, and consumption. These differences generate not only complexity but the dynamics of consumption. Contemporary research in history and the social sciences needs to examine both what people do practically and what people are thought to be normatively. It requires an imaginative use of sources to capture the interplay between practice and discourse, as well as further analytical work at the interface of history, sociology and anthropology.

BIBLIOGRAPHY

Baudrillard, J. (1998) *The Consumer Society: Myths and Structures*, London: Sage.

Bordo, S. (1993) *Unbearable Weight: Feminism, Western Culture and the Body*, Berkeley: University of California Press.

Bourdieu, P. (1984) *Distinction: A Social Critique of the Judgement of Taste*, London: Routledge.

Brewer, J. and Porter, R. (1993) *Consumption and the World of Goods*, London: Routledge.

Elias, N. and Dunning, E (1986) *The Quest for Excitement: Sport and Leisure in the Civilizing Process*, Oxford: Basil Blackwell.

Ewen, S. (1976) *Captains of Consciousness: Advertising and the Social Root of Consumer Culture*, New York: McGraw Hill.

Fox, W. and Lears, T. J. J. (1983) *The Culture of Consumption: Critical Essays in American History 1880–1980*, New York: Pantheon Books.

Giddens, A. (1991) *Modernity and Self-Identity*, Cambridge: Polity Press.

Sassatelli, R. (2007) *Consumer Culture: History, Theory, Politics*, London: Sage.

Wernick, A. (1991) *Promotional Culture: Advertising, Ideology and Symbolic Expression*, London: Sage.

CHAPTER 34

··

CONSUMPTION AND
WELL-BEING

··

AVNER OFFER

> He who binds himself to a joy
> Doth the winged life destroy.
> But he who kisses the joy as it flies,
> Lives in eternity's sun rise.
>
> William Blake, 'Eternity'

Consumption holds out a promise that does not always fulfil. It defines the standard of living—whether food is hot or cold, whether walls are dry or damp. It is the stuff of desires and dreams. It signals superiority, but also community. It drives policy and vexes scholars. But consumption is not consummation. Its purpose recedes even as it is being realized. This chapter opens with some standard assumptions about the benefits of consumption, and competing ones about its futility. It reports on social and behavioural research, and concludes with the insights of sages through the ages.

I

··

The historian Bill Rubinstein once said to me, 'there is no problem that cannot be cured by 50,000 dollars'. Sophie Tucker, the American cabaret singer, quipped, 'I've been rich and I've been poor; believe me honey, rich is better'. In the musical *Fiddler on the Roof*, Tevye the Milkman muses 'If I were a rich man...'. Those words express a commonplace and common-sense truism. They are endorsed by standard consumer theory in economics, which assumes that individuals can rank their different wants consistently, that they want as much as they can get, and that they act on their preferences. Wants become less compelling the more they are satisfied, so people shift their preferences sequentially to more pressing ones. But Want in general is insatiable, and the craving continues. It sustains a state of anticipation and consummation, it drives the modern economy and delivers a cornucopia of riches. Modern cornucopians justly claim that on a large number of dimensions, *It's Getting Better All the Time*.[1]

This serial fulfilment of transient desires may represent most people's sense of well-being. For many, perhaps most, this is good enough. In affluent countries, average consumption per head of market goods and services has increased by more than ten times over the last two centuries, and in Britain the United States between three to more than four times respectively since 1900. Outstanding progress has been made in life expectancy, education, nutrition, health, housing, transport, and many other aspects of material well-being. Consumer goods have improved even more: the digital music players of today are many times more capable than the gramophones of a century ago.

The substitution of one desire for another is plain to see. This progression can be expressed as the effect of a change of income on the demand for a commodity. The succession of wants can then be followed in the broad sweep of consumption broken down into a few main categories. Figure 34.1 shows this for the UK and the USA over the last century. Think of the nation as a single person. Although most consumption is done by the better off, consumption is more equally distributed than either wealth or income.

One of the few regularities in economics is that food outlays decline in proportion to consumption as income increases (Engel's Law). Figure 34.1 confirms that the appetite for food has physiological limits. Clothing is also an 'inferior good' in that sense (consumption rises less than income), due to rising efficiency in production, and declining value as a signifier of rank. Housing and transport have risen to fill the gap, and their share of consumption outlays has increased by some 15 percentage points over the century. Housing and transport need to be considered jointly, since there is a trade-off: outlying houses are cheaper, but are more costly to reach. Shelter is a necessity, but housing conveys a status signal. Two of its components are in limited supply: good location and social standing. As income rises, the supply of good locations and of social status does not keep pace, and so their relative price increases. In absolute terms, the rise has been much greater: housing has taken a larger bite of a much larger income. Quality improved as well, but the most important driver was land rent, that is, the price of location. Unlike many market commodities, the cost of shelter has actually risen with economic growth, and shelter is much the largest item of consumption.

In the United States after 1945, medical costs emerged from behind and eventually took second place to housing and transport (in the UK, these costs were mostly government rather than market expenditure). Of the other categories, 'recreation', at about one-tenth of outlays in the USA, remained stable, but shifted from the older consolations of alcohol and tobacco, to recreation and eating out, travel, culture, and books. The two countries' curves are not strictly comparable—the exclusion of healthcare increased the relative share of 'recreation' in the UK. And some minor categories are included for one country but not the other. But overall the patterns are similar.

---

[1] The title of a book by Stephen Moore and Julian L. Simon (Washington, DC, 2000).

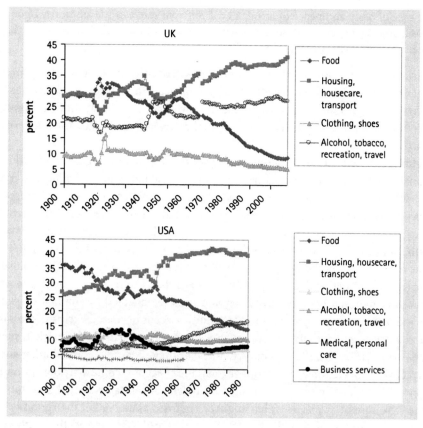

FIGURE 34.1 Percentage shares of consumer expenditure in the UK and USA.

Note: The two figures are not strictly comparable. US data are derived from constant 1987 prices, while the UK data are from current prices. The USA has much higher private spending on health care, though government spending in the two countries (in recent years at least) is comparable. Note also the data break in the series the UK in for 1966, when shifting from Feinstein to Office of National Statistics estimates (see sources below).

(*Sources:* United Kingdom: C. H. Feinstein, *National Income, Expenditure and Output of the United Kingdom, 1855–1965* (Cambridge, 1972), table 22, and UK Office of National Statistics, National Accounts: Household Final Expenditure at Current Prices, dataset natpe1 (electronic source, downloaded 30 June 2009), http://www.statistics. gov.uk/STATBASE/tsdataset.asp?vlnk=630&More=N&All=Y; United States: Stanley Lebergott, *Pursuing Happiness: American Consumers in the Twentieth Century* (Princeton, 1993), Appendix A, Personal Consumption Table.)

II

It is almost an alternative truism that happiness does not depend on wealth. 'Anybody who thinks money will make you happy, hasn't got money,' says David Geffen, a rich American media agent. 'Who wants to be a millionaire?' warbles the woman in Cole Porter's song—'I don't'. Adam Smith, the advocate of economic growth, wrote that

In ease of body and peace of mind, all the different ranks of life are nearly upon a level, and the beggar, who suns himself by the side of the highway, possesses that security which kings are fighting for.[2]

Two truisms are in conflict. Is the sustained growth of consumption necessary for well-being? During the last three decades, a large empirical effort in social science has tried to answer this question. We consider the findings first, then what they say about the benefits of consumption. Finally, we reflect on the 'wisdom of the ages', the legacy of millennia of discussion and debate.

Figure 34.1 used national income aggregates to estimate the growth of affluence. National income measurement came into common use in the 1950s. Politicians, economists, and the general public all embraced economic growth as a measure of prosperity. Maximizing it became the policy norm.[3] For example, the first President Bush stated his priority in 1989 as being 'to achieve the highest possible rate of sustainable economic growth'. But those who first devised the national accounts said that they were not suitable as measure of well-being. Simon Kuznets, doyen of the field, wrote, 'For those not intimately acquainted with this type of work it is difficult to realize the degree to which estimates of national income have been and must be affected by implicit or explicit value judgments.'[4] Already in 1933 he stressed that accounts based exclusively on market and government activity left out much welfare created outside the market, such as housework, leisure, and life expectancy, and that they measured some market payoffs incorrectly, by, for example, neglecting the psychic effect of income distribution, and the atrophy of individual human physical and intellectual capital. National accounts also counted as output many flows which might be regarded as bad rather than good.[5]

The public pursuit of growth after the Second World War ran together with public qualms about its futility, as in such bestselling works as J. K. Galbraith's post-materialist manifesto, *The Affluent Society* (1958). By the 1968 it was possible for the idealist Robert Kennedy, at that point a serious presidential candidate, to express such doubts in public:

Gross National Product counts air pollution and cigarette advertising, and ambulances to clear our highways of carnage...It counts the destruction of the redwood and the loss of our natural wonder in chaotic sprawl...Yet the Gross National Product does not allow for the health of our children, the quality of their education or the joy of their play. It does not include the beauty of our poetry or the strength of our marriages, the intelligence of our public debate or the integrity of our public officials...it measures everything in short, except that which makes life worthwhile.[6]

[2] Adam Smith, *Theory of Moral Sentiments* (Edinburgh, 1759), IV.I.10.
[3] Robert M. Collins, *More: The Politics of Economic Growth in Postwar America* (New York, 2000).
[4] Simon Smith Kuznets, Lillian Epstein and Elizabeth Jenks, *National Income and Its Composition, 1919–1938* (New York, 1941), p. 5.
[5] Simon Kuznets, 'National Income', in Edwin Seligman and Alvin Johnson (eds), *Encyclopaedia of the Social Sciences* (New York, 1933), vol. 11, pp. 207–11; Simon Kuznets, *National Income: A Summary* (New York, 1946), pp. 121–8.
[6] Robert F. Kennedy Address, University of Kansas, Lawrence, Kansas, 18 March 1968.

III

The national accounts measure all market exchange and government activity. They do not measure everything useful, and do measure some things which are not. A reasonable corrective was to 'extend' them beyond markets and government, and to impute a dollar value to the sort of goods and bads highlighted by Kuznets and Kennedy. This has been calculated repeatedly since the 1970s.[7] Extension begins by adding non-traded goods, primarily the product of housework and the value of leisure. The most striking result is that, taken together, the imputed dollar value of housework and leisure is much larger than market and government activity. Another step is to deduct 'bads'. The list commonly includes the cost of law enforcement, defence, commuting, and, more controversially, unemployment and divorce. Other large negative items are the cost of pollution and the depletion of natural resources.

Extending the national accounts has commonly converted the aggregate trajectory of economic growth into stagnation and even decline since the 1970s, mostly due to environmental degradation and resource depletion.[8] Modern economic growth is two centuries old, and it is easy to assume that it will just continue. In 1798 Malthus argued that the resources of subsistence placed a limit on the satisfaction of human wants. So far, so good—it hasn't happened yet. But growth over these two centuries was powered by a windfall of fossil fuels, by coal, oil, and gas. It is doubtful whether there is another two-centuries' worth of these resources, and the crisis of oil may arrive sooner. Most natural resources are finite, as is the planet's surface. But ingenuity is open-ended. Can it find a way to release solar and fusion power, which are potentially limitless? If the experience of well-being depends on continued economic growth, then the experience may not be sustainable.[9]

More optimistic extended accountants incorporate life expectancy, which continues to grow. This is usually done by estimating the financial value of life and adding it as income. When done this way, the aggregate extended income exceeds the rate of economic growth, although advocates of this procedure rarely undertake a complete goods-and-bads estimate. An alternative procedure would be (as in the case of other imputations of the financial value of life) to measure the value of extended life in terms of earned income. Since most of the extension of life takes place after the end of working years, it delivers little additional income. This is a criticism of valuing life financially, not of the desirability of longer lives. Another potential criticism (discussed further below), is that life expectancy has increased, but that this is not due entirely to economic growth, or at least not to consumption.

An implication of extended accounting is that people work for pay in order to support their well-being outside the market. Two items dominate the accounts: the imputed

---

[7] Avner Offer, *The Challenge of Affluence* (Oxford, 2006), pp. 16–21.

[8] Ibid., pp. 18–20.

[9] Erik Assadourian, 'The Rise and Fall of Consumer Cultures', in Erik Assadourian (ed.), *2010 State of the World: Transforming Cultures: From Consumerism to Sustainability* (New York, 2010), pp. 3–20.

value of leisure time (estimated in terms of the earnings sacrificed), and the value of household production, calculated in similar terms. Typically, the aggregate imputed dollar value of leisure is of the same order of magnitude as GDP, and household production adds another 25 to 45 per cent. So about two-thirds of the dollar value of satisfaction is deliberately sought in non-earning activities. Furthermore, in affluent countries like the UK and the USA, the public sector allocates between 30 and 50 per cent of GDP—citizens have chosen to pursue their interests increasingly in political rather than economic markets, in the form of public goods paid for by taxation, or of private ones produced within household. The share of market consumption in GDP in the UK has declined from about 80 per cent in the interwar period, to around 60 per cent since the 1970s, mostly due to the rise of the public sector. In the USA the share of consumption is higher (at around 70 per cent), but that includes private outlays on healthcare.

Market and non-market consumption complement and compete with each other. Under affluence, the rising component of expenditure, housing, and transport was largely spent on 'nesting', securing and equipping a home where the satisfactions of leisure and reproduction could find a place beyond the reach of market exchange: a haven from a heartless world. This is also captured by time-budgets: for more than a century, as people have grown wealthier, men have spent less time working for pay, while in recent decades, women have spent more. Overall, in the UK, average paid work per adult declined by almost a fifth between 1961 and 1984.[10] This implies a rising preference for non-market goods.[11] So one consequence of abundance is the rising cost of non-market goods. 'Rising real and shadow wages have made both leisure and unpaid household labour more expensive. Rising incomes have also made such normal goods as safety, health, a temperate climate, and the environment, more valuable.'[12]

A different approach to well-being is that it requires not abundance but adequacy—some goods are preconditions of well-being. Adequacy is taken to be an inventory of basic goods, such as access to nutrition, living space, clean water, sanitation, education, and health care. Such 'social indicators' are mostly physical rather than financial quantities, and they are not set out in an aggregate balance sheet of benefit and cost.[13] Instead, progress is measured over time, by means of household surveys. After the early household surveys of Frederick Morton Eden and David Davies in eighteenth-century Britain, investigation became more extensive and rigorous, with such familiar landmarks as the poverty surveys of Charles Booth, Arthur Bowley, and Seebohm Rowntree before the First World War, and more recent fixtures such the British government's Food and Family Expenditure Surveys. Such surveys express an impulse towards redistribution and social uplift.

---

[10] Calculated from Jonathan Gershuny, *Changing Times* (Oxford, 2000), table 8.1, pp. 224–5.

[11] Ronald Inglehart has argued that rising affluence has encouraged an increase with affluence of non-materialistic attitudes (e.g. in *Modernization and Postmodernization: Cultural, Economic, and Political Change in 43 Societies* (Princeton, 1997)).

[12] Dora L. Costa and Matthew E. Kahn, 'The Rising Price of Non-Market Goods', *American Economic Review*, 93.2 (2003): 227.

[13] Between the 1930s and the 1970s these were often called 'level-of-living indicators'.

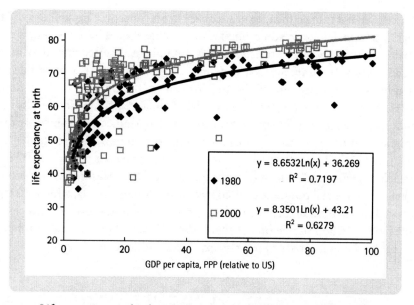

FIGURE 34.2 Life expectancy at birth, 1980 (173 countries), and 2000 (191 countries).

(*Source:* World Bank, *World Development Indicators* (Washington, DC, 2003). Accessed online via the Economic and Social Data Service International, through the Oxford University subscription.)

'There is no wealth but life,' wrote Ruskin.[14] A typical social indicator is life expectancy at birth. Figure 34.2 plots it at two points in time, 1980 and 2000, against income per head. This figure captures a typical feature of social indicators: that growing material abundance is associated with diminishing returns to well-being. Under indigence, a small improvement in material abundance delivers a large extension of life, but this almost ceases at quite low levels of income. Life expectancy rose for most countries between 1980 and 2000, for the poor as well as the rich. But thirty countries had better life expectancy than the United States (the richest country) in 2000, and a few achieved this at one-fifth of what American income per head had been twenty years earlier. American ranking in infant mortality was similarly low. This suggests that life expectancy is not driven by average levels of national income per head, and that it may depend less on consumer discretionary spending, and more on relevant knowledge, some of it quite simple, such as personal hygiene, eating habits, exercise, public health regulation, and primary health care. 'Rather than income, technology and the growing power of the state appeared to be the driving forces for improved welfare across countries.'[15] Equity and equality may count for more than income: some determinants of ill-being are social, like the overconsumption of food, alcohol, tobacco, and drugs, gun possession, and crime.

[14] John Ruskin, *Unto This Last: Four Essays on the First Principles of Political Economy* (London, 1862). Ruskin meant the quality of life, but the phrase can serve for quantity as well.
[15] Anthony Kenny and Charles Kenny, *Life, Liberty and the Pursuit of Utility* (St Andrews, 2006), p. 100.

Amartya Sen has framed the idea of adequacy in his concept of 'capabilities and functionings'. The principle of freedom implies that people should have discretion on how they arrange their lives (their 'functionings'), but to have that freedom, they require a set of 'capabilities'. These are not easy to define operationally, but they constitute a set of social indicators. This idea influenced the formation of the UN's Human Development Index (HDI), made up of life expectancy, education, and income. The results of such exercises are not consistent with market cornucopia. Higher incomes do not map directly onto higher well-being. In 2008, for example, fourteen countries scored higher on the HDI than the United States, which had the highest income per head.[16] Most recently, the French government has formed a commission on the measurement of economic performance and social progress, chaired by Sen and Joseph Stiglitz, which attempts to bring together the extended accounts and social indicator approaches.[17] At the other end, the bottom billion subsist on less than a dollar a day. At that level, consumption is not a luxury—the concept of poverty also expresses the idea of inadequacy.

IV

A completely different approach is that well-being is not an inventory of goods but a state of mind, a dynamic experience. All satisfactions, all incentives, all rewards, are ultimately in the mind. But other people's minds are not directly accessible. One way of probing them is to ask directly. This begins with a survey in which people are questioned about their happiness or life satisfaction, for example, 'Taking one thing with another, how would you describe your feeling today? Very satisfied, quite satisfied or not so satisfied?' The response is placed on scale of subjective well-being. When the question is about mood, the response is called 'happiness', when it is an evaluation of life, it is called 'satisfaction'.[18] Individual responses are then checked for their co-variance with personal attributes such as gender, income, employment, education, residence, and health. More than 3 million replies to this type of question have been collected in scores of countries, over sixty years.[19] The question itself may sound simple-minded, but the results are robust and revealing. The correlates of subjective well-being, their coefficients, and their signs replicate reliably and consistently across space and time.

Subjective well-being is related to income in a way similar to social indicators: it rises rapidly with income under conditions of indigence, but flattens out at low-to-middling

[16] This result may be attributable to higher inequality in the United States, which exacerbates the social and personal symptoms of low incomes (Richard Wilkinson and Kate Pickett, *The Spirit Level* (London, 2009)).

[17] Joseph Stiglitz, Amartya Sen, and Jean-Paul Fitoussi, *Report by the Commission on the Measurement of Economic Performance and Social Progress* (Paris, 2009).

[18] Richard Layard, *Happiness: A New Science* (London, 2005).

[19] Ruut Veenhoven, 'World Database of Happiness', http://worlddatabaseofhappiness.eur.nl/.

levels of income by international standards. Gender makes little difference. Women and men are approximately equally happy, and women at home and at work also have the same levels of happiness. Happiness is U-shaped with age, declining in the middle years and then rising again. Educated people are moderately happier. Small towns are happier places than big cities. Health and financial security make a difference, but are noticed more in their absence. The importance of income under affluence is not how much it can buy, but how it compares with what other people can spend ('relative' is more important than 'absolute' income). The level of a country's average income per head has only a very small influence on subjective well-being once other attributes are controlled for. The largest effect appears to be local history and culture. In international comparison (controlling for income), there are a large coefficients for particular countries. Latin American countries score highly on happiness despite low standards of living. Germany, Italy, and Spain score surprisingly low. The former countries of the Soviet Union are among those that come lowest. Some of the highest scores are found in the Nordic countries, which also score highly in social indicators.

Current Western affluent societies, with high levels of income, also have high levels of consumption, so we can use the two terms interchangeably. Reported subjective well-being is also high. The percentage saying they are 'happy' or 'very happy' is usually between the mid-80s and the mid-90s. That percentage is also quite robust over time. This is the 'paradox of happiness'. Over periods of decades, during which consumption has grown several times over, countries registered little change in the average level of reported subjective well-being. Furthermore, when particular individuals were followed over time, rising income also made no lasting change to the level of subjective well-being. At the same time, income continued to rise, in single-figure percentages, year after year—income has to rise exponentially for satisfaction to persist. One metaphor for this paradox is 'the hedonic treadmill'. This metaphor is consistent with standard consumption theory. Particular wants might be satisfied by incremental doses of arousal, but not 'Want' overall. It is also a feature of time use: the largest claim on discretionary time since 1960s has been television, whose output is ordered as a sequence of episodes structured as narrative. Before that, a visit to the cinema once or twice a week was a high point of daily life. Even earlier was following competitive sports, which provide sequential doses of anticipation. Betting on the outcomes has the same structure of commitment, arousal, and climax, often repeated week after week. Arousal was promised and provided by a progression of technologies, each partly displacing the other: music hall, gramophone, cinema, radio, black and white television, high-fidelity recordings, colour TV, video recorder, optical disk, personal computer, Internet, i-pod, and so on. The evidence of reported subjectivity is that people on the whole experience this consumption sequence as well-being. They also support the parties and policies that promise to sustain it.

In many respects we live today in the best of all present and previous worlds. Economic growth has lifted billions out of poverty. Income per head has never been higher. Life has never been more comfortable, healthier, and longer. Consumption is celebrated in such works as Stanley Lebergott's *Pursuing Happiness*, which take increasing material wealth as synonymous with well-being.[20] Basic material needs are indeed a high priority for society, and form the precondition of both contentment and dignity. There is also a more ideological agenda. If material affluence is the source of individual well-being, then it should be the highest social priority as well. Market advocates assert the invisible hand doctrine, namely that the pursuit of self-interest delivers maximum aggregate wealth. The material consumption view of well-being implies, in their view, a preference for market-and-business-friendly policies. But during the last hundred years government and taxation have grown even faster than markets, and much of the increase of well-being may be attributed to services such as education, health, and social insurance, that are typically public. Other views of well-being remain even more sceptical about unfettered market competition, and seek the sources of happiness elsewhere.

V

In social science research, the main qualms about individual consumption as the prime source of well-being arise out of the dynamics of hedonic experience. Once out of indigence (and in some instances even within it), the rise of consumption does not consistently and reliably increase sustained reported subjective well-being, and is also associated with a range of disorders. Taking these qualms in sequence, we consider relative income, habituation, materialism, history and culture, advertising, myopia, narcissism, and individualism.

In economics, what people are supposed to maximize is absolute levels of income. Economic man is regarded as autonomous and impervious to the opinion of others, unless he chooses voluntarily to take them into account. This runs counter to common sense, and, since the 1970s, a broad movement of psychologists and dissident 'behavioural' economists has rejected this a priori reasoning in favour of empirical investigation of individual choices, both in laboratory settings and in questionnaire surveys of population samples. The findings are that, contrary to the assumptions of standard economic consumer theory, income is valuable largely for comparison. In defining their aspirations, people usually selected targets about one-third higher than their current income. If these aspiration curves are plotted, they are concave, like the relation between income and subjective well-being.[21] Rising income relative to that of others reliably increases subjective well-being. The rich are happier than the poor. But an absolute improvement for everybody over time, a rise in national income per head, has no such effect. Social psychologists have identified an 'endowment effect', in which mere possession raises the subjective value of artefacts above their market value. A corollary of this is 'loss aversion'—people experience a loss more intensely than a gain of the

---

[20] Stanley Lebergott, *Pursuing Happiness* (Princeton, 1993). Also Moore and Simon, cited n. 1.
[21] Richard Coleman, Lee Rainwater, and Kent A. McClelland, *Social Standing in America: New Dimensions of Class* (1978), ch. 17.

same objective magnitude, as measured in dollars. For example, over a sample of forty countries, being in the lower third of the income distribution, decreased happiness by twice as much as being in the top third increased it.[22] This places economic growth in a somewhat different light: it is not a matter of gaining satisfactions, but of avoiding loss: any lapse of economic growth is likely to pull satisfaction down.

Social relations count in other ways. Subordination depresses subjective well-being. A lower social rank is associated with shorter life expectancy, higher morbidity, obesity, probability of crime, and teen pregnancies.[23] This would seem to contradict Adam Smith's view that the beggar is as happy as the prince. His views can be saved by noting that people of lower income and status still remain remarkably happy despite their objective adversities.

One clue about well-being is provided by the evidence of ill-being. In affluent societies, about one-tenth of people report low satisfaction scores in well-being surveys. Unhappiness is associated with the absence or loss of social connection. The highest likelihood of low subjective well-being is among the unemployed, the separated, the divorced, widowed, and single. Mental disorder, another source of intense unhappiness, is also a form of social disconnection. Its social incidence is inversely related to the level of average income per head, and is higher in wealthy market societies. Racial and ethnic minorities also suffer. Inter-personal regard appears to be a condition of well-being. The consumer of economic theory is solitary, but no punishment is worse than solitary confinement. No wonder that people invest so much in domesticity—the family is the most enduring and reliable source of interpersonal relations.

By the 1970s scepticism about the benefits of growth had become widespread, even in the United States, the most materialist of affluent societies. In his 'malaise' speech on 15 July 1979, President Carter said that

> We've discovered that owning things and consuming things does not satisfy our longing for meaning. We've learned that piling up material goods cannot fill the emptiness of lives which have no confidence or purpose.

His opponent, Reagan, soon won an electoral landslide, but this should not be taken as a blanket endorsement of materialism. Thirty-six millions still voted for Carter (83 per cent of the Reagan vote), and 47 per cent did not vote at all.

We have seen that consumption signals status. It can also help to define self-identity, and to signal social connection. Through the medium of reciprocal exchange, emulation, and gifting, commodities underpin social bonds. The anthropologist Daniel Miller affirms 'the centrality of relationships to modern life, and the centrality of material culture to relationships'.[24] Consumption is a dialect of affinity, and goods are its vocabulary.

---

[22] Offer, *Challenge of Affluence*, pp. 276–278.

[23] M. Marmot, *The Status Syndrome* (London, 2004); R. Wilkinson and K. Pickett, *The Spirit Level* (London, 2009); R. Sapolsky, 'Social Status and Health in Humans and Other Animals', *Annual Review of Anthropology*, 33 (2004): 393–418.

[24] Daniel Miller, *The Comfort of Things* (Cambridge, 2008), p. 287.

Another social dimension is captured by the notion of 'Keeping up with the Joneses', a term which originated as the title of a comic strip that ran in American newspapers between the wars.

At the individual level, 'materialists' are defined as those who value possessions and money higher than human relations. Several studies have found such people are likely to score lower on subjective well-being and other measures of satisfaction than people with a more social, reciprocal, or altruistic orientation. The hypothesis is that for such people consumption is used as a substitute for human relations, essentially as a substitute for love.[25] Advertising certainly strives to suggest that the purchase of goods will provide the emotional fulfilment of human interaction. It is full of cues of relationship and reciprocity. I found, for example, in a sample of more than 1,000 ads in American magazines in the 1950s–1960s that almost two-thirds communicated smiles. Economics assumes that people make autonomous consumption choices. The existence of advertising suggests that they are open to persuasion. Advertising has an informative function (although that function is in conflict with the theoretical assumption of a fully informed consumer). But a good deal of advertising appeals to interpersonal comparisons and emotional cues.

The standard economic model of consumption invokes the sort of desires that motivate Roald Dahl's children's book *Charlie and the Chocolate Factory*, where unlimited chocolate is the ultimate fantasy of consumerist fulfilment. Economics assumes that satisfaction is an individual matter of getting more. But if that is not the true road to fulfilment, then consumption is likely to disappoint. There is some evidence that young people in the USA in recent decades have increasingly embraced the primacy of individual self-regard, and have formed exaggerated views of their own ability, prospects, and talent. The corollary is an increasing amount of disappointment and heartbreak, with a large rise in recent decades of anxiety, drug addiction, and mental disorder.[26] Not Charlie though. In the *Chocolate Factory*, the owner grants him the keys to the factory, but Charlie will not take them unless his family can join him too.

Families are the locus of connection. In the 1950s, in the first flush of post-war affluence, families in the affluent West invested in domesticity as never before. Education and birth control soon gave women more of a choice between occupational and domestic satisfactions. This discretion (and the freedom to leave an oppressive relationship) enhanced the autonomy of adults, who increasingly had the choice of avoiding domestic commitment or dissolving it, but there is evidence that family instability undermined the prospects of children. English-speaking countries have experienced rising divorce, increase in family breakdown, worse outcomes for children of divorce, and the rise of anxiety, depression, and other symptoms of mental distress. If secure interpersonal relations are the key to well-being, then the possessive individualism of recent consumer societies may produce some unhappiness as well.

[25] Tim Kasser, *The High Price of Materialism* (Cambridge, MA, 2002).

[26] Jean M. Twenge, *Generation Me: Why Today's Young Americans Are More Confident, Assertive, Entitled—and More Miserable Than Ever Before* (New York, 2006).

VI

If insatiability is the vortex at the heart of consumption, there are other problems too. In standard economic theory consumers rank preferences in the present, but the most significant choices arise not between two immediate substitutes (say coffee or tea) but between the present and the future. Consumption is experienced over time—reward can be immediate, but may also require waiting. Compare the purchase of recorded music with learning to play an instrument. The economic discounting algorithm that provides the standard solution is to 'maximize net present value', but, in reality, choice over time is a difficult problem to solve.

An immediate passion can override permanent interests. With no direct access to the intensities involved, there is no objective method of choosing between a preference between 'one houre' of bliss, and 'all else ever' (as in John Donne's poem 'The Feaver'). This is the problem of 'time-inconsistency'. This type of choice is algorithmically intractable. Choice over time is also hard for other reasons. There seems to be an intrinsic myopic bias for immediate payoffs. 'Now has emotional power, and delay does not.'[27] The future is more inscrutable further out. Circumstances change. The calculating brain is overridden by its emotional parts. Time-inconsistency is pervasive.[28]

The implications are radical: no calculation can work out the optimal choice. But choices still have to be made. It is difficult to make a sacrifice now for the sake of something better later. Call this the commitment problem. Take a degree or apply for a job? Get married, or walk away? When calculation is intractable, people fall back on ready-made solutions evolved by society: call them 'commitment devices'. Conventions, norms, and institutions provide guidance in recurring situations. There are personal strategies of self-control, like willpower and personal rules ('no eating between meals'). Social commitment devices are more extensive, and rely on third-party monitoring. Numbers and time also provide commitment devices. A weekly rest day controls the compulsion to work. Commitment devices evolve, develop, and decline. Paper money is efficient, but is tempting to print. The Victorian gold standard provided a commitment device. Gold is a hard constraint, 'difficult to make and difficult to fake'. Private insurance and compulsory taxation are mandatory prudential payments. Statutory law restricts choice. Constitutions bind legislators. 'The great use of Government is as a restraint', wrote Edmund Burke.[29] Commitment forms the fabric of civilization. In contrast to the hedonics of indulgence, it may be commitment that underpins well-being.

Personality, class, family, culture, ideology, policy, national character all define priorities and obligations at different ranges of time. For the individual, society helps to achieve self-control. For society, the failure to commit is a nuisance. Defection does not

---

[27] David Laibson.
[28] Avner Offer, *The Challenge of Affluence*, chs 3–4. A valuable resource is George Loewenstein, Daniel Read and Roy F. Baumeister (eds), *Time and Decision* (New York, 2003).
[29] Edmund Burke, *Thoughts and Details on Scarcity* (London, 1800).

only harm the defector, but also those who might have gained from his cooperation. The criminal, the truant, the latecomer impose costs ('externalities') on others. By analogy, a harmful myopic preference can be seen as 'internality', an inconsistency (e.g. addiction) which consumers inflict on themselves. People vary in their capacity for commitment, and also in their access to its tools. Those who have more education and more wealth find self-control easier, and, with more to anticipate, also more worthwhile.

Myopia suggests that in contrast to economic consumption theory, what people end up choosing cannot be taken as a reliable measure of their welfare. Choice is fallible. The 'hedonic treadmill' may be why surveys fail to detect rising satisfaction as income rises in affluent societies. The psychic mechanism that diminishes pleasure is habituation: continued arousal reduces its effect. This is also familiar from economic consumption theory as the concept of 'diminishing returns'.

A second reason is comparison—if everyone is improving equally, no one gets ahead. 'When everybody is somebody, then nobody is anybody.'[30] Losing status is more painful than gaining it is pleasurable, so economic growth with rising inequality can generate more pain than pleasure. Competition is compelling and imparts a warm glow to the winner, but can be painful to others.

One notion of well-being is purely hedonic, not of maximizing arousal, but a comfortable bodily and mental state. The flow of inputs should match the capacity to absorb them. True prosperity is a good balance between short-term arousal, and long-term security.[31] One writer calls this experience 'flow', another calls it 'pacing'.[32] In economics, consumers are assumed to be insatiable. In reality, the flow of new rewards can swamp the capacity to enjoy them. The challenge is not to maximize consumption, but to pace it back to the level of optimal satisfaction. That means a little slack. It means preferring quality (scarce by definition) over quantity. Creating such collective capacity is partly a task for government. For example, the legacy of high culture, theatre, visual arts, music, inherited from the past, requires re-investment, to reproduce existing assets and create new ones, and to teach people to enjoy them.

The cornucopian flow of novelty contains both goods and bads. It is difficult to evaluate the long-term consequences of innovations. Cigarettes were taken up avidly when they became cheap around 1900, and by the mid-century, about three-quarters of UK men were smoking. Moore and Simon, in their cornucopian book, hail the decline of smoking, but they might as well have hailed its increase as well, since it increased consumer satisfaction. Other satisfactions in their book may yet follow the trajectory of smoking. It takes time to form commitment devices, and if the pace of novelty is fast, then choice will acquire an increasingly short-term bias. The flow of new rewards can undermine the capacity to enjoy them.

---

[30] W. S. Gilbert, *The Mikado*.

[31] D. E. Berlyne, *Conflict, Arousal, and Curiosity* (New York, 1960); Tibor Scitovsky, *The Joyless Economy: The Psychology of Human Satisfaction* (rev. edn., New York, 1992).

[32] Mihaly Csikszentmihalyi, *Flow: The Psychology of Happiness* (London, 1992); George Ainslie, *Picoeconomics: The Strategic Interaction of Successive Motivational States within the Person* (Cambridge, 1992).

Economic historians as a group are particularly keen on the merits of growth. More than other historians they tend to judge the past by current economic yardsticks. From this perspective consumption is the latest form of the 'idea of progress'. Most periods of history had lower levels of income than affluent societies today, with all the attendant suffering, so the focus on growth is justified. Other historians are more aware of the tragic dimension (we all die), and the pervasiveness of intractable dilemmas. Economic growth has raised the standard of living, but there is no certain way of achieving it. It may, like happiness, arrive in the process of working for something else. Striving for status seems to be a constant of history, which is not easy to change, not even by increasing equality, which makes even the small advantages of others more salient. That may be why the futility of affluence has concerned writers so early in history. Improving one's own economic position is more rewarding than raising prosperity for everyone. Economists argue that the first is a condition of the second. But that view is counterintuitive and has gained more acceptance in the United States than elsewhere. Modern economic growth is only about two hundred years old. For long periods before, levels of income and consumption did not change much. In those conditions, it is the mobility of individuals, rather than non-existent growth, that attracts attention from historians.

VII

Social and behavioural research in the last three decades has found that 'there is much more to well-being than simply being well-off.'[33] This resonates with our second truism about the futility of affluence, and also captures the 'wisdom of ages' over three millennia. Most sages lived in times when standards of living were lower than today. We regard them as wise since their thoughts are still read. They might, however, be biased, with personal attributes and endowments that were different from most, and also unrepresentative in a more mundane sense, as being either wealthier, or poorer.

Social science writers about well-being are not much concerned with ethics, but writers on ethics have a good deal to say about well-being. There is no agreement about the Good, and none may be possible. Morality is less clear-cut than fact. Conceptions of the Good divide roughly into those who emphasize pleasure, and those that assign priority to fulfilment of duty. The association of well-being with duty and virtue is an ethical dimension of the pursuit of well-being. Good personal relations require reciprocity. Reciprocity is voluntary, and requires trust—which is a virtue. Social standing has been shown to be one of the main sources of well-being. It requires conformity with social norms. In ancient Greece, this involved being a good citizen, ready to sacrifice time, treasure, and blood for the *polis*.

Unlike social science, the 'wisdom of the ages' is not empirical but speculative. It is a sequence of opinions. The whole range of views emerged in antiquity. Aristotle held that

[33] Angus Campbell, *The Sense of Well-Being in America* (New York, 1981), p. 71.

well-being is achieved when man is true to his nature. Humans are by nature social beings, who are bound to society in a web of obligation. Well-being constitutes the exercise of virtue. The highest virtue is that of disinterested reflection, which is given only to the wise. In contrast, the Epicureans equated hedonic experience with the good life, but this was more passive than active, and laid some stress on restraint. The Cynics, and after them the Stoics, took virtue to be the precondition of well-being. True wisdom would overcome destructive desires. They dismissed the relevance of material provision to these ends.

Religion typically sets other-worldly objectives. Buddhism scorned worldly pleasure. Christianity taught acceptance and resignation. Fast-forward through the centuries, the Enlightenment (reacting to the passivity of religion) specified personal freedom as the highest good. The focus on pleasure at the core of modern consumption theory goes back to Bentham and the eighteenth century. Adam Smith had a social utilitarian conception of the Good, but he admired the Stoics, and had his own theory of virtue. This was his concept of the 'impartial spectator'. According to Smith, the main purpose of wealth was to attract the good opinion of other people. This good opinion needed to be earned by praiseworthy behaviour. It needed to pass muster with an hypothetical impartial spectator, whose viewpoint the individual was urged to adopt. Even if he failed to obtain the recognition he deserved, he would 'be more indifferent about the applause, and, in some measure, despise the censure of the world; secure, that however misunderstood or misrepresented, [he] was the natural and proper object of approbation.'[34]

Enlightenment thinkers who accepted pleasure as the final end still left a role for virtue, albeit of a more circumscribed form. Not the other-directed virtues of altruism or reciprocity, but the Epicurean ones of self-control, moderation, temperance, and prudence, which are necessary in order to experience the satisfactions of pleasure. Enlightenment writers understood the problem of time-inconsistency: the need to sacrifice immediate satisfactions for the sake of future ones, and to adjust the flow of stimulation to the capacity to enjoy it. They did not fancy the chocolate-factory hedonics of modern consumption theory. A striking example is the teaching of Malthus: succumbing to the 'passion between the sexes' would lead to over-population, and would depress living standards to the level of subsistence. These passions would eventually be checked by pervasive misery and vice. Hence well-being required the prudential check of sexual moderation.

This tension between the individual and society pervades Enlightenment thinking. Jeremy Bentham reduced human motivation to the pursuit of pleasure and avoidance of pain. Bentham, and the utilitarians in general, then made a leap from individual maximizing to the social kind, and proclaimed that the pleasure that counted was 'the greatest good of the greatest number'. This altruistic orientation was not self-serving but virtuous, which may be regarded as an inconsistency. This inconsistency was discarded by twentieth-century libertarians and egotists, who (in various guises) asserted that a person's only obligation was to himself. In the guise of rational choice, this doctrine has largely displaced utilitarianism as the dominant ethic. But amoral self-regard may ultimately be self-defeating, due to the centrality of social connection, reciprocity, and

---

[34] Adam Smith, *The Theory of Moral Sentiments*, (6th edn. London 1790), Bk III, i. 5.

approbation in the experience of well-being. It also goes against many people's ethical intuitions. At the other extreme, the philosopher Peter Singer has questioned whether affluence can be regarded as ethical so long as indigence continues in other parts of the world and recommended that ten per cent of income should be voluntarily transferred to the poor by every person of average income or above.[35]

Democratic institutions and political rights are associated with higher subjective well-being, controlling for wealth.[36] This highlights two other dimensions of well-being, namely freedom and justice. During the Cold War a common catchword was 'better dead than red'.[37] License plates in the State of New Hampshire proclaim 'live free or die'. Without probing too deeply into the concept of freedom, these sentiments are another claim that there are values higher than wealth, indeed higher than life itself. Amartya Sen has argued that even in a state of indigence, individual discretion ranks above basic needs, although (in a contradiction which is not resolved), the satisfaction of basic needs is also a condition of freedom. The dilemma arose starkly under 'development dictator-ships' such as those of the Soviet Union, Communist China, and the Asian Tigers, all of which combined decades of sustained economic and consumption growth with a denial of political and individual freedoms, and always in the name of the common good. The craving for freedom can be at odds with the quest for justice. Social science experiments have demonstrated that people value fairness and are willing to make material sacrifices in order to satisfy a desire for justice. The issue is addressed in the most influential work of post-war political philosophy, John Rawls's *Theory of Justice* (1971). Rawls regards ine-quality as undesirable and unjust, but is willing to tolerate as much of it as will maximize the position of the worse off. This begs a question: how is the position of the poor to be measured given the findings of social scientists about the priority of relative over abso-lute income? It may be surmised, however, that Rawls has been popular because he justi-fies the inequality that people accept as part of their own quest for wealth and status.

In general, the work of Enlightenment writers, from the eighteenth century to the present, strove to underpin morality by reason. Although these efforts have had an impact, they cannot be said to have succeeded. Likewise, the pursuit of well-being, whether by means of consumption or by means of restraint, gives rise to intractable dilemmas.

VIII

The pleasures of life are more equally distributed than income and wealth. A glass of wine, a cup of coffee, a puff of tobacco, affection, romantic love, the sounds of music and contemplation of art, a gripping novel, the joy of children, a view of the clouds, the sunset or the sea, are within reach of almost everyone. 'Sur le plus haut trône du monde, on n'est jamais assis que sur son cul', wrote Montaigne. In an engaging and learned survey of

[35] Peter Singer, *Practical Ethics* (2nd edn., Cambridge, 1993), ch. 8.
[36] John Helliwell and H. F. Huang, 'How's Your Government? International Evidence Linking Good Government and Well-Being', *British Journal of Political Science*, 38. 4 (2008): 575–93.
[37] Originating in Nazi Germany.

conceptions of well-being through the ages Władyslaw Tatarkiewicz says nothing about consumption. All the more extraordinary (or perhaps understandable), given that he wrote it in German-occupied Warsaw during the Second World War, while being cut off from the most basic comforts.[38]

A preference for high thinking and plain living implies that the damaging detriments of materialism can offset its benefits. One repository of this tradition is the monastic and hermetic tradition, which continues unbroken from early Christianity to the present, and which has parallels in other cultures. Christian monasticism managed to combine plain living with trappings of grandeur. Buddhist monasticism (sometimes grand too) is even more demanding: every day is a new quest for alms. The Enlightenment has sought the equivalent in nature, which stands for untrammelled simplicity. Rousseau celebrated the noble savage and sought solace out of doors. Well-being requires an inner freedom from the compulsion to consume. This brings together the virtues of self-control and the benefit of freedom. This rejection of craving can be conservative or radical. Here it is from Edmund Burke, responding to the excesses of the French Revolution, which Rousseau had inspired:

> those are qualified for civil liberty in exact proportion to their disposition to put moral chains upon their own appetites...Society cannot exist unless a controlling power upon will and appetite be placed somewhere, and the less of it there is within, the more there must be without. It is ordained in the eternal constitution of things, that men of intemperate minds cannot be free. Their passions forge their fetters.[39]

Similar thoughts have engaged the American transcendentalists, European romantics, Tolstoyan ascetics, and contemporary downshifters.[40] Both John Stuart Mill and Maynard Keynes thought there was a prudential limit to craving, and that economies would settle at a steady state. The basic intuition may simply be that well-being consists of pitching expectations lower than endowment. It is told of Alexander the Great that he went to pay homage to the philosopher Diogenes, whose abode was a wooden tub by the roadside. Alexander enquired of the philosopher whether he could do anything for him. Diogenes asked him to stop obstructing the sunlight. Alexander responded, 'if I were not Alexander, then I should wish to be Diogenes.' This captures something of the intractable duality of well-being.

BIBLIOGRAPHY

De Botton, Alain, *Status Anxiety* (London, 2004).
Diener, Ed, and Biswas-Diener, Robert, *Happiness: Unlocking the Mysteries of Psychological Wealth* (Oxford, 2008).

[38] Władyslaw Tatarkiewicz, *Analysis of Happiness* (The Hague, 1976).
[39] Edmund Burke, *A Letter from Mr Burke, to a Member of the National Assembly* (London, 1791).
[40] For the USA, see David E. Shi, *The Simple Life: Plain Living and High Thinking in American Culture* (rev. edn, Athens, GA, 2007).

Kasser, Tim, *The High Price of Materialism* (Cambridge, MA, 2002).

Kenny, Anthony and Kenny, Charles, *Life, Liberty, and the Pursuit of Utility: Happiness in Philosophical and Economic Thought* (Exeter, 2006).

Layard, Richard, *Happiness: Lessons from a New Science* (London, 2005).

Lebergott, Stanley, *Pursuing Happiness: American Consumers in the Twentieth Century* (Princeton, 1993).

Miller, Daniel, *The Comfort of Things* (Cambridge, 2008).

Moore, Stephen and Simon, Julian Lincoln, *It's Getting Better All the Time: 100 Greatest Trends of the 20th Century* (Washington, DC, 2000).

Offer, Avner, *The Challenge of Affluence: Self-Control and Well-Being in the United States and Britain since 1950* (Oxford, 2006).

Tatarkiewicz, Władyslaw, *Analysis of Happiness* (The Hague, 1976).

INDEX
....

Activism *see* **Consumer activism**
Advertising
  children's consumption 590
  luxury as common parlance 173
  modern colonialism 472, 476
  modern Japan 491
  Nazi Germany 436–437, 439
  seventeenth-century Britain 66
  urban consumption 192
Africa
  impact of pre-colonial Africa on
    globalization
  accommodation of consumer demand in
    East Africa 102–106
  consumer trends before 19th
    century 89–91
  importance of pre-colonial
    consumption 106–107
  introduction 7
  marketing consumer objects in East
    Africa 91–96
  social relations of consumption in East
    Africa 96–102
  value of pre-colonial study
    86–89
  Indian cotton trade 153
  man and animal power 310
  supermarkets 275
Asia *see* **China; India; Japan**
Athens
  abundance of goods 26–28
  clothes 37–38
  constraints on consumption 39–41
  effect of power struggles 25
  food as a status symbol 34
  household spending 37
  lack of previous study of
    consumption 23–24
  need for provisional assumptions 25
  organization of market-place 28–30
  place of special interest 42–45
  public consumption 35
  sexual services 36–37
  social activity in the marketplace
    32–34
  source of modern inspiration 24–25

Barter
  early modern Europe 245
  early reliance 634
  possibilities for future study 124
  pre-colonial East Africa 92
  transatlantic goods 118–119
  waste 334, 339
Body *see* **Self and body**
Boycotts
  American Revolution 505
  Chinese shops 283
  consumer activism 400, 404–406
  economic and political weapon 424
  emergence of consumer-oriented national
    history 2
  ethical consumer behaviour 515
  link between nationalism and
    consumerism 419–422
  mixed motives 509
  modern popularity 514–517
  slave-grown sugar 545
  State actions 410, 416
Branding
  ancient Athens 30–32
  luxury as common parlance 173
  nationalist China
    impact of global exchange 426–429
    national obsession 431–432

Britain
  consumer movements 512
  everyday life 540
  history of retail trade
    co-operative stores 271–272
    self-service and supermarkets 274
  impact of India on food 129
  impact on East Africa 105
  Indian cotton consumption 164
  material culture in seventeenth-century
      Britain
    attitudes to preservation and
        durability 78–83
    dangers of seeking point of take-off 83
    focus on materialism 67–70
    impact of technological change 71–73
    need for re-working of values 64–65
    new cultural practices 73–76
    re-statement of consumption as an
        active force 66–67
    supply of necessities 76–78
  saving habits 368–372
  transatlantic consumption
    changing profiles of consumers 119–121
    commodification 113–114
    growth in importance of economic
        history 112–113
    importance 111–112
    possibilities for future study 124–125
    relationship between consumption and
        production 122–124
    slave trade 115–119
    'staples theory' 114–115
    therapeutic and recreational
        drugs 140–142
  youth's golden age 615
Budgeting
  eating habits 385
  everyday life 538–539
  gender and family 573
  indication of values 355–356
  limitation of waste 127
  modern Japan 490, 494
  prioritization of food and clothing 356–357
  rural consumption 195
  source of social life 13
  standards of living 211, 214–215

  use of cotton 148
  working-class households 354–355
  youth consumption 602

Children's consumption
  see also **Youth consumption**
  children defined 586–587
  differing frames of reference 588–589
  early drinking habits 207
  everyday life 540, 545
  future avenues of research 597–599
  importance 585–586
  market recognition 592–595
  material culture 596–597
  modern Japan 496
  nationalist China 427
  parents as primary consumers 589–592
  place of children in family 587–588
  saving and spending 356
China
  consumption in a nationalist society
    link between consumerism and
        commodity spectacles 422–423
    link with consumerism via
        boycotts 419–422
    obsession with branding 431–432
    period 1949–76 423–431
    useful basis for comparison 418–419
  debates over luxury goods 180
  everyday life 540
  hunger for scrap 327
  impact of growth on waste 342–343
    market reform 342
    MSW 343
    overview 341–342
    recycling 343–346
  impact on food 129–130
  imports of luxuries 183
  Indian cotton trade 150–153
  Ming China
    association of consumption with
        morality 51–52
    clothes and fashion 53
    continuously developing
        literature 60–63
    cultural abundance 50

distaste of ostentation 53–54
elite values 54–56
impact of Marxism 59
intertwining of trade, commodities and
    social status 49
luxuries and necessities
    distinguished 56–58
negative side of consumption 52–53
profusion of goods in marketplace 50–51
relevance to modern study 47–48
need for critical attention 17
pre-modern waste 330
small shops 269
standards of living 216
therapeutic and recreational
    drugs 140–142

Choice
'addict identities' 650
assumed autonomous consumption 664
comfort and convenience 303, 310–311
consumer politics 519
democratic societies 577
department stores 278
dominant ethic 668
early modern Europe 193–194, 200, 203,
    205, 206
East African trade 94, 101, 104, 107
eating out 385
energy consumption 308–309
everyday habit 535, 539, 544
global trends 622
individual stylization 643
luxury goods 175–176
measure of welfare 666
measurement of well-being 665–666
Nazi Germany 444–447
needs for further legitimation 649
rise of mass consumption 532
self-responsibility 644
seventeenth-century Britain 73
standardization and homogeneity 616
standards of living 220, 222
symbolic power 3–5

Cities see **Urban consumption**

Class
consumer activism 406
consumer movements 509

consumption as an instrument of social
    power 9
distinctiveness and social change 560–562
eating habits 381, 388
importance of middle class in modern
    colonialism 473–478
intertwining of trade, commodities and
    social status in Ming China 49
modern Japan
    emergence of modern
        consumer 489–490
    wartime modernity 497
sociable elites 253–255
youth consumption 608–609

Clothes
ancient Athens
    constraints on consumption 41
    status symbols 37–38
convenience 300–301
everyday life 540, 545
fashion
    form of modern social change 631–632
    impact of globalization 619–620
    link with urban life 622–628
    male fashionability of Indian cotton 155
    power to transform self 618–619
    relevance to consumption 628–630
    theoretical approaches 620–621
    US influences 621–622
Indian cotton trade
    diversity of production 147–148
    Europe and transatlantic trade 157–163
    exports to Africa and Asia 150–156
    global reach 160–166
    importance 145–147
    luxury and fashion 148–150
luxuries and necessities
    distinguished 185–188
Ming China
    cultural visibility 58
    negative side of consumption 53
modern Japan
    early modern consumption 486
    emergence of modern
        consumer 495–496
pre-colonial East Africa
    diversity 93–95

Clothes (*cont.*)

   modern and religious

      influences 101–102

   politics of consumption 89–91

  prioritization of spending 356–357

  rural consumption 205–206

  seventeenth-century Britain

   maintenance and durability 78

   re-statement of consumption as an

     active force 66

  Soviet Union 455

  standards of living

   movers of change 222–223

   pre-industrialization trends 215–217

  transatlantic goods 121

  urban consumption 201–205

Co-operatives 271–272

Colonial societies

  see also **Africa**

  alteration of trade routes in late 19th

     century 104–105

  India

   diversity of cotton production 147–148

   Europe and transatlantic trade 157–163

   exports to Africa and Asia 150–156

   global reach 160–166

   impact on British food 129

   impact on East Africa 103–104

   impact on luxury and fashion 148–150

   importance of cotton trade 145–147

   waste control 338–340

  modern colonialism

   flawed assumptions about culture and

     social impact 480–484

   importance of middle class 473–478

   post-colonial consumers 470–472

   relationship with particular

     commodities 478–479

   revisionist approach 467–470

  modern Japan

   emergence of modern

     consumer 488–497

   wartime modernity 497–500

  shift in perspective of consumption 2

  tobacco trade with 17th century Britain 74

  trade in food and drugs 128–130

  transatlantic consumption

   changing profiles of consumers 119–121

   commodification 113–114

   growth in importance of economic

     history 112–113

   importance 111–112

   Indian cotton 161–163

   possibilities for future study 124–125

   relationship between consumption and

     production 122–124

   slave trade 115–119

   'staples theory' 114–115

   therapeutic and recreational

     drugs 140–142

Comfort

  changing patterns of

     consumption 303–306

  cleanliness 542

  department stores 576

  domestic environment 579

  domestic lighting 315

  eating, dressing, and dwelling 545

  eating habits 390

  everyday life

   early studies 535

   global exchange and diffusion 545–546

   post-war studies 526, 528, 532

  flows of influence 6

  function of credit 365

  impact on environment 295–297

  interpretation and development of

     standards 292–295

  meaning and scope 290–292

  modern Japan 499

  Nazi Germany 434, 436, 443–447

  new approach to consumption 289–290

  Renaissance Italy 14, 535

  seventeenth-century Britain 70

  travel 317

  waste 339

Commodification

  alternative approaches

   capitalist manipulation of taste and

     lifestyle 10–11

   symbolic communication 11

  effects on study of food 380–381

  modern colonialism

   post-colonial consumers 471

revisionist approach 468
movement of people 381
role of pre-colonial Africa 85
sexual services in ancient Athens 36–37
transatlantic consumption
    growth in importance of economic
        history 113–114
    slaves 115–119
victim of post-modernism 17
'Conspicuous consumption'
    instrument of social power 9
    luxury goods 174–175
    post-Communist Russia 464
Consumer activism
    core political element 400
    new wave 14
Consumer movements
    boycotts 514–517
    concerns for people 508–513
    core political element 400
    eating habits 379
    emerging studies 507–508
    future avenues of research 517–519
    importance 506
    modern China 424
    organized activities 505–506
    protection and promotion of
        interests 407–408
    shift to rights-based approach 513–514
    United States 417
Consumer regimes
    challenge to individual autonomy 410–411
    core political element 400
    dilemmas for consumers 413–414
    emergence 513
    Government boycotts 409–410
    lack of study 408–409
    protective measures 414–416
    public spending 411–412
    shaping of consumer practices 412–413
'Consumer society'
    chronological preoccupations with 3–6
    emergence in Europe 23
    gender and family 569
    Ming China 62, 64
    questioning of terms 433
    unhelpful model 16

Consumerism
    Americanization 5
    ancient Athens 37, 42–45
    appeal of comparative testing 513
    consumption distinguished 418
    immorality 367
    importance of credit 351
    luxury goods 173, 186
    Ming China 62
    modern colonialism
        importance of middle class 476
        revisionist approach 468
    modern Japan
        beginnings 488
        post-war ascendance 500–503
    nationalist China
        link with commodity
            spectacles 422–423
        link with nationalism via
            boycotts 419–422
    Nazi Germany 448
    pervasive promise 178
    politics of consumption 403
    public anxieties 10
    questioning of terms 433
    Renaissance Italy 231
    waste production 339, 344
    youth's golden age 611–617
Consumption
    alternative approaches
        capitalist manipulation of taste and
            lifestyle 10–11
        significance of materiality 17–18
        status 9–10
        symbolic communication 11–14
    chronological preoccupations with two
        particular periods 3–8
    consumerism distinguished 418
    creative consumption
        design and media 628
        everyday life 546
        housewife's power 571
        shift in perspective of
            consumption 11–14
        source of study 8
    diversity of economic theories 15–17
    early modern Japan 485–488

Consumption (*cont.*)

importance of financial conduct 351–352

importance of sociability 252

semantic roots 376–377

shift in perspective 1–3

significance of public spending 14

Convenience

association with time-saving 298–299

changing patterns of
  consumption 303–306

clothes 300–301

early modern Europe 199–200

eating, dressing, and dwelling 545

eating habits 379

everyday life 535–536, 538, 545–546

food 299–301

luxury goods 180

meaning and scope 297

new approach to consumption 289–290

relation between material culture and
  social practice 301–303

United States 411

warm food 73

waste 339

Cotton

comfort and convenience 290

energy consumption 309

fashion 621

Indian production and trade

  diversity of production and 147–148

  Europe and transatlantic trade 157–163

  exports to Africa and Asia 150–156

  global reach 160–166

  importance 145–147

  luxury and fashion 148–150

Japanese consumption 487

luxury goods 189–190

Ming China 55

pioneering histories 7

relationship with slavery 412

role in East Africa 90–95, 99, 101, 103

seventeenth-century Britain 67, 82

small shops 269

standards of living 216, 222

Western European consumption
  203–205

widespread 4

Creative consumption

design and media 628

everyday life 546

housewife's power 571

shift in perspective of consumption 11–14

source of study 8

Credit

early modern Europe

  developing system 244–249

  the Priuli family in Venice 230

importance 14–15

modern Japan

  early modern consumption 487

  emergence of modern
    consumer 492–495

  post-war ascendance of
    consumers 501–502

not the only path to affluence 6

pre-colonial East Africa 92–93, 97

public consumption 17

regional contrasts 16

retail trade 277

United States 360–361, 362–365

Cultural values

alternative approaches

  capitalist manipulation of taste and
    lifestyle 10–11

  instrument of social power 9

  symbolic communication 11–14

ancient Athens

  clothes 37–38

  food 34

  settlement of accounts 29

depictions of consumption in early modern
  Europe 236–244

eating habits 386

everyday life 529

fashion

  form of modern social change
    631–632

  impact of globalization 619–620

  link with urban life 622–628

  male fashionability of Indian cotton 155

  power to transform self 618–619

  relevance to consumption 628–630

  theoretical approaches 620–621

  US influences 621–622

gender and family
  revisionist approach 578–580
  tension between public spheres
    575–578
importance of middle class in modern
  colonialism 474
Indian cotton 155
lifestyle
  early modern Europe 246
  everyday life 531, 542
  importance 7
  luxuries 174–177
  Ming China 58
  modern Japan 489, 496
  nationalist China 422, 424
  Nazi Germany 448
  Renaissance Italy 230
  saving and spending 356
  shopping 273, 280
  Soviet Union 454, 458, 463
  supermarkets marketing strategies 516
  transatlantic consumption 123
  urban consumption 193, 207
luxury goods 176–177
Ming China 50, 58–59
modern colonialism 481–482
modern Japan
  emergence of modern consumer 489
  post-war ascendance of
    consumers 502–503
  wartime modernity 498
possibilities for future study 125
pre-colonial East Africa 89
'public sphere'
  importance 256–259
  post-Habermasian movement 259–264
self and body 641–649
seventeenth-century Britain
  focus on materialism 68–69
  tobacco-smoking 73–76
significance of public spending 14
Soviet Union 457–460, 462
  post-Stalin era 460–462
  privileged access 455–457
status
  complex moral and political
    baggage 557

distinctiveness and social
    change 560–564
early modern Europe 235
elite values in Ming China 54–56
general approach to consumption 9–10
importance 551–552
importance of middle class in modern
  colonialism 473–478
Indian cotton 148
intertwining with trade and
    commodities in Ming China 49
luxury goods 174–175
modern Japan 488
pre-colonial East Africa 90, 99–100
sociable elites 253–255
urban and rural communities
    compared 197–201
Weberian approach 552–556
taste
  capitalist manipulation of taste and
    lifestyle 10–11
  energy consumption 308–309
  impact of transatlantic trade 121–122
  Indian cotton 148–149, 155
  instrument of social power 9
  Nazi Germany 435
  pre-colonial East Africa 94–95
  role of imperialism 129
  self and body 641–649
  shift in perspective of consumption 1
  Soviet Union 457–460
  urban consumption 192
youth consumption
  films 607
  golden age of consumerism 611–617
  impact of gang culture 603–606
  presentation of self 606–607

Democratic societies
  see also Britain; Europe; United States
ancient Athens
  abundance of goods 26–28
  clothes 37–38
  constraints on consumption 39–41
  food as a status symbol 34
  household spending 37

Democratic societies (*cont.*)
   luxuries and necessities
      distinguished 30–32
   need for provisional assumptions 23–25
   organization of market-place 28–30
   place of special interest 42–45
   pleasures of consumption 35–36
   public consumption 35
   sexual services 36–37
   social activity in the marketplace 32–34
  association with well-being 669
  choice 577
  consumer movements 512–513
  everyday life 522, 526, 531, 536, 542
  luxury goods 177
  new emphasis on living conditions 581
  standards of living 218
  status 554–555
  waste infrastructures 338
Department stores
  comfort 576
  confrontation with small shops 272–274
  modern Japan 490
  origins and development 270–272
  part of global exchange 284
  politics of retailing 281–282
  tensions created by family and gender 576
Diet *see* **Food and drink**
Diffusion *see* **Global exchange and diffusion**
Disposable goods
  downplay of interconnectedness 124
  Ming China 49
  modern China 343
  tobacco-smoking in 17th century Britain 75–76
  waste 335–336
Diversity
  distinctiveness and social change 560–564
  food and drink 131
  historical perspectives 8
  Indian cotton 147–148
  Ming China 50–51
  pre-colonial East Africa 93–94
  quality and branding in ancient Athens 30–32

  tobacco-smoking in 17th century Britain 75
  youth consumption 608–609
Domesticity
  see also **Gender and family; Household consumption**
  African women 472
  central element 568
  comfort and convenience 300
  innovative approach 569–570
  Western investment 664
Drugs
  areas of future research 144
  determinants of ill-being 659
  global exchange
    development of global role 143
    psychotic beverages 138–139
    role of imperialism 128–130
    significance 127–128
    therapeutic and recreational drugs 140–142
  new approach to health 633
  quasi-mythic status as generators of addiction 650
  US controls 411, 417
Durables
  ancient Athens 37
  debates over luxury goods 181
  transatlantic goods 121, 123

East Africa
  accommodation of consumer demand 102–106
  marketing of consumer objects 91–96
  social relations of consumption 96–102
Eating *see* **Food and drink**
Elites *see* **Status**
Emulation
  children's consumption 590
  civilizing process 253
  colonial societies 475
  comfort and convenience 291
  early modern Europe 208
  explanation of consumer culture 10
  'female vice' 178
  luxury 180
  'Veblenesque' desire 569

well-being 663
youth consumption 608
Energy consumption
  areas for future research 320–323
  changes in transport 316–318
  changing approach to
    consumption 307–309
  Chinese heavy industry 425–426
  comfort and convenience 293, 295
  everyday life 537, 544
  factories 312–313
  households
    early changes 314–315
    universal electricity supplies 318–320
  man and animal power 309–311
  nationalist China 425–426
  private consumption 16
  public lighting 313–314
  reactions to high consumption 315–316
  significance of materiality 18
  urban communities 311–312
Europe
  ancient Athens
    abundance of goods 26–28
    clothes 37–38
    constraints on consumption 39–41
    effect of power struggles 25
    food as a status symbol 34
    household spending 37
    lack of previous study of
      consumption 23–24
    need for provisional assumptions 25
    organization of market-place 28–30
    place of special interest 42–45
    public consumption 35
    sexual services 36–37
    social activity in the marketplace 32–34
    source of modern inspiration 24–25
  Britain
    co-operative stores 271–272
    consumer movements 512
    everyday life 540
    impact of India on food 129
    impact on East Africa 105
    Indian cotton consumption 164
    saving habits 368–372
    self-service and supermarkets 274

    youth's golden age 615
  consumer movements 512, 514
  consumption in early modern Europe
    gender divisions 232–237
    importance of social and material
      negotiations 249
    mobility between country and
      city 237–244
    the Priuli family in Venice 229–230
    pushing the consumer revolution back
      in time 231–232
    role of credit 244–249
  decline of influence on lifestyle 563
  energy consumption 320
  gender and family 573
  historical culture of consumption 7
  history of retail trade
    'active' and 'passive' consumers 278
    co-operative stores 271–272
    department stores 271
    impact on urban environment 279–280
    part of global exchange 283–284
    politics of retailing 282–283
    small shops 269
  imports of luxuries from Asia 182–185
  Indian cotton trade 156–163
  luxury goods 178
  material culture in seventeenth-century
    Britain
    attitudes to preservation and
      durability 78–83
    dangers of seeking point of take-off 83
    focus on materialism 67–70
    impact of technological change 71–73
    need for re-working of values 64–65
    new cultural practices 73–76
    re-statement of consumption as an
      active force 66–67
    supply of necessities 76–78
  Nazi Germany
    importance of consumption 434–438
    legacies of fascism 447–449
    politics of consumption 438–441
    relationship between consumption and
      consent 444–447
    relevance 433–434
    role of producer 441–444

Europe (*cont.*)
    politicization of everyday life in twentieth
        century 580–583
    rise of 'public sphere' 256–259
    saving habits 368–372
    seventeenth-century Britain
        attitudes to preservation and
            durability 78–83
        dangers of seeking point of take-off 83
        focus on materialism 67–70
        impact of technological change 71–73
        need for re-working of values 64–65
        new cultural practices 73–76
        re-statement of consumption as an
            active force 66–67
        supply of necessities 76–78
    shift in perspective of consumption 2
    studies of everyday life 525–526
    transatlantic consumption
        changing profiles of consumers 119–121
        commodification 113–114
        growth in importance of economic
            history 112–113
        importance 111–112
        possibilities for future study 124–125
        relationship between consumption and
            production 122–124
        slave trade 115–119
        'staples theory' 114–115
        therapeutic and recreational drugs 140–142
    youth's golden age 612–615
Everyday life
    comfort and convenience 297, 545–546
    concerns over resistance 543
    early history 532–539
    extension of aesthetic value 380
    future studies 546
    'governmentality' 540–541
    historical approach 8
    impact of socialism 544–545
    impact of urban water supplies 541–542
    luxuries 191
    meaning and scope 522–524
    methodological questions 542–543
    new source of study 522
    politicization in twentieth-century
        Europe 580–583

    post-war history 522–524
    practices 543–544
    relevance 521–522
    revolutionary life 540
    seventeenth-century Britain 83
    Soviet Union 454
Exchange of goods *see* **Barter**

Family *see* **Gender and family**
Fascist societies
    Nazi Germany
        importance of consumption 434–438
        legacies of fascism 447–449
        politics of consumption 438–441
        relationship between consumption and
            consent 444–447
        relevance 433–434
        role of producer 441–444
        support for Marxist view 10
        youth consumption 608–609, 610
Fashion
    see also **Taste**
    form of modern social change 631–632
    impact of globalization 619–620
    link with urban life 622–628
    male fashionability of Indian cotton 155
    power to transform self 618–619
    relevance to consumption 628–630
    theoretical approaches 620–621
Female consumption *see* **Gender
        and family**
Financialization 372–374
Food and drink
    ancient Athens
        organization of market-place 29
        as a status symbol 34
    areas of future research 144
    convenience 299–301
    eating habits
        eating out 385–386
        effects of commodification 380–381
        effects of globalization 379–380
        future avenues of research 389–391
        gastronomy 386–387
        grounds for study 376–379
        international movement of people 382–383

nutritional information and advice 386
suburbanization 383–384
use of cookery books 388–389
everyday life 528–529, 545
global exchange
  development of global role 142–143
  role of imperialism 128–130
  salt 130–132
  significance 127–128
  spices 132–135
  sugar 135–138
modern Japan
  early modern consumption 486
pre-colonial East Africa 89
prioritization of spending 356–357
rituals of symbolic communication 12
rural consumption
  preparation and service 207–208
  urban communities compared 195–196
salt
  contribution to the creation of new food
    cultures 133
  early modern Europe 248
  East African trade 92
  eating habits 389
  global exchange and diffusion 130–132
  new focus on ornamentation 199
  slave labour 118
seventeenth-century Britain 72–73
shift in perspective of consumption 1
Soviet Union
  scarcity and privilege 455–457
spices
  eating habits 383
  global exchange and diffusion 132–135
  Indian trade 150
  Ming China 55
  retailing 283
  Western European diet 206
standards of living
  movers of change 222–223
  pre-industrialization trends 215–217
sugar
  American consumption 413
  East African trade 91
  eating habits 378, 389
  energy consumption 309

global exchange and diffusion 135–138
Indian trade 150
luxuries 176, 181
model of a commodity biography 7
relationship with slavery 478, 545
seventeenth-century Britain 74
Soviet consumption 452
standards of living 223
transatlantic consumption 113, 117, 121
transatlantic goods 121
urban consumption
  limited data 206–207
  rural communities compared 195–196

Gender and family
see also **Domesticity**
children's consumption
  children defined 586–587
  differing frames of reference 588–589
  early drinking habits 207
  everyday life 540, 545
  future avenues of research 597–599
  importance 585–586
  market recognition 592–595
  material culture 596–597
  modern Japan 496
  nationalist China 427
  parents as primary consumers 589–592
  place of children in family 587–588
  saving and spending 356
confrontation between small shops and
    department stores 273
consumer movements 510–511
domesticity
  innovative approach 569–570
early modern Europe
  divisions of labour 232–237
  grounds for debate 231
  the Priuli family in Venice 230
everyday life 530
female shoppers
  ancient Athens 29
  source of social life 13
impact of transatlantic trade 119–120
impact of universal energy supplies on the
    role of women 319

Gender and family (*cont.*)

importance 568–569

innovative approach 569–570

linkage between concepts 571–575

luxury as a female vice 181–182

male fashionability of Indian cotton 148

modern colonialism

importance of middle class 475–476

modern Japan 490–491

Nazi Germany 442–443

politicization of everyday life 580–583

revisionist approach 578–580

rural clothes 205

symbolic sources of identity 13

tension between public spheres 575–578

urban clothes 204–205

urban consumption

importance 192

youth consumption 601

Generational identities

children's consumption

children defined 586–587

differing frames of reference 588–589

early drinking habits 207

everyday life 540, 545

future avenues of research 597–599

importance 585–586

market recognition 592–595

material culture 596–597

modern Japan 496

nationalist China 427

parents as primary consumers

589–592

place of children in family 587–588

saving and spending 356

youth consumption

Africa 101

golden age of consumerism 611–617

impact of films 607

impact of gang culture 603–606

nationalist China 427

presentation of self 606–607

Renaissance Italy 253

self and body 645

significance 602–603

Soviet Union 462

towards mass consumption 609–611

Global exchange and diffusion

consumer activism 406

drugs

development of global role 143

psychotic beverages 138–139

role of imperialism 128–130

significance 127–128

therapeutic and recreational

drugs 140–142

Eastern Europe 462

food

development of global role 142–143

role of imperialism 128–130

salt 130–132

significance 127–128

spices 132–135

sugar 135–138

impact of China's growth 342–343

market reform 342

MSW 343

overview 341–342

recycling 343–346

impact on eating habits

movement of goods 379–380

movement of people 381

impact on everyday life 545–546

impact on fashion

link with urban life 626

US influences 619–620

import and export of goods by ancient

Athens 26–28

importance of foreign rarities in Ming

China 57

Indian cotton trade

diversity of production and 147–148

Europe and transatlantic trade 157–163

exports to Africa and Asia 150–156

global reach 160–166

importance 145–147

luxury and fashion 148–150

luxuries

importance 173–174

scramble for world

commodities 188–190

modern colonialism

flawed assumptions about culture and

social impact 480–484

importance of middle class 473–478
post-colonial consumers 470–472
relationship with particular
    commodities 478–479
revisionist approach 467–470
nationalist China 424–430
need for ongoing analysis 16
problems of financialization 372–374
retail trade 283–285
role of pre-colonial Africa
    accommodation of consumer demand in
        East Africa 102–106
    consumer trends before 19th
        century 89–91
    importance of pre-colonial
        consumption 106–107
    marketing consumer objects in East
        Africa 91–96
    overview 85–86
    social relations of consumption in East
        Africa 96–102
    value of pre-colonial study 86–89
role of pre-colonial Africa in global flow of
    goods 7
tobacco trade with 17th century Britain 74
transatlantic consumption
    changing profiles of consumers
        119–121
    commodification 113–114
    growth in importance of economic
        history 112–113
    importance 111–112
    possibilities for future study 124–125
    relationship between consumption and
        production 122–124
    slave trade 115–119
    'staples theory' 114–115
'Governmentality' 540–541

Habits
comfort and convenience 290, 303–304
'cultured socialist trade' 458
early modern Europe 193, 199
eating
    eating out 385–386
    effects of commodification 380–381

effects of globalization 379–380
future avenues of research 389–391
gastronomy 386–387
grounds for study 376–379
international movement of
    people 382–383
nutritional information and
    advice 386
suburbanization 383–384
use of cookery books 388–389
energy consumption 322
everyday life
    early studies 534–536, 539
    impact of water supplies 542–543
    post-war studies 526, 528–529
    revolutionary period 540
fashion 620
impact on waste 333, 336–338
Indian cotton 150
modern Japan 498
relevance 15
self and body 643
sociability 261
standards of living 213
well-being 659
youth 616
'Hedonic indices' 175–176
Household consumption
see also Domesticity
ancient Athens 37
energy
    early changes 314–315
    universal electricity supplies 318–320
luxuries and necessities
        distinguished 187–188
pre-colonial East Africa 96–97
seventeenth-century Britain
    impact of technological change 71–73
    maintenance and durability of
        goods 78–83
    re-statement of consumption as an
        active force 67
shift in perspective of consumption 1
source of social life 12–13
standards of living 211–212
urban and rural communities
        compared 196

Identity
see also **Generational identity**
Athens as an historical source 25
crisis in France 528
debates over luxury goods 180
eating habits 382
fashion
  link with urban life 623
  power to transform self 618–619
food and drink 378–379, 388
gender and family
  linkage between concepts 573
  tension between public spheres 575
importance of food and drugs 127
Indian cotton 148
new approach to consumption 12
pre-colonial East Africa 96–97
self and body
  African dress 101
  ancient Athens 25
  attention to females 575–576
  comfort and convenience 296, 303
  consuming dualis 649–652
  cultural values 641–649
  energy consumption 315, 316
  European clothing 102
  everyday life 538
  fashion 616, 631
  Islamic dress 95
  luxuries 175, 180
  notions of consumption 634–637
  objects of consumption 637–641
  saving and spending 350, 363–367, 370
  seventeenth-century Britain 79
  Soviet Union 454, 464
  standards of living 219
  threefold relationship with
    consumption 633–634
  traditions of critical reason 18
  waste 339
  women's domestic life 574
  youth consumption 606–607
  youth culture 606
shift in perspective of consumption
  1–2
symbolic sources of women's identity 13
youth consumption 601

India
cotton trade
  diversity of production 147–148
  Europe and transatlantic trade 157–163
  exports to Africa and Asia 150–156
  global reach 160–166
  importance 145–147
  luxury and fashion 148–150
impact on British food 129
impact on East Africa 103–104
waste control 338–340
Industrial consumption
historical significance 14
seventeenth-century Britain
  impact of technological change 71–73
  re-statement of consumption as an
    active force 67

Japan
everyday life 538–539
history of retail trade
  co-operative stores 271–272
  department stores 271
impact on food 129
modern Japan
  early modern consumption 485–488
  emergence of modern
    consumer 488–497
  post-war ascendance of
    consumers 500–503
  wartime modernity 497–500
saving habits 368–372
standards of comfort 293
trade with East Africa 105
waste
  pre-modern waste 330
  sanitary control 338

Lifestyle
Bourdieu's approach 557–560
capitalist manipulation of taste and
  lifestyle 10–11
chequered and complex history 556
complex moral and political baggage 557
early modern Europe 246

everyday life 531, 542
importance 7, 551–552
luxuries 174–177
Ming China 58
modern Japan 489, 496
nationalist China 422, 424
Nazi Germany 448
Renaissance Italy 230
saving and spending 356
shopping 273, 280
Soviet Union 454, 458, 463
supermarkets marketing strategies 516
transatlantic consumption 123
urban consumption 193, 207
Luxuries
ancient Athens
    constraints on consumption 41
    as a source of study 24
continuing debates 179–182
economic theories 174–177
gastronomy 386–387
global trade in ancient world 177
importance 173–174
imports from Asia 182–185
instrument of social power 9
intertwining of trade, commodities and
        social status in Ming China 49
Ming China
    continuously developing literature 61
    necessities distinguished 56–58
    negative side of consumption 52–53
modern Japan 499
as the mother of slavery 11
nationalist China 425–426
necessities distinguished 185–188
political framework 177
post-war golden age 177–178
quality and branding in ancient
        Athens 30–32
recreational drugs 140–142
scramble for world commodities 188–190
'sensuous luxury' 178–179
seventeenth-century Britain
    focus on materialism 68–70
    re-statement of consumption as an
        active force 66–67
Soviet critique 463

spices 132, 138
standards of living 211–213

Male consumption *see* **Gender and family**
Marketplaces
see also **Shopping**
ancient Athens
    abundance of goods 26
    centre of social activity 32–34
    organization and specialization 28–30
    place of special interest 42–45
consumption in early modern Europe
    gender divisions 232–237
    importance of social and material
        negotiations 249
    mobility between country and
        city 237–244
    the Priuli family in Venice 229–230
    pushing the consumer revolution back
        in time 231–232
    role of credit 244–249
Ming China 50–51
tensions created by family and gender 577
urban consumption 194
Marxism
capitalist manipulation of taste and
        lifestyle 10–11
everyday life
    early studies 533–534
    post-war studies 525
food and drink 378
impact on Chinese history 59
marginalization of gender and family 571
underlying principles 451–452
Mass consumption
changes over time 17
luxury goods 177
Marxist approach 10–11
resilience of American model 8
tensions created by family and gender 575
tobacco-smoking in 17th century Britain 75
waste
    disposability of MSW through the
        1980s 335
    significance 326–327
youth market 609–611

Materialism
  children's consumption 596–597
  effects on study of food 380–381
  fashion 628–629
  freed slaves 98–99
  importance of sociability 252
  modern colonialism 478–480
  relationship with convenience 301–303
  seventeenth-century Britain 67–70
  shift in perspective of consumption 1
  significance 17–18
  Soviet Union 457
  urban and rural communities
      compared 197–201
Medicines *see* **Therapeutic drugs**
Ming China
  association of consumption with
      morality 51–52
  clothes and fashion 53
  continuously developing literature 60–63
  cultural abundance 50
  distaste of ostentation 53–54
  elite values 54–56
  impact of Marxism 59
  intertwining of trade, commodities and
      social status 49
  luxuries and necessities distinguished 56–58
  negative side of consumption 52–53
  relevance to modern study 47–48
Monetization
  absence of study 352
  explanations for absence of study 352–353
  history of money 350–351
  importance of financial conduct 351–352
  modern China 342
  modern Japan 489, 492
  money as dominant means of
      exchange 348–350
  moralistic approaches 358–359
  need for fresh interpretations 354–361, 374
  new age of financialization 372, 374
  problems of financialization 372–374
  revisionist histories 366
Municipal Solid Waste
  disposability through the 1980s 334–341
  emergence as concept 333
  impact of China's growth 343

Nationalist societies
  China
    link between consumerism and
        commodity spectacles 422–423
    link with consumerism via
        boycotts 419–422
    obsession with branding 431–432
    period 1949–76 423–431
    useful basis for comparison 418–419
  Nazi Germany
    importance of consumption 434–438
    legacies of fascism 447–449
    politics of consumption 438–441
    relationship between consumption and
        consent 444–447
    relevance 433–434
    role of producer 441–444
Nazi Germany
  importance of consumption
      434–438
  legacies of fascism 447–449
  politics of consumption 438–441
  relationship between consumption and
      consent 444–447
  relevance 433–434
  role of producer 441–444
  source of 'Konsumterror' 530–531
Necessities
  determinants of standard of living
      211–213
  energy 307–308
  luxuries distinguished 185–188
  Ming China 56–58
  quality and branding in ancient
      Athens 30–32
  rituals of symbolic communication 12
  salt 131
  seventeenth-century Britain 76–78
  Soviet Union
    scarcity and privilege 455–457

Obsolescence
  impact on waste 329, 335–336
  luxury goods 174
  rural consumption 208
  urban consumption 198

Patterns of spending 1, 356, 378
Pleasures of consumption
 ancient Athens
  constraints on consumption 39–41
  food 35–36
 debates over luxury goods 180
 everyday life 526
 function of credit 365
 'hedonic indices' 175–176
 historical approach 8
 method of analysis 10
 new approach 12
 'sensuous luxury' 178–179
 spices 135
 well-being
  choice 665–666
  citizenship and the home 582
  comfort and convenience 290–291
  comparison 666
  conflicting truisms 655–656
  disciplined bodywork 638
  equal distribution of pleasures 669–670
  ethical considerations 667–669
  growth 667
  inventory of goods approach 657–660
  limiting consumption 211–213
  nationalist China 432
  novelty 666
  picture of 'normality' 650
  saving and spending 349, 367
  social science research 662–664
  standard assumptions 653–655
  state of mind 660–662
  women's responsibility for family 573
Politics of consumption
 consumer activism
  core political element 400
  networked solidarity 404–406
  new wave 14
 consumer movements
  boycotts 514–517
  concerns for people 508–513
  core political element 400
  eating habits 379
  emerging studies 507–508
  future avenues of research 517–519
  importance 506

 modern China 424
 organized activities 505–506
 protection and promotion of
  interests 407–408
 shift to rights-based approach 513–514
 United States 417
consumer regimes
 challenge to individual
  autonomy 410–411
 dilemmas for consumers 413–414
 Government boycotts 409–410
 lack of study 408–409
 protective measures 414–416
 public spending 411–412
 shaping of consumer practices
  412–413
distinct forms 416–417
energy 320–321
everyday life 454
 comfort and convenience 545–546
 concerns over resistance 543
 early history 532–539
 future studies 546
 'governmentality' 540–541
 impact of socialism 544–545
 impact of urban water supplies 541–542
 meaning and scope 522–524
 methodological questions 542–543
 new source of study 522
 post-war history 524–532
 practices 543–544
 relevance 521–522
 revolutionary life 540
history of retail trade 281–283
impact of transatlantic trade 121
Indian cotton 154
luxury goods 177, 179–180
modern colonialism
 flawed assumptions about culture and
  social impact 480–484
 importance of middle class 473–478
 post-colonial consumers 470–472
 relationship with particular
  commodities 478–479
 revisionist approach 467–470
modern Japan
 early modern consumption 485–488

Politics of consumption (*cont.*)
    emergence of modern
      consumer 488–497
    post-war ascendance of
      consumers 500–503
    wartime modernity 497–500
    nationalist China
    link between consumerism and
      commodity spectacles 422–423
    link with consumerism via
      boycotts 419–422
    obsession with branding 431–432
    period 1949–76 423–431
    useful basis for comparison 418–419
    Nazi Germany
    importance of consumption 434–438
    juxtaposition of enticement and
      deprivation 438–441
    legacies of fascism 447–449
    relationship between consumption and
      consent 444–447
    relevance 433–434
    role of producer 441–444
    politicization of everyday life in
      twentieth-century Europe 580–583
    pre-colonial Africa
    access to imported goods 97–98
    clothes 89–91
    importance 86–87
    Soviet Union
    collapse of communism 464–466
    early practice 452–454
    post-Stalin era 460–462
    rediscovery of good taste 457–460
    role of Eastern Europe 462–464
    scarcity and privilege 455–457
    underlying principles 451–452
    spices 133
    standards of living
    emergence of political debate
      213–215
    luxuries and necessities
      distinguished 212–213
    'three-phase' model 399–404
'Positional goods' 173, 176
Practices 543–544
  see also Habits

Production
    ancient Athens 30, 45
    early modern Europe
      gender divisions 233–234
    effects of mass production 4
    factory consumption of energy 312–313
    food and drink 379
    impact of industrialization on standards of
      living 213–215
    impact of transatlantic trade 122–123
    Indian cotton 147–148
    luxuries
      effects of world trade 189–190
      significance 174
    Marxist approach 10–12, 17
    Ming China 49, 51, 59
    modern colonialism 478
    modern Japan 491
    Nazi Germany 441–444
    new approach to consumption 1–2
    seventeenth-century Britain
      necessities 76–78
      technological and industrial
        change 71–73
    Soviet Union 452–454
Psychotic beverages 138–139
Public consumption
    energy for lighting 313–314
    historical significance 14
    need for ongoing analysis 16–17
    sacrifices in ancient Athens 35
'Public sphere'
    everyday life 536
    importance 256–259
    post-Habermasian movement 259–264
    tensions created by family and
      gender 575–578

Recreational drugs 140–142
Retailing *see* Shopping
Rural consumption
    see also Urban consumption
    Bourdieu's approach to lifestyle 558–559
    clothing 205–206
    early modern Europe 237–244
    energy 319

food and drink
  preparation and service 207–208
  urban communities compared
    195–196
  importance 208
  modern colonialism 477
  modern Japan
    early modern consumption 487
    wartime modernity 497–498
  nationalist China 424
  ownership of goods 197–201
  revisionist approach 192–193
  small shops 269–270
  Soviet Union 455–456
  standards of living 213
  urban consumption compared 195–197

Salt
  contribution to the creation of new food
    cultures 133
  early modern Europe 248
  East African trade 92
  eating habits 389
  global exchange and diffusion 130–132
  new focus on ornamentation 199
  slave labour 118
Saving
  comparative perspectives
    G7 nations 368–372
    importance 367–368
  history of thrift 361–367
  indication of values 355–356
  need for fresh interpretations 374
  new source of study 14–15
  regional contrasts 16
  working-class households 354–355
'Scuttlers' 605
Second-hand goods
  early modern Europe
    the Priuli family in Venice 230
    role of credit 246
    significance 249
  impact of China's growth on
    recycling 343–346
  possibilities for future study 124
  seventeenth-century Britain 78–83

Self and body
  African dress 101
  ancient Athens 25
  attention to females 575–576
  comfort and convenience 296, 303
  consuming dualis 649–652
  cultural values 641–649
  energy consumption 315, 316
  European clothing 102
  everyday life 538
  fashion 616, 631
  Islamic dress 95
  luxuries 175, 180
  notions of consumption 634–637
  objects of consumption 637–641
  saving and spending 350, 363–367, 370
  seventeenth-century Britain 79
  Soviet Union 454, 464
  standards of living 219
  threefold relationship with
    consumption 633–634
  traditions of critical reason 18
  waste 339
  women's domestic life 574
  youth consumption 606–607
  youth culture 606
Self-service stores 274–275
'Sensuous luxury' 178–179
Sexual services
  ancient Athens 35–37, 44–45
  modern Japan 491
Shopping
  see also **Marketplaces**
  'active' and 'passive' consumers 277–278
  ancient Athens
    place of special interest 42–44
  Athens a source of study 24
  department stores
    confrontation with small shops
     272–274
    origins and development 270–272
  early modern Europe
    the Priuli family in Venice 229
  gender and family
    linkage between concepts 574
    tension between public spheres 576
  impact on urban environment 278–280

Shopping (*cont.*)
interactive process between buyers and
    sellers 275–277
Ming China 52
modern Japan
    early modern consumption 487
    wartime modernity 498–499
Nazi Germany 442–443
organization of market-place in ancient
    Athens 28–30
part of global exchange 283–285
politics of retailing 281–283
self-service and supermarkets 274–275
small shops
    confrontation with department
        stores 272–274
    new approach 267–268
    statistical predominance 268–270
Slaves
ancient Athens 27–30
consumer movements 509
as consumers 118–119
impact of transatlantic trade 115–118
luxury as the mother of slavery 11
materialism of freed slaves 98–99
replacement by energy consuming
    appliances 314–315
Small shops
confrontation with department
    stores 272–274
new approach 267–268
politics of retailing 281
statistical predominance 268–270
Sociability
connection with urban luxury 181–182
department stores 272
eating habits
    eating out 385–386
    future avenues of research 390
    grounds for study 378
female shoppers 575
focus on elites 253–255
food and clothing 186–187
new approach to consumption 12–13
post-Habermasian movement 259–264
pre-colonial East Africa 96–102
restaurants and cafés 208
rise of 'public sphere' 256–259

'scuttlers' 605
seventeenth-century Britain 73, 83
various meanings and significances 264–265
Socialist societies
impact on everyday life 544–545
need for critical attention 17
Soviet Union
    collapse of communism 464–466
    early practice 452–454
    post-Stalin era 460–462
    rediscovery of good taste 457–460
    role of Eastern Europe 462–464
    scarcity and privilege 455–457
    underlying principles 451–452
Soviet Union
collapse of communism 464–466
early practice 452–454
everyday life
    early studies 537
    post-war studies 527
    revolutionary period 540
history of retail trade
    'active' and 'passive' consumers 278
    department stores 271
    impact on urban environment 279
    part of global exchange 284
increasing influence on lifestyle 563
post-Stalin era 460–462
rediscovery of good taste 457–460
role of Eastern Europe 462–464
scarcity and privilege 455–457
small shops 269
underlying principles 451–452
Spices
eating habits 383
global exchange and diffusion 132–135
Indian trade 150
Ming China 55
retailing 283
Western European diet 206
Standards of living
changes in measurement 220–221
changing approaches 210–211
consumer movements 512
emergence of political debate 213–215
focus on demographic changes 217–220
impact of transatlantic trade 123
luxuries and necessities distinguished 211–213

new movers of change 222–224
pre-industrialization trends 215–217
Soviet Union 460
urban and rural communities
    compared 195–197
'Staples theory' 114–115
Status
    ancient Athens
        clothes 37–38
        food 34
        settlement of accounts 29
    complex moral and political baggage 557
    distinctiveness and social change 560–564
    early modern Europe 235
    elite values in Ming China 54–56
    general approach to consumption 9–10
    importance 551–552
    importance of middle class in modern
        colonialism 473–478
    Indian cotton 148
    instrument of social power 9
    intertwining with trade and commodities
        in Ming China 49
    luxury goods 174–175
    modern Japan 488
    pre-colonial East Africa 90, 99–100
    self and body 641
    sociable elites 253–255
    Soviet Union
        post-Stalin era 460–462
        privileged access 455–457
    urban and rural communities
        compared 197–201
    Weberian approach 552–556
Sugar
    American consumption 413
    East African trade 91
    eating habits 378, 389
    energy consumption 309
    global exchange and diffusion 135–138
    Indian trade 150
    luxuries 176, 181
    model of a commodity biography 7
    relationship with slavery 478, 545
    seventeenth-century Britain 74
    Soviet consumption 452
    standards of living 223
    transatlantic consumption 113, 117, 121

Supermarkets 274–275
Symbolic communication
    ancient Athens
        as an historical source 25
        social activity in the marketplace 32–34
    Bourdieu's approach to lifestyle 558
    early modern Europe 242–244
    food and drink 378, 384
    Indian cotton 154–155
    luxury goods 176–177
    shift in perspective of consumption 2, 11–14
    youth's golden age 615–616

Taste
    see also Fashion
    alternative approaches
        capitalist manipulation of taste and
            lifestyle 10–11
        instrument of social power 9
    decline of highbrow taste 564–566
    energy consumption 308–309
    impact of transatlantic trade 121–122
    Indian cotton 148–149, 155
    Nazi Germany 435
    pre-colonial East Africa 94–95
    role of imperialism 129
    self and body 641–649
    shift in perspective of consumption 1
    Soviet Union 457–460
    urban consumption
        importance 192
Taxation
    ancient Athens 28, 39–41
    costs of parish relief 213
    department stores 281
    early modern Europe 249
    goods legally imported into the towns 206
    Indian cotton 154
    itinerant traders 270
    luxuries 174, 187
    luxuries and necessities distinguished 187
    modern Japan 488
    nationalist China 425
    Nazi Germany 444
    revenue purposes 212
    salt 131
    United States 412–413, 415

Taxation (*cont.*)
on villages 211
water 542
well-being 658, 662, 665
Technology
abolition of man and animal power 310
impact on everyday life 542
impact on food and drugs trade 142–143
luxuries
effects of world trade 189–190
imports from Asia 182
modern Japan 497, 500–503
Nazi Germany 434
nineteenth century concerns over urban
waste 332–333
seventeenth-century Britain
household goods 71–73
necessities 76–78
standards of comfort 292–293
urban consumption
importance 192
rural communities compared 196–197
Therapeutic drugs
early modern Europe 240
global exchange 140–142
Tobacco
determinants of ill-being 659
smoking in 17th century Britain
disposable goods 75–76
first mass-consumption 75
luxury consumption 73–74
mercantile impact 74
transatlantic consumption 117
Towns *see* **Urban consumption**
Transatlantic consumption
changing profiles of consumers
119–121
commodification 113–114
growth in importance of economic
history 112–113
importance 111–112
Indian cotton 161–163
possibilities for future study 124–125
relationship between consumption and
production 122–124
slave trade 115–119
'staples theory' 114–115

sugar 136
therapeutic and recreational
drugs 140–142
Transport
access to energy 71, 316–318
disposability of MSW through the 1980s 334
impact on eating habits 380
location of department stores 279
modern Japan 491
Nazi Germany 435
role of cities 192
rural consumption of luxuries 176
standards of living 214
status 237
waste disposal 331, 334

United States
children's consumption 589–592
chronological preoccupations with
'consumer society' 3–6
consumer activism 404–406
consumer movements 512–514
consumer regimes
challenge to individual autonomy 410–411
dilemmas for consumers 413–414
Government boycotts 409–410
lack of study 408–409
protective measures 414–416
public spending 411–412
shaping of consumer practices 412–413
decline of highbrow taste 565
energy consumption 320
everyday life 536
fashion influences 621–622
history of retail trade
department stores 271
impact on urban environment 280
part of global exchange 284
self-service and supermarkets 274–275
history of thrift 361–367
impact of transatlantic trade 119–121
impact on pre-colonial East Africa 103–104
increasing influence on lifestyle 563
luxury goods 178
politics of consumption 416–417
shift in perspective of consumption 2

shift to 'consumer ethic' 357
standards of comfort 293
use of credit 360–361
waste production 327, 336–337
youth's golden age 611–613
Urban consumption
see also **Rural consumption**
clothing 201–205
debates over luxury goods 181
department stores
    origins and development 270–272
early modern Europe
    mobility between country and city 237–244
    the Priuli family in Venice 229–230
energy 311–312, 318
food and drink
    limited data 206–207
    rural communities compared 195–196
    suburban eating habits 383–384
history of retail trade 269–270
impact of China's growth 342–343
impact of retail shopping 278–280
importance 192
importance of fashion 622–628
lifestyle
    Bourdieu's approach 558–559
    distinctiveness and social change 563
modern Japan
    early modern consumption 486
    wartime modernity 497–498
nationalist China 424
ownership of goods 197–201
rural consumption compared 195–197
Soviet Union 456
waste
    disposability of MSW through the
        1980s 334–341
    nineteenth century concerns 331–334

Waste
defined 328
disposability
    MSW through the 1980s 334–341
    nineteenth century concerns 331–334
    nineteenth century concerns over urban
        waste 331–334

impact of China's growth 342–343
    market reform 342
    MSW 343
    overview 341–342
    recycling 343–346
Ming China 52–53
pre-modern human and animal
        waste 329–331
shift in perspective of consumption 1
significance 326–329
topics for further examination 344–345
Well-being
alternative approaches
    inventory of goods approach 657–660
    social science research 662–664
    state of mind 660–662
choice 665–666
citizenship and the home 582
comfort and convenience 290–291
comparison 666
conflicting truisms 655–656
disciplined bodywork 638
equal distribution of pleasures 669–670
ethical considerations 667–669
growth 667
limiting consumption 211–213
nationalist China 432
novelty 666
picture of 'normality' 650
saving and spending 349, 367
standard assumptions 653–655
women's responsibility for family 573

Youth consumption
see also **Children's consumption**
Africa 101
golden age of consumerism 611–617
impact of films 607
impact of gang culture 603–606
nationalist China 427
presentation of self 606–607
Renaissance Italy 253
self and body 645
significance 602–603
Soviet Union 462
towards mass consumption 609–611

Lightning Source UK Ltd.
Milton Keynes UK
UKOW02f0058200314

228433UK00003B/5/P